A CATALOGUE OF PAMPHLETS ON ECONOMIC SUBJECTS

published between 1750 and 1900 and now housed in Irish Libraries

by

R. D. COLLISON BLACK

Professor of Economics, The Queen's University Belfast

AUGUSTUS M. KELLEY · PUBLISHERS
NEW YORK 1969

First published 1969 by
Queen's University, Belfast

© 1969 *R. D. Collison Black*

Published in the United States by
Augustus M. Kelley · Publishers
New York, New York 10010

Library of Congress Catalog Card No. 79–81989

SBN 678 08002 X

Printed in Great Britain by
William Clowes and Sons, Limited, London and Beccles

To
FRANCES

Table of Contents

Introduction

THE historian of economic thought has never been particularly well served with bibliographical aids, even for the classical period of English economic writing. The period from 1750 to 1848 is reasonably, though not exhaustively, covered by Higgs' *Bibliography of Economics, 1751–1775* and the five volumes of the *Catalogue of the Kress Library of Business and Economics*, but the period after 1848 still remains very nearly that trackless desert to which Professor Jacob Viner referred in his review of the first volume of the Kress Catalogue more than twenty-five years ago.[1]

It hardly needs to be emphasised that many of the most important ideas in the development of Economics were not first put forward in major treatises but in pamphlets; the Bullion controversy and the formulation of the theory of rent in 1815 are obvious cases in point. Pamphlets are ephemeral things, and their preservation is often a matter of chance. While the better known items have usually been reprinted in collections of one sort or another, many pamphlets which are now recognised as having considerable significance in the development of economic thought have never been so reprinted and have become extremely scarce with the passage of time, as is the case, for example, with some of the early works of Robert Torrens. It is often a matter of great difficulty for a research worker to discover where a copy of any given pamphlet is to be found; many libraries with excellent collections of pamphlet material have never had the time or resources to produce catalogues for their own use, much less for publication.

In the course of my own research in the history of economic ideas I came to realise that copies of almost all the well-known economic pamphlets of the classical period existed in Irish libraries, and a great many lesser known but valuable pamphlets as well. Unfortunately, what has been said in the previous paragraph about the absence of adequate catalogues is particularly true for most of these Irish collections, and the present work is an attempt to make known to scholars in economics and economic history the extent of the riches to be found in the many collections of pamphlets in libraries throughout Ireland.

This work is in fact a Union Catalogue of pamphlets of economic interest published anywhere between the 1st January, 1750 and the 31st December, 1900, of which at least one copy is now housed in one or more of the seventeen major Irish libraries listed on page xi. I believe that no major collection of pamphlets now existing in any library in Ireland open to the public has been omitted, but on the other hand, no attempt has been made to cover private collections.

In preparing a bibliography of this kind, it was necessary to decide the meaning to be given to the words 'economic' and 'pamphlet'. I have deliberately given to them a connotation somewhat wider than that which a purist might desire. Thus, I have included works on land tenure, tithes, bankruptcy, and similar subjects which lie on the borderline between Economics and other social sciences. Nor have I adhered strictly to the librarian's definition of a pamphlet as a printed work containing not more than one hundred pages. Although normally no work of more than two hundred and fifty pages has been included, my basic rule has only been that where a work has been found bound up with others in a volume of pamphlets, and is not known to be widely available separately in hard covers, then it has been included.

On the other hand, certain items which are frequently to be found bound up in volumes of pamphlets have been deliberately excluded from this catalogue. Copies of speeches delivered in Parliament or elsewhere, which are known to be fully reported in the columns of either Hansard or contemporary newspapers have not been catalogued, nor have offprints from well-known

[1] In the *Journal of Political Economy*, Vol. 49, August 1941, pp. 629–31, reprinted in *The Long View and the Short* (Glencoe, 1958), pp. 413–15.

periodicals, such as the various quarterly reviews of the nineteenth century. Items which appeared in *The Pamphleteer* have also been excluded. Papers read before learned societies have likewise been omitted when it is known that they are obtainable in bound volumes of the transactions of the Society concerned without particular difficulty. For example, papers read before the Dublin Statistical Society subsequent to January 1855 have been omitted since its Journal is fairly complete and readily obtainable after that date; papers read before January 1855 have been included, since the earlier volumes of the Journal of the Dublin Statistical Society are frequently incomplete and difficult to obtain.

The entries in the catalogue are arranged by years, and alphabetically within each year. This method raises a problem with undated items; where no date appears on the title page of a pamphlet, every effort has been made to date it accurately, by comparisons with other catalogues and bibliographies, and on the basis of internal evidence. Many libraries enter dates of acquisition on their pamphlets, and while these may often correspond closely with publication dates this certainly cannot be taken for granted. Acquisition dates have therefore never been used as a basis for dating without a cross-check of some kind. In some few cases, it has not proved possible to assign a firm date to an item, and in these cases they have been placed under the first year of what appears to be the appropriate decade. Thus if a pamphlet seems to have appeared between 1750 and 1759, but cannot be placed more accurately, it is entered here under 1750.

In general, the form of each entry follows that adopted by the National Library of Ireland for the compilation of the Irish National Bibliography. Where the author is known his family name appears first, followed by his given name or names, and style and titles where appropriate. Where an author had a number of titles (as in the case of a cleric who was, say, first a dean and subsequently a bishop) the title given is the last held; but where an author was well-known under one name and later received a title which altered it, the well-known form is here used throughout. For example, all the works of Sir Henry Parnell are entered under that name, even though he ultimately became Baron Congleton.

Every effort has been made to ascertain the authorship of anonymous items, and to penetrate behind pseudonyms and other literary disguises. Most of the attributions given here are to be found in the standard dictionaries of anonyma and pseudonyma[2] but some have been taken over from other catalogues and bibliographies, including those attached to standard monographs.[3] In many cases manuscript attributions have been found on the pamphlets: where these cannot be confirmed from any other source the attribution is given here, but followed by a question mark.[4]

Titles are given in full throughout, followed by pagination, details of edition where applicable, place of publication and publisher or printer where known, with date of publication if this appears on the title-page. When date of publication is known, or can be inferred, but does not appear on the title-page it has been entered within square brackets. Where more than one edition of a pamphlet has been found, published in the same year, the editions are listed under the main entry, with any variations of pagination noted. If there are considerable differences between the titles of editions, or if they appeared in different years, separate entries are given for each.

[2] The dictionaries employed for this purpose were:
Cushing: *Anonyms*: a Dictionary of Revealed Authorship
———— : *Initials and Pseudonyms*: a Dictionary of Literary Disguises
Halkett & Laing: *Dictionary of Anonymous and Pseudonymous English Literature* (New and enlarged edition)
Stonehill (Block & Stonehill): *Anonyma and pseudonyma*
Barbier: *Dictionnaire des ouvrages anonymes*
Evans: *American Bibliography*
Watt: *Bibliotheca Britannica*

[3] For this purpose the British Museum and Library of Congress catalogues have been extensively used, in addition to the *Catalogues of the Kress Library*; *The London Bibliography of the Social Sciences*; Higgs: *Bibliography of Economics, 1751–1775*; Wagner: *Irish Economics, 1700–1783*; Clarke: *A Bibliography of the Publications of the Royal Dublin Society from 1731 to 1951*, and Williams: *Guide to the Printed Materials for English Social and Economic History, 1750–1850*. Monographs whose bibliographies have been consulted include: Barnes: *History of the English Corn Laws*; Furniss: *Position of the Labourer in a System of Nationalism*; McDowell: *Irish Public Opinion*, 1750–1800; idem: *Public Opinion and Government Policy in Ireland 1800–1846*; Seligman: *Shifting and Incidence of Taxation*; Fetter: *The Irish Pound 1797–1826*.

[4] In one or two instances where a contemporary manuscript attribution has been found on a pamphlet, it has been cited here in preference to disputed attributions given in other sources. Thus the pamphlets numbered 896 and 937 (*Traité sur la mendicité* and *Supplement au Traité*) are attributed by various authorities to Francois Joseph Tainteneur and Francois Xavier de Feller; but the copies listed in this catalogue both have manuscript inscriptions (probably by John Foster) on the title-page: 'Mr. Tamlini, proc. d'Oudenarde'.

The library or libraries in which each pamphlet may be found is indicated by a series of code-letters, as listed on page xi. The catalogue has both an author and a title index, each of which is complete. Thus where a pamphlet has no known author, it will be entered in the title index; where its authorship is known, it will be entered in both author and title index, whether its authorship was acknowledged or not. Pseudonyms are listed in the author index, with the author's real name where known. For the user wishing to find material such as annual reports of societies, a separate index to societies and institutions has been provided, for although these items are listed separately in the title index many societies published reports under varying titles over the years.

The need for a catalogue of this kind was borne in on me by a number of years of research in the history of economic thought; but the idea of carrying it out, specifically for Irish libraries, developed out of discussions with Professor Frank Whitson Fetter as long ago as 1955. Preliminary investigations of the amount of material involved made it clear that the task could not be carried out, even over a number of years, without full-time research assistance and funds to cover travel and other expenses. An approach was therefore made to the Rockefeller Foundation, which generously agreed to cover half the estimated cost of the project for a period of three years, subsequently extended to five. The remainder of the cost was financed by the Queen's University of Belfast. I should like to take this opportunity of expressing my gratitude to the authorities of both these institutions for their continued and generous support.

That support enabled me to have the help of a full-time Research Assistant from the commencement of the project in September 1958 until the collection of material was completed in December 1963. This position was held in 1958–59 by Mr. R. P. Davis; from September 1959 until the end of 1961 by Mr. S. A. Barcroft, and throughout 1962 and 1963 by Mr. W. G. Fuge. To all three I am greatly indebted, but especially to Mr. Fuge, who participated not only in the collection of material but also in the final indexing and editing of the catalogue. This process of editing has occupied a period as long as that taken in the original collection of the material, partly because of the necessity for detailed checking and correction of every entry, partly because of many other demands on my time. In the process of checking the main entries and completing the indexes I have benefited greatly from the help of Mr. W. J. Vennard. Completion of the catalogue within the scheduled time would not have been possible without further part-time assistance, and here I should like to acknowledge the help given by Mrs. D. Barrington and Dr. Maire de Paor, as well as by Mr. Liam Byrne, Mr. G. Burns, Mr. R. B. McCarthy, Mr. A. MacLaughlin, Mr. G. F. Ruddock, Mr. H. R. S. White, Mr. J. F. Young and Mr. R. Kennedy.

Throughout the preparation of the catalogue my Research Assistants and myself have received ready co-operation and assistance from the staffs of all the libraries in which we have worked. It is difficult to acknowledge our indebtedness fully but particular mention should be made of the help which we have had from Mr. J. J. Graneek and Mr. P. Havard-Williams, of the Library of Queen's University, Belfast; Mr. J. Vitty, of the Linenhall Library, Belfast; Miss. E. Power, Librarian of University College, Dublin; Mr. F. J. E. Hurst, Librarian of Trinity College, Dublin, and now Librarian of the New University of Ulster; Miss M. Pollard, of Marsh's Library, and Trinity College, Dublin; Miss M. Donnelly of the Royal Irish Academy; Mr. T. P. O'Neill, formerly Keeper of Printed Books in the National Library of Ireland; Father Sean Corkery of St. Patrick's College, Maynooth; Mr. D. J. Clarke, of the Royal Dublin Society; Mrs. P. Mac-Menamin, of the Library of King's Inns; Miss A. M. McAulay, then Librarian of Magee University College, Londonderry, and Very Rev. E. Rennison, formerly Dean of Armagh.

While the catalogue has been in preparation for the printer, Mr. Donald Wing, of Yale University, and Mr. P. R. Lewis of the School of Library Studies at Queen's University, have given valuable advice on its format. I am also much indebted to Mr. P. Havard-Williams, Librarian of Queen's University, for his assistance in arrangements for printing and publication.

For those errors and imperfections which remain, the responsibility is mine alone.

R. D. COLLISON BLACK

Department of Economics,
Queen's University,
Belfast.
September, 1968.

Code of Identification Letters for Libraries

A   Royal Irish Academy, Dublin

B   Belfast City Library

C   University College, Cork

D   Royal Dublin Society

E   Magee University College, Londonderry

G   Pearse Street Library, Dublin, Gilbert Collection

K   King's Inns Library, Dublin

L   Linenhall Library, Belfast (Belfast Library and Society for promoting knowledge)

M   Marsh's Library, Dublin

N   National Library of Ireland, Dublin

P   St. Patrick's College Library, Maynooth, Co. Kildare

Q   Queen's University, Belfast

R   Primate Robinson's Library, Armagh

RM County Museum, Armagh

S   Presbyterian Assembly's College, Belfast

T   Trinity College, Dublin

U   University College, Dublin.

1750

1 Advice to a newly elected member of parliament: inscribed to the right honble William Fitzgerald, commonly called marquess of Kildare.
24 pp. Dublin, [175?]

A.

T.p. mutilated. This edition is bound in a volume of pamphlets published in 1756 but it does not appear to differ from the edition of 1769. See 713.

2 Animadversions upon the present laws of England; or an essay to render them more useful & less expensive to all his majesty's subjects. To which is added, a proposal for regulating the practice and reducing the number of attornies, sollicitors, etc. with a supplement, humbly submitted to the consideration of both houses of parliament.
68 pp. London, M. Cooper, 1750

A.

3 [BARNARD, Sir John.]   Considerations on the proposal for reducing interest on the national debt.
36 pp. London, J. Osborn, 1750

K, P, Q.

4 BERKELEY, George, bishop of Cloyne. The querist, containing several queries, proposed to the consideration of the public.
68 pp. 2nd ed. Dublin, George Faulkner, 1750

A.

——.   68 pp. 4th ed. Dublin, George Faulkner, 1750

A.

"These editions differ considerably from the original, there being now 595 queries; besides a number that appeared in the first edition have been omitted, the subjects that they discussed having lost their importance." Wagner, p. 62.

5 BINDON, David. A scheme for supplying industrious people with money to carry on their trades: and for the better providing for the poor of Ireland.
fold. tables. 28 pp. 3rd ed. Dublin, George Faulker, 1750

A., N.

6 BOYD, Hugh. A letter from Hugh Boyd, esq., of Ballycastle, to a member of parliament, on the late scarcity of coals in the city of Dublin.
12 pp. Dublin, 1749–50

A.

7 COLE, Thomas. A short narrative of the proceedings, of the society appointed to manage the British white herring fishery, established by act of parliament. Shewing the names of the managers; the course of the several shoals of herrings:

the prime cost: the methods of catching, curing and packing: what the same sell for at foreign markets; the bulk and dimensions of the herring busses and yangers, &c. with seasonable hints for improving and extending the British white herring fishery, on the coast of Wales.
26 pp. London, W. Owen, 1750

A., T.

8 A conversation between a blacksmith and a merchant, upon the subject of passing guineas by weight only.
8 pp. Dublin, 1750

A., N.

9 Cox, Sir Richard, bart.   The case of Edward lord bishop of Elphin, in relation to money, part of the rents of the Ranelagh Charity, lodged in a public bank in Dublin.
16 pp. Dublin, Peter Wilson, 1750

Q.

10 DELANY, Patrick, dean of Down. An essay towards evidencing the divine original of tythes.
32 pp. 5th ed. Dublin, 1750

A., Q.

11 A description of the English and French territories, in North America: being, an explanation of a new map of the same. Shewing all the encroachments of the French, with their forts, and usurpations on the English settlements; and the fortifications of the latter. Done from the newest maps published in London. And compared with Dr. Mitchell's, F.R.S. and every omission carefully supplied from it.
28 pp. Dublin, J. Exshaw, 1750

G.

12 [EGMONT, John Percival, 2nd earl of.]   A representation of the state of the trade of Ireland, laid before the house of lords of England on Tuesday, the 10th of April, 1750, on occasion of a bill before that house, for laying a duty on Irish sail cloth imported into Great Britain.
tables. 28 pp. Dublin, Esdall, 1750

N.

——.   28 pp. 2nd ed. Dublin, Faulkner, Esdall, 1750

A., N., T.

13 The fisheries revived: or, Britains hidden treasure discovered. Proving that not only our future wealth, but security, will depend upon that inestimable trade.
map. 64 pp. London, J. Robinson and J. Millan, 1750

Q.

14 A genuine account of Nova Scotia: containing, a description of its situation, air, climate, soil and its produce: also rivers, bays, harbours, and fish, with which they abound in very great plenty. To which is added, his majesty's proposals, as an encouragement to those who are willing to settle there.
16 pp. Dublin [etc.], reprinted for Philip Bowes, 1750
A.

15 The junior's precedence and the senior's succession; or the younger going before the elder. Inscribed in a new impression of two acts of parliament, made in Ireland, in the second of his late majesty King George, & in the first of his present majesty, for the recovery of small debts. With an explanation of the utility & practice thereof. And likewise of sundry acts for establishing a public registry in Dublin, to record all deeds, &c. affecting lands and tenements; whereby it will be evident, that the trading, and other subjects of that kingdom, are favoured with better laws for recovering small debts, and with more effectual ones for securing their property, than those of South-Britain. To which is added, an appendix shewing the necessity of erecting courts of conscience, & of reforming county or sheriffs courts throughout the kingdom.
64 pp. London, W. Owen, 1750
A.

16 A letter to a member of parliament, concerning the free British fisheries; with draughts of a herring-buss and nets, and the harbour and town of Peterhead.
fold. map, diag. 40 pp. London, R. Spavan, 1750
A.

17 A letter to a proprietor of the East India Company.
tables, appendices. 124 pp. London, T. Osborne, 1750
T.

18 [MONTESQUIEU, Charles Louis de Secondat, baron de La Brède et de]. Two chapters of a celebrated French work, intitled, De L'Esprit Des Loix, (sic) translated into English. One, treating of the constitution of England; another, of the character and manners which result from this constitution.
32 pp. Edinburgh, Hamilton and Balfour, 1750
Q.

19 [PERRY, —, of Penshurst, Kent.] A treatise on trade or, the antiquity and honour of commerce. Shewing how trade was esteemed by the Egyptians, Jews, Greeks and Romans, and on what footing of worship it stands with us. Addressed to the country-gentlemen of England.
appendix. 72 pp. London, John Clarke, 1750
K.
See 121.

20 The placeman's estimate: in a letter from a member of parliament, to his brother. To which is added, his brother's answer.
tables. 18 pp. London printed and Dublin reprinted, 1750
A.

21 [POEKRICH, Richard.] A letter to a member of parliament, complaining of some public grievances, relating to the kingdom in general, and this city in particular. With proper schemes for redressing them. By a lover of his country.
16 pp. Dublin, the author, 1750
A., K., N.

22 PULLEIN, Samuel. Some hints intended to promote the culture of silkworms in Ireland. Addressed to the Dublin Society.
18 pp. Dublin, printed by S. Powell, 1750
A.

23 Some considerations on the British fisheries. With a proposal for establishing a general fishery, on the coasts of Ireland. Addressed to the rt. honourable the lord —.
16 pp. Dublin, Peter Wilson, 1750
A., N., T.

24 The state of the trade of Ireland, etc. no t.p.
28 pp. n.p., [1750?]
M.

25 [TUCKER, Josiah.] A brief essay on the advantages & disadvantages which respectively attend France & Great Britain, with regard to trade. With some proposals for removing the principal disadvantages of Great Britain. In a new method.
174 pp. 2nd ed. London, T. Trye, 1750
A.
See 136, 340 and 465.

26 The vindication of Dominick Molloy, merchant, against the false and scandalous aspersions of John Crump and Hosea Coates, merchants.
30 pp. Dublin, 1750
A.

27 WRIGHT, Martin. An introduction to the law of tenures.
224 pp. 3rd ed. Dublin, Mary Owen, 1750
Q.

1751

28 An abstract of the acts of parliament, now in force, relating to the linen manufacture, distinguished under proper heads, according to the progress of the manufacture; and an alphabetical index of such words as seem most likely to lead to any particular article. Published by order of the commissioners and trustees appointed by his majesty for improving the linen manufacture of Scotland.
tables. 34 pp. Edinburgh, 1751
Q.

29 An answer to a late proposal for uniting the kingdoms of Great-Britain and Ireland, with some occasional remarks thereon, shewing, that these kingdoms may be best preserved disunited.
68 pp. Dublin printed and London reprinted for Marshal Sheepey, 1751
N., Q.

30 An answer to the late proposal for uniting the kingdoms of Great Britain and Ireland; in some occasional remarks upon the proposal itself.
48 pp. Dublin, J. Exshaw, 1751
A., N., U.

31 ARCHDALL, Nicholas. An alarum to the people of Great-Britain and Ireland: in answer to a late proposal for uniting these kingdoms. Shewing, the fatal consequences of such a union, to the constitution, laws, trade and manu-

factures of both kingdoms; how destructive to the protestant religion established in Ireland and how little beneficial to England.
40 pp. Dublin, printed by George Faulkner, 1751
A., G., N., Q., T.

32 BARTON, Richard. A dialogue, concerning some things of importance to Ireland; particularly to the county of Armagh. Being part of a design to write the natural, civil and ecclesiastical history of that county.
28 pp. Dublin, Oli. Nelson, 1751
B.

33 A brief narrative on the late campaigns in Germany and Flanders. In a letter to a member of parliament.
48 pp. London, J. Lion, 1751
Q.

34 [DAWSON, Thomas.] A dissertation on the inlargement of tillage, the erecting of public granaries, and the regulating, employing and supporting the poor in this kingdom. Addressed to his grace the lord primate of all Ireland. By Publicola.
72 pp. Dublin, T. Moore, 1751
Q.

35 DECKER, Sir Matthew. An essay on the cause of the decline of the foreign trade, consequently of the value of the lands of Britain, and on the means to restore both, begun in the year 1739. To which is added serious considerations on the several high duties which the nation in general (as well as its trade in particular) labours under: etc.
210 pp. 4th ed. Dublin, printed by G. Faulkner, 1751
D.

36 Farther considerations upon a reduction of the land-tax: together with a state of the annual supplies of the sinking-fund, and of the national debt, at various future periods and in various suppositions.
tables. 114 pp. London, R. Griffiths, 1751
T.

37 FIELDING, Henry. An enquiry into the causes of the late increase of robbers, etc. With some proposals for remedying this growing evil. In which the present reigning vices are impartially exposed and the laws that relate to the provision for the poor and to the punishment of felons are largely and freely examined.
112 pp. Dublin, G. Faulkner [etc.], 1751
A., N., Q.

38 HOOKE, Andrew. An essay on the national debt, and national capital: or the account truly stated, debtor and creditor, wherein is shown that the former is but a diminutive part of the latter; and a practicable scheme exhibited, whereby the whole may, with great facility, be paid off, at once, exclusive of the aid of the sinking fund, and without any diminution of the present revenues of the crown, or annual expenses of the people.
tables. 86 pp. 2nd ed. London, W. Owen, 1751
K., T.

39 An humble address to the nobility, gentry and freeholders of the kingdom of Ireland.
26 pp. Dublin, printed by George Faulkner, 1751
A., N., Q.

40 LABELYE, Charles. A description of Westminster bridge. To which are added, an account of the methods made use of in laying the foundations of its piers. And an answer to the chief objections that have been made thereto. With an appendix containing several particulars, relating to the said bridge or to the history of the building thereof as also its geometrical plans, and the elevation of one of the fronts, as it is finished, correctly engraven on two large copper plates.
appendix. 86 pp. Dublin, Ewing, 1751
A., K., T.

There are no illustrations.

41 A letter from an English gentleman to a member of parliament: shewing the hardships, cruelties and severe usage with which the Irish nation has been treated . . .
172 pp. London, printed by T. Hill, 1751
B.

42 A letter to a member of parliament, concerning the laws which disable papists from purchasing in this kingdom.
16 pp. Dublin, 1751
A., N., Q.

43 A letter to T... P... esq. concerning a new bridge.
8 pp. Dublin, 1751
A., N.

Signed 'M.B.'

44 Plan of the universal register office now opened, opposite to the parliament house in College-green.
16 pp. Dublin, printed by S. Powell, 1751
A.

45 A proposal for uniting the kingdoms of Great Britain and Ireland.
46 pp. 2nd ed. London printed and Dublin reprinted for Richard James, 1751
A., D., G., N., P., Q.

Attributed by some to Wills Hill, 1st marquess of Downshire.

46 The reply examined; or, a supplement to the vindication of Dominick Molloy, merchant, against the false and scandalous aspersions of John Crump and Hosea Coates, merchants.
34 pp. Dublin, 1751
A.

47 A reply to Dominick Molloy's libel (miscall'd a vindication) against John Crump, merchant, & his friends.
40 pp. Dublin, 1751
A.

48 [ROBERTS, Robert.] A state of the case of the creditors of Burton's bank. In which is contained, a narrative of the proceedings relative to the demands of the said creditors, against the estate of Francis Harrison, esq; deceased. Together with a collection of the papers published, both for and against the proposal, lately made by Abraham Creichton, esq; to the said creditors.
52 pp. Dublin, 1751
A. (part missing), G., N., Q.

49 Rules and directions for raising flax and preserving the seed in Ireland, after the Flanders and other approven

methods. Published at the request of Robert McDougald*
millwright from Scotland.
12 pp. Belfast, printed by Blow, 1751

A. (Imperfect.)

[* The author?]

50 A scheme humbly offered to the consideration of the
parliament of Ireland, to make the inhabitants of that
kingdom a happy and flourishing people, without interfering
with anything that might affect the people of England.
24 pp. Dublin, printed by Rider, 1751

A.

51 A second letter from N... N..., a creditor of Burton's
bank, to A... C..., esq.
8 pp. Dublin, 1751

A., G., Q.

A... C... was Abraham Creichton.

52 Some considerations on the laws which incapacitate
papists from purchasing lands, from taking long or beneficial leases, and from lending money on real securities.
40 pp. 3rd ed. Dublin, G. Faulkner, 1751

A.

53 Some seasonable thoughts, relating to our civil and
ecclesiastical constitution: wherein is occasionally consider'd, the case of the professors of popery.
28 pp. Dublin, 1751

N., Q.

54 [TUCKER, Josiah.] An impartial inquiry into the benefits
and damages arising to the nation, from the present very great
use of low-priced spirituous liquors: with proper estimates
thereupon, and some considerations humbly offered for
preventing the introduction of foreign spirits not paying the
duties. By J. T. of Bristol., author of the brief essay on the
advantages which respectively attend France and Great
Britain, with regard to trade.
40 pp. London, T. Trye, 1751

Q.

55 ——. Reflections on the expediency of a law for the
naturalization of foreign protestants: Part 1. containing
historical remarks on the disposition and behaviour of the
natives of this island, in regard to foreigners; occasioned by
the rejection of the late Naturalisation Bill.
80 pp. London, T. Trye, 1751

Q.

See 81 for Part II.

56 A visionary letter to the freemen of the city of Bagdad
on a late election of cailiff and scapins. By a pupil of Alexander
the coppersmith.
24 pp. 'Bagdad' (Cork?) printed by the successor of Culty
Marny, 1751

G.

The preface is signed W.B. (William Boles?)

1752

57 Abstract of the by-laws, rules and orders, made by the
governors of the Royal hospital of King Charles II. near
Dublin, for the relief and maintenance of antient and maimed
officers and soldiers, of the army of Ireland. Collected from
the registry books of the said hospital, by order of the
governors.
86 pp. Dublin, printed by George Faulkner, 1752

A.

58 An act for finishing and regulating the hospital founded
by Richard Stephens, esq. doctor of physick.
16 pp. Dublin, 1752

A., Q.

59 BELLONI, Jerome. A dissertation on commerce clearly
demonstrating the true sources of national wealth and power,
together with the most rational measures for acquiring and
preserving both. The whole deduced from the nature of trade,
industry, money and exchanges. Translated from the
Italian.
110 pp. London, R. Manly, 1752

K., Q., T.

60 BERKELEY, George, bishop of Cloyne. Miscellany,
containing several tracts on various subjects.
266 pp. Dublin, printed by George Faulkner, 1752

A.

Comprising: An ode to the author of Siris. By the
R.R.T.L.B.O.N.; Farther thoughts on tar-water; An essay
towards preventing the ruin of Great Britain: A discourse
addressed to magistrates and men in authority, occasioned
by the enormous licence and irreligion of the times; A word
to the wise; or an exhortation to the roman catholic clergy of
Ireland; A letter from the roman catholic clergy; A letter to
the roman catholics of the diocese of Cloyne, published in the
late rebellion; Maxims concerning patriotism; The querist.
Containing several queries proposed to the consideration of the
public [version comprising 595 queries]; Verses by the
author, on the prospect of planting arts and learning in
America; A proposal for the better supplying of churches in our
foreign plantations, and for converting the savage Americans
to Christianity, by a college to be erected in the Summer
islands, otherwise called the isles of Bermuda; A sermon
preached before the incorporated society for the propagation
of the gospel in foreign parts; De Motu; sive, de motus
principio et natura et de causa communicationis motuum.

61 BROOKS, John. England's interest; or, free thoughts on
the starch duty. Wherein is set forth, the advantages that will
attend the farmers and landholders; and also some observations relating to the powder, and the hardships and inconveniences that the barbers and peruke-makers are subjected to
thereby. Together with a recital of what will be laid before the
parliament. Also an address to his royal highness, the duke of
Cumberland, relating to the army. To which is added, a
letter to a member of the honourable house of commons.
tables. 40 pp. London. R. Baldwin, 1752

K.

62 Considerations on the case of the bakers in Dublin. By a
citizen.
32 pp. Dublin, 1752

A., Q.

——. 34 pp. 2nd ed. Dublin, 1752

A.

63 Cox, Sir Richard, bart. A letter from Sir Richard Cox, bart. to Thomas Prior, esq. shewing, from experience, a sure method to establish the linen-manufacture; & the beneficial effects, it will immediately produce . . . To which is added, an appendix. Containing a further account of the increase of the linen manufacture, in the years 1749 & 1750.
tables. 44 pp. 3rd ed. Dublin, Peter Wilson, 1752
A.

64 Coyer, Abbé. A supplement to lord Anson's voyage round the world. Containing a discovery & description of the island of Frivola. By the abbé Coyer. To which is prefixed an introductory preface by the translator.
46 pp. Dublin, P. Wilson & M. Williamson, 1752
A.

65 [Dawson, Thomas.] The Irish collieries and canal defended, in answer to a pamphlet entitled, a letter to a commissioner of the inland navigation, concerning the Tyrone collieries. Signed by Publicola.
22 pp. Dublin, G. & A. Ewing, 1752
A., K., N.

66 A discourse on the advantages resulting from the arts and sciences, pronounced in a public assembly of the academy of sciences & belles-lettres of Lyons, on the 22d of June 1751. Translated from the French original by Mr. D...
36 pp. Dublin, printed by George Faulkner, 1752
A.

67 Dodd, James Solas. An essay towards a natural history of the herring.
196 pp. London, T. Vincent, 1752
A.

68 [Dorset, Charles Sackville, 2nd duke of.] A treatise concerning the militia, in four sections. I. Of the militia in general. II. Of the Roman militia. III. The proper plan of a militia for this country. IV. Observations upon this plan. by C. S.
64 pp. London, J. Millan, 1752
Q.

——. Another issue.
56 pp. Dublin, George Faulkner, 1752
Q.

69 Honesty the best policy: or, the history of Roger.
24 pp. London, T. Freeman, 1752
K., Q.
'Roger' is Henry Boyle later earl of Shannon.

70 Honesty the best policy: or, the history of Roger, the seventh edition, wherein the characters and passages, omitted by the editor of the former editions, are restored. To which is prefixed a letter from the author to the printer.
24 pp. London, Dublin, 1752
G., K., Q., U.

71 La Touche (James Digges). Mr. La Touche's address to his grace the duke of Dorset.
24 pp. Dublin, printed by Richard James, 1752
A., M., T.

2—C.P.E.S.

72 A letter to a commissioner of the inland navigation; concerning the Tyrone collieries.
24 pp. Dublin, R. Main, 1752
A., K.

73 Letters from Belfast from John Freeman and James Picken.
16 pp. Belfast, 1752
A., N., Q.

74 Nelson, Robert. An address to persons of quality and estate. To which is added, a representation of the several ways and methods of doing good, with some reflections upon the necessity and excellency of christian beneficence.
150 pp. Dublin, Peter Wilson, 1752
A., G., Q.

75 Remarks on a pamphlet lately published intitled, reasons against the establishment of a bank in the town of Belfast. In a letter from a gentleman in Dublin, to his friend in Belfast.
36 pp. n.p., 1752
B.

76 [Roberts, Robert.] A first letter from R... R...s, esq; to the creditors of Burton's bank. Containing part of his answer to two letters, lately printed and addressed to them, and signed A. Z.
16 pp. Dublin, 1752
A., Q., T.

77 ——. A second letter from R... R...s, esq; to the creditors of Burton's bank.
16 pp. Dublin, 1752
A., Q.

78 [Rousseau, Jean-Jacques.] The discourse which carried the praemium at the academy of Dijohn, in MDCCL. On this question proposed by the said academy, whether the re-establishment of arts and sciences has contributed to the refining of manners. By a citizen of Geneva. Translated from the French original.
48 pp. 4th ed. Dublin, printed by Richard James, 1752
A.

79 Some considerations concerning the revenue of the customs. With some proposals for effectually preventing frauds and abuses in that revenue.
36 pp. London, 1752
T.

80 [Thornton, W.] The counterpoise. Being thoughts on a militia and a standing army. By W... T..., esq.
64 pp. London, M. Cooper, 1752
Q.

81 Tucker, Josiah. Reflections on the expediency of a law for the naturalisation of foreign protestants. Part II. Containing important queries relating to commerce—the employment of the poor—the landed and national interest—taxes of all kinds, particularly the poor tax—the real interest of tradesmen—reformation of morals—constitution both in church and state, the duties of humanity and the principles of the Christian religion.
80 pp. London, T. Trye, 1752
Q.

82 A vindication of the r...t h...e and h...e l...ds and gentlemen, who have been basely aspersed, and scandalously misrepresented, in a late anonimous work, intitled, the history of Roger. By a lover of truth.
22 pp. Dublin, 1752

Q., T.

83 WEEKS, James Eyre. A new geography of Ireland.
72 pp. 3rd ed. Dublin, printed by J. Hoey, 1752

A. (some missing), N.

84 WILLS, Michael. A scheme for enlarging Essex-bridge: whereby, not only three fourths of the expence [sic] of a new bridge will be saved: but the public shall enjoy the benefit in six months. Together with a plan for building a new bridge.
15 pp. Dublin, printed by Augustus Long, 1752

A., K., N., Q.

1753

85 The advantages of the revolution illustrated, by a view of the present state of Great Britain. In a letter to a member of parliament. By G... B..., esq.
appendix, 40 pp. London, Owen, 1753

N.

86 An answer to a late pamphlet, intituled, a free and candid inquiry, addressed to the representatives, etc. of this kingdom.
46 pp. Dublin, 1753

A., G., N., Q., T.

87 [ARCHDALL, Nicholas?] A letter to H. E. Henry Boyle esq., speaker of the honourable house of commons in Ireland, with remarks on the linen trade and manufactures of this kingdom, and some hints for promoting the same.
16 pp. Dublin, printed by G. Faulkner, 1753

N.

88 [BINDON, David.] A letter from a merchant who has left off trade to a member of parliament, in which the case of the British and Irish manufacture of linen, threads and tapes, is fairly stated; and all the objections against the encouragement proposed to be given to that manufacture, fully answered.
tables. 84 pp. 2nd ed., London, 1753

U.

89 [BRISTOW, —.] Modern observations on antient history, chap. 1, on patriotism.
16 pp. n.p., 1753

Q.

90 [BRUCE, William.] Some facts and observations relative to the fate of the late linen bill, last session of parliament in this kingdom.
34 pp. Dublin, 1753

A., G., N., Q., T.

91 CAMPBELL, John. Full & particular description of the Highlands of Scotland, its situation & produce, the manners & customs of the natives through the various periods of life, from their births to their graves; to which is annex'd, a scheme, which, if executed according to the authors system, will prove effectual in bringing in the most disaffected amongst them, &

those of England & Ireland & render them, in all time coming zealously affected to his reigning majesty, & his discendants [sic] to latest posterity, and which will entirely extirpate all those evils which have so long prevailed in these kingdoms through their intestine divisions, and render them the admiration and glory of christendom. Humbly addressed to the brave & worthy inhabitants of Great Britain & Ireland.
46 pp. London, 1753

A.

92 The case of the infantry in Ireland. Humbly addressed to the right honourable Richard, lord viscount Molesworth; general and commander in chief; and to the general officers on the establishment of Ireland.
18 pp. Dublin, printed by John Butler, 1753

Q.

93 Considerations on the case of the bakers in Dublin. By a citizen.
36 pp. 3rd ed. Dublin, 1753

Q.

94 [Cox, Sir Richard, bart.] A letter from Sir R...d C...x, to a certain great man and his son. On the present state of affairs in Ireland.
8 pp. Dublin, 1753

A., Q.

95 ——. The true life of Betty Ireland with her birth, education and adventures. Together with some account of her elder sister Blanch of Britain, containing sundry very curious particulars.
36 pp. Dublin, Peter Wilson, 1753

A., G., K., T.

96 ——. The true life of Betty Ireland. With her birth, education and adventures. Together with some account of her elder sister Blanch of Britain. Containing sundry very curious particulars.
28 pp. London, J. Robinson, 1753

A., T.

97 Dedication on dedication: or, a second edition of a dedication to his grace the d... of D.... Wherein some curious anecdotes are brought to light. Very necessary to be known at this time.
23 pp. London, J. Swan, 1753

N., Q., T.

98 A dialogue between Dean Swift and Tho. Prior, esq; In the isles of St. Patrick's church, Dublin, on that memorable day, Oct. 9th, 1753. By a friend to the peace and prosperity of Ireland.
136 pp. Dublin, G. and A. Ewing, 1753

G., Q.

99 FIELDING, Henry. A proposal for making an effectual provision for the poor, for amending their morals, and for rendering them useful members of the society. To which is added, a plan of the buildings proposed, with proper elevations. Drawn by an eminent hand.
96 pp. London, A. Millar, 1753

T.

100 ——. A proposal for making an effectual provision for the poor, for amending their morals, and for rendering them useful members of the society.
56 pp. Dublin, John Smith and Richard James, 1753
A., Q.

101 A fragment of the history of Patrick.
16 pp. London, 1753
G.

102 A free and candid inquiry humbly addressed to the representatives of the several counties and boroughs in this kingdom: and proper at this time to be read by their several electors, in a letter to a person of distinction in the north from a gentleman in town.
44 pp. Dublin, printed by S. Powell, 1753
A., G., N., Q., T.
MS note on Academy copy: 'By the Revd. Mr. Britt a creature of J[?]P.'

103 HENRY, William. An earnest address to the people of Ireland against the drinking of spirituous liquors.
46 pp. Dublin, Peter Wilson, 1753
Q.

104 The history of the Dublin election in the year 1749. With a sketch of the present state of parties in the kingdom of Ireland. By a Briton.
174 pp. London, John Swan, 1753
M.

105 [HOWARD, Gorges Edmond.] A short account of his majesty's hereditary revenue and private estate in the kingdom of Ireland.
22 pp. Dublin, 1753
A., Q., T.

106 A letter from a free citizen of Dublin, to a freeholder in the county of Armagh.
16 pp. 2nd ed. Dublin, 1753
A., G., N., Q.

107 A letter from George the first in Aungier-street to William the third on College-green.
14 pp. Dublin, 1753
A., G., N.

108 A letter to a member of the h[ous]e of c[ommon]s of I[relan]d, on the present crisis of affairs in that kingdom.
24 pp. London, Robert Scot, 1753
A., C., G., N., T.

109 A letter to a member of parliament concerning the Money-bill.
16 pp. Dublin, 1753
A., N., Q., T., U.

110 A letter to a member of parliament, containing observations on a pamphlet, intitled, considerations on the case of the bakers in Dublin. By a baker.
32 pp. 2nd ed. Dublin, printed by S. Powell, 1753
A., K., N., Q.
See 603.

111 A letter to a person of distinction in town, from a gentleman in the country, Containing some remarks on a late pamphlet, intitled, A free and candid inquiry, etc.
48 pp. Dublin, 1753
A., G., N., Q., T.

112 A letter to his excellency Henry Boyle, esq., speaker of the honourable house of commons in Ireland. With remarks on the linen trade and manufactures of this kingdom, and some hints for promoting the same.
16 pp. Dublin, George Faulkner, 1753
A., K., T.

Signed N. A., B. M. copy—Wagner.

113 [LUCAS, Charles.] An address to the inhabitants of Ireland. By C. L--as, M.D.
24 pp. Dublin, 1753
A.

114 A Memorial by the earl of K-ld--e to his m-j---y, the 26th of May, 1753. Containing an account and reasons of the discontents and divisions that at present subsist among your m-j---y's most dutiful, faithful, loyal h--e of c-mm-ns, and devoted protestant s-bj-cts of I--l--d: humbly offered to your m-j---y's consideration. With the e--l of H--ld-ss's letter, by his majesty's command to the l--d ch-n--ll-r of I--l--d in answer to the earl of K-ld--e's memorial.
8 pp. London, 1753
Q.

115 NEWCASTLE-UPON-TYNE, Thomas Pelham-Holles, 4th duke of. The duke of Newcastle's letter by his majesty's order, to Monsieur Michell, the king of Prussia's secretary of the embassy, in answer to the memorial, and other papers, deliver'd, by Monsieur Michell, to the duke of Newcastle, on the 23d of November, and 13th of December last.
40 pp. folding tables. Dublin, W. Smith and R. James, 1753
K., Q.

116 Observations on the rebuilding of Essex-bridge. Showing, how far the situation thereof, when enlarged, may conduce to the advantage of commerce, in this trading city, if properly executed. Address'd to the right honourable Sir Charles Burton, lord mayor: to the right honourable and honourable the chief commissioners and governors of his majesty's revenue: & to the venerable body of merchants in the city of Dublin.
16 pp. Dublin, printed by Augustus Long, 1753
A., K.

117 Observations on the table of assize. By a journeyman baker.
20 pp. Dublin, 1753
A., K., N., Q.

118 [O'CONOR, Charles.] Seasonable thoughts relating to our civil and ecclesiastical constitution.
52 pp. Dublin, 1753
N., Q.

119 The patriot; or, the Irish packet open'd Nos. 1–7.
48 pp. London, W. Webb, 1753
N., Q.

120 The patriot, Nos. 1–2.
16 pp. Dublin, 1753

A., G., Q.

121 [PERRY, —— of Penshurst, Kent.] A treatise on trade; or, the antiquity and honour of commerce. Shewing how trade was esteemed by the Egyptians, Jews, Greeks and Romans, and on what footing of worship it stands with us.
76 pp. London, W. Owen, 1753

K.

See 19.

122 Political pastime: or faction displayed. In a letter to the author of the candid inquiry. By a lover of liberty, and a true friend to his country.
54 pp. Dublin, printed by S. Powell, 1753

G., N., Q., T.

123 Queries relative to the present crisis of affairs, humbly addressed to all true patriots.
8 pp. London, 1753

T.

124 Reflections upon naturalization, corporations and companies; supported by the authorities of both ancient and modern writers. By a country gentleman.
92 pp. London, M. Cooper, [etc.], 1753

K.

125 Scheme of a bill to facilitate compositions with insolvent debtors; and to prevent frauds committed by bankrupts.
16 pp. Dublin, Peter Wilson, 1753

Q.

126 A scheme to pay the national debt at the small expence of a farthing. To which is added, a remedy to render the said proposal entirely useless.
44 pp. London, J. Powell, 1753

K.

127 Seasonable advice to the freeholders of the county of Armagh. By a brother freeholder.
28 pp. 2nd ed. n.p. 1753

A., Q.

128 A second letter to a person of distinction in town from a gentleman in the country, containing among other things, some remarks on a late pamphlet, entitled, political pastime or faction displayed.
54 pp. Dublin, 1753

G., T.

129 A second number of queries, relative to the present crisis of affairs, humbly addressed to all true patriots.
8 pp. Dublin, 1753

Q.

130 A short view of the rise, progress and establishment of the woolen manufacture in England, and of the continual attempts of the manufacturers to monopolize wool, and lower its price. In which their late complaints, relating to the marking sheep, and winding wool, are candidly considered.
76 pp. London, W. Owen, 1753

K.

131 Some advice to the gentlemen members of the late instituted society of attorneys, from one of their members: with some general hints, humbly offered to the public, for regulating and improving the profession of an attorney.
22 pp. Dublin, Peter Wilson, 1753

Q.

132 Some further advice to the gentlemen, members of the late instituted society of attornies, with some further hints, humbly offered to the consideration of the publick, for regulating and improving the profession of an attorney, and also some hints for remedying and correcting several of the abuses, errors and defects which have happened in the practice and execution of the laws. By one of their members.
28 pp. Dublin, Peter Wilson, 1753

N., Q.

133 The spirit of the party. Address'd to the people of Ireland, by the farmer. Chap. the first.
8 pp. London, 1753

Q.

134 The state of the corn trade considered in answer to all the objections against the bounty granted to encourage the exportation of corn and its influence on the landed and navigation interest clearly and fully explained.
30 pp. London, S. Birt, 1753

A., Q.

135 The state of the question in relation to the alteration in the money-bill. Humbly submitted to the friends of Ireland.
8 pp. Dublin, 1753

A., L., N., Q., T,

136 TUCKER, Josiah. A brief essay on the advantages & disadvantages which respectively attend France & Great Britain with regard to trade. With some proposals for removing the principal disadvantages of Great Britain. In a new method.
174 pp. 3rd ed. London, T. Trye, 1753

A., T.

See 25, 340 and 465.

137 ——. A letter to a friend concerning naturalizations: shewing, I, what a naturalization is not; II, what it is; III, what are the motives for the present clamours against the Bill passed last sessions for enabling the parliament to naturalize such Jews as they shall approve of; IV, setting forth the nature of this affair considered in a religious light; V, proposing a scheme for the prevention of all future naturalizations, by explaining how the same ends may be obtained in a way much more efficacious, and altogether popular. With a hint relating to the orphan fund in the city of London.
34 pp. 2nd ed. London, T. Trye, 1753

Q.

138 ——. A second letter to a friend concerning naturalizations: wherein the reasons are given why the Jews were antiently considered as the immediate vassals and absolute property of the crown; but are now in a state of liberty and freedom like other subjects. To which are added, the opinions of the most eminent lawyers, together with proofs and arguments drawn from divers important facts and statutes of the realm relating to the same subject.
48 pp. London, T. Trye, 1753

Q.

1754

139 An abridgment of the several statutes for promoting and carrying on an inland navigation in Ireland. With an alphabetical table of the principal matters.
84 pp. Dublin, printed by George Abraham Grierson, 1754

A.

140 An account of the revenue and national debt of Ireland. With some observations on the late bill for paying off the national debt. In which is contained, a speech to the parliament of Henry lord viscount Sidney, lord lieutenant in the year 1692, as also an order of council, and several resolutions of the house of commons, extracted from their journals, parallel to the present juncture of affairs in that kingdom.
tables. 48 pp. London, H. Carpenter, 1754

C., N., T.

141 An address from the free electors of the pro...nce of Ul...er, to Anthony Malone, esq., the right honourable Thomas Carter &c. and Bell-ngham Boyle, esqurs. wherein their dislocations, the distribution of pensions and places, corruption in p-t and at elections, influenced sh-ffs, invasions on the liberties of the people, power of high priests, &c. are duly considered. With a general review of two hundred and sixty six I-r-h places, offices and employments, their uses and applications in a cor-pt go-nt. A dissertation on the emperor Caligula's horse, whom he made his prime minister, &c. And Mr. Wentworth's speech in queen Elizabeth's reign, in order to shew the freedom of speech in that glorious parliament. Taken from Fog's journal, June 14th, no. 345. To which is added, a clear and reasonable answer to that disingenuous pamphlet call'd, Considerations on the late bill, for payment of the remainder of the national debt.
32 pp. London, printed at the sign of the Irish ram, butting corruption with his patriotic horns, 1754

A., N., P., T.

142 An answer to a letter, published in the [Dublin] Gazette, relating to the money-bill, February 16th 1754.
2 pp. [Dublin] 1754

N.

143 An answer to a pamphlet intitled, The proceedings of the honourable house of commons of Ireland, in rejecting the altered money bill, on December 17, to the argument of a pamphlet intitled, considerations on the late bill for payment of the remainder of the national debt, etc.
32 pp. Dublin, printed by Richard James, 1754

G.

144 [BINDON, David.] An answer to part of a pamphlet intitled, 'The proceeding of the honourable house of commons of Ireland, in rejecting the altered money-bill on Dec. 17th, 1753, vindicated.' By the author of the observations, &c.
tables. 30 pp. Dublin, 1754

A., K., N., Q., T.

145 [——.] Some observations relative to the late bill for paying off the residue of the national debt of Ireland, humbly submitted to the consideration of the true friends of this country.
tables. 40 pp. Dublin, 1754

A., K., N., Q., T.

——. 40 pp. 2nd ed. Dublin, 1754

G., K., T.

146 The Bristol contest: being a collection of all the papers published by both parties on the election, 1754.
76 pp. Bristol, J. Palmer, 1754

B.

147 [BURGESS, James.] A letter from a gentleman at Cork, to his friend in Dublin. Concerning the loan-bill, rejected on the 17th December, 1753.
16 pp. Dublin, 1754

A., N., P.

148 The cabinet, containing, a collection of curious papers relative to the present political contests in Ireland, some of which are now first published. viz. The earl of K...e's memorial. Barrack resolutions. Commons address to the king in 1752—to the lord lieutenant in 1752. Lord lieutenant's answer, earl of H...s's letter to the lord ch...r, duke of D...t's letter to the same. Observations on a letter from somebody to somebody. Account of an extraordinary overture made to the earl of K...e. Parson's letter to Sir R...d C...x. The answer. A letter from the spy to the candid inquirer. Lord lieutenant's speech in 1753. Commons address to the king in 1753.—lord lieutenant in 1753. Ax laid to the root of the tree. Letter from the p...y c...l of England. Money-bill. Letter to the author of the queries to the people of Ireland. Lat-he's letter to lord Ch...d. Dr. B...d's letter to the bishop of O...y. Considerations on query-writing. Constitutional queries relating to Ireland. Tobias Wilcox's letter to Obadiah Oldbottom. Moderation moderated.
92 pp. (pages 85 and 86 missing). London, printed by William Durham, 1754

G., K.

149 The charter-party: or articles of agreement of the Social annuity-company of Dublin.
30 pp. Dublin, printed by Saunders, 1754

A., N.

150 A clear and reasonable answer to the disingenuous pamphlet called, Considerations on the late bill for payment of the national debt.
18 pp. n.p., [1754?]

N.

151 Common sense: in a letter to a friend.
80 pp. Dublin, 1754

A., B., G., N., Q., T.

152 [Cox, Sir Richard, bart.] A letter from Dionysius to the renowned triumvirate.
24 pp. Dublin, Peter Wilson, 1754

A., B., G., N., Q., T.

153 ——. The proceedings of the honourable house of commons of Ireland in rejecting the altered money bill, on December 17, 1753, vindicated by authorities taken from the law and usage of parliament. Wherein are occasionally exposed the fallacies of two pamphlets intitled, 'Considerations on the late bill, &c.'—and 'Observations relative to the late bill for paying off the residue of the national debt.'
tables. 96 pp. Dublin, Peter Wilson, 1754

A., K., N., Q., R., S., T., U.

154 [DAWSON, Thomas?] The great importance & necessity of increasing tillage by an act of parliament, in Ireland, in proportion to the number of its inhabitants, demonstrated: together with the usefulness & advantages of erecting public granaries, & granting praemiums on the exportation of corn: in a letter addressed to the right honourable John, earl Grandison.
52 pp. Dublin, Peter Wilson, 1754

A.

Signed Publicola, probably Thomas Dawson

——. 52 pp. 2nd ed. Dublin, Peter Wilson, 1754

A.

155 A dialogue between a banker and a merchant of the city of Dublin.
8 pp. Dublin, 1754

A., Q., T.

156 A dialogue between Dick —— and Tom ——, esqrs; relating to the present divisions in I(relan)d.
16 pp. Dublin, 1754

A., N., Q.

157 DODSLEY, R. Public virtue: a poem in three books. I, Agriculture. II, Commerce. III, Arts.
76 pp. Dublin, printed by Faulkner, 1754

A.

158 The finishing stroke, being a supplement to the queries to the people of Ireland. By another hand.
16 pp. Dublin, 1754

G., N., T.

159 The free citizens address to Sir Samuel Cooke, bart. For his unshaken attachment to the true interest of Ireland this session of parliament.
16 pp. London, 1754

G., Q.

160 A full account of the present dispute in Ireland between the prerogatives of the crown and the rights of the people: together with reflections on the present political contest in that kingdom.
16 pp. Dublin, 1754

A., G., K., N., Q.

161 [GAST, John.] A letter to the tradesmen, farmers and the rest of the good people of Ireland. Very proper to be read in all families, at this critical juncture. By L. B. haberdasher and citizen of Dublin.
36 pp. Dublin, 1754

G., K., N., Q., T.

162 [——.] A second letter to the tradesmen, farmers and the rest of the good people of Ireland. Very proper to be read in all families, at this critical juncture. By L. B. haberdasher and citizen of Dublin.
28 pp. Dublin, 1754

A., G., K., N., P., Q., T.

163 The history of the ministerial conduct of the chief governors of Ireland, (so far as relates to that kingdom,) from the glorious revolution in 1688, to the never-to-be forgotten 17th of December, 1753. With a general review, of the most remarkable proceedings in parliament during that period of time. To which is prefix'd, an introductory survey of the English ministry, from the reign of Henry VIIIth, to the abdication of James IInd, wherein the tyranny, avarice and ambition of prime ministers and court-favourites are impartially display'd.
appendix. 96 pp. London, W. Browne, 1754

A., N., Q., T.

164 The honest mans apology to his country for his conduct. Humbly submitted to the impartial of all sides, with his reasons for acting as he did and for his accepting a place from the crown.
14 pp. Dublin, the author, 1754

G., K., N., Q., T.

165 [HOWARD, Gorges Edmond.] A letter to the publick, on the present posture of affairs. With some quaeries, humbly offered to their consideration.
36 pp. Dublin, 1754

A., G., N., T.

This edition has a quotation from Horace between 'affairs' and 'With'.

166 [——.] A letter to the publick: with some quaeries, humbly offered to it's consideration.
36 pp. Dublin, 1754

K., T.

This edition has an ornamental cut on t.p. after 'consideration'.

167 [——.] A letter to the publick: with some quaeries, humbly offered to its consideration.
36 pp. Dublin, 1754

Q.

168 [——.] A second letter to the publick on the present posture of affairs.
32 pp. Dublin, 1754

A., G., K., T.

169 [——.] A short account of such parts of his majesty's hereditary revenue in the kingdom of Ireland as are unappropriated; and of his private estate therein.
22 pp. Dublin, 1754

N., Q., T.

——. 24 pp. 2nd ed. Dublin, 1754

G., K., T.

170 [——.] A third letter to the publick, on the present posture of affairs with some quaeries proposed to certain modern authors and submitted to the consideration of the publick.
30 pp. Dublin, 1754

A., G., K., Q., T.

Signed Philo Hibernicus.

171 [JEFFERYS, Thomas.] The conduct of the French with regard to Nova Scotia, Virginia, and other parts of the continent of North America. From its first settlement to the present time. In which are exposed the falsehood and absurdity of their arguments made use of to elude the force of the

treaty of Utrecht, and support their unjust proceedings. In a letter to a member of parliament.
80 pp. London, T. Jefferys, Dublin, R. James, 1754
G.

172 The last shift. A modest proposal; being a sequel to the advertisement of June the 4th. To which is annexed, a letter from the author of truth against craft, earnestly recommending the case of the unhappy sufferer, to the consideration of the public.
8 pp. n.p. 1754?
A., G., N., Q., T.

173 LEE, Weyman. A valuation of annuities and leases certain for a single life.
tables. 108 pp. 2nd ed. London, Shuckburgh, 1754
A.

174 [LELAND, John.] The case fairly stated or, an inquiry how far the clause lately rejected by the honourable house of commons, would, if it had passed, have affected the liberties of the people of Ireland.
56 pp. Dublin, R. Main, 1754
A., G., N., Q., R., T.

175 [——.] A defence of The case fairly stated, against a late pamphlet, intitled, Truth against craft, or sophistry and falsehood detected. By the author of The case fairly stated.
26 pp. Dublin, R. Main, 1754
G., Q., T.

176 A letter from a burgess of Monaghan, to the parish-clerk of Ardbraccan.
14 pp. Dublin, 1754
A., N., Q., T.

177 A letter from a gentleman at Cork, to his friend in Dublin. Concerning the loan-bill rejected on the 17th December, 1753.
16 pp. Dublin, 1754
Q.

178 A letter to the right honourable James, earl of Kildare, on the present posture of affairs. With some occasional reflections on the conduct of a certain justice of peace, on Friday the 10th instant. By a patriot.
28 pp. Dublin, 1754
A., N., Q., T.

——. 28 pp. 2nd ed. Dublin, 1754
G.

179 Moderation recommended to the friends of Ireland, whether of the court or country party. In a letter to the publick. By an honest Irishman.
48 pp. Dublin, 1754
A., G., K., N., Q., T.

——. 48 pp. 2nd ed. Dublin, 1754
K.

180 [OLDBOTTOM, Obadiah?] The quaker's answer to the weaver's letter.
8 pp. Dublin, 1754
G., T.

181 Queries to the querist. Or a series of 141 queries. In vindication of the conduct and characters of the patriots of Ireland, who have been most scandalously traduced in a scurrilous, malicious libel lately published by Dr. B...tt, entitled 'Queries to the people of Ireland', wherein the fallacy of this church attorney is justly exposed, and a scene of affairs opened, affording the public an opportunity of judging who are enemies to national liberty, and peace and happiness and tranquility of their country. To which are added, six humourous toasts, by Moll Walker, and some necessary groans of the midwives., who have been sufferers by So-o-m-cal Ga-ny-e-dism, piously imported and promoted in I-d.
16 pp. Dublin, 1754
Q.

182 A question to be considered, previous to the rejection of the bill for paying off the national debt, upon account of inserting to the preamble, his majesty's previous consent. Humbly address'd to all his majesty's faithful subjects of Ireland.
32 pp. Dublin, 1754
A., E., K., N.

183 Remarks on a pamphlet intitled, considerations on the late bill for paying the national debt, etc.
16 pp. Dublin, 1754
A., G., K., Q., T., U.

184 Remarks on a pamphlet intitled, considerations on the late bill for paying the national debt, etc.
Number II. 16 pp. 'Dublin printed; and Belfast reprinted'. 1754
A., G., K., Q., T., U.

185 Remarks on a pamphlet intitled, considerations on the late bill for paying the national debt, etc.
Number III. 16 pp. 'Dublin printed; and Belfast reprinted'. 1754
A., G., K., Q., T., U.

186 Remarks on a pamphlet intitled, considerations on the late bill for paying the national debt, etc.
Number IV. 50 pp. Dublin, 1754
A., K., T.

187 The review; being a short account of the doctrine, arguments and tendency, of the writings offered to the publick, by the c(our)t advocates, since last September; together with an humble address to the worthy patriots of Ireland, on the happy and providential events, which have crowned their labours in defence of their country. By the author of a letter to a member of the Irish h(ous)e of c(om mon)s on the present crisis of affairs.
table. 52 pp. Dublin, 1754
G.

188 [ROBINSON, Christopher.] An answer to a pamphlet, intitled, 'The proceedings of the honourable house of commons of Ireland, in rejecting the altered money bill, on Dec. 17th, 1753, vindicated etc.' So far as the same relates to the argument of a pamphlet, intitled, 'Considerations on the late bill for payment of the remainder of the national debt, &c.'
32 pp. Dublin, printed by Richard James, 1754
A., K., N., P., Q., T.

——. 32 pp. 2nd ed. Dublin, 1754

N., T.

189 [——.] Considerations on the late bill for payment of the remainder of the national debt, in which the occasion of inserting the clause relative to his majesty's consent, and the arguments in support of such right in the crown, are impartially stated.
appendix. 60 pp. Dublin, printed by R. James, 1754

A., G., K., N., P., T.,
U.

——. 60 pp. 2nd ed. Dublin, 1754

N.

——. 60 pp. 3rd ed. Dublin, 1754

N., T.

——. 60 pp. 4th ed. Dublin, 1754

T.

——. 60 pp. 5th ed. Dublin, 1754

D., K., T.

190 [——.] Considerations on the late bill for payment of the remainder of the national debt, in which the occasion of inserting the clause relative to his majesty's consent, and the arguments in support of such right in the crown are impartially stated.
appendix. 60 pp. 'Dublin, printed: London, re-printed; and sold by William Owen.' 1754

C., P., Q., T.

191 Scheme of a bill to facilitate compositions with insolvent debtors, and to prevent frauds committed by bankrupts. Revised and amended and humbly offered to the consideration of the honourable house of commons.
8 pp. Dublin, 1754

Q.

192 A second letter to the public on the present posture of affairs.
32 pp. Dublin, 1754

Q.

193 Some thoughts on lowering the water of Lough Neagh and other great lakes in Ireland. Without prejudice to their navigation, or fisheries.
32 pp. Dublin, S. Powell, 1754

RM.

194 The state of Ireland, laid open to the view of his majesty's subjects.
folding table. 72 pp. London, 1754

A., D., G., N., Q., T.

195 [STEPHENSON, Robert.] Considerations on the present state of the linen manufacture. Humbly addressed to the trustees of the linen-board.
32 pp. Dublin, 1754

A.

196 A supplement to the remarks on a pamphlet intitled, Considerations on the late bill for paying the national debt, etc.
28 pp. Dublin, 1754

A., G., K., N., T.

197 Thoughts on some late removals in Ireland, in a letter to the right honourable the earl of Kildare. (To which is annexed a list of the members who voted for and against the rejected money-bill, and the expulsion of the surveyor-general). By Hiberno-Britannus.
56 pp. London, M. Cooper, 1754?

N., Q.

198 Thoughts on the affairs of Ireland: with the speeches of the lord chancellor, cardinal Wolsey and Gerald, earl of Kildare.
30 pp. London, W. Owen, 1754

A., N., Q.

199 To all the serious honest and well-meaning people of Ireland. The following queries are affectionately addressed and recommended to their serious perusal. To which is prefixed, a letter from the editor to the printer. And at the end is added, An epistle dedicatory to Sir R...d C...x, b...t.
42 pp. Dublin, 1754

Q.

200 Truth against craft: or, sophistry and falsehood detected. In answer to a pamphlet intitled, The case fairly stated; and likewise to the defence of the considerations.
86 pp. Dublin, 1754

G., K., Q., T.

K. copy has ms. note 'This pamphlet was wrote by Bruce who soon afterwards died mad.'

201 A vindication of Truth against craft; in answer to the defence of the Case fairly stated: in a letter to the author of said case and defence.
76 pp. Dublin, 1754

B., K., N.

202 The weaver's letter to the tradesmen and manufacturers of Ireland.
8 pp. Dublin, 1754

G., K., Q., T.

1755

203 [BROCKLESLY, Richard]. A letter to a member of the Irish parliament relative to the present state of Ireland. Wherein, many advantages are laid down which would arise to the province of Munster in particular, and to the kingdom in general, from improving and farther extending the navigation of the Blackwater river thro' the counties of Waterford and Corke.
32 pp. Cork [etc.] reprinted by Eugene Swiney, 1755

A.

Signed Philo-Ierne.
——. Another issue, 32 pp. London, Mrs. Kingman and G. Woodfall, 1755

P., T.

Author's name given in this issue.

204 [BROWN, St. John?] A just and true answer to a scandalous pamphlet call'd, a genuine letter from a freeman of Bandon to George Faulkner.
16 pp. Dublin, 1755

A., N., Q.

MS note on Q. copy: 'By St. John Brown DD. vicar of Bandon alias Bray, Archsychopant [sic] to the Prince & partly by George Faulkner.'

205 [——.] A letter to the people of Ireland, relative to our present feuds & jealousies.
32 pp. Dublin, 1755
A., N.
MS note on A. copy t.p.: 'By the Rev. St. John Browne all egregious nonsense'.

206 BURKITT, ——. Burkitt's observations on the inland navigation of loughs, making entrances into ports, & a bridge over the ferry of Waterford, & the benefits to be had by sowing of cole-seed.
10 pp. Dublin, printed by Sarah Cotter, 1755
A.

207 The case of the Roman-catholics of Ireland. Wherein the principles and conduct of that party are fully explained and vindicated.
80 pp. Dublin, P. Lord, 1755
A., R., T.
——. 80 pp. 2nd ed. Dublin, P. Lord, 1755
A., N., Q.

208 [CLARKE, Barney?] A letter to the right honourable the earl of Chesterfield, upon the present posture of affairs in Ireland, with some remarks on a late anonimous paper, without a title, but in the manner of a letter, to some right honourable.
24 pp. n.p., 1755
A., N.

209 The conduct of a certain member of parliament, during the last session and the motives on which he acted explain'd in a letter to a friend.
50 pp. Dublin, 1755
A., G., N., Q.

210 Cox, Sir Richard, bart. A charge delivered to the grand jury at the general quarter sessions for the county of Cork, held at Bandon-Bridge, on Jan. 14, 1755. Published at the request of the justices of the peace.
30 pp. Dublin, printed by Matthew Williamson, 1755
A., G., L., N., Q.

211 [DAWSON, Thomas]. The great importance and necessity of increasing tillage, by an act of parliament, in Ireland, in proportion to the number of its inhabitants, demonstrated: together, with the usefulness and advantage of erecting public granaries, and granting praemiums on the exportation of corn: in a letter addressed to the right honourable John, earl Grandison.
52 pp. 2nd ed. Dublin, Peter Wilson, 1755
T.

212 A description of the English & French territories, in North America: being, an explanation of a new map of the same. Shewing all the encroachments of the French with their forts, and usurpations on the English settlements; and the fortifications of the latter.
28 pp. Dublin, J. Exshaw, 1755
A.

213 A dialogue between Roger and Caiaphas, concerning a land-tax in regard to Ireland; towards the expence of a war.
8 pp. n.p., 1755
C.

214 [DORSET, Lionel Cranfield Sackville, 1st duke of.] Common sense: in a letter to a friend. By Major Sawney M'Cleaver.
48 pp. 4th ed. Dublin, 1755
A., K.
——. 84 pp. 4th ed. London, reprinted by Cox
G., N., T.

215 [——.] Ireland in tears; or a letter to St. Andrew's eldest daughter's youngest son. By Major Sawney M'Cleaver.
44 pp. London, M. Cooper, 1755
A., N.
——. 56 pp. 2nd ed. London, M. Cooper, 1755
G., K., T.

216 [EGMONT, John Percival, 2nd earl of.] A representation of the state of the trade of Ireland, laid before the house of lords of England, on Tuesday the 10th of April, 1750, on occasion of a bill before that house, for laying a duty on Irish sail-cloth imported into Great-Britain.
24 pp. 3rd ed. Dublin, printed by James Esdall, 1755
A.

217 An essay towards a method of speedily manning a fleet upon any sudden emergency.
46 pp. London printed, Dublin re-printed by Richard James, 1755
K.

218 A few thoughts on the present posture of affairs in Ireland.
24 pp. Dublin, 1755
G., K.

219 A few words to all true patriots & protestants or mock-patriotism displayed.
8 pp. n.p., 1755
A., G., N.

220 [GAST, John]. Faction's overthrow: or, more fair warning, and good advice, to the nobility, gentry, & commonalty of Ireland. Very fit to be read in families.
16 pp. Dublin, printed by S. Powell, 1755
A., G., N.

221 Great importance of the Shannon navigation to the whole kingdom of Ireland: humbly submitted to the serious consideration of his excellency, the lord lieutenant, both houses of parliament, and the trustees of the tillage and inland navigation of Ireland.
11 pp. 2nd ed. Dublin, Price, 1755
N.
Signed Philo-Senensis.

222 HENRY, William. A letter to Arthur Gore, esq; relating to the present abuse of spirituous liquors; and a method to remedy the evil.
16 pp. Dublin, Peter Wilson, 1755
A., N., Q., T.

223 Hezekiah Oldbottom to the adviser of the people of Ireland.
16 pp. Dublin, 1755
A., G., N.

224 Huske, John. The present state of North America. Lately presented to the lords of the regency of Great Britain. Part I. 80 pp. Dublin, printed by George Faulkner, 1755

A., K.

——. Another issue.
92 pp. London, R. & J. Dodsley, 1755

K.

225 J... P...'s answer to N... A...'s letter.
8 pp. Dublin, 1755

Q.

226 A layman's sermon preached at the patriot club of the county of Armagh, which met at Armagh, the 3d of September, 1755.
34 pp. Dublin, 1755

A., N.

227 A letter concerning prerogative addressed to C...r N...n, esq.—[signed] S... X....
52 pp. Dublin, printed by T. Cooper, 1755

A., G., N., T.

228 A letter from a member of parliament to his grace the Duke of —— upon the present situation of affairs.
26 pp. London, M. Cooper, 1755

T.

229 A letter from a merchant of Dublin, to the author of the remarks on the conduct of messrs. W...cks [Willcocks] and D...n [Dawson]. To which is added the remarker's answer containing an impartial examination into the proceedings of the late bankers and their friends. With some general observations on the meeting of the banker's friends, debtors and a few creditors, at the musick-hall in Fishamble St., on the 6th of this instant. To which are annexed, a few queries highly interesting to the creditors of the bank.
28 pp. Dublin, J. Samuel, [1755]

N.

The letter is signed Ch: M:

230 A letter to a member of parliament concerning the inland navigation of Ireland and the many advantages arising from it. By Iernus Cambrensis.
16 pp. Dublin, 1755

A., G., N., Q.

231 A letter to the creditors of messrs. W[illco]cks & D[awso]n, late bankers of the city of Dublin. By the author of the remarks.
14 pp. Dublin, J. Samuel, 1755

A., N.

232 A letter to the right hon. J.P. esq: in relation to a national affair in the house of commons, on the 1st of November 1755.
8 pp. Dublin, 1755

A., N.

233 Lyndon, William. The case of W. Lyndon, late of the city of Dublin, merchant.
32 pp. Dublin, George and Alexander Ewing, 1755

G., N.

234 McCannon, John. A vindication of the conduct of Mr. John McCannon, lately of this city, woollen-draper. Written by himself.
16 pp. Dublin, children of James Esdall, 1755

A., N.

235 Maxwell, Henry. Reasons offered for erecting a bank in Ireland; in a letter to Hercules Rowley esq.
tables. 60 pp. 3rd. ed., Dublin, Faulkner, 1755

A., D., K.

236 Mr. Omer's letter to the public comptroller of the inland navigations examined; and the observations on the said letter observed upon.
tables. 36 pp. Dublin, William Smith, 1755

A., N., Q.

237 The naked truth. Numb. I. The second edition, with additions.
appendix. 40 pp. London: A. Price, 1755

T.

238 A new system of agriculture; or, A plain, easy and demonstrative method of speedily growing rich: proving, by undeniable arguments, that every land-owner, in England, may advance his estate to a double value, in the space of one year's time. Together with several very curious instructions, how to feed oxen, cows, and sheep, to much greater profit, than has ever yet been known in England. By a country gentleman.
112 pp. Dublin, George Faulkner, and Peter Wilson, 1755

N., Q.

239 Observations on the conduct of messrs. W...cks [Willcocks] and D...n [Dawson], late bankers of the city of Dublin, towards Mr. R...d B...r [Richard Brewer] their cashier.
8 pp. Dublin, J. Samuel, [1755]

A., N.

240 Observations on the linen manufacture of Ireland. By J...n G...ne, esq.
30 pp. Dublin, George Faulkner, 1755

K.

241 Omer, Thomas. Mr. Omer's letter to the public. [sic] Comptroller of the inland navigation.
16 pp. Dublin, 1755

A., K., N., Q., U.

p. 4 has another title: 'A few observations on Mr. Omer's letter.'

242 Peters, Matthew. A reply to some assertions published in a pamphlet, entitled, the schemes for inland navigation from Dublin to the Shannon.
16 pp. Dublin, 1755

A.

243 Petty, Sir William. Several essays in political arithmetick. The fourth edition, corrected. To which are prefixed memoirs of the author's life.
tables. 194 pp. London, D. Browne; J. Shuckburgh [etc.] 1755

U.

244 Policy & justice: an essay. Being a proposal for augmenting the power, & wealth of Great Britain, by uniting Ireland.
50 pp. Dublin, 1755

A., L., N., T.

245 Remarks on the conduct of Messrs. W...cks [Willcocks] and D...n [Dawson], late bankers of the city of Dublin, and Mr. R...d B...r [Richard Brewer] their cashier. By a country gentleman.
60 pp. Dublin, printed by G. Harrison [1755]

A., N.

246 Remarks on a late pamphlet, entituled, the case of the Roman catholics of Ireland. By a protestant.
54 pp. Dublin, booksellers in Dame-Street, 1755

A., G., N.

247 The schemes for inland navigation from Dublin to the Shannon, submitted to the consideration of the public.
12 pp. Dublin, William Smith, 1755

K.

248 Seasonable advice to the friends of Ireland, on the present crisis of affairs.
24 pp. Dublin, 1755

A., K., N., Q., T.

249 SHARP, R. A letter to the people of Ireland; on the present state of the kingdom. Relative to the banks, etc.
12 pp. Dublin, 1755

A., T.

250 A short and easy method of establishing paper credit on a solid foundation by means of a national land-bank.
8 pp. Dublin, George Faulkner, 1755

K.

251 Some thoughts on the interest of money in general, and particularly in the publick funds. With reasons for fixing the same at a lower rate, in both instances, with regard especially to the landholders.
116 pp. London, J. Roberts, [1755?]

Q.

252 To all the good people of Ireland. Friendly and seasonable advice.
8 pp. n.p. [1755?]

A., G.

253 [TUCKER, Josiah.] Reflections on the expediency of opening the trade to Turky. [sic] New edition, with an appendix. By a sincere well-wisher to the trade and prosperity of Great Britain.
32 pp. London, T. Trye, 1755

Q.

254 A vindication of the ministerial conduct of his grace the duke of Dorset in Ireland. By a servant of the crown in that kingdom.
22 pp. London, printed by M. Griffiths, 1755

A., G., N., Q., T.

255 WHYTE, Michael. An inquiry into the causes of our want of tillage in Ireland, with some hints for establishing a yeomanry.
30 pp. Dublin, the author, 1755

A., N., Q.

1756

256 An account of the life, character and parliamentary conduct of the right honourable Henry Boyle, esq; speaker of the honourable house of commons, one of his majesty's most honourable privy council, and twelve times sworn one of the Lords justices of Ireland. Dedicated to his grace the duke of Dorset, with a curious dedication to whom it may concern: to which is added a general answer to the pamphlet intitled Moderation recommended to the friends of Ireland, whether of the court or country party, in a letter to the public. Printed from the London edition, which underwent five impressions in six weeks; containing valuable materials and additions never before printed in this kingdom.
48 pp. Dublin, printed by G. Harrison, [1756?]

G.

257 The Acts of that short session of parliament held in Dublin, May 7, 1689, under the late King James II. Which more fully discover the genius, interests, views, etc. of the then sitting members than any thing hitherto taken notice of by the historians of that time. To which is prefixed, the speech of the late K. James II, at the opening of the said session. The whole taken from authentic MSS. & published for the entertainment of the curious.
84 pp. Dublin, Michael North, 1756

A.

258 A bill for the better ordering of the militia forces in the several counties of that part of Great Britain called England. Absolutely necessary to be perused by all people at this juncture.
48 pp. London, David Hookham, [1756?]

Q.

259 BRISTOW, Rev. —— Modern observations on antient history, chap. 2. On secret agreements.
24 pp. n.p. 1756

A., G., K., Q.

This and the subsequent chapters are concerned with Irish affairs.

260 ——. Modern observations on antient history, chap. 3. Of public spirit.
16 pp. n.p. 1756

A., G., K., Q.

261 ——. Modern observations on antient history, chap. 4. On popularity.
22 pp. n.p. 1756

A., G., K., Q.

262 ——. Modern observations on antient history, chap. 5. On Platonic love.
22 pp. n.p. 1756

A., G., K., Q.

263 ——. Modern observations on antient history, chap. 6. On the love of our country, with index.
56 pp. n.p. 1756

A., G., K., Q.

264 The conduct of the ministry impartially examined in a letter to the merchants of London. In which amongst other things, the arguments made use of, in two pamphlets lately published, entitled 'A letter', and 'An appeal to the people of England', in defence of Admiral Byng, are answered, and the sophistry of those performances fully confuted.
tables. 48 pp. Dublin, A. Bradley, J. Exshaw, [etc.] 1756
A., N., Q., U.

265 Considerations on the utility and necessity of a marine in every trading country. To which is annexed a new scheme for augmenting the royal navy of Great Britain: with a plan of operation in time of war with France.
22 pp. London, M. Hunt, 1756
T.

266 The crisis.
48 pp. Dublin, Peter Wilson, 1756
A.

267 DECKER, Sir Mathew, bart. Serious considerations on the several high duties which the nation in general (as well as its trade in particular) labours under: with a proposal for preventing the running of goods, discharging the trader from any search, and raising all the public supplies, by one single tax.
32 pp. 7th ed. London, Johnson, Davey and Law, 1756
A., T.

268 A description of the rival lines for an inland navigation from Dublin to the Shannon, with some remarks upon them.
8 pp. Dublin, 1756
A., N., Q.

269 ELLWOOD, Thomas. An appendix, giving an account of tithes in general.
78 pp. Dublin, Jackson, 1756
P.
See 293.

270 An essay on the present state of our public roads; shewing the absolute necessity of a total prohibition of the use of narrow wheels, on all carriages drawn by more than one horse lengthways, and the benefit that will accrue thereby to farmers and carriers, to trade and manufactures, as well as ease, pleasure and safety to travellers.
sketch. 38 pp. London, R. Baldwin, 1756
T.

271 An essay towards a method of speedily manning a fleet upon any sudden emergency.
46 pp. Dublin, reprinted by Richard James, 1756
A.

272 The expediency of giving the civil bill to the city of Dublin.
40 pp. Dublin, printed by G. Faulkner, [1756]
G., L., Q.

273 [FAUQUIER, Francis.] An essay on ways and means for raising money for the support of the present war, without increasing the public debts. Inscribed to the right honourable George Lord Anson, first lord commissioner of the admiralty, &c. by F. F.
tables. 68 pp. 2nd ed. London, Cooper, 1756
A., T.

274 [FERGUSON, Adam.] Reflections previous to the establishment of a militia.
56 pp. London, R. and J. Dodsley, 1756
Q.

275 The French king's letter to marshal D'Richlieu, before Fort St. Philip's castle.
16 pp. London printed, Dublin reprinted, 1756
Q.

276 Ireland's deliverance from invasion, by the confession, last speech & dying words of Roadmoney Presentment, esq.; who with many of his relations were tried, condemned & executed, for levying money extorted above & contrary to limitation of law, for his high roads, & sundry high crimes and misdemeanours, at the prosecution of Mr. Statute Labour, the legal officer, April 25, 1756. Thanks to the judges & grand jury at M...gh.
8 pp. Dublin, 1756
A.

277 A letter from a citizen of Port-Royal in Jamaica, to a citizen of New York; relating to some extraordinary measures, lately set on foot in that Island.
16 pp. London, J. Johnson, 1756
Q.

278 A letter from a cobbler to the people of England, on affairs of importance.
18 pp. London, 1756
A.

279 A letter from a member of parliament on the plate-tax.
32 pp. London, J. Scott, 1756
T.

280 A letter from a young gentleman in town, to his friend in the country.
8 pp. Dublin, 1756
K.

281 A letter from the side of the Shannon, to Roger. Concerning the late change of affairs; by a gentleman patriot, & humbly inscribed to all lovers of Ireland.
24 pp. Dublin, printed by Honest Blunt, 1756
A., G., N.

282 Letter to a friend in the country concerning the Work-House.
8 pp. [No t.p.,] [1756?]
N.

283 LITLE, Joseph. To the right honourable John, earl of Rothes as general in chief of his majesty's forces in Ireland. The case of Joseph Litle, late manager at the side of the dragoons and infantry of the kingdom of Ireland. Is most humbly inscribed to your lordship. And humbly submitted to the lieutenants, cornets and quartermasters and dragoons; as also to the captains, subalterns and foot soldiers of the kingdom of Ireland. Whereunto is adjoined, considerations offered for the provision of the children of soldiers, whose ancestors die or are called away in their country's service; with remarks to the field-officers, etc. and militia of this kingdom.
16 pp. Dublin, the author, 1756
A.

284 LUCAS, Charles. An appeal to the commons & citizens of London. By Charles Lucas, the last free citizen of Dublin. 104 pp. London, 1756

A., G., L., N.

285 ——. Charles Lucas's prophecy, concerning the mock-patriots of Ireland; humbly addressed to the free-citizens of the city of Dublin.
8 pp. London, 1756

A., G., N.

286 [MASSIE, Joseph.] Calculations of taxes for a family of each rank, degree, or class: for one year.
tables. 46 pp. London, Thomas Payne, 1756

T.

287 ——. Observations on Mr. Fauquier's 'Essay on ways and means for raising money for the support of the present war without increasing the public debts.' To which is added, an account of several national advantages derived from the nobility and gentry of the present age living in London a greater part of the year than their ancestors used to do. by J. M.
70 pp. London, Payne, 1756

A., T.

288 A new scheme for increasing the protestant religion and improving the kingdom of Ireland. With some occasional observations on heads of a bill for a register of popish priests.
48 pp. Dublin, 1756

A., Q.

289 Observations on a pamphlet lately published, entitled, 'A description of the rival lines for inland navigation', etc.
24 pp. Dublin, Smith, 1756

A., N.

290 Observations on the embargo lately laid on the exports of beef, pork and butter, from Ireland.
26 pp. London, Griffiths, 1756

N.

291 PARISOT, Peter. The humble representation of Peter Parisot of Lorrain, to the English nation, concerning the new establishment of arts and manufactures, formed under his direction, by the order, and through the generosity of, the royal family, and the first nobility of the kingdom; and afterwards supported at his own expense. Containing a brief account of this establishment, its rise in 1750, to December 20, 1755. In French and English.
72 pp. London, printed by Woodfall, 1756

T.

292 PEARSON, Anthony. The great case of tithes truly stated, clearly open'd, and fully resolv'd.
appendix. 146 pp. Dublin, Isaac Jackson, 1756

A., K., N.

This was first published in 1657.

293 —— and ELLWOOD, Thomas. A premonition to the reader on the great case of tithes truly stated, clearly open'd, and fully resolv'd. With an appendix giving an account of tithes in general. By Thomas Ellwood.
94 pp. Dublin, Isaac Jackson, 1756

P.

See 269.

294 The question of previous consent discussed. By a gentleman of the bar.
52 pp. Dublin, printed by Matt. Williamson, 1756

A., G., K., N., Q., T.

295 Reasons for an agent in England to take care of the interest of Ireland in the parliament of England, in a letter to a member of parliament.
24 pp. Dublin, – S. Price –, 1756

T.

296 Reasons why the canal for the inland navigation, from the Shannon to Dublin, should be cut thro' the Bog of Allen, rather than any part of the kingdom.
10 pp. Dublin, printed by W. Sleater, 1756

N., Q.

297 Remarks on the first and second chapter of a late work, intitled 'Modern observations on antient history', being a candid inquiry into the nature and tendency of occasional writings on fictitious conjunctures; to serve for an explanation where it may be wanted.
16 pp. Dublin, 1756

G.

298 [SHEBBEARE, John.] Three letters to the people of England. Letter I on the present situation and conduct of national affairs. Letter II on foreign subsidies, subsidiary armies and their consequence to the nation. Letter III on liberty, taxes and the application of public money.
96 pp. London, 1756

G., T.

——. 100 pp. 6th ed. London, 1756

A., K., N., Q., T.

299 [——.] A fourth letter to the people of England, on the conduct of the m...rs, in alliances, fleets, and armies, since the first differences on the Ohio, to the taking of Minorca by the French. To which are added numbers LII and LIII of the Monitor, applicable to the letter.
88 pp. 6th ed. London, M. Collier, 1756

G., K., Q., T.

300 [——.] A fifth letter to the people of England. On m...l influence. And management of national treasure.
32 pp. London, 1756

A., G., K.

301 Some queries relative to the present state of popery in Ireland.
16 pp. Dublin, 1756

A., N., Q.

——. 16 pp., 2nd ed., Dublin, 1756

A.

302 The speech of a patriot prince: or, a Christmas-box for the publick.
24 pp. London, printed by J. H., 1756

A., N.

303 A sixth letter to the people of England. On the love of our country.
30 pp. London, 1756

A., N.

304 A seventh letter to the people of England. On annual parliaments, public addresses, a general militia, and the danger of foreign mercenaries.
36 pp. London, 1756

A., N., Q.

305 The trial of Roger, for the murder of Lady Betty Ireland, late of Medals-town, in the county of Bogland, on Wednesday the 23rd of March, 1756.
16 pp. Dublin, 1756

Q.

——. 16 pp. 2nd ed. Dublin, 1756

G., K.

306 A vindication of the case of the corporation of Bakers; in answer to a memorial presented by the masters of some other corporations, to the right honourable the lord mayor, and also containing observations on an essay made by his lordship. By a Baker.
32 pp. Dublin, printed by Alex. M'Culloh, 1756

G., K., N., Q.

1757

307 An alarm to the people of England; shewing their rights, liberties, & properties, to be in the utmost danger from the present destructive, and unconstitutional association, for the preservation of the game all over England, which is proved to be illegal. With a list of the associators.
50 pp. London, J. Scott, 1757

A.

308 [ARBUCKLE, James?] A letter from a citizen of Dublin, to a member of parliament. Containing a political scheme for the relief of the poor of Ireland; for easing the nation of beggars, and other burthensome members; and for increasing the commerce and strength of his majesty's dominions, particularly the British colonies, in North America.
40 pp. Dublin, printed by S. Powell, 1757

A., T.

sgd. p. 40, 'Hibernicus'.

309 BAKER, John Wynn. A short description and list, with the prices of the instruments of husbandry, made in the factory at Laughlinstown, near Celbridge.
32 pp. Dublin, printed by S. Powell, for the author, 1757

Q.

310 The case of Richard Toler, esq.; late surveyor, of the Cove of Cork.
40 pp. London, 1757

A.

311 Collections of cases, memorials, addresses and proceedings in parliament, relating to insolvent debtors, customs and excises, Admiralty-courts, and valuable liberties of citizens—to which are added, observations on the embargo in Ireland.
190 pp. Dublin, R. Griffiths, 1757

Q.

312 Considerations on the case of the bakers in Dublin.

First published in the year 1751 and now reprinted with amendments and large additions, and a proposal for a new table of assize.
tables. 70 pp. Dublin, G. and A. Ewing, 1757

A., K., L., N., Q., T.

313 [COSTELLO, Edmund.] A proposal for the better supplying the city of Dublin, with corn and flour; being, heads of a bill intended to be laid before the parliament, at their next meeting.
14 pp. Dublin, Richard Watts, 1757

A.

314 An essay on the expediency of a national militia. With proposals for raising and supporting a military force sufficient for our security at home: to be furnished by the several counties, after the manner of militia, and continually employed in the service of the public, without any additional expence to the subject.
52 pp. London, R. Griffiths, 1757

A.

315 A fifth letter, by the author of four former letters to the people of England; in which some new lights are thrown on particular affairs; & contains an answer to a court pamphlet, intitled, the conduct of the ministry impartially examined. Also, a letter, showing the reasons of the misconduct and miscarriages of the navy.
96 pp. London, M. Collier, 1757

A.

316 [HARRIS, Joseph.] An essay upon money and coins. Part I. The theories of commerce, money, and exchanges.
136 pp. London, G. Hawkins, 1757

T.

See 352.

317 [HELLEN, Robert.] Letters from an Armenian in Ireland, to his friends at Trebisond, etc. Translated in the year 1756.
124 pp. London, 1757

K., L.

——. Another issue, 250 pp. London, 1757

G.

Attributed also to Edmund Sexton Pery and to Francis Andrews.

318 HOME, Francis. The principles of agriculture and vegetation.
188 pp. Edinburgh, G. Hamilton and J. Balfour, 1757

Q.

319 A letter from a gentleman in the city, to a member of parliament in the north of Ireland.
14 pp. n.p., 1757

A., D., G., K., N.

320 A letter from a merchant of the city of London to the rt. hon. W[illiam] P[itt] esq., upon the affairs and commerce of North America, and the West Indies; our African trade; the destination of our squadrons and convoys; new taxes, and the schemes proposed for raising the extraordinary supplies for the current year.
tables 98 pp. 2nd ed., London, Scott, 1757

A.

321 A letter to his gr...e the d...e of B...d, l...d l...t of Ir...d.
44 pp. London, 1757

A.

——. 44 pp. 2nd ed. London, 1757

A., N., Q.

322 A letter to the publick, concerning bogs.
32 pp. Dublin, G. & A. Ewing, 1757

A., D., K., N.

323 MASSIE, Joseph. The proposal, commonly called Sir Matthew Decker's scheme, for one general tax upon houses, laid open; and shewed to be a deep concerted project to traduce the wisdom of the legislature; disquiet the minds of the people; and ruin the trade and manufactures of Great Britain.
two folding tables. 124 pp. London, J. Shuckburgh, 1757

T.

324 MAULE, Henry, bishop of Dromore: God's goodness visible in our deliverance from popery. With some fit methods to prevent the further growth of it in Ireland. In a sermon preached at Christ Church, Dublin, 1733. (Also) A brief account of the proceedings of the incorporated society in Dublin for protecting and promoting English protestant schools in Ireland. To which is prefixed, an abstract of his majesty's royal charter.
108 pp. 6th ed. Dublin, Samuel Price, 1757

N., Q.

325 Maxims relative to the present state of Ireland, 1757. Humbly submitted to the consideration of the legislative powers.
24 pp. Dublin, 1757

A., K., N.

326 Memoirs concerning the city of Dublin, in 1755 and 56.
46 pp., n.p., 1757

A.

327 [MORGAN, Maurice.] An enquiry concerning the nature and end of a national militia. Wherein, from first principles and a short review of our present condition both at home and abroad is deduced the practicability and immediate necessity of such an establishment.
61 pp. London, R. & J. Dodsley, [1757?]

A.

328 MORRIS, Corbyn. A letter balancing the causes of the present scarcity of our silver coin, and the means of immediate remedy, and future prevention of this evil. Addressed to the right honourable the earl of Powis.
20 pp. London, 1757

A.

329 Northern revolutions: or, The principal causes of the declension and dissolution of several once flourishing Gothic constitutions in Europe. From the ghost of Trenchard.
100 pp. Dublin, L. Finn, 1757

Q.

330 The practice of the court of admiralty in England and Ireland. To this edition is added, an act of parliament for the encouragement of seamen, etc. Made in the XXIXth year of the reign of his present majesty. Together with the proclamation for the distribution of prizes: which regulates the practice in the crown & prize causes; also articles relative to perquisites. Necessary for all practitioners, merchants, insurers, seamen, & others that may have any business in the court of admiralty.
130 pp. Dublin, Richard Watts, 1757

A.

331 Premiums offered by the society, instituted at London, for the encouragement of arts, manufactures, and commerce.
appendix, various paging, 10 pp. London: printed by order of the society by W. Adlard, 1757

K.

332 A proposal for lessening the excessive price of bread corn in Ireland.
36 pp. 3rd ed. Dublin, Sam Price, 1757

A., N., T.

333 Proposals for uniting the English colonies on the continent of America so as to enable them to act with force and vigour against their enemies.
46 pp. London, Wilkie, 1757

A.

334 The protestant interest: considered relatively to the operation of the Popery-acts in Ireland.
64 pp. Dublin, 1757

A., Q.

335 ROBINSON, Bryan. An essay on coin.
tables, appendix. 112 pp. Dublin, G. and A. Ewing, 1757

G., K.

336 [ROBINSON Christopher.] The case of the exclusive liberty claimed by the dean and chapter of St. Patricks, Dublin stated for publick consideration.
22 pp. Dublin, 1757

K., Q.

337 Serious thoughts concerning the true interest and exigencies of the state of Ireland in a letter humbly addressed to his grace the d... of B...d.
60 pp. Dublin, 1757

G., K., Q., U.

338 Some proceedings of the Freeholder's-society, now collected and re-published at their desire. Together with some further queries from that society, never published before.
28 pp. Dublin, printed by Matthew Williamson, 1757

G., Q.

339 [STEPHENSON, Robert.] An inquiry into the state and progress of the linen manufacture of Ireland. In which will be introduced remarks on the principal transactions of the trustees of the linen board. To be published monthly.
208 pp. Dublin, S. Powell, 1757

A., K., L., N., Q.

Published in three parts.

340 TUCKER, Josiah. A brief essay on the advantages and disadvantages which respectively attend France and Great Britain, with regard to trade. With some proposals for

removing the principal disadvantages of Great Britain. In a new method.
tables. 124 pp. 3rd ed. Dublin, printed by George Faulkner, 1757

A., K., P., Q., T.

See 25, 136 and 465.

341 WELDON, Walter. Hints for erecting county granaries in this kingdom, as the sure means to lower the exorbitant price of corn at the latter end of the year; to preserve a sufficiency for homeward consumption, to the great relief of the poor, and the preservation of all our manufactures.
36 pp. Dublin, William Sleater, 1757

A., N.

1758

342 An address to the people of Ireland, on the present state of public affairs, and their constitutional rights.
20 pp. Dublin, 1758

A., K.

343 BAILEY, William. A treatise on the better employment, and more comfortable support, of the poor in workhouses. Together with some observations on the growth and culture of flax, with divers new inventions neatly engraved on copper, for the improvement of the linen manufacture, of which the importance and advantages are considered and evinced.
plates and tables. 94 pp. London, R. & J. Dodsley, 1758

Q.

344 [BIZOTT, Dr.?] The true interest and exigencies of the state of Ireland. In a letter to his grace the d... of B...d.
60 pp. Dublin, 1758

A.

——. 60 pp. 2nd ed. Dublin, 1758

T.

345 [BROWN, John, vicar of Newcastle.] An explanatory defence of the Estimate of the manners and principles of the times, being an appendix to that work, occasioned by the clamours lately raised against it among certain ranks of men. Written by the author of the Estimate in a series of letters to a noble friend.
86 pp. London, L. Davies and C. Reymers, 1758

Q.

346 CALLAN, Peter. A dissertation on the practice of land-surveying in Ireland, and an essay towards a general regulation therein. In two parts.
48 pp. Drogheda, 1758

N., Q.

347 The case of the five millions, fairly stated. In regard to taxes, law, lawyers, etc. Addressed to the guardians of our liberty.
34 pp. London, John Millan, 1758

K.

348 Considerations on the effects which the bounties granted on exported corn, malt, and flour, have on the manufactures of the kingdom, and the true interests of the state, with a postscript, containing remarks on a pamphlet lately published, intituled, 'Thoughts on the causes and consequences of the present high price of provisions.'
112 pp. London, T. Cadell, 1758

Q.

349 [COX, Sir Richard?] Ireland disgraced, or the island of saints become an island of sinners; clearly proved in a dialogue between doctor B-tt and doctor B-ne, in Dublin.
86 pp. London, S. Hooper and A. Morley, 1758

A.

350 A farewell to the duke of B...d. An extract from a letter to a noble lord in England.
16 pp. London printed and Dublin re-printed, 1758

A., N., Q.

351 [GRATTAN, James.] The recorder's second letter to the gentry, clergy, freemen & free holders, of the city of Dublin.
16 pp. Dublin, G. Faulkner & P. Wilson, 1758

A., T.

352 [HARRIS, Joseph.] An essay upon money and coins. Part II. Wherein is shewed that the established standard of money should not be violated or altered, under any pretence whatsoever.
table of contents, table. 144 pp. London, Hawkins, 1758

A., T.

See 316.

353 A letter to the people of Ireland, on the subject of tythes. By a friend to the constitution.
20 pp. Dublin, S. Powell, 1758

A., L., N., P., Q.

354 The management of the revenue; with queries relative thereto.
36 pp. Dublin, 1758

A., K., N., T.

355 The management of the revenue with queries relative thereto.
18 pp. Dublin, 1758

U.

356 [MASON, I. M.?] Remarks upon Poynings law and the manner of passing bills in the p...t of I...d. By a gentleman of Ireland.
48 pp. Dublin, 1758

Q.

357 MASSIE, J. (ed.) Orders appointed by his majestie (King Charles I) to be straitly observed, for the preventing and remedying of the dearth of graine and victuall: with his majesties proclamation, declaring his royal pleasure and further commandment therein.
32 pp. London, Payne, 1758

A.

358 The present constitution of the city of Dublin, addressed to the citizens of Dublin. By a citizen.
20 pp. Dublin, printed by S. Powell, 1758

G., K., N., Q.

359 Rules and orders of the society, established at London, for the encouragement of arts, manufactures and commerce. 24 pp. London, printed by order of the society, 1758

K., Q.

360 A second letter to the people of Ireland, on the subject of tythes. With a particular address to the dissenters. To which is added, a state of the case of the inhabitants of the province of Ulster, in relation to the demands of the clergy. By a friend to the constitution. appendix. 36 pp. Dublin, S. Powell, 1758

A., N., P., Q.

361 Serious thoughts concerning the true interest and exigencies of the state of Ireland. In a letter humbly addressed to his grace the d... of B...d. 60 pp, Dublin, 1758

A., N.

362 [SMITH, Charles.] A short essay on the corn trade and the corn laws. Containing a general relation of the present method of carrying on the corn trade and the purport of the laws relating thereto in this kingdom. 60 pp. London, 1758

Q.

363 Some hints for the advancement of tillage, and for supplying the city of Dublin with coals constantly at a moderate price. Humbly inscribed to the right honourable Hercules Langford Rowley, esq. 40 pp. Dublin, W. Sleater, 1758

L.

364 Some thoughts on the general improvement of Ireland with a scheme of a society for carrying on all improvements, in a more extensive and effectual manner than has hitherto been done. Humbly submitted to the consideration of the rt. hon. and hon. the lords and commons in parliament assembled. 50 pp. Dublin, S. Powell, 1758

A., N., Q.

365 Some thoughts on the present state of our trade to India, with a dedication, humbly addressed to the freeholders of Great Britain. By a merchant of London. tables. 46 pp. 2nd. ed. London, Brotherton, 1758

N.

366 A third letter to the people of Ireland, on the subject of tythes. Wherein the farmers complaints, and other objections against them, are particularly considered. By a friend to the constitution. 20 pp. Dublin, S. Powell, 1758

A., N., P., Q., T.

367 A treatise on the inland navigation of the ancients and moderns. 40 pp. Dublin, John Smith, 1758

A., K.

368 TUCKER, Josiah. Instructions for travellers. 96 pp. Dublin, William Watson, 1758

A., K., N., Q.

369 [WALLACE, Robert.] Characteristics of the present political state of Great Britain. 154 pp. Dublin, L. Flin, 1758

A., K., T.

1759

370 Advice to the patriots of the Coomb, the liberties, and the suburbs of Dublin, lately assembled in parliament. Of whatever trade, sex, or denomination. By a faithful Irishman. 14 pp. Dublin, 1759

A.

371 [BROOKE, Henry?] An essay on the antient and modern state of Ireland with the various important advantages thereunto derived under the auspicious reign of his most sacred majesty, King George II. 104 pp. Dublin, P. Lord, 1759

A., K., N.

372 ——. The interests of Ireland considered, stated and recommended particularly with respect to inland navigation. plan. 168 pp. Dublin, Geo. Faulkner, 1759

G.

373 ——. Supplement to the interests of Ireland. A proposal for raising an annual fund, to be appropriated to inland navigation, from a tax upon dogs. 12 pp. Dublin, printed by George Faulkner, 1759

Q.

374 CANTILLON, Philip. The analysis of trade, commerce, coin, bullion, banks and foreign exchanges. Wherein the true principles of this useful knowledge are fully but briefly laid down and explained, to give a clear idea of their happy consequences to society when well regulated. Taken chiefly from a manuscript of a very ingenious gentleman deceased, and adapted to the present situation of our trade and commerce. 240 pp. London, the author, 1759

Q.

This is in fact by Richard Cantillon: cf. Jevons: *Richard Cantillon and the nationality of political economy*, reprinted in Higgs' edition of Cantillon (1931) pp. 333–339.

375 The clothier's letter to the inhabitants of the liberties. 16 pp. Dublin, 1759

A., K., N.

376 The conduct of messrs. Daniel Mussenden, James Adair, & Thomas Bateson & the other managers of the Belfast charitable scheme, impartially examined. 40 pp. n.p. 1759

A., N.

377 Considerations on the present scarcity of silver coins, etc. 40 pp. London, 1759

A.

378 Cox, Sir Richard, bart. A letter from Sir Richard Cox, bart. to the high-sheriff of the county of Cork. Relative to the present state of the linen-manufacture in that county; and further means of improving it. 44 pp. Dublin, Peter Wilson, 1759

A., K.

379 DUNKIN, William. An epistle to the right honourable Philip earl of Chesterfield. To which are added Lawson's obsequies: an eclogue.
60 pp. Dublin, George Faulkner, 1759
L.

380 HOME, Francis. The principles of agriculture and vegetation.
216 pp. 2nd ed. London, and Edinburgh. A. Miller, A. Kincaid and J. Bell, 1759
Q.

——. 104 pp. 3rd ed. Dublin, G. & A. Ewing, 1759
A.

381 A letter to the inhabitants of Dublin, and the liberty. By T. B. Journeyman Weaver.
8 pp. Dublin, 1759
A.

382 A plea for the poor: in which I. Their inexpressible hardships and sufferings are verified from undeniable facts. II. Their maintenance is evidently shewn to be an intolerable burthen upon the public. III. Methods are proposed for making beggars, vagrants, and vagabonds useful to their country, and providing for the impotent and disabled. IV. A summary is given of the several schemes of judge Hale, Sir Josiah Child, Mr. Fielding, and others, for that purpose. Humbly submitted to the consideration of parliament. By a merchant of the city of London.
60 pp. London, J. Townsend, 1759
K.

383 Populousness with oeconomy, the wealth and strength of a kingdom. Most humbly addressed to both houses of parliament, in behalf of the poor.
table. 36 pp. London, J. Buckland, 1759
K.

384 Some considerations on the present methods, used for the relief and employment of the poor. In a letter to a member of parliament.
40 pp. London, 1759
K.

385 Some thoughts on lowering the water of Lough Neagh, and other great lakes in Ireland. Without prejudice to their navigation or fisheries.
32 pp. Dublin, printed by Powell, 1759
A., N.
See 193.

386 Some thoughts on the nature of paper-credit, relative to the late failures of bankers and receivers in Ireland. By a free citizen.
24 pp. Dublin, 1759
A., G., K., N., T.
See 438.

387 STEPHENSON, Robert. A letter to the right honourable and honourable the trustees of the linen manufacture.
tables. 24 pp. Dublin, printed by James Hunter, 1759
A., L., N., Q.

388 Thoughts on the pernicious consequences of borrowing money: with a proposal for raising a supply for the current service. And also for taking off part of our present load of taxes. To which are added some estimates to shew the advantages that would arise from an equal land-tax. And also, a method proposed, for discharging the national debt.
tables. 40 pp. 2nd ed. London, Payne, 1759
N.

1760

389 An account of certain proceedings and depositions relative to the case of squire Pam. From the notes and observations of William Singleton, parish clerk. And published by order of the parish clerks of the city of Dublin.
28 pp. Dublin, 1760
A.

——. 28 pp. 2nd ed. Dublin, 1760
A., G.

390 An answer to a pamphlet intitled Previous promises inconsistent with a free parliament.
16 pp. Dublin, printed by James Hunter, 1760
A., K.

391 [BROOKE, Henry.] The case of the Roman catholics of Ireland. In a course of letters from a member of the protestant church, in that kingdom, to his friend in England. Letter 1.
22 pp. Dublin, Pat. Lord, 1760
A., Q.

392 [——.] The case of the Roman catholics of Ireland in a course of letters from a member of the protestant church, in that kingdom to his friend in England. Letter II: The famous case of the R.C's in Ireland.
22 pp. Dublin, Pat. Lord, 1760
Q.

393 [——?] An essay on the antient & modern state of Ireland, with the various important advantages thereunto derived, under the auspicious reign of his most sacred majesty King George the second. Including a particular account of the great & glorious St. Patrick.
80 pp. London [etc.], R. Griffiths, 1760
A.

394 ——. The farmer's case of the Roman catholics of Ireland. In a course of letters from a member of the protestant church in that kingdom, to his friend in England. Wherein the popery-laws are considered, and arguments drawn to shew how far they are prejudicial to the protestant interest in particular, as well as that of the nation in general, and that the reason and motives, which gave rise to those laws, no longer subsist. Letter II.
24 pp. Dublin, Pat. Lord, 1760
A.

395 ——. The farmer's case of the Roman catholics of Ireland. In a course of letters . . . Letter III.
22 pp. Dublin, Pat. Lord, 1760
A.

396 ——. The farmer's case of the Roman catholics of Ireland. In a course of letters . . . Letter IV.
20 pp. Dublin, Pat. Lord, 1760.
A.

397 A comment on a late extraordinary letter from the e. of C... to the d. of B... lately handed about in London; in which an Union between the two kingdoms is impartially considered. By a nobleman.
26 pp. London, 1760

A., N., Q., T.

398 A comparative view of the nominal value of the silver coin in England & France, and of their influence on the manufactures & commerce of each respective kingdom.
22 pp. London, J. Burd, 1760

A., K.

399 Considerations on the present calamities of this kingdom; and the causes of the decay of public credit with the means of restoring it.
18 pp. Dublin, 1760

A., K., N., Q.

400 A course of experiments and improvements in agriculture, made by a person who lately occupied many hundred acres of land of all sorts; now published by him, for the use of country gentlemen.
118 pp. Dublin, printed by James Hoey, 1760

A.

401 Cox, Sir Richard, bart. The case of Edward lord bishop of Elphin, in relation to money, part of the rents of the Ranelagh charity, lodged in a public bank in Dublin. With notes, critical and explanatory, by Sir Richard Cox, bart.
16 pp. Dublin, Peter Wilson, 1760

A., N., Q.

402 ——. Previous promises inconsistent with a free parliament and an ample vindication of the last parliament.
50 pp. Dublin, P. Wilson, 1760

A., G., N., Q.

403 [DAWSON, Thomas?] A letter to the author of a pamphlet entitled some thoughts on the nature of paper credit. By Publicola.
24 pp. Dublin, 1760

A., K., Q.

404 [——.] Reasons for and against lowering the gold and silver of this kingdom: or rather to estimate all gold and silver here at the price of bullion, as we have no mint: The silver is to be the rule or standard of gold, as 1 to 15, that is 15 ounces of silver to constitute the value of 1 ounce of gold: The silver at 5s. 4d. and the gold at £3 18s. 6d. per ounce English; which was the average price of both, at a medium, these ten years last past.
In three letters directed to J. P. J. and one letter to a friend. And humbly inscribed and dedicated to Hely Hutchinson, esq. the darling of the people, by his most obedient humble servant, Publicola.
34 pp. Dublin, 1760

A., Q.

405 ——. Reasons for and against lowering the gold and silver of this kingdom: or rather to estimate all gold and silver here at the price of bullion, as we have no mint: the silver to be the rule or standard of gold, as 1 to 15; that is, 15 ounces of silver to constitute the value of 1 ounce of gold: The silver at 5s. 4d. and the gold at 3l. 18s. 6d. per ounce, English; which was the average-price of both, at a medium, these ten years past. Part II.
16 pp. Dublin, 1760

Q.

406 The draper's ghost's answer to the clothier's letter.
16 pp. Dublin, 1760

A., Q.

407 [EYRE, Thomas.] A reply to the report of the commissioners and others, upon the condition of the Dublin barracks.
16 pp. Dublin, 1760

A., G., Q.

408 [FRANKLIN, Benjamin.] The interest of Great Britain considered, with regard to her colonies, and the acquisition of Canada and Guadeloupe. To which are added, observations concerning the increase of mankind, peopling of countries, etc.
tables, appendix. 46 pp. Dublin, P. Wilson and J. Potts, 1760

A., K., T.

——. 46 pp. 2nd ed. London, T. Becket, 1760

K.

409 [GRATTAN, James.] A letter to a member of the honourable house of commons of Ireland.
24 pp. Dublin, Peter Wilson, 1760

A., G., K., N., Q.

410 ——. A second letter to a member of the honourable house of commons of Ireland. Containing a scheme for regulating the corporation of the city of Dublin.
40 pp. Dublin, Peter Wilson, 1760

A., K., Q., T.

411 HENRY, William. A letter to the right honourable John Ponsonby, esq; speaker of the honourable house of commons; concerning the abuse of spirituous liquors.
24 pp. Dublin, Peter Wilson, 1760

A., N., Q.

412 Honest advice to the electors of Ireland, on the present most critical occasion. By a patriot. M.S.
8 pp. Dublin, 1760

G., Q.

413 [LATOUCHE, James Digges.] A short but true history of the rise, progress and happy suppression of several late insurrections commonly called rebellions in Ireland. By a late eminent citizen of Dublin. Well known for his spirited writings and extraordinary attachment to the liberties of this country.
46 pp. London and Dublin, 1760

A., K., N., Q.

414 A letter from a commoner in town, to a noble lord in the country.
32 pp. London, J. Swan, 1760

A., G., K., Q., T.

——. 32 pp. 2nd ed. London, J. Swan, 1760

A., N.

415 A letter from a free citizen in Limerick to his friend in Dublin.
8 pp. Limerick, 1760
A.

416 A letter from a shop-keeper in Dublin, to his grace the duke of Bedford, lord lieutenant of Ireland, etc. On public credit.
20 pp. Dublin, 1760
A., C., K., N.

417 A letter from some of the principal citizens to the aldermen of Dublin.
168 pp. Dublin, 1760
Q.

418 A letter to the people of England on the necessity of putting an immediate end to the war; and the means of obtaining an advantageous peace.
56 pp. Dublin, J. Potts, 1760
A., T.

419 LUCAS, Charles. Seasonable advice to the electors of members of parliament at the ensuing general election. Addressed to the free and independent electors of the kingdom of Ireland in general, to those of the city of Dublin in particular.
32 pp. Dublin, printed by James Hunter, 1760
A., Q.

———. Another issue. 74 pp. London, T. Davies, 1760
A.

420 Lysimachus: or, a dialogue concerning the union of Great-Britain and Ireland.
68 pp. Dublin, G. Faulkner, 1760
A., K., Q.

421 M'CORMICK, Pat. Thunder and lightning!—or the second address of Pat. M'Cormick, attorney at law, to the people of Ireland.
8 pp. Dublin, printed by Cusack Greene, 1760
Q.

422 McDONNELL, Thomas. The eighth commandment considered in its full extent; and particularly, as applicable to the present reigning spirit of gameing: A sermon. Preached in the parish church of St. Ann, Dublin, March the ninth, 1760. Addressed to the right honourable the earl of Shelburne. By the rev. Thomas McDonnell, D.D. late fellow of Trinity College, Dublin.
30 pp. Dublin, 1760
Q.

423 MERCHANT, C. S. Informations to the people of Ireland concerning the linen trade of Spain, Portugal, and the Spanish West Indies. Printed with the allowance and at the expence of the linen board.
16 pp. Dublin, Richard Watts, 1760
A., Q.

424 The new bankers proved bankrupts, in a dialogue between themselves and a free-citizen. With some second thoughts on the nature of paper-credit in Ireland.
24 pp. n.p. 1760
Q.

425 NORTH, Richard. An account of the different kinds of grasses propagated in England, for the improvement of corn and pasture lands, lawns and walks: with many useful directions for sowing them manuring &c. and some remarks upon the perennial red flowering clover and saving hay-seeds from fine meadows. And the best directions for raising turnips, rape cabbage &c., for feeding horses, cattle and sheep, and to save their seeds continually pure from degenerating. Also, an account of the manures, natural and made, how they are used, and the prices they are sold for about town. With directions for trench-plowing.
48 pp. London, W. Prat, [1760]
Q.

426 [NUGENT, Robert.] The act for permitting the free imporation of cattle from Ireland, considered with a view to the interests of both kingdoms.
48 pp. London, Dodsley, 1760
A., K.

427 Observations on, and a short history of, Irish banks and bankers. By a gentleman in trade.
40 pp. Dublin, 1760
A., D., K., N., Q.

428 The pedlar's letter to the bishops and clergy of Ireland.
30 pp. Dublin, 1760
A., K., N.

429 Perpetual supplies for the state; by annuities and reversions: in two numbers of subscribers. I. The full number effecting ample supplies, and a ceasing of the land-tax, window-money, and other unnecessary duties; and raising many spare millions for public utility. II. The half of that full number, effecting as above, except the spare millions, resulting from that double subscription. Either of the two numbers are very easily carried into execution by the legislature and subjects, and both extremely benefited by it; and also unhurtful to any part of the community. With an approximation of five millions yearly, from either number of subscribers, for the discharge of the national debt. To which is prefixed, a preparatory letter referring to the plans.
table, appendix. 56 pp. London, J. Wilkie. 1760
K.

430 A proposal for the restoration of public wealth and credit, in a letter to a truely honourable member of the house of commons.
20 pp. Dublin, printed by Dillon Chamberlaine, 1760
K., Q.

431 Proposals humbly offered to parliament for the restoration of cash and public credit to Ireland.
16 pp. Dublin, G. Faulkner, 1760
A., Q.

———. 16 pp. 2nd ed. Dublin, G. Faulkner, 1760
A., N.

432 The question relative to the petitions of the cities of Dublin & Corke, & the town of Belfast, for a new regulation of the Portugal gold coin. Humbly addressed to the publick, by a citizen of Dublin. To which is added, a letter to the merchants.
22 pp. Dublin, 1760
A., K., N.

433 Remarks on the letter addressed to two great men. In a letter to the author of that piece.
38 pp. Dublin, G. Faulkner, [etc., etc.] 1760
Q.

434 The representation of the L...s J...s of Ireland, touching the transmission of a privy council money-bill previous to the calling of a new parliament. In two letters. Addressed to the duke of Bedford. To which is annexed Mr. Sloane's narrative in defence of the conduct and resolutions of the House of Commons in 1692.
51 pp. Dublin, printed by Milliken, 1760
A.

435 ROBINSON, Christopher. A charge given to the grand juries of the county of the city of Dublin and county of Dublin; at a sitting of his majesty's commissions of Oyer and Terminer, and general gaol delivery for the said counties, on Monday the 15th day of December 1760. By the hon. Christopher Robinson, second justice of his majesty's court of king's bench. Published at the request of the city grand jury.
38 pp. Dublin, George and Alexander Ewing, 1760
G., Q., S., T.

436 [RUFFHEAD, Owen.] Reasons why the approaching treaty of peace should be debated in parliament: as a method most expedient and constitutional. In a letter addressed to a great man. And occasioned by the perusal of a letter addressed to two great men.
44 pp. Dublin, James Hoey, 1760
A.

437 A short address to the electors of the city of Dublin.
16 pp. Dublin, 1760
A.

438 Some thoughts on the nature of paper-credit, relative to the late failures of bankers and receivers in Ireland. By a free-citizen.
24 pp. Dublin, 1760
A., G., N., Q., T.
See 386.

439 STEPHENSON, Robert. A review of part of the schemes proposed at different times, by Robert Stephenson, merchant, to parliament, and the trustees of the linen board, towards extending and improving the linen manufacture of Ireland, distinguishing the periods and success of the scheme for making linen markets in the twenty-five counties.
8 pp. n.p., [1760?]
T.

440 TILSON, James. The multitude of holydays detrimental to the publick, and not advantageous to religion. Being part of the 1st discourse of the 6th volume of Father Feijoo's works, translated from the Spanish, and published with a view to the benefit of Ireland; and addressed to the roman catholic clergy of that kingdom.
20 pp. Dublin, printed by George Faulkner, 1760
A.

441 The true state of the British malt-distillery. Being a defence of Mr. M--wh--y's queries. In which is shewn, the great importance of that trade to the land-holders of Great Britain. And the present dispute between the malt-distiller and sugar-planter is fully opened and explained. In a letter to a member of parliament. By a British freeholder.
tables. 44 pp. London, R. Stevens, 1760
K.

442 Unanswerable arguments against a peace. By a British freeholder.
24 pp. Dublin, S. Smith, 1760
T.

443 VOLTAIRE, François Marie Arouet de. An essay on the age of Lewis XIV. By Mr. De Voltaire. Being his introduction to the work. Translated from the French by Mr. Lockman.
48 pp. 4th ed. Dublin, George Faulkner, 1760
A., Q.

——. 48 pp. 5th ed. Dublin, George Faulkner, 1760
A.

1761

444 An address to the committee of the merchants society.
16 pp. Dublin, 1761
A., G., Q.

445 An answer to the comments on a letter from the e... of Cl...e, to the d... of B...d. With some occasional thoughts upon the remarks relative to an union between the two kingdoms.
24 pp. Dublin, 1761
A., G., Q., T.

446 The benefits of an inland navigation to Ireland. Estimated in a dialogue between a gentleman in the country and a citizen of Dublin, in spring, 1761. Occasioned by the great scarcity of coals then in the city.
27 pp. Dublin, printed by George Faulkner, 1761
A., Q.

447 [CAMPBELL, John.] Memoirs of the revolution in Bengal, anno. dom. 1757. By which Meer Jaffeir was raised to the government of that province, together with those of Bahar & Orixa. Including the motives to this enterprise; the method in which it was accomplished; & the benefits that have accrued from thence to that country, our united company trading to the East Indies, & to the British nation.
88 pp. Dublin, printed by George Faulkner, 1761
A.

448 The compleat city and country brewer. Containing an account, I. of the nature of barley-corn and of the proper soils and manures for the improvement thereof. II. Of making malts. III. To know good from bad malts. IV. Of the use of the pale, amber and brown malts. V. Of the nature of several waters and their use in brewing. VI. Of grinding malts. VII. Of brewing in general. VIII. Of the London method of brewing stout butt beer, pale and brown ales. IX. Of the country or private way of brewing. X. Of the nature and use of the hop. XI. Of boiling malt liquors, and to brew a quantity of drink in a little room, and with a few tubs. XII. Of foxing or tainting of malt liquors, their prevention and cure. XIII. Of fermenting and working of beers and ales, and the unwholesome practice of beating in the yeast detected. XIV. Of

several artificial lees for feeding, fineing preserving and relishing malt liquors. XV. Of several pernicious ingredients put into malt liquors to increase their strength. XVI. Of the cellar or repository for keeping beers and ales. XVII. Of sweetning and cleaning casks. XVIII. Of bunging casks and carrying them to some distance. XIX. Of the age and strength of malt liquors. XX. Of the profit and pleasure of private brewing and the charge of buying malt liquors. To which is added a philosophical account of brewing strong October beer, by an ingenious hand. By a person formerly concerned in a common brewhouse at London, but for near twenty years past has resided in the country. Recommended by the Dublin society.
104 pp. Dublin, Laurence Flin, 1761
G.

449 Considerations on the expediency of a Spanish war: containing reflections on the late demands of Spain; and on the negotiations of Mons. Bussy.
28 pp. Dublin, W. Whitestone & J. Potts, 1761
A., N.

450 [DOUGLAS, John, bishop of Salisbury.] Seasonable hints from an honest man on the present important crisis of a new reign and a new parliament.
48 pp. Dublin, G. and A. Ewing, 1761
A., K., N., Q., T.

451 A full and candid answer to a pamphlet, entitled, considerations on the present German war.
52 pp. Dublin, Faulkner, 1761
Q., T.

452 HITT, Thomas. A treatise of husbandry on the improvement of dry & barren lands. Shewing, I. The many advantages which would arise to the nation in general, by destroying of warrens & converting the lands into tillage, pasture, etc. II. Pointing out new & cheap methods to make growing fences upon the most barren soils, & how to till and manure the same at a low expence. III. How to prepare the land, & raise upon it various sorts of plants, to produce both poles & timber.
fold. diag. 132 pp. Dublin, Richard Watts & William Whitestone, 1761
A., N.

453 [HOWARD, Gorges Edmond.] Queries relative to several defects and grievances in some of the present laws of Ireland, and the proceedings thereon, most humbly offered to the consideration of the gentlemen of the profession, now in parliament. With an appendix containing particularly, a few observations and queries on the several acts of parliament here, against the further growth of popery.
48 pp. Dublin, printed by Oli. Nelson, 1761
A., G., K., N., Q., T.
See also 497.

454 MASSIE, Joseph. Calculations of the present taxes yearly paid by a family of each rank, degree, or class.
tables. 58 pp. 2nd ed. London, T. Payne, W. Owen, C. Henderson, 1761
T.

455 [MAUDUIT, Israel.] Considerations on the present German war.
112 pp. Dublin, printed by George Faulkner, 1761
N., Q., T.

456 [O'CONNER, ——?] The danger of popery to the present government, examined. To which are annexed, queries, relative to the same subject, by Dr. Berkley, bishop of Cloyne.
40 pp. Dublin, printed by George Faulkner, 1761
A.

457 The question about septennial, or, frequent new parliaments, impartially examined in two letters to Charles Lucas, esq; M.D. To which are added, instructions, from a constituent, to a representative.
42 pp. Dublin, 1761
Q.

458 Reasons for a new bridge.
16 pp. Dublin, 1761
A., N., Q.

459 A serious and affectionate call to the electors of Ireland.
8 pp. Dublin, 1761
A., T.

460 A short appeal to common sense, addressed to the citizens of Dublin.
16 pp. n.p. [1761 ?]
A.

461 Some considerations relative to the coal trade in Dublin.
12 pp. Dublin, printed by Geo. Faulkner, 1761
A., Q.

462 Some observations and queries on the present laws of this kingdom, relative to papists. By a true church of England-man.
24 pp. 2nd ed. Dublin, printed by Oli. Nelson, 1761
A., N., K., Q.

463 The speech of a young member of parliament on the debate of the septennial bill.
16 pp. Dublin, 1761
A.

464 The trial of the cause of the roman catholics; on a special commission directed to lord chief justice Reason, lord chief baron Interest, and mr. justice Clemency. Wednesday, August 5th, 1761. Mr. Clodworthy Common-sense, foreman of the jury, Mr. Serjeant Statute, council for the crown, Constantine Candour, esq. council for the accused.
302 pp. Dublin, printed by George Faulkner, 1761
A.

465 TUCKER, Josiah. A brief essay on the advantages and disadvantages which respectively attend France & Great Britain, with regard to trade. With some proposals for removing the principal disadvantages of Great-Britain. In a new method.
116 pp. 3rd ed. tables. Dublin, printed by G. Faulkner, 1761
A.
See 25, 136 and 340.

1762

466 The abuse of standing parliaments, and the great advantage of frequent elections in a letter to a noble lord.
32 pp. London, [1762?]

A., Q.

467 BAKER, John Wynn. Some hints for the better improvement of husbandry and reducing it to a rational and intelligible system. In a letter humbly submitted to the consideration of his excellency the right honorable the earl of Halifax lord lieutenant of Ireland, and president of the Dublin society for the encouragement of husbandry, etc. And the rest of the members of that respectable body.
90 pp. Dublin, Laurence Flin, 1762

A., Q., T.

468 The case of Christopher Byron, late an officer in his majesty's post-office, Dublin. Submitted to the consideration of his friends, & the public.
62 pp. Dublin, 1762

A., G.

469 The case of Ireland in 1762. Submitted to the consideration of the people of that kingdom.
8 pp. n.p., 1762

A.

470 [Cox, Sir Richard, bart.] The present state of his majesty's revenue, compared with that of some late years.
tables. 16 pp. Dublin, Peter Wilson, 1762

A., K., N., Q., T.

471 [DEBAUFRE, Peter.] A scheme by which great advantages are proposed for the government as well as for the people of Great Britain.
10 pp. London, 1762

N.

472 A dialogue between an English nobleman and a gentleman of Middlesex, on the affairs of Ireland; particularly the bill for limitting [sic] the duration of parliaments.
38 pp. Dublin, reprinted from London edition, [1762?]

A., G.

473 An examination of the commercial principles of the late negotiation between Great Britain and France in MDCCLXI. In which the system of that negotiation with regard to our colonies and commerce is considered.
tables, 110 pp. 2nd ed. London, R. and J. Dodsley, 1762

K.

474 A hint for lessening the national debt of Great-Britain.
24 pp. Dublin, Peter Wilson, 1762

A.

475 LONG, John. The golden fleece: or, some thoughts on the cloathing trade of Ireland. With a proposal for its advancement, so far as to supply our own consumption; employ our idle hands; prevent their going for the future into France & Spain for work; & put an entire stop to the clandestine exportation of wool.
40 pp. Dublin, printed by T. Dyton, 1762

A., N., Q.

476 [MACAULAY, Alexander?] Septennial parliaments vindicated; or, freedom against oligarchy.
20 pp. Dublin, 1762

A., N., Q.

477 [NEVILL, Arthur Jones.] Some hints on trade, money & credit: humbly addressed, to the true friends of Ireland.
24 pp. Dublin, 1762

A.

478 Observations on a paper intitled A review of the evils that have prevailed in the linen manufacture of Ireland.
8 pp. Dublin, 1762

A.

479 One more letter to the people of England, by their old friend.
76 pp. London, J. Pridden, 1762

T.

By J. Shebbeare?

480 A review of the evils that have prevailed in the linen manufacture of Ireland.
48 pp. Dublin, Peter Wilson, 1762

Q., T.

481 A review of the evils that have prevailed in the linen manufacture of Ireland. Arising from a neglect of the original laws.
Part II. 50 pp. Belfast, printed by Henry and Robert Joy, 1762

A., Q.

482 A slight review of the transactions of the long parliament, with some observations on the rise and progress of the septennial bill.
40 pp. Dublin, 1762

A., Q.

483 Some additional queries on the present laws in this kingdom, against the further growth of popery and particularly relative to the heads of a bill, which lately passed the house of commons of Ireland.
8 pp. Dublin, printed by Oli. Nelson, 1762

A., Q.

484 Some reasons against raising an army of Roman catholics in Ireland. In a letter to a member of parliament.
16 pp. Dublin, 1762

A., T.

485 STACPOOLE, George. Some short historical anecdotes with remarks relative to Ireland. In four parts. Part I.
94 pp. Corke, printed by Eugene Swiney, 1762

A.

486 STEPHENSON, Robert. The reports and observations of Robert Stephenson made to the right hon. and honourable the trustees of the linen manufacture for the years 1760 and 1761. Distinguishing the state of the spinning and weaving in each county respectively; as also what species of the manufacture they are employed in, the progress of the inhabitants, and how the most immediate and effectual improvements are likely to be obtained, in the several branches thereof throughout the kingdom.
104 pp. By order of the board. Printed by Alex. McCulloh, Dublin, 1762

A., N., Q., T.

487 Sufficient reasons against the naturalizing of foreign protestants: wherein is shewn, the eminent danger to which our religious and civil liberties are exposed by this pernicious and destructive measure: together with some particular observations of the bad effects of that predominancy of foreign interests, which prevail'd in the reigns of King William & Queen Anne; whereby the present affair is eludicated [*sic*] & explained, & entirely expos'd by the force of argument.
26 pp. London, M. Mechell, [1762?]

A.

1763

488 ASTON, Richard. A charge given to the grand juries of the county of the city of Dublin and county of Dublin at a sitting of his majesty's commissions of oyer and terminer, and general gaol delivery for the said counties, on Saturday the 3rd day of December, 1763.
30 pp. Dublin, Sarah Cotter, 1763

K., N., Q.

489 A brief state of the debate concerning the sealing of brown linens, and exposing them to sale in open folds: wherein is contained everything that has been offered to the public against those regulations. Together with answers to the same.
34 pp. Dublin, P. Wilson, 1763

A., T.

490 The charter-party, or articles of agreement of the Concordia-annuity-company of Dublin.
36 pp. Dublin, printed by W. Sleater, 1763

A.

491 Charter-party: or, articles of agreement of the Unanimous annuity-company of Dublin.
36 pp. Dublin, Bradley, 1763

A.

492 Considerations on the fatal effects to a trading nation of the present excess of public charities. In which the Magdalene asylum, foundling hospitals for sick and lame, lying in hospitals, charity schools, and the dissenting fund, are particularly considered, and a plan for a new system of poors laws proposed.
60 pp. London, S. Hooper, 1763

K.

493 Copies of the several memorials presented to the linen-board, by the merchants of Dublin, London, Bristol, Liverpoole and Chester, and different parts of England; concerning the late regulations of the board, and the present design of making a new body of laws, for the better order and regulation of the linen manufacture, of Ireland.
appendix. 26 pp. Dublin, P. Wilson, 1763

A., T.

494 An essay on the means of discharging the public debt; in which the reasons for instituting a national bank, and disposing of the forest-lands, are more fully considered. With a method proposed of raising money to answer the expenses of any future war, without creating new funds. By the author of the proposal for establishing a national bank.
tables. 78 pp. London, Payne, 1763

N.

495 A few hints towards a scheme for employing & decently supporting our forces in this kingdom when a reduction shall take place. Directed to the consideration of every gentleman who may think such a scheme necessary for the honour & security of this kingdom.
8 pp. Dublin, printed by Alex. McCulloh, 1763

A., N.

496 FORSTER, Sir Michael. An examination of the scheme of church-power, laid down in the Codex Iuris Ecclesiastici Anglicani, &c.
118 pp. 5th ed. Dublin, Elizabeth Watts, 1763

K.

497 HOWARD, Gorges Edmond. Queries, relative to several defects and grievances in some of the present laws of Ireland, and the proceedings thereon, most humbly offered to the consideration of the gentlemen of the profession, now in parliament.
48 pp. 3rd ed. Dublin, printed by Oli. Nelson, 1763

Q., T.

See 453.

498 [HOWARD, Gorges Edmond?] The way to mend and grow better; or, thoughts on the present posture of affairs. In a letter to his e...y the lord l...t. [By Phil-Hibernicus.]
52 pp. Dublin, 1763

A., D., Q.

499 Impartial considerations on the danger of multiplying banks here; how far they may be injurious to trade and commerce, affect the merchant and manufacturer, and consequently the landed interest of this kingdom. By a member of the guild of merchants and a real lover of his country.
20 pp. Dublin, Faulkner, 1763

A., K.

500 A letter to the rt. hon. the lord mayor, aldermen, sheriffs, and clergy of the city of Dublin.
24 pp. Dublin, 1763

A., K.

501 M'AULAY, Alexander. An inquiry into the legality of pensions on the Irish establishment.
16 pp. London, printed for J. Wilkie, 1763

A., K., N., Q., T., U.

——. Another issue. 16 pp. Dublin, James Hoey, 1763

A.

——. 16 pp. 2nd ed. Dublin, James Hoey, 1763

K.

502 Observations on the parochial charity-schools in the city of Dublin. With some hints for the rendering of them more effectual.
28 pp. Dublin, printed by William Sleater, 1763

A., N.

503 Observations on the several matters offered to the linen board as materials for a linen bill; particularly on a paper, called, Observations on the linen trade. Together with some humble hints with regard to the proposed amendment of our linen laws. By the linen-weavers and manufacturers of the

towns of Belfast, Lisburn, Hillsborough, and country adjacent.
68 pp. Dublin, P. Wilson, 1763
A.

504 Observations upon the linen trade. Humbly submitted to the consideration of the rt. hon. and hon. the trustees of the linen-manufacture. By the draper of Belfast.
appendix. 56 pp. Belfast, printed by H. & R. Joy, 1763
A.

505 Papers, collected, and seriously deliberated upon, by a number of linen-drapers in and near Lisburn and Belfast, humbly presented to the rt. hon. and hon. trustees of the linen-manufacture, as materials for a linen-bill; and humbly submitted to their consideration, preparatory to a new act of parliament for the better order, regulation, and improvement of the said manufacture.
116 pp. 2nd ed. Belfast, printed by H. & R. Joy, 1763
A.

506 A proposal for selling part of the forest lands and chaces and disposing of the produce towards the discharge of that part of the national debt, due to the bank of England; and for the establishment of a national bank; by which there would be a saving to the public of one per cent. on so much of the national debt, as is immediately redeemable by parliament. Which, with the produce of the sinking fund, would, it is imagined, be sufficient to pay off the national debt in a reasonable time. And also to defray the extraordinary expenses of any war the nation should hereafter engage in, without borrowing.
tables. 36 pp. London, T. Payne, 1763
N.

507 A proposal for the support and regulation of the poor, by subjecting them to the care and maintaining them at the charge of their respective parishes.
38 pp. Belfast, printed by H. and R. Joy, 1763
Q.

508 Reflections on the domestic policy, proper to be observed on the conclusion of a peace.
96 pp. London, A. Millar, 1763
A., N., K.

509 A review of Mr. Pitt's administration, or, an impartial account of the glorious successes that attended our arms in the last war, when conducted by the wise and animated counsels of that able and patriotic statesman, lord Chatham; with a short retrospect on the state of the nation, previous to his administration. And general Wolfe's letter of Sept. 2, 1759, being one of the clearest and most elegant accounts of a series of military operations that has perhaps ever been published.
152 pp. 5th ed. London, J. Bew [etc.], 1763
A.

Preface signed "John Almon".

510 ROBINSON, Christopher and TENISON, Thomas. The respective charges given to the grand jury of the county of Armagh, at the general assizes held there, July 23, 1763, by the then going judges of assize, Mr. Justice Robinson and Mr. Justice Tenison, on occasion of the late commotions in several of the northern counties.

42 pp. Dublin, George and Alexander Ewing, 1763
K., N., Q.

511 A scheme for utterly abolishing the present heavy and vexatious tax of tythe. In a letter to a member of parliament. First published in the year 1742. With a letter to the printer, relative to the present circumstances of affairs.
20 pp. 2nd ed. Dublin, Faulkner, 1763
A., N.

512 STEPHENSON, Robert. The reports and observations of Robert Stephenson made to the right hon. and honourable the trustees of the linen manufacture, for the years 1762 and 1763. Distinguishing the state of the spinning and weaving in each county, respectively; also what species of the manufacture they are employed in, the progress made by the inhabitants and how the most immediate and effectual improvements are likely to be obtained in the several branches thereof throughout the kingdom.
50 pp. Dublin, Peter Wilson, [1763?]
Q.

513 WALPOLE, Sir Robert, afterwards earl of Orford. A short history of that parliament which committed Sir Robert Walpole to the tower, expelled him the house of commons, and approved of the infamous peace of Utrecht.
62 pp. 2nd ed. London, J. Almon, J. Williams, 1763
K.

514 The weavers address to the citizens of Dublin; or Dean Swift's advice to the good people of Ireland; together with his apparition occasioned by the importation of wrought silks from France.
20 pp. Dublin, 1763
A., K.

1764

515 Advice to both the protestants and papists of this kingdom. In a letter to a great lord and remarks on the circumstances of each.
14 pp. Dublin, 1764
A., K., Q.

516 The ancient right of the English nation to the American fishery; and its various diminutions; examined and stated. With a map of the lands, islands, gulphs, seas and fishing-banks comprising the whole. Humbly inscribed to the sincere friends of the British naval empire.
map. 106 pp. London, printed by Baker, 1764
A.

517 An annual abstract of the sinking fund, from Michaelmas 1718, when it was first stated to parliament, to the 10th of October, 1763. By a member of parliament many years in the treasury. Collected for his private amusement, and now made publick.
tables. 76 pp. London, Davis, 1764
A.

518 An answer to Father O'Fogherty's letter to a count of Milan of the most holy Roman empire, and fellow of the Royal society, etc. etc.
16 pp. n.p., 1764
A.

519 The application of eight thousand pounds granted by parliament to the Dublin Society, for the encouragement of certain trades & manufactures, 1764.
16 pp. Dublin, printed by S. Powell, [1764?]

A.

520 [ASHBURTON, John Dunning, 1st baron.] A letter to the proprietors of East-India stock, on the subject of lord Clive's jaghire; occasioned by his lordship's letter on that subject.
56 pp. London, Ch. Bathhurst, 1764

T.

521 [BUSH, John.] Hibernia curiosa. A letter from a gentleman in Dublin, to his friend at Dover in Kent. Giving a general view of the manners, customs, dispositions, etc. of the inhabitants of Ireland.
62 pp. London, W. Flexney, 1764

A., D.

522 CALDWELL, Sir James, bart. A brief examination of the question whether it is expedient either in a religious or political view, to pass an act to enable papists to take real securities for money which they may lend.
35 pp. Dublin, printed by S. Powell, 1764

A., C., N., Q., T.

523 ——. A proposal for the increase of apiaries in Ireland, addressed to the Dublin Society.
16 pp. Dublin, printed by S. Powell, 1764

N.

524 CLIVE of Plassey, Robert Clive, 1st baron. A letter to the proprietors of the East India stock, from lord Clive.
appendix. 94 pp. London, J. Nourse, 1764

T.

525 Considerations on the acts of parliament relative to the highways in Scotland, and on the new scheme of a tax in lieu of statute-labour. Together with an abstract of these acts, and a plan for a new general act.
68 pp. Edinburgh, A. Kincaid, J. Bell, 1764

Q.

526 Considerations on the merchantile character and conduct.
22 pp. London, J. Scott, [1764?]

Q.

527 Considerations which may tend to promote the settlement of our new West-India colonies, by encouraging individuals to embark in the undertaking.
52 pp. London, James Robson, 1764

K.

528 COOPER, Samuel. Definitions and axioms relative to charity, charitable institutions and the poor laws. In a series of letters to William Fellowes, esq., occasioned by a pamphlet, entitled 'Considerations on the fatal effects of the present excess of public charity to a trading nation.'
180 pp. London, W. Sandby, 1764

K.

529 DARCY, Patricke. An argument delivered by Patricke Darcy, esq; by the expresse order of the House of Commons in the parliament of Ireland, 9. Iunii, 1641.

176 pp. Waterford, printed by Thomas Bourke. Dublin, reprinted [by George Faulkner?] 1764

A., G., N.

530 DRAPER, William. Colonel Draper's answer, to the Spanish arguments, claiming the Galeon, and refuting payment of the ransom bills, for preserving Manila from pillage and destruction, in a letter addressed to the earl of Halifax, his majesty's principal secretary of state for the southern department.
42 pp. London, J. Dodsley, 1764

T.

531 An essay on paper circulation, and a scheme proposed for supplying the government with twenty millions, without any loan or new tax.
48 pp. London, W. Nicoll, 1764

K., P., T.

532 Essays. I. On the populousness of Africa. II. On the trade at the forts on the Gold Coast. III. On the necessity of erecting a fort at Cape Appolonia. Illustrated with a new map of Africa from Cape Blanco to the kingdom of Angola.
76 pp. London, T. Lowndes, 1764

A.

533 A few remarks on a pamphlet (written by Sir James Caldwell), entitled, A brief examination of the question: whether it is expedient, either in a religious or political view; to pass an act to enable papists to take real securities, for money which they may lend?
16 pp. Dublin, 1764

A., K., N., Q.

534 [HARTLEY, David?] The budget. Inscribed to the man who thinks himself minister.
tables. 24 pp. 7th ed. London, Almon, 1764

A.

535 The honour and advantage of agriculture. Translated from the Spanish of Feijos. By a farmer in Cheshire.
72 pp. Dublin, William Williamson, 1764

A., Q.

536 [HOUGHTON, Benjamin.] A faithful narrative of the conduct of Benjamin Houghton, a freeman of the city of Dublin; & one of the present commons, on the late rising & tumults in the said city. Humbly addressed to the right honourable the lord mayor, and to the worshipful the recorder, board of aldermen, sheriffs, commons, and citizens of the city of Dublin.
105 pp. Dublin, Sarah Cotter, 1764

A., G., N.

——. Another issue. 28 pp. Dublin, Sarah Cotter, 1764

G.

537 The importance of the northern collieries in a letter to a noble lord.
16 pp. Dublin, printed by George Faulkner, 1764

Q.

538 A letter to Sir James Caldwell, fellow of the Royal Society. Occasioned by his brief examination of the question,

whether it is expedient, either on a religious, or political view, to pass an act to enable papists to take real securities for money which they may lend.
8 pp. Dublin, 1764

Q.

539 MARCANDIER, — of Brouges. A treatise on hemp. In two parts. Containing I. Its history, with the preparations & uses made of it by the antients. II. The methods of cultivating, dressing, and manufacturing it, as improved by the experience of modern times.
94 pp. London, T. Beckett & P. A. de Hondt, 1764

A.

540 Observations upon a bill for augmenting the salaries of the curates.
16 pp. Dublin, 1764

A., K., Q.

541 RANDALL, John, pseud. 'Ladnar'. The farmer's new guide for raising excellent crops of pease, beans, turnip or rape (sown in narrow or wide rowes, with a seed-plough, in the power of every wright to make at any easy expence) and cleaning the ground, while they are growing, to prepare it for raising good crops of wheat, barley, or oats, in the common way of sowing the seeds, clear of those weeds which so often ruin the farmer, or keep him poor. Being experiments made on the various soils of stiff and light.
diagrams. 44 pp. London, Sandby [1764?]

N.

542 A scheme for the better relief and employment of the poor; humbly submitted to the consideration of his majesty and the two houses of parliament. By a member of parliament.
28 pp. London, 1764

Q.

543 Some arguments for limiting the duration of parliament in addition to those urged last session. Humbly submitted to the consideration of the public.
16 pp. Dublin, 1764

A.

544 STEPHENSON, Robert. The reports and observations of Robert Stephenson, made to the right hon. and honourable the trustees of the linen manufacture, for the years M, DCC, LXII, and M, DCC, LXIII distinguishing the state of the spinning and weaving in each county respectively; as also what species of the manufacture they are employed in, the progress made by the inhabitants and how the most immediate and effectual improvements are likely to be obtained, in the several branches thereof throughout the kingdom. Printed by order of the board.
88 pp. Dublin, Peter Wilson, 1764

A.

545 The tour of his royal highness Edward duke of York, from England to Lisbon, Gibralter, Minorca, Genoa, Alexandria, Asti, Turin, Milan, Parma, Florence, Leghorn, Pisa, Lucca, Pistoja, Sienna, Rome, Bologna, Mantua, Verona, Vicenza, Padua, Venice, etc. etc. etc. With an introduction, and a circumstantial & historical detail of each place through which he passed: also a particular account of a bull fight. Most humbly dedicated to his royal highness.
46 pp. Dublin, P. Wilson [&c.], 1764

A., N.

546 [YOUNGHUSBAND, Israel.] Directions for the better cultivation of land for flax-seed and for the management of flax.
20 pp. Dublin, printed by John Murphy, 1764

A., Q., T.

1765

547 BAKER, John Wynn. Experiments in agriculture, made under the direction of the right honourable and honourable Dublin Society, in the year 1764.
fold. tabs., 194 pp. Dublin, G. Faulkner, 1765

A., D., N., P.

548 ——. A plan for instructing youths in the knowledge of husbandry, published at the request of the right honourable and honourable Dublin Society.
16 pp. Dublin, printed by S. Powell and son, 1765

A., N., Q., T.

549 CALDWELL, Sir James. A letter to the Dublin Society, from Sir James Caldwell, fellow of the Royal Society. Giving an account of the culture and quality of several kinds of grass lately discovered. To which is added, the second edition of his proposal for the increase of apiaries in Ireland. Addressed to the Dublin society.
38 pp. Dublin, S. Powell, 1765

A.

550 Considerations on the present state of the silk manufacture in Ireland. Humbly submitted to the members of both houses of parliament and the Dublin Society. By a lover of his country.
16 pp. Dublin, 1765

A., N., Q.

551 [CUNNINGHAM, J.] Considerations on taxes, as they are supposed to affect the price of labour in our manufacturies: also, some reflections on the general behaviour and disposition of the manufacturing populace of this kingdom; shewing by arguments drawn from experience that nothing but necessity will enforce labour and that no state ever did, or ever can, make any considerable figure in trade, where the necessaries of life are at a low price.
64 pp. London, J. Johnson, 1765

G.

——. 72 pp. 2nd ed. London, J. Johnson, 1765

Q.

552 [CUNNINGHAM, Timothy?] A new treatise on the laws concerning tithes: containing all the statutes, adjudged cases, resolutions and judgements relative thereto. By a gentleman of the Middle Temple.
table of contents. 176 pp. London, Griffin, Kearsby, Richardson & Urquhart, 1765

A., Q.

553 Descriptions of the harbours etc.
maps. 24 pp. Dublin? 1765

A.

Part of a larger work.

554 [DICKINSON, John.] The late regulations respecting the British colonies on the continent of America considered, in a letter from a gentleman in Philadelphia to his friend in London.
tables. 38 pp. Philadelphia, William Bradford, 1765
T.

555 DUMMER, Jeremiah. A defense of the New-England charters.
88 pp. London, J. Almon, [1765]
Q., T.

556 [GRENVILLE, George.] The regulations lately made concerning the colonies, and the taxes imposed upon them, considered.
114 pp. London, J. Wilkie, 1765
K.

557 [HARTLEY, David.] The right of appeal to juries, in causes of excise asserted.
28 pp. 2nd ed. London, J. Almon, 1765
A.

558 ——. The state of the nation with a preliminary defence of the budget.
tables. 40 pp. 2nd ed. London, J. Almon, 1765
A.

559 [JENYNS, Soame.] The objections to the taxation of our American colonies, by the legislature of Great Britain, briefly consider'd.
20 pp. London, J. Wilkie, 1765
T.

560 A letter to the public, containing some important hints relating to the revenue.
42 pp. London, S. Bladon, 1765
Q.

561 LUCAS, Charles. To the right honourable, the lord-mayor, aldermen, sheriffs, commons, citizens, and freeholders of Dublin. The address of Charles Lucas, M.D. one of their representatives in parlement [sic].
16 pp. Dublin, printed by Alex. McCulloh, 1765
A., N., Q.

562 A new address to the rt. hon. the lord mayor, and the citizens of Dublin.
16 pp. Dublin, [1765]
Q.

563 [NUGENT, Robert?] The act for permitting the free importation of cattle from Ireland, considered with a view to the interests of both kingdoms.
50 pp. London, J. Dodsley, 1765
A., Q.

564 Observations on the number and misery of the poor; on the heavy rates levied for their maintenance; and on the general causes of honesty including some cursory hints, for the radical cure of these growing evils, humbly submitted to public consideration.
48 pp. London, T. Becket, 1765
Q.

565 [OTIS, James.] Considerations on behalf of the colonists. In a letter to a noble lord. By F. A.
54 pp. London, J. Almon, 1765
Q., T.

566 ——. The rights of the British colonies asserted & proved.
120 pp. London [etc.], J. Williams, 1765
A.

567 The political balance in which the principles and conduct of the two parties are weighed.
68 pp. London, T. Becket and P. A. De Hondt, 1765
Q.

568 The principles of the late changes impartially examined; in a letter from a son of Candor to the Public Advertiser.
88 pp. London, J. Almon, 1765
Q.

569 Reasons humbly offered to public consideration, against the present scheme of reducing the interest of money in Ireland.
48 pp. Dublin, Thomas Ewing, 1765
A., Q.

570 SCALÉ, Bernard and RICHARDS, William. Directions for navigating into the Bay of Dublin from Wicklow Head and from Balbriggen. With a particular account of the bays, roads, harbours, rocks, banks, swashes, landmarks, the setting and flowing of the tides, etc. from an actual survey taken by Bernard Scalé and William Richards, land surveyors and hydrographers.
maps. 36 pp. Dublin, printed by Powell, 1765
G., N.

571 A short account of the great benefits which have already arisen to the public, by means of the society instituted in London, in the year 1753, for the encouragement of arts, manufactures and commerce. By a member of the same.
22 pp. London, S. Hooper, 1765
Q.

572 Thoughts on a question of importance proposed to the public, whether it is probable that the immense extent of territory acquired by this nation at the late peace, will operate towards the prosperity, or the ruin of the island of Great Britain?
48 pp. London, J. Dixwell, 1765
K.

1766

573 An account of the institution and proceedings of the guardians of the Asylum or house of refuge, situated on the Surrey side of Westminster-bridge for the reception of orphan girls having resided six months within the bills of mortality. Whose settlements cannot be found.
table of contents, tables. 36 pp. London, 1766
A.

574 The adventures of a bale of goods from America in consequence of the stamp act.
24 pp. London, J. Almon, 1766
T.

575 The analysis of a new quack-medicine, called an antidote, etc. By a member of one of the inferior corporations.
30 pp. Dublin, 1766

N., Q.

576 An antidote to Dr. L...s's address; addressed to the merchants of the city of Dublin.
12 pp. Dublin, 1766

A., K., N., Q., T.

577 An application of some general political rules to the present state of Great Britain, Ireland and America. In a letter to the right honourable earl Temple.
88 pp. London, J. Almon, 1766

Q.

578 The application of the money granted by parliament in the year 1765, to the Dublin Society, for the encouragement of certain trades and manufactures.
22 pp. Dublin, printed by S. Powell, 1766

A., T.

579 BAKER, John Wynn. Experiments in agriculture, made under the direction of the right honourable and honourable Dublin society, in the year 1765. And now published at their request.
104 pp. Dublin, S. Powell and son, 1766

A., D., N., Q., S., T.

580 BLACKWOOD, John. A letter to his excellency Francis, earl of Hertford, lord lieutenant of Ireland, etc. on the growing of winter flax.
16 pp. Dublin, 1766

A.

581 [BRINDLEY, James.] A history of inland navigations particularly those of the duke of Bridgwater, in Lancashire and Cheshire; and the intended one promoted by earl Gower and other persons of distinction in Staffordshire, Cheshire and Derbyshire. Illustrated with geographical plans, shewing the counties, townships and villages, through which these navigations are carried, or are intended to be. The whole shewing the utility and importance of inland navigations.
106 pp. London, T. Lowndes, 1766

P.

582 [——.] History of inland navigations particularly those of the duke of Bridgwater, in Lancashire and Cheshire; and the intended one promoted by earl Gower & other persons of distinction, in Staffordshire, Cheshire & Derbyshire. Part the second. Containing the different essays which have been lately wrote, some to establish others to prevent, a navigable canal being made from Witton bridge to Knutsford, Macclesfield, Stockport & Manchester. Illustrated with a whole sheet geographical plan, showing at one view, the counties, townships and villages through which these navigations are or will be carried.
table of contents, tables. 108 pp. London, Lowndes, 1766

N.

583 [CALDWELL, Sir James.] Debates relative to the affairs of Ireland; in the years 1763 and 1764. Taken by a military officer. To which are added, an enquiry how far the restrictions laid upon the trade of Ireland, by British acts of parliament, are a benefit or disadvantage to the British dominions in general, and to England in particular, for whose separate advantage

they were intended. With extracts of such parts of the statutes as lay the trade of Ireland under those restrictions.
416 pp. London, 1766

B., G.

584 CAMDEN, Charles Pratt, 1st earl. Lord Camden's argument in Doe on the demise of Hindson, & Ux. & al. v. Kersey. Wherein lord Mansfield's argument in Wyndham v. Chetwynd, is considered and answered.
96 pp. Dublin, G. Faulkner, 1766

A.

585 A candid enquiry into the causes and motives of the late riots in the province of Munster; together with a brief narrative of the proceedings against these rioters, anno 1766. In a letter to a noble lord in England.
76 pp. London, 1766

A.

586 The case fairly stated, relative to an act, lately passed in this kingdom against the exportation of corn. By a friend to the country.
16 pp. Dublin, 1766

A., N., Q., T.

587 The case of the curates and how far it affects the established religion, considered.
38 pp. Dublin, Thomas Ewing, 1766

A., Q.

588 The celebrated speech of a celebrated commoner.
22 pp. London, Austin, 1766

A., Q.

589 Considerations on public granaries.
8 pp. Dublin, 1766

N.

590 Considerations on the American stamp act, and on the conduct of the minister who planned it.
38 pp. London, W. Nicoll, 1766

K.

591 Correct copies of the two protests against the bill to repeal the American stamp act, of last session. With lists of the speakers and voters.
24 pp. Paris, chez J. W., Imprimeur, 1766

Q.

592 [COTES, Humphrey.] An enquiry into the conduct of a late right honourable commoner.
40 pp. Dublin, G. Faulkner, [etc.], [1766?]

A.

593 The counter address of a free citizen, to the right honourable the lord mayor of the city of Dublin.
8 pp. Dublin, 1766

N., Q.

594 The crisis. Or, a full defence of the colonies. In which it is incontestibly proved that the British constitution had been flagrantly violated in the late stamp act, and rendered indisputably evident, that the mother country cannot lay any arbitrary tax upon the Americans, without destroying the essence of her own liberties.
32 pp. London, W. Griffin, 1766

T.

595 [DEAN, Sir Robert.] A dialogue between Mr. Demagogue, and a sober citizen.
8 pp. Dublin, John Butree, 1766

A., Q.

596 DOWLING, Daniel. Mercantile arithmetic: or, compendious methods for performing the principal arithmetical calculations, practised by merchants & exchangers.
2nd ed., fold table, 256 pp. Dublin, J. Exshaw & H. Saunders, 1766

A., N.

597 [DULANEY, Daniel.] Considerations on the propriety of imposing taxes in the British colonies, for the purpose of raising a revenue, by act of parliament.
tables, appendix. 88 pp. North-America printed, London re-printed for J. Almon, 1766

K., P., Q.

——. 88 pp. 2nd ed. London, J. Almon, 1766
T.

598 An essay to state some arguments relative to publick granaries, submitted with all humility to the nation which they concern.
22 pp. Dublin, 1766

A., N., Q.

599 An examination of the rights of the colonies, upon principles of law. By a gentleman at the bar.
42 pp. London, R. Dymott, J. Almon, 1766
K.

600 Free and candid remarks on a late celebrated oration; with some few occasional thoughts on the late commotions in America. In a letter to ——.
32 pp. London, B. Law, 1766

A.

601 The general opposition of the colonies to the payment of the stamp duty; and the consequence of enforcing obedience by military measures; impartially considered, also a plan for uniting them to this kingdom in such a manner as to make their interest inseparable from ours, for the future. In a letter to a member of parliament.
40 pp. London, T. Payne, 1766

K.

602 A letter from Richard in the country, to Dick in the city. On the subject of publick granaries.
14 pp. Dublin, 1766

A., G.

603 A letter to a member of parliament. Containing observations on a pamphlet, intituled, Considerations on the case of the bakers in Dublin. By a baker.
48 pp. Dublin, reprinted by Ewing, 1766
A.
See 110.

604 A letter to Charles Lucas, M.D. relative to the annual stipend, proposed to be paid him, during the city's pleasure.
8 pp. Dublin, News-Hawkers, [1766?]
A.

605 Lord mayor of the city of Dublin. The counter address of a free citizen.
8 pp. Dublin, 1766

A.

606 [LUCAS, Charles.] An answer to the counter address of a pretended free-citizen. Humbly addressed to the right honourable Sir James Taylor, knt. Lord mayor of the city of Dublin by a true citizen.
20 pp. Dublin, 1766

Q.

607 ——. A second address to the right hon. the lord mayor, the aldermen, sheriffs, commons, citizens, and freeholders of the city of Dublin from Charles Lucas, M.D. one of their representatives in parlement. Containing, an answer to a new address to his lordship and the citizens.
38 pp. Dublin, Alex. McCulloh, 1766

A., Q.

608 ——. A third address to the right hon. the lord mayor, the board of aldermen, and the sherifs, commons, and citizens of Dublin, from Charles Lucas, M.D. one of their representatives in parlement. Relative to the late proceedings of the board and the commons.
appendix. 64 pp. Dublin, printed by Alex. McCulloh, 1766

A., N.

609 McAULAY, Alexander. Septennial parliaments vindicated.
44 pp. 2nd ed. Dublin, Peter Wilson, 1766

A., N., Q.

610 [MAUDUIT, Jasper.] The legislative authority of the British parliament, with respect to north America, and the privileges of the assemblies there, briefly considered. By J. M. of the Inner Temple.
20 pp. London, W. Nicoll, 1766

T.

611 Memorials of the British Consul and factory at Lisbon, to his majesty's ambassador at that court and the secretaries of state of this kingdom.
appendix. 136 pp. London, Wilkie, 1766

T.

612 Morning amusements of the K... of P...: or, the modern system of regal policy, religion, justice, etc. Translated from the Paris edition.
60 pp. London, G. Robinson and J. Roberts, 1766

Q.

613 The necessity of repealing the American stamp-act demonstrated; or, a proof that Great Britain must be injured by that act. In a letter to a member of the British house of commons.
46 pp. London, J. Almon, 1766

T.

614 A new address to the rt. hon. the lord mayor and the citizens of Dublin.
16 pp. 2nd ed. Dublin, [1766?]

A., N., Q.

615 NEWENHAM, Sir Edward. A charge given to the grand jury of the county of Dublin, at the quarter-sessions held for the said county at Kilmainham, on the 9th day of April, 1766. By Sir Edward Newenham, knight, one of his majesty's justices of the peace for the county of Dublin. Published at the request of the grand jury.
14 pp. Dublin, printed by Sarah Cotter, 1766
Q.

616 A parallel; drawn between the administration in the four last years of Queen Anne and the four first of George III. By a country gentleman.
36 pp. London, J. Almon, 1766
A., Q.

617 A plain and seasonable address to the freeholders of Great-Britain on the present posture of affairs in America.
24 pp. London, Richardson and Urquhart, 1766
T.

618 Political speculations; or, an attempt to discover the causes of the dearness of provisions, and high price of labour, in England: with some hints for remedying those evils.
44 pp. various paging. London, J. Almon, 1766
P.

619 Protest against the bill to repeal the American stamp act of last session.
tables. 16 pp. Paris 'chez J. W.' 1766
A., P., Q.

620 Quaeries proposed to the consideration of the public, on the reduction of the interest of money in Ireland.
16 pp. Dublin, printed by W. Sleater, 1766
A., Q.

621 Reasons against passing into law a bill now depending in parliament for erecting public granaries in Dublin, Corke and Belfast. With a new plan for the improvement of tillage in Ireland. Humbly proposed to the legislature.
14 pp. Dublin, printed by J. Potts, 1766
A.

622 Reflections on the post-master's demand of a halfpenny for the delivery of each letter at the houses of the persons they are directed to: being an attempt to shew that such demand is illegal. By a citizen.
28 pp. Bath, printed by J. Keene, 1766
Q.

623 ROCQUE, B. A practical treatise on cultivating lucern grass. Improved & enlarged. And some hints relative to Burnett & Timothy grasses. Most humbly presented to the honourable society for the encouragement of arts, manufactures & commerce.
56 pp. London, R. Davis & T. Caston, 1765
A.

624 The royal charter of the Dublin society. To which are added, the society's by-laws & ordinances, for the good government of the corporation.
22 pp. Dublin, printed by S. Powell, 1766
A., T.

625 Second protest with a list of the voters against the bill to repeal the American stamp act, of last session.
16 pp. Paris, printed by J. W., Imprimeur, 1766
N., P., Q., R.
Published at London according to Sabin.

626 [SMITH, Charles, a miller.] Three tracts on the corn trade and corn laws: viz. 1. a short essay on the corn-trade & the corn-laws containing, a general relation of the present method of carrying on the corn-trade, & the purport of the laws relating thereto in this kingdom, first printed in 1758. 2. Considerations on the laws relating to the importation & exportation of corn, being an inquiry what alteration may be made in them for the benefit of the public, wrote in the beginning of the year 1759. 3. A collection of papers relative to the price, exportation, & importation of corn . . . To which is added, a supplement containing several papers & calculations which tend to explain & confirm what is advanced in the foregoing tracts.
214 pp. London, J. Brotherton, 1766.
A.

627 SNELLING, Thomas. The doctrine of gold and silver computations, in which is included, that of the par of money: the proportion in value between gold and silver; and the valuation of gold, silver, and parting assays; with useful tables and copper-plates.
tables, illustrations. 152 pp. London, T. Snelling, 1766
K.

628 Some hints for the better promoting the due execution of the laws in this kingdom, and for putting a speedy stop to the many outrages and violences which have been so frequent of late, and are increasing every day. And for improving at the same time considerably by these means, one of the most ancient branches of the revenue, for the benefit of the publick. By a real lover of liberty, and the author of the case fairly stated.
16 pp. Dublin, S. Powell, 1766
A., K., Q.

629 The speech of Mr. P... & several others, in a certain august assembly on a late important debate: with an introduction of the matters preceding it.
32 pp. n.p. [17]66
A., G.

630 [STEELE, Joshua.] An account of a late conference on the occurrences in America. In a letter to a friend.
table. 40 pp. London, J. Almon, 1766
T.

631 STEPHENSON, Robert. The reports and observations of Robert Stephenson, made to the right hon. and hon. the trustees of the linen manufacture, for the years 1764 and 1765. Distinguishing the state of the spinning and weaving in each county, respectively; as also what species of the manufacture they are employed in, the progress made by the inhabitants, and how the most immediate and effectual improvements are likely to be obtained in the several branches thereof throughout the kingdom.
152 pp. Dublin, printed by order of the board, 1766
Q.

632 TAAFFE, Nicholas, 6th viscount. Observations on affairs in Ireland, from the settlement in 1691, to the present time.
48 pp. 2nd ed. Dublin, printed by James Hoey, jr., 1766
A., K., N., Q., T., U.

633 THICKNESSE, Philip. Observations on the customs and manners of the French nation, in a series of letters, in which that nation is vindicated from the mis-representations of some late writers.
118 pp. London, Robert Davis [etc.], 1766
A.

634 The true interest of Great Britain, with respect to her American colonies, stated and impartially considered. By a merchant of London.
tables. 56 pp. London, G. Kearsley, 1766
K.

635 TUCKER, Josiah. A letter from a merchant in London to his nephew in North America, relative to the present posture of affairs in the colonies: in which the supposed violation of charters, and the several grievances complained of, are particularly discussed, and the consequences of an attempt towards independency set in a true light.
58 pp. London, J. Walter, 1766
K., P., T.

636 A vindication of the present ministry, from the many flagrant calumnies, gross mis-representations and evident falsities, contained in a book, intitled, the history of the late minority, &c. &c. &c. In a letter to the supposed authors of that piece.
72 pp. London, J. Cooke, 1766
T.

637 [WARD, Samuel.] The grievances of the American colonies candidly examined.
48 pp. (printed by authority, Providence, Rhode Island), reprinted London for J. Almon, 1766
K., T.

638 [WHATELY, Thomas.] Considerations on the trade and finances of this kingdom, and on the measures of administration, with respect to those great national objects since the conclusion of peace.
tables. 120 pp. London, Wilkie, 1766
A., T.

639 [WOODWARD, Richard, bishop of Cloyne.] A scheme for establishing county poor-houses, in the kingdom of Ireland. Published by order of the Dublin Society.
16 pp. Dublin, printed by S. Powell and son, 1766
A., N., Q., R., T.

See 711.

1767

640 An address to the freeholders of Ireland.
20 pp. Dublin, 1767
A.

641 The art of dying wool and woollen stuffs. By M. Hellot, member of the Royal Academy of Sciences. Translated from the French by order of the Dublin Society, and published at their expence, for the use of the dyers of Ireland.
106 pp. Dublin, printed by S. Powell, 1767
A.

642 BAKER, John Wynn. Experiments in agriculture, made under the direction of the right honourable & honourable Dublin Society, in the year 1766. And now published at their request.
98 pp. Dublin, S. Powell & G. Faulkner, 1767
A., D., N.

643 ——. A short description and list, with the prices of the instruments of husbandry, made in the factory at Laughlinstown, near Celbridge, in the county of Kildare. Established & conducted by Mr. John Wynn Baker, under the patronage & encouragement of the right honourable & honourable Dublin Society.
36 pp. Dublin, S. Powell & G. Faulkner, 1767
A.

See 716.

644 [BINGHAM, Sir Charles.] An essay on the use and necessity of establishing a militia in Ireland, and some hints towards a plan for that purpose. By a country gentleman.
46 pp. Dublin, printed by W. G. Jones, 1767
A., N., Q.

645 A brief account of the Hibernian nursery for the support and education of the orphans and children of mariners only. With the present state of that charitable institution, which the governors think their duty to lay before the public.
tables. 18 pp. Dublin?, 1767
A., N.

646 CALDWELL, Sir James, Bart. Two letters to the Dublin Society. The first proposing the encouragement of a manufacture, and the second of a commerce.
24 pp. Dublin, printed by S. Powell, 1767
A., N.

647 A candid enquiry into the causes and motives of the late riots in the province of Munster in Ireland; by the people called white-boys or levellers. With an appendix containing other papers on the same subject. In a letter to a noble lord in England.
77 pp. London, W. Flexney, [etc.] 1767
A.

648 Charter of incorporation for working collieries.
14 pp. Dublin, printed by John Abbot Husband, 1767
Q.

649 The conduct of the late administration examined, with an appendix, containing original and authentic documents.
appendices. 214 pp. London, J. Almon, 1767
Q.

650 ESPIE, Comte d'. The manner of securing all sorts of buildings from fire or, a treatise upon the construction of arches, adorned with two copper-plates serving to illustrate the whole work.
illus. 62 pp. London, H. Piers and Partner [etc.,] [1767]
Q.

651 FENN, Joseph. Proposals for printing by subscription, the instructions given in the drawing schools established in England, Scotland and other parts of Europe. To enable the youth of those countries to become proficient in the different branches of that art, and to pursue with success, geographical, nautical, mechanical, commercial and military studies.
76 pp. Dublin, George Cecil, 1767
A., Q.

652 [GRENVILLE, GEORGE.] Speech against the suspending and dispensing prerogative, etc.
62 pp. 5th ed. Dublin, E. Watts, 1767
A., T.

653 HOMER, Henry. An enquiry into the means of preserving and improving the publick roads of this kingdom. With observations on the probable consequences of the present plan.
92 pp. Oxford, S. Parker, 1767
Q.

654 [JENYNS, Soame.] Thoughts on the causes and consequences of the present high price of provisions.
28 pp. London, J. Dodsley, 1767
P., Q.

655 Letters from a merchant in England to a gentleman in Ireland. On matters highly interesting to the commerce of both kingdoms, with an account of some affairs lately transacted in the latter of a very singular nature.
138 pp. London, J. Dodsley, [etc., etc.], 1767
Q.

656 A letter to a member of the honourable the house of commons of Ireland. Shewing the utility and necessity of making the canals from the sea, below Newry, to Drumglass colliery, in the county of Tyrone, navigable for sea vessels according to a plan laid down by that honourable house, in the session of 1759. By a friend to the manufacturers of Ireland.
31 pp. Dublin, 1767
A.

657 A letter to the right honourable J... P..., speaker of the house of commons in Ireland.
38 pp. 'London pr. & Dublin re-pr. for J.P.' 1767
A., K.

658 A letter to the right honourable J..n P...y, s...r of the h...e of c...s in I...d.
46 pp. London, J. Wilkie, 1767
G., N., Q.

——. 44 pp. 3rd ed. London, J. Wilkie, 1767
A., N.
——. Another issue, 36 pp. Dublin, 1767
A.

659 A letter to the right honourable J...n P...y, speaker of the House of Commons in Ireland.
46 pp. London, J. Wilkie, 1767
Q., R.

660 A list of the absentees of Ireland and an estimate of the yearly value of their estates and incomes spent abroad. With observations on the trade and manufactures of Ireland,

and the means to encourage improve, and extend them; with some reasons why Great Britain should be more indulgent to Ireland, in particular points of trade. Also some reasons and observations why absentees should be obliged to contribute to the support and welfare of the country they derive their honours, estates and incomes from. Humbly submitted to the consideration of the legislature of Ireland.
appendix. tables. 76 pp. Dublin, Faulkner, 1767
A., K., N., Q., T.

——. 80 pp. 2nd ed. Dublin, Faulkner, 1767
A., N., T.

The original *List of the absentees of Ireland* was written by Thomas Prior (1681–1751) and published in Dublin by R. Gunne in 1729. This 1767 edition is one of a number of later versions based on Prior's. See also 725 and 1261, below.

661 [LLOYD, Charles.] The conduct of the late administration examined relative to the American Stamp Act: with an appendix containing original and authentic documents.
218 pp. 2nd ed. London, J. Almon, 1767
T.
'Much of this pamphlet was dictated by Grenville himself'— D. N. B.

662 A modest vindication of the character and conduct of a great officer of state. In answer to a letter to the right honourable J... P...; in a letter to a noble lord in England. By an English gentleman, now in Ireland.
30 pp. Dublin, [etc.], 1767
A., N.

663 Political speculations; or an attempt to discover the causes of the dearness of provisions, and high price of labour in England, with some hints for remedying those evils. Part the second.
64 pp. London, J. Almon, 1767
T.

664 Premiums offered by the Dublin society, in the year 1767, for the encouragement of agriculture, manufactures, and useful arts, in Ireland.
30 pp. Dublin, printed by S. Powell, 1767
A., T.

665 Protest against rescinding the East India dividend, voted by a general court, on the 6th of May, 1767; and confirmed by three several general courts held afterwards.
14 pp. London, 1767
N.

666 The rights of the clergy of Ireland candidly considered. By a friend to the constitution.
76 pp. Dublin, printed by G. Faulkner, 1767
A., N., P., T.

667 Serious thoughts concerning the true interest and exigencies of the state of Ireland.
60 pp. Dublin, 1767
A., Q.

668 A short examination of the laws lately made for the amendment and preservation of the publick highways and turnpike-roads; clearly showing that the various restraints

4

and penalties laid upon the farmers, respecting their carriages, must ever inhance the necessaries of life, without having the least tendency to amend and preserve the publick roads of this kingdom.
44 pp. London, B. White, 1767
                                        A., Q.

669 A speech, in behalf of the constitution, against the suspending and dispensing prerogative, etc.
140 pp. London, J. Almon, 1767
                                        A., T.

670 Thoughts on the causes and consequences of the present high price of provision.
26 pp. London, J. Dodsley, 1767
                                        Q.

671 Two papers on the subject of taxing the British colonies in America.
22 pp. London, Almon, 1767
                                        N.
Written 'by a Club of American merchants', 1739.

672 VARLEY, Charles. Some hints to the right honourable and honourable the trustees of the linen manufactory, for promoting the growth of flax and seed in Ireland by establishing a free flax-farmer's school or academy to learn twenty apprentices each and one hundred servants sent by gentlemen and farmers, each nine weeks in the year at proper seasons.
16 pp. Dublin, the author, 1767
                                        Q.

673 A view of the advantages of inland navigations: with a plan of a navigable canal, intended for a communication between the ports of Liverpool and Hull.
Diag. 44 pp. 2nd ed. London, T. Becket and P. A. De Hondt, 1766
                                        P.

1768

674 An abridgment of the several statutes for promoting and carrying on an inland navigation in Ireland. With an alphabetical table of the principal matters.
84 pp. Dublin, printed by Boulter Grierson, 1768
                                        A., N.

675 The account of alderman Benjamin Geale, treasurer of the city of Dublin for the receipts, issues and profits, accrueing to the said city, commencing Michaelmas, 1766, and ending Michaelmas, 1767; and for the casualties ending at the same time. To which is prefixed a rental of the said city and arrears of rent, due the 29th of September, 1767.
tables. 46 pp. Dublin, printed by O. Nelson, 1768
                                        T.

676 An Act for directing the application of the sum of seven thousand pounds granted to the Dublin Society for the encouragement of such trades and manufactures as should be directed by parliament.
8 pp. Dublin, printed by Boulter Grierson, 1768
                                        A., D.

677 Animadversions on a pamphlet lately published; entitled The Rights of the Clergy of Ireland, &c. By a friend to the civil and religious rights of mankind.
40 pp. Dublin, Alex McCulloh, 1768
                                        K.

678 An answer to a pamphlet, intituled, 'Thoughts on the causes and consequences of the present high price of provisions;' in a letter, addressed to the supposed author of that pamphlet. By a gentleman of Cambridge.
36 pp. London, Bingley, 1768
                                        N.
See 654, 691.

679 CALDWELL, Sir James, Bart. Proposals for the relief of the blind poor in & about the city of Dublin, by Sir James Caldwell, fellow of the Royal Society. To which is added, an ode, as it is to be performed at an assembly to be held at the rotunda of the lying-in hospital, as an aid for establishing a fund to provide for this charity. Written by a gentleman who most sincerely wishes for its success.
16 pp. Dublin, printed by S. Powell, 1768
                                        A., N.
See also 778.

680 CANNING, George, Senior. A letter to the right honourable Wills, earl of Hillsborough, on the connection between Great Britain and her American colonies.
40 pp. Dublin, Elizabeth Lynch, 1768
                                        A., N., Q., T.

681 The case of his grace the duke of Portland, respecting two leases lately granted by the lords of the treasury to Sir James Lowther, bart. with observations on a motion for a remedial bill, for quieting the possession of the subject. And an appendix, consisting of authentic documents and observations, etc.
appendices. 105 pp. London, J. Almon, 1768
                                        Q.

——. 54 pp. 7th ed. London, J. Almon, 1768
                                        G., T.

——. 54 pp. 7th ed. Dublin, J. Exshaw, 1768
                                        T.

682 A caveat on the part of public credit, previous to the opening of the budget for the present year, 1768.
tables. 20 pp. London, J. Almon, 1768
                                        N.

683 Considerations on the present state of the military establishment of this kingdom, addressed to the knights, citizens and burgesses of Ireland, in parliament assembled.
52 pp. Dublin, printed and sold by the booksellers, 1768
                                        A., N., Q.

684 CUNNINGHAM, Richard. Experiments on lime, united with weed-ash and kelp, in different proportions. Together, with observations on the qualities of different kinds of foreign ash. With their different effects in bleaching of linen.
34 pp. Dublin, printed by John Murphy, 1768
                                        A.

685 A defence of the amendments proposed in the corn laws: being an answer to a pamphlet, entitled, 'Observations on the acts of parliament, of the thirty-first of George II. Chap. 3, and of the thirty-third of George II. Chap. 12 &c.,' Humbly submitted to the consideration of the right hon. and hon. the House of Commons.
tables. 30 pp. Dublin, G. Faulkner, 1768
Q., T.

686 FLEETWOOD, Everard. An enquiry into the customary-estates & tenant-rights of those who hold lands of church and other foundations, by the tenure of three lives and twenty-one years. With some considerations for restraining excessive fines. To which is added, the copy of a bill, drawn and perused by divers eminent lawyers, for settling of church-fines.
72 pp. 3rd ed. London printed and Dublin re-printed, 1768
A., K., P.

687 FOSTER, Edward. An essay on hospitals, or, succinct directions for the situation, construction, & administration of country hospitals. With an appendix, wherein the present scheme for establishing public county hospitals in Ireland, is impartially considered.
128 pp. Dublin, printed by W. G. Jones, 1768
A.

688 Hibernia to her favourite sons: A letter on a very interesting and important occasion, the increase of the military establishment of this kingdom.
24 pp. Dublin, printed by W. G. Jones, 1768
Q.

689 Important considerations upon the act of the thirty-first of George II relative to the assize of bread. Wherein are introduced several experiments that have been made on the manufacturing of wheat into bread.
58 pp. 2nd ed. London, T. Becket and P. A. De Hondt, 1768
Q.

690 [JACKSON, George, afterwards Sir George Duckett.] Reasons for an augmentation of the army on the Irish establishment, offered to the consideration of the public.
tables. 32 pp. Dublin, printed by and for S. Powell, 1768
A., Q., T.

691 [JENYNS, Soame.] Thoughts on the causes and consequences of the present high price of provisions.
32 pp. Dublin, E. Watts, 1768
K., Q.

692 [JEPHSON, Robert.] Considerations upon the augmentation of the army. Address'd to the publick.
23 pp. Dublin, H. Bradley, 1768
A., N., Q.

693 [KNOX, William, and GRENVILLE, George.] The present state of the nation: particularly with respect to its trade, finances, etc., etc. Addressed to the king and both houses of parliament.
tables. 46 pp. London, J. Almon, 1768
T.

——. Another issue. 74 pp. Dublin, Watson, 1768
K., Q., T.

694 Letters from a farmer in Pennsylvania to the inhabitants of the British colonies; regarding the right of taxation, and several other important points. To which are added as an appendix the speeches of lord Chatham, and lord Camden, the one on the stamp act, the other on the declaratory bill, with a preface by the Dublin editor.
158 pp. Dublin, Sheppard, 1768
A., G., K.

695 [LOWE, George.] Considerations on the effects which the bounties granted on exported corn, malt, and flour, have on the manufactures of the kingdom and the true interests of the state. With a postscript, containing remarks on a pamphlet lately published, intituled, Thoughts on the causes and consequences of the present high price of provisions.
112 pp. London, T. Cadell, 1768
P., Q.

696 LUCAS, Charles. The liberties & customs of Dublin asserted & demonstrated upon the principles of law, justice, & good policy: with a comparative view of the constitutions of London & Dublin. And some considerations on the customs of intrusion & quarterage.
50 pp. Dublin, Thomas Ewing, 1768
A., G.

——. 50 pp. 2nd ed. Dublin, Thomas Ewing, 1768
N.

697 ——. Seasonable advice to the electors of members of parlement at the ensuing general election. Addressed to the free & independent electors of the kingdom of Ireland in general, to those of Dublin in particular, upon the present critical conjuncture of affairs.
50 pp. Dublin, Thomas Ewing, 1768
A., N.

698 ——. To the right honorable the lord mayor, the worshipful the board of aldermen, the sherifs, commons, citizens, and freeholders of Dublin, the address of C. Lucas, M.D. one of their representatives in parlement. Upon the proposed augmentation of the military establishment.
tables. 36 pp. Dublin, Thomas Ewing, 1768
A., N., Q., T.

699 MACQUER, Pierre Joseph. The art of dying silk by M. Macquer, member of the Royal Academy of Sciences. Translated from the French by order of the Dublin society and published at their expence, for the use of the dyers of Ireland.
174 pp. Dublin, printed by S. Powell, 1768
A.

700 [MORTIMER, Thomas.] The national debt no national grievance; or the real state of the nation, with respect to its civil and religious liberty, commerce, public-credit and finances. Interspersed with, critical remarks on a pamphlet lately published, intitled: The present state of the nation; to which are added, proposals for improving the public revenue, and for providing a fund for the exigencies of war, without laying additional taxes on the public. By a financier.
176 pp. London, J. Wilkie, 1768
Q.

701 A new address to the rt. hon. lord Mayor, and the citizens of Dublin.
16 pp. second edition with corrections. Dublin, [1768]

C.

702 No liberty! No life! Proper wages, and down with oppression. In a letter to the brave people of England. By John Englishman.
28 pp. London, Harris, 1768

P.

703 Observations on the acts of parliament of the thirty-first George II, Chap. 3, and of the thirty-third George II, Chap. 12 (which grant premiums on the carriage of corn and flour to Dublin) and the advantages that have accrued to the kingdom of Ireland thereby. Occasioned by a letter to Mr. Faulkner, published in the Dublin Journal of December the 8th and 12th, 1767.
22 pp. Dublin, 1768

A., Q.

704 Premiums offered by the Dublin society in the year 1768, for the encouragement of agriculture, manufactures and useful arts in Ireland.
table of contents, 40 pp. Dublin, printed by Powell, 1768

N., T.

705 Queries upon liberty, the freedom of the press, independency, &c. By a real friend to the constitution, in Church and state.
28 pp. Dublin, printed by James Hoey, 1768

G.

706 Reasons humbly offered, why heads of a bill for the regulating trades and manufactures in Ireland, should not pass into a law.
14 pp. Dublin, 1768

N., Q.

707 Some impartial observations on the proposed augmentation. By a country gentleman.
8 pp. Dublin, 1768

A., Q.
Refers to augmentation of the army on the Irish establishment.

708 State of the charitable loan, for the relief of the poor industrious tradesmen of the city of Dublin, who are supplied with the sum generally of £5 never less than £3 (English) interest free, which is repaid weekly in forty weeks.
tables. 16 pp. Dublin, printed by John Abbot Husband, 1768

K., T.

709 [WESTON, Edward.] Popular considerations on the dearness of provisions in general, and particularly of bread-corn: occasioned by the late riots. In a letter to a member of parliament. By a country gentleman.
36 pp. London, J. and F. Rivington, 1768

P.

710 WOODWARD, Richard, Bishop of Cloyne. An argument in support of the right of the poor in the kingdom of Ireland, to a national provision; in the appendix to which, an attempt is made to settle a measure of the contribution due from each man to the poor, on the footing of justice.
56 pp. Dublin, S. Powell, 1768

A., N.

711 [——.] Scheme for establishing county poor-houses, in the kingdom of Ireland. Published by order of the Dublin Society.
tables. 14 pp. 2nd ed. Dublin, printed by Powell, 1768

N.

See 639.

1769

712 An address to the noblemen and other the landed proprietors of Ireland. By a gentleman who has gathered his wisdom from experience.
68 pp. Dublin, Samuel Watson, 1769

A., N., Q.
Sub-title on p. 3: 'The defects in having improper persons for the cultivation of lands, and the prejudice that arises therefrom to the owners of estates.'

——. 64 pp. 2nd ed. Dublin, 1769 [Incomplete; mutilated t.p.]

N.

713 Advice to a newly elected member of parliament: inscribed to the right honble William Fitzgerald, commonly called marquess of Kildare.
24 pp. Dublin, 1769

Q.

714 BAKER, John Wynn. Experiments in agriculture, made under the direction of the right honourable and honourable Dublin Society, in the year 1767.
122 pp. Dublin, printed by S. Powell, 1769

A., Q.

715 ——. Experiments in agriculture, made under the direction of the right honourable and honourable Dublin Society, in the year 1768. To which is added, A plan for a new constructed barn.
diags. 76 pp. Dublin, printed by S. Powell, for the author and G. Faulkner, 1769

A., Q.

716 ——. A short description and list, with the prices of the instruments of husbandry, made in the factory at Laughlinstown, near Celbridge, in the county of Kildare. Established and conducted by Mr. John Wynn Baker, under the patronage and encouragement of the right honourable and honourable Dublin Society.
tables. 56 pp. 3rd edition with large additions and amendments. Dublin, S. Powell, 1769

A., N., P., Q.

See 643.

717 ——. To his excellency, the right honourable, lord visc. Townshend, lieutenant general, & general governor of Ireland, president, vice-presidents. And to the rest of the lords & gentlemen, composing that highly respectable body,

the Dublin Society, the following remonstrance is most humbly addressed.
104 pp. Dublin, printed by S. Powell, 1769
A., D., N.

718 [BURKE, Edmund.] Observations on a late state of the nation.
appendix. 116 pp. Dublin, A. Leathly, [etc. etc.], 1769
C., K., Q.

——. Another issue, 160 pp. London, J. Dodsley, 1769
A., N., Q.

719 [BUSHE, Gervase Parker.] The case of Great Britain & America addressed to the king, & both houses of parliament.
38 pp. London, T. Becket & P. A. de Hondt, 1769
A., N., Q.

——. 48 pp. 2nd ed. London, T. Becket, 1769
A.

——. 46 pp. 3rd ed. London, T. Becket, 1769
A.

——. 48 pp. 3rd ed. Dublin, James Williams, 1769
K., Q., T.

720 The charter-party of the friendly-annuity-company of the city of Londonderry.
32 pp. Dublin, Lynch, 1769
N.

721 [KNOX, William.] An appendix to the present state of the nation containing a reply to the observations on that pamphlet. By the author of the state of the nation.
44 pp. Dublin, John Exshaw & Wm. Watson, 1769
A., C., Q.
Another issue, 66 pp. London, J. Almon, 1769
A.

722 [——.*] The controversy between Great Britain and her colonies reviewed; the several pleas of the colonies, in support of their right to all the liberties & privileges of British subjects, & to exemption from the legislative authority of parliament, stated & considered; & the nature of their connection with, & dependence on, Great Britain, shewn, upon the evidence of historical facts & authentic records.
appendix. 268 pp. London, J. Almon, 1769
A., T.
* [Aided by George Grenville & Thomas Whitely.]

——. Another issue. 250 pp. Dublin, W. Watson, 1769
N.

723 [KNOX, William, and GRENVILLE, George.] The present state of the nation: particularly with respect to its trade, finances, etc. addressed to the king, and both houses of parliament.
tables. 56 pp. the fourth edition. Dublin, John Milliken, 1769
U.

——. Another issue. 105 pp. London, J. Almon, 1769
A., Q.

724 [LANGRISHE, Sir Hercules, Bart.] Considerations on the dependencies of Great Britain. With observations on a pamphlet, intitled, The present state of the nation.
90 pp. London, J. Almon, 1769
A., Q., T.

——. Another issue. 92 pp. Dublin, J. Williams, 1769
A., K., Q., T.

725 A list of the absentees of Ireland, and an estimate of the yearly value of their estates and incomes spent abroad, with observations on the trade and manufactures of Ireland, and the means to encourage, improve, and extend them; with some reasons why Great Britain should be more indulgent to Ireland, in particular points of trade. Also some reasons, and observations why absentees should be obliged to contribute to the support and welfare of the country they derive their honours, estates, and incomes from. Humbly submitted to the consideration of the legislature of Ireland. The third edition. In this edition the list of the absentees are greatly amended, and set forth as they stand in the present year 1769. To which is added, notes and an appendix, containing some material transactions that have occurred since the publication of the former editions, in 1767. With observations upon them, and an act of parliament, passed the last session for laying a tax of 4 sh. in the pound on absentees.
table. appendix. 108 pp. Dublin, George Faulkner, 1769
A., K., N., Q.
See 660.

726 [NEVILLE, Arthur Jones?] A state of the public revenues and expence, from the year 1751 to 1767.
tables. 12 pp. [Dublin, 1769]
K., N.

727 Observations on the review of the controversy between Great Britain and her colonies.
48 pp. London, T. Becket and P. A. de Hondt, 1769
T.

728 PHIPPS, Joseph. Brief remarks on the common arguments now used in support of divers ecclesiastical impositions in this nation, especially as they relate to dissenters.
26 pp. London, printed by Mary Hindle, 1769
A.

729 Premiums offered by the Dublin society, in the year 1769, for the encouragement of agriculture, manufactures, & useful arts, in Ireland.
58 pp. Dublin, printed by S. Powell, 1769
A., T.

730 Remarks on the review of the controversy between Great Britain and her colonies. In which the errors of its author are exposed, and the claims of the colonies vindicated, upon the evidence of historical facts and authentic records. To which is subjoined, a proposal for terminating the present unhappy disputes with the colonies; recovering their commerce; reconciliating their affection; securing their dependence on a just and permanent basis. Humbly submitted to the consideration of the British legislature.
130 pp. London, T. Becket and P. A. de Hondt, 1769
T.

731 SHERIDAN, Thomas.   A plan of education for the young nobility & gentry of Great Britain. Most humbly addressed to the father of his people.
124 pp. Dublin, printed by George Faulkner, 1769
A.

732   To the publisher of the London Chronicle, or any other of the common conveyancers of intelligence, ordinary and extraordinary. A letter from a gentleman in Ireland.
24 pp. Dublin, S. Powell, 1769
K.

733   The true constitutional means for putting an end to the disputes between Great Britain and the American colonies.
40 pp. London, T. Becket and P. A. de Hondt, 1769
T.

734   The way to be wise & wealthy, or the excellency of industry & frugality in sundry maxims. Suitable to the present times.
36 pp. Dublin, Isaac Jackson, 1769
A.

735   [WHATELY, Thomas.]   Considerations on the trade and finances of this kingdom, and on the measures of administration, with respect to those great national objects since the conclusion of the peace.
240 pp. 3rd ed. London, J. Wilkie, 1769
Q.

——.   Another issue. 240 pp. Dublin, Charles Ingham, 1769
A., P., Q., T., U.

1770

736   An answer to observations on a speech, delivered the 26th day of December, 1769, in the house of lord's, in Ireland. By a member of the house of commons.
20 pp. Dublin, J. Hoey, Jun., 1770
A., K., N., Q., T.

737   BRETT, John. The judgment of truth: or common sense & good nature, in behalf of Irish Roman Catholics. Occasioned by an apology printed for them in London. And an answer intituled, considerations, etc. by the Rev. Mr. Blackburne, archdeacon of Cleveland.
278 pp. Dublin, printed by S. Powell, 1770
L.

738   BURKE, Edmund.   Thoughts on the cause of the present discontents.
80 pp. London, J. Dodsley and Dublin, G. Faulkner, J. Exshaw [etc.] 1770
N., Q., T.

739   A candid enquiry into the present ruined state of the French monarchy. With remarks on the late despotick reduction of the interest of the national debt of France, 1770.
120 pp. London, J. Almon, 1770
A.

740   Copies of, and extracts from, some authentick papers for the consideration of the public. In regard to the late prorogation.
40 pp. Dublin, 1770
A., N., Q., T.

741   [DENNIS, William.]   A stricture upon observations on a speech. By an impartial observer.
20 pp. Dublin, 1770
A.

742   An essay on the East-India trade, and its importance to this kingdom, with a comparative view of the Dutch, French, and English East-India companies, and the privileges and support that have been granted to each, by its respective state; also the rights of the East India Company to the revenues they are possessed of in India; impartially considered.
70 pp. London, T. Payne, 1770
N.

743   [FRENCH, Robert?]   The constitution of Ireland, & Poyning's laws explained. By a friend to his country.
44 pp. Dublin, G. Faulkner, 1770
A., N., K.

744   [HARRIS, Walter, ed.]   Hibernica: or, some antient pieces relating to Ireland. Part 1. To which is added. An essay on the defects in the histories of Ireland, and remedies proposed for the improvement thereof. In a letter to the right honourable the lord Newport, lord chancellor of Ireland, and president of the Physico-historical Society established in Dublin.
288 pp. Dublin, J. Milliken, 1770
B., G.

745   [HELLEN, Robert.]   Observations on a speech, delivered (by lord Townshend), the 26th day of December, 1769, in the House of Lords in Ireland.
appendix. 28 pp. Dublin, R. Moncrieff, 1770
K., N., Q., T.

——.   26 pp. 3rd ed. Dublin, 1770
A., T.

746   [HOWARD, Gorges Edmond.]   Some questions upon the legislative constitution of Ireland, proposed to the several pamphleteers and other writers against the late prorogation; for their candid answers thereto; but chiefly for the consideration of the public.
22 pp. Dublin, S. Powell, 1770
A., K., N., Q.

747   A letter to Sir L...s O'...n, Bart. on the late prorogation; and in answer to his letter to Mr. Faulkner, on the subject of the rejected money-bill.
40 pp. Dublin, 1770
A., N.

748   A letter to the people of Ireland. [Signed "Posthumus".]
16 pp. London, 1770
D., N., Q.

——.   16 pp. 2nd ed. London, 1770
K.

——.   16 pp. 3rd ed. London, 1770
A.

749 LODGE, John. The usage of holding parliaments; & of preparing and passing bills of supply, in Ireland, stated from record.
72 pp. Dublin, printed by Boulter Grierson, 1770
A., T.

750 LUCAS, Charles. The great charter of the liberties of the city of Dublin, transcribed and translated into English, with explanatory notes addressed to his majesty, and presented to his lords justices of Ireland.
80 pp. Dublin, re-published by L. Flin, 1770
A., Q.
First ed. 1749.

751 ——. The rights and privileges of parliaments asserted upon constitutional principles, against the modern anti-constitutional claims of chief governors, to take notice of, animadvert upon and protest against the proceedings of either house of parliament. Humbly addressed to his excellency George, lord visc. Townshend lord lieutenant general and general governor of Ireland.
80 pp. Dublin, Tho. Ewing, 1770
A., B., N., Q., T.

752 ——. The usage of holding parliaments & of passing bills of supply, in Ireland, stated from record.
78 pp. Dublin, Thomas Ewing, 1770
A., D., N., T.

753 MACAULAY, Catharine. Observations on a pamphlet, entitled, thoughts on the cause of the present discontents.
34 pp. Dublin, G. Faulkner, [etc.], 1770
A., N., T.

754 [MOLYNEUX, William.] The case of Ireland being bound by acts of parliament in England, stated. With a new preface.
156 pp. London, re-published by J. Almon & M. Hingeston, 1770
A.

755 Observations on the finances and trade of Ireland, humbly addressed to the immediate consideration of gentlemen of landed interest, more particularly to members of the house of commons.
tables. 50 pp. n.p., [1770?]
G., Q.

756 Of the herring fishery, translated from an essay in Dutch, entitled, Beschryving Van de Haringvisscherye.
Of the herring fishery, translated from the French of M. Duhanvel and others.
tables. 56 pp. n.p., [1770?]
N., Q., R.

757 Parliamentary premiums offered by the [Royal] Dublin society, 1770.
14 pp. Dublin, S. Powell, 1770
T.

758 The policy of Poynings law, fairly explained & considered: with seasonable advice to the people of Ireland.
16 pp. Dublin, R. Moncrieff, 1770
A.

759 [POWER, Richard.] A comparative state of the two rejected money bills, in 1692 and 1769. With some observations on Poynings Act, and the explanatory statute of Philip and Mary. By a Barrister.
92 pp. Dublin, James Williams, 1770
N., P., T.

——. 92 pp. 2nd ed. Dublin, 1770
G., T.

——. 92 pp. 3rd ed. Dublin, 1770
G., A.

760 Reasons for an amendment of the statute of 28 Henry VIII. C. 11. ¶ 3. Which gives to the successor in ecclesiastical benefices all the profits from the day of the vacancy: in a letter to a friend, from a country clergyman.
56 pp. London, T. Payne, 1770
A.

761 State of the poor peasant.
tables. 60 pp. n.p., [1770?]
A.

762 STEELL, Isaac. Tables for computing the value of leases, & fines to be paid. Together with rules for valuing freeholds, cathedral, church, & college leases. To which is added, a section, containing the methods of estimating the value of annuities upon lives. To which is also added, a compendious method of computing simple interest.
68 pp. Dublin, printed by H. Saunders, 1770
A., T.

763 [STONE, George, & MALONE, Anthony.] The representation of the L...s J...s of Ireland, touching the transmission of a privy-council money-bill previous to the calling of a new parliament. In two letters address'd to his grace the duke of Bedford. To which is annexed, Mr. Sloane's narrative in defence of the conduct & resolutions of the house of commons in 1692.
52 pp. Various paging. Dublin, John Milliken, 1770
A., G., K., N., T.

764 Thoughts, English & Irish, on the pension-list of Ireland.
44 pp. London, George Kearsly, 1770
A., D., G., K., N., T.

765 [YOUNG, Arthur.] The expediency of a free exportation of corn at this time: with some observations on the bounty and its effects. To which is added an appendix, in answer to a pamphlet lately published, entitled 'Thoughts upon several interesting subjects'. 2nd ed. By the author of the farmer's letters to the people of England.
74 pp. London, printed for W. Nicoll, 1770
Q.

766 ——. Rural oeconomy: or essays on the practical parts of husbandry. Designed to explain several of the most important methods of conducting farms of various kinds, including many useful hints to gentlemen farmers relative to the oeconomical management of their business. To which is added the rural Socrates, being memoirs of a country philosopher. By the author of the farmer's letters.
tables. Appendix. 368 pp. Dublin, Exshaw etc., 1770
A.

1771

767 Address to the representatives of the people; upon subjects important and interesting to the kingdom of Ireland. By a freeholder.
tables. 40 pp. Dublin, 1771

N.

768 AIKIN, John, & PERCIVAL, Thomas. Thought on hospitals, by John Aikin surgeon with a letter to the author, by Thomas Percival, M.D., F.R.S.
98 pp. London, Joseph Johnson, 1771

Q.

769 BAKER, John Wynn. An abridgment of the six weeks, and six months tour's of Arthur Young, Esq.; through the southern & northern counties of England & part of Wales. Containing, all the most important articles of information relating to agriculture, now in practice in the best cultivated counties, with some accounts of the successful culture of lucerne, cabbages, etc. etc. Intended for the use of the common farmers of Ireland. Abridged at the request of the Dublin society.
fold. frontisp. 328 pp. Dublin, printed by S. Powell, 1771

A., G.

770 [——.] An address to the representatives of the people upon subjects of moment, to the well-being and happiness of the kingdom of Ireland. By a friend to the nation.
46 pp. Dublin, 1771

A., N., Q.

771 ——. Considerations upon the exportation of corn; written at the request of the Dublin Society.
tables. 48 pp. Dublin, printed by S. Powell, 1771

A., D., G., K., N., Q., T.

772 ——. Experiments in agriculture, made under the direction of the right honourable and honourable Dublin society, in the year 1769. In which cabbage husbandry is particularly explained and the cheap maintenance of cattle, both in summer and winter etc.
134 pp. Dublin, G. Faulkner, 1771

A., D., Q.

773 ——. Experiments in agriculture, made under the direction of the right honourable and honourable Dublin society, in the year 1770. In which the cabbage husbandry is further pursued; the culture of rape in various methods as food for cattle, the culture of clover, wheat etc.
diag. 92 pp. Dublin, G. Faulkner, 1771

D., Q.

774 ——. Practical agriculture epitomized, and adapted to the tenantry of Ireland; with considerations upon the Dublin society's premiums for husbandry, and a plan for an entire change of form therein; interspersed with occasional reflections, upon variety of interesting subjects. Particularly, the French nation near ruined by Colbert's rage for manufactures. Wisdom of the English nation at that period. The astonishing spirit now in France, amongst all ranks of people to promote agriculture. The spirited exportation of corn, a true principle for increasing the quantity and lowering the price. Manufacturers working upon foreign materials, hurtful to the nation. A spirited culture of the land, the only source of riches to the kingdom. Misery of the lower tenantry. The present course of husbandry, and its unprofitableness to the farmer, and lessening of produce to the nation. Improved courses of husbandry proposed. Ameliorating and impoverishing crops distinguished. Instruction of country labourers in useful arts of cultivation, one capital foundation of improved husbandry. Primary and secondary objects distinguished in a national view. The insufficient population, and hints for improving it. Waste lands to be improved. Growth of timber and planting, whose immediate province. Humbly submitted to the consideration of the Dublin society.
tables. folding table. appendix.
168 pp. Dublin, G. Faulkner, 1771

A., D., Q., T.

775 [CALDWELL, Sir James, bart.] An address to the house of commons of Ireland: By a freeholder.
44 pp. n.p., 1771

A., K., N., Q.

——. 44 pp. 2nd ed., 1771

A.

——. 44 pp. 3rd ed., 1771

A., G., N., T.

776 [——.] An essay on the character and conduct of his excellency lord visc. Townshend, lord lieutenant general, and general governor of Ireland, etc. etc. etc.
26 pp. n.p., 1771

A., K., N., Q.

777 ——. A proposal for employing, cloathing, & furnishing, with implements of husbandry, children, from the age of ten to sixteen; with a view to agriculture, the improvement of land, and gardening.
8 pp. Dublin, printed by S. Powell, 1771

A., G., P.

778 ——. Proposals for the relief of the blind poor in and about the city of Dublin, by sir James Caldwell, fellow of the royal society. To which is added, an ode, as it is to be performed at an assembly to be held at the rotunda of the lying-in hospital, as an aid for establishing a fund to provide for this charity. Written by a gentleman who most sincerely wishes for its success.
16 pp. Dublin, S. Powell, 1771

G., P., U.

See 679.

779 The charter-party; or, articles of agreement of the Belfast annuity company.
56 pp. Belfast, H. & R. Joy, 1771

P.

780 The charter-party: or, articles of agreement of the Benevolent annuity-company of Dublin.
60 pp. Dublin, S. Watson, 1771

G.

781 [CLARKE, S.?] Sentiments offered to the public for the coining of forty thousand pounds worth of silver.
30 pp. London, Evans, Woodfall & Co. [etc.], 1771

A.

782 [CURRY, John, and O'CONNOR, Charles.] Observations on the popery laws.
54 pp. Dublin, printed by T. Ewing, 1771
A., Q.

783 [DALRYMPLE, Alexander.] Observations on the present state of the East India Company; and on the measures to be pursued for ensuring its permanency and augmenting its commerce.
92 pp. London, J. Nourse, 1771
T. [Imperfect copy.]

784 An essay on the theory of money.
tables. 180 pp. London, J. Almon, 1771
A., K., Q.
Sometimes attributed to Henry LLOYD.

785 FORDYCE, George. Elements of agriculture and vegetation. To which is added, an appendix for the use of practical farmers.
diags. 114 pp. 2nd ed. London, J. Johnson, 1771
Q.

786 Hints for improving the kingdom of Ireland in a letter to his excellency George lord viscount Townshend, lord lieutenant of Ireland. By a lover of his country.
16 pp. Dublin, printed by Charles Ingham, 1771
A., K.

787 John Pimlico's letter to the people. To which is added, Lord M--sf--ld's speech on the second reading of the bill for the further preventing delays of justice, by reason of privilege of parliament, after the 24th of June, 1770.
32 pp. Dublin, George Faulkner, 1771
K.

788 A letter to the members in parliament, on the present state of the coinage: with proposals for the better regulation thereof.
20 pp. London, Browne, 1771
A.

789 Money of England, reduced into money of Portugal, and the money of Portugal, reduced into English money, at the exchange of sixty-seven pence halfpenny per mill rea which is the par of exchange between these kingdoms. Also, the coins, measures, and weights of both kingdoms, compared.
tables. 12 pp. London, printed by Blyth and Beevor, 1771
N.

790 A narrative of facts, respecting the Tyrone collieries & canals. In a letter to a member of parliament.
20 pp. Dublin, 1771
A.

791 The protest of the lords. December 18, 1771.
20 pp. Dublin, 1771
A., G.

792 [RAMSAY, Allan, Jun.] An historical essay on the English constitution: or, an impartial inquiry into the elective power of the people, from the first establishment of the Saxons in this kingdom. Wherein the right of parliament, to tax our distant provinces, is explained, & justified, upon such constitutional principles as will afford an equal security to the colonists, as to their brethren at home.
156 pp. Dublin, R. Moncrieffe, 1771
A., G., N.

——. Another issue, 220 pp. London, Edward & Charles Dilly, 1771
A.

793 A representation of the progress of the linen & hempen manufactures of Ireland, & her title to encouragement & precedence in those manufactures.
4 pp. Dublin, trustees of the linen-manufacture of Ireland, 1771
A.

794 RIGGE, Ambrose. A brief and serious warning to such as are concerned in commerce and trading, who go under the profession of truth, to keep within the bounds thereof, in righteousness, justice and honesty towards all men. Now reprinted, together with the advices of several yearly meetings of like tendency.
24 pp. London, printed by Mary Hinde, 1771
A.

795 Serious thoughts upon a subject truly interesting to the welfare of Ireland, submitted to the consideration of both houses of parliament; but more particularly to the country gentlemen. By a friend to the yeomanry.
14 pp. n.p., 1771
A., N.

796 The standing orders of the right honourable and honourable the trustees of the linen-board.
12 pp. Dublin, printed by John Murphy, 1771
A., Q.

797 TRAIL, John. The report of J. Trail, engineer, concerning the practicability and expense of compleating the Grand Canal from Dublin to Tullamore in the King's County, and making the Maiden and Brusna Rivers navigable from thence to the River Shannon, with collateral cuts to the Rivers Barrow and Boyn.
map. appendix. diagrams. tables. 48 pp. Dublin, printed by O. Nelson, 1771
N., T.

798 WELDON, Patrick. A new manner of distilling by which the distillers shall all have as sweet and good spirits, as any imported and as large produce as in their present method, with half the consumption of corn.
11 pp. n.p., printed by order of the lord chancellor of Ireland, 1771
Q.

799 [YOUNG, Arthur.] Proposals to the legislature for numbering the people containing some observations on the population of Great Britain and a sketch of the advantages that would probably accrue from an exact knowledge of its present state.
52 pp. London, W. Nicoll, 1771
Q.

1772

800 The advantages and disadvantages of inclosing waste lands and open fields, impartially stated and considered. By a country gentleman.
86 pp. London, J. Almon, 1772

A.

801 An attempt to shew the cause of the present risings in the north and south: in which the state of the nation is briefly considered. Published originally in the 'Batchelor', in the 'Dublin Mercury'.
60 pp. Dublin, printed by James Hoey, Jr., 1772

A., L.

802 BAKER, John Wynn. Experiments in agriculture, made under the direction of the right honourable and honourable Dublin society, in the year 1771. In which three comparative methods for the culture of wheat are particularly explained; the importance to the community and the farmer, of sowing wheat upon clover-hay, exemplified by experiment, upon a large scale; the culture of carrots upon stiff ground; the culture of horse-beans, preparatory to wheat; further experiments upon cabbages and clover; and other subjects, interesting to the husbandry of Ireland.
tables. diags. 126 pp. Dublin, G. Faulkner, 1772

A., Q.

803 [BELDAM, ——.] Considerations on money, bullion and foreign exchanges; being an enquiry into the present state of the British coinage; particularly with regard to the scarcity of silver money.
160 pp. London, Lockyer Davies, 1772

Q.

804 BROOKE, Henry. A brief essay on the nature of bogs, & the method of reclaiming them. Humbly addressed to the right honourable & honourable the Dublin society, by their grateful & faithful servant, Henry Brooke.
16 pp. Dublin, printed by S. Powell, 1772

A., N.

805 BURGH, William. Report of the committee, to whom it was referred to examine the matter of the petition of Michael Keating, Esq., and others, for and on behalf of themselves and the several other creditors of William Howard, late of the city of Dublin, merchant.
tables. 84 pp. Dublin, printed by Abraham Bradley, 1772

Q.

806 The bye-laws for the better regulation of the rates or fares of carriages plying for hire, in and about the city of Dublin, made by the governors of the workhouse of the said city.
16 pp. Dublin, printed by David Hay, 1772

A.

807 The charter party: or, articles of agreement of the Provident Annuity Company of Dublin.
64 pp. Dublin, printed by S. Powell, 1772

A.

808 A collection of the protests of the lords of Ireland, from 1634 to 1771.
134 pp. Dublin, J. Milliken, 1772

A., N.

809 COMBER, T. Real improvements in agriculture (on the principles of A. Young, Esq.) recommended to accompany improvements of rents; in a letter to Reade Peacock, Esq; alderman of Huntingdon. To which is added, A letter to Dr. Hunter, physician in York, concerning the rickets in sheep.
86 pp. London, W. Nicoll, 1772

Q.

810 CUNNINGHAM, Richard. Experiments on lime united with weed ash and kelp [in linen manufacture (in MS)] in different proportions together with a process for making potash.
diagrams. tables. 32 pp. Dublin, printed by Murray, 1772

N.

811 [CURRY, John, & O'CONNOR, Charles.] Observations on the popery laws.
80 pp. London, J. Murray & T. Ewing, 1772

A.

812 [DALRYMPLE, Alexander.] The measures to be pursued in India, for ensuring the permanency, and augmenting the commerce, of the company, farther considered, with the heads of a plan for carrying those measures into execution. By the author of Observations on the present state of the East India Company, etc.
48 pp. London, J. Nourse, 1772

T.

813 DOYLE, James. The expeditious discounter, being a correct interest-book, on an entire new principle, from any before published. Together with sundry other useful tables of exchanges, etc. Particularly adapted to the trade of Ireland.
102 pp. Various paging, Dublin, William Sleater, 1772

A., K.

814 HAMILTON, Hugh, dean of Armagh. A sermon occasioned by the late disturbances in the north of Ireland, preached before the judges of assize in the cathedral church of Armagh, on Sunday, April 12, 1772.
32 pp. Dublin, George Faulkner, 1772

A., N.

815 HARGRAVE, Francis. An argument in the case of James Sommersett a negro, lately determined by the court of king's bench: wherein it is attempted to demonstrate the present unlawfulness of domestic slavery in England. To which is prefixed a state of the case.
82 pp. London, W. Otridge, 1772

A.

816 Imprisonment for debt considered with respect to the bad policy, inhumanity and evil tendency of that practice. Translated from the Italian.
54 pp. London, F. Newbery, 1772

Q.

817 An inquiry into the late mercantile distresses in Scotland and England; with a few thoughts on the causes of the difficulties that now prevail amongst the greatest part of the inhabitants of the whole island; in a letter to the earl of ——.
198 pp. London, T. Evans, [1772]

K., P., Q.

818 Justice & policy. An essay on the increasing growth & enormities of our great cities. Shewing the breaches thereby occasioned in the constitution & through the means of morality & industry, to place it upon a more firm basis, by the bands of union; that Britain may become the asylum of worth, and the empire, with the commerce of it, justly established, instead of exchanging religion for trade. Also, considerations upon the state of Ireland, with a proposal for the relief of it, & a scheme for its benefit, by employing the poor universally; together with reflections on police in general, & on the exportation of provisions from Ireland in particular. To which is added thoughts on conquests, trade, & military colonies etc. etc. By a freeholder in Ireland, & a stockholder in England.
84 pp. Dublin, the author, 1772

A., T.

See 921.

819 [LANGRISHE, Hercules.] The substance of a speech made by H...s L...she, Esq.; in a debate on the bill for enabling papists to take building leases.
28 pp. Dublin, 1772

A.

820 [MASERES, Francis, baron.] A proposal for establishing life-annuities, in parishes for the benefit of the industrious poor.
68 pp. London, Bery White, 1772

Q.

821 POSTLETHWAYTE, Malachy. The national and private advantages of the African trade considered. With a correct map of Africa and the European settlements.
map. 132 pp. 2nd ed. London, William Otridge, 1772

Q.

822 Premiums offered by the Dublin Society, for the encouragement of agriculture, planting and other articles in husbandry.
48 pp. [Dublin], 1772

Q.

823 Premiums offered by the society instituted at London, for the encouragement of arts, manufactures and commerce.
44 pp. London, the society, 1772

Q.

824 PRICE, Richard. An appeal to the public on the subject of the national debt. 2nd ed. with an appendix, containing explanatory observations and tables and an account of the present state of population in Norfolk.
106 pp. London, T. Cadell, 1772

A., N., Q.

825 [——.] A supplement to the second edition of the treatise on reversionary payments, etc. Containing additional observations and tables.
62 pp. London, T. Cadell, 1772

Q.

826 Remarks on Dr. Price's observations on reversionary payments, etc. Particularly on the national debt, and his proposed method for discharging the same. To which is added, a scheme for the making a sure provision for the posterity of private persons, at an easy expence.
68 pp. London, T. L. Lowndes, 1772

Q.

827 Reports of the lords commissioners for trade and plantations on the petition of hon. T. Walpole, Benjamin Franklin, John Sargent, and Samuel Wharton, Esquires, and their associates; for a grant of lands on the River Ohio, in N. America; for the purpose of erecting a new government. With observations and remarks.
appendices. table. 109 pp. London, Almon, 1772

N.

828 Rules and orders of the society instituted at London, for the encouragement of arts, manufactures and commerce.
20 pp. London, the society, 1772

Q.

829 Social Annuity Company, Dublin. Deed for preventing any advantage by survivorship in the Social Annuity Company.
8 pp. Dublin, printed by Dyton, 1772

N.

830 Some reasons humbly offered to the consideration of parliament for preventing the delays of justice, occasioned by their privilege in suits; for building courts and public offices; for ascertaining their fees. And the redressing of some material inconveniences in the proceedings in courts of equity, as contained in the preface to Mr. Howard's practice of the high court of chancery in Ireland, just published.
38 pp. Dublin, Elizabeth Lynch, 1772

K., Q.

831 [WELDON, C.] Proposals humbly offered to his excellency lord Townshend; and to the present parliament, for the improvement of trade and restoration of cash and public credit to Ireland, now sinking for want of trade and her late troubles in the north of Ireland.
tables. 16 pp. Dublin, printed by James Hunter, 1772

Q.

832 WOODWARD, Richard, bishop of Cloyne. An argument in support of the right of the poor in the kingdom of Ireland to a national provision; in the appendix to which, an attempt is made to settle a measure of the contribution due from each man to the poor, on the footing of justice.
56 pp. Dublin, printed by S. Powell, 1772

A., D., G., N., P.

1773

833 [ARBUTHNOT, John, of Mitcham?] An inquiry into the connection between the present price of provisions, and the size of farms. With remarks on population as affected thereby. To which are added, proposals for preventing future scarcity. By a farmer.
tables. 154 pp. London, T. Cadell, 1773

Q.

834 [BAYLEY, Thomas Butterworth.] Observations on the general highway and turnpike acts passed in the seventh year of his present majesty: and also upon the report of the

committee of the House of Commons, who were appointed upon the twenty-eighth of April, 1772, to consider the above acts.
70 pp. London, Joseph Johnson, 1773
A., Q.

835 BAKER, John Wynn. The reclaiming and cultivation of a bog in the county of Kildare, by Wentworth Thewles, Esq; viewed and examined in August last, by desire of the Dublin society, and now reported in pursuance thereof.
table. 26 pp. Dublin, S. Powell, 1773
Q.

836 A bill for the retrenchment of the national expences and for the reduction of useless offices and boards, sinecure places, pensions, and additional salaries, and more economical receipt of the revenues of Ireland, presented by the earl of Aldborough, 17th Dec., 1773.
8 pp. n.p., [1773?]
T.

837 BROOKE, Henry. A letter to the universal fishing company of the kingdom of Ireland.
16 pp. Dublin, James Williams, 1773
A.

838 Considerations on the act of parliament commonly called the Nullum Tempus-Act. With some reasons why such a statute of limitation ought not to be extended to ecclesiastical persons.
34 pp. London, Lockyer Davis, 1773
A.

839 Considerations on the state of the Sugar Islands, and on the policy of enabling foreigners to lend money on real securities in those colonies. In a letter addressed to the right hon. lord North; by a West India planter.
28 pp. London, Bladon, 1773
A.

840 [COOPER, Samuel.] A letter to the clergy of the county of Norfolk. In which the necessity for the abolition of tithes is plainly proved, and the propriety of other plans is fully evinced. By No-Tithe-Gatherer.
30 pp. Norwich, printed by Chase, 1773
A.

841 [DICKSON, Adam, of Whittingham.] An essay on the causes of the present high price of provisions, as connected with luxury, currency, taxes and national debt.
112 pp. London, E. and C. Dilly, 1773
Q.

842 [FORTESCUE, James.] Some hints on planting. By a planter.
24 pp. Newry, printed by George Stevenson, 1773
A., Q., R.

843 An inquiry into the practice of imprisonment for debt, and a refutation of Mr. James Stephen's doctrine. To which is added, A hint for relief of both creditor and debtor.
56 pp. London, J. Towers, 1773
Q.

844 The letters of Georgicus, upon the iniquity of tythes, intended for the benefit of the English farmer, with additions.
96 pp. London, J. Wilkie and others, 1773
Q.

845 Letters which passed in Great Britain, relative to the absentee tax. 12 pp. Various paging. Dublin, 1773.
A., C., K., N., P.

846 A letter to the right honourable J...n L...d A...y.
15 pp. Dublin, 1773
A., K., N., Q.
On Tithe-Farmers.

847 Letter upon the subject of taxing the estates of absentees.
8 pp. Dublin, 1773
A., K., N., P.
Signed: A Real Lover of his Country.

848 [MASERES, Francis, baron.] Considerations on the bill now depending in the house of commons, for enabling parishes to grant life-annuities to poor persons, upon purchase, in certain circumstances and under certain restrictions. Being an appendix to the pamphlet, intitled, 'A proposal for establishing Life-Annuities in Parishes for the benefit of the industrious poor'.
60 pp. London, B. White, 1773
Q.

849 MOORE, Francis. Considerations on the exorbitant price of provisions, setting forth the pernicious effects which a real scarcity of the necessaries of life must eventually have upon the commerce, population and power of Great Britain. To which is added, a plan to remove the cause of our present national distress.
104 pp. London, T. Cadell [etc.] 1773
Q.

850 [MOUNTMORRES, Hervey Redmond Morres, 2nd viscount?] Plan of an universal fishing company, in Ireland.
32 pp. Dublin, printed by Husband, 1773
N., Q., T.
Signed Themistocles.

851 Observations on the conduct and management of the twelve commissioners of the revenue, since February 1772, addressed to the right honourable the earl of Lanesborough, and every virtuous member of the legislature.
30 pp. Dublin, 1773
K.

852 Rules & regulations of the company of undertakers of the Grand Canal, for the better carrying on the navigation, & regulating the proceedings of the company. Printed by the order of the company.
32 pp. Dublin, printed by Oliver Nelson, 1773
A.

853 SCOTT, J. A digest of the present act for amendment of the highways: with a calculation of the duty, composition and contribution for every rent from 1 l. to 400 l. per annum. For the use of surveyors etc. Also a list of forfeitures and penalties, with a schedule of forms and remarks.
tables. 104 pp. n.p., printed by W. Strahan and M. Woodfall 1773
Q.

854 [Scott, John, of Amwell.] Observations on the present state of the parochial vagrant poor.
136 pp. London, Edward and Charles Dilly, 1773
Q.

855 [Scrope, John (Rector of Castle Combe).] Reflection upon tithes, seriously addressed in behalf of the clergy, to the gentlemen associated for the purpose of considering of an equivalent for the payment of tithes in kind: demonstrating that no equivalent can be devised, which these same gentlemen will not think liable to the same complaints and objections. By a clergyman of Wiltshire.
32 pp. Salisbury, printed by Easton, 1773
A., Q.

856 Serious considerations on the present alarming state of agriculture and the linen trade. By a farmer.
38 pp. Dublin, W. Watson, 1773
A.

857 Some thoughts on lowering the water of Lough-Neagh, & other great lakes in Ireland: without prejudice to their navigation or fisheries.
24 pp. Dublin, printed by S. Powell, 1773
A.

See 193, 385.

858 Tucker, Josiah. Four letters on important national subjects, addressed to the right honourable the earl of Shelburne, his majesty's first lord commissioner of the treasury.
128 pp. 2nd ed. London, T. Cadell, 1773
G., Q.

859 Whitehouse, Thomas, and Whitehouse, Joshua. An address to the people of Ireland.
36 pp. Dublin, printed by Messrs. Whitehouse, 1773
A., N., Q.

On imprisonment for debt.

860 [Young, Arthur.] Observations on the present state of the waste lands of Great Britain. Published on occasion of the establishment of a new colony on the Ohio. By the author of Tours through England.
84 pp. London, W. Nicoll, 1773
Q., T.

1774

861 An account of the proceedings, & state of the fund of the corporation instituted for the relief of the poor, & for punishing vagabonds & sturdy beggars in the county & city of Dublin.
10 pp. [Dublin], by order of corporation, 1774
A., K.

862 An appeal to the public, stating and considering the objections to the Quebec bill. Inscribed and dedicated to the patriotic society of the bill of rights.
60 pp. London, T. Payne and M. Hingeston 1774
Q.

——. 78 pp. 2nd ed. London, printed for T. Payne and M. Hingeston, 1774
A.

863 An argument in defence of the exclusive right claimed by the colonies to tax themselves with a review of the laws of England relative to representation and taxation to which is added an account of the rise of the colonies and the manner in which the rights of the subjects within the realm were communicated to those that went to America, with the exercise of those rights from their first settlement to the present time.
172 pp. London, Brotherton and Sewell [etc.], 1774
Q.

864 Baker, John Wynn. Experiments in agriculture, made under the directions of the right honourable and honourable Dublin Society, in the year 1772. In which further comparative methods are carried on in the culture of wheat, and the importance to the community and the farmer of sowing wheat, upon clover-hay, confirmed by further experiments; the same compared with beans as a preparation for wheat; the culture of carrots and parsnips, horse-beans, clover and cabbages with a numerous set of minute experiments, taking in all the articles of cultivation within the farmers department, ultimately tending to discover the most advantageous courses of crops, for the production of wheat and other grain, independent of fallow.
diagrams. 124 pp. Dublin, G. Faulkner, 1774
Q.

865 Bernard, Sir Francis. Select letters on the trade and government of America; and the principles of law and polity, applied to the American colonies. Written by governor Bernard at Boston, in the years 1763, 4, 5, 6, 7 and 8. Now first published: To which are added the petition of the assembly of Massachuset's Bay against the governor, his answer thereto, and the order of the king in council thereon.
138 pp. 2nd ed. London, T. Payne, 1774
A.

866 Blackhall, John. Hints for encouraging a more extensive & beneficial culture of that most useful of all roots, the potatoe. Humbly offered to the right honourable and honourable the Dublin society.
8 pp., [1774?]
A.

867 A collection of rules and standing orders of the house of commons; relative to the applying for and passing bills, for enclosing and draining of lands, making turnpike roads, navigations and other purposes.
24 pp. London, M. Hingeston, 1774
A.

868 [Cooper, Myles.] The American querist: or, some questions proposed relative to the present disputes between Great Britain, and her American Colonies. By a North-American.
32 pp. 11th ed. New York, printed by James Rivington, 1774
K.

869 [——.] A friendly address to all reasonable Americans, on the subject of our political confusions: in which the necessary consequences of violently opposing the king's troops, and of a general non-importation are fairly stated.
56 pp. New York, 1774
K.

See 910.

870 DE PINTO, ——. An essay on circulation and credit, in four parts; and a letter on the jealousy of commerce. From the French of Monsieur De Pinto. Translated, with annotations, by the Reverend S. Baggs, M.A.
272 pp. London, Ridley, 1774

A.

871 [DICKINSON, John.] Letters from a farmer in Pennsylvania to the inhabitants of the British Colonies.
136 pp. Philadelphia, and London, J. Almon, 1774

K., T.

872 [——.] A new essay [by the Pennsylvanian farmer] on the constitutional power of Great Britain over the colonies in America; with the resolves of the committee for the province of Pennsylvania, and their instructions to their representatives in assembly.
32 pp. Philadelphia & London, J. Almon, 1774

A., K.

873 ELLIS, John. An historical account of coffee. With an engraving and botanical description of the tree. To which are added sundry papers relative to its culture and use, as an article of diet and of commerce.
plates. table of contents. 76 pp. London, E. & C. Dilly, 1774

A.

874 Extracts from the votes and proceedings of the American continental congress, held at Philadelphia, on the fifth of September, 1774 containing, the bill of rights, a list of grievances, occasional resolves, the association, an address to the people of Great-Britain, and a memorial to the inhabitants of the British American colonies. Published by order of the Congress.
84 pp. Philadelphia & London, J. Almon, 1774

T.

875 FORSTER, Edward. Observations on the evidence relating to the Russia trade: as delivered at the bar of the honourable the House of Commons, on the 5th of May, 1774; to a committee of the whole House, appointed to enquire into the present state of the linen trade of Great Britain and Ireland.
table. 24 pp. London, the Russia Company, 1774

T.

876 GLOVER, Richard. A short account of the late application to parliament made by the merchants of London upon the neglect of their trade: with the substance of the evidence thereupon; as summed up by Mr. Glover.
72 pp. 6th ed. London, J. Wilkie, 1774

A.

877 [GRAY, John.] An essay concerning the establishment of a national bank in Ireland.
54 pp. London, G. Robinson, 1774

Q.

878 HYNDMAN, C. A new method of raising flax; by which it is proved, that Ireland may raise annually many thousand pounds worth more flax from the usual quantity of land, & from one fourth less seed than by the common method. With tables, shewing what quantity of seed will sow any lot or quantity of ground. The whole containing many useful and curious remarks on that valuable plant, never before made publick.
tables, diag. 40 pp. Belfast, printed by James Magee, 1774

A.

879 [KNOX, William.] The interest of the merchants and manufacturers of Great Britain, in the present contest with the colonies, stated and considered.
52 pp. London, T. Cadell, 1774

K.

880 [——.] The justice and policy of the late act of parliament, for making more effectual provision for the government of the province of Quebec, asserted and proved; and the conduct of administration respecting that province, stated and vindicated.
90 pp. London, J. Wilkie, 1774

A., Q.

881 A letter occasioned by the application to parliament, for farther encouragement to the linen manufacturers of Great Britain and Ireland.
18 pp. London, 1774

T.

882 Letters of governor Hutchinson and lieutenant governor Oliver, etc. printed at Boston. And remarks thereon with the assembly's address, and the proceedings of the lords committee of council. Together with Mr. Wedderburn's speech relating to those letters.
98 pp. Dublin, Gilbert, 1774

K., N.

883 Letters to men of reason and the friends of the poor, on the hardships of the excise laws relating to malt and beer, more especially as they affect the inhabitants of cities and great towns. With a few remarks on the late regulations in the corn trade.
62 pp. London, J. Almon, 1774

Q.

884 POWNALL, Thomas. The administration of the British colonies. Part the second. Wherein a line of government between the supreme jurisdiction of Great Britain, & the rights of the colonies is drawn, & a plan of pacification is suggested. To which is added, a postscript, being remarks on the Pennsylvania instructions, the 'New essay on the constitutional power of the parliament over the colonies'. With an appendix, containing papers referred to in both the first & second parts.
182 pp. London, J. Waller, 1774

A.

885 Proceedings of the corporation instituted for the relief of the poor, etc. in the county of Dublin etc.
24 pp. Dublin, Wilson, 1774

N.

886 QUINCY, Josiah, Jun. Observations on the act of parliament commonly called the Boston port-bill; with thoughts on civil society and standing armies.
184 pp. Boston, and London, Edward and Charles Dilly, 1774

Q.

887 Reasons, humbly submitted to the honourable members of both houses of Parliament, for introducing a law, to prevent unnecessary and vexatious removals of the poor; thereby to reduce parish expenses, by letting the poor live where they can best earn their bread.
20 pp. Cambridge, Fletcher and Hodson, 1774

Q.

888 Remarks on the decay of the linen manufacture of Ireland; with methods proposed for its re-establishment & farther improvement.
32 pp. Dublin, printed by Spotswood, 1774

A.

889 Report from the committee appointed to consider of the methods practised in making flour from wheat; the prices thereof; and how far it may be expedient to put the same again under the regulations of an assize. In this report are set forth several experiments and computations, relative to what quantity of flour for the different sorts of bread in use, is equivalent to a quarter of wheat, and the manner of dressing the flour, and making the different sorts of bread for sale.
96 pp. Dublin, printed by George Faulkner, 1774

A., Q.

890 [ROKEBY, Matthew Robinson, Baron.] Considerations on the measures carrying on with respect to the British Colonies in North America. 2nd ed. With additions and an appendix relative to the present state of affairs on that continent.
224 pp. London, R. Baldwin [etc.], 1774

Q.

891 Rules, ordinances, bye-laws and regulations made and established by the governors of the foundling hospital and work-house. Dublin, 6th July 1774.
32 pp. [+folding diet chart.] Dublin, Dyton, 1774

T.

892 SHIPLEY, Jonathan, Bishop of St. Asaph. A speech intended to have been spoken on the Bill for altering the charters of the colony of Massachusett's Bay.
44 pp. 4th ed. London, T. Cadell, 1774

N., Q.

893 Some observations on the proceedings in the Dublin society, in the granting and disposing of premiums and bounties for some years past, submitted to their consideration. With some hints for the improvement and enriching of the kingdom. By a fellow member.
80 pp. Dublin, Thomas Walker, 1774

A., K., N., Q.

894 Some observations upon libels and laws relating thereto. As also on the late Stamp Act. By a friend to society.
24 pp. Dublin, Samuel Price, 1774

A., K., Q.

895 Some thoughts on the present state of the linen trade, of Great Britain & Ireland.
20 pp. London, 1774

A., N.

896 [TAMLINI...?] Traité sur la mendicité avec les projets de réglement propres à l'empêcher dans les villes et villages, dédié à messieurs les officiers de justice et de police. Par un citoyen.
76 pp. n.p., 1774

Q.

897 Thoughts on the act for making more effectual provision for the government of the province at Quebec.
40 pp. London, T. Becket, 1774

Q.

898 Tontine-tables; or, calculations respecting the loan of £265,000; on which are to be granted life annuities of £6 per cent. With benefit of survivorship. For the information of the present subscribers and future purchasers, and sellers. Shewing distinctly, what lives may be most advantageously nominated; the chance of survivorship; the numbers that must die, to produce each increment of annuity; the time in which according to the probabilities of human life those numbers will die; and the consequent gain or loss of each subscriber at each stage of the annuity. By J. Y., mathematician.
32 pp. Dublin, Watson, 1774

K., N.

899 TUCKER, Josiah. Four tracts on political and commercial subjects. [Tract I. A solution of the important question, whether a poor country, where raw materials & provision are cheap and wages low, can supplant the trade of a rich manufacturing country, where raw materials & provision are dear and the price of labour high—with a postscript obviating objections. Tract II. The case of going to war for the sake of trade, considered in a new light, being the fragment of a greater work. Tract III. A letter from a merchant in London, to his nephew in America, concerning the late and present disturbances in the colonies. Tract IV. The true interest of Great Britain set forth in regard to the colonies; and the only means of living in harmony with them.]
224 pp. 2nd ed. Gloucester, R. Raikes, 1774

P.

1775

900 The address of the people of Great Britain to the inhabitants of America.
62 pp. Dublin, printed by Mary Hay, 1775

A., K.

901 An address to the people of Great-Britain, from the delegates, appointed by the several English colonies of New-Hampshire, Massachusett's-Bay, Rhode-Island & Providence Plantations, Connecticut, New York, New-Jersey, Pennsylvania, the lower counties on Delaware, Maryland, Virginia, North-Carolina, & South Carolina, to consider their grievances, in general congress, at Philadelphia, September 5, 1774.
56 pp. Philadelphia & Dublin, J. Porter, 1775

A.

902 Authentic papers from America: submitted to the dispassionate consideration of the public.
36 pp. London, T. Becket, 1775

K.

903 [BROOKE, Arthur.] An inquiry into the policy of the laws, affecting the popish inhabitants of Ireland, preceded by a short political analysis of the history and constitution of Ireland, in which the rights of colonists and planters are briefly mentioned, the nature of the connection between England and Ireland deduced from the time of Henry II. and a few observations made on the policy of the laws that restrain the trade of Ireland,—with some hints respecting America.
131 pp. Dublin, Elizabeth Lynch, 1775
A., N., Q.

904 BURKE, Edmund. The history of American taxation from the year 1763 to the end of last session. In which is introduced an account of the official abilities of the following ministers and how far they have been concerned either in pursuing or receding from the present scheme of governing America. The rt. hon. George Grenville; lord Rockingham; lord Chatham; and the rt. hon. Charles Townshend. With an account of the act asserting the entireness of British legislative authority. 3rd ed. By Edmund Burke [Paginated with] the speech of the right honourable the earl of Chatham in the House of Lords on Friday the 20th of January, 1775.
102 pp. London and Dublin, John Exshaw and others, 1775
A., K., N., Q., T.

905 BURKE, Edmund. Speech of Edmund Burke, Esq., on American taxation, April 19, 1774.
96 pp. 4th ed. London, J. Dodsley, 1775
A.

906 ——. The speech of Edmund Burke, Esq., on moving his resolutions for conciliation with the colonies, March 22, 1775.
90 pp. Dublin, J. Exshaw & R. Moncrieffe, 1775
A.

907 BURNABY, Andrew. Travels through the middle settlements in North-America. In the years 1759–1760. With observations upon the state of the colonies.
214 pp. 2nd ed. London, T. Payne, 1775
Q.

908 CLOSSY, William. An appeal to the public, relative to the steeple lotteries for the years 1770, 1771, & 1772 & the deficiencies of the funds thereof.
62 pp. Dublin, printed by M. Mills, 1775
A.

909 Common sense: in nine conferences between a British merchant and a candid merchant of America, in their private capacities as friends.
table of contents. 128 pp. London, J. Dodsley, Brotherton and Sewell, 1775
A.

910 [COOPER, Myles.] A friendly address to all reasonable Americans, on the subject of our political confusions: in which the necessary consequences of violently opposing the king's troops, and of a general non-importation are fairly stated.
56 pp. 'New York: printed and Cork re-printed for Mary Edwards by Dennis Donnoghue', 1775
K.

'New York: printed & Dublin reprinted by Mary Hay', 1775
T.
See 869.

911 DONALDSON, William. Agriculture considered as a moral and political duty, in a series of letters inscribed to his majesty and recommended to the perusal and attention of every gentleman of landed property in the three kingdoms, as they are calculated for the entertainment, instruction and benefit of mankind.
204 pp. London, T. Becket, 1775
Q.

912 [ELIBANK, Patrick Murray, 5th Baron.] Eight sets of queries, submitted, with an unusual degree of humility, to the nobility, lairds, fine gentlemen, fine ladies, tenants, merchants' manufacturers, clergy and people of Scotland. Upon the subject of wool and of the woolen manufacture. By a peer of the realm.
44 pp. Edinburgh, William Creech, 1775
Q.

913 ELLIS, John. A description of the mangostan and the bread-fruit: the first, esteemed one of the most delicious; the other, the most useful of all the fruits in the East Indies. To which are added, directions to voyagers, for bringing over these and other vegetable productions, which would be extremely beneficial to the inhabitants of our West India Islands.
plates. 48 pp. London, Edward and Charles Dilly, 1775
A.

914 [EVANS, Caleb.] A letter to the Rev. Mr. John Wesley, occasioned by his calm address to the American Colonies.
24 pp. London, Edward and Charles Dilly, 1775
Q.

915 [GALLOWAY, Joseph.] A candid examination of the mutual claims of Great Britain, and the Colonies with a plan of accommodation on constitutional principles.
64 pp. New York, James Rivington, 1775
K.

916 GLOVER, Richard. The evidence delivered on the petition presented by the West-India planters and merchants to the House of Commons, as it was introduced at the bar, and summed up. By Mr. Glover.
98 pp. n.p., 1775
A., N.

917 ——. The substance of the evidence on the petition presented by the West-India planters and merchants to the hon. House of Commons, as it was introduced at the bar and summed up by Mr. Glover on Thursday the 16th of March, 1775.
49 pp. London, T. Cadell, 1775
Q.

918 HOWARD, Gorges Edmond. Several special cases on the laws against the further growth of popery in Ireland.
368 pp. Dublin, Elizabeth Lynch, 1775
A.

919 [HOWARD, George.] Some hints to the Dublin society, on the most important subject now before them in relation to

a new list of premiums to take place after the present year 1775, for the encouragement of agriculture, manufactures and arts. By a member of the society.
14 pp. Dublin, Samuel Price, 1775

G., Q.

920 [JOHNSON, Samuel.] Taxation no tyranny; an answer to the resolutions and address of the American congress.
92 pp. 3rd ed. London, T. Cadell, 1775

P.

921 Justice and policy. An essay on the increasing growth and enormities of our great cities. Shewing the breaches thereby occasioned in the constitution; and to place it upon a more firm basis, by uniting Ireland, instead of exchanging religion for trade. With a plan of an union—the publication of state of the nation in regard to America, of the Isle of Man, on policy, and a new scheme of annuities for the benefit of the poor, by employing them universally; with miscellaneous reflections. Addressed to a noble peer. By a freeholder in Ireland, and a stockholder in England. Part II.
38 pp. 3rd ed. London and Dublin, the author, 1775

T.

This is a continuation of the pamphlet with similar title written in 1772.
See 818.

922 [KNOX, William.] The interest of the merchants and manufacturers of Great Britain, in the present contest with the colonies, stated and considered.
24 pp. Dublin, printed by executors of David Hay, 1775

K., P.

923 [LEE, Arthur?] An appeal to the justice and interests of the people of Great Britain, in the present disputes with America. By an old member of parliament.
tables. 68 pp. 2nd ed. corrected. London, Almon, 1775

N.

924 [——.] A second appeal to the justice and interests of the people, on the measures respecting America. By the author of the first.
90 pp. London, J. Almon, 1775

Q.

925 [——.] A speech intended to have been delivered in the House of Commons, in support of the petition from the General Congress at Philadelphia. By the author of an appeal to the justice and interests of Great Britain.
70 pp. London, J. Almon, 1775

Q.

926 [LEEDS, Francis Godolphin Osborne, 5th duke of.] A short hint, addressed to the candid and dispassionate, on both sides of the Atlantic.
20 pp. London, J. Almon, 1775

Q.

927 LOCH, David, of Over Cambie. Essay on the trade, commerce and manufactures of Scotland.
104 pp. Edinburgh, the author, 1775

Q.

928 MACAULAY, Catherine. An address to the people of England, Scotland, and Ireland, on the present important crisis of affairs.
30 pp. London, Edward and Charles Dilly, 1775

K.

929 MAHON, Charles Stanhope, styled viscount Mahon. Considerations on the means of preventing fraudulent practices on the gold coin. Written at Geneva in 1773.
diagrams. 18 pp. London, Shropshire, 1775

A.

930 Observations on the state and condition of the poor, under the institution, for their relief, in the city of Dublin; together with the state of the fund, etc. published by order of the corporation, instituted for the relief of the poor, & for punishing vagabonds & sturdy beggars, in the county of the city of Dublin, March 25th, 1775.
table. 118 pp. Dublin, printed by William Wilson, 1775

A., G., N., P., R.

931 The pamphlet entitled, 'Taxation no tyranny', candidly considered, and it's arguments, and pernicious doctrines, exposed and refuted.
134 pp. London, Davis, Evans, [1775]

N.

932 POTTER, Robert. Observations on the poor laws, on the present state of the poor and on houses of industry.
76 pp. London, J. Wilkie, 1775

Q.

933 Premiums offered by the society instituted at London for the encouragement of arts, manufactures and commerce.
94 pp. London, the society, 1775

Q.

934 A proposition for the present peace and future government of the British Colonies in North America.
60 pp. London, the author, 1775

Q.

935 Reflections upon the present state of affairs, at home and abroad, particularly with regard to subsidies, and the differences between Great Britain and France. In a letter from a member of parliament to a constituent.
60 pp. London, J. Payne, 1775

T.

936 The supremacy of the British legislature over the colonies, candidly discussed.
42 pp. London, J. Johnson, 1775

T.

937 [TAMLINI, ——?] Supplement au Traité sur la Mendicité avec les objections qui ont été faites contre les projets de réglement, qui y sont proposés pour l'abolir, et les réponses.
56 pp. Bruxelles, R. Varle (Tourrai), 1775

Q.

938 Three letters to a member of parliament, on the subject of the present dispute with our American colonies.
74 pp. London, T. Lowndes, 1775

K.

939 Transactions of the committee, appointed the 20th of March, 1775, in St. Mary's vestry room, to examine into the accounts of the steeple schemes for the years 1770, 1771, & 1772.
24 pp. Dublin, printed by M. Mills, 1775
A.

940 TUCKER, Josiah. An humble address and earnest appeal to those respectable personages in Great-Britain and Ireland, who, by their great and permanent interest in landed property, their liberal education, elevated rank, and enlarged views, are the ablest to judge, and the fittest to decide, whether a connection with, or a separation from the continental colonies of America, be most for the national advantage, and the lasting benefit of these kingdoms.
tables. 96 pp. 3rd ed. Glocester [sic], printed by Raikes, 1775
K., N.

See also 986.

941——. A letter to Edmund Burke, Esq., member of parliament for the city of Bristol and agent for the colony of New York, etc. in answer to his printed speech said to be spoken in the House of Commons on the twenty-second of March, 1775.
58 pp. Gloucester, R. Raikes, London, T. Cadell, 1775
A., G., K., T.

——. 48 pp. Dublin, printed by Mary Hay, 1775.
K., N.

942 ——. Tract V. The respective pleas & arguments of the mother country, & of the colonies, distinctly set forth; & the impossibility of a compromise of differences, or a mutual concession of rights, plainly demonstrated. With a prefatory epistle to the plenipotentiaries of the late congress at Philadelphia.
60 pp. London, T. Cadell & J. Walters, 1775
A., N., T.

943 WESLEY, John. A calm address to our American colonies.
24 pp. London, printed by R. Hawes, [1775]
Q., T.

944 WOODWARD, Richard, bishop of Cloyne. An address to the public on the expediency of a regular plan for the maintenance and government of the poor: in which its utility with respect to industry morals and public oeconomy is proved from reason; and confirmed by the experience of the house of industry lately established in Dublin. With some general observations on the English system of poor laws; and an examination of the chapter in lord Kaims's sketches of the history of man relative to the poor. To which is added an argument in support of the right of the poor in the kingdom of Ireland to a national provision.
165 pp. Dublin and London, reprinted for G. Robinson, 1775
A., N., Q.

945 ——. An address to the public on the expediency of a regular plan for the maintenance and government of the poor: in which its utility with respect to industry, morals, and publick economy is proved from reason; and confirmed by the experience of the house of industry lately established in Dublin. With some general observations on the English system of poor laws; and an examination of the chapter in lord Kaims's sketches of the history of man relative to the poor. Written at the particular request of the corporation instituted for the relief of the poor, and the punishment of vagabonds, &c. in the county of the city of Dublin.
tables. 96 pp. Dublin, E. Lynch, 1775
G., K., T.

946 ZUBLY, John J. The law of liberty. A sermon on American affairs, preached at the opening of the provincial congress of Georgia. Addressed to the right honourable the earl of Dartmouth. With appendix, giving a concise account of the struggles of Swisserland to recover their liberty.
74 pp. Philadelphia and London, J. Almon, 1775
Q.

1776

947 ADAMS, Samuel. An oration delivered at the state-house, in Philadelphia, to a very numerous audience; on Thursday the 1st of August, 1776.
44 pp. Philadelphia & Dublin, reprinted by J. Exshaw, 1776
A.

948 An appeal to the understanding of the electors of Ireland.
30 pp. Dublin, printed by George Bonham (successor to S. Powell), 1776
A., Q.

949 [BOYD, Hugh.] Letters addressed to the electors of the county of Antrim. By a freeholder. Published previous to the general election.
72 pp. Belfast, 1776
A., G.

950 The builders price-book; containing a correct list of the prices allowed by the most eminent surveyors in London, to the several artificers concerned in building. Collected by an experienced surveyor.
tables. 124 pp. London, I. Taylor, 1776
Q.

951 BURN, Richard. Observations on the bill intended to be offered to Parliament for the better relief and employment of the poor. In a letter to a member of Parliament.
56 pp. London, T. Cadell, 1776
Q.

952 Bye-laws and orders of the corporation instituted for the relief of the poor, etc. in the county of the city of Dublin.
24 pp. Dublin, W. Wilson, 1776
N.

953 The charters of the British colonies in America.
144 pp. Dublin, John Beatty, 1776
A., Q.

954 An essay on the rights of the East India company to the perpetuity of their trade, possessions and revenue in India; and to the appointment of their officers and servants, without the interference of government. In which the dangers to be apprehended from the dissensions in their council at Bengal are considered; and a short plan proposed, for a division of the

profits that may arise from their trade and revenues. By the author of an essay on the East India trade, and its importance to this kingdom.
tables. 60 pp. London, T. Payne, 1776
T.

955 [FERGUSON, Adam.] Remarks on a Pamphlet lately published by Dr. Price, entitled, Observations on the nature of civil liberty, the principles of government, and the justice and policy of the war with America, etc. In a letter from a gentleman in the country to a member of parliament.
64 pp. London, T. Cadell, 1766
Q.

——. Another edition, 72 pp. Dublin, Whitestone, 1776
A.

956 [GRENVILLE, George.] A speech, against the suspending & dispensing prerogative etc.
74 pp. 6th ed. London, J. Almon, 1776
A.

957 HEY, Richard. Observations on the nature of civil liberty and the principles of government.
74 pp. London, T. Cadell, and T. and J. Merill, 1776
Q.

958 [HUTCHINSON, Thomas?] Experience preferable to theory. An answer to Dr. Price's observations on the nature of civil liberty, and the justice & policy of the war with America.
104 pp. London, T. Payne, 1776
A.

959 [LEE, Arthur.] An appeal to the justice and interests of the people of Great Britain, in the present disputes with America, by an old member of parliament.
47 pp. 4th ed. London, J. Almon, 1776
Q.

960 [LEONARD, Daniel.] Massachusettensis: or a series of letters, containing a faithful state of many important and striking facts, which laid the foundation of the present troubles in the province of Massachusetts-bay; interspersed with animadversions & reflections, originally addressed to the people of that province, & worthy the consideration of the true patriots of this country. By a person of honor upon the spot.
124 pp. 3rd ed. Boston & London, J. Mathews, 1776
A.

——. 124 pp. 4th ed. Boston & London, J. Mathews, 1776
N.

961 A letter to the Rev. Dr. Richard Price, on his observations on the nature of civil liberty, the principles of government and the justice and policy of the war with America. By T. D.
30 pp. London, Evans and Wallis and Stonehouse, [1776?]
Q.

962 [LIND, John.] An answer to the declaration of the American congress.
130 pp. 4th ed. London, T. Cadell, [etc.], 1776
N.
See 1001.

——. 130 pp. 5th ed. London, T. Cadell, [etc.], 1776
A.

963 [——.] Three letters to Doctor Price, containing remarks on his observations on the nature of civil liberty, the principles of government, and the justice and policy of the war with America. By a member of Lincoln's Inn, F.R.S., F.S.A.
188 pp. London, T. Payne, J. Sewell, [etc.], 1776
A., Q.

964 [MACPHERSON, James.] The rights of Great Britain asserted against the claims of America: being an answer to the declaration of the General Congress.
table. 96 pp. London, T. Cadell, 1776
Q.

——. 96 pp. 2nd ed. London, printed for T. Cadell
N.

965 ——. The rights of Great Britain asserted against the claims of America; being an answer to the declaration of the general congress. 8th ed. To which is now added, a refutation of Dr. Price's state of the national debt table.
128 pp. London, T. Cadell, 1776
K., Q.

——. fold. tabl. 100 pp. 3rd ed. London, T. Cadell, 1776
A.

——. fold tabl. 62 pp. 3rd ed. Dublin, printed by Caleb Jenkin, 1776
A., K., R.

966 [MADAN, Martin.] Strictures upon the declaration of the congress at Philadelphia; in a letter to a noble lord, etc.
32 pp. London, 1776
T.

967 MAUDUIT, Israel. A short view of the history of the New England colonies, with respect to their charters and constitution. 4th ed. To which is now added, an account of a conference between the late Mr. Grenville and the several colony agents, in the year 1764, previous to the passing of the stamp act. Also the original charter granted in the 4th of Charles I. and never before printed in England.
100 pp. London, J. Wilkie, 1776
Q.

968 MOLYNEUX, William. The case of Ireland's being bound by acts of parliament in England stated.
105 pp. Belfast, John Hay, 1776
B., N.

969 [O'BRIEN, Sir Lucius Henry.] The substance of two speeches in the House of Commons of Ireland, on the 25th and 26th of March, 1776, on the subject of fisheries. With some additions necessary more fully to explain the fishing trade.
80 pp. Dublin, William Watson, 1776
A., Q.

970 [PAINE, Thomas.] Common sense; addressed to the inhabitants of America, on the following interesting subjects. I. Of the origin and design of government in general, with concise remarks on the English constitution. II. Of monarchy and hereditary succession. III. Thoughts on the present state

of American affairs. IV. Of the present ability of America, with some miscellaneous reflections. A new edition, with several additions in the body of the work. To which is added an appendix; together with an address to the people called Quakers. N.B. The new addition here given increases the work upwards of one-third.
58 pp. Philadelphia, printed; London, re-printed, for J. Almon, 1776

A., Q.

971 The plain question upon the present dispute with our American colonies.
24 pp. 2nd ed. London, J. Wilkie, 1776

Q.

——. 24 pp. 6th ed. Dublin, James Hoey, 1776

R.

972 Premiums offered by the Dublin society, for the encouragement of agriculture, planting, & other articles in husbandry.
22 pp. n.p., Dublin society, 1776

A.

973 PRICE, Richard. Observations on the nature of civil liberty, the principles of government and the justice and policy of the war with America. To which are added an appendix and postscript, containing a state of the national debt, an estimate of the money drawn from the public by the taxes and an account of the national income and expenditure since the last war.
134 pp. 2nd ed. diags. London, T. Cadell, 1776

A.

——. 138 pp. 6th ed. London, T. Cadell, 1776

Q.

974 ——. Observations on the nature of civil liberty, the principles of government, and the justice and policy of the war with America. To which is added, an appendix, containing a state of the national debt, an estimate of the money drawn from the public by the taxes, and an account of the national income and expenditure since the last war. With the amount of the capitals at the bank, South-sea, and India-houses, not inserted in the London edition of this work.
tables, appendix. 186 pp. Dublin, J. Exshaw, [etc.], 1776.

P.

975 [RAMSAY, Alan.] A plan of reconciliation between Great Britain and her colonies; founded in justice, and constitutional security: by which the rights of Englishmen, in matters of taxation, are preserved to the inhabitants of America, and the islands beyond the Atlantic. By the author of the historical essay on the English constitution.
62 pp. London, J. Johnson, P. Elmsly, 1776

K.

976 Reflections on the state of parties; on the national debt, and the necessity and expediency of the present war with America.
70 pp. London, W. Davies, [1776?]

Q.

977 ROBINSON, William. The gentleman and builder's director; containing plain and familiar instruction for erecting

every kind of building according to their respective classes as regulated by an Act of Parliament, passed the last sessions, for the better regulating of buildings and more effectually preventing mischiefs by fire. To which is added, a plate shewing at the first view the external and party-walls for each class of building. Also a section of a stack of chimneys with directions to build them to prevent their smoking.
54 pp. London, G. Kearsley, W. Shropshire, [etc.], [1776]

Q.

978 [SERLE, Ambrose.] Americans against liberty: or, an essay on the nature & principles of true freedom, shewing that the designs & conduct of the Americans tend only to tyranny and slavery.
44 pp. 2nd ed. London, James Matthews, 1776

A.

——. 48 pp. 3rd ed. London, James Matthews, 1776

A.

979 SHEBBEARE, J. An answer to the queries, contained in a letter to Dr. Shebbeare printed in the Public Ledger, August 10. Together with animadversions on two speeches in defence of the printers of a paper, subscribed a South Briton. The first pronounced by the right. hon Thomas Townshend, in the house of commons, & printed in the London Packet of February 18. The second by the right learned councellor Lee, in Guildhall, & printed in the Public Ledger of August 12.
180 pp. London, S. Hooper, T. Davies, [1776]

A.

980 ——. An essay on the origin, progress and establishment of national society; in which the principles of government, the definitions of physical, moral, civil and religious liberty contained in Dr. Price's observations, etc. are fairly examined and fully refuted; together with a justification of the legislature, in reducing America to obedience, by force. To which is added an appendix on the excellent and admirable in Mr. Burke's second printed speech of the 22nd of March, 1775.
216 pp. London, J. Bew, 1776

A., Q.

981 A short appeal to the people of Great Britain; upon the unavoidable necessity of the present war with our disaffected colonies.
24 pp. 2nd ed. Dublin, J. Hoey, 1776

A.

'Said to be by Dr. Samuel Johnson'—Sabin.

982 SLOAN, John and others. A short treatise upon improvements made in the linen manufacture of Ireland.
By John Sloan, John O'Brien, J. Privat, Terence Byrne.
16 pp. Dublin, Forde, 1776

A.

See 1030.

983 [SMITH, William.] Plain truth: addressed to the inhabitants of America containing remarks on a late pamphlet intitled Common Sense: wherein are shown, that the scheme of independence is ruinous, delusive and impracticable; that were the author's assertions, respecting the power of America, as real as nugatory, reconciliation on liberal principles with Great Britain would be exalted policy; and that circumstanced as we are, permanent liberty and true happiness can only be obtained by reconciliation with that kingdom. Written by Candidus.

52 pp. printed Philadelphia; reprinted London for J. Almon, 1776

A., N., Q., T.

984 STAIR, John Dalrymple, earl of. The state of the national debt, the national income, and the national expenditure. With some short inferences and reflexions applicable to the present dangerous crisis.

tables. 30 pp. Dublin, Chamberlaine, Whitestone, [etc.], 1776

A., K., N., P., Q., T.

985 TUCKER, Josiah. Four tracts, on political and commercial subjects. Tract I. A solution of the important question, whether a poor country, where raw materials & provision are cheap and wages low, can supplant the trade of a rich manufacturing country, where raw materials & provisions are dear, & the price of labour high.—with a postscript obviating objections. Tract II. The case of going to war for the sake of trade, considered in a new light, being the fragment of a greater work. Tract III. A letter from a merchant in London, to his nephew in America, concerning the late and present disturbances in the colonies. Tract IV. The true interest of Great Britain set forth in regard to the colonies; and the only means of living in peace & harmony with them.

222 pp. 3rd ed. London, T. Cadell, 1776

A., K.

986 ——. An humble address and earnest appeal to those respectable personages in Great Britain and Ireland who, by their great and permanent interest in landed property, their liberal education, elevated rank, and enlarged views, are the ablest to judge, and the fittest to decide, whether a connection with, or a separation from the continental colonies of America, be most for the national advantage, and the lasting benefit of these kingdoms. The third ed. corrected.

tables. 94 pp. London, T. Cadell, 1776

K., T.

987 TWISS, Richard. Tour in Ireland in 1775. With a view of the salmon-leap at Ballyshannon.

fold. frontisp. 232 pp. Dublin, Sheppard, [etc.], 1776

A.

988 WATSON, Richard. An essay on civil liberty: or the principles of the revolution vindicated. Delivered before the university of Cambridge, on Wednesday, May 29, 1776.

22 pp. 2nd ed. Cambridge and Dublin, W. Wilson, 1776

N., Q.

——. 24 pp. 3rd ed. Cambridge and Dublin, W. Wilson, 1776

A.

989 WHITWORTH, Sir Charles. A register of the trade of the port of London; specifying the articles imported and exported, arranged under the respective countries; with a list of the ships entered inwards and cleared outwards. Number I. for January, February, and March, 1776; to be continued. By Sir Charles Whitworth, member of parliament.

142 pp. London, Flexney, Robinson, [etc.], 1776

Q.

1777

990 ABINGDON, Bertie Willoughby, 4th earl of. Thoughts on the letter of Edmund Burke, esq; to the sheriffs of Bristol, on the affairs of America.

64 pp. Oxford, W. Jackson, [1777]

A., Q.

——. Another issue. 48 pp. Dublin, company of booksellers, [1777]

K.

——. Another issue. 36 pp. Newry, printed by Joseph Gordon, [1777]

E.

991 An account of Mr. Thomas Johnston's improvement of the live stock, of the kingdom of Ireland.

44 pp. Dublin, printed by M. Mills, 1777

A., K., P.

992 [ANDERSON, Sir James?] An enquiry into the nature of the corn-laws; with a view to the new corn-bill proposed for Scotland.

60 pp. Edinburgh, Mrs. Mundell, 1777

Q.

993 An answer to the letter of Edmund Burke, esq., one of the representatives of the city of Bristol, to the sheriffs of that city.

62 pp. London, T. Cadell, 1777

Q.

994 [BERESFORD, John?] Observations on the brewing trade of Ireland, submitted to the public, by an officer of the revenue. (Also) report from the committee appointed to take into consideration the petition of the master, wardens and brethren of the Corporation of Brewers, etc. 1773.

2+130+18 pp. (separately paginated). n.p., [1777?]

A., K., N., Q.

Only the K. and Q. editions include the report.

995 BURKE, Edmund. A letter from Edmund Burke, esq., one of the representatives in Parliament for the city of Bristol, to John Farr and John Harris, esqrs., sheriffs of that city, on the affairs of America.

76 pp. 2nd ed. London, J. Dodsley, 1777

A., Q.

——. 80 pp. 4th ed. London, 1777

A., N.

——. Another issue, 60 pp. Dublin, W. Whitestone, 1777

A., K.

996 The case stated, on philosophical ground, between Great Britain and her colonies: or the anology between states and individuals, respecting the term of political adultness, pointed out.

168 pp. London, G. Kearsly, 1777

Q.

997 [CLARE, John Fitzgibbon, 1st earl of.] Commerce not a fit subject for an embargo. By an emminent barrister, member of the late parliament, etc.
42 pp. Dublin, T. Walker, [etc.], 1777
A., K., N., T.

998 DODD, A. Charles. The contrast; or, strictures on select parts of Doctor Price's additional observations on civil liberty, etc. Forming, a concise state of the present currency; an impartial view of the trade and government of the kingdom; the cause and consequences of the war with America; and a sketch of the dedts [sic] and revenues of France.
64 pp. London, Fielding and Walker, 1777
Q.

999 Essays commercial and political, on the real and relative interests of imperial and dependent states, particularly those of Great Britain and her dependencies; displaying the probable causes of, and a mode of compromising the present disputes between this country and her American colonies. To which is added, an appendix, on the means of amancipating slaves, without loss to their proprietors.
160 pp. Newcastle, the author, 1777
Q.

1000 FOSTER, Edward. A letter to Sydenham Singleton, esq., chairman of the committee appointed by the hon. House of Commons to inquire into the state of lunatics in this city, and on the present state of the insane poor in this kingdom.
16 pp. Dublin, printed by M. Mills, 1777
Q.

1001 [LIND, John.] An answer to the declaration of the American congress.
96 pp. 4th ed. Dublin, printed by P. Higly, 1777
Q.
See 962.

1002 [MORGAN, William.] Special rules on the revenue side of the court of the exchequer.
32 pp. Dublin, printed by William Kidd, 1777
A., T.

1003 PRICE, Richard. Additional observations on the nature & value of civil liberty, & the war with America: also observations on schemes for raising money by public loans; an historical deduction & analysis of the national debt; & a brief account of the debts & resources of France.
192 pp. London, T. Cadell, 1777
A., N.

1004 Reasons for the late increase of the poor-rates; or, a comparative view of the price of labour and provisions.
46 pp. London, J. Dodsley, 1777
Q.

1005 A short account of the institution, rules and proceedings of the Cork Society, for the relief and discharge of persons confined for small debts.
tables. 40 pp. Cork, printed by Flyn, 1777
A.

1006 [STEVENS, William.] Strictures on a sermon, The principles of the revolution vindicated.
36 pp. 3rd ed. Dublin, W. Hallhead, 1777
N., Q.

1007 TRANT, James Phillip. The extraordinary case of James Ph. Trant.
22 pp. Cork, the author, 1777
A.
On Catholic tenures.

1008 [TRUSLER, John.] The way to be rich and respectable, addressed to men of small fortune. In this pamphlet is given an estimate, shewing that a gentleman, with a wife, four children, and five servants, may, residing in the country, with a few acres of land, live as well as, and make an appearance of life equal to, a man of 1000l. a year, and yet not expend 400l. including the rent both of house and land; and still be able, in the course of 20 years, to lay by 2500l.
48 pp. Dublin, printed by James Hoey, [1777]
A.

1009 An unconnected whig's address to the public upon the present civil war, the state of public affairs and the real cause of all the national calamities.
84 pp. London, G. Kearsley, 1777
Q.

1010 WITHERSPOON, John. The dominion of providence over the passions of men. A sermon preached at Princeton, on the 17th of May, 1776. Being the general fast appointed by the congress through the united colonies. To which is added, an address to the natives of Scotland, residing in America.
48 pp. 4th ed. Glasgow & Belfast, Robert Smith, 1777
A.

1778

1011 BURKE, Edmund. Speech of Edmund Burke, esq., on moving his resolutions for conciliation with the colonies, March 22, 1775.
109 pp. 3rd ed. London, J. Dodsley, 1778
A.

1012 ——. Two letters from Mr. Burke to gentlemen in the city of Bristol, on the bills depending in parliament relative to the trade of Ireland.
34 pp. London, J. Dodsley, 1778
A., N.

——. 34 pp. 2nd ed. London, J. Dodsley, 1778
N.

1013 [CLARKE, J. ——.] The neglected wealth of Ireland explored or a plain view of the great national advantages which may be obtained by compleating the navigation of the river Shannon, the uniting of other rivers to it, the working of mines, and, the establishment of various manufactures in the kingdom of Ireland. With some observations on the means of carrying these plans into execution, and of removing every restriction on the trade and commerce of the Irish: upon principles of national equity to Great Britain and her sister country.
tables. 50 pp. Dublin, printed by M. Mills, 1778
A., N., P., T., U.

1014 Consideration on the silk trade of Ireland. With useful hints for the extension thereof, addressed to the Dublin society.
24 pp. Dublin, 1778

A.

1015 The Cork by-laws, of the corporation for the relief of the poor, and the punishment of sturdy beggars and vagrants.
16 pp. Cork, printed by William Flyn, 1778

A.

1016 [EARDLEY-WILMOT, John.] A short defense of the opposition; in answer to a pamphlet intitled, 'A short history of the opposition'.
82 pp. London, J. Almon, [etc.], 1778

A.

1017 Extract of rules on the revenue side of the exchequer, from 1685, also, authorities of law produced in support of heads of a bill proposed for the more effectual execution of the green wax process.
8 pp. Dublin, printed by W. Kidd, 1778

A., Q.

1018 [GROSSETT, Charles.] Hints preparatory to the serious consideration and discussion, of the sundry fisheries of this kingdom. Most humbly addressed to his excellency John earl of Buckingham lord lieutenant general and general governor of Ireland: the right honourable the lords spiritual and temporal: the right honourable and honourable the knights, citizens, and burgesses, in parliament assembled.
78 pp. Dublin, printed by John Exshaw, 1778

A.

1019 [HOLWELL, J. J.] An address to the proprietors of East India stock. In consequence of the errors and mistakes in some late publications, relative to their shipping.
tables. 124 pp. London, F. Nourse, 1778

Q.

1020 Humble remonstrance, for the repeal of the laws against the Roman Catholics. With judicious remarks, for the general union of christians.
40 pp. Dublin, B. Corcoran, 1778

A.

1021 An inquiry into the conduct of the commissioners for paving the streets of Dublin. Addressed to the right honourable the knights, citizens, and burgesses in parliament assembled.
tables. 68 pp. Dublin, the booksellers, 1778

Q.

1022 [KNOX, William.] Considerations on the state of Ireland.
72 pp. Dublin, William Watson, 1778

K., N., Q.

1023 A linen draper's letter to the friends of Ireland.
fold. tab. 28 pp. Dublin, 1778

A., N.

1024 MORGAN, Richard. Observations on heads of a bill for the amendment of the laws with respect to custodians. Committed in the sessions of 1773. With amendments pro-

posed for the extending the advantages of the custodian laws.
24 pp. Dublin, printed by John Hillary, 1778

A., Q.

1025 Premiums offered by the Dublin society, 1778.
24 pp. Dublin, printed by W. Sleater, [1778?]

A.

1026 PULTENEY, William. Thoughts on the present state of affairs with America, and the means of conciliation. By William Pulteney, esq., representative in parliament for the town of Shrewsberry; and brother to governor Johnstone, one of the commissioners to negotiate peace with America to which are added, two appendixes, containing letters wrote by Mr. Franklyn. Also extracts from the works of Dr. Tucker, dean of Gloucester. The fourth edition.
appendix. 104 pp. Dublin, William Hallhead, 1778

A., K., Q., T.

1027 A Roman Catholic's address to parliament. With an appendix, containing, the address of the Roman Catholics of Great Britain, to his majesty; and the act lately passed in the British parliament for the relief of the Roman Catholics of England.
48 pp. London & Dublin, Wogan, Bean, and Pike, 1778

A.

1028 Rules and regulations of the company of undertakers of the Grand Canal, for the better carrying on the navigation: and the proceedings of the company. Amended and agreed to in February 1778. Printed by order of the company.
44 pp. Dublin, printed by Wogan, Bean, and Pike, 1778

T.

1029 A sketch of the history of two acts of the Irish parliament, of the 2nd and 8th of Queen Anne, to prevent the further growth of popery; in a letter to a member of the House of Commons in Ireland. To which are added, the civil and military articles of Limerick.
84 pp. London, printed for J. Murray, 1778

A., N., Q.

1030 SLOAN, John and others. A short treatise upon improvements made in the linen manufacture of Ireland.
14 pp. Carlow, printed by Kinnier, 1778

N.

See 982.

1031 [TICKELL, Richard.] Anticipation: containing the substance of his m...y's most gracious speech to both H...s of P...l...t, on the opening of the approaching session, together with a full and authentic account of the debate which will take place in the H...e of C...s, on the motion for the address and the amendment. With notes.
82 pp. 2nd ed. London, T. Becket, 1778

A., Q.

1779

1032 The alarm; or, the Irish spy. In a series of letters on the present state of affairs in Ireland, to a lord high in the opposition. Written by an ex-Jesuit, employed by his lordship for the purpose.
72 pp. Dublin, printed by R. Marchbank, 1779

A., G., K., L., N., Q.

1033 An appeal from the protestant association to the people of Great Britain; concerning the probable tendency of the late act of parliament in favour of the papists.
62 pp. London, J. Dodsley, [etc.], 1779
A.

1034 AUCKLAND, William Eden, 1st baron. Four letters to the earl of Carlisle from William Eden esq.,
On certain perversions of political reasoning; and on the nature, progress, and effect of party spirit and of parties.
On the present circumstances of the war between Great Britain and the combined powers of France and Spain. On the public debts, on the public credit, and on the means of raising supplies.
On the representations of Ireland respecting a free-trade.
163 pp. 2nd ed. London, B. White & T. Cadell, 1779
A., N.

1035 ——. A letter to the earl of Carlisle from William Eden esq. on the representations of Ireland respecting a free trade.
tables. 48 pp. Dublin, the company of booksellers, 1779
A., K., N., P., Q., T.

1036 ——. Three letters to the earl of Carlisle. On certain perversions of political reasoning; and on the nature, progress and effect of party spirit and of parties. On the present circumstances of the war between Great Britain and the combined powers of France and Spain. On the public debts, on the public credit, and on the means of raising supplies.
tables. 98 pp. Dublin, printed by W. Spotswood, 1779
A., N., Q., T.

1037 BOSWELL, George. A treatise on watering meadows: wherein are shown some of the many advantages arising from that mode of practice, particularly on coarse, boggy or barren land: with four copper plates.
114 pp. London, J. Almon, 1779
D., Q.

1038 BURKE, Edmund. Two letters from Mr. Burke to gentlemen in the city of Bristol, on the bills depending in Parliament, relative to the trade of Ireland.
32 pp. Dublin, printed by Talbot, 1779
A., K.

1039 BUTTER, Samuel. A sermon preached in the parish church of St. Michan, Dublin, on Sunday the 17th day of October, 1779, by the Rev. Samuel Butter, L.L.B. curate of said parish, before the goldsmith's company of volunteers in Dublin, & printed at their unanimous request.
15 pp. Dublin, M. Mills, 1779
A.

1040 CALDWELL, Sir James, bart. An enquiry how far the restrictions laid upon the trade of Ireland, by British Acts of Parliament, are a benefit or disadvantage to the British dominions in general, and to England in particular; for whose separate advantage they were intended. With an address to the gentlemen concerned in the woollen commerce of Great Britain, and particularly to the members of parliament for the several counties, cities, and boroughs connected with those manufactures. To which is prefixed a letter to Sir John Duntze, bart., member of parliament for Tiverton, on the same subject; in which a union between the two kingdoms is

discussed. With extracts of such parts of the statutes as lay the trade of Ireland under those restrictions.
100 pp. Dublin, the company of booksellers, 1779
A., K., L., N., Q., T.

——. Another issue, 113 pp. Exeter, T. Beckett, 1779
A.

——. Another issue, 100 pp. Dublin, 1779
A.

1041 ——. [MS. t.p.]
[On the trade of Ireland. The first reporter of Irish parliamentary debates.]
64 pp. n.p., 1779
N.

1042 CARVER, Jonathan. A treatise on the culture of the tobacco plant; with the manner in which it is usually cured. Adapted to Northern climates, and designed for the use of the landholders of Great-Britain and Ireland.
58 pp. Dublin, White, 1779
N.

1043 [CAWTHORNE, Joseph?] Terms of conciliation: or, considerations on a free trade in Ireland; on pensions on the Irish establishment; & on an union with Ireland. Addressed to his grace, the duke of Northumberland.
90 pp. London, J. Milliken, 1779
A.

1044 A concise abstract of the most important clauses in the following interesting acts of parliament, passed in the session of 1779; by which the public in general are more immediately affected, than by any passed in any former session, viz.
1. Act for the suppression of smugglers, and the protection and encouragement of fair traders.
2. Act for preventing personal arrests under ten pounds.
3. Act for raising, embodying, and regulating the militia in England, and fencible men in Scotland.
4. Act for impressing seamen.
5. Act for erecting penitentiary houses for the confinement of offenders convicted of transportable crimes.
6. Act for imposing taxes on dwelling-houses, and hired servants.
7. Act for imposing taxes on post and other hired horses and carriages.
8. Act for additional stamp duties wherein are ascertained the quantity of chancery and common-law sheets.
9. Act for licensing auctioneers, and taxing estates and goods sold by auction.
With preface, notes, and observations, by a gentleman of the Inner-Temple.
London, Fielding and Walker, 1779
P.

1045 Considerations on the state of the Roman Catholics in Scotland.
23 pp. London, J. P. Coghlan, 1779
A.

1046 A defence of Great Britain, against a charge of tyranny in the government of Ireland, by an Irishman. To which are

added two letters in answer, by Lucius Hibernicus and Sarsfield. And a reply, by a real Irishman.
32 pp. Dublin, printed by C. Talbot, 1779
A., K., Q.

1047 Essays commercial and political on the real and relative interests of imperial and dependent states, particularly those of Great Britain and her dependencies displaying the probable causes of, and a mode of compromising the present disputes between this country and her American colonies. To which is added an appendix, on the means of emancipating slaves without loss to their proprietors. The second edition.
tables, appendix. 158 pp. London, J. Johnson: York, Wilson: Edinburgh, W. Creech: Newcastle, Whitfield, 1779
K.

1048 An examination into the conduct of the present administration, from the year 1774 to the year 1778. And a plan of accommodation with America. By a member of parliament.
71 pp. 2nd ed. London, J. Almon, 1779
A.

1049 Extracts from a pamphlet, entitled, observations on the brewing trade of Ireland. With some observations on those sections of the revenue law, passed last session of parliament, that relate to this subject.
22 pp. Dublin, 1779
A.

See 994.

1050 The first lines of Ireland's interest in the year one thousand seven hundred and eighty.
83 pp. Dublin, R. Marchbank, 1779
A., G., K., L., N., Q.

1051 [FLOOD, Henry or GRATTAN, Henry.] A letter to the people of Ireland, on the expediency and necessity of the present associations in Ireland, in favour of our own manufactures. With some cursory observations on the effects of a union.
78 pp. Dublin, sold by Isaac Colles, 1779
A., L., N., Q., T.

1052 [GALLOWAY, Joseph.] A letter to the right honourable lord viscount H(ow)e, on his naval conduct in the American war.
54 pp. London, J. Wilkie, 1779
Q.

1053 [GRAY, John.] A comparative view of the public burdens of Great Britain and Ireland. With a proposal for putting both islands on an equality, in regard to the freedom of foreign trade.
64 pp. London and Dublin, reprinted by R. Burton, 1779
A., K., L., N., P., Q., T.

Wagner believes that the first edition of this pamphlet was in 1772.

1054 [——.] An essay concerning the establishment of a national bank in Ireland.
60 pp. Dublin, W. Hallhead, 1779
A., K., N., Q., T.

1055 [HASLER, Sir John.] Cursory observations on Ireland. By a member of the Dublin society.
appendix. 64 pp. Dublin, printed by T. T. Faulkner, 1779
A., K., N., Q., T.

1056 [HELY-HUTCHINSON, John.] The commercial restraints of Ireland considered. In a series of letters to a noble lord. Containing an historical account of the affairs of that kingdom, so far as they relate to this subject.
240 pp. Dublin, printed by William Hallhead, 1779
A., G., N., T.

See 1104.

1057 HODGSON, P. Levi. The complete measurer, adapted to timber and building, agreeable to the Irish standard. The seventh edition.
tables, 128 pp. Dublin, R. Marchbank, 1779
A., Q.

1058 Impartial thoughts on a free trade to the kingdom of Ireland, in a letter to the right hon. Frederick, lord North, first lord commissioner of the treasury. Recommended to the consideration of every British senator, merchant, and manufacturer in this kingdom.
26 pp. London, J. Millidge, 1779
P.

1059 [JEBB, Frederick.] The letters of Guatimozin, on the affairs of Ireland, as first published in the Freeman's Journal, and which having been since re-printed in London, have gone through several editions there; to which are added, the letters of Causidicus, that accompanied the essays of Guatimozin in their first appearance.
84 pp. Dublin, Marchbank, 1779
A., D., G., K., T.

According to Gilbert, Causidicus was Robert Johnson.

1060 The people of Ireland not a parcel of lazy, incorrigible scoundrels. By G... B..., gent.
44 pp. Dublin, W. Wilson, 1779
Q.

1061 [POLLOCK, Joseph.] Letters of Owen Roe O'Nial.
48 pp. Ireland, 1779. [Dublin, W. Jackson.]
A., K., L., N.
On Irish legislative independence.
Place of publication and publisher's name on half-title page only.

1062 PULTENEY, William. Considerations on the present state of public affairs, & the means of raising the necessary supplies.
tables. 54 pp. London, J. Dodsley & T. Cadell, 1779
A., N., P.

——. Another issue, 54 pp. Dublin, William Hallhead, 1779
A.

1063 Renovation without violence yet possible.
46 pp. Dublin, printed by William Hallhead, 1779
N., Q.

1064 A scheme to prevent the running of Irish wools to France, and Irish woollens goods to foreign countries by

prohibiting the importation of Spanish wools into Ireland and permitting the people of Ireland to send their woollen goods to England (not for consumption but re-exportation) under a duty at importation to be drawn back on exportation from England to foreign countries. Humbly offered to the consideration of parliament. By a merchant of London.
tables. 50 pp. London, R. Franklin, [1779]
Q.

1065 SHERIDAN, Richard. A letter to William Eden, esq., on the subject of his to the earl of Carlisle; the Irish trade.
37 pp. Dublin, printed by M. Mills, 1779
A., N., Q., T.

1066 A short account of the reasons of the intended alteration of the value of the coins current in this kingdom.
8 pp. Dublin, printed by A. Rhames, 1779
A., Q.

1067 Substance of political debates on his majesty's speech, on the address, & the amendment: November 25th, 1779. With remarks on the state of the Irish claim to a free trade.
40 pp. London, R. Faulder, 1779
A.

1068 Thoughts on the inexpediency of continuing the Irish woollen ware-house, as a retail shop, humbly offered to the consideration of the members of both houses of parliament, and those of the Dublin society in particular.
tables. 20 pp. Dublin, printed by P. Wogan, 1779
A., C., N., Q., T.

1069 Thoughts on the present alarming crisis of affairs: humbly submitted to the serious consideration of the people of Ireland. Dedicated to the right honourable lord Naas. To which are added two letters formerly written to the popish inhabitants of this kingdom. By a grazier.
31 pp. Dublin, printed by W. Spotswood, 1779
K., Q., S.

1070 [TICKELL, Richard.] Anticipation: (for the year MDCCLXXIX) containing the substance of his m...y's most gracious speech to both H...s of P...l...t, on the opening of the approaching session. Together with a full and authentic account of the debate which will take place in the H...e of C...s on the motion for the address and the amendment. With notes. (First published five days before the opening of the session.)
64 pp. Dublin, for the company of booksellers, 1779
K.
See 1031.

1071 [——.] The green box of Monsieur de Sartine, found at Mademoiselle Du Thé's lodgings, from the French of the Hague edition. Revised & corrected by those of Leipsic & Amsterdam.
73 pp. Dublin, company of booksellers, 1779
A., N., K.

1072 YOUNG, Arthur. Political arithmetick. Part II. Containing considerations on the means of raising the supplies within a year. Occasioned by Mr. Pulteney's pamphlet on that subject.
tabs. 81 pp. London, T. Cadell, 1779
A., N.

1780

1073 Advice to a newly elected member of parliament, with observations on the legislative constitution, and the contract relating thereto, between the representatives of the people in parliament and their constituents. By a friend to the public.
31 pp. Dublin, printed by Robert Burton, 1780
L., N.

1074 An appeal from the protestant association to the people of Great Britain: concerning the probable tendency of the late act of parliament in favour of the papists.
64 pp. Dublin, printed by William Hallhead, 1780
A.

1075 AUCKLAND, William Eden, 1st baron. A fifth letter to the earl of Carlisle from William Eden, esq. on population; on certain revenue laws and regulations connected with the interests of commerce; and on public œconomy.
tables, appendices. 72 pp. Dublin, W. and H. Whitestone, 1780
A., K., U.

——. Another issue. 72 pp. London, B. White and T. Cadell, 1780
A., N., Q., T.

1076 Authentic minutes of the proceedings of a very respectable assembly, on 20th of December, 1779, to which are added, (in order to preserve them) the speeches of some noble lords, spoken the day following, some of which have already appeared in print.
76 pp. Dublin, printed by J. Potts, 1780
A., N.

——. Another issue. 78 pp. London, H. Payne and C. Dilly, 1780.
A.
See 1129.

1077 BAYLY, Edward. A plain and affectionate address to the shop-keepers, manufacturers, artificers, and traders, of this city and kingdom.
20 pp. Dublin, printed by James Williams, 1780
P.

1078 BIRD, Robert. Proposals for paying great part of the national debt and reducing taxes, immediately.
tables. 48 pp. London, J. Dodsley, 1780
U.

1079 BURKE, Edmund. Letter from a gentleman in the English House of Commons, in vindication of his conduct, with regard to the affairs of Ireland, addressed to a member of the Irish Parliament.
56 pp. London, J. Bew, 1780
N.

1080 ——. A letter from Edmund Burke, esq; in vindication of his conduct with regard to the affairs of Ireland. Addressed to Thomas Burgh, esq., member of parliament for Athy.
58 pp. London, J. Bew: Dublin, re-printed by C. Jackson, 1780
A., K., L., N., Q., T.

1081 ——. Speech of Edmund Burke, esq. on presenting to the House of Commons (on the 11th of February, 1780) a plan for the better security of the independence of parliament, and the oeconomical reformation of the civil and other establishments.
100 pp. Dublin, printed by R. Marchbank, for the company of booksellers, 1780
A., K., N., Q., T.

——. 100 pp. 4th ed. Dublin, 1780
A.

——. Another issue, 100 pp. Dublin, 1780
A.

1082 [CAMPBELL, Thomas?] A view of the present state of Ireland, containing observations upon the following subjects, viz., Its dependence, linen trade, provision trade, woollen manufactory, coals, fishery, agriculture. Of emigration, import trade of the city of Dublin. Effect of the present mode of raising the revenue. On the health and happiness of the people. The revenue. A national bank: and an absentee tax. Intended for the consideration of Parliament, on the approaching enlargement of the trade of that kingdom. To which is added, a sketch of some of the principal political characters in the Irish House of Commons.
134 pp. London, R. Faulder, Luke White, 1780
A., G., K., N., P., Q.

1083 A candid display, of the reciprocal conduct of Great Britain & her colonies; from the origin of the present contest, to the claim of independency. With a seasonable memento to the ruling powers of Great Britain and Ireland.
48 pp. Dublin, printed by P. Higly, 1780
A.

1084 CARYSFORT, John Joshua Proby, 1st earl of. Copy of a letter from the right honourable lord Carysfort, to the Huntingdonshire committee: to which is added, the report of the Westminster sub-committee, respecting the duration of parliament, and the representation of this country; with the resolutions of the committee.
16 pp. [London], society for constitutional information, 1780
A.

1085 Considerations upon the sugar & mutiny bills. Addressed to the people of Ireland in general, & the citizens of Dublin in particular.
32 pp. Dublin, Pat. Byrne, 1780
A., P.

1086 Debates of the house of commons of Ireland, on a motion whether the king's most excellent majesty, & the lords & commons of Ireland, are the only power competent to bind or enact laws in this kingdom. Taken in short hand, verbatim & literatim, by a gentleman.
26 pp. Dublin, 1780
A., T.

1087 A defense of the act of parliament lately passed for the relief of Roman Catholics; containing a true state of the laws now in force against popery: in answer to a pamphlet entitled, An appeal from the protestant association to the people of Great Britain, etc. In a letter to a friend. By a protestant.
48 pp. London & Dublin, Wogan, Bean & Pike, 1780
A., T.

1088 DOBBS, Francis. A letter to the right honourable lord North, on his propositions in favour of Ireland.
24 pp. Dublin, printed by M. Mills, 1780
A., G., K., Q.

——. Another issue. 28 pp. Dublin, 1780
N.

——. Another issue. 23 pp. London, S. Bladon, 1780
T.

1089 [D'OUTREPONT, Charles-Lambert.] Essai Historique sur l'Origine des Dixmes. Pour parvenir à l'examen de la question, si les décimateurs ont leur intention fondée en droit pour exiger la Dixme des fruits nouveaux.
116 pp. n.p., 1780
Q.

1090 [DRENNAN, William?] A letter to Edmund Burke, esq., by birth an Irishman, by adoption an Englishman. Containing some reflections on patriotism, party-spirit, and the union of free nations. With observations upon the means on which Ireland relies for obtaining political independence.
37 pp. Dublin, printed by William Hallhead, 1780
A., K., L., N., Q., T.

1091 [DUNN, John] Thoughts on news-papers and a free trade.
32 pp. Dublin, printed by William Hallhead, 1780
A., K., N., Q., T.

1092 An enquiry into the advantages and disadvantages resulting from bills of inclosure. In which objections are stated and remedies proposed; and the whole is humbly recommended to the attentive consideration of the legislature, before any more bills (for that purpose) be enacted into laws.
75 pp. London, T. Cadell, 1780
T.

1093 The examination of Joseph Galloway, esq; late speaker of the house of assembly of Pennsylvania. Before the house of commons, in a committee on the American papers. With explanatory notes.
88 pp. 2nd ed. London, J. Wilkie, 1780
Q.

1094 Facts: addressed to the landholders, stockholders, merchants, farmers, manufacturers, tradesmen, proprietors of every description, & generally to all the subjects of Great Britain & Ireland.
117 pp. 2nd ed. London, J. Johnson & J. Almon, [1780]
A.

1095 [FERGUSON, Anthony?] A volunteer's queries, in spring, 1780; humbly offered to the consideration of all descriptions of men in Ireland.
88 pp. Dublin, Pat. Byrne, 1780
A., K., N., P., Q.

1096 Fragment of a letter to a friend, relative to the repeal of the test.
32 pp. Dublin, 1780
K., Q.

1097 [GALLOWAY, Joseph.] A candid examination of the mutual claims of Great-Britain and the colonies: with a plan

of accommodation, on constitutional principle. By the author of letter to a nobleman on the conduct of the American war. [Paginated with] A reply to an address to the author of a pamphlet, entitled, 'A candid examination of the mutual claims of Great Britain and her colonies', etc.
116 pp. London, G. Wilkie, and R. Faulder, 1780

Q.

Reprinted from the New York edition, J. Rivington, 1775.

1098 [——.] Cool thoughts on the consequences to Great Britain of American independence. On the expence of Great Britain in the settlement and defense of the American colonies. On the value and importance of the American colonies and the West Indies to the British empire.
75 pp. London, J. Wilkie, 1780

Q.

1099 [——.] Historical and political reflections on the rise and progress of the American rebellion. In which the causes of that rebellion are pointed out and the policy and necessity of offering to the Americans a system of government founded in the principles of the British constitution, are clearly demonstrated. By the author of letters to a nobleman on the conduct of the American war.
144 pp. London, G. Wilkie, 1780

A., K., Q.

1100 [——.] Letters to a nobleman, on the conduct of war in the middle colonies.
112 pp. 3rd ed. London, J. Wilkie, 1780

Q.

1101 [——.] Plain truth: or, a letter to the author of dispassionate thoughts on the American war. In which the principles and arguments of that author are refuted and the necessity of carrying on that war clearly demonstrated. By the author of letters to a nobleman on the conduct of the American war, and of cool thoughts on the consequences of American independence.
86 pp. London, G. Wilkie and R. Faulder, 1780

Q.

1102 [GRAY, John.] A letter to the earl of Nugent, relative to the establishment of a national bank in Ireland.
34 pp. London, John Donaldson, 1780

A., K., N.

1103 [GRIFFITH, Amyas?] Six letters: addressed to the right honourable the countess of G....
frontisp. 24 pp. Dublin, 1780

A.

1104 [HELY-HUTCHINSON, John.] The commercial restraints of Ireland considered in a series of letters to a noble lord. Containing an historical account of the affairs of that kingdom, so far as they relate to this subject.
table of contents, tables, appendix. 256 pp. London, Longman, 1780

N.

See 1056.

1105 [JEBB, David.] A dissertation, on the present Bounty laws, for the encouragement of agriculture in Ireland. Submitted to the consideration of Parliament.
tables. 32 pp. Dublin, printed by Hallhead, 1780

A., N., Q.

1106 JEBB, Frederick. Considerations on the expediency of a national circulation bank at this time in Ireland.
appendix. 32 pp. Dublin, R. Marchbank, 1780

A., K., N., Q., T.

1107 LAW, Robert. Moral duties necessary to secure the advantages of a free trade: With a caution against some abuses to which the beginnings of manufactures and commerce are peculiarly exposed. A sermon in two parts. Published at the request of the parishioners [of St. Mary's].
36 pp. Dublin, Hallhead, 1780

N.

1108 A letter from a gentleman of the Middle Temple, to his friend in Dublin, relative to the present crisis of affairs in this kingdom.
40 pp. Dublin, William Hallhead, 1780

K., Q.

1109 A letter to lord North, on his re-election, into the house of commons. By a member of the late parliament.
50 pp. London, G. Wilkie & R. Faulder, 1780

A.

1110 A letter to the new parliament; with hints of some regulations which the nation hopes & expects from them.
60 pp. London, John Francis & Charles Rivington, 1780

A.

1111 A letter to the right honourable the earl of Hillsborough, secretary of state for the southern department, on the present state of affairs in Ireland. And an address to the people of that kingdom.
38 pp. Dublin, company of booksellers, 1780

A., N., T.

1112 A letter to Travers Hartley, esq; on the sugar bill, & the resolutions of the body of merchants.
126 pp. Dublin, printed by Pat. Byrne, 1780

A.

1113 LEYAL, P..., [pseud.?] Letters lately printed in the Freeman's & Hibernian journals, under the signature of P. Leyal: addressed to his grace the duke of Leinster. And now republished at the desire of the Apollo society, & of several respectable citizens.
48 pp. Dublin, printed by James Porter, 1780

A., N.

1114 Moderation unmasked; or, the conduct of the majority impartially considered. By the author of a scheme for a constitutional association.
80 pp. Dublin, printed by William Hallhead, 1780

A., K.

1115 [MOLYNEUX, William Philip, styled viscount, later 1st baron Sefton.] Some thoughts on the bill for the relief of tenants holding leases for lives, renewable for ever. Addressed to lord Lifford, lord chancellor of Ireland.
46 pp. Dublin, Elizabeth Lynch, 1780

A., K., N., T.

1116 [MORRES, Hervey Redmond, 2nd viscount Mountmorres.] Considerations on the intended modification of Poyning's Law. By a member of the Irish parliament.
30 pp. London, J. Almon, 1780

A., Q.

1117 [O'BEIRNE, Thomas Lewis, bishop of Meath.] Considerations on the late disturbances by a consistent whig.
30 pp. London, J. Almon, 1780
A.

1118 [——?] Four letters from the country gentleman, on the subject of the petitions.
24 pp. London, J. Almon, 1780
A.

1119 [——.] A short history of the last session of parliament, with remarks.
100 pp. London, J. Almon & J. Debrett, 1780
A.

1120 Observations on the finances and trade of Ireland, humbly addressed to the immediate consideration of gentlemen of landed interest, more particularly to members of the House of Commons.
tables. 70 pp. Dublin, printed by W. Sleater, 1780
A., K., N., P., Q., T.

1121 A plain and affectionate address to the shopkeepers, manufacturers, artificers and traders of this city and kingdom. (By) a firm friend of Ireland.
16 pp. Dublin, printed by James Williams, 1780
A., Q.

1122 PRICE, Richard. An essay on the population of England, from the revolution to the present time, with an appendix containing remarks on the account of the population, trade and the resources of the kingdom, in Mr. Eden's letters to lord Carlisle.
74 pp. 2nd ed. London, T. Cadell, 1780
A., Q., T.

1123 Prices to be paid by the manufacturers to the undertakers or journeymen for weaving the different articles in the silk, silk and worsted and riband branches, as mutually agreed to, and to commence 24th June, 1780.
tables. 56 pp. n.p., 1780
Q.

1124 Proposals for printing by subscription a plan of reform for the public affairs of Ireland, built upon the four following articles: Art. I. What is an actual violation of the constitution? Art. II. What respects the vital nerve of commerce? Art. III. What would equal the protecting duty bill in national benefits? Art. IV. And what is the disgrace and bane of the kingdom?
3 pp. Dublin, printed by D. Graisberry, [1780?]
Q.

1125 [RAMSBOTHAM, Dorning.] Thoughts on the use of machines, in the cotton manufacture. Addressed to the working people in that manufacture, and to the poor in general. By a friend of the poor.
22 pp. Manchester, printed by J. Harrop, 1780
T.

1126 Seasonable advice to the people of Ireland, during the present recess of Parliament.
31 pp. Dublin, printed by Pat Byrne, 1780
A., N., Q.

1127 [SHARP, James.] Description of some of the utensils in husbandry, rolling carriages, cart rollers, and divided rollers for land or gardens, mills, weighing engines, etc. etc. made and sold by James Sharp, No. 15 Leadenhall St., London; which may be seen at his manufactory in Southwark.
plates (not paginated), London, White, Dilly, [1780]
A.

1128 A slight sketch of the connection between Great Britain and Ireland. In a letter from a gentleman in Dublin to his friend in the country.
24 pp. Dublin, printed by William Hallhead, 1780
Q.

1129 Some authentic minutes of the proceedings of a very respectable assembly, on the 20th of December, 1779. To which are added (in order to preserve them) the speeches of some noble lords, spoken the day following, some of which have already appeared in print.
72 pp. Dublin, printed by J. Potts, 1780
A., K., N., Q.
See 1076.

1130 Some thoughts on the general improvement of Ireland, with a scheme of a society for carrying on all improvements, in a more extensive & effectual manner, than has hitherto been done. Humbly submitted to the consideration of the right-honourable & honourable the lords & commons in parliament assembled.
49 pp. 2nd ed. Dublin, 1780
A., G., N.

1131 The strong-box opened: or, a fund found at home, for the immediate employment of our people, & for preventing emigration. Inscribed to D-n-s D-l-y, esq.
28 pp. Dublin, printed by T. T. Faulkner, 1780
A., K., N.

1132 [STUART, Andrew] and [MORRES, Hervey Redmond, 2nd viscount Mountmorres.] The propriety of extending the trade of Ireland; and the advantages that will thereby accrue to the manufactures of England, and the state in general. By one of his majesty's commissioners for trade and plantations. [Signed A.S.] To which is added an enquiry into the legality and consequences of an embargo. By a member of the Irish parliament.
30 pp. London, T. Cadell and Dublin, C. Jackson, 1780
G., K., N., Q., T.

1133 Thoughts on a fund for the improvement of credit in Great Britain: & the establishment of a national bank in Ireland. By a friend to Ireland in the British parliament.
32 pp. Dublin, printed by Michael Mills, 1780
A., K., T.

——. Another issue. 36 pp. London, T. Murray, 1780
Q.

1134 The times: addressed to the virtuous and spirited freemen of Ireland. Dedicated to the most disinterested patriot.
68 pp. Dublin, printed by William Hallhead, 1780
A., N., Q.

1135 Traité touchant la suppression de la mendicité et l'administration des pauvres dans la ville d'Anvers.
tables. 96 pp. Anvers, J. Grange, 1780
Q.

1136 Turgot, Anne Robert Jacques, baron de l'Aulne. M. Turgot à. M. Necker. & sur l'administration de M. Necker, par un citoyen françois.
86 pp. Londres, Paris, 1780

P.

1137 The usurpations of England the chief sources of the miseries of Ireland; & the legislative independence of this kingdom, the only means of securing & perpetuating the commercial advantages, lately recovered. By a native of Ireland & a lover of the British empire.
34 pp. Dublin, printed by R. Burton, 1780

A., G., K., T.

1138 [Wilson, Hill?] Some remarks on Dr. Jebb's considerations on the expediency of a national circulation bank in Ireland.
24 pp. Dublin, printed by James Hunter, 1780

A., G., K., N., Q., T.

1781

1139 An answer to a pamphlet, entitled, observations on the mutiny bill. By a member of the house of commons.
58 pp. Dublin, printed by James Hoey, 1781

A., N.

1140 [Auckland, William Eden, 1st baron.] Considerations submitted to the people of Ireland, on their present condition with regard to trade and constitution. In answer to a pamphlet, lately published, entitled 'Observations on the Mutiny Bill, etc.'
74 pp. Dublin, W. Wilson, 1781

A., N., P., Q., T.

——. 74 pp. 2nd ed. Dublin, W. Wilson, 1781

K.

See 1149.

1141 Authentic rebel papers seized at St. Eustatius, 1781.
tables. 32 pp. London, Lambert, Kearsley, [etc.], 1781

A.

1142 [Bruhl, Hans Moritz, graf von.] Recherches sur divers objets de l'économie politique. par M. Le C. de B.
154 pp. Dresden, Walther, 1781

T.

1143 Burke, Edmund. A speech of Edmund Burke, Esq. at the Guildhall, in Bristol, previous to the late election in that city, upon certain points relative to his parliamentary conduct.
70 pp. 4th ed. London, J. Dodsley, 1781

A.

1144 Candid thoughts; or, an enquiry into the causes of national discontents and misfortunes since the commencement of the present reign.
74 pp. London, W. Nicoll, 1781

A.

1145 Considerations on the removal of the custom-house humbly submitted to the public.
48 pp. Dublin, 1781

A., G., K., N., Q., T.

1146 Directions for raising flax: originally published by order of the commissioners and trustees for fisheries, manufactures, and improvements, in Scotland; and now re-printed by order of the lords commissioners for trade and plantations, for the benefit and instruction of those farmers who may cultivate flax, and become intitled to the bounties granted on that article, by a late Act of Parliament.
24 pp. London, 1781

T.

1147 [Drennan, William.] An address to the volunteers of Ireland. By the author of a letter to Edmund Burke, Esq. containing reflections on patriotism, party spirit, & the union of free nations.
40 pp. Dublin, William Hallhead, 1781

L., Q.

1148 Faithful copies of all the letters that have appeared in the General Advertiser, under the signatures of Scourge, and W. Bennett, Camberwell; and relate to the transactions of the Commissioners of Victualling and Christopher Atkinson, Esq; their corn-factor, in the supplying government with wheat, malt, etc. etc.
96 pp. London, J. Debrett, 1781

Q.

1149 [Grattan, Henry.] Observations on the mutiny bill, with some strictures on Lord Buckinghamshire's administration in Ireland.
78 pp. Dublin, W. Wilson, 1781

A., K., Q.

See 1140.

——. 78 pp. 2nd ed. Dublin, W. Wilson, 1781

A., N.

——. 78 pp. 2nd ed. London, J. Stockdale, 1781

N.

1150 Hartley, David. An address to the committee of the county of York, on the state of public affairs.
64 pp. London, J. Stockdale, 1781

A.

1151 ——. Considerations on the proposed renewal of the bank charter.
tables. appendix. 42 pp. London, J. Stockdale, 1781

P.

1152 The history of lord North's administration, to the dissolution of the thirteenth parliament of Great Britain.
174 pp. London, G. Wilkie, 1781

A.

——. Another issue. 192 pp. Dublin, printed by P. Byrne, 1781

A.

1153 Howlett, John. An examination of Dr. Price's essay on the population of England and Wales, and the doctrine of an increased population in this kingdom, established by facts. To which is added an appendix, containing remarks on

Dr. Price's argument of a decreased population deduced from the decreased produce of the hereditary and temporary excise.
188 pp. Maidstone, the author, 1781
N., Q., T.

1154 [JEBB, Frederick.] Thoughts on the discontents of the people last year, respecting the sugar duties. With an appendix, containing a report from the committee of the British House of Commons, to whom the petition of the sugar refiners of London was referred, etc. etc.
164 pp. Dublin, printed by William Wilson, 1781
A., N., Q.
Sometimes attributed to Jebb and Robert Johnson as joint authors.

1155 JONES, William. An essay on the law of bailments.
130 pp. London, Charles Dilly, 1781
A.

1156 A letter to William Eden, Esq. occasioned by a pamphlet commonly attributed to him and entitled, Considerations submitted to the people on their present condition, with regard to trade and constitution.
64 pp. Dublin, printed by William Hallhead, 1781
A., K., N., Q.

1157 Memoire sur l'éstablissement des administrations provinciales; présenté au roi par M. Necker, Directeur-General des Finances. Suivi d'un discours adressé à S.M., sur la retraite de M. Necker.
40 pp. n.p., 1781
Q.

1158 NECKER, Jacques. Compte rendu au Roi par M. Necker, directeur général des finances, au mois de Janvier, 1781.
tables. table of contents. maps. 120 pp. à Paris, de l'Imprimerie Royale, 1781
A.

1159 ——. State of the finances of France, laid before the king, by Mr. Necker, director-general of the finances, in the month of January, 1781.
tables. maps. 118 pp. London, G. Kearsley, T. Becket, [etc.], 1781
G.

1160 On the debt of the nation and the impossibility of carrying on the war without public oeconomy.
table of contents. tables. folding table. 138 pp. London, Debrett, 1781
A.

1161 [PACEY, Henry Butler.] Considerations upon the present state of the wool trade, the laws made concerning that article, & how far the same are consistent with true policy, & the real interest of the state. By a gentleman resident on his estate in Lincolnshire.
38 pp. London, P. Elmsly, 1781
A., N.

1162 The people nearly brought to ruin by a law, intended to save them from it.
20 pp. Dublin, 1781
L., N.
On civil bill legislation.

1163 The provincial bounty, or a plan for the encouragement of female servants, who have lived three years in friends' families, in the province of —— and have preserved good characters.
12 pp. Dublin, printed by Robert Jackson, 1781
A.
[Gap in title.]

1164 A review of the conduct of his excellency John, earl of Buckinghamshire, lord lieutenant general, and general governor of Ireland, during his administration in that kingdom; in a letter addressed to a noble lord.
40 pp. Dublin, L. Flin, 1781
Q., T.

——. Another issue. 55 pp. Dublin, 1781
A.

1165 Seasonable and affecting observations on the mutinybill, articles of war and abuse of a standing army. In a letter from a member of parliament to a noble lord.
52 pp., Dublin, booksellers, 1781
A.

1166 [SHERIDAN, Charles Francis.] A review of the three great national questions relative to a Declaration of Right, Poyning's Law and the Mutiny Bill.
128 pp. Dublin, printed by M. Mills, 1781
A., N., Q.

1167 TIGHE, W. A letter to the earl of Darnley, on the state of the poor in Ireland.
24 pp. Dublin, W. and H. Whitestone, 1781
K.

——. Another issue. 20 pp. London, T. Payne, 1781
A.

1168 A translation of the memorial to the sovereigns of Europe upon the present state of affairs, between the old and the new world, into common sense and intelligible English.
46 pp. London, J. Stockdale, 1781
A.

1169 WALES, William. An inquiry into the present state of population in England & Wales; & the proportion which the present number of inhabitants bears to the number of former periods.
82 pp. London, C. Nourse, 1781
A., T.

1782

1170 ABINGDON, Bertie Willoughby, 4th earl. The earl of Abingdon's two late speeches in the house of lords, upon the affairs of Ireland: with his lordship's celebrated bill upon the same occasion.
19 pp. London, J. Debrett, 1782
A.

1171 The account of alderman Benjamin Geale, treasurer to the honourable the city of Dublin for the receipts, issues, and profits, accruing, to the said city (commencing, Michaelmas 1780, and, ending, Michaelmas 1781) and for the casualties

ending at the same time. To which is prefixed a rental of the estate of the said city; and arrears of rent, due the 29th of September 1781.
tables. 70 pp. Dublin, printed by Thomas Todd Faulkner, 1782

G.

1172 ANDERSON, Sir James. The interest of Great Britain, with regard to her American colonies, considered. To which is added an appendix, containing the outlines of a plan for a general pacification.
tables. appendix. 180 pp. London, T. Cadell, 1782

K., P.

1173 An answer addressed to those who have read Sir John Dalrymple's pamphlet, in support of a tax and permission to export raw wool, by a plain matter of fact man.
24 pp. London, R. Faulder, 1782

Q.

1174 Answer to a pamphlet, written by C. F. Sheridan, Esq., entitled, a review of the three great national questions, relative to a declaration of right, Poyning's law, and the mutiny bill. Part the first, declaration of right.
40 pp. Dublin, John Cash, 1782

A.

1175 Answer to a pamphlet written by C. F. Sheridan, Esq., entitled, a review of the three great national questions, relative to a declaration of right, Poyning's law, and the mutiny bill. Part the third, mutiny bill.
40 pp. Dublin, John Cash, 1782

A., N.

1176 [BANKS, Sir Joseph.] The propriety of allowing a qualified exportation of wool discussed historically. To which is added an appendix; containing a table, which shews the value of the woolen goods of every kind, that were entered for exportation at the Custom House, from 1697 to 1780 inclusive, as well as the prices of wool in England, during all that period.
92 pp. London, P. Elmsly, 1782

A., Q.

1177 [BEAUCHAMP, Francis Ingram-Seymour-Conway, styled viscount, later 5th marquess of Hertford.] A letter to the first Belfast company of Volunteers, in the province of Ulster.
40 pp. Dublin, printed by P. Byrne, 1782

A., L., N., Q.

1178 [BENTLEY, Thomas.] Letters on the utility and policy of employing machines to shorten labour; occasioned by the late disturbances in Lancashire: To which are added some hints for the further extension and improvement of our woollen trade and manufactures.
44 pp. London and Dublin, reprinted by William Sleater, 1782

Q.

1179 [CAMPBELL, Thomas.] A letter to his grace the duke of Portland, lord lieutenant of Ireland, touching internal regulation: with particular strictures upon the linen board, excise laws, etc. etc. To which is added A series of aphorisms, tracing, the progress of society through every stage, from its most rude to its most refined state; and connecting, in one demon-

strative chain, the elementary principles of political oeconomy.
62 pp. Dublin, R. Marchbank, 1782

A., N.

1180 CARTWRIGHT, John. Give us our rights! or, a letter to the present electors of Middlesex and the metropolis, shewing what those rights are: and that according to a just and equal representation, Middlesex and the Metropolis are intitled to have fifty members in the commons' house of parliament; forty of whom are now placed there by decayed cinque ports and almost unpeopled boroughs; to the perpetual nurture of corruption, and the ruin of the state.
64 pp. London, Dilly & Stockdale, 1782

A.

1181 ——. A summary of a treatise by major Cartwright, entitled the people's barrier against undue influence: or the commons' house of parliament, according to the constitution.
6 pp. [London?], Society for constitutional information, 1782

A.

1182 [CAWTHORNE, Joseph.] A plan of reconciliation with America; consistent with the dignity and interests of both countries. Humbly inscribed to the king.
52 pp. London, G. Wilkie, 1782

Q.

1183 [CHEPLIN, Thomas, the Younger.] A letter from a grower of long combing wool to the manufacturers of that valuable staple.
8 pp. London, 1782

A., Q.

1184 DALRYMPLE, Sir John. The question considered whether wool should be allowed to be exported when the price is low at home on paying a duty to the public?
28 pp. 2nd ed. London, T. Cadell, 1782

A., Q.

See 1240

1185 DAY, Thomas. Reflexions upon the present state of England, and the independence of America.
108 pp. London, J. Stockdale, 1782

Q.

1186 DESCA, Antoine. Reflexions politiques, sur la paix conclue en 1762, entre l'Angleterre & la France.
48 pp. Dublin, printed by J. Hill, 1782

A.

1187 A dispassionate examen of the most popular objections against the sugar and mutiny acts. With some conclusive arguments on the propriety of the one, and the expediency and constitutionality of the other; in a letter to the right honourable Lord B—.
88 pp. 2nd ed. Dublin, printed by James & William Porter, 1782

A.

1188 DOBBS, Francis. A history of Irish affairs, from the 12th of October, 1779, to the 15th September, 1782, the day of lord Temple's arrival.
172 pp. Dublin, printed by M. Mills, 1782

A., K., L., N., T.

1189 [EFFINGHAM, Thomas Howard, 3rd earl.] An essay on the nature of a loan being an introduction to the knowledge of the public accounts.
30 pp. York, printed by A. Ward, 1782
Q.

1190 The English woollen manufacturers remarks, humbly offered on the present declining state of their trade for exportation, and the necessity there is of preventing the Irish wool being run.
11 pp. n.p., [1782]
Q.

1191 An enquiry into the nature and qualities of English wools and the variations in sheep. With some short remarks on the dean of Gloucester's pamphlet on coarse wools and proposals for relieving the wool-growers, by a mode which will not prejudice the manufacturers. By a gentleman farmer.
52 pp. London, T. Evans, 1782
Q.

1192 [FLETCHER, William.] Junius Secundus's letters to the people of Ireland, against the establishment of a national bank.
48 pp. Dublin, printed by R. Marchbank, 1782
K., N.

1193 FLOOD, Henry. The celebrated speeches of colonel Henry Flood, on the repeal of the declaratory act of the 6th George 1st. As delivered in the house of commons of Ireland, on the 11th & 14th of June, 1782. Also, the speech of Lord Abingdon, in the English house of peers the 5th of July 1782, on introducing his bill for a declaration of right over every part of the British dependencies.
40 pp. Dublin, printed by C. Campbell, 1782
A., N.

1194 ——. The two speeches of Henry Flood, Esq. on the repeal of the declaratory act of the sixth of George I. To which are added, lord Abingdon's bill for a declaration of right over all the dependencies of Great Britain, brought into the house of lords, on the 5th of July, 1782. And his lordship's speech thereupon.
36 pp. Dublin, printed by J. Chambers, 1782
A., N.

1195 FORSTER, Nathaniel. An answer to Sir John Dalrymple's pamphlet upon the exportation of wool.
48 pp. Colchester, W. Keyner, 1782
Q.

1196 [GLOVER, R.] A letter to the landed gentlemen and graziers of Lincolnshire: in which are pointed out the principal causes of the present redundancy of wool and the exportation of it, proved to be impolitic and dangerous; together with the proposal of a more safe and certain remedy, occasioned by, and interspersed with observations upon, Sir John Dalrymple's question on that subject. By a friend and neighbour.
34 pp. Cambridge, printed by J. Archdeacon for J. & J. Merril and others, 1782
A., Q.

1197 [GRIFFIN, George, later STONESTREET.] Prize sugars not foreign: An essay intended to vindicate the rights of the public to the use of the prize sugars; and to show the impolicy, as well as injustice of forcing the prize cargoes out of the kingdom, at a time when the manufactory is languishing through the want of due employment, and the people are aggrieved by the excessive price of the commodity. With observations on the export trade of raw and refined sugars, on the draw backs and bounties; and on enquiry into the proper means of moderating the price of this necessary article.
table. 62 pp. London: T. Cadell and J. Sewell, 1782
Q.

1198 HARDY, Thomas. Reflections upon the present state of England, and the independence of America.
108 pp. London, J. Stockdale, 1782
Q.

1199 HOULTON, Robert. A selection of political letters, which appeared during the administrations of the earls of Buckinghamshire and Carlisle, under the signatures of Junius-Brutus, Hampden, The Constitutional Watchman, and Lucius Hibernicus.
100 pp. Dublin, printed by Wilson, 1782
A., N., Q.

1200 The Irish protest to the ministerial manifesto, contained in the address of the British parliament to the king.
24 pp. Dublin, printed by P. Cooney, [1782?]
A.

1201 [JEBB, Fred.] Strictures on a pamphlet lately published, entitled, 'Considerations submitted to the people of Ireland, in answer to a pamphlet, entitled, observations on the mutiny-bill'.
77 pp. Dublin, W. & H. Whitestone, 1782
A.

1202 A letter to the right honorable [sic] William Pitt, from a Presbyterian of the kirk of Scotland, to which is added, a short epistle to Wm. Pulteney, Esq., on his pamphlet, entitled, 'Effects to be expected from the East India Bill upon the constitution'.
44 pp. London, J. Debrett, [1782?]
A.

1203 A letter to the right honourable the earl of Shelburne, first lord of the treasury.
43 pp. London, Charles Dilly, 1782
A., N.

——. Another issue. 36 pp. Dublin, C. Jenkin [etc.], 1782.
A.

——. Another issue, 38 pp. Dublin, C. Jenkin, 1782.
K.

1204 [LEWIS, R.] Common sense, & common humanity: or, the cruelty & impolicy of the penal laws against the Roman Catholics demonstrated. Most humbly addressed to the legislature of Ireland. By an English protestant.
40 pp. Dublin, R. Lewis, 1782
A.

1205 MOLYNEUX, William. The case of Ireland's being bound by acts of parliament made in England, stated. By

William Molyneux, of Dublin, Esq. Also, a small piece on the subject of appeals to the lords of England, by the same author, never before published. To which are added, letters to the men of Ireland, by Owen Roe O'Nial.
93 pp. Dublin, 1782

A., K., L., N.

See 1061

1206 [MOORE, Francis.] The contrast; or, a comparison between [sic] our woollen, linen, cotton, and silk manufactures: shewing the utility of each, both in a national and commercial view; whereby the true importance of the fleece, the first and great staple of our land, will appear evident; the effect that must naturally arise from the system we now pursue, and the consequences we may rationally hope from a contrary policy: together with such facts and remarks as may claim the attention of every Englishman, who is a friend to the freedom and prosperity of his country.
52 pp. London, J. Buckland, Seagood [etc], 1782

Q.

1207 MOORE, John. Army estimates for the Irish establishment.
tables. 148 pp. Dublin, printed by Robert Marchbank, 1782

A.

1208 MUGLISTON, William. A letter on the subject of wool, interspersed with remarks on cotton, addressed to the public at large but more particularly to the committee of merchants and manufacturers at Leeds.
20 pp. Nottingham, the author, 1782

Q.

1209 A narrative of the proceedings of the lords of Ireland. In the years 1703 and 1719, in consequence of the attempts made at those periods by the lords of Great Britain, to enforce their authority in this kingdom. Together with the representation of the Irish lords to the king upon that subject, in which the independent legislative and judicial rights of this kingdom are ably stated, which representation caused the British parliament to pass the Declaration act of the 6th of George the First. Inscribed to the lords of parliament and the peers of Ireland, by a friend to the constitutional rights of both kingdoms.
52 pp. Dublin, all the booksellers, 1782

A., G.

1210 Observations on the Paving Acts, reports, execution of work, etc. Addressed to those whom it may concern.
tables. 16 pp. Dublin, 1782

T.

1211 PAINE, Thomas. Letter addressed to the Abbé Raynal on the affairs of North America. In which mistakes in the abbé's account of the revolution of America are corrected and cleared up.
84 pp. Philadelphia, reprinted London, J. Stockdale, 1782

N.

See 1270, 1717 and 1778

1212 Plain reasons addressed to the people of Great Britain, against the (intended) petition to parliament from the owners and occupiers of land in the county of Lincoln, for leave to export wool. With some remarks on Sir John Dalrymple's

treatise, lately published, in favour of a general exportation of wool.
45 pp. Leeds, printed by Wright & Son, 1782

Q.

1213 [PORTLAND, William Henry Cavendish Bentinck, 3rd duke.] Observations on a pamphlet entitled A letter to his grace the duke of Portland, lord lieutenant of Ireland, so far as the same relates to the subject of revenue; in which is considered the state of the distilling trade of Ireland.
tables. 98 pp. Dublin, 1782

A., K., Q., T.

1214 Resolutions of the committee of owners and occupiers of lands in the county of Lincoln, aggrieved by the present low price of long and coarse wool—unanimously agreed to, at the St. Albans Tavern, on Tuesday the 12th of February, 1782.
13 pp. n.p., 1782

Q.

1215 The saddle put on the right horse; or, some thoughts, on a more equitable mode of taxing the inhabitants of the British dominions, whereby much greater sums might be annually raised than at present, and the burthens of the poor either wholly removed, or considerably lightened, without the least additional expense to government. Most humbly submitted to the legislatures of Great-Britain and Ireland.
24 pp. Dublin, William Spotswood, 1782

A., N., K.

1216 SINCLAIR, John. Thoughts on the naval strength of the British Empire.
62 pp. London, T. Cadell, 1782

Q.

1217 ——. Thoughts on the strength of the British Empire, Part 2. Tending to point out what steps might be taken at this time for a speedy and effectual increase of the navy.
tables. Part II. 55 pp. London, T. Cadell, 1782

Q.

1218 STAIR, John Dalrymple, 5th earl of. Facts and their consequences, submitted to the consideration of the public at large; but more particularly to that of the finance minister and of those who are or mean to become creditors of the state.
38 pp. London, J. Stockdale, 1782

Q.

1219 Thoughts on the present situation of Ireland. In a letter from the north, to a friend in Dublin; in which the late extraordinary meeting at Dungannon is considered.
66 pp. Dublin, all the booksellers, [1782]

A., K., L., N., T.

1220 TUCKER, Josiah. Cui Bono? or, an inquiry, what benefits can arise either to the English or the Americans, the French, Spaniards, or Dutch from the greatest victories, or successes in the present war? Being a series of letters addressed to Monsieur Necker, late controller general of the finances of France. With a plan for a general pacification.
144 pp. Gloucester, printed by R. Raikes, for T. Cadell (etc.), 1782

K., Q.

1221 ——. Reflections on the present low price of coarse wools, its immediate causes and its probable remedies.
48 pp. London, T. Cadell, 1782

A., N., Q.

1222 TURNER, Edmund. A short view of the proceedings of the several committees and meetings held in consequence of the intended petition to parliament from the county of Lincoln, for a limited exportation of wool; together with Mr. R. Glover's letter on that subject. To which is added a list of the pamphlets on wool lately published, with some extracts.
20 pp. London, J. Stockdale, 1782

A., Q.

1223 [WESKETT, John.] Plan of the Chamber of Commerce, (in the building late the King's Arms Tavern, Cornhill) or office, for consultation, opinion and advice, information and assistance, in all commercial, insurance and maritime affairs and matters of trade in general.
32 pp. London, Richardson and Urquhart, [etc.], 1782

Q.

1224 A word at parting to the earl of Shelburne.
43 pp. London, J. Debrett, 1782

Q.

1783

1225 An address to the Dungannon and Leinster Volunteer delegates, on the matter of parliamentary reform.
26 pp. Dublin, R. Moncrieffe, 1783

A., N.

1226 Address to the right honourable the lords commissioners of the admiralty: upon the degenerated, dissatisfied state of the British navy; with ways and means to put the navy upon a formidable and respectable footing, both as to ships and men. Also a proposition, to establish a new mode of caulking the king's ships. With a proposed regulation, for maintaining an extra-establishment of marines in time of peace: and a recommendation, to establish a general naval register office. To which is added, a proposition for establishing commissaries on board the king's ships; and various other strictures upon the naval service in general, by a sailor.
100 pp. London, J. Stockdale, 1783

A.

1227 [ALDBOROUGH, Edward Augustus Stratford, 2nd earl of.] An essay on the true interests & resources of the empire of the king of Great-Britain & Ireland, etc. etc.
28 pp. Dublin, printed by P. Byrne, 1783

A., T.

1228 ARBUTHNOT, John. To the right honourable and honourable, the trustees of the linen board. The report of John Arbuthnot, Esq., inspector-general for the provinces of Leinster, Munster and Connaught.
tables. diagram. index. 96 pp. Dublin, 1783

N.

1229 Arguments to prove the interposition of the people to be constitutional and strictly legal; in which the necessity of a more equal representation by the people in parliament is also proved and a simple unobjectionable mode of equalizing the representation is suggested.
36 pp. Dublin, P. Byrne, 1783

G., Q., T.

1230 BALLARD, John. Gauging unmasked. Which shews all the necessary rules in vulgar and decimal arithmetic, with several contractions in both. The extraction of the square and cube roots: stereometry, or the whole art of gauging, by the pen and sliding-rule; with the forms and definitions: the method of keeping the stock book for ale and x-waters: tables of cylinders and areas of circles and squares. The whole designed for the use and service of the revenue officers, being calculated according to 217.6 the solid inches contained in the liquid gallon, now used in Ireland.
tables. 152 pp. Dublin, printed by Bart. Corcoran, 1783

A.

1231 [BELLAMONT, Charles Coote, 1st earl of.] A letter to lord viscount Beauchamp, upon the subject of his 'letter to the first Belfast Company of volunteers, in the province of Ulster'.
30 pp. Dublin, W. Wilson [&c] 1783

L.

——. Another issue. 50 pp. London, John Debrett, 1783

A.

——. 56 pp. 2nd ed. London, John Debrett, 1783

A.

1232 [BEAUCHAMP, Francis Ingram-Seymour-Conway, styled viscount, later 5th marquess of Hertford.] A letter to the first Belfast company of Volunteers, in the province of Ulster. By a member of the British parliament.
56 pp. London, John Debrett, 1783

Q.

1233 [BLAKE, Sir Francis, 2nd bart.] A proposal for the liquidation of the national debt; the abolition of tithes; and the reform of the church revenue.
30 pp. London, W. Flexney, 1783

Q.

1234 BUCKINGTON, Nathaniel. Serious considerations on the political conduct of lord North, since his first entry into the ministry; with a deduction of positive facts, shewing clearly, that his lordship's system was, and is, not only the best, but the only one which could or can be pursued with the least hopes of effecting the great national points, of making us respected abroad, and a free, easy, and happy people at home; by converting the present national debt into permanent landed property; which would destroy the pernicious practice of stock-jobbing, reduce the oppressive taxes, and cause the necessity of borrowing in future to be totally done away for ever.
84 pp. London, J. Stockdale, 1783

A., N.

1235 [CAMPBELL, Thomas.] A remedy for the distilleries of Ireland, which, at present, labour under such disadvantages, as to be called a disease, in an official pamphlet, just published, intitled, Observations on a letter to the duke of Portland,

lord lieutenant of Ireland, so far as the same relates to the subject of revenue, etc. By the author of the letter to the duke of Portland.
88 pp. Dublin, P. Byrne, and R. Marchbank, 1783
A., C., E., G., N., Q.

1236 A capital mistake of the legislature respecting the taxes on receipts. Which must either produce an immediate repeal of these unprecedented duties, or convince the world that the subjects of Great Britain are now entirely lost to every sense of their own interest. By a gentleman conversant in revenue affairs.
26 pp. London, the author, 1783
Q.

1237 The case of the earl of Newburgh, and lord viscount Kinnaird.
24 pp. London, printed by R. Ayre, 1783
A.

1238 [CHALMERS, George?.] The case and claim of the American loyalists impartially stated and considered.
40 pp. London, by order of their agents, [1783]
N., Q.

1239 A copy of the charter of the corporation of the governor and company of the bank of Ireland.
appendix. 24 pp. Dublin, printed by Wilson, 1783
A., N.

1240 DALRYMPLE, Sir John, Bart. The question considered, whether wool should be allowed to be exported, when the price is low at home, on paying a duty to the public? By Sir John Dalrymple, bart. Also, an answer to Sir John Dalrymple's pamphlet upon the exportation of wool. By Nathaniel Forster, D.D. chaplain to the countess dowager of Northington.
66 pp. Dublin, P. Byrne, 1783
A., N., P., T.

See 1184

1241 DAY, Thomas. Reflections on the present state of England, and the independence of America.
130 pp. 4th ed. London, J. Stockdale, 1783
A., Q.

——. 134 pp. 3rd ed. London, J. Stockdale, 1783
A.

1242 DEASE, Michael. Observations on the linen manufacture, particularly bleaching, pointing out the source of the damage linens sustain in that process, including strictures on an act of parliament, made last session prohibiting the admixture of lime and potash and experimentally shewing it to be founded in error. To which are added, some new remarks on agricultural knowledge and a few on mineral waters.
76 pp. Dublin, P. Byrne, 1783
Q.

1243 A defence of the conduct of the court of Portugal; with a full refutation of the several charges alleged against that kingdom, with respect to Ireland. Originally written in Portuguese, by a gentleman of distinction, and faithfully translated from that language, signed Lusitania.
64 pp. London, J. Stockdale, 1783
A., N.

——. Another issue. 68 pp. Dublin, A. Fox, 1783
A.

1244 DOBBS, Francis. The true principles of government, applied to the Irish constitution, in a code of laws. Humbly submitted to the king, lords and commons of Ireland, for their adoption, in lieu of the many thousand volumes, which now contain the laws of the land.
72 pp. Dublin, printed by J. Chambers, 1783
A.

1245 DROUGHT, Thomas. Letters on subjects interesting to Ireland, and addressed to the Irish volunteers.
48 pp. Dublin, W. Colles, 1783
A., L., N.

1246 [DUIGENAN, Patrick.] The alarm: or, an address to the nobility, gentry, and clergy of the Church of Ireland, as by law established.
44 pp. Dublin, Henry Watts, 1783
A., N., Q., T.

1247 An examination into the principles, conduct and designs of the minister.
64 pp. London, J. Stockdale, 1783
A.

1248 A full and faithful report of the debates in both Houses of Parliament, on Monday the 17th February, and Friday the 21st of February, 1783, on the articles of peace.
192 pp. London, S. Bladon, 1783
Q.

1249 [GALLOWAY, Joseph.] Political reflections on the late colonial governments: in which their original constitutional defects are pointed out, and shown to have naturally produced the rebellion, which has unfortunately terminated in the dismemberment of the British Empire. By an American.
266 pp. London, G. Wilkie, 1783
Q.

1250 General tariff of the customs for all ports and frontiers of the Russian empire, except Astrachan, Orenburgh, and Siberia, as settled by the commissioners of commerce, 1782.
tables. 100 pp. London, the Russia company, 1783
T.

1251 GRAYDON, Robert. Thoughts on the expediency of forwarding the establishment of manufactures in Ireland. In which is comprehended the sketch of a design for promoting and extending them.
tables. 40 pp. Dublin, P. Byrne, 1783
A., K., L., N., P., Q., T.

1252 [JOHNSON, Robert?] Considerations on the effects of protecting duties. In a letter to a newly-elected member of parliament.
48 pp. Dublin, W. Wilson, 1783
A., N., P.

1253 KING, John. Thoughts on the difficulties and distresses in which the peace of 1783, has involved the people of England; on the present disposition of the English, Scots, and Irish, to emigrate to America; and on the hazard they run (without certain precautions) of rendering their condition more deplorable. Addressed to the right hon. Charles James Fox.
50 pp. London, J. Fielding, T. Davies, [etc.] 1783
A., Q.

1254 [KIPPIS, Andrew.] Considerations on the provisional treaty with America, and the preliminary articles of peace with France and Spain.
tables in appendices. 164 pp. London, T. Cadell, 1783
K., Q.

1255 A letter on parliamentary representation, in which the propriety of triennial and septennial parliaments is considered, inscribed to John Sinclair, Esq., M.P.
36 pp. 2nd ed. London, J. Stockdale, 1783
A.

1256 Letter from the committee of Ulster Volunteers to the duke of Richmond, the duke of Richmond's answer; together with his bill for a parliamentary reform.
90 pp. n.p., 1783
A.

1257 A letter to a member of parliament, on a tax upon absentees.
28 pp. Dublin, printed by William McKenzie, 1783
A., Q.

1258 A letter to Henry Flood, Esq., on the present state of representation in Ireland.
26 pp. Belfast, printed by Henry & Robert Joy, 1783
A.

1259 A letter to the author of a pamphlet entitled free parliaments.
24 pp. London, 1783
A.

1260 A letter to the earl of Shelburne, on the peace.
44 pp. 3rd ed. London, J. Debrett, 1783
Q.

1261 A list of the absentees of Ireland. And an estimate of the yearly value of their estates and incomes, spent abroad. With observations on the trade and manufactures of Ireland, and the means to encourage, improve, and extend them; with some reasons why Great Britain should be more indulgent to Ireland, in particular points of trade. Also, some reasons and observations why absentees should be obliged to contribute to the support and welfare of the country they derive their honours, estates, and incomes from. Humbly submitted to the consideration of the legislature of Ireland. The sixth edition. In this edition the lists of the absentees are greatly amended, and set forth, as they stood in the year 1782. To which is appended, notes and an appendix, containing some material transactions that have occurred since the publication of the former edition, 1769. With observations upon them, and the several acts of parliament passed since.
tables. appendix. 120 pp. 6th ed. Dublin, printed by T. T. Faulkner, 1783
A., C., K., L., M., N., Q., T.

A further version of the list of absentees originally produced by Thomas Prior in 1729.

1262 MCDOWEL, Benjamin. A charity sermon, preached in St. Mary's Abbey meeting-house.
25 pp. Dublin, printed by W. Gilbert, [1783]
A.

1263 M'GREGOR, George. Tables calculated for the use of the revenue officers of Ireland.
72 pp. Dublin, printed by Bartholomew Corcoran, 1783
A.

1264 [MCGRUGAR, Thomas.] Letters of Zeno, addressed to the citizens of Edinburgh, on parliamentary representation; and, particularly, on the imperfect representation for the city of Edinburgh, and the other burghs of Scotland.
62 pp. new ed. Edinburgh, the committee of citizens, 1783
L.

1265 [MENDICANT, Benjamin.] An essay on the necessity of Protecting Duties.
50 pp. Dublin, P. Byrne, 1783
A., C., G., K., N., P., Q., T.

1266 NEVILL, John. Seasonable remarks on the linen-trade of Ireland. With some observations on the present state of that country.
98 pp. Dublin, printed by P. Byrne, 1783
N., Q.

1267 [O'BRYEN, Denis.] A defence of the rt. hon. the earl of Shelburne, from the reproaches of his numerous enemies; in a letter to Sir George Saville, bart. and intended for the direction of all other members of parliament whose object is rather to restore the glory of the British empire, than administer to the views of a faction. To which is added, a postscript, addressed to the rt. hon. John Earl of Stair. By the author of Junius's letters.
98 pp. 6th ed. London, J. Stockdale, 1783
A.

———. 84 pp. 9th ed. Dublin, R. Moncrieffe [etc.], 1783
A., N., T.

———. 90 pp. 9th ed. Dublin, W. Wilson, 1783.
K.

1268 Observations on the commerce of the American states with Europe and the West Indies; including, the several articles of import and export; and on the tendency of a bill now depending in parliament.
78 pp. London, J. Debrett, 1783
A.

1269 O'CONNOR, Roderick, and BREAKEY, James. To the right honourable and honourable the trustees of the linen and hempen manufacture (including) Roderick O'Connor, Esquire's letter and observations on ashes. (and) James Breakey's process and affidavit, as also his remarks.
20 pp. n.p. 1783
A., Q.

1270 PAINE, Thomas. Letter addressed to the Abbé Raynal on the affairs of North America. In which the mistakes in the abbé's account of the revolution of America are corrected and cleared up.
86 pp. Philadelphia and London, J. Stockdale, 1783
Q.

See 1211, 1717, and 1778.

1271 ——. A letter to the earl of Shelburne on his speech, July 10, 1782, respecting the acknowledgement of American Independence.
24 pp. Philadelphia and Dublin, W. Wilson, 1783
A., K., N., Q.

1272 PETERSON, Peter. Addressed to his grace the duke of Portland. A memorial concerning the woollen manufactory, and the exportation of wool, unmanufactured, into foreign countries. To which is added a plan to prevent so destructive a commerce.
32 pp. London, T. Hookham, 1783
Q.

1273 A plain letter to the common people of Great Britain and Ireland, giving some fair warning against transporting themselves to America.
24 pp. London, J. Dixwell, T. Egerton, [etc.], 1783
T.

1274 Plan of the general dispensary in Aldersgate-street, London, for the relief of the poor. Instituted 1770.
tables. 58 pp. London, printed by James Phillips, 1783
T.

1275 [POWIS, ——.] A dialogue on the actual state of parliament.
38 pp. Dublin, P. Byrne, 1783
G., Q., T.

——. Another issue. 56 pp. London, J. Stockdale, 1783
A.

1276 POWNALL, Thomas. A memorial addressed to the sovereigns of America, by T. Pownall, late governor, captain-general, vice-admiral, etc. of the provinces, now states, Massachusetts-Bay and South-Carolina; and lieutenant-governor of New-Jersey.
142 pp. London, J. Debrett, 1783
A., N.

1277 Preliminary articles of peace, between his Britannick majesty, and the most Christian king, the king of Spain, and the commissioners of the United States of America. Signed at Versailles, the 20th of January, 1783.
30 pp. London and Dublin, reprinted by William Wilson, 1783
A.

1278 The present state of the East-India Company's affairs; containing the estimates and accounts delivered by the directors of the east-India Company to the lords of the treasury, and laid before the secret committee appointed by the House of Commons to enquire into East-India affairs. To which are added, the different plans proposed by several of the directors, and others, for the re-establishment of the credit and circumstances of the company. Together with remarks on each plan.
tables 36 pp. London, S. Bladon,, [1783?]
T.

1279 [PRICE, Joseph.] Five letters from a free merchant in Bengal, to Warren Hastings, Esq. governor general of the honorable [sic] East India company's settlements in Asia; conveying some free thoughts on the probable causes of the decline of the export trade of that kingdom; & a rough sketch, or outlines of a plan, for restoring it to its former splendor [sic].
220 pp. London, 1783
A.

1280 ——. A letter from captain Joseph Price, to Philip Francis, Esq. late a member of the supreme council at Bengal.
36 pp. London, 1783
A.

1281 [——.] A letter to Sir Phil. Jen. Clerke, chairman of the committee of the house of commons, to whom the petition of Benjamin Lacam, sole proprietor of New Harbour in Bengal, was referred.
222 pp. London, the author, 1783
A.

1282 [——.] A letter to the proprietors & directors of East India stock. Together with an epistle dedicatory to Robert Gregory, Esq. chairman of the court of directors for the management of the affairs of the East India Company.
32 pp. London, 1783
A.

1283 [——.] The saddle put on the right horse; or, an enquiry into the reason why certain persons have been denominated nabobs; with an arrangement of those gentlemen into their proper classes, of real, spurious, reputed, or mushroom, nabobs. Concluding with a few reflections on the present state of our Asiatic affairs. By the author of the vindication of gen. Richard Smith.
114 pp. London, 1783
A.

1284 [——.] A series of facts, shewing the present political state of India, as far as concerns the powers at war; & the probable consequences of a general pacification in Europe, before we shall have decided our contests in the Carnatic. Addressed (for form's sake) to the earl of Shelburne, but recommended to the serious consideration of all his majesty's ministers, & the members of both houses of parliament.
54 pp. London, 1783
A.

1285 [——.] A vindication of gen. Richard Smith, chairman of the select committee of the house of commons, as to his competency to preside over & direct, an investigation into the best mode of providing the investment for the East India company's homeward-bound Bengal ships. To which are added some instances to prove, that the general is not that proud, insolent, & irascible man, his enemies would induce the public to believe him to be. As also, a few serious hints to the select committee, tending to shew, that they are wasting

their time in the minutiae of Asiatic commerce, whilst the great outlines and consequential branches, are in danger of being overlooked.
146 pp. London, 1783

A.

1286 [PRICE, Richard.] Postscript to a pamphlet by Dr. Price on the state of the public debts and finances at signing the preliminary articles of peace in January, 1783.
16 pp. London, T. Cadell, 1784

Q.

This copy marked "1783" by John Foster

1287 ——. The state of the public debts and finances at the signing of the preliminary articles of peace in January 1783. With a plan for raising money by public loans, and for redeeming the public debts.
40 pp. London, T. Cadell, 1783

A., N., Q.

1288 Proceedings relative to the Ulster assembly of volunteer delegates: on the subject of a more equal representation of the people in the parliament of Ireland. To which are annexed, letters from the duke of Richmond, Dr. Price, Mr. Wyvill, & others. Published by the committee of correspondence.
8 pp. Belfast, printed by Henry & Robert Joy, 1783

A., L.

1289 A reform of the Irish house of commons, considered.
36 pp. Dublin, Henry Watts, 1783

A.

1290 Sequel to an essay, on the origin and progress of government.
54 pp. London, T. Cadell, 1783

A.

1291 A short account of the institution, rules, and proceedings, of the Cork Society for the relief and discharge of persons confined for small debts.
80 pp. Cork, by order of Society, 1783

A.

1292 SINCLAIR, John. Hints addressed to the public on the state of our finances.
tables. 60 pp. 2nd ed. London, T. Cadell, 1783

Q.

1293 Some observations and remarks on a late publication, entitled travels in Europe, Asia and Africa, in which the real author of that new and curious Asiatic Atlantis, his character and abilities, are fully known to the public.
142 pp. London, 1783

A.

1294 STAIR, John Dalrymple, 5th earl of. An argument to prove, that it is the indispensible duty of the creditors of the public to insist, that government do forthwith bring forward the consideration of the state of the nation; in order to ascertain, as near as may be, the annual receipts & expenditure of the state; & by providing efficient & adequate funds for the sum in which the latter shall be found to exceed the former, to strengthen the public credit, & to restore public confidence.
54pp. London, J. Stockdale, 1783

A., N.

1295 ——. An attempt to balance the income and expenditure of the state: with some reflections on the nature and tendency of the late political struggles for power.
22 pp. London, J. Stockdale, 1783

Q.

1296 ——. State of the public debts, and of the annual interest and benefits paid for them; as they will stand on the 5th of January, 1783, likewise as they will stand (if the war continues) on the 5th of January, 1784. To which the attention of the public is humbly requested, before they decide as to peace or war. Together with some thoughts on the extent to which the state may be benefited by oeconomy; and a few reflections on the conduct and merit of the parties contending for power.
32 pp. Dublin, P. Byrne, 1783

A., K., T.

——. 32 pp. 3rd ed. London, J. Stockdale, 1783

N., Q.

1297 Thoughts on the conduct and continuation of the volunteers of Ireland.
38 pp. Dublin, James Williams, 1783

A., L., N.

1298 Thoughts on the establishment of new manufactures in Ireland, occasioned by the late freedoms we have obtained. With an account of the Manchester manufactury, established by Mr. Brooke. Written by a friend of his in the county of Kildare.
48 pp. Dublin, printed by P. Higly, 1783

A., G., N.

1299 Thoughts on the peace in a letter from the country.
38 pp. London, J. Debrett, 1783

Q.

1300 TUCKER, Josiah. Four letters on important national subjects, addressed to the right honourable the earl of Shelburne, his majesty's first lord commissioner of the treasury.
78 pp. Dublin, W. & H. Whitestone, [etc.], 1783

A., K., N., T.

1301 [WALLER, John Thomas.] An address to the people of England and Ireland. In which is submitted to their consideration, a plan for restoring the freedom and vigour of our constitution, the independence of parliament and the happiness of the people. More particularly adapted to the electors of the county of Limerick, by a freeholder of that county.
36 pp. Dublin, T. Walker & J. Ferrar, [1783?]

A.

1302 WASHINGTON, George. A circular letter from George Washington, commander in chief of the armies of the United States of America, to his excellency William Greene, Esq., governor of the state of Rhode Island.
28 pp. London, J. Stockdale, 1783

A.

1303 WATSON, Richard, bishop of Llandaff. A letter to his grace the archbishop of Canterbury.
80 pp. new edition, Dublin, printed by P. Byrne, 1783

A., N.

1304 YOUNG, Arthur. An enquiry into the legality and expediency of increasing the Royal Navy by subscriptions for building county ships. Being the correspondence on that subject between Arthur Young and Capel Lofft, Esqrs. With a list of the subscribers to the Suffolk Man of War, to which are added observations on the state of the taxes and resources of the Kingdom on the conclusion of the peace.
tables. 100 pp. Bury St. Edmund's, printed by Green and Gedge, [1783]

N.

1784

1305 Articles of association, for establishing the Royal Exchange Insurance Company of Ireland, for insuring ships, merchandize, and lives, in the city of Dublin.
32 pp. Dublin, printed by J. Hunter, 1784

A.

1306 [BRUCE, William.] The history of the last sessions of parliament, addressed to the right hon. the earl of Charlemont.
44 pp. Dublin, printed by T. Henshall, 1784

A., Q.

1307 [———.] A vindication of government. Addressed to the people of Ireland, dedicated (by permission) to the majority in both Houses of Parliament. By ———, chaplain to his grace the duke of ———.
40 pp. Dublin, printed by T. Henshall, M,DCC,XXXXIV [1784?]

A., Q.

1308 BURKE, Edmund. Mr. Burke's speech, on the 1st December, 1783. Upon the question for the speaker leaving the chair, in order for the house to resolve itself into a committee on Mr. Fox's East India bill.
108 pp. Dublin, L. White, 1784

A., L., N., Q., T.

1309 ———. A representation to his majesty, moved in the House of Commons, by the right honourable Edmund Burke and seconded by the right honourable William Windham, on Monday, June 14, 1784 and negatived. With a preface and notes.
52 pp. Dublin, Luke White and other, 1784

N., Q.

1310 [CHALMERS, George.] The beauties of Fox, North, & Burke, selected from their speeches, from the passing of the Quebec Act, in the year 1774, down to the present time. With a copious index to the whole, and an address to the public.
58 pp. London, J. Stockdale, 1784

A.

1311 ———. Opinions on interesting subjects of public law and commercial; arising from American independence.
tables. 200 pp. London, J. Debrett, 1784

A., Q.

1312 CLINTON, Sir Henry. A letter from lieut. gen. Sir Henry Clinton, K.B. to the commissioners of public accounts, relative to some observations in their seventh report, which may be judged to imply censure on the late commanders in chief of his majesty's army in North America.
32 pp. London, J. Debrett, 1784

Q.

1313 Considerations on the national debt, & nett produce of the revenue: with a plan for consolidating into one rate the land & all other taxes by which more money will be raised; individuals not pay half the present taxes; smuggling altogether prevented; the Revenue Officers provided for during life: farther burthens rendered unnecessary; the poor exempted from every contribution: the public debt gradually discharged, & a commercial union with Ireland recommended. By a merchant of London.
tables. 66 pp. London, C. Dilly & other, 1784

Q.

1314 The contrast, a political pasticcio, with recitative, cantatas, etc. chaunted, with variations, in the opera-house of St. Stephens, by Signor Carlo Reynardo, etc.
frontisp. 86 pp. 3rd ed. Dublin, printed by P. Byrne, 1784

A., Q., T.

1315 CUNNINGHAM, Richard. To the right honourable and honourable, the trustees of the linen manufacture of Ireland. The case of Richard Cunningham.
tables. 24 pp. Newry, 1784

Q.

1316 DALRYMPLE, Sir John, bart. Address & proposals from Sir John Dalrymple, bart. on the subject of the coal tar and iron branches of trade.
12 pp. Edinburgh, 1784

Q.

1317 DEANE, Silas. An address to the United States of America. To which is added, a letter to the hon. Robert Morris, esq. with notes and observations.
100 pp. London, J. Debrett, 1784

Q.

1318 DOBBS, Francis. Thoughts on the present mode of taxation in Great Britain.
26 pp. London, J. Stockdale, 1784

A., P., Q.

1319 DUNDONALD, Archibald Cochrane, 9th earl of. Thoughts on the manufacture and trade of salt on the herring fisheries, and on the coal-trade of Great Britain, submitted to the consideration of the right honourable William Pitt, chancellor of the exchequer, etc. and of every lover of his country.
56 pp. Edinburgh, William Creech, 1784

Q.

1320 EDWARDS, Brian. Thoughts on the late proceedings of government, respecting the trade of the West India Islands with the United States of North America. [2nd ed.] To which is now first added a postcript, addressed to the right honourable lord Sheffield.
96 pp. London, T. Cadell, 1784

A.

1321 Emigration, earnestly recommended to the catholics of Ireland, in a letter addressed to the nobility, clergy and gentry, of that persuasion.
32 pp. Dublin, printed by Mathew Doyle, 1784
K., Q.

1322 [FERGUSON, Anthony.] A volunteer's queries, humbly offered to the consideration of all descriptions of men in Ireland.
84 pp. 2nd ed. Dublin, printed by P. Byrne, 1784
A., K., Q.

1323 FOX, Charles James. Substance of the speech of the right honourable Charles James Fox, on Monday, December 1, 1783. Upon a motion for the commitment of the bill 'for vesting the affairs of the East India Company in the hands of certain commissioners, for the benefit of the proprietors, and of the public.'
40 pp. Dublin, printed by P. Byrne, 1784
A., N., Q., T.

1324 FRANCIS, Sir Philip. Speech in the House of Commons, on Friday July 2, 1784.
56 pp. London, Debrett, 1784
N.
On moving certain papers relative to the state of East India Company's affairs.

1325 FRANKLIN, Benjamin. Two tracts; information to those who would remove to America, and remarks concerning the advantages of North America.
40 pp. 2nd ed. London, J. Stockdale, 1784
A., L., Q.

1326 [GORDON, Thomas.] General remarks on the British fisheries. By a North Briton.
64 pp. London, Murray, Wilkie, [etc.], 1784
A., C., P.

1327 GRAYDON, Robert. The practical arrangement of a design lately published, for promoting and extending the establishment of manufactures in Ireland.
tables. 40 pp. Dublin, P. Byrne, 1784
K., Q.

1328 GREER, John and ARBUTHNOT, John. The respective reports of John Greer, inspector-general for the province of Ulster and of John Arbuthnot, inspector-general for the provinces of Leinster, Munster & Connaught, on Mr. Robert Stephenson's schemes and proposed premiums for the province of Ulster and Munster, which are annexed.
appendices. 40 pp. n.p., 1784
A.

1329 GRIFFITH, Richard. Thoughts on protecting duties.
tables. 44 pp. Dublin, Luke White, 1784
A., N., Q.

1330 HEY, J. V. D. Observations politiques, morales & experimentées, sur les vrais principes de la finance. Suivies d'un essay sur les moyens de reforme, pour les finances de la Grande Bretagne: et d'une Ébauche, pour un plan d'emprunt, selon lequel le gouvernement Britannique, pourra d'abord trouver les fonds nécessaires, & leurs intérêts, pour payer les arrérages de la dernière guerre; sans imposer d'avantage le peuple, par de nouveaux droits, taxes ou accises.
144 pp. Londres, H. Reynell [etc.], 1784
Q.

1331 The history of the proceedings and debates of the volunteer delegates of Ireland, on the subject of parliamentary reform. Containing the plan of parliamentary reform, the names of the delegates, and the state of borough representation, etc. etc.
164 pp. Dublin, W. Porter and others, 1784
A., L., N., Q.

——. Another issue. 144 pp. Dublin, 1784
K.

1332 HOPE, John. Letters on credit. With a postscript and a short account of the bank at Amsterdam. Second edition.
72 pp. London, J. Debrett, 1784
Q.

1333 KEOGH, John. Thoughts on equal representation; with hints for improving the manufactures and employment of the poor in Ireland.
14 pp. Dublin, printed by T. Heery, 1784
A., Q., T., U.

1334 [KNOX, John.] A view of the British empire, more especially Scotland; with some proposals for the improvement of that country, the extension of its fisheries and the relief of the people.
186 pp. London, J. Walter, 1784
A., Q.

1335 A letter from an American to a member of parliament, on the subject of the restraining proclamation; and containing strictures of lord Sheffield's pamphlet on the commerce of the American states.
24 pp. Dublin, reprinted by James Potts, 1784
T.

1336 A letter to the linen-manufacturers of Ireland, on the subject of protecting duties.
tables. 78 pp. Dublin, printed by W. Porter, 1784
A., K., L., M., N., Q.

1337 A letter to the right honourable William Brownlow, on the present administration. By a citizen.
28 pp. Dublin, printed by A. Roche, 1784
N., Q.

1338 Letters of a Dungannon and Munster delegate, which appeared shortly after the publication of the plan of parliamentary reform, proposed by the grand national convention; are now first collected, and earnestly recommended to the perusal of the public, previous to the agitation of the question of reform in the house of commons.
86 pp. Dublin, R. Marchbank, 1784
A., N.

1339 MABLY, Gabriel Bonnot de. Remarks concerning the government and laws of the United States of America: in four letters addressed to Mr. Adams, plenipotentiary from the United States of America to those of Holland, and one of the

negotiators for the purpose of concluding a general peace, from the French of the Abbé de Mably: with notes by the translator.
284 pp. London, J. Debrett, 1784

A., Q.

See 1397

1340 MOLYNEUX, Capel. A warm appeal to the freemen of Ireland, on the present interesting crisis of affairs.
26 pp. Dublin, printed by P. Byrne, 1784

A., C., N., Q.

1341 Observations on Doctor Forster's answer to Sir John Dalrymple.
20 pp. 1784

Q.

On the export of textiles.

1342 Observations on the parliamentary conduct of the right hon. John Foster; as also on the liberty of the press, the Volunteers and Roman Catholics of Ireland. By a private gentleman.
44 pp. Dublin, printed by R. Marchbank, 1784

N., Q., T.

1343 ODELL, William Butler. Impartial thoughts on party and parliamentary reform.
40 pp. Limerick, printed by Edward Flin, 1784

A.

1344 Oppression unmasked; being a narrative of the proceedings in a case between a great corporation and a little fishmonger. Relative to some customs for fish, demanded by the former as legal, but refused by the latter, as exactions and extortions. By an advocate for justice.
30 pp. Dublin, 1784

Q.

1345 Plain arguments in defence of the people's absolute dominion over the constitution. In which the question of Roman Catholic enfranchisement is fully considered.
64 pp. Dublin, printed by Thomas Webb, 1784

L., N., T.

1346 PRICE, Richard. Questions relating to schemes for granting reversionary annuities, together with some observations on annuity schemes. Particularly that established by act of parliament, for raising and establishing a fund, for a provision for the widows and children of the ministers of the church of Scotland. On which was grounded a plan lately proposed to be established by act of parliament for raising and establishing a fund, for a provision for the widows and children of the church of Ireland. Extracted from observations on reversionary payments, etc.
tables. 58 pp. Dublin, printed by William McKenzie, [1784]

A.

1347 Remarks on a bill for the relief of clergymen's widows; with reasons for postponing the same to the next sessions of parliament. By a clergyman of the church of Ireland.
16 pp. Dublin, P. Byrne, 1784

Q.

1348 SHEFFIELD, John Baker Holroyd, 1st earl of. Observations on the commerce of the American states by John Lord Sheffield. A new edition, much enlarged. With an appendix, containing tables of the imports and exports of Great Britain to and from all parts, from 1700 to 1782. Also, the exports of America, etc. With remarks on those tables, on British navigation, and on the late proclamations, etc.
fold. tables. 328 pp. Dublin, Luke White, 1784

A.

1349 A short account of the institution, rules, and proceedings of the Cork Society for the relief and discharge of persons confined for small debts.
tables. 60 pp. Cork, printed by W. Flyn, 1784

N.

1350 Short state of the present situation of the India company, both in India and in Europe; with an examination into the probable prospects of extricating it from its present difficulties.
tables. 56 pp. London, Debrett, 1784

N.

1351 The source of the evil: or, the system displayed. Addressed to the gentry, Yeomanry, Freeholders and Electors of England and Ireland. By a Freeholder. In four letters.
72 pp. Dublin, printed by P. Byrne, 1784

A., N., Q.

1352 STAIR, John Dalrymple, 5th earl of. Address to and expostulation with the public.
52 pp. London, J. Stockdale, 1784

Q.

1353 STEPHENSON, Robert. Observations on the present state of the linen trade of Ireland: in a series of letters addressed to the right honourable and honourable the trustees of the linen manufacture. In which the reports, libel and British examination of Mr. John Arbuthnot inspector general of Leinster, Munster and Connaught are considered and refuted.
table of contents, tables. 108 pp. Dublin, 1784

A., T.

1354 STEVENSON, John. An address to Brian Edwards, esq., containing remarks on his pamphlet, entitled, 'Thoughts on the late proceedings of government, respecting the trade of the West India islands with the United States of America.' Also observations on some parts of a pamphlet, lately published by the West India planters and merchants, entitled, 'Considerations on the present state of the intercourse between his majesty's sugar colonies and the dominions of the United States of America.'
94 pp. London, W. Nicoll, 1784

A.

1355 A summary view of the East-India company of Great Britain. Exhibiting a sketch of its origin, progress and constitution, in abstracts from its charters, from proceedings in parliament, and from other documents, briefly stated.
152 pp. Dublin, printed by W. Foster, 1784

Q.

1356 [TAYLOR, Benjamin Ogle & BRUCE, William.] Letters of Neptune and Gracchus, addressed to the P... of

W..., and other distinguished characters; now first collected from their original publication in the Morning Post.
2nd ed. London, M. Smith, 1784

A.

1357 TWINING, Richard. Observations on the tea and window act, and on the tea trade.
72 pp. London, Cadell, 1784

T.

1358 ——. Remarks on the report of the East India directors, respecting the sale and prices of tea.
tables and appendices. 80 pp. London, Cadell, 1784

T.

1785

1359 The account settled! or a balance struck between the Irish propositions agreed to in the house of commons of Ireland on the 12th of February, 1785, and the English resolutions entered into by the house of commons of England on the 30th of May, 1785
64 pp. Dublin, printed by P. Byrne, 1785

A., N., T.

1360 An address to the king and people of Ireland, upon the system of final adjustment contained in the twenty propositions which have passed the British House of Commons and are now before the British House of Lords.
28 pp. Dublin, R. Marchbank, 1785

A., N., Q.

——. Another issue. 26 pp. London, J. Desborough, 1785

A.

1361 The arrangements with Ireland considered.
98 pp. London, John Stockdale, 1785

Q.

1362 An authentic statement, faithfully extracted from the report of the privy council appointed by his majesty, for the consideration of all matters relating to the intended system of commerce between Great Britain and Ireland. To which are added, observations resulting from the facts, as stated by the committee. Addressed to the merchants and manufacturers of Great-Britain.
30 pp. London, J. Debrett, 1785

Q., T.

1363 [BURGH, William.] Defense of opposition with respect to their conduct on Irish affairs, with explanatory notes. Dedicated to the right honourable C. J. Fox. By an Irish gentleman, a member of the whig club.
56 pp. Dublin, L. White, 1785

A., Q.

——. Another issue. 61 pp. London, Stockdale, 1785

A., N., T.

1364 [——.] Defence of opposition with respect to their conduct on Irish affairs, with explanatory notes. Dedicated to the right honourable C. J. Fox. By an Irish gentleman, a member of the whig club. (Also) appendix. The commercial resolutions of the Irish parliament, in their present session,

vindicated. To which is added an authentic copy of the resolutions.
118 pp. London, John Stockdale, 1785

Q., T.

1365 [BURKE, Edmund.] A reply to the treasury pamphlet entitled 'The proposed system of trade with Ireland explained'.
98 pp. London, J. Debrett, 1785

A., Q., T., U.

1366 ——. Mr. Burke's speech, on the motion made for papers relative to the directions for charging the Nabob of Arcot's private debts to Europeans, on the revenues of the Carnatic. February 28th, 1785. With an appendix, containing several documents.
203 pp. Dublin, P. Byrne, 1785

A., N., Q., T.

1367 [CHALMERS, George?] An answer to the reply to the supposed treasury pamphlet.
88 pp. London, John Stockdale, 1785

A., Q., T., U.

1368 CHAPMAN, William. Observations of the advantages of bringing the Grand canal round by the Circular road into the river Liffey. Addressed to the right honourable and honourable the commissioners appointed by parliament, for making wide and convenient the streets of Dublin.
32 pp. Dublin, P. Byrne, 1785

A., G., N., P., Q.

1369 The charter-party: or articles of agreement of the Brotherly-Annuity company of Dublin.
46 pp. Dublin, printed by John Hillary, 1785

A.

1370 The charter party: or, articles of agreement of the Provident Annuity Company of Dublin.
68 pp. Dublin, printed by Brett Smith, 1785

A.

1371 The commercial regulations with Ireland, explained and considered, in the speech of the right hon. Mr. Orde upon the opening of the same in the House of Commons of Ireland; with an authentic copy of the propositions and of the observations, made upon them by the committee of merchants and traders of the city of London.
32 pp. London, J. Debrett, 1785

A., Q.

1372 The commercial resolutions of the Irish parliament, in their present session, vindicated. To which is added, an authentic copy of the resolutions.
34 pp. London, John Stockdale, 1785

Q.

——. Another issue, 62 pp. London, J. Stockdale, 1785

T.

1373 Considerations on the woollen manufactory of Ireland, in a letter addressed to his grace Charles duke of Rutland, lord lieutenant general and general governor of Ireland. By a friend to Ireland.
26 pp. Dublin, printed by W. Porter, 1785

A., K., N., Q.

1374 CRAUFURD, George. An essay on the actual resources for reestablishing the finances of Great Britain.
table of contents. 110 pp. London, J. Debrett, 1785
N., P.

1375 The crisis; or immediate concernment of the British empire.
76 pp. London, C. Dilly, 1785
T.

1376 Cursory remarks on lord Sheffield's pamphlet, relative to the trade and manufactures of Ireland.
40 pp. Cork, printed by William Flyn, 1785
A., N., P., Q.

1377 [DRENNAN, William.] Letters of Orellana, an Irish helot, to the seven northern counties not represented in the national assembly of delegates, held at Dublin, October, 1784, for obtaining a more equal representation of the people in the parliament of Ireland, originally published in the Belfast News-Letter.
76 pp. Dublin, printed by J. Chambers & T. Heery, 1785
A., G., L.

1378 [——.] Letters of an Irish helot, signed Orellana, republished by order of the constitution society of the city of Dublin.
32 pp. Dublin, 1785
L.

1379 [DUNDONALD, Archibald Cochrane, 9th earl of] Account of the qualities and uses of coal tar and coal varnish. With certificates from ship masters and others.
43 pp. London, Tand & Wilkie, 1785
Q.

1380 ——. The present state of the manufacture of salt explained; and a new mode suggested of refining British salt, so as to render it equal, or superior to the finest foreign salt. To which is subjoined, a plan for abolishing the present duties and restrictions on the manufacture of salt and for substituting other duties less burthensome to the subjects, more beneficial to the revenue and better qualified to promote the trade of Great Britain.
appendix, 118 pp. 2nd ed. London, T. Cadell and others, 1785
A., Q.

1381 EATON, Richard. A daily and alphabetical arrangement of all imports and exports, at the port of Dublin, in the quarter ending the 25th March, 1785. Containing the particulars of such import and export, and the net duty annexed to each article with which the same stands chargeable according to the Acts of Parliament in force since the 25th March, 1785. By Richard Eaton, esq., equalizer of duties and inspector of the hereditary revenue of Ireland &c.
unpaged, tables. 114 pp. Dublin, Carrick, [1785?]
G.

1382 The emperor's claims. Being a description of the city of Antwerp and the river Schelde. With a concise history of the Austrian Netherlands. Together with extracts from the articles of the treaty of Munster and those of the Barrier treaty, whereby the Dutch found their right to the blocking up of the Schelde. Interspersed with remarks on the rise and fall of the trade of Antwerp. And everything tending to elucidate the present subject of dispute between the emperor and the Dutch. With a preface, containing different views of the emperor's designs, and an admonition to the British government, relative to their behaviour in the contest. Adorned with an elegant map of the river Schelde; a view of the city of Antwerp, and all the adjacent imperial and Dutch territories. Dedicated to the emperor.
64 pp. London, J. Stockdale, 1785
Q.

1383 [FORBES, William?] A candid review of Mr. Pitt's twenty resolutions. Addressed to the people of Ireland.
48 pp. Dublin, Pat. Byrne and P. Cooney, 1785
N., Q., T.

——. Another issue. 74 pp. Dublin, 1785
A.

1384 [FOSTER, Sir Michael?] An examination of the scheme of churchpower, laid down in the codex juris ecclesiastici anglicani, &c.
102 pp. Dublin, J. Smith and W. Bruce, 1785
T.

1385 Fox, Charles James. Mr. Fox's reply to Mr. Pitt, upon reporting the fourth proposition of the Irish system; purporting that all laws for the regulation of trade and navigation shall have equal force in Ireland as in England on Tuesday, May 31, 1785.
22 pp. Dublin, printed by P. Byrne, 1785
A., N.

1386 ——. The speech of the right hon. Charles James Fox, in the House of Commons, on the Irish resolutions, on Thursday, May 12, 1785, to which is added an authentic copy of the resolutions, as originally proposed and now altered by Mr. Chancellor Pitt.
104 pp. London, J. Debrett, 1785
A., D., N., Q.

——. Another issue. 106 pp. London, 1785
T.

1387 ——. The heads of Mr. Fox's speech: containing the arguments he opposed to the fourth Irish proposition, in a committee of the whole house of commons, May 23, 1785. To which is added a correct list of the minority in the house of commons, on Mr. Chancellor Pitt's Irish propositions.
58 pp. London, J. Debrett, Wilson [etc.] 1785.
A., G., T.

——. Another issue, 63 pp. Dublin, Wilson, [etc.] 1785
A.

1388 FRASER, Archibald Campbell. Certain arrangements in civil policy, necessary for the further improvement of husbandry, mines, fisheries, and manufacture in this kingdom, in a letter to the gentlemen assembled in quarter session, in a large northern county.
appendix [written 1766]. 46 pp. London, T. Cadell, 1785
N.

1389 [GEALE, ——?] Short observations on the necessity of admitting Dublin to participate in the corn bounties, in

order to remove a present great discouragement to the agriculture and corn trade of Ireland, particularly addressed to the landed interest of the kingdom.
tables. 48 pp. Dublin, printed by Richard Moncrieffe, 1785
A., N., Q.

1390 GIBBONS, William. A reply to Sir Lucius O'Brien, bart, in which that part of his letter to the author which most particularly respects the present state of the iron trade between England and Ireland is considered.
72 pp. Bristol, J. B. Beckett and others, 1785
N., Q., T.

1391 [GRAY, J...?] A plan for finally settling the government of Ireland upon constitutional principles, and the chief cause of the unprosperous state of that country explained.
75 pp. Dublin, L. White & P. Byrne, 1785
A., L., N.

——. Another issue. 77 pp. London, J. Stockdale, 1785
A.

1392 HELY-HUTCHINSON, John. A letter from the secretary of state to the mayor of Cork, on the subject of the bill presented by Mr. Orde on the 15th August, 1785, for effectuating the intercourse and commerce between Great Britain and Ireland, on permanent and equitable principles for the mutual benefit of both kingdoms.
56 pp. Dublin, printed by P. Byrne, 1785
A., K., N., P., Q., T.

1393 Historical account of the laws respecting Roman Catholics, & of the laws passed for their relief; with observations on the laws remaining in force against them: being the last note in that part of the new edition upon Coke Littleton, which is executed by Mr. Butter.
50 pp London, J. P. Coghlan, 1785
A.

1394 HOWARD, Gorges Edmond. Queries, relative to several defects and grievances in some of the present laws of Ireland, and the proceedings thereon, and especially as to custodians in civil actions between party and party.
60 pp. Dublin, printed by Mrs. Elizabeth Lynch, 1785
A.

1395 KEMEYS, John Gardner. Free and candid reflections occasioned by the late additional duties on sugars and on rum; submitted to the consideration of the British ministry, the members of both Houses of Parliament and the proprietors of sugar estates in the West-India colonies.
127 pp. Dublin, printed by Byrne, 1785
A., N., P., Q.

1396 LAFFAN, James. Political arithmetic of the population, commerce and manufactures of Ireland, with observations on the relative situation of Great Britain and Ireland.
56 pp. Dublin, printed by P. Byrne, 1785
A., N., Q., T., U.

1397 MABLY, Gabriel Bonnot de. Remarks concerning the government and laws of the United States of America: in four letters addressed to Mr. Adams, plenipotentiary from the United States of America to those of Holland, and one of the negotiators for the purpose of concluding a general peace, from the French of the Abbé de Mably: with notes by the translator.
280 pp. Dublin, Moncrieffe [etc.], 1785
A.

See 1339

1398 MARSHALL, Humphrey. Arbustrum Americanum: The American grove, or, an alphabetical catalogue of forest trees and shrubs, natives of the American United States ... also, some hints of their uses in medicine, dyes, and domestic oeconomy.
index. 196 pp. Philadelphia, printed by Cruikshank, 1785
A.

1399 MERIDYTH, Sir William, bart. Political letters written in March and April 1784.
72 pp. Dublin, printed by P. Byrne, 1785
Q.

——. Another issue. 86 pp. London, J. Stockdale, 1785
A.

1400 Minutes of the evidence taken before a committee of the House of Commons, being a committee of the whole House, to whom it was referred to consider of so much of his majesty's most gracious speech to both Houses of Parliament, on the 25th day of January, 1785, as relates to the adjustment of the commercial intercourse between Great Britain and Ireland.
tables. 216 pp. Dublin, printed by P. Byrne, 1785
A., Q., T.

1401 MOUNTMORRES, Hervey Redmond Morres, 2nd viscount. Impartial reflections upon the question, for the equalizing of the duties, upon the trade, between Great Britain and Ireland.
77 pp. London, J. Almon, 1785
A., Q., T.

1402 [O'BEIRNE, Thomas Lewis, bishop of Meath.] A gleam of comfort to this distracted empire in despite of faction, violence and cunning, demonstrating the fairness and reasonableness of national confidence in the present ministry. Addressed to every Englishman, who has at heart the real happiness of his country.
152 pp. London, J. Debrett, 1785
Q.

——. 150 pp. 3rd ed. London, J. Debrett, 1785
A.

——. 95 pp. 7th ed. Dublin, Chambers, 1785
A.

1403 [——.] A letter from an Irish gentleman in London to his friend in Dublin, on the proposed system of commerce.
35 pp. Dublin, P. Byrne, 1785
A., N., Q., T., U.

1404 O'BRIEN, Sir Lucius, bart. Letters concerning the trade and manufactures of Ireland, principally so far as the same relates to the making Iron in this kingdom, and the manufacture and export of iron wares, in which certain facts

and arguments set out by lord Sheffield in his observations on the trade and present state of Ireland are examined.
128 pp. Dublin, Luke White, 1785

A., N., P., Q., T.

1405 ——. Letters concerning the trade and manufactures of Ireland, principally so far as the same relate to the making iron in this kingdom, and the manufacture and export of iron wares, in which certain facts and arguments set out by lord Sheffield, in his observations on the trade and present state of Ireland, are examined.
With a letter from Mr. William Gibbons of Bristol to Sir Lucius O'Brien, bart., and answer, to which is added, the resolutions of England and Ireland relative to a commercial intercourse between the two kingdoms.
72 pp. London, John Stockdale, 1785

N.

1406 [O'FLATTERY, Patrick.] The beauties of Mr. Orde's bill; being extracts from certain private speeches of the following gentlemen in opposition: Mr. Grattan, Mr. Flood, Mr. Conolly, Mr. Forbes, Mr. Ogilivie, Mr. Corry, Mr. Hardy, Mr. Burgh, Mr. Curran, Mr. John O'Neill, Major Doyle, Mr. Browne (M. Univ.), Mr. Smith, Mr. Hartley, Mr. J. Wolfe, Mr. O'Hara, Mr. Kearney, etc. . . . Dedicated with all due respect, to the right honourable Thomas Orde.
74 pp. Dublin, P. Brady, 1785

A., G., Q.

1407 Mr. Pitt's reply to Mr. Orde: being a correct abstract of the speeches of those two right honourable gentlemen, as delivered in the different senates of Great Britain and Ireland, on the subject of the new commercial regulations between the two countries; with a defence of both.
40 pp. Dublin, printed by P. Byrne, 1785

A., L., N., Q.

——. Another issue. 50 pp. London, J. Jarvis and J. Debrett 1785

N., Q., U.

1408 [PLAYFAIR, William.] The increase of manufactures, commerce and finance, with the extension of civil liberty, proposed in regulations for the interest of money.
124 pp. London, Robinson, 1785

A.

1409 PRICE, Richard. Observations on the importance of the American revolution and the means of making it a benefit to the world. To which is added, a letter from M. Turgot, late comptroller-general of the finances of France: with an appendix, containing a translation of the will of M. Fortuné Ricard, lately published in France.
tables in appendix. 164 pp. London, T. Cadell, 1785

A., L., N., P., Q.

1410 Reflections on the policy and necessity of encouraging the commerce of the citizens of the United States of America.
16 pp. Virginia, 1785

A.

1411 The report of the resolutions of the committee on the affairs of Ireland; with the remarks of the general chamber of manufacturers of Gt. Britain. Also a complete abridgment of the debates in the British house of commons on the whole of the commercial propositions. To which is added a correct copy of the resolutions, respecting the commercial propositions. Together with an authentic and copious sketch of the elegant speech of the rt. hon. Charles James Fox, on Monday, the 30th of May, 1785.
80 pp. Dublin, printed by P. Cooney, 1785

A., K., N., P., T.

1412 [ROSE, George.] The proposed system of trade with Ireland explained.
58 pp. London, John Nichols, [etc.], 1785

N., Q., T.

——. Another issue. 56 pp. Dublin, P. Byrne, 1785

A., N., P.

1413 A second address from the association for the support of the rights and interests of the fishermen, Dublin, on occasion of the glorious victory obtained by justice, and the death-wound given to extortion, by the Act of Parliament for regulating the payment of bounties, and exempting them from fees.
34 pp. Dublin, printed by W. Porter, 1785

N.

1414 SHEFFIELD, John Baker Holroyd, 1st earl of. Observations on the manufactures, trade, and present state of Ireland. Part the first.
table. 58 pp. Dublin, the company of booksellers, 1785

E., K., P., Q., T., U.

1415 ——. Observations on the manufactures, trade and present state of Ireland. Part the first.
table. 64 pp. London, J. Debrett, 1785

A., Q., U.

1416 ——. Observations on the manufactures, trade and present state of Ireland.
411 pp. Dublin, R. Moncrieffe, 1785

A.

——. Another issue. 401 pp. tables. London, J. Debrett, 1785

A.

1417 [SHERIDAN, Charles Francis?] Free thoughts upon the present crisis, in which are stated the fundamental principles upon which alone Ireland can, or ought to agree to any final settlement with Great Britain. In a letter from a county gentleman to the people of Ireland.
72 pp. Dublin, R. Marchbank, 1785

A., N., Q., T.

1418 [SHERIDAN, Richard Brinsley.] The legislative independence of Ireland vindicated: in a speech of Mr. Sheridan's on the Irish propositions, in the British House of Commons. To which is annexed an authentic copy of the twenty resolutions, on the Irish commercial intercourse; as they passed that House, on the 30th of May, 1785; and were sent up to the House of Lords. Taken from the votes of the English House of Commons.
28 pp. Dublin, printed by P. Cooney, 1785

A., L., N., Q., T.

1419 A short address to the disinterested and unprejudiced citizens, merchants and manufacturers of Great Britain, on

the importance of the trade of this country with the United States of America; also, reasons why as customers they should not be restricted, like other foreign nations, from sending raw materials to this country in payment of British goods. By a manufacturer.
32 pp. London, J. Stockdale, 1785
Q.

1420 A short view of the proposals lately made for the final adjustment of the commercial system between England and Ireland.
30 pp. London, John Stockdale, 1785
A., Q., U.

1421 The speech of the rt. hon. Thomas Orde, on his moving for leave to bring in the bill, for a commercial adjustment between Great Britain and Ireland, on the 12th of August, 1785. Taken in short-hand by a member of the House.
48 pp. Dublin, printed by P. Byrne, 1785
A., N., Q., U.

1422 Summary abstract of the evidence given by the manufacturers, before the committee of the house of lords of Great Britain against the Irish propositions. Being a continuation of the minutes of the evidence given before the house oe [sic] commons.
58 pp. Dublin, printed by P. Byrne, 1785
A., N.

1423 Thoughts on the commercial arrangements with Ireland; addressed to the people of Great Britain.
66 pp. London, J. Janis and others, 1785
P., Q.

1424 Three letters to the people of Great Britain and particularly those who signed the addresses on the changes of administration and the dissolution of Parliament.
123 pp. London, J. Debrett, 1785
Q.

1425 TUCKER, Josiah. Reflections on the present matters in dispute between Great Britain and Ireland; and on the means of converting these articles into mutual benefits to both kingdoms.
48 pp. London, T. Cadell, 1785
A., C., K., P., Q., T., U.

1426 ——. Reflections on the present matters in dispute between Great Britain and Ireland; and on the means of converting these articles into mutual benefits to both kingdoms.
appendix. 48 pp. Dublin, Wilson, White, [etc.], 1785
A., K., Q., T.

1427 ——. Reflections on the present matters in dispute between Great Britain and Ireland, and on the means of converting these articles into benefits to both kingdoms.
appendix. 50 pp. Dublin, printed by R. Marchbank, 1785
K.

1428 To guard against misrepresentation. An authentic statement faithfully extracted from the report of the committee of the privy council, appointed by his majesty, for the consideration of all matters relating to the intended system of commerce between Great-Britain and Ireland. To which are added, observations resulting from the facts, as stated by the committee. Addressed to the merchants and manufacturers of Great-Britain.
tables. 92 pp. London, J. Debrett, 1785
Q., T.

1429 TRUSLER, John. Practical husbandry; or, the art of farming with a certainty of gain, as practised by judicious farmers in this country.
tables. 172 pp. 2nd ed. London, the author, 1785
D.

1430 TWINING, Richard. An answer to the second report of the East India directors, respecting the sale and prices of tea. By Richard Twining. To which is added Mr. Twining's letter to Robert Preston, esq.
tables, appendix. 112 pp. London, T. Cadell, 1785
P.

1431 ——. Observations on the tea and window act and on the tea trade.
tables, appendix. 76 pp. 2nd ed. London, T. Cadell, 1785
P.

1432 WILLIAMS, Joseph. Loose thoughts on the very important situation of Ireland, containing a distinction between the catholics and protestants: and strictures on the conduct of ministers. Addressed to the right honourable lord Thurlow.
44 pp. London, J. Southern, 1785
A.

1433 WOODFALL, William. An impartial sketch of the debate in the House of Commons of Ireland, on a motion made on Friday, August 12, 1785, by the rt. hon. Thomas Orde, secretary to the rt. hon. Charles Manners, duke of Rutland, lord lieutenant, for leave to bring in a bill for effectuating the intercourse and commerce between Great Britain and Ireland, on permanent and equitable principles. for the mutual benefit of both countries. Together with an impartial sketch of the principal speeches on the subject of the bill that were delivered in the house on Monday, August 15, 1785. With a copy of the bill presented to the house of commons of Ireland, the eleven Irish propositions, of the twenty resolutions of the British parliament, the address to the king and his majesty's answer.
228 pp. Dublin, Luke White, 1785
B., N., Q., T., U.

——. Another issue. 228 pp. London, Woodfall, 1785
A., C., P., T.

1434 WRIGHT, John. An address to the members of both Houses of Parliament on the late tax laid on fustian, and other cotton goods; setting forth that it is both reasonable and necessary to annul that impost: Also, that it may be both politic and wise, to leave every species of manufacture and commerce free from every restraint or tax whatever, particularly from excise laws. To which is annexed, a few strictures on separate clauses of the same Act of Parliament.
64 pp. Warrington, printed by W. Eyros, 1785
Q.

1435 WYVILL, Christopher. A summary explanation of the principles of Mr. Pitt's intended Bill for amending the representation of the people in Parliament.
32 pp. 2nd ed. London, John Stockdale, 1785
Q.

1786

1436 An abstract of the number of Protestant and Popish families in the several provinces and counties of Ireland, taken from the returns, made by the hearthmoney collectors, to the hearthmoney office in Dublin, in the years 1732 and 1733. Those being reckoned Protestant or Popish families, where the heads of families are either Protestants or Papists. With observations.
16 pp. Dublin, R. Gunne (?), 1786
A., Q.

See 1571.

1437 Advice to the servants of the crown in the House of Commons of Ireland. The first number; containing advice to a lord lieutenants secretary.
53 pp. Dublin, printed by P. Byrne, 1786
A., N., Q., T.

1438 The anti-tyther. A memorial and remonstrance of the commonwealth of Virginia, against a bill proposed in their provincial assembly, entitled 'A bill establishing a provision for teachers of the Christian religion.'
30 pp. Dublin, printed by J. Chambers, 1786
T.

1439 Articles of agreement of the Liberal Annuity Company, of Dublin.
50 pp. printed by T. McDonnel, 1786
A.

1440 At a meeting of the right honourable and honourable the trustees of the linen manufacture, at their house at the linen-hall, on Tuesday the 24th of January, 1786.
72 pp. Dublin, printed by Mat. Williamson, 1786
A.

1441 AUCKLAND, William Eden, 1st baron. Letter to the earl of Carlisle, from the right honourable William Eden, on the subject of the late arrangement.
30 pp. Dublin, Burret [etc.], 1786
A., N., Q., T.

1442 BARING, Sir Francis. The principle of the Commutation-Act, established by facts.
tables. 60 pp. London, 1786
P., Q.

——. 60 pp. 3rd ed. London, 1786
Q.

1443 BATES, David. A treatise of mercantile arithmetic; published for the use of the young gentlemen of the Royal academy, at Belmont, on Summer-hill, Dublin.
409 pp. Dublin, the author, 1786
A.

1444 [BLAKE, Sir Francis, 2nd bart.] A proposal for the liquidation of the national debt; the abolition of tythes; and the reform of the church revenue.
tables. 124 pp. 3rd ed. Dublin, P. Byrne, 1786
A., N., P., T.

1445 BROOKE, Robert. A letter from Mr. Brooke, to an honourable member of the house of commons.
43 pp. Dublin, printed by B. Dugdale, 1786
A., N.

1446 BROUGH, Anthony. Considerations on the necessity of lowering the exorbitant freight on ships employed in the service of the East India company.
52 pp. London, Robinson, 1786
N.

1447 CHALMERS, George. An estimate of the comparative strength of Great Britain, during the present and four preceding reigns; and of the losses of her trade from every war since the revolution.
263 pp. London, John Stockdale, 1786
A., K., T.

1448 CLARKE, Thomas Brooke. The crisis; or, immediate concernments of the British Empire. Addressed to the lord Loftus, by the Rev. T. B. Clarke.
38 pp. London & Dublin, W. McKenzie, 1786
Q.

1449 CLARKSON, Thomas. An essay on the slavery and commerce of the human species, particularly the African. Translated from a Latin dissertation, which was honoured with the first prize in the university of Cambridge for the year 1785, with additions.
288 pp. Dublin, P. Byrne, 1786
T.

1450 Charter of the Hibernian Society, Dublin.
19 pp. Dublin, 1786
Q.

1451 The charter party of the Beneficent Annuity Company of the city of Dublin.
40 pp. Dublin, printed by J. Fleming, 1786
A.

1452 Charter party of the Irish insurance company, for ships, merchandize, and lives.
27 pp. Dublin, printed by R. Marchbank, 1786
A.

1453 A comparative view of the Portland administration in Ireland. In four numbers.
32 pp. Dublin, printed by P. Cooney, 1786
A.

1454 A congratulatory address to his majesty, from the peasantry of Ireland, vulgarly denominated White Boys, or, Right Boys.
20 pp. Dublin, printed by P. Byrne, 1786
A., N.

1455 CORRY, James. Charts of the revenue and debts of Ireland.
tables. 24 pp. n.p. [1786?]
N.

1456 DUIGENAN, Patrick. An address to the nobility and gentry of the church of Ireland, as by law established. Explaining the real causes of the commotions and insurrections in the southern parts of this kingdom, respecting tithes. And the real motives and designs of the projectors and abettors of those commotions and insurrections: and containing a candid inquiry into the practicability of substituting any other mode of subsistence and maintenance for the clergy of the church established, consistent with the principles of reason and justice, in place of tithes. By a layman.
114 pp. Dublin, printed by Henry Watts, 1786
A., G., N., Q., T.
See 1151.

1457 [——?] A project for a better regulation in collecting the income of the clergy, and for the ease and advantage of the laity, particularly the poorer orders. By a beneficed clergyman.
23 pp. Dublin, printed by P. Byrne, 1786
A., N., P., Q., T.

1458 A farmer's letter addressed to the gentlemen of landed property in Ireland.
30 pp. Dublin, printed by Robert Bell, 1786
A.

1459 [GARDINER, Luke?] Remarks on the principle of a bill now pending in parliament, for the establishment of turnpikes round the city of Dublin.
30 pp. Dublin, P. Byrne, 1786
K., P., Q.

1460 GILBERT, T. Heads of a bill for the better relief and employment of the poor, and for the improvement of the police of this country. Submitted to the consideration of the members of both houses of parliament.
36 pp. Manchester, printed by Harrop, 1786
N.

1461 GIRVIN, John. A letter to Adam Smith, esq., one of the commissioners of his majesty's customs and salt duties in Scotland, and author of an enquiry into the causes of the wealth of nations, from John Girvin, wherein the accounts respecting the bounties on the white-herring buss-fishery are examined and proved to be mis-stated in the inquiry.
tables. 18 pp. Dublin, printed by P. Byrne, 1786
A., Q.

1462 HASTINGS, Warren. A letter from Warren Hastings, esq., dated 21st of February, 1784. With remarks and authentic documents to support the remarks.
74 pp. London, James Ridgway, 1786
A.

1463 [HOLLINGSWORTH, S....] An account of the present state of Nova Scotia.
table of contents. 164 pp. Edinburgh, Creech: London, Longman, 1786
N.

1464 HOWLETT, John. An essay on the population of Ireland.
16 pp. Dublin, printed by P. Byrne, 1786
A., N., Q.

——. Another issue. 16 pp. London, 1786
A.

1465 An impartial discussion on the subject of tithes: containing a paralell [sic] between the tythes paid in England and those in Ireland. A history of the origin thereof. A history of the real causes of the present disturbances. And a plan for the abolition of tithes. Addressed to the members of both houses of parliament. By a clergyman of the established church.
56 pp. Dublin, printed by P. Byrne, 1786
A., P., Q., T.

1466 Instructions for the gaugers of excise in Ireland.
tables, folding tables. 66 pp. Dublin, printed by Rhames, 1786
A.

1467 LAFFAN, James. Political arithmetic of the population, commerce and manufactures of Ireland, with observations on the relative situation of Great Britain and Ireland.
48 pp. London, John Stockdale, 1786
Q.

1468 Letters addressed to parliament; and to the public in general; on various improvements of the metropolis; which appeared in the Dublin Journal, in December last. With remarks on the public buildings, now conducted by that eminent architect, James Gandon, esq. Showing the impropriety of expending the revenues and the public's money, so profusely, on a custom-house; and courts of law, of equity and justice, which will be the most superb, the most whimsical, and most expensive building, of the kind, in Europe. To which is added Mr. Gandon's most extraordinary reply, with notes, and critical remarks on it; by the author; an admirer of general, of useful, and necessary improvements.
78 pp. Dublin, printed by Thomas Byrne, 1786
A.

1469 Letters to the people of Ireland, on the subject of an union with Great Britain. Letter the first.
52 pp. Dublin, the author, 1786
A., N.

1470 LUSON, Hewling. Inferior politics: or, considerations on the wretchedness and profligacy of the poor, especially in London and its vicinity:— On the defects in the present system of parochial and penal laws:— On the consequent increase of robbery and other crimes:— And on the means of redressing these public grievances. With an appendix, containing a plan for the reduction of the national debt.
144 pp. London, S. Bladon, 1786
A.

1471 [MACKENZIE, J.] A woollen draper's letter on the French treaty, to his friends and fellow tradesmen all over England.
48 pp. London, J. French, 1786
A., N.

1472 The necessity of founding villages contiguous to harbours, for the effectual establishment of fisheries on the

west coast of Scotland and the Hebrides. With a refutation of the reasoning on that subject of Robert Fall, esq., of Dunbar, in a pamphlet addressed to the committee of the House of Commons on the fisheries. By a member of the Highland Society in London.
40 pp. London, printed by C. Macrae, 1786
N.

1473 [NEWHAVEN, William Mayne, baron.] A short address to the public; containing some thoughts how the national debt may be reduced, and all homes taxes, including land-tax, abolished.
24 pp. London, J. Debrett, 1786
N., Q.

——. Another issue. 24 pp. Dublin, printed by P. Byrne, 1786
Q.

1474 O'LEARY, Arthur. The Rev. Mr. O'Leary's address to the common people of Ireland: particularly, to such of them as are called Whiteboys; revised and corrected by himself.
30 pp. Dublin, printed by P. Cooney, 1786
A.

1475 PICKERING, Thomas Abree. A discourse on the use and doctrine of attachments. With a report of proceedings in his majesty's Court of Common Pleas, at Westminster, against an attorney, collaterally, during the terms of Trinity and Michaelmas, 1784, and Hilary & Easter, 1785. Which proceedings were enforced by writ of attachment; and a proposal for an act of Parliament.
54 pp. London, J. Fielding, 1786
A.

1476 Premiums offered by the Dublin Society, for agriculture and planting, 1786.
30 pp. Dublin, printed by W. Sleater, 1786
N., Q.

1477 The present politics of Ireland: consisting of I. The right honourable Mr. Hutchinson's letter to his constituents at Cork. II. Parliamentary discussions of the Irish arrangements; by Messrs. Connolly, Grattan and Flood, against them, Fitzgibbon, Mason, Forster, Hutchinson, for them. III. Mr. Laffan's observations on the relative situation of Great Britain and Ireland; with notes thereon by an English editor.
100 pp. London, John Stockdale, 1786
A., N., Q.

1478 Property inviolable: or, some remarks upon a pamphlet entitled, Prescription sacred.
48 pp. Dublin, 1786
Q.

1479 ROE, Robert. An answer to a pamphlet published by the earl of Dundonald, entitled, Thoughts on the manufacture and trade of salt and on the coal-trade of Great Britain, etc. With a particular examination of his mode of refining British salt. Together with remarks on the writings of Dr. Anderson and others on the same subjects.
tables. 80 pp. Dublin, Luke White, 1786
A., N., Q.

1480 [ROKEBY, Matthew Robinson-Morris, 2nd baron.] An address to the landed, trading and funded interests of England on the present state of public affairs.
154 pp. London, J. Stockdale, 1786
Q.

Reprinted in 1786 as second edition with title: The dangerous situation of England. cf. Sabin.

1481 ——. The dangerous situation of England or an address to our landed, trading and funded interests on the present state of public affairs.
154 pp. 2nd ed. London, John Stockdale, 1786
Q.

1482 A short answer to earl Stanhope's observations on Mr. Pitt's plan for the reduction of the national debt.
52 pp. London, T. Cadell, 1786
A.

1483 The sixth edition, much improved, being a more minute & particular account of that arch-imposter, Charles Price, otherwise Patch, otherwise Wilmot, otherwise Powel, otherwise Brant, &c. &c. &c. many years a stock-broker and lottery-office-keeper in London and Westminster: in this edition the whole of his various forgeries and frauds are circumstantially related; together with his origin, and all the material occurrences of his life, including that desperate undertaking of forgeries on the Bank of England.
frontisp. 56 pp. Dublin, printed by P. Cooney, 1786
A.

1484 [STEPHENSON, Robert?] Examinator's letters, or, a mirror for British monopolists and Irish financiers.
106 pp. Dublin, 1786
A., N., Q.

1485 Thoughts concerning the constitutional principles in points of finance and personal service, that ought to be adopted in future, for the support of the British navy and army, prior to, and during the establishment of a commercial union between Great Britain and Ireland.
tables. 78 pp. n.p., 1786
A.

1486 Thoughts upon a bill, lately offered to parliament, for regulating the export and import of corn: with observations upon Dean Tucker's reflections, so far as they relate to this subject. By a country gentleman.
36 pp. London, J. Pridden, 1786
A.

1487 Tracts on tithes. I. Brief and serious reasons why the people called Quakers do not pay tithes. Published by said people in 1768. II. Plain reasons why the people called Quakers may in conscience, and ought in duty, to pay tithes. Published in 1786, and said to be written by a prelate of this kingdom. III. A vindication of the brief and serious reasons, in reply to the last. By J. G. one of said people.
76 pp. Dublin, printed by Robert Jackson, 1786
T.

1488 A treaty of amity and of commerce between the United States of America, and his majesty the king of Russia.
35 pp. n.p., 1786
N., Q.

1489 Treaty of navigation and commerce between his Britannick majesty and the most Christian king. Signed at Versailles, the 26th of September, 1786. Published by authority. 33 + 33 pp. (doubly paginated in French and English). Dublin, printed by Watson [etc.], 1786

A., N., P., Q.

1490 The two treaties between Great Britain & France, the former ratified in the reign of Queen Anne, 1713, the latter signed by Mr. Eden, in the year 1786, compared article by article in opposite columns. Together with the substance of forty-six petitions presented against the former treaty, by the manufacturing interests of Great Britain, faithfully transcribed from the journals of the house of commons, and likewise a brief narrative of the reception of the same treaty by the public, and the final decision upon it in parliament. 18 pp. London, J. Debrett, 1786

A.

1787

1491 Advice to the protestant clergy of Ireland; in which the present dispositions of the public towards them are considered, the pretended and real causes of these dispositions enquired into, and some measures suggested that seem most necessary and expedient at the present juncture to redress the injuries and secure the rights of the clergy. By a layman of the church of England. 72 pp. Dublin, printed by P. Byrne, 1787

A., G., L., N., T.

1492 The American museum, or repository of ancient and modern fugitive pieces, etc. prose and poetical. For July, 1787. 104 pp. Vol. II, Numb. 1. Philadelphia, printed by Mathew Carey, 1787

Q.

1493 An answer to the complete investigation of Mr. Eden's treaty. 38 pp. London, John Stockdale, 1787

A.

1494 BARBER, Samuel. Remarks on a pamphlet, entitled the present state of the Church of Ireland. By Richard, lord bishop of Cloyne. 60 pp. Dublin, printed by P. Byrne, 1787

A., N., Q., T.

——. 48 pp. 2nd ed. Dublin, printed by P. Byrne, 1787

A., N., T.

1495 ——. A reply to the Revd. Mr. Burrowes's remarks, etc. 22 pp. Dublin, printed by P. Byrne, 1787

A., N., Q., T.

1496 BARKER, Thomas Michael. The merchant's and traders guide, or new and complete tables of the net duties payable, and drawbacks allowed, on certain goods, wares, and merchandize, imported, exported, or carried coastwise: together with a list of the bounties. Published under the inspection of Mr. Thomas Michael Barker, of the Custom House, London. Likewise a table of net duties, allowances, bounties, and drawbacks, in the Excise; together with the licences necessary to be taken out by those persons dealing in exciseable commodities: together with an enumeration of the stamp duties, agreeable to the consolidation act of 27 Geo. III. with the alterations and amendments of the last session. The whole alphabetically arranged. To which is added, for convenience of the merchant, a complete table of the duties of customs and excise on wine; calculated from a gallon to a tun: with a table of the duty customs on vinegar. tables. 80 pp. London, Thomas Michael Barker & Philip Wicks, 1787

Q.

1497 A brief and candid vindication of the doctrine and present appropriation of tithes. Deduced from the principles of reason. Their real origin, nature and signification represented—the true reasons assigned, why Christ could not (with any degree of consistency) have ordained their payment & use—with many suitable observations on the subject, in various lights—meriting the attention equally of all sects. In a letter from a gentleman in Munster to a friend in Dublin. 68 pp. Dublin, Grierson, 1787

A., K., N., P., T.

1498 The British merchant, for 1787. Addressed to the chamber of manufactures. Part I. On the commercial policy of any treaty with France; and in, particular, of the present treaty. With an appendix, containing, the French tariffs of duties inwards in 1664 and 1669. And a table of the alterations in our own duties, affected by the VIIth article of the present treaty. 148 pp. London, J. Debrett, 1787

A.

1499 BURROWES, Robert. A letter to the Rev. Samuel Barber, minister, of the Presbyterian congregation of Rathfryland, containing: a refutation of certain dangerous doctrines advanced in his remarks on the bishop of Cloyne's present state of the church of Ireland. 72 pp. Dublin, printed by George Grierson, 1787

A., G., N., T.

——. Another edition. 70 pp. Dublin, printed by George Grierson, 1787

C.

1500 [CAMPBELL, ——?] The choice of evils, or which is best for the kingdom of Ireland, the commercial propositions or a legislative union with Great Britain? containing a full answer to the secretary of state's letter to the mayor of Cork. The whole pointing to the original source and secondary causes of those disorders, which have, for so many years, infested the south of Ireland—If the causes be not well understood, the application of remedies is the more precarious. 111 pp. Dublin, Luke White, 1787

A., C., N., Q.

1501 CLARKE, Thomas Brooke. The second edition of Junius Alter's letter to Mr. O'Leary. With a short examination into the first causes of the present lawless spirit of the Irish peasantry; and a plan of reform. 32 pp. Dublin, printed by William McKenzie, 1787

T.

1502 A congratulatory address to his majesty, from the peasantry of Ireland, vulgarly denominated White Boys, or, Right Boys.
tables. 20 pp. Dublin, printed by P. Byrne, 1787
T.

1503 Considerations on the negotiation for reducing the rate of interest on the national debt of Ireland. Addressed to the holders of four per cent. debentures, and treasury bills at 3d. per day.
34 pp. Dublin, printed by J. Chambers, 1787
A.

1504 Considerations on the political and commercial circumstances of Great-Britain and Ireland, as they are connected with each other; and on the most probable means of effecting a settlement between them; tending to promote the interests of both, and the advantages of the British Empire.
84 pp. Dublin, printed by P. Byrne, 1787
A., K., N., Q., T.

——. Another issue. 106 pp. London, J. Debrett, 1787
A., Q.

1505 A critical review of the B. of Cloyne's publication; with occasional remarks on the productions of some other writers, particularly those of Trinity College, and on the conduct of the present ministry. Addressed to his lordship, by an unbiassed Irishman.
102 pp. Dublin, printed by Chambers, 1787
A., L., N., T.

1506 [DAWSON, Thomas.] The mirror: or cursory observations, on the licentious pamphlets of Theophilus, etc. etc. etc. wherein the subject of tithes is candidly discussed, and the real cause of the late disturbances in the south faithfully developed. By Publicola.
68 pp. Dublin, printed by P. Cooney, 1787
A.

1507 DE CALONNE, Charles Alexandre. Abridgment of the memorial addressed to the king of France, by M. de Calonne, minister of state. Translated from the French by W. Walter.
136 pp. London, Robson and Clarke [etc.], 1787
A.

1508 ——. The speech delivered, by the order and in the presence of the king, in the assembly of the notables, held at Versailles the 22nd of Feb., 1787. By M. De Calonne, comptroller general of the finances.
48 pp. Dublin, printed by P. Byrne, 1787
A., K., N., Q.

1509 DELOLME, John Lewis. The British empire in Europe: part the first, containing an account of the connection between the kingdoms of England and Ireland, previous to the year 1780. To which is prefixed, an historical sketch of the state of rivalry between the kingdoms of England and Scotland, in former times.
160 pp. Dublin, printed by P. Byrne, 1787
N., Q.

——. Another issue. 160 pp. Dublin, Moncrieffe, Culbert, 1787
A., G.

1510 A digest of the excise laws of Ireland.
48 pp. n.p., [1787?]
Q.

1511 [DUIGENAN, Patrick.] An address to the nobility and gentry of the church of Ireland, as by law established. By Theophilus.
120 pp. 2nd ed. Dublin, printed by Henry Watts, 1787
A., N., T.
See 1456.

1512 An earnest address to both Houses of Parliament, on the subject of the intended application for a reform of the Police Act.
16 pp. Dublin, printed by P. Byrne, 1787
Q.

1513 Extracts relative to the fisheries on the north-west coast of Ireland from the reports of the committee of the British House of Commons, appointed to inquire into the state of the British fisheries, and from the publications of Mr. Knox, Dr. Anderson and others: with some observations, and authentic papers, to corroborate what is there asserted, of the advantage of establishments on the north west coast of Ireland. For the purpose not only of carrying on the Irish home fishery, but likewise those of Greenland, Newfoundland and Iceland.
tables, appendix. 76 pp. London, 1787
C.

1514 A few serious and seasonable observations on some matters that engage now the public attention: in which, the subject of tithes, the disturbances in the south, and the present state and conduct of the established clergy of Ireland, are fairly considered. By a curate.
72 pp. Dublin, printed by B. Smith, 1787
A., N., T.

1515 FLOOD, Henry. Speech of the right hon. Henry Flood, in the House of Commons of Great Britain, February 15, 1787, on the commercial treaty with France.
27 pp. Dublin, printed by P. Byrne, 1787
A., N., Q., T.

1516 [GARDINER, Luke?] Remarks on the principle of a Bill for the establishment of turnpikes round the city of Dublin. Printed in 1786, and now re-printed with several additions. To which is added a brief abstract of the material clauses of the bill now pending in parliament.
30 pp. Dublin, printed by P. Byrne, 1787
A., N., Q.

1517 GRACE, George. A short plea for human nature and common sense. In which it is attempted to state a few general principles for the direction of our judgment of the present state of the church of Ireland, as described by the lord bishop of Cloyne.
62 pp. Dublin, printed by P. Byrne, 1787
T.

1518 GRIFFITH, Amyas. Observations on the bishop of Cloyne's pamphlet: in which the doctrine of tithes is candidly considered, and proved to be oppressive and impolitic; his

lordship's arguments for the insecurity of the protestant religion, are also demonstrated to be groundless and visionary.
72 pp. Dublin, printed by T. Byrne, 1787

A., G., N.

1519 Helps to a right decision upon the merits of the late treaty of commerce with France. Addressed to the members of both houses of parliament.
44 pp. London, J. Debrett, 1787

A.

1520 HOWLETT, John. Enclosures, a cause of improved agriculture, of plenty and cheapness of provisions, of population, and of both private and national wealth. Being an examination of two pamphlets, entitled, the one, a political enquiry into the consequences of enclosing waste lands and the cause of the present high price of butcher's meat, the other, cursory remarks upon enclosures, by a country farmer, together with some slight observations upon the report of the London committee, appointed the 16th July, 1786, to consider the causes of the present high prices of provisions.
table of contents, tables, 108 pp. London, P. Richardson, 1787

N.

1521 HUTCHESON, Francis. A short introduction to moral philosophy. In three parts. Containing the elements of ethicks, and the law of nature.
298 pp. Dublin, printed by William McKenzie, 1787

A.

1522 An inquiry into the justice and policy of an union between Great Britain and Ireland, with an answer to the supposed 'Practicability' of such a measure, consistent with the welfare of the latter, in reply to the arguments of John Williams, Esq. late of Merton College, Oxon.
128 pp. Dublin, printed by P. Byrne, 1787

A., P., Q., T.

1523 The insurrection, or, a faithful narrative of the disturbances which lately broke out in the province of Munster, under the denomination of the white or right-boys.
46 pp. Dublin, W. Sleater, 1787

A., K.

1524 [JACKMAN, John?] A candid review of the most important occurrences that took place in Ireland, during the last three years: in which is comprised, 1. The proceedings of the national convention assembled in Dublin, November 1783, & the succeeding year. 2. Rise and progress of the bill for effectuating a commercial intercourse between the two nations, on permanent & equitable principles. 3. His grace of Portland's reasons for opposing the twenty propositions sent from the commons to the lords of England, for their consideration. 4. Proceedings of the Irish legislature on the twenty propositions transmitted from England. 5. Opinion of Mr. Fox's ministerial character. 6. The probable consequences of any proposition in the British parliament tending to an union with the sister nation. 7. The present state of the press in Ireland considered in a letter addressed to George Stackpole, Esq.
64 pp. Dublin, Printed by P. Byrne, 1787

A., K., Q., T.

——. Another issue, 93 pp. London, J. Bell, 1787

A., N.

1525 A letter addressed to the public, on the subject of tithes, and the late outrages. In which the propositions and plan of Theophilus, in his late address to the lords and commons, are amicably discussed. By a friend to equity and moderation.
40 pp. Dublin, R. Marchbank, 1787

A., N., P., T.

1526 A letter from a Munster layman, of the established church, to his friend in Dublin, on the disturbances in the south.
30 pp. Dublin, Luke White, 1787

A., T.

1527 Letters by a farmer: originally published in The Belfast Evening Post; with several alterations and additions.
146 pp. Belfast, printed by James Magee, 1787

A., L., N.

1528 A list of the proprietors of licences on private sedan chairs, at 25th March, 1787, alphabetically ranged; with their respective residences, published as required by law. To which are prefixed, a list of the subscribers to the six annual assemblies, intended to be held in the new rooms in Rutland Square. And also, the motives which induced such undertaking. There are likewise added, certain tables explanatory of the receipts, expenditures, and state of the lying-in hospital.
frontisp. tables. fold. tables. diags. 38 pp. [Dublin], by order of the governors of the said hospital, [1787]

A.

1529 MAGEE, John. An Irishman's reception in London; or, the adventures of two days and a night.
88 pp. London, the author, 1787

Q.

A proposal to replace the shop tax by a lottery.
See 1591.

1530 MASCALL, Edward-James. Tables of the net duties payable, and drawbacks allowed on certain goods, wares and merchandise, imported, exported, or carried coastwise. Together with a list of the bounties. To which are added, a table of the duties, allowances, bounties and drawbacks in the excise; together with the licences necessary to be taken out by those persons dealing in exciseable commodities—and an alphabetical arrangement of the various stamp-duties in Great Britain. The whole agreeable to the consolidation act of the 27th of George III. [Also introduction comprising Pitt's speech 26 Feb., 1787, on simplifying duties].
108 pp. London, W. Lowndes, 1787

A.

1531 NECKER, Jacques. Mr. Necker's answer to Mr. De Calonne's charge against him in the assembly of the notables.
114 pp. London, J. Debrett, 1787

A.

1532 [O'BRYEN, Dennis.] A view of the treaty of commerce with France: signed at Versailles, Sept. 20, 1786, by Mr. Eden.
tables. 140 pp. London, J. Debrett & J. Bew, 1787

A., P.

1533 Observations on the agricultural and political tendency of the commercial treaty.
32 pp. London, J. Debrett, 1787

A.

1534 Observations on the indecent and illiberal strictures against the lord bishop of Cloyne, contained in a pamphlet lately published under the title of Mr. O'Leary's defence, etc.
34 pp. Dublin, printed by W. Sleater, 1787
A., N., T.

1535 [O'DRISCOL, William.] A letter to the Rev. Doctor O'Leary. Found on the great road leading from the city of Cork to Cloughnakilty.
30 pp. Dublin, printed by W. Sleater, 1787
A., G., N., T.

1536 O'LEARY, Arthur. Mr. O'Leary's defence; containing a vindication of his conduct and writings during the late disturbances in Munster; with a full justification of the Catholics, and an account of the risings of the Whiteboys. In answer to the false accusations of Theophilus and the ill-grounded insinuations of the Right Reverend Doctor Woodward, lord bishop of Cloyne.
appendices. 178 pp. Dublin, printed by P. Byrne, 1787
Q., T.

——. 152 pp. 2nd ed. Cork, printed by William Flyn, 1787
A., L., T.

1537 ——. Mr. O'Leary's letter to the monthly reviewers.
16 pp. Dublin, printed by P. Byrne, 1787
A., T.
On the Whiteboy disturbances.

1538 ORDE, Thomas. Mr. Orde's plan of an improved system of education in Ireland; submitted to the house of commons, April 12, 1787; with the debate which rose thereon. Reported by John Gifford, Esq.
178 pp. Dublin, printed by W. Porter, [1787]
A., L., N.

1539 [PEEL, Sir Robert, 1st baronet.] The national debt productive of national prosperity.
56 pp. Warrington, printed by W. Eyres, London, J. Johnson, 1787
P.

1540 The people's answer to the court pamphlet. Entitled A short review of the political state of Great Britain.
52 pp. Dublin, printed by P. Byrne, 1787
N., Q.

——. 62 pp. 2nd ed. London, J. Debrett, 1787
A.

——. 62 pp. 2nd ed. Dublin, L. White [etc.], 1787
A.

——. 52 pp. 4th ed. London, J. Debrett, 1787
Q.

1541 PITT, William. The speech of the right honourable William Pitt, in the house of commons, February 12, 1787, in a committee of the whole house, to consider of so much of his majesty's most gracious speech to both houses of parliament as relates to the treaty of navigation and commerce between his majesty and the most Christian king.
62 pp. Dublin, printed by P. Byrne, 1787
A., N., Q.

1542 Premiums offered by the Dublin Society, for agriculture and planting, 1787.
30 pp. Dublin, printed by W. Sleater, 1787
N., Q.

1543 The principles of British policy; contrasted with a French alliance; in five letters, from a whig member of parliament to a country gentleman.
68 pp. London, J. Debrett, 1787
A.

1544 Remarks on a letter lately published, signed Arthur O'Leary, stiled An address to the protestant nobility and gentry of Ireland, by a friend to truth and the publick.
22 pp. Dublin, W. Slater, 1787
T.

1545 [RICHARDSON, Joseph.] A complete investigation of Mr. Eden's treaty, as it may effect the commerce, the revenue, or the general policy of Great Britain.
tables. 174 pp. London, J. Debrett, 1787
N., P.

——. Another issue. 174 pp. Dublin, W. Colles, L. White [etc.], 1787
N., Q., U.

1546 The rights of Ireland vindicated, in an answer to the secretary of state's letter to the mayor of Cork, on the subject of Mr. Orde's bill, presented the 15th of August, 1785.
88 pp. Dublin, S. Watson, 1787
A., N., U.

1547 ROBINSON, Christopher, & TENISON, Thomas. The respective charges given to the grand jury of the county of Armagh, at the general assizes held there July 23, 1763, by the then going judges of assize, Mr. Justice Robinson, and Mr. Justice Tenison; on occasion of the late commotions in several of the northern counties.
32 pp. Dublin, William McKenzie, 1787
A., G., T.

1548 RYAN, Edward. Remarks on the pamphlet of Mr. Barber, dissenting minister of Rathfriland, by the Rev. Edward Ryan, D.D.
56 pp. Dublin, printed by P. Bryne, 1787
A., T.

1549 [SCHOMBERG, Alexander C.] Historical and political remarks upon the tariff of the commercial treaty: with preliminary observations.
172 pp. London, T. Cadell, 1787
K.

1550 A short, plain, civil answer to a long, laboured and illiberal pamphlet, intitled "An address to the nobility and gentry of the church of Ireland, etc. etc. by a layman'.
50 pp. Dublin, printed by P. Byrne, 1787
A., N., Q., T.

1551 A short refutation of the arguments contained in doctor Butler's letter to lord Kenmare. By a clergyman. [To which is added, a reply to the third section of Mr. O'Leary's defence.]
36 pp. Dublin, printed by W. Sleater, 1787
T.

1552 A short vindication of the French treaty, from the charges brought against it in a late pamphlet, entitled, A view of the treaty of commerce with France, signed at Versailles, Sept. 28, 1786, by Mr. Eden.
49 pp. London, John Stockdale, 1787

A.

1553 SINCLAIR, Sir John, bart. State of alterations which may be proposed in the laws for regulating the election of members of Parliament for shires in Scotland.
48 pp. London, T. Cadell, 1787

Q.

1554 Some reflections, concerning the reduction of gold coin in Ireland. Upon the principles of the dean of St. Patrick's and Mr. Lock humbly submitted to the good people of Ireland.
16 pp. Dublin, 1787

Q.

1555 [STOKES, J... W...?] An address to both Houses of Parliament, in which some parts of the present system of revenue law are considered; and some observations and strictures, are submitted to their consideration, on the powers vested in, and exercised by, the courts of commissioners, sub-commissioners, and commissioners of appeals. By a barrister.
86 pp. Dublin, printed by P. Brady, 1787

A., N., Q.

1556 Strictures on a pamphlet signed Theophilus explaining the real causes of the discontents in every part of this kingdom, respecting tithes, and containing reasons why tithes ought to be abolished entirely, and the practicability of substituting a better mode of subsistence and maintenance for the clergy of the church established, consistent with the principles of reason and justice. By a farmer.
tables. 80 pp. Dublin, Luke White, 1787

A., K., N., T.

1557 Strictures on the bishop of Cloyne's present state of the church of Ireland; with appendices, containing passages alluded to in the bishop's pamphlet.
appendices, 96 pp. London, C. Dilly, Dublin, P. Byrne, 1787

A., N., Q., T.

1558 Temperate, unborrowed animadversions, on the pamphlet lately published by Richard, bishop of Cloyne, on the subject of tythes: Wherein this writer proposes plain radical remedies, not only for the evils now complained of, but for the abuses introduced into primitive Christianity by ecclesiasticks of all denominations. Also, a cool statement of Mr. O'Leary's conduct, in which the charge of duplicity against that gentleman, is honestly done away. By a sincere unbiassed protestant.
64 pp. Dublin, printed by J. M. Davis, 1787

A., G., Q.

1559 THOMAS, Daniel. Observations on the pamphlets published by the bishop of Cloyne, Mr. Trant and Theophilus, on one side; and on those by Mr. O'Leary, Mr. Barber and Doctor Campbell on the other. To which are added remarks on the cause of the late insurrection in Munster, a consideration of the grievances under which the peasantry of Ireland

labours, with a proposal of an adequate compensation for tithes.
82 pp. Dublin, the author, 1787

A., N., Q., T.

1560 [TIGHE, Robert Stearne.] Melantius: a letter addressed to Mr. Orde, upon the education of the people.
40 pp. Dublin, printed by P. Byrne, 1787

A., N., Q.

1561 To the reverend doctor James Butler, a titular archbishop, from a friend.
16 pp. Dublin, printed by W. Sleater, 1787

T.

1562 TOWNSEND, Joseph. A dissertation on the poor laws.
104 pp. 2nd ed. London, C. Dilly, 1787

P.

1563 TRANT, Dominick. Considerations on the present disturbances in the province of Munster, their causes, extent, probable consequences and remedies.
table. 78 pp. Dublin, printed by P. Byrne, 1787

A., C., G., N., Q., T., U.

——. 94 pp. 2nd ed. Dublin, 1787

A., N., T.

——. 94 pp. 3rd ed. Dublin, 1787

K., N., T.

1564 TUCKER, Josiah. A brief essay on the advantages and disadvantages which respectively attend France and Great Britain with regard to trade.
54 pp. Dublin, printed by P. Byrne, 1787

A., N., Q., U.

1565 ——. A brief essay on the advantages and disadvantages which respectively attend France and Great Britain, with regard to trade. (Re-pr. from the 3rd ed. of 1753. With three essays. I On the balance of trade. II On the jealousy of trade. III On the balance of power. By David Hume, Esq.)
96 pp. London, J. Stockdale, 1787

N.

1566 The utility of an union between Great Britain and Ireland, considered, by a friend to both countries.
24 pp. Dublin, printed by P. Byrne, 1787

A., Q., T.

——. Another issue. 32 pp. London, J. Stockdale, 1787

A.

1567 A view of the policy and methods of government established in the United Provinces; particularly in Holland.
64 pp. Dublin, printed by P. Byrne, 1787

A., N., Q.

1568 A vindication of the conduct of the clergy; who petitioned the house of lords against two bills relative to tithes, in the session of parliament held in 1788. By a southern clergyman. With an appendix containing his former answers to certain 'Allegations' with additions.
tables. appendix. 56 pp. Dublin, William Sleater, 1788

K.

1569 WILLIAMS, John. An union of England and Ireland proved to be practicable and equally beneficial to each kingdom. With supplementary observations, relative to the absentees of Ireland, pointing out the constitutional means of removing complaints arising from that and other causes of present discontent, and finally for conciliating the desires of each country. To which is added, a collateral reply to the dean of Gloucester's advice to the Irish, to trade with foreign in preference to the British colonies.
58 pp. Dublin, P. Byrne, 1787

A., Q., T.

——. Another issue, 52 pp. London, G. Kearsly, 1787

N.

1570 WOODWARD, Richard, bishop of Cloyne. The present state of the church of Ireland: containing a description of it's precarious situation: and the consequent danger to the public. Recommended to the serious consideration of the friends of the protestant interest. To which are subjoined some reflections on the impracticability of a proper commutation for tithes; and a general account of the origin and progress of the insurrections in Munster.
appendices. 128 pp. Dublin, W. Sleater, jun., 1787

A.

——. 128 pp. 2nd ed. Dublin, W. Sleater, 1787

A., K., R.

——. 128 pp. 3rd ed. Dublin, W. Sleater, 1787

A., T.

——. 318 pp. 4th ed. Dublin, W. Sleater, 1787

A.

——. 140 pp. 5th ed. Dublin, W. Sleater, 1787

G., K., M., N.

——. 132 pp. 6th ed. Dublin, W. Sleater, 1787

A., L., N.

——. 136 pp. 7th ed. London, T. Cadell, 1787

A., N.

——. 132 pp. 8th ed. Dublin, W. Sleater, 1787

Q.

——. 138 pp. 9th ed. Dublin, W. Sleater, 1787

A., Q., T.

See also 1606.

1788

1571 An abstract of the number of Protestant and Popish families in the several provinces and counties of Ireland. Taken from the returns made by the hearthmoney collectors, to the hearthmoney office in Dublin, in the years 1732 and 1733. Those being reckon'd Protestant and Popish families, where the heads of the families are either Protestants or Papists. With observations.
16 pp. Dublin, reprinted by W. Sleater, 1788

Q.

See 1436.

1572 An address to the inhabitants in general of Great Britain, and Ireland; relating to a few of the consequences which must naturally result from the abolition of the slave trade.
32 pp. Liverpool, Mrs. Egerton Smith; (etc.), 1788

A.

1573 Astraea: or, a letter addressed to an officer of the court of exchequer, on the abuses committed in his majesty's casual revenue, as well as in the administration and execution of public justice in Ireland. Together with a plan for the better execution of public justice in counties at large. By an attorney at law.
85 pp. Dublin, printed by P. Byrne, 1788

A., N., Q., T.

1574 [BROWN, Arthur.] A full display of some late publications on the subject of tithes and the sufferings of the established clergy in the south of Ireland, attributed to those dues. With strictures necessary for the further elucidation of that subject. By Candidus.
182 pp. Dublin, printed by W. Sleater, 1788

A., N., P., T.

1575 CLARKSON, Thomas. An essay on the impolicy of the African slave trade. In two parts.
tables. 11 + 127 pp. 2nd ed. London, J. Phillips, 1788

A., Q.

1576 COMMERELL, Abbé de. An account of the culture and use of the mangel wurzel, or root of scarcity. Translated from the French of the Abbé de Commerell, corresponding member of the Royal Society of Arts and Sciences at Metz.
34 pp. 3rd ed. Dublin, printed by J. Moore, 1788

A.

This edition has 'Advertisement' and 'Preface to the Second Edition', signed John Coakley Lettsom.

——. 92 pp. 4th ed. London, C. Dilly and J. Phillips, 1788

N.

1577 Considerations on the negotiation for reducing the rate of interest on the national debt of Ireland. To which is added, a postscript. Addressed to the holders of four per cent, debentures, and treasury bills at 3d. per day.
34 pp. 2nd ed. Dublin, printed by J. Chambers, 1788

A., N.

1578 A copy of the charter of the corporation of the governor and company of the bank of England.
84 pp. London, John Bell, 1788

Q.

1579 CROFT, John. A treatise on the wines of Portugal; and what can be gathered on the subject and nature of the wines, etc., since the establishment of the English factory at Oporto, Anno 1727: also a dissertation on the nature and use of wines in general, imported into Great Britain, as pertaining to luxury and diet. In two parts.
32 pp. York, J. Todd, 1788

Q.

1580 A defence of the Protestant clergy in the south of Ireland, in answer to the charges against them, contained in the rt. hon Henry Grattan's speeches relating to tithes, as they

are printed, and said to have been delivered in the House of Commons, on Thursday the 14th, and Tuesday the 19th of February 1788. With a postscript containing some remarks on his last speech on the re-agitation of tithes, delivered on the 11th of April, 1788. By Authenticus.
tables. 134 pp. Dublin, printed by P. Byrne, 1788

A., N., Q., T.

1581 [DUIGENAN, Patrick.] A letter to Amyas Griffith, Esq., late surveyor of the Bean-Walk, Stephen's Green, and formerly inspector general of the Monitor, and of the polite conversation of Dodderige and Vanthrump. Occasioned by his late scurrilous pamphlet against the bishop of Cloyne, Theophilus, and the dignitaries of the established church. With some observations on the recent conduct of the firm 'of the barbarous sirname'. By Theophilus.
60 pp. Dublin, printed by C. Lewis, [1783?]

Q.

1582 The economist. Shewing, in a variety of estimates from fourscore pounds a year to upwards of 800L. how comfortably and genteely a family may live with frugality for a little money. Together with the cheapest method of keeping horses and carriages. By a gentleman of experience.
32 pp. Dublin, printed by James Hoey, [1788?]

A.

1583 Extravagance supported on the principles of policy and philosophy.
90 pp. London, the Trusters, 1788

A.

1584 FALCONBRIDGE, Alexander. An account of the slave trade on the coast of Africa.
56 pp. London, printed by Phillips, 1788

N.

1585 GRATTAN, Henry. A full report of the speech of the rt. hon. Henry Grattan, in the house of commons, on Thursday the 14th February, 1788, in the debate on tithes. Taken in shorthand by Mr. Franklin.
56 pp. Dublin, printed by P. Byrne, 1788

A., N., T.

1586 ——. Speech of the right honorable Henry Grattan, relative to tithes, in the house of commons, on Thursday, February 14, 1788.
52 pp. Dublin, Printed by M. Graisberry, 1788

A.

——. 58 pp. 2nd ed. Dublin, printed by M. Graisberry, 1788

L., N.

——. 60 pp. 3rd ed. Dublin, printed by R. Graisberry, 1788

A.

——. Another issue, 78 pp. 3rd ed. Dublin, printed by R. Graisberry, 1788

A.

1587 ——. Speech of the rt. hon. Henry Grattan, on the re-agitation on the subject of tithes, in the house of commons, Friday, April 11, 1788.
28 pp. Dublin, W. Gilbert, 1788

A., N., T.

1588 A hint to the established clergy of the kingdom of Ireland; in answer to two letters lately addressed to the right reverend bench, by a reformer high in office, and which contained a plan for the entire subversion of the ecclesiastical establishment. This hint is recommended to the serious attention of the clergy and laity. By Clericus.
64 pp. Dublin, printed by William McKenzie, 1788

T.

1589 HODGSON, P. Levi, and Son. The complete measurer, adapted to timber and building, agreeable to the Irish standard.
tables. 116 pp. 8th ed. Dublin, the author, 1788

Q.

1590 HOWLETT, John. The insufficiency of the causes to which the increase of our poor, and of the poor's rates have been commonly ascribed; the true one stated; with an enquiry into the mortality of country houses of industry, and a slight general view of Mr. Acland's plan for rendering the poor independent.
London, W. Richardson, 1788

P.

1591 MAGEE, John. An Irishman's reception in London; or the adventures of two days and a night. The necessity of supporting the exigencies of the state should be impressed on every mind—much clamour, and perhaps, justly, has been excited against the shop-tax; as not less partial in operation than oppressive in collection, to retail traders and shop keepers of London. A mode is now suggested of a substitute for that tax; or, if the pressure of the times will not suffer the premier to abandon an established tax, the chancellor of the exchequer is now enabled to raise annually £322,600, and that without the expence of a single new office, by a mode no less productive to the treasury of the nation, than promoting decency and enforcing law among stock-jobbers and stock-brokers, as well as preserving the morals of the most useful part of the community, the faithful domestic and industrious mechanic.
70 pp. Dublin, W. Gilbert, 1788

A.

See 1529.

1592 NECKER, Jacques. The speech of Mr. Necker, director general of the finances, at a meeting of the assembly of notables, held at Versailles, November 6, 1788. To which is added, the king's and the keeper's speeches.
42 pp. London, J. Debrett, 1788

A.

1593 Observations on the late increase of the dividend on bank stock.
20 pp. London, J. Sewell, 1788

A.

1594 Observations on the pernicious consequences of the excessive use of spiritous liquors, and the ruinous policy of permitting distillation in this country.
52 pp. Dublin, printed by John Chambers, 1788

A.

1595 [PAINE, Thomas.] Prospects on the Rubicon: or an investigation into the causes and consequences of the politics to be agitated at the meeting of Parliament.
60 pp. Dublin, Printed by P. Byrne, 1788

A., Q.

1596 PICKETT, William. An apology to the public, for a continued intrusion on their notice; with an appeal to the free and independent proprietors of bank stock; demonstrating that it is highly proper for them to examine into the state of their affairs.
50 pp. London, J. Sewell (etc.), 1788
A.

1597 Premiums offered by the Dublin Society, for agriculture and planting, 1788.
34 pp. Dublin, printed by W. Sleater, [1788?]
Q.

1598 Reflections on national reformation; with the probable means of effecting it, seriously addressed to the parliament, and people of Ireland, and humbly inscribed to the author of Melantius. . . . To which are prefixed, congratulatory lines to the Marquis of Buckingham, on his re-assumption of the vice-regal power.
44 pp. Dublin, printed by Luke White, 1788
A.

1599 A report of the case, which some time since depended in the consistorial court of Dublin, between the late rev. Smyth Loftus, vicar of Coolock, and Peter Callage, one of his parishioners, for the subtraction of tithes; with the arguments of the civilians and common lawyers in that court—the sentence—and appeal therefrom to delegates; together with the opinions of the most eminent civilians and common lawyers in Great Britain and Ireland upon that case, and the propriety of an appeal from that sentence. This report contains the whole of the law, as to the time and manner of setting out tithes of all kinds, and particularly of hay and corn—the state in which tithes are to be set out—the form of legal notice to the incumbent—the respective duties of minister and parishioner in respect to saving, keeping, and removing tithes—and the consequence of the incumbent's not removing them in time; and, therefore, must necessarily be extremely useful to all persons liable to payment of tithes.
appendix. 78 pp. Dublin, Caleb Jenkin, 1788
T.

1600 SHERIDAN, Richard Brinsley. A comparative statement of the two bills, for the better government of the British possessions in India, brought into parliament by Mr. Fox and Mr. Pitt. With explanatory observations.
54 pp. Dublin, printed by P. Byrne, 1788
A., N., Q.

1601 TOOKE, John Horne. Two pair of portraits, presented to all the unbiassed electors of Great Britain and especially to the electors of Westminster.
30 pp. London, J. Johnson, 1788
Q.

1602 TOWNSEND, Joseph. Observations on various plans offered to the public, for the relief of the poor.
table in appendix. 50 pp. London, C. Dilly, 1788
P.

1603 The utility of an union between Great Britain and Ireland, considered by a friend to both countries.
32 pp. London, John Stockdale, 1788
A., N.

1604 A vindication of the conduct of the clergy, who petitioned the house of lords against two bills relative to tithes, in the session of parliament held in 1788. By a southern clergyman. With an appendix, containing his former answers to certain 'allegations'. With additions.
56 pp. Dublin, printed by William Sleater, 1788
A., N., T.

1605 WOODWARD, Richard, bishop of Cloyne. An argument in support of the right of the poor in the kingdom of Ireland, to a national provision; in the appendix to which, an attempt is made to settle a measure of the contribution due from each man to the poor, on the footing of justice.
appendix. 56 pp. Dublin, S. Powell, 1788
K.

1606 ——. The present state of the church of Ireland: containing a description of it's precarious situation; and the consequent danger to the public. Recommended to the serious consideration of the friends of the protestant interest. To which are subjoined, some reflections on the impracticability of a proper commutation for tithes; and a general account of the origin and progress of the insurrections in Munster.
128 pp. Dublin, printed by W. Sleater, 1788
Q.

1789

1607 Abecedarian Society, instituted Thursday, March the 26th, 1789.
12 pp. [Dublin?], 1789
A.

Prospectus of a charitable society.

1608 Ab[st]ract of the premiums offered by the society, instituted at London for the encouragement of arts, manufactures, and commerce.
8 pp. London, printed by Nichols, 1789
N.

1609 BAYLEY, John. A short treatise on the law of bills of exchange, cash bills, and promissory notes.
88 pp. Dublin, E. Lynch [etc.], 1789
A., N.

1610 BEATTY, J. Interesting facts respecting the loans and lotteries of the years of 1788 and 1789, submitted to the consideration of the public.
38 pp. n.p., printed by John Beatty, 1789
A.

1611 A call of the holders of government securities to a review of the negotiation for the loans and lotteries for the years 1788 and 1789. Especially as they apply to debentures bearing an interest of 4 per cent. and treasury bills at three-pence per day. Addressed to his excellency, the marquis of Buckingham. By a stock holder.
48 pp. Dublin, P. Byrne, [etc.], 1789
A., N., Q.

1612 CHAPMAN, William, engineer. Estimate of the expences of completing the navigation of the river Barrow from St. Mullin's to Athy. Report on the means of perfecting the navigation of the river Barrow from St. Mullin's to Athy.
tables. 62 pp. Dublin, printed by Sleator, 1789
N.

1613 Charter of the Hibernian marine society, Dublin.
20 pp. Dublin, 1789

A.

1614 The charter of the royal canal company, with their rules and extracts from the act of the 29th of his present majesty George III. With an index. To which is prefixed, A list of subscribers.
60 pp. Dublin, printed by John Chambers, 1789

A., N.

1615 [COOKE, Thomas.] A letter to the rt. hon. Thomas Conolly, secretary to the Whig club. To which are added, the declarations and resolutions of that society.
66 pp. Dublin, printed by W. Porter, 1789

A., N., Q.

1616 Common sense in vindication of his excellency the marquess of Buckingham, during his government of Ireland; dedicated to the right honourable the earl of Bellamont. By a candid inquirer.
44 pp. Dublin, printed by M. Graisberry, 1789

A., Q.

1617 CULLEY, George. Observations on livestock, containing hints for choosing and improving the best breeds of the most useful kinds of domestic animals.
176 pp. Dublin, printed by P. Byrne, 1789

A., Q.

1618 DALRYMPLE, Sir John, bart. Queries concerning the conduct which England should follow in foreign politics in the present state of Europe. Written in October, 1788.
fold. tables. tables. 96 pp. London, J. Debrett, 1789

A.

1619 DEMPSTER, George, & GRAY, John. A discourse containing a summary of the proceedings of the directors of the society for extending the fisheries and improving the sea coasts of Great Britain, since 25th March, 1788. And some thoughts on the present emigrations from the highlands. By George Dempster, Esq. one of directors. Together with some reflections intended to promote the success of the said society. By John Gray Esq. author of the plan for finally settling the government of Ireland upon constitutional principles, and other political tracts.
diag. 90 pp. London, G. & T. Wilkie & J. Debrett, 1789

Q.

1620 Extra official state papers. Addressed to the right hon. lord Rawdon, and the other members of the two houses of parliament, associated for the preservation of the constitution and promoting the prosperity of the British empire. By a late under secretary of state.
306 pp. London and Dublin, 1789

A.

1621 FALCONER, William. An essay on the preservation of the health of persons employed in agriculture, and on the cure of the diseases incident to that way of life.
96 pp. Bath, printed by Cruttwell, 1789

A., T.

1622 FORDYCE, George. Elements of agriculture and vegetation, to which is added an appendix for the use of practical farmers.
diagrams. 112 pp. 4th ed. London, Johnson, 1789

D.

1623 [GRATTAN, Henry.] A few hasty observations on the barren-land bill.
16 pp. Dublin, printed by P. Byrne, 1789

A., N., Q.

Signed H. G.

1624 ———. Speech of the right hon. Henry Grattan, relative to tythe, in the house of commons on Friday, May 8, 1789. To which is annexed, a bill to appoint commissioners for the purpose of enquiring into the state of tithes, etc. Also, a manifesto of the parochial clergy of Munster.
78 pp. Dublin, M. Graisberry, 1789

A., B., G., N., T.

1625 KIRWAN, Richard. Observations on coal mines.
tables. 16 pp. Dublin, printed by Bonham, 1789

A.

1626 LOCKER, John. Observations and reasons for the establishment of a mint in Ireland.
17 pp. Dublin, printed by P. Byrne, 1789

A., N., Q.

1627 MERREY, Walter. Remarks on the coinage of England from the earliest to the present times; with a view to point out the causes of the present scarcity of silver for change and to shew the only proper way to make it plentiful. To which is added an appendix, containing observations upon the ancient Roman coinage; and a description of some medals and coins found near Nottingham.
table of contents. appendix. 112 pp. Nottingham, printed by Tupman, 1789

A., K.

1628 MONTESQUIOU-FEZENSAC, Anne Pierre, Marquis de. Rapport fait a l'Assemblée nationale, au nom du Comité des finances, par M. le marquis de Montesquiou; le 26 septembre 1789.
24 pp. (no t.p.) Paris, Baudouin, 1789

N.

1629 Observations on the frauds committed by the bakers of the city of Dublin; with some hints at the proper modes of prevention as well as punishment; in a letter addressed to Travers Hartley, Esq., M.P.
26 pp. Dublin, Grueber & McAllister, 1789

A.

1630 Preliminary observations, on our happy and free constitution; encomiums on our patriotic and independent representatives in parliament. With general, and political remarks, on several important subjects, relative to the state of this country, and the ensuing election, which deserve the attention both of the public and legislature. By a citizen.
62 pp. Cork, James Jones, 1789

B.

1631 Premiums offered by the Dublin Society, for agriculture and planting, 1789.
tables. 40 pp. Dublin, printed by W. Sleater, 1789
                                        Q.

1632 PRICE, Richard. A discourse on the love of our country, delivered on Nov. 4, 1789, at the meeting-house in the old Jewry, to the society for commemorating the revolution in Great Britain. With an appendix, containing the report of the committee of the society: an account of the population of France: and the declaration of rights by the national assembly of France.
66 pp. 2nd ed. London, T. Cadell, 1789
                                        A., N.

1633 STEPHENSON, Robert. A letter to the right hon. and honourable the trustees of the linen manufacture.
tables. 36 pp. Dublin, printed by Corbett, 1789
                                        N.

1634 Remarks, upon the circumstances attending the drawing of the late Irish state lottery, being an enquiry what has been the alteration in the chance of the holders of tickets, produced by a number having been accidentally left out of the wheel.
34 pp. Dublin, printed by H. Watts, 1789
                                        A., N.

1635 The royal interview: a fragment.
48 pp. Dublin, Exshaw and others, 1789
                                        A., N., Q.

——. Another issue, 64 pp. London, J. Walker, 1789
                                        A.

1636 A short but particular and impartial account of the treatment of slaves in the island of Antigua, so far as came within the writer's knowledge, during a residence of eight years. Wherein are considered, the arrival and sale of slaves, and their first treatment, their allowance of provisions previous to, and during the war in America, clothes allowed to slaves, and the dress of negroes in general, in what the work of slaves consists, and their punishments and amusements. With anecdotes and notes. By S. K.
70 pp. Cork, printed by John Cronin, 1789
                                        A.

1637 Some thoughts on the importance of the linnen-manufacture [sic] to Ireland, & how to lessen the expence of it.
128 pp. Dublin, printed by George Faulkner, 1789
                                        L.

1638 The speeches of Mr. Wilberforce, Lord Penrhyn, Mr. Burke, Sir W. Young, Alderman Newnham, Mr. Dempster, Mr. Martin, Mr. Pitt, Mr. Grenville, Mr. Fox, Mr. Gascoigne, Alderman Sawbridge, Mr. Smith, etc. etc. on a motion for the abolition of the slave trade, in the house of commons, May the 12th, 1789. To which are added, Mr. Wilberforce's twelve propositions.
30 pp. London, John Stockdale, 1789
                                        Q.

1639 Strictures on two late publications of Messrs. Graisberry & Franklin; purporting to be 'full & faithful reports of the speech of the rt. hon. Henry Grattan, in the house of commons, on Thursday, 14th February 1788'. With notes. And an appendix: containing observations on the barren-land bill. By a clergyman.
52 pp. Dublin, printed by R. M. Butler, 1789
                                        A.

1640 TENCH, Watkin. A narrative of the expedition to Botany Bay; with an account of New South Wales, its productions, inhabitants, etc. To which is subjoined, a list of the civil and military establishments at Port Jackson.
156 pp. Dublin, H. Chamberlaine and others, 1789
                                        Q.

1641 WADSTROM, C... B.... Observations on the slave-trade, and a description of some part of the coast of Guinea, during a voyage, made in 1787, and 1788, in company with doctor A. Sparrman and captain Arrehenius.
68 pp. London, James Phillips, 1789
                                        P.

1642 WILBERFORCE, William. The speech of William Wilberforce, Esq. representative for the county of York, on Wednesday the 13th May, 1789, on the question of the abolition of the slave trade. To which are added, the resolutions then moved, and a short sketch of the speeches of the other members.
76 pp. London, J. Walter, [1789]
                                        Q.

1790

1643 Address from the National Assembly of France to the people of Ireland.
32 pp. Paris and Dublin, re-printed by J. Chambers, 1790
                                        A.

1644 An address to the electors of Southwark, on the following subjects: 1. Their late petition to parliament. 2. The conduct of their representatives on that occasion. 3. The state of the British nation. 4. Their duty under the present circumstances. By an elector.
32 pp. London, J. Smith, [1790 ?]
                                        A.

1645 AINSLIE, John. Tables for computing the weight of hay, cattle, sheep, and hogs, etc. by measurement, with a comparative table of the weight used at Edinburgh to those in use at Smithfield and elsewhere.
tables, illus. 24 pp. Edinburgh, Constable [c. 1790]
                                        N.

1646 [BOOTHBY, Sir Brooke.] A Letter to the right hon. Edmund Burke, in reply to his 'Reflections on the revolution in France, etc.' By a member of the Revolution society.
60 pp. London, John Stockdale, 1790
                                        A.

——. Another issue.
60 pp. Dublin, J. Sheppard, 1790
                                        A.

1647 [BURGESS, Sir James Bland.] Letters lately published in the Diary, on the subject of the present dispute with Spain. Under the signature of Verus.
108 pp. London, G. Kearsley, 1790
                                        A., N.

1648 BURKE, Edmund. Reflections on the revolution in France, and on the proceedings in certain societies in London relative to that event. In a letter intended to have been sent to a gentleman in Paris.
360 pp. Dublin, W. Watson, 1790
A.

——. 368 pp. 6th ed. London, J. Dodsley, 1790
N.

1649 A candid statement of the case of the insolvent debtors of the kingdom of Ireland. Humbly submitted to the consideration of the lords spiritual and temporal and dedicated to the rt. hon. lord Donoughmore. [Signed Civis.]
32 pp. Dublin?, printed by Cooney, [1790]
N.

1650 CLARKE, John. To the right honorable and honorable the trustees of the linen manufacture, the report of John Clarke. Printed by order of the board.
39 pp. Dublin, printed by M. Williamson, 1790
A., N., T.

1651 The conduct of the present parliament considered, previous to its dissolution.
44 pp. Dublin, printed by P. Byrne, 1790
A.

1652 [COOKE, Edward.] A Letter to the rt. hon. Thomas Conolly, secretary to the Whig club. To which are added, the declarations and resolutions of that society.
66 pp. 2nd ed. Dublin, printed by W. Porter, 1790
A., B., N., R., T.

1653 COURTENAY, John. Philosophical reflections on the late revolution in France, and the conduct of the dissenters in England; in a letter to the Rev. Dr. Priestly.
98 pp. 3rd ed., London, T. Becket, 1790
A.

——. Another ed. 54 pp. Dublin, W. Wilson, 1790
A.

1654 The debate in the British house of commons, on the repeal of the corporation and test acts, March 2, 1790. Containing Mr. Fox's speech compleat; also the speeches of Sir Henry Houghton, Mr. Pitt, etc.
76 pp. Dublin, P. Byrne [etc.] [1790]
N., Q.

1655 DUHIGG, Bartholomew Thomas. Observations on the operation of insolvent laws, and imprisonment for debt. Dedicated to Lord Yelverton.
48 pp. n.p. [c. 1790]
A., G., N., Q.

1656 EDWARDS, Bryan. A speech delivered at a free conference between the honourable the council and assembly of Jamaica, held the 19th of November, 1789. On the subject of Mr. Wilberforce's propositions in the house of commons concerning the slave trade.
tables, appendices. 72 pp. London, Debrett, Kingston, 1790
N.

1657 Essays on agriculture and planting founded on experiments made in Ireland. By a country gentleman.
148 pp. Dublin, William Jones, 1790
A., N., Q., T.

1658 A fair exposition of the principles of the Whig club; with some cursory observations on a pamphlet, entitled, 'Thoughts on a letter to Mr. Conolly,' by an Irishman.
52 pp. Dublin, printed by P. Byrne, 1790
B., N., Q.

1659 FITZPATRICK, Sir Jeremiah. Thoughts on penitentiaries.
folding tables. 48 pp. Dublin, printed by H. Fitzpatrick, 1790
A.

1660 HENLEY, Michael. States of the pay of the several regiments of dragoon guards, dragoons, foot and royal artillery on the peace establishment of Ireland.
tables of contents, tables. 86 pp. Dublin, printed by Stewart, 1790
A.

1661 A letter to the Royal canal company.
24 pp. Dublin, 1790
Q.

1662 MACAULAY-GRAHAM, Catherine, Mrs. Observations on the reflections of the right hon. Edmund Burke, on the revolution in France, in a letter to the right hon. the earl of Stanhope.
94 pp. London, C. Dilly, 1790
A.

1663 MAY, Edward. Remarkable extracts, selected from a work printed in the year 1687, by Peter Jurien, entitled the accomplishment of the scripture prophecies, etc. In which are pointed out, in an extraordinary manner, many things analogous to the present changes in France; particularly the equalization of mankind; the fall of the pope's authority; of tyranny; of the nunneries, etc. & of titles of honour. To which are added, several acts and decrees of the national assembly of France similar thereto.
50 pp. London, Darton, 1790
A.

1664 Meetings of the trustees of the linen manufacture at their house at the Linen Hall [reports of 21 meetings.] [no tp.]
100 pp. Dublin, printed by Williamson, 1790
N.

1665 MERCHANT, C.... S.... Informations to the people of Ireland, concerning the linen trade of Spain, Portugal, and the Spanish West Indies.
12 pp. Dublin, printed by Mat. Williamson, at expense of the linen board, 1790
N., Q.

1666 MILLER, Sir John Riggs. Speeches in the house of commons upon the equalization of the weights and measures of Great Britain; with notes, observations, etc. etc. Also a general standard proposed for the weights and measures of Europe. With brief abstracts of the most material acts of the British legislature, and other ordinances and regulations, for the equalization of our weights and measures from Magna

Charta to the present time, &c. &c. Together with two letters from the bishop of Autun to the author upon the uniformity of weights and measures; that prelates proposition, respecting the same, to the national assembly, and the decree of that body, of the 8th May conformable to the bishop's proposition. —With English translations.
146 pp. London, J. Debrett, 1790

A.

1667 A new dialogue between Monsieur François & John English, on the French Revolution. London printed by order of the Association for preserving liberty & property against republicans & levellers.
14 pp. London, J. Pridden & Debrett, [1790]

A.

1668 Official papers relative to the dispute between the courts of Great Britain and Spain, on the subject of the ships captured in Nootka sound, and the negotiation that followed thereon; together with the proceedings in both houses of parliament on the King's message: to which are added the report of M. De Mirabeau, and the subsequent decrees of the national assembly of France on the Family Compact.
108 pp. London, J. Debrett [1790?]

Q.

1669 Premiums offered by the Dublin Society, for agriculture and planting. 1790.
tables. 42 pp. Dublin, printed by W. Sleater, 1790

A., Q.

1670 PRICE, Richard. A discourse on the love of our country, delivered on Nov. 4, 1789, at the meeting-house in the old jewry, to the society for commemorating the revolution in Great Britain. With an appendix, containing the report of the committee of the society; an account of the population of France: and the Declaration of rights by the national assembly of France.
appendix. 2nd ed. 70 pp. Dublin, H. Chamberlaine, P. Byrne, [etc., etc.] 1790

A., N.

See 1632

1671 RAYMENT, Robert. The corn-trade of Great Britain, for eighteen years, from 1748 to 1765 compared with the eighteen years, from 1771 to 1788. Shewing the national loss in the latter period to have been above twenty millions of money.
62 pp. London, T. Whieldon, 1790

Q.

1672 Reflections on the causes and probable consequences of the late revolution in France; with a view of the ecclesiastical and civil constitution of Scotland, and the progress of its agriculture and commerce. Translated from a series of letters, written originally in French, and dedicated to the National Assembly, by Mons. B... de.
144 pp. Dublin, W. Wilson & others, 1790

A., Q.

1673 Report of the committee of the Highland society of Scotland, to whom the subject of Shetland wool was referred, with an appendix containing some papers, drawn up by Sir John Sinclair and Dr. Anderson, in reference to the said report.
86 pp. Edinburgh, the Society, 1790

Q.

1674 Representation of the lords of the committee of council, appointed for the consideration of all matters relating to trade and foreign plantations, upon the present state of the laws for regulating the importation and exportation of corn: and submitting to his Majesty's consideration some further provisions which are wanting to amend and improve the said laws.
tables, appendices. 40 pp. London, J. Stockdale, 1790

A.

1675 A short and impartial statement of facts relative to the house of industry, respectfully addressed to the right hon. Mr. Secretary Hobart, by a member of the Royal College of Surgeons in Ireland.
14 pp. Dublin, printed by William Gilbert, 1790

Q.

See 1728

1676 Short observations on the right hon. Edmund Burke's reflections.
44 pp. London, G. Kearsley, 1790

A.

1677 SINCLAIR, Sir John, Bart. The code of legislation and political economy founded on the basis of political and statistical researches. Chapter VII. On value, and its elements, cost and price.
34 pp. London, printed by Warr, [1790?]

P.

Another issue, 34 pp. n.p., [1790?]

P.

1678 ——. The code of political economy, founded on the basis of statistical researches. [No t.p.]
tables. 82 pp. London, printed by E. H. Blagdom, [1790?]

P.

1679 [STACK, Richard.] Thoughts on a letter addressed to the right hon. Thomas Conolly, as secretary to the whig club. By a whig.
58 pp. Dublin, P. Byrne, 1790

A., N., Q., R., T.

1680 To the sportsmen and inhabitants of the county of Meath.
15 pp. Dublin, printed by P. Byrne, 1790

Q.

Signed: A Friend to the Poor. Discusses the problem of poverty.

1681 [TONE, Theobald Wolfe.] A Review of the conduct of administration, during the seventh session of parliament. Addressed to the constitutional electors and free people of Ireland, on the approaching dissolution. Signed: An Independent Irish Whig.
60 pp. Dublin, printed by P. Byrne, 1790

A., B., N., Q., T.

1682 [——.] Spanish war. An enquiry how far Ireland is bound, or right, to embark in the impending contest on the side of Great Britain? Addressed to the members of both houses of parliament. Signed Hibernicus.
table, 46 pp. Dublin, printed by P. Byrne, 1790

A., Q., T.

1683 [WOLLSTONECRAFT, Mary] A vindication of the rights of men, in a letter to the right honourable Edmund Burke; occasioned by his reflections on the revolution in France. 154 pp. London, J. Johnson, 1790

A.

1791

1684 An abstract of the evidence delivered before a select committee of the house of commons in the years 1790, and 1791: on the part of the petitioners for the abolition of the slave-trade. 172 pp. London, printed by Phillips, 1791

T.

1685 Agricola's letters to the right hon. the chancellor of the exchequer, demonstrating the pernicious effects of the cheapness of spiritous liquors upon the morals, health, industry and peaceable demeanour of the people of Ireland; and the great necessity of applying a remedy to the evil. And shewing the great advantages to be derived to the revenue, from the discouragement of distilleries, by the encouragment of the breweries of Ireland. Strongly recommended to the perusal and attention of the members of the legislature. 62 pp. Dublin, printed by W. Porter, 1791

A., N.

1686 Another sketch of the reign of George III. From the year 1780 to 1790. Being an answer to A Sketch, etc. Part the first. 86 pp. Dublin, P. Byrne and others, 1791

A., N., Q.

1687 An answer to the right hon. Edmund Burke's Reflections on the revolution in France, with some remarks on the present state of the Irish constitution. By an Irishman. 68 pp. Dublin, James Moore, 1791

A.

1688 ARBUTHNOT, John & CLARKE, John. Report on experiments made by order of the right honorable and honorable the trustees of the linen and hempen manufactures, to ascertain the comparative merits of specimens of oxygenated muriatic bleaching liquids, sent by different persons, in claim of a bounty offered by the trustees, to the person who should produce the best liquids. tables. 32 pp. Dublin, printed by M. W. Williamson and Son, [1791]

Q.

1689 Articles of agreement entered into by & between the subscribers to the Dublin tontine company, & concluded upon the 25th day of March, 1791. 44 pp. Dublin, 1791

A.

1690 BAGOT, Daniel. A treatise of the law & practice concerning the summary remedy by civil bill at the assizes in Ireland. 142 pp. Dublin, printed by James Mehain, 1791

A.

1691 Bills of exchange. A full and correct report of the great commercial cause of Minet and Fector, versus Gibson and Johnson; decided in the house of lords, on Monday the 14th of February, 1791: including the speeches of the lord chancellor, Lord Kenyon, Lord Loughborough, Lord Chief Baron, etc. 122 pp. London, J. Walter, 1791

P.

See 1723

1692 BOUSFIELD, Benjamin. Observations on the right hon. Edmund Burke's pamphlet, on the subject of the French Revolution. 46 pp. Dublin, P. Byrne, 1791

N., Q.

1693 BURKE, Edmund. An abridgement of the letter of the right honourable Edmund Burke to a gentleman in Paris, on the revolution in France. 32 pp. London, J. Debrett, 1791

A.

1694 CHRISTIE, Thomas. Letters on the revolution of France, & on the new constitution established by the national assembly. Occasioned by the publications of the right hon. Edmund Burke, M.P. & Alexander de Calonne, late minister of state. To which is added, an appendix containing original papers & authentic documents relative to the affairs of France. Addressed to Sir John Sinclair, Bart. M.P.—Vol. II. part 1, containing the French constitution. 64 pp. Dublin, printed by William Porter for P. Wogan & others, 1791

A., N., Q.

1695 CLARKE, John. A concise view of the house of industry, with respect principally, to some interesting particulars in the internal state and regulation of it. By a member of the Corporation. 32 pp. Dublin, printed by Porter, 1791

A.

1696 [COXE, Tench.] Brief examination of Lord Sheffield's observations on the commerce of the United States. tables. 48 pp. Philadelphia, printed by Carey and Stewart, 1791

N.

1697 DE CALONNE, Charles Alexander. Considerations on the present and future state of France. By M. de Calonne, minister of state. Translated from the French. 538 pp. London, J. Evans, 1791

A.

1698 DEPONT. Answer to the reflections of the right hon. Edmund Burke. By M. Depont. With the original notes. 38 pp. Dublin, P. Byrne, 1791

A., N.

1699 Extracts from the several laws which have been at any time enacted in this kingdom, for the protection of trees and encouragement of planting. With a few cursory observations. By a member of the committee of agriculture of the Dublin society. 48 pp. Dublin, printed by W. Sleater, 1791

A., N., Q.

1700 Free remarks on the present system of our corn laws, and on the necessity of altering it.
22 pp. Dublin, R. White, 1791
N.

1701 A free trade between Ireland and the East Indies, submitted to the consideration of the people of this country, by a free merchant of the East Indies, a native of this kingdom. March 1, 1791.
22 pp. Dublin, printed by Robert Crosthwaite, 1791
A.

1702 [GEALE, Frederick?] Observations on the present state of the corn laws of Ireland, so far as they partially relate to the metropolis.
32 pp. Dublin, R. Marchbank, 1791
A., Q., T.

1703 [GIBSON, J.?] Hints for providing residencies for the parochial clergy. Humbly submitted to the consideration of the arch-bishops and bishops of Ireland. By one of the body.
50 pp. Drogheda, printed by Evans, 1791
A.

1704 GOLBORNE, James. Report in pursuance of several resolutions passed at a meeting of the committee of landowners, and others, interested in the improvement of the outfall of the River Ouse, at the Crown and Anchor, in the Strand, on Thursday, the 16th of June, 1791; And read before the same committee, at the Rose Tavern in Cambridge, on Wednesday the 31st of August, in the same year; and which is now printed by order of the said Committee.
tables. 44 pp. Lynn, printed by Whitlingham, 1791
N.

1705 HAMILTON, Alexander. Report of the secretary of the treasury of the United States on the subject of manufactures. Presented to the house of representatives, December 5, 1791.
88 pp. Dublin, reprinted by P. Byrne, 1791
A.

1706 KIRWAN, Richard; Perceval, Robert; Dickson, Stephen; Deane, William. An address to the royal society of Ireland, on the answer of their committee of science to Mr. Clarke's analytic enquiry into the nature and component principles of an alkaline salt, wherein a comparative state is drawn of the philosophical principles of modern chemysts contrasted with those by which he was governed in the enquiry. To this address Mr. Clarke has annexed his analytic enquiry and reply to the attempt which the committee of science made to answer that performance.
pls., tables. 158 pp. Dublin, printed by P. Byrne, 1791
Q.

1707 KYD, Stewart. Treatise on the law of bills of exchange and promissory notes.
index. 172 pp. Dublin, Burnett, Lynch [etc.,] 1791
N.

1708 LANGRISHE, Sir Hercules. Sir Hercules Langrishe's speech, in the Irish house of commons, April 7th, 1791, on the corn laws; containing a state of the benefits this country has derived from the present system and the evils that must result from any material alteration in it.
tables. 74 pp. Dublin, printed by P. Byrne, 1791
A., N., Q.

1709 LEACH, Edmund. A treatise of universal inland navigations, and the use of all sorts of mines. A work entirely new. Recommended to the inhabitants of Great Britain & Ireland.
folding tables. 40 pp. London, Alex. Hamilton, 1791
A., T.

1710 Letter to Luke White Esq. on the provision trade and new established company by an unbiassed Irishman.
34 pp. n.p., [1791?]
A., N., P.

1711 LOUGHBOROUGH, Alexander Wedderburn, baron. Lord Loughborough's charge to the grand jury of Wilts, at the late assizes at Salisbury, August 6, 1791.
2 pp., n.p., 1791
A.
Condemning riots against machinery.

1712 MACKENZIE, Henry. The letters of Brutus to certain celebrated political characters.
74 pp. Dublin, P. Byrne [etc.], 1791
A., N., Q.

1713 MACKINTOSH, James. Vindiciae Gallicae. Defense of the French Revolution and its English admirers against the accusations of the right hon. Edmund Burke; including some strictures on the late production of Mons. de Calonne.
176 pp. Dublin, R. Gross and others, 1791
A., N., Q.

——. 356 pp. 2nd ed., London, G. G. J. & J. Robinson, 1791
Q.

1714 Minutes of the Barrow navigation company.
34 pp. Dublin, 1791
A.

1715 MITFORD, William. Considerations on the opinion stated by the committee of council, in a representation to the King, upon the corn laws, that Great Britain is unable to produce corn sufficient for its own consumptions and on the Corn-Bill now depending in Parliament.
78 pp. London, John Stockdale, 1791
Q.

1716 PAINE, Thomas. Common sense; addressed to the inhabitants of America on the following interesting subjects. I. Of the origin and design of government in general, with concise remarks on the English constitution. II. Of monarchy and hereditary succession. III. Thoughts on the present state of American affairs. IV. Of the present ability of America, with some miscellaneous reflections. To which is added an appendix: together with an address to the people called Quakers.
100 pp. Philadelphia, W. & T. Bradford, 1791
A., N.
Reprint of 1776 pamphlet. See 970.

1717 ——. A letter addressed to the Abbé Raynal, on the affairs of North-America: in which the mistakes in the Abbé's account of the revolution of America are corrected and cleared up.
96 pp. London, J. S. Jordan, 1791
A., N.
See also 1211, 1270 and 1778

1718 ——. Rights of man: being an answer to Mr. Burke's attack on the French revolution.
72 pp. Dublin, Issued by the Whigs of the capital, 1791
A., B., N.

——. 72 pp. 4th ed. Dublin, Issued by the Whigs of the capital, 1791
N.

——. 104 pp. 13th ed. Dublin, P. Byrne, 1791
A.

——. Another ed. 72 pp. Dublin, G. Burnet, 1791
A.

——. Another ed. 162 pp. Dublin, G. Burnet, 1791
A.

——. Another ed. 162 pp. Dublin, P. Byrne, 1791
A.

1719 Premiums offered by the Dublin society, for agriculture and planting, 1791.
tables. 44 pp. Dublin, printed by W. Sleater, 1791
Q.

1720 PRIESTLEY, Joseph. A discourse on occasion of the death of Dr. Price; delivered at Hackney, on Sunday, May 1, 1791.
48 pp. London, J. Johnson, [1791]
A.
[Contains a bibliography of Price's publications.]

1721 PRUJEAN, John. A treatise upon the laws of England now in force for the recovery of debt, pointing out the many abuses of them, together with a plan for administering more speedy & equitable justice to creditors & to debtors.
130 pp. Dublin, printed by James Mehain, 1791
A., N.

1722 RAWDON, Francis Rawdon-Hastings, baron. Substance of observations on the state of the public finances of Great Britain, by lord Rawdon, in a speech on the third reading of the bank loan bill in the house of lords, on Thursday, June 9, 1791.
48 pp. Dublin, Arthur Grueber, [1791]
A.

1723 Report of the great commercial cause of Minet and Fector versus Gibson and Johnson; decided in the house of lords on Monday the 14th of February, 1791, including the speeches of the Lord Chancellor, Lord Kenyon, Lord Loughborough, Lord Chief Baron etc.
122 pp. Dublin, printed by Moore, 1791
N.
See 1691.

1724 ROUS, George. Thoughts on government: occasioned by Mr. Burke's reflections etc. in a letter to a friend. To which is added a postscript, in reply to a vindication of Mr. Burke's reflections.
84 pp. 4th ed. London, J. Debrett, 1791
Q.

1725 SAINT-JUST, Louis Leon. Esprit de la revolution et de la constitution de France.
188 pp. Paris, Beuvin, 1791
N., Q.

1726 SHEFFIELD, John Baker-Holroyd, 1st baron. Observations on the corn bill, now depending in Parliament.
86 pp. London, J. Debrett, 1791
Q.

——. 86 pp. 2nd ed. London, J. Debrett, 1791
T.

1727 ——. Observations on the project for abolishing the slave trade, and on the reasonableness of attempting some practicable mode of relieving the negroes. The second edition, with additions.
74 pp. London, J. Debrett, 1791
T.

1728 A short and impartial statement of facts, relative to the house of industry. Respectfully addressed to Mr. Secretary Hobart, by a member of the Royal College of Surgeons in Ireland.
14 pp. Dublin, printed by Gilbert, 1791
A., Q.
See 1675

1729 A short review of Mr. Pitt's administration.
60 pp. London, J. Ridgway, 1791
A.

1730 SINCLAIR, Sir John, bart. Address to the landed interest, on the Corn-Bill now depending in Parliament.
40 pp. London, T. Cadell, 1791
Q.

1731 ——. Specimen of the statistical account of Scotland. Drawn up from the communications of the ministers of the different parishes.
56 pp. Edinburgh, 1791
N., Q.

1732 STEPHENSON, Robert. A letter to the right honourable and honourable the trustees of the linen manufacture, and also, to the trustees for distributing bounties, etc., etc.
20 pp. Dublin, printed by John Rea, 1791
N., Q.

1733 Strictures on a pamphlet, entitled, a short and impartial statement of facts relative to the house of industry. In a letter to the right hon. Henry Grattan, one of the representatives in parliament for the city of Dublin.
16 pp. Dublin, printed by P. Byrne, 1791
A.

1734 Strictures on the letter of the right hon. Edmund Burke, on the Revolution in France, and remarks on certain occurrences that took place in the last session of that parliament relative to that event.
62 pp. London, J. Johnson, 1791
Q.

1735 Substance of the report of the court of directors of the Sierra Leone company to the general court held at London on Wednesday the 19th of October, 1791.
68 pp. London, printed by James Phillips, 1791
P.

1736 Sundry papers and reports, relative first, to the defense of the estate of Cherry Cobb Sands against the Humber: secondly, the draining of Keyingham Marshes: and, thirdly, the eventual improvement and accretion of the fore-shore, opposite Foul Holme Sands.
fold. map. 48 pp. London, printed by C. Clarke, 1791
Q.

1737 [Tone, Theobald Wolfe.] An argument on behalf of the catholics of Ireland.
32 pp. [Belfast], re-printed by order of society of United Irishmen of Belfast, 1791
B., T.

1738 Towers, Joseph. Thoughts on the commencement of a new parliament. With an appendix, containing remarks on the letter of the right hon. Edmund Burke, on the revolution in France.
118 pp. Dublin, P. Wogan, 1791
A., N.

1739 [Truss, Charles.] Considerations on the present state of the navigation of river Thames from Maidenhead to Isleworth; and also on the utility and advantage of a navigable canal from Boulter's Lock, near Maidenhead to Isleworth; proposed by the Corporation of the City of London, and the commissioners of the upper district in the year 1770; agreeable to the survey of Messieurs Brindley and Whitworth.
30 pp. n.p., 1791
N.

1740 [Wansey, Henry.] Wool encouraged without exportation; or practical observations on wool and the woollen manufacture. In two parts. Part I. containing strictures on appendix no IV to a report made by a committee of the highland society, on the subject of Shetland wool. Part II. Containing a brief history of wool, and the nature of the woollen manufacture as connected with it. By a Wiltshire Clothier, F.A.S.
88 pp. London, T. Cadell, 1791
A.

1792

1741 Alley, Jerom. Observations on the government and constitution of Great Britain, including a vindication of both from the aspersions of some late writers, particularly Dr. Price, Dr. Priestley and Mr. Paine; in a letter to the right hon. Lord Sheffield.
94 pp. Dublin, printed by W. Sleater, 1792
A., N.

1742 Anderson, George. A general view of the variations which have been made in the affairs of the East-India company, since the conclusion of the war, in India, in 1784.
fold. tables. 110 pp. n.p., 1792
Q.

1743 An appeal to the candour and justice of the people of England, on behalf of the West India merchants and planters, founded on plain facts and incontrovertible arguments.
134 pp. London, J. Debrett, 1792
P.

1744 Appendix. Result of a meeting held Dec. 15, 1792, respecting the present exorbitant price of sugar.
6 pp. London, printed by G. Woodfall, [1792]
Q.

1745 Archard, T. Suppression of the French nobility vindicated, in an essay on their origin, & qualities, moral & intellectual. By the Rev. T. A., a Paris. To which is added, A comparative view of Dr. Smith's system of the wealth of nations, with regard to France & England.
84 pp. London, J. Debrett, 1792
A.

1746 Bentley, Thomas. A short view of some of the evils & grievances which at this time oppress the British empire, through the corruption of its government: & which are utterly contrary to the spirit & precepts of reason & Christianity.
8 pp. n.p., 1792
A.

1747 Birkett, M. A poem on the African slave trade. Addressed to her own sex by M. Birkett. Part I & II.
44 pp. Dublin, J. Jones, 1792
Q.

1748 Black, William. Reasons for preventing the French, under the mask of liberty, from trampling upon Europe.
54 pp. London, J. Debrett, 1792
A.

1749 Boothby, Sir Brooke. Observations on the Appeal from the new to the old whigs, and on Mr. Paine's rights of man. In two parts.
292 pp. Dublin, W. Jones, 1792
A.

1750 Boswell, George. A treatise on watering meadows: wherein are shewn some of the many advantages arising from that mode of practice, particularly on coarse, boggy, or barren lands; & the method of performing the work. Also remarks on a late pamphlet upon that subject. With six copperplates, 3rd ed.
fold. diags. 128 pp. Dublin, printed by J. Moore, 1792
A.

1751 Chapman, William. Report on the improvement of the harbour of Arklow, and the practicability of a navigation from thence by the vales of the various branches of the Ovoca. Copy of Petition to Parliament, on behalf of the subscribers for improving the harbour of Arklow, and making from thence an interior navigation to the Meeting's-bridge at the junction of the rivers Avonmore & Avonbeg.
map, tables. 22 pp. Dublin, printed by Chambers, 1792
A., N., Q.

1752 ——. Report on the practicability and expense of making a navigable canal from Thomas-town, Co. Kilkenny. Addressed to the rt. hon. the earl of Ormonde.
tables. 24 pp. Kilkenny, printed by Finn, 1792
N.

1753 [COBBETT, William?] The soldier's friend; or, considerations on the late pretended augmentation of the subsistence of the private soldiers.
22 pp. London, J. Ridgway, 1792

P.

1754 [COOMBE, William.] A word in season to the traders and manufacturers of Great Britain.
24 pp. Glasgow, 1792

A.

1755 A country gentleman's reasons for voting against Mr. Wilberforce's motion for a bill to prohibit the importation of African negroes into the colonies.
tables. 80 pp. London, Debrett, 1792

N.

1756 Décret de l'Assemblée Nationale, du 16 Août 1792, l'an quatrième de la liberté.
16 pp. Paris, de l'imprimerie nationale, [1792]

A.

1757 A Dissertation on the querulousness of statesmen.
118 pp. London, T. Longman, 1792

N., Q.

1758 DOBBS, Francis. A history of Irish affairs from the 12th of October, 1779, to the 15th September, 1782, the day of lord Temple's arrival.
172 pp. Dublin, M. Mills, 1792

R.

1759 Farther reasons of a country gentleman for opposing Mr. Wilberforce's motion on the 15th day of May last, for prohibiting British subjects trading to Africa to procure negroes for the British Colonies.
26 pp. London, Debrett, 1792

T.

1760 [Fox, William.] An address to the people of Great Britain, (respectfully offered to the people of Ireland) on the utility of refraining from the use of West India sugar and rum. The sixth edition.
12 pp. Dublin, W. Sleater, 1792

A., N., U.
['Also ascribed to William Bell Crafton'—Kress, B.2296.]

1761 Free thoughts on the measures of opposition, civil & religious, from the commencement of the last parliament to the present period; with a modest plea for the rights of ascendency of episcopal protestantism. Humbly addressed to his excellency the lord lieuttenant [sic], lords and commons of Ireland. By Candidus Redintegratus.
132 pp. Dublin, printed by James Moore, 1792

A., N.

1762 [GILBERT, Sir Jeffrey.] A treatise on rents. By a late lord chief baron of his majesty's court of exchequer.
124 pp. Dublin, W. Jones, 1792

A.
[First published in 1758.]

1763 GRATTAN, Henry. Mr. Grattan's speech in the house of commons of Ireland, on Thursday the 19th January, 1792, on the address to the King: to which is added, the Speech delivered by the Lord Lieutenant to both Houses of Parliament and the Address.
36 pp. Dublin, printed by James Moore, 1792

A., N., Q., T.

1764 HAMILTON, William. Letters on the principles of the French democracy, and their application and influence on the constitution and happiness of Britain and Ireland. Letter I.
20 pp. Dublin, J. Archer & W. Sleater, 1792

Q.

1765 ——. Letters on the principles of the French democracy, and their application and influence on the constitution and happiness of Britain and Ireland. Letter 2.
20 pp. Dublin, J. Archer and W. Sleater, 1792

N., Q.

1766 KEITH, George Skene. Tracts on the corn laws of Great Britain, containing, I. an inquiry into the principles by which all corn laws ought to be regulated. II. Application of these principles to the corn laws of Great Britain, now collected into one act of parliament. III. Inquiry into the expediency of repealing all our corn laws, & laying the corn trade entirely open. IV. Outlines of a new corn bill, or of a bill to amend the late corn act, which commenced Nov. 15, 1791.
fold. tabs. 48 pp. London, J. Murray, 1792

A.

1767 LAURENT, Charles. A scheme for establishing general charitable loans throughout Ireland, humbly submitted to the consideration of the right honourable and honourable the lords and gentlemen governors of the incorporated charitable musical society in Dublin, by their registrar, Charles Laurent and now published by their order.
14 pp. Dublin, W. Watson, 1792

A., N., Q.

1768 Liberty & property preserved against republicans & levellers. A collection of tracts. Number II. containing one penny worth of answer from John Bull to his brother Thomas —John Bull's second answer to his brother Thomas.—A letter from John Bull to his countrymen.—The mayor of Paris's speech on the murders of the 2nd & 3rd September.
London, J. Sewell & others, [1792]

Q.

1769 Liberty & property preserved against republicans & levellers. A collection of tracts. Number V. containing an antidote against French politics—A picture of true & false liberty.
16 pp. London, J. Sewell [&c] [1792]

Q.

1770 MCKENNA, Theobald. Address to the Roman catholics of Ireland relating to the late proceedings, & on the means and practicability of a tranquil emancipation.
56 pp. Dublin, J. Rice, 1792

A., N., Q., T.

1771 ——. A review of the catholic question, in which the constitutional interests of Ireland, with respect to that part of the nation, are investigated. To which is annexed, the declaration of the Catholic society of Dublin, and a vindication thereof.
100 pp. Dublin, printed by J. Moore, 1792

A., N., Q.

1772 MIRABEAU, Honoré Gabriel Riquetti, Comte de. Speeches of M. de Mirabeau the elder, Pronounced in the national assembly of France. To which is prefixed, a sketch of his life and character. Translated from the French edition of M. Mejan. By James White, Esq.
132 pp. Dublin, P. Byrne, [etc.], 1792

A., Q.

1773 A mirror for the times; or a serious address to the people of Ireland. On the situation of their own country, comparatively considered with that of Europe in general, and particularly France.
32 pp. Dublin, William McKenzie, 1792

Q., T.

1774 MOLLOY, Tobias. An appeal from man in a state of civil society to man in a state of nature; or, an inquiry into the origin & organization of those political incorporations most productive of human happiness. Being an appeal to reason: containing parallels between the acceptation of the French Magna Charta by Lewis XVI and the acceptation of the English one by John, and his son Henry III. Also between the French constituting national assembly and the English convention; in which the fallacy of certain positions respecting the rights of man and the rights of the people, as promulgated by an Ancient Whig, is detected and exposed; and which also includes strictures on Mr. Pain's Rights of man; and points out the true origin of hereditary monarchy.
262 pp. Dublin, printed by P. Byrne, 1792

A.

1775 MORGAN, William. A review of Dr. Price's writings, on the subject of the finances of this kingdom: to which are added the three plans communicated by him to Mr. Pitt in the year 1786, for redeeming the national debt: and also an enquiry into the real state of the public income and expenditure, from the establishment of the consolidated fund to the year 1791.
appendix. tables. 80 pp. London, T. Cadell, 1792

P.

1776 MULLALLA, James. A compilation on the slave trade, respectfully addressed to the people of Ireland.
30 pp., Dublin, printed by William McKenzie, 1792

A., N.

1777 The Orphan-house: being a brief history of that institution, & of the proceedings of the founders & directors of that asylum or place of refuge for destitute female children, situate at No. 42 Prussia-street.
32 pp. Dublin, George Bonham, 1792

A.

1778 PAINE, Thomas. A letter addressed to the Abbé Raynal, on the affairs of North-America. In which the mistakes in the Abbé's account of the revolution of America are corrected & cleared up.
46 pp. London, J. Ridgway, 1792

A.

See also 1211, 1270 and 1717.

1779 ——. A letter to Mr. Secretary Dundas, in answer to his observations in the house of commons, May 25th, on the Rights of man & the late proclamation.
16 pp. Dublin, printed by James Moore, 1792

A.

1780 ——. Letters addressed to the addressers, on the late proclamation.
54 pp. Dublin, G. Burnet, 1792

A., N.

1781 ——. Miscellaneous articles, by Thomas Paine consisting of a letter to the marquess of Lansdowne. A letter to the authors of the Republican. A letter to the Abbé Syeyes. Thoughts on the peace, and on the probable advantages thereof. First letter to Mr. Secretary Dundas. Letter to lord Onslow. Second letter to Mr. Dundas. And a letter to the people of France.
frontisp. 36 pp. London, J. Ridgway, 1792

A.

1782 PITT, William. The speech of the right hon. William Pitt, chancellor of the exchequer, on Friday, the 17th day of February 1792, on proposing the application of an additional sum for the reduction of the public debt, & the repeal of certain duties on malt, on female servants, on carts & waggons, on houses, & on candles.
48 pp. London, G. G. J. & J. Robinson & J. Stockdale, 1792

A., T.

1783 Postscript to the report of the court of directors of the Sierra Leone Company to the general court, held at London on Wednesday the 19th of October, 1791.
London, printed by James Phillips, 1792

P.

1784 Premiums offered by the Dublin society, for agriculture and planting. 1792.
tables, 42 pp. Dublin, printed by W. Sleater, 1792

Q.

1785 [ROSE, George.] A brief examination into the increase of the revenue, commerce and navigation of Great Britain, January, 1792.
tables. 20 pp. London, J. Stockdale, 1792

A., P.

1786 [——.] A brief examination into the increase of the revenue, commerce, and navigation, of Great Britain, since the conclusion of the peace in 1783.
fold. tables. 56 pp. Dublin, P. Wogan, [etc. etc.], 1792

A., K., N., T., U.

See 1827

1787 Short strictures upon the constitution, manufactures, & commerce of Ireland. By an inhabitant of Belfast.
12 pp. Belfast, printed by John Tisdall, 1792

A., P.

1788 Sketch of the debates in the house of commons of Ireland, on Wednesday, February 9th, 1792, including the discussion, on the reception of the Belfast protestant petition, on behalf of the Roman catholics of Ireland; and the debate on Mr. Ponsonby's motion for leave to introduce a bill for the repeal of all existing restrictions on the right of this country to trade beyond the cape of Good Hope.
40 pp. Dublin, P. Byrne & J. Moore, 1792

A.

1789 SWEETMAN, Edward. The speech of Edward Sweetman, captain of a late independent company, at a meeting of

the freeholders of the county Wexford, convened by the sheriff, on September 22, 1792, to take into consideration 'Mr. Edward Byrne's letter recommending a plan of delegation to the catholics of Ireland, in order to prepare an humble petition to the legislature'.
36 pp. Dublin, printed by P. Byrne, 1792

M.

1790 To every moderate man in Ireland; the following ideas on the relative situation of protestants & catholics are submitted.
58 pp. Dublin, [R.] White, 1792

A.

1791 TONE, Theobald Wolfe. An argument on behalf of the catholics of Ireland.
5th ed. 16 pp. Dublin, re-printed by order of the United Irishmen, 1792

A., B., G.

1792 The transactions of the Parliament of Ireland, 1792.
38 pp. Dublin, Richard White, 1792

U.

1793 Trials at large. On prosecutions for the crown at the king's commissions of Oyer & Terminer, & quarter sessions of the peace, held for the city and county of the city of Dublin. No. I. containing the proceedings at the commission commencing Tuesday, July 9th, 1792, in the mayoralty of the right honourable Henry Gore Sankey, before the honourable judge Downes, fourth justice of his majesty's court of King's Bench.
242 pp. Dublin, V. Dowling, 1792

A., N.

1794 Two letters to the whigs of the capital. Letter 1.
36 pp. Dublin, the author, 1792

A.

1795 The utility of an early dispatch, of the inland mails, proved by a statement of facts, submitted to the consideration of the people of Ireland.
16 pp. Dublin, James Moore, 1792

N., Q.

1796 WRIGHT, T. The advantages and method of watering meadows by art with two descriptive plates, and with occasional extracts and remarks upon Wimpey, Forbes, Boswell, and other writers on this subject.
diags. 48 pp. Dublin, printed by W. Sleater, 1792

A., N., Q.

1793

1797 Abridgement of the new Act for the Government and trade of India, and for the appropriation of the revenues and profits of trade, between the public and the East India Company.
24 pp. n.p., 1793

A.

1798 An abstract of the laws now in force, relating to dealers in coffee. Including the several clauses upon that subject, contained in the act of 32 G. 3.c. 17. As also an appendix, containing several precedents of informations, etc.
36 pp. Dublin, printed by George Grierson, 1793

A.

1799 ADAMS, John. An answer to Paine's rights of man.
46 pp. Dublin, P. Byrne, [etc.], 1793

A., N.

1800 BENTHAM, Jeremy. A protest against law taxes, shewing the peculiar mischievousness of all such impositions as add to the expense of an appeal to justice.
48 pp. Dublin, printed by P. Byrne, 1793

A., N., Q.

1801 [BOWLES, John.] Dialogues on the rights of Britons, between a farmer, a sailor, & a manufacturer.
Dialogue the second. 22 pp. 2nd ed. London, T. Longman [etc.], 1793

A.

1802 [——.] Three dialogues on the rights of Britons, between a farmer, a sailor, & a manufacturer.
24 pp. 3rd ed. London, G. Nicol, [etc.], 1793

A.

1803 Case of the proprietors of India annuities, on the notice given by the right honourable the speaker of the house of commons, March 25, 1791; and the renewal of the charter of the East India company; now under discussion; submitted to the consideration of his majesty's ministers, and both houses of parliament.
36 pp. London, John Stockdale, 1793

A.

1804 CHAPMAN, William. Report of William Chapman, engineer, on the means of making Woodford river navigable, from Lough-Erne to Woodford-Lough, as an off-branch from the Lough–Erne & Ballyshannon navigation. (With observations on the practicability of carrying it forward to the Shannon.) Published by order of the subscribers to this branch.
16 pp. Limerick, printed by A. Watson, 1793

A.

1805 Comments on the proposed war with France, on the state of parties, and on the new act respecting aliens. With a postscript: containing remarks on lord Granville's Answer of Dec. 31, 1792, to the note of M. Chauvelin. By a lover of peace.
116 pp. London, C. Dilly, [etc.], 1793

A., K.

1806 [CURRIE, James.] A letter, commercial & political, addressed to the right hon. William Pitt, in which the real interests of Britain in the present crisis are considered, & some observations are offered on the general state of Europe. By Jasper Wilson.
70 pp. Dublin, P. Byrne, 1793

A., K., N., T., U.

1807 Dialogue between a linen merchant and a weaver.
16 pp. Dublin, 1793

A., K., Q.

1808 DORNFORD, Josiah. The motives and consequences of the present war impartially considered.
54 pp. London & Dublin, re-printed by Thomas Stewart, 1793
A.

1809 EVANS, Richard. To the right honorable [sic] & honorable [sic] the Royal canal company. The address of Richard Evans, engineer.
28 pp. Dublin, 1793
A.

1810 FRANCIS, Phillip. Letter from Mr. Francis to lord North, late earl of Guilford. With an appendix.
112pp. London, J. Debrett, [1793]
A.

[Written 1777.]

1811 FREND, William. Peace and union recommended to the associated bodies of republicans and anti-republicans.
68 pp. 2nd ed. London, G. G. J. & J. Robinson, 1793
A.

——. Another issue. 52 pp. St. Ives, printed by P. C. Croft, 1793
A.

1812 HARDIE, David. Taxation of coals, considered in an address to the inhabitants of the cities of London & Westminster, & all places supplied with coals from the port of London.
41 pp. n. p., [1793]
A.

1813 An humble address to the most high, most mighty, & most puissant, the sovereign people.
40 pp. [London?], printed by I. Colles, 1793
A., K., N.

1814 KING, Anthony. Thoughts on the expediency of adopting a system of national education, more immediately suited to the policy of this country: with certain brief remarks on that class of free schools, commonly distinguished by the name of diocesan schools.
tables in appendix. 156 pp. Dublin, printed by George Bonham, 1793
R.

1815 Letters of an impartial observer, on the affairs of Ireland. Addressed to a gentleman in Dublin.
28 pp. Dublin, T. Clarke, 1793
A., N., Q., T.

1816 McKENNA, Theobald. Address to the Roman catholics of Ireland, relative to the late proceedings, and on the means and practicability of a tranquil emancipation.
54 pp. 2nd ed. Dublin, J. Rice, 1793
A., T.

1817 MELVILLE, Henry Dundas, 1st viscount. Heads of the speech of the rt. hon. H. Dundas, in the house of commons, Febr. 25, 1793, on stating the affairs of the East India Company.
tables. appendices. 74 pp. London, Debrett, 1793
N.

1818 ——. Letter to the Chairman (of the East India Company) dated the 15th April, 1793.
16 pp. n.p., 1793
A.

1819 [MORE, Hannah.] Village politics. Addressed to all the mechanics, journeymen, & day labourers, in Great Britain. By Will Chip, a country carpenter.
24 pp. London, F. and C. Rivington, 1793
A.

1820 NICHOLS, Thomas. Methods proposed for decreasing the consumption of timber in the navy by means of prolonging the duration of our ships of war; with observations on fastening ships with iron knees: to which are added some general remarks on the present timbered state of the kingdom, in a letter addressed to the right hon. John, earl of Chatham, first Lord Commissioner of the Admiralty, together with a letter addressed to the honourable commissioners of the navy, on the way of keeping, seasoning, and converting timber, before it is used in ship-building. With observations on the sap of oak trees.
80 pp. Southampton, T. Baker [etc.], 1793
Q.

1821 PAINE, Thomas. The case of the officers of excise; with remarks on the qualifications of officers; & on the numerous evils arising to the revenue, from the insufficiency of the present salary. Humbly addressed to the hon. & right hon. the members of both houses of parliament.
42 pp. London, J. S. Jordan, 1793
A.

1822 ——. Prospects on the war & paper currency.
74 pp. London, J. Ridgway, 1793
A., P.

1823 Plan for establishing a board of agriculture and internal improvement; as intended to be proposed in parliament by Sir John Sinclair. May, 1793.
table 8 pp. n.p., 1793
A.

1824 The poor man's answer to the rich associators.
8 pp. n.p., 1793
A.

1825 Report of the committee, appointed by the Royal canal company, 12 June, 1793. To which are annexed, the proceedings of said committee, the reports of Mr. Brownrigg, & Mr. Evans, & a letter from Sir Thomas Hyde Page, thereon.
60 pp. n.p., 1793
A.

1826 [ROSCOE, William.] Thoughts on the causes of the present failures.
30 pp. 2nd ed. London, J. Johnson, 1793
K.

1827 [ROSE, George.] A Brief examination into the increase of the revenue, commerce, and navigation, of Great Britain, since the conclusion of the peace in 1783.
fold. tables. 64 pp. 4th ed. London, John Stockdale, 1793
A., Q., T.

See 1786

1828 [ROSSE, Lawrence Parsons, 4th earl of.] Thoughts on liberty & equality. By a member of parliament.
60 pp. Dublin, James Moore, 1793
A.

——. Another ed. 66 pp. Dublin, Moore, 1793
A.

1829 [RUSSELL, Francis.] A short history of the East India company: exhibiting a state of their affairs, abroad and at home, political and commercial; the nature and magnitude of their commerce, and its relative connection with the government & revenues of India; also remarks on the danger and impolicy of innovation, and the practical means of ensuring all the good effects of a free trade to the manufacturers of Great Britain and Ireland, by means of regulations without disturbing the established system.
table of contents. tables. 88 pp. n.p., 1793
A.

1830 Speculations on the state of Ireland: shewing the fatal causes of her misery, the evil influence under which she languishes, and the power thereof to reduce her to the last extreme of human wretchedness and woe.
32 pp. Dublin, J. Mehain, 1793
N.

1831 SPENCE, Thomas. The rights of man, as exhibited in a lecture, read at the Philosophical society in Newcastle, to which is now first added, an interesting conversation, between a gentleman and the author, on the subject of his scheme. With the queries sent by the Rev. Mr. J. Murray, to the society in defense of the same. And a song of triumph for the people, on the recovery of their long lost rights.
42 pp. 4th ed. London, the author, 1793
A.

1832 [TIGHE, Robert Stearne, ed.] Letters addressed to Mrs. Peter La Touche by Melantius. Containing a state of the orphan-houses of England, Ireland, Zealand and Holland.
38 pp. Dublin, Bernard Dornin, 1793
A., Q.

1833 VANSITTART, Nicholas, baron Bexley. Reflections on the propriety of an immediate conclusion of peace.
fold. tabs. 132 pp. London, John Stockdale, 1793
A. N.

1834 [VAUGHAN, William?] On wet docks, quays, and warehouses, for the port of London; with hints respecting trade. Part I.
tables. appendices. 32 pp. London, 1793
T.

1835 [WALKER, John.] Thoughts on the misery of a numerous class of females: particularly addressed to those of their own sex, whom God has entrusted with affluence; for which they must shortly give account.
12 pp. Dublin, B. Dugdale, 1793
A.

1836 YOUNG, Arthur. The example of France, a warning to Britain.
96 pp. Dublin, P. Byrne, J. Moore and W. Jones, 1793
N., Q., T.

1794

1837 An account of the institution & regulations of the Sunday & daily school, North-Strand. Addressed more particularly to the inhabitants of the parishes of St. Mary's, St. Thomas & St. George. With reflections on the importance of affording gratuitous education to the children of the poor.
26 pp. Dublin, printed by W. Sleater, 1794
N., Q.

1838 An address to the friends of liberty. Shewing the peculiar situation of France which rendered a revolution necessary & unavoidable. The safety of England in that respect, and the most likely means of putting Ireland on the same secure footing. By the curate of Mullavilly.
80 pp. Newry, printed by R. Moffet, 1794
A.

1839 BAGOT, Daniel. The law & practice concerning the summary remedy by civil bill, before the judges of assize in Ireland, with an appendix and a general alphabetical index.
140 pp. 2nd ed. Dublin, printed by James Mehain & Henry Watts, 1794
A. N.

1840 BOWLES, John. Objections to the continuance of the war examined & refuted.
76 pp. 2nd ed. London, J. Debrett & T. N. Longman, 1794
A.

1841 CAMPBELL, Thomas. A discourse delivered in the new church of St. Luke's Gallown, on Sunday the 6th of October 1793; when a collection was made, in order to extend the benefits of a charitable loan of fifty guineas, already lent out to industrious house-keepers of the parish of Gallown.
frontisp. 72 pp. Dublin, Mercier & Co., 1794
A., Q.

1842 COOPER, Thomas. Some information respecting America, collected by Thomas Cooper, late of Manchester.
244 pp. Dublin, P. Wogan, 1794
A.

1843 FOX, William. On the renewal of the East India charter.
18 pp. [not paginated.] London, Gurney, 1794
N.

1844 HALES, William. Observations on the present state of the parochial clergy of the church of Ireland.
42 pp. Dublin, printed by George Grierson, 1794
A., M., N., R.

1845 ——. Observations on tithes, shewing the inconveniences of all the schemes that have been proposed for altering that antient manner of providing for the clergy of the established church of Ireland. To which is annexed, a second edition of the moderate performer, or a proposal for abolishing some of the most obvious and gross abuses that have crept into the church of England, and are the occasion of frequent complaints against it. By a friend to the church of England.
76 pp. London, B. and J. White, 1794
T.

1846 [HAYES, Samuel.] Practical treatise on planting & the management of woods & coppices. By S. H. Esq. M.R.I.A. & member of the committee of agriculture of the Dublin Society, etc. etc.
pls. 190 pp. Dublin, 1794

A., D., N.

1847 LAUDERDALE, James Maitland, 8th earl of. Letters to the peers of Scotland.
322 pp. London, G. G. & J. Robinson, 1794

A.

1848 MADISON, James. The following resolutions were proposed by Mr. Madison in the house of representatives of the United States, January 3, 1794.
tables. 72 pp. (t.p. missing)

Q.

1849 MORNINGTON, Richard Wellesley, 2nd earl of. Substance of lord Mornington's speech in the house of commons, on Tuesday, January 21, 1794, on a motion for an address to his majesty at the commencement of the sessions of parliament.
154 pp. Dublin, P. Byrne, 1794

A., N.

1850 MORTIMER, Thomas A treatise on the law of bills of exchange and promissory notes. With all the new cases relative to bills of exchange and promissory notes, and an abridgment of the statutes relative thereto down to the present time.
104 pp. Dublin, John Rice, 1794

P.

1851 PALLAS, Peter Simon and ANDERSON, James. An account of the different kinds of sheep found in the Russian dominions, and among the tartar hordes of Asia: by Dr. Pallas. Illustrated with six plates. To which is added, five appendixes tending to illustrate the natural and economical history of sheep and other domestic animals. By James Anderson LL.D., F.R.S., F.A.S. Member of different academies, and author of several performances.
col. frontisp. plates. 216 pp. Edinburgh, T. Chapman, 1794

Q.

1852 Remarks on the propriety & expediency of the agreement entered into between the commissioners for making wide & convenient streets in the city of Dublin, & Mr. Henry Ottiwell, grounded on the evidence laid before the committee of the house of lords, appointed in the session of 1794, to enquire into the conduct of said commissioners.
40 pp. Dublin, 1794

A., N., P.

1853 Spectacles for sans-culottes of full age; or a dialogue on government between a gentleman & a farmer.
66 pp. Dublin, printed by John Bettson, 1794

A.

1854 [STUART, Daniel.] Peace and reform, against war & corruption. In answer to a pamphlet written by Arthur Young Esq. entitled, 'The example of France, a warning to Britain'.
104 pp. London, J. Ridgway, 1794

A., N.

1855 Thoughts on the present state of the cottiers & day labourers of this kingdom: addressed to the landlords & landholders, of the county of Meath. By a native of that county.
16 pp. Dublin, W. Watson, 1794

A., N.

1856 [VAUGHAN, William.] Plan of the London-dock, with some observations respecting the river immediately connected with docks in general, and of the improvement of navigation. Part II.
tables. 14 pp. London, 1794

T.

1857 YORKE, Henry. Thoughts on civil government: addressed to the disfranchised citizens of Sheffield.
76 pp. London, D. I. Eaton, 1794

A.

1858 YOUNG, John. Essays on the following interesting subjects: viz. I. Government. II. Revolutions. III. The British constitution. IV. Kingly government. V. Parliamentary representation and reform. VI. Liberty and equality. VII. Taxation and, VIII. The present war and the stagnation of credit connected with it.
164 pp. Glasgow, David Niven, 1794

Q.

1795

1859 Account of the experiments tried by the board of agriculture, in the composition of various sorts of bread.
tables. diagrams. 32 pp. London, Nicol, 1795

A.

1860 [AUCKLAND, William Eden, 1st baron.] Some remarks on the apparent circumstances of the war in the fourth week of October, 1795.
42 pp. Dublin, printed by J. Chambers, 1795

A., Q.

——. Another ed. 68 pp. London, J. Walter, 1795

Q.

See 1903

1861 BOND, Sir Thomas, bart. A digest of foreign exchanges, containing an abstract of the existing laws and custom of merchants relative to bills and notes. A short method of calculation with correct tables of exchange of the monies, weights and measures of foreign nations compared with ours of interest at one per cent and of the value of goods, from one to ten thousand pounds, gallons, yards, ells etc. being an epitome of all that is useful in every similar publication.
tables. 308 pp. Dublin, printed by Alex Stewart, 1795

G.

1862 BOWLES, John. The dangers of premature peace. With cursory strictures on the declaration of the king of Prussia. Inscribed to William Wilberforce, Esq. M.P.
72 pp. London, T. N. Longman & J. Debrett, 1795

A.

1863 The case of tithes truly stated, with some observations on a commutation. To which is added, a postscript, containing the resolutions of the tithe meeting in Devonshire, on the 25th day of May, 1795. By a country gentleman.
tables. 158 pp. Canterbury, all the booksellers in Kent & London, J. Johnson, 1795

A., T.

1864 [COBBETT, William.] A bone to gnaw, for the democrats, containing, 1st observations on a patriotic pamphlet. Entitled, 'Proceedings of the United Irishmen'. 2dly. democratic principles exemplified by example. 3dly. democratic memoires: or an account of some recent feats performed by the Frenchified citizens of the United States of America. (Signed) 'Peter Porcupine'.
76 pp. Philadelphia, printed by Thomas Bradford, 1795

Q.

Headed, Part II.

1865 County of Kildare presentments lent assizes, March 23rd 1795.
20 pp. Carlow, printed by G. Cooke, 1795

A.

1866 [CURRAN, John Philpot.] A letter to the right honourable Edmund Burke, on the present state of Ireland.
50 pp. Dublin, printed by J. Chambers, 1795

N., P., Q., T.

1867 D'IVERNOIS, Sir Francis. Coup-d'oeil sur les assignats, et sur l'état où la convention actuelle laisse les finances à ses successeurs, le 6 Septembre 1795. Tiré de ses débats.
96 pp. London, 1795

A.

1868 ——. A cursory view of the assignats, and remaining resources of French finance. (September 6, 1795.) Drawn from the debates of the convention. Translated from the original French by F. D'Ivernois, Esq.
86 pp. Dublin, printed by P. Byrne, 1795

A., L., N., Q.

1869 ——. Réflexions sur la guerre. En réponse aux Réflexions sur la paix, addressées à Mr. Pitt et aux Français.
164 pp. London, P. Elmsley, 1795

A.

1870 DOWNES, William. The charge of the hon. William Downes, one of the justices of his majesty's Court of King's Bench, delivered to the grand jury of the county of the city of Dublin, & the grand jury of the county of Dublin, at an adjournment of the commission of oyer & terminer, on Saturday the 13th day of December, 1794, & published at the request of those grand juries.
16 pp. Dublin, printed by John Exshaw, 1795

A. N.

1871 [DRENNAN, William.] A letter to his excellency earl Fitzwilliam, lord lieutenant, etc. of Ireland.
54 pp. Dublin, printed by J. Chambers, 1795

L., N., U.

1872 Facts relative to a banking connexion between Thellusson Brothers, and Co., of London, and Thomas and Richard Walker, of Manchester.
tables. appendices. 24 pp. n.p., 1795

N.

1873 FERRAR, John. A plan for clothing and educating the destitute orphans and poor children of soldiers, labourers, and others, humbly submitted to the consideration of his excellency the lord lieutenant.
8 pp. Dublin, printed by J. Chambers, 1795

N., Q.

1874 [FITZWILLIAM, William Wentworth, 4th earl of.] A [second] letter from a venerated nobleman, recently retired from this country to the earl of Carlisle, explaining the causes of that event.
32 pp. Dublin, 1795

T.

1875 Fox, Charles James. The speech of the right hon. Charles James Fox, in the house of commons, on Tuesday, March 24, 1795. On a motion 'That the house do resolve itself into a committee of the whole house to consider of the state of the nation.' To which is added a correct list of the minority.
52 pp. Dublin, P. Wogan, [etc.], 1795

A., N.

1876 GIFFORD, John. A Letter to the earl of Lauderdale, containing strictures on his lordships letters, to the peers of Scotland.
184 pp. London, T. N. Longman, 1795

A., N.

1877 [GRAYDON, Robert.] An inquiry into the expenses of the collection of the revenue of Ireland, and the examination of the principal merchants of Dublin, respecting fees of office in the custom-house, etc. From the report of the committee of the house of commons of the last session.
tables. 34 pp. Dublin, printed by J. Chambers, 1795

A., Q., T.

1878 The grievances of Ireland, an address to all ranks of the people.
42 pp. Dublin, printed by B. Smith, 1795

A.

1879 GRIFFITH, Richard. Thoughts and facts relating to the increase of agriculture, manufactures, and commerce, by the extension of inland navigation in Ireland. Wherein is considered, the propriety of directing into channels, more productive of permanent improvement, the bounties now paid on the inland and coast carriage of corn to Dublin.
map. 54 pp. Dublin, printed by P. Byrne, 1795

A., C., N., Q.

——. map. 60 pp. 2nd ed. Dublin, printed by Campbell and Shea, 1795

A., K., N., Q.

1880 HAMILTON, Alexander. Report of the secretary of the treasury, read in the house of representatives of the United States January 19th, 1795; containing a plan for the further support of public credit.
fold tables. 90 pp. n.p., printed by John Fenno, by order of the house of representatives, 1795

Q.

1881 [HARBORNE, W. C.] Observations on the advantages which would arise to this country from opening a trade with

the coast of Africa; with a plan for the same, by which the slave trade may be ultimately abolished.
32 pp. Dublin, J. Chambers, 1795

T.

1882 [HOLMES, William.] A sketch on the chancellor's budget is here humbly offered.
16 pp. Exeter, 1795

Q.

1883 KIRWAN, Richard. Essay, in answer to the following question proposed by the Royal Irish Academy; 'What are the manures most advantageously applicable to the various sorts of soils, & what are the causes of their beneficial effect in each particular instance?'
80 pp. Dublin, printed by W. Sleator, 1795

A., P.

[Signed Agricola.]

1884 A letter to his excellency earl Camden. President. The rt. hon. Lord Yelverton, the rt. hon. the Lord Mayor, and the rest of the members of the association for discountenancing vice and promoting the practice of virtue and religion. By a member of that association.
24 pp. Dublin, J. Jones, 1795

A., N., Q.

1885 MORRIS, Edward. A short inquiry into the nature of monopoly & forestalling. With some remarks on the statutes concerning them.
30 pp. London, T. Cadell jun. & W. Davies, 1795

A.

1886 MOUNTMORRES, Henry Redmond Morres, 2nd viscount. The crisis. A collection of essays written in the years 1792 & 1793, upon toleration, public credit, the elective franchise in Ireland, the emancipation of the Irish Catholics, with other interesting & miscellaneous subjects.
200 pp. Dublin, printed by P. Byrne, 1795

A., N.

1887 ——. An historical dissertation upon the origin, suspension, & revival of the judicature & independency of the Irish parliament. With a narrative of the transactions in 1719, relative to the celebrated declaratory law; extracted from the papers of the late earl of Egmont: & a comment on his lordship's opinion, upon the legislative union of these kingdoms. To which is annexed the standing orders of the house of lords. Transcribed from a copy printed by authority, the 11th Feb. 1790. Accurately compared with the leading cases: the dates & causes of their origin, construction & application, extracted from the journals of parliament, in Gt. Britain & Ireland.
128 pp. London, J. Debrett, 1795

A.

1888 MUSGRAVE, Sir Richard. A letter on the present situation of public affairs. Dedicated to his grace the duke of Portland.
60 pp. Dublin, printed by P. Byrne, 1795

A., N., P., R.

1889 The parish priests legacy, to his parishioners.
32 pp. Dublin, 1795

A.

On agriculture.

1890 PEARSON, George. Experiments and observations on the constituent parts of the potato root.
20 pp. n.p., [1795?]

A.

1891 Plan and Regulations of the society for promoting the comforts of the poor.
14 pp. Dublin, printed by William Watson, 1795

Q.

1892 A refutation of the 'remarks, on the agreement between the commissioners for making wide streets and Mr. Ottiwell', founded on that part of the evidence produced, which the writer of 'the remarks' hath misrepresented, mutilated, or suppressed.
48 pp. Dublin, 1795

A., N., Q.

1893 Report of the Committee of the board of agriculture, appointed to extract information from the county reports and other authorities, concerning the culture and use of potatoes. table of contents. plates. tables. appendix. 188 pp. London, Nicol, 1795

A.

1894 RICHMOND, Charles Henry Gordon-Lennox, 11th duke of. A letter from his grace the duke of Richmond to Lieutenant Colonel Sharman, chairman to the committee of correspondence appointed by the delegates of forty-five corps of volunteers, assembled at Lisburn in Ireland. With notes, by a member of the society for constitutional information.
16 pp. 8th ed. London, London Corresponding Society, 1795

B.

1895 Six letters, addressed to his excellency earl Fitzwilliam, lord lieutenant of Ireland. By Bolingbroke.
72 pp. Dublin, printed by G. Folingsby, 1795

A., N.

1896 SOMERVILLE, Robert. Outlines of the fifteenth chapter of the proposed general report from the board of agriculture. On the subject of manures.
table of contents. appendices. 126 pp. London, printed by Bulmer, 1795

A.

1897 Speculations on our prospects under the present administration: including thoughts on the propriety & practicability of a parliamentary reform.
42 pp. Dublin, printed by James Moore, 1795

A.

1898 [TAAFFE, Denis.] Ireland's mirror, exhibiting a picture of her present state, with a glimpse of her future prospects. Also, cursory observations on the alarming measures now going forward . . . By D. T.
64 pp. Dublin, author, 1795

A., N.

1899 [THOMPSON, Thomas.] Tithes indefensible: or, observations on the origin and effects of tithes. With some remarks on the tithe laws. Addressed to country gentlemen.
108 pp. 2nd ed. London, T. Cadell [etc.], York, Wilson & Co., 1795

A., Q.

1900 [VAUGHAN, William.] Reasons in favour of the London-docks.
8 pp. London, 1795

T.

1901 [VOGHT, Kaspar, freiherr von.] Account of the management of the poor in Hamburgh, since the year 1788. In a letter to some friends of the poor in Great Britain.
table. 64 pp. Edinburgh, 1795

Q.

See 1941

1902 [WILLIAMS, David?] A letter to the prince of Wales, in consequence of a second application to parliament, for the payment of debts *wantonly* contracted since May 1787.
40 pp. London, J. Owen, [1795]
[MS. attribution to David Williams on 1st ed.—also attributed to William Augustus Miles - Kress B.2997.]

A., N.

——. 2nd ed. 48 pp. and 5th ed. 58 pp. London, J. Owen, 1795

A.

1796

1903 [AUCKLAND, William Eden, 1st baron.] Some remarks on the apparent circumstances of the war in the fourth week of October, 1795.
40 pp. London, 1796

A., N.

See 1860

1904 ——. The substance of a speech made by Lord Auckland, on Monday the second day of May, 1796, on the occasion of a motion made by the Marquess of Lansdown [sic].
42 pp. London, J. Walter, 1796

P., Q., T.

1905 AUSTIN, Gilbert. A sermon for the support of Mercer's hospital. Preached at St. Anne's Church, Dublin, January 31st, 1796. And published at the request of the governors of the hospital.
40 pp. Dublin, printed by J. Chambers, 1796

A.

1906 BAYLEY, Thomas B. Thoughts on the necessity and advantages of care and œconomy in collecting and preserving different substances for manure.
24 pp. 2nd ed. Manchester, George Nicholson, 1796

P.

1907 [BENTLEY, Richard.] Considerations upon the state of public affairs at the beginning of the year 1796.
100 pp. 4th ed. London, J. Owen, 1796

A.

1908 [BOWLES, John.] Two letters addressed to a British merchant, a short time before the expected meeting of the new parliament in 1796; and suggesting the necessity and facility of providing for the public exigencies, without any augmentation of debt, or accumulation of burdens.
98 pp. 2nd ed. London, T. N. Longman & J. Owen, 1796

Q.

——. 102 pp. 4th ed. London, 1796

T.

1909 BROOME, Ralf. Observations on Mr. Paine's pamphlet, entitled the decline and fall of the English system of finance; in a letter to a friend, June 4, 1796.
76 pp. London, J. Debrett, (1796?)

A., N., Q.

——. Another edition. 39 pp Dublin, J. Milliken, 1796

A.

1910 [CAREY, Matthew.] Look before you leap; or a few hints to such artizans, mechanics, labourers, farmers and husbandmen, as are desirous of emigrating to America, being a genuine collection of letters, from persons who have emigrated; containing remarks, notes, and anecdotes, political, philosophical, biographical and literary, of the present state, situation, population, prospects and advantages, of America, together with the reception, success, mode of life, opinions and situations of many characters who have emigrated, particularly to the federal city of Washington. Illustrative of the prevailing practice of indenting, and demonstrative of the nature, effects and consequences of that public delusion.
144 pp. London, W. Row, 1796

T.

1911 Considerations respecting the necessity of increasing the circulating medium: & the most easy & safe method by which that may be done.
8 pp. London, printed by J. Bateson, 1796

A.

1912 CORRIE, Edgar. Letters on the subject of the Scotch distillery laws.
24 pp. Liverpool, printed by J. M'Creery, 1796

Q.

1913 (Descriptions of various pieces of textile machinery which have been patented.)
plates. 32 pp. n.p., 1796

A.

1914 D'IVERNOIS, Sir Francis. Histoire de l'administration des finances de la République Française, pendant l'année 1796.
244 pp. London, P. Elmsley [etc.], 1796

A.

1915 FAIRMAN, William. The stocks examined & compared: or, a guide to purchasers in the public funds. Containing an introduction, in which the origin & nature of the public debts are explained, & useful information is given relative to the management of business in the funds. An account of the public funds, from the times of their creation to the year 1796; including the imperial & Irish annuities, transferable at the bank of England, & the stock of public companies. And six new, useful, & extensive tables, illustrated by observations & examples. Also, a statement of the national debt, & an account of the present plan for liquidating the same.
128 pp. 2nd ed. London, J. Johnson [etc.], 1796

A.

1916 FERRAR, John. The prosperity of Ireland displayed in the state of fifty-four charity schools, in Dublin, containing 7416 children.
64 pp. Dublin, printed by Campbell & Shea, 1796
A., N., R.

1917 GRATTAN, Henry. Right honourable Henry Grattan's answer to the Rev. Michael Sandys.
32 pp. n.p. [1796]
A.

1918 GRAVES, Richard. A sermon in aid of the United charitable society for the relief of indigent room-keepers. Preached in St. Werburgh's Church, February 21st, 1796.
40 pp. Dublin, printed by W. Watson and Son, 1796
A., N., Q.

1919 HARPER, Robert Goodloe. An address from Robert Goodloe Harper, of South Carolina, to his constituents; containing his reasons for approving of the treaty of amity, commerce and navigation, with Great Britain.
36 pp. Boston, printed by Young and Minns, 1796
N.

1920 [JOERSSON, S. A.] Adam Smith author of an inquiry into the wealth of nations and Thomas Paine author of the decline and fall of the English system of finance. A critical essay published in all languages.
120 pp. Germany, 1796
Q.

1921 KIRKPATRICK, H. An account of the manner in which potatoes are cultivated and preserved, and the uses to which they are applied in the counties of Lancaster and Chester, together with a description of a new variety of the potato, peculiarly convenient for forcing in hot-house and frames.
50 pp. Warrington, J. Johnson, 1796
Q.

1922 LEDWICH, Edward. A statistical account of the parish of Aghaboe in the Queen's county, Ireland.
frontisp. map. fold. map. tables. 96 pp. Dublin, John Archer, 1796
A., N., P.

1923 A letter to his excellency earl Camden, on the present causes of discontent in Ireland. By a yeoman.
30 pp. Dublin, P. Byrne, 1796
A.

1924 MONKS, Daniel. A report laid before the River Boyne Company, October 19th 1796, by Daniel Monks, engineer.
16 pp. Dublin, printed by J. and A. B. King, 1796
Q.

1925 MORGAN, William. Additional facts, addressed to the serious attention of the people of Great Britain, respecting the expences of the War, & the state of the national debt.
54 pp London, J. Debrett, [etc.], 1796
A., P.

1926 ——. Facts addressed to the serious attention of the people of Great Britain respecting the expense of the war, and the state of the national debt.
56 pp. 2nd ed. London, J. Debrett, [etc.], 1796
A., N., Q.

——. 38 pp. 4th ed. Dublin, P. Byrne, 1796
A.

1927 MOUNTMORRES, Hervey Redmond Morres, 2nd viscount. Impartial reflections upon the present crisis; comprised in four essays upon the economy of the present stock of corn—the assize of bread—tithes—and a general system of inclosures. With an appendix, containing the system of inclosures introduced in 1732 by Arthur Dobbs, in the Irish Parliament.
appendix. 64 pp. London, G. Nichol (etc.), 1796
N.

——. Another issue. 64 pp. Kilkenny, reprinted by M. Finn, 1796
T.

1928 PAINE, Thomas. The decline and fall of the English system of finance.
46 pp. 2nd ed. Paris, Hartley Adlard and London, D. I. Eaton, 1796
P., Q.

44 pp. 4th ed. Dublin, printed by H. B. C. Clarke, 1796
A., N., P., Q.

32 pp. 7th ed. London, D. I. Eaton, 1796
A.

1929 PLUMMER, Thomas. A letter to the right hon. the lord mayor, on the subject of the intended new docks to be established at Wapping.
appendices. 46 pp. London, J. Johnson, 1796
P.

1930 Premiums offered by the Dublin society, for agriculture and planting, manufactures and fine arts, 1796.
56 pp. Dublin, printed by W. Sleater, 1796
Q.

1931 [RUMFORD, Benjamin Thompson, count.] An account of an establishment for the poor at Munich. Together with a detail of various public measures, connected with that institution, which have been adopted and carried into effect for putting an end to mendicity, and introducing order, and useful industry, among the more indigent of the inhabitants of Bavaria (Essay I).
116 pp. n.p. [1796?]
Q.

1932 ——. Count Rumford's experimental essays, political, economical & philosophical. Essay I. An account of an establishment for the poor in Munich. Together with a detail of various public measures, connected with that institution, which have been adopted & carried into effect for putting an end to mendicity, & introducing order, & useful industry, among the more indigent of the inhabitants of Bavaria.
194 pp. 3rd ed. Dublin, printed by W. Porter & J. Archer, 1796
B., L., P.

1933 ——. Essay II. Of the fundamental principles on which general establishments for the relief of the poor may be formed in all countries.
76 pp. n.p., [1796]
Q.

1934 ——. Essay III. Of food: and particularly of feeding the poor.
152 pp. n.p., [1796]
Q.

1935 ——. Count Rumford's experimental essays, political, economical, & philosophical. Essay III. Of food; & particularly of feeding the poor.
116 pp. 3rd ed. Dublin, printed by W. Porter & J. Archer, 1796
A., P.

1936 RUSSELL, Thomas. A letter to the people of Ireland on the present situation of the country.
26 pp. Belfast, Northern Star office, 1796
A., B., L., N.

1937 SANDYS, Michael. A letter to the rt. hon. Henry Grattan, on the state of the labouring poor in Ireland. From the Rev. M. Sandys, A.M., Minister of Powerscourt with Mr. Grattan's answer.
tables. 38 pp. Dublin, Dugdale, 1796
A., N., T.

1938 VANSITTART, Nicholas. later 1st baron Bexley. An inquiry into the state of the finances of Great Britain; in answer to Mr. Morgan's Facts.
fold. tables. 80 pp. London, J. Owen, 1796
A., Q.

1939 [VAUGHAN, William.] A letter to a friend on commerce and free ports, and London docks.
map. 28 pp. London, 1796
T.

1940 A Visit to the Philadelphia prison, etc.
fold. tables. 94 pp. Philadelphia, [1796?]
L.

1941 VOGHT, Kaspar, freiherr Von. Account of the management of the poor in Hamburgh, since the year 1788. In a letter to some friends of the poor, in Great Britain.
tables. 62 pp. Dublin, Dugdale, 1796
A., N., P.
See 1901

1942 WAKEFIELD, Daniel. A letter to Thomas Paine, in reply to his decline & fall of the English system of finance.
table. 36 pp. London, F. & C. Rivington, 1796
A.

1943 WINCHILSEA, George Finch, Ninth Earl of. Letter to the President of the board of agriculture, on the advantage of cottagers renting land. Drawn up for the consideration of the board of agriculture and internal improvement.
20 pp. London, Nicol, 1796
A.

1944 [WINTER, Pratt?] Reflections on the best means of securing tranquillity. Submitted to the consideration of country gentlemen.
88 pp. Dublin, printed by J. Chambers, 1796
A., N.

1797

1945 An account of the rise & progress of the Royal canal in Ireland, & also of the opposition thereto.
26 pp. Dublin, printed by N. Kelly, 1797
A., N., T.

1946 ALLARDYCE, A. An address to the proprietors of the Bank of England.
46 pp. 2nd ed. London, W. J. & J. Richardson, 1797
Q.

1947 ANDERSON, James. Essays relating to agriculture and rural affairs.
table of contents. 412 pp. Dublin, 1797
A.

1948 [ANDERSON, William.] The iniquity of banking: or, bank notes proved to be injurious to the public, & the real cause of the present exorbitant price of provisions.
44 pp. London, J. S. Jordan, 1797
A.

1949 [——?] The iniquity of banking; or, bank notes proved to be the real cause of the present exorbitant price of provisions. To which is now added, an enquiry concerning the nature and probable effects of the Bank Indemnity Bill and a plan for removing (or at least alleviating) the evils produced by the paper system. (In 2 parts.)
102 pp. 5th ed. London, J. Jordan, [1797?]
A.

1950 ASHE, Isaac. A sermon, preached on Sunday the 25th of June, for the relief of the distressed manufacturers.
30 pp. Dublin, printed by W. Watson & Son, 1797
Q.

1951 AUSTIN, Gilbert. A charity sermon for the sick & indigent room keepers. Preached at St. Peter's Dublin, before the Countess of Camden, February 19th 1797.
36 pp. Dublin, printed by J. Chambers, 1797
A.

1952 BARING, Sir Francis. Observations on the establishment of the Bank of England, and on the paper circulation of the country.
86 pp. London, Sewell and others, 1797
N., Q., T.

1953 BURROUGHS, Francis. Strictures on the present state of public credit and public security: containing a summary review of Mr. Pitt's administration.
66 pp. Dublin, printed by H. Fitzpatrick, 1797
A., N., P.

1954 The case of the traders of London, in 1674 and in 1705, as it now stands since the copartnership of the Wharfingers.
tables. 42 pp. London, Samuel Crouch, 1797
T.
Originally published 1705.

1955 CHAPMAN, William. Observations on the various systems of canal navigation, with inferences practical and mathematical; in which Mr. Fulton's plan of wheel-boats,

and the utility of subterraneous and of small canals are particularly investigated, including an account of the canals and inclined planes of China.
diagrams. table of contents. map. 106 pp. London, I. & J. Taylor, 1797

A.

1956 DAY, Robert. An address delivered to the grand jury of the county of Dublin, on Tuesday, the 10th of January, 1797. To which are added, introductory observations, recommended to the attention of the people of Great Britain.
26 pp. North Allerton & Dublin, Graisberry & Campbell, 1797

A.

1957 EDGEWORTH, Richard Lovell. A letter to the rt. hon. the earl of Charlemont, on the tellograph, and on the defence of Ireland.
52 pp. Dublin, P. Byrne, 1797

N.

1958 ERSKINE, Thomas. A view of the causes and consequences of the present war with France.
140 pp. London, J. Debrett, 1797

A., T.

——. Another issue. 110 pp. Dublin, P. Wogan, 1797

A., N.

——. 72 pp. 2nd ed. Dublin, P. Wogan, 1797

A.

——. 92 pp. 10th ed. London, J. Debrett, 1797

T.

1959 FAIRMAN, William. An appendix to the stocks examined & compared: containing the amount of each stock brought forward from midsummer, 1796, with the particulars of the additions that have been made to midsummer, 1797. Including the funding of navy & exchequer bills, the several loans, etc. With a continuation of tables.
40 pp. London, J. Johnson, [etc.], 1797

A.

1960 FITZPATRICK, Sir Jeremiah. Suggestions on the slave trade, for the consideration of the legislature of Great Britain.
74 pp. London, John Stockdale, 1797

A.

1961 FRY, Thomas. A new system of finance: proving the defects of the present system; that a saving may take place in the public income and expenditure to the amount of near ten millions annually! Exposition of the consequences to the public through their connection with the Bank of England; the baneful consequence of stock-jobbing; astonishing losses sustained by the public, that have enabled the minister to carry on the deception of lessening the public debt; the unparalleled advantages given by the minister to the loan mongers for paper credit, in order to support the present ruinous war; one hundred pounds securities in the three per cents given by the minister to receive 41l. 10s. 8d. to be sent to Germany for the support of the emperor's loan. Together with a reply to Messrs. Morgan and Vansittart on the subject of finance. Some remarks on Simon the stockbroker's letter to Mr. Alderman Curtis, late lord mayor of London. On the

iniquity of private tontines. Schemes for the benefit of age, on the most reputable establishments. A reasonable compromise between debtor and creditor. A perfect establishment for national credit in future; and the people relieved from the most burthensome of their taxes.
124 pp. London, J. S. Jordan, 1797

P.

1962 HAYES, Samuel. Essays in answer to all the queries on the culture of potatoes. With memoirs, & remarks, letters, etc. By James Anderson, L.L.D. By Mr. Somerville, of Haddington. By James Crowe, Esq., of Norwich, Thomas King, Esq., of Kingston, County of Wicklow.
152 pp. Dublin, printed by W. Sleater, 1797

A., P.

1963 HERRIES, Sir Robert, bart. Sketch of financial and commercial affairs in the autumn of 1797. In which, among other things, the mode of conducting the loyalty loan is fully considered; and means of redress to the subscribers to that loan suggested, without prejudice to the state.
110 pp. London, J. Wright, 1797

Q.

1964 Hints for a speedy reduction of a large proportion of the national debt, and a gradual decrease of taxes, addressed to the nation at large, and more particularly the public creditors.
24 pp. London, R. H. Westley, 1797

Q.

1965 HORAN, George. A sermon for the relief of the distressed manufacturers. Preached on Sunday the 25th of June, 1797, in the parish church of St. Catherine's.
24 pp. Dublin, printed by W. Watson, 1797

A., N.

1966 An Irishman's letter to the people called defenders.
8 pp. n.p., [1797?]

A., N.

1967 KENNEDY, P. A short defense of the present men and present measures, with occasional strictures on some recent publications of democratic notoriety. In a letter to a friend in the country; including thoughts on war, expenses, taxes, France, negotiation, emigration, Spain, invasion, etc.
102 pp. 3rd ed. London, the author, 1797

A., Q.

1968 LAUDERDALE, James Maitland, 8th earl of. Thoughts on finance, suggested by the measures of the present session.
tables. 58 pp. London, Robinson, 1797

A.

1969 [McKENNA, Theobald?] The interests & present state of the nation, considered: with thoughts on the British connexion. By a barrister.
64 pp. Dublin, printed by J. Rice, 1797

A.

1970 MONKS, Daniel. A report laid before the river Boyne company, April 20th 1797, by Daniel Monks, engineer. To which is prefixed the resolutions of the grand jury of the county Meath, at Lent assizes. 1797.
42 pp. Dublin, printed by J. and A. B. King, 1797

A., Q.

1971 O'CONNOR, Arthur. An address to the free electors of the county of Antrim.
10 pp. Belfast, 1797
A., L.

1972 OLIVARI, Francis. An essay on aerostation: wherein is exhibited the easiest method of constructing and directing aerostats, a plan for reconnoitering balloons, and a new hint for aerostatical telegraphs.
diagrams. 32 pp. Dublin, Bonham, 1797
A. N.

1973 The oppression of tithe exemplified; or, a review of a late contest between conscientious scruple & ecclesiastical exaction.
54 pp. Belfast, printed at Public printing office, 1797
A.

1974 PAINE, Thomas. Agrarian justice, opposed to agrarian law, and to agrarian monopoly; being a plan for meliorating the condition of man by creating in every nation a national fund, to pay to every person, when arrived at the age of twenty-one years, the sum of fifteen pounds sterling, to enable him, or her, to begin the world; and also ten pounds sterling per annum during life to every person now living of the age of fifty years, and to all other persons when they shall arrive at that age, to enable them to live without wretchedness, and go decently out of the world.
16 pp. Cork, 'printed at the late Gazette-Office', [1797]
P.

1975 ——. A letter to George Washington, president of the United States of America, on affairs public & private.
46 pp. Dublin, printed by J. Stockdale, 1797
A.

——. Another ed. 50 pp. Dublin, printed by J. Chambers, 1797
A.

——. Another ed. 78 pp. n.p., 1797
A.

1976 Papers relative to the agreement made by government with Mr. Palmer, for the reform and improvement of the posts.
tables. appendices. 92 pp London, Cadell and Davies, 1797
A.

1977 PATJE, C. L. A. An essay on the English national credit: or, an attempt to remove the apprehensions of those who have money in the English funds.
40 pp. London, R. Marsh, 1797
Q.

1978 PLUMMER, Thomas, junior. The inconsistencies of Mr. Pitt, on the subject of the war, and the present state of our commerce, considered, and fairly stated. Addressed, by permission to the right hon. Charles James Fox.
92 pp. London, J. Debrett, 1797
P.

1979 PRESTON, Richard. Tracts on I. The definition and nature of cross remainders. II. Fines and recoveries by tenant in tail. III. Difference between merger, remitter and ex-

tinguishment. IV. Estates executed, executory, vested and contingent. V. Contingencies with a double aspect. VI. The succession by a parent to a child. VII. The language of powers.
diag. index. 138 pp. London, R. Pheney, 1797
K.

1980 Read or be ruined! Containing some few observations on the causes of the commencement, of the disastrous progress,—and of the ruinous expences of the present war; with a serious call on the stockholders in the British funds, to forgo the receipts of a part of their dividends for a stated period, as the only possible mode of rendering their property secure, as well as of saving their country. Also a plan for discharging the national debt in 55 years, and yet immediately ameliorating the distressed situation of the middling, and inferior classes of the people of Great Britain, by commencing its operation with the abolition of taxes to the amount of ten millions per annum.
82 pp. London, J. S. Jordan, 1797
A.

1981 Reasons for extending the public wharfs in the port of London; and for settling a table of rates for wharfage and cranage; to which are added some observations relating to lighters and lighterage. Together with the case of the traders of London, in relation to the wharfingers: printed in the year 1705, and now reprinted.
18 pp. London, 1797
T.
[Reprint attributed by Foxwell to William Vaughan - Kress, B.3492.]

1982 A short account of the institution, rules, and proceedings of the Cork society for the relief and discharge of persons confined for small debts.
tables. 40 pp. Cork, printed by W. Flyn, 1797
N.

See also 1005 and 1349

1983 Short considerations upon some late proceedings of the Irish parliament, and upon the present crisis of public affairs. March, 1797.
34 pp. Dublin, printed by P. Byrne, 1797
A., N.

1984 SINCLAIR, Sir John, bart. Address to the board of agriculture, by Sir John Sinclair, 20th June, 1797: stating the progress that had been made by the board, during the fourth session since its establishment.
8 pp. n.p., 1797
A.

1985 ——. Letters written to the governor & directors of the bank of England, in September, 1796, on the pecuniary distresses of the country, & on the means of preventing them. With some additional observations on the same subject, & the means of speedily re-establishing the public & commercial credit of the country.
34 pp. London, G. Nicol, [etc.], 1797
A.

1986 SPENCE, Thomas. The rights of infants: or the imprescriptable rights of mothers to such a share of the elements as is sufficient to enable them to suckle and bring up

their young. In a dialogue between the aristocracy and a mother of children. To which are added, by way of preface and appendix, strictures on Paine's Agrarian justice.
16 pp. London, the author, 1797

A.

1987 TATHAM, Edward. A third letter to the right honourable William Pitt, chancellor of the exchequer, on the state of the nation, and the prosecution of the War.
36 pp. London, Rivington, [etc.], 1797

Q.

1988 Thoughts on the projected union between Great Britain and Ireland.
48 pp. Dublin, J. Moore, 1797

A., N., P.

1989 To the tradesmen, farmers, shopkeepers, and country people in general of the kingdom of Ireland.
20 pp. Dublin, 1797

A., K., N., P., T.

1990 VAUGHAN, William. Reasons in favour of the London-docks.
12 pp. London, 1797

A.

1991 Vindicators remarks on Sarsfield's letters, which appeared in four numbers of the Dublin Evening Post, beginning 26th August, and ending 2nd of September.
40 pp. Dublin, J. Milliken, 1797

A., Q.

1992 WARREN, William. A political & moral pamphlet, by William Warren, of Lisgoold, Esq., county of Cork, addressed to the rt. hon. earl of Camden, his excellency the lord lieutenant of, & to the people of Ireland.
180 pp. Cork, printed by James Haly, 1797

A.

1798

1993 An account of the proceedings of the acting governors of the house of industry. (In Dublin.) Annexed to their petition to the hon. the house of commons of Ireland.
36 pp. Dublin, printed by W. Corbet, [1798]

A., Q.

1994 BALL, Charles. An union neither necessary nor expedient for Ireland: being an answer to the author of arguments for and against an union, between Great Britain and Ireland, considered.
66 pp. Dublin, printed by William Porter, 1798

A., B., N., Q., T.

1995 BARNES, George. Strictures on 'An account of the proceedings of the acting governors of the house of industry'.
tables. appendices. 72 pp. Dublin, J. Chambers, 1798

A., P.

1996 BENTLEY, Richard. Considerations upon the state of public affairs, at the beginning of the year MDCCXCVIII. Part the first, France. Part the second, upon the instructions of his majesty's plenipotentiary at Lille, and the indemnity of

Great Britain at the peace. By the author of 'Considerations, etc. at the beginning of the year MDCCXCVI'.
112 pp. Dublin, J. Milliken, 1798.

A., Q., T.

1997 [BOWDLER, John.] Reform or ruin: take your choice! In which the conduct of the king, the lord lieutenant, the Parliament, the ministry, the opposition, the nobility, and gentry, the bishops and clergy of all denominations, the lawyers, the merchants, the lower classes, etc. etc. is considered: and that reform pointed out, which alone can save the country.
46 pp. Dublin, J. Milliken, 1798

A., K., N., Q., T.

1998 [BUSHE, Charles Kendal.] The Union. Cease your funning. Or, the rebel detected.
46 pp. Dublin, printed by James Moore, 1798

A., D., K., L., N., Q., T.

1999 The Charter-party of the Clonmel annuity company.
56 pp. n.p., 1798

N.

2000 CLARE, John Fitzgibbon, 1st earl of. The speech of the right honourable John, earl of Clare, lord high chancellor of Ireland, in the house of lords of Ireland, on a motion made by the earl of Moira, Monday, February 19, 1798.
106 pp. 3rd ed. Dublin, J. Milliken, 1798

A., B., N., Q., T.

2001 [COOKE, Edward.] Arguments for and against an union, between Great Britain and Ireland, considered.
60 pp. Second edition. Dublin, printed, London: reprinted for J. Wright, 1798

A., L., M., T.

——. 60 pp. 8th ed. Dublin, J. Milliken, 1798

G., K., T.

2002 [——.] Arguments for and against a union between Great Britain and Ireland considered. To which is prefixed a proposal on the same subject, by Josiah Tucker D. D., Dean of Gloucester.
32 pp. new ed. London, reprinted for Stockdale, 1798

T.

2003 [COTTINGHAM, James Henry?] Some observations on the projected union between Great Britain and Ireland, and the inexpediency of agitating the measure at this time. By J. H. C. Esq., barrister at law.
36 pp. Dublin, printed by Wm. McKenzie, 1798

A., K., N., T.

2004 A dialogue between a gentleman and a mechanic, reduced to writing, & published. By Philopolites.
26 pp. Dublin, John Rice, 1798

A., N.

2005 Essays on the political circumstances of Ireland, written during the administration of earl Camden; with an appendix containing thoughts on the will of the people. And a postscript, now first published. By a gentleman of the north of Ireland.
254 pp. Dublin, printed by Graisberry & Campbell, 1798

A.

2006 The friends of an union the enemies of Ireland.
32 pp. Cork, printed by J. Connor, 1798
A., L., N., T.

2007 HARPER, Robert Goodloe. Observations on the dispute between the United States and France, addressed by Robert Goodloe Harper, Esq. one of the delegates of South Carolina (a state, at one time, the most devoted to the French interests, of any in the union) to his constituents, in May 1797.
160 pp. 4th ed. Philadelphia printed, Dublin, reprinted by P. Byrne, 1798
A., M.

——. 96 pp. 4th ed. Philadelphia and Dublin, William Watson, 1798
Q.

——. 104 pp. 10th ed. Philadelphia printed and Dublin reprinted by J. Milliken, 1798
L.

2008 [HUMPHREY, John.] Strictures on a pamphlet, entitled 'Arguments for and against an union between Great Britain & Ireland, considered'.
24 pp. Dublin, printed by William Porter, 1798
A., N., Q., T.
See 2001.

2009 HUNTER, C. A general view of a plan of universal and equal taxation.
8 pp. London, Cadell and Davies, 1798
Q.

2010 JEBB, Richard. A reply to a pamphlet, entitled, arguments for and against an union.
72 pp. Dublin, William Jones, 1798
A., K., N., Q.

——. 72 pp. 2nd ed. Dublin, William Jones, 1798
T.

——. 72 pp. 3rd ed. Dublin, William Jones, 1798
T.

2011 [JENOUR, Joshua.] Observations on the taxation of property. Chiefly extracted from the Daily Advertiser of the 6th, 9th, 16th, 21st, 27th and 30th of December, 1797.
48 pp. London, the author, 1798
Q.

2012 JERVIS, Sir John Jervis White, bart. A letter addressed to the gentlemen of England and Ireland, on the inexpediency of a federal-union between the two kingdoms.
72 pp. Dublin, printed by John Whitworth, 1798
A., D., K., L., N., T.

2013 [JOHNSTONE, William.] Letter to Joshua Spencer, Esq., occasioned by his thoughts on an union. By a barrister.
42 pp. Dublin, John Archer, 1798
A., K., L., N., T.

——. Another issue. 42 pp. Cork, Haly, 1798
P.
See 2031.

9

2014 KERR, Charles. Strictures upon the union betwixt Great Britain and Ireland. By an officer.
46 pp. Dublin, Bernard Dornin, 1798
A., T.

2015 LAUDERDALE, James Maitland, 8th earl of. A letter on the present measures of finance; in which the bill now depending in parliament is particularly considered.
tables. appendices. 50 pp. London, J. Debrett, 1798
T.

2016 [LE FANU, Alicia?] The guilt and baseness of absentees, fully displayed; or, strictures on emigration.
24 pp. Dublin, J. Milliken, 1798
A., N.

2017 A letter addressed to the right honorable [sic] Sir John Parnell, bart. By a citizen.
12 pp. Dublin, J. Milliken, 1798
A.

2018 A letter to his excellency Marquess Cornwallis, on the proposed union. In which his excellency's political situation is candidly discussed. By an Irishman.
38 pp. Dublin, printed by James Moore, 1798
A., B., K., N., T.

2019 [MAGENS, Magens Dorrien.] Thoughts on a new coinage of silver, more especially as it relates to an alteration in the division of the pound troy. By a banker.
112 pp. London, John Sewell & J. Debrett, 1798
Q.

2020 NICHOLLS, John. The speech of John Nicholls, Esq. in the house of commons, Wednesday, January 3, 1798, on the bill for augmenting the assessed taxes.
28 pp. London, J. Wright, 1798
Q.

2021 O'BEIRNE, Thomas Lewis, bishop of Ossory. A sermon preached before his excellency John Jefferies, earl Camden, lord lieutenant, president, and the members of the Association for discountenancing vice, and promoting the practice of virtue and religion, in St. Peter's Church, on Tuesday 22nd May, 1798.
74 pp. Dublin, William Watson & Son, 1798
N., Q.

2022 O'CONNOR, Arthur. The state of Ireland. To which are added his addresses to the electors of the county of Antrim.
120 pp. 2nd ed. London, 1798
A., K., M., N., P.

2023 [OGILVIE, J.] A proposal for liquidating 66,666,666⅔ of the three per cents, by converting the land tax into a permanent annuity; with cursory observations humbly submitted to both houses of parliament.
52 pp. London, J. Wright, 1798
Q.

2024 PHIPPS, Joseph. Animadversions on the practice of tithing under the gospel; including remarks on the common arguments now used in support of ecclesiastical impositions in this nation, especially as they relate to dissenters.
58 pp. London, James Phillips, 1798
A.

2025 Proceedings at a meeting of the bankers and merchants, of Dublin, convened by the rt. hon. the Lord Mayor, on Tuesday—December, 18th—1798, for the purpose of considering the subject of an union.
16 pp. Dublin, V. Dowling, 1798
A., K., N., T.

2026 Reasons against a union. In which 'Arguments for and against a union', supposed to have come from a person in high station, are particularly considered; by an Irishman.
34 pp. Dublin, G. Folingsby, 1798.
A., Q.

——. 34 pp. 2nd ed. Dublin, G. Folingsby, 1798
K., L., N., T.

2027 The reports of the society for bettering the condition and increasing the comforts of the poor. Vol. I.
table of contents. tables. index. 324 pp. London, printed by Bulmer, 1798
A.

2028 SCARTH, Michael. The rules and regulations of the Castle Eden friendly society; with extracts from the proceedings, etc. to which are added, explanatory notes and observations.
66 pp. London, W. Clarke, 1798
Q.

2029 A schedule of inland duties of excise for and upon several articles therein mentioned.
30 pp. Dublin, printed by Grierson, 1798
D.

2030 A second letter to the earl of Moira on the commercial situation of Ireland. By the author of a letter to his lordship in defence of the conduct of his majesty's ministers and of the army in Ireland.
52 pp. London, printed J. Bell, 1798
A., Q.

2031 SPENCER, Joshua. Thoughts on an union.
36 pp. 2nd ed. Dublin, William Jones, 1798
A., D., L., N., Q., T.

——. 36 pp. 3rd ed. Dublin, William Jones, 1798
K., N.

——. 36 pp. 4th ed. Dublin, William Jones, 1798
K., N., T.

2032 A statistical account of the parish of Kilronan, in Ireland, and of the neighbouring district.
18 pp. Edinburgh, 1798
Q.

2033 TAAFFE, Denis. The probability, causes, and consequences of an union between Great Britain and Ireland, discussed: with strictures on an anonymous pamphlet, in favour of the measure, supposed to be written by a gentleman high in office.
appendix. 48 pp. Dublin, printed by J. Hill, 1798
A., K., L., N., P., T.

2034 Union or separation. By R. F.
42 pp. Dublin, Bernard Dornin, 1798
A., K., N., T.

2035 WALLACE, Thomas. An essay on the manufactures of Ireland, in which is considered, to what manufactures her natural advantages are best suited; and what are the best means of improving such manufactures.
table of contents. 362 pp. Dublin, printed by Campbell and Shea, 1798
A.

2036 WATSON, Richard, bishop of Landaff. An address to the people of Great Britain.
30 pp. Dublin, printed by John Exshaw, 1798
B.

——. 44 pp. 4th ed. Dublin, J. Milliken, 1798
A., N.

——. 46 pp. 8th ed. Dublin, J. Milliken, 1798
A., N.

2037 [——.] Hints towards an improved system of taxation, extending to all persons in exact proportion to their property, & without any kind of investigation or disclosure of their circumstances. With an appendix, recommending a plan, arising from this system, for the institution of a national bank.
56 pp. London, J. Murray & S. Highley (etc.), 1798
A.

2038 WILMOT, Edward Coke. A succinct view of the law of mortgages. With an appendix, containing a variety of scientific precedents of mortgages.
appendix. 222 pp. London, W. Clarke, 1798
K.

2039 YOUNG, Arthur. An enquiry into the state of the public mind amongst the lower classes: and on the means of turning it to the welfare of the state. In a letter to William Wilberforce, Esq., M.P.
38 pp. Dublin, J. Milliken, 1798
A., N., T.

1799

2040 An account of the proceedings of the acting governors of the house of industry for two years.
fold. table. 68 pp. Dublin, printed by W. Corbet, 1799
A., K.

2041 An account of the rise and progress of the dispute between the masters and journeymen printers exemplified in the trial at large with remarks thereupon, and the speeches of Messrs. Knapp, Raine and Hovell both in the trial and at the time of passing sentence.
68 pp. London, J. Ridgway, 1799
N.

2042 Address to the publick from the committee of the Cork Society for bettering the condition and increasing the comforts of the poor.
24 pp. Cork, printed by A. Edwards, 1799
A.

2043 An address to the Roman catholics of Ireland, on the conduct they should pursue at the present crisis; on the subject of an union. By an Old Friend.
36 pp. Dublin, J. Moore, 1799
B., N., T.

2044 An answer to some of the many arguments made use of against a pamphlet, [by Edward Cooke] entitled Arguments for and against an union. By an attorney.
22 pp. Dublin, Milliken, 1799
T.

2045 An argument for independence in opposition to an union, etc. [no tp.].
52 pp. n.p., [1799]
N.

2046 AUCKLAND, William Eden, 1st baron. The substance of a speech made by Lord Auckland, in the house of peers, on Tuesday, the 8th day of January, 1799, on the third reading of the 'Bill for granting certain duties upon income'.
tables. 44 pp. London, J. Wright, 1799
Q., T.

——. 44 pp. 3rd ed. London, J. Wright, 1799
N.

2047 ——. Substance of the speech of Lord Auckland, in the house of peers, April 11, 1799, on the proposed address to his majesty, respecting the resolutions adopted by the two houses of parliament, as the basis of an union between Great Britain and Ireland.
fold. tabs. tabs. 98 pp. Dublin, J. Milliken, 1799
A., D., L., N.

——. Another issue. 66 pp. Dublin, J. Milliken, 1799
B., Q., S., T.

——. Another issue, 42 pp. London, J. Wright, 1799
A.

2048 BALL, Charles. An union neither necessary nor expedient for Ireland: being an answer to the author of Arguments for and against an union, between Great Britain and Ireland, considered.
56 pp. 3rd ed., Dublin, printed by William Porter, 1799
A., L., T.

2049 BARNES, George. The rights of the imperial crown of Ireland asserted and maintained, against Edward Cooke, Esq. reputed author of a pamphlet, entitled, 'Arguments for and against an union, etc.' In a letter to that gentleman.
96 pp. Dublin, W. Gilbert, 1799
A., K., N., Q., T.

——. 100 pp. 2nd ed. Dublin, W. Gilbert, 1799
B., P., Q., T.

2050 [BENTLEY, Richard.] Considerations upon the state of public affairs, at the beginning of the year MDCCXCVIII. Part the third. The domestic state and general policy of Great Britain. By the author of 'Considerations, etc. At the beginning of the year MDCCXCVI'.
74 pp. Dublin, J. Milliken, 1799
A., N., Q., T.

2051 [——.] Considerations upon the state of public affairs, in the year MDCCXCIX. Ireland.
104 pp. Dublin, J. Milliken, 1799
L., T.

2052 BETHEL, Isaac Burke. A reply to the gentleman who has published a pamphlet, entitled 'Arguments for and against an union' in which Mr. McKenna's Memoire is taken into consideration.
30 pp. Dublin, printed by W. Gilbert, 1799
A., N., Q., T.

2053 [BOND, Sir Thomas, bart.] National advantages to be derived from adopting the following plans: viz. I. A land tax in place of tithes. II. Extension of woollen and cotton manufactures. III. Setting the kings commons. IV. Encreasing the revenue on malt and spirits. V. Relief of persons confined for debt. VI. Supplying the poor with coals cheap. VII. Lending money to the poor at ten per cent. VIII. Cutting a canal from Dublin to Drogheda. IX. Improving the harbour of Dublin. X. Supplying the city of Dublin with water at two-thirds of the present expense. By a citizen of Dublin.
24 pp. Dublin, printed by Morton Bates, 1799
A., C., K., P., Q., T., U.

2054 BOUSFIELD, Benjamin. A letter from Ben Bousfield Esq. to the citizens of Cork.
32 pp. Cork, printed by Haly, 1799
A., D., N., T.

——. 32 pp. 2nd ed. Cork, printed by Haly, 1799
K., T.

2055 [BUSHE, Charles Kendal.] Cease your funning: or, the rebel detected.
48 pp. 7th ed. Dublin, printed by James Moore, 1799
G., L., N.

2056 [——.] Tit for tat, or the reviewer reviewed; being an examination of Mr. Smith's review of the speech of the rt. hon. John Foster, in a letter addressed to him by an old correspondent.
40 pp. Dublin, printed by Moore, 1799
A., N., T.

2057 Calm considerations on the probable consequences of an union of the kingdom of Ireland with that of Great Britain. By Conciliator.
40 pp. Dublin, J. Milliken, 1799
L., T.

2058 CASTLEREAGH, Robert Stewart, viscount. A report of two speeches delivered by the rt. hon. lord Viscount Castlereagh, in the debate on the regency bill, on April 11th, 1799.
38 pp. Dublin, J. Milliken, 1799
A., N., Q.

2059 A caution to the loyal inhabitants of Dublin. By a freeman of Dublin. (No. 1).
20 pp. Dublin, 1799
A., N., T., U.

2060 A caution to the inhabitants of Dublin. By a freeman of Dublin, (No. II).
24 pp. Dublin, 1799

A., N., T.

2061 A caution to the inhabitants of Dublin. By an Irishman (No. III).
24 pp. Dublin, 1799

A., N.

2062 CLARKE, Thomas Brooke.   Dean Tucker's arguments on the propriety of an union between Great Britain & Ireland; written some years since, and now first published in this tract upon the same subject.
68 pp. Dublin, J. Milliken, 1799

A., K., L., N., T.

2063 ——. Misconceptions of facts, and mistatements of the public accounts by the rt. hon. John Foster, speaker of the Irish house of commons—proved and corrected, according to the official documents and authentic evidence of the Inspector-General of Gt. Britain, in a letter to Wm. Johnson Esq., M.P.
appendix. tables. 82 pp. London, J. Hatchard, 1799

N., T.

See 2205

2064 ——. The political, commercial and civil, state of Ireland. By the Rev. Dr. Clarke, secretary for the library and chaplain to His Royal Highness the Prince of Wales. Being an appendix to 'Union or separation'.
82 pp. London, J. Hatchard, 1799

A., D., L., N., P., Q., S.

——. Another issue. 72 pp. Dublin, J. Milliken, 1799

A., K., L., P., T.

2065 COFFEY, Andrew.   Observations on Mr. James Lynch's report on the pipe-water works of the city of Dublin.
16 pp. Dublin, printed by Thomas Morton Bates, 1799

A., N.

2066 COLLIS, John.   An address to the people of Ireland, on the projected union.
18 pp. Dublin, James Moore, 1799

C., K., L., N., T.

——. Another issue. 18 pp. Cork, 1799

N.

2067 Competency of the Parliaments of Great Britain and Ireland to incorporate their legislatures; with some remarks upon the debate in the Irish house of commons upon the address. By the author of the 'Necessity of an incorporate union between Great Britain and Ireland'.
28 pp. Dublin, J. Milliken, 1799

T.

2068 A complete state of the British revenue for the year ending on the 5th day of January 1799: being an authentic copy of the several official accounts presented to the house of commons, placed under the following heads: Public income, Public expenditure, Public funded debt, and reduction of the same. Unfunded debt, & outstanding demands. Exports & imports. Arrears & balances of public accountants. Account of the hereditary & temporary revenues of the crown, & of the civil-list grants. Account of the revenues which would have been applicable to the civil list, had they been reserved by his present majesty,—of the amount of the annuity reserved by his majesty in lieu of those revenues, & of the difference to the public. And of the expenditure of the money granted for the service of the year 1798.
tables. 256 pp. London, J. Debrett, 1799

Q.

2069 Considerations on the state of Ireland; and on the impolicy, and impracticability of separation.
104 pp. Limerick, printed by Richard Peppard, 1799

A., Q.

2070 [COOKE, Edward.] Arguments for and against an union between Great Britain and Ireland considered.
4th ed. 60 pp. Dublin, J. Milliken, 1799

K., N., Q.

——. 60 pp. 5th ed. Dublin, J. Milliken, 1799

K.

——. 60 pp. 8th ed. Dublin, J. Milliken, 1799

A., T.

——. 60 pp. 9th ed. Dublin, J. Milliken, 1799

T.

2071 CURTIUS, Marcus (pseud.) The melancholy consequences of a union displayed. In a series of letters, originally addressed to the right honourable the Lord Chancellor of Ireland. By Marcus Curtius.
92 pp. London, J. Wright, 1799

A., N., T.

2072 DE FOE, Daniel.   The history of the union between England and Scotland. To which is added the articles of Union, etc.
220 pp. Dublin, reprinted by Exshaw, 1799

A.

2073 Detached thoughts on an union, offered, with all due respect, to the Irish nation. By a citizen of Cork.
18 pp. Cork, M. Harris, 1799

P.

2074 DOBBS, Arthur.   Speech in the house of commons of Ireland, 5th March 1799, on submitting five propositions for tranquillizing the country.
16 pp. Dublin, printed by Moore, 1799

A., N., P.

2075 DONOUGHMORE, Richard Hely Hutchinson, 1st viscount.   The substance of a speech delivered in the Irish house of lords, by Lord viscount Donoughmore on Tuesday, 26th of February, 1799, on the subject of a bill, introduced by the earl of Clare. 'To restrain the negotiation of *small* notes, and inland bills of exchange, under a *limited* sum'.
54 pp. Dublin, printed by William Sleater, 1799

A., N., T.

2076 [DOWNES, Joseph.] Observations on the speech of the Rt. Hon. John Foster speaker of the House of commons of Ireland, delivered there, April 11th, 1799. By a gentleman at the Bar.
64 pp. London, J. Downes, J. Hatchard, 1799
A.

2077 DRENNAN, William. A letter to the Right Honourable William Pitt.
48 pp. Dublin, printed by James Moore, 1799
A., L., N., T.
On the act of union.

2078 DRENNAN, William. A second letter to the Right Honourable William Pitt.
50 pp. Dublin, printed by George Folingsby, 1799
A., L., N., T.

2079 DUIGENAN, Patrick. A fair representation of the political state of Ireland; in a course of strictures on two pamphlets, one entitled: 'The case of Ireland reconsidered'; the other entitled 'Considerations on the state of public affairs 1799—Ireland'; with observations on the other modern publications on the subject of an incorporating Union of Great Britain and Ireland, particularly on a pamphlet entitled 'The speech of Lord Minto in the House of Peers, April 11, 1799'.
appendices. 258 pp. London, J. Wright, 1799
T.
See 2213.

2080 Extracts from the reports of the English society for bettering the condition of the poor, and from other papers on the same subject: to serve as hints as to the best means of relieving the poor during the present scarcity.
36 pp. Dublin, printed by William Watson, 1799
A.

2081 FEAGAN, Dennis (pseud.) The answer of Dennis Feagan, breeches-maker at Edenderry, to the letter of Darby Tracey, chairman in St. James St., London. Wherein is clearly proved the bad effects and misfortunes an union with Great Britain, will have on the interest and happiness of the common people of Ireland.
12 pp. Dublin, J. Moore, 1799
A., T.

2082 Fares of hackney coaches and chaises, by the day, hour, etc. And also for the carriage of coals and turf; as appointed by William Alexander, Esq., superintendent magistrate of the district of the metropolis. And approved of by the Right Hon. the lord chancellor and chief judges.
8 pp. Dublin, printed by J. Exshaw, 1799
A., N.

2083 A few thoughts on an union, with some observations upon Mr. Weld's pamphlet of 'no union'. Addressed to the yeomanry of Dublin. By a wellwisher of Ireland.
38 pp. Dublin, J. Milliken, 1799
A., K., L., N., P., T.

2084 The first report of the society for bettering the condition and increasing the comforts of the poor.
370 pp. 5th ed. London, J. Hatchard, (etc., etc.), 1799
A.

2085 Form of notices necessary to be given before the first of July, 1799, of proceeding for the recovery of the value of tithes of the years 1797 and 1798, under the tithe compensation act of 39 Geo. 3. and of the petitions, schedules and affidavits, if the proceeding be in a court of equity; and of the notices and schedules, if the proceedings be by civil bill; with instructions in both cases, from which the clergy and lay impropriators will, in a considerable part of the business, be enabled to act for themselves.
30 pp. Dublin, J. Milliken, 1799
A.

2086 [FOSTER, John?] The commercial system of Ireland reviewed and the question of union discussed, in an address to the merchants, manufacturers, and country gentlemen of Ireland.
102 pp. Dublin, James Moore, 1799
A., K., N., P., T.

[——?] Second edition, with an introductory preface, of the commercial system of Ireland reviewed, and the question of union discussed, in an address to the merchants, manufacturers, and the country gentlemen of Ireland.
108 pp. Dublin, printed by J. Moore, 1799
L., T., U.

2087 ——. Speech of the Right Honourable John Foster, speaker of the house of commons of Ireland, delivered in committee of the whole house. On Thursday the 11th day of April, 1799.
46 pp. Dublin, James Moore, 1799
A., B., L., N., Q., T.

2088 Free thoughts on the misconception of the superiority of natural advantages possessed by this country over England.
14 pp. Dublin, James Moore, 1799
A., K., L., P., T.

2089 GAY, Nicholas. Strictures on the proposed union between Great Britain and Ireland with occasional remarks.
44 pp. Dublin, printed by J. Exshaw, 1799
A., T.

2090 GERAGHTY, James. The consequences of the proposed union with respect to Ireland, considered: in a second letter to the Marquess Cornwallis.
60 pp. London, Stockdale, 1799
A., N.

2091 ——. The present state of Ireland, and the only means of preserving her to the empire, considered. In a letter to the Marquess Cornwallis.
52 pp. London, J. Stockdale, 1799
A., K., L., N., T.

2092 [GIFFARD, Harding.] Union or not? By an orangeman.
42 pp. Dublin, printed by J. Milliken, 1799
A., T.

2093 GLENBERVIE, Sylvester Douglas, baron. Speech of the Right Honourable Sylvester Douglas, in the house of commons, Tuesday, April the 23rd, 1799, on seconding the motion of the Right Honourable the chancellor of the exchequer, for

the house to agree with the lords in an address to his majesty, relative to a union with Ireland.
196 pp. Dublin, John Milliken, 1799
L., N.

———. Another issue. 198 pp. London, J. Wright, 1799
A., T.

2094 GOOLD, Thomas. An address to the people of Ireland, on the subject of the projected union.
112 pp. Dublin, printed by James Moore, 1799.
A., L., N., T.

———. 109 pp. 3rd ed. Dublin, 1799
T.

———. 109 pp. 4th ed. Dublin, 1799
T.

2095 HAMILTON, John. A letter to Theobald McKenna, Esq. occasioned by a publication, entitled A memoire on some questions respecting the projected union.
64 pp. Dublin, printed by James Moore, 1799
A., K., L., N., T.

2096 HARDIE, James. An account of the malignant fever lately prevalent in the city of New-York.
tables. 152 pp. New York, printed by Hurtin and McFarlane, 1799
A.

2097 HARPER, Robert Goodloe. A short account of the principal proceedings of congress, in the late session, and a sketch of the state of affairs between the United States and France in July, 1798: in a letter from Robt. Goodloe Harper, Esq., of South Carolina, to one of his constituents.
24 pp. Dublin, J. Milliken, 1799
A.

2098 [HOLMES, Robert.] A demonstration of the necessity of a legislative union of Great Britain and Ireland, involving a refutation of every argument which can be urged against that measure. By a philosopher.
40 pp. Dublin, 1799
A., L., N., P., T.

2099 HUMPHREY, John. Strictures on a pamphlet, entitled arguments for and against a union between Great Britain and Ireland, considered.
32 pp. 2nd ed. Dublin, printed by William Porter, 1799
A., L., N., T.

2100 Impartial remarks, on the subject of an union. In answer to the arguments in favour of that measure. In which the sentiments of the catholic body, are vindicated from the charge of favouring the project. With a reply to Mr. McKenna's Memoire. By a farmer.
50 pp. Dublin, William Jones, 1799
A., C., K., L., T.

2101 An impartial view of the causes leading this country to the necessity of an union; in which the two leading characters of the state are contrasted; and in which is contained, a reply to Cease your funning, and Mr. Jebb.
54 pp. Dublin, Bernard Dornin, 1799
P., T.

2102 JEBB, Richard. A reply to a pamphlet entitled, arguments for and against an union.
tables. 72 pp. London, J. Debrett, 1799
M.

2103 ———. A reply to a pamphlet, entitled, arguments for and against an union.
tables. 54 pp. 3rd ed. Dublin, William Jones, 1799
K.

2104 [JOHNSON, William.] The probable consequences of a union impartially considered. By a barrister.
40 pp. Dublin, J. Milliken, 1799
P.

2105 ———. Reasons for an union between Ireland and Great Britain.
64 pp. Dublin, J. Milliken, 1799
A., K., N., P., Q., R., T.

———. 64 pp. 2nd ed. Dublin, J. Milliken, 1799
A., D., N., Q.

———. 62 pp. 4th ed. Dublin, J. Milliken, 1799
A., N.

———. 64 pp. 5th ed. Dublin, J. Milliken, 1799
T.

———. 64 pp. 6th ed. Dublin, J. Milliken, 1799
P.

2106 Keep up your spirits, or huzza for the empire!! being a fair, argumentative defence of an union, addressed to the people of Ireland, by a citizen of the Isle of Man.
28 pp. Dublin, J. Moore, 1799
A., B., K., N., P., T.

2107 KENNEDY, Henry. A few remarks on the affairs at the house of industry, and on the conduct of some of the present acting governors; in a letter to Henry Alexander, Esq., chairman of the committee of the house of commons, which sat to enquire into the management of that institution.
12 pp. Dublin, printed by J. Moore, 1799
A.

2108 [KERR, Charles.] Strictures upon the union betwixt Great Britain and Ireland. By an officer.
46 pp. Dublin, Bernard Dornin, 1799
A., N., T.

2109 [LATOUCHE, James Digges.] English union, is Irelands ruin! or an address to the Irish nation. By Hibernicus.
32 pp. Dublin, James Moore, 1799
A., K., L., N., P., T.

2110 [LATTIN, Patrick.] The case of Ireland reconsidered, in answer to a pamphlet, entitled Arguments for and against an union, considered.
92 pp. London, the author, 1799
T.

———. Another issue. 64 pp. Dublin, H. Fitzpatrick, 1799
A., D., K., N., T.
See 2238.

2111 A letter addressed to a gentleman in England, concerning the principal arguments against an union, and deciding in favour of the measure.
54 pp. Dublin, printed by Fitzpatrick, 1799
A., N., T.

2112 Letter from a retired barrister in London, to a practicing barrister in Dublin.
30 pp. Dublin, J. Milliken, 1799
A., K., L., T.
[On the union.]

2113 A letter to his excellency Charles Marquess Cornwallis: in which the leading measures of his administration are considered. By a friend to Ireland.
42 pp. Dublin, J. Milliken, 1799
L.

2114 A letter to the electors of Ireland, on the projected measure of an union. With some friendly hints to the borough patrons of Ireland. By a freeholder.
20 pp. Dublin, J. Moore, 1799
A., L., N., P., T.

2115 A letter to the people of Ireland, which they all can understand, and ought to read. By a real friend.
32 pp. Dublin, J. Milliken, 1799
A., L., N., P., T.

2116 A letter to William Smith, Esq., in answer to his address to the people of Ireland; in which his assertion of an absolute despotic power being acknowledged by our constitution is particularly examined. By one of the people.
40 pp. Dublin, printed by James Moore, 1799
A., L., N., T.

2117 LOCKER, John. Timely application to the people of Ireland: or, remarks on the necessity of a most effectual reformation in the state of the coin, being essential to the completion of national prosperity, wealth, trade, commerce, peace, and independence of Ireland. Also extracts from a pamphlet published in the year 1729, entitled, A scheme of the money-matters of Ireland.
56 pp. Dublin, printed by William Porter, 1799
A., Q., T.

2118 A loyal subject's thoughts on an union between Great Britain & Ireland.
38 pp. Dublin, J. Milliken, 1799
A., K., L., N., T.

2119 [McDOUGALL, Henry.] Sketches of Irish political characters, of the present day, shewing the parts they respectively take on the question of the union, what places they hold, their characters as speakers, etc. etc.
324 pp. London, printed by T. Davison, 1799
G., R.

2120 McKENNA, Theobald. Constitutional objections to the government of Ireland by a separate legislature, in a letter to John Hamilton, Esq., occasioned by his remarks on A Memoire on the projected union.
92 pp. Dublin, printed by H. Fitzpatrick, 1799
A., L., N.

——. 92 pp. 2nd ed. Dublin, 1799
N.

——. 94 pp. 3rd ed. Dublin, 1799
N.

2121 ——. A memoire on some questions respecting the projected union of Great Britain & Ireland.
40 pp. Dublin, John Rice, 1799
A., N., Q., T.

2122 [MacNEVEN, W. J.] An argument for independence, in opposition to an union. Addressed to all his countrymen. By an Irish catholic.
54 pp. Dublin, printed by J. Stockdale, 1799
A., K., L., N., T.

2123 MARSHALL, William. Proposals for a rural institute, or college of agriculture and other branches of rural economy.
46 pp. London, G. & W. Nicol and others, 1799
Q.

2124 MELVILLE, Henry Dundas, 1st viscount. Substance of the speech of the right hon. Henry Dundas, in the house of commons, Thursday, Feb. 7, 1799, on the subject of the legislative union with Ireland.
68 pp. Dublin, printed by John Exshaw, 1799
L.

——. 70 pp. 2nd ed. London, 1799
N.

——. 68 pp. 3rd ed. Dublin, 1799
T.

——. 68 pp. 4th ed. London, J. Wright, 1799
A.

2125 MOLYNEUX, William Philip, styled viscount, later 1st baron Sefton. A reply to the memoire of Theobald McKenna Esq., on some questions touching the projected union of Great Britain and Ireland.
36 pp. Dublin, Fitzpatrick, 1799
K., T.

2126 More thoughts on an union.
16 pp. Dublin, printed by J. Moore, 1799.
L., N., P., T.

2127 Necessity of an incorporate union between Great Britain and Ireland proved from the situation of both kingdoms. With a sketch of the principles upon which it ought to be formed.
90 pp. Dublin, J. Milliken, 1799
A., B., K., L., N., P., T.

——. 90 pp. 2nd ed. Dublin, J. Milliken, 1799
D., N., T.

2128 [NEWBERRY, Francis.] Thoughts on taxation: in the course of which the policy of a tax on income is impartially investigated.
56 pp. Dublin, J. Milliken, 1799
A., N., P.

2129 No flinching or a persevering opposition to the measure of an incorporate union, strongly recommended by an eminent barrister.
36 pp. Dublin, J. Milliken, 1799
A., K., L., N., P., T.

2130 Observations on a pamphlet, supposed to be written by an Englishman, entitled, arguments for and against an union. By a student of Trinity College.
32 pp. Dublin, printed by J. Milliken, 1799
A., K., N., Q., T.

2131 Observations on arguments for and against an union between Great Britain and Ireland.
16 pp. Dublin, printed by J. Stockdale, 1799
N., Q., T.

2132 Observations on Bailie Smith's address, and on the answer thereto by an old magistrate. By an inhabitant of Edinburgh.
20 pp. Edinburgh, printed by George Reid, 1799
L.
[On Edinburgh municipal finances.]

2133 Observations on that part of the speaker's speech, which relates to trade.
fold. tables. 42 pp. Belfast, printed by E. Black, [1799]
A., C., L., N., U.

——. Another issue. 58 pp. Dublin, T. Burnside, 1799
N., P.

——. 56 pp. 3rd ed. Dublin, John Rea, 1799
L., N., T.
[Maynooth copy has Mss. attribution to John Beresford.]

2134 [ORR, Robert.] An Address to the people of Ireland, against an union: in which a pamphlet entitled arguments for and against that measure is considered. By a friend to Ireland.
46 pp. Dublin, J. Stockdale, 1799
A., K., N., P., Q., T.

——. 54 pp. 2nd ed. Dublin, J. Stockdale, 1799
A., B., K., L., M., N., T.

2135 ——. A review of the speech of the right hon. William Pitt, in the British house of commons, on Thursday, January 31st, 1799.
48 pp. Dublin, J. Stockdale, 1799
A., D., L., M., N., T.

2136 PEEL, Robert. The substance of the speech of Robert Peel, Esquire, in the house of commons, on Thursday, the 14th February, 1799, on the question for receiving the report of the committee on the resolutions respecting an incorporate union with Ireland. With a correct copy of the resolutions, as they were finally amended by the house of commons.
4 pp. Dublin, printed by John Exshaw, 1799
L., N., T.

2137 The philleleu, or an arithmetical calculation of the losses which the trade and property of Ireland, and of the empire, in general must sustain by an union.
tables. 8 pp. Dublin, printed by Joseph Mehain, 1799
A., K., N., T.

2138 PITT, William. The speech of the Right Hon. William Pitt, in the British house of commons, on Thursday, January 31, 1799.
54 pp. Dublin, printed by George Grierson, 1799
A., B., N., Q., T.

2139 ——. Speech of the Right Honourable William Pitt, in the house of commons, Thursday, January 31, 1799, on offering to the house the resolutions which he proposed as the basis of an union between Great Britain and Ireland, to which are added the speeches of the Right Honourable John Foster, on the 12th and 15th of August, 1785, on the bill for effectuating the intercourse between Great Britain and Ireland, on permanent and equitable principles for the mutual benefit of both countries.
16 pp. Dublin, printed by John Exshaw, 1799
L., N., T.

2140 ——. Substance of the speeches of the Right Honourable William Pitt, on the 23rd & 31st of January, 1799: including a correct copy of the plan, with the debate which took place in the house of commons on the proposal for an union between Great Britain & Ireland. To which are annexed, the celebrated speeches of the Right Honourable John Foster, late Chancellor of the exchequer, now speaker of the house of commons of Ireland, on the 12th & 15th days of August 1785, upon the commercial propositions.
48 pp. Dublin, printed by John Exshaw, 1799
A., N., T.

2141 Pitt's union.
24 pp. Dublin, printed by J. Stockdale, 1799
A., K., L., N., T.

2142 Plan and regulations of the society for promoting the comforts of the poor.
14 pp. Dublin, printed by William Watson & Son, 1799
A., N., Q.

2143 The probable consequences of a union, impartially considered. By a barrister.
18 pp. Dublin, J. Milliken, 1799
A., N., T.

2144 Proceedings at a meeting of the gentlemen, clergy & freeholders, of the county of Dublin, on Friday, January the 4th, 1799, to take into consideration the measure of a legislative union between this country & Great Britain. Alexander Kirkpatrick, Esq., high sheriff, in the chair. In which is a correct report of Mr. Spencer's speech.
30 pp. Dublin, William Jones, 1799
A., D., N., T.

2145 Proofs rise on proofs, that the union is totally incompatible with the rights of the ancient, self-legislative, & independent kingdom, of Ireland, however embellished & flattering its introduction may appear.
44 pp. Dublin, Marchbank & others, 1799
D., K., L. N., T.

2146 Remarks on a pamphlet, entitled 'Arguments for and against an union'. By a Farmer.
52 pp. Dublin, 1799
A.

2147 Report of the committee of secrecy of the house of commons, to whom the several papers, referred to in His Majesty's message of the 2nd of January 1799, and which were presented (sealed up) to the house by Mr. Secretary Dundas, upon the 23rd day of the said month, by His Majesty's command, were referred; and who were directed to examine the matters thereof, and report the same, as they shall appear to them, to the house. Ordered to be printed 15th March 1799.
124 pp. London, J. Wright, 1799

Q.

2148 A report of the debate of the Irish bar, on Sunday, the 9th of December, 1798, on the subject of an union of the legislatures of Great Britain and Ireland. To which is added, the resolution and protest.
90 pp. J. Moore, 1799

A., L., S., T.

2149 A report of the debate in the house of commons of Ireland, on Tuesday and Wednesday the 22nd and 23rd of January, 1799, on the subject of an Union.
94 pp. Dublin, James Moore, 1799

A., T.

2150 A report of the important debate in the house of commons of Ireland, on Thursday, April 11, 1799, on the regency bill, including the admirable speech of the Right Hon. John Foster, (speaker).
52 pp. Dublin, 1799

A.

2151 ROSE, George. A brief examination into the increase of the revenue, commerce, and manufactures of Great Britain, from 1792–1799.
fold. tables. 86 pp. 2nd ed. London, J. Wright & others, 1799

C., M., N., P., Q., T.

——. Another issue, 'from the corrected London edition, with an introduction by the Irish editor'.
fold. tabs. 86 pp. Dublin, J. Milliken & D. Graisberry, 1799

A., K., N., Q., T., U.

2152 RUDD, Pemberton. An answer to the pamphlet, entitled Arguments for and against an union, etc. etc. In a letter addressed to Edward Cooke, Esq., secretary at war.
36 pp. Dublin, J. Milliken, 1799

A., D., K., N., Q., T.

2153 ——. An answer to the pamphlet, entitled Arguments for and against an union, etc., etc. In letters addressed to Edward Cooke, Esq., secretary at war. Letter the second.

A., K., L., N., Q., T.

2154 RUDING, Rogers. A proposal for restoring the antient constitution of the mint, so far as relates to the expence of coinage. Together with the outline of a plan for the improvement of the money: & for increasing the difficulty of counterfeiting.
38 pp. London, Sewell, [etc.], 1799

A.

2155 RUMFORD, Benjamin Thompson, count. Proposals for forming by subscription in the metropolis of the British Empire, a public institution for diffusing the knowledge and facilitating the general introduction of useful mechanical inventions and improvements, and for teaching by courses of philosophical lectures and experiments the applications of science to the common purposes of life.
56 pp. London, 1799

A.

2156 A second letter to the electors of Ireland, on the projected measure of an union. By a freeholder.
16 pp. Dublin, J. Moore, 1799

L., N., P., T.

2157 SHEEHY, P. Union a plague. In answer to Counsellor McKenna's memoire on the projected union.
52 pp. Dublin, printed by J. Hill, 1799

A., B., K., L., N., T.

2158 SHEFFIELD, John Baker-Holroyd, earl of. Substance of the speech of the Right Honourable Lord Sheffield, Monday, April 22, 1799, upon the subject of union with Ireland. Printed from a copy corrected by his lordship.
40 pp. Dublin, J. Milliken, 1799

L., N., T.

——. Another issue. 66 pp. London, J. Debrett, 1799

A.

2159 SHERIDAN, Richard Brinsley. Speech of Richard Brinsley Sheridan, Esq., in the house of commons of Great Britain, on Thursday, January 31st, 1799, in reply to Mr. Pitt's speech on the union with Ireland.
28 pp. Dublin, James Moore, 1799

A., N.

2160 A short address to the people of Ireland, on the subject of an union; by a freeholder.
26 pp. Dublin, William Jones, 1799

A., K., L., N., T.

2161 A sketch of a plan, addressed to the beneficed clergy, curates, etc. for establishing a fund for the relief of the widows of the clergy.
16 pp. Cork, printed by A. Edwards, 1799

A.

2162 A sketch of the most obvious causes of the poverty, ignorance and general want of civilisation amongst the peasantry of Ireland, and a comparison between their situation and that of the peasantry of Great Britain, with a practicable plan for improving their manners and for making their circumstances more eligible than they have ever been chiefly by a liberal attention to the education of the rising generation and by establishment of poors laws and taxes for their permanent relief. To which are annexed, impartial strictures on the proposed legislative union between Ireland and Britain: questions relative to it, and to the English minister, to a probable land tax, city of Dublin trade and manufactures, excess of our population, lawyers, attornies, absentees, reduction of the rates of provisions, house and land rents, places, pensions, &c. By a sincere friend to humanity, to peace, and the constitution.
38 pp. Dublin, J. Milliken, 1799

A., T.

2163　SMITH, Sir William Cusac, bart.　Letters on the subject of an union, addressed to Messrs. Saurin and Jebb, in which Mr. Jebb's 'Reply' is considered. By a Barrister.
82 pp. Dublin, J. Milliken, 1799

A., K., L., P., Q., T.

2164　——.　Review of a publication, entitled, the speech of the Right Honourable John Foster, speaker of the house of commons of Ireland; in a letter, addressed to him by William Smith, Esq.
68 pp. Dublin, Marchbank, 1799

B., Q., T.

——.　68 pp. 2nd ed. Dublin, Marchbank, 1799

K.

——.　70 pp. 3rd ed. Dublin, Marchbank, 1799

A., L., N., Q., T.

2165　——.　The substance of Mr. William Smith's speech on the subject of a legislative union between this country and Great Britain; delivered in the house of commons, on Thursday, January, 24th, 1799, and now reduced to the form of an address to the people of Ireland.
108 pp. 3rd ed. Dublin, Marchbank, 1799

N., Q., T.

——.　108 pp. 4th ed. Dublin, Marchbank, 1799

Q.

——.　108 pp. 5th ed. Dublin, Marchbank, 1799

A.

——.　60 pp. 6th ed. Dublin, Marchbank, 1799

L., T.

2166　SMYTH, Giles S.　First letter to a noble lord, on the subject of the union.
34 pp. Dublin, printed by J. Moore, 1799

A., K., L.

——.　34 pp. 2nd ed. Dublin, 1799

T.

2167　STEVENS, William.　Hints to the people, especially to the inhabitants of Dublin: in which the effects of an union on the trade and property of Dublin are investigated.
30 pp. Dublin, printed by H. Fitzpatrick, 1799

A., K., L., P., U.

2168　STOKES, Whitley.　Projects for re-establishing the internal peace and tranquility of Ireland.
54 pp. Dublin, James Moore, 1799

A., K., N.

2169　SWIFT, Theophilus.　Hear Him! Hear Him! in a letter to the Right Hon. John Foster.
72 pp. Dublin, printed by J. Stockdale, 1799

A., L., N.

2170　TAAFFE, Dennis.　The second part of Taaffe's reflections on the Union.
48 pp. Dublin, printed by Joseph Mehain, 1799

A., K., N., T.

2171　Tempora mutantur; or, reasons for thinking that it is inconsistent with the welfare of this kingdom to persist in witholding from the Roman catholics, the political power, offices and honours exclusively enjoyed by protestants; and that the admission of the Roman catholics to a suitable participation of these would not render them predominant in the political system, nor consequently be followed by those pernicious effects which are generally apprehended.
10 pp. Dublin, printed by J. Moore, 1799

A.

2172　Three letters to a noble lord on the projected legislative union of Great Britain and Ireland. By a Nobleman.
62 pp. London, J. Wright, Richardson, 1799

N., P.

2173　[TITTLER, colonel.]　Ireland profiting by example; or, the question, whether Scotland has gained or lost, by an union with England, fairly discussed. In a letter, from a gentleman in Edinburgh, to his friend in Dublin.
38 pp. Dublin, J. Milliken, 1799

A., N., Q., T.

——.　32 pp. 3rd ed. Dublin, J. Milliken, 1799

A., L., P., T.

2174　To be, or not to be, a nation: that is the question?
34 pp. Dublin, printed by Joseph Mehain, 1799

A., K., N., T.

2175　TRACY, Darby (pseud.)　A letter from Darby Tracy, Chairman, in London, to Mr. Denis Feagan, breeches-maker, at Edenderry, wherein is clearly proved the effects which an Union with Great Britain, will have on the interests and happiness of the common people of Ireland.
16 pp. Dublin, printed by Folds. 1799

A., K., N., T.

2176　TROTTER, John Benard.　An investigation of the legality and validity of a union.
42 pp. Dublin, printed by H. Fitzpatrick, 1799

A., L., N.

2177　TUCKER, Josiah.　Union or separation, written some years since by the Rev. Dr. Tucker dean of Gloucester now first published in this tract upon the same subject by the Rev. Dr. Clarke.
88 pp. 2nd ed. London, J. Hatchard and J. Wright, [etc.], 1799

A., N.

2178　Unconnected hints, and loose ideas upon the union, with two propositions. By a mimber [sic].
34 pp. Dublin, Marchbank, 1799

P., T.

2179　An union to be subjection, proved from Mr. C's own words in his arguments for and against. In two parts. Part I. This contains a strong refutation of all the abstract or metaphysical reasoning, and is conclusive in itself. The next part will discuss fully all the arguments, metaphysical and practical. By an Irish logician.
44 pp. Dublin, J. Rice, 1799

L., N., T.

2180 The union. The debate in the house of commons of Great Britain, on the subject of an union with Ireland. To which is added, the king's message, and the proceedings of the lords.
40 pp. Dublin, printed by J. Moore, 1799
A., L.

2181 The vaticination. As you will find it written in the 110th no. of Pue's Occurrences, Redivivus! The fifth year of the incorporation.
14 pp. Dublin, printed by H. Fitzpatrick, 1799
A., N., T.

2182 [VAUGHAN, William.] A comparative statement of the advantages and disadvantages of the docks in Wapping and the docks in the isle of Dogs, with general remarks on the advantages of making the port of London a great depot.
tables. 46 pp. 2nd ed. London, printed by H. L. Galabin, 1799
T.

2183 Verbum sapienti; or a few reasons for thinking that it is imprudent to oppose and difficult to prevent the projected union.
14 pp. Dublin, J. Milliken, 1799
T.

2184 WESTON, Ambrose. A method of increasing the quantity of circulating money: upon a new and solid principle. Letter I. 24 pp. [London, 1799]
Q.

2185 [——.] Two letters, describing a method of increasing the quantity of circulating money: upon a new and solid principle.
64 pp. London, printed by A. Strahan, 1799
Q.
See 3105.

1800

2186 An account of the mode and expense of cultivating moss and peat lands, copied from The Edinburgh Advertiser, of May 2, 1800.
16 pp. Bristol, printed by Biggs and Cottle, 1800
Q.

2187 An account of the proceedings of the acting governors of the house of industry (in Dublin) annexed to their petition to the Hon. the House of Commons of Ireland.
tables. appendix. 38 pp. Dublin, printed by Corbet, [1800?]
A.

2188 An account of the proceedings of the merchants, manufacturers and others, concerned in the wool and woollen trade of Great Britain, in their application to parliament, that the laws respecting the exportation of wool might not be altered, in arranging the Union with Ireland, but left to the wisdom of the Imperial Parliament, if such a measure should hereafter appear to be just and expedient.
326 pp. London, printed by Phillips, 1800
A.

2189 An address to proprietors of Irish estates, residing in Great Britain.
18 pp. n. place, (1800?)
A.

2190 An appeal to the loyal citizens of Dublin. By a freeman of Dublin.
42 pp. Dublin, printed by John Milliken, 1800
A., N., Q., T.

2191 ASHWORTH, Samuel. A statement of the trial of Mr. S. Ashworth [for Forestalling], at an adjournment of the Quarter Sessions held on Tuesday the twenty-first of Oct., 1800, before the worshipful the recorder and bench of Justices.
16 pp. Dublin, Halpen, 1800
N.

2192 AVONMORE, Barry Yelverton, 1st viscount. The speech of the Right Honourable Barry, Lord Yelverton, chief baron of his majesty's court of exchequer, in the House of Lords of Ireland, on Saturday, March 22, 1800; in the debate on the fourth article of a legislative union between Great Britain & Ireland. Published by authority.
40 pp. Dublin, printed by J. Milliken, 1800
A., N., Q., T.

2193 BARLOW, Joel. Joel Barlow to his fellow citizens of the United States of America. A Letter on the system of policy hitherto pursued by their government. Paris, 4 March, 1799.
28 pp. Philadelphia, re-printed at the Aurora office, 1800
A.

2194 ——. Joel Barlow to his fellow citizens of the United States. Letter II. On certain political measures proposed to their consideration.
72 pp. Philadelphia, 1800
A.

2195 BEEKE, Henry. Observations on the produce of the income tax and on its proportion to the whole income of Great Britain. A new and corrected edition, with considerable additions respecting the extent, commerce, population, division of income, and capital of this kingdom.
190 pp. London, J. Wright, 1800
Q.

2196 BERESFORD, John. Speech of the Right Honourable John Beresford, on his moving the sixth article of the union in the house of commons of Ireland, March 27th, 1800.
42 pp. Dublin, J. Milliken, 1800
A., P., Q., T.

2197 [BOUSTEAD, ——?] A letter from Rusticus to a young member of the Irish house of commons.
24 pp. Cork, printed by J. Haly, 1800
K., T.

2198 BRAND, John. A determination of the average depression of the price of wheat in war, below that of the preceding peace; and of its relevance in the following; according to its yearly rates from the revolution to the end of the last peace: with remarks on their greater variations in that entire period.
tables. 100 pp. London, F. and C. Rivington, 1800
Q.

2199 BROWNE, Arthur. Remarks on the terms of the union.
24 pp. Dublin, 1800
A., G., N.

2200 BURKE, Edmund. Thoughts and details on scarcity, originally presented to the right hon. William Pitt, in the month of November, 1795.
64 pp. London, F. & C. Rivington, and J. Hatchard, 1800
A., N., Q.

2201 CASTLEREAGH, Robert Stewart, viscount. (T)he speech of the Right Honourable Lord Viscount Castlereagh, upon delivering to the house of commons of Ireland his excellency the lord lieutenant's message on the subject of an incorporating union with Great Britain, with the resolutions; containing the terms on which it is proposed to carry that measure into effect. February 5, 1800.
56 pp. Dublin, printed by J. Rea, 1800
A., N., Q., T.

2202 The cause of the present threatened famine traced to its real source, viz. an actual depreciation on our circulating medium, occasioned by the paper currency, with which the war, the shock given to public credit in 1794, the stoppage of the bank in 1797, and the bankruptcies of Hamburgh in 1799, inundated the country, to accommodate government and enable the merchants to keep up the price of their merchandize. Shewing, by an arithmetical calculation, founded on facts, the extent, nay, the very mode of the progress, which the paper system has made in reducing the people to paupers. With its only apparent practicable remedy. By Common Sense, author of the letter which appeared under that signature in the Morning Chronicle of September 27, on this subject.
42 pp. London, R. B. Scott, (etc.), 1800
A., N.
See 2211.

2203 CHAPMAN, William. Report of William Chapman, engineer, on the means of draining the low grounds in the vales of the Derwent and the Hertford, in the North and East Ridings of the county of York.
fold map. 22 pp. Newcastle, printed by E. Walker, 1800
Q.

2204 CLARE, John Fitzgibbon, 1st earl. The speech of the Right Honourable John, Earl of Clare, Lord high chancellor of Ireland, on a motion made by him on Monday, February 10, 1800.
98 pp. Dublin, printed by J. Milliken, 1800
N., Q., T.

——. appendix. 106 pp. 2nd edition. Dublin, printed by J. Milliken, 1800
A., D., N.

——. 106 pp. 7th edition. Dublin, J. Milliken, 1800
T.

2205 CLARKE, Thomas Brooke. Misconceptions of facts, and mistatements of public accounts, by the right hon. John Foster speaker of the Irish house of Commons, proved and corrected according to the official documents and authentic evidence of the Inspector General of Great Britain. In a letter to Wm. Johnson, Esq. member of the Irish parlia-

ment, from the Rev. Dr. Clarke, secretary for the library, & chaplain in ordinary to his royal highness the prince of Wales.
64 pp. Dublin, J. Milliken, 1800
A., K., L., N., P., Q.
See 2063

2206 A compendium of the laws of forestalling, engrossing and regrating. With some observations thereon.
40 pp. Dublin, W. Jones, 1800
A.

2207 Corn trade. An examination of certain commercial principles, in their application to agriculture and the corn trade, as laid down in the fourth book of Mr. Adam Smith's treatise on the wealth of nations. With proposals for revival of the statutes against forestalling, etc.
38 pp. London, John Stockdale, 1800
A.

2208 CORRY, Isaac. Substance of the speech of the Right Honourable Isaac Corry, Chancellor of the Exchequer, delivered in committee on the loan bil[l] on Tuesday the 15th July, 1800, on the petition to parliament of Luke White, Esq. respecting the loan, with the documents referred to in the speech.
78 pp. Dublin, printed by John Rea, 1800
A., N., P., Q., T.

2209 The crisis of the monied and commercial interest.
16 pp. London, J. Ridgway, 1800
A.

2210 Deed of co-partnership, fof [sic] the commercial insurance company, Dublin.
28 pp. Dublin, printed by John Barlow, 1800
A.

2211 The discharge of 37,000,000l. of the national debt, demonstrated to be part of the cause of the rapid dearness of provisions that has taken place within the last ten years; proving on the same compound principle upon which the debt is discharged, the extent of that part, viz. that the first four millions discharged had the pernicious effect of depreciating each annual income of 26l., to the amount of 1l. 14s. 8d. that is, to 24l. 5s. 4d. and so on progressively: with some thoughts on the principles that must be adopted to save the nation from the impending ruin attendant on such a disaster. Being part the second of 'The cause of the threatened famine traced to its real source'. By Common Sense author of the letters which have appeared under that signature in the Morning Chronicle.
60 pp. London, R. B. Scott (etc.), 1800
A., N.
See 2202.

2212 [DOWNSHIRE, Arthur Hill, 2nd marquess?] A proposal for uniting the kingdoms of Great Britain and Ireland.
40 pp. London, J. Hatchard, 1800
A.

2213 DUIGENAN, Patrick. A fair representation of the present political state of Ireland: in a course of strictures on two pamphlets, one entitled 'The case of Ireland re-considered'; the other entitled 'Considerations on the state of public affairs in the year 1799,—Ireland' with observations

on other modern publications on the subject of an incorporating union of Great Britain and Ireland, particularly on a pamphlet entitled 'The speech of Lord Minto in the house of peers, April 11, 1799'.
260 pp. Dublin, J. Milliken, 1800

A., B., D., L., N., T.

——. 'Genuine edition, corrected by the author.' 258 pp. Dublin, J. Milliken, 1800

A., L., M.

See 2079.

2214 ——. The speech of Patrick Duigenan, Esq., L.L.D. in the house of commons of Ireland, February 5, 1800, on his excellency the lord lieutenant's message on the subject of an incorporating union with Great Britain. Earnestly recommended to the serious consideration of the loyal citizens of Dublin.
30 pp. Dublin, J. Milliken, 1800

A., L., N., T.

2215 The economy of an institution, established in Spitalfields, London. For the purpose of supplying the poor with a good meat soup, at one penny per quart. Principally extracted from the papers of the society, and published with a view to the establishment of similar institutions, in towns, villages, and populous neighbourhoods. To which is added an account of the soup establishment at Westminster.
fold. diag. 24 pp. Dublin, printed by W. Watson, 1800

A.

2216 EDEN, Sir Frederick Morton, bart. An estimate of the number of inhabitants in Great Britain and Ireland.
98 pp. London, J. Wright, 1800

A., P., Q., T.

2217 EDWARDS, George. Effectual means of providing, according to the exigencies of the evil, against the distress apprehended from the scarcity and high prices of different articles of food.
44 pp. London, J. Johnson, 1800

A.

2218 The evidence of Messrs. Joshua Pim; John Orr; Thomas Abbot, Jacob Geoghegan; Leland Crosthwaite; Denis Thomas O'Brien; Harry Sadleir; John Duffy; Francis Kirkpatrick; John Anderson; Nicolas Grimshaw, James Dickey; John Houston; Daniel Dickinson; Thomas Blair; George Binns; John Locker; James Williams, and Thomas Kenny, as delivered before the committee of the whole house, on his excellency the Lord Lieutenant's message, respecting a legislative union with Great Britain.
28 pp. Cork, James Haly, 1800

B., N.

2219 An exposition of the principal terms of Union, and its probable effects on Ireland.
tables. 26 pp. Dublin, printed by J. Milliken, 1800

A., N.

2220 FARNBOROUGH, Charles Long, baron. A temperate discussion of the causes which have led to the present high price of bread. Addressed to the plain sense of the people.
46 pp. London, T. Wright, 1800

Q.

2221 FARNHAM, Barry Maxwell, 1st earl of. An examination into the principles contained in a pamphlet, entitled the speech of Lord Minto, with some remarks upon a pamphlet, entitled observations on that part of the Speaker's speech which refers to trade.
tables. 64 pp. Dublin, J. Moore, 1800

A., K., N., T.

2222 FEAGAN, Murtagh (pseud.) A letter from Murtagh Feagan, cousin german to Denis Feagan, of Edenderry: in answer to Darby Tracy of London, Chairman. Showing (nothing but truth).
8 pp. Dublin, printed by J. Stockdale, 1800

A., T.

2223 The first number of the reports of the society for promoting the comforts of the poor. Vol. 1.
134 pp. Dublin, William Watson, 1800

A., N.

2224 First part of the report of the sub-committee of the society for promoting the comforts of the poor, on the charitable institutions of Dublin.
26 pp. Dublin, W. Watson, 1800

A., N., T.

2225 FOSTER, John. Speech etc. [MS note 'Rt. Hon. John Foster, answer to Lord Castlereagh, 5th Feb. 1800'].
38 pp. Dublin, 1800

A.

2226 ——. Speech of the Right Honorable John Foster, speaker of the house of commons of Ireland, delivered in committee, on Monday the 17th day of February, 1800.
fold. table. 50 pp. Dublin, James Moore, 1800

A., L., N., T.

2227 ——. Speech of the Right Honorable John Foster, speaker of the house of commons of Ireland, delivered in committee, on Wednesday the 19th March, 1800.
40 pp. Dublin, J. Moore, 1800

L., N.

2228 GENTZ, Friedrich von. Essai sur l'état actuel de l'administration des finances et de la richesse nationale de la Grande Bretagne.
tables. 256 pp. London, Debrett, Hamburg, Perthes, 1800

T.

2229 GLENBERVIE, Sylvester Douglas, baron. Speech in the House of Commons, April 23rd, 1799, relative to a union with Ireland.
table of contents. 182 pp. 2d. ed. London, Wright, 1800

A.

2230 GRATTAN, Henry. An answer to a pamphlet entitled, the speech of the Earl of Clare, on the subject of a legislative union, between Great Britain and Ireland.
48 pp. 2nd edition. Dublin, J. Moore, 1800

A., D., N., Q., T.

——. 48 pp. 3rd ed. Dublin, J. Moore, 1800

N., T.

——. 56 pp. 4th ed. Dublin, J. Moore, 1800

T.

——. 48 pp. 5th ed. Dublin and London, G. G. & J. Robinson, 1800

A., B., D., N., Q., T.

2231 ——. The speech (at length) of the Honourable Henry Grattan, in the Irish house of commons, against the union with Great Britain.
36 pp. London, J. S. Jordan, 1800

A.

2232 ——. The speech of Henry Grattan, Esq., on the subject of a legislative union with Great Britain. The resolutions of the Roman catholics of the city of Dublin; the guild of merchants; the freeman and freeholders of the city of Dublin, at an aggregate meeting held on the 16th of January last; the celebrated speech delivered on that occasion by John Philpot Curran, Esq., and the resolutions of the county of Dublin, etc. etc.
34 pp. Dublin, printed by J. Stockdale, 1800

A., N.

2233 GRAY, John. Practical observations on the proposed treaty of union of the legislatures of Great Britain & Ireland; showing, in some particulars, how that treaty may be rendered acceptable to the people of Ireland, and beneficial to the British Empire in general.
108 pp. London, Bennet, [etc.], 1800

A.

2234 A hint to the inhabitants of Ireland by a native.
tables. 62 pp. Dublin, 1800

A., N., T.

2235 HULL, John Simpson. Remarks on the United States of America; drawn up from his own observations, and from the observations of other travellers.
70 pp. Dublin, printed by William McKenzie, [c. 1800.]

A.

2236 Irish independence or the policy of union.
88 pp. Dublin, printed by J. Milliken, 1800

K., P., T.

2237 JOHNSON, William. Reasons for adopting an union, between Ireland and Great Britain. With a preface now first published.
90 pp. 6th ed. Dublin, J. Milliken, 1800

L.

2238 [LATTIN, Patrick.] The case of Ireland re-considered, in answer to a pamphlet entitled 'Arguments for and against an union, considered'.
72 pp. London, printed by J. Stockdale, 1800

L., T.

See 2110.

2239 ——. Observations on Dr. Duigenan's fair representation of the present political state of Ireland; particularly, with respect to his strictures on a pamphlet, entitled the case of Ireland reconsidered.
132 pp. London, J. Debrett, 1800

A., T.

2240 LEADER, Nicholas Philpot. An address to the merchants, manufacturers and landed proprietors of Ireland in which the influence of an Union on their respective pursuits is examined, and in which the real reciprocal interests of Great Britain and Ireland are candidly and impartially discussed.
102 pp. Dublin, James Moore, 1800

M.

——. 102 pp. 2nd ed. Dublin, James Moore, 1800

P.

——. 102 pp. 3rd ed. Dublin, James Moore, 1800

A., K., N., T.

2241 A letter from Major Pitt, of the Dorset regiment to the society for promoting the comforts of the poor, established at Carrick-on-Suir, in the county of Tipperary.
14 pp. Dublin, William Watson, 1800

A.

2242 A letter to the farmers and traders of Ireland, on the subject of union. By a farmer and trader. May 1st, 1800.
18 pp. Dublin, the author, 1800

A., N.

2243 A letter to the Honourable Thomas Erskine, on the subject of forestalling hops; including a plan for the reduction of the price of corn, porter, etc. with an exposition of the fraudulent practices of the planters. Earnestly recommended to the consideration of Sam. Ferrand Waddington, Esq.
18 pp. London, Macpherson, 1800

T.

2244 [MACARTNEY, Sir George?] Facts and arguments respecting the great utility of an extensive plan of inland navigation in Ireland. With an appendix, containing the report of William Jessop, Esq., civil engineer, respecting the practicability, and expence of making an artificial harbour, for large vessels, in the bay of Dublin. By a friend to national industry.
78 pp. Dublin, printed by William Porter, 1800

A.

2245 [MALTHUS, Thomas Robert.] An investigation of the causes of the present high price of provisions. By the author of the essay on the principle of population.
28 pp. London, J. Johnson, 1800

P.

2246 MARTIN, Richard. The speech of Richard Martin, Esq., in the house of commons on the 21st day of May, 1800. On the motion that leave be given to bring in the union bill.
64 pp. Dublin, B. Dornin, 1800

A., N.

2247 MOORE, George. Observations on the union, orange associations and other subjects of domestic policy; with reflections on the late events on the continent. A new edition, to which is added an appendix, suggested by the late debates in the Irish Parliament, and the resolutions of certain public bodies of the city of Dublin.
104 pp. Dublin printed, and London, J. Debrett, 1800

T.

2248 MORRIS, Edward. A short enquiry into the nature of monopoly and forestalling.
58 pp. 3rd ed. London, T. A. Adell [sic] Jun. & W. Davies, 1800

Q.

2249 The ninth and tenth reports of the society for bettering the condition and increasing the comforts of the poor.
104 pp. London & Dublin, W. Watson, 1800
A.

2250 Observations on a pamphlet entitled, the speech of the Right Hon. John Beresford, on his moving the sixth article of the union. By a friend of the speaker's.
34 pp. Dublin, J. Moore, 1800
A., N.

2251 Observations on the commercial principles of the projected union; or, a free examination of the sixth resolution; being the only one that touches upon commerce, and carrying a direct commission to appropriate Ireland, and for ever, as a consuming colony to the British manufacturer.
68 pp. London, R. Pitkeathley, 1800
L., N., T.

2252 O'NEILL, H. A fair and honest statement of the several humane institutions established within these last twenty-five years 'for the comfort and relief of the poor of Chapelizod parish, Phoenix Park, and environs', addressed to the inhabitants thereof, by their affectionate friend and parish curate, H. O'Neill.
12 pp. Dublin 1800
T.

2253 Patriotic competition against self-interested combination, recommended; by a union between the nobility, the landed, and independent, interest, the clergy, and consumer; with a view of reducing commodities from their money, or market, price, to their real, or labour, price.
40 pp. London, James Ridgway, 1800
A., T.

2254 PATTERSON, William. An analytical view of a popular work, on a new plan, entitled fountains at home, for the poor as well as the rich; with an appendix, containing a short address to the colleges of physicians and surgeons at Dublin.
64 pp. Dublin, W. Watson, 1800
A.

2255 PERCY, William. Irish salvation promulged; or, the effects of an union with Great Britain, candidly investigated: in an evenings conversation between a farmer and schoolmaster.
24 pp. Belfast, printed by J. Smyth, 1800
A., N.

2256 Premiums offered by the Dublin society, for agriculture, planting, and fine arts. 1800.
32 pp. (Dublin), printed by W. Sleater, 1800
A., N., Q.

2257 Pro and con; being an impartial abstract of the principal publications on the subject of a legislative union, between Great Britain and Ireland, in which the arguments for and against that measure, by the following writers are fairly contrasted; Earl of Clare, Lord Auckland, Lord Minto [and others]. By a searcher after truth.
table of contents, 98 pp. Dublin, Marchbank, 1800
A., N., T.

2258 Protestant ascendancy and catholic emancipation reconciled by a legislative union; with a view of the trans-actions in 1782, relative to the independence of the Irish parliament, and the present political state of Ireland, as dependent on the crown, and connected with the parliament of Great Britain.
With an appendix. 56 pp. London, J. Wright, 1800
A., N.

2259 [REDFOORD, Archibald.] Union necessary to security. Addressed to the loyal inhabitants of Ireland. By an independent observer.
106 pp. Dublin, J. Archer, 1800
A., N., P., T.

2260 Refutation of Dr. Duigenan's appendix; or an attempt to ascertain the extent, population, and wealth, of Ireland, and the relative numbers, as well as property of its protestant and Roman catholic inhabitants.
80 pp. London, J. Stockdale, 1800
A.

2261 A reply to the speech of the speaker, as stated to have been delivered on the 17th of February, 1800.
tables. 66 pp. Dublin, printed by John Rea, 1800
A., L., N., T.

2262 Report from the committee appointed to enquire into the state of the copper mines, and copper trade of this kingdom.
98 pp. London, printed by G. Woodfall, 1800
A.

2263 Report of the debate in the house of commons of Ireland, on Friday the 14th of February, 1800, on the subject of a legislative union with Great Britain and the reply of Henry Grattan, Esq., also the petitions from the County of Carlow, county of the town of Carrickfergus [etc.].
86 pp. Dublin, printed by J. Stockdale, 1800
B.

2264 A report of the debate in the house of commons of Ireland on Wednesday and Thursday, the 5th and 6th of February 1800 on the King's message recommending a legislative union with Great Britain.
96 pp. Dublin, Milliken and Rice, 1800
T.

2265 A report of the debate in the house of commons of Ireland, on Wednesday and Thursday the 15th and 16th of January, 1800. On an amendment to the address moved by Sir Laurence Parsons, Bart. on the subject of an union.
142 pp. Dublin, James Moore, 1800
A., Q.

2266 The reports of the society for bettering the condition and increasing the comforts of the poor. Vol. II.
376 pp. London, J. Hatchard, (etc., etc.), 1800
A.

2267 A review of Mr. Grattan's answer to the earl of Clare's speech. Part the first. In which the merits of the constitution of 1782 and its aptness to the circumstances of Ireland are investigated.
36 pp. Dublin, J. Milliken, 1800
A., N., Q., T.

2268 ROGERS, Thomas. Remarks on a road or safe anchorage between Ireland's Eye and Howth, with a plan for an harbour and a canal from thence to Dublin for large ships; also, a short description of Dalkey Sound.
fold. maps. 28 pp. Dublin, printed by Thomas Burnside, 1800
A., N., P.

2269 ROSE, George. A brief examination, into the increase of the revenue, commerce, and manufactures, of Great Britain, from 1792 to 1799.
fold. tabs., 92 pp. 7th ed. Dublin, printed by John Exshaw, 1800
A.

2270 Rules for conducting the education of the female children in the foundling hospital. Drawn up by order of the board of governors, and by them ordered to be printed.
24 pp. Dublin, printed by William Porter, 1800
A.

2271 The rules of the Strangers' Friend society, as established in Dublin, 1790
index. 20 pp. Dublin, printed by Jones [1800]
A., N.

2272 SAURIN, William. An accurate report of the speech of William Saurin, Esq. in the Irish house of commons, on Friday, the 21st of February, 1800, on the question of a legislative union with Great Britain.
24 pp. Dublin, printed by J. Moore, 1800
A., N., Q.

2273 [SHEFFIELD, John Baker-Holroyd, 1st earl of.] Appendix. (I have great pleasure in being permitted to add to these observations, the following satisfactory and interesting proof, that wool, as fine and as valuable as that imported from Spain, may be grown in this island.)
12 pp. n. place, [1800?]
Q.

2274 ——. Observations made on the objections made to the export of wool from Great Britain to Ireland.
72 pp. London, J. Debrett, 1800
A.

2275 ——. Remarks on the deficiency of grain, occasioned by the bad harvest of 1799; on the means of present relief, and of future plenty. With an appendix containing accounts of all corn imported and exported, with the prices from 1697 to the 10th October 1800; and also several other tables.
126 pp. London, J. Debrett, 1800
A., Q.

2276 A short abstract of the evidence given before the committee of the house of commons, appointed in April, 1799, to enquire into the state of the copper mines, and copper trade, of this kingdom. With observations.
66 pp. London, printed by G. Woodfall, 1800
A.

2277 A short enquiry into the causes of the present alarming dearth of coals; in which are suggested, the probable means of reducing the price of that article upwards of thirty per cent. Interspersed with some cursory remarks on the benefits that would accrue from such reduction to the trade and manu-

factures of Ireland, particularly by its relieving the pressing wants of the poor: Respectfully submitted to his excellency the Lord Lieutenant and the right honorable and honorable the members of both houses of parliament. By a friend to national industry.
36 pp. Dublin, John Barlow, 1800
A., N., P., Q.

2278 SINCLAIR, Sir John, bart. Abstract of the proposals for establishing by subscription a new institution to be called the Plough or joint stock farming society, for the purpose of ascertaining the principles of agricultural improvement; submitted to the consideration of the friends to agricultural and other public improvements.
diagrams. 8 pp. London, printed by Bulmer, 1800
A.

2279 SMITH, Sir William Cusac, bart. Animadversions on the speeches of Mr. Saurin & Mr. Bushe, etc. etc.
48 pp. Dublin, Marchbank, 1800
N., Q., T.

2280 Some strictures on the conduct of administration during the session of parliament, that opened under Charles, Marquess Cornwallis, on the 22nd of January and closed on the 1st of June, 1799.
56 pp. Dublin, printed by J. Milliken, 1800
A., L., Q.

2281 The spirit calculator; or, merchant, grocer, distiller, and dealers, daily companion.
24 pp. Dublin, Thomas Wilkinson, [1800?]
A.

2282 The state of his majesty's subjects in Ireland professing the Roman catholic religion. Part II. Containing the refutation of two libels, the one entitled, 'An answer to Henry Grattan,' the other, 'A fair representation', and both published under the false name of Pat. Duigenan, a doctor of the laws.
160 pp. Dublin, printed by H. Fitzpatrick, 1800
A., N.

2283 [SYMMONS, John.] Thoughts on the present prices of provisions, their causes & remedies; addressed to all ranks of people. By an independent gentleman.
88 pp. London, T. Reynolds, 1800
B., T.

2284 Union, prosperity, and aggrandisement.
84 pp. London, West & Hughes, Wright, 1800
A., N.

2285 WALKER, William. A charge delivered to the grand jury of the city of Dublin, upon the subject of forestalling.
16 pp. Dublin, 1800
A.

2286 WALLACE, Thomas. View of the present state of the manufactures of Ireland, in which is considered to what manufactures her natural advantages are best suited; and what are the best means of improving such manufactures.
table of contents. 344 pp. Dublin, printed by Shea, 1800
N.

1801

2287 An account of the proceedings of the governors of the house of industry in Dublin.
fold. diags. 72 pp. Dublin, printed by T. M. Bates, 1801
A., K., L., N., P.

2288 Analytical hints relative to the process of Ackermann, Suardy & Co's. Establishments for waterproof clothes and wearing apparel, at Belgrave Place, Chelsea, and at Mill-Hill, Leeds, for cloth in ends and pieces only.
32 pp. London, printed by Spragg, [1801 ?]
A.
See 2333.

2289 ANDERSON, James. A calm investigation of the circumstances that have led to the present scarcity of grain in Britain: suggesting the means of alleviating that evil, and of preventing the recurrence of such a calamity in future. (Written December 1800.)
98 pp. 2nd ed. London, John Cumming, 1801
Q.

2290 The annual report of the Strangers' friend society, as established in Dublin in 1790
20 pp. Dublin, printed by Jones, 1801
A.

2291 BARCLAY, David. An account of the emancipation of the slaves of Unity Valley Pen in Jamaica.
tables. 20 pp. London, printed by Phillips, 1801
N., T.

2292 BARING, Sir Francis. Observations on the publications of Walter Boyd M.P.
32 pp. London, J. Sewell, etc., 1801
N.

2293 BOND, Sir Thomas, bart. The sure road to prosperity; or the way to obtain wealth and increase it: demonstrated by arguments which cannot be controverted; and proved by a system of accounts as necessary for private gentlemen as for merchants and traders.
32 pp. Dublin, sold by the author, 1801
A.

2294 [BOSWELL, George.] A treatise on watering meadows: wherein are shewn some of the many advantages arising from that mode of practice, particularly on coarse boggy or barren lands; and the method of performing the work. Also remarks on a late pamphlet upon that subject. Illustrated with five copper-plates.
diags. 150 pp. 4th ed. London, J. Debrett, 1801
P.
[First published 1779.]

2295 BOYD, Walter. A letter to the right honourable William Pitt on the influence of the stoppage of issues in specie at the Bank of England, on the prices of provisions and other commodities.
2nd ed., with additional notes, and a preface, containing remarks on the publication of Sir Francis Baring. 192 pp. London, J. Wright, [etc.] 1801
N.

10

2296 BUTLER, Charles. A Letter to a nobleman on the proposed repeal of the penal laws which now remain in force against the Irish Roman catholics.
12 pp. London, Coghlan, (etc.), 1801
A., N.

——. 16 pp. 2nd ed. Dublin, printed by John Shea, 1801
A.

2297 DALRYMPLE, William. A treatise on the culture of wheat, with an appendix; containing an account of the growth of beans with wheat, and a plan of improved seed harrows. By William Dalrymple, Esq. Dedicated to his royal highness the Duke of Clarence.
fold. diag. 84 pp. 2nd ed. London, T. Becket, 1801
Q.

2298 DODD, James Solas. The traveller's director through Ireland; being a topographical description not only of all the roads but of the several cities, towns, villages, parishes, cathedrals, churches, abbeys, castles, rivers, lakes, mountains, harbours, and the seats of noblemen and gentlemen on these roads; their antiquities and present state respecting parliamentary representation, patronage, trade, manufacturers, commerce, markets, fairs, distances from each other, and natural curiosities; with an account of their foundations, vicissitudes, battles, sieges, and other remarkable events that have occurred at them in so much, that his work comprehends in itself, an accurate Irish itinerary, an extensive Irish gazetteer, and Irish chornological remebracer [sic] an epitome of the ecclesiastical, civil, military and natural history of Ireland, from the earliest accounts to the present year, and every information necessary for the resident, or stranger.
maps. 232 pp. Dublin, printed by J. Stockdale, 1801
A.

2299 EDEN, Sir Frederick Morton, bart. Observations on friendly societies, for the maintenance of the industrious classes, during sickness, infirmity, old age and other exigencies.
32 pp. London, J. White and J. Wright, 1801
Q.

2300 The fifteenth report of the society for bettering the condition and increasing the comforts of the poor.
table of contents. 44 pp. Dublin, reprinted for Wm. Watson, 1801
A.

2301 FULLARTON, William. A letter addressed to the Right Hon. Lord Carrington, president of the board of agriculture.
104 pp. London, printed by J. Debrett, 1801
Q.

2302 GIBNEY, John, and others. A report of John Gibney, M.D.—Mr. John Fay, & Mr. Matthew Codd, who were appointed as a committee by the river Boyne company, to enquire into the advantages expected to derive from a navigation to extend from Dublin to the northern counties of Ireland, and to the south by a communication with the Grand Canal.
fold. map. 24 pp. Drogheda, printed by Charles Evans, 1801
A., N., Q.

2303 GRAVES, Thomas. A sermon preached before his excellency Charles Marquess Cornwallis, lord lieutenant,

president and the members of the association for discountenancing vice, and promoting the practice of virtue and religion in St. Peters Church, on Thursday, 12th June, 1800.
56 pp. Dublin, William Watson and Son, 1801
Q.

2304 [GRIEVE, John.] Report of the Arigna iron works, in Ireland. May 1800.
24 pp. Dublin, printed by J. Jones, 1801
A.

2305 HAMILTON, John. An essay on the subserviency of improved agriculture to the proper feeding of stock, and the mutual support they may derive from each other.
40 pp. Dublin, printed by Samuel Watson, 1801
A., N.

2306 HEADRICK, James. Essay on the various modes of bringing waste lands into a state fit for cultivation, and improving their natural productions. Extracted from the communications to the board of agriculture in England, and approved by that body.
136 pp. Dublin, printed by H. Fitzpatrick, under the patronage of the Dublin Society, 1801
A.

2307 HODGSON, Peter. The Commercial revenue guide for transacting business in the port of Dublin, etc. containing instructions relative to entries, drawbacks, repayments, bounties etc. Sundry extracts and observations from the Revenue laws, countervailing duties, and other tables of duties, drawbacks, bounties, &c. Directions to masters of ships, including the whole substance of the Manifest act.
index. tables. 162 pp. Dublin, printed by Carrick, 1801
A.

2308 HODGSON, Ph. Levi & son. The modern measurer, particularly adapted to timber and building, according to the present standard of the Kingdom of Ireland.
table of contents. tables. 120 pp. 10th ed. with alterations & additions. Dublin, printed by Stewart, 1801
N.

2309 KENNEDY, Henry. A few observations on the nature and effect of fever, to which the poor of Dublin are liable: and on the proposed plan of a receiving house for the accommodation of those labouring under it.
22 pp. Dublin, Gilbert and Hodges, 1801
A., K.

2310 KIRWAN, Richard. Report of the gold mines in the county of Wicklow; with observations thereon.
tables. 30 pp. (paginated 131–158). Dublin, 1801
A.

2311 LAWN, Buxton. The corn trade investigated, and the system of fluctuations exposed: with a proposition most humbly offered for the consideration of the legislature, which will effectually remedy the alarming fluctuating prices of bread corn. And an investigation of the import and export laws: with some remarks on the landed interest and agriculture of this kingdom; clearly justifying the farmers; vindicating the dealers and merchants, and affixing the stigma on the proper objects.
120 pp. 'New ed.' Salisbury, J. Easton, 1801
P.

2312 [McARTHUR, John.] Financial facts of the eighteenth century; or, a cursory view, with comparative statements, of the revenue, expenditure, debts, manufactures, and commerce of Great Britain.
tables. 92 pp. London, J. Wright, 1801
Q.

2313 MALHAM, John. An historical view of the unavoidable causes of the non-residence of the parochial clergy on their respective livings; wherein more than one hundred acts of parliament are referred to, and many of them amply discussed, during an interval of near six hundred years: with a particular investigation of the act, 21 Henry 8, cap. 13, on the subjects of residence, farming, etc., and remedies proposed for improving the condition of the clergy.
100 pp. Salisbury, J. Easton & others, 1801
Q.

2314 MORGAN, William. A comparative view of the public finances, from the beginning to the close of the late administration.
80 pp. London, J. Debrett, 1801
Q.

2315 Observations on the commerce of Great Britain with the Russian and Ottoman empires and on the projects of Russia against the Ottoman and British dominions.
tables. 66 pp. London, J. Debrett, 1801
P.

2316 PAGE, Sir Thomas Hyde. Reports relative to Dublin harbour and adjacent coast, made in consequence of orders from the Marquess Cornwallis, lord lieutenant of Ireland, in the year 1800.
56 pp. Dublin, 1801
A., N., P., T.

2317 PALMER, James Bardin. Mr. Palmer's address (on his debts).
40 pp. Dublin, 1801
A.

2318 Plan of St. Georges dispensary for administering advice and medicines to the poor, at the dispensary, Upper Dorset-Street, or, their own habitations, instituted 1801.
20 pp. Dublin, printed by William Sleater, 1801
A.

2319 PLAYFAIR, William. A statement of facts in opposition to loose reports: showing the cause of the failure of the original security bank; contained in a letter to a friend. To which is prefixed a short letter to Richard Brinsley Sheridan, Esq., with explanatory notes.
52 pp. London, printed by James Bateson, 1801
A.

2320 PRUSHAW, Thomas, and MOYALLON, S. M. A compendium of book-keeping. Designed for the use of those who wish to acquire the knowledge of that art, without much loss of time & at a small expense.
58 pp. Dublin, the authors, 1801
L.

2321 Remarks on Mr. Morgan's comparative view of the public finances, from the beginning to the close of the late administration.
82 pp. London, J. Wright, 1801
A.

2322 Remarks on the situation of the poor in the metropolis, as contributing to the progress of contagious diseases: with a plan for the institution of houses of recovery, for persons infected by fever. Published by the desire, and at the expence of the society for bettering the condition of the poor.
36 pp. London and Dublin, William Watson, 1801
A., N.

2323 Report of the proceedings of the general committee of the society in Cork for bettering the condition and increasing the comforts of the poor in the year 1801.
appendix. 26 pp. Dublin, Watson, 1802
A.

2324 ROSBOROUGH, Samuel. Observations on the state of the poor of the metropolis: humbly suggesting a general system of practical charity; for the alleviation of misery, encouragement of industry, and the repression of mendicancy.
42 pp. Dublin, the author, 1801
A.

2325 SHEFFIELD, John Baker Holroyd, 1st earl. Part III. of remarks on the deficiency of grain; on the means of present relief and of future plenty.
128 pp. London, J. Debrett, 1801
A., Q.
Paginated 121 to 246.

2326 Some account of the origin and plan of an association, formed for the establishment of a house of recovery, or fever hospital, in the city of Dublin, with extracts shewing the necessity and utility of such an institution.
32 pp. Dublin, printed by T. M. Bates, 1801
A.

2327 A summary view of the principal measures relating to Ireland, which were discussed in the late session of parliament. With a table and index of statutes, passed in the first session of the United Kingdom of Great Britain and Ireland, 41 G. 3 A.D. 1801.
tables. 56 pp. London, printed by Luke Hansard, 1801
A., Q.

2328 Third number of the reports of the society for promoting the comforts of the poor.
164 pp. Dublin, Wm. Watson, 1801
A., N.

2329 A treatise on the culture of potatoes. Shewing, the best means of obtaining productive crops, a matter of national importance. By a practical farmer.
52 pp. Launceston, W. Bray, 1801
T.

2330 A treatise on the culture of potatoes, showing the best means of obtaining productive crops, a matter of national importance. By a practical English farmer. With notes by an eminent experimental farmer and land-holder of the county of Dublin. To which are added three letters of Thomas King,

Esq., of Kingston, in the County of Wicklow. To Samuel Hayes, Esq., of Avondale on the culture of potatoes.
table of contents. appendix. 76 pp. Dublin, printed by Shea, 1801
A.

2331 WAKEFIELD, Daniel. An investigation of Mr. Morgan's comparative view of the public finances, from the beginning to the close of the late administration.
72 pp. London, F. & C. Rivington, 1801
Q.

1802

2332 An address to the people of Ireland, with a brief report of parliamentary proceedings on Irish affairs: containing a summary view of the principal measures discussed, and an abstract and index of all the statutes passed, for that part of the United Kingdom, in the second session of the first united parliament, 42 Geo. III, 1802.
98 pp. London, T. Cadell, Jun. and W. Davies, 1802
A.

2333 Analytical hints relative to the process of Ackermann, Suardy and Cos. Waterproof cloths, for wearing apparel, as now established by the Irish Company; under the immediate patronage of His Majesty, the Royal Family, and His Excellency the Earl of Hardwicke.
16 pp. Dublin, T. McDonnel, 1802
Q., T.
See 2288.

2334 An appeal to experience and common sense, by a comparison of the present with former periods.
52 pp. London, J. Hatchard, 1802
A.

2335 [ATKINSON, Jasper.] Considerations on the propriety of the bank of England resuming its payments in specie at the period prescribed by the act 37th, George III.
112 pp. London, J. Hatchard and J. Sewell, 1802
A., N., Q.

2336 Bank notes. A concise statement of the nature and consequences of the restriction of paying in specie at the Bank of England: addressed to the public in general; and respectfully recommended in particular to the serious attention of the members of the New Parliament. By a merchant.
28 pp. London, Jordan, 1802
A.

2337 BARNES, George. A defence of the parliamentary institution of Ireland. Being a brief historical sketch of the acts of parliament from the year 1753.
32 pp. Dublin, printed by H. Fitzpatrick, 1802
A., N.

2338 [BOASE, Henry.] Guineas an unnecessary and expensive incumbrance on commerce; or, the impolicy of repealing the bank restriction bill considered.
124 pp. London, G. & W. Nicol, (etc.), 1802
A.

2339 CAMPBELL, Peter. Essay upon the practice of canaling.
28 pp. Dublin, printed by Graisberry and Campbell, 1802
A., K., N.

2340 CLARKE, Thomas Brooke. The case of Ireland, setting forth various difficulties experienced in its commercial intercourse with Great Britain since the Union, in a letter to the Rt. Hon. Henry Addington, Chancellor of the Exchequer &c, &c.
42 pp. London, Cadell & Davies, 1802
A., N., Q., T.

2341 Considerations on the probable commerce and revenue, that may arise on the proposed canal, between Newcastle and Maryport. Published in 1796; now reprinted, with a preface shewing the great national utility of the proposed canal.
30 pp. Newcastle, printed by Edward Walker, 1802
Q.
[MS. attribution to William Chapman in Kress Library copy.]

2342 Cox, Walter. Advice to emigrants, or observations made during a nine months residence in the middle states of the American union.
36 pp. Dublin, printed for the author, 1802
A., N.

2343 Directions to the inspectors of flax-seed and hemp-seed. Printed by order of the trustees of the linen and hempen-manufactures of Ireland.
18 pp. Dublin, B. and J. Williamson, [1802]
T.

2344 DUDLEY, Sir Henry Bate. A few observations respecting the present state of the poor; and the defects of the poor laws: with some remarks upon parochial assessments, and expenditures.
fold. table. 42 pp. London, T. Cadell, Jun., and W. Davies, 1802
Q.

2345 EDEN, Sir Frederick Morton, bart. Eight letters on the peace; and on the commerce and manufactures of Great Britain and Ireland.
tables. 110 pp. 2nd ed. London, J. White, and J. Stockdale, 1802
P., Q., T.

——. Another issue. 138 pp. London, J. Wright, 1802
A.

2346 An English country gentleman's address to the Irish members of the imperial parliament, on the subject of the slave trade.
104 pp. London, J. Hatchard, 1802
Q.

2347 A few brief hints on the subject of tithes. Addressed to the Kentish farmers. By No Bigot.
26 pp. Maidstone, J. Blake, 1802
T.

2348 Fifth number of the reports of the society for promoting the comforts of the poor.
table of contents. appendix. 74 pp (paginated 93–160) Dublin, Watson, 1802
A

2349 Fourth number of the reports of the society for promoting the comforts of the poor.
table of contents. appendix. 42 pp. (paginated 53–92). Dublin, Watson, 1802
A., N., T.

2350 FRANKLIN, Benjamin. The way to wealth, and how to use it.
28 pp. Dublin, printed by Jones, 1802
A.

2351 FRASER, Robert. Gleanings in Ireland; particularly respecting its agriculture, mines, and fisheries.
table of contents. appendices. 94 pp. London, G. & W. Nicol, 1802
A., D., L., N., Q.

2352 HARDY, Joseph. An essay on drill husbandry, by Lt. Col. Hardy, of Westmead, Carmarthenshire, giving an account of the mode of culture, practised by Mr. Ducket, of Esher.
fold. diags. 48 pp. n. place, 1802
N., P., Q.

2353 HINCKS, Thomas Dix. A short account of the different charitable institutions of the City of Cork, with remarks.
appendix. 62 pp. Cork, printed by J. Haly, 1802
A., N.

2354 Impartial thoughts on the intended bridges over the Menai and the Conway, with remarks on the different plans which are now in contemplation for improving the communication between Great Britain and Ireland through the principality of Wales: to which are prefixed, sketches of the bridges and a map of the roads. By a country gentleman.
76 pp. London, John Stockdale, 1802
Q.

2355 IRVINE, Alexander. An inquiry into the causes and effects of emigration from the highlands and Western Islands of Scotland, with observations on the means to be employed for preventing it.
158 pp. Edinburgh, Hill, London, Longmans, 1802
N.

2356 KIRWAN, Richard. Essay in answer to the following question proposed by the Royal Irish Academy. 'What are the manures most advantageously applied to the various sorts of soils, and what are the causes of their beneficial effect in each particular instance?'
tables. 90 pp. Dublin, printed by Graisberry & Campbell, 1802
D.

2357 LIDWILL, John. The history and memoirs of John Lidwill, eldest son of Thomas Lidwill, Esq. late of Clonmore, in the county of Tipperary: containing an account of his industry, experiments, and success; his travels, observations, and providential escapes; also, his misfortunes, vicissitudes, sufferings, and losses, interspersed with a variety of other occurrences useful and entertaining, from his birth to his present age of near sixty years. Written and selling by himself.
64 pp. Dublin, author, 1802
A., B., K., N.

2358 MAUNSELL, William. An essay on raising potatoes from shoots, by the Rev. Dr. Maunsell: and a letter from alderman Alexander, on potatoes, addressed to the Dublin society.
8 pp. Dublin, printed by Graisberry and Campbell, 1802
A.

2359 Memoire, or, detailed statement of the origin and progress of the Irish union: delivered to the Irish government, by Messrs. Emmett, O'Connor, and McNevin: together with the examinations of these gentlemen before the secret committees of the houses of lords and commons, in the summer of 1798.
102 pp. London, P. Robinson, 1802
A., B., G., L., N.

2360 New agreement, between the members of the Royal exchange insurance company of Dublin, for insuring against fire, and for the purchase and sale of annuities for lives and years, in addition to the insurance of ships, merchandise and lives; and for applying for a Charter of Incorporation in the city of Dublin.
14 pp. Dublin, printed by J. Barron, 1802
A.

2361 POPE, Simeon. Considerations, political, financial, and commercial, relative to the important subject of the public funds. Addressed to the stockholders in general, and more particularly to the holders of omnium.
tables. 36 pp. London, printed by Wilson & Co., 1802
N.

2362 Premiums offered by the Dublin society for agriculture, planting, and fine arts. Also, premiums of the board of agriculture and London society, extending to Ireland.
58 pp. Dublin, printed by Graisberry and Campbell, 1802
A., N.

2363 Report of St. George's dispensary and fever hospital; addressed to his excellency earl of Hardwicke, etc. etc.
36 pp. Dublin, William Watson, 1802
A.

2364 Report of the proceedings of the general committee of the society for bettering the condition and increasing the comfort of the poor in the year 1801.
table. appendix. 28 pp. Cork, A. Edwards, 1802
A., N., P.

2365 The sixteenth report of the society for bettering the condition and increasing the comforts of the poor.
appendix. 113 pp. London & Dublin, William Watson, 1802
T.

2366 The seventeenth report of the society for bettering the condition and increasing the comforts of the poor.
table of contents. appendix. 56 pp. (paginated 163–210). Dublin, William Watson, 1802
A., N.

2367 A short statement of various measures, calculated for the improvement of the county of Caithness, carrying on in the course of the year 1802.
104 pp. Edinburgh, printed by David Willison, 1802
Q.

2368 [SINCLAIR, Sir John, bart.] Hints regarding certain measures calculated to improve an extensive property, more especially applicable to an estate in the northern parts of Scotland.
appendix, tables. 52 pp. London, printed by Bulmer, [1802]
A.

2369 [——.] Sketch of an introduction to the proposed analysis of the statistical account of Scotland. As drawn up for the consideration of a few intelligent friends.
diagrams. 20 pp. London, printed by Bulmer, [1802]
A.

2370 THORNTON, Henry. On the probable effects of the peace, with respect to the commercial interests of Great Britain: being a brief examination of some prevalent opinions.
80 pp. London, J. Hatchard, (etc.), 1802
A.

2371 The utility of country banks considered.
tables. 86 pp. London, J. Hatchard, 1802
A., P.

2372 WADE, Walter. Syllabus of a course of lectures on botany, and its connexion with agriculture, rural economy, and the useful arts. In four parts. 1. Introductory, 2. Theoretical, 3. Practical, 4. Demonstrative, and conclusion.
54 pp. Dublin, printed by Graisberry and Campbell, 1802
A.

2373 WAKEFIELD, Edward. A letter to the land owners and other contributors to the poor's rates in the hundred of Dangye in Essex.
72 pp. London, J. Johnson, 1802
Q.

2374 WALKER, James. Hints to consumers of wine: on the abuses which enhance the price of that article: their nature and remedy.
56 pp. Edinburgh, Peter Hill, (etc.), 1802
A.

1803

2375 Address to the tenants of small farms on the lands of Springfield, County Waterford.
36 pp. Dublin, printed by William Porter, 1803
A.

2376 BARNES, George. The rights of the imperial crown of Ireland asserted and maintained, against Edward Cooke, Esq., reputed author of a pamphlet, entitled, 'Arguments for and against an union, etc.' In a letter to that gentleman.
100 pp. 3rd ed. Dublin, Gilbert, 1803
N., T.

2377 BELLEW, Robert. Hibernica trinoda necessitas. A regulation of tithes, a provision for the catholic clergy, and catholic emancipation. Thoughts on the foregoing heads, together with observations on the opinions of Doctor Patrick Duigenan.
128 pp. London, J. Ginger, 1803
P.

2378 [——?] Hints on the policy of making a national provision for the Roman catholic clergy of Ireland; as a necessary means to the amelioration of the state of the peasantry. Addressed to John Bagwell.
48 pp. London, J. Ginger, Dublin, Archer, 1803
N.

2379 [BOASE, Henry.] Guineas an unnecessary and expensive incumbrance on commerce; or, the impolicy of repealing the bank restriction bill considered. The second edition, To which has been added an appendix, shewing the influence that the restriction bill has upon our foreign exchange and commerce.
146 pp. London, G. & W. Nicol, [etc.], 1803
A.

2380 BOND, Sir Thomas, bart. Hints, tending to increase the wealth, and promote the peace and welfare of the Irish nation.
28 pp. Dublin, the author, 1803
A., D., N.

2381 [BURDON, William.] The question, why do we go to war? temperately discussed, according to the official correspondence.
32 pp. 2nd ed. London, J. Wallis, 1803
A.

2382 Bye-laws made and established by the Barrow navigation company, for the regulation of boats, collection of the tolls, etc. on the navigation. 25th day of April, 1803.
table of contents. 28 pp. Dublin, 1803
A.

2383 Carlow charitable society, instituted for the support of the sick poor of the parish of Carlow, of all religious persuasions; founded the first day of January, in the year of our Lord God, 1803.
8 pp. Dublin, printed by P. Wogan, 1803
A.

2384 Case on the act for the relief of the poor, submitted to the opinion of Mr. Serjeant Snigge.
14 pp. n. place, [1803?]
A.

2385 CLARKE, Thomas Brooke. An historical and political view of the disorganisation of Europe: wherein the laws and characters of nations, and the maritime and commercial system of Great Britain and other states are vindicated against the imputations and revolutionary proposals of M. Talleyrand and M. Hauterive, secretaries of state to the French Republic.
224 pp. London, T. Cadell and W. Davies, 1803
A.

2386 Considerations on the silver currency.
56 pp. n. place, [1803?]
A.

2387 Considerations upon a bill for repealing the code of laws respecting the woollen manufacture of Great Britain: and for dissolving the ancient system of apprenticeship, by the abrogation of laws relating thereto, as far as they respect the clothing trade, in certain countries, mentioned in the said bill.
tables. 58 pp. London, C. Stower, 1803
P.

2388 Considerations upon a bill now before parliament, for repealing (in substance) the whole code of laws respecting the woollen manufacture of Great Britain: and for dissolving the ancient system of apprenticeship, by the abrogation of the laws relating thereto, as far as they respect the clothing trade, in certain counties, mentioned in the said bill.
62 pp. London, C. Stower, 1803
P., Q.

2389 COURTENAY, Thomas Peregrine. Observations upon the present state of the finances of Great Britain; suggested by Mr. Morgan's supplement to his 'comparative view' and by Mr. Addington's financial measures.
tables. appendices. 96 pp. London, J. Budd, 1803
P.

2390 Essays on the population of Ireland, and the characters of the Irish. By a member of the last Irish parliament.
58 pp. London, C. & R. Baldwin, 1803
A., C., P., T.

2391 An exposition of the act for a contribution on property, professions, trades and offices; in which the principles and provisions of the Act are fully considered, with a view to facilitate its execution, both with respect to persons chargeable, as persons liable to the tax by way of deduction, and the officers chosen to carry it into effect. Part the first.
68 pp. London, I. Gold, 1803
T.

2392 FINLAY, Andrew. A view of the interests of Ireland. as connected with Great Britain, or France.
40 pp. Dublin, printed by D. Graisberry, 1803
B., N., T.

2393 FRASER, Robert. A letter to the Rt. Hon. Charles Abbot, speaker of the house of commons, containing an inquiry into the most effectual means of the improvement of the coasts and western isles of Scotland, and the extension of the fisheries. With a letter from Dr. Anderson to the author, on the same subject.
fold. map. 108 pp. London, G. & W. Nicol, 1803
N., Q.

2394 GORDON, James. An address to the people of Ireland.
28 pp. Dublin, printed by John Jones, 1803
A., N., T.

2395 HARRISON, George. An abstract of the Act lately passed for consolidating the former acts for the Redemption of the Land Tax; and for removing doubts respecting the right of persons to vote for the election of members of Parliament; showing the disposition and arrangement of the subject matter of it. With occasional notes explanatory of the object and effect of the new provisions. To which are prefixed a few observations on the nature and extent of the advantages resulting to the public, and to the landed proprietor, from the measure.
tables. 118 pp. 3rd ed. London, I. Gold, 1803
N.

2396 Hints for those who may be desirous of introducing the manufacture of split straw in country towns, villages, schools, workhouses, etc.
8 pp. Dublin, printed by W. Watson, 1803
A.

2397 Howison, William. An investigation into the principles and credit of the circulation of paper money, or bank notes, in Great Britain: as protected or enforced by legislative authority under the suspension of paying them in cash; in the extent of such paper money, the responsibility attached to it, and its effects upon prices of commodities, individual income, agriculture, manufactures, commerce, and upon the course of exchange with foreign countries. Together with a discussion of the question, whether the restraining law in favour of the Bank of England from paying notes in money, ought or ought not to be continued as a measure of state?
76 pp. London, John Stockdale, 1803
A., N., T.

2398 Kemp, John. Extract from an account of the funds, expenditure, and general management of the affairs of the society in Scotland for propagating Christian knowledge: contained in a report, published by order of said society, in 1796. Together with an extract from a sermon, delivered 17 May, 1801, before the corresponding board in London.
tables. 54 pp. Dublin, printed by W. Watson, 1803
T.

2399 King, Peter King, 7th baron. Thoughts on the restriction of payments in specie at the Banks of England and Ireland.
tables. 110 pp. London, Cadell & Davies (etc.), [1803]
A., T.

2400 McArthur, John. Financial & political facts of the eighteenth & present century; with comparative estimates of the revenue, expenditure, debts, manufactures, and commerce of Great Britain. . . . Fourth edition. With an appendix of useful & interesting documents. The whole revised, corrected, & considerably enlarged.
244 pp. London, W. Miller, 1803
A.

2401 The nineteenth report of the society, for bettering the condition and increasing the comforts of the poor.
72 pp. London and Dublin, re-printed for W. Watson, 1803
A.

2402 Observations on an act passed in the last session of parliament, respecting apprentices employed in cotton, and other factories, and the report of a select committee of the society thereon.
24 pp. London and Dublin, re-printed by W. Watson, 1803
A.

2403 Observations on woollen machinery.
24 pp. Leeds, printed by Edward Baines, 1803
A.

2404 Old truths and established facts.
14 pp. n. place, [1803]
A.

Concerns slavery.

2405 Plan of the St. Mary-le-bone General Dispensary, Margaret Street, Cavendish Square, instituted 1785 for the relief of the poor of the parishes of St. Mary-le-bone; St. George, Hanover Square; St. Anne, Soho; St. Martin; St. Pancras; St. Giles; St. George, Bloomsbury; St. James,

Paddington; and places adjacent. Supported by the voluntary contributions of the nobility, gentry and others.
40 pp. London, J. Smeeton, 1803
T.

2406 Rawson, Thomas James. On the culture of potatoes.
16 pp. Dublin, printed by William Porter, 1803
Q.

2407 The reason why. In answer to a pamphlet entitled, 'Why do we go to war?'
66 pp. London, John Stockdale, 1803
A.

2408 The reason why. In answer to a pamphlet entitled, 'Why do we go to war?' to which is affixed, a rejoinder to the reply of the author of 'Why do we go to war?'
114 pp. 2nd ed. London, John Stockdale, 1803
A.

2409 The report of the strangers' friend society, for the year 1803. Instituted in the year 1790.
16 pp. Dublin, printed by J. Jones, 1803
A.

2410 The Royal exchange insurance company of Ireland, for insurance of ships, merchandise & lives; & houses & goods against fire, etc.
14 pp. Dublin, printed by J. Barlow, 1803
A.

2411 Townsend, Horatio. Essay on the agriculture of the county of Cork, by the Rev. Horatio Townsend. To which is added an appendix, containing an analysis of several species of calcareous manures, with some observations thereon, by William Meade, M.D.
illustr. table in appendix. 88 pp. Cork, Edward Henry Morgan, 1803
P.

2412 Westminster society for insurance on lives and survivorships and granting annuities. London, and opposite the commercial buildings in Dame Street, Dublin.
tables. 16 pp. London, printed by T. Collins, 1803
T.

2413 Whately, George N. Hints for the improvement of the Irish fishery.
48 pp. London, J. Hatchard, 1803
Q.

1804

2414 An abstract of the presentments of the grand jury, of the County Meath, at summer assizes, 1804.
70 pp. Dublin, printed by Graisberry and Campbell, 1804
A.

2415 Annual report of the house of recovery of the city of Cork, from Nov. 8th, 1802, to Nov. 8th, 1803.
24 pp., Dublin, W. Watson, 1804
A.

2416 Appendix to the concise statement of the question regarding the abolition of the slave trade.
30 pp. London, J. Hatchard & others, 1804
Q.

2417 An argument as to the exchange between England and Ireland; and a suggestion by which the aberration which has taken place is proposed to be remedied, upon certain principles applicable to the issue of paper currency and of coin.
35 pp. Bath, T. Gibbons, [etc.], 1804
Q.
[The copy in the Seligman collection at Columbia University has mss. attribution to Stephen Edward Rice. Cf. Fetter: *The Irish Pound*, p. 126.]

2418 The bank note, or remarks on the influence paper currency has on society. By an Observer.
24 pp. Dublin, at the head of Abraham Newland [c. 1804]
A.

2419 BELL, Robert. A description of the condition and manners as well as the moral and political character, education, etc. of the peasantry of Ireland, such as they were between the years 1780 and 1790, when Ireland was supposed to have arrived at its highest degree of prosperity and happiness.
48 pp. London, Vernon and Hood and others, 1804
A., N., Q., T.

2420 BOASE, Henry. A letter to the Right Hon. Lord King, in defense of the conduct of the directors of the banks of England and Ireland, whom his lordship (in a publication entitled, 'Thoughts on the restriction of payments in specie', etc. etc.) accuses of abuse of their privilege. With remarks on the cause of the great rise of the exchange between Dublin and London, and the means of equalizing it.
56 pp. London, G. & W. Nicol, 1804
A., N., Q.

2421 A brief state of facts, respecting the proposed improvements to be made in the bay and harbour of Dublin, Addressed to his excellency, Philip, Earl Hardwick, K.G. lord lieutenant general, and general governor of Ireland, etc.
18 pp. Dublin, 1804
A.

2422 [BROUGHAM and VAUX, Henry Peter Brougham, first baron.] A concise statement of the question regarding the abolition of the slave trade.
2nd ed. 78 pp. London, J. Hatchard, 1804
N.

2423 A candid cobler's cursory and critical conjectures on ex-change and small-change, on balance of trade, on balance of remittance, on circulating medium and kite-flying. Interspersed with certain schemes more fair and friendly, than feasible; calculated for those who are more in the habit of hearing than reading.
48 pp. [Dublin?] Hibernian Press, 1804
A., N., Q.

2424 CHAMBERLAINE, William. History of the proceedings of the committee appointed by the general meeting of apothecaries, chemists, and druggists in London for the purpose of obtaining relief from the hardships imposed on the dealers in medicine by certain clauses and provisions contained in the new Medicine Act passed June 3, 1802.
60 pp. London, Highly, 1804
A.

2425 CHETTLE, John. The public taxes of England and Scotland, for the year ending 5th January, 1804; shewing, at one view, what each article produced, expence of management, etc.
16 pp. London, T. Tegg, 1804
Q.

2426 Considerations on the late and present state of Ireland, in refutation of observations and reflections thereon, by Robert Stearne Tighe, Esq. of Mitchelstown, in the Co. Westmeath; and on a letter to the earl of Wycombe, from Mr. Miles, on the present state of Ireland.
56 pp. Dublin, M. N. Mahon, 1804
A., N., Q.

2427 Copy of a paper, printed in the Monthly Magazine, on the manufacture and quality of Cheshire salt, in reply to a paper circulated in America, in the Medical Repository, printed at New York, ascribing the Yellow Fever, etc. to the salt brought from Liverpool.
16 pp. Liverpool, W. Robinson, 1804
Q.

2428 DIXON, John. Improvement of the fisheries; Letter V. on a plan for establishing a nursery for disbanded seamen and soldiers and increasing the strength of the British Empire.
60 pp. London, G. & W. Nicol, 1804
T.

2429 An enquiry into the depreciation of Irish bank paper, its effects and causes, and a remedy proposed.
96 pp. Dublin, M. N. Mahon, 1804
A., N., P., Q., T.

2430 ESTCOURT, Thomas. An account of the result of an effort to better the condition of the poor in a country village: and some regulations suggested, by which the same might be extended to other parishes of a similar description. Presented to the Board of agriculture.
20 pp. London, printed by B. McMillan, 1804
A.

2431 FOSTER, John Leslie. An essay on the principle of commercial exchanges, & more particularly of the exchange between Great Britain & Ireland: with an inquiry into the practical effects of the bank restrictions.
appendix. tables. 224 pp. [pagination irregular] London, J. Hatchard, 1804
A., N., P., T.

2432 FREND, William. The principles of taxation: or contribution according to means; in which it is shewn, that if every man pays in proportion to the stake he has in the country, the present ruinous and oppressive system of taxation, the custom house and the excise office may be abolished, and the national debt gradually and easily paid off.
appendix. 76 pp. London, J. Mawman, 1804
N.

2433 [GILBERT, Davies.] Cursory observations on the act for ascertaining the bounties, and for regulating the exportation and importation of corn. By a member of parliament.
16 pp. London, John Stockdale, 1804
Q.

2434 Grand canal company. At the half-yearly meeting of the company of undertakers of the grand canal, at their house in Dawson Street, 28 Sept. 1804, Richard Griffith, Esq., in the chair: the report of the court of directors having been read, & the same being taken into consideration, Resolved unanimously that the company highly approve of every part of the conduct of the directors, in the transactions relative to the pipe-water, & that their sincere thanks be presented to the directors for the same. Ordered, that so much of the said report, as relates to the subject of pipe-water, be printed for the use of the company, & distributed among the proprietors.
42 pp. Dublin, printed by R. & E. Maturin, 1804
A.

2435 HIBBARD, John. Statements on the great utility of a circular and other inland, etc. canal navigation, and drainage; with the great interest locally arising therefrom, to the improvement of agriculture, cattle, manufacture, commerce, and fisheries, of Britain and Ireland. Also, the present reduction of the prices of grain; and further improvements attending the growth of wheat and use of oats in bread, with the general advantage arising therefrom, to the land-owner, occupier, and the community at large, of the United Kingdom. Shewing, likewise the great revenue that might accrue to government from such without the least expence to state or subject.
64 pp. London, printed by A. Kemmish, 1804
Q.

2436 KING, Peter King, 7th baron. Thoughts on the effects of the bank restrictions. The second edition enlarged, including some remarks on the coinage.
186 pp. London, T. Cadell [etc.], 1804
A., T.

2437 LAUDERDALE, James Maitland, 8th earl of. An inquiry into the nature & origin of public wealth, & into the means & causes of its increase.
490 pp. Edinburgh, Arch. Constable, [etc.], 1804
A.

2438 A letter (on the) bankrupt laws of Ireland, to the lord high chancellor of Ireland. By Philanthropos.
32 pp. n. place, 1804
Q.

2439 MAGENS, Magens Dorrien. An inquiry into the real difference between actual money, consisting of gold and silver, and paper money of various descriptions. Also an examination into the constitution of banks; and the impossibility of their combining the two characters of bank and exchequer.
76 pp. London, J. Asperne and T. Maiden, 1804
A., Q.

2440 MILES, William Augustus. A letter to the earl of Wycombe, &c &c from Mr. Miles, on the present state of Ireland.
88 pp. London, R. Faulder, 1804
A., N., P.

2441 [MILLAR, J.?] Observations on the defects of the port of Dublin, in which the former proposals for remedying them are considered, and new, and comparatively cheap means of permanent improvement are suggested. Addressed to the Rt. Hon. & Hon. the directors of inland navigation. [Signed J.M.]
66 pp. Dublin, printed by Charles Brown, 1804
A., N.

2442 Observations on the exchange between London and Dublin. By a merchant of Dublin.
tables. 14 pp. Dublin, printed by M. N. Mahon, 1804
A., P., Q.

2443 O'CONNOR, Arthur. The present state of Great-Britain.
146 pp. Paris, 1804
A., N.

2444 [O'NEIL, Peter.] Letters to the farmers, tradesmen, shopkeepers, & labourers of Ireland.
62 pp. Dublin, printed by Graisberry & Campbell, 1804
A., N.

2445 PARNELL, Sir Henry Brooke, bart. (later first baron Congleton). An additional appendix to the second edition of the observations on the state of currency in Ireland, & upon the course of exchange between Dublin & London.
table. 38 pp. London and Dublin, re-printed by M. N. Mahon, 1804
A., P.

2446 ——. Observations upon the state of currency in Ireland, and upon the course of exchange between Dublin and London.
66 pp. Dublin, M. N. Mahon, 1804
A., N., P., Q.

——. 72 pp. 2nd ed. Dublin, M. N. Mahon, 1804
A., T.

——. 96 pp. 3rd ed. Dublin, M. N. Mahon, London, J. Johnson, 1804
N.

——. Another issue of 3rd ed. 92 pp. Dublin, M. N. Mahon; London, J. Johnson, 1804
A., N.
[This issue has the Abridgement of the Report of the committee on currency and exchange in Ireland, pp. 81–92, not in all copies.]

2447 [PARNELL, William.] An inquiry into the causes of popular discontents in Ireland. By an Irish country gentleman.
74 pp. London, J. Wallis, 1804
A., B., N.

2448 A pindaric epistle: addressed to the Right Hon. Sir Evan Nepean, Bart, occasioned by his letter to the lord mayor on the subject of bad silver.
20 pp. Dublin, printed by M. N. Mahon, 1804
A.

2449 Remarks addressed to the country, not to parties. By a national observer.
44 pp. London, Debrett and others, 1804
Q.

2450 A series of letters signed landlord and tenant, which appeared in the Chelmsford Chronicle, between December 30, 1803 and April 13, 1804.
tables. appendix. 72 pp. Chelmsford: Meggy, Chalk, 1804
T.

2451 SHEFFIELD, John Barker Holroyd, 1st earl of. Strictures on the necessity of inviolably maintaining the navigation and colonial system of Great Britain.
72 pp. London, J. Debrett, 1804
N., Q.

2452 Sixth number of the report of the society for promoting the comforts of the poor.
60 pp. [Paginated from 161 to 216.] Dublin, William Watson, 1804
A.

2453 [SMITH, Thomas.] The Real causes of the high rate of exchange and the only true remedies.
80 pp. Dublin, printed by D. Graisberry for the author, 1804
A., Q.

2454 [TAAFFE, Denis.] Antidotes to cure the catholicophobia, & lernephobia: efficacious to eradicate the horrors against catholics, Irishmen, early instilled prejudices; & incessant inoculation of calumnies, lately circulated in various forms. Correspondence between two noble lords, etc. etc. etc. Calculated to promote conciliation, peace, & harmony, between all sects & parties, by Julius Vindex.
108 pp. Dublin, the author, 1804
A.

2455 A treatise on practical husbandry, collected from the most approved writers on that subject, and digested into a regular system, wherein the different subjects are distinctly treated and discussed, with directions for the management of stock, &c. &c.
tables. 168 pp. Dublin, Peter Moore, 1804
P.

2456 [VAVASOUR, William?] A letter addressed to his excellency Philip, Earl of Hardwicke, lord lieutenant of Ireland, upon the improvement of the harbour of Dublin.
64 pp. Dublin, William Watson, 1804
A., N.

2457 WAKEFIELD, Daniel. An essay upon political oeconomy; being an inquiry into the truth of the two positions of the French Economists; that labour employed in manufactures is unproductive; and that all taxes ultimately fall upon, or settle in the surplus produce of land.
Second ed. table. appendix. 128 pp. London, F. C. and J. Rivington, 1804
T.

2458 West India dock company. The important trial John & George Cowell versus George Smith, Esquire, treasurer to the said company, upon the question of cooperage on rums. Tried in the Court of King's Bench, Guildhall, before Lord Ellenborough & a special jury, March 7th 1804. In which Mr. Garrow's speech, taken in shorthand, is given verbatim.
28 pp. London, W. J. & J. Richardson, 1804
A.

2459 A word of advice to the trading & monied interests of Ireland, upon the momentous subject of the alarming scarcity of the smaller denominations of silver coin. With some suggestions upon the most feasible mode of regulating the application for a new coinage, so as permanently to secure the people of Ireland from a repetition of this calamity.
28 pp. Dublin, printed by J. Shea, 1804
A.

1805

2460 An address to the land owners, corn growers, maltsters, and malt distillers, of Ireland, upon the subject of the Irish revenue as immediately connected with their own private interests.
tables. 48 pp. Dublin, Holmes and Charles, 1805
T.

2461 BOND, Sir Thomas, bart. Pro bono publico; or, public good considered & promoted.
32 pp. Dublin, the author, 1805
A., P., U.

2462 [BRINKLEY, John.] Considerations on the silver currency relative to both the general evil as affecting the Empire, and the present enormous particular evil in Ireland: With an Appendix containing a report of Sir Isaac Newton on the state of the gold and silver coin in 1717 and also some tables relative to the same subject.
60 pp. Dublin, J. Milliken, 1805
A., Q.

2463 Considerations on the expediency of adopting certain measures for the encouragement and extension of the Newfoundland fishery.
72 pp. London, printed by G. Auld, 1805
Q.

2464 DAVY, Sir Humphry, bart. On the analysis of soils, as connected with their improvement.
20 pp. London, W. Bulmer, 1805
A.

2465 DAWSON, William. Plan for a complete harbour at Howth-town, for the use of His Majesty's mail packet-boats. Merchants ships, in case of storm, and fishing vessels to supply Dublin market: with remarks on all the plans for the improvement of the harbour or Bay of Dublin for the shipping: no plan for either of these purposes having been fully recommended or approved of as likely, if executed to improve either of them: and shewing, that neither the harbour or Bay of Dublin are capable of further improvement for the safety or convenience of the shipping, except a little east of Dunleary Pier, where there should be a good pier.
24 pp. Dublin, R. Gibson, 1805
A., T.

——. enlarged. plan. 30 pp. 2nd ed. Dublin, R. Gibson, 1805
G.

2466 Essay on the present state of manners and education among the lower class of the people of Ireland and the means of improving them.
40 pp. 3rd ed. Dublin, printed by Wm. Watson, 1805
A., N.

2467 GRELLIER, J. J. The terms of all the loans which have been raised for the public service: with observations on the rates of interest paid for the money borrowed. And an account of navy & exchequer bills funded at different periods.
96 pp. 3rd ed. London, W. J. and J. Richardson, 1805
A.

2468 GUEST, Thomas. Report of the Arigna iron-works, in Ireland.
52 pp. Dublin, printed by John Jones, 1805
A.

2469 HAUTENVILLE, H. B. A digest of the duties of Customs & Excise.
table of contents. tables. appendices. 366 pp. 2nd ed. Dublin, printed by John Barlow, 1805
A.

2470 HOPKIN, Evan. An abstract of the particulars contained in a perambulatory survey of above two hundred miles of turnpike-road through the counties of Carmarthen, Brecknock, Monmouth, and Glocester [sic]. Pointing out the most obvious defects, and also the improvements which may be made along this line of road.
16 pp. Swansea, printed by T. Jenkins, 1805
Q.

2471 The horrors of the negro slavery existing in our West Indian islands, irrefragably demonstrated from official documents recently presented to the house of commons.
40 pp. London, J. Hatchard [etc. etc.], 1805
Q.

2472 LANCASTER, Joseph. A letter to John Foster, Esq. Chancellor of the Exchequer for Ireland, on the best means of educating and employing the poor, in that country.
40 pp. London, Darton and Harvey and J. Hatchard, 1805
A., Q., T.

2473 LAUDERDALE, James Maitland, 8th earl of. Hints to the manufacturers of Great Britain, on the consequences of the Irish union; and the system since pursued, of borrowing in England, for the service of Ireland.
52 pp. Edinburgh, Arch. Constable and co., [etc., etc.], 1805
A., N., Q., T.

2474 ——. Thoughts on the alarming state of the circulation, and on the means of redressing the pecuniary grievances in Ireland.
124 pp. Edinburgh, A. Constable, [etc., etc.,] 1805
A., Q., T.

2475 A letter from an Irish member of parliament, upon the report of the select committee of the house of commons, appointed March 2nd, 1804, to take into consideration the circulating paper, the specie, and current coin of Ireland; and also the exchange between that part of the United Kingdom and Great Britain.
52 pp. London, John Stockdale, 1805
A., N., T.

2476 Letter from J... R..., Esq. to his friend in England, on the rise, progress and present state of the corporation for paving and lighting the city of Dublin.
14 pp. Dublin, printed by John Shea, 1805
A., Q.

2477 MILLER, Joseph. The articles of association of the chamber of commerce of the city of Dublin, adopted at a public meeting of merchants, manufacturers and traders at the Royal Exchange, on Tuesday, the 16th day of April, 1805, with an index annexed.
24 pp. Dublin, Graisberry and Campbell, 1805
A., P., Q.

2478 Observations on Lord Castlereagh's speech of the 19th of July 1804, and on the state of the East India Company's affairs.
56 pp. London, J. Budd, 1805
A., Q.

2479 [PARNELL, William.] An enquiry into the causes of popular discontents in Ireland. By an Irish country gentleman. With a preface and notes, by a friend to the constitution.
112 pp. London and Dublin, re-printed by J. Milliken, 1805
A., N., T.

2480 Premiums offered by the Dublin society, for agriculture, planting, and fine arts. Also, premiums of the board of agriculture, extending to Ireland.
26 pp. Dublin, printed by Graisberry and Campbell, 1805
A.

2481 Report of the court of directors of the Grand canal, to the proprietors, at a meeting held on Saturday the 2nd of February, 1805, pursuant to public notice.
24 pp. Dublin, printed by R. and E. Maturin, 1805
A.

2482 Reports of the committee of the house of commons respecting the Caledonian canal. With an introduction containing observations on the importance of that navigation to the commerce of Ireland.
120 pp. Dublin, M. N. Mahon, 1805
A.

2483 ROGERS, Thomas. Observations on the reports laid before the right hon. & hon. the directors general of inland navigation in Ireland, for the improvement of Dublin harbour. This work contains, a correct view of the tides & currents in the bay & harbour, etc. etc. assisted by ten engravings. With the general outlines of a plan for the improvement of the harbour of Dublin, & that at Ireland's Eye.
fold. diags. 94 pp. Dublin, printed by T. Burnside, 1805
A., N., T., S.

2484 Seventh number of the report of the society for promoting the comforts of the poor.
table of contents. tables. 100 pp. Dublin, Watson, 1805
A.

2485 A short account of the ladies society for the education and employment of the female poor.
24 pp. Dublin, William Watson, 1805
A.

2486 Some observations on the subject of the debate in the house of commons, on Indian affairs, on the 5th of April 1805.
24 pp. London, J. Hatchard, 1805
A.

2487 Statement relative to the Parish of St. George's, Dublin. tables. appendices. 16 pp. Dublin, printed by Shea, 1805
A.
[Shows how funds were raised for church building.]

2488 The state of county infirmaries in Ireland considered, & hints thrown out for their improvement. By a governor. 86 pp. Dublin, printed by William McKenzie, 1805
A.

2489 TALLEYRAND-PÉRIGORD, Charles Maurice de, Prince de Bénévent. Memoire sur les relations commerciales des États-Unis avec l'Angleterre. Par le citoyen Talleyrand. Lu à l'institut national, le 15 Germinal, an. V., suivi d'un essai sur les avantages à retirer de colonies nouvelles dans les circonstances présentes, par le même auteur, lu à l'institut, le 15 Messidor, an V.
48 pp. London, W. Spilsbury, 1805
P.

2490 The twenty-fifth report of the society for bettering the condition and increasing the comforts of the poor. 84 pp. London, J. Hatchard [etc, etc.], 1805
Q.

——. Another issue, 56 pp. Dublin, W. Watson, 1805
A.
[Containing a letter from William Wilberforce.]

2491 WHITELAW, James. An essay on the population of Dublin. Being the result of an actual survey taken in 1798, with great care and precision, and arranged in a manner entirely new. To which is added, the general return of the district committee in 1804, with a comparative statement of the two surveys. Also, several observations on the present state of the poorer parts of the city of Dublin. tables. fold. tabs. 72 pp. Dublin, printed by Graisberry and Campbell, 1805
A., N.

2492 [——.] Population tables of the nineteen parishes and two deaneries of the city of Dublin, in the summer of 1798. Shewing what streets, and parts of streets, etc. are comprehended in each parish; with the number of inhabitants, whether male or female; and of houses, whether inhabited or waste.
104 pp. n. place, [1805]
A.

1806

2493 An Abridgment of the report of the commissioners appointed to enquire into the mode of collecting the revenue of Ireland.
table of contents. 42 pp. Dublin, printed by John Boyce, 1806
A., N., Q.

2494 ADAMS, Philip. A letter to the Rt. hon. Lord Erskine, Lord High Chancellor of Gt. Britain, &c concerning the bill now pending in the Imperial parliament for the relief of certain insolvent debtors, with observations upon the decisions of some of the Irish judges.
24 pp. Dublin, printed by J. Shea, 1806
A., P.

2495 ALLEY, Jerome. A vindication of the principles and statements advanced in the strictures of the Right Hon. Lord Sheffield, on the necessity of inviolably maintaining the navigation and colonial system of Great Britain: with tables, and an appendix.
102 pp. London, H. D. Symonds, 1806
Q.

2496 Authentic papers relating to the expediency of importing salted beef, pork, butter, & fish, into the island of Jamaica, either freely from neutral and other states in amity with Great Britain, or exclusively from the British dominions, in British vessels, and by British subjects. Transmitted from Jamaica to the chamber of commerce of Dublin.
40 pp. Dublin, printed by R. E. Mercier, 1806
A.

2497 COLQUHOUN, Patrick. A new and appropriate system of education for the labouring people; elucidated and explained, according to the plan which has been established for the religious and moral instruction of male and female children admitted into the free school, No. 19, Orchard Street, in the city of Westminster; containing an exposition of the nature and importance of the design, as it respects the general interest of the community: With details, explanatory of the particular economy of the institution, and the methods prescribed for the purpose of securing and preserving a greater degree of moral rectitude, as a means of preventing criminal offences by habits of, temperance, industry, subordination, and loyalty, among that useful class of the community comprising the labouring people of England. To which are added, concluding observations on the importance of extending the system generally, under the aid and sanction of the legislature.
94 pp. London, J. Hatchard, 1806
Q.

2498 First report on the object and effects of the house of recovery in Cork-street, by the physicians to that institution. fold. table. 48 pp. Dublin, printed by Charles Downes, 1806
A.

2499 [FOX, Charles James.] The state of the negotiation [between Britain & France] with details of its progress & causes of its termination, in the recall of the earl of Lauderdale. To which is added, a copious supplementary review, & exposition of the direct falsehoods & disingenious suppressions of the French official papers.
112 pp. 5th ed. London, John Stockdale, 1806
A.

2500 General remarks on our commerce with the continent, shewing our commercial and political influence on the states of Russia, Prussia, Sweden and Denmark. To which is added observations on British expeditions to Germany; and on our diplomatique agents abroad, etc. etc. respectfully dedicated to the merchants and manufacturers of Great Britain and Ireland.
54 pp. London, J. Parsons; W. J. and J. Richardson; Ridgway; [1806]
K.

2501 HOPKIN, Evan. An abstract of the particulars contained in a perambulatory survey of the turnpike-road from

Milford to Carmarthen, as directed to be done by the South-Wales association for the improvement of roads, in June, 1806.
10 pp. Swansea, T. Jenkins, 1806
Q.

2502 A key to the papers which have been presented to the house of commons, upon the subject of the charges preferred against the earl of St. Vincent by Mr. Jeffrey, M.P. for Poole.
202 pp. London, 1806
Q.

2503 A letter to the Right Honourable Sir John Newport, Bart. on the embarrassing situation and prospects of the present ministry: with particular reflections on the distressed state of Ireland. By an Irishman.
80 pp. Dublin, printed by John King, 1806
A., N., T.

2504 Observations explanatory & critical on a pamphlet, entitled, an inquiry into the causes of popular discontents in Ireland. By an Irish country gentleman. Serving to elucidate some mysterious passages, & develop the genuine meaning & intention of the author. By another Irish country gentleman.
144 pp. Dublin, 1806
A., K., N.

2505 Observations on the present method of making and repairing of roads, etc. Addressed to Grand Juries and road makers. By an overseer of roads.
18 pp. Armagh, T. Stevenson, 1806
T.

2506 Observations on the proposed tax on pig-iron. By an iron-master.
24 pp. London, printed by I. and I. Walter, 1806
Q.

2507 Peace or war, considered. By a barrister of the honourable society of Lincoln's Inn.
64 pp. London, J. Ridgway, 1806
T.

2508 Plan of the re-printed reports of the board of agriculture. With preliminary observations, by the president of that board.
36 pp. London, B. McMillan, 1806
Q.

2509 The present claims and complaints of America briefly and fairly considered.
72 pp. London, Hatchard, 1806
T.

2510 RANDOLPH, John. The speech of the hon. J. Randolph, representative for the state of Virginia, in the general congress of America; on a motion for the non-importation of British merchandize, pending the present disputes between Great Britain and America. With an introduction by the author of 'War in disguise'.
78 pp. London, J. Butterworth, 1806
P., Q.

2511 Remarks on the trade with Germany, respectfully submitted to the merchants and others, both here and abroad,

interested in this important branch of commerce, March, 1806.
140 pp. London, W. J. and J. Richardson, 1806
Q.
[English and German versions on facing pages.]

2512 Report from the trustees, the managing committee, and the physicians, concerning the house of recovery or fever hospital, Cork-street, Dublin.
24 pp. Dublin, printed by Charles Downes, 1806
A.

2513 ROSE, George. A brief examination into the increase of the revenue, commerce and navigation of Great Britain, during the administration of the right Hon. William Pitt, with allusions to some of the principal events which occurred in that period, and a sketch of Mr. Pitt's character.
table. appendices. 126 pp. 2nd ed. London, J. Hatchard, 1806
P., T.

2514 SHARKEY, Richard F. A proposal for the more speedy relief of the poor of Ireland, in seasons of scarcity; addressed to the rt. hon. Sir John Newport, Bart., Chancellor of the Irish exchequer.
32 pp. Dublin, J. Milliken, 1806
Q., T.

2515 SINCLAIR, Sir John, bart. Address to the Board of agriculture, on Tuesday the 22nd April, 1806.
tables. 12 pp. London, W. Bulmer, 1806
A.

2516 A state of the allegations and evidence produced, and opinions of merchants and other persons given, to the committee of council; extracted from their report of the 31st May, 1784, on his majesty's order of reference of the eighth of March last, made upon the representation of the West India planters and merchants, purporting to show the distressed state of his majesty's sugar colonies by the operation of his majesty's order in council of the 2nd of July, 1783, and the necessity of allowing a free intercourse between the sugar colonies and the United States of America, in American bottoms.
table. 186 pp. London, printed by T. Davidson, 1806
Q.

2517 [STEPHEN, James.] War in disguise; or, the frauds of the neutral flags.
260 pp. 3rd ed. London, J. Hatchard, [etc.], 1806
A.

1807

2518 BERNARD, Sir Thomas, bart. A letter to the honourable and right reverend the Lord Bishop of Durham, president of the society for bettering the condition of the poor, on the principle and detail of the measures now under the consideration of parliament, for promoting and encouraging industry, and for the relief and regulation of the poor.
66 pp. London, J. Hatchard, 1807
T.

2519 [Bosanquet, Charles.] A letter to W. Manning, Esq., M.P. on the causes of the rapid and progressive depreciation of West India property.
54 pp. London, printed by S. and C. McDowall, 1807
A.

2520 [Burke, Edmund.] A short account of a late short administration.
14 pp. 2nd ed. London, James Ridgway, 1807
A.

2521 Corrie, Edgar. A letter on the subject of the duties on coffee.
20 pp. Liverpool, the West India Association, 1807
Q.

2522 [Ellice, Edward.] Letters concerning the abolition of the Slave-Trade and other West India affairs. By Mercator.
32 pp. London, printed by Galabin, 1807
N.

2523 [Farnborough, Charles Long.] Short remarks upon recent political occurrences; and, particularly, on the new plan of finance.
54 pp. London, J. Hatchard, 1807
Q., T.

2524 Jarrold, Thomas. A letter to Samuel Whitbread, Esq. M.P. on the subject of the Poor's laws.
32 pp. London, T. Cadell and W. Davies, 1807
A.

2525 Ladies society for the education and employment of the female poor, an Account of an institution for training young women for nursery-maids, or schoolmistresses for the poor, or qualifying them for assistants in shops. Established and superintended by the Ladies committee.
12 pp. Dublin, William Watson, 1807
A.

2526 Ladies society for promoting the education and employment of the female poor. Outlines of instruction for the mistress of a charity school, to explain the nature of her duty, and to assist her in the performance of it.
12 pp. Dublin, William Watson, [1807?]
A.

2527 A letter on the nature, extent and management of the poor rates in Scotland; with a review of the controversy respecting the abolition of poor laws.
38 pp. Edinburgh, John Park, 1807
P.

2528 A letter to William A. Maddock, Esq. M.P. etc. etc. containing principally, observations on a publication of documents and letters addressed to him relative to the building of a pier, at a Cove called Porthdynllaen in Carnarvon Bay. By Investigator.
22 pp. Dublin, printed by J. Parry, 1807
A.

2529 [Lloyd, Charles.] A true history of a late short administration.
24 pp. London, John Stockdale, 1807
T.

2530 Malthus, Thomas Robert. A letter to Samuel Whitbread, Esq., M.P. on his proposed bill for the amendment of the poor laws.
42 pp. London, J. Johnson, [etc.], 1807
Q., T.

2531 Miller, Joseph. The memorial and suggestions of the merchants and traders of the city of Dublin, for the amendment of the laws and practice relative to bankrupts. Humbly presented to the Right Hon. George Ponsonby, Lord High Chancellor of Ireland. With a prefatory address to William Saurin, Esq. his majesty's premier counsel at law.
58 pp. Dublin, printed by J. and J. Carrick, 1807
A., C., Q.

2532 [Monck, John Berkeley.] General reflections on the system of the poor laws, with a short view of Mr. Whitbread's bill, and comment on it.
48 pp. London, R. Bickerstaff, 1807
Q.

2533 Notifications, orders, and instructions, relating to prize subjects, during the present war.
92 pp. London, J. Butterworth, [etc.], 1807
Q.

2534 The panorama; or, a journey to Munster, a serio-comic poem: with historical, national and natural sketches of Ireland, from the days of Queen Bess to the forty-seventh year of the present reign.
84 pp. Dublin, printed by J. and J. Carrick, 1807
A., N.

2535 Proceedings of the trustees of the linen and hempen manufactures of Ireland, from the 3rd of June, 1806, to the 5th of January, 1807.
fold. table. 118 pp. Dublin, printed by Williamson and Folds, 1807
A.

2536 Proceedings of the trustees of the linen and hempen manufactures of Ireland, from the 5th of January to the 5th of July, 1807.
appendix. 102 pp. Dublin, printed by Williamson and Folds, 1807
A., D.

2537 Remarks on the British treaty with the United States; and reflections on the characters of the president, and other leading members of the government. Written by an American.
64 pp. New York and Liverpool, Woodward and Alderson, 1807
K., Q.

2538 Return of all Charitable donations and bequests contained in the Wills registered in the Prerogative and consistorial offices of Dublin from 1st Jan. to the end of the year, 1806 also a return of all those entered in the Registry Offices of the several Dioceses in Ireland, from the 1st Jan 1805–1st Oct 1806.
56 pp. Dublin, printed by W. Watson, 1807
N.

2539 Richardson, William. An essay on the improvement of the great flow bogs of Ireland; particularly the Bog of Allen, and the Montaghs in the north; suggesting a cheap and

expeditious mode of converting these unprofitable wastes into valuable meadow: in a letter addressed to the grand juries of Antrim, Armagh and Tyrone.
22 pp. Dublin, printed by William Porter, 1807
G., N., Q.

2540 ROGERS, Thomas. Documents addressed to W. A. Maddocks, Esq. M.P. relating to Portdynllaen harbour, Caernarvonshire, with a view to its improvement, for the better security of trade, & a shorter & safer communication, between Ireland & England. With a report & plans.
fold. map. 52 pp. Dublin, printed by J. Shea, 1807
A., N.

2541 Second report on the object and effects of the house of recovery, and Fever Hospital, in Cork-street, Dublin, by the physicians to that institution.
fold. tabl. 14 pp. Dublin, printed by Charles Downes, 1807
A.

2542 SPENCE, William. Britain independent of commerce; or, proofs, deduced from an investigation into the true causes of the wealth of nations, that our riches, prosperity and power, are derived from resources inherent in ourselves, and would not be affected, even though our commerce were annihilated.
92 pp. London, T. Cadell and W. Davies, 1807
Q.
See 2588

2543 ——. The radical cause of the present distresses of the West-India planters pointed out; and the inefficiency of the measures which have been hitherto proposed for relieving them, demonstrated; with remarks on the publications of Sir William Young, Bart. Charles Bosanquet Esq., and Joseph Lowe, Esq.; relative to the value of the West India trade.
106 pp. London, T. Cadell and W. Davies, 1807
Q.

2544 Statement of a plan of finance, proposed to parliament in the year 1807.
tables in appendices. 94 pp. (Appendix not paginated) London, E. Jeffrey and J. Budd, 1807
P.

2545 [STEPHEN, James.] The dangers of the country. By the author of war in disguise.
232 pp. London, J. Butterworth, [etc.], 1807
A.

2546 Thoughts on a late advertisement in the Dublin Evening Post, relative to a meeting to be held in Cashel, on the 22nd of August, 1807; on the subject of a modification of tithes. By a clergyman of the established church.
22 pp. Clonmel, printed by Gorman, 1807
N.

2547 The trial of Mr. H. Malone, on a charge of fraud & embezzlement of notes, etc. etc. of the Bank of Ireland, on Monday, November 2nd at the Commission of Oyer & Terminer, with the speech of the solicitor general, & the luminous charge of Mr. Baron Smith to the jury. The whole compiled from notes, accurately taken & enlarged by an eminent barrister.
60 pp. Dublin, printed by J. Martin, [1807]
A., N.

2548 WEYLAND, John. Observations on Mr. Whitbread's poor bill, and on the population of England; intended as a supplement to A short inquiry into the policy, humanity, and past effects of the poor laws, etc.
68 pp. London, J. Hatchard, 1807
Q.

2549 WHITBREAD, Samuel. Substance of a speech on the poor laws: delivered in the house of commons, on Thursday, February 19, 1807. With an appendix.
112 pp. London, J. Ridgway, 1807
N., Q.

1808

2550 Address to the tenants on Mr. De Salis's estate in the county of Armagh.
tables. 30 pp. Dublin, printed by Fitzpatrick, 1808
A.

2551 Annual report of the managing committee of the house of recovery, and Fever Hospital, in Cork Street, Dublin, for the year ending 4th January, 1808.
8 pp. Dublin, printed by Charles Downes, 1808
A.

2552 ASHBURTON, Alexander Baring, 1st baron. An inquiry into the causes and consequences of the orders in council; and an examination of the conduct of Great Britain towards the neutral commerce of America.
184 pp. 2nd ed. London, J. M. Richardson, (etc.), 1808
P.

2553 BELLEW, Robert. Thoughts and suggestions on the means apparently necessary to be adopted by the legislature, towards improving the condition of the Irish peasantry. Dedicated to the earl of Shannon.
94 pp. 2nd ed. London, J. Ridgway, 1808
N., P.

2554 BUSHE, Gervase Parker. A digested abridgment of the laws relating to the linen & hempen manufactures of Ireland.
178 pp. Dublin, printed by W. Folds, 1808
A.

2555 Commutation of tythes in Ireland injurious not only to the Church establishment, but to the poor. Addressed, without permission, to the gentry of Kerry, Galway and Tipperary.
60 pp. London, F. C. and J. Rivington, 1808
N., T.

2556 Considerations on the nature and objects of the intended light and heat company. Published by authority of the committee.
30 pp. London, James Ridgway, 1808
Q.

2557 CORRIE, Edgar. Letters on the subject of the duties on coffee.
70 pp. 2nd ed. London, T. Cadell and W. Davies, 1808
Q.

2558 ——. A second letter on the subject of the duties on coffee.
table. 26 pp. Liverpool, printed by J. Lang, 1808
Q.

2559 ——. Letter fourth. To the Right Hon. Spencer Percival, Chancellor of the Exchequer, etc. etc. etc.
8 pp. Liverpool, 1808
Q.

2560 ——. Letters on the subject of the duties on coffee (5th letter).
14 pp. London, T. Cadell and W. Davies, 1808
Q.

2561 ——. Proof copy of preface to the second edition of letters on the subject of the duties on coffee.
8 pp. n. place, 1808
Q.

2562 [COURTENAY, Thomas Peregrine.] Observations on the American treaty, in eleven letters. First published in 'The Sun', under the signature of Decius.
84 pp. London, J. Budd, [etc.], 1808
Q.

2563 [CROKER, John Wilson.] A sketch of the state of Ireland, past and present.
68 pp. Dublin, M. N. Mahon, 1808
A., B., D., N., T.

——. 68 pp. 2nd ed. Dublin, M. N. Mahon, 1808
A.

——. 68 pp. 4th ed. Dublin, M. N. Mahon, 1808
A., M.

——. 68 pp. 5th ed. Dublin, M. N. Mahon, 1808
T.
See also 3301.

2564 DEALTRY, Robert. A sermon preached in the parish church of Stillorgan, on Sunday, October 30th, 1808 & published at the request of the Stillorgan charitable institution, for promoting the comforts of the poor.
34 pp. Dublin, William Watson, 1808
A., N.

2565 DUDLEY, Sir Henry Bate, bart. A short address to the most reverend, & honourable William, lord primate of all Ireland; recommendatory of some commutation, or modification of the tythes of that country: with a few remarks on the present state of the Irish church.
30 pp. London, Cadell and Davies, 1808
A., B., N., Q.

2566 [DUIGENAN, Patrick.] An address to the nobility and gentry of the church of Ireland, as by law established: explaining the real causes of the commotions, and insurrections in the southern parts of this kingdom, respecting tithes; the real motives and designs of the projectors and abettors of those commotions and insurrections: and containing a candid inquiry into the practicability of substituting any other mode of subsistence and maintenance for the clergy of the church established, consistent with the principles of reason and justice, in the place of tithes. By Theophilus.
120 pp. 3rd ed. Dublin, printed and London re-printed, J. Hatchard, 1808
Q.

2567 [ELRINGTON, Thomas.] Letters on tythes, published in the Dublin journal and correspondent, under the signature of N. in reply to a speech made at the meeting held at Cashell, 22nd August, 1807; with a postscript, containing observations on a pamphlet, lately published, in which the subject of tythes is discussed.
42 pp. 2nd edition. Dublin, J. Brooke, 1808
P., R.

2568 ELSAM, Richard. The gentleman and builders assistant; containing a list of prices of the several artificers works, usually employed in building, together with some observations on the customs of measuring in Ireland which, in many instances, tend to injure not only the employer but the employed.
table of contents. tables. 176 pp. Londonderry, printed by Samuel Boyd, 1808
N., R.

2569 Extracts from publications relating to the culture and management of hemp. Published by order of the trustees of the linen and hempen manufactures of Ireland.
58 pp. Dublin, printed by William Folds, 1808
A., N., Q.

2570 FAIRMAN, William. The stocks examined & compared: or, a guide to purchasers in the public funds containing an account of the different funds, from the times of their creation to the year 1807, including the imperial & Irish annuities, transferable at the Bank of England, & the stock of the public companies. With useful & extensive tables, illustrated by observations & examples. Also, statements of the national debt, a view of the progress of the sinking fund, & an account of the American funds.
196 pp. 5th ed. London, Joseph Johnson, [etc.], 1808
A.

2571 FORTUNE, E. F. Thomas. National life annuities: comprizing all the tables, and every necessary information contained in the Act of Parliament, for granting the same, both on single and joint lives, with benefit of survivorship; also additional tables, annexed to the former throughout; calculated to shew what annuity can be purchased for one hundred pounds sterling, at the same rates upon the same lives.
tables. 94 pp. London, T. Boosey, 1808
T.

2572 INGRAM, Robert Acklom. Disquisitions on population; in which the principles of the essay on population, by the Rev. T. R. Malthus, are examined and refuted.
136 pp. London, J. Hatchard, 1808
Q.

2573 A letter addressed to the late Grand Jury of Armagh with some observations on the subject of tithes. By a Killeavy Weaver.
16 pp. Dublin, King, 1808
N.

2574 A letter to his excellency the Duke of Richmond, on the abolition of tythes, and maintenance of the Roman catholic clergy in Ireland.
24 pp. 2nd ed. Dublin, John Jones, 1808
A., Q.

2575 LUSHINGTON, William. The interests of agriculture and commerce, inseparable.
76 pp. London, Edmund Lloyd, 1808
A., Q.

2576 MANN, Abraham. Mr. Mann's letter etc. to the merchants, manufacturers, and others, interested in the trade to the United States of America.
20 pp. London, Richard Taylor and Co., 1808
Q.

2577 MASON, James. A brief statement of the present system of tythes in Ireland.
32 pp. Shrewsbury, printed by Eddowes, 1808
N.

2578 MILL, James. Commerce defended. An answer to the arguments by which Mr. Spence, Mr. Cobbett, and others, have attempted to prove that commerce is not a source of national wealth.
158 pp. London, C. and R. Baldwin, 1808
Q.

——. 158 pp. 2nd ed. London, C. & R. Baldwin, 1808
P.

2579 [NOLAN, Michael, and HARTIGAN, ...] An enquiry into the history of tithe, its influence upon the agriculture, population and morals of Ireland: with a plan for modifying that system, and providing an adequate maintenance for the catholic and presbyterian clergy.
tables. 132 pp. Dublin, Gilbert and Hodges, 1808
B., N., P., Q.

2580 O'FLANAGAN, Phelim. The ensanguined strand of Merrion: or, a stuffing for the pillow of those, who could have prevented the recent calamity in the Bay of Dublin.
70 pp. Dublin, John King, 1808
A., T.

2581 Orders in council, or an examination of the justice, legality, and policy of the new system of commercial regulations, with an appendix of state papers, statutes, and authorities.
118 pp. London, Longman, Hurst, Rees and Orme, [etc.], 1808
Q.

2582 PARNELL, Sir Henry Brooke, bart (later 1st baron CONGLETON.) A history of the penal laws against the Irish catholics; from the Treaty of Limerick to the Union.
188 pp. London, J. Harding, 1808
A.

——. Another issue. 260 pp. Dublin, H. Fitzpatrick, 1808
A., N.

2583 Premiums offered in 1808, by the society instituted at London, A.D. 1754, for the encouragement of arts, manufactures, and commerce, with a list of the present officers.
20 pp. [London], printed by C. Whittingham, 1808
A.

2584 Proceedings of the trustees of the linen and hempen manufactures of Ireland, from the 5th of January, to the 5th of July, 1808.
appendix. 226 pp. Dublin, printed by Williamson and Folds, 1808
A., D.

2585 Pursuits of agriculture; a satirical poem, in three cantos, with notes. Canto the second.
212 pp. London, John Joseph Stockdale, 1808
Q.

See 2657

2586 South Wales association, for improvement of roads, 1st June, 1808.
tables. 56 pp. London, printed by William Phillips, 1808
Q.

2587 SPENCE, William. Agriculture: the source of the wealth of Britain; a reply to the objections urged by Mr. Mill, the Edinburgh reviewers, and others, against the doctrines of the pamphlet, entitled 'Britain independent of commerce'. With remarks on the criticism of the monthly reviewers upon that work.
114 pp. London, T. Cadell and W. Davies, 1808
P., Q.

2588 ——. Britain independent of commerce; or, proofs, deduced from an investigation into the true causes of the wealth of nations, that our riches, prosperity and power, are derived from resources inherent in ourselves, and would not be affected, even though our commerce were annihilated.
92 pp. 3rd ed. London, T. Cadell and W. Davies, 1808
N.

See 2542

2589 ——. The radical cause of the present distresses of the West-India planters pointed out; and the inefficiency of the measures which have been hitherto proposed for relieving them, demonstrated: with remarks on the publications of Sir William Young, Bart. Charles Bosanquet, Esq. and Joseph Lowe, Esq.; relative to the value of the West India trade.
110 pp. 2nd ed. London, T. Cadell and W. Davies, 1808
A., Q.

2590 TALLEYRAND-PÉRIGORD, Charles Maurice de, Prince de Bénévent. Memoire sur les relations commerciales des États-Unis avec l'Angleterre. Lu à l'Institut National, le 15 Germinal, An. V. Suivi d'un essai sur les avantages à retirer de colonies nouvelles dans les circonstances présentes. Par le même auteur. Lu à l'Institut, le 15 Messidor, An V.
48 pp. 2e ed. Londres, printed by J. Dean, 1808
N.

2591 TORRENS, Robert. The economists refuted; or, an inquiry into the nature and extent of the advantages derived from trade: with observations on the expediency of making

peace with France. And an appendix, discussing the policy of prohibiting corn in the distilleries.
112 pp. London, S. A. and H. Oddy, Dublin, C. La Grange, 1808

P., Q.

2592 Tracts, relating to the culture and management of hemp. Published by order of the trustees of the linen and hempen manufactures of Ireland.
42 pp. Dublin, printed by William Folds, 1808

Q.

2593 WOODWARD, Richard, bishop of Cloyne. The present state of the Church of Ireland: containing a description of its precarious situation; and the consequent danger to the public. Recommended to the serious consideration of the friends of the protestant interest. To which are subjoined, some reflections on the impracticability of a proper commutation for tythes; and a general account of the origin and progress of the insurrections in Munster.
128 pp. Dublin, printed by John Brooke, 1808
(New edition.)

A., D., Q., T.

1809

2594 BAILLIE, George. A most interesting case proving the necessity of the bill now before parliament for altering the bankrupt laws: in a letter addressed to Sir Samuel Romilly.
pull out tables. 16 pp. London, S. Chapple and Bell, 1809

Q.

2595 BEARBLOCK, James. A treatise upon tithes; containing an estimate of every titheable article in common cultivation, with the various modes of compounding for the same. 3rd ed., much enlarged. To which are prefixed, observations on a pamphlet written by Rich. Flower, recommending the abolition of tithes.
tables. 180 pp. London, J. Hatchard, [etc.], 1809

A.

2596 BOYD, Charles. A Georgic of modern husbandry. In twelve parts; each corresponding with a month, beginning the year at Michaelmas.
table of contents. index. 132 pp. Dublin, Gilbert and Hodges, 1809

N.

2597 Cases and opinions relative to flax-seed.
16 pp. n. place, [1809]

L., Q.

2598 Clothing Wool.
tables. 8 pp. (t.p. missing) [Dublin?], 1809

N.

[Farming Society of Ireland pamphlet.]

2599 DAWSON, William. Plan for three harbours, one, easterly from Howthtown, one due-east from the island at Holyhead, and one about three hundred yards easterly of Dunleary. Subjoined are remarks on the work, said to be for an harbour, at the northern side of the ruined abbey, at Howth-town, and reasons against the continuation of it any longer.
fold. map. 32 pp. Dublin, printed by R. Gibson, 1809

A., Q.

2600 D'IVERNOIS, Sir Francis. Effets du blocus continental sur le commerce, les finances, le credit et la prosperité des Isles Britanniques.
166 pp. London, B. Dulau & Co., [etc.], 1809

A., Q.

———. fold. tables. 140 pp. 2nd ed. London, B. Dulau & Co., [etc.], 1809

Q.

2601 FLOWER, Richard. Abolition of tithe recommended, in an address to the agriculturalists of Great Britain; in which the increasing and unjust claims of the clergy are fully examined and disputed: with some observations on the present construction of the law of tithing and its dangerous consequences to the landed interest of this country.
tables. 52 pp. Harlow, printed by B. Flower, 1809

A.

2602 GREG, Thomas. A letter to Sir John Sinclair, Bt., M.P., President of the board of agriculture; containing a statement of the system, under which a considerable farm is profitably managed in Hertfordshire. Given at the request of the Board.
plates. tables. 22 pp. London, printed by W. Bulmer, 1809

A.

2603 HANSON, Joseph. The whole proceedings on the trial of an indictment against Joseph Hanson, Esq., for a conspiracy to aid the weavers of Manchester in revising their wages, before Mr. Justice Le Blanc, and a special jury, at the Lancaster Spring Assizes, 1809. Taken in short hand by Mr. Jones, Liverpool.
appendix. 132 pp. London, T. Gillet, 1809

P.

2604 A letter to his grace the duke of Richmond, Lord lieutenant of Ireland, stating the case of certain officers in the custom department of Ireland, claiming compensation under the act of the 48th of the king for abolishing fees, etc. etc. By Asellus.
26 pp. Dublin, printed by Charles Lagrange, 1809

L., Q.

2605 LOCKER, John. Address to the King, the Ministry, and the people of Great Britain and Ireland, on the present state of the money system of the United Kingdoms. With an Appendix, containing letters of His Majesty's subjects to the author, and some important documents farther explanatory of the system, and the means of amendment.
appendices. tables. 82 pp. London, S. Tipper, 1809

N.

2606 McCALLUM, P. F. Eleven millions income tax. The statement made by G. L. Wardle, Esq., M.P. respecting the abolition of the £11,000,000 income tax; in a speech delivered in the house of commons on the 19th day of June, 1809: together with the speech of Wm. Huskisson, Esq. secretary of the treasury, and the able reply of Henry Parnell, Esq.
tables. 44 pp. London, Blacklock, 1809

N.

2607 McMENAMY, William. A plan for the improvement of Dublin harbour, together with a project for a new one, denominated Dublin Life Harbour etc.
72 pp. Dublin, Stewart, 1809

A.

2608 MORGAN, William. Address delivered by Mr. Morgan, the actuary, to the members of the society for equitable assurances on lives and survivorships, at a general court holden the seventh of December, M.DCCC.IX.
24 pp. London, the society, 1809

T.

2609 MURDOCK, William. A letter to a member of parliament, from Mr. William Murdock, in vindication of his character and claims; in reply to a recent publication, by the committee for conducting through parliament a bill for incorporating a gas-light and coke company.
15 pp. London, printed by Galabin and Marchant, 1809

Q.

2610 [ORSON, B.] Facts and experiments on the use of sugar in feeding cattle: with hints for the cultivation of waste lands. And for improving the condition of the peasantry in Great Britain & Ireland.
140 pp. London, J. Harding, 1809

A., N.

2611 The practical Norfolk farmer; describing the management of a farm throughout the year with observations founded on experience. Dedicated to Thomas W. Coke, Esq., enlarged. tables. 174 pp. 2nd ed. Norwich, Stevenson, Matchett and Stevenson, 1809

N., T.

2612 Premiums offered by the board of agriculture, 1809.
14 pp. London, B. McMillan, 1809

Q.

2613 [PRICE, Richard Hope.] Remarks proving the use of tea to be against the interests of Ireland, and shewing that its manufactures and produce would be increased by substituting coffee.
8 pp. Dublin, R. H. Price, 1809

A., D., Q.

2614 Proceedings of the trustees of the linen and hempen manufactures of Ireland.
appendix. index. 92 pp. Dublin, Williamson and Folds, [1809]

D.

2615 Questions relative to milch cows and dairy-management, proposed by the farming society of the County of Cork.
16 pp. Cork, Henry Denmead, 1809

T.

2616 Remarks upon the bill for incorporating the gas light and coke company.
22 pp. London, printed by George Sidney, 1809

Q.

2617 RICHARDSON, William. Plan for reclaiming the Bog of Allen, and the other great morasses, in Ireland; addressed to the Right Honourable Earl of Rosse.
34 pp. Dublin, printed by Porter, 1809

N.

2618 SHEFFIELD, John Baker-Holroyd, 1st earl of. The orders in council and the American embargo beneficial to the political and commercial interests of Great Britain.
56 pp. London, G. and W. Nichol, 1809

A., Q.

2619 SINCLAIR, Sir John, bart. An account of the systems of husbandry adopted in the more improved districts of Scotland; & a general view of the principles on which they are respectively founded. Drawn up for the consideration of the board of agriculture, with a view of explaining how far those systems are applicable to the less cultivated parts of England.
36 pp. Edinburgh, Alex Smellie, 1809
[Includes one-page tract, 'Hints regarding a special grain called Escanda'.]

Q.

2620 TRIMMER, Joshua Kirby. A brief inquiry into the present state of agriculture in the southern part of Ireland, and its influence on the manners and conditions of the lower classes of the people: with some considerations upon the ecclesiastical establishment of that country.
84 pp. London, J. Hatchard, 1809

A., N., Q.

2621 [YOUNG, Arthur.] On the advantages which have resulted from the establishment of the board of agriculture: being the substance of a lecture read to that institution, May 26th, 1809. By the secretary to that board.
72 pp. London, Richard Phillips, 1809

N., Q.

1810

2622 (Abolition of tithes.) A short letter to the Rev. T. C. Munnings; exposing the futility of his pretended agricultural improvements, and proposing a very simple but very efficacious plan for ameliorating the condition of the farmers by a gradual abolition of tithes.
12 pp. 9th ed. London, J. J. Stockdale, 1810

Q.

2623 Analysis of the money situation of Great Britain, with respect to its coins and bank notes.
28 pp. London, J. Mackinlay, 1810

T.

2624 At a general court of proprietors of the west-India dock company, held at their house in Billiter Square, on Friday the 5th January, 1810, George Hibbert, Esq. in the chair the chairman read to the meeting a report from a committee of directors, on benefits resulting from the establishment to the public revenue, proprietors of produce, and others; which was ordered to be printed, for the use of the proprietors.
appendices. 34 pp. London, printed by J. Bryan, [1810]

T.

2625 ATKINSON, Jasper. A letter to a member of parliament occasioned by the publication of the report from the select committee on the high price of gold bullion.
106 pp. London, J. J. Stockdale, 1810

Q.

2626 BARRINGTON, Jonah, and BATTERSBY, Leslie. Correspondence of the Reverend Leslie Battersby, clerk—master of arts—rector and vicar of Skreen in the county of Sligo—vicar general of the diocese of Killala and Achonry—one of his majesty's justices of the peace, and quorum for the county of Sligo;—and first lieutenant in the corps of Tyreragh infantry, with Sir Jonah Barrington, L.L.D. judge of the high court of admiralty of Ireland: on the subject of family-money; with the documents referred to by both gentlemen in their correspondence.
48 pp. Dublin, William Figgis, 1810

A., B., N., P.

2627 BLAKE, William. Observations on the principles which regulate the course of exchange; and on the present depreciated state of the currency.
tables. 132 pp. London, Edmund Lloyd, 1810

Q.

2628 BOSANQUET, Charles. Practical observations on the report of the bullion-committee.
114 pp. London, J. M. Richardson, 1810

A., N.

2629 Cursory observations upon the proposed application to the legislature of these kingdoms for the grant of a charter to effect marine insurances.
18 pp. London, E. Wilson, 1810

Q.

2630 Dangers from the policy of England in the depression of Ireland.
120 pp. London, 1810

A., U.

2631 D'IVERNOIS, Sir Francis. Effects of the continental blockade upon the commerce, finances, credit, and prosperity of the British Islands. Translated from the third French edition, revised, corrected & enlarged. To which are added observations on certain statements contained in a late work, entitled 'A view of the natural and commercial circumstances of Ireland, by Thomas Newenham Esq.'
tables. appendix. 208 pp. Dublin, Corbet, 1810

A., U.

2632 DIXON, William. An inquiry into the impolicy of the continuance of distillation from grain, in Great Britain; in which its injurious effects on agriculture, and its tendency to produce a deficiency of national subsistence, are particularly considered.
110 pp. Liverpool, Wright and Cruickshank, [etc.], 1810

Q.

2633 DOYLE, John. Speech of major general Doyle, lieutenant governor of Guernsey, delivered in St. Peter's Church, on the question of levying a general tax, for the formation of good military roads in that island. To which is added his animated reply, on receiving the unanimous vote of thanks from the states of the island.
28 pp. 2nd ed. London, Lane, Newman and Co., [1810?]

Q.

2634 DRURY, Charles. A farmer's recent and important discovery of a system for improving land, and augmenting the crops of corn, etc. at not more than one-fourth of the

expense which is now incurred by the present mode of manuring land.
24 pp. London, Taylor and Hessey, [etc.], 1810

T.

2635 DUIGENAN, Patrick. The nature and extent of the demands of the Irish Roman Catholics fully explained; in observations and strictures on a pamphlet, entitled, a history of the penal laws against the Irish Roman Catholics.
248 pp. London, J. J. Stockdale, 1810

B.

2636 [ELRINGTON, Thomas, Bishop of Leighlin and Ferns.] A letter to the right honorable William Wellesley Pole, chief secretary to his grace the lord lieutenant; on the proposal for a commutation of tythes in Ireland. By a clergyman.
54 pp. Dublin, R. E. Mercier, 1810

R.

2637 Fourth report of the directors of the African institution, read at the annual general meeting.
table of contents. appendices. 128 pp. London, J. Hatchard, 1810

A.

2638 FRANCIS, Sir Philip. Reflections on the abundance of paper in circulation and the scarcity of specie.
tables. appendix. 68 pp. 2nd ed. London, J. Ridgway, 1810

T.

2639 GRENFELL, John. Defence of bank notes. Second Edition. With two letters to Francis Horner, Esq. M.P., chairman of the Bullion committee.
54 pp. London, J. Walker, 1810

N.

2640 HINCKS, Thomas Dix. An account of the progress of the Cork Institution laid before the Dublin society, on November the 25th, 1810, by order of the managers of the institution, as a mark of respect entertained by them for the parent society.
36 pp. Dublin, Graisberry and Campbell, 1810

A., L.

Another issue. 38 pp. Dublin, Graisberry and Campbell, 1810

Q.

2641 Hints to the legislature, for removing the causes of the discontents in Ireland. By a Landholder of Ireland.
24 pp. London, T. Reynolds & Son, 1810

N., P.

2642 HOPKINS, Thomas. The cause of the disappearance of guineas and of the cause of exchange being against us, whilst the balance of trade is in our favour: with practicable means suggested to enable the Bank of England to resume its payments in specie, without sustaining any loss.
78 pp. London, T. Murray, [1810]

T.

2643 HUSKISSON, William. The question concerning the depreciation of our currency stated and examined.
176 pp. London, John Murray, 1810

A., N., P., Q.

2644 [KELLY, William.] Strictures on bankruptcy, insolvency and on the state of the nation.
60 pp. n. place [1810]

A.

2645 A letter from a gentleman farmer, in Ireland, to O. P. Esq.
8 pp. London, 1810

Q.

2646 A letter to Jasper Vaux, Esq. Chairman of the meeting at Lloyds, on Monday, the 29th January last, in which the nature and principles, and the past and present extent of marine assurance are examined; the necessity of a new company to examine marine assurance pointed out; and the opposition displayed to its establishment, especially by the underwriters at Lloyd's coffee-house, is considered and refuted. By a subscriber to Lloyd's.
80 pp. London, J. M. Richardson, 1810

Q.

2647 A letter to the Right Honourable Spencer Perceval, on the augmentation of a particular class of poor livings without burthening the public.
64 pp. London, J. Hatchard, 1810

N., Q.

2648 McGIBBON, Alexander. Reports as to improving the navigation of the river Forth etc. and the advantages of small canals demonstrated.
tables. map. 100 pp. Edinburgh, Menzies, 1810

A.

2649 MARRYAT, Joseph. Observations upon the report of the committee on marine insurance, with a few incidental remarks on a pamphlet lately published, entitled 'A letter to Jasper Vaux, Esq.' To which is added, copy of a report, proposed as an amendment to the report adopted by the committee on marine insurance.
68 pp. London, J. M. Richardson, 1810

Q.

2650 A method of improving the condition of the Irish poor. Suggested in a letter to Samuel Whitbread, Esq. M.P.
26 pp. Dublin, printed by W. Folds, 1810

N.

2651 MUSHET, Robert. An enquiry into the effects produced on the national currency and rates of exchange, by the Bank restriction bill; explaining the cause of the high price of bullion; with plans for maintaining the national coins in a state of uniformity and perfection.
table of contents. tables. 116 pp. 2nd ed. with additions. London, C. and R. Baldwin, 1810

A.

2652 NEWENHAM, Thomas. A letter to Sir Francis D'Ivernois, in reply to his observations on certain statements, in Mr. Newenham's view of the natural, political and commercial circumstances, of Ireland.
16 pp. Dublin, Keene, 1810

A.

——. Another issue. 16 pp. London, Cadell and Davies, [etc.], 1810

Q.

2653 Observations on the sinking fund, humbly recommended to the attention of members of parliament, previous to the passing of a new loan bill.
42 pp. London, R. Bickerstaff, 1810

T.

2654 PARNELL, Sir Henry Brooke, bart. (later 1st baron CONGLETON). Tythes. A corrected report of the speech of H. Parnell, Esq. in the House of Commons on Friday 13th of April, 1810, on a motion for a select committee to inquire into the collection of tythes in Ireland.
46 pp. London, Budd, 1810

N.

2655 Premiums offered by the Dublin society in 1810, for agriculture and fine arts. Also, premiums of the London society extending to Ireland.
32 pp. Dublin, printed by Graisberry and Campbell, 1810

A., L.

2656 Proceedings of the trustees of the linen and hempen manufactures of Ireland from the 5th of January to the 5th July, 1810.
appendix. index. 232 pp. Dublin, printed by Williamson and Folds, [1810]

D.

2657 Pursuits of agriculture; a satirical poem, in three cantos, with notes. Canto the third.
108 pp. London, John Joseph Stockdale, 1810

Q.

See 2585

2658 RICARDO, David. The high price of bullion, a proof of the depreciation of bank notes.
60 pp. 3rd ed. London, John Murray, 1810

Q.

2659 ROSE, George. Observations respecting the public expenditure and the influence of the Crown.
tables. 84 pp. 3rd ed. London, Cadell and Davies, 1810

T.

2660 Rules & regulations for the house of industry, Belfast, to be laid before a general meeting of the town, for their approbation. Together with a list of the original subscribers to this institution. (Published by order of the committee.)
fold. table. 36 pp. Belfast, printed by Alexanedr [sic] Mackay, 1810

L.

2661 [RUSSELL, W. P.] Suggestions on the entire discharge of the national debt. By Patrioticus.
26 pp. Colchester, J. Chaplin; London, Baldwin, Cradock, and Joy [c. 1810]

T.

2662 SINCLAIR, Sir John, bart. A letter from the Right Honourable Sir John Sinclair, Bart, M.P., to the chancellor of the exchequer in Ireland; on the proceedings which have lately taken place for dissolving the union between the two kingdoms.
26 pp. Edinburgh, printed by John Brown, 1810

Q.

2663 ——. Observations on the report of the Bullion committee. The second edition.
tables. appendix. 72 pp. London, T. Cadell and W. Davies; J. Stockdale; J. M. Richardson, 1810

T.

2664 SINCLAIR, John. Thoughts on circulation and paper currency.
20 pp. London, printed by B. McMillan, [1810]

Q.

2665 A singular case, arising out of the sale of flax-seed.
18 pp. Dublin, printed by B. Dugdale, 1810

Q.

2666 State of Ireland considered, with an enquiry into the history and operation of tithe: and a plan for modifying that system, and providing an adequate maintenance for the catholic and presbyterian clergy. 2nd ed., with an appendix, containing the rev. Mr. Howlett's plan of commutation and a proposition for taxing absentees.
tables. diagrams. 178 pp. Dublin, Downes and Reilly, 1810

N., P., R.

'W. R(obertson), the author?'—Bradshaw, 2949.

2667 The state of the established church; in a series of letters to the Right Hon. Spencer Perceval, chancellor of the exchequer, etc. etc. etc. … second edition, corrected & enlarged; with an appendix of official documents,
tables. 151 pp. London, J. J. Stockdale, 1810

Q.

2668 SWIFT, Edmund L. The indissolubility of union.
tables. 42 pp. Dublin, printed by Corbet, 1810

D., N.

2669 Thoughts on the expediency and means of improving the agriculture of Ireland.
tables. 40 pp. Cork, J. Haly, 1810

P., Q.

2670 TROTTER, Sir Coutts, bart. The principles of currency and exchanges applied to the report from the Select Committee of the house of commons appointed to inquire into the high price of gold bullion.
80 pp. 2nd ed. London, Cadell and Davies, 1810

N.

1811

2671 Additional remarks on an intended asylum port near Dun Leary, comprising several observations on the last grant made by parliament of £40,000, British, for Howth Harbour, which, with 25% for collecting, will make the neat sum £50,000. By a Seaman.
32 pp. Dublin, Callaghan, 1811

A., N.

2672 ATKINSON, Jasper. A Letter to a member of parliament, occasioned by the publication of the Report from the select committee on the high price of gold bullion.
tables. 108 pp. 2nd ed. London, J. J. Stockdale, 1811

N.

2673 BARNES, George. A statistical account of Ireland, founded on historical facts.
82 pp. Dublin, Gilbert and Hodges, 1811

A., L., M., N., P., T.

2674 BOASE, Henry. Remarks on the new doctrine concerning the supposed depreciation of our currency.
118 pp. London, printed by W. Bulmer, 1811

T.

2675 [CAREY, James.] A few facts stated in answer to the report of the Bullion committee etc. by an Annuitant.
28 pp. London, J. M. Richardson, 1811

N.

2676 The case of James McAnally, formerly of New York, but now of the city of Dublin, merchant, a case of singular severity and distress, arising from the construction of the laws relative to the sale of flax-seed in Ireland.
24 pp. Dublin, printed by Graisberry and Campbell, 1811

N., Q.

2677 CASTLEREAGH, Robert Stewart, viscount. The substance of a speech delivered by Lord Viscount Castlereagh, in a committee of the house of commons, May 8, 1811; on the report of the bullion committee.
52 pp. London, J. J. Stockdale, 1811

N., Q.

2678 CHALMERS, George. Considerations on commerce, bullion and coin, circulation and exchanges, with a view to our present circumstances.
fold. tables. 238 pp. London, J. J. Stockdale, 1811

N., Q.

——. 238 pp. 2nd ed. London, J. J. Stockdale, 1811

T.

2679 Considerations on a pamphlet lately published on the proposed pier and harbour at Dunleary, by a Citizen.
8 pp. Dublin, Callaghan, 1811

A.

2680 Considerations on the necessity and importance of an asylum port in the bay of Dublin, including remarks on the harbour erecting at Howth; and that (which is the object of various petitions) proposed for Dunleary, by a Seaman.
map, appendix. 70 pp. Dublin, J. Bull, 1811

A., N.

2681 Considerations on the present state of bank notes, specie and bullion; in a series of letters, addressed to the Right Honourable ——. In two parts, by Mercator.
32 pp. London, David Arnot, 1811

Q.

2682 COPPINGER, William, bishop of Cloyne and Ross. A letter to the right honorable and honorable the Dublin society from the right rev. Doctor Coppinger, titular bishop of Cloyne and Ross, occasioned by certain observations and misstatements of the rev. Horatio Townsend, in his statistical survey of the county Cork, executed and published by the direction and under the patronage of this society.
48 pp. Cork, James Haly, 1811

P., R.

2683 ——. The rt. rev. Dr. Coppinger's letter to the Dublin society, with such additional documents and explanatory remarks as seem called for by the rev. Horatio Townsend's observations upon this letter, and with a supplement to his appendix.
appendix. 92 pp. Cork, J. Haly, 1811

P.

2684 COURTENAY, Thomas Peregrine. A view of the state of the nation, & of the measures of the last five years; suggested by Earl Grey's speech in the house of lords, 13th June, 1810.
188 pp. London, J. J. Stockdale, 1811

B., Q.

2685 CRUICKSHANK, James. Observations on money, as the medium of commerce, showing the present circulating medium of this country to be defective in those requisites which a medium of currency ought to possess, and pointing out in what manner the defect may be remedied; and also the real effect that a greater or less quantity of circulating medium has on the country: together with remarks on the present State of the Nation: to which are subjoined a few practical inferences.
138 pp. London, J. M. Richardson, [etc.], 1811

N.

2686 Cursory observations on the evidence and report of the Bullion committee and on the pamphlets of Sir John Sinclair and Mr. Huskisson on the subject matter thereof, by an Irish trader.
42 pp. Dublin, 1811

A.

2687 DAWSON, William. Holyhead & roads to it from Shrewsbury & Chester.
8 pp. Dublin, 1811

A., T.

2688 ELIOT, Francis Perceval. Observations on the fallacy of the supposed depreciation of the paper currency of the kingdom; with reasons for dissenting from the report of the bullion committee.
180 pp. London, J. J. Stockdale, 1811

A., Q.

2689 A few reflections on passing events.
32 pp. London, J. J. Stockdale, 1811

Q.

2690 [GILBERT, Davies.] A plain statement of the bullion question, in a letter to a friend. By Davies Giddy (pseud.)
48 pp. London, J. J. Stockdale, 1811

N.

2691 HAMILTON, Joseph. Proposals for the establishment of a pottery in Ireland, by subscription shares of £100 each: with observations on the many local advantages of the country. Dedicated to the right hon. & hon. the Dublin society.
16 pp. Dublin, Graisberry and Campbell, 1811

D., Q.

2692 [HERRIES, John Charles.] A review of the controversy respecting the high price of bullion and the state of our currency.
tables. 126 pp. London, J. Budd, 1811

A., T.

2693 An humble address to the members of the honourable house of commons, etc. etc. etc. respecting the insufficiency of the present pay of the captains and commanders of his majesty's navy.
36 pp. London, Egerton and others, 1811

Q.

2694 HUNTER, William. Thoughts on the present political state of affairs, in a letter to a friend.
110 pp. London, J. J. Stockdale, 1811

Q.

2695 KING, John. A report of the cases of the King v Wright and the King v De Yonge, who were severally tried for exchanging guineas for bank notes.
112 pp. London, Butterworth, Dublin, Cooke, 1811

N.

2696 [KINGSMAN, William.] A letter to the right honourable Sir John Sinclair, Bart. (author of the history of the revenue, and other fugitive pieces,) on the subject of his remarks on Mr. Huskisson's pamphlet, by a country gentleman.
30 pp. 2nd ed. London, J. Ridgway, 1811

T.

2697 A letter to the Right Hon. Henry Grattan, on the deplorable consequences resulting to Ireland, from the very low price of spirituous liquors; pointing out the causes of the aggravated increase of those evils, and entreating his attention to the necessity and means of remedying them.
20 pp. Dublin, J. Parry, 1811

A., P., Q., T.

2698 [MACHENRY, James.] It would be so. A vision. By Solomon Second Sight.
16 pp. Dublin, 1811

Q.

2699 MARTIN, Matthew. Substance of a letter, dated Poet's Corner, Westminster, 3d. March, 1803, to the Right Hon. Lord Pelham, on the state of mendicity in the metropolis.
fold. tables. 28 pp. London, J. Hatchard (for the society for bettering the condition of the poor), 1811

Q.

2700 MORTON, Edward Augustus. Observations on sundry subjects, considered so far as they are supposed to have influence on the present spirit and temper of the times in a letter addressed to R. L. Esq. M.P.
72 pp. London, printed by B. R. Howlett, 1811

A.

2701 Multum in parvo: or, a reform catechism; in three parts: (which appeared in the Times of the 5th, 10th and 17th May, 1811) with additional notes. To which is added, a bullion catechism; in two parts: (which appeared in the Times of the 23rd April and 15th May, 1811).
40 pp. London, J. M. Richardson; [etc.], 1811

T.

2702 NOWLAN, Thomas. Address to the creditors of Williams & Finn, bankrupts: with some reflections on the present administration of the bankrupt code.
appendices. 34 pp. Dublin, 1811

A., N.

2703 Observations on the intended Stamford junction canal, and on the bill now before parliament.
8 pp. London, printed by Barry, 1811
Q.

2704 [O'CONNELL, Daniel.] Historical account of the laws against the Roman catholics of England.
52 pp. London, Keating, Brown & Co. [etc.], 1811
Q.

2705 On the state of Ireland, in a letter to a friend, written in 1811, by an Irish Landlord.
16 pp. Bristol, Barry, [1811?]
A.

2706 PHILLIMORE, Joseph. Reflections on the nature and extent of the licence trade.
appendix. 126 pp. 2nd ed. London, J. Budd, [etc., etc.], 1811
T.

2707 PITT, William. The bullion debate: a serio-comic satiric poem.
appendix. 88 pp. London, Longman, Hurst, Rees, Orme, and Brown, 1811
T.

2708 Premiums offered by the farming society of Ireland, for the year 1812.
12 pp. Dublin, printed by William Porter, 1811
Q.

2709 Proceedings of the trustees of the linen and hempen manufactures of Ireland.
appendix. tables. index. 366 pp. Dublin, Williamson and Folds, 1811
A.

2710 Proposals for fire and life insurance and for granting annuities. Eagle insurance company, 23 Dame-street Dublin, and Cornhill, London.
14 pp. Dublin, R. Smith, 1811
A.

2711 Proposals for insurance of lives. The Commercial insurance company for insuring ships, merchandise, & lives; and against fire.
10 pp. Dublin, Barlow, 1811
A.

2712 Prospectus of the Patriotic Fishing Company, to be incorporated by act of parliament, for which application is making in the present sessions of parliament.
16 pp. London, 1811
Q.

2713 RADCLIFFE, William. Exportation of cotton yarns. The real cause of the distress that has fallen upon the cotton trade for a series of years past: with hints, as to the only remedy to bring this trade to its former flourishing state, pointed out: in a letter to Lord Sydmouth, when Chancellor of the Exchequer: in minutes of evidence before a committee of the house of commons, when enquiring into the merits of Dr. Cartwright's invention of the power loom; and in two letters to the right honourable Spencer Percival, Chancellor of his majesty's exchequer.
46 pp. Stockport, D. Dean, 1811
P.

2714 READE, John. Observations upon tythes, rents and other subjects, with a peculiar reference to Ireland; an appendix and postscript upon catholic emancipation.
appendix. 124 pp. Dublin, printed by Henshall, 1811
A., C., E., N., R.

2715 Remarks and reflections on the intended Liverpool dock bill, now before parliament, and also on the statement and plan circulated by the dock trustees for filling up the old dock, and various proposals to provide additional dock space, etc. etc. With a plan of the docks. Respectfully addressed to the inhabitants of Liverpool, by Mercator.
fold. plan. 40 pp. Liverpool, Wright and Cruickshank, 1811
Q.

2716 Remarks on the supposed depreciation of paper currency in England, by a merchant.
appendix. 38 pp. London, J. M. Richardson, 1811
T.

2717 A replication to all the theorists and abstract reasoners on bullion, coins, exchanges and commerce; in a letter addressed to the legislature of the United Kingdom of Great Britain and Ireland.
90 pp. London, printed for the author by J. Gillet, 1811
Signed: C. R. B. H.
T.

2718 RICARDO, David. Reply to Mr. Bosanquet's observations on the report of the Bullion Committee.
appendix. 150 pp. London, Murray, Edinburgh, Blackwood, Dublin, Mahon, 1811
T.

2719 ROSE, George. Substance of the speech delivered in the house of commons by the Right Honorable George Rose, on Monday the sixth of May 1811, in the committee of the whole house on the report of the bullion committee.
136 pp. London, T. Cadell (etc.), 1811
A.

2720 ROSSE, Sir Lawrence Parsons, 2nd earl of. Observations on the present state of the currency of England.
96 pp. London, J. J. Stockdale, 1811
A., T.

2721 Rules & regulations to be observed by the member of the Shipwright society in the City of Dublin.
8 pp. Dublin, J. and J. Carrick, 1811
A.

2722 [RUSSELL, W. P.] Animating hints; for British statesmen; British merchants; and Britons in general: on going to war with America. By a Briton.
34 pp. London, Blacklock, 1811
K.

2723 RUTHERFORD, A. W. Hints from Holland; or, Gold bullion as dear in Dutch currency as in bank notes, in a letter to two merchants ....
tables. 88 pp. London, J. M. Richardson, etc., 1811
A., N., T.

2724 ——. Observations on the letter of Davies Giddy, Esq., M.P. entitled a plain statement of the Bullion question.
32 pp. London, J. M. Richardson, 1811
T.

2725 SHEFFIELD, John Baker-Holroyd, 1st earl of. Lord Sheffield's present state of the wool trade.
30 pp. Dublin, printed by Graisberry and Campbell, 1811
N., Q.

2726 SHOLL, Samuel. A short historical account of the silk manufacture in England, from its introduction down to the present time: with some remarks on the state of the trade, before the act of parliament was granted, to empower the magistrates to settle the price of labour in the different branches of the manufacture. Also the methods resorted to by the journeymen to raise the money to pay the expence of law, as pointed out in the said act. To which is added, a faithful account of the first cause of the introduction of the grand national flag. By Samuel Sholl, Journeyman Weaver, inventor of the improved silk looms, founder of the silk flag, etc. To which will be subjoined a sketch of the first 58 years of his life, written by himself, and assisted by a gentleman of the first celebrity.
tables. 52 pp. London, M. Jones, 1811
T.

2727 SIORDET, J. M. A letter to the right hon. Sir John Sinclair, Bart, M.P. supporting his arguments in refutation of those advanced by Mr. Huskisson, on the supposed depreciation of our currency. Including a letter to Sir Charles Price, Bart. M.P. in August last, on the report of the bullion committee.
56 pp. [London], H. K. Causton, 1811
N., Q., T.

2728 A sketch of the present state of Ireland.
58 pp. Dublin, H. Fitzpatrick, 1811
L., N.

2729 Sketches of Irish history, and considerations on the catholic question. Together with an answer to the misrepresentations of Messrs. Newenham and Cobbett, respecting the affairs of Ireland.
114 pp. London, John Murray, 1811
M.

2730 SMITH, Thomas. An essay on the theory of money and exchange. Second edition with considerable additions including an examination of the report of the Bullion-committee.
254 pp. Edinburgh, Manners and Miller, London, J. M. Richardson, (etc.), 1811
N.

2731 Sur la Banque de France, les causes de la crise qu'elle a éprouvée, les tristes effets qui en sont resultés, et les moyens d'en prévenir le retour; avec une théorie des banques. Rapport fait à la Chambre de Commerce par une commission spéciale.
80 pp. Paris, 1806; London, reprinted by J. Breteil, 1811
T.
Signed by Pierre Samuel Dupont de Nemours.

2732 TAYLOR, J. N. Prospectus of the National floating breakwater and Refuge Harbour Co.
sketches. plans. 4 pp. London, printed by Hancock, [1811?]
A.

2733 THORNTON, Sir Edward. Observations on the report of the committee of the house of Commons, appointed to inquire into the high price of gold bullion, etc. etc. together with some remarks on the work of Francis Blake, Esq. F.R.S. entitled, 'Observations on the principles which regulate the course of exchange, and on the present depreciated state of the currency.'
166 pp. London, John Stockdale, 1811
Q.

2734 Two reports of the Commissioners of the Thames Navigation (publ. by order of general meeting at Oxford 1810).
54 pp. Oxford, Munday, 1811
A.

2735 A view of the comparative state of Great Britain and France in 1811. Preceded by observations on the spirit and measures of the successive administrations since the decease of Mr. Pitt, in January, 1806.
192 pp. London, John Stockdale, 1811
Q.

2736 WILSON, Robert. Observations on the depreciation of money and the state of our currency.
tables. table of contents. appendix. 84 pp. Edinburgh, J. Anderson, London, Longman, Hurst, Rees, Orme and Brown, 1811
N.

1812

2737 An Abstract of the Evidence lately taken in the house of commons against the orders in council: being a summary of the facts there proved, respecting the present state of the commerce and manufactures of the country.
tables. index. appendices. 76 pp. London, J. M'Creery, 1812
A.

2738 An abstract of the presentments, of the Grand Jury of the County Meath, Summer assizes, 1812.
tables. 58 pp. Dublin, printed by Smith, 1812
A.

2739 Appeal to common sense on the bullion-question. By a merchant.
72 pp. London, J. M. Richardson, [etc.], 1812
N.

2740 An appeal to the public from the committee of the intended new Dublin female penitentiary.
24 pp. Dublin, Jones, 1812
A.

2741 Authentic narrative of the aerial voyage of Mr. Sadler across the Irish Channel from Belvedere House, Drumcondra; in the neighbourhood of Dublin on Thursday October 1st, 1812.
map. illustration. 32 pp. Dublin, printed by Tyrrell, 1812
N.

2742 BLACK, Robert. Substance of two speeches, delivered in the general synod of Ulster, at its annual meeting in 1812: by the Rev. Robert Black, D.D. senior Presbyterian minister of Londonderry; with an abstract of the proceedings of the synod relative to the Rev. Doctor Dickson.
80 pp. Dublin, printed by Stewart and Hopes, 1812
L.

2743 Brief thoughts on the present state of the currency of this country. By a merchant.
46 pp. Edinburgh, A. Constable & Co., 1812
A.

2744 Contract of agreement, the Lord Provost, Magistrates, and Town Council, and the Minister & Kirk Session, of the City of Edinburgh, for building and endowing the charity workhouse, 1740.
8 pp. Edinburgh, printed by Browne, 1812
A.

2745 CRUMP, T. V. A practicable plan for abolishing tithes in England and Ireland.
60 pp. London, Sherwood, Neely, Jones, 1812
A.

2746 DABBADIE, M. An impartial view of the Royal canal company's affairs, in reply to the report of their committee. with a full statement of the several sums appropriated and due by the company, and some directors, to the canal fund; together with a computation of interest thereon.
tables. 114 pp. Dublin, printed by Graisberry and Campbell, 1812
N.

2747 Hints to all classes on the state of the country in this momentous crisis. By one of the people.
28 pp. London, J. J. Stockdale, 1812
Q.

2748 HOLMES, William Anthony. An examination of Mr. Parnell's arguments and plan for a commutation of tithe in Ireland; as submitted to the house of commons, in the year 1812; in a letter to the rt. hon. Lord Viscount Castlereagh.
44 pp. Belfast, printed by Joseph Smyth, 1812
A., K., Q.

2749 Institution for administering medical aid to the sick poor, and assisting them and their families with the necessaries of life during sickness; and for preventing the spreading of contagious diseases. [Report by J. F. Kearney, M.D.]
32 pp. Dublin, printed by Charles Downes, 1812
L.

2750 [McDONNEL, Robert.] Observations on the present state of the paper currencies of Great Britain and Ireland.
28 pp. Belfast, S. Archer; London, Longman, Hurst, Rees, Orme and Brown, 1812
A., L., P., Q.

2751 MINCHIN, W. R. Present state of the debtor and creditor law: being an essay on the effects of imprisonment; or, a consideration of creditors' rights and debtors' wrongs: and an analysis of the Lords' Committee's report on imprisonment for civil debt. With an abstract of Lord Redesdale's bill; and other measures, proposed to effect amendments. Dedicated by permission to His Royal Highness the Duke of Kent.
176 pp. London, James Collins, 1812
T.

2752 MULOCK, Thomas. Short practical considerations on scarcity; and on the plans for remedying deficient subsistence in Great Britain and Ireland.
appendix. 58 pp. Dublin, Archer, 1812
N.

2753 Observations upon the past and present state of our currency. By a citizen of Dublin.
112 pp. London, P. Murray, 1812
A.

2754 O'DEDY, U. A view of the laws of landed property in Ireland, of the relation of landlords and tenants, and of the condition of the latter actually, morally and politically considered: with a mode suggested of attaching the mass of the people to British interests.
144 pp. London, W. Reed, [etc.], 1812
N., Q., U.

2755 [O'REILLY, Edward?] A letter to the magistrates of the police districts of the city of Dublin, upon enforcing the laws which prohibit the grocers selling spirits in small quantities. By a publican.
18 pp. Dublin, 1812
A., Q.

2756 PARNELL, Sir Henry Brooke, bart., later 1st baron Congleton. Substance of a speech made by Henry Parnell Esq. on the 9th of May, 1811, in the committee of the whole house of commons, to which the report of the bullion committee was referred.
tables. 60 pp. London, J. Budd, 1812
A.

2757 Premiums offered by the farming society of Ireland, for 1812, and 1813.
16 pp. Dublin, printed by W. Porter, 1812
Q.

2758 RICHARDSON, William. Observations on a report [by Rev. T. Radcliff for the farming society of Ireland] of the agriculture and live stock of the county of Wicklow. With a recommendation of the culture of fiorin grass, on the Wicklow mountains, for winter food. [With postscript.]
58 pp. Dublin, printed by W. Porter, 1812
N.

2759 Rules to be observed by the United brothers of the flower and independent society of Belfast.
24 pp. Belfast, printed by H. K. Gordon, 1812
A.

2760 SINCLAIR, Sir John, bart. An account of improvements carried on by Sir John Sinclair, Bart. founder and first president of the board of agriculture, on his estates in Scotland. Extracted from the agricultural report of the county of Caithness.
fold. map and diags. 44 pp. London, B. McMillan, 1812
Q.

2761 Sixth annual report of the Stillorgan charitable institution for promoting the comforts of the poor.
tables. 32 pp. Dublin, Watson, 1812
A.

2762 SMITH, Thomas. The bullion-question impartially discussed; an address to the editors of the Edinburgh review.
96 pp. (48–64 missing), London, J. M. Richardson, (etc.), 1812
A.

2763 SUGDEN, Edward Burtenshaw (afterwards baron St. Leonards). Cursory inquiry into the expediency of repealing the Annuity act, and raising the legal rate of interest. In a series of letters.
table of contents. 64 pp. London, J. Murray, [etc.], 1812
A.

2764 Third report of the Meath charitable loan.
30 pp. Dublin, Jones, 1812
A.

2765 TRIMMER, Joshua Kirby. Further observations on the present state of agriculture, and condition of the lower classes of the people in the southern parts of Ireland: with an estimate of the agricultural resources of that country and a plan for carrying into effect a commutation for tithe, and a project for poor laws.
122 pp. London, F. C. and J. Rivington, etc., 1812
N.

2766 WILSON, Glocester. A further defence of abstract currencies.
116 pp. London, John Murray, (etc.), 1812
A.

2767 YOUNG, Arthur. An enquiry into the progressive value of money in England, as marked by the price of agricultural products; with observations upon Sir G. Shuckburgh's table of appreciation: the whole deduced from a great variety of authorities, not before collected.
tables. 70 pp. (paginated 65–128), London, printed by B. McMillan, 1812
A.

1813

2768 Annual report of the charitable association for the year 1812.
36 pp. Dublin, printed by Napper, 1813
A.

2769 The annual report of the managers and auditors of the Cork institution, previous to the general meeting at the Spring assizes, 1813.
60 pp. Cork, printed at the Stanhope-Press, 1813
A.

2770 [BEXLEY, Nicholas Vansittart, 1st baron.] Outlines of a plan of finance: proposed to be submitted to parliament.
tables. 40 pp. London, Luke Hansard & sons, 1813
Q.

2771 Considerations on the proposed Southwark bridge, from Bankside to Queen Street, Cheapside; addressed to the subscribers. By a subscriber.
20 pp. London, Sherwood, Neely & Jones, 1813
Q.

2772 CORRIE, Edgar. Letters on the subject of the duties on beer, malt, and spirits.
tables. appendix. 28 pp. Liverpool, printed by J. Lang, 1813
T.

2773 DE SALIS, Jerome, count. Considerations on the propriety of a general draining bill for the whole British Empire and of a commutation of tithes for Ireland.
20 pp. Armagh, Stevenson, 1813
A.

2774 Fourth report of the Meath charitable loan.
34 pp. Dublin, Watson, 1813
A.

2775 A full report with notes, of the trial of an action, wherein the hon. Fred Cavendish was plaintiff and the Hope Assurance Coy. of London were defendants; held before the rt. hon. Lord John Norbury, Chief Justice of the Common Pleas in Ireland, and a special jury 18th–23rd Feb. 1813, wherein a verdict was found for the defendants. To which is added, a copy of the reports of the inspectors, appt. to view the premises immediately subsequent to the fire.
306 pp. Dublin, printed by Fitzpatrick, 1813
N.

2776 GALTON, S. Tertius. A chart, exhibiting the relation between the amount of Bank of England notes in circulation the rate of foreign exchanges, and the prices of gold and silver bullion and of wheat.
chart. 32 pp. London, J. Johnson, 1813
A.

2777 GRAHAM, John. An account of the town and parish of Maghera, in the diocese of Derry, drawn up for the first volume of Mr. Shaw Mason's Statistical Account, or parochial survey of Ireland.
40 pp. Dublin, Graisberry and Campbell, 1813
A.

2778 HODGSON, Peter J. A book of rates of customs duties, payable in Ireland, upon all goods imported and exported also the drawbacks bounties and allowances, on goods exported. With tables of storage and tares. The whole brought up to the latest period.
table of contents. tables. 160 pp. Dublin, printed at the Hibernia-Press Office, 1813
A.

2779 HOWE, James. A work on leasing lands, perused by Lords Erskine and Somerville; which is presumed will be found to be a complete definition of the law between landlord and tenant.
30 pp. London, J. Williams, 1813
T.

2780 HUSKISSON, William. Substance of the speech of Wm Huskisson in the house of commons in a committee of the whole house upon the resolutions proposed by the Chancellor of the Exchequer respecting the state of the finances and the Sinking Fund of Great Britain, on Thursday, 25th March, 1813.
82 pp. London, Murray, 1813
A.

2781 A letter to Sir Henry Parnell Bart. in reply to his 'Arguments and plan for a commutation of tithes in Ireland', by a beneficed clergyman.
30 pp. London, J. Hatchard, 1813
A., N., P.

2782 Letters on Ireland: to refute Mr. George Barnes' statistical account, by a Citizen of Waterford.
142 pp. Waterford, printed by W. Smith, 1813
A., N.

2783 MASON, William Shaw. Reprint of the statistical account of the town and parish of Thurso in Scotland, and of the parish of Aghaboe in Ireland, with a short introduction containing a plan for the arrangement of the statistical account of Ireland.
maps. tables. illustrations. 94 pp. Dublin, Graisberry and Campbell, 1813
A.
[The survey of Thurso was by Sir John Sinclair, that of Aghaboe by Edward Ledwich.]

——. Reprint of the statistical account of ... Thurso [only].
40 pp. Dublin, Graisberry and Campbell, 1813
N.

2784 MELVILLE, Henry Dundas, 1st viscount. Letters from the Right Hon. Henry Dundas to the chairman of the Court of Directors of the East-India Company, upon an open trade to India.
appendix. 50 pp. London, J. Richardson, 1813
K.

2785 ——. Opinions of the late Lord Melville and Marquess Wellesley upon an open trade to India.
20 pp. London, E. Cox and son, 1813
K.

2786 On the state of Ireland, in a second letter to a friend, written in 1813, by an Irish Landlord.
10 pp. Bristol, Barry, [1813?]
A.

2787 The preliminary debate at the East-India house, on Tuesday, the 5th January, 1813, on the negociation with his majesty's ministers relative to a renewal of the charters; with an appendix containing all the letters and documents referred to upon the subject. By an impartial reporter.
appendices. 70 pp. London, Black, Parry, 1813
K.

2788 Proposals for reducing the price of silver, and raising the value and diminishing the amount of our paper currency.
76 pp. London, J. M. Richardson, 1813
N.

2789 Report of the directors of the Royal Canal company, to a court of proprietors, held at the Brod Stone, on 26th of July, 1813, announced to them the dissolution of the corporation by Parliament.
28 pp. Dublin, printed by J. & J. Carrick, 1813
A., M.

2790 Resolutions and regulations of the committee for managing the Charitable Fund raised in the Parish of St. Peter.
12 pp. Dublin, printed by W. Watson, 1813
N.

2791 Rules and orders to be observed by members of the Phoenix society in the city of Dublin.
12 pp. Dublin, Coyne, 1813
A.

2792 Rules and regulations agreed to by the Imokilly district farming society, at a general meeting held at Castlemartyr, on Tuesday, 7th December, 1813.
10 pp. Cork, printed by Odell, Campbell and Laurent, 1813
A.

2793 [SCHLEGEL, August Wilhelm von.] Sur le système continental et sur ses rapports avec la Suède.
100 pp. London, Schulze and Dean, 1813
A.
[This copy has MS note: 'said to be by Mme. de Stael'.]

2794 SHEFFIELD, John Baker-Holroyd, 1st earl of. On the trade in wool and woollens, including an exposition of the commercial situation of the British Empire. Extracted from the reports addressed to the Wool-meetings at Lewes, in the years 1809, 1810, 1811, 1812.
24 pp. Dublin, printed by Graisberry and Campbell, 1813
A., N.

2795 A short conversation on the present crisis of the important trade with the East Indies.
32 pp. London, Black, Parry, 1813
K.

2796 THOM, Walter. Letter to W. Shaw Mason of Dublin, (and a short essay on political economy).
32 pp. Dublin, [Thom?], 1813
A.

2797 The toll-collectors' terror! or Farmers' Guide, to prevent extortion and imposition.
18 pp. Dublin, Tyrrell, [1813?]
A., D., N.

1814

2798 Annual report of the charitable repository and school of industry, Bandon.
20 pp. Cork, Edwards and Savage, 1814
A.

2799 An authentic report of the charge delivered by the Rt. Hon. Wm. Downes, Lord Chief Justice of the Court of King's Bench in Ireland, to a special Jury on 18 March 1814 in a cause in which the Hon. Frederick Cavendish was plaintiff and the Globe Insurance Co. of London were defendants.
12 pp. Dublin, printed by A. O'Neill, 1814
A., N.

2800 BOOTH, George. Observations on lowering the rent of land, and on the corn laws.
50 pp. Liverpool, Robinson, London, Longman, Hurst, Rees, Orme and Brown, [1814]
K., T.

2801 BROADHURST, J. Speech against the proposed alteration of the Corn laws, intended to have been spoken in the house of commons.
70 pp. London, Colburn, 1814
A.

2802 The calumnious aspersions contained in the report of the sub-committee of the stock-exchange, exposed and refuted,

in so far as regards Lord Cochrane, K.B. and M.P., the Hon. Cochrane Johnstone, M.P. and R. G. Butt, Esq. to which are added, under the authority of Mr. Butt, copies of the purchases and sales of omnium and consols, referred to in the report of the sub-committee.
66 pp. 2nd ed. London, Jones, [etc.], [1814?]

Q.

2803 A comparative view of the present depreciated currency with the sterling money of England... also a project for rendering & preserving that currency of equal value with the standard coin of the realm.
32 pp. Bath, Meyler, 1814

A.

2804 A description of the collieries of Killenaule, in the barony of Slevardagh and county of Tipperary, now to be let, the estate of Edward Worth Newenham, Esq., containing upwards of 3150 acres, statute measure.
map. 10 pp. Dublin, T. Courtney, 1814

A., P.
See 2860.

2805 A description of the silver and lead mines of Shalee, in the barony of Upper Ormond, and county Tipperary, now to be let, the estate of Sir Edward Newenham and his son and heir Edward Worth Newenham, Esq.
map. 4 pp. Dublin, T. Courtney, 1814

A.

2806 DUMBELL, John.   Letter to the Rt. Hon. Wm. Donville Bt., the Lord Mayor of London.
112 pp. and postscript of 36 pp. London, printed by R. and A. Taylor, 1814

A.

2807 ELIOT, Francis Perceval.   Letters on the political and financial situation of the country in the year 1814; addressed to the earl of Liverpool.
tables. 22 pp. London, 1814

P.

2808 ENSOR, George.   Observations on the present state of Ireland.
table of contents. 128 pp. Dublin, printed by H. Fitzpatrick, 1814

N., R., U.

2809 An essay on the nature of credit, as it is connected with the bankrupt law.
20 pp. London, printed by the Philanthropic Society, 1814

T.

2810 Fifth report of the Meath charitable loan, instituted July 1809.
20 pp. Dublin, W. Watson, 1814

A., N.

2811 First report of the Society for the suppression of beggars.
tables. 68 pp. Edinburgh, Smellie, 1814

A., N.

2812 GRIFFITH, Richard, Jr.   Geological and mining report on the Leinster coal district.
tables. 160 pp. Dublin, Graisberry and Campbell, 1814

A., T.

2813 HARRISON, William.   The substance of the reply of Wm. Harrison Esq., before the select committee of the house of commons, on East India-built shipping, on Tuesday, June 28th, 1814, in reply on the whole case.
60 pp. London, printed by T. Davison, 1814

A.

2814 ——.   The substance of the speech of William Harrison, Esq. before the select committee of the house of commons, on East India built shipping, on Monday, April 18, 1814. Sir Robert Peel, Bart. in the chair.
28 pp. London, J. M. Richardson, 1814

Q.

2815 An inquiry into the policy, efficiency, and consistency, of the alterations in our corn laws; which have been lately proposed to parliament in a letter to Sir Henry Parnell, Bart.
50 pp. London, 1814

P.

2816 Interesting extracts from the minutes of evidence taken before the committee of the whole house, to whom it was referred to consider of the affairs of the East India company, in the session of 1813; illustrative of the improvements in the manufacture of iron, steel, brass, tin, copper, hemp, cordage, etc. by the natives of India.
46 pp. London, J. M. Richardson, 1814

Q.

2817 JACOB, William.   Considerations on the protection required by British agriculture and on the influence of the price of corn on exportable productions.
198 pp. London, Johnson, 1814

A.

2818 KILLALY, John.   Papers respecting surveys made for lines of navigation from Lough Erne to Strabane, and from Lough Erne to Ballyshannon, by order of the directors general of inland navigation, upon the approbation of the Lord Lieutenant of Ireland.
maps. 12 pp. Dublin, printed by La Grange, 1814

A.

2819 ——.   Plans respecting a survey made for a navigation and railroad from the River Barrow at Gore's Bridge, by the City of Kilkenny, to Castlecomer, by order of the directors general of inland navigation with the approbation of H. E. the Lord Lieutenant of Ireland.
map. 8 pp. Dublin, printed by La Grange, 1814

A.

2820 LAUDERDALE, James Maitland, 8th earl of.   A letter on the corn laws by the Earl of Laudersale.
tables. appendix. 96 pp. London, Longman, Hurst, Rees, Orme and Brown; Edinburgh, Constable, 1814

U.

2821 A letter to the Earl of Liverpool on the probable effect of a great reduction of corn prices, by importation; upon the relative condition of the state and its creditors, and of debtors and creditors in general.
110 pp. London, Black, Parry, 1814

A., K., T.

2822 MALTHUS, Thomas Robert. Observations on the effects of the corn laws and of a rise or fall in the price of corn on the agriculture and general wealth of the country.
46 pp. London, J. Johnson, 1814

A.

2823 MASON, William Shaw. Prospectus and review of the Statistical account or parochial survey of Ireland.
16 pp. Dublin, 1814

A.

2824 NAISMITH, John. An inquiry concerning the propriety of increasing the import duty on foreign corn.
44 pp. London, 1814

P.

2825 O'REGAN, Maurice. The present state of Ireland, as delineated in the hon. Justice Fletcher's charge to the grand jury of the county of Wexford, together with some observations on Mr. Peel's Acts.
38 pp. Dublin, 'printed by James Cuming', 1814

P.

2826 PARNELL, Sir Henry Brooke, bart. (later 1st baron CONGLETON). The substance of the speeches of Sir [Henry] Parnell in the house of commons, with additional observations on the corn laws.
tables. 40 pp. 3rd Edition. London, 1814

P.

2827 PEMBERTON, Benjamin. Letter to William Walker, Esq., Recorder of the City of Dublin, on the primary cause of combination among the tradesmen of Dublin.
16 pp. Dublin, 1814

N.

2828 Report of the committee appointed to distribute relief to the poor of Dublin (Jan.–March 1814).
24 pp. Dublin, Exshaw, 1814

A.

2829 Report of the Grand Jury of county Cork on the nature of the expenditures and deviations on the main-coach line of road, Cork to Skibbereen.
136 pp. Cork, Edwards and Savage, 1814

A.

2830 Review & examination of the statements, reasoning, & opinions contained in the mis-reported charge of the Hon. Mr. Justice Fletcher to the grand jurors of Wexford.
46 pp. Dublin, printed by L. Tute, 1814

B.

2831 The right and practice of impressment, as concerning Great Britain and America, considered.
70 pp. London, J. Murray, 1814

A., Q.

2832 The second report of the society, instituted in Edinburgh on 25th January, 1813, for the suppression of beggars, for the relief of occasional distress, and for the encouragement of industry among the poor.
tables. 32 pp. Edinburgh, printed by Smellie, 1813

A.

2833 [SIMPSON, Thomas.] A defence of the land-owners and farmers of Great Britain; and an exposition of the heavy parliamentary and parochial taxation under which they labour; combined with a general view of the internal and external policy of the country; in familiar letters from an agricultural gentleman in Yorkshire to a friend in parliament.
tables. 120 pp. London, R. Bickerstaff, Stockton-upon-Tees, Christopher and Jennett, 1814

K., T.

2834 SMITH, Thomas. Letter to the Earl of Lauderdale, in reply to his 'Depreciation of paper-currency proved'.
appendix. 116 pp. London, J. M. Richardson, [etc.], 1814

N.

2835 St. George's Parochial charitable loan society: St. George's Parish; resolutions of the committee for managing the charitable fund, for the relief of the Industrious poor in St. George's Parish.
12 pp. Dublin, printed by White, 1814

N.

2836 TALLEYRAND-PÉRIGORD, Charles Maurice de, Prince de Bénévent. Memoir concerning the commercial relations of the United States with Great Britain. (Also) An essay on the advantages to be derived from new colonies in the existing circumstances.
26 pp. [1814]

P.

2837 [THOM, Walter?] A synopsis of the science of political economy. By W. T.
28 pp. Dublin, printed by Cumming, 1814

N.

2838 WESTERN, Charles Callis Western, baron. Letter to his constituents on the subject of the foreign corn trade.
table. 32 pp. London, Budd and Calkin, 1814

A.

2839 WILBERFORCE, William. A letter to His Excellency the Prince of Talleyrand-Périgord, &c. &c. &c. on the subject of the slave trade.
appendix. 86 pp. London, J. Hatchard, 1814

T.

2840 WILKS, Charles. Observations on the height of carriage wheels, on the comparative advantages of employing one or two horses with one carriage, and on repairing roads.
diagrams. 26 pp. Cork, Odell and Laurent, 1814

A., N.

1815

2841 An account of the improvements on the estate of Sutherland.
22 pp. London, Macleish, 1815

A.

2842 An address to the nation, on the relative importance of agriculture and manufactures, and the means of advancing them both to the highest degree of improvement of which they are capable; together with remarks on the doctrines lately advanced by Mr. Malthus, on the nature of rent, and the

relation it has to the amount of national income; and a prefatory letter to C. M. Talleyrand Périgord, Prince of Benevento, on his late exposé of the financial state of the French nation. By the author of 'Observations on the National debt'; 'Thoughts on peace; with an appendix, concerning the theory of Money,' Etc. Etc.
144 pp. London, Longman, Hurst, Rees, Orme and Brown, 1815

K., T.

2843 An address to the public on the impolicy of the new corn-bill and of the alarming tendency of a late compromise. By Civis.
20 pp. London, J. M. Richardson, 1815

K.

2844 Address to the two houses of parliament on the importance of the corn laws to the national revenue.
20 pp. London, J. J. Stockdale, 1815

K., T.

2845 BAGOT, Daniel. To the proprietors of Grand canal stock. List of proprietors.
38 pp. Dublin, W. Porter, 1815

A.

2846 BALL, John. An address to the public on behalf of the poor; with an appendix containing extracts from various writings relative to their condition.
appendix. 66 pp. Dublin, printed by Nolan, 1815

A., N., T.

2847 BOOTH, George. Observations on paper currency, the bank of England notes, and on the principles of coinage, and a metallic circulating medium.
42 pp. Liverpool, Robinson; London, Longman, Hurst, Rees. Orme and Brown, 1815

T.

2848 Bosman's balance for weighing a corn law.
20 pp. London, T. Underwood, 1815

K.

2849 BUCHANAN, Robertson. A treatise on the economy of fuel, and management of heat, especially as it relates to heating and drying by means of steam. In four parts. With many useful tables. (Part four and appendix only.)
plates. appendix. 140 pp. Glasgow, the author, 1815

T.

2850 CHAPMAN, William. Observations on the effects that would be produced by the proposed corn laws on the agriculture, commerce, and population of the United Kingdom.
tables. appendices. 38 pp. London, J. M. Richardson; Winchester, W. Jacob; Edinburgh, Archibald Constable; Glasgow, Brash and Reid, 1815

K., T.

2851 Charter of incorporation of the chambers of commerce of the City of Waterford, granted in the year 1815.
28 pp. Waterford, Bull, 1815

A., N.

2852 CLARK, William. Thoughts on the commutation, or abolition, of tithes.
32 pp. Bath, Richard Cruttwell; London, Longman, Hurst, Rees, Orme and Brown, 1815

T.

2853 ——. Thoughts on the management and relief of the poor; on the cause of their increase; and on the measures that may be best calculated to amend the former, and check the latter.
tables. 68 pp. Bath, Richard Cruttwell, 1815

K., T.

2854 CLARKSON, William. An inquiry into the cause of the increase of pauperism and poor rates; with a remedy for the same, and a proposition for equalizing the rates throughout England and Wales.
tables. 78 pp. London, Baldwin, Cradock, and Joy, 1815

K., T.

2855 [COLLINS, J.] An address to the people of Ireland, and particularly to the inhabitants of those counties, wherein some atrocities have lately occurred, with remarks on the present posture of affairs, and on Mr. Peele's [sic] bill, lately passed into a law, for the preservation of the peace of the country. By a compatriot.
50 pp. Dublin, Espy & Cross, 1815

A., N.

2856 Considerations upon the Corn bill; suggested by a recent declaration from high authority, that it was calculated 'To throw the burden from those upon whom it ought to rest, to those upon whom it ought not'.
tables. appendices. 52 pp. London, Longman, Hurst, Rees, Orme, and Brown, [etc.], 1815

K., T.

2857 COOKE, Henry. A sermon preached in the Meeting-House of the third Presbyterian Congregation, Belfast on Sunday the 18th December, 1814 in aid of the funds of the House of Industry.
3rd ed. Belfast, printed by Finlay, 1815

A.

2858 Copy of the charter of the Farming society of Ireland.
24 pp. Dublin, printed by W. Porter, 1815

N.

2859 [DAYMAN, John.] Observations on the justice and policy of regulating the trade in corn. By J. D. Dedicated, by permission, to the Right Honorable William Huskisson.
34 pp. Exeter, printed by R. Cullum, 1815

K.

——. Another issue. 34 pp. Exeter, E. Upham, 1815

T.

2860 A description of the collieries of Killenaule, in the barony of Sleverdagh and County of Tipperary, now to be let, the estate of Edward Worth Newenham, Esq. containing upwards of three thousand, one hundred and fifty acres, statute measure.
map. 18 pp. Dublin, printed by T. Courtney, 1815

A.

See 2804.

2861 DUNDONALD, Thomas Cochrane, 10th earl of.   A letter to Lord Ellenborough from Lord Cochrane.
appendix. 176 pp. 2nd ed. London, pr. for the author [by T. C. Hansard] and sold by W. Jackson, 1815
T.

2862 DUPPA, Richard.   Observations on the price of corn as connected with the commerce of the country and the public revenue.
22 pp. London, J. Murray, 1815
K., T.

2863 EDYE, John.   A letter to William Wilberforce, Esq., M.P. on the consequences of the unrestrained importation of foreign corn.
24 pp. London, Longman, Hurst, Rees, Orme and Brown, [etc.], 1815
K., T.

2864 An enquiry into the causes that have impeded the increase and improvement of arable farms and that have principally depressed the landed interest with some suggestions for establishing a system of permanent relief.
44 pp. Bath, R. Cruttwell, 1815
A.

2865 [GOURLAY, Robert Fleming.] The right to church property secured, and commutation of tythes vindicated, in a letter to the rev. William Coxe, archdeacon of Wilts.
42 pp. London, Highley & son, 1815
K.

2866 Grand canal company. To the proprietors of Grand canal stock. 1815.
20 pp. Dublin, printed by W. Porter, 1815
N.

2867 [GREGOIRE, Henri, constitutional bishop of Blois.] De la traité et de l'esclavage des noirs et des blancs; par un ami des hommes de toutes les couleurs.
84 pp. Paris, Adrien Égron, 1815
U.

2868 HALL, George Webb.   Letters on the importance of encouraging the growth of corn and wool, in the United Kingdom of Great Britain and Ireland.
82 pp. London, Evans and Ruffy, [1815]
A., K., T.

2869 HUME, James Deacon.   Thoughts on the corn laws, as connected with agriculture, commerce, and finance.
tables. 80 pp. London, F. C. and J. Rivington, 1815
T.

2870 JACOB, William.   A letter to Samuel Whitbread, Esq. M.P. being a sequel to considerations on the protection required by British agriculture; to which are added remarks on the publications of a fellow of University College, Oxford; of Mr. Ricardo, and Mr. Torrens.
tables. appendix. 38 pp. London, J. Johnson, [etc.], 1815
K.

2871 KILLALY, John.   Papers respecting a survey for a navigation between Lough Erne and Lough Neagh, Made by order of the Directors General of Inland Navigation, and

published with the approbation of H. E. the Lord Lieutenant of Ireland.
map. 12 pp. Dublin, printed by La Grange, 1815
A.

2872 A letter to the Rt. Hon. Samuel Birch, Lord Mayor of London, on the subject of the corn laws, by an Essex Farmer.
22 pp. London, J. Cawthorn, 1815
A.

2873 MACAULAY, Zachary.   A letter to his royal highness the duke of Gloucester, president of the African institution, from Zachary Macaulay, Esq., occasioned by a pamphlet published by Dr. Thorpe, late judge of the colony of Sierra Leone, entitled 'A letter to William Wilberforce, Esq.' etc., etc.
appendices. 126 pp. 2nd ed. London, J. Hatchard, 1815
T.

2874 McRAE, Alexander.   A disclosure of the hoax practised upon the Stock Exchange, 21st February, 1814; with some remarks on the extraordinary letter of Lord Cochrane to Lord Ellenborough.
appendix. 60 pp. London, S. Cotterell, 1815
T.

2875 MAJOR, Henry.   Observations demonstrative of the necessity to Ireland's welfare and to the character of England, of a tax upon absentees.
68 pp. Dublin, Graisberry and Campbell, 1815
A.

2876 MALTHUS, Thomas Robert.   The grounds of an opinion on the policy of restricting the importation of foreign corn; intended as an appendix to 'Observations on the corn laws'.
50 pp. London, J. Murray, [etc.], 1815
K., T.

2877 ——.   An inquiry into the nature and progress of rent and the principles by which it is regulated.
66 pp. London, J. Murray, 1815
A., T.

——.   Another issue. 66 pp. London, J. Murray and J. Johnson, 1815
K.

2878 —— Observations on the effects of the corn laws and of a rise or fall in the price of corn on the agriculture and general wealth of the country.
50 pp. third edition. London, J. Murray, 1815
A., K., T.

2879 MASON, Henry J. M.   Address to the nobility and gentry upon the necessity of using every exertion at the present to promote the education of the poor of Ireland.
76 pp. Dublin, Folds, 1815
A., N.

2880 [MEDWYN, John Hay Forbes, baron.] A short account of the Edinburgh savings bank, containing directions for establishing similar banks, with the mode of keeping accounts and conducting the details of business.
tables in appendix. 20 pp. Edinburgh, John Anderson, 1815
T.

See 2949

2881 Minutes of the trustees of the linen and hempen manufactures of Ireland, respecting the mode of preparing and dressing Hemp and Flax. Introduced by Mr. James Lee. table of contents. appendices. 44 pp. Dublin, printed by Folds, 1815

N.

2882 MIRABEAU, Victor de Riquetti, marquis de. On the corn laws; being a digest of extracts from the oeconomical table: An attempt towards ascertaining and exhibiting the source, progress, & employment of riches, with explanations by the friend of mankind, the celebrated Marquis De Mirabeau.
110 pp. London, W. Clarke, 1815

T.

2883 MONTEAGLE, Thomas Spring Rice, baron. An inquiry into the effects of the Irish grand jury laws, as affecting the industry, the improvement and the moral character of the people of Ireland.
map. tables. 124 pp. London, J. Murray, 1815

A.

Final page contains list of errata—all corrected in copy listed below.

2884 ——. An inquiry into the effects of the Irish grand jury laws, as affecting the industry, the improvement and the moral character, of the people of England.
map. tables. 122 pp. London, J. Murray, 1815

A.

[Mss. note on t.-p.: '2nd edition.']

2885 O'REARDON, John. Institution for administering medical aid to the sick poor, and assisting them and their families with the necessaries of life during sickness; and for preventing the spreading of contagious diseases.
tables. 28 pp. Dublin, Wm. Watson, 1815

P.

2886 A pat from the lion's paw, inflicted in the name of common sense, upon the opponents of the property tax. By Leo Britannicus.
24 pp. 2nd edition, London, Longman, Hurst, Rees, Orme and Brown; [etc.], 1815

T.

2887 POPE, Charles. A practical abridgment of the customs and excise laws, relative to the import, export, and coasting trade of Gt. Britain and her dependencies; including tables of the duties, drawbacks and bounties. The whole interspersed with the regulations of the several companies; proclamations touching war and peace; orders in council; treaties with foreign powers; reports of adjudged cases; and various matters of official information: the statutes brought down to the adjournment of parliament in 55 Geo. 3 and other parts to 2nd January, 1815.
tables. 60 pp. (pagination irregular). 2nd ed. London, Robert Baldwin, [etc.], 1815

T.

2888 PRESTON, Richard. An address to the fund holder, the manufacturer, the mechanic, and the poor on the subject of the corn laws.
64 pp. London, W. Clarke, 1815

T.

2889 Rates and regulations of the Grand canal company's floating and graving docks at Ringsend.
index. 20 pp. Dublin, Porter, 1815

A.

2890 Remarks on the commercial policy of Great Britain, principally as it relates to the corn trade.
104 pp. London, M. Stockdale, [etc.], 1815

K., T.

2891 RICARDO, David. An essay on the influence of a low price of corn on the profits of stock; shewing the inexpediency of restrictions on importation: with remarks on Mr. Malthus' two last publications: 'An inquiry into the nature and purpose of rent'; and 'The grounds of an opinion on the policy of restricting the importation of foreign corn'.
tables. 52 pp. 2nd ed. London, J. Murray, 1815

K., T.

2892 RICHARDSON, Townley. Letter to the Dublin society, referring to 'the late wheel-carriage experiments'.
6 pp. Dublin, 1815

A.

2893 ——. Observations on wheel carriage experiments submitted to the consideration of the Dublin Society.
18 pp. Dublin, Graisberry and Campbell, 1815

A., D.

2894 RICHARDSON, William. Observations on Mr. Townsend's plan of a canal between Lough Neagh and Lough Erne etc. etc.
12 pp. Newry, printed by Alexander Wilkinson, 1815

R.

[On this copy 'Lough Erne' has been crossed out and 'the sea' written in in ms.]

2895 ROSE, George. Speech on the subject of the property tax.
24 pp. London, J. Hatchard, 1815

A.

2896 A second letter to the Rt. Hon. Samuel Birch, Lord Mayor of London, on the subject of the corn laws and the price of bread, by an Essex Farmer.
24 pp. London, Cawthorn, 1815

A.

2897 Second report of the committee for managing St. Peter's Parochial Charitable Loan, 27th May, 1815.
12 pp. Dublin, Watson, 1815

N.

2898 Sergeant Johnson's statement, Mr. Dickson's reply, with Mr. Bruce's answer, Mr. Stephen Dickson's address to the public, and Mr. Bruce's answer; together with the last resolution of the creditors of Arthur Dickson, bankrupt, and Mr. Dickson's refusal to fulfill his first proposal to them etc. etc.
48 pp. Limerick, printed by MacDonnell, 1815

A.

2899 SHEFFIELD, John Baker Holroyd, 1st earl of. A letter on the corn laws, and on the means of obviating the mischiefs and distress, which are rapidly increasing.
46 pp. London, J. Murray, 1815

N.

——. 64 pp. 2nd ed., 'corrected and considerably enlarged'. London, J. Murray, 1815

K., T.

2900 SINCLAIR, Sir John, bart. Hints regarding the agricultural state of the Netherlands, compared with that of Great Britain; and some observations on the means of diminishing the expence of growing corn; of preventing the mildew of wheat, the rot in sheep, and the introduction of other improvements into British agriculture.
tables. appendix. 130 pp. London, G. & W. Nicol, [etc., etc.], 1815

K.

2901 SMITH, Sir Wm. Cusac, bart. Grand Canal. Defence of the court of directors, including a statement of the true state of the company's affairs.
58 pp. Dublin, W. Porter, 1815

A., N.

2902 Some observations on the original and late and present state of the excise establishment and on the laws and regulations of the excise of Ireland, by Publicanus.
130 pp. Dublin, Goodwin, 1815

A.

2903 Special report of the directors of the African institution, made at the annual general meeting, on the 12th of April, 1815, respecting the allegations contained in a pamphlet entitled 'A letter to William Wilberforce, Esq. etc. by R. Thorpe, Esq. etc.'
tables in appendices. 162 pp. London, J. Hatchard, 1815

T.

2904 SPENCE, William. The objections against the corn bill refuted; and the necessity of this measure to the vital interests of every class of the community demonstrated.
50 pp. 4th ed. London, Longmans, Hurst, Rees, Orme, and Brown, 1815

E., K., T.

2905 [STEPHEN, James?] Reasons for establishing a registry of slaves in the British colonies: being a report of a committee of the African institution.
120 pp. London, J. Hatchard, 1815

T.

2906 STOWELL, Kermotte. Letter, addressed to the Hon. John Moore (one of the Hon. Commissioners of Harbours) embracing various subjects. Appendix - Duties, import and export, in the Isle of Man.
32 pp. Dublin, Espy, 1815

A.

2907 THORPE, Robert. A letter to William Wilberforce, Esq. M.P. Vice president of the African institution, etc. etc. containing remarks on the reports of the Sierra Leone company, and African institution: With hints respecting the means by which an universal abolition of the slave trade might be carried into effect.
appendices. 112 pp. 3rd ed. London, F. C. and J. Rivington, 1815

T.

2908 ——. Postscript to the reply 'point by point'; containing an exposure of the misrepresentation of the treatment of the captured negroes at Sierra Leone; and other matters arising from the ninth report of the African Institute.
66 pp. London, F. C. and J. Rivington, 1815

T.

2909 ——. A reply 'point by point' to the special report of the directors of the African Institution.
116 pp. London, F. C. and J. Rivington, 1815

T.

2910 To the Rt. Hon. and Hon. Dublin society. The Memorial of the undersigned silk manufacturers of the city of Dublin.
14 pp. Dublin, [1815]

A., D.

2911 [URQUHART, Thomas.] Substance of a letter to Lord Viscount Melville, written in May, 1815, with the outlines of a plan to raise British seamen, and to form their minds to volunteer the naval service when required; to do away with the evils of impressment, and man our ships effectively with mercantile seamen.
16 pp. London, W. Phillips, 1815

K.

2912 [WEST, Sir Edward.] Essay on the application of capital to land, with observations shewing the impolicy of any great restriction on the importation of corn, and that the bounty of 1688 did not lower the price of it. By a fellow of University College, Oxford.
tables. appendix. 72 pp. London, T. Underwood, 1815

K., T.

2913 WEYLAND, John. The principle of the English poor laws illustrated from the evidence given by Scottish proprietors, (before the corn committee,) on the connexion observed in Scotland between the price of grain and the wages of labour.
82 pp. London, J. Hatchard, 1815

K., T.

2914 WILSON, Robert. An enquiry into the causes of the high prices of corn and labour, the depressions on our foreign exchanges and high prices of bullion, during the late war; and consideration of the measures to be adopted for relieving our farming interest from the unprecedented difficulties to which they are now reduced, in consequence of the great fall in the price of their produce since the peace; with relative tables and remarks, etc.
tables in appendix. 92 pp. Edinburgh, Constable, 1815; London, Longman, Hurst, Rees, Orme and Brown, 1815

K., T., U.

1816

2915 An address to the honourable house of commons of Great Britain and Ireland, on the state of the nation. By a Yorkshire freeholder.
table. 18 pp. London, Longman, Hurst, Rees, Orme and Brown, 1816

T.

2916 The annual report of the managers and auditors of the Cork institution, previous to the general meeting at the Spring Assizes 1816.
32 pp. Cork, printed by Edwards and Savage, 1816
A., N.

2917 Antidote to West-Indian sketches, drawn from authentic sources. Nos. I–VII.
92 pp. London, Whitmore and Fenn, 1816–17
N.

2918 BALBERNIE, Arthur. Reflections on the Bank paper currency, with a plan how to prevent forgeries, either on Bank of England, Royal or provincial banks.
24 pp. Glasgow, Chapman, 1816
A.

2919 BANNATYNE, Dugald. Observations on the principles which enter into the commerce in grain, and into the measures for supplying food to the people; being the substance of an essay read to the Literary and commercial society of Glasgow.
32 pp. Glasgow, J. Smith, 1816
K., T.

2920 BEAUMONT, John Thomas Barber. An essay on provident or parish banks for the security and improvement of the savings of tradesmen, artificers, servants, etc. until required for their future wants, or advancement in life; containing a brief history of the several schemes for the above purpose; and developing the causes which have promoted or prevented their success; to which is added, a detailed account of the plan, regulations, and routine of management of the provident bank in the parish of St. Paul, Covent Garden.
tables. 70 pp. London, Cadell and Davies, 1816
K., T.

2921 [——.] Letters on public-house licensing; shewing the errors of the present system; (originally printed in the Times newspaper) together with a proposal for their cure. By a magistrate of Middlesex.
32 pp. London, T. Cadell and W. Davies, 1816
T.

2922 Brief remarks on the slave registry bill; and upon a special report of the African institution, recommending that measure.
tables in appendices. 70 pp. London, J. M. Richardson, 1816
K., T.

2923 [BURNABY, Edwyn Andrew.] England may be extricated from her difficulties consistently with the strictest principles of policy, honour, and justice. By a country gentleman.
60 pp. London, J. Hatchard, 1816
T.

2924 BUXTON, Sir Thomas Fowell. The speech of T. F. Buxton at the Egyptian Hall, on the 26th Nov., 1816, on the subject of the distress in Spitalfields. To which is added the report of the Spitalfields Association, read at the meeting. Publ. by order of the Committee then appointed and for the benefit of its funds.
16 pp. London, printed by W. Phillips, 1816
N.
[The Report of the Spitalfields Association missing.]

2925 CHALMERS, George. The state of the United Kingdom, at the peace of Paris, Nov. 20, 1815, respecting the people; their domestic energies; their agriculture; their trade; their shipping; and their finances.
16 pp. London, J. J. Stockdale, 1816
A.

2926 The charter party or the articles of agreement of the Farmers' Tontine company of Ireland.
32 pp. Dublin, W. Porter, 1816
A.

2927 CHRISTIAN, Edward. A plan for a county provident bank. With observations upon provident institutions already established.
88 pp. London, Clarke, 1816
K.

2928 [COLQUHOUN, Patrick.] Epitome of a scheme of finance; whereby a considerable revenue may be obtained, without taxation or any burthen on the country, while it would afford great relief to the agricultural, commercial, trading and manufacturing interests of the country, at this particular and most important crisis, by lending money on mortgages, and by issuing notes as a circulating medium, where every note so issued, shall represent the fraction of a mortgage on freehold, copyhold and leasehold property, and pass into the hands of the public, through the medium of such loans. With observations on the means of improving and extending the general resources of the British Empire.
24 pp. London, J. Hatchard, 1816
T.

2929 Commutation of Tythe, by an acreable charge upon land, calculated to prevent the necessity of Tythe Proctors, etc., etc. By a Beneficed clergyman of the established church.
46 pp. London, Sherwood, Neely, Jones; Dublin, Cuming, 1816
N.

2930 CROMBIE, Alexander. Letters on the present state of the agricultural interest addressed to Charles Forbes, Esq., M.P.
86 pp. London, R. Hunter, 1816
K., T.

2931 EDGEWORTH, Richard Lovell. A letter to the Dublin society relative to the experiments on wheel carriages.
22 pp. Dublin, Graisberry and Campbell, 1816
A., D.

2932 EDMEADS, William. National establishment, national security. Or thoughts on the consequences of commuting the tithes.
38 pp. Oxford, R. Bliss, 1816
K.

2933 The emigrant's guide: or a picture of America: exhibiting a view of the United States, divested of democratic colouring, taken from the original now in the possession of James Madison and his twenty-one governments. Also a sketch of the British provinces delineating their native beauties and superior attractions. By an old scene-painter.
78 pp. London, W. Simpkin and R. Marshall, 1816
T.

2934 An essay on the propriety of permitting the free exportation of British wool.
32 pp. London, Thomas and George Underwood, 1816

K., T.

2935 HAYGARTH, John. An explanation of the principles and proceedings of the provident institution at Bath for savings.
tables. appendix. 120 pp. Bath, R. Cruttwell, for Longman, Hurst, Rees, Orme, and Brown, 1816

K., T.

2936 [HUBAND, Joseph.] Letters to the right honorable Robert Peel, chief secretary to the Lord lieutenant of Ireland, relating to the improvement of 'The district of the metropolis,' and principally the earl of Meath's liberties; by making therein wide and convenient streets. By Viator.
78 pp. Dublin, A. O'Neil, 1816

A., N.

2937 An inquiry into the present agricultural distresses of this country, with suggestions for their relief.
56 pp. Colchester, Swinborne and Walter, 1816

A.

2938 The interference of the British legislature, in the internal concerns of the West India Islands, respecting their slaves deprecated. By a zealous advocate for the abolition of the slave trade.
62 pp. London, J. Mawman, 1816

K., T.

2939 JORDAN, Gibbes Walker. An examination of the principles of the slave registry bill, and of the means of emancipation, proposed by the authors of the bill.
152 pp. London, T. Cadell and W. Davies, 1816

K., T.

2940 KEARNEY, Richard. A plan for the payment of the national debt and for the immediate reduction of taxation.
40 pp. Dublin, Charles, 1816

A.

2941 A letter to the members of the imperial parliament referring to the evidence contained in the proceedings of the house of assembly of Jamaica, and shewing the injurious and unconstitutional tendency of the proposed slave registry bill. By a colonist.
26 pp. London, J. M. Richardson, 1816

K.

2942 A list of all places, pensions, and sinecures, &c. With the various salaries and emoluments arising therefrom. Exhibiting also a complete view of the national debt, with an account of the receipts and expenditure of the public money. With notes, critical and explanatory. The whole comprising the strongest body of evidence to prove the necessity of retrenchment which can possibly be laid before the nation. By a commoner.
appendix. tables. 230 pp. London, J. Blacklock, 1816

A.

2943 McCULLOCH, John Ramsay. An essay on a reduction of the interest of the national debt, proving, that this is the only possible means of relieving the distresses of the commercial and agricultural interests; and establishing the justice of that measure on the surest principles of political economy.
54 pp. London, Joseph Mawman, 1816

K., T.

2944 ——. An essay on the question of reducing the interest of the national debt; in which the justice and expediency of that measure are fully established.
tables. 222 pp. Edinburgh, David Brown, [etc.]; London, T. and C. Underwood, 1816

T.

2945 [MADDEN, Samuel.] Reflections and resolutions proper for the gentlemen of Ireland. As to their conduct for the service of their Country, as landlords, As masters of families, As protestants, As descended from British ancestors, As country gentlemen and farmers, As justices of the peace, As merchants, As members of parliament.
table of contents. 250 pp. Dublin, G. Ewing, 1738, *reprinted* 1816

A.

[Thomas Pleasants' 1816 reprint of Madden's tract of 1738.]

2946 MARRYAT, Joseph. More thoughts occasioned by two publications which the authors call 'An exposure of some of the numerous mis-statements and misrepresentations contained in a pamphlet, commonly known by the name of Mr. Marryat's pamphlet, entitled Thoughts &c.' and 'A defence of the bill for the registration of slaves'.
146 pp. second edition. London, J. M. Richardson; [etc.], 1816

K., T.

2947 [——.] Thoughts on the abolition of the slave trade, and civilization of Africa; with remarks on the African institution, and an examination of the report of their committee, recommending a general registry of slaves in the British West India islands.
244 pp. 3rd ed. London, J. M. Richardson, [etc.], 1816

K., T.

2948 MATHISON, Gilbert. A short review of the reports of the African Institution, and of the controversy with Dr. Thorpe, with some reasons against the registry of slaves in the British colonies. Second edition, with additions and notes.
appendix. 122 pp. London, Wm. Stockdale, [etc.], 1816

T.

2949 MEDWYN, John Hay Forbes, baron. A short account of the Edinburgh savings bank, containing directions for establishing similar banks with the mode of keeping the accounts and conducting the details of business.
tables. 26 pp. Dublin, Hodges and McArthur, 1816

A.

See 2880

2950 National difficulties practically explained. By a member of the Lowestoft book-club.
52 pp. London, Baldwin, Cradock and Joy; [etc.], 1816

T.

2951 A new system of practical political economy adapted to the peculiar circumstances of the present times: pointing out the means of dieting the inhabitants of the metropolis and

its vicinity to upwards of a million sterling per annum better advantage in their housekeeping expenses; opening new sources of advantageous commercial enterprise; and creating new objects of lucrative investment of capital. Illustrated by copper plates of the structure and machinery of the improved hydrostatic ship.
diagrams. tables. 92 pp. London, Longman, [1816?]

N.

2952 The New Year: An essay, re-printed, with additions and corrections, from *The Liverpool Courier*.
62 pp. Liverpool, T. Kaye; London, Baldwin, Cradock and Joy, [etc.], 1816

T.

2953 NIGHTINGALE, Joseph. The bazaar, its origin, nature, and objects explained, and recommended as an important branch of political economy; in a letter to the rt. hon George Rose, M.P. To which is added a postscript, containing an account of every establishment, bearing this name, in the metropolis.
appendix. 70 pp. London, the author, 1816

T.

2954 Observations on the bill introduced last session, by Mr. Wilberforce, for the more effectually preventing the unlawful importation of slaves, and the holding free persons in slavery in the British colonies.
28 pp. London, J. M. Richardson, 1816

K., T.

2955 Observations on the present difficulties of the country, contained in strictures on two pamphlets lately published by J. H. Moggridge. By Cambriensis.
table. 32 pp. London, Black, Parbury and Allen, 1816

T.

2956 Observations on the subject of the Dunleary Asylum Harbour, as connected with the trade and general interests of the city of Dublin. By Censor.
8 pp. n. p., 1816

A.

2957 Observations upon our present system of commercial intercourse with the continent of Europe; shewing the necessity of a change of our commercial policy, during a state of peace.
22 pp. London, John Murray, 1816

K.

2958 On the policy of throwing open the transit trade in foreign linens, and on the importance of that trade to the manufactures and general commerce of the British Empire.
22 pp. London, [J. Bryan,] 1816

A.

2959 OSBORNE, Ebenezer. Observations on a pamphlet entitled A few plain facts etc. etc.
62 pp. Cork, M'Mullen, 1816

A.

[On fire insurance.]

2960 PARKER, William. Observations on the intended amendment of the Irish Grand Jury laws, now under the consideration of the honourable the house of commons, to

which is added a plan for the general survey and valuation of Ireland, and for the commutation of tithes, with several important hints relative to the internal economy of Ireland, and the distressed state of the poor.
table of contents. tables. appendix. 208 pp. Cork, Edwards and Savage, 1816

A., N., P.

2961 ———. A plan for the general improvement of the state of the Poor in Ireland (dedicated to the Rt. Hon. Robert Peel, Chief Secretary to the Lord Lieutenant of Ireland).
166 pp. Cork, Benber, 1816

A., N.

2962 PARRY, Charles Henry. The question of the necessity of the existing corn laws, considered, in their relation to the agricultural labourer, the tenantry, the landholder, and the country.
tables. 238 pp. Bath, printed by Richard Cruttwell; London, Longman, Hurst, Rees, Orme and Brown, 1816

A., K.

2963 PHILLIPS, M. Suggestions for producing public improvements, and affording employment for the distressed manufacturers and the labouring poor, to enable them to procure the necessary articles of food and clothing by industry and economy, to relieve, support, and re-establish the middling classes of the community, and to place before them a much greater share of the comforts of life; and for the wealthy and the great to enjoy their several possessions in a superior degree.
20 pp. Stroud, F. Vigurs, 1816

T.

2964 A plan for a general enclosure bill, for commons of a limited extent, in which the practicability and advantages of such a bill are fully and clearly explained, and some further improvements, connected with the agriculture of the country, are humbly submitted to the consideration of parliament. By a country gentleman, formerly a member of the house of commons.
46 pp. London, Payne and Foss, 1816

K., T.

2965 PRESTON, Richard. Further observations on the state of the nation, the means of employment of labor [sic] the sinking fund and its application, pauperism, protection requisite to the landed and agricultural interests.
48 pp. London, printed by A. J. Valpy, 1816

A.

2966 PRINSEP, Charles Robert. Letter to the Earl of Liverpool, on the cause of the present distresses of the country, and the efficacy of reducing the standard of our silver currency towards their relief.
48 pp. London, J. Ridgway, 1816

N.

2967 Proposal concerning a society for the abolition of mendicity and for the relief and encouragement of the industrious poor in the town of Belfast.
12 pp. Belfast, Smith and Lyons, 1816

A.

2968 Remedies proposed as certain, speedy, and effectual, for the relief of our present embarrassments. By an independent gentleman.
56 pp. London, J. Hatchard, 1816

T.

2969 A reply to the examined case and trial of Mr. Sherson, of the Madras anonymous establishment; to Marsh's Review of the administration of Sir G. Barlow, Bart. By the author of 'a reply to the fairly-stated case of Mr. Cooke'.
90 pp. London, J. M. Richardson, 1816

K.

2970 A reply to the 'Fairly-stated case' of Mr. Cooke, of the Madras civil establishment.
tables. 54 pp. London, J. M. Richardson, 1816

K.

2971 Report of the court of directors of the Grand Canal company, at their half-yearly meeting.
18 pp. Dublin, W. Porter, 1816

A.

2972 RICARDO, David. Proposals for an economical and secure currency; with observations on the profits of the Bank of England, as they regard the public and the proprietors of Bank stock.
tables. appendix with tables. 130 pp. second edition. London, J. Murray, 1816

A., K., T.

2973 ROSE, George. Observations on banks for savings.
tables. appendix. 60 pp. London, Cadell and Davies, 1816

A., K., T.

2974 SIMPSON, Thomas. Letter to the right honorable Lord Castlereagh upon the subject of the present state of Great Britain; describing the origin, the causes, the progress, and the real and probable consequences of the distress, in which the whole kingdom is involved, suggested principally by the speeches of His Lordship and of Henry Brougham, Esq., M.P. on the 9th April.
tables. appendix. 270 pp. Stockton, Christopher and Jennett, [etc.], 1816

T.

2975 SMITH, Thomas. A letter to the right honourable the earl of Liverpool on the proposed new coinage.
table in appendix. 42 pp. London, J. M. Richardson, 1816

T.

2976 ——. A reply to Mr. Ricardo's proposals for an economical and secure currency.
44 pp. London, J. M. Richardson, 1816

T.

2977 ——. A second letter to the right honourable the earl of Liverpool, on the proposed new coinage.
26 pp. London, J. M. Richardson, 1816

T.

2978 Société Centrale d'Agriculture, Paris: Avis aux cultivateurs ['rédigé sur la demande de S. Ex. Le Ministre Secrétaire d'État au département de l'Intérieur par une Commission de la Société Royale et Centrale d'Agriculture'. Dated Paris, 13 août 1816].
20 pp. Paris, printed by Hazard, 1816

N.

2979 Suggestions submitted to the consideration of the nobility, gentry and magistrates of Ireland, anxious to support unemployed people, until work shall be provided for them. Also arguments in favour of continuing distillation from corn in Ireland; remarks on domestic economy, as practised in France, recommended to the consideration of persons whose limited means of support renders economy peculiarly necessary at this eventful crisis. With a plan for national improvement, which may be carried on at a small expense, and afford employment to many thousands of the labouring class. By a Member of the Dublin Society.
32 pp. Dublin, printed by O'Neil, 1816

A.

2980 SUTCLIFFE, John. A treatise on canals and reservoirs, and the best mode of designing and executing them; with observations on the Rochdale, Leeds and Liverpool, and Huddersfield canals, and a comparative view of them; and also on the Bridgewater, the Lancaster, and the Kennett and Avon canals. Likewise observations on the best mode of carding, roving, drawing, and spinning all kinds of cotton twist. Also instructions for designing and building a corn mill, and how to grind corn upon the best principle; with a new and simple mode of preserving grain from the consequences of a wet or soft harvest, and rendering useful grain that has become foul and fusty; together with important directions on public drains.
tables. 432 pp. Rochdale, J. Hartley; London, Law and Whittaker, 1816

T.

2981 Third agreement between members of the Royal exchange insurance company of Dublin, established for the insurance of ships, merchandise, and lives.
14 pp. Dublin, printed by J. Carrick, 1816

A.

2982 Three letters of Paul Silent to his country cousins.
82 pp. second edition. London, J. Ridgway, [etc.], 1816

T.

2983 TORRENS, Robert. A letter to the right honourable the earl of Liverpool, on the state of the agriculture of the United Kingdom, and on the means of relieving the present distress of the farmer, and of securing him against the recurrence of similar embarrassment.
34 pp. London, J. Hatchard, 1816

K., T.

2984 TOWSEND, Horatio. A view of the agricultural state of Ireland, in 1815; with observations on the causes of its depression, and the means of relief.
table. appendix. 52 pp. Cork, Edwards and Savage, 1816

A., T.

2985 Two letters to the Right Honourable Viscount Castlereagh, principal secretary of State &c. &c. on the present

situation of the landed interest, and the intended partial repeal of the Income Tax.
table. 20 pp. London, printed by Ellerton and Henderson, 1816
T.

2986 [URQUHART, Thomas.] A letter to Wm. Wilberforce, Esq., M.P. on the subject of impressment; calling on him and the philanthropists of this country to prove those feelings of sensibility they expressed in the cause of humanity on negro slavery, by acting with the same ardour and zeal in the cause of British seamen.
24 pp. London, R. S. Kirby, 1816
K.

2987 ——. Letters on the evils of impressment, with the outline of a plan for doing them away, on which depend the wealth, prosperity, and consequence of Great Britain.
100 pp. 2nd ed. London, J. Richardson, 1816
K.

1817

2988 Address of the American society for the encouragement of domestic manufactures to the people of the United States.
32 pp. New York, Van Winkle, Wiley & Co., 1817
A.

2989 An address to the legislature; including the substance of a letter to the Honorable George Rose, M.P. on subjects connected with the vital interests of the empire.
16 pp. London, J. Hill, 1817
T.

——. Another issue. 16 pp. London, J. Hatchard, [etc.], 1817
T.
[On poor laws.]

2990 Annual report of the strangers' friend society (instituted in 1790) for year 1817. With their address to the public.
table. 16 pp. Dublin, printed by Jones, 1817
N.

2991 ATTWOOD, Thomas. A letter to the right honourable Nicholas Vansittart on the creation of money and on its action upon national prosperity.
112 pp. Birmingham, R. Wrightson, 1817
T.

2992 [——.] Prosperity restored; or, reflections on the cause of the public distresses, and on the only means of relieving them. By the author of the remedy, or thoughts on the present distresses.
appendix. 222 pp. London, Baldwin, Cradock and Joy, [etc.], 1817
T.

2993 BERNARD, Sir Thomas, bart. On the repeal of the salt duties, and its effects in relieving the present distresses of the poor, being a second postscript to a letter addressed to the Rt. Hon. Nicholas Vansittart.
14 pp. London, J. Murray, 1817
N.

2994 ——. On the supply of employment and subsistence for the labouring classes, in fisheries, manufactures and the cultivation of waste lands; with remarks on the operation of the salt duties, and a proposal for their repeal. Addressed to the right hon. Nicholas Vansittart.
72 pp. London, J. Murray, 1817
T.

2995 BICHENO, James Ebenezer. An inquiry into the nature of benevolence, chiefly with a view to elucidate the principles of the poor laws, and to show their immoral tendency.
tables. 150 pp. London, Rowland Hunter, 1817
K., T.

2996 BOWLES, John. Reasons for the establishment of provident institutions, called savings' banks; with a word of caution respecting their formation: and an appendix, containing a model for the formation of savings' banks, according to the plan adopted by the provident institution established in the western part of the metropolis, and by that for the city of London, and its vicinity.
appendix. 46 pp. 3rd ed. London, J. M. Richardson, [etc.], 1817
K.

2997 A brief exposé which every person who insures life or property in Ireland should carefully read and perfectly understand.
tables. 24 pp. Dublin, Kelly, 1817
A., N.

2998 BROWNE, John. A treatise on irrigation, or the watering of land. With some observations on cattle, tillage, and planting.
plates. table. 100 pp. London, J. Harding, 1817
T.

2999 CANTWELL, John. A practical treatise on the law of tolls and customs, as well as those payable in the city of Dublin, as in every city, corporate town, fair and market in Ireland. Enabling the farmer, merchant, factor, citizen, dealer, carman, etc. to detect any imposition which may be attempted. To which is added an appendix, comprising all the acts of parliament on this very important subject; several adjudged cases, various resolutions of the Irish house of commons and a copy of the docket of the tolls claimed by the city of Dublin.
116 pp. Dublin, Barlow, 1817
A., M., N., P.

3000 CHAINE, William. Letter to the most noble, the Marquess of Downshire, in reply to the letter of Robt. Williamson esquire on the proposed repeal of the transit duty on foreign linens.
notes. appendix. 40 pp. Belfast, Mackay, 1817
A.

3001 The character of passing events.
46 pp. London, J. Hatchard, 1817
T.
[Comments on the post-1815 depression.]

3002 CLARKE, Christopher. Observations on the importance of Gibraltar to Great Britain, as the means of promoting

the intercourse with the states of the Mediterranean; particularly with Morocco: to which is added a description of the part of Spain immediately connected with Gibraltar.
102 pp. London, J. Hatchard, 1817

K.

3003 Considerations on a commutation of tithes with strictures on the church establishment of the British isles, and on some other subjects. By a lay protestant.
46 pp. Dublin, Keightley, 1817

A., D.

3004 Correspondence on the usury laws, between a writer under the signature of '* * *' and 'a Belfast Merchant'. Originally published in the *Belfast Newsletter*, in 1817.
52 pp. Belfast, printed by Mackey, 1817

A.

3005 CRAUFURD, Sir Charles Gregan. Observations on the state of the country since the peace: with a supplementary section on the poor laws.
84 pp. London, W. Stockdale, 1817

T.

3006 ——. Reflections upon circulating medium; currency; prices; commerce; exchanges, etc. With immediate reference to the present state of the country.
appendix. 230 pp. London, W. Stockdale, 1817

T.

3007 ——. A supplementary section on the poor laws; and a list of errata and omissions in the pamphlet entitled, 'Observations on the state of the country since the peace'.
48 pp. London, W. Stockdale, 1817

T.

3008 CROMBIE, Alexander. A letter to D. Ricardo, Esq., containing an analysis of his pamphlet on the depreciation of bank notes.
144 pp. London, R. Hunter, 1817

K., T.

3009 DAVIS, William. Friendly advice to industrious and frugal persons recommending provident institutions or savings Banks.
table. appendix. 32 pp. fourth edition—enlarged. London, printed by Bensley and Son, 1817

U.

3010 DAVISON, John. Considerations on the Poor Laws.
126 pp. Oxford, J. Parker; London, J. Murray; [etc.], 1817

K.

3011 [DOUGLAS, Thomas?] The state of the country discussed in a number of questions and answers; by which some principles of Political Oeconomy are explained and enforced. The whole being an argument for the abolition of sinecures and for parliamentary reform; and is addressed to all who feel an interest in the welfare and prosperity of the country. By Mercator.
52 pp. London, R. Hunter, 1817

T.

3012 ENSOR, George. Observations on the present state of Ireland.
124 pp. n.p., [1817?]

A.

3013 Exposition of one principal cause of the national distress, particularly in manufacturing districts; with some suggestions for its removal.
42 pp. London, Darton Harvey, 1817

T.

3014 [FELLOWES, Robert.] Thoughts on the present depressed state of the agricultural interest of this kingdom; and on the rapid increase of the poor-rates; with observations on Mr. Curwen's plan for bettering the condition of the poor; and a proposal for the gradual abolition of the poor laws, till they are reduced within the scope and intention of the forty-third of Elizabeth; as the only effectual remedy in the present alarming state of pauperism.
48 pp. London, Payne and Foss, 1817

K., T.

3015 Fifth report of the society for promoting the education of the poor of Ireland.
60 pp. Dublin, Jones, 1817

A.

3016 The fifth report of the society, instituted in Edinburgh on 25th January, 1813, for the suppression of beggars, for the relief of occasional distress, and for the encouragement of industry among the poor.
tables. 40 pp. Edinburgh, printed by Smellie, 1817

A.

3017 FISHER, John. A letter to Frankland Lewis Esq., M.P., on commutation of tithes.
32 pp. London, F. C. and J. Rivington, 1817

K., T.

3018 FREND, William. The national debt in its true colours, with plans for its extinction by honest means.
table. 38 pp. London, J. Mawman, 1817

T.

3019 GASCOIGNE, Henry Barnet. Suggestions for the employment of the poor of the metropolis, and the direction of their labours to the benefit of the inhabitants: with hints on mendicity. Respectfully addressed to the Right Hon. The lord mayor and citizens of London.
32 pp. London, Baldwin, Cradock, and Joy, 1817

T.

3020 GOUGH, John. Account of two journies southward in Ireland.
50 pp. Dublin, West, 1817

A.

3021 GOURLAY, Robert. The village system, being a scheme for the gradual abolition of pauperism, and immediate employment and provisioning of the people.
40 pp. Bath, H. Gye, 1817

T.

3022 GRAHAME, James. Defence of usury laws against the arguments of Mr. Bentham and the Edinburgh reviewers.
38 pp. Edinburgh, A. Constable, 1817

T.

3023 Grand canal. Report of the court of directors at the half-yearly meeting of the company. 29.IV.1817. Schedule of retrenchments.
24 pp. Dublin, W. Porter, 1817
A., N.

3024 Hints to radical reformers, and materials for true.
164 pp. London, J. Hatchard, 1817
T.

3025 KEITH, George Skene. Different methods of establishing a uniformity of weights and measures stated and compared.
illustration. table. 32 pp. London, Longman, Hurst, Rees, Orme, and Brown, 1817
T.

3026 LAFFITTE, Jacques. Opinion de M. Laffitte sur le projet de loi relatif aux finances pour 1817, prononcée a la séance du 10 fév. 1817.
46 pp. Paris, Bossange, 1817
N.

3027 A letter addressed to C. C. Curwen, Esq. M.P. on the poor laws, containing a safe, easy, and economical substitute for the present system.
32 pp. Warwick, Henry Sharpe, 1817
T.

3028 The letter, to Mr. Peel and Mr. Vansittart, of a projector; on two objects of practicable retrenchment.
12 pp. Dublin, 1817
A.

3029 M'GUIRE, John. A plan, of general and perpetual employment, for the working orders, of every description, by the management and application of the funds and subscriptions, for the relief of the working poor, of the city of Dublin; and also throughout all parts of the British Empire; Whereby the distressed working orders, in cities, towns, and in the country,—whether artisans, labourers or servants, males or females,—may be employed, especially in the distressing season of winter, at their respective trades and avocations of industry;—and will also stimulate them by an encouraging principle, to secure a provision against sickness, and become parties to perpetuate a system of industry, advantageous in its results to the employers, to the employed, and to the British Empire at large.
20 pp. Dublin, printed by William Henry Tyrrell, 1817
A., M.

3030 MARRYAT, Joseph. An examination of the report of the Berbice commissioners, and an answer to the letters of James Stephen, respecting the crown estates in the West Indies, published in the Courier, under the signature of 'Truth'.
124 pp. London, J. M. Richardson, [etc.], 1817
A., P., T.

3031 MILLS, James. The simple equation of tithes, prepared for the consideration of the members of both houses of parliament, previous to any legislative enactment as to leasing the same. With some remarks on the unequal operation of the poor laws—the impolicy of allowing foreign wool to be imported duty free—the injurious effects upon agriculture of the tax on water-borne coal and on the necessity of future responsibility in country banks.
tables. plate. 112 pp. London, J. Hatchard, [etc.], 1817
K., T.

3032 NICOLL, S. W. An account of the York saving bank, instituted, June, 1816. Drawn up and published, at the request of the directors.
appendix. 56 pp. York, W. Alexander, [etc.], 1817
T.

3033 Observations for the use of landed gentlemen on the present state, and future prospects, of the British farmer. By Rusticus.
table. 88 pp. Edinburgh, William Blackwood, [etc.], 1817
K., T.

3034 Observations on the Grand jury laws of Ireland, with remarks on some of the clauses in the bill proposed and now in progress through Parliament for their amendment, respectfully addressed to the legislature by an old grand juror.
32 pp. Cork, printed by Edwards and Savage, 1817
N.

3035 Observations on the use of machinery in the manufactories of Great Britain; proving it to be the cause of the present stagnation of trade; and of the distress now prevailing amongst the industrious classes of the people. With remarks on climbing boys, and the treatment of children employed in cotton manufactories: and on the Rev. Mr. Malthus's plan for preventing the poor from intermarrying. By a mechanic.
16 pp. London, W. Peart, 1817
T.

3036 Observations on the window tax, with some hints for its better collection.
22 pp. Dublin, 1817
A.

3037 On the present state of public affairs.
102 pp. London, J. Murray, 1817
T.

3038 OWEN, Robert. Plan for the relief of the poor and the emancipation of mankind. New state of society.
diagram. 4 pp. London, 1817
A.

3039 The picture of Dublin, being a description of the city, and a correct guide to all public establishments, curiosities, amusements, exhibitions, and remarkable objects, in and near the city of Dublin.
map. illustrated. 208 pp. Dublin, J. E. W. Gregory, [1817?]
A.

3040 Proceedings of the trustees of the linen and hempen manufactures of Ireland for the year 1816.
appendix. index. 370 pp. Dublin, printed by Folds, [1817?]
D.

3041 READE, John. The second annual report of the Clondalkin Institution, for bettering the condition and promoting the comforts of the poor of that parish; with an account of receipts and disbursements.
tables. 14 pp. Dublin, Watson, 1817
A.

3042 A short account of Scottish money and coins, with tables of their value at different periods, and the price of commodities etc.
tables. 16 pp. Edinburgh, Webster, 1817

A.

3043 Sketch of the origin and progress of the Merino Factory, Co. Kilkenny, presented to the Dublin society.
12 pp. Dublin, Graisberry and Campbell, 1817

A.

3044 SOUTHEY, Robert. A letter to William Smith, Esq., M.P. from Robert Southey, Esq.
48 pp. 2nd edition, London, J. Murray, 1817

T.

3045 [STEPHENSON, George.] A description of the safety lamp, invented by George Stephenson, and now in use in Killingworth colliery. To which is added, an account of the lamp constructed by Sir Humphrey Davy.   With engravings.
plates. 16 pp. London, Baldwin, Cradock and Joy, 1817

T.

3046 [TOWNSEND, Joseph.] A Dissertation on the poor laws. By a well-wisher to mankind. 1786
120 pp. London, J. Ridgway, 1817

A.

3047 A vindication of the present order of friendly benefit societies, and their general conduct and government defended from the illiberal observations and unjust aspersions of the rev. J. W. Cunningham, vicar of Harrow and domestic chaplain to the right honourable lord Northwick. By a secretary and member of a friendly benefit society.
96 pp. London, printed by Brimmer, 1817

A.

3048 WILLIAMSON, Robert. Letter to the most noble, the Marquess of Downshire on the proposed repeal of the transit duty on foreign linens.
Notes. tables. appendix. 36 pp. Belfast, Mackey, 1817

A., N.

3049 YATES, John Ashton. A letter on the distresses of the country; addressed to His Royal Highness The Duke of Kent, in consequence of his motion respecting 'The revulsion of trade, and our sudden transition from a system of extensive war to a state of peace;' in which the supposed influence of our debt and taxes upon our manufactures and foreign trade, is investigated.
appendix with tables. 238 pp. second edition. London, Longman, Hurst, Rees, Orme, and Brown, 1817

T.

1818

3050 An address to the electors of the United Kingdom, containing an inquiry into the real causes of the present distress; with observations on the corn laws, the income tax, the poor laws, a general inclosure bill, and a reform in parliament. By a Glocestershire [sic] freeholder.
tables. appendix. 56 pp. Stroud and Cheltenham, F. Vigurs, [etc.], 1818

T.

3051 Articles of agreement of the Liberal Annuity Company of Dublin.
Index. 58 pp. Dublin, Kelly, 1818

A.

3052 An attempt towards a plan for rendering the charitable institutions of Dublin more effective by cooperation.
index. 72 pp. Dublin, Jones, 1818

A., N.

3053 ATTWOOD, Thomas. Observations on currency, population and pauperism in two letters to Arthur Young, Esq.
appendix. 264 pp. Birmingham, R. Wrightson, 1818

T.

3054 BEAUMONT, John Thomas Barber. Substance of a speech on the best means of counteracting the existing monopoly in the supplying of beer; exemplifying the evil, and tracing its source to the system of arbitrary licensing of victualling houses, peculiar to Great Britain: delivered at a public meeting holden at the Crown and Anchor tavern in the Strand, on January the 26th, 1818.
32 pp. London, Longman, Hurst, Rees, Orme, and Brown, 1818

T.

3055 The benevolent Society of St. Patrick patronized, according to his majesty's royal pleasure, by his Royal highness the duke of Kent. Instituted in March, 1784
58 pp. London, Philanthropic Society, 1818

A.

3056 BIGNOLD, Thomas. An exposure of the unjustifiable proceedings and unworthy motives of Mr. Thorpe and others, holding the late meetings at the George and Vulture tavern, refuting the fabricated reports which they have lately issued, and shewing the effect which calumny so malignant and premeditated is calculated to produce on society.
44 pp. London, Pinnock and Maunder, 1818

A.

[Defence of the directors and secretary of the Norwich Union insurance office; see 3083 and 3092.]

3057 BRUN, J. Ant. A plan for the detection and prevention of forgery, by which the bank may be enabled to exhibit to the public the proofs of the forgery of its notes without offering any advantage to forgers. Followed by a demonstration proving the existence of a radical but curable evil attached to the present mode of relief in recovering bank notes.
diag. 34 pp. London, Boosey, 1818

T.

3058 CARR, George. Rational reform on constitutional principles: addressed to the good sense of the English nation.
270 pp. London, Baldwin, Cradock and Joy, 1818

T.

3059 CAYLEY, Sir George, bart. A letter on the subject of parliamentary reform, addressed to Major Cartwright.
30 pp. York, T. Sotheran, 1818

T.

3060 CHICHESTER, Edward. Documents illustrative of the oppressions and cruelties of Irish revenue officers.
46 pp. London, T. Wood, 1818

A., B., N.

3061 ——. Oppressions and cruelties of Irish revenue officers. Being the substance of a letter to a British member of Parliament.
table in appendix. 126 pp. London, John Grinsted, 1818
A., N.

3062 ——. A second letter to a British member of parliament, respecting the oppressions and cruelties of Irish revenue officers, wherein the observations on a former letter are considered and refuted.
56 pp. London, T. Wood, 1818
B., N.

——. Another issue, with appendix. 72 pp. London, printed by Thomas Wood, 1818
A.

3063 CLARKE, Christopher. An examination of the internal state of Spain: to which is prefixed a brief sketch of her history to the late invasion by the French.
236 pp. London, J. Hatchard, 1818
T.

3064 [COCKBURN, ——.] Commercial oeconomy: or, the evils of a metallic currency. By an old country gentleman.
28 pp. London, J. Hatchard, 1818
T.

3065 COFFEY, Aeneas. Observations on the Rev. Edward Chichester's pamphlet, entitled oppressions and cruelties of Irish revenue officers.
tables. 98 pp. London, W. Clowes, 1818
A., B., N.

3066 COLEBROOKE, Henry Thomas. On the import of colonial corn.
tables. appendices. 234 pp. London, J. Murray, 1818
K.

3067 COOKE, Edward. Thoughts on the expediency of repealing the usury laws.
26 pp. London, 1818
P.

3068 COURTENAY, Thomas Peregrine. A treatise upon the poor laws.
tables in appendices. 176 pp. London, J. Murray, 1818
K., T.

3069 CRAVEN, Charles. A plan calculated to reduce the expenditure of the nation, and to enable Officers of all ranks, on halfpay, (who choose to accept it) to realise the greater part of the purchase-money of their commissions.
tables. 32 pp. London, Egerton, 1818
N., P.

3070 A freeman's letter to the rt. hon. Robert Peel on the present state of the City of Dublin.
30 pp. Dublin, Kempston, 1818
A.

3071 HALL, Frederick. An appeal to the poor miner, and to every nobleman, gentleman and tradesman in the kingdom, who feels interested in a miner's fate.
46 pp. 2nd edition, London, Longman. Hurst, Rees, Orme & co. 1818
T.

3072 Important tea trial. Report of the proceedings before the Commissioners of Customs upon an information against Mr. Thomas Naylor, of Great-Britain Street, grocer, with a copy of the information, speeches of counsel, and an appendix, containing the several memorials, affidavits, and notices attendant upon the seizure and trial.
appendix. 64 pp. Dublin, Warrick, 1818
A.

3073 An inquiry into the principle and tendency of the bill now pending in parliament, for imposing certain restrictions on cotton factories.
70 pp. London, Baldwin, Cradock, and Joy, 1818
T.

3074 An inquiry into the state of the currency of the country, its defects and remedy.
tables. 56 pp. London, Longmans, Hurst, Rees, Orme, and Brown, 1818
T.

3075 IRELAND, John. A letter to Henry Brougham, esq., M.P. from John Ireland, D.D. formerly Vicar of Croydon, now Dean of Westminster.
appendix. 32 pp. London, J. Murray, 1818
T.

[On charitable trusts.]

3076 KNIGHT, John. The emigrants best instructor, or, the most recent and important information respecting the United States of America, selected from the works of the latest travellers in that country: particularly Bradbury, Hulme, Brown, Birkbeck &c. containing a topographical and statistical account of the states of Ohio, Indiana, and Illinois; with their constitution, population, climates, temperature and the manners and dispositions of their inhabitants; also, the prices of land, provisions, labour and taxes, soil, productive minerals, arts and manufactures. The English laws on emigration together with the form of a certificate and every other information needful to the emigrant.
tables. 72 pp. second edition. London, Souter; Manchester, J. Knight, 1818
K.

3077 ——. Important extracts from original and recent letters: written by Englishmen, in the United States of America, to their friends in England: containing unquestionable information respecting the temperature and fertility of that country; together with the price of land, labour, and provisions, the manners and dispositions of its inhabitants, &c. &c.
tables. 48 pp. Manchester, J. Knight, 1818
K.

3078 MAITLAND, John. Observations on the impolicy of permitting the exportation of British wool, and of preventing the free importation of foreign wool.
appendix. 68 pp. London, W. Phillips, 1818
T.

3079 Minutes of the trustees of the linen and hempen manufactures of Ireland, containing the reports of the Inspector-General of Ulster, on the brown seals of that province.
38 pp. Dublin, Folds, 1818
A.

3080 [Moggridge John H.] Remarks on the report of the select committee of the house of commons, on the poor-laws; in which the proposed alteration of the laws of settlement; and pauperism, its causes, consequences, and remedies, are distinctly considered. By a Monmouthshire magistrate.
64 pp. Bristol, Brown & Manchee, 1818
T.

3081 Nicoll, S. W. A summary view of the report and evidence relative to the poor laws, published by order of the house of commons, with observations and suggestions.
appendix. 112 pp. York, W. Alexander, 1818
T.

3082 Nimmo, Alexander. Report and estimates on draining and cultivating the bogs on the Cashen, or northern division of Kerry.
30 pp. Dublin, Thom, 1818
A., N.

3083 Norwich Union, fire and life insurance. The report of the London committee appointed to investigate the late charges made against the Norwich Union fire and life office, presented to a meeting of insurers on 25th September, 1818.
tables. appendix. 146 pp. London, Bensley, 1818
A.
See 3056 and 3092.

3084 Observations on banks for savings; shewing the expediency of making the principle on which they are founded applicable to clerks in public offices, and all large establishments of labourers, mechanics, and others.
30 pp. (pagination irregular). London, Black, Kingsbury, Parbury, and Allen, 1818
K.

3085 Observations on the house of industry, Dublin, and on the plans of the association for suppressing mendicity in that city.
32 pp. Dublin, Napper, 1818
A.

3086 Papps, Thomas. By His Majesty's royal letters patent. Papp's patent system of book-keeping: being the second part. The first part is adapted for merchants, wholesale dealers, and manufacturers; the second, which is the present, is applicable to all descriptions of trade. This work presents to either the retail dealer, or wholesale and retail together, a degree of perfection hitherto supposed impossible. A retail tradesman's books kept by this system will produce all the satisfaction at present obtained by double entry, with the additional advantage of a perpetual balance, whether the accounts are, or are not posted; which may not improperly be termed a tradesman's sheet anchor.
tables. 164 pp. London, T. Hodgson, 1818
T.

3087 Prinsep, Charles Robert. An essay on money.
158 pp. London, J. Ridgway, 1818
T.

3088 Purdon, Freeman. Suggestions on the best mode of relieving the present prevailing distress in the south of Ireland,

for the consideration of Mr. Grant and Sir John Newport, and the members for Ireland.
22 pp. Dublin, Graisberry & Campbell, 1818
A., N.

3089 Read, Samuel. The problem solved: in the explication of a plan, of a safe, steady and secure government paper currency, and legal tender.
16 pp. Edinburgh, Macreadie, Skelly, 1818
T.

3090 Reade, John. Observations upon tithes and rents, addressed to the clergy and impropriators of Ireland.
92 pp. 2nd ed. Dublin, Archer, 1818
A., N.

3091 Remarks on the projected abolition of the usury laws, and the probable effects of the measure upon the commerce and general prosperity of the nation.
52 pp. London, T. & G. Underwood, 1818
T.

3092 Report of the committee appointed to enquire into the funds and conduct of the Norwich Union society, presented to a general meeting of the London insurers, held at the George and Vulture tavern on the 27th August, 1818.
36 pp. London, Graves, 1818
A.
See 3056 and 3083.

3093 Report of the committee of directors of the association for the suppression of mendicity in Dublin.
2 pp. (broadsheet). Dublin, Thom, 1818
A.

3094 Report, presented at the first annual general meeting of the association for promoting the employment of the poor and ameliorating their condition in Co. Kilkenny and the adjoining counties, by encouraging therein agriculture, fisheries, manufactures and commerce.
24 pp. Dublin, Thom, 1818
A.

3095 Rigby, Edward. Holkham, its agriculture, etc.
146 pp. 3rd ed. enlarged. Norwich, printed by Burks and Kinnebrook, 1818
A.

3096 A schedule of the assessed taxes on hearths, windows, servants, carriages, horses and dogs, payable in Ireland under the act of 58 George III.
30 pp. Dublin, Woodmason & Procter, 1818
A.

3097 Sheffield, John Baker Holroyd, 1st earl of. Observations on the impolicy, abuses, and false interpretation of the poor laws, and on the reports of the two houses of parliament.
62 pp. London, J. Hatchard, 1818
N.

3098 Sketches of the Merino factory, descriptive of its origin and progress and of its system of discipline and moral government. By an English Traveller and K. W. of Belfast.
illustration. 54 pp. Dublin, Graisberry & Campbell, 1818
A., N., T., U.

3099 Some account of the establishment of the Savings Bank, School Street, Dublin, with the rules and regulations for its management.
tables. 32 pp. Dublin, Printed by Jones, 1818
A.

3100 A statement of facts, relating to the maximum of legal interest on all loans of money; addressed to the trading, commercial and landed interest of the kingdom.
16 pp. London, Baldwin, Cradock and Joy, 1818
T.

3101 [STEVEN, Robert.] An inquiry into the abuses of the chartered schools in Ireland. With remarks upon the education of the lower classes in that country. Second edition.
212 pp. London, T. and G. Underwood, 1818
T.

3102 Suppression of street-begging; report.
20 pp. Dublin, the Association for suppressing street-begging, 1818
A., N.

3103 THORPE, Robert. A view of the present increase of the slave trade, the cause of that increase, and suggesting a mode for effecting its total annihilation: with observations on the African institution and Edinburgh review, and on the speeches of Messrs. Wilberforce and Brougham, delivered in the house of commons, 7th July 1817: also, a plan submitted for civilising Africa, and introducing free labourers into our colonies in the West Indies.
132 pp. London, Longman, Hurst, Rees, Orme, and Brown, 1818
T.

3104 WALKER, Chamberlen Richard. A treatise upon the assessed and local taxes, payable by the householders of Dublin, in their capacity of householders. First part: window, hearth, pipe water, and metal main taxes.
tables. 102 pp. Dublin, Mosse, 1818
A.

3105 WESTON, Ambrose. Two letters, describing a method of increasing the quantity of circulating money upon a new and solid principle. Printed for private circulation in 1799, and now published from the author's corrected copy. With a short preface by the editor.
table of contents. 60 pp. London, Taylor and Hessey, 1818
N.
See 2185

3106 WILLIAMS, Charles Wye. Considerations on the alarming increase of forgery on the Bank of England and the neglect of remedial measures, with an essay on the remedy for the detection of forgeries and an account of the measures adopted by the Bank of Ireland.
198 pp. London, Longman, Hurst, Rees, Orme & Brown, 1818
A., N.

3107 WRAY, John. Dangers of an entire repeal of the bank restriction act: and a plan suggested for obviating them.
24 pp. London, F. C. and J. Rivington, [1818]
T.

1819

3108 An address to the nobility and gentry of Ireland on the subject of distillation, as affecting the agriculture and revenue of that part of the United Kingdom.
42 pp. Dublin, printed by M. Goodwin, 1819
A.

3109 Annual report for the year 1818 of the benevolent or Stranger's friend society (originated in the year 1790).
24 pp. Dublin, Keene, 1819
A.

3110 Appendix to the report respecting the Merino factory; containing the evidence adduced before the committee.
26 pp. Dublin, printed by Graisberry, 1819
A., D.

3111 BLAKEMORE, Richard. A letter to the right honourable Charles B. Bathurst, M.P. on the subject of the poor laws.
32 pp. London, Taylor & Hessey, 1819
N., T.

3112 BOLLMANN, Erick. A letter to Thomas Brand, esq., M.P. for the county of Hertford; on the practicability and propriety of a resumption of specie payments.
100 pp. London, J. Murray, 1819
T.

3113 ——. A second letter to the honourable Thomas Brand, M.P. for the county of Hertford; in which doubts are suggested on the practicability of the new system of bullion-payments; and on its efficacy to regulate and control the amount of bank notes in circulation, by their convertibility.
46 pp. London, J. Murray, 1819
T.

3114 CHAMBERS, Abraham Henry. Comments on some recent political discussions, with an exposure of the fallacy of the sinking fund.
table. 56 pp. London, T. Egerton, & J. M. Richardson, 1819
T.

3115 ——. Thoughts on the resumption of cash payments by the bank; and on the corn bill, as connected with that measure: in a letter addressed to the right honourable the Chancellor of the Exchequer.
40 pp. London, T. Egerton and J. M. Richardson, 1819
N.

3116 CLARK, J. Plan of the European company for life insurances, the sale and purchase of annuities, endowments for children, and the investment of money for accumulation; calculated to accommodate the landed interest and others who can furnish adequate security with pecuniary advances 'on equitable terms' and to procure for the monied interest 'a great and increasing income for the capitals they possess'.
tables. 48 pp. 3rd ed. London, printed by Sydney, 1819
N.

3117 CONGREVE, Sir William, bart. Of the impracticability of the resumption of cash payments; of the sufficiency of a

representative currency in this country, under due regulations; and of the danger of a reduction of the circulating medium in the present state of things.
46 pp. London, J. Hatchard, 1819

T.

3118 Considerations on the sinking fund. Appendix with tables.
144 pp. London, J. Hatchard, 1819

A., K., T.

3119 COOKE, Edward. An address to the public on the plan proposed by the secret committee of the house of commons for examining the affairs of the bank.
appendix. 52 pp. London, J. J. Stockdale, 1819

A.

3120 ——. The real cause of the high price of gold bullion.
appendix. 52 pp. 2nd ed. London, J. J. Stockdale, 1819

A.

3121 [COPLESTON, Edward, bishop of Llandaff.] A letter to the right hon. Robert Peel, M.P. for the university of Oxford, on the pernicious effects of a variable standard of value, especially as it regards the condition of the lower orders and the poor laws. By one of his constituents.
108 pp. 3rd ed. Oxford, J. Murray, 1819

T.

3122 [——.] A second letter to the right hon. Robert Peel, M.P. for the university of Oxford, on the causes of the increase of pauperism, and on the poor laws. By one of his constituents.
tables. 116 pp. 2nd ed. Oxford, J. Murray, 1819

T.

3123 [CURTIS, C. G.] An account of the colony of the Cape of Good Hope, with a view to the information of emigrants. And an appendix, containing the offers of government to persons disposed to settle there.
map. tables. appendix. 176 pp. London, Rest Fenner, 1819

T.

3124 DAWSON, James. Canal extensions in Ireland, recommended to the Imperial legislature, as the best means of promoting the agriculture—draining the bogs—and employing the poor, of Ireland; and also, as the surest means of supplying the British markets with corn, reducing the rates of foreign exchanges, and facilitating the general resumption of cash payments.
table in appendices. 56 pp. Dublin, Printed by William Porter, 1819

A., M.

3125 DENNIS, Jeffrey. A systematic plan for bettering the condition of British seamen, in which are submitted, new dresses for sailors, rules for serving out their daily provisions, manning our ships, and paying mariner's permanent wages in the merchant sea service, being an attempt to renovate completely, this national and important concern.
plates. appendix. tables. 12 pp. 2nd ed. London, Dennis, 1819

A.

3126 DUFRENE, John. A treatise of immediate utility to merchants and traders, showing some of the principal defects in the present bankrupt system; and proving them by several interesting cases in bankruptcy; with extracts of importance from the evidence of the late Sir Samuel Romilly, and other witnesses, taken before the select committee of the house of commons on the Bankrupt laws, last session. Also containing most serious objections to several parts of the two bills lately brought into parliament for altering and amending the Bankrupt laws; and earnestly recommending a simple legislative enactment, which would produce the most beneficial effects to both debtors and creditors, and, in a great degree, prevent bankruptcy, with its frequent lamentable consequences of waste of property, etc.
84 pp. London, J. Swan, 1819

T.

3127 [DUNN, William.] The soul of Mr. Pitt; developing that eighteen millions of taxes may be taken off, and the three per cent. consols be constantly at 100.
table. 16 pp. 2nd ed. London, J. M. Richardson [etc.], 1819

T.

3128 Essay on the theory of money, with a reference to present circumstances, June 1819.
32 pp. London, J. Hatchard, 1819

T.

3129 The financial house that Jack built.
12 pp. London, J. M. Richardson, 1819

N.
A satire on the British public finances of the time.

3130 FFRENCH, Charles Austin Ffrench, 3rd baron. The letter of the Lord Ffrench, to the Lord Manners, lord high chancellor of Ireland, etc., etc., etc.
16 pp. Dublin?, 1819

N.
Concerning the failure of a bank with which the author was connected.

3131 FRY, Joseph Storrs. A concise history of tithes, with an inquiry how far a forced maintenance for the ministers of religion is warranted by the examples and precepts of Jesus Christ and his apostles.
36 pp. 2nd ed. London, John and Arthur Arch [etc.], 1819

K., T.

3132 GRAY, Andrew. A treatise on spinning machinery; illustrated with plans of different machines.... With some preliminary observations, tending to shew that the arts of spinning, weaving, and sewing, were invented by the ingenuity of females. And a postscript, including an interesting account of the mode of spinning yarn in Ireland.
plates, 88 pp., Edinburgh, A. Constable, [etc., etc.] 1819

B.

3133 GRIFFITH, Richard. Practical domestic politics; being a comparative and prospective sketch of the agriculture and population of Great Britain and Ireland, including some suggestions on the practicability and expediency of draining and cultivating the bogs of Ireland, and thereby to afford employment to the numerous poor of that country, and to provide corn for the increasing population of the United Kingdom.
appendix. 108 pp. London, Sherwood, Neely & Jones, 1819

A., N., U.

3134 [HALL, George Webb.] The origin and proceedings of the agricultural associations in Great Britain in which their claims to protection against foreign produce, duty free, are fully and ably set forth. Printed for the use of the members of both houses of parliament, and published for the information of the subscribers and the public.
tables. 40 pp. London, printed at the office of the Farmers' Journal, 1819

N.

3135 HALL, Walter. A view of our late and of our future currency.
80 pp. London, J. M. Richardson, 1819

N.

3136 HEATHFIELD, Richard. Elements of a plan for the liquidation of the public debt of the United Kingdom; being the draught of a declaration; submitted to the attention of the landed, funded, and every other description of proprietor, of the united kingdom.
table. supplement. 50 pp. 4th ed. London, Longman, Hurst, Rees, Orme and Brown, 1819

A., P., T.

3137 [KER, Henry Bellenden.] A vindication of the enquiry into charitable abuses, with an exposure of the misrepresentations contained in the Quarterly Review.
132 pp. London, Longman, Hurst, Rees, Orme, and Brown, 1819

T.

3138 KNIPE, James. A letter to the right hon. N. Vansittart, chancellor of the exchequer, &c. &c. and to common carriers in general; tracing the insecurity of property while in the hands of carriers to the present state of the law, and suggesting a remedy.
92 pp. London, the author, 1819

T.

3139 A letter to the Rt. Hon. Frederick Robinson, president of the board of trade, etc., etc., on the policy and expediency of further protection to the corn trade of Great Britain: and on the necessity of revising and amending the last corn bill; particularly as regards the mode of making the returns and of striking the averages, etc., etc. By a corn factor.
40 pp. London, Longman, Hurst, Rees, Orme, and Brown, 1819

T.

3140 A letter to the Right Hon. Robert Peel, on the report of the bank committee, showing the unavoidable consequences of the measure on the issues of country bankers.
18 pp. London, printed by Darton Harvey and Darton, 1819
T.
Kress copy has attribution to Henry Burgess, made by H. S. Foxwell. See Kress C. 344.

3141 MACDOUGALL, Archibald. A treatise on the Irish fisheries and various other subjects connected with the general improvement of Ireland.
table of contents, prospectus for a new work, appendix. 226 pp. Belfast, Printed by J. Smith, 1819

A., N.

3142 MACNAB, Henry Grey. The new views of Mr. Owen of Lanark impartially examined, as rational means of ultimately promoting the productive industry, comfort, moral improvement, and happiness of the labouring classes of society, and of the poor; and of training up children in the way in which they should go: also observations on the New Lanark school, and on the systems of education of Mr. Owen, of the Rev. Dr. Bell, and that of the new British and foreign system of mutual instruction. Dedicated (by permission) to His Royal Highness the Duke of Kent and Strathearn, &c. &c.
tables. appendix. 238 pp. London, J. Hatchard, 1819

T.

3143 NOBLE, John. Noble's instructions to emigrants. An attempt to give a correct account of the United States of America; and offer some information which may be useful to those who have a wish to emigrate to that republic; and particularly to those of the poorer class.
map. tables. appendix. 118 pp. Boston, John Noble, London, Baldwin, Cradock and Joy, 1819

T.

3144 Notices on the claims of the Hudson's Bay Company: to which is added, a copy of their royal charter.
70 pp. London, J. Murray, 1819

K.

3145 Observations on the reports of the committees of both houses of parliament, on the expediency of resuming cash payments at the Bank of England, in a letter to a friend.
tables. 60 pp. Bath, Meyler and Sons, London, J. M. Richardson, 1819

N.

3146 On the relation of corn and currency.
44 pp. London, J. Murray, 1819

T.

3147 The oppressed labourers, the means for their relief, as well as for the reduction of their number, and of the poor-rates, presented to public notice.
48 pp. London, Darton, Harvey, 1819

K., T.

3148 [OWEN, Robert.] Mr. Owen's proposed arrangements for the distressed working classes, shown to be consistent with sound principles of political economy: in three letters addressed to David Ricardo, esq. M.P.
tables, 102 pp. London, Longman, Hurst, Rees, Orme, and Brown, 1819

A., P., T.

3149 PARKER, William An essay on the employment which bridges, roads, and other public works may afford the labouring classes, by the general and effectual amendment of the Grand Jury laws.
48 pp. Cork, Bolster, 1819

A., N.

3150 ——. A plea for the poor and industrious. Part first, the necessity of a national provision for the poor in Ireland; deduced from the argument of the rt. rev. R. Woodward, late lord bishop of Cloyne: and from the present deplorable state of the lower orders.
appendices, index. 202 pp. Cork, Bolster, 1819

A.

3151 PHILLPOTTS, Henry. A letter to the right honourable William Sturges Bourne, M.P. on a bill introduced by him into parliament, 'To amend the laws respecting the settlement of the poor.'
24 pp. second edition. London, J. Hatchard [etc.], 1819
K., T.

3152 Proceedings of the trustees of the linen and hempen manufactures of Ireland for the year 1818.
appendix. index. 532 pp. Dublin, printed by W. Folds [1819?]
D.

3153 Remarks on the practicability of Mr. Robert Owen's plan to improve the condition of the lower classes.
tables. 96 pp. London, Samuel Leigh, 1819
P.

3154 Report of the association for the suppression of Mendicity in Dublin for the year 1818.
tables in appendix. 42 pp. Dublin, printed by A. Thom, 1819
A., K., N., P.

3155 Report of the committee of the society for relief of the industrious poor to the annual meeting of subscribers, held second of January, 1819.
tables, 12 pp. Dublin, printed by Napper, 1819
N.

3156 Report of the committee of the society of arts etc., together with the approved communications and evidence upon the same relative to the mode of preventing the forgery of bank notes.
illustrated. 74 pp. London, Howard, 1819
A.

3157 RICARDO, David. Proposals for an economical and secure currency, with observations on the profits of the Bank of England, as they regard the public and the proprietors of bank stock.
128 pp. 3rd. ed. London, J. Murray, 1819
A.

3158 RIGBY, Edward. Holkham, its agriculture, &c.
76 pp. 3rd ed. London, 1819
P.

3159 ROGAN, Francis. Observations on the condition of the middle and lower classes in the north of Ireland, as it tends to promote the diffusion of contagious fever, with the history and treatment of the late epidemic disorder. . . .
appendix, 178 pp. London, Whitmore & Fenn, 1819
A.

3160 [ROOKE, John.] Remarks on the nature and operation of money with a view to elucidate the effects of the present circulating medium of Great Britain; intended to prove that the national distresses are attributable to our money system. By Cumbriensis.
76 pp. London, Baldwin, Cradock and Joy, 1819
T.

3161 ——. A supplement to the remarks on the nature and operation of money &c by Cumbriensis.
104 pp. London, Baldwin, Cradock and Joy, 1819
T.

3162 RUDING, Rogers. A supplement to the annals of the coinage of Britain, &c. containing the corrections and additions, and five new plates, published with the edition in octavo.
plates. tables. appendix. 106 pp. London, Lackington, Hughes, Harding, Mavor, and Jones, 1819
T.

3163 SHEFFIELD, John Baker Holroyd, 1st earl of. Remarks on the Bill of the last parliament for the amendment of the poor laws; with observations on their impolicy, abuses, and ruinous consequences; together with some suggestions for their amelioration, and for the better management of the poor.
table of contents. tables. appendices. 116 pp. London, J. Hatchard, 1819
N.

3164 [TAUNTON, Sir William Elias.] Hints towards an attempt to reduce the poor rate; or, at least, to prevent its further increase.
16 pp. Oxford, W. Baxter [etc. etc.], 1819
T.

3165 Things as they are; or, America in 1819. By an Emigrant, just returned to England.
table. 16 pp. Manchester, printed by J. Wroe, 1819
N.

3166 THORPE, Robert. A commentary on the treaties entered into between his Britannic majesty, and his most faithful majesty, signed at London, the 28th of July, 1817; between his Britannic majesty, and his catholic majesty, signed at Madrid, the 23rd of September, 1817; and between his Britannic majesty, and his majesty the king of the Netherlands, signed at the Hague, the 4th of May, 1818. For the purpose of preventing their subjects from engaging in any illicit traffic in slaves.
64 pp. London, Longman, Hurst, Rees, Orme and Brown, 1819
K., T.

3167 TORRENS, Robert. A comparative estimate of the effects which a continuance and a removal of the restriction upon cash payments are respectively calculated to produce: with strictures on Mr. Ricardo's proposal for obtaining a secure and economical currency.
84 pp. London, R. Hunter, and Ridgways, 1819
K., T.

3168 Treatise on the commutation of tithes.
8 pp. Dublin, Alexander Thom, 1819
P.

3169 TROTTER, Thomas. A practicable plan for manning the royal navy, and preserving our maritime ascendancy, without impressment: addressed to Admiral Lord Viscount Exmouth, K.G.B.
92 pp. London, Longman, Hurst, Rees, Orme and Brown, 1819
K.

3170 TURNER, Samuel. A letter addressed to the right hon. Robert Peel, &c. &c. late chairman of the committee of

secrecy, appointed to consider of the state of the Bank of England, with reference to the expediency of the resumption of cash payments at the period fixed by law.
tables. 88 pp. London, the author, 1819

R.

3171 A very short letter to the Right Hon. R. Peel.
18 pp. London, J. Robins, 1819

T.

On the resumption of specie payments.

3172 WENTWORTH. William Charles. A statistical, historical and political description of the colony of New South Wales, and its independent settlements in Van Diemen's Land: with a particular enumeration of the advantages which these colonies offer for emigration, and their superiority in many respects over those possessed by the United States of America.
tables. appendix. 476 pp. London, G. and W. B. Whittaker, 1819

T.

3173 WILLIAMS, Charles Wye. Exposure of the fallacies contained in the letter to the Rt. Hon. Robert Peel M.P. with remarks on the late auspicious change in the sentiments of the Earl of Lauderdale on paper currency.
70 pp. London, J. Hatchard, 1819

A., T.

Cf. 3121.

1820

3174 BAYLY, William Davis. The state of the poor and working classes considered, with practical plans for improving their condition in society, and superseding the present system of compulsory assessment.
128 pp. London, Hatchard & Son, 1820

T.

3175 BESNARD, Peter. Report of a tour of inspection through the counties in charge of Peter Besnard, esq., inspector-general of Leinster, Munster & Connaught.
24 pp. appendix of 16 pp. Dublin, printed by Wm. Folds, 1820

A., P.

[deals with linen industry]

3176 BURGOYNE, Montagu. A letter to the Rt. Hon. Sturges Bourne, M.P., from M.B. on the subject of the removal of the Irish by the 59 Geo. III Cap. XII sec. 33. London, 1820.
54 pp. London, printed by Shaw, 1820

N.

3177 Considerations on the expediency of an improved mode of treatment of slaves in the West Indian Colonies, relatively to an increase of population; with a plan of a religious establishment, suited to their capacities; with other objects of colonial policy.
64 pp. London, printed by E. Spragg, 1820

K.

3178 Elementary propositions illustrative of the principles of currency. Second edition, corrected. To which are added, outlines of political economy.
22 pp. London, J. Hatchard, 1820

T.

3179 FORTUNE, E. F. Thomas. Fortune's epitome of the stocks and public funds; containing every necessary information for perfectly understanding the nature of those securities, and the mode of doing business therein; also a copious equation table, exhibiting at one view, not only the exact value the different stocks and funds bear, or ought to bear, in respect to each other, but also with the value of land; and likewise the several prices at which the same interest is made in either upon the money laid out. With an appendix containing a full account of the bank stock and funds of the United States of America, and also of the French funds.
table. index. 106 pp. London, T. Boosey, 1820

A.

3180 The ground of national grievances examined; with a proposal for the liquidation of the national debt. Intended for the use of the present generation, and the benefit of posterity. By a friend to national reformation.
10 pp. 2nd ed. Newcastle, J. Clark, 1820

T.

3181 [HEATHFIELD, Richard.] Addenda to Mr. Heathfield's second publication, on the liquidation of the national debt, entitled, 'Further observations on the propriety and expediency of liquidating the public debt of the united kingdom.'
tables. 22 pp. London, Longman, Hurst, Rees, Orme, and Brown [etc., etc.], 1820

T.

3182 ——. Elements of a plan for the liquidation of the public debt of the United Kingdom.
50 pp. London, Longman, Hurst, Rees, Orme & Brown, 1820

A.

3183 ——. Further observations on the practicability and expediency of liquidating the public debt of the united kingdom; with reference, particularly, to the landed proprietor: including some considerations on population and the poor.
tables. appendices. 126 pp. London, Longman, Hurst, Rees, Orme, and Brown, 1820

P., T.

3184 HICKEY, William. The state of the poor in Ireland briefly considered and agricultural education recommended to check redundant population and to promote national improvement.
appendix with tables. 46 pp. Carlow, printed by R. Price, 1820

A., D., N.

3185 Hints on the duties and qualifications of land stewards and agents, comprising directions for conducting repairs, alterations, buildings and other improvements, with a plan for the management of neglected estates, beneficial to landlord and tenant. By a Steward.
44 pp. Faversham, printed by Z. Warren, 1820

A.

3186 HUBBERSTY, J. L. Brief observations on the necessity of a renewal of the property tax, under certain modifications.
44 pp. 2nd ed. London, F. C. & J. Rivington, 1820

T.

3187 Interesting particulars, relative to that great national undertaking, the breakwater, now constructing in Plymouth

sound; together with a copy of the order in council, and approval of his royal highness the Prince Regent (now King of Great Britain) in the name and on the behalf of his late majesty George III when estimate for carrying on the said work, amounted to one million one hundred and seventy one thousand pounds.
plates. tables. 38 pp. Devon, J. Johns [etc.], [1820?]

K.

3188 Justice to the poor; and justice to every other class of the people, as respects the situation of the poor, and the state of agriculture and commerce.
tables. 92 pp. Northampton, T. E. Dicey and R. Smithson, 1820

T.

3189 KING, William H. Report. Account of the Fisheries on the western entrance of the River Shannon, extending from Killala Bay to Kerry Head. [dated Oct. 21, 1820.]
tables. 14 pp. n.p. 1820

N.

3190 A letter to the right hon. Robert Peel, M.P. for the university of Oxford, on the comparative operation of the corn laws, and of public taxation, as causes of the depression of trade, and of the distressed state of the industrious classes. By a Briton.
70 pp. 2nd ed. London, J. Hatchard, 1820

T.

See 3207.

3191 Observations on Ireland by an Irishman.
34 pp. Kilkenny, printed by A. Denroche, 1820

B.

3192 Observations on the injurious consequences of the restrictions upon foreign commerce: addressed to the president of the board of trade, by a member of the late parliament.
tables. 96 pp. London, J. Murray, 1820

T.

3193 RADCLIFF, Thomas. Reports on the fine-wooled flocks of the Messrs Nolan, at Merino Cottage, in the county of Kilkenny: on the Merino factory of Messrs Nolan & Shaw, in the county of Kilkenny; and on the fine-wooled flocks of lord viscount Lismore, at Shanbally Castle, in the county of Tipperary.
appendix. 40 pp. Dublin, William Porter, 1820

A., P.

3194 Remarks on the waste lands of Ireland.
68 pp. Dublin, 1820

A.

3195 Reply to a recent publication which has abused the Linen board, their officers, and the government of Ireland.
138 pp. Dublin, 1820

A.

3196 Report of a committee of the Dublin society respecting the spinning of worsted yarn by hand established in this city by Bernard Coyle and John Kirby, and the comments of the Dublin prints thereon.
table. 14 pp. Dublin, printed by D. Graisberry, 1820

A.

3197 Second report of the association for the suppression of mendicity in Dublin, 1819.
tables in appendix. 40 pp. Dublin, printed by M. Keene, 1820

K., N., P.

3198 Report of the Institution established at Fenagh, Co. Carlow by the association formed for the purpose of promoting industry, neatness, and comfort amongst the poor of that village and its vicinity, and relieving their distress by affording employment etc. for the year ending July 1820.
24 pp. Carlow, printed by R. Price, 1820

A.

3199 RIGBY, Edward. Framingham, its agriculture etc. including the economy of a small farm.
diagrams. 116 pp. Norwich, R. Hunter, 1820

A., T.

3200 Rules & regulations to be observed by members of the Elishan society.
18 pp. Dublin, printed by J. Harvey, [1820?]

A.

3201 SALISBURY, William. A treatise on the practical means of employing the poor, in cultivating and manufacturing articles of British growth, in lieu of foreign materials, as practised in the royal school of economy in London. Also, a plan for forming county asylums for the industrious, as communicated to the author, by his late royal highness Edward duke of Kent and Stratherne.
tables. 46 pp. London, T. Cadell and W. Davies, 1820

T.

3202 Sketch of a plan for the effectual and permanent removal of the public distresses.
28 pp. London, T. & G. Underwood, 1820

T.

3203 The state of the poor of Ireland briefly considered and agricultural education recommended, to remedy redundant population and to promote national improvement.
tables. appendix. 46 pp. Dublin, 1820

A., N., P.

3204 Summum bonum; or, a sponge for the taxes: in a letter addressed to his majesty's ministers. By a yeoman of Herts.
20 pp. London, J. Hatchard, 1820

T.

3205 [SYMES, —.] The absentee, or a brief examination into the habits and condition of the people of Ireland, and the causes of the discontent and disorganized state of the lower classes, by an officer of the customs of Ireland.
46 pp. London, Rodwell & Martin, 1820

A., C., N., P.

3206 Thoughts on a radical remedy for the present distresses of the country.
tables. 40 pp. London, J. Hatchard & Son, 1820

T.

3207 TRENOR, Keating. Letter to the rt. hon. Robert Peel, M.P. for the university of Oxford: in answer to a letter (by a writer who styles himself a Briton) on the comparative operation of the Corn Laws and public taxation as causes of the depression of trade, and in relation to the prohibitory measures under the consideration of the Congress of the United

States as connected with the commercial, manufacturing and shipping interest, and the provisionment of the West India colonies from the western part of Ireland.
80 pp. London, W. Wright, 1820

A.

See 3190.

3208 A view of the British and Irish fisheries with recommendations for the establishment of an Irish national fishing company, by an old sailor.
110 pp. Dublin, printed by W. Underwood, 1820

A., N.

3209 A vindication of Mr Owen's plan for the relief of the distressed working classes, in reply to the misconceptions of a writer in No. 64 of the Edinburgh Review.
tables. appendix. 72 pp. London, Longman, Hurst, Rees, Orme and Brown, 1820

T.

[The 'writer in No. 64' was Robert Torrens.]

3210 WILKINSON, Harrison. The principles of an equitable and efficient system of finance, founded upon self-evident, universal and invariable principles, capable of diminishing taxes and poor-rates; reviving and permanently supporting agriculture, trade, commerce, wealth and happiness. Demonstrating that the existing system of Finance, is capricious, impolitic and improvident; injurious to liberty, property and legislation; proving the necessity of repealing all existing taxes, both general and local; and adopting one, simple, equitable and efficient, grounded upon a scale, just, wise, and unchangeable. By the adoption of this plan the dread of the rich would be removed, the distress of the poor relieved, and the confidence of all restored; founded upon the same system, (and with a view of exciting the energy of agricultural industry) a commutation of tithes is proposed, by which the property of the Church would be guaranteed, the dignity of the Clergy augmented, and the irritation of the people tranquilised; connected with the same plan, are more equitable and easy modes of collecting parochial and County assessments; a proposition for removing turnpike gates, educating the poor, etc. Together with an appendix, containing numerous tables and calculations, corollaries etc. an introductory address to the members of both Houses of Parliament, and a preface.
appendix. tables. 112 pp. London, C. Chapple, 1820

N.

3211 WILLIAMS, William. A correspondence with the right Hon. Robert Peel; the right Hon. Charles Grant, and William Gregory esq., several of whose letters were written by command of the Lord Lieutenant, with observations on the proceedings of the Linen Board; intended to prove, by a statement of facts, that the constitution of that board is defective, and its administration injurious to the linen manufacture and to public morals.
72 pp. Dublin, the author, 1820

A., N.

1821

3212 [ATTWOOD, Thomas.] Thoughts on the report of the Committee appointed by the house of commons to inquire into the Agricultural distress; By a Proprietor of land.
tables. appendices. 72 pp. Dublin, Hodges & M'Arthur, 1821

A.

3213 BOYES, John. Observations addressed to the Right Hon. Lord Stourton, occasioned by his two letters to the earl of Liverpool.
tables. appendix. 58 pp. York, Thomas Wilson; London, Longman, Hurst, Rees, Orme and Brown, 1821

T.

3214 Brief thoughts on the agricultural report. By a musing bee within the hive.
tables. 46 pp. London, Effingham Wilson, [etc.], 1821

K.

3215 BURROUGHS, Edward. Essays on practical husbandry and rural economy.
90 pp. London, Longman, Hurst, Rees, Orme and Brown, [etc., etc.], 1821

A., P., T.

3216 ——. A view of the state of agriculture in Ireland, with some remarks on the impediments to its prosperity.
62 pp. Dublin, printed by Gannon & Co., 1821

A., N.

3217 Causes of the variations in the public stocks and funds payable in Ireland.
tables, 80 pp. Dublin, R. Milliken, 1821

A.

3218 CRAIG, John. Remarks on some fundamental doctrines in political economy; illustrated by a brief inquiry into the commercial state of Britain, since the year 1815.
tables. 256 pp. Edinburgh, A. Constable, London, Hurst, Robinson, 1821

T.

3219 DAVIS, William. Hints to philanthropists; or, a collective view of practical means for improving the condition of the poor and labouring classes of society.
table. 172 pp. Bath, Binns and Robinson, London, J. and A. Arch, [etc.], 1821

T.

3220 ELLMAN, John, jr. Consideration on the propriety of granting protection to the agriculture of the United Kingdom, with remarks on the report of the select committee of the house of commons thereon.
52 pp. London, printed by Ruffy & Evans, [c. 1821]

A.

3221 The Farmer's Friend; or a new system of farming and managing land, laid down upon a scale of thirty acres; whereby farming, dairying, feeding, &c. &c. may be combined, and carried on upon new principles, even upon a small farm. Also, the means of procuring manure, by a new and simple process, &c. &c. Designed for the use of small farmers, to enable them to pay their rents, and to gain independence.
16 pp. Dublin, printed by Joshua Porter, 1821

A.

3222 Foreign slave trade. Abstract of the information recently laid on the table of the house of commons on the subject of the slave trade; being a report made by a committee specially appointed for the purpose to the directors of the

African institution, 8th May, 1821, and by them ordered to be printed, as a supplement to the annual report of the present year.
table of contents. 180 pp. London, Ellerton and Henderson, 1821

N.

3223 HANNAH, Charles. Remarks and sketches taken in an excursion through part of the counties of Antrim, Down, and Derry, in the summer and autumn of 1820.
70 pp. Belfast, printed by F. D. Finlay, 1821

A.

3224 An inquiry into those principles, respecting the nature of demand and the necessity of consumption, lately advocated by Mr. Malthus, from which it is concluded, that taxation and the maintenance of unproductive consumers can be conducive to the progress of wealth.
130 pp. London, R. Hunter, 1821

T.

3225 The laws and regulations of the chamber of commerce of the city of Dublin, adopted at a general meeting of its members at the Royal Exchange on Thursday 16th November 1820.
8 pp. Dublin, printed by C. Bentham, 1821

A.

3226 A letter addressed to the Honourable John Frederick Campbell, M.P. on the poor laws, and the practical effect to be produced by the Act of 59 Geo. III c. 12. commonly called the select vestry act. By a magistrate of the county of Pembroke.
tables. 64 pp. London, Longman, Hurst, Rees, Orme, and Brown, 1821

T.

3227 A letter to the right honourable Sir John Newport, bart. M.P. &c. &c., in consequence of his proposition in the house of commons for the appointment of a parliamentary commission to inquire into the abuses in the collection, management and conduct of the revenue in Ireland, by Hibernicus.
40 pp. Dublin, Milliken, 1821

A., C., N., P.

3228 LONG, George. Observations on a bill to amend the laws relating to the relief of the poor in England, lately introduced into the house of commons by James Scarlett, esq.
58 pp. London, J. & W. T. Clarke, 1821

T.

3229 McADAM, John Loudon. Remarks on the present system of road-making; with observations, deduced from practice and experience, with a view to a revision of the existing laws, and the introduction of improvement in the method of making, repairing and preserving roads, and defending the road funds from misapplication.
4th ed., carefully revised, with considerable additions, and an appendix. 196 pp. London, Longman, Hurst, Rees, Orme and Brown, 1821

A.

3230 MILL, James. Elements of political economy.
244 pp. London, Baldwin, Cradock and Joy, 1821

T.

3231 Monopoly and taxation vindicated against the errors of the legislature. By a Nottinghamshire farmer.
72 pp. Newark, M. Hage, London, Longman, Hurst, Rees, Orme & Brown, 1821

T.

3232 Observations on certain verbal disputes in political economy, particularly relating to value, and to demand and supply.
86 pp. London, R. Hunter, 1821

T.

Sometimes attributed to Samuel Bailey; but see Rauner: Samuel Bailey and the Classical Theory of Value (London, 1961) p. 89.

3233 On the expediency and necessity of striking off a part of the national debt; with observations on its practicability, with the least possible injury.
24 pp. London, 1821

P.

3234 PLAYFAIR, William. A letter on our agricultural distresses, their causes and remedies; accompanied by tables and copper-plate charts, showing and comparing the prices of wheat, bread and labour from 1565–1821. Addressed to the lords and commons.
tables. graphs. 80 pp. London, W. Sams, 1821

A.

3235 Proceedings of the trustees of the linen and hempen manufactures of Ireland for the year ended 5th January 1821.
332 pp. & appendix and index of 118 pp. Dublin, printed by W. Folds, [1821]

A.

3236 Protection to agriculture, or universal ruin. Further considerations on the corn question, etc.
24 pp. London, 1821.

P., T.

3237 Remarks on the impolicy of restrictions on commerce; with a particular application to the present state of the timber trade.
34 pp. London, R. Hunter, 1821

R.

3238 Report of the committee appointed by the Royal Dublin society to inquire and report upon the expense of draining, and the practicability of permanently reclaiming the bogs and waste lands of Ireland, to which is annexed an appendix.
44 pp. Dublin, printed by D. Graisberry, 1821

A.

3239 Report of the Council of the chamber of commerce of Dublin to the annual assembly of the members of the association.
32 pp. Dublin, printed by C. Bentham, 1821

A.

3240 Report of the general committee for the association for the suppression of mendicity in Dublin for the year 1820
56 pp. Dublin, the mendicity association, 1821
A., P.

3241 SAUNDERS, William Herbert. An address to the Imperial parliament, upon the practical means of gradually abolishing the poor-laws, and educating the poor systematically. Illustrated by an account of the colonies of Fredericks-Oord, in Holland, and of the Common mountain, in the south of Ireland. With general observations.
126 pp. London, W. Sams, 1821
A.

3242 Sketch of a plan for a reformation in the system of provincial banking, by which the notes of country bankers may be rendered as secure as those of the Bank of England, and the agriculturists, manufacturers, etc. etc. relieved from the distress and inconvenience occasioned by the want of a secure circulating medium. With an abstract of the chancellor of the exchequer's bill to authorise bankers in England and Ireland to issue and circulate promissory notes, secured upon a deposit of public funds, or other government securities.
appendix. 16 pp. London, 1821
P.

3243 The source and remedy of the national difficulties deduced from principles of political economy in a letter to Lord John Russell.
42 pp. London, Rodwell & Martin, 1821
A.

3244 State of Ireland.
26 pp. appendix 58 pp. Dublin, printed by Gannon, 1821
A., N.

3245 Statement on the present timber and deal trade, as regards Europe and the British American colonies, resting on plain and undeniable facts.
28 pp. London, 1821
P.

3246 STOKES, Whitley. Observations on the population and resources of Ireland.
tables. appendix. 104 pp. Dublin, J. Porter, 1821
A., C., N., T.

3247 Sun Assurance Company. Report of a trial wherein Bernard Burgess was plaintiff, and Charles B. Forde, Chas. Bolton, and William Burnie, three of the directors of the Sun Assurance Company, were defendants, to recover the amount of a policy of insurance, effected by the plaintiff in the office of the defendants, for £500, on the life of the late Philip Henry Godfry, esq., deceased.
34 pp. Dublin, printed by J. Nolan, 1821
A.

3248 [TAYLOR, John.] The restoration of national prosperity, shewn to be immediately practicable. By the author of 'Junius Identified'.
tables. appendix. 94 pp. London, Taylor and Hessey, 1821
P.

3249 TOWNSEND, Horatio, the elder. A tour through Ireland and the northern parts of Great Britain, with remarks... respecting...the coal formation in Ireland.
80 pp., Cork, Edwards and Savage, 1821
A.

3250 TUCKER, Henry St. George. Remarks on the plans of finance lately promulgated by the honourable court of directors, and by the supreme government of India.
100 pp. London, J. Hatchard, 1821
K.

3251 A warning voice to the legislators and land-owners of the United Kingdom.
40 pp. London, J. and A. Arch, 1821
T.

3252 WILKS, Jonathan. A practical scheme for the reduction of the public debt and taxation, without individual sacrifice.
tables. 46 pp. London, Hurst, Robinson, [etc.], 1821
T.

3253 YOUNG, Thomas. The annual tour of inspection of Thomas Young, Inspector-General of Fisheries; his district extending from Annalong to the West Point of Killala Bay. Commenced the 7th of July and finished the 8th of August, 1821.
26 pp. (no t.p.) n.p., 1821
N.

1822

3254 An address to the members of the house of commons upon the necessity of reforming our financial system, and establishing an efficient sinking fund for the reduction of the national debt; with the outline of a plan for that purpose. By one of themselves.
appendix. 82 pp. London, J. M. Richardson, G. Cowie, and A. Constable, 1822
R.

3255 The annual report of the managers and auditors of the Royal Cork Institution, previous to the general meeting at the Spring Assizes, 1822.
tables. 36 pp. Cork, Edwards & Savage, 1822
A.

3256 An answer to the state of the nation at the commencement of the year 1822 and the declarations and conduct of His Majesty's Ministers fairly considered.
tables. 106 pp. London, J. Ridgway, 1822
T.

3257 An appeal to the King on the present state of Ireland.
52 pp. London, Simpkin & Marshall; Dublin, Graham, 1822
A., T.

3258 At a meeting of the trustees of the Linen and Hempen Manufactures of Ireland, at their house at the Linen Hall, on Tuesday, the 5th of February, 1822.
16 pp. Dublin, 1822
A.

3259 [BLESSINGTON, Charles John Gardiner, earl of?] A letter to His Excellency the marquess of Wellesley, on the state of Ireland. By a representative peer.
54 pp. London, printed by Valpy, 1822
N.

3260 ——. Observations addressed to his excellency the marquess Wellesley, K.G., K.C., &c., &c., on the state of Ireland.
98 pp. London, Longman, Hurst, Rees, Orme & Brown; Dublin, R. Milliken, 1822
A., K., N.

3261 ——. Observations on the proposed North of Ireland Canal, under the patronage of H.R.H. the duke of Sussex. List of proprietors of Grand Canal Stock.
32 pp. London, printed by E. Beckett, 1822
A.

3262 BRAMSTON, Thomas Gardiner. A practical inquiry into the nature and extent of the present agricultural distress, and the means of relieving it.
58 pp. 2nd ed. London, J. Hatchard, 1822
K.

3263 BROWNE, Denis. A letter from the right hon. Denis Browne, M.P. for Kilkenny, to the most noble the marquess Wellesley on the present state of Ireland.
24 pp. London, J. Nichols, 1822
G.

3264 Catalogue of the library, Royal Irish Academy house, 114, Grafton street, Dublin.
66 pp. Dublin, M. Goodwin, 1822
A.
Contains section on 'Economics and statistics', p. 27.

3265 CLEGHORN, James. On the depressed state of agriculture, being the essay for which the Highland Society of Scotland, at their general meeting on 1st July, 1822, voted a piece of plate of 50 gns. value.
table of contents. 144 pp. Edinburgh, A. Constable & co.; London, Hurst and Robinson, 1822
N.

3266 CLONCURRY, Valentine Browne Lawless, 2nd baron. A letter to the duke of Leinster on the police and present state of Ireland.
24 pp. Dublin, Nolan, 1822
A., N.

——. 22 pp. 2nd ed. Dublin, printed by William Corbet, 1822
N.

3267 [CROKER, John Wilson.] A sketch of the state of Ireland, past and present.
72 pp. 8th ed. Dublin, M. N. Mahon, 1822
A., T.

——. Another issue. 74 pp. London, J. Murray, 1822
A., N., T.

3268 CROPPER, James. Letters addressed to William Wilberforce, M.P. recommending the encouragement of the cultivation of sugar in our dominions in the East Indies, as the natural and certain means of effecting the total and general abolition of the slave trade.
tables. appendix. 62 pp. London, Longman, Hurst, Rees, Orme & Brown, 1822
K., T.

3269 Cursory suggestions on naval subjects, with the outline of a plan for raising seamen for his majesty's fleets in a future war, by ballot.
102 pp. London, F. C. and J. Rivington, 1822
K.

3270 DALLAS, Alexander. A sermon upon the present distress in Ireland, preached to a country congregation, principally of the labouring class at Highclere in the county of Hants.
26 pp. London, Baldwin, Cradock & Joy, 1822
A.

3271 DENNIS, Jeffery. A systematic plan for bettering the condition of merchants, owners, underwriters, commanders, officers, seamen, &c. in the merchant sea service; in which the new principles of government are exemplified, under the following important heads:—initiation, manning, victualling, permanent wages in commanders and mariners; proposing relief to subscribers when unemployed, or shipwrecked; and an annual allowance, or pension, to decayed owners, commanders, officers, seamen, &c. and their widows; and wherein uniforms for commanders and officers, and appropriate dresses for seamen and sailors, are submitted, by which the rank and qualification of each may be distinguished.
illust. appendix. 44 pp. London, M. Dennis, 1822
K.

3272 DOYLE, Wesley. Ostensible causes of the present state of Ireland considered and remedies suggested inscribed to the members of the imperial parliament.
36 pp. Scarborough, printed by Sedman & Weddill, 1822
A., T.

3273 DUDLEY, Sir Henry Bate, bart. A short address to the most reverend and honourable William Lord Primate of all Ireland recommendatory of some commutation or modification of the tythes of that country.
32 pp. London, Cadell, 1822
A.

3274 ELLIS, Henry. A few words of money and of taxation.
24 pp. London, W. Reynolds, 1822
T.

3275 [ERLINGTON, Thomas, bishop of Leighlin & Ferns.] An inquiry whether the disturbances in Ireland have originated in tithes or can be suppressed by a commutation of them. By S. N.
50 pp. Dublin, R. Milliken, 1822
A., P., T.

3276 Emigration recommended as a means of improving the condition of the unemployed and the unproductively employed. By a Retired Officer.
52 pp. Dublin, printed by Courtney, 1822
A.

3277 An enquiry into the consumption of public wealth by the clergy, in which it is shown that the church of England

and Ireland consumes more than all the clergy of the whole Christian world, abridged from a pamphlet published by E. Wilson, Royal Exchange.
24 pp. London, T. J. Wooler, 1822
A.

See 3314

3278 ENSOR, George. Addresses to the people of Ireland on the degradation and misery of their country, and the means which they (in themselves) possess, not only to save it from utter ruin, but to raise it to its proper rank and consequence amongst nations.
54 pp. Dublin, printed by Nolan, [1822?]
A., N.

3279 An essay on the tithe system, shewing its foundation on the laws of the land; its advantages and disadvantages.
52 pp. Oxford, W. Baxter, 1822
K. T.

3280 An exposition of the real causes and effective remedies of the agricultural distress. By an impartial looker-on.
42 pp. London, Sherwood, Neely, Jones, 1822
A.

3281 FINLAY, John. Letters addressed to the Irish government on local taxes, the Irish collieries etc.
92 pp. London, C. Bentham, 1822
A., N., P.

3282 First annual report of the association for the suppression of mendicity in the city of Waterford.
tables. 46 pp. Waterford, printed by J. Bull, 1822
A., P.

3283 FRASER, Robert. Examination of Captain Mathew Luke, respecting the Cappagh Copper Mine, and the veins adjacent thereto, for the information of the hon. the Board of Commissioners for the issue of public money.
8 pp. Dublin, Mullen, 1822
A.

3284 ———. Review of the state of Ireland, with regard to the best means of employing the redundant population, in useful and productive labour, drawn up for the consideration of His Excellency, the most noble, Lord Lieutenant General and General Governor of Ireland.
appendices. 30 pp. Dublin, Carrick, 1822
A.

3285 ———. Sketches and essays on the present state of Ireland, particularly regarding the bogs, waste-lands, and fisheries, with observations on the best means of employing the population in useful and productive labour.
106 pp. Dublin, R. Milliken, London, Longman, Hurst, Rees, Orme & Brown, 1822
A., N.

3286 [GRACE, I., archdeacon?] Lachrymae Hibernicae; or grievances of the peasantry of Ireland, especially in the Western counties. By a resident native.
24 pp. Dublin, printed by M. Goodwin, 1822
A., B., N., T.

3287 HEATHFIELD, Richard. Observations on trade considered in reference, particularly, to the public debt, and to the agriculture of the United Kingdom.
tables. appendices. 74 pp. London, Longman, Hurst, Rees, Orme and Brown [etc., etc], 1822
A., N., P.

3288 [HODSON, Hartly?] A letter to his grace the archbishop of Armagh, and a letter to his grace the duke of Devonshire, with observations on the system of tithing. By an Irish Volunteer.
52 pp. London, Sherwood, Neely, & Jones, 1822
A.

3289 HOPKINS, Thomas. Economical enquiries relative to the laws which regulate rent, profit, wages, and the value of money.
tables. 120 pp. London, J. Hatchard, 1822
T.

3290 An impartial review of the true causes of existing misery in Ireland.
50 pp. Dublin, R. Milliken, 1822
A.

3291 January 1822. Observations upon the peace establishments of the army, produced by the discussions upon the army estimates in the last session of parliament; and by the proposals then made, and at subsequent periods repeated at public meetings, &c. that the peace establishment of 1821–22 should be assimilated to that of 1792.
56 pp. London, John Hatchard, 1822
T.

3292 JOPLIN, Thomas. An essay on the general principles and present practice of banking in England & Scotland, with observations upon the justice and policy of an immediate alteration in the charter of the Bank of England and the measures to be pursued in order to effect it.
78 pp. 2nd ed. London, J. Ridgway; Edinburgh, Hill, 1822
A.

3293 ———. Supplementary observations to the third edition of an essay on the general principles and present practice of banking etc.
20 pp. London, J. Ridgway; Edinburgh, Hill, 1822
A.

3294 KING, W. H. Account of the fisheries in 1822 on the western coast of Ireland.
14 pp. Galway, 1822
A.

3295 The laws and regulations of the Chamber of Commerce, of the City of Dublin. Adopted at a general meeting of its members, held on Thursday, 3rd day of January, 1822.
10 pp. Dublin, printed by C. Bentham, 1822
A.

3296 Letter from an Irish beneficed clergyman, concerning tithes.
30 pp. London, F. C. and J. Rivington, 1822
K.

3297 A letter to his excellency the lord lieutenant of Ireland on the present state of that kingdom; with brief remarks on the advantages of catholic emancipation.
38 pp. London, Miller, 1822

T.

3298 Letter to Rt. Hon. William Conyngham Plunket, attorney-general for Ireland, on the subject of Tithes; and particularly the great vital question, whether they are to be regarded like any other private property. By an Irish landlord.
46 pp. London, printed by Gosnell, 1822

N.

3299 A letter to the earl of Liverpool, on agricultural distress; its extent, cause and remedy. By an old tory.
32 pp. London, J. Hatchard, 1822

K.

3300 MCADAM, John Loudon. Remarks on the present system of road making with observations, deduced from practice and experience, with a view to a revision of the existing laws, and the introduction of improvement in the method of making, repairing, and preserving roads, and defending the road funds from misapplication. Fifth edition carefully revised, with considerable additions, and an appendix.
tables. appendix. 196 pp. London, Longman, Hurst, Rees, Orme and Brown, 1822

R., T.

3301 MCCAY, John. A general view of the history and objects of the bank of England; with extracts from the charter, acts of parliament and bye-laws regulating that corporation, accompanied by observations upon the most important clauses, in a series of letters to a friend.
appendix. 114 pp. London, Longman, Hurst, Rees, Orme and Brown, 1822

A., T.

3302 [MONTEAGLE, Thomas Spring Rice, 1st baron.] Considerations on the present state of Ireland and on the best means of improving the condition of its inhabitants, by an Irishman.
40 pp. London, R. & A. Taylor, 1822

A.

3303 [O'BEIRNE, Thomas Lewis.] A letter from an Irish dignitary to an English clergyman on the subject of tithes in Ireland, written during the administration of the duke of Bedford, with the addition of some observations and notes, suggested by the present state of this momentous question.
36 pp. Dublin, R. Milliken, 1822

A., G., K., N., P., T.

3304 Observations on the interests of landlords, affected by the local taxes of Dublin, with the outline of a plan for their future management and collection.
16 pp. Dublin, the Booksellers, 1822

U.

3305 On our commercial system; shewing the cause of the present fall of prices, &c. &c.
28 pp. London, Longman, Hurst, Rees, Orme, and Brown, 1822

T.

3306 OWEN, Robert. Mr. Owen's Plan for the amelioration of the population of Ireland, illustrated by statements and calculations proving the practicability of such an amelioration affording permanent security to the possessors of every description of property in Ireland.
14 pp. Dublin, printed by J. Nolan, 1822

A.

3307 PAGE, Frederick. The principle of the English poor laws illustrated and defended, by an historical view of indigence in civil society; with observations and suggestions relative to their improved administration.
114 pp. London, J. Hatchard, 1822

T.

3308 PAGET, Thomas. Letter addressed to David Ricardo, esq. M.P. on the true principle of estimating the extent of the late depreciation in the currency, and on the effect of Mr. Peel's Bill for the resumption of cash payments by the Bank.
tables. 36 pp. London, J. Richardson, 1822

N.

3309 ——. The price of gold an imperfect index of the depreciation in the currency. A letter addressed to Sir Francis Burdett, bart. upon the occasion of his presenting the petition of the inhabitants of Westminster, to the house of commons.
10 pp. [pag. 39–48]. London, J. Richardson, 1822

N.

3310 Proposal for the modification of the Irish tithe system by a resident landed proprietor.
16 pp. Cork, Edwards & Savage, 1822

A.

3311 Reasons why the bank of England ought not to reduce the rate of discount to four per cent, to which are added, some observations on a recent publication entitled 'A [sic] protection to agriculture'. By an impartial observer.
62 pp. 2nd ed. enlarged. London, T. Cadell, etc., 1822

A.

The publication referred to is Ricardo's *On Protection to Agriculture*.

3312 Reflections on the State of Ireland in the nineteenth century, the progressive operation of the causes which have produced it; and the measures best calculated to remove some, and to mitigate the effects of others of them.
294 pp. [various paging.] London, Ridgway, 1822

A.

3313 Remarks on a letter from lord Cloncurry to the duke of Leinster on the police and present state of Ireland.
22 pp. Dublin, printed by W. Corbet, 1822

A., D.

3314 Remarks on the consumption of public wealth by the clergy of every Christian nation, and particularly by the established church in England and Wales, and in Ireland; with a plan for altering its revenues, subject to existing interests, whereby the episcopal body would be provided for, on a scale to make them the richest episcopal body in the world. The working clergy of the establishment, would be much better provided for than at present. The working clergy of all other denominations would be equally provided for with those of the establishment, and both on a scale to make them

the richest working clergy in the world, and upwards of £100,000,000 obtained to extinguish so much of the national debt, and relieve the nation from four millions of annual taxes.
tables. 86 pp. London, Effingham Wilson, 1822
A., P.

3315 A reply to Mr Hale's appeal to the public in defence of the Spitalfields act. By the author of 'Observations on the ruinous tendency of the Spitalfields act'.
60 pp. 2nd ed. London, J. & A. Arch, 1822
N.

3316 Report of the general committee of the association for the suppression of mendicity in Dublin for the year 1821.
98 pp. Dublin, printed by Carrick, 1822
A., N.

3317 Report of the proceedings of the committee of management for the relief of the distressed districts in Ireland, appointed at a general meeting, held at the mansion-house, Dublin, on the 16th May, 1822 with an Abstract of Accounts and an appendix.
appendix. table. 28 pp. Dublin, printed by R. Beere, 1822
A., U.

3318 A report to the Farming society of Ireland, upon the improvement or deterioration of wool of Irish growth; and as to the best means of enabling the Irish farmer to grow fine wool, with advantage to himself, and to the British manufacturer. By the Society's Secretary.
tables. 80 pp. [last page torn]. Dublin, printed by Porter, 1822
N.

3319 A review of the existing causes which at present disturb the tranquillity of Ireland, recommended to the serious attention of land holders, the established clergy, and the Hibernian Sunday School Society.
24 pp. Dublin, Watson, Tims [etc.], 1822
A., N.

3320 REYNOLDS, John Stuckey.   Practical observations on Mr. Ricardo's principles of political economy and taxation.
104 pp. London, Longman, Hurst, Rees, Orme, and Brown, 1822
T.

3321 RICARDO, David.   On protection to agriculture.
appendices. folding table. 100 pp. 4th ed. London, J. Murray, 1822
A., K., T.

3322 RICHARDS, James. A letter to the earl of Liverpool, on the agricultural distress of the country; its cause demonstrated in the unequal system of taxation; and a just system suggested.
tables. 54 pp. London, J. and A. Arch, [etc.], 1822
K., T.

——.   58 pp. 2nd ed. London, J. & A. Arch, 1822
K., T.

3323. SINCLAIR, Sir John, bart.   Address to the owners and occupiers of land in Great Britain and Ireland; pointing out effectual means, for remedying the agricultural distresses of the country.
tables. 26 pp. Edinburgh, A. Constable, 1822
N.

3324 SLANEY, Robert A.   An essay on the employment of the poor, by Robert A. Slaney, esq., second edition, with additions. To which is prefixed a letter to the author, by James Scarlett, esq., M.P. published by his permission.
102 pp. London, J. Hatchard, 1822
A., T.

3325 Society for bettering the condition of the poor in Ireland, by means of employment.
16 pp. London, printed by Beckett, 1822
A.

3326 STANSFELD, Hamer.   Reasons for thinking that Free Trade will raise the rent of land as well as the profit of capital and the wages of labour; and that it would be foolish in the landlords to incur the odium of enacting a corn law to protect the value of their property, when the effect will be the reverse; as any duty which they impose on foreign produce falls ultimately with increased pressure on their own.
table, appendix with table. 26 pp. London, Henry Hooper, [1822?]
U.

3327 The state of the nation at the commencement of the year 1822. Considered under the four departments of the finance, foreign relations, home department, colonies, and board of trade.
appendix. 222 pp. 6th ed. London, J. Hatchard, 1822
A., P., T.
Attributed by Barbier to the marquess of Londonderry, and by the British Museum to baron Lyndhurst.

3328 STEVEN, Robert.   Remarks on the present state of Ireland; with hints for ameliorating the condition, and promoting the education and moral improvement, of the peasantry of that country. The result of a visit during the summer and autumn of 1821.
96 pp. London, Smith and Elder, 1822
A., P., T.

——.   Second edition, with an appendix; containing an outline of the system of education pursued in the schools of the London Hibernian society.
80 pp. London, Smith & Elder etc., 1822
A., L., N., T.

3329 A stitch in time saves nine.
32 pp. Dublin, R. Milliken, 1822
A., K., N.
Supports the position of the Church of Ireland clergy on the tithe question.

3330 STOURTON, William Joseph Stourton, 18th baron.   Further considerations, addressed to the right honourable the earl of Liverpool on agricultural relief, and the extent of the national resources.
116 pp. London, J. Mawman, 1822
T.

3331 THACKERAY, Francis.   A defence of the clergy of the Church of England, stating their services, their rights and their revenues, from the earliest ages to the present time and showing the relation in which they stand to the community and to the agriculturalist.
202 pp. London, F. C. & J. Rivington, 1822
A., T.

3332 Townsend, Edmund.   A view of the injurious effects of the present bankrupt system, in regard to property and public morals: with remarks on the lord chancellor's late bills; and suggestions of improvements, different to the provisions of those bills.
24 pp. 2nd ed. London, Sherwood, Neely, Jones, 1822
A.

3333 A treatise relative to the effect of an increase of current money in promoting the growth of population.
194 pp. London, J. Murray, 1822
T.

3334 Trenor, Keating.   An inquiry into the political economy of the Irish peasantry, as connected with the commissariat resources of Ireland.
52 pp. London, Egerton, 1822
A., T.

3335 Trimmer, Joshua Kirby.   Observations on the state of agriculture, and condition of the lower classes of the people, in the southern parts of Ireland, in the year 1812. To which are added further observations relating to the same subjects, in the year 1822.
tables. 148 pp. London, F. C. and J. Rivington, [etc., etc], 1822
K., T.

3336 Turner, Samuel.   Considerations upon the agriculture, commerce, and manufactures of the British empire; with observations on the practical effect of the bill of the right hon. Robert Peel, for the resumption of cash payments by the Bank of England; and also upon the pamphlet lately published by David Ricardo, esq., entitled, Protection to agriculture.
tables in appendices. 112 pp. London, J. Murray, 1822
K., T.

3337 Watson, William.   The emigrants' guide to the Canadas.
36 pp. Dublin, printed by G. Bull, 1822
A.

3338 Western, Charles Callis Western, 1st baron.   Second address to the landowners of the United Empire. Second edition.
tables. appendix. 60 pp. London, J. Ridgway, [etc.], 1822
T.

3339 Whitmore, William Wolryche.   A letter on the present state and future prospects of agriculture. Addressed to the agriculturists of the county of Salop.
tables. 88 pp. London, J. Hatchard, 1822
K., T.

3340 Whyte, Henry.   Statement of the late tithe occurrences at New Ross.
52 pp. Dublin, 1822
A., N.

3341 [Wiggins, John.]   A letter to the absentee landlords of the south of Ireland; on the means of tranquillizing their tenantry, and improving their estates.
62 pp. London, J. Hatchard, 1822
R.

3342 [Wilmot, Mrs. —.?]   A word to the landholders of Ireland.
22 pp. Cork, Edwards and Savage, 1822
K.

1823

3343 An account of the proceedings of the committees of the journeymen silk weavers of Spitalfields; in the legal defence of the acts of parliament, granted to their trade, in the 13th, 52nd and 51st years of the reign of his late majesty, King George the third.
68 pp. London, printed by E. Justins, 1823
P.

3344 Animadversions on the repeal of the act for regulating the wages of labour among the Spitalfield weavers; and on the combination law: with original remarks on free trade, contained in two letters, one addressed to the Spitalfield weavers; and the other addressed to the representatives in parliament for the city of Coventry by a Coventry freeman.
20 pp. London, R. Brown, 1823
P.

3345 Articles of Agreement of the National Assurance Company of Ireland, dated 9th January, 1823.
34 pp. Dublin, printed by C. Bentham, 1823
A.

3346 An attempt to collect materials for a statistic history of Ireland.
40 pp. Dublin, printed by Graisberry, 1823
A.

3347 Baldwin, Walter J.   An appeal to common sense and to religion on the catholic question, with a word on tithes.
168 pp. London, J. Ridgway, 1823
A., N.

3348 Barham, Joseph Foster.   Considerations on the abolition of negro slavery, and the means of practically effecting it.
tables. appendices. 92 pp. second ed. London, J. Ridgway, 1823
T.

3349 Barrow: Agricultural School: The report of their secretary respecting the agricultural school of Barrow in the Barony of Bargie, and County of Wexford as ordered by the board.
18 pp. Dublin, printed by Porter, 1823
A., D., N.

3350 Bayldon, J. S.   The art of valuing rents and tillages; wherein is explained the manner of valuing the tenant's right on entering and quitting farms, in Yorkshire and the adjoining counties. The whole is adapted for the use of landlords, land agents, appraizers, farmers and tenants.
diag. 204 pp. London, Longman, Hurst, Rees, Orme and Brown, 1823
T.

3351 BEATSON, Jasper. An examination of Mr. Owen's plans, for relieving distress, removing discontent, and 're-creating the character of man': showing that they are directly calculated to root out all the virtuous affections of the human mind; and to destroy all that is valuable in the institutions, the manners, and the laws, of human society.
68 pp. Glasgow, William Turnbull, 1823
T.

3352 BLAKE, William. Observations on the effects produced by the expenditure of Government during the restriction of cash payments.
126 pp. London, J. Murray, E. Lloyd, 1823
T.

3353 [BLOMFIELD, Charles James, afterwards bishop of London.] A remonstrance addressed to H. Brougham, esq., M.P. by one of the 'Working Clergy'.
56 pp. London, J. Mawman; F. C. and J. Rivington, 1823
T.

3354 BOOTH, David. A letter to the Rev. T. R. Malthus, M.A., F.R.S. being an answer to the criticism on Mr. Godwin's work on population, which was inserted in the LXXth number of the Edinburgh Review; to which is added An examination of the censuses of Great Britain and Ireland.
tables. 128 pp. London, Longman, Hurst, Rees, Orme and Brown, 1823
K., T.

3355 CAMPBELL, Augustus. An appeal to the gentlemen of England, on behalf of the Church of England.
61 pp. Liverpool, G. F. Harris's widow and brothers, 1823
T.

3356 ——. A reply to the article on Church establishments, in the last number of The Edinburgh Review.
42 pp. London, J. Hatchard, 1823
T.

3357 CAREY, Matthew. View of the very great natural advantages of Ireland; and of the cruel policy pursued for centuries, towards that island, whereby those advantages have been blasted. To which is added, a sketch of the present deplorable condition of the Irish peasantry. Extracted from the Vindiciae Hibernicae.
24 pp. Philadelphia, H. C. Carey & I. Lea, 1823
L.

3358 [CARMALT, William.] A letter to the Right Honourable George Canning, on the principle and administration of the English poor laws. By a select vestryman of the parish of Putney, under the 59 Geo. 3. cap. 12.
112 pp. London, T. Cadell, 1823
T.

3359 The Case of Ireland in 1823; an argument for the repeal of the Union between that country and Great Britain. By the author of the Answer to Mr. Peel's speech on the Catholic question, in 1817.
70 pp. London, J. Murray, 1823
A., P.

3360 The causes of discontent in Ireland and remedies proposed.
90 pp. Dublin, printed by Graisberry, [1823?]
A.

3361 CLARKSON, Thomas. Thoughts on the necessity of improving the condition of the slaves in the British colonies with a view to their ultimate emancipation, and on the practicability, the safety and the advantages of the latter measure.
64 pp. London, printed by R. Taylor, 1823
N.

3362 The contractor unmasked; being letters to one of the contractors of the Colombian loan, occasioned by his recent pamphlet; comprising authentic information respecting the loan and debentures, never before published. With a postscript on the new loan hoax. By a member of the honourable society of Lincoln's inn.
40 pp. London, Hurst, Robinson, [etc.], 1823
K.

3363 CROPPER, James. A letter addressed to the Liverpool society for promoting the abolition of slavery, on the injurious effects of high prices of produce, and the beneficial effects of low prices, on the condition of slaves.
32 pp. London, Hatchard; J. & A. Arch, 1823
K.

3364 ——. Relief for West-Indian distress; shewing the inefficiency of protecting duties on East-India sugar, and pointing out other modes of certain relief.
tables. appendix. 38 pp. London, Hatchard, 1823
A., K., N.

3365 DOYLE, Sir John. Speech of General Doyle, president of the first anniversary meeting of the society for improving the condition and increasing the comforts of the Irish peasantry.
22 pp. London, the Philanthropic Society, [1823?]
A.

3366 DU THON, Adele. An account of the principal charitable institutions of the parish of St. Mary-le-bone.
64 pp. London, J. Murray, 1823
T.

3367 [EMERSON, John Swift.] One year of the administration of his excellency the marquess of Wellesley in Ireland.
137 pp. 2nd ed. London, J. Hatchard, Dublin, Neary Mahon, 1823
B., K., N., T.

3368 ENSOR, George. The poor and their relief.
table of contents. 384 pp. London, Effingham Wilson, 1823
N.

3369 Errors in our funding system, and the management of our money concerns, with the mode of retrieving them; as pointed out in the New Edinburgh Review, for January, 1823.
tables. 20 pp. Edinburgh, Waugh & Innes [etc.], 1823
A.

Review of: 'A plan for reducing the capital and the annual charge of the national debt', by John Brickwood, jr. [1820].

3370 ERSKINE, Thomas Americus Erskine, 3rd baron. A letter to the proprietors and occupiers of land, on the cause of, and the remedies for, the declension of agricultural prosperity.
48 pp. London, J. Murray, 1823
K., T.

3371 The first report of the British-Irish Ladies Society for improving the condition and promoting the industry and welfare of the female peasantry in Ireland.
70 pp. London, W. Phillips, 1823
A.

3372 FORDAL, James. A letter to the Right Honourable the earl of Liverpool on the present state of the nation.
tables. 78 pp. London, Longman, Hurst, Rees, Orme, and Brown, 1823
T.

3373 HAUTENVILLE, H. B. Digest of the duties of Customs & Excise upon all articles imported into or exported from Ireland.
176 pp. Dublin, W. Underwood, 1823
A.

3374 HENDERSON, James. Observations on the great commercial benefits that will result from the Warehousing-Bill, particularly as regards the free transit of foreign linens, silks and woollens. Respectfully addressed to the consideration of the members of the British parliament.
48 pp. London, J. M. Richardson, [etc.], 1823
A., P.

3375 [HINCKS, William.] The claims of the clergy to tithes and other Church revenues, so far as they are founded on the political expediency of supporting such a body; on divine right; on history; or on the notion of unalienable property, examined.
40 pp. London, R. Hunter, Effingham Wilson, 1823
T.

3376 Hints on the danger of unsettling the currency, invading the funds, or giving way to visionary reformers.
tables. 76 pp. London, J. Hatchard, 1823
T.

3377 HODGSON, Adam. A letter to M. Jean-Baptiste Say, on the comparative expense of free & slave labour.
60 pp. 2nd ed. Liverpool, W. Grapel [&c], 1823
B., K.
Appendix contains reply from Say.

3378 HUMPHREYS, William. To the proprietors of the National Assurance company of Ireland, assembled at an extraordinary general meeting of the company. 1st Feb. 1823.
4 pp. Dublin, C. Bentham, 1823
A.

3379 The impolicy of imprisonment for debt; considered in relation to the attempts at present made to procure a repeal of the Insolvent Debtors' Act. Dedicated to Mr. Sergeant Onslow.
24 pp. London, Wilson, 1823
N., T.
Signed: a Merchant.

3380 Inordinate taxes and not Mr. Peel's Bill, the cause of the present distress: illustrated in three letters, written in answer to Mr. Western, and originally published in the Kent and Essex Mercury. By Gracchus. With prefatory remarks, by the editor of that Journal.
40 pp. London, R. Hunter, 1823
T.

3381 LAURENCE, Richard, archbishop of Cashel. Remarks upon certain objections published in the Dublin newspaper called the Warder, against the tithe composition bill now pending in parliament.
16 pp. London, A. & R. Spottiswoode, 1823
T.

3382 A letter containing some observations on the delusive nature of the system proposed by Robert Owen, esq. for the amelioration of the condition of the people of Ireland: as developed by him at the public meetings held for that purpose in Dublin, on the 18th March, and 12th, 19th, and 24th April 1823.
44 pp. Dublin, Richard Moore Tims, 1823
A., N., T.

3383 A letter to Mr. Canning, on agricultural distress. By a country gentleman.
32 pp. London, Longman, Hurst, Rees, Orme and Brown, 1823
K., T.

3384 Letter to the Right Honourable the Chancellor of the Exchequer, on the repeal of the assessed taxes.
32 pp. London, William Phillips, [etc., etc.], 1823
T.

3385 A letter to the Rt. Hon. the earl of Liverpool on the origin, title, effects and commutation of tithes.
160 pp. London, T. Cadell, 1823
A., K., T.

3386 Letters addressed to the marquess Wellesley on the means of ameliorating the condition of the Irish peasantry. By Clericus.
50 pp. Cork, Bolster [etc., etc.], 1823
A.

3387 Letters of Laelius on various topics connected with the present state of Ireland, as published in the Carlow Morning Post in the years 1822 and 1823.
62 pp. Carlow, Richard Price, [1823]
A., P.

3388 Low, David. Observations on the present state of landed property, and on the prospects of the landholder and the farmer.
134 pp. Edinburgh, Constable, London, Hurst, Robinson, 1823
U.

3389 [LYNDHURST, John Singleton Copley, baron.] Administration of the affairs of Great Britain and Ireland and their dependencies at the commencement of the year 1823 stated under the heads of finance, national resources, foreign relations, colonies, trade and domestic administration.
206 pp. 2nd ed. London, Hatchard, 1823
A.

3390 [MACAULAY, Zachary.] East and West India sugar; or, a refutation of the claims of the West Indian colonists to a protecting duty on East India sugar.
appendices. 134 pp. (various paging). London, Lupton Relfe, 1823
K.

3391 [——.] A letter to William W. Whitmore, esq., M.P. pointing out some of the erroneous statements contained in a pamphlet by Joseph Marryat, esq., M.P. entitled 'a reply to the arguments contained in various publications recommending an equalization of the duties on East and West India sugars'. By the author of a pamphlet entitled 'East and West India sugar'.
tables. 40 pp. London, Lupton Relfe, 1823
K., T.

3392 [MacDonnell, Eneas.] Practical views and suggestions on the present condition and permanent improvement of Ireland. By Hibernicus author of the letters published under the same signature in the Courier, London, Paper.
tables. folding tables, 178 pp. Dublin, printed by J. Carrick, 1823
A., N., P., U.

3393 Malthus, Thomas Robert. The measure of value stated and illustrated, with an application of it to the alterations in the value of the English currency since 1790.
table. 88 pp. London, J. Murray, 1823
T.

3394 Marryat, Joseph. A reply to the arguments contained in various publications, recommending an equalization of the duties on East and West Indian sugar.
tables. 110 pp. London, J. M. Richardson, 1823
N.

3395 Meason, Gilbert Laing. A letter to William Joseph Denison, esq., M.P. on the Agricultural Distress, and on the necessity of a silver standard.
appendix. 54 pp. London, John Harding, 1823
T.

3396 Monopoly unmasked, and shewn to be the primary cause of pauperism and agricultural distress; from a statement of facts never before published. January, 1823.
tables. 42 pp. London, Sherwood, Neely, 1823
T.

3397 National Assurance Co. of Ireland. Rules and Regulations supplementary to the deed of Copartnership, as passed at a meeting of the proprietary, 8th March, 1823.
16 pp. Dublin, 1823
A.

3398 [Ormsby, J. W.?] Remarks on the address of the arch-bishops and bishops to the Lord Lieutenant on the subject of Mr. Goulburns Bill on Tithes, in a letter to his excellency, by a beneficed clergyman.
18 pp. Dublin, 1823
A., N.

3399 Owen, Robert. An explanation of the cause of the distress which pervades the civilised parts of the world and of the means whereby it may be removed.
plate. 16 pp. London, A. Applegarth, 1823
A.

3400 ——. Permanent relief for the agricultural and manufacturing labourers and the peasantry of Ireland.
24 pp. Dublin, printed by Nolan, 1823
N.

3401 ——. A report of the British and foreign philanthropic society with other statements and calculations explanatory of Mr. Owen's plan for the relief of Ireland and of the poor and working classes generally in all other countries.
tables. 118 pp. Dublin, R. Milliken, 1823
A., P., T.

3402 ——. Report of the proceedings at the several public meetings held in Dublin by Robert Owen esq.... preceded by an introductory statement of his opinions and arrangements at New Lanark, extracted from his 'Essays on the formation of the human character'.
plates. tables. 161 pp. Dublin, J. Carrick, 1823
A., P.

3403 Park, J. J. Suggestions addressed to the legislature and the landed interest: occasioned by the bills submitted to parliament by the government of Ireland for a composition and commutation of tithes.
46 pp. London, Butterworth [etc., etc.], 1823
A., N.

3404 Payne, Daniel Beaumont. A letter to the marquess of Lansdowne, on the reputed excess and depreciation of bank notes, and on the consequences of the new metallic currency.
28 pp. London, Taylor and Hessey, 1823
T.

3405 ——. A second letter to the marquess of Lansdowne, on the reputed excess and depreciation of bank notes, on the nature and operation of coins, and on the consequences of the new metallic currency.
62 pp. London, Taylor and Hessey, 1823
T.
The pagination follows on, after previous pamphlet, 31–92 inclusive.

3406 [Phelan, William.] The case of the church of Ireland stated, in a letter respectfully addressed to his excellency the marquess Wellesley and in reply to the charges of J.K.L. by Declan.
96 pp. Dublin, R. Milliken, 1823
A., G.

3407 [——.] Sketch of an amendment to Mr Goulburn's bills for the composition of tithes in Ireland. Respectfully addressed to Mr. Wilberforce.
table. 16 pp. London, J. Hatchard, 1823
A., K., T.

3408 Plan for tranquillizing Ireland; by devising a fund that will authorise abolishing tithes, and taking off the taxes on the necessaries of life; also a legal provision for the poor of Ireland: accounting, at the same time, for the distresses presently felt by the people of Great Britain and Ireland, and suggesting how these may be relieved.
12 pp. Edinburgh, Abernethy and Walker, 1823
A.

3409 Prinsep, G. A. Remarks on the external commerce and exchanges of Bengal, with appendix of accounts and estimates.
tables. appendices. 122 pp. London, Kingsbury, Parbury, and Allen, 1823
T.

3410 Proposal for the formation of a clerical provident fund, in a letter addressed to the clergy of Great Britain and Ireland. By a rector.
18 pp. Oxford, Parker [etc.], 1823
A., N.

3411 [RENNELL, Thomas.] A letter to Henry Brougham, esq., M.P., upon his Durham speech, and the three articles in the last Edinburgh review, upon the subject of the clergy.
106 pp. London, C. & J. Rivington, 1823
A., K., T.

3412 Report of the Committee for the relief of the distressed districts in Ireland, appointed at a general meeting held at the city of London tavern, 7th May, 1822.
appendix with tables. 360 pp. London, printed by W. Phillips, 1823
A., T.

3413 Report of the council of the chamber of commerce of Belfast, 19th November, 1823.
8 pp. Belfast, printed by F. Finlay, [1823?]
A.

3414 Report of the council of the chamber of commerce of Dublin, to the annual assembly of the members of the association.
36 pp. Dublin, printed by C. Bentham, 1823
A.

3415 [Fifth] Report of the general committee of the association for the suppression of mendicity in Dublin, for the year 1822.
84 pp. Dublin, printed by Chambers & Hallagan, 1823
A.

3416 Report of the proceedings of the North-West of Ireland society, established for promoting agriculture, arts, manufactures, and fisheries.
44 pp. Derry, printed by M. Hempton, 1823
A.

3417 Reports of the committee of St. Mary's parish, on local taxation.
tables. appendix. 104 pp. Dublin, printed by J. Carrick, 1823
A., N., P.

3418 [ROSSER, Archibald.] Credit pernicious.
44 pp. London, J. Hatchard, 1823
T.

3419 RYAN, Richard. Directions for proceeding under the tithe act, with observations and an appendix, containing precedents of applications, notices, certificates, etc. required under this act.
74 pp. Dublin, printed by Grierson & Keene, 1823
A., N.

3420 Second annual report of the association for the suppression of mendicity in the city of Waterford.
16 pp. Waterford, printed by S. Smith [jr.], 1823
A.

3421 [SEELEY, Robert Benton.] The case of the landed interests, and their just claims.
tables. 42 pp. London, Rodwell and Martin, 1823
T.

3422 SEELY, John B. A few hints to the West-Indians on their present claims to exclusive favour and protection at the expense of the East-India interests with some observations and notes on India. Respectfully inscribed to the right hon. president of the board of controul.
table. 100 pp. London, Kingsbury, Parbury and Allen, 1823
K.

3423 [SMITH, Sir William Cusac.] Recent scenes and occurrences in Ireland; or animadversions on a pamphlet, entitled 'One year of the administration of the marquess Wellesley'. In a letter to a friend in England.
202 pp. London, Longman, Hurst, Rees, Orme and Brown [etc.], 1823
K., L., T.
See 3367.

3424 [SOAMES, Henry.] A vindication of the church and clergy of England from the misrepresentations of the Edinburgh Review. By a beneficed clergyman.
68 pp. London, C. & J. Rivington, 1823
T.

3425 Society for improving the condition of the Irish peasantry. Charitable Loan Institutions.
table. 8 pp. [Dublin? 1823?]
N.

3426 Society for improving the condition of the Irish peasantry. Report transmitted to the committee from parish of Barrow, Wexford. Through Thomas Boyse esq.
tables. 10 pp. [no t.p.]. London, printed by Marshall, 1823
N.

3427 Society for improving the condition of the poor in Ireland. [First report.]
8 pp. London, the Philanthropic Society, 1823
A.

3428 Society for the encouragement of arts, manufactures, and commerce. Premiums offered in the session 1823–1824.
40 pp. London, printed by Hansard, 1823
N.

3429 SOLLY, Edward. Remarks on the policy of repealing Mr. Peel's bill.
table. 40 pp. London, J. Ridgway, 1823
T.

3430 A statement of the charitable society for the relief of sick and indigent roomkeepers of all religious persuasions, in the city of Dublin.
20 pp. Dublin, printed by J. Nolan, 1823
A.

3431 A statement of the claims of the West India colonies to a protecting duty against East India sugar.
tables. 124 pp. London, Whitmore and Fenn, 1823
N., T.

3432 Substance of the debate in the house of commons, on the 15th May, 1823, on a motion for the mitigation and gradual abolition of slavery throughout the British Dominions. With a preface and appendixes, containing facts and reasonings illustrative of colonial bondage.

appendix. 288 pp. London, the Society for the mitigation and gradual abolition of slavery throughout the British Dominions, 1823

T.

3433 Sun Life Assurance Society for effecting assurances on lives and survivorships.
tables. 16 pp. London, Norris and Son, 1823

N.

3434 THACKERAY, Francis. Some observations upon a pamphlet entitled, 'Remarks on the consumption of public wealth by the clergy of every Christian nation'. And also upon an attack in the 74th number of the Edinburgh Review, upon the Church of England. With a few remarks upon the injustice and inexpedience of a general commutation of tithes; the whole being supplementary to 'A defence of the clergy of the Church of England'.
tables. 52 pp. London, C. & J. Rivington, 1823

T.

3435 Thoughts on the expediency of legalizing the sale of game. By a country gentleman, author of three letters on the 'game laws'.
34 pp. London, J. Murray, 1823

T.

3436 Tithes no Tax, in a letter to a friend, wherein the arguments of Mr. O'Driscoll, Hume, etc. etc. are particularly considered. By Mediensis.
36 pp. Dublin, J. Jones, 1823

A., P.

3437 WAKE, Bernard John. Turnpike roads: lenders of money on mortgage of tolls, etc. cannot, under the present acts, have any legal security:—A reply, in support of this doctrine, to William Knight Dehany, esq. barrister-at-law, the avowed draftsman of the recent turnpike road acts, and who has attempted to refute it, in answer to a former publication by the author of this.
16 pp. London, J. & W. T. Clarke, 1823

T.

3438 WARRE, James. The past, present, and probably the future state of the wine trade; proving that an increase of duty caused a decrease of revenue; and a decrease of duty, an increase of revenue. Founded on parliamentary and other authentic documents. Most respectfully submitted to the right honourable the president and members of the Board of trade.
tables. appendices. 110 pp. London, J. Hatchard; J. M. Richardson, 1823

T.

See 3504

3439 [WHITE, GEORGE & HENSON, Gravener.] A few remarks on the state of the laws at present in existence, for regulating masters and work-people, intended as a guide for the consideration of the house, in their discussions on the bill for repealing several acts relating to combinations of workmen, and for more effectually protecting trade, and for settling disputes between masters and servants.
tables. 146 pp. London, the authors, 1823

T.

3440 WRIGHT, John. Remarks on the erroneous opinions which led to the new corn law; and also on those of the bullionists, on a circulating medium; and pointing out the only protection to agriculture.
50 pp. (various paging.) London, J. Hatchard, 1823

K., T.

1824

3441 Anti-negro emancipation. An appeal to Mr. Wilberforce.
30 pp. London, J. M. Richardson, 1824

T.

3442 BARTON, E. Irish tracts and topics; a soliloquy by E. Barton. Part the first.
158 pp. Dublin, R. Milliken, 1824

A., N., R., T.

On tithes; comments on the writings of Thomas Elrington, bishop Doyle and William Phelan. See also 3448.

3443 [BLANE, William Newnham.] Bread for all. A plan for doing away with the poor's rates; or, parochial, agricultural, and national hints. By an English gentleman.
24 pp. London, printed by E. Thomas, 1824

P.

3444 BRERETON, Charles David. A practical inquiry into the number, means of employment, and wages, of agricultural labourers.
tables. appendix. 110 pp. Norwich, Burks & Kinnebrook, London, J. Hatchard, [1824?]

T.

3445 CHALMERS, Thomas. On the parliamentary means for the abolition of pauperism in England.
34 pp. Glasgow, Chalmers & Collins, 1824

A.

3446 CORNISH, James. A view of the present state of the salmon and channel-fisheries, and of the statute laws by which they are regulated; showing, that it is to the defects of the latter that the present scarcity of the fish is to be attributed. Comprehending also the natural history and habits of the salmon, with some of its peculiarities hitherto undescribed. Together with the forms of a new act, designed to remedy the evils so generally complained of; and an abstract of the evidence before the committee of the house of commons upon the subject.
with notes. 230 pp. London, Longman, Hurst, Rees, Orme, Brown and Green, 1824

T.

3447 CULLEN, Michael. A letter to James Grattan, esq., M.P., in which the subject of the poor laws being introduced in Ireland is considered.
36 pp. Dublin, Pickering, 1824

A., N.

3448 DANIER, F., Ed. Letters from literary characters to E. Barton, edited by F. Danier: with a prefatory notice, by

E.B., of Captain Rock; and a summary passage, by him, north about.
178 pp. Dublin, R. Milliken, 1824

A., K., R., T.

On tithes. T.C.D. copy has 'Baron Smith', i.e., Sir William Cusac Smith, in ms. after 'by E.B.'.

3449 The deed of agreement of the Patriotic assurance company of Ireland.
56 pp. Dublin, Chambers & Hallagan, 1824

A.

3450 The deed of agreement of the Saint Patrick assurance company of Ireland.
64 pp. Dublin, Porter, 1824

A.

3451 Digest of the Acts 4 George IV. c. 99. and 5 George IV. c. 63. providing for the establishing of composition for tithes in Ireland.
index. tables. 70 pp. London, W. Clowes, 1824

A.

3452 [DOYLE, James Warren, bishop of Kildare and Leighlin.] A defence by J.K.L. of his vindication of the religious & civil principles of the Irish catholics.
120 pp. Dublin, Richard Coyne; London, Keating, Brown & Keating, 1824

B., L., N., T.

3453 DOYLE, Wesley. Considerations vitally connected with the present state of Ireland, particularly in reference to the Roman catholic question, the Orange system, and the forfeited estates: inscribed, with great respect, to the earl of Liverpool.
table. 90 pp. Scarborough, Sedman and Weddill, 1824

T.

3454 East India sugar or an inquiry respecting the means of improving the quality and reducing the cost of sugar raised by free labour in the East Indies. With an appendix containing proofs and illustrations.
tables. appendix with tables. 44 pp. London, J. Hatchard [etc.], 1824

K., T.

3455 Eighteenth annual report of the Charitable Association for the year 1823.
30 pp. Dublin, Underwood, 1824

A.

3456 Epitome of the evidence on grand jury cess, taken before a select committee of the house of commons, appointed to enquire into the local taxation of Dublin, in the session of 1823: with notes and illustrations by the Officers of the Prisons.
198 pp. Dublin, R. Graisberry, 1824

A.

3457 First annual report of the County of Roscommon Ladies' Association, auxiliary to the British and Irish Ladies' Society, for ameliorating the condition of the female peasantry of Ireland.
tables. 48 pp. Boyle, Bromell, 1824

A.

3458 HASTINGS, Francis Rawdon-Hastings, 1st marquess of. Summary of the administration of the Indian government by the marquess of Hastings during the period that he filled the office of Governor General.
tables. appendix. 124 pp. London, William Earl, 1824

K., T.

3459 An inquiry, but not a parliamentary inquiry into the past and present abuses of the Irish revenue, and into the plunder of the Irish patronage.
96 pp. Dublin, P. Byrne, 1824

A., P.

3460 KENNEDY, John. On the exportation of machinery. A letter addressed to the Hon. E. G. Stanley M.P. by John Kennedy of Manchester.
26 pp. London, Longman, Hurst & co., 1824

A.

3461 A letter to the archbishop of Canterbury, on the subject of the church property. By a clergyman.
104 pp. London, Baldwin, Cradock, and Joy, 1824

K.

3462 A letter to the right honourable George Canning, secretary of state for foreign affairs: on the composition of the Austrian loan, the West India question and other material points. By Nero.
16 pp. London, D. MacDonald, 1824

T.

3463 LOW, George Augustus. The Belise merchants unmasked; or, a review of their late proceedings against Poyais; from information and authentic documents gained on the spot, during a visit to those parts in the months of August and September, 1823.
64 pp. London, Effingham Wilson, 1824

T.

3464 McCULLOCH, John Ramsay. A discourse on the rise, progress, peculiar objects, and importance, of political economy: containing an outline of a course of lectures on the principles and doctrines of that science.
116 pp. Edinburgh, A. Constable, 1824

K., T.

3465 McDONNELL, Alexander. Considerations on negro slavery. With authentic reports, illustrative of the actual condition of the negroes in Demerara. Also, an examination into the propriety and efficacy of the regulations contained in the late order in council now in operation in Trinidad. To which are added, suggestions on the proper mode of ameliorating the condition of the slaves.
tables. 350 pp. London, Longman, Hurst, Rees, Orme, Brown, and Green, 1824.

T.

3466 [McSWEENY, Joseph.] An essay on aerial navigation, with some observations on ships. By J.McS.
40 pp. Cork, King & Co., 1824

A.

3467 MADDEN, William. Expert calculator; or counting house companion. Containing the concisest methods of the most general and necessary mercantile transactions.
68 pp. Dublin, W. J. Battersby, 1824

A.

3468 MAUGHAM, Robert. A treatise on the principles of the usury laws; with disquisitions on the arguments adduced against them by Mr. Bentham and other writers, and a review of the authorities in their favour.
82 pp. London, Longman, Hurst, Rees, Orme, Brown and Green, 1824

A., P.

3469 [MOORE, Thomas.] A letter to Daniel O'Connell esq., occasioned by the petition adopted at the late aggregate meeting of the Catholics of Ireland. By a Munster farmer.
36 pp. Dublin, R. Milliken, 1824

A., S., T.

3470 [——.] A letter to the Hon. Pierce Somerset Butler, occasioned by his speech at the Lisdowney meeting on the subject of tithes, together with observations on J.K.L.'s defence of his vindications. By a Munster farmer.
30 pp. Dublin, R. Milliken, 1824

A., K., N., S., T.

3471 [O'DRISCOL, J.] Letter to the Hon. J. Abercrombie, M.P. on the new Irish Tithe Bill. By —.
94 pp. Dublin, R. Milliken, London, Longman, Hurst, Rees, Orme and Brown, 1824

A., N., P., R., T.

3472 [PHELAN, William.] The case of the Church of Ireland stated, in a letter, respectfully addressed to His Excellency the marquess Wellesley, and in reply to the charges of J. K. L. By Declan.
116 pp. 2nd ed. Dublin, R. Milliken, 1824

K., R., T.

3473 [——.] The case of the Church of Ireland stated in a second letter respectfully addressed to his Excellency the marquess Wellesley, and in reply to the charges of J.K.L. By Declan.
100 pp. Dublin, R. Milliken, London, C. & J. Rivington, 1824

A., K., R., T.

3474 [——.] The case of the Church of Ireland, stated, in a second letter, respectfully addressed to His Excellency the marquess of Wellesley, and in reply to charges of J.K.L.
110 pp. Dublin, R. Milliken, 1824

K., T.

3475 Plain statement of facts connected with the proposed St. Katharine Dock in the Port of London, to be established upon the principle of open and general competition.
30 pp. London, J. M. Richardson, 1824

A.

3476 POWELL, John. A letter addressed to weavers, shop-keepers, and publicans, on the great value of the principle of the Spitalfield Acts: in opposition to the absurd and mischievous doctrines of the advocates for their repeal.
8 pp. London, E. Justins, 1824

P.

3477 The practicability and expediency of abolishing direct taxation, by repealing, in the present year, the remaining moiety of the assessed taxes, considered, in a letter to the Right Hon. the Chancellor of the Exchequer, and to the

members of the house of commons. By a magistrate of the county of * * * * *.
tables. 16 pp. London, B. J. Holdsworth, 1824

T.

3478 Proceedings of an inquiry and investigation, instituted by major general Codd, his majesty's superintendent and commander-in-chief at Belize, Honduras, relative to Poyais, &c. &c. &c.
tables. 172 pp. London, Lawler and Quick, 1824

T.

3479 PURDON, R. E. Coote. Turnips, sheep, wool and prosperity versus flax, potatoes, mud hovels and poverty. Being a series of letters in which the soundness of the policy of extending the growth of wool and permitting its free export is clearly demonstrated. By an Irish landlord.
52 pp. Bristol, Barry, 1824

A.

3480 RAVENSTONE, Piercy. Thoughts on the funding system and its effects.
tables. 80 pp. London, J. Andrews, 1824

T.

3481 Remarks on making and repairing roads and for correcting the abuses which exist under the present system of road-making in Ireland.
20 pp. Kilkenny, Reynolds, 1824

D.

3482 Remarks on the Tithe Composition Bill, in reply to the letter of * * * to the Honorable J. Abercrombie, M.P. and some observations on Hibernicus. By Vindex.
24 pp. Dublin, R. Milliken, 1824

A.

3483 Report of Association for the Suppression of Mendicity in Dublin for the year 1823.
96 pp. Dublin, 1824

N., P.

3484 Review of the Quarterly Review; or an exposure of the erroneous opinions promulgated in that work on the subject of colonial slavery: Being the substance of a series of letters which appeared in the 'New Times' of September and October 1824. With notes and an appendix.
appendix. 104 pp. London, J. Hatchard, 1824

T.

3485 RICARDO, David. Plan for the establishment of a national bank.
36 pp. London, J. Murray, 1824

A., T.

3486 ROBINSON, Samuel. Remarks on the culture and management of flax; proposed as a means to assist the Irish poor by giving them employment, thus rendering their situations more comfortable, and increasing the national wealth.
12 pp. Dublin, Bentham & Gardiner, 1824

A., N., R.

3487 ROGERS, John Cooke? Thoughts for the total abolition of tythes in Ireland, submitted with the utmost respect to the consideration of the lords spiritual and temporal, in

parliament assembled, and of the archbishops, bishops, clergy, and people in that part of the united kingdom called Ireland.
20 pp. Dublin, 1824

A., T.

3488 RYAN, Richard. Prize essay. An essay upon the following subject of enquiry, 'What are the best means of rendering the national sources of wealth possessed by Ireland effectual for the employment of the population?' Proposed by the Royal Irish Academy, 1822.
94 pp. London, J. Hatchard, 1824

A., N.

3489 SAY, Jean Baptiste. Historical essay on the rise, progress and probable results of the British dominion in India.
36 pp. London, Treuttel and Wurtz, Treuttel Jun. and Richter, 1824

T.

3490 Second report from the committee of the county of Limerick Agricultural Association, establ. 6 May, 1822.
34 pp. Limerick, E. McAuliff, 1824

A.

3491 The second report of the British & Irish Ladies society, for improving the condition and promoting the industry and welfare of the female peasantry in Ireland, 1823. With an appendix and list of subscribers.
106 pp. London, W. Phillips, 1824

A.

3492 SHACKLETON, Ebenezer. Proposal of a public provision for the poor of Ireland, on a principle conducive at once to the interests of all classes.
20 pp. Dublin, Bentham & Gardiner, 1824

A.

3493 Short statement relative to the bishops' court in Ireland and the conduct of tithe proctors in that country.
16 pp. London, Rodwell & Martin, 1824

A., P., T.

3494 [SMITH, Sir William?] Reflections on the lieutenancy of the marquess Wellesley, in a letter to a friend.
appendix. 116 pp. London, J. Murray, 1824

A., R., T.

3495 A statement of the charitable society, for relief of sick and indigent room-keepers, of all religious persuasions, in the city of Dublin, for the year 1823.
36 pp. Dublin, printed by A. O'Neil, 1824

A.

3496 Statements illustrative of the nature of the slave-trade to which are subjoined, some particulars respecting the colony at Sierra Leone. Published by a committee appointed by the religious society of Friends, to aid in promoting the total abolition of the slave-trade.
40 pp. London, printed by Harvey, Darton & Co., 1824

T.

3497 [STAUNTON, Michael.] Tracts on Ireland, political & statistical. Containing No. I. Lists of absentees formed at different periods; peers & commoners now resident in Dublin,

& those who were resident at the period of the union. No. II. peculiar causes relating to Ireland, which produce absenteeism; laws against absentees: arguments for & against these laws. No. III. Sketch of the various insurrections, with a review of the calumnies & misrepresentations of factious writers. No. IV, history of the Treaty of Limerick; articles of the treaty; arguments of Sir Theobald Butler, & others, against their violation. No. V. Famine of 1822, intended to show how much we are 'Envy of surrounding nations & admiration of the world'. To which is added, Mr Scullys celebrated statement of penal laws.
233 pp. Dublin. H. Fitzpatrick, 1824

B.

——. Another issue.
354 pp. Dublin. C. J. Wilkinson, 1824

B., N.

——. Another issue.
352 pp. Dublin, M. Staunton, 1824

A.

3498 STEWART, William. Comments on the Act 1 George IV chap. 87 for enabling landlords more speedily to recover possession of lands and tenements unlawfully held over by tenants in England, Wales, and Ireland. With practical forms of the notices, affidavit, consent, orders, recognizances, posted, &c. required by, or incident to that statute.
56 pp. London, Butterworth [etc.], 1824

A.

3499 A succinct history of tithes in London; shewing the progress of that portion of the ecclesiastical revenues, from a very early period: drawn from original records, and respectfully inscribed to the inhabitants of St. Botolph, Aldgate. By a parishioner.
tables. 44 pp. London, John Letts, jun., 1824

A., T.

3500 Suggestions for the improvement of Ireland. By the author of 'Civil disabilities on account of religion, considered with reference to the christian dispensation, history, and policy'.
tables. 46 pp. London, Sherwood, 1824

T.

3501 Third annual report of the association for the suppression of mendicity, in the city of Waterford.
tables. 26 pp. Waterford, printed by John Bull, 1824

P.

3502 [THOM, Walter.] Plan for the improvement of the condition of the people of Ireland, By W-- T--.
36 pp. Dublin, 1824

A., P.

3503 [TRENOR, Keating.] A letter to John Charles Herries, esq., M.P. One of the joint secretaries of His Majesty's treasury, and late Commissary in chief. Upon the causes of famine in the south and west of Ireland, and decline of the Irish export trade to the British colonies and foreign countries, as connected with the commissariat resources of Ireland.
tables. 28 pp. Dublin. Milliken, 1824

A., P., T.

3504 WARRE, James. The past, present, and probably the future state of the wine trade; proving that an increase of duty caused a decrease of revenue; and a decrease of duty, an increase of revenue. Founded on parliamentary and other authentic documents. Most respectfully submitted to the right honourable the President and members of the Board of Trade. Second edition, with supplementary observations.
tables. appendices, 134 pp. London, J. Hatchard, and J. M. Richardson, 1824

T.

See 3438

3505 Ways & Means; or, every man his own financier. Explaining the various modes of raising money, and the practicability of arranging and combining securities, so as to accommodate every individual, even of remote but solid pretensions; with hints to monied men on the best mode of employing dormant capital.
30 pp. London, the author, 1824

A.

3506 WHEATLEY, John. A letter to his grace the duke of Devonshire on the state of Ireland, and the general effects of colonisation.
148 pp. Calcutta, Baptist Mission Press, 1824

A.

3507 WIGGINS, John. South of Ireland. Hints to Irish landlords, on the best means of obtaining and increasing their rents; improving their estates; and bettering the condition of the people. By a land agent. With an appendix exemplifying the measures recommended.
table. appendix. 72 pp. London, John and Henry L. Hunt, 1824

A., N., P., T.

3508 [WILMOT, Mrs. ——?] Glympses across the Irish channel by a friend, not a flatterer.
116 pp. (various paging). London, J. Hatchard, 1824

A., K., T.

1825

3509 Analysis of the memorial presented by the secretary of the treasury to the first constitutional congress of the united Mexican states: being the substance of a report of the financial committee of the chamber of senators, and printed by order of the same. Translated from the official copy published in Mexico.
tables. 100 pp. London, G. Cowie, 1825

T.

3510 Annual report of the Stranger's Friend Society, founded in 1790, for visiting and relieving distressed strangers, and the resident sick poor, at their habitations, in Dublin and its vicinity: with an account of some of the cases relieved, and a list of subscribers, for 1824.
24 pp. Dublin, printed by R. Napper, 1825

A.

3511 An appeal for Ireland, in a letter to the Rt. Hon. Geo. Canning.
appendix. 20 pp. London, T. & J. Allmann, 1825

T.

3512 The Bank of England case, under Marsh and company's commission briefly stated and discussed by a solicitor.
36 pp. London, Lupton Relfe, 1825

T.

3513 The Bank of England claim, under Marsh and company's commission, further discussed, in reply to Mr. Wilkinson's report upon the facts, and, to a letter, to the author, upon the law of the case. By the author of 'The Bank of England case, under Marsh and Co's commission, briefly stated and discussed'.
72 pp. London, Lupton Relfe, 1825

T.

3514 BROWN, William Keer. A letter to the right honourable George Canning, M.P. etc., relative to a free trade in corn in Great Britain.
tables. appendix. 76 pp. Canterbury, Henry Ward, 1825

K., T.

3515 BUCHANAN, G. C. Ireland as she ought to be: or a serious and impressive call to the nobility, gentry, agricultural and trading interests of Ireland.
34 pp. Dublin, Grace, 1825

A., N.

3516 CALLAGHAN, G. Observations on the grand jury system.
30 pp. Cork, Edwards and Savage, 1825

A., U.

3517 A case against the junction of the English and Bristol channels by a ship canal, with a preface and notes. By a subscriber of one share.
140 pp. London, J. Chappell, 1825

T.

3518 [CHICHESTER, Edward.] A letter to a British member of parliament on the state of Ireland in the year 1825. By an Irish magistrate.
178 pp. Dublin, R. Milliken, London, C. & J. Rivington, 1825

A., K., N.

3519 Considerations submitted in defence of the orders in council for the melioration of slavery in Trinidad: and upon the probable effect of sudden emancipation on agricultural industry, and British capital in the West Indies, in a series of letters which appeared in the Star newspaper under the signature of Vindex. To which is annexed the thirteenth article in the sixtieth number of the Quarterly Review; and the observations thereon in a series of letters, which appeared in the New Times newspaper, under the signature of Anglus.
tables. appendix. 272 pp. London, J. Murray, 1825

T.

3520 CROPPER, James. Present state of Ireland: with a plan for improving the condition of the people.
60 pp. Liverpool, G. Smith, 1825

A., K.

3521 CUNDY, Nicholas Wilcox. Reports on the grand ship canal, from London to Arundel Bay and Portsmouth, with plan and section, notice to parliament, and prospectus.
maps. 48 pp. London, F. C. & J. Rivington [etc., etc.], 1825

T.

3522 [DAVENPORT, Edward Davies.] The corn question; in a letter addressed to the right hon. W. Huskisson. By one of the proscribed class.
34 pp. London, J. Ridgway, 1825
T.

3523 The deed of agreement of the mining company of Ireland.
78 pp. Dublin, J. Carrick, 1825
A., M., R.

3524 [DRUMMOND, Henry.] Cheap corn best for farmers, proved in a letter to George Holme Sumner, esq., M.P. for the county of Surrey. By one of his constituents.
38 pp. London, J. Ridgway, 1825
T.

3525 ENGLISH, Henry. A general guide to the companies formed for working foreign mines, with their prospectuses, amount of capital, number of shares, names of directors, &c. and an appendix, shewing their progress since their formation, obtained from authentic sources; with a table of the extent of their fluctuations in price, up to the present period.
tables. 112 pp. London, Boosey, 1825
A., T.

3526 ENSOR, George. A defence of the Irish and the means of their redemption.
appendices. 164 pp. Dublin, J. C. Scully, 1825
A., M., N., R.

3527 An essay on the management and mismanagement of the currency.
42 pp. London, James Duncan, 1825
T.

3528 EXETER, John. Causes of the present depression in our money market, with a suggestion for its relief.
tables. 22 pp. London, J. M. Richardson, 1825
T.

3529 First half yearly report presented to the Mining Co. of Ireland by the board of directors, 26th July, 1825, with an abstract of the accounts, from the formation of the company on 5th February, 1824, to the 5th July, 1825.
16 pp. Dublin, 1825
A.

3530 [FISHER, Thomas.] The negro's memorial, or, abolitionist's catechism; by an abolitionist.
tables. appendix. 134 pp. London, J. Hatchard, [etc.], 1825
T.

3531 Free commerce with India. A letter addressed to the right honourable president of the Board of Trade, with reference to his late propositions in parliament for the improvement of the colonial mercantile policy of Great Britain. By a Madras Civil Servant.
16 pp. London, Kingsbury, Parbury and Allen, 1825
K.

3532 GEORGE, John. A view of the existing law, affecting unincorporated joint stock companies.
74 pp. London, S. Sweet, 1825
T.

3533 GRANT, Alexandre. Observations sur le papier-monnoie [sic] de la Russie.
88 pp. Londres, chez J. M. Richardson, 1825
T.

3534 Highways improved. A letter to a member of parliament, on the expediency of appointing county or district surveyors of highways.
18 pp. London, Charles Knight, 1825
T.

3535 HILLARY, Sir William, bart. An appeal to the British nation on the humanity and policy of forming a national institution for the preservation of lives and property from shipwreck.
68 pp. 3d. ed. London, Whittaker, 1825
A.

3536 ——. A sketch of Ireland in 1824: the sources of her evils considered and their remedies suggested.
40 pp. London, Simpkin & Marshall, 1825
A., C.

3537 Hints to philanthropists; or, a collective view of practical means of improving the condition of the poor, and labouring classes of society.
22 pp. Dublin, R. Graisberry, 1825
A., N.
An abridged version of the pamphlet published in 1821 by William Davis, of Bath; see 3219.

3538 JOPLIN, Thomas. An illustration of Mr. Joplin's views on currency, and plan for its improvement; together with observations applicable to the present state of the money-market; in a series of letters.
tables. appendix. 152 pp. London, Baldwin, Cradock and Joy, 1825
T.

3539 KING, Edward. An essay on the creation and advantages of a cultural and commercial triform stock as a counter-fund to the national debt, and for unlimited investment of capital at £5 per cent per annum.
132 pp. London, Lupton Relfe, 1825
T.

3540 Letter to John Taylor, esq. respecting the conduct of the directors of the Real del Monte company, relative to the mines of Tlalpuxuahua.
20 pp. London, Hurst, Robinson, 1825
T.

3541 A letter to the author of the Bank of England case, under Marsh and Co's commission, briefly stated and discussed. By a solicitor.
16 pp. London, J. & W. T. Clarke, 1825
T.

3542 Limerick Agricultural Association: Third report of the committee of the County of Limerick Agricultural Association (established 6th May, 1822) for the year ending 1st March, 1825.
appendix. table. 42 pp. Limerick, Canter, 1825
A. N.

3543 MCADAM, John Loudon. Observations on the management of trusts for the care of turnpike roads, as regards the repair of the road, the expenditure of the revenue, and the appointment and quality of executive officers. And upon the nature and effect of the present road law of this kingdom, illustrated by examples from a practical experience of nine years.
tables. appendices. 152 pp. London, Longman, Hurst, Rees, Orme, Brown and Green, 1825
T.

3544 MCCONNELL, Patrick. Tables shewing the value in British money of any sum of Irish money, from one farthing to £10,000, agreeably to the Act of Parliament lately passed for assimilating the currency and moneys of account throughout Great Britain and Ireland. Also, the value of bankers' notes in each currency.
tables. 34 pp. Dublin, M. Goodwin, 1825
N.

3545 MACDOUGALL, A. A plan for improving the condition of the peasantry, etc. of the county of Antrim.
37 pp. Belfast, Luke M. Hope, 1825
B.

3546 MACNEVEN, William J. Introductory discourse to a few lectures on the application of chemistry to agriculture, delivered before the New-York Athenaeum in the winter of 1825.
40 pp. New-York, G. & C. Carvill, 1825
N.

3547 MASON, W. Monck. Suggestions relative to the project of a survey and valuation of Ireland: together with some remarks on the report of the committee of the house of commons; Sess. 1824.
20 pp. Dublin, Folds, 1825
N., P.

3548 [MENDHAM, Joseph.] Taxatio Papalis; being an account of the tax-books of the united church and court of modern Rome; or, of the taxae cancellariae apostolicae, and taxae sacrae poenitentiariae apostolicae. By Emancipatus.
64 pp. London, C. and J. Rivington, 1825
P., T.

3549 MOLINA, Giovanni Ignazio. Report of the soil and mineral productions of Chili, being an extract from the work by the abbé don John Ignatius Molina originally published in Italian.
46 pp. London, Effingham Wilson, 1825
T.

3550 MONTAGU, Basil. Inquiries respecting the court of commissioners of bankrupts, and Lord Chancellor's court.
tables. 132 pp. London, J. and W. T. Clarke, 1825
T.

3551 MOUNTENEY, Barclay. Selections from the various authors who have written concerning Brazil; more particularly respecting the captaincy of Minas Geraës, and the gold mines of that province.
tables. map. appendix. 194 pp. London, Effingham Wilson, 1825
T.

3552 [MUNDELL, Alexander.] The influence of interest and prejudice upon proceedings in parliament stated, and illustrated by what has been done in matters relative to education —religion—the poor—the corn laws—joint stock companies —the Bank of England and banking companies—and taxes.
tables. 230 pp. London, J. Murray, 1825
T.

3553 MUSSON, John P. A letter to ministers suggesting improvements in the trade of the West Indies and the Canadas; in which are incidentally considered, the merits of the East and West India sugar question, reasons in favour of the independence of Spanish America, and a liberal and practical plan of forwarding slave emancipation.
tables. 110 pp. London, J. M. Richardson, 1825
T.

3554 NIMMO, Alexander. The report of Alexander Nimmo, civil engineer, on the proposed railway between Limerick & Waterford.
26 pp. Dublin, Thom & Johnston, 1825
A.

3555 Observations on the West-India Company bill as printed and read a second time on Tuesday, March 29, 1825
32 pp. London, J. Hatchard, 1825
K., T.

3556 O'CALLAGHAN, Jeremiah. Usury or interest proved to be repugnant to the divine and ecclesiastical laws, and destructive to civil society.
192 pp. London, C. Clement, 1825
A.

3557 O'DRISCOLL, John. Review of the evidence taken before the Irish committees of both houses of parliament.
108 pp. Dublin, R. Milliken [etc.], 1825
A., M., N.
attacks J. R. McCulloch.

3558 On the advantages of a high remunerating price for labour.
8 pp. Leicester, A. Cockshaw, 1825
A.
extract from an essay on the Combination Laws.

3559 On the employment of the peasantry in Ireland, from the Irish peasantry society.
50 pp. London, Hetherington, 1825
A., N.

3560 One more specific for Ireland. Containing observations on corn laws—tythes—taxes—courts of law—corporations— catholic emancipation—plan for converting the farmer into a proprietor of the soil—and proposed arrangement with respect to forfeited estates. By R.T.H.
38 pp. London, Harvey & Co., 1825
A., N.

3561 ORPEN, Emanuel H. An authentic exposure of Irish affairs, calculated to elucidate the chief causes of the present condition of that unhappy country.
82 pp. London, J. Hatchard, 1825
K.

3562 PARNELL, Sir Henry Brooke, bart., later first baron Congleton.   Observations on the Irish Butter Acts.
46 pp. London, J. Ridgway, Dublin, R. Milliken, 1825
A.

3563 [PIKE, James M.]   Statement of some of the causes of the disturbances in Ireland, and of the miserable state of the peasantry; with a plan for commencing on sound principles an amelioration of their condition, thereby removing the causes of the disturbances, and bringing the country into a state of peace and quietness.
34 pp. Dublin, Bentham and Hardy, 1825
A., N.
Quaker plan to found a company to promote land purchase.

3564 POPE, Charles.   A lecture on the origin, progress, and present state of shipping, navigation, and commerce, read before the Bristol Philosophical and Literary Society; on Thursday evening, February 10, 1825. Together with an abstract of the net produce of the revenue of the United Kingdom, in the years ended 5 January 1824 and 5 January 1825.
abstract. 38 pp. London, Baldwin, Cradock, and Joy, 1825
T.

3565 [POWELL, John.]   Statistical illustrations of the territorial extent and population; commerce, taxation, consumption, insolvency, pauperism and crime, of the British Empire.
index. 120 pp. London, J. Miller, 1825
A.

3566 The present state of Mexico: as detailed in a report presented to the general congress, by the secretary of state for the home department and foreign affairs, at the opening of the session in 1825. With notes, and a memoir of Don Lucas Alaman.
130 pp. London, J. Murray, 1825
T.

3567 PRESTON, E. W.   An abstract of the act for assimilating the currency, throughout the United Kingdom of Great Britain and Ireland. To which is added a table of Irish money reduced to British.
table. 16 pp. Dublin, Underwood, 1825
N.

3568 Prospectus of a joint stock company for steam navigation from Europe to America and the West Indies.
24 pp. London, Gunnell, 1825
A.

3569 Prospectus of a plan for the extension of a southern canal from Monastereven to Roscrea, Limerick, Cashel and Mallow, uniting the Liffey with the Suir—the Shannon—and the Blackwater.
map. 14 pp. Dublin, Smith, 1825
N.

3570 RAWSON, Sir William, originally William Adams.   The present operations and future prospects of the Mexican mine associations analysed. By the evidence of official documents, English and Mexican. And the national advantages expected from joint stock companies, considered; in a letter to the right hon. George Canning.
tables. appendix. 88 pp. 2nd ed. London, J. Hatchard, [etc.], 1825
K., T.

3571 Reasons against the repeal of the usury laws.
146 pp. London, J. Murray, 1825.
A.

3572 Remarks on joint-stock companies. By an old merchant.
tables. 108 pp. London, J. Murray, 1825
T.

3573 Report of a deputation from the directors of the National Fishing Co. on the subject of the fisheries on the south and western coasts of Ireland.
56 pp. Dublin, M. Goodwin, 1825
A., N.

3574 A report of a deputation to Ireland in the year 1825. Printed by order of the court.
map. appendix. tables. 38 pp. London, Skipper, 1825
A.
addressed 'to the Honourable Society of the Governor and assistants of London, of the New Plantation of Ulster, within the realm of Ireland'.

3575 Report of the council of the chamber of commerce of Dublin, to the annual assembly of the members of the association.
34 pp. Dublin, Bentham and Hardy, 1825
A.

3576 Report of the trustees for bettering the condition of the poor in Ireland. With an appendix.
36 pp. Dublin, John Jones, 1825
A., N., U.

3577 Report presented to the general constituent sovereign congress of Mexico, by their commissions upon the systems of finance and mines; on the inexpediency of augmenting the duties on the exportation of gold and silver. Translated from the Spanish.
20 pp. London, G. Cowie, 1825
T.

3578 ROBINSON, Samuel.   Remarks on the culture and management of flax proposed as a means to assist the Irish poor by giving them employment, with the memorial of a scutch miller [i.e. S. Robinson], complaining of the present mode of preparing flax in the provinces of Leinster, Munster and Connaught, which drew forth from Peter Besnard, inspector general of Munster and Connaught strong animadversions and assertions, refuted by a variety of facts collected from 1600 square miles of country.
34 pp. Dublin, Bentham and Gardiner, 1825
A., N.

3579 RYAN, Richard.   Directions for proceeding under the tithe composition acts. With remarks on the averages.
94 pp. 2nd ed. Dublin, W. Underwood, 1825
A.

3580 A schedule of tonnage rent on vessels entering the Dublin docks, and a table of charges upon goods landed and housed there.
tables. 50 pp. Dublin, Thom and Johnson, 1825
A.

3581 Second report of the committee of the society for the mitigation and gradual abolition of slavery throughout the British Dominions. Read at the general meeting of the society held on the 30th day of April, 1825.
56 pp. London, Ellerton & Henderson, 1825
T.

3582 Seventh report of the general committee of the association for the suppression of mendicity in Dublin, for the year 1824.
118 pp. Dublin, J. Jones, 1825
A.

3583 A short examination of the Hyderabad papers, as far as they relate to the House of William Palmer & Co., in a letter addressed to the proprietors of East India stock. By an enemy to oppression.
tables. 114 pp. London, J. M. Richardson, 1825
T.

3584 A simple and effectual mode of providing for the labouring classes; and, at the same time, of promoting the landed interest. By Eight Seven.
50 pp. Dublin, Bentham & Gardiner, 1825
A., N., U.

3585 A sketch of the proceedings connected with certain pecuniary transactions of Messrs. Palmer and Co. with the government of his highness the Nizam.
64 pp. London, W. Simpkin and R. Marshall, 1825
K., T.

3586 The slave colonies of Great Britain; or a picture of negro slavery drawn by the colonists themselves; being an abstract of the various papers recently laid before parliament on that subject.
168 pp. London, The society for the mitigation and gradual abolition of slavery throughout the British dominions, 1825
K., T.

3587 A statement of the charitable society for relief of sick and indigent room keepers, of all religious persuasions in the city of Dublin, for the year 1824.
28 pp. Dublin, printed by R. Grace, 1825
A.

3588 SYLVESTER, Charles. Report on railroads and locomotive engines addressed to the chairman of the committee of the Liverpool and Manchester projected railroad.
tables. 50 pp. 2nd ed. Liverpool, T. Kaye, 1825
A.

3589 TAYLOR, John. Statements respecting the profits of mining in England considered in relation to the prospects of mining in Mexico. In a letter to Thomas Fowell Buxton, esq., M.P.
tables. 58 pp. London, Longman & co., 1825
K., T.

3590 TUCKER, Henry St. George. A review of the financial situation of the East-India Company, in 1824.
appendix. tables. 250 pp. London, Kingsbury, Parbury, and Allen, 1825
T.

3591 TURNER, Samuel. A letter addressed to Charles Rose Ellis, esq., M.P. chairman of the standing committee of the West India Planters and Merchants, in consequence of the unanimous resolution of a sub-committee that it was not expedient to apply to parliament for a reduction of the present duty on sugar.
tables. 40 pp. second ed. London, J. McCreery, 1825
T.

3592 [WALSH, Robert.] Account of the Levant company; with some notices of the benefits conferred upon society by its officers, in promoting the cause of humanity, literature, and the fine arts; &c. &c.
68 pp. London, J. and A. Arch [etc.], 1825
T.

3593 WESTERN, Charles Callis Western, 1st baron. A letter to the earl of Liverpool on the cause of our present embarrassment and distress: and the measures necessary for our effectual relief.
appendix. 44 pp. London, J. Ridgway, 1825
T.
See 3696

3594 WHITE, George. A digest of the evidence in the first report from the select committee on the state of Ireland.
166 pp. London, Onwhyn, 1825
A., N.

3595 WILKINSON, Robert. Mr. Robert Wilkinson's reply to 'Observations on his report to the assignees of the late banking-house of Marsh Stracey, and Co.'
16 pp. London, J. M. Richardson, 1825
T.

1826

3596 An address to the members of the new parliament, on the proceedings of the colonial department in furtherance of the resolutions of the house of commons of the 15th May 1823, 'For ameliorating the condition of the slave population in his majesty's colonies'; and on the only course that ought now to be pursued by his majesty's government.
42 pp. London, Longman, Rees, Orme, Brown, and Green, 1826
T.

3597 AINSWORTH, William H. Considerations on the best means of affording immediate relief to the operative classes in the manufacturing districts.
24 pp. London, John Ebers, 1826
T.

3598 ALLEN, William. Colonies at home, or the means for rendering the industrious labourer independent of parish relief and for providing for the poor population of Ireland by the cultivation of the soil.
plates. 32 pp. London, Longman, Rees, Orme, Brown and Green [etc.], 1826.
A.

3599 [ANDERSON, William.] The iniquity of the landholders, the mistakes of the farmers and the folly and

mischievous consequences of the unaccountable apathy manifested by all the other classes of the community, in regard to the corn laws, clearly demonstrated by a simple statement of indisputable facts, or intuitive inferences.
48 pp. London, Effingham Wilson, 1826
T.

3600   Articles of agreement of the Liberal Annuity Company of Dublin.
index. 60 pp. Dublin, Kelly, 1826
N.

3601   ATHERLEY, Edmond Gordon.   A letter to the earl of Liverpool, shewing that the objections which are made to the admission of foreign corn are either totally unsound, or may easily be obviated.
24 pp. London, Ridgway and sons, 1826
T.

3602   [BAILEY, Samuel.]   A letter to a political economist; occasioned by an article in the Westminster Review on the subject of value. By the author of the *Critical dissertation on value* therein reviewed.
102 pp. London, R. Hunter, 1826
T.

3603   BEAUMONT, Augustus Hardin.   Compensation to slave owners fairly considered in an appeal to the common sense of the people of England.
24 pp. 2nd ed. London, Effingham Wilson, 1826
T.

3604   [BLANSHARD, Richard.]   Thoughts on the present commercial distress, and on the means to prevent its recurrence. By a merchant.
24 pp. London, J. M. Richardson, 1826
T.

3605   [BLISS, Henry.]   Consideration of the claims and conduct of the United States respecting their north-eastern boundary, and of the value of the British colonies in north America.
appendices. 114 pp. London, J. Hatchard, 1826
K.

3606   BLOUNT, William.   A letter to the Protestants of England, on the unjust surcharge to which their estates are liable, by the law intending to relieve the Roman catholics of the double land-tax.
48 pp. London, J. Ridgway, 1826
A.

3607   The cause of our present distresses; and the remedies that have been suggested for their relief, shortly considered.
34 pp. London, J. M. Richardson, 1826
T.

3608   CAYLEY, Edward.   Corn, trade, wages and rent; or observations on the leading circumstances of the present financial crisis.
48 pp. London, J. Ridgway, 1826
T.

3609   CHALMERS, Thomas.   A few thoughts on the abolition of colonial slavery.
16 pp. Glasgow, Chalmers & Collins [etc.], 1826
T.

3610   CHARLES, J. J.   Charles's tables of currency coins, weights and measures, shewing in a most ready, correct, and comprehensive form, the exchange of English money into Irish, in regular and systematic progression, from one farthing to the highest sum may be required. With new tables of sovereigns and guineas. Also, the act of parliament explained in a familiar way, respecting the new weights and measures of distance, land, and capacity, with their comparative proportions: the new regulations adopted by the lord mayor, agreeable to the act of parliament for the measure and delivery of coals in the city of Dublin, with a copious dissertation, explaining the different government funds; joint stock, and other public securities of Great Britain and Ireland, with their rates of interest—where and when payable—when first established and for what purpose—mode of purchase and selling out in do.—brokers' fees; with a most useful table, explaining the proper method of dealing in the several public securities, &c. &c. &c.
32 pp. Dublin, J. Charles, 1826
A., N.

3611   CLONCURRY, Valentine Browne Lawless, 2nd baron.   Letter from lord Cloncurry to the most noble the marquess of Downshire on the conduct of the Kildare Street Education Society and the employment of the poor.
16 pp. Dublin, T. Reilly, 1826
N.

3612   The corn laws considered, in their effect on the labourer, tenant, landlord, &c.
tables. 36 pp. London, J. Hatchard, 1826
K.

3613   COURT, Major Henry.   Theory and facts in proof, that the laws for the imposition of tithes are attended with the most calamitous consequences to the country, with plans for the redemption of tithes, and a comparison of the effects of a repeal of the tithe laws, with the proposed repeal of the corn laws.
tables. appendix. 50 pp. London, J. Hatchard, 1826
K., T.

3614   COYLE, Thomas.   A new treatise on practical arithmetic, showing a simple and concise method of finding the amount sterling of any quantity of merchandise, by one figure.
16 pp. Dublin, W. Espy, 1826
A.

3615   [CROKER, John Wilson.]   Two letters on Scottish affairs from Edward Bradwardine Waverly, esq., to Malachi Malagrowther, esq.
66 pp. London, J. Murray, Edinburgh, Oliver & Boyd, 1826
A., T.

———.   64 pp. 2nd ed. London, J. Murray, 1826
A.

3616   [DALLAS, Alexander R. C.]   Protestant Sisters of Charity; a letter addressed to the lord bishop of London, developing a plan for improving the arrangements at present existing for administering medical advice, and visiting the sick poor. [By a country clergyman.]
38 pp. London, Charles Knight, 1826
T.

3617 Deed of settlement of the Hibernian Joint Stock Company. Printed by order of a general meeting of proprietors, held the 5th June, 1826.
90 pp. Dublin, Chambers & Hallagan, 1826
A.
Company to deal in annuities, loans, funds, stock, etc.

3618 DRUMMOND, Henry. Elementary propositions on the currency with additions showing their application to the present times.
70 pp. 4th ed. London, J. Ridgway, 1826
N., T.

3619 An Edict of Diocletian fixing a maximum of prices throughout the Roman empire. A.D. 303.
50 pp. London, J. Murray, 1826
A.

3620 ENGLISH, Henry. A compendium of useful information relating to the companies formed for working British mines, containing copies of the prospectuses, amount of capital, number of shares, names of directors, &c. with general observations on their progress, detailing their operations, mines in their possession, and original information, obtained from authentic sources; and a table of the payments made, fluctuations in prices &c., up to the present period.
tables. 134 pp. London, Boosey, 1826
A., T.

3621 An enquiry into the origin and increase of the paper currency of the kingdom, a subject deserving and requiring the serious consideration of the legislature and of every man in England.
tables. 36 pp. London, Longmans, Rees, Orme, Brown, and Green, 1826
T.

3622 ENSOR, George. Irish affairs at the close of 1825.
appendix. 80 pp. Dublin, Joseph C. Scully, 1826
K., R., RM.

3623 Eunomia. With brief hints to country gentlemen, and others of tender capacity, on the principles of the new sect of political philosophers, termed Eunomians: which principles are applied to the grand question, 'What is money, its office and effects in society?' The question again 'set at rest for ever'. With some strictures upon banks and the banking system, in answer to the right hon. Sir John Sinclair, bart., Malachi Malagrowther, Sir Robert Peel, bart., and all the rest of the philosophers, advocating 'cheap currency', which 'gives your districts the impetus'. Under Sir John Sinclair's grand plan, hereunto appended.
88 pp. London, Effingham Wilson, 1826
T.

3624 Fifth annual report of the association for the suppression of mendicity in the city of Waterford.
tables. 28 pp. Waterford, John Bull, 1826
P.

3625 Fourth report of the committee of the county of Limerick agricultural association, for year ending March, 1826.
20 pp. Limerick, R. P. Canter, 1826
A.

3626 Freedom of trade. By a public counsellor.
58 pp. London, J. Murray, 1826
T.

3627 GRAHAM, Sir James Robert George, bart. Corn and currency; in an address to the landowners.
tables. 116 pp. 2nd edition. London, J. Ridgway, 1826
T.

3628 GRATTAN, Richard. Observations on the causes and prevention of fever and pauperism in Ireland.
56 pp. Dublin, Hodges and M'Arthur [etc.], 1826
P.

3629 GREGG, Francis. The law and practice in bankruptcy: relative to public and private meetings, meetings for the audit and dividend, and the certificate.
90 pp. London, J. Butterworth, 1826
T.

3630 GRIFFITH, Richard. Second report on the proposed rail-road from Cork to Limerick.
tables. 30 pp. Cork, Edwards and Savage, 1826
M.

3631 [GROOM, Richard.] The Bank of England defended, or the principal cause of the high prices demonstrated, by an inquiry into the origin of the present system of coinage, also by an examination of certain opinions in regard to a metallic currency, the foreign exchanges, and the effects of our paper currency; with suggestions for forming a more accurate monetary system.
86 pp. London, J. Hatchard, 1826
T.

3632 HALE, William Hale. Observations on clerical funds. A letter addressed to the right rev. the lord bishop of Chester by the Rev. William Hale Hale, M.A. his lordship's domestic chaplain, and preacher at the Charter House.
tables. 22 pp. (various paging.) London, J. Mawman, 1826
K.

3633 HIGGINS, Godfrey. An address to the houses of lords and commons, in defence of the corn laws.
appendices. 60 pp. London, A. J. Valpy, 1826
T.

3634 HOME, George. Suggestions for giving employment and permanent relief to the manufacturers now so distressed in the Liberty.
tables. 20 pp. Dublin, J. & M. Porteous, 1826
A., N., P.

3635 [HORTON, Sir Robert John Wilmot, bart.] The West India question practically considered.
appendices. 124 pp. London, J. Murray, 1826
K., T.

3636 Irish tenancy exemplified in the case of Mr. John Peters, which it is submitted is of particular hardship, and great wanton and unnecessary oppression.
16 pp. Dublin, W. Underwood, 1826
A.

3637 JENNYNS, J. Clayton. An appeal to the earl Bathurst, when colonial minister, on the unconstitutional continuance

of foreign laws in the colonies ceded to Great Britain. With a preface on the direful revolution projected in England, and excited in the British Antilles, by the advocates of negromania. Addressed to field marshal his grace the duke of Wellington, K.G. etc.
table. appendices. 68 pp. London, Sams, Richardson, 1826
T.

3638 KEATING, M. I. Suggestions for a revision of the Irish grand jury laws.
14 pp. Limerick, R. P. Canter, [1826?]
N.

3639 LEAHY, Patrick. New and general table of weights and measures; with ample calculations, and suitable examples under each head; all reduced agreeable to the act of the 6th Geo. IV, chap. 12.
72 pp. Dublin, Bentham and Hardy, 1826
A.

3640 LEES, Sir Harcourt, bart. The free traders, or the fatal effects of cabinet incapacity. Being a popish and financial romance of the 19th century.
42 pp. Dublin, G. P. Bull, 1826
A., P.

3641 A letter to James John Farquharson, esq., on the subject of the late meeting at Blandford, Dorset, on the corn laws. By Artophagos.
16 pp. London, J. Ridgway, 1826
T.

3642 Letter to Robert Wilmot Horton, esq., M.P., under secretary of state for the colonial department; containing strictures on a pamphlet entitled 'The West-India question practically considered'.
16 pp. London, J. Hatchard, 1826
K.

3643 A letter to Sir Charles Forbes, bart., M.P. on the administration of Indian affairs. By a civil servant.
56 pp. London, J. Murray, 1826
K., T.

3644 A letter to the right hon. Robert Peel, M.P., etc. etc. upon the necessity of adopting some parliamentary measure to control the issues of country bankers, and to prevent the recurrence of the late shock to public and private credit with the heads of a bill for that purpose.
76 pp. London, J. Hatchard, 1826
T.

3645 Letters on the necessity of a prompt extinction of British colonial slavery; chiefly addressed to the more influential classes. To which are added, thoughts on compensation.
224 pp. London, J. Hatchard, Leicester, T. Combe, 1826
T.

3646 LYNE, Charles. A letter to the lord high chancellor on the nature and causes of the late and present distress in commercial, manufacturing and banking concerns, with proposed partial remedies.
24 pp. London, E. Lloyd, 1826
T.

3647 McCLINTOCK, John. Observations on Grand Jury Laws, affecting Ireland.
12 pp. 2d. ed. with additions. Dublin, R. M. Tims, 1826
A., N.

3648 M'DONNELL, Alexander. The West India legislatures vindicated from the charge of having resisted the call of the mother country for the amelioration of slavery.
104 pp. London, J. Murray, 1826
K., T.

3649 MACKENZIE, George. Letter to the members both houses of parliament, on the resources of the country. Machinery, currency, taxation, the corn laws, English and Scotch banking, the navigation laws, the silk trade, and the commercial system generally.
24 pp. London, G. Cowie, 1826
T.

3650 MATHISON, Gilbert. A critical view of a pamphlet, intitled 'The West India Question practically considered' with remarks on the Trinidad Order in Council, in a letter addressed to the Rt. Hon. Robert Wilmot Horton.
tables. appendices. 84 pp. London, Smith, Elder, 1826
T.

3651 MILFORD, John. Observations on the proceedings of country bankers during the last thirty years and on their communications with government: together with a remedy proposed against the alarming consequences arising from the circulation of promissory notes; in a letter addressed to the chancellor of the exchequer.
46 pp. London, Longman, Rees, Orme, Brown and Green, 1826
T.

3652 MOORE, Richard. The outline of a plan for bringing the Scotch and English currency to the same standard bullion value and producing a sterling country bank note of exchangeable value, convertible in every place to gold coin.
80 pp. London, J. Murray, 1826
T.

3653 MUSHET, Robert. An attempt to explain from facts the effect of the issues of the Bank of England upon its own interests, public credit, and country banks.
tables. appendix. 220 pp. London, Baldwin, Cradock and Joy, 1826
T.

3654 NEALE, Francis. An essay on money-lending; containing a defence of legal restrictions on the rate of interest, and an answer to the objections of Mr. Bentham.
94 pp. London, William Pickering, 1826
T.

3655 NIMMO, Alexander. The report of Alexander Nimmo, civil engineer, on the proposed railway between Limerick and Waterford.
40 pp. Dublin, Thom & Johnston, 1826
A.

3656 No colonies no funds!!! Proving that the present certain destruction of the West India colonies will yet involve the

national debt ! ! ! Addressed to the abettors of injustice. By a West Indian.
24 pp. London, Effingham Wilson, 1826
T.

3657 On the increasing importance of the British West-Indian possessions.
30 pp. London, J. M. Richardson, 1826
T.

3658 Opinions of Henry Brougham, esq. on negro slavery: with remarks.
50 pp. London, Whitmore and Fenn, 1826
T.

3659 A practical plan for alleviating the distress of the poor of Ireland in a letter addressed to the lord lieutenant etc. by Howard.
24 pp. Dublin, Bentham & Hardy, 1826
A.

3660 The progress of colonial reform; being a brief view of the real advance made since May 15th, 1823, in carrying into effect the recommendations of his majesty, the unanimous resolutions of parliament, and the universal prayer of the nation, with respect to negro slavery. Drawn from the papers printed for the house of commons, prior to the 10th April, 1826.
52 pp. London, J. Hatchard, 1826
T.

3661 RAWSON, Sir William. The present operations and future prospects of the Mexican mine associations analysed. By the evidence of official documents, English and Mexican. And the national advantages expected from joint stock companies, considered; in a letter to the right hon. George Canning.
tables. appendix. 88 pp. 3rd ed. London, J. Hatchard, [etc., etc.], 1826
K.

3662 Reasons and plans for the encouragement of agriculture. No. III.
table of contents. tables. 26 pp. [pag. 35–60]. London, Effingham Wilson, 1826
N.

3663 Reflections on slavery: in reply to certain passages of a speech recently delivered by Mr. Canning. Addressed to the Right Hon. Lord Dacre. By a barrister.
28 pp. London, J. Hatchard, [etc.], 1826
T.

3664 Reflections upon the value of the British West Indian colonies and of the British North American provinces 1825.
40 pp. London, Egerton, 1826
N.

3665 Remarks on an address to the members of the new parliament, on the proceedings of the colonial department, with respect to the West India question. By a member of the late parliament.
plate. appendices. 80 pp. London, J. Murray, 1826
K., T.

3666 Report of the board of directors of the mining company of Ireland, to the proprietary for the half year ending January, 1826.
8 pp. Dublin, Chambers & Hallagan, 1826
A.

3667 Report of the board of directors of the mining company of Ireland, to the proprietary, for the half-year, ending 5th July, 1826.
table. 8 pp. [no t.p.] Dublin, 1826
N.

3668 Report of the proceedings at a general meeting of the friends and subscribers to the Dublin mechanics' institution.
30 pp. Dublin, Bentham & Hardy, 1826
A.

3669 Rules and regulations for the North-East Society of Ireland for the encouragement of agriculture and rural improvement and domestic economy.
22 pp. Belfast, A. Mackay jr., 1826
A.

3670 Safe banks: a proposal to the landed interest. By a member of parliament.
20 pp. London, J. Murray, 1826
T.

3671 SCOTT, Sir Claude, bart. Some brief observations relative to the practical effect of the corn laws; being the substance of two letters addressed to a member of the house of commons.
16 pp. London, Nornaville and Fell, 1826
T.

3672 [SCOTT, Sir Walter, bart.] A letter to the editor of the Edinburgh Weekly Journal from Malachi Malagrowther esq. on the proposed change of currency and other late alterations, as they affect or are intended to affect the kingdom of Scotland.
60 pp. 3rd. ed. Edinburgh, W. Blackwood, 1826
A.

3673 [——.] A second letter to the editor of the Edinburgh Weekly Journal from Malachi Malagrowther on the proposed change of currency and other late alterations, as they affect, or are intended to affect the kingdom of Scotland.
86 pp. 3rd ed. Edinburgh, W. Blackwood, 1826
A.

3674 [——.] A third letter to the editor of the Edinburgh Weekly Journal from Malachi Malagrowther on the proposed change of currency and other late alterations, as they affect or are intended to affect the kingdom of Scotland.
40 pp. 2nd. ed. Edinburgh, W. Blackwood, 1826
A., P.

3675 SCOTT, William. Mr. Scott's speech and letters upon the currency in answer to Malachi Malagrowther.
24 pp. Edinburgh, Lizars; London, Highley, 1826
A.

3676 Second report of the Trustees for bettering the condition of the poor of Ireland.
36 pp. Dublin, J. Jones, 1826
A.

3677 SEDGWICK, James. Twelve letters addressed to the Rt. Hon. Thomas Wallace, M.P. chairman of the commission of revenue inquiry.
tables. 202 pp. London, J. Ridgway, 1826
T.

3678 SLEIGH, W. W. A letter to the independent governors of St. George's Hospital proving a loss to the poor, by mismanagement, of (even in eight items), ninety thousand pounds!
tables. 8 pp. London, Fores, 1826
T.

3679 Some practical remarks on the effect of the usury laws on the landed interests, in a letter to John Calcraft, esq., M.P. By a solicitor.
London, J. Ridgway, 1826
T.

3680 STANHOPE, Philip Henry Stanhope, 4th earl. A letter from earl Stanhope on the corn laws.
46 pp. London, J. Ridgway, 1826
T.

3681 The state of our circulation and currency briefly considered in a letter to a friend.
tables. appendix. 40 pp. London, J. Hatchard, 1826
T.

3682 STEPHEN, James. England enslaved by her own slave colonies. An address to the electors and people of the United Kingdom.
table in appendix. 92 pp. London, J. and A. Arch, 1826
K.

3683 STEWART, William. Comments on the Act I George IV c. 87 for enabling landlords more speedily to recover possession of lands and tenements unlawfully held over by tenants in England, Wales and Ireland.
appendix. 70 pp. 2nd ed. London, J. Butterworth, 1826
A.

3684 STURCH, William. The grievances of Ireland, their causes and their remedies, in a letter to Sir Francis Burdett, bart., M.P.
64 pp. London, Rowland Hunter, 1826
A., K., L., N., T.

3685 [SURR, Thomas Skinner.] The present critical state of the country developed; or, an exhibition of the true causes of the calamitous derangement of the banking and commercial system, at the present alarming crisis; shewing the essential distinction between the solidity of the national bank of England and that of country banks. By an individual of thirty years' practical experience in banking and commercial affairs.
84 pp. London, Thomas Kelly, 1826
T.

3686 Third annual report of the Cork ladies society in connections with the British and Irish society, for bettering the condition of the female peasantry of Ireland.
52 pp. Cork, Edwards & Savage, 1826
A.

3687 Third report of the committee of the society for the mitigation and gradual abolition of slavery throughout the British dominions. Read at a special meeting of the members and friends of the society, held (on the 21st of December, 1825) for the purpose of petitioning parliament on the subject of slavery. With notes and an appendix.
36 pp. London, printed by Ellerton & Henderson, 1826
T.

3688 [THOMPSON, Thomas Perronet.] An exposition of fallacies on rent, tithes etc. Containing an examination of Mr. Ricardo's theory of rent and of the arguments brought against the conclusion that tithes and taxes on the land are paid by the landlords, the doctrine of the impossibility of a general glut, and other propositions of the modern school, with an enquiry into the comparative consequences of taxes on agricultural and manufactured produce. Being in the form of a review of the third edition of Mr. Mill's Elements of political economy. By a Member of the University of Cambridge.
64 pp. London, F. & C. Rivington, 1826
N.

3689 TOOKE, Thomas. Considerations on the state of the currency.
156 pp. London, J. Murray, 1826
T.

——. tables. appendices. 204 pp. 2nd ed. London, J. Murray, 1826
T.

3690 TRENCH, William. A plan for lessening pauperism.
4 pp. Parsonstown, Legge, 1826
A.

3691 True cause of the late panic, and present distress fairly stated. By an observer.
26 pp. London, Henry Stokes, 1826
T.

3692 [WADE, John.] New parliament. An appendix to the Black Book; containing a list and analysis of the new house of commons with strictures on their parliamentary conduct and principles: also remarks on the reduction of the national debt, with the best means of relieving public distress; with documents, from the last session of parliament, of the 'dead weight', and public expenditure.
tables. 56 pp. 3rd ed. London, J. Fairburn, 1826
A.

3693 WALKER, Thomas. Observations on the nature, extent and effects of pauperism and on the means of reducing it.
96 pp. London, J. Hatchard, 1826
A., N., T.

3694 WALLER, Sir Charles Townshend, bart. A plan for the relief of the poor in Ireland in a letter addressed to his grace the duke of Devonshire.
24 pp. Bath, J. Keene, 1826
A., N.

3695 WEST, Sir Edward. Price of corn and wages of labour with observations upon Dr. Smith's, Mr. Ricardo's and Mr. Malthus's doctrines upon those subjects; and an attempt at

an exposition of the causes of the fluctuation of the price of corn during the last 30 years.
chart. 158 pp. London, J. Hatchard, 1826
A., T.

3696 WESTERN, Charles Callis Western, 1st baron. A letter to the earl of Liverpool on the cause of our present embarrassment and distress: and the measures necessary for our effectual relief.
50 pp. London, J. Ridgway, 1826
A.
See 3593

3697 WHITMORE, William Wolryche. A letter to the electors of Bridgnorth, upon the corn laws.
tables. 84 pp. Edinburgh, W. Blackwood, 1826
K., T.

3698 [WILSON, John.] Some illustrations of Mr. McCulloch's principles of political economy. By Mordecai Mullion, private secretary to Christopher North.
tables. 74 pp. Edinburgh, W. Blackwood, London, T. Cadell, 1826
T.

3699 WINTER, John Pratt. Suggestions for the regulations of the office of justice of the peace in Ireland and of the powers of grand juries in levying money; accompanied with observations on the situation of country gentlemen, and some notices relative to the state of the rural population.
128 pp. Dublin, Archer, 1826
A., N.

3700 WYATT, J. Observations on the question of the corn laws and free trade, shewing the disadvantages of the present system, particularly to the landed interest, and the propriety and necessity of altering it, at the same time pointing out the evils of too sudden a change, and suggesting a means of effecting it with the least disadvantage: to which is added, a short account of Mr. Jacob's report on foreign corn and agriculture.
table. 44 pp. London, J. Hatchard, 1826
K., T.

1827

3701 ADAMSON, Laurence. A letter to the rt. hon. the lord mayor of the city of Dublin on the abuses in the coal trade.
table. 48 pp. Dublin, W. Underwood, 1827
A., N.

3702 [ALLEN, William.] Colonies at home: or, the means for rendering the industrious labourer independent of parish relief; and for providing for the poor population of Ireland, by the cultivation of the soil.
tables. plates. 32 pp. 2nd ed. London, Longman & co. [etc., etc.], 1827
T.
See 3598.

3703 The annual report of the managers and auditors of the Royal Cork Institution, previous to the general meeting at the spring assizes, 1827.
tables. 32 pp. Cork, Edwards & Savage, 1827.
A.

3704 Annual report of the Stranger's Friend Society, founded in 1790 for visiting and relieving distressed strangers and the resident sick poor.
24 pp. Dublin, R. Napper, 1827
A., N.

3705 BEARE, John. A letter to the king on the practical improvement of Ireland.
92 pp. London, Clerc Smith, 1827
A., N., P., U.

3706 BRAMSTON, Thomas Gardiner. The principle of the corn laws vindicated.
tables. 94 pp. London, J. Hatchard, 1827
T.

3707 BRERETON, Charles David. The subordinate magistracy and parish system considered, in their connexion with the causes and remedies of modern pauperism, with some observations on the relief of the poor in England, Scotland, and Ireland, and on parochial emigration.
table of contents. appendix. 222 pp. London, J. Hatchard, [1827]
N., T.

3708 BUNSTER, Grosvenor. Observations on captain F. B. Heads' 'reports relative to the failure of the Rio de la Plate mining association'; with additional remarks, and an appendix of original documents.
appendix. 150 pp. 2nd ed. London, E. Wilson, 1827
T.

3709 BURGESS, Henry. A memorial, addressed to the right honourable lord viscount Goderich, on the fitness of the system of the bank of England,—of the country banks,—and of the branch banks of England,—to the wants of the people: and on the ample means of protection, which private bankers and the public have, against the monopoly of the Bank of England.
appendix. 54 pp. 2nd edition. London, J. Ridgway, 1827
T.

3710 BURROUGHS, Edward. Essays on practical husbandry and rural economy.
80 pp. Dublin, J. Porter, 1827
A.
See 3215.

3711 Cheap bread injurious to the working classes, and gold unnecessary as a circulating medium. By no landowner.
22 pp. London, J. Ridgway, 1827
T.

3712 CHRISTIE, Jonathan Henry. A letter to the right hon. Robert Peel, one of his majesty's principal secretaries of state, &c. &c. &c. on the proposed changes in the laws of real property, and on modern conveyancing.
52 pp. London, J. Murray, 1827
T.

3713 COHEN, Bernard. Supplement to the seventh edition of Fairman on the funds.
tables. 54 pp. London, John Richardson, 1827
T.

3714 Common sense on colonial slavery. A review of the chief objections, urged against the speedy manumission of our British slaves; under distinct heads: with notes, appendix, etc. By the author of the letters on the same subject, lately published, under the signature of 'Oculus', in the *New Times* newspaper.
tables. appendix. 76 pp. London, J. Hatchard, 1827
T.

3715 CRUTTWELL, Richard. Petition to his majesty the king, on the currency, or standard of value, as connected—with taxation—the corn laws—free trade—existing sufferings among manufacturing-operatives—trading embarrassments generally—scarcity of money—low prices—great injustice to bankers—risks and inconveniences occasioned to bankers, from the present monetary-system—the corn-bill and Peel's bill, collision of and violent counteraction between them— Cobbett's ignorance, false statements, ferocious brutality, &c.
50 pp. London, J. Hatchard, 1827
T.

3716 The distribution of the national wealth considered in its bearings upon the several questions now before the public, more especially those of the corn laws and restriction in general. By Cedric.
tables in appendices. 106 pp. London, Robert Jennings, 1827
T.

3717 DIXON, Robert. Observations on the proposed new code relating to real property.
64 pp. London, J. & W. T. Clarke, 1827
T.

3718 England's prosperity. Considerations on the present depressed state of England; and various suggestions for its amendment and future prosperity. By a gentleman.
tables. appendix. 94 pp. London, Havell, 1827
P., T.

3719 ENGLISH, Henry. A complete view of the joint stock companies, formed during the years 1824 and 1825; being six hundred and twenty-four in number: shewing the amount of capital, number of shares, amount advanced, present value, amount liable to be called, fluctuations in price, names of bankers, solicitors, &c. with a general summary and remarks. And an appendix, giving a list of companies formed, antecedent to that period; with amount of capital, number of shares, dividends, &c.
tables. tables in appendix. 42 pp. London, Boosey, 1827
A., T.

3720 FERNANDEZ, John. An address to his majesty's ministers, recommending efficacious means for the most speedy termination of African slavery.
36 pp. London, the author, 1827
K., T.

3721 A few practical observations upon the existing bankrupt law. By a man of business.
48 pp. London, Sherwood, Gilbert and Piper, 1827
T.

3722 Fifth report of the committee of the county of Limerick agricultural association (established 6th May, 1822) for the year ending 1st March, 1827. To which is subjoined, the report

and statement of accounts of the trustees for the promotion of industry, with whom the committee act in conjunction.
44 pp. Limerick, R. Canter, 1827
A.

3723 FLETCHER, M. Reflexions on the causes which influence the price of corn.
tables in appendix. 98 pp. London, Black, Young & Young, 1827
P., T.

3724 The forty-shilling freeholder, containing an account of the persons entitled to exercise the elective franchise at the time of passing the eighth Henry the Sixth; the former and present value of the estate of qualification contrasted; the difference of the effects resulting from the restraining statutes in England and Ireland, and the situation of the English and Irish forty-shilling freeholders compared; to which is prefixed a short history of the mode of electing knights of the shire, and who were the electors prior to the eighth Henry the Sixth, which introduced the present system of representation in counties. By a barrister.
28 pp. Dublin, Richard Milliken, 1827
U.

3725 FRY, Elizabeth and GURNEY, Joseph John. Report addressed to the Marquess Wellesley, lord lieutenant of Ireland by Elizabeth Fry and Joseph John Gurney, respecting their late visit to that country.
100 pp. London, J. & A. Arch, 1827
A., N., RM., T., U.

3726 The further progress of colonial reform; being an analysis of the communication made to parliament by his majesty, at the close of the last session, respecting the measures taken for improving the condition of the slave population in the British colonies. Comprising the period from January 1826, to May, 1827. [In continuation of two pamphlets, 'The slave colonies of Great Britain', etc. and 'The progress of colonial reform', containing a view of the advance made in carrying into effect the recommendations of his majesty, with respect to negro slavery, between May 1823, and December 1825.]
tables. 82 pp. London, Bagster and Thoms, 1827
T.

3727 GARDINER, Henry. Essays on currency and absenteeism &c. &c. With strictures on Mr. Drummond's pamphlet entitled 'Elementary propositions on the currency'.
188 pp. Liverpool, G. & J. Robinson, 1827
T.

3728 GILBART, James William. A practical treatise on banking, containing an account of the London and country banks; exhibiting their system of book-keeping—the terms on which they transact business—their customs in regard to bills of exchange—and their method of making calculations. Also a view of joint stock banks, and the branch banks of the bank of England: likewise ample information respecting the banks of Scotland and Ireland: with a summary of the evidence delivered before the parliamentary committees, relative to the suppression of notes under five pounds in those countries.
tables. 80 pp. London, Effingham Wilson, [etc., etc.], 1827
A., T.

3729 [GRAHAM, Sir James Robert George, bart.] A compendium of the laws, passed from time to time, for regulating and restricting the importation, exportation, and consumption of foreign corn, from the year 1660, and a series of accounts, from the date of the earliest official records; showing the operation of the several statutes, and the average prices of corn: presenting a complete view of the corn trade of Great Britain. Compiled from public documents.
tables. 66 pp. 2nd ed. London, J. Ridgway, 1827
A.

3730 GRATTAN, Richard and FARRAN, Charles. The report of doctors Grattan & Farran to the King & Queen's College of Physicians in Ireland, relative to the estates of Sir Patrick Dun in co. Waterford.
36 pp. Dublin, Bentham & Hardy, 1827
A.
College of Physicians was trustee for these estates.

3731 [HAUGHTON, Jeremiah?] A letter to the Rt. Hon. Mr. Lamb, containing a few practical hints for the improvement of Ireland. By a land owner.
12 pp. Dublin, Bentham & Hardy, 1827
A., U.
Royal Irish Academy version contains also letters 'to the committee lately appointed on combination' and 'to employers and employed' by 'a workman and employer' and 'a manufacturer' respectively bound in as an appendix.

12 pp. 2nd edition. Dublin, Bentham & Hardy, 1827
N., P.

3732 The high price of bread shown to be the result of commercial prosperity, not the cause of national distress; and the dangers of free trade in corn pointed out. By a warning voice.
202 pp. London, J. Hatchard, 1827
T.

3733 HUSKISSON, William. A letter on the corn laws by the right hon. W. Huskisson to one of his constituents. In 1814.
16 pp. London, J. Ridgway, 1827
T.

3734 ——. Shipping interest. Speech of the right hon. W. Huskisson in the house of commons, Monday, 7th May 1827 on general Gascoyne's motion, 'That a select committee be appointed, to inquire into the present distressed state of the British commercial shipping interest.' With an appendix, containing the several accounts referred to.
appendix. tables. 94 pp. London, J. Hatchard, 1827
A.

3735 An inquiry into the present state and means of improving the salmon fisheries: including a digest of the evidence taken by a select committee of the house of commons.
214 pp. London, J. Ridgway, 1827
T.

3736 JAMES, Edward. Remarks on the mines, management, ores, &c. &c. of the district of Guanaxuato, belonging to the Anglo Mexican mining association.
52 pp. London, Effingham Wilson, 1827
T.

3737 Jones, William. Observations on the insolvent debtors' act; miscalled "An act for the relief of insolvent debtors.'
20 pp. London, J. Hatchard, 1827
T.

3738 KENNEDY, James. England and Venice compared. An argument on the policy of England towards her colonies.
50 pp. London, J. Hatchard, 1827
A., T.

3739 LARDNER, Dionysius. Syllabus of a few lectures on the steam-engine, to be delivered by desire of the Royal Dublin Society, in order to exhibit the advantages of a new apparatus, designed for the illustration of popular lectures on mechanical science.
12 pp. Dublin, R. Graisberry, 1827
A.

3740 A letter addressed to the Rt. Hon. Henry Goulburn, secretary of state for Ireland, on the miseries of the 40/- freehold system of that unhappy country with suggestions for its removal. By Patricius.
46 pp. Bath, Samuel Gibbs, 1827
A.

3741 A letter to the Rt. Hon. Lord Goderich on the deplorable condition of the helpless poor in Ireland, with a plan of relief, as at present partly in operation in several districts of the province of Ulster. By a member of a parochial poor relief committee.
tables. 30 pp. Dublin, 1827
A., N.

3742 MCCAFFRY, J. Leger [sic] lessons, designed chiefly for the use of schools. It is particularly recommended to agents, merchants, clerks, extensive shop-keepers, and all others desirous of balancing and closing accounts, in an easy, familiar, and satisfactory manner.
Cavan, O'Brien, 1827
A.

3743 MCDONALD, John. Emigration to Canada. Narrative of a voyage to Quebec and journey from thence to New Lanark in Upper Canada, detailing the hardships and difficulties which an emigrant has to encounter before and after his settlement, with an account of the country as it regards its climate, soil, and the actual condition of its inhabitants.
36 pp. 10th ed. Dublin, printed by J. Scott, 1827
A.

3744 M'DONNELL, Alexander. Compulsory manumission; or an examination of the actual state of the West India Question.
94 pp. London, J. Murray, 1827
K., T.

3745 Mining company of Ireland. Report for half year ending 1st Dec. 1826.
10 pp. Dublin, J. Carrick, 1827
A., N.

3746 Mining company of Ireland. Report for half year ending 1st June, 1827.
14 pp. Dublin, Bentham & Hardy, 1827
A.

3747 MONTEATH, Robert. Miscellaneous reports on woods and plantations shewing a method to plant, rear, and recover all woods, plantations and timber trees on every soil and situation in Britain and Ireland; containing demonstrative proof of the great profits to be derived from planting; means of ascertaining the comparative tanning principles of all kinds of barks; with plans for employing the operatives, and improving the waste lands of Great Britain and Ireland. In a letter to the Rt. Hon. Robert Peel, secretary of state.
illustrations. 168 pp. Dundee, James Chalmers, 1827
A.

3748 National polity and finance; plan for establishing a sterling currency, and relieving the burdens of the people. Extracted from the Literary Gazette, by the editor.
78 pp. interleaved. London, Longman, Rees, Orme, Brown, and Green, [etc., etc.], 1827
T.

3749 Ninth report of the general committee of the association for the suppression of mendicity in Dublin, for 1826.
60 pp. Dublin, J. Jones, 1827
A.

3750 Observations on the corn laws. By Atticus.
tables, 22 pp. London, J. Hatchard, 1827
K., T.

3751 Observations on the corn laws addressed to W. W. Whitmore, esq., M.P. in consequence of his letter to the electors of Bridgnorth.
48 pp. London, Longmans, Rees, Orme, Brown, and Green, 1827
T., U.

3752 O'CONNELL, Daniel. A full report of the speech of Daniel O'Connell, on the subject of Church rates and parish cess, as delivered at a meeting of catholics, on Wednesday, the 10th of January, 1827. By James Sheridan.
74 pp. Dublin, Richard Coyne, 1827
L., N., P., T.

3753 The petition and memorial of the planters of Demarara and Berbice, on the subject of manumission examined: being an exposure of the inaccuracy of the statements, and the fallacy of the views, on which they have proceeded in their recent application to his majesty in council.
table. 64 pp. London, Bagster and Thomas, 1827
T.

3754 A proposal for steam navigation from Europe to America and the West Indies.
30 pp. London, Gunnell and Shearman, 1827
A.

3755 Prosperity of the labourer the foundation of universal prosperity. By Eight-Seven.
148 pp. Dublin, J. Porter, 1827
A., N.

3756 Remarks on a letter to the electors of Bridgnorth upon the Corn Laws by W. W. Whitmore, M.P. by Cincinnatus.
46 pp. Dublin, Curry, 1827
A.

3757 A remedy to meet or plan to cure the evils of combination, addressed to the Rt. Hon. Robert Peel by a tradesman.
16 pp. Dublin, Shaw, 1827
A.

3758 Report of the committee of investigation appointed by a resolution of the half-yearly general meeting of the shareholders of the Arigna Iron & Coal Company.
52 pp. London, E. Justin, 1827
A.

3759 Report of the committee of the Carrickfergus Mendicity Association, for the year ending May 1st, 1827
8 pp. Belfast, Finlay, 1827
A.

3760 Report of the council of the chamber of commerce of Dublin to the annual assembly of the members of the association, 12th April, 1827.
78 pp. Dublin, J. Carrick, 1827
A.

3761 Report of the court of directors to the company of undertakers of the Grand Canal.
tables. 26 pp. Dublin, J. Porter, 1827
A.

3762 Rights of the poor. Charities of Bristol. An account of public charities, digested and arranged from the reports of H.M. Commissioners on charitable foundations in England and Wales, with notes and comments. By the editor of 'The cabinet lawyer'.
table of contents. 62 pp. London, Simpkin & Marshall, 1827
A.
pp. 65–128 only.

3763 Rules and regulations of the Irish Commercial Clerks Society established in Dublin 1827 under the sanction of the council of the chamber of commerce.
22 pp. Dublin, Bentham & Hardy, 1827
A.

3764 Rules, &c. for the government and observance of the Aldham and united parishes institution or insurance society.
Tables. 50 pp. Colchester, the society, 1827
K.

3765 SEDGWICK, James. Two letters from Godfrey Sykes, esq., solicitor of stamps in England; and two letters from Charles Bremner, esq., writer to the signet, and assistant of the late solicitor of stamps in Scotland.
table. 80 pp. London, A. Maxwell, 1827
T.

3766 SENIOR, Nassau William. An introductory lecture on political economy, delivered before the University of Oxford, on the 6th of December, 1826
42 pp. London, J. Mawman, 1827
T.

3767 Shipping interest. Two letters in reply to the speech of the right hon. W. Huskisson, in the house of commons, Monday, May 7, 1827, on general Gascoyne's motion, 'That a select committee be appointed to inquire into the present distressed state of the British commercial shipping interest.'

To which are added, three letters previously published in the 'Morning Post' on the same subject.
with notes. tables. 78 pp. London, Effingham Wilson, 1827
                                        T.

3768 STANHOPE, Philip Henry, 4th earl. A letter from earl Stanhope, on the proposed alteration of the corn laws.
30 pp. London, J. Ridgway, 1827
                                        T.

3769 A statement of the charitable society for relief of sick and indigent room keepers in the city of Dublin, for the year 1826.
38 pp. Dublin, J. Coyne, 1827
                                        A.

3770 STRACHAN, John. Remarks on emigration from the United Kingdom, addressed to Robert Wilmot Horton, esq., M.P. chairman of the select committee of emigration in the last parliament.
tables. appendix. 94 pp. London, J. Murray, 1827
                                        K.

3771 STRICKLAND, George. A discourse on the poor laws of England and Scotland, on the state of the poor of Ireland, and on emigration.
tables. 134 pp. London, J. Ridgway, 1827
                                        T.
Strickland later assumed the name of Cholmley, and became Sir George Cholmley, bart.

3772 Thoughts on taxation. By an humble patriot.
tables. 32 pp. London, Richard Long, 1827
                                        T.

3773 Thoughts on the policy of the proposed alteration of the corn laws.
62 pp. London, J. Ridgway, 1827
                                        T.

3774 [THOMPSON, Alexander?] The real state of Ireland.
112 pp. London, J. Murray, 1827
                                        A., K., N.

3775 [THOMPSON, Thomas Perronet.] Catechism on the corn laws with a list of fallacies and the answers: by a member of the University of Cambridge.
64 pp. 10th ed. revised and corrected. London, 'Westminster Review', 1827
                                        N.

3776 TOOKE, Thomas. Considerations on the state of the currency.
tables in appendix. 176 pp. 3rd ed. London, J. Murray, 1827
                                        T.

3777 TORRENS, Robert. Substance of a speech delivered by colonel Torrens in the house of commons, 15th February, 1827, on the motion of Sir Robert Wilmot Horton, for the re-appointment of a select committee on emigration from the United Kingdom.
24 pp. 2nd ed. London, Brettell, 1827
                                        A., N.

3778 The trial of the English farmer; or, his real character and situation faithfully delineated from practical experience;
15

exhibiting the various conflicting opinions, as to the immediate cause of agricultural distress; and refuting the fallacious sentiments of illiberal and selfish men, on the conduct of that loyal and respectable body, the British yeomen: also shewing, by apposite reasoning, the futile invention, and baneful tendency of the new corn laws: by an old farmer.
62 pp. London, Effingham Wilson, 1827
                                        T.

3779 TWIGG, J. A. Report on the iron works and collieries at Arigna, Roscommon, Ireland; the property of the Arigna Iron and Coal Company: furnished to the committee of investigation.
tables, diagrams. 58 pp. London, printed by E. Justins, 1827
                                        A.

3780 [WAVELL, Arthur Goodall?] Notes and reflections on Mexico, its mines, policy, &c. by a traveller, some years resident in that and the other American states.
appendix. 72 pp. London, J. M. Richardson, 1827
                                        T.

3781 WESTERN, Thomas Burch. Hints to agriculturists and others. Residing in the neighbourhood of Colchester, upon the advantages which may be derived from benefit societies, established on scientific principles; together with observations on the injuries often inflicted on the members of benefit societies. To which are added directions, rules, &c. for the use of those who may wish to establish insurance societies for the poor.
tables. 88 pp. Colchester, Swinborne and Walter [etc.], 1827
                                        K.

3782 [WILLOUGHBY, Sir Henry Pollard, bart.] The apology of an English landowner, addressed to the landed proprietors of the county of Oxford. By one of them.
tables. 44 pp. Oxford, J. Parker, 1827
                                        T.

3783 WOODCOCK, William. Prize essay. An essay on the state of the poor among the ancient and modern nations. To which was adjudged a prize by the Royal Irish Academy.
118 pp. Dublin, R. Milliken, [etc.], 1827
                                        A.

3784 WRENFORD, W. O. An abstract of the malt laws, containing all the regulations affecting maltsters, and dealers in malt; and including the provisions of the act of 7 & 8 Geo. IV. chap. 52, called the malt consolidation act; with a copious index.
64 pp. London, J. Richardson, 1827
                                        T.

3785 WYATT, Harvey. An address to the owners and occupiers of land on the importance of an adequate protection to agriculture.
tables. 52 pp. London, J. Hatchard, 1827
                                        K.

3786 YATES, John Ashton. Essays on currency and circulation, and on the influence of our paper system on the industry, trade, and revenue of Great Britain.
tables. appendix. 200 pp. Liverpool, G. and J. Robinson, [etc.], 1827
                                        T.

1828

3787 Abstracts of the evidence taken before the select committee of the house of lords, appointed to take into consideration the state of the British wool trade, classed under different heads.
70 pp. London, J. Ridgway, 1828

T.

3788 An address to the members of trade societies and to the working classes generally, being an exposition of the relative situation, condition and future prospects of the working people in the U.S.A., together with a suggestion and the outlines of a plan by which they may gradually and indefinitely improve their condition. By a Fellow Labourer.
32 pp. Dublin, Shaw, 1828

A., N.

Reprinted from the original edition published in Philadelphia, 1827.

3789 An address to the proprietors of bank stock, the London and country bankers and the public in general on the affairs of the Bank of England.
tables. appendices. 124 pp. London, Saunders and Otley, 1828

T.

3790 [ALEXANDER, William.] Address to the public, on the present state of the question relative to negro slavery in the British colonies.
16 pp. York, printed by W. Alexander; London, Harvey & Darton, [etc., etc.]., 1828

K., T.

3791 ALLEN, William. Colonies at home, or means for rendering the industrious labourer independent of parish relief and for providing for the poor population of Ireland by the cultivation of the soil.
54 pp. London, Longman, Rees, Orme, Brown and Green, 1828

A.

See 3598.

3792 An analysis of the artificial wealth of England in reply to lord Grenville's essay on the supposed advantages of the sinking fund.
52 pp. London, J. Hatchard, 1828

K., T.

3793 ANDREWES, George Payne. An abridgment of the new act of parliament to amend the corn laws.
tables. 58 pp. London, Shackell, 1828

T.

3794 An appeal to England against the new Indian stamp act; with some observations on the condition of British subjects in Calcutta, under the government of the East India Company.
appendices. 142 pp. London, J. Ridgway, 1828

T.

3795 ATTWOOD, Thomas. The Scotch banker; containing articles under that signature on banking, currency, etc. republished from the Globe newspaper with some additional articles.
192 pp. London, J. Ridgway, 1828

T.

3796 BADNALL, Richard. A view of the silk trade.
tables. 108 pp. n.p. [1828?]

P.

3797 BARRET, ——, of Jamaica. A reply to the speech of Dr. Lushington in the house of commons on 12th June, 1827 on the condition of the free coloured people of Jamaica.
62 pp. London, Shackell & Baylis, 1828

N.

3798 BECHER, John Thomas. The anti-pauper system; exemplifying the positive and practical good, realised by the relievers and the relieved, under the frugal, beneficial and careful administration of the poor laws, prevailing at Southwell and in the neighbouring district, with plans of the Southwell workhouse, and of the Thurgartion Hundred workhouse, and with instructions for bookkeeping.
table of contents. plans. appendix. tables. 64 pp. London, Simpkin, Marshall, 1828

N., T.

3799 ——. The constitution of friendly societies, upon legal and scientific principles, exemplified by the rules and tables adopted for the government of the Southwell Friendly Institution, examined, authenticated and recommended for general use, by William Morgan and Arthur Morgan.
table of contents. tables. 86 pp. 4th ed. London, Simpkin, Marshall, 1828

N.

3800 BISCHOFF, James. The wool question considered: being an examination of the report from the select committee of the house of lords, appointed to take into consideration the state of the British wool trade, and an answer to earl Stanhope's letter to the owners and occupiers of sheep farms.
tables. 112 pp. London, J. Richardson; Leeds, John Baines, 1828

P., T.

3801 BOYD, Walter. Observations on lord Grenville's essay on the sinking fund.
16 pp. London, J. Hatchard, 1828

K., T.

3802 ——. Reflections on the financial system of Great Britain, and particularly on the sinking fund. Written in France in the summer of 1812.
tables. 72 pp. second edition. London, J. Hatchard, 1828

K., T.

3803 BRICKWOOD, John. A plan for reducing the capital, and the annual charge of the national debt humbly suggested to the consideration of his majesty's government.
tables. appendix. 60 pp. 4th ed. London, Marchant, 1828

P.

3804 BRUCE, W. Poor rates the panacea for Ireland.
20 pp. 2d. ed. Bristol, Mills, 1828

A., N.

3805 BUCHANAN, A. C. Emigration practically considered, with detailed directions to emigrants proceeding to British North America, particularly to the Canadas; in a letter to the right hon. R. Wilmot Horton, M.P.
table of contents. appendix. 156 pp. London, H. Colburn, 1828

A.

3806 BUNN, Thomas. Remarks on the necessity and the means of extinguishing a large portion of the national debt. appendix. 100 pp. Bath, George Wood, 1828

T.

3807 [BURGESS, Henry.] A letter to his grace the duke of Wellington, containing practical suggestions, founded on simple principles, for the regulating of the currency; the relieving of the country from pauperism and a redundant population; and for the preventing, detecting, and correcting of crime. By an Englishman.
68 pp. London, J. Ridgway, 1828

P.

3808 CANTWELL, John. A compendious abstract of the statutes passed in the session of 1827 relating to Ireland, with an appendix of statutes of former sessions; viz., wilful destruction of houses act—all the manor courts acts—and the subletting act, with the opinions of eminent lawyers on the billeting of soldiers throughout Ireland, and on bills of exchange and promissory notes, and other useful matter: with notes and comments.
82 pp. Dublin, J. Blundell, 1828

A.

3809 The Catholic Question discussed and decided, particularly as it regards the admission of catholics into parliament. With a preface in refutation of Mr. M'Culloch's opinion on absenteeism, as stated before the committee of the house of commons.
36 pp. London, J. Hatchard, 1828

K.

3810 The Charter of the National Assurance Company of Ireland, incorporated on the 10th day of November, 1828.
54 pp. Dublin, Bentham & Hardy, 1828

A.

3811 COURTENAY, Thomas Peregrine. A letter to lord Grenville on the sinking fund.
142 pp. London, John Murray, 1828

K., T.

3812 CRAWFURD, John. A view of the present state and future prospects of the free trade and colonisation of India.
126 pp. London, J. Ridgway, 1828

T.

3813 CRUTTWELL, Richard. The system of country-banking defended; with reference to corn, currency, panic, population, bankruptcy, crime, pauperism and so forth. A letter to lord Goderich, first lord of his majesty's treasury, etc., etc., etc. appendix. 36 pp. London, J. Hatchard, 1828

T.

3814 DOUGLAS, John. Observations on the necessity of a legal provision for the Irish poor, as the means of improving the condition of the Irish people, and protecting the British landlord, farmer, and labourer.
40 pp. London, Longman, Rees, Orme, Brown and Green, 1828

A., N.

3815 DWARRIS, Fortunatus. The West Indian question plainly stated; and the only practical remedy briefly considered in a letter to the Right Hon. Henry Goulburn, Chancellor of the exchequer.
table. notes. 84 pp. London, J. Ridgway, 1828

T.

3816 FARREN, George. Letter to the earl of Eldon, on the report of the finance committee.
10 pp. London, J. M. Richardson, 1828

T.

3817 Fifth annual report of the Cork ladies society, in connection with the British and Irish Society, for bettering the condition of the female peasantry of Ireland.
54 pp. Cork, Edwards & Savage, 1828

A.

3818 FLETCHER, M. Reflexions on the causes which influence the price of corn. Part II.
tables. 28 pp. London, Black, Young & Young, 1828

P.

3819 GILBART, James William. Practical treatise on banking containing an account of the London and country banks; exhibiting their system of book-keeping and the terms on which they transact business—their customs in regard to bills of exchange and their method of making calculations. Also a view of the joint stock banks and the branch banks of the Bank of England: likewise ample information respecting the banks of Scotland and Ireland, with a summary of the evidence delivered before the parliamentary committees relative to the suppression of notes under five pounds in those countries.
tables, table of contents. 116 pp. 2nd ed. London, Effingham Wilson, 1828

N.

3820 GRAHAM, Sir James Robert George, bart. Corn and currency, in an address to the land owners.
tables. 118 pp. new ed. London, J. Ridgway, 1828

A.

3821 [GRAHAM, Sir James Robert George.] Free trade in corn the real interest of the landlord, and the true policy of the state. By a Cumberland landholder.
tables. 88 pp. London, J. Ridgway, 1828

P.

3822 GRANT, A. W. Remarks on the influence attributed to the state of the currency on prices and credit, and on the suppression of small notes.
46 pp. London, J. M. Richardson, 1828

N., T.

3823 GRENVILLE, William Wyndham Grenville, baron. Essay on the supposed advantages of a sinking fund.
98 pp. London, J. Murray, 1828

P.

——. 100 pp. 2nd ed. London, J. Murray, 1828

K., T.

3824 GRIFFITH, Richard. Report on the metallic mines of the province of Leinster in Ireland.
30 pp. Dublin, R. Graisberry, 1828

A., C., N.

3825 HEAD, F. B. A few practical arguments against the theory of emigration.
70 pp. London, J. Murray, 1828
K., T.

3826 Hints on emigration as the means of effecting the repeal of the poor laws.
58 pp. London, J. Hatchard, 1828
K., T.

3827 [HOLT, Francis Ludlow.] A letter to his grace the duke of Wellington, first lord of the treasury, etc. etc. in answer to lord Grenville's essay on the supposed advantages of the sinking fund. In four parts. I. Answer to the fallacies of lord Grenville's argument. II. The efficacy of the sinking fund. III. Obligation to maintain it from public faith. IV. Necessity of a surplus fund.
82 pp. London, J. Hatchard, 1828
K., T.

3828 HOPKINS, Thomas. On rent of land, and its influence on subsistence and population: with observations on the operating causes of the condition of the labouring classes in various countries.
148 pp. London, Hunt and Clarke, 1828
T.

3829 HORTON, Sir Robert John Wilmot. Protestant securities suggested in an appeal to the clerical Members of the University of Oxford. Appendices.
198 pp. London, J. Murray, 1828
K.

3830 ——. Speech of the right honble. R. Wilmot Horton, in the house of commons on the 6th of March, 1828, on moving for the production of the evidence taken before the privy council, upon an appeal against the compulsory manumission of slaves in Demerara and Berbice. With notes and appendix.
92 pp. London, J. Murray, 1828
K.

3831 HOYTE, Henry A treatise on agriculture addressed to the noblemen and gentlemen of landed property in Ireland; with hints, the practical application of which must ultimately ameliorate the condition of the peasantry, and greatly improve the landed interest of this kingdom.
table of contents. 48 pp. Dublin, Bentham & Hardy, 1828
A., N.

3832 HUDDART, Joseph. Piloting directions for the Bristol channel, St. George's channel and all the coast of Ireland......
table of contents. 120 pp. London, Laurie, 1828
A.

3833 JACOB, William. Observations upon the benefits arising from the cultivation of poor soils, by the application of pauper labour, as exemplified in the colonies for the indigent and for orphans in Holland.
44 pp. Lindfield, Sussex, Charles Greene, 1828
A., N.

3834 [JAMES, Paul Moon.] A summary statement of the one pound note question.
tables. 24 pp. London, G. B. Whitaker, 1828
T.

3835 JOPLIN, Thomas. Views on the corn bill of 1827, and other measures of government; together with a further exposition of certain principles on corn and currency before published.
table in appendix. 124 pp. various paging. London, J. Ridgway [etc.], 1828
T.

3836 ——. Views on the currency, in which the connection between corn and currency is shown; the nature of our system of currency explained; and the merits of the corn bill, the branch banks, the extension of the bank charter, and the small note act examined.
254 pp. London, J. Ridgway, 1828
A., N.

3837 KEATING, M. I. A letter to Wilmot Horton esq. M.P. on emigration from Ireland.
16 pp. Limerick, R. Canter, [1828]
A., N.

3838 A letter to Sir James Graham, bart., M.P., alias 'A Cumberland landowner'; in reply to certain positions contained in a pamphlet entitled 'Free trade in Corn the real interest of the landlord and the true policy of the state; By a Cumberland Landowner.'
32 pp. London, Poole and Edwards, 1828
K., T.

3839 A letter to the Rt. Hon. Mr. Lamb, containing a few practical hints for the improvement of Ireland. By a landowner.
12 pp. 3rd. Dublin, Bentham and Hardy, 1828
N., P.

3840 Letters to a friend in England on the actual state of Ireland.
126 pp. London, J. Ridgway, 1828
A., N.

3841 [MAILLARD DE CHAMBURE, Charles-Hip.] Coup-D'Oeil historique et statistique sur l'état passé et présent de l'Irlande, sur le rapport de son gouvernement, de sa religion—de son agriculture, de son commerce et de son industrie. par C.-H.M.D.C.
98 pp. Paris, Mongie Diné [etc.], 1828
A.

3842 [MANGIN, Edward.] Parish settlements and pauperism.
62 pp. London, J. Hatchard, 1828
T.

3843 MEREWETHER, Francis. A letter to the editor of the Quarterly Review, in furtherance of the subjects of three articles in No. 72 of that review, entitled On agriculture and rent: Substitution of savings' banks for poor laws: On planting waste lands.
36 pp. London, F. C. & J. Rivington, Leicester, Combe, 1828
K., T.

3844 Mining company of Ireland. List of proprietors, 24 Dec. 1828.
4 pp. Dublin, J. Chambers, 1828
A.

3845 Mining company of Ireland. Report from the board of directors for the half-year ending 1st December, 1827.
10 pp. Dublin, J. Chambers, 1828
                                        A., N.

3846 Mining company of Ireland. Report from the board of directors of the mining company of Ireland, for the half-year ending 1st June, 1828.
16 pp. Dublin, J. Carrick, 1828
                                        A.

3847 MUNDELL, Alexander. Reasons for a revision of our fiscal code; arising from the continuing defalcation in the supply of gold and silver from the mines, and the consequent depression of money prices. Addressed to the finance committee.
plate. tables. 104 pp. 2nd ed. London, Longman, Rees, Orme, Brown and Green [etc.], 1828
                                        T.

3848 No emigration. The testimony of Experience, before a committee of agriculturists and manufacturers, on the report of the emigration committee of the house of commons: Sir John English in the chair.
60 pp. London, Longman, Rees, Orme, Brown & Green, etc., 1828
                                        K., N., T.

3849 NOLAN, George. Practical observations upon the projected alterations of the law for regulating the import of corn into the United Kingdom of Great Britain and Ireland: in a letter addressed to his grace the duke of Wellington.
table. appendix. 30 pp. London, W. Ruffy, 1828
                                        N.

3850 Observations upon the importation of foreign corn: with the resolutions moved by lord Redesdale in the house of lords, March 29, 1827; and his speech thereupon, May 15, 1827 (with some notice of observations then made on those resolutions;) and also remarks upon an act permitting importation of corn, meal, and flour, until May 1, 1828.
140 pp. London, John Hatchard, 1828
                                        K., T.

3851 On the advantages derived from the establishment of branch banks; in a letter to his grace the duke of Wellington, K.G. first lord of the treasury, etc. etc. etc.
24 pp. London, T. and G. Underwood, 1828
                                        T.

3852 PARNELL, Sir Henry Brooke, bart., afterwards first baron Congleton. Observations on paper money, banking and over-trading; including those parts of the evidence taken before the committee of the house of commons, which explains the Scottish system of banking.
table of contents. 182 pp. 2nd ed. London, J. Ridgway, 1828
                                        A.

3853 [PETTMAN, William Robert Ashley.] An essay on political economy; shewing in what way fluctuations in the price of corn may be prevented, and the means by which all the advantages of a free trade in corn may be attained; an ample remunerating price secured to the British grower, and good permanent rents to land-owners. Part I.
tables. 88 pp. London, G. B. Whittaker, 1828
                                        T.

3854 A plain statement of some particulars of the financial situation of the United Kingdom; with brief remarks on the inutility of the sinking fund in the present state of the revenue.
tables. appendix. 50 pp. London, J. Ridgway, 1828
                                        T.

3855 POWELL, John. Two letters addressed to the chairman of the delegates of the general union of trades at Derby, on the progress of the general union in London, and the circumstances which affect the wages of labour etc. published at the request of the delegates at Derby, and with the concurrence of the London committee.
no. t.p. 8 pp. n.p. 1828
                                        P.

3856 Practice opposed to theory; or, an inquiry into the nature of our commercial distress, with a view to the development of its true causes, and the suggestion of a suitable remedy. By a practical man.
tables. appendix. 216 pp. London, J. M. Richardson, 1818 [1828?]
                                        T.
T.p. dated 1818—text gives references to 1827.

3857 Principles of coinage: intended as an answer to the reported speech of the right hon. Robert Peel, one of his majesty's principal secretaries of state, for the home department, delivered by him, in reply to Sir James Graham, bart., of Netherby, who moved, in the house of commons, for a select committee, to inquire into the circulation of promissory notes, under the value of five pounds, on the 3rd June, 1828.
60 pp. London, C. and J. Rivington, 1828
                                        T.

3858 PUSEY, Philip. An historical view of the sinking fund; in a letter addressed to the earl of Carnarvon.
86 pp. London, J. Ridgway, 1828
                                        T.

3859 ———. A letter to the earl of Carnarvon, on the right hon. the home secretary's financial statement of Friday, the 15th of February, 1828.
tables. appendix. 82 pp. London, J. Ridgway, 1828
                                        T.

3860 RADCLIFFE, William. Origin of the new system of manufacture, commonly called 'power-loom weaving' and the purposes for which this system was invented and brought into use fully explained in a narrative, containing William Radcliffe's struggles through life to remove the cause which has brought this country to its present crisis. Written by himself.
216 pp. Stockport, James Lomax, 1828
                                        P.

3861 Remarks on 'Observations on the necessity of a legal provision for the Irish poor, as the means of improving the condition of the Irish people, and protecting the British landlord, farmer and labourer, by John Douglas esq.' with an epitome of the poor laws of England and proving their superiority over those of Scotland. Illustrated by contrasted cases in both countries, by T.B.
40 pp. Edinburgh, Guthrie, Lizars and Shields, 1828
                                        A.

3862 Remarks on the leading principles contained in lord Grenville's essay on the sinking fund; offered for the consideration of the national creditor. By a public functionary.
24 pp. London, Effingham Wilson, [etc.], 1828
T.

3863 Report of the committee of the Liverpool East India Association, on the subject of trade with India. Presented to the association at a general meeting, 21st March, 1828.
tables. 40 pp. Liverpool, George Smith, 1828
T.

3864 Report of the council of the chamber of commerce of Dublin to the annual assembly of the members of the association, 4th March, 1828.
50 pp. Dublin, Bentham & Hardy, 1828
A.

3865 RICHMOND, William. A letter addressed to the right honorable the president and vice-president of the board of trade; suggesting certain measures for the relief of the shipping interest of Great Britain. Written at their request.
16 pp. London, J. J. Metcalfe, 1828
P.

3866 RYAN, Richard. Directions for proceeding under the tithe composition acts. With forms of applications, notices, summonses, agreements, certificates, qualifications, &c., &c. Third edition, containing the 7th & 8th George IV, chap. 69 and notices of some cases which have not already been published.
84 pp. Dublin, A. & W. Watson, 1828
A.

3867 ——. Practical remedies for the practical evils of Ireland.
34 pp. Dublin, Moore Tims, 1828
A.

3868 [SAWBRIDGE, H. H. B.] A letter on restrictions and fetters in trade.
36 pp. London, C. and J. Rivington, 1828
T.

3869 Scarcity a fiction: or high price and misery exemplified in the fictitious scarcity of 1800; its cause and cure. Being a sort of elegy on the death of small farms, and growth of paper credit. Written in the year aforesaid, by a native of a common, now no more.
18 pp. London, E. Bridgewater, 1828
K.

3870 [SCROPE, George Julius Duncombe Poulett.] A letter to the magistrates of the south and west of England, on the expediency and facility of correcting certain abuses of the poor laws. By one of their number.
table. 30 pp. London, J. Ridgway, 1828
T.

3871 SENIOR, Nassau William. Three lectures on the transmission of the precious metals from country to country and the mercantile theory of wealth, delivered before the University of Oxford, in June, 1827.
100 pp. London, John Murray, 1828
T.

3872 Sketch of the proceedings of the Society for the improvement of Ireland, in the year 1828.
100 pp. Dublin, R. Graisberry, 1828
A.

3873 Slave law of Jamaica: with proceedings and documents relative thereto.
appendix. 280 pp. London, J. Ridgway, 1828
T.

3874 Society for the improvement of Ireland.
12 pp. Dublin, A. Thom, 1828
A.

Includes statement of objects of the society, and report on disadvantages sustained by manufacturers in Ireland.

—— Another issue, containing only the report on disadvantages sustained by manufacturers.
no t.p. 8 pp. Dublin, A. Thom, 1828
N.

3875 Society for the improvement of Ireland. Statement of the proceedings of the society for the improvement of Ireland for the year 1828. With an appendix, containing its rules and regulations, names of members, and other illustrative documents. By order of the society.
tables. 32 pp. Dublin, printed by A. Thom, 1828
A., D., K., N., P., U.

3876 STANHOPE, Philip Henry, 4th earl. A letter to the owners and occupiers of sheep farms, from earl Stanhope.
38 pp. London, J. Ridgway, 1828
T.

3877 STAPYLTON, Martin. A defence of the petition of the debtors in Horsham jail, from the misconceptions of the honourable member for Sussex.
42 pp. London, J. Hatchard, 1828
T.

3878 A statement of the charitable society for the relief of sick and indigent room-keepers, of all religious persuasions, in the city of Dublin, for the year 1827.
36 pp. Dublin, printed by J. Kirkwood, 1828
A.

3879 STEELE, Thomas. Practical suggestions on the general improvement of the navigation of the Shannon between Limerick and the Atlantic; and more particularly of that part of it named by pilots, the Narrows. With some remarks intended to create a doubt of the fairness of not keeping faith with the Irish Roman catholics, after they had been lured into a surrender of Limerick, (their principal fortress), by a treaty.
160 pp. London, Sherwood, Gilbert, Piper, 1828
A.

3880 STEWART, William. Comments on the sub-letting act, 7 Geo. 4, Chap 29; entitled 'An act to amend the laws in Ireland, respecting the assignment and sub-letting of lands and tenements,' detailing the entire course of proceeding under its provisions, and containing several recent and important decisions.
94 pp. London, H. Butterworth and J. Clarke [etc., etc.], 1828
A., N., T., U.

3881 Suggestions with a view to ameliorate the condition of the poor, and to open a permanent channel for the employment of the labouring classes, and thereby to diminish the poor's rates; together with a plan for the introduction of foreign corn, unattended with disadvantages to the landholder. Inscribed (by permission) to the most noble the marquess of Lansdowne by a commoner.
tables. 66 pp. London, J. Ridgway [etc., etc.], 1828
T.

3882 TAYLOR, James. A view of the money system of England, from the conquest; with proposals for establishing a secure and equable credit currency.
194 pp. London, John Taylor, [etc.] 1828
T.

3883 Tenth report of the general committee of the association for the suppression of mendicity in Dublin, for the year 1827.
appendices. tables. 130 pp. Dublin, J. Carrick, 1828
A.

3884 The Thames tunnel. Report of the court of directors and of M. J. Brunel, esq., the engineer of the Thames Tunnel Company.
16 pp. London, printed by Teape, 1828
A.

3885 The third report from the select committee on the public income and expenditure of the United Kingdom, examined and answered by a civil servant of the crown.
36 pp. London, J. Ridgway, 1828
T.

3886 [THOMPSON, Thomas Perronet.] A catechism on the corn laws; with a list of fallacies and the answers. By a member of the University of Cambridge.
128 pp. 4th ed. London, J. Ridgway, 1828
P.

3887 TRIMMER, Joshua Kirby. Practical observations on the improvement of British fine wool, and the national advantages of the arable system of sheep husbandry.
88 pp. London, J. Ridgway, 1828
T.

3888 VYVYAN, Sir Richard. The promissory note question, considered as a case between the great capitalist and the daily labourer, or the monied interest and the nation at large.
table of contents. 76 pp. London, J. Nicholls, 1828
A., P.

3889 WALLER, Sir Charles Townshend, bart. Letters containing a plan for the general relief of the poor of Ireland, addressed to the members of the house of commons.
16 pp. Bath, Bennett, 1828
A.

1829

3890 Annual report of the stranger's friend society, founded in 1790 for visiting and relieving distressed strangers, and the resident sick poor, at their habitations, in Dublin and its vicinity; with an account of some of the cases relieved, and a list of subscribers, for 1828
24 pp. Dublin, R. Napper, 1829
A., N.

3891 BADNALL, Richard. Mr. Badnall's reply to the remarks of Mr. Ballance on his recent publication, entitled 'A view of the silk trade': containing most accurate information on the real comparative state of the silk manufacture of Great Britain and France.
tables. appendices. 46 pp. London, Effingham Wilson, 1829
P.

3892 BALLANCE, John. A brief reply to the second pamphlet of Mr. R. Badnall, jun., on the silk trade; addressed to the rt. hon. W. Vesey Fitzgerald, &c. &c. &c.
tables. 28 pp. London, J. M. Richardson, 1829
P.

3893 ——. Remarks on some of the important errors contained in Mr. Badnall's pamphlet entitled 'A view of the silk trade'.
tables. 40 pp. London, J. M. Richardson [etc.], 1829
P., T.

3894 Brief statement of facts connected with the scientific pursuits of the late Charles Broderip, esq., more especially as they regarded the improvement of steam navigation.
62 pp. London, W. Mason, 1829
A.

3895 BRUCE, W. Poor rates for Ireland.
24 pp. London, Thomas, 1829
N.
Includes also his 'Poor rates the panacea for Ireland', first publ. 1826. See 3804.

3896 BURGESS, Henry. A petition to the honourable the commons house of parliament, to render manifest the errors, the injustice and the dangers of the measures of parliament respecting currency and bankers; suggesting more just and practicable arrangements, and praying for an investigation: accompanied with illustrations and reflections, which shew the utter impracticability of perfecting the present policy and the danger of further attempts to enforce that policy.
152 pp. London, J. Ridgway [etc.], 1829
N., P.

3897 CARTWELL, J. A treatise on tolls and customs, by J. Cartwell, esq., edited by W. C. McDermott.
182 pp. 2nd ed. Dublin, Cumming, 1829
A.

3898 A christian view of the present state of the country, its causes and consequences.
table. 92 pp. London, J. Hatchard, 1829
T.

3899 Christianity and slavery. An address to the British clergy, showing that the two are most improperly blended as a controversial question.
44 pp. London, Charles Tilt, 1829
T.

3900 COFFEY, Andrew. A view of the past and present state of the works for supplying Dublin with water.
36 pp. Dublin, A. B. King, 1829

A., S.

3901 COGHLAN, John Armstrong. Prospectus of plan of providing for the support of superannuated clergymen—and the widows and orphans of deceased clergymen.
tables. 12 pp. Dublin, Underwood, 1829

N.

3902 [CRAWFURD, John.] An inquiry into some of the principal monopolies of the East India Company.
appendix. 82 pp. London, J. Ridgway, 1829

P.

3903 [——.] A view of the present state and future prospects of the free trade and colonisation of India.
108 pp. 2nd ed. enlarged. London, J. Ridgway [etc.], 1829

A., P., T.

3904 DALY, Robert. A letter to the editor of the Christian Examiner on the subject of a legal provision for the poor of Ireland.
20 pp. Dublin, Curry, 1829

A., N., T.

3905 DANCE, Henry. Remarks on the practical effect of imprisonment for debt, and on the law of insolvency.
16 pp. London, J. Ridgway, 1829

T.

3906 DARNLEY, John Bligh, 4th earl of. Speech of the Rt. Hon. the earl of Darnley on the state of the poor in Ireland delivered in the house of lords on Thursday, May 1st, 1828, on his lordship's motion for a select committee to inquire into the distressed state of the people of that country.
appendix. 56 pp. London, J. Hatchard, 1829

A., K.

3907 EDE, John. Reflections on the employment, wages, and condition of the poor, showing the fallacy and injustice of recommending emigration, as a remedy for the lamentable state of the English labourer, and tracing the evils of insufficient wages and ruinous poor's rates to their natural causes; particularly addressed and recommended to parish officers and landowners, and to all those who take an interest in the good management of the poor.
44 pp. London, J. M. Richardson [etc.], 1829

T.

3908 Enquiries relating to negro emancipation.
100 pp. London, J. Hatchard, 1829

K., T.

3909 Essay on currency; being a serious research into the various bearings and morbid views of the subject. By an old practitioner.
44 pp. London, J. M. Richardson, 1829

N., T.

3910 EVANS, G. H. Remarks on the policy of introducing the system of poor rates into Ireland, addressed to the society for the improvement of that country.
48 pp. London, J. Ridgway, 1829

A.

3911 Facts relating to Chinese commerce; in a letter from a British resident in China to his friend in England.
74 pp. London, J. M. Richardson, 1829

T.

3912 GRIFFITH, Richard. Geological and mining surveys of the coal districts of the counties of Tyrone and Antrim in Ireland.
table of contents. tables. plans. 88 pp. Dublin, R. Graisberry, 1829

A.

3913 HAWORTH, B. A dissertation on the English poor, stating the advantages of education with a plan for the gradual abolition of the poor laws.
104 pp. London, J. Ridgway, 1829

A., T.

3914 HEATHFIELD, Richard. Thoughts on the liquidation of the public debt, and on the relief of the country from the distress incident to a population exceeding the demand for labour.
appendices. 36 pp. London, Longman, Rees, Orme, Brown and Green, [1829?]

T.

3915 [HICKEY, William.] Hints originally intended for the small farmers of the county of Wexford, but suited to the circumstances of many parts of Ireland. By Mr. Martin Doyle.
plan. table of contents. tables. 106 pp. 2nd ed. Dublin, W. Curry, 1829

A.

3916 HORTON, Sir Robert John Wilmot. The causes & remedies of pauperism in the United Kingdom considered: Part 1. Being a defence of the principles & conduct of the emigration committee, against the charges of Mr. Sadler.
158 pp. London, John Murray, 1829.

L., N., T.

3917 JACKSON, John. A treatise on the capability of our eastern possessions to produce those articles of consumption, and raw material for British manufacture, for which we chiefly depend on foreign nations; and the incalculable advantages of a free trade to and settlement in India, to all classes of his majesty's subjects.
tables. appendix. 38 pp. London, Smith, Elder, 1829

T.

3918 KINAHAN, Daniel. An outline of a plan for relieving the poor of Ireland, by an assessment on property.
30 pp. Dublin, Milliken, 1829

A., N.

3919 KIRCHOFF, Chevalier T. R. L. de. Memoire on the colonies of beneficence of Fredericks Oord and Wortel, in the Kingdom of the Netherlands.
Translated from the French by the Revd. Edward Groves, secretary to the society for the improvement of Ireland.
26 pp. Dublin, 1829

A.

3920 LAMBERT, Joseph. Observations on the rural affairs of Ireland or a practical treatise on farming, planting &

gardening adapted to the circumstance, resources, soil and climate of the country; including some remarks on the reclaiming of bogs and wastes, and a few hints on ornamental gardening. tables of contents. 352 pp. Dublin, W. Curry jr., 1829

A.

3921 LAUDERDALE, James Maitland, 8th earl of. Three letters to the duke of Wellington, on the fourth report of the select committee of the house of commons, appointed in 1828 to enquire into the public income and expenditure of the United Kingdom; in which the nature and tendency of a sinking fund is investigated, and the fallacy of the reasoning by which it has been recommended to public favour is explained. appendix. 136 pp. London, J. Murray, 1829

T.

3922 A letter to the duke of Wellington, on the expediency of an income tax. By a wholesale grocer.
16 pp. London, Effingham Wilson, 1829

T.

3923 LINCOLN, Levi. Speech of his excellency Levi Lincoln, before the honourable council, and both branches of the legislature, May 30, 1829. [Senate no. 1.]
22 pp. Boston, True & Greene, 1829

Q.

On railways.

3924 MACGREGOR, John. Observations on emigration to British America.
appendix with tables. 58 pp. London, Longman, Rees, Orme, Brown and Green, 1829

K.

3925 MACKONOCHIE, Alexander. Thoughts on the present state and future commercial policy of the country; with the plan of a periodical work, to be confined exclusively to commercial subjects.
22 pp. London, J. M. Richardson, 1829

P.

3926 MALTHUS, Thomas Robert. The measure of value stated and illustrated, with an application of it to the alterations in the value of the English currency since 1790.
tables. 88 pp. London, John Murray, 1829

K.

3927 Mining company of Ireland. Report from the board of directors of the mining company of Ireland to the proprietary for the half year ending 1st December, 1828.
14 pp. Dublin, J. Chambers, 1829

A.

3928 Mining company of Ireland. Report...for the half year ending 1st June, 1829.
16 pp. Dublin, J. Chambers, 1829

A.

3929 MONTEATH, Robert. A new and easy system of draining and reclaiming the bogs and marshes of Ireland: with plans for improving wastelands in general, to which are added miscellaneous reports of recent surveys of woods and plantations; also an equitable method of valuing woods, plantations, and timber trees of all ages, when sold with estates.
plates. table of contents, 258 pp. Edinburgh, W. Blackwood, [etc.], 1829

A.

3930 MOORE, Richard. The case of the currency with its remedy.
192 pp. London, J. Ridgway, 1829

T.

3931 ——. Outline of a plan for raising provincial capital, and establishing public country banks, in addition to the existing country banks, to meet the expenses of a gold and sterling mint note currency.
68 pp. London, Ridgways, 1829

T.

3932 On the territorial government and commerce of the East India Company.
tables. 48 pp. London, J. Murray, 1829

K., T.

3933 Outlines of a plan for the establishment of an agricultural model school in the province of Munster, recommended by the London Irish Relief Committee of 1822, who appropriated three thousand pounds of their remaining funds, to aid in carrying this object into effect. Approved of by the committee appointed by the trustees for the encouragement of industry in the county of Cork.
tables. appendix. 50 pp. Cork, Edwards and Savage, 1829

U.

3934 PAGE, Frederick. The principle of the English poor laws, illustrated and defended by an historical view of indigence in civil society etc.
148 pp. 2nd ed. London, Longman, Rees, Orme, Brown & Green, Dublin, R. Milliken, 1829

A.

See 4083.

3935 PLAYFAIR, Henry William. Remarks on the East India Company's charter, as connected with the interests of this country, and the general welfare of India.
tables. 88 pp. London, Lupton Relfe, 1829

K., T.

3936 The present degraded state of trade, its cause and effects considered; in a letter to the right hon. W. F. Vesey Fitzgerald, president of the board of trade, &c. &c. &c. By Veritas.
24 pp. London, J. Bowen, 1829

P., T.

3937 The protestant colonization society of Ireland.
4 pp. Dublin, Harman, 1829

A.

Report of a meeting held 18th December, 1829. The society's object was the reclamation and settlement of waste lands. Cf. William Jacob's pamphlet, 3833 above.

3938 PROUT, John. A practical view of the silk trade, embracing a faithful account of the result of the measures enacted in 1824, for the encouragement of that manufacture.
tables. 68 pp. Macclesfield,J. Swinnerton, 1829

P.

3939 Reform of the bankrupt court. By a commissioner of bankrupts.
58 pp. London, Stevens, 1829

T.

3940 Report of the committee of the Carrickfergus Mendicity association, for the year ending May the 1st, 1829.
8 pp. no t.p. Appendix. [1829?]

M.

3941 Report of the council of the chamber of commerce of Dublin to the annual assembly of the members of the associa‧tion, held on the 4th of March, 1829.
appendix. 52 pp. Dublin, Bentham & Hardy, 1829

A.

3942 Report of the proceedings at Liverpool, connected with Mr. Buckingham's lectures on the trade to India and China. Compiled for the Oriental Herald.
48 pp. London, Lewer, 1829

A.

3943 Report of the sub-committee to whom was referred the superintendent's report of 3rd December, 1828, to report whether they would recommend any, and what alterations in the rates and modes of payment, and distribution of rations.
14 pp. Dublin, Walsh, 1829

A.

Refers to the Dublin Mendicity Institution.

3944 The report on the taxation of Dublin and the petition to parliament adopted at a general meeting of the inhabitants held at the royal exchange on the 24th March 1829, the Rt. Hon. the Lord Mayor in the chair; to which are added a preface, appendices and tables, proving and illustrating the several allegations and complaints therein contained.
appendices. tables. 60 pp. Dublin, Porteous, 1829

A., N.

3945 A review of the arguments and allegations which have been offered to parliament against the renewal of the East-India Company's charter.
tables. 74 pp. London, Effingham Wilson, 1829

T.

3946 Reflections on the importance of the domestic growth of tobacco, with directions for its culture. By the editor of the late Irish Farmers' Journal.
26 pp. Dublin, J. Porter, 1829

A.

3947 Rules and regulations to be observed and kept by the Friendly Brothers of St. Joseph's Society in the city of Dublin.
12 pp. Dublin, 1829

A.

3948 SAINTSBURY, George. East India slavery. Second edition, with an appendix.
52 pp. London, Charles Tilt, 1829

T.

3949 SCROPE, George Julius Duncombe Poulett. Plea for the abolition of slavery in England, as produced by an illegal abuse of the poor law, common in the southern counties.
48 pp. London, J. Ridgway, 1829

A., T.

3950 SENIOR, Nassau William. Two lectures on population, delivered before the University of Oxford in Easter term, 1828,

by Nassau William Senior, late Fellow of Magdalen College, A.M., professor of political economy. To which is added, a correspondence between the author and the Rev. T. R. Malthus.
appendix, 94 pp. London, Saunders and Otley, 1829

T.

3951 SHERLEY, Frederick. Practical observations on the poor laws, describing their demoralizing tendency on the habits of the poor, with a suitable remedy suggested.
tables. appendix. 44 pp. London, W. R. Dyson, 1829

T.

3952 SINCLAIR, Sir John, bart. Thoughts on currency, and the means of promoting national prosperity, by the adoption of 'an improved circulation' founded on the security of solid property and adapted to the wants and necessities of the country. With an appendix 'on the doctrines of free trade'. Earnestly submitted to the immediate consideration of the government and public.
table of contents. tables. appendix. 152 pp. London, Hatchard & Son [etc.], 1829

N., P.

3953 Society for the improvement of Ireland.
no t.p. 8 pp. Dublin, printed by A. Thom, 1829

A.

3954 State of the poor, with the outline of the plan of a society for bettering their condition. Extracted from 'The Philanthropist'.
14 pp. Dublin, R. & A. Taylor, 1829

A.

3955 TAZEWELL, Littleton Waller. A review of the negociations between the United States of America and Great Britain, respecting the commerce of the two countries, and more especially concerning the trade of the former with the West Indies.
134 pp. London, J. Murray, 1829

K.

3956 The tenth report of the society, instituted in Edinburgh on 25th January, 1813, for the suppression of beggars, for the relief of occasional distress and for the encouragement of industry among the poor.
34 pp. Edinburgh, A. Smellie, 1829

A.

3957 [THOMPSON, Thomas Perronet.] Catechism on the corn laws; with a list of fallacies and the answers. By a member of the University of Cambridge. Thirteenth edition. Revised and corrected.
64 pp. London, Robert Heward [etc.], 1829

K., L., U.

3958 [———.] Catechism on the corn laws with a list of fallacies and the answers. Fourteenth edition, revised and corrected. To which is added the article on free trade, from the Westminster Review, No. XXIII. With a collection of objections and the answers. By a member of the University of Cambridge.
80 pp. London, Robert Heward, 1829

A., N.

3959 [——.] The true theory of rent, in opposition to Mr. Ricardo and others, being an exposition of fallacies on rent, tithes etc., in the form of a review of Mr. Mill's elements of political economy. By the author of the catechism on the corn laws.
32 pp. 4th ed. London, proprietors of Westminster Review, 1829

K.

——. 32 pp. 5th ed. London, proprietors of Westminster Review, 1829

A.

3960 Thoughts explanatory of the pressure experienced by the British agriculturist and manufacturer. By one of both vocations.
diag. 48 pp. London, T. Cadell, 1829

K., T.

3961 TOOKE, Thomas. A letter to lord Grenville on the effects ascribed to the resumption of cash payments on the value of the currency.
tables. appendix. 136 pp. London, J. Murray, 1829

K., T.

3962 ——. On the currency in connexion with the corn trade; and on the corn laws. To which is added a postscript on the present commercial stagnation.
tables. appendix. 122 pp. London, J. Murray, 1829

P., T.

——. 122 pp. 2nd. ed. London, J. Murray, 1829

K.

3963 TUNNARD, Charles Keightley. Employment of the poor. An address to the grand jury of the hundreds of Kirton and Skirbeck, in the parts of Holland, in the county of Lincoln, at the general quarter sessions of the peace, held at Boston, October 20th, 1829
16 pp. Boston, John Noble, 1829

T.

3964 WEDDERBURN, Sir James W., bart. A reply to Mr. Gally Knight's letter to the earl of Aberdeen, on the foreign policy of England; with remarks upon the present state of the nation.
58 pp. London, C. J. G. and F. Rivington, [1829?]

K.

3965 WESTERN, Charles Callis Western, 1st baron. A letter on the present distress of the country, addressed to his constituents.
16 pp. Chelmsford, Meggy and Chalk, 1829

A.

3966 WHITE, John Meadows. Some remarks on the statute law affecting parish apprentices, with regulations applicable to local districts and parishes, for allotting and placing out poor children, in conformity to the 43 Eliz. c. 2, and subsequent statutes.
tables. appendix. 108 pp. Halesworth, the author, 1829

T.

1830

3967 Cultivation of the grasses best suited to Ireland with the quantity and variety of seed to be sown.
table of contents. illustrations. 34 pp. Dublin, 'Farmer's Gazette', [183?]

A.

3968 First report of the committee of the Limerick Board of Trade, appointed to inquire into the present state and prospects of Irish manufactures, especially those carried on in Limerick, and its vicinity.
table. 24 pp. Limerick, Browne, [183?]

N.

3969 A letter to the rt. hon. lord Althorp, chancellor of the exchequer, etc., etc., on the subject of the duty on printed cottons. By a calico printer.
table. appendix. 48 pp. London, J. Ridgway, Manchester, T. Forrest, [183?]

T.

3970 Political calculations.
24 pp. n.p. [183?]

A.

Attack on landlords, written in the form of a dialogue; ends 'Well, my friend Eight-Seven, for the present adieu.' See 3980.

3971 Poor laws the panacea for Ireland.
16 pp. London, Baldwin, Cradock & Joy, [183?]

A.

3972 PURCELL, Peter. The Irish poor law bill and an agricultural substitute.
2 pp. (broadsheet) Dublin, N. Walsh, [183?]

A.

3973 The tea trade. A full and accurate report of the extraordinary proceedings at the East India House, on the commencement of the March sale. Containing also copies of the correspondence between the East India Company and the committee of the tea trade; together with the correspondence of the committee of wholesale tea-dealers with Government and the East India Company, relative to the repeal of the new scale of tea duties, and other matters of interest to the tea trade.
44 pp. London, Effingham Wilson, [183?]

K.

3974 WHITLAW, Charles. A short review of the causes and effects of the present distress, and its dreadful consequences on the labouring, manufacturing and commercial classes.
52 pp. London, Effingham Wilson, [183?]

T.

3975 Absenteeism: the union considered, after 30 years. In two chapters. By J. C. Esq.
16 pp. n.p. 1830

A.

3976 An abstract of the British West Indian statutes, for the protection and government of slaves.
table. 52 pp. London, J. Ridgway, 1830

T.

3977 An address to the men of Hawkhurst, (equally applicable to the men of other parishes) on their riotous acts and purposes.
12 pp. 2nd ed. London, Longman, Rees, Orme, Brown and Green, 1830
T.

3978 Alarming state of the nation considered; the evil traced to its source, and remedies pointed out. By a country gentleman.
107 pp. London, J. Ridgway, 1830.
T.

3979 Annual report of the Strangers Friend Society (founded in 1790) for visiting and relieving distressed strangers and the resident sick poor in Dublin and its vicinity, with an account of some of the cases relieved, and list of subscribers for 1829.
24 pp. Dublin, printed by R. Napper, 1830
A.

3980 An antidote to revolution or a practical comment on the creation of privilege for quadrating the principles of consumption with production. By Eight-Seven.
16 pp. Dublin, M. Goodwin, 1830
A., N., U.
Scheme for turning labourers into small farmers.

3981 ASSER, John. Communications to T. G. Bramston, esq., M.P. and members of both houses, for preventing frauds to the manufacturers and growers of wheat.
table. 8 pp. London, the author, 1830
K.

3982 BADNALL, Richard. Letter to the lords and commons, on the present commercial and agricultural condition of Great Britain.
200 pp. London, Whittaker, Treacher & Co. [etc.], 1830
K., T.

3983 BAINES, Sir Edward. On the moral influence of free trade, and its effects on the prosperity of nations: a paper read before the Leeds philosophical and literary society, on the 19th February, 1830.
56 pp. London, Ridgway, 1830
P.

3984 BARNES, Ralph. A letter to Sir Thomas Dyke Acland, baronet, on the Tithe Composition Bill.
74 pp. Exeter, Roberts, 1830
A.

3985 BATTERSBY, W. J. Repeal or ruin for Ireland: or a speech delivered in the royal exchange on Thursday, the 18th November, 1830 at a most numerous meeting of the bookbinders of Dublin, to petition for the repeal of the union, by their chairman, Mr. W. J. Battersby: to which are added, the resolutions, proceedings, and petitions of the meeting.
36 pp. Dublin, printed by J. Byrn, 1830
A.

3986 BENTHAM, Sir Samuel. Financial reform scrutinized, in a letter to Sir Henry Parnell, bart., M.P.
82 pp. London, J. Hatchard, 1830
P., T.

3987 BENWELL, James B. New formulae in the valuation of annuities on lives, etc., and in deducing the rate of interest. Also supplemental tables, adapted to estates certain and lifehold, with their practical applications illustrated.
tables. 62 pp. London, J. M. Richardson, 1830
T.

3988 BRENTON, Edward Pelham. A letter to the committee of management of the society for the suppression of mendicity, in Red Lion Square.
48 pp. London, C. Rice, 1830
T.

3989 BRICKWOOD, John. Further remarks on the superiority of the new five per cent stock.
tables. 16 pp. London, J. M. Richardson, 1830
P.

3990 ——. A plan for redeeming the new four per cents. Humbly suggested to the consideration of his majesty's government.
tables. 48 pp. London, printed by Marchant, 1830
T.

3991 BRIGGS, John. The present land-tax in India considered as a measure of finance in order to show its effects on the government and people of that country, and on the commerce of Great Britain. In 3 parts.
358 pp. London, Longman, Rees, Orme, Brown & Green, 1830
N.

3992 British colonial slavery, compared with that of pagan antiquity.
tables. appendix. 72 pp. London, J. Ridgway, 1830
T.

3993 BUCKINGHAM, James Silk. Explanatory report on the plan and object of Mr. Buckingham's lectures on the oriental world, preceded by a sketch of his life, travels and writings, and on the proceedings on the East India monopoly, during the past year.
table of contents. table. 40 pp. London, Hurst, Chance, 1830
A.

3994 ——. History of the public proceedings on the question of the East India monopoly, during the past year. With an outline of Mr. Buckingham's extempore descriptions of the oriental world.
80 pp. London, Hurst, Chance, 1830
T.

3995 BURGES, G. An address to the misguided poor of the disturbed districts throughout the kingdom.
42 pp. London, Rivingtons, 1830
T.

3996 A call to women of all ranks in the British Empire, on the subject of the national debt.
66 pp. London, Smith Elder, 1830
T.

3997 Causes and cure of the present distress.
30 pp. London, J. Ridgway, 1830
T.

3998 CAYLEY, Edward Stillingfleet. On commercial economy, in six essays; viz. machinery, accumulation of capital, production, consumption, currency, and free trade.
tables. 268 pp. London, J. Ridgway, 1830
T.

3999 Chinese monopoly examined.
tables. appendix with tables. 100 pp. London, J. Ridgway, 1830
T.

4000 CLISSOLD, Henry. Prospectus of a central national institution of home colonies, designed to instruct and employ distressed unoccupied poor on waste lands in spade husbandry.
12 pp. London, C. J. G. & F. Rivington, 1830
T.

4001 Considerations on some of the more popular mistakes and misrepresentations on the nature, extent, and circumstances of church property in a letter to a friend. By the incumbent of a country parish.
32 pp. London, J. Cochran and J. M. Key [etc.], 1830
T.

4002 COVENTRY, George. On the revenues of the church of England, exhibiting the rise and progress of ecclesiastical taxation.
214 pp. London, E. Wilson, 1830
A.

4003 Defence of the licensed victuallers and retail dealers in malt liquor and spirits. By a member of a county committee.
36 pp. London, J. Owen, 1830
T.

4004 A dispassionate appeal to the legislature, magistrates and clergy, of the United Kingdom, against Mr. Calcraft's proposed bill, for throwing open the retail trade in malt liquor. By a county magistrate.
36 pp. London, Effingham Wilson, 1830
T.

4005 DONNELL, J. Observations concerning the working class of the Irish population.
18 pp. Dublin, W. Underwood, 1830
U.

4006 ELGIN, Thomas Bruce, 7th earl of. View of the present state of pauperism in Scotland.
appendix. 82 pp. London, J. Murray, 1830
T.

4007 ELLIS, Henry. A series of letters on the East India question. Addressed to the members of the two houses of parliament. Letter I.
appendices. 82 pp. second edition. London, J. Murray, 1830
K., T.

4008 An enquiry as to the practicability and policy of reducing the duties on malt and beer, and increasing those on British spirits. With suggestions for an equitable adjustment of the land tax.
tables. 52 pp. London, J. Ridgway, 1830
T.

4009 EVELYN, John. Co-operation. An address to the labouring classes, on the plans to be pursued and the errors to be avoided in conducting trading unions.
28 pp. London, J. Souter, 1830
K., T.

4010 An examination of the currency question, and of the project for altering the standard of value.
72 pp. London, John Murray, 1830
T.
Originally published in the Quarterly Review of April, 1822.

4011 FAIRFAX, ——. Wrongs of man: in a series of observations on taxes, tithes, and trinity, national debt, church rates, poor rates, and poor laws, with other miscellanies.
80 pp. Windsor, the author, 1830
T.

4012 FARISH, William Milner. A plan for immediately ameliorating the present distressed condition of the agricultural poor, and permanently improving their moral character: contained in a letter addressed to the right hon. viscount Melbourne, secretary of state for the home department.
appendices. 14 pp. London, C. and J. Rivington, [1830]
T.

4013 FEILD, Edward. An address on the state of the country, read to the inhabitants of Kidlington, in the parish schoolroom, Nov. 28, 1830.
22 pp. 2nd ed. Oxford, J. Parker, London, C. J. G. & F. Rivington, 1830
T.

4014 A few words in a country village.
22 pp. Dorking, Edward Langley, 1830
T.

4015 A few words on the licensing system, and the proposed unlimited increase of public houses.
32 pp. London, Chapman and Hall, Richmond, F. H. Wall, 1830
T.

4016 FLOOD, Henry. Poor laws. Arguments against a provision for paupers if it be parochial or perpetual.
16 pp. Dublin, P. D. Hardy, 1830
A.

4017 FORMAN, Walter. A letter to Mr. Cobbett, in refutation of his promulgated opinions, respecting the consequence of a contraction of the currency.
30 pp. London, Longman, Rees, Orme, Brown, and Green, Shepton Mallet, Wason and Foxwell, 1830
T.

4018 ——. The present commercial distress traced up to the true cause; and the best, if not the only, means of removing it pointed out. In seven letters, addressed to the editor of the Times.
40 pp. London, Longman, Rees, Orme, Brown, and Green, Shepton Mallet, Wason and Foxwell, 1830
T.
The letters were not published in *The Times*.

4019 FORSYTH, Robert. Political fragments.
table of contents. 228 pp. Edinburgh, W. Blackwood, [etc.],
1830
                          A.

4020 GREGSON, Henry. Suggestions for improving the condition of the industrious classes, by establishing friendly
societies and savings' banks, in co-operation with each other;
accompanied by a set of rules and regulations for each; and
also by abstracts from the two last acts of parliament which
regulate the same.
tables. appendix. 194 pp. London, J. Hatchard, 1830
                        K., T.

4021 GRIERSON, George A. The circumstances of Ireland
considered with reference to the question of the poor laws.
tables. 66 pp. London, J. Ridgway, Dublin, Moore Tims, 1830
                        A., N.

4022 HALIDAY, Charles. An inquiry into the influence of
the excessive use of spiritous liquors in producing crime,
disease and poverty in Ireland, and into the causes which have
tended to render malt liquor the more general drink of the
labouring classes of England.
table of contents. 134 pp. Dublin, R. Milliken, [etc.], 1830
                          A.

4023 Have slave-holders any right to be compensated on
being deprived of the power to continue to steal men's personal liberty?
12 pp. Dublin, R. Webb, 1830
                          A.

4024 [HEYWOOD, T.] An enquiry into the impediments to
a free trade with the peninsula of India.
48 pp. London, T. Rodd, 1830
                          T.

4025 [HICKEY, William.] Hints addressed to the small-
holders and peasantry of Ireland on road-making and on
ventilation. By Martin Doyle.
90 pp. Dublin, Wm. Curry jr., 1830
                        A., N.

4026 [——] Hints to small holders on planting and on
cattle, &c. &c. By Martin Doyle.
94 pp. illustr. Dublin, William Curry jr., 1830
                      A., RM., T.

4027 [——.] Irish cottagers. By Martin Doyle.
table of contents. 148 pp. Dublin, Wm. Curry, jr., 1830
                          A.

4028 HILL, Adam. A pamphlet containing reflections upon
subjects suited to the nature of the present times.
27 pp. Belfast, H. Clark, 1830
                          B.

4029 Hints from a hermit; or, plain politics for plain people.
72 pp. London, Effingham Wilson, 1830
                          T.

4030 Hints on emigration to the new settlement on the Swan
and Canning rivers on the west coast of Australia. Fourth
edition.
tables. map. plan. appendix. 98 pp. London, J. Cross, 1830
                          K.

4031 Hints on licensing publicans.
tables. 29 pp. London, G. Cowie, 1830
                          T.

4032 HODGSON, John. Proposed improvements in friendly
societies, upon the Southwell system or any other similar to
it, by the introduction into them of an 'early pay plan',
adopted by a 'society', called 'the upper division of the lath
of Scray friendly society', established at Sittingbourne in
and for the country [sic] of Kent.
tables. appendix. 58 pp. London, Rivingtons, [1830]
                        K., T.

4033 HORTON, Sir Robert John Wilmot. An enquiry into
the causes and remedies of pauperism. First Series. Containing correspondence with C. Poulett Thomson, esq. M.P. upon
the conditions under which colonization would be justifiable
as a national measure.
36 pp. London, E. Lloyd, 1830
                        N., P., T.

4034 ——. Causes and remedies of pauperism. Second
series. Containing correspondence with M. Duchatel, author
of an essay on charity; with an explanatory preface.
46 pp. London, E. Lloyd, 1830
                        N., P., T.

4035 ——. An inquiry into the causes and remedies of
pauperism. Third series. Containing letters to Sir Francis
Burdett, bt., M.P. upon pauperism in Ireland.
90 pp. London, E. Lloyd, 1830
                        N., P., T.

4036 ——. Causes and remedies of pauperism. Fourth
series. Explanation of Mr. Wilmot Horton's bill, in a letter
and queries addressed to N. W. Senior esq., with his answers:
Dedicated to the rate-payers of England and Wales.
tables. appendix. 140 pp. London, E. Lloyd, 1830
                          N.

4037 ——. Correspondence between the Right Honourable
R. Wilmot Horton and a select class of the members of the
London Mechanics' Institution, formed for investigating the
most efficient remedies for the present distress among the
labouring classes in the United Kingdom; together with the
resolutions unanimously adopted by the class. Also a letter
from the right hon. R. Wilmot Horton to Dr. Birkbeck,
president of the institution: and his answer.
table of contents. 22 pp. London, Baldwin & Cradock, 1830
                          N.

4038 The humble petition of the beggars of Ireland. With
notes.
42 pp. Liverpool, Wright, 1830
                          A.

4039 HUME, Joseph. Copy of a letter received by the ballast
master of the corporation for preserving and improving the
Port of Dublin from Joseph Hume, esq., M.P., chairman of a
select committee on lighthouses; with reply thereto.
16 pp. Dublin, P. D. Hardy, 1830
                          A.

4040 An inquiry into the causes of the long-continued stationary condition of India and its inhabitants; with a brief

examination of the leading principles of two of the most approved revenue systems of British India. By a civil servant of the Honourable East India Company.
appendix. 138 pp. London, Parbury, Allen, 1830
K., T.

4041 Instructions for establishing friendly institutions upon the improved principle, and in conformity with the act.
tables. 16 pp. 2nd ed. London, Simpkin and Marshall, 1830
T.

4042 Ireland in 1829; or, the first year's administration of the duke of Northumberland. By the author of 'A sketch of the Marquis of Anglesey's administration', of which it forms a continuation.
50 pp. Dublin, Webb [etc.], 1830
A.

4043 JAGO, Robert Howlett. A letter to Thomas Greene, esq., M.P. on his bill for the commutation of tithes into corn rents. Revised and enlarged from the letter published in 'The Times' newspaper of April 14th, 1830. With a letter to the editor of 'The Times', on the remarks in his leading article, on the letter to Mr. Greene.
table. 44 pp. London, W. Joy, 1830
T.

4044 LAW, James Thomas. The poor man's garden; or, a few brief rules for regulating allotments of land to the poor, for potatoe gardens. With remarks, addressed to Mr. Malthus, Mr. Sadler, and the political economists: and a reference to the opinions of Dr. Adam Smith, in his 'Wealth of Nations'.
24 pp. 3rd ed. London, C. J. G. & F. Rivington, 1830
T.

4045 A letter to a member of the Dublin Temperance Society on the supposed value of ardent spirits in relation to national wealth, government revenue, rent and agricultural profits.
68 pp. Dublin, T. I. White, 1830
A., N.

4046 A letter to the holders of the Greek bonds; with some remarks on the official correspondence between the allied ministers and Prince Leopold. By Philogordo.
28 pp. London, Longman, Rees, Orme, Brown, & Green, 1830
T.

4047 A letter to the most honourable the marquis of Chandos. By a West Indian planter.
tables. appendix. 92 pp. London, J. Ridgway, [etc.], 1830
T.

4048 [Letter] to the rt. hon. lord Cloncurry, Lyons, Celbridge.
tables. 14 pp. [no t.p.] Limerick, R. Canter, 1830
N.
On land reclamation.

4049 Letter to Sir Henry Parnell shewing the unsoundness of the doctrines laid down in his work on financial reform and proving that free trade will eventually produce the ruin of the country. By an ultra tory.
tables. 72 pp. London, T. Cadell, 1830
N., T.

4050 A letter to the right hon. the lord mayor of the city of Dublin proposing a wholesome and improved system of poor-laws for Ireland, best calculated to ameliorate and better the condition of the people, and to encourage the industry and prosperity of the country. By Patricious.
14 pp. Dublin, printed by W. Espy, 1830
A.

4051 LIGHT, Alexander W. A plan for the amelioration of the condition of the poor of the United Kingdom (more particularly Ireland); and for their permanent establishment, by means at once simple and economical; from the adoption of which an immense expenditure would be saved to the country, and the original outlay returned, with four per cent per annum interest, in the short period of four years, from the time the plan was called into operation.
frontisp. tables. plates. 190 pp. London, Effingham Wilson, 1830
T.

4052 [LONG, Charles Edward.] Negro emancipation no philanthropy: a letter to the duke of Wellington. By a Jamaica proprietor.
54 pp. London, J. Ridgway, 1830
T.

4053 McCORMAC, Henry. An appeal on behalf of the poor; submitted to the consideration of those who take an interest in bettering their condition.
28 pp. Belfast, Archer, Hodgson & Jellett, 1830
A.

4054 ——. On the best means of improving the moral and physical condition of the working classes, being an address delivered on the opening of the first monthly scientific meetings of the Belfast Mechanics' Institute.
24 pp. London, Longman, Rees, Orme, Brown & Green, 1830
A., B., T.

4055 ——. Plan for the relief of the unemployed poor.
32 pp. Belfast, Stuart & Gregg, 1830
A., N.

4056 [McCULLOCH, John Ramsay.] Observations on the duty on sea-borne coal, and on the peculiar duties and charges on coal in the Port of London. Founded on the reports of parliamentary committees, and other official documents.
tables. 24 pp. London, Longman, Rees, Orme, Brown & Green, 1830
N.

4057 M'CULLOCH, Paddy (pseud.?). Absentee tax. (Letter to the editors of the Dublin press.)
2 pp. Dublin, 1830
A.

4058 M'DONNELL, Alexander. Rum and British spirit duties. A statement of the arguments for and against an equalization of the duties on British spirits, and West India rum.
tables. 52 pp. London, Effingham Wilson, 1830
T.

4059 Machine-breaking, and the changes occasioned by it, in the village of Turvey Down. A tale of the times, November, 1830.
38 pp. Oxford, J. Parker, and London, C. J. G. & F. Rivington, 1830

T.

4060 McKee, David. The real grievances of Ireland, with the most likely modes of redress as understood by the middle and lower orders in the north of that kingdom.
78 pp. Belfast, Simms & McIntyre, 1830

A.

4061 Macqueen, T. Potter. Thoughts and suggestions on the present condition of the country.
54 pp. London, J. Ridgway, 1830

T.

4062 MacVickar, John. Introductory lecture to a course of political economy; recently delivered at Columbia College, New York.
38 pp. London, John Miller, 1830

P.

4063 Mangles, Ross Donnelly. A brief vindication of the honourable East India Company's government of Bengal, from the attacks of Messrs. Richards & Crawfurd.
182 pp. London, J. Ridgway, 1830

T.

4064 Marriage, Joseph. Letters on the distressed state of the agricultural labourers, and suggesting a remedy, addressed to the nobility of England and other large landed proprietors.
18 pp. Chelmsford, Meggy & Chalk, 1830

A., P.

4065 Martin, Robert Montgomery. Remarks on the East India Company's administration over 100 millions of British subjects, considered in reference to its political effects on India and Great Britain.
tables. 32 pp. Dublin, Gardiner, London, Hurst, Chance, 1830

A.

4066 Mining company of Ireland. The board of directors' report for the half year ending 1st December, 1829.
12 pp. Dublin, J. Chambers, 1830

A.

4067 Mining company of Ireland. The board of directors' report for the half year ending 1st June, 1830.
8 pp. Dublin, J. Chambers, 1830

A.

4068 Morgan, Hector Davies. The expedience and method of providing assurances for the poor, and of adopting the improved constitution of friendly societies, constructed upon principles calculated to ensure their stability and prevent their insolvency and governed by regulations in conformity with the act 10 Geo. IV. c. 56. Submitted to the consideration of the bank for savings for the hundred of Hinckford in the county of Essex.
tables. appendix. 58 pp. Oxford, J. Parker, 1830

K., T.

4069 Morris, William. A demonstration that Great Britain & Ireland have resources to enrich the subjects of the state by manufacturing labour, through the medium of a free trade, which will necessarily supercede the collection of poor's rates or, if the legislature neglect that mode, the soil of the state affords means to employ all the idle poor profitably, and to enrich both the aristocracy and the revenue.
82 pp. London, Simpkin & Marshall, 1830

A.

4070 Mundell, Alexander. The principle and operation of gold and silver in coin; of paper in currency; and of gold and silver in buying and selling; stated in the shape of substantive propositions.
16 pp. London, Longman, Rees, Orme, Brown and Green, 1830

T.

4071 Naper, James Lenox William. A plan of a labour rate, submitted to the consideration of the rt. hon. Sir Henry Hardinge.
10 pp. Dublin, Hodges & Smith, 1830

A.

4072 The national debt considered as to the obligation to pay. By X.Y.Z.
appendix. 16 pp. London, Effingham Wilson, 1830

T.

4073 A new and easy introduction to the principles of political economy.
48 pp. London, Effingham Wilson, [1830?]

A.

4074 O'Brien, William Smith. Considerations relative to the renewal of the East India Company's charter.
tables. appendix. 76 pp. London, J. M. Richardson, 1830

A., N., T., U.

4075 ——. Plan for the relief of the poor in Ireland with observations on the English and Scotch poor laws, addressed to the landed proprietors of Ireland.
60 pp. London, J. M. Richardson, 1830

A., N., T.

4076 Observations on the state of the country, and on the proper policy of administration.
30 pp. London, Longman, Rees, Orme, Brown, and Green, 1830

T.

4077 Ocharik, Desh-u-Lubun, 'of Calcutta'. Letter to the author of a 'View of the present state and future prospects of the free trade and colonization of India'; or, a plain and practical review of the above important subjects.
tables. appendix. 88 pp. 2nd ed. London, Smith Elder, 1830

T.

4078 O'Connell, Daniel. Letters on the repeal of the legislative Union between Great Britain & Ireland.
34 pp. Dublin, J. Harvey, [1830]

A., N.

4079 On the injurious effects of tithe; with suggestions for its commutation. By a magistrate for the county of Somerset.
32 pp. London, Longman, Rees, Orme, Brown and Green, 1830

K., T.

4080 ORMATHWAITE, John Benn Walsh, 1st baron. Poor laws in Ireland, considered in their probable effects upon the capital, the prosperity and the progressive improvement of that country.
table of contents. 128 pp. London, J. Ridgway, 1830
A., N.

——. 128 pp. 2nd ed. London, J. Ridgway, 1830
T.

4081 OWEN, Robert. The addresses of Robert Owen, (as published in the London journals), preparatory to the development of a practical plan for the relief of all classes, without injury to any.
50 pp. London, Stephen Hunt, 1830
T.

4082 PAGE, Frederick. Observations on the state of the indigent poor in Ireland, and the existing institutions for their relief: being a sequel to 'The principle of the English poor laws illustrated and defended'.
tables in appendices. 74 pp. London, Longman, Rees, Orme, Brown and Green [etc.], Dublin, R. Milliken, 1830
T.

4083 ——. The principle of the English poor laws illustrated and defended by an historical view of indigence in civil society; with suggestions relative to their improved administration to which are added observations on the state of the indigent poor in Ireland, and the existing institutions for their relief.
216 pp. 3rd ed. London, Longman, Rees, Orme, Brown and Green, Dublin, R. Milliken, 1830
A., N.
See 3934.

4084 PETTMAN, William Robert Ashley. Resources of the United Kingdom; or, the present distresses considered; their causes and remedies pointed out; and an outline of a plan for the establishment of a national currency, that would have a fixed money value, proposed.
310 pp. London, J. Ridgway, 1830
T.

4085 PICKERING, Joseph. Emigration or no emigration; being the narrative of the author, (an English farmer) from the year 1824 to 1830; during which time he traversed the United States of America, and the British province of Canada, with a view to settle as an emigrant: containing observations on the numbers and customs of the people—the soil and climate of the countries; and a comparative statement of the advantages and disadvantages offered in the United States and Canada: thus enabling persons to form a judgment on the propriety of emigrating.
tables. appendix. 144 pp. London, Longman, Rees, Orme, Brown, and Green, 1830
T.

4086 Plan for forming parochial committees or boards, auxiliary to the managing committee of the mendicity association.
8 pp. Dublin, J. Folds, 1830
A.

4087 POPPY, Charles. Practical hints on burning clay, sods, surface soil of fallows etc. and on the employment of the poor. illustrations. 30 pp. Ipswich, King & Garnod, 1830
A.

4088 Practicability of a legislative measure for harmonizing the conflicting interests of agriculture and by this means enabling Great Britain to obtain great additional benefits from her great resources. By Eight-Seven.
18 pp. Dublin, Moore Tims, 1830
A.
Plan for settling every family who wishes it on a small acreage of land.

4089 Probable effects of the allotment system upon the agricultural labourers.
14 pp. London, C. J. G. & F. Rivington, 1830
K., T.

4090 Protestant colonies on the waste lands of Ireland.
4 pp. (no t.p.) n.p., [1830?]
N.

4091 The protestant colonisation society of Ireland.
folding sheet. 16 pp. Dublin, Bull, [1830?]
A.
Contains list of subscribers, accounts of two meetings.

4092 RANKIN, Robert. A familiar treatise on life assurance and annuities, comprising an historical sketch of the science, and of life assurance offices, with observations on the duration of human life, and other objects of interest connected with the subject: to which are appended original tables of the probabilities and expectations of life in the city of Bristol, etc.
tables in appendix. 116 pp. London, Simpkin & Marshall, [etc.], 1830
T.

4093 Remarks on free trade to China.
20 pp. London, C. J. G. & F. Rivington, 1830
K., T.

4094 Remarks on the question of again permitting the issue of one pound notes by the Bank of England, and also by country banks.
table of contents. 68 pp. London, Saunders & Otley, 1830
N., T.

4095 Report of a trial held in the court of exchequer, Ireland, on the 15th, 16th, 17th, & 18th days of December, 1829, before the hon. baron Smith and a special jury, to recover the amount of a life insurance policy, wherein William Abbott, esq., merchant was plaintiff, and Grant Allen, esq., one of the directors of the Imperial Insurance Company, was the defendant.
102 pp. Dublin, R. Milliken, 1830
A., N.

4096 Report of the Benevolent Strangers' Friend Society for the year 1829.
16 pp. Dublin, printed by N. Martin, 1830
A.

4097 Report of the committee of the Carrickfergus Mendicity Association, for the year ending May the 1st, 1830.
no t.p. appendix. 8 pp. [n.p., 1830?]
M.

4098   Report of the committee of the Commerce and Navigation of the United States. Submitted to congress February 8th, 1830.
tables. 76 pp. Washington, published, London, republished by Miller, 1830

N., P.

4099   Report of the council of the chamber of commerce of Dublin to the annual assembly of the members of the association.
44 pp. Dublin, P. D. Hardy, 1830

A.

4100   Report of the late committee together with a list of subscribers who contributed to the support of the house of industry, Belfast, for the year 1829.
18 pp. Belfast, printed by Finlay, 1830

A.

4101   Report of the mansion house relief committee, appointed at a public meeting, held on the 25th September, 1829, at the royal exchange, for the relief of the distressed manufacturers of the city of Dublin and its vicinity, the Rt. Hon. Jacob West, lord mayor, chairman.
appendices. tables. 28 pp. Dublin, A. Thom, 1830

A., N.

4102   Report on the affairs of the Arigna Iron and Coal Company.
tables. 42 pp. London, E. Justins, 1830

A.

4103   Report presented to the managing committee of the Mendicity Association of Dublin respecting the powers of levying money for the support of the poor.
18 pp. Dublin, Folds, 1830

A.

4104   The result of the change of administration; or, what the new ministry has to look to.
38 pp. London, Longman, Rees, Orme, Brown, and Green, 1830

T.

4105   The result of the pamphlets or, what the Duke of Wellington has to look to.
36 pp. London, Longman, Rees, Orme, Brown and Green, and J. Ridgway, 1830

A., K.

The pamphlets referred to were:–
  1. "The result of the General Election; or, what has the Duke of Wellington gained by the Dissolution?"
  2. "Reply to a pamphlet entitled 'What has the Duke of Wellington gained by the Dissolution?' By a Graduate of the University of Oxford." "The authors of both pamphlets are Party men and they write for Party purposes."

4106   The revenues of the Church of England not a burden on the public.
106 pp. London, J. Murray, 1830

A.

4107   Rules of the friendly society, established at Sittingbourne, in the upper division of the lath of Scray, for the county of Kent: with improvements.
tables. 56 pp. London, J. McGowan, 1830

K., T.

4108   Rules etc. of the Irish Musical Fund Society for the relief of distressed musicians, their widows and orphans.
20 pp. Dublin, Rorke, 1830

N.

4109   SADLER, Michael Thomas.   A refutation of an article in the Edinburgh Review, (No. CII) entitled 'Sadler's law of population, and disproof of human superfecundity', containing also, additional proofs of the principle enunciated in that treatise, founded on the censuses of different countries recently published.
tables. 112 pp. London, J. Murray, 1830

K., T.

4110   [SCROPE, George Julius Duncombe Poulett.]   The currency question freed from mystery, in a letter to Mr. Peel, showing how the distress may be relieved without altering the standard.
50 pp. London, James Ridgway, 1830

T.

4111   [——.]   A letter to the agriculturists of England, on the expediency of extending the poor law to Ireland. By a landowner.
24 pp. London, J. Ridgway, 1830

N.

4112   [——.]   On credit-currency, and its superiority to coin, in support of a petition for the establishment of a cheap, safe and sufficient circulating medium.
table of contents. 92 pp. London, J. Murray, 1830

N., T.

4113   SENIOR, Nassau William.   Three lectures on the cost of obtaining money, and on some effects of private and government paper money; delivered before the University of Oxford, in Trinity Term, 1829.
106 pp. London, J. Murray, 1830

T.

4114   ——.   Three lectures on the rate of wages, delivered before the University of Oxford, in Easter Term, 1830. With a preface on the causes and remedies of the present disturbances.
82 pp. London, J. Murray, 1830

K., N., T.

4115   ——.   Three lectures on the transmission of precious metals from country to country, and the mercantile theory of wealth. Delivered before the University of Oxford, in June, 1827.
100 pp. 2d. ed. London, J. Murray, 1830

A.

4116   SLADE, John.   Notices on the British trade to the port of Canton; with some translations of Chinese official papers relative to that trade, &c. &c. &c.
108 pp. London, Smith, Elder, 1830

T.

4117 SOLLY, Edward. The present distress in relation to the theory of money.
16 pp. London, J. Ridgway, 1830
A., T.

4118 A statement of the management of the Farnham estates.
table. illustrations. 56 pp. Dublin, Wm. Curry, jr., 1830
A., N.

4119 Statement on behalf of the manufacturers of Ireland shewing that the existence of the present rate of duty on the importation of coal into Ireland is a violation of the treaty of union between Great Britain and Ireland.
third edition. appendices. 28 pp. Dublin, Joseph Blundell, 1830
A., N., U.

4120 STAUNTON, Michael. Hints for Hardinge, being a series of political essays published originally in the Dublin Morning Register, with an appendix containing observations on the report of Mr. Spring-Rice's committee on the state of the poor in Ireland, and letters to the editors of the Times, Globe, and Courier.
table of contents. 138 pp. Dublin, the author, 1830
A., N.

4121 STRICKLAND, George. A discourse on the poor laws of England & Scotland, on the state of the poor in Ireland, and on emigration.
table of contents. 152 pp. 2d. ed. London, J. Ridgway, 1830
A.

4122 TAYLOR, James. A letter to his grace the duke of Wellington, on the currency.
appendices. 112 pp. London, John Taylor, 1830
T.

4123 TENNANT, Charles. Letter to the rt. hon. Sir George Murray—on systematic colonization.
appendix. 54 pp. London, J. Ridgway, 1830
N., T.
Has appendix 'containing the written controversy between the rt. hon. Robert Wilmot Horton and Col. Torrens, and the other members of the committee of the National Colonization Society'.

4124 [——.] A statement of the principles and objects of a proposed national society, for the cure and prevention of Pauperism, by means of a systematic colonization.
76 pp. London, J. Ridgway, 1830
N., P., T.

4125 THOMPSON, Thomas Perronet. The true theory of rent, in opposition to Mr. Ricardo and others. Being an exposition of fallacies on rent, tithes etc. In a form of a review of Mr. Mill's 'Elements of political economy'. By the author of the Catechism on the corn laws. N.B. This pamphlet was published before the Catechism on the corn laws and is in fact its groundwork and foundation.
32 pp. 7th ed. additions. London, R. Heward, 1830
N.

4126 Twelfth report of the managing committee of the association for the suppression of mendicity in Dublin for the year 1829.
100 pp. Dublin, M. Goodwin, 1830
A.

4127 TWIGG, T. Twigg's corrected list of the country-bankers of England and Wales; with the Christian and surnames of all such as take out licences for issuing promissory-notes payable on demand.
84 pp. London, T. Twigg, 1830
T.

4128 [VICARS, Richard.] Representation of the state of government slaves and apprentices in the Mauritius; with observations. By a resident, who has never possessed either land or slaves in the colony.
tables. 76 pp. London, J. Ridgway, 1830
T.

4129 WOOD, Joseph. Proposals for the immediate reduction of eight millions and a half of taxes, and the gradual liquidation of the national debt in a letter addressed to the Rt. Hon. Henry Goulburn, chancellor of the exchequer.
tables. 42 pp. London, J. Ridgway [etc.], 1830
N.

4130 A word to the white horse men. By a Berkshire magistrate.
20 pp. Oxford, J. Parker, and London, C. J. G. & F. Rivington, 1830
T.

1831

4131 Alarming distress in Ireland (letters).
4 pp. London, Gunnell & Shearman, 1831
A.

4132 ALLEN, William. A plan for benefitting [sic] the agricultural labourers, by William Allen, late of Hartley Tower & All Stretton Hall, in the county of Salop.
46 pp. London, Effingham Wilson, 1831
T.

4133 BAXTER, Stafford Stratton. Poor laws, stated and considered; the evils of the present system exposed, and a plan suggested, founded on the true principles of political economy, for placing such laws on a firm and equitable basis.
42 pp. London, Longman, Rees, Orme, Brown & Green, [etc.], 1831
N., T.

4134 Belgium in 1830.
48 pp. London, Henry Corburn and Richard Bentley, 1831
T.

4135 BENTHAM, George. Observations on the registration bill now pending before the house of commons, addressed to the commissioners on the law of real property.
appendix. 164 pp. London, J. Ridgway, 1831
T.

4136 BLAKISTON, Peyton. Hints for the improvement of the condition of the labouring classes by the Rev. Peyton Blakiston, M.A., late fellow of Emmanuel College, Cambridge.

With an appendix containing practical plans for the reduction of poor rates and for restoring the comforts and independence of the peasantry, by their own means.
appendix. 72 pp. London, Longman, Rees, Orme, Brown & Green [etc.], 1831

T.

4137 BLANE, Sir Gilbert, bart. Reflections on the present crisis of publick affairs, with an enquiry into the causes and remedies of the existing clamours, and alleged grievances, of the country, as connected with population, subsistence, wages of labourers, education etc., most respectfully submitted to both houses of parliament, on occasion of their assembling on the 18th of April, 1831, for the further consideration of the question of reform.
table of contents. 78 pp. London, J. Ridgway [etc.], 1831

A., T.

4138 BOOTH, Henry. An account of the Liverpool and Manchester railway, comprising a history of the parliamentary proceedings preparatory to the passing of the act, a description of the railway, in an excursion from Liverpool to Manchester, and a popular illustration of the mechanical principles applicable to railways, also an abstract of the expenditure from the commencement of the undertaking, with observations on the same.
plates. chart. tables. 104 pp. Liverpool, Wales & Baines, 1831

A.

4139 BRENTON, Edward Pelham. A letter to the rt. hon. R. W. Horton, shewing the impolicy, inefficacy, and ruinous consequences of emigration, and the advantages of home colonies.
appendix. 40 pp. London, C. Rice, 1831

T.

4140 Brief observations on the proposed measure for promoting the employment of the labouring classes in Ireland and suggestions for rendering the plan available to the encouragement of the Irish Fisheries. By an officer of the late board of Irish fisheries.
18 pp. Cork, Jackson, 1831

A.
Possibly by William Stanley; cf. 4952.

4141 BRIGGS, William. A letter to John Wood, esq., M.D. on the principle of taxation, as connected with the liberty of the subject.
46 pp. London, J. Ridgway, 1831

P.

4142 Bristol chamber of commerce. Report from the board of directors to the chamber, at the annual meeting held January 31st, 1831 at the Commercial Rooms, Bristol, and the resolutions consequent thereon.
tables. 18 pp. Bristol, printed by T. J. Manchee, 1831

U.

4143 British connexion and tithe property; in two letters addressed to the Roman catholic peasantry in the south of Ireland. By Reuben.
56 pp. Dublin, W. Curry, jr., 1831

A.

4144 [BROWNE, Thomas.] The parson's horn-book.
cartoons. 68 pp. London, the booksellers, 1831

A.

4145 [——.] The parson's horn-book, Part II. By the comet literary and patriotic club.
table of contents. 116 pp. Dublin, Brown & Sheehan, 1831

A.
A satire on ecclesiastical wealth and tithes, also attributed to Samuel Lover. See 4249.

4146 BUCKINGHAM, James Silk. Outlines of a new budget, for raising eighty millions, by means of a justly graduated property tax.
62 pp. London, Effingham Wilson, 1831

T.

4147 BURGES, George. Remarks on a commutation of the tithe-system.
48 pp. London, C. J. G. & F. Rivington, 1831

K., T.

4148 [BURGOYNE, Sir John Fox, bart.] Ireland in 1831. Letters on the state of Ireland.
48 pp. London, Bain, 1831

A., N., T.

4149 BURGOYNE, Montagu. A letter to the right honourable the lord Duncannon and the lords commissioners of his majesty's woods and forests; shewing the necessity of the removal of the deer from the forests of Waltham and Hainault, and also of an enclosure of parts of these forests, in order to protect his majesty's rights, preserve the timber belonging to the crown, and the crops of the farmers; to find employment and provision for the labouring poor, and above all to suppress the vice and immorality which are encouraged and sheltered by the present state of these forests.
tables. appendices. 78 pp. London, C. J. G. & F. Rivington, 1831

T.

4150 BURTON, Edward. Thoughts upon the demand for church reform.
42 pp. Oxford, J. Parker, and London, C. J. G. & F. Rivington, 1831

K.

4151 CAPPER, Charles Henry. Observations on 'Investigator's' pamphlet, relative to railways.
tables. 32 pp. London, Longman, Rees, Orme, Brown, and Green, 1831

T.
See 4232.

4152 The case of the agriculturalists considered, in connection with the commercial and manufacturing interests and free trade. By a friend to national prosperity.
appendices. 108 pp. London, J. Hatchard, 1831

P.

4153 Church of Ireland. Tithes!!! A most important dialogue between a bishop and a judge. Being a complete answer in anticipation to a reply from the redoubted champion of the

church's temporalities. The Rev. Mr. McGhee to the Rt. Revd. Doctor Doyle.
12 pp. Dublin, J. Byrne, 1831

A., N.

Appears to be a popularised version of 'The Church of Ireland, a dialogue between a bishop and a judge on tithes'. See 4168.

4154 The claims of the clergy; being a review of a pamphlet entitled 'The claims of the clergy to tithes and other church revenues, so far as they are founded on the political expediency of supporting such a body, on divine right, on history, or on the notion of unalienable property examined'. By a layman.
37 pp. London, printed for C. J. G. and F. Rivington, 1831

K., T.

4155 CLINCH, James Bernard. On the spirit, nature and effects of Irish independence, 1782, and on the act of union, 1800, with the danger of further agitating its repeal.
66 pp. Dublin, Blundell, 1831

A.

4156 CLONCURRY, Valentine Browne Lawless, 2nd baron. Suggestions on the necessity, and on the best mode of levying assessments for local purposes, in Ireland.
20 pp. Dublin, R. Milliken, 1831

K., N.

4157 COCKBURN, G. Six letters on subjects very important to England.
table of contents. 204 pp. Edinburgh, Blackwood, Tait [etc., etc.], 1831

A., N., T.

4158 CONNERY, James. The reformer; or, an infallible remedy to prevent pauperism and periodical returns of famine with other salutary measures for the support of the destitute poor, the enforcement of cleanliness, and suppression of usury, and establishing the futility of the plan of William Smith O'Brien (M.P.) to mitigate any of those grievances in Ireland.
16 pp. Cork, Jackson, 1831

N.

4159 A consideration of the population of Ireland with a view to bettering the condition of the people by means of an improvement of the agriculture of the country, in a letter to the rt. hon. lord Cloncurry; also extracts from a work entitled 'Practical hints for establishing work-farms for the employment of the poor, and as models for improving the agriculture of the country generally, by the introduction of the Flemish system of making manure', &c.
76 pp. Dublin, Joshua Porter, 1831

A.

4160 Considerations addressed to the clergy and laity, shewing the advantages of leases on corn rents, as composition for tythes, and their preferableness to a commutation of tythes for land or money payments.
8 pp. London, C. J. G. & F. Rivington, 1831

K., T.

4161 COURT, Major Henry. Tithes. Commutation versus composition: the rights of the laity, and the rights of the church, illustrated, and proved not to be the same; in a letter to the lord chancellor Brougham.
46 pp. London, J. Ridgway, 1831

T.

4162 DAVIS, Hewitt. On foreign corn importation; more particularly addressed to agriculturists, and the members of both houses of parliament.
18 pp. London, F. Waller, 1831

T.

4163 DAWSON, Edmund. An attempt to develope [sic] the causes of pauperism and distress, with a few suggestions for their removal or mitigation.
tables. 48 pp. London, Roake & Varty, 1831

T.

4164 DAWSON, W. Observations communicated to his majesty's commissioners, appointed to inquire into the law of real property, in England and Wales, on the delays and difficulties which occurred to the author in the practice of conveyancing, and, on the outline of a plan for general metropolitan registration, of deeds, wills, and judgments, proposed by those commissioners: with an appendix, comprising a plan for general provincial register offices, and for a docquet or index office, to be established in London, as a substitute for, and to answer every purpose of a general registry there.
tables. appendix. 68 pp. London, Baldwin & Cradock, [etc., etc.], 1831

T.

4165 DOOLAN, Thomas. Munster: or the memoirs of a chief constable.
78 pp. London, W. Davy, 1831

A.

4166 DOUGLAS, Sir Howard, bart. Considerations on the value and importance of the British North American provinces, and the circumstances on which depend their further prosperity, and colonial connection with Great Britain.
36 pp. London, J. Murray, 1831

T.

See 4239.

——. 42 pp. 2nd ed. London, J. Murray, 1831

K.

4167 DOUGLAS, James. The prospects of Britain.
104 pp. Edinburgh, Adam Black, London, Longman, Rees, Orme, Brown and Green, 1831

T.

4168 [DOYLE, James Warren, bishop of Kildare & Leighlin.] The church of Ireland. A dialogue between a bishop and a judge on tithes.
22 pp. Dublin, T. Reilly, 1831

A., N.

See 4153.

4169 ——. Letter to Thomas Spring Rice esq. M.P. on the establishment of a legal provision for the Irish poor, and on the nature and destination of church property.
132 pp. Dublin, R. Coyne, London, J. Ridgway, 1831

A., B., N., T.

4170 ——. The Rt. Rev. Dr. Doyle's letter on poor law in reply to Mr. Senior, of London.
12 pp. Dublin, Byrne, 1831

N.

4171 ——. The Rt. Rev. Dr. Doyle's reply to lord Farnham, relative to the observations made on him by his lordship in the house of lords.
12 pp. Dublin, J. McMullen, 1831

A., N.

4172 DUNCALF, J. The political scales; or the elements of policy; designed as a key to unlock the latent powers, and promote the wealth of England in particular; and the world in general.
120 pp. London, Baldwin and Cradock, [1831?]

T.

4173 EAGLE, William. A legal argument showing that tithes are the property of the public and of the poor.
48 pp. 2nd ed. London, Saunders & Benning, 1831

A.

——. 20 pp. 4th ed. London, Saunders & Benning, 1831

A., N.

4174 The East India question fairly stated. Comprising the views and opinions of some eminent and enlightened members of the present board of control.
56 pp. London, J. Ridgway, 1831

N.

4175 [ENDERBY, Charles.] England in 1830; being a letter to earl Grey, laying before him the conditions of the people as described by themselves in their petitions to parliament.
156 pp. London, J. Ridgway, 1831

T.

4176 ENSOR, George. Anti-union. Ireland as she ought to be.
168 pp. Newry, Morgan & Dunlop, 1831

A., N., RM.

4177 An equitable property tax: a financial speculation: and a fair rate of wages to the labouring poor. By a loyal Briton.
24 pp. London, Longman, Rees, Orme, Brown, and Green, [etc.], 1831

T.

4178 The evils political and moral arising out of the unnatural union of church and state. A letter to the right hon. lord Brougham and Vaux, lord high chancellor of Great Britain.
42 pp. London, Frederick Westley and A. H. Davis, 1831

T.

4179 FAIRBAIRN, Sir William, bart. Remarks on canal navigation, illustrative of the advantages of the use of steam, as a moving power on canals. With an appendix, containing a series of experiments, tables, &c. on which a number of proposed improvements are founded. Also, plans and descriptions of certain classes of steam boats, intended for the navigation of canals and the adjoining branches of the sea.
appendix. tables. illusts. 94 pp. London, Longman, Rees, Orme, Brown & Green, [etc., etc., 1831]

T.

4180 The Federalist; or a series of papers showing how to repeal the union so as to avoid a violent crisis, and, at the same time, secure and reconcile all interests. By a minister of peace. (Signed T.B.O.M.)
tables. 176 pp. Dublin, 1831

A.

4181 GALLATIN, Albert. Considerations on the currency and banking system of the United States.
tables. 108 pp. Philadelphia, Carey & Lea, 1831

P.

4182 GRAHAME, Thomas. A letter addressed to Nicholas Wood, esq. on that portion of Chapter IX of his treatise on railroads entitled, 'Comparative performances of motive power on canals and railroads'.
tables. 40 pp. Glasgow, John Smith, [etc., etc.], 1831

K., T.

4183 [HALLIBURTON, Sir Brenton.] Observations on the importance of the north American colonies to Great Britain. By an old inhabitant of British America.
48 pp. London, J. Murray, 1831

K., T.

4184 HANNINGTON, C. M. Registration made easy; or, a concise plan for a general register of all instruments to be made affecting land in England, without requiring even the production of any deed or instrument, by the simple additions of a date and number to every impression of stamp duty.
forms. 10 pp. London, Shackell and Carfrae, 1831

T.

4185 Has Ireland gained or lost by the union with Great Britain?
22 pp. London, J. Ridgway, 1831

T.

4186 [HICKEY, William.] An address to the landlords of Ireland, on subjects connected with the melioration of the lower classes, by Martin Doyle.
appendix. tables. 162 pp. Dublin, W. Curry, jr., [etc., etc.], 1831

T.

4187 [——.] Hints on emigration to Upper Canada; especially addressed to the lower classes in Great Britain and Ireland. By Martin Doyle.
table of contents. appendix. 112 pp. Dublin, W. Curry, jr., 1831

A., N.

4188 HILL, Waldron. Irish residence, with suggestions for its partial adoption.
60 pp. London, Longman, Rees, Orme, Brown & Green, 1831

K., T.

4189 Hints for the establishment of charitable loan funds. By F.T.
32 pp. Dublin, W. Curry, jr., 1831

A.

4190 HODGSON, John. A letter to the members of the amicable society: comprising the substance of a speech delivered at

the special general court on December 18, 1830 with additional observations.
54 pp. London, J. & W. T. Clarke, 1831

T.

4191 HORTON, Sir Robert John Wilmot. Lecture I delivered at the London Mechanics' Institution, on the 15th of December, 1830: being the first of a series of lectures on statistics & political economy, as affecting the condition of the operative and labouring classes. With notes.
table of contents. tables. appendix. 32 pp. London, E. Lloyd, 1831

N.

——. Lecture II.
32 pp. London, E. Lloyd, 1831

N.

——. Lecture III.
32 pp. London, E. Lloyd, 1831

N.

4192 JEREMIE, John. Four essays on colonial slavery.
128 pp. London, J. Hatchard, 1831

K., T.

4193 KINAHAN, Daniel. Outline of a plan for employing the poor of Ireland.
36 pp. London, J. Ridgway, Dublin, R. Milliken, 1831

N.

4194 A letter to the most reverend father in God the lord archbishop of Canterbury, in relation to the final adjustment of the tithe system. By a clergyman, of the diocese of Bath and Wells.
20 pp. London, C. J. G. & F. Rivington, 1831

K., T.

4195 A letter to the people on the revenues of the church. By a layman. Being a reply to Mr. Cobbett's address to the labourers of England, on the measures which ought to be adopted with regard to the tithes, and with regard to the other property, commonly called church property.—No. 7 of his 'Two-penny trash'.
36 pp. Cardiff, W. Bird, London, Longman, Rees, Orme, Brown & Green, 1831

K., T.

4196 A letter to the rt. hon. E. G. Stanley on the state of church property in Ireland. From a country clergyman.
18 pp. Dublin, R. Milliken, 1831

A., N.

signed 'R.T.'

4197 A letter to the rt. hon. the earl of Darnley on the introduction of a labour rate, for the employment of the poor in Ireland.
80 pp. Dublin, J. Chambers, 1831

N.

signed 'A well-wisher to Ireland'.

4198 Letters to the duke of Wellington from 1828 to 1830 on currency. By a citizen of London.
30 pp. London, Effingham Wilson, 1831

T.

4199 LIVINGSTONE, J. Lennox. Mr. Livingstone's letters to the king, and to lord Brougham and Vaux, on the subject of a plan for the formation of a society for the abolition of poor's rate in England, and the prevention of it in Ireland, and for other most desirable objects, which will relieve distress, employ the poor, assist farmers, benefit the landlords, stimulate trade, increase the revenue, and strengthen the government. Mr. Livingstone's petition to the house of commons on the same subject, and his observations on a bill for the relief of the aged, helpless and infirm poor of Ireland, pointing out not only the defects, but the inutility of that bill.
18 pp. London, H. Baylis, 1831

A.

4200 [McCULLOCH, John Ramsay.] Historical sketch of the Bank of England: with an examination of the question as to the prolongation of the exclusive privileges of that establishment.
table of contents. appendix with tables. 78 pp. London, Longman, Rees, Orme, Brown and Green, 1831

A., K., T.

4201 [——.] Observations on the influence of the East India Company's monopoly on the price of tea, and on the commerce with India, China etc., reprinted (by permission of the publishers), with corrections and amendments, from the Edinburgh Review No. CIV.
42 pp. London, Longman, Rees, Orme, Brown, and Green, 1831

A., P., T.

4202 MALET, Sir Alexander, bart. The Canadas: the onerous nature of their existing connexion with Great Britain stated, the discontents of these colonies discussed, and a remedy proposed; in a letter to lord viscount Howick, under secretary for the colonial department.
32 pp. London, J. Ridgway, 1831

T.

4203 MILLER, James. A letter to the right hon. the earl Grey, first lord of the treasury &c. &c. &c. on the origin and nature of church property, and the connexion of tithes with the existing agricultural distress; and on improvements which may be safely adopted without the introduction of a new principle.
84 pp. London, Hatchard; Durham, Andrews, 1831

K., T.

4204 Mining company of Ireland. The board of directors' report for the half year ending 1st December, 1830.
10 pp. Dublin, J. Chambers, 1831

A.

4205 MOLLOY, Philip. On popular discontent in Ireland.
126 pp. Dublin, R. Milliken, London, J. Ridgway, 1831

A., K., U.

4206 [MORGAN, Ashburner.] Remarks on the national debt; the principal cause of the present distress; and statement of a plan for effectual relief from its pernicious effects.
tables. 28 pp. London, William March, 1831

T.

4207 MORRIS, Patrick. Six letters intended to prove that the repeal of the union and the establishment of a local

legislature in Ireland are necessary to cement the alliance with Great Britain; and continuing a short view of the trade, manufactures, and agriculture of Ireland. Addressed to the rt. hon. Sir John Newport, bt. M.P.
190 pp. Waterford, T. Hanton, 1831

A., N.

4208 Moss, Samuel. Some considerations of the benefits and evils of steam power in a letter addressed to his excellency the lord lieutenant.
24 pp. Dublin, P. D. Hardy, 1831

A., N.

Suggests a tax on steam-engine power to replace taxes affecting the poor.

4209 Mullins, Bernard. Observations upon the Irish grand jury system.
34 pp. Dublin, C. Hope, 1831

A., U.

4210 Mundell, Alexander. The necessary operation of the corn laws: in driving capital from the cultivation of the soil; diminishing the means of employing agricultural labour; rendering Great Britain dependent upon foreign countries for a supply of grain; and endangering her manufacturing superiority. With a remedy for those evils.
tables. 68 pp. London, Longman, Rees, Orme, Brown and Green, [etc.], 1831

K.

——. 92 pp. 2nd ed. enlarged. London, Longman, Rees, Orme, Brown & Green [etc.], 1831

A., K., N., T.

4211 Naper, James Lenox William. Practical hints for the relief and employment of the poor of Ireland in continuation of a 'plan of a labour rate'.
12 pp. Dublin, Hodges & Smith, 1831

A.

4212 The national debt, its evils, and their remedy. By a land and fund holder.
tables. 46 pp. London, Effingham Wilson, 1831

T.

4213 [Neale, Erskine?] A letter to the king, on the unjust distribution of church property. By a country curate.
26 pp. 2nd ed. London, J. Ridgway, 1831

P., T.

4214 The new bankrupt act, 1 and 2 William IV Chapter LVI with an introduction, notes, and index. By a barrister.
tables. 42 pp. London, Simpkin and Marshall [etc.], 1831

T.

4215 Notes relative to the condition of the Irish peasantry, especially in the province of Ulster. Addressed to lord viscount Melbourne, by an Ulster landlord.
table. 28 pp. London, Edward Bull, 1831

T.

4216 O'Brien, William Smith, and others. Considerations addressed to the landed proprietors of the county of Clare.
128 pp. Limerick, R. Canter, 1831

A., N.

4217 ——. Plan for the relief of the poor in Ireland with observations on the English and Scotch poor laws, addressed to the landed proprietors of Ireland.
48 pp. Dublin, J. S. Folds, 1831

A., N.

——. Another issue.
64 pp. Dublin, R. Milliken, 1831

A., N., U.

4218 Observations on the causes of the evils resulting from the tithe system with suggestions for a remedy. By a barrister.
22 pp. London, Butterworth, 1831

N.

4219 O'Neill, P. C. A brief review of the Irish post office from 1784 to 1831, when Sir Edward Lees was removed from that establishment, in a letter to the rt. hon. lord Melbourne.
104 pp. n.p. 1831

A.

4220 Opinions of the Hon. Mountstuart Elphinstone upon some of the leading questions connected with the government of British India; examined and compared with those of the late Sir Thomas Munro and Sir John Malcolm, as taken from their evidence before parliament, &c. By the author of 'An inquiry into the causes of the stationary condition of India', &c.
70 pp. London, Parbury, Allen, 1831

K.

4221 Ormathwaite, John Benn Walsh, 1st baron. On reform of parliament; and on poor laws for Ireland.
tables. 120 pp. London, J. Ridgway, 1831

T.

4222 ——. Poor laws in Ireland, considered in their probable effects upon the capital, the prosperity and the progressive improvement of that country.
table of contents. 128 pp. 3rd ed. London, J. Ridgway, 1831

T.

4223 ——. Popular opinions on parliamentary reform considered.
table of contents. 148 pp. 3rd. ed., with additions. London, J. Ridgway, 1831

A.

4224 [Osborne, Robert Boyse.] Plan or proposed system by which above 150,000 poor in Ireland may not only be supported but lodged in comfort and made useful members of society; promote the national peace and prosperity of the kingdom, without any additional taxation. By an Irish magistrate and landed proprietor.
22 pp. Wexford, Price & Breen, 1831

A.

4225 [Perrin, ——.] The desideratum, or Ireland's only remedy; 'Poor laws and education', proved on social, political and christian principles. Addressed to the citizens of Dublin.
24 pp. Dublin, W. Curry, jr., 1831

N.

4226 Plan of a company to be established for the purpose of founding a colony in Southern Australia purchasing land therein, and preparing the land so purchased for the reception of immigrants.
maps. tables. appendix. 72 pp. London, J. Ridgway, 1831
A.

4227 [PLUMPTRE, Edward Hayes?] Dr. Doyle, and the tithes. An address to the landlords and farmers of Ireland, in reply to Dr. Doyle's letter to lord Farnham. By P.E.H.
20 pp. Dublin, R. Moore Tims, [etc.], 1831
A., N.

4228 [——.] Dr. Doyle and the tithes. An address to the landlords and farmers of Ireland proving that though Dr. Doyle now denounces tithes, he has sworn, as a Roman catholic prelate, to maintain them; and that they are equally a fair and just as well as a legal demand: in reply to Dr. Doyle's letter to lord Farnham. By P.E.H.
20 pp. 3rd. ed. Dublin, R. Moore Tims [etc.], 1831
A.

4229 Poor colonies at home! showing how the whole of our pauper population may be profitably employed in England. By a magistrate and a clergyman of Chichester.
28 pp. Chichester, J. Hackman, 1831
A.
Recommends land reclamation as an alternative to emigration

4230 POSTANS, Thomas. Letter to Sir Thomas Baring, bart. M.P. &c. &c. &c. on the causes which have produced the present state of the agricultural labouring poor; to which are added practical hints for bettering their condition. With a drawing and plan for a double cottage.
plate. 32 pp. London, Michael Staunton, 1831
K.

4231 Remarks on an article in the Quarterly Review for Feb. 1831 entitled 'Poor law for Ireland', with anecdotes of the Irish character. To which are added observations on poor laws and absenteeism.
22 pp. Dublin, R. Milliken, 1831
A., U.

4232 Remarks on the proposed railway between Birmingham and London, proving by facts and arguments that that work would cost seven millions and a half; that it would be a burden upon the trade of the country, and would never pay. By Investigator.
tables. 120 pp. London, J. M. Richardson, [etc.], 1831
T.
See 4151.

4233 The repeal of the legislative union of Great Britain and Ireland considered.
38 pp. 2nd ed. London, J. Ridgway, 1831
T.

4234 The repeal of the union between Great Britain and Ireland compared with the separation of Belgium and Holland. By Frank Fairplay.
24 pp. London, J. M. Richardson, 1831
T.

4235 A repeal of the union the ruin of Ireland. By R.B.G.
58 pp. Dublin, W. Curry, jr., London, J. Ridgway, 1831
A.

4236 Report on the affairs of the Arigna Iron and Coal Company, presented to the proprietors at a special general meeting, held on the 14th April, 1831.
16 pp. London, printed by E. Justins, 1831
A.

4237 Report on the state of the River Shannon, both as to the navigation and the drainage of the adjoining lands; together with a report on the lakes of Galway and Mayo.
64 pp. London, S. W. Fores, 1831
A., N.

4238 Reports of the board of managers of the Pennsylvania colonization society, with an introduction and appendix.
tables. appendix. 48 pp. Philadelphia, the society, London, John Miller, 1831
T.

4239 REVANS, John. Observations on the proposed alteration of the timber-duties, with remarks on the pamphlet of Sir Howard Douglas.
tables. 34 pp. London, J. M. Richardson, 1831
T.
See 4166.

4240 Rules and regulations to be strictly observed by members of the Bedford Society.
24 pp. Dublin, J. Harvey, 1831
A.

4241 RYAN, Richard. A letter to the rt. hon. E. G. Stanley &c. &c. in answer to Dr. Doyle's letter to Thomas Spring Rice, esq. M.P. on the subject of poor laws and the nature and destination of church property.
32 pp. Dublin, A. & W. Watson, 1831
A., N., T.

4242 SALMON, John. A letter to the marquess of Downshire, chairman of the committee for the improvement of Ireland on the subject of lowering the waters of the Shannon, with a view to draining the bog and callow lands in its vicinity, and improve its navigation.
24 pp. Westminster, T. Vacher, 1831
A.

4243 SCROPE, George Julius Duncombe Poulett. A letter to the magistrates of the south of England, on the urgent necessity of putting a stop to the illegal practice of making up wages out of rates, to which alone is owing the misery and revolt of the agricultural peasantry.
26 pp. London, J. Ridgway, 1831
N.

4244 ——. A second letter to the magistrates of the south of England, on the propriety of discontinuing the allowance system, the means of employing or disposing of the excess of labour, and for diminishing the unequal pressure of the poor rate.
54 pp. London, J. Ridgway, 1831
N.

4245 A second dialogue on rick-burning, rioting, tithes, &c. between Squire Wilson, Hughes, his steward, Thomas, the bailiff, and Harry Brown, a labourer.
24 pp. London, C. J. G. & F. Rivington, 1831
T.

4246 Second report of the nourishment and clothing society, in cooperation with the South-East general dispensary near Sir Patrick Dun's Hospital, Grand Canal-Street, Denzille-Street, for the year ending 1st November, 1831.
18 pp. Dublin, printed by P. D. Hardy, 1831
A.

4247 SENIOR, Nassau William. A letter to lord Howick, on a legal provision for the Irish poor; commutation of tithes, and a provision for the Irish Roman catholic clergy.
tables in appendices. 104 pp. 2nd ed. London, J. Murray, 1831
A., B., K., N., T.

4248 SISSON, Jonathan. Letter to the rt. hon. earl Grey proposing the appointment of a board of trade for Ireland.
24 pp. Dublin, W. Espy, 1831
A., U.

4249 SMITH, Thomas. The parson's horn-book examined, and its concealed, cowardly author exposed.
16 pp. Dublin, R. Moore Tims, 1831
A., T.
See 4144-5.

4250 SOLLY, Edward. The Belgic question in reference to British interference.
19 pp. London, J. Ridgway, 1831
T.

4251 Some notices touching the present state of Ireland. By C.C.C.
40 pp. London, J. Ridgway, 1831
A.

4252 A statement of the proceedings of the western committee for the relief of the Irish poor.
appendix. 128 pp. London, Seeley; Dublin, Carson, [etc.], 1831
A.

4253 STAUNTON, Michael. 'Case of Ireland', or a speech delivered at a meeting of the Dublin Political Union, held on Saturday, 10th December, 1831. With an appendix. Published in pursuance of an unanimous vote of the Dublin Political Union, proposed by D. O'Connell, esq., and seconded by James Nugent, esq.
tables. appendix. 102 pp. Dublin, Edward Bull, 1831
A., N., U.

4254 STEPHENSON, George. Report on the practicability and utility of the Limerick and Waterford railway, or of such parts thereof as ought to be completed immediately.
table. 16 pp. London, Walton and Mitchell, 1831
N.

4255 STEWART, Matthew. Some remarks on the present state of affairs; respectfully addressed to the marquess of Lansdowne. Second edition.
appendix. 130 pp. 2nd edition. London, J. Murray, 1831
T.

4256 STEWART, William. Comments on the Magistrates' Replevin Act 7 & 8 George IV c. 69 'For the relief of persons aggrieved by unlawful or excessive distresses for rent in Ireland'.
104 pp. 2nd. ed. Dublin, R. Milliken, 1831
A.

4257 STROMBOM, Isaac. Remarks and suggestions on the actual commercial and financial state of Great Britain, with observations on the currency.
50 pp. London, George Horne, 1831
T.

4258 Suggestions for employing the peasantry of the western districts of Ireland. By W.S.
8 pp. Dublin, Porter, 1831
A.

4259 Suggestions on the abolition of slavery in the British colonies; or, slavery gradually starved to death upon a low diet, v: strangulation. By a member of the University of Cambridge.
48 pp. Cambridge, J. & J. J. Deighton, [etc., etc.], 1831
K.

4260 TENNANT, Charles. Letters forming part of a correspondence with Nassau William Senior, esq. concerning systematic colonization, and the bill now before parliament for promoting emigration; also, a letter to the Canada land company, and, a series of questions in elucidation of the principles of colonization.
appendix. 98 pp. London, J. Ridgway, 1831
T.

4261 Third report of the Cove Sick and Indigent Room-keepers and Sailors' Friend Society. Established Jan. 17th 1828.
16 pp. Cork, W. Scraggs, 1831
A.

4262 Third quarterly report of the Protestant Colonization Society of Ireland.
8 pp. (no t.p.) Dublin, Courtney, 1831
A., N.

4263 Thirteenth report of the managing committee of the association for the suppression of mendicity in Dublin for the year 1830.
196 pp. Dublin, W. Holden, 1831
A.
The series continues for later years in the Haliday collection.

4264 [THOMPSON, Thomas Perronet.] The true theory of rent, in opposition to Mr. Ricardo and others; being an exposition of fallacies on rent, tithes, etc., in the form of a review of Mr. Mill's Elements of political economy. By the author of 'The catechism on the corn laws'.
32 pp. 8th ed. London, R. Heward, 1831
D., U.

4265 [THORN, William.] The history of tithes patriarchal, levitical, catholic and protestant with reflections on the extent and evils of the English tithe system, and suggestions for abolishing tithes, and supporting the clergy without them. By Biblicus.
68 pp. London, Dinnis, 1831
A.

——. another ed. 68 pp. London, Dinnis, 1831
A.

4266 Thoughts on emigration as the means of surmounting our present difficulties.
46 pp. London, C. J. G. & F. Rivington, 1831
K., T.

4267 Thoughts on the poor of Ireland and means of their amelioration. By a barrister. In 2 parts.
100 pp. Dublin, R. Graisberry, 1831
N.

4268 Tithes: a mine of national wealth. By a poor layman.
tables. 22 pp. London, Effingham Wilson, 1831
T.

4269 TORRENS, Robert. Address to the farmers of the United Kingdom, on the low rates of profit in agriculture and in trade.
tables. 16 pp. 2nd ed. London, Longman & co., 1831
K., T.

4270 To the proprietors of dock stock, in the port of London. By a proprietor.
16 pp. London, J. M. Richardson, 1831
T.

4271 [TRUEMAN & COOK.] The state of the commerce of Great Britain with reference to colonial and other produce, for the year 1830.
tables in appendices. 44 pp. 2nd edition. London, J. M. Richardson, 1831
T.

4272 The ultimate remedy for Ireland.
76 pp. London, Thomas Hookham, 1831
T.

4273 WALLER, Zepheniah. Seven letters from an emigrant, to his friends in England; containing remarks on the manners, customs, laws, and religion of the United States of America, with a description of the city of New York, and observations on emigration.
38 pp. Diss, E. E. Abbott, 1831
T.

4274 [WARE, William.] Sketch of a petition proper to be presented to the legislature of the United Kingdom of Great Britain and Ireland by the friends of peace and justice in Ireland. By X.
24 pp. Belfast, Stuart & Gregg, 1831
A., N.

Proposes abolition of established church in Ireland and of tithes.

4275 WARNER, Richard. Great Britain's crisis! Reform: retrenchment: and economy: the hard case of the farmers: and the distressed condition of the labouring poor: a letter to the rt. hon. Sir James Graham, bart.
40 pp. 2nd ed. London, Longman, Rees, Orme, Brown, and Green, 1831
K., T.

4276 WATSON, Peter. The law of tithes, offerings, oblations, etc. shewing their nature, kinds, properties, and incidents; by whom, and to whom, when, and in what manner payable; what thing, lands, or persons are charged or exempted therefrom; with the compositions, modus decimandi libels, suggestions, prohibitions, declarations, citations, allegations, consultations, the writ decontumacie capiendo, pleas of abatement in answer thereto; and how to extricate yourselves out of the ecclesiastical court without the assistance of a proctor, and the ecclesiastical law clearly understood so that every person may do their own law business themselves, at a small charge, and save the very heavy law expences attending that court; also, copies of answers to libels, etc. wherein, all the statutes and adjudged cases relative to the subject in the common law are introduced and considered.
appendix. 86 pp. London, Effingham Wilson, 1831
T.

4277 WELD, Isaac. Observations on the Royal Dublin Society and its existing institutions in the year 1831.
34 pp. Dublin, R. Graisberry, 1831
A., N.

4278 WILDMAN, Richard. The right of tithes, and its consequences, considered.
24 pp. London, J. Ridgway, 1831
T.

4279 WILLIAMS, Charles Wye. Observations on an important feature in the state of Ireland, and the want of employment of its population; with a description of the navigation of the River Shannon. Suggested by the report of the select committee of the house of commons on the state of the poor in Ireland, and the remedial measures proposed by them.
map. tables. 68 pp. Westminster, T. Vacher, 1831
A., C., K., N., U.

4280 WILLIAMS, David. 'Tithes', 'justified and explained', in a letter from the Rev. David Williams, A.M., F.G.S., rector of the parishes of Bleadon and Kingston Seamoor, Somersetshire, to one of his parishioners.
24 pp. Bristol, Barry, Norton, Bulgin and Chilcott, [1831]
K., T.

4281 WRIGHT, William. Slavery at the cape of Good Hope.
appendices. 116 pp. London, Longman, Rees, Orme, Brown & Green, [etc.], 1831
T.

1832

4282 Administration of the poor laws.
tables. 40 pp. London, James and Luke G. Hansard, 1832
P.

4283 The age of gold not a golden age. Paper and gold compared. Also, plan for a [a] national bank, to which is added, a plan for a new system of taxation.
30 pp. London, Bowdery and Kerby, 1832
T.

4284 ALLEN, William. Colonies at home; or, means for rendering the industrious labourer independent of parish

relief, and for providing for the poor population of Ireland by the cultivation of the soil. A new edition with additions.
tables. appendix. 60 pp. 6th edition. London, Longman, Rees, Orme, Brown, Green & Longman, 1832

K., T.

see 3598, 3702.

4285 Annual report of the charitable society for relief of sick and indigent room-keepers of all religious persuasions, in the city of Dublin, for the year 1831.
48 pp. Dublin, J. Coyne, 1832

A.

4286 Annual report of the Strangers' Friend Society.
30 pp. Dublin, R. Napper, 1832

A.

4287 [ARCHER, Thomas.] A plan for relieving the pressure of the poor rates, affording employment to the agricultural poor, and improving their condition. By a solicitor.
tables. 74 pp. 2nd edition. London, Pelham Richardson, 1832

T.

4288 BOURNE, Richard. To his excellency the lord lieutenant, the memorial of Richard Bourne, a principal proprietor of steamers, plying between Dublin and London.
4 pp. (2 large sheets.) Dublin, 1832

A.

4289 BRENTON, Edward Pelham. Letters to his majesty, to earl Grey,—the duke of Richmond, the bishop of London,—lord Melbourne,—lord Kenyon, and captain the hon. George Elliot, R.N.—secretary to the admiralty, on population, agriculture, poor laws, and juvenile vagrancy.
appendix. 68 pp. London, C. Rice, 1832

T.

4290 CHATFIELD, Francis. Review illustrative of various bearings peculiar to interests and discounts, and demonstrative of two systems in commercial transactions, which are herein denominated simple interest and discount interest; comprehending, also, instructions on specific profits in trade, influenced by discounts, cash advanced in part payment, and goods by barter; with some useful hints on discounts off bills, and discounts off list prices in business, which pertain to bankruptcy accounts, etc. Accompanied by tables explanatory of discounts and interests, or profits and losses, as relative to each other.
tables. 16 pp. London, H. K. Causton jun., 1832

K.

4291 Commissioners for emigration: information published by his majesty's commissioners for emigration respecting the British colonies in North America.
tables. 18 pp. London, C. Knight, 1832

N.

4292 CONNER, William. The speech of William Conner, esq., against rack-rents, &c. delivered at a meeting at Inch, in the Queen's county, convened for the purpose of taking into consideration the condition of the farming and labouring classes, and of petitioning parliament for a bill for the applotment or valuation of land, by a sworn jury.
32 pp. Dublin, 1832

A.

4293 CORT, Richard. Letter to British Iron Company, with proofs that the shareholders have been sold by their own servants, extracted from the sworn records of the court of exchequer, in the case of Small versus Attwood.
tables. 32 pp. London, Sears and Trapp, 1832

P.

4294 CROMBIE, Alexander. A letter to lieut. col Torrens, M.P., in answer to his address to the farmers of the United Kingdom.
tables. 24 pp. London, R. Hunter, 1832

K., T.

4295 D'ALTON, John. A history of tithes, church lands and other ecclesiastical benefices, with a plan for the abolition of the former and the better distribution of the latter.
148 pp. Dublin, R. Coyne, 1832

A.

4296 Deed of agreement of the Liberal Annuity Company of Dublin, establ. 1780, with a copious index, containing all the rules of the company.
table of contents. 84 pp. Dublin, N. Kelly, 1832

A.

4297 DICKSON, Stephen Fox. A translation of the charters of the corporation of merchants, or, guild of the Holy Trinity, Dublin. Addressed to the rt. hon. Thomas S. Rice, M.P.
24 pp. Dublin, L. McDermott, 1832

A., N.

Concerns a levy on coal imports by the guild.

4298 DOYLE, James Warren, bishop of Kildare & Leighlin. Letter of the Rt. Revd. Doctor Doyle to the marquess of Anglesey on tithe meetings, etc.
12 pp. Dublin, T. O'Flanagan, 1832

A.

4299 DUCPETIAUX, Edouard. Des moyens de soulager et de prévenir l'indigence, et d'éteindre la mendicité. Extrait d'un rapport addressé au ministre de l'intérieur, suivi d'un projet de loi pour l'extinction de la mendicité, et de renseignemens statistiques sur l'état des établissemens de bienfaisance, en Belgique.
116 pp. Brussells, Laurent, 1832

B.

See 4547

4300 [DUNLOP, William.] Statistical sketches of Upper Canada, for the use of emigrants: by a backwoodsman.
tables. 124 pp. London, J. Murray, 1832

T.

4301 EDEN afterwards HENLEY, Robert Henley, 2nd baron. A plan of church reform.
82 pp. 2nd ed. London, Roake and Varty, 1832

T.

——. 88 pp. 3rd ed. London, Roake and Varty, 1832

N.

4302 The emigrants' guide: containing practical and authentic information, and copies of original and unpublished letters

from emigrants, to their friends in the counties of Mayo, Galway and Roscommon.
table of contents. tables. appendix. 140 pp. Westport, Hoban, 1832

A.

4303 Emigration and the condition of the labouring poor. A letter, addressed to the gentlemen of the grand jury, and other land-owners of the county of Essex. Lent Assizes, 1832. appendix. 34 pp. Colchester, Swinborne, Walter and Taylor, [etc., etc.], [1832]

K., T.

4304 [EYRE, Henry Townsend.] A plan for improving the condition of the Irish peasantry, by combining these with a profitable investment of capital. By a friend to Ireland. illustrations. 46 pp. Dublin, W. Underwood, 1832

A., N., U.

4305 Extracts from letters written by a gentleman lately established on the Swan River in Western Australia. map. 46 pp. Dublin, W. Underwood, 1832

A.

4306 First report and statement of accounts of the Sandymount Loan-Fund committee, January, 1832. 16 pp. Dublin. W. Underwood, 1832

A., N.

4307 FITZWILLIAM, Charles William Wentworth-Fitzwilliam, 5th earl, at this time styled 'viscount Milton'. Address to the landowners of England, on the corn laws. tables. 50 pp. 4th edition. London, J. Ridgway, 1832

A., T.

4308 The foreign trade of China divested of monopoly, restriction, and hazard, by means of insular commercial stations. appendix. 110 pp. London, Effingham Wilson, 1832

T.

4309 Fourteenth report of the managing committee of the association for the suppression of mendicity in Dublin, for the year 1831. 157 pp. Dublin, W. Holden, 1832

A.

4310 FUGE, Robert. An essay on the turnpike roads of the kingdom, and the practicability of uniting them with the department of the general post-office. Also, shewing the advantages of abolishing the tolls now collected on all public roads, and substituting a rate on each county, for the maintenance and repairs, etc. etc. etc. tables in appendices. 40 pp. London, T. Hurst, 1832

T.

4311 GIRDLESTONE, Charles. A letter on church reform addressed to the Regius professor of divinity in the University of Oxford; with one remark on the plan of lord Henley. appendix. 16 pp. London, C. J. G. & F. Rivington, [etc., etc.], 1832

K.

4312 GORDON, Alexander. An historical and practical treatise upon elemental locomotion, by means of steam carriages on common roads: showing the commercial, politi-

cal, and moral advantages; the means by which an elementary power is obtained; the rise, progress, and description of steam carriages; the roads upon which they may be made to travel; the ways and means for their general introduction. Illustrated by plates, and embodying the report of, and almost the whole evidence before, the select committee of the house of commons.
with an appendix. tables. illustrations & diagrams. appendix. 196 pp. London, B. Steuart, 1832

T.

4313 GRAULHIÉ, Gerard. An outline of a plan for a new circulating medium; in three letters addressed to the chancellor of the exchequer.
table. 32 pp. London, J. Ridgway, 1832

T.

4314 GURNEY, Sir Goldsworthy. Mr. Gurney's observations on steam carriages on turnpike roads. With returns of the daily practical results of working; the cause of the stoppage of the carriage at Gloucester; and the consequent official report of the house of commons, ordered to be printed, 12th October, 1831.
table. illustration. 48 pp. London, Baldwin and Cradock, 1832

T.

4315 HALE, William Hale, prebendary of St. Paul's. An essay on the supposed existence of a quadripartite and tripartite division of tithes in England, for maintaining the clergy, the poor, and the fabric of the church.
appendix. 52 pp. London, C. J. G. & F. Rivington, [etc.], 1832

K., T.

4316 HALL, George Webb. Letter to the right hon. viscount Milton; being a review of the various sources of national wealth and a reply to the recent publication of his lordship against the corn laws.
56 pp. London, J. Ridgway, 1832

T.

4317 [HANCOCK, George.] A conversation in political economy; being an attempt to explain familiarly to the understanding of every man the true causes of the evil operation of any general system of poor laws; and to point out the only effectual means of raising the condition of the labouring classes. By Philo-Malthus.
tables in appendix. 72 pp. London, T. Cadell 1832

A., T.

4318 HENEKEY, George. A letter to the rt. hon. lord Althorp, chancellor of the exchequer, etc. etc. on the wine duties' bill, clearly demonstrating the impolicy, injustice and unconstitutional tendency of retrospective taxation by exacting an increased duty on any article on which a tax has been already paid, and the government declared itself satisfied. To which is added an abstract of the wine duties' act.
tables. 22 pp. London, Pelham Richardson, 1832

T.

4319 [HICKEY, William.] Hints on emigration to Upper Canada; especially addressed to the middle and lower classes in Great Britain and Ireland ... by Martin Doyle.
map. table of contents. 100 pp. 2nd. ed. Dublin, W. Curry, jr. [etc., etc.], 1832

A., N.

4320 ——. Hints to small-holders on planting, cattle, poultry, agricultural implements, flax, etc. By Martin Doyle. table of contents. 92 pp. 2nd ed. revised. Dublin, W. Curry, jr., 1832

A.

4321 HILL, Sir Rowland. Home colonies. Sketch of a plan for the gradual extinction of pauperism and for the diminution of crime.
52 pp. London, Simpkin & Marshall, 1832

A., P., T.

4322 HULL, William Winstanley. Thoughts on church reform.
16 pp. London, B. Fellowes, 1832

K.

4323 Information published by his majesty's commissioners for emigration, respecting the British colonies in North America, with supplementary instructions added by the Limerick Emigrants' Friend Society.
tables. 20 pp. Limerick, C. O'Brien, 1832

N.

4324 KAY, James Phillips. The moral and physical condition of the working classes employed in the cotton manufacture in Manchester. 2nd edition enlarged and containing an introductory letter to the rev. Thomas Chalmers.
tables. appendix. 120 pp. London, J. Ridgway, 1832

T.

4325 KENTISH, W. A. A plan for the redemption of the public debt.
no t.p. tables. 16 pp. n.p., 1832

P.

4326 LAMBERT, Henry. A letter on the currency, to the right hon. the viscount Althorp, chancellor of the exchequer, etc. etc. etc.
appendix. 52 pp. London, W. H. Dalton, 1832

T.

4327 LAW, George Henry, bishop of Bath & Wells. Reflections upon tithes, with a plan for the general commutation of the same.
30 pp. Wells, B. Backhouse, 1832

A.

30 pp. 2nd ed., n.d.:

T.

4328 LAW, James Thomas, chancellor of Lichfield and Coventry. A letter to lord King, controverting the statements lately delivered in parliament by his lordship, Mr. O'Connell and Mr. Sheil, as to the fourfold division of tithes.
appendix. 28 pp. London, C. J. G. & F. Rivington, 1832

K., T.

4329 Letters of Philodemus on the political degradation of Mayo—the parliamentary conduct of its representatives Messrs. Dominick and John Denis Browne; and the means of establishing its independence. 1st series.
46 pp. Castlebar, printed at 'The Telegraph' Office, 1832

A.

4330 LITCHFIELD, Francis. Three years' results of the Farthinghoe clothing society, with a few remarks on the policy of encouraging provident habits among the working classes.
tables. 22 pp. Northampton, J. Freeman, 1832

K., T.

4331 LUBÉ, Denis George. An argument against the gold standard, with an examination of the principles of the modern economists, theory of rent, corn laws, etc. Addressed to the landlords of England.
table of contents. 196 pp. London, J. Ridgway, 1832

A.

4332 [MARTIN, Robert Montgomery.] British relations with the Chinese empire in 1832. Comparative statement of the English and American trade with India and Canton.
tables and appendix. 148 pp. London, Parbury, Allen, 1832

K., N., T.

4333 ——. The past and present state of the tea-trade of England and of the continents of Europe and America; and a comparison between the consumption, price of, and revenue derived from tea, coffee, sugar, wine, tobacco, spirits, etc.
tables. appendix. tables of contents. 234 pp. London, Parbury, Allen, 1832

A., T.

4334 A memorial from the lessees of the Dublin docks to the lords of the treasury, praying for a renewal of their lease of those premises on terms particularly advantageous to the merchant and trader, and giving a comparative statement of the former and present system under which the business of the Dublin docks has been conducted.
50 pp. Dublin, 1832

A.

4335 MEREWETHER, Francis. An appeal to the nobility and gentry of the county of Leicester, in behalf of the Church of England. Dedicated by permission to the duke of Rutland.
78 pp. Ashby-de-la-Zouch, W. Hextall [etc., etc.], 1832

T.

4336 MILLER, James. A letter to the right hon. the earl Grey, on church property and church reform. Second edition, with additions.
120 pp. London, Baldwin and Cradock, 1832

T.

4337 MOORE, Richard. A treatise on paper and gold money shewing the necessity for instituting an imperial, paper, standard, mint note, to be made co valuable and co current, with our gold standard money:—as become indispensable, for the purposes of arresting our general financial distresses;—for the more universally commanding the use of gold sovereigns, in the remote, as in the near localities of the metropolis:—for producing the pecuniary means in every locality, possessing capital in gross, of employing its population;—for putting an end to the necessity of colonisation, for that purpose;—and by these means, securing our future prosperity.
208 pp. 2nd ed. London, J. Ridgway, 1832

T.

4338 MULLINS, Bernard. Thoughts on inland navigation, with a map, and observations upon propositions for lowering

the waters of the Shannon and of Lough Neagh, addressed to the Rt. Hon. E. G. Stanley, chief secretary for Ireland.
map. 52 pp. Dublin, Hope, 1832

A.

4339 MUNDELL, Alexander. A comparative view of the industrial situation of Great Britain, from the year 1775 to the present time. With an examination of the causes of her distress.
tables. 150 pp. London, Longman, Rees, Orme, Brown, Green & Longman, [etc.], 1832

T.

4340 ———. An examination of the evidence taken before the committee of secrecy on the Bank of England charter.
tables. 88 pp. London, Longman, Rees, Orme, Brown, Green and Longman, 1832

T,

4341 ———. Supplement to an examination of the evidence taken before the committee of secrecy on the Bank of England charter.
tables. 24 pp. London, Longman, Rees, Orme, Brown, Green and Longman, 1832

T.

4342 MURRAY, John. A letter to the right honorable earl Grey, on colonial slavery.
20 pp. London, Holdsworth and Ball, 1832

K., T.

4343 National Association for the encouragement, promotion and consumption of Irish produce and manufacture. The appeal of the national association for the encouragement, promotion and consumption of Irish produce and manufacture. Founded, June 29th, 1832.
12 pp. Dublin, Coyne, 1832

A.

4344 NEWLAND, Henry. An examination of the evidence and arguments adduced by Dr. Doyle before the committee on tithes in Ireland, in defence of the supposed quadripartite or tripartite division.
156 pp. Dublin, W. Curry, jr., [etc.], 1832

A.

4345 Nykterhet och Statshushållning saurt Bank—Mynt— och Diskontsystem, Tillämpadt på sverige of J.L.S....dt.
table of contents. appendix. tables. 224 pp. Stockholm, Westerberg, 1832

N.

4346 Observations on pauperism. By R. F.
22 pp. London, Longman, Rees, Orme, Brown and Green, 1832

T.

4347 Observations on the state of Ireland. Addressed to impartial inquirers.
36 pp. London, Saunders & Otley, 1832

A.

4348 O'CONNOR, Feargus. A letter from Feargus O'Connor, esq., barrister at law to his excellency the marquis of Anglesey.
32 pp. Cork, 1832

U.

On rents, tithes and taxes.

4349 The opinions of lords Wellesley and Grenville, on the government of India, compared and examined.
98 pp. London, J. Hatchard, 1832

K., T.

4350 ORPEN, Charles Edward Herbert. Address to the public on the state of the poor of Dublin, especially as connected with the prevention of cholera.
12 pp. Dublin, M. Goodwin, 1832

A., N.

4351 OWEN, Robert. Report to the county of Lanark, of a plan for relieving public distress and removing discontent, by giving permanent, productive employment to the poor and working classes, under arrangements which will essentially improve their character, and ameliorate their condition; diminish the expenses of production and consumption, and create markets co-extensive with production.
table of contents. 76 pp. London, C. Vandrant, 1832

A., N., P.

4352 [PAGE, Frederick.] A letter to a friend, containing observations on the comparative merits of canals and railways, occasioned by the reports of the committee of the Liverpool and Manchester railway.
tables. diag. 40 pp. London, Longman & co., [etc.], 1832

K., T.

4353 [PARNELL, Sir Henry Brooke, later 1st baron Congleton.] A plain statement of the power of the Bank of England, and of the use it has made of it; with a refutation of the objections made to the Scotch system of banking: and a reply to the 'Historical sketch of the Bank of England'.
tables. 100 pp. London, J. Ridgway, 1832

A., T.

4354 Parochial rates and settlements considered; being a reply to queries nos. 11 & 58, proposed by the commissioners appointed to inquire into the poor laws. By a county justice.
tables. 58 pp. London, J. Hatchard, 1832

T.

4355 PERCEVAL, Arthur P. A letter to lord Henley, respecting his publication on church reform.
32 pp. London, C. J. G. & F. Rivington, 1832

K.

See 4301.

4356 PIGGOTT, Grenville. A letter on the nature of the protection afforded by the present corn laws, and on the probable results of a free trade in corn, addressed to the land-owners, farmers, and electors of Buckinghamshire.
tables in appendix. 68 pp. London, Roake and Varty, 1832

T.

4357 PRENTICE, Henry L. A short address to the tenantry on the estates of the Rt. Hon. the earl of Caledon in the counties of Tyrone and Armagh by his lordship's agent, Henry L. Prentice, esq.
38 pp. Belfast, printed by Stuart & Gregg, 1832

A.

4358 Reasons for a revision of the rate raised upon the county of Derby.
24 pp. London, C. J. G. & F. Rivington, 1832

T.

4359 [REID, William.] The life and adventures of the old lady of Threadneedle street; containing an account of her numerous intrigues with various eminent statesmen, of the past and present times. Written by herself.
62 pp. London, Relfe and Unwin, 1832
A., T.

4360 Report &c. &c., relating to the management of the Dublin dock premises.
28 pp. Dublin, P. D. Hardy, 1832
A.

4361 Report of a deputation to Ireland in the year 1832.
fold. table. 44 pp. London, A. Taylor, 1832
A.

The deputation, from the honourable the Irish society, inspected the society's property, fisheries, charities and schools, in Londonderry and Coleraine.

4362 Report of the committee to the annual meeting of the society for promoting the education of the poor in Ireland; held at Kildare-place, Dublin, 1st February, 1832.
tables. 22 pp. Dublin, P. D. Hardy, 1832
T.

4363 Report of the council of the chamber of commerce of Dublin to the annual assembly of the members of the association, held on the 6th of March 1832.
30 pp. Dublin, P. D. Hardy, 1832
A.

4364 A retrospective view of West India slavery; together with its present aspect: submitted at a public meeting of the Hibernian Negroes' Friend Society.
56 pp. Dublin, P. D. Hardy, 1832
A.

4365 Rules and regulations of the Equitable Labour Exchange. Gray's Inn road, London. For the purpose of relieving the productive classes from poverty, by their own industry, and for the mutual exchange of labour for equal value of labour. Established 1832.
14 pp. London, Equitable Labour Exchange Association, 1832
N.

4366 St. Peter's parish savings bank or provident institution for the city of Dublin and its vicinity, first opened 23rd February, 1818 at no. 46 Cuffe-street, Stephen's Green.
12 pp. 34th ed. Dublin, P. D. Hardy, 1832
A.

4367 SAWBRIDGE, H. B. A letter addressed to Michael Thomas Sadler M.P. on the subject of emigration.
50 pp. London, C. J. G. & F. Rivington, 1832
A., T.

4368 SENIOR, Nassau William. A letter to lord Howick on a legal provision for the Irish poor; commutation of tithes, and a provision for the Irish Roman catholic clergy. 3rd ed. With a preface containing suggestions as to the measures to be adopted in the present emergency.
124 pp. London, J. Murray, 1832
A.

4369 ——. Preface to the third edition of Mr. Senior's letter to lord Howick.
20 pp. London, W. Clowes, 1832
A.

4370 SHACKLETON, Ebenezer. Poor laws the safest, cheapest and surest cure for Boyism of every kind in Ireland.
8 pp. Dublin, Webb, 1832
N.

4371 SINCLAIR, Sir John, bart. On the corn laws, and the necessity of protecting the landed and farming interests, from the ruin with which they are now threatened.
no t.p. table. 8 pp. Edinburgh, [1832]
P.

4372 SISSON, Jonathan. Second letter to the Rt. Hon. earl Grey on the necessity of the appointment of a board or council at Dublin for the internal interests of Ireland, similar in principle to that found under the duke of Ormonde's viceroyalty, 1664, and as a remedy for Ireland's present political state in relation to England.
table of contents. 86 pp. London, J. Ridgway, Dublin, Hodges & Smith, 1832
A., N.

4373 The sixty-first report of the Belfast Charitable Society, for the year ending November 24, 1832, with an account of the proceedings at the annual meeting of the general board, a list of subscribers and a statement of receipts & expenditure.
tables. 26 pp. Belfast, Thomas Mairs, 1832
N.

4374 Sketch of the province of New Brunswick, published for the use of emigrants, by the Limerick Emigrants' Friend Society.
table. 10 pp. [no t.p.] Limerick, C. O'Brien, [1832?]
N.

4375 [SMITH, Thomas Sharpe.] On the economy of nations. A sketch by Britannicus.
130 pp. London, James Carpenter, 1832
T.

4376 Society for the encouragement of arts, manufactures, and commerce. Premiums for the sessions 1832–33, 1833–34.
26 pp. London, Moyes, 1832
N.

4377 Some reflections of a Church of England man, on the conduct of a chief secretary for Ireland.
48 pp. London, J. Hatchard, 1832
K., T.

4378 STANLEY, William. Facts on Ireland.
tables. 28 pp. 2nd. ed. Dublin, R. Milliken, London, J. Ridgway, 1832
A., N., U.

4379 Table of rates and charges of the St. Katharine Dock Company, with an abstract of the principal regulations applicable to ships and goods.
table of contents. tables. 84 pp. London, Marchant, 1832
A.

4380 [TAYLOR, John.] An attempt at an analysis of the subjects of currency, and the merits of the Bank of England.
32 pp. London, Pelham Richardson, 1832
T.

4381 THIRLWALL, Thomas Wigzell, B.D. The effect of the repeal of the corn laws.
16 pp. London, R. Hunter, 1832
K., T.

4382 TOWNSEND, T. S. Facts and circumstances relating to the condition of the Irish clergy of the established church, and to the present state of Ireland.
145 pp. Dublin, W. Curry, jr., London, Simpkin & Marshall, 1832
A.

4383 Transactions of the Protestant Colonization Society of Ireland, reported at a public meeting of subscribers on Thursday, May 24, 1832.
appendix. tables. 44 pp. Dublin, J. Hoare, 1832
A., N.

4384 Visit to the Irish poor in the Borough, addressed to the marquess of Lansdowne and the proprietors of the Irish soil resident in London.
no t.p. 8 pp. London, C. J. G. and F. Rivington, 1832
T.

4385 The voice of the West Indies, and the cry of England; or, compensation or separation considered.
tables. 22 pp. London, Effingham Wilson, 1832
T.

4386 WELLS, Samuel. Continuance of the bank charter. A legal statement of the real position of the government, with relation to the Bank of England.
58 pp. 2nd ed. London, Effingham Wilson, 1832
P.

4387 WHATELY, Richard, archbishop of Dublin. Introduction to political economy, lecture IX, delivered at Oxford, in Easter term, MDCCCXXXI.
36 pp. London, B. Fellowes, 1832
A.

4388 WINTER, John Palmer. An address to the proprietors of bank stock, on the subject of the charter, the exclusive privilege of banking, the production of accounts, and an increase of dividend.
tables. appendix. 42 pp. London, Pelham Richardson, 1832
T.

4389 WODEHOUSE, Charles Nourse. A petition to the house of lords for ecclesiastical improvements, with explanations.
94 pp. London, Longman, Rees, Orme, Brown, Green and Longman; Norwich, Matchett, Stevenson and Matchett, 1832
K.

4390 WOOD, Sir George. Observations on tithes and tithe laws. By the late Sir George Wood, knight, one of the barons of his majesty's court of exchequer.
24 pp. London, Longman, Rees, Orme, Brown & Green, 1832
K., T.

4391 WOODWARD, Henry. A letter to the Rt. Hon. E. G. Stanley on tithes in Ireland.
12 pp. Dublin, R. Moore Tims, 1832
A., K., T.

1833

4392 The abolition of the poor laws, the safety of the state. Considerations on the calamitous results of the present system of pauperism to the labourer himself, the agriculturist, and to society at large. With an appendix; containing an account of the labourers' friend society, with extracts from its publications.
40 pp. London, Jackson & Walford, 1833
N.

4393 ALLEN, William. A plan for diminishing the poor's rates in agricultural districts, being a brief account of the objects and plans pursued upon 'Gravely Estate' in the parish of Lindfield, Sussex, by John Smith M.P., and Wm. Allen, for bettering the condition of the agricultural poor.
tables. appendix. 28 pp. London, Longmans, 1833
A., N., T.

4394 Annual report of the Stranger's Friend Society, (founded in 1790) for visiting and relieving distressed strangers, and the resident sick poor, in Dublin and its vicinity: with an account of some of the cases relieved and list of subscribers for 1832.
30 pp. Dublin, Thomas I. White, 1833
N.

4395 The Bank of England and its charter considered in a letter to the right hon. lord Althorp, etc. etc. etc.
table. appendix. 60 pp. London, Bailey, 1833
T.

4396 BARTON, John. An inquiry into the expediency of the existing restrictions on the importation of foreign corn: with observations on the present social and political prospects of Great Britain.
tables. 140 pp. (various paging). London, J. Ridgway, 1833
K., T.

4397 BATHURST, Henry. A letter to the archbishop of Canterbury proposing a satisfactory adjustment, under the mediation of his grace and the episcopal bench, of the Irish Church Bill, so as to redeem the popularity of the measure in general, and ensure the approbation of the people, without separating from the government object of an efficient bill, and without alarming the conservative opponents of Government, and to send it back remodelled to the more perfect satisfaction of the commons house of parliament.
16 pp. London, J. Ridgway, 1833
T.

4398 BLISS, Henry. The colonial system. Statistics of the trade, industry and resources of Canada, and the other plantations in British America.
tables. 172 pp. London, J. M. Richardson, 1833
N.

4399 BLOOMFIELD, S. T.   An analytical view of the principal plans of church reform; with a full and impartial examination of their respective merits and practicability, and a statement of the true principles of church reform.
appendix. 60 pp. London, A. J. Valpy, 1833
K.

4400 BOOTH, Henry.   Substance of Mr Henry Booth's pamphlet on free trade, as it affects the people. Addressed to a reformed parliament.
tables. 16 pp. London, The Westminster Review, 1833
P.

4401 [BREED, ——, of Liverpool.]   An impartial inquiry into the bank question; with observations on banking and currency. By a merchant.
90 pp. London, J. Ridgway, 1833
A., D., T.

4402 A brief inquiry into the state and prospects of India. By an eye-witness in the military service of the company.
68 pp. Edinburgh, Blackwood, London, T. Cadell, 1833
K., T.

4403 [BUNN, Thomas.]   An essay on the abolition of slavery throughout the British dominions, without injury to the master or his property, with the least possible injury to the slave, without revolution and without loss to the revenue.
106 pp. Frome, W. P. Penny, 1833
K.

4404 CHURCH, Charles.   An essay on the repeal of the Act of Irish legislative union.
80 pp. Dublin, printed by MacDonnell, 1833
A.

4405 A concise statement of the proceedings of the Ballast Corporation and the consequent state of the harbours; an inquiry into the promised and probable consequences to the trade and commerce of Dublin from the proposed railway between Dublin and Kingstown; and an investigation into the project of constructing a ship-canal connecting the Asylum Harbour at Kingstown with a floating dock in the river Liffey.
Maps. 62 pp. Dublin, Ponsonby, [1833]
A., N., U.

4406 A concise treatise on the wealth, power and resources of Great Britain, showing the means by which the country may be restored to its former vigour and prosperity; respectfully submitted to the consideration of the members of his majesty's privy council, and of both houses of parliament, and to the notice of all others who take an interest in the welfare of the community. By Cosmopolite.
176 pp. London, Treuttel, Würtz and Richter, [etc.], 1833
A., T.

4407 CONDY, George.   An argument for placing factory children within the pale of the law.
60 pp. London, Longman, Rees, Orme, Browne, Green & Longman, Manchester, T. Sowler, 1833
T.

4408 CONNERY, James.   The reformer, or, an infallible remedy to prevent pauperism and periodical returns of famine, with other salutary measures for the support of the destitute poor, the enforcement of cleanliness, suppression of usury, and establishing the futility of the plan of William Smith O'Brien...to mitigate any of those evils in Ireland. Also, several amendments...which lay open at one view the evils of the Irish nation.
62 pp. 5th ed. Limerick, G. & J. Goggin, 1833
A., N., R.

——.   62 pp. 6th ed. Limerick, G. & J. Goggin, 1833
A.
See 4158.

4409 Considerations on joint-stock banking, chiefly with reference to the situation and liabilities of shareholders.
16 pp. London, J. Frazer [etc.], 1833
T.

4410 Constitution of the Dublin Typographical Provident Society; to which is added a list of the members.
24 pp. Dublin, 1833
A.

4411 CRAWFORD, William Sharman.   The expediency and necessity of a local legislative body in Ireland, supported by a reference to facts and principles.
table of contents.   88 pp. Newry, printed at the Examiner Office, 1833
A., B.

4412 ——.   A review of circumstances connected with the past and present state of the protestant and catholic interests in Ireland; also, of the principal arguments for and against the legislative union, particularly as connected with those interests; and suggestions with reference to the necessity of constituting a national body to manage the local interests and local taxation of Ireland, in connection with the Imperial parliament.
50 pp. Dublin, John Cumming, Belfast, S. Archer, 1833
A., N.
Suggests local representative body for Ireland

4413 [CROSTHWAITE, John Clarke.]   A letter to the lords on the subject of the Irish Church Reform Bill. By a presbyter of the Church of Ireland.
28 pp. Dublin, R. Milliken, 1833
K.

4414 Cui Bono? or, the prospects of a free trade in tea. A dialogue between an antimonopolist and a proprietor of East India stock.
tables. 40 pp. London, J. Hatchard, 1833
K., T.

4415 DANIEL, Edward.   An appeal to the landed, manufacturing, and trading, and professional interests of Great Britain, both great and small, which, in a natural and well-modelled state of society, would be identified, but which, in its present unnatural and ill-concerted state, are ranged in opposition to each other, and therefore in greater danger than the subjects of the following fable.
30 pp. London, Mills, Jowett and Mills, 1833
N.

4416 DAWSON, Edmund.   Spade husbandry; or, an attempt to develope the chief causes of pauperism and distress, with

suggestions for their removal, or mitigation. Most respectfully inscribed to the Right Hon. lord Willoughby de Eresby, the poor man's indulgent benefactor. Second edition, with additions.
tables. 64 pp. London, C. J. G. & F. Rivington; Alford, J. J. Brian, 1833

K.

4417 DAY, William. An enquiry into the poor laws and surplus labour, and their mutual reaction: with a postscript, containing observations on the commutation of tithes, and remarks on lord Milton's address on the corn-laws.
tables. 112 pp. 2nd ed. London, James Fraser, 1833

T.

4418 DOUGLAS, James. Address on slavery, sabbath protection, and church reform.
appendix. 70 pp. Edinburgh, Adam and Charles Black, London, Longman, Rees, Orme, Brown, Green and Longman, 1833

K.

4419 Draft of a petition to the king, against lord Althorp's proposed bill, for church-reform in Ireland: plainly proving that bill to be in open breach of the coronation oath. With a prefatory address and an appendix.
22 pp. London, Roake and Varty, 1833

T.

4420 Dublin docks. A letter from Messrs. Scovell to the Dublin merchants, on a minute of the lords of the treasury, dated 20th November, 1832.
appendix. table. 18 pp. Dublin, Page, 1833

A.

4421 Dublin Printers Asylum, instituted May, 1832. A report delivered at a general meeting of subscribers together with an abstract of the proceedings, the rules and regulations and a list of subscribers.
40 pp. Dublin, Pettigrew and Oulton, 1833

A.

4422 [DUNLOP, William.] Statistical sketches of Upper Canada, for the use of emigrants. By a backwoodsman.
128 pp. 3rd ed. London, J. Murray, 1833

N.

4423 DWYER, George. A view of evidence on the subject of tithes in Ireland, given before the committee of lords and commons in 1832; vindicating the protestant clergy of that country; exposing the schemes of the agitators; and shewing the necessity of a firm maintenance of the protestant church in Ireland, to prevent a dissolution of the union.
table. appendix. 216 pp. London, T. Cadell [etc., etc.], 1833

A.

4424 Effectual remedies for the general distress. By a man of no party.
16 pp. Derby, William Bemrose, London, J. Hatchard, 1833

T.

4425 Emigration: letters from Sussex emigrants who sailed from Portsmouth in April, 1832, on board the ships Lord Melville and Eveline for Upper Canada. Extracts from various writers on emigration to Canada, and from Canadian newspapers with references to the letters. Capt. Hale's instructions to emigrants, and a Gazetteer of the places named in the letters.
tables. 114 pp. [42 pp. supplement.] Petworth, J. Phillips, London, Longman, Rees, Orme, Brown, Green & Longman, 1833

N.

See 4516.

4426 An essay on the national debt and finance of Great Britain; wherein is shown the ruinous tendency of the public debt and the serious evil of connecting the revenue with trade and commerce, the practicability of liquidating the national debt; and the necessity of adopting a more simple system of finance.
table. 92 pp. London, Effingham Wilson, 1833

A., T.

4427 EVANS, Eyre. The evils which afflict Ireland referred to primogeniture, the laws of entail and the legislative union of that country with England.
46 pp. Liverpool, printed by T. Bean, 1833

A., N.

4428 EVANS, G. Remarks on the expediency of introducing poor rates into Ireland.
75 pp. London, J. Ridgway, 1833

N., P.

4429 Facts and illustrations for the labourer's friend society.
tables. maps. appendix. 12 pp. n.p., 1833

U.

4430 Facts (founded upon parliamentary returns) illustrative of the great inequality of the taxes on houses and windows, showing how unjustly and oppressively they bear upon the middle and industrious classes.
36 pp. London, G. Neal, [1833]

A.

4431 FARREN, George. Hints by way of warning on the legal, practical and mercantile difficulties attending the foundation and management of joint stock banks.
34 pp. London, P. Richardson, 1833

A., T.

4432 A few facts and reasons in favour of joint stock banks in a reply to the pamphlet of George Farren, esq., By Civis.
tables. 22 pp. London, Effingham Wilson, 1833

T.

4433 FINLAY, Kirkman. Letter to the rt. hon. lord Ashley on the cotton factory system, and the ten hours factory bill.
appendix. 24 pp. Glasgow, E. Khull, 1833

A., T.

4434 FRANKS, Robert H. Corporation abuses. A letter to the right honourable lord viscount Althorp etc. etc. etc., on the justice and necessity of reforming the livery companies of the city of London, by Robert H. Franks; also, a copy of his petition to the house of commons, presented by M. D. Hill, esq., M.P. with the authorities upon which its allegations are founded.
tables. 44 pp. London, Effingham Wilson, 1833

P., T.

4435 GIRDLESTONE, Charles. A second letter on church reform, in justification of church reformers; with a proposal for the abolition of pluralities.
20 pp. London, C. J. G. & F. Rivington, 1833
K.

4436 GLOVER, George. An historical argument on the origin and property of tithes, with remarks on the expediency of a fair and equitable commutation, in a letter to earl Grey.
42 pp. London, J. Ridgway; Norwich, Bacon and Kinnebrook, 1833
T.

4437 GOUGER, Robert. Emigration for the relief of parishes practically considered.
tables. 16 pp. London, J. Ridgway, E. Wilson, 1833
N.

4438 GOULD, Nathaniel. Sketch of the trade of British America. Written originally for the Nautical Magazine; with a few alterations and additions.
tables. 20 pp. London, Fisher, Fisher & Jackson, 1833
A., N.

4439 HALE, William Hale. An essay on the supposed existence of a quadripartite and tripartite division of tithes in England, for maintaining the clergy, the poor, and the fabric of the church. Part II. With a supplement containing an inquiry into the origin of the quarta pars episcopalis of the Irish church.
tables. appendix. 62 pp. London, C. J. G. & F. Rivington [etc.], 1833
K., T.

4440 HANCOCK, John. Plan for the reconciliation of all interests in the emancipation of West India slaves.
16 pp. London, J. Hatchard, [etc.], 1833
K.

4441 Have the present ministers any claims on the future confidence of the nation? By a friend of the people.
16 pp. London, J. Hatchard, 1833
T.

4442 HEATHFIELD, Richard. Observations occasioned by the motion in the house of commons, on the 26th March, 1833, by Geo. R. Robinson, esquire, for a select committee, 'To consider and revise our existing taxation, with a view to the repeal of those burthens which press most heavily on productive industry, and the substitution of an equitable property tax in lieu thereof.' Addressed to the landed proprietors of the United Kingdom.
tables. 20 pp. London, Longman, Rees, Orme, Brown, Green and Longman, 1833
T., U.

4443 HERON, John. An abstract of the custom laws, duties, regulations, prohibitions and restrictions, inwards and outwards, for the United Kingdom, with the bounties on exportation and countervailing duties between Gt. Britain and Ireland.
tables. 80 pp. Dublin, W. Underwood, 1833
A., P.

4444 [HICKEY, William.] Hints originally intended for the small farmers of Co. Wexford; but suited to the circumstances of most parts of Ireland. By Martin Doyle.
illustration. table of contents. 126 pp. new ed. Dublin, W. Curry, jr., 1833
A.

4445 Hints on the practical effects of commercial restriction on production, consumption, and national wealth. With remarks on the claims of the silk trade. By a consumer.
32 pp. London, J. Hatchard, 1833
T.

4446 Hints to legislators, upon the subject of a commutation of tithes. By an Essex freeholder.
tables. 60 pp. London, Sherwood, Gilbert, and Piper, 1833
T.

4447 HODGKIN, Thomas. An inquiry into the merits of the American colonization society; and a reply to the charges brought against it. With an account of the British African colonization society.
62 pp. + map. London, J. & A. Arch [etc.], 1833
A., K.

4448 Impartial thoughts on the late calamitous fire, (Custom-House stores); in which the true cause of the same is sought to be accounted for on philosophical principles; the imperfections of the building noticed; and the claims of the sufferers upon the government considered. [signed D.C.]
Dublin, M. Goodwin, 1833
A., N.

4449 Information respecting the eastern townships of lower Canada, in which the British American Land Co. intend to commence operations for the sale and settlement of lands in the ensuing spring. 3rd Dec. 1833.
map. tables. 22 pp. London, C. Ruffy, 1833
N.

4450 Important to every person who rents a house! A caution to tenants against the injustice and legal chicanery to which they are exposed, under the existing state of the law of landlord and tenant, shewing in certain cases its absurdity and iniquity and proving from a recent verdict that almost every outgoing tenant is at the mercy of his landlord, and may be forced into a law-suit and saddled with all the costs, notwithstanding he may have offered to pay more than the amount due, and that the sum recovered should be only one farthing! Intended to point out the necessity for a reform in the law, and to put tenants on their guard while it continues in its present state.
tables. 42 pp. 2nd ed. London, E. Wilson, 1833
T.

4451 Inquiry into the navigation laws, and the effects of their alteration; with tables of shipping and trade compiled from official documents.
tables. 114 pp. London, Pelham Richardson, 1833
P., T.

4452 Ireland. Ignorance. 'Repeal.'
20 pp. London, J. Ridgway, 1833
A., N.

4453 JAGO, Richard Howlett. General and equitable commutation of tithes. A plan for the general commutation of lay and ecclesiastical tithes into corn rents: being a self-adjusting mode of payment in exact ratio to the half yearly average price of agricultural produce; proposed and exemplified in three letters, addressed to Thomas Greene, esq., M.P. for Lancaster, the editor of the Times newspaper, and to the right rev. the bishop of Bath and Wells. the second edition. table. 52 pp. London, C. Chapple, 1833
K., T.

4454 JONES, Richard. A few remarks on the proposed commutation of tithe, with suggestions of some additional facilities. 20 pp. London, J. Murray, 1833
A., K., N., T.

4455 ——. An introductory lecture on political economy, delivered at King's College, London, 27th February, 1833. To which is added a syllabus of a course of lectures on the wages of labor, to be delivered at King's College, London, in the month of April, 1833. 64 pp. London, J. Murray, 1833
K., N., T.

4456 ——. Syllabus of a course of lectures on the wages of labor, proposed to be delivered at King's College, London. 46 pp. London, J. Murray, 1833
K., T.

4457 JOPLIN, Thomas. The advantages of the proposed national bank of England, both to the public and its proprietory, briefly explained. tables. 30 pp. London, J. Ridgway, 1833
P.

4458 KINAHAN, Daniel. A digest of the Irish Temporalities and Ecclesiastical Commission Act, with notes and an index. Dublin, R. Milliken, 1833
A.

4459 LARPENT, George G. de H. Some remarks on the late negotiations between the board of control and the East India Company. tables. 62 pp. London, Pelham Richardson, 1833
T.

4460 [LE MARCHANT, Sir Denis, bart., ed.] The reform ministry and the reformed parliament. tables. 110 pp. 4th ed. London, J. Ridgway, 1833
A., T.

4461 A letter to his grace the archbishop of Canterbury, on church reform, in which is suggested a plan of alterations both safe and efficient, by a non-beneficed clergyman. 54 pp. London, Roake and Varty, 1833
K.

4462 Letters of Philodemus on the political degradation of Mayo, the parliamentary conduct of its representatives Messrs. Dominick and John Denis Browne; and the means of establishing its independence. 2nd series. 40 pp. Castlebar, printed at 'The Telegraph' Office, 1833
A.

4463 [LLOYD, Francis.] A letter to the right hon. the viscount Althorp, chancellor of the exchequer, etc., on his proposed interference with the present system of country banking. By a country banker. table. 72 pp. London, J. Ridgway, 1833
T.

4464 LLOYD, William Forster. Two lectures on the checks to population, delivered before the University of Oxford, in Michaelmas term 1832. 76 pp. Oxford, S. Collingwood, 1833
K., T.

4465 MCCREA, J. B. The principle of the Irish Church Reform Bill introduced by viscount Althorp the real cause of the embarrassments of the empire. A speech delivered in the conservative society of Ireland on the 26th of February, 1833. tables. 24 pp. Dublin, R. M. Tims, [1833?]
T.

4466 MALCOLM, Sir John. Speech of major-gen. Sir John Malcolm, G.C.B., &c. &c. in the court of proprietors, on Monday, the 15th April, 1833, on the preliminary papers respecting the East India company's charter. 38 pp. London, J. Murray, 1833
K., T.

4467 MARJORIBANKS, Charles. Letter to the right hon. Charles Grant, president of the board of controul on the present state of British intercourse with China. 68 pp. London, J. Hatchard, 1833
K., T.

4468 MARTIN, Robert Montgomery. Ireland, as it was, -is, -& ought to be; with a comparative statistical chart of the population-houses-value of agricultural produce; number of schools & scholars, protestant & Roman catholic; number of baronies & parishes, number of newspapers & stamps issued; representatives in parliament; grand jury presentments; savings banks & amount of deposits; proprietors income from land; renting, rate of land to landlords & middlemen, area in square miles & acres; proportion of inhabitants to land, etc. etc. of each county. tables. fold. tables. 184 pp. London, Parbury, Allen, 1833
B., K., L., N., Q., T., U.

——. 2nd ed. 188 pp. London, Parbury and Allen, 1833
A.

4469 ——. Poor laws for Ireland, a measure of justice to England; of humanity to the people of both islands; and of self-preservation for the empire. With a practical development of an improved system of settlement, assessment, and relief. 54 pp. London, Parbury, Allen, 1833
A., K., N., T., U.

4470 Memoranda, deduced from official and public documents, and intended to show the comparative advantages derivable to the trade and commerce of Dublin from the works carrying on for the improvement of the navigation of the river; from the project of a railway for commercial purposes: and from the plan of a ship canal, connecting the harbour of Kingstown with a floating dock in the Liffey. map. 44 pp. Dublin, 1833
A., N.

4471 MEREWETHER, Francis. A letter to the right honorable Edward G. Stanley, M.P., chief secretary for Ireland, on a recently reported declaration of his in parliament.
8 pp. London, C. J. G. and F. Rivington [etc.], 1833
K.

4472 MONCK, Charles Atticus. An address to the agricultural classes of Great Britain on the evils which are the consequence of restricting the importation of foreign corn.
64 pp. London, J. Ridgway, 1833
K., T.

4473 MOORE, Richard. Important notices of that which concerns the pecuniary credit of a state and in particular that of England.
52 pp. London, Longman & co., 1833
T.

4474 MOORSOM, Richard. Thoughts on the changes which have taken place in the navigation laws of England, and their effects on the shipping interest: together with observations on a trade of export, and the benefits to be derived by British ships from the termination of the East India Company's charter.
tables. 80 pp. London, J. Ridgway, 1833
T.

4475 MULCASTER, Samuel. Tables for friendly societies, agreeable to their old usage and customs; complied [sic] from the existing data, arising from the practice of the various benefit societies in the metropolis; extracted from their books, annual statements, and records, for the last half century, from societies of 2 years to nearly 100 years standing, for the allowances on sickness, superanuation, [sic] mortality of members, mortality of member's wives, lyings-in, loss by fire, imprisonment for debt, and substitute for the militia.
tables. 16 pp. London, Berger [etc., etc.], 1833
K.

4476 MUNDELL, Alexander. The danger of the resolutions relative to the bank charter, as proposed by the chancellor of the exchequer, succinctly pointed out.
table. 16 pp. London, Longman, Rees, Orme, Brown, Green and Longman, 1833
T.

4477 ——. The operation of the corn laws during the last sixty years, stated in the shape of substantive propositions.
tables. 20 pp. London, Longman, Rees, Orme, Brown, Green & Longman, [etc.], 1833
K., N., T.

4478 NEWNHAM, Henry. East India question. Facts and observations intended to convey the opinions of the native population of the territory of Bengal respecting the past and the future.
appendices. 125 pp. London, J. Ridgway, 1833
T.

4479 [NORTON, Eardley.] Letters to lord Althorp, chancellor of the exchequer, etc. on his proposed change of the tithe system, the working of the poor laws with plan of extensive relief for the landed interest.
34 pp. London, J. Hatchard, 1833
K., T.

4480 O'BRIEN, William Smith. Thoughts upon ecclesiastical reform, with suggestions for the conciliatory adjustment of the tithe question.
Limerick, R. Canter, 1833
A., N., U.

4481 Observations on the rejected local court jurisdiction bill, addressed to the trading interests.
30 pp. London, Effingham Wilson, 1833
T.

4482 Observations upon the proposed measure for altering the tenure of the leases of church-lands in Ireland.
tables. 30 pp. Dublin, Richards, 1833
A.

4483 [OGILVIE, Henry.] Suggestions for the improvement of the domestic policy of the British government.
tables. 124 pp. London, J. Ridgway, 1833

4484 On pluralities: a third letter addressed to the right reverend father in God, Edward, lord bishop of Llandaff. By a clergyman.
20 pp. London, C. J. G. & F. Rivington, 1833
K., T.

4485 Outline of a plan for the general commutation of tithes in England and Wales. By H.S.
34 pp. London, J. Hatchard, 1833
K., T.

4486 PENNY, John. Practical retrenchment the legitimate object of reform.
table. 58 pp. London, J. Ridgway, [etc.], [1833?]
T.

4487 [PERCEVAL, Arthur Philip.] The king and the church vindicated and delivered or, the prime minister convicted of counselling to the crown, a violation of the coronation oath: in an address to the house of lords, and in a plain, solemn, and faithful appeal to his grace the lord archbishop of Canterbury. By a minister of the Church of Ireland.
52 pp. London, Hatchard, Dublin, R. M. Tims, 1833
T.

4488 [——.] A letter to the Right Honourable earl Grey, on the obligation of the coronation oath. By one of his majesty's chaplains.
16 pp. London, C. J. G. & F. Rivington, 1833
T.

4489 PHILLIPS, Joseph. West India question. The outline of a plan for the total, immediate, and safe abolition of slavery throughout the British colonies.
14 pp. London, J. and A. Arch, 1833
K., T.

4490 Plain words addressed to members of the Church of England. By one of themselves.
20 pp. London, C. J. G. & F. Rivington, 1833
T.

4491 A plan for procuring the residence of ministers of the established church, without interfering with vested interests, contained in a letter to lords Brougham and Althorp, and

respectfully submitted to the consideration of both houses of parliament. By the son of a lawyer.
14 pp. London, C. J. G. & F. Rivington, 1833
K.

4492 [PLAYFAIR, Arthur.] Outlines of a plan for the immediate settlement of the question of church reform, without disturbing the rights and interests of the present holders of church property.
16 pp. London, J. Hatchard, 1833
K.

4493 PRATT, John Tidd. The law relating to the purchase of government annuities through the medium of savings banks and parochial societies comprising the stat. 3W. IV. c. 14. with explanatory notes and references; An appendix containing the different sections of the several statutes referred to and applicable to a society formed for the above purpose and a copious index with a form of rules.
84 pp. London, Shaw, 1833
A., T.

4494 Public economy concentrated; or a connected view of currency, agriculture, and manufactures. By an enquirer into first principles.
96 pp. Carlisle, Hudson Scott, 1833
T.

4495 REID, William. An inquiry into the causes of the present distress with an attempt to explain the theory of national wealth.
34 pp. Edinburgh, William Tait, 1833
T.

4496 [——.] Strictures on the evidence taken before the committee of secrecy of the house of commons on the Bank of England charter. By Scotus.
tables. 64 pp. London, Relfe and Unwin, 1833
T.

4497 Remarks on the importance of preserving the existing scale of duties on North American and foreign wood; with an appendix, containing evidence taken before a select committee of the house of commons, on manufactures, commerce and shipping.
tables. appendix. 142 pp. Glasgow, Hedderwick, 1833
N.

4498 Remarks on the propriety and necessity of making the factory bill of more general application.
appendix with tables. 10 pp. London, Longman, Rees, Orme, Brown, Green and Longman; Leeds, Robinson, 1833
T.

4499 Repeal or no repeal. Repeal of the union considered in its practical bearings.
36 pp. London, J. Ridgway, 1833
A., N.

4500 Report by the directors of the Provincial Bank of Ireland to the proprietors assembled at the eighth yearly general meeting on Thursday, the 16th day of May 1833, with a list of the directors, office-bearers, branches and agents, together with an alphabetical list of the proprietors, at 30th April, 1833.
48 pp. London, Thomas & Co., 1833
A.

4501 Report of the agricultural seminary at Templemoyle for 1833.
16 pp. Londonderry, Hempton, 1833
A.

4502 The report of the Strangers' Friend Society, instituted in the year 1786, for the purpose of visiting and relieving sick and distressed strangers, and other poor, at their respective habitations; for the year ending June 24th, 1833, with its rules and a list of subscriptions and donations.
44 pp. Bristol, the society, 1833
A.

4503 A report of the committee appointed at a meeting of gentlemen, merchants and traders, held in Dublin 11th August 1833, with a view to promote and ensure the construction of a ship canal from Kingstown harbour to Dublin.
24 pp. Dublin, E. Ponsonby, 1833
A., N.

4504 Report of the council of the chamber of commerce of Dublin to the annual assembly of the members of the association, held on the 6th of March, 1833.
26 pp. Dublin, P. D. Hardy, 1833
A.

4505 Report of the proceedings of the committee of the relief association for the suffering peasantry in the West of Ireland.
tables. appendix. 40 pp. Dublin, P. D. Hardy, 1833
A.

4506 RICKMAN, John. Poor laws in Ireland.
16 pp. London, L. Hansard, 1833
A., N.

4507 RUDKIN, Henry. Remarks humbly submitted to the right hon. lord Althorp, chancellor of the exchequer, and the right hon. Sir Henry Parnell, M.P., etc., on the insufficiency of the system now in use for determining and securing the spirit revenue, arising from the licensed distilleries of the United Kingdom; with a proposed plan for superseding the saccharometer, and all other fallacious implements applicable to the present mode of estimating the duty on the attenuation, or primary processes; shewing, by an exposition of official facts, supported by some of the first authorities, scientific, legal, and practical, that by abolishing that instrument, and its consequent presumptive calculations on the ingredients; and by estimating the duty as proposed, on positive principles on the spirit, exempt from the usual loss by evaporation, that a sum, exceeding one million sterling, stated by official report to parliament to be lost by the fallacy of the present system, may be added to the annual finances of the state, as clearly illustrated by experiments lately prosecuted by command of the right honorable the lords commissioners of his majesty's treasury, at the revenue distillery.
36 pp. London, W. Gilbert, 1833
P.

4508 A scheme for a general taxation on property, income, and trade; and for saving expence in its collection: and to afford the means of bringing about reciprocal free trading. To which is added, a proposal addressed to Mr. Secretary

Stanley, on the subject of the abolition of negro slavery; with a plan for carrying that object into effect, to the satisfaction of the abolitionist, the planter, and the slave population. appendix. 22 pp. London, Dean and Munday, [1833?]

T.

4509 SCROPE, George Julius Duncombe Poulett. An examination of the bank charter question, with an enquiry into the nature of a just standard of value, and suggestions for the improvement of our monetary system.
table of contents. 78 pp. London, J. Murray, 1833

K., N., T.

4510 ——. Plan of a poor-law for Ireland, with a review of the arguments for and against it.
94 pp. London, J. Ridgway, 1833

A., N., U.

4511 SEDGWICK, James. A letter to the rate-payers of Great Britain, on the repeal of the poor-laws; to which is subjoined the outline of a plan for the abolition of the poor-rates at the end of three years.
table. appendix. 172 pp. London, J. Ridgway, 1833

T.

4512 The seventh report of the Belfast society for relief of the destitute sick adopted at the annual general meeting of the society, on Thursday, the 29th of August, 1833; with a list of subscribers.
18 pp. Belfast, Mairs, 1833

N.

4513 SHEAHAN, Thomas. 'Articles' of Irish manufacture, or, portions of Cork history.
228 pp. Cork, Higgins, 1833

A.

4514 SINCLAIR, Sir John, bart. Plan for the establishment of a small note circulation in England, to the amount of ten millions.
no t.p. 10 pp. n.p., [1833]

P.

4515 Sketch on an association for gathering and diffusing information on the condition of the poor.
14 pp. London, S. W. Fores, 1833

A.

4516 [SOCKETT, Thomas.] Emigration. A letter to a member of parliament, containing a statement of the method pursued by the Petworth committee, in sending out emigrants to Upper Canada in the years 1832 and 1833 and a plan upon which the sums required for defraying the expense of emigration may be raised.
tables. 22 pp. Petworth, J. Phillips, London, Longman, Rees, Orme, Brown, Green & Longman, 1833

K., N.

See 4425.

4517 A statement from and on behalf of the retail grocers of Dublin. To the members of the imperial parliament, indiscriminately.
8 pp. Dublin, 1833

A.

4518 STAUNTON, Michael. Exposition of facts and fallacies concerning Ireland (extracted from the Irish Monthly Magazine for April 1833).
tables. 28 pp. Dublin, J. Blundell, 1833

A., N.

4519 ——. Lights for Littleton; being a series of letters published in the Dublin Morning Register in September, 1833, and addressed to the Rt. Hon. E. J. Littleton, chief secretary for Ireland.
tables. 44 pp. Dublin, E. Bull, 1833

A., N.

4520 STEPHEN, George. A letter to the proprietors and occupiers of land in the parish of Bledlow, in Buckinghamshire, on their system of giving bread-money in aid of wages.
32 pp. London, J. Hatchard, 1833

T.

4521 STODDART, George H. Evidence on the necessity of church reform, compiled from the publications of lord Henley, archdeacon Wilkins, and Berens, Doctors Arnold, and Burton, the rev. prebendaries C. Wodehouse, and G. Townsend, reverends W. Wilkinson, Riland, Cox, Girdlestone, Miller, E. Duncombe, Storer; Winstanley Hull, esq.; Uvedale Price, esq.; and others; with additional remarks by the Rev. George H. Stoddart, A.M. of Queen's College, Oxford.
86 pp. London, W. H. Dalton, 1833

K.

4522 Strictures on a proposition contained in a letter from C. E. Branfill, esq., of Upminster Hall, in Essex, to the right hon. lord Althorp, on tithe-commutation.
20 pp. London, J. Hatchard, [etc.] 1833

K., T.

4523 [TAYLOR, Edgar.] Lord Brougham's local courts bill examined. By H. B. Denton.
appendix. 68 pp. London, Williams Crofts, 1833

T.

4524 TEYNHAM, Henry Francis Roper-Curzon, 14th baron. How it must work: in an address to the freeholders and electors of the United Empire.
tables. 62 pp. 2nd ed. London, J. Ridgway, 1833

T.

4525 TORRENS, Robert. Letters on commercial policy.
table. 80 pp. London, Longman & Co., 1833

K., T.

4526 TOWNSEND, George. A plan for abolishing pluralities, and non-residence, in the church of England, by increasing the value of poor livings, without spoliation. In a letter to lord Henley: with a postscript to the church reformation society, and the draft of an act of parliament.
100 pp. [various paging.] London, C. J. G. and F. Rivington, 1833

K.

4527 VIVIAN, Sir Hussey. Opinions on tithes, and on the state of Ireland, expressed, at different times, in the house of commons.
60 pp. London, J. Ridgway, 1833

N.

4528 WALTER, Henry. A letter to the Rev. H. F. Yeatman, Ll.B. acting magistrate for Dorset and Somerset, etc. etc. etc. tables. 66 pp. London, C. J. G. & F. Rivington, Cambridge, J. & J. J. Deighton, 1833

K.

On poor laws; see also 4537.

4529 WALTERS, William Clayton. Notes historical and legal on the endowments of the Church of England.
64 pp. London, B. Fellowes, 1833

T.

4530 WETHERELL, B. J. Church reform. A letter to the viscount Althorp, M.P., chancellor of the exchequer, &c. &c. &c. on ecclesiastical leases.
46 pp. London, Longman, Rees, Orme, Brown, Green and Longman, 1833

K.

4531 WETHERELL, Charles. The present state of the poor-law question, in letters to the marquis of Salisbury.
tables. table of contents. 52 pp. London, J. Murray, 1833

A., N.

4532 WHATELY, Thomas. The evidence of the Revd. Thomas Whately before the committee of the house of lords on the state of the poor in the years 1830, 1831; with introductory remarks on poor laws in Ireland and on an article in the XCVII No. of the Quarterly Review.
tables. 56 pp. London, B. Fellowes, 1833

A., N.

4533 WHITE, Francis. Report and observations on the state of the poor of Dublin.
32 pp. Dublin, J. Porter, 1833

A., D., N.

4534 [WILLIAMS, Charles Wye.] Observations on the inland navigation of Ireland and the want of employment for its population, with a description of the River Shannon. 2nd. ed. Comprising an examination of the application of money grants in aid of public works.
table of contents. 116 pp. London, Vacher & Son, Dublin, W. Curry, jr., 1833

A., N., Q.

4535 WOODROW, John. An outline of a plan for the formation of a savings and annuity bank, also a general parochial friendly society together with the general extermination of pauperism at sixty years of age, and a few observations regarding the original plan, and the Savings Banks Annuity Act. Now before parliament.
appendix. 38 pp. London, Castell, 1833

N.

4536 WORTLEY, John Stuart. A brief inquiry into the true award of an 'Equitable adjustment' between the nation and its creditors. With tables.
tables. 42 pp. London, J. Hatchard, 1833

T.

4537 YEATMAN, Harry Farr. An inquiry into the merits of the poor law report of D. O. P. Okeden, esquire, assistant

commissioner; by the Rev. H. F. Yeatman, L.L.B. acting magistrate for Dorset and Somerset.
tables. 42 pp. Sherborne, Toll, 1833

N.

See 4528.

1834

4538 Annual report of the charitable society for relief of sick and indigent room-keepers (of all religious persuasions), in the city of Dublin for the year 1833.
tables. 60 pp. Dublin, printed by Grean, 1834

A.

4539 An appeal to all who can conscientiously declare themselves to be real friends and supporters of the church of England, especially to the nobility, gentry, land and tithe owners of England, and to members of her legislature. By one of themselves.
24 pp. London, C. J. G. and F. Rivington, 1834

K.

4540 An appeal to his majesty's government and the honorable East India Company, for justice to the claims of the hon. E. I. company's maritime service, to compensation, under clause 7 of the new India act, out of the commercial assets late belonging to the hon. company, but now to be applied to the use of India. To which is added, an equitable scale of pensions, suggested to be granted in order to carry the intention of the clause into effect. By an officer of the service.
plate. 88 pp. London, Pelham Richardson, 1834

K., T.

4541 Animadversions on the conflicting interests of the Church in Ireland as a chief cause of her disturbed state, with the recommendation of a remedy. By an Irish Landowner.
68 pp. London, J. Ridgway, 1834

T.

4542 BERMINGHAM, Thomas. Additional statements on the subject of the River Shannon to the reports published in 1831.
16 pp. London, S. W. Fores, 1834

A., T.

———. Another issue. 16 pp. London, S. W. Fores, 1834

A., N.

4543 BISH, Thomas. A plea for Ireland; submitting the outline of a proposition for holding the court and parliament at occasional intervals in Dublin. In a letter to the Rt. Hon. lord Althorp, chancellor of the exchequer.
50 pp. London, J. M. Richardson, Dublin, Cumming, 1834

A., N., RM.

4544 BLACKER, William. An essay on the improvements to be made in the cultivation of small farms by the introduction of green crops, and house-feeding the stock thereon: originally published in an address to the small farmers on the estates of the earl of Gosford and colonel Close, in the county of Armagh.
landlords' edition. 92 pp. Dublin, W. Curry, jr., 1834

A., D.

tenants' edition. 96 pp. Dublin, W. Curry, jr., 1834

A., B., U.

4545 ——. Prize essay, addressed to the agricultural committee of the Royal Dublin Society, on the management of landed property in Ireland; the consolidation of small farms, employment of the poor etc. etc. for which the gold medal was awarded.
table of contents. 44 pp. Dublin, R. Graisberry, 1834
A., D., N., T.

4546 BLIGH, Richard. Bellum Agrarium. A foreview of the winter of 1835; suggested by the poor law project: with observations on the report and the bill.
40 pp. London, J. Hatchard, 1834
T.

4547 BRENTON, Edward Pelham. Observations on the training and education of children in Great Britain: a letter to Sir James Graham on impressment: and a translation from the French of M. Ducpetiaux's work on mendicity. With an appendix.
tables. appendix. 26 pp. London, C. Rice, 1834
K., T.
See 4299.

4548 Brief remarks on lord Althorp's bill for the amendment of the poor laws, and hints for its improvement, by a country magistrate.
16 pp. London, J. Ridgway, 1834
A.

4549 Case of the bread manufacturers of the city of Dublin.
8 pp. Dublin, 1834
A.

4550 The cause of the evils existing in Ireland with a plain and simple remedy whereby agitation may be put down, the people may be pacified and employed, the country improved and enriched, life and property made secure, and the natural resources greatly augmented. By one of the people.
16 pp. London, T. Drury, 1834
A., N.

4551 CLONCURRY, Valentine Broune Lawless, 2nd baron. The design of a law for promoting the pacification of Ireland, and the improvement of the Irish tenantry and population, submitted to his majesty's government, the legislature and the public. By lord Cloncurry.
40 pp. Dublin, Folds, 1834
A., N., U.

4552 COBBETT, William. Three lectures on the political state of Ireland delivered in the Fishamble St. Theatre, Dublin, by Wm. Cobbett esq. M.P., faithfully reported with an analysis and some notes appended by T. Hughes, esq.
46 pp. Dublin, Byrne, 1834
A., N.

4553 [COLEBROOKE, Sir William Macbean George.] A plan for the improvement of Ireland by the union of English and Irish capital, and the co-operation of the people in both countries; with a map and appendix, containing extracts from parliamentary reports and other publications.
tables. appendix. 158 pp. London, J. Ridgway, 1834
U.

——. Another issue, without appendix. 88 pp. London, J. Ridgway, 1834
A., K., N., T.

4554 COWELL, John Welsford. A letter to the rev. John T. Becher, of Southwell, in reply to certain charges and assertions made in the introduction to a second edition of his anti-pauper system, recently published.
appendix. 62 pp. London, J. Ridgway, 1834
T.

4555 CROLY, David O. An essay religious and political on ecclesiastical finance, as regards the Roman catholic church in Ireland; interspersed with other matter not irrelevant to the subject.
appendix. 96 pp. Cork, Barry Drew [etc., etc.], 1834
T.

4556 CROPPER, James. Outline of a plan for an agricultural school, and for the employment of agricultural labourers by spade cultivation, at Fearnhead, near Warrington.
12 pp. Liverpool, Smith, 1834
N.

4557 DALY, Thomas. Outline of a plan for the abolition of the tithes, and for making a provision for the ministers of the protestant established and Roman catholic churches.
32 pp. Dublin, Wakeman, London, Hatchard, 1834
N.

4558 DICKSON, Stephen Fox. Minutes of the evidence given by Stephen F. Dickson before the select committee of the house of commons, on manufactures, commerce and shipping, copied from the report printed by order of the house of commons with some explanatory observations.
20 pp. Dublin, L. McDermott, 1834
A.

4559 ——. Rules and regulations for ships loading lord Lowther's coal, at the port of Whitehaven.
8 pp. Dublin, L. McDermott, 1834
A.

4560 The East-India company and the maritime service.
28 pp. London, J. Hatchard, 1834
K., T.

4561 Facts for the repealers. Originally published in the Dublin Evening Post, during the months of January and February, 1834.
24 pp. Dublin, W. Page, 1834
A., N.

4562 FARRELL, H. Outline of a plan to pay off the national debt progressively, without a forfeiture of public credit or a breach of national faith. Analysis of the causes which led to the first French revolution: their striking resemblance with the elements of our present crisis: advice to the minister, how to avert such a catastrophe. Irish absenteeism examined, with suggestion of remedial measures for Ireland. Analysis of the repeal question.
24 pp. Dublin, the author, 1834
A.

4563 FERGUSSON, Adam. Practical notes made during a second visit to Canada, in MDCCCXXXIII.
tables. 48 pp. + map. Edinburgh, William Blackwood, London, T. Cadell, 1834
T.

4564 FITZMAURICE, Gerald. The rights of the people of Ireland, an integral part of the United Kingdom, under a reformed parliament. In a letter to earl Grey, K.G.
tables. 68 pp. London, J. Ridgway, Dublin, R. Milliken, 1834
N.

4565 FITZWILLIAM, Charles William Wentworth-Fitzwilliam, 5th earl, at this time styled 'viscount Milton'. Address to the landowners of Great Britain on the corn laws. Published, by permission, by friends to free trade, and particularly to an open trade in corn, essential, in their opinion, to the best interests of Great Britain.
tables. appendix. London, Effingham Wilson, 1834
N., P.

4566 FLYNN, Henry E. A glance at the question of a ship-canal connecting the asylum harbour at Kingstown with the River Liffey.
maps. tables. 88 pp. Dublin, Folds, 1834
A., N.

4567 Four years of a liberal government.
tables. 16 pp. London, H. Hooper, 1834
N.

4568 GILBART, James William. A practical treatise on banking.
128 pp. 3rd ed. London, Effingham Wilson, 1834
N., T.
See 3819 for full title.

4569 [GOULD, Nathaniel.] Emigration. Practical advice to emigrants, on all points connected with their comfort and economy from making choice of a ship to settling on and cropping a farm.
tables. appendix with tables. 120 pp. London, Effingham Wilson, 1834
K.

——. 128 pp. 2nd ed. London, E. Wilson, 1834
N.

4570 GRAHAME, Thomas. A treatise on internal intercourse and communication in civilised states, and particularly in Great Britain.
tables. 174 pp. London, Longman, Rees, Orme, Brown, Green and Longman, 1834
K.

4571 Great Western Railway, England: An account of the proceedings of the Great Western Railway company, with extracts from the evidence given in support of the bill, before the committee of the house of commons, in the session of 1834.
122 pp. London, Smith & Ebbs, 1834
N.

The extracts of evidence are printed separately, by Gutch & Martin, Bristol.

4572 GREG, Samuel and GREG, William Rathbone. Analysis of the evidence taken before the factory commissioners, as far as it relates to the population of Manchester and the vicinity engaged in the cotton trade. [Paper] read before the Statistical society of Manchester, March, 1834.
34 pp. Manchester, Bancks, 1834
T.

4573 HALL, Robert Gream. Observations addressed to a member of parliament on the inexpediency of a general metropolitan registry for deeds and other assurances affecting lands in England and Wales.
appendix. 78 pp. London, J. Murray [etc.], 1834
T.

4574 HINCHY, John. A plan for a modified system of poor laws, and employment for the people of Ireland. In a letter to his excellency the most noble Richard Colley Wellesley, marquis Wellesley, K.G. lieutenant general and general governor of Ireland.
8 pp. Dublin, printed by Joseph Blundell, 1834
A., N.

4575 Hints on the mal-administration of the poor laws with a plan for bringing the collection and appropriation of the poor rates under the immediate superintendence and control of his majesty's government.
table. 26 pp. London, Charles Skipper and East, 1834
T.

4576 Hints on the unlimited diffusion of useful knowledge, at no expense to the reader through the medium of the mercantile and trading classes, practically illustrated by a history of printing, specimen of types and guide to authors in correcting the press.
20 pp. Edinburgh, Neill & co., 1834
N.

4577 HULL, John. The philanthropic repertory of plans, for improving the condition of the labouring poor. Comprising education: 1. Popular education. 2. Schools of industry. 3. Agricultural schools. 4. Locomotive school rooms. 5. Cheap village schools de Fellenberg's schools. Provident societies: 6. District visiting societies. 7. Loan funds. 8. Self-supporting dispensaries. Of general benefit: 9. Allotment of land. 10. Erection of cottages. 11. Temperance societies. 12. Juvenile guardian societies. 13. Village libraries. 14. Circulating libraries. 15. Trust societies.
tables. 40 pp. 5th ed. Dublin, R. Milliken, 1834
R.

4578 Instructions given by the commissioners appointed to enquire into the state of the poor of Ireland to the assistant commissioners.
56 pp. Dublin, A. Thom, 1834
A., P.
Contains: Copy of commission, instructions, copies of the queries circulated by the commissioners.

4579 KENNEDY, John Pitt. I. Rules of Loughash national and agricultural day school.
4 pp. Dublin, A. Thom, 1834
U.

4580 KERR, George. Kerr's exposition of legislative tyranny and defence of the trades' union.
22 pp. Belfast, J. Smith, 1834
A.

4581 KNIGHT, Thomas Andrew. Upon the necessity of a commutation of tithes, and upon the means of rendering the soil of the British islands capable of abundantly supporting

twice the amount of their present population: addressed to the right hon. viscount Althorp, chancellor of the exchequer, &c. &c.
44 pp. London, Longman, Rees, Orme, Brown, Green and Longman, Ludlow, R. Jones, 1834
K., T.

4582 The law, practice and principles of church-rates, (including Dr. Lushington's opinion); being a report of the proceedings of a numerous vestry meeting in Louth, October 2nd, 1834, when a church rate was refused. Published under the superintendence of the committee for opposing the rate.
tables. 166 pp. Louth, H. Hurton, [1834]
T.

4583 LEFROY, Christopher Edward.   Letter to Sir Thomas Baring, baronet, on the subject of allotments of land to the poor, containing his experience of that system for four years, upon a very small scale, at West Ham, near Basingstoke, from Christopher Edward Lefroy, esquire.
16 pp. London, Hatchard & son, 1834
T.

4584 Legislative reports on the poor laws, from the years 1817, to 1833, inclusive, with remedial measures proposed.
58 pp. London, J. Ridgway, 1834
T.

4585 A letter on the repeal of the union, addressed to Sir Wm. Gosset, under secretary of state, by a protestant dissenter.
32 pp. Dublin, Pettigrew & Oulton, 1834
A., N.

4586 A letter to earl Fitzwilliam on the corn laws. By J. R. T.
24 pp. London, Simpkin and Marshall, Thirsk, R. Peat, 1834
K., T.

4587 A letter to the Right Honourable earl Grey, premier, chiefly respecting the established Church of Ireland. By a member of the established Church of Scotland.
10 pp. Aberdeen, D. Chalmers, 1834
T.

4588 A letter to the Right Honourable lord Althorp, on the bill for amending the poor laws. By a chairman of quarter sessions.
16 pp. London, J. Hatchard, 1834
T.

4589 LONGFIELD, Mountifort.   Four lectures on the poor laws.
appendix. 106 pp. Dublin, R. Milliken, 1834
A., K., N., T.

4590 ——. Lectures on political economy, delivered in Trinity and Michaelmas terms, 1833.
appendix. 278 pp. Dublin, R. Milliken, 1834
T.

4591 McCULLOCH, John Ramsay. A dictionary, practical, theoretical and historical, of commerce and commercial navigation: illustrated with maps and plans.
16 pp. 2nd. ed. corrected. enlarged. London, Longman, Rees, Orme, Brown, Green & Longman, 1834
A.
This contains only the Preface to the two editions.

4592 MACDONNELL, Eneas.   Letter to the right hon. Charles Grant, president of the board of commissioners for the affairs of India.
appendix. 148 pp. London, J. Ridgway, 1834
K., T.

4593 MacKENNA, Theobald. A familiar summary of the rights and liabilities of the tenant, the landlord and the incumbent, under the last two tithe acts viz., the 2 and 3 William the Fourth, Chap. 119; and the 3 and 4 William the Fourth, chap. 100.
appendix, index. table of contents. 112 pp. Dublin, R. Milliken, 1834
A.

4594 MAHONY, Pierce. Letters from Mr. Mahony to the Rt. Hon. E. J. Littleton M.P., chief secretary of state for Ireland, on the Irish Tithe or Land-Tax Bill of 1834.
64 pp. London, J. L. Cox & son, 1834
A., D., N., U.

——.   90 pp. 4th ed. London, J. L. Cox & son, 1834
T.

4595 ——. Observations by Mr. Mahony on the Tithe Bill (Ireland), for the Right Hon. E. J. Littleton, M.P. &c. &c.
tables. 12 pp. London, J. L. Cox & son, 1834
U.

4596 [MAXWELL, Sir John, 8th bart.]   Manual labour, versus machinery, exemplified in a speech, on moving for a committee of parliamentary enquiry into the condition of half-a-million hand-loom weavers, in reference to the establishment of local guilds of trade; with an appendix: containing affidavits of general distress, rates of wages and prices of provisions for a series of years, and a demonstration of the effects of heavy taxation on human industry when subjected to competition with untaxed machinery. By the member for Lanarkshire.
tables. 46 pp. London, Cochrane & M'Crone, 1834
A.

4597 Memorials to the lords of the treasury relative to the claims of the merchants of Dublin, whose property was destroyed by the fire in the government stores, 9th August, 1833. To which are appended, the legal opinions taken upon the subject.
46 pp. Dublin, P. D. Hardy, 1834
A., N.

4598 [MORGAN, Hector Davies.]   The beneficial operation of banks for savings, affirmed in an address to the trustees, managers and friends of the bank for savings for the hundred of Hinckford, in the county of Essex, by whose liberal subscriptions a splendid memorial of their approbation was presented to the secretary of the institution, Nov. 28, 1833. Annexed is a brief memoir of the late Lewis Majendie, esq. of Hedingham Castle.
tables in appendix. 70 pp. London, Henry Wise, 1834
K.

4599 MURRAY, John Fisher. Repeal no remedy: or, the union with Ireland completed; addressed at this crisis to every Englishman.
44 pp. London, J. Ridgway, 1834
A., N.

4600 National Benevolent Institution (Bristol District), for the relief of distressed persons in the middle ranks of life, of whatever country or persuasion; established in Bristol in 1810: report and statement of account as balanced to December 31, 1833,
30 pp. Bristol, J. Wansbrough, 1834
A.

4601 New Brunswick and Nova Scotia Land Company. Practical information respecting New Brunswick, including details relevant to its soil, climate, productions and agriculture, published for the use of persons intending to settle upon the lands of the company.
20 pp. [map missing.] London, Taylor, 1834
N.

4602 North American Colonial Association of Ireland. prospectus. 16 pp. Dublin, Shaw, 1834
N.

4603 Notice of the silver mines of Fresnillo, in the state of Zacatecas, Mexico, now working for account of that state, and of their present condition, production, and prospects. With the basis of the conditions upon which the government of Zacatecas offers to grant the rights of possession, and of working these mines for a term of years.
map. plate. table. 46 pp. London, Cochrane and McCrone, 1834
T.

4604 Observations on a pamphlet entitled, brief examination of the bishop of Exeter's recent charge to his clergy concerning tithes, church reform, unitarianism, &c. By an unitarian clergyman.
40 pp. London, C. J. G. & F. Rivington, [etc., etc.], 1834
K., T.

4605 Observations on the present state of the poor laws.
30 pp. London, J. Ridgway, 1834
T.

4606 Observations on tithes: shewing their oppressive operation on the cultivation of land; and their want of accordance, under their present interpretation, with the acknowledged principles of law. By a voice from Kent.
tables. appendices. 54 pp. London, J. J. Welsh, [etc.], 1834
K., T.

4607 O'KELLY, P. Advice and guide to emigrants, going to the United States of America.
map. table of contents. 100 pp. Dublin, Folds, 1834
A.

4608 O'LEARY, Joseph. The law of statutable composition for tithes in Ireland, with an appendix containing the necessary parts of the tithe acts, and some precedents of pleadings.
table of contents. 298 pp. Dublin, Hodges & Smith, 1834
A.

4609 On combinations of trades.
appendix. 94 pp. new ed. London, J. Ridgway, 1834
A.

First published 1831.

4610 On the corn laws. By an Essex farmer.
tables. appendix. 44 pp. London, John and Arthur Arch, 1834
T.

4611 PHILIPS, Francis. Analysis of the defective state of turnpike roads and turnpike securities, with suggestions for their improvement.
appendices. 72 pp. London, Longman, Rees, Orme, Brown, Green, and Longman, 1834
K., T.

4612 A plea for the church in Ireland, or, a protest against sacrilege.
40 pp. London, Roake and Varty, 1834
K.

4613 The poor laws: their present operation, and their proposed amendment. Chiefly drawn from the evidence and reports of the poor law commissioners. Section I.
52 pp. London, C. Knight, 1834
A.

4614 PRATT, John Tidd. Preface to the second edition of Mr. Tidd Pratt's poor law bill.
40 pp. n.p., [1834?]
A.

4615 PURDON, Simon. Practicability of improving Ireland; and great encouragement for joint-stock companies. A lecture delivered in the Atheneum of the Plymouth Institution, 6th March, 1834.
18 pp. Plymouth, G. Hearder, 1834
A.

4616 Remarks on British relations and intercourse with China. By an American merchant.
56 pp. London, Edward Suter, 1834
K.

4617 Remarks on Mr. Robert Steele's report to the chamber of commerce of Greenock, on the bill now before parliament for the measurement of tonnage. By a member of the late committee.
tables. 28 pp. London, J. Murray, 1834
K.

4618 Remarks on the report of the poor law commissioners. (By) an observer in an agricultural district.
table. no t.p. 16 pp. London, B. Fellowes, [1834?]
T.

4619 The repeal of the assessed taxes and malt duty, and the imposition of a property tax, in a letter to the Rt. Hon. the earl Grey. [by] Philo Justiciae.
18 pp. Glasgow, Robertson, [etc., etc.], 1834
N.

4620 Report by the directors of the Provincial Bank of Ireland to the proprietors, assembled at the ninth yearly general meeting, on Thursday, May 15, 1834; with a list of the directors, office bearers, branches, and agents; together with an alphabetical list of proprietors, at the 30th of April, 1834.
46 pp. London, printed by Thomas, 1834
A.

4621 Report of a visit to the estates of the honorable the Irish Society, in Londonderry and Coleraine in the year 1834. fold. maps. 48 pp. London, Charles Skipper & East, 1834

A., B.

4622 Report of the council of the chamber of commerce of Dublin to the annual assembly of the members of the association, held 4th March, 1834. 42 pp. Dublin, P. D. Hardy, 1834

A.

4623 Reports of a committee of proprietors of the New Royal Canal Company, inculpatory of the management of the board of directors of that concern, with replies to the several allegations contained in those reports vindicatory of the board's management. 66 pp. Dublin, Hope, 1834

A., N.

4624 Rules and articles of agreement to be observed by the members of the second Dog and Partridge Building Society, established at the house of Mr. Thos. Nabb, the Dog and Partridge, behind the Exchange, Manchester. 18 pp. Manchester, Wilkinson, 1834

N.

4625 RYAN, Richard. A digest of the law for collecting and enforcing tithe composition etc. as it will stand on 1st Nov. 1834, with observations on Mr. Goulburn's and Mr. Stanley's acts, and the rejected bill. 58 pp. Dublin, Gibton & Overend, 1834

A.

4626 [SCOTT, A.] A clue to the cause of dear bread and fallen rents: submitted to the consideration of members of parliament, by a landed proprietor. August, 1834. tables. 8 pp. London, Hearne, 1834

N.

4627 SCROPE, George Julius Duncombe Poulett. Friendly advice to the peasantry of Ireland. 8 pp. Dublin, Folds, 1834

A., U.

4628 ——. How is Ireland to be governed? A question addressed to the new administration. 34 pp. London, J. Ridgway, 1834.

A., N.

4629 ——. Plan of a poor law for Ireland, with a review of the arguments for and against it. 24 pp. 2nd. ed. London, J. Ridgway, 1834

A., K., N.

4630 Settlement of the tithe question in Ireland. August 24th, 1834. tables. 18 pp. n.p., 1834

A., N.

4631 The spirit of the press and of the proprietors of East India stock, shewn in extracts from the leading newspapers and magazines, and the debates at the India house, relative to the compensations to be granted to the East India Company's maritime service; together with testimonials from the presidents of the company's factory in China; to which is prefixed the dissent of John Forbes, esq. a member of the court of directors. 98 pp. 2nd ed. with appendix. London, Pelham Richardson, 1834

T.

——. Another issue. 98 pp. London, Pelham Richardson, 1834

K.

4632 STEELE, Robert. Report to the chamber of commerce of Greenock, on the admeasurement of shipping for tonnage. Diagrams. tables. 24 pp. Greenock, printed in the Advertiser Office, 1834

A.

4633 The strike; or, a dialogue between Andrew Plowman and John Treadle. 24 pp. London, Thomas Hookham, 1834

T.

4634 SUMNER, Charles Richard, bishop of Winchester. A charge delivered to the clergy of the diocese of Winchester, in October, 1833. tables. appendix. 84 pp. London, J. Hatchard, 1834

T.

4635 The tea trade. A full and accurate report of the extraordinary proceedings at the East India House, on the commencement of the March sale. Containing also, copies of the correspondence between the East India Company and the committee of the tea trade: together with the correspondence of the committee of wholesale tea-dealers with government and the East India Company, relative to the repeal of the new scale of tea duties, and other matters of interest to the tea trade. tables. 44 pp. London, Effingham Wilson, [1834]

T.

4636 [THOMPSON, Thomas Perronet.] Catechism on the corn laws; with a list of the fallacies and the answers. Eighteenth edition. Stereotype. To which is added the article on *Free Trade*, from the Westminster Review, No. XXIII, with the article on the *Silk and Glove Trades*, from No. XXXII; and the supplements from No. XXXIII, XXXIV and XXXV. With a collection of objections and the answers. By a member of the University of Cambridge. 92 pp. London, R. Heward, 1834

N.

4637 TORRENS, Robert. On wages and combination. table of contents. 144 pp. London, Longman, Rees, Orme, Brown, Green and Longman, 1834

A., T.

4638 Trades' unions and strikes. 102 pp. London, C. Knight, 1834

N.

4639 [TUFNELL, Edward Carleton.] Character, object and effects of trades' unions: with some remarks on the law concerning them. 142 pp. London, J. Ridgway, 1834

A., K.

4640 URMSTON, Sir James Brabazon. Observations on the China trade, and on the importance and advantages of removing it from Canton, to some other part of the coast of that empire.
tables. appendices. 156 pp. London, A. H. Baily & Co., 1834
T.

4641 VOUSDON, P. Special directions for the government of persons interested in the new License Act regulating the sale of beer, cider, spirits, wine etc. in Ireland.
16 pp. 2nd ed. Dublin, R. Carrick, 1834
A.

4642 WALTER, John. A letter to the electors of Berkshire, on the new system for the management of the poor, proposed by the government.
tables. appendix. 74 pp. London, J. Ridgway, 1834
T.

4643 WHITE, John Meadows. Remarks on the Poor Law Amendment Act, as it affects unions, or parishes, under the government of guardians, or select vestries.
index. 52 pp. London, B. Fellowes, 1834
T.

4644 [WILLIAMS, Charles Wye.] The policy of joint stock companies considered, and a comparison drawn between 'the return system' and the system of high dividends and a high share list. To which are added some letters of correspondents, for and against, with a communication from C. W. Williams, esq., on the principle of the city of Dublin Joint Stock Steam Packet Co.
20 pp. (reprinted from 'The Albion'.) Liverpool, Bean, 1834
N.

4645 WOODHOUSE, J. O. Observations on the overflowing of Lough Neagh, and its rivers, in winter, and the present state of the navigation thereof; and suggestions for preventing the overflow and improving the navigation.
26 pp. Dublin, Corbet, 1834
A., N.

4646 YOUNG, George R. The British North American colonies. Letters to the right hon. E. G. S. Stanley, M.P. upon the existing treaties with France and America as regards their 'rights of fishery' upon the coasts of Nova Scotia, Labrador, and Newfoundland; the violations of these treaties by the subjects of both powers, and their effect upon the commerce, equally of the mother country and the colonies; with a general view of the colonial policy, shewing that the British dependencies are now prepared to pay the expenses of their local governments; that the military expenditure, if chargeable to them, is fully counterbalanced by the commercial advantages derived from them; and that their preservation, as integral parts of the empire, is essential to the commercial prosperity and political supremacy of the British nation.
tables. map. 198 pp. London, J. Ridgway, 1834
K., T.

1835

4647 Agricultural employment institution, founded 1832, for allotting small portions of land to the deserving poor for cultivation during their unemployed time, in the parishes where they reside. Second report.
64 pp. London, the Society, 1835
N.

4648 The alarming state of the country considered, and the causes thereof fully explained. With observations upon the poor law amendment bill. Shewing that if something be not effected to relieve the agricultural interest, the landowner must be deprived of his estate, the clergy of their tithes, the farmer and tradesman must be ruined, and the poor and working classes reduced to the utmost state of destitution and distress. A plan is submitted to the public, shewing how employment may be found for both the agricultural and manufacturing population, so that the landowner may save his estate, the clergy their tithes, the ruin of the farmer and tradesman be prevented, and the country restored to a state of prosperity and happiness. By a friend of the people.
66 pp. London, Simpkin Marshall, 1835
T.

4649 BEAUMONT, George. An inquiry into the origin of copyhold tenure.
72 pp. London, J. and W. T. Clarke, 1835
T.

4650 BERMINGHAM, Thomas. The social state of Great Britain and Ireland considered with regard to the labouring population, dedicated by permission to her royal highness the duchess of Kent.
tables. diagrams. 244 pp. London, S. W. Fores, 1835
A., N., T.

4651 BEWLEY, Samuel. Hints for consideration concerning Ireland, 1835
2 pp. [manuscript letter.]
A.

4652 BLACK, Adam. View of the financial affairs of the city of Edinburgh, with suggestions for a compromise with the creditors.
tables. 24 pp. Edinburgh, Adam & Charles Black, 1835
N.

4653 BOWEN, John. A letter to the king, in refutation of some of the charges preferred against the poor: with copious statistical illustrations demonstrative of the injustice with which that body has been assailed.
tables. 114 pp. London, J. Hatchard, [1835]
T.

4654 BRADY, W. E. A letter and suggestions for the employment of the people and the amelioration of the poor of Ireland addressed to the rt. hon. lord Morpeth, chief secretary of Ireland, for the favourable consideration of H.M. government.
38 pp. London, Rudd, 1835
N.

4655 [BRIDGES, George W.] Emancipation unmasked in a letter to the right honourable the earl of Aberdeen, secretary of state for the colonies. By the author of 'The annals of Jamaica', &c. &c.
28 pp. London, Edward Churton, 1835
K.

4656 A brief address on mining in Cornwall, demonstrating some of the advantages resulting to commerce, and the profit to capitalists, by investment in these national undertakings. By the secretary to the Kellewerris and West Tresavean mining companies, 55, Old Broad Street.
tables. 24 pp. London, F. Waller, 1835
T.

4657 BROADHURST, John. Letter to lord Melbourne on the Irish church and Irish tithes.
72 pp. London, Thomas Hookham, 1835
K.

4658 Cheap corn, but no bread: or the results of free corn trade.
48 pp. London, C. & J. Rivington, [etc., etc.], 1835
T.

4659 CHAPMAN, Henry S. The Act for the regulation of municipal corporations in England and Wales. 6 William IV, cap. LXXVI. With a complete index and notes, practical and explanatory; also the order in council, issued September 11, 1835, for delaying certain proceedings directed by the act to be done, and the reasons given in the conferences between the houses of parliament, for several of the provisions of the act.
tables. 166 pp. London, Charles Ely, 1835
T.

4660 [COBDEN, Richard.] England, Ireland and America. By a Manchester manufacturer.
168 pp. London, J. Ridgway, 1835
A.

4661 CONNER, William. The true political economy of Ireland: or rack-rent the one great cause of all her evils, with its remedy, being a speech delivered at a meeting of the farming and labouring classes at Inch in Queen's County.
76 pp. Dublin, Wakeman, 1835
A., B., N., U.

4662 [COOKE, W. B.] Colonial policy, with hints upon the formation of military settlements. To which are added observations on the boundary question now pending between this country and the United States.
52 pp. 2nd ed. London, James Cochrane, 1835
K.

4663 Cottage husbandry, the utility and national advantage of alloting land for that purpose; being a selection from the publications of the Labourers' Friend Society and re-issued under their direction.
tables. appendix. index. 316 pp. London, John W. Parker, 1835
T.

4664 COTTON, Henry, archdeacon of Cashel. Fiat justitia. A letter to the right hon. Sir H. Hardinge on the present circumstances of the established church in Ireland.
80 pp. Dublin, R. M. Tims, [etc., etc.], 1835
R., T.

4665 CRAWFORD, William Sharman. Observations on the Irish Tithe Bill passed by the house of commons, in the last session of the imperial parliament submitted to the considera-

tion of the electors of Dundalk, in letters, addressed to William Brett esq. by Wm. Sharman Crawford esq. M.P.
57 pp. Dundalk, J. Coleman, 1835
A.

4666 [CROSTHWAITE, John Clarke.] The Irish church bill, or facts for the consideration of the lords.
20 pp. London, Roake and Varty, 1835
K., T.

4667 Deed of settlement of the Agricultural and Commercial Bank of Ireland.
64 pp. Dublin, R. Carrick, 1835
A.

4668 DYMOND, Jonathan. The church and the clergy: showing that religious establishments derive no countenance from the nature of Christianity, and that they are not recommended by public utility: with some observations on the church establishment of England and Ireland and on the system of tithes.
52 pp. sixth edition. London, E. Couchman, 1835
U.

4669 Fifth annual report for the year 1835, of the Children's Friend Society founded by Capt. E. P. Brenton, R.N. in 1830, for the prevention of juvenile vagrancy with an account and plan of the institution, its rules and regulations, and list of subscribers.
tables. 48 pp. London, the Society, 1835
U.

4670 Final report of the Irish Distress Committee.
16 pp. Dublin, M. Porter, 1835
A.

4671 FINLAY, John. Miscellanies. The foreign relations of the British Empire: the internal resources of Ireland: sketches of character; dramatic criticism: etc. etc. etc.
table of contents. 290 pp. Dublin, J. Cumming, 1835
A., S.

4672 FLEMING, Alexander. An historical lecture on teinds, or tithes; shewing them to be funds set apart for the worship of God, upholding sacrifice, and maintaining the clergy, whether before, during, or after the law of Moses, down to the present time.
78 pp. Glasgow, W. R. McPhun, 1835
T.

4673 [FREESE, John Henry.] Remarks upon the objects and advantages of the Imperial Anglo-Brazilian canal, road, bridge, and land improvement company, protector, his imperial majesty Don Pedro II. To which are prefixed, translated copies of the decree of the provisional legislative assembly of Rio de Janeiro, conceding certain exclusive rights and privileges to Mr. John Henry Freese,—and of his memorial to the general legislative assembly, praying for further concessions. As also a map of the province of Rio de Janeiro, showing the lines of intended operations. And a colored view of the colony of New Friburg.
plate. map. tables. appendix. 72 pp. London, Wacey, Dean & Munday, [1835?]
T.

4674 GARNIER, Thomas (jun.), dean of Lincoln. Plain remarks upon the new Poor Law Amendment Act, more particularly addressed to the labouring classes.
36 pp. Winchester, Jacob and Johnson, [etc., etc.], 1835
T.

4675 GASKELL, P. Prospects of industry, being a brief exposition of the past and present conditions of the labouring classes. With remarks on the operation of the Poor Law Bill, workhouses etc.
42 pp. London, Smith, Elder & Co., 1835
A., N.

4676 GORDON, Alexander. The fitness of turnpike roads and highways for the most expeditious, safe, convenient and economical internal communication.
tables. 32 pp. London, Roake and Varty, 1835
T.

4677 GRAHAM, Sir James Robert George, bart. The speech of the Right Honourable Sir James R. G. Graham, bart., M.P. on lord John Russell's motion relative to the revenues of the Church of Ireland. March 30th, 1835. Thoroughly corrected and revised.
48 pp. London, John Macrone, 1835
T.

4678 HANCOCK, John. Observations on the climate, soil and productions of British Guiana, and on the advantages of emigration to, and colonising the interior of, that country: together with incidental remarks on the diseases, their treatment and prevention; founded on a long experience within the tropics.
table of contents. 98 pp. London, J. Hatchard, [etc.], 1835
N.

4679 [HICKEY, William.] An address to the landlords of Ireland on subjects connected with the melioration of the lower classes. By Martin Doyle.
136 pp. 2nd ed. enlarged. Dublin, W. Curry, jr., 1835
A.

4680 [——.] Common sense for common people, or illustrations of proverbs, designed for the use of the peasantry of Ireland. By Martin Doyle.
108 pp. Dublin, W. Curry, jr., 1835
B.

4681 HINCHY, John. General observations on the state of Ireland and plans for its improvement, with remarks on the poor laws.
18 pp. Dublin, Kirkwood, 1835
A., N.

4682 [HUME, James Deacon.] Letters on the corn laws, and on the rights of the working classes; originally inserted in the Morning Chronicle; shewing, the injustice, and also the impolicy of empowering those among a people, who have obtained the proprietary possession of the lands of a country, to increase, artificially, the money value of their exclusive estates, by means of arbitrary charges, made on the rest of the people, for the necessaries of life. By H.B.T.
48 pp. London, Hooper, 1835
A.

4683 INNES, John. Letter to the lord Glenelg, secretary of state for the colonies, containing a report from personal observation on the working of the new system in the British West India colonies.
table of contents. tables. 124 pp. London, Longman, Rees, Orme, Brown, Green & Longman, 1835
A., K., T.

4684 Instructions for the establishment of friendly societies, with a form of rules and tables applicable thereto.
tables. index. 32 pp. London, His Majesty's Stationery Office, 1835
A.

4685 KENNEDY, John Pitt. Instruct; employ; don't hang them: or, Ireland tranquilized without soldiers, and enriched without English capital. Containing observations on a few of the chief errors of Irish government and Irish land proprietors, with the means of their correction practically illustrated.
tables. diagrams. appendix. 176 pp. London, T. & W. Boone, [etc.], 1835
A.

4686 A letter to a new member of the new parliament, on church-rates, registration, tithes, etc. etc.
24 pp. London, J. G. & F. Rivington, 1835
K.

4687 A letter to his grace the archbishop of Canterbury, on tithes. By a clerical tithe-holder.
table. 20 pp. Ashby-de-la-Zouch, W. Hextall, London, J. G. & F. Rivington, 1835
K., T.

4688 Letter to the people, on the protestant established church, and the Irish tithe question. By a late member of parliament.
50 pp. London, J. G. & F. Rivington, 1835
K., T.

4689 A letter to the right honourable lord John Russell. By a beneficed clergyman of the protestant church of Ireland.
52 pp. London, J. Ridgway, 1835
K.

On tithes.

4690 List of the local agricultural societies in Ireland extracted from the correspondence of the Agricultural Society of Ireland.
62 pp. Dublin, the Society, 1835
D.

4691 LESLIE, John. A practical illustration of the principles upon which the poor law amendment is founded, as exhibited in the administration of the poor rates in the parish of St. George, Hanover square, for the year ending Lady Day, 1835.
tables. appendix. 36 pp. London, J. Ridgway [etc.], 1835
T.

4692 LLOYD, William Forster. Four lectures on poor-laws, delivered before the University of Oxford, in Michaelmas term, 1834.
130 pp. London, Roake and Varty, Oxford, J. H. Parker, 1835
A., K., T.

18

4693 LONGFIELD, Mountifort. Three lectures on commerce, and one on absenteeism, delivered in Michaelmas term, 1834, before the University of Dublin.
appendix. 114 pp. Dublin, R. Milliken, 1835
A., N., T.

4694 MACKLIN, James. Agricultural Society of Ireland. Essay on the recent failure of the potato crop, and the best mode of averting a recurrence of the evil: recommended by the sub-committee of husbandry, for an extra prize, February, 1835.
16 pp. Dublin, J. Hoare, 1835
A.

4695 The Malthusian Boon unmasked. With remarks upon 'The Poor Law Amendment Bill', as connected with it, and in which the real cause of the oppressive burden of our poor rates is fully developed. By a friend to the poor.
16 pp. London, Whittaker, 1835
K., T.

4696 [MASSINGBERD, Francis Charles]. A letter to his grace the archbishop of Canterbury, on the right of the convocation to tax the clergy for the service of the church.
18 pp. London, J. G. & F. Rivington, 1835
K.

4697 Meath St. Savings' Bank Annuity Society, established 1835 for granting government annuities.
16 pp. Dublin, Shaw, 1835
A.

4698 MILLS, James. Letters addressed to earl Grey in the early part of his administration, on the absolute necessity for the extinction of the tythe of agricultural produce as a clerical revenue; most humbly dedicated to the king.
28 pp. London, McGowan, 1835
A.

4699 National Provident Institution. Enrolled under the acts of parliament, passed the 10th of George IV, and 4th and 5th of William IV relating to friendly societies. Established in London 1835, on the plan of the Friends' Provident Institution, King William street, corner of Nicholas Lane, No. 13.
tables. 48 pp. London, Edward Couchman, 1835
U.

4700 National Provident Institution, for assurance of lives, endowments, and annuities, on the principle of mutual assurance, and an equitable division of profits amongst all its members. Enrolled under the acts of parliament, passed the 10th of George IV, and 4th and 5th of William IV, relating to friendly societies. Established in London, 1835. Agents for Dublin: Messrs. Thomas Williams & Co., Lower Sackville street.
tables. 16 pp. London, printed by Bradbury and Evans, 1835
U.

4701 NIVEN, Ninian. Agricultural Society of Ireland. Essay on the recent failure of the potato crop, and the best means of averting a recurrence of the evil; to which a prize of 20 guineas was awarded by the subcommittee of husbandry, February, 1835
16 pp. Dublin, J. Hoare, 1835
A., D.

4702 Observations and documents respecting the petitions presented to parliament from the parish of Stoke Poges, in the county of Bucks.
40 pp. London, James Frazer, 1835
T.

4703 O'FLYNN, James. The present state of the Irish poor with the outlines of a plan of general employment.
32 pp. London, Hooper, 1835
A., B.

4704 On the culture and management of green crops, with some observations on the plan proved in the north of Ireland, and the successful results of that plan.
no t.p. 16 pp. Roscrea, Eggers, [1835?]
D.

4705 The origin and principles of the Agricultural and Commercial Bank of Ireland.
70 pp. Dublin, R. Carrick, 1835
A., N.

4706 PERCEVAL, Arthur Philip. A letter to the right hon. Sir Robert Peel, bart. on the present state of the Church of England.
46 pp. London, J. G. & F. Rivington, 1835
K.

4707 PHELAN, Denis. A statistical inquiry into the present state of the medical charities of Ireland; with suggestions for a medical poor law, by which they may be rendered much more extensively efficient.
table of contents. tables. 360 pp. Dublin, Hodges & Smith, London, Longman & Co., 1835
A.

4708 PHIPPS, J. Brief remarks on the common arguments now used in support of divers ecclesiastical impositions in this nation, especially as they relate to dissenters.
24 pp. London, reprinted by R. Clay, 1835
A., N.
See 733.

4709 Report of a deputation to Ireland in the year 1835.
104 pp. London, Taylor, 1835
A.
Headed...'To the honourable society of the governor and assistants of London, of the New Plantation in Ulster.'

4710 Report of a sub-committee of the chamber of commerce, Dublin, on the facts connected with the building of the Royal Exchange.
8 pp. printed for reference, not published. Dublin, 1835
A.

4711 The report of the Bristol Samaritan Society, its rules, and a list of subscribers for 1834.
20 pp. Bristol, Wansbrough, 1835
A.

4712 Second annual exhibition of articles of Irish manufacture, produce and invention, at the Royal Dublin Society's house, May, 1835. Catalogue.
20 pp. Dublin, R. Graisberry, 1835
A., N.

4713 Selection of parochial examinations relative to the destitute classes in Ireland, from the evidence received by H.M. commissioners for enquiring into the condition of the poorer classes in Ireland.
436 pp. Dublin, R. Milliken, London, B. Fellowes, 1835
A., N.

4714 [SENIOR, Nassau William.] On national property and on the prospects of the present administration and of their successors.
114 pp. London, B. Fellowes, 1835
A., K., T.

4715 ——. Statement of the provision for the poor and of the condition of the labouring classes in a considerable portion of America and Europe. Being the preface to the foreign communications contained in the appendix to the poor-law report.
tables. 246 pp. London, B. Fellowes, 1835
A.

4716 SHUTE, Hardwicke. Proposed plan for the commutation of tithes, and all other existing ecclesiastical demands, submitted to the consideration of the legislature, and of the clergy, and laity in general.
tables. 48 pp. London, J. G. & F. Rivington, [etc., etc.], 1835
K., T.

4717 SILVER, Thomas. A memorial to his majesty's government on the danger of intermeddling with the church rates.
74 pp. Oxford, J. H. Parker, London, J. G. and F. Rivington, 1835
K.

4718 STANLEY, William. The policy of a poor law for Ireland analytically examined.
30 pp. Dublin, Page, 1835
A., N.

4719 STOKER, William. Sketch of the medical and statistical history of epidemic fevers in Ireland from 1798, and of pestilential diseases since 1823.
tables. 62 pp. Dublin, R. Milliken, 1835
A., N.

4720 A substitute for Sir J. Campbell's summary law for obtaining judgments on bonds, bills, and notes, applicable to all other debts, as well as debts on those securities. By an attorney.
28 pp. London, H. Dixon, 1835
T.

4721 Suggestions for a satisfactory arrangement of tithes in Ireland. By a land proprietor.
8 pp. Bristol, Gutch and Martin, 1835
A., N.

4722 SWABEY, Maurice. A practical explanation of the duties of parish officers for unions of parishes and places under the poor law amendment act, and of the duties of guardians when elected.
16 pp. London, B. Fellowes, 1835
T.

4723 [TAYLOR, William Cooke.] On the nature and objects of statistical science. From the Foreign Quarterly Review, No. XXXI.
tables. 28 pp. London, C. Roworth & Sons, 1835
N.

4724 Third report of the Scottish Benevolent Society of St. Andrew adopted at the anniversary meeting of the society, held on Monday, 1st December, 1834, with rules, by-laws, &c. &c.
36 pp. Dublin, G. Folds, 1835
A.

4725 WESTERN, Charles Callis Western, 1st baron. A letter to the president and members of the Chelmsford Agricultural Society, upon the causes of the distressed state of the agricultural classes of the United Kingdom of Great Britain & Ireland.
20 pp. 4th ed. London, J. Ridgway & Sons, 1835
A., N.

4726 ——. Lord Western's second letter to the president and members of the Chelmsford and Essex Agricultural Society.
tables. 16 pp. Bath, S. Simms [etc.], 1835
N.

4727 WHITE, John Meadows. Parochial settlements an obstruction to poor law reform.
tables. appendix. 30 pp. London, B. Fellowes, 1835
T.

4728 WILLIAMS, Charles Wye. The policy of joint-stock companies considered and a comparison drawn between the system of high dividends with a high share list, and 'the return system' as illustrated on the principle of the city of Dublin Joint Stock Steam-Packet Company, and the insurance companies.
14 pp. Liverpool, Bean, 1835
A.

4729 [——.] A speech on the improvement of the Shannon, being in continuation of the debate in the house of commons, 12th May, 1835, giving a comparative view of the navigation of the Rideau canal in Canada, and the River Shannon in Ireland; with observations on the value of a connection by steam-packets, with British America.
maps. tables. table of contents. appendix. 80 pp. London, Bain, Dublin, Curry, 1835
A.

4730 [WONTNER, Thomas.] Abolition of pauperism. A discovery in internal national polity. Independence for every man, woman and child in the country; developed in the heads of a plan recently submitted to lord Brougham, through which every individual in the kingdom may be raised out of the mine of positive poverty. To cause the abrogation of the poor laws, and to concentrate the benefits of all charities, while it removes the degradation inflicted on the recipients. By the author of 'Old Bailey Experience', etc.
24 pp. London, B. Stein, 1835
T.

1836

4731 ABITBOL, M. An original financial plan for the conversion of the foreign debt of Spain without interest, into active fund with interest.
tables. 22 pp. London, Effingham Wilson, 1836
T.

4732 The act of incorporation of the North American Colonial Association of Ireland. With an index and notes. To which is prefixed, the prospectus of the association.
appendix. index. 52 pp. Dublin, G. Folds, 1836
N.

4733 An address to the honorable the commons of the United Kingdom of Great Britain and Ireland, in parliament assembled, on the sugar duties. By a West Indian.
16 pp. Woolwich, E. Jones, 1836
N.

4734 Agricultural Society of Ireland. Report of the gentlemen who formed a deputation to inspect, and enquire into the success of the bog improvements executed by John Fetherston H., [sic] in the county of Westmeath.
tables. 14 pp. Dublin, J. Hoare, 1836
A., N.

4735 Association for the suppression of mendicity: eighteenth annual report of the managing committee of the association in Dublin for the year 1835.
appendix. tables. 140 pp. Dublin, W. Holden, 1836
N.

4736 An authentic report of the highly important motion in the court of exchequer, in the case of the venerable Edmond Dalrymple H. Knox, archdeacon of Killaloe, versus John Gavin and others, on the 29th and 30th January, and 1st of February, 1836, with the judgments of the learned barons, awarding attachments against major Miller, inspector of police, and chief constable Malone, for refusing to aid in arresting parties under a writ of commission of rebellion issued in a suit for recovery of tithes. Taken in short-hand. By a barrister.
92 pp. Dublin, R. Milliken, London, Saunders and Benning, 1836
T.

4737 BALD, William and HENRY, David J. Report upon the proposed railways between Dublin, Navan and Drogheda.
16 pp. Dublin, Porter, 1836
A.

4738 BARNES, Ralph. Remarks on the tithe commutation act. Addressed to the clergy of the diocese of Exeter and inscribed, by permission, to the lord bishop of Exeter.
table. 28 pp. London, J. G. & F. Rivington, 1836
T.

4739 BARRINGTON, Mathew. An address to the inhabitants of Limerick on the opening of the Mont de Piété, or Charitable Pawn Office, for the support of Barrington's hospital, in that city.
28 pp. Dublin, Holden, 1836
A., N., U.

4740 BIGSBY, John Jeremiah. A lecture on mendicity; its ancient and modern history and the policy of nations and individuals in regard to it; as delivered before the Worksop Mechanics Institute, 14th April, 1836
48 pp. Worksop, F. Sissons, 1836
A.

4741 BLACKER, William. The claims of the landed interests to legislative protection considered; with reference to the manner in which the manufacturing, commercial, & agricultural classes contribute to national wealth & prosperity & suitable remedies for relieving the distress of the latter, suggested: addressed to the most noble the marquess of Chandos, & the committee of the central agricultural society.
313 pp. London, J. Ridgway, Dublin, William Curry, 1836
B., N.

4742 BRIDE, Arthur Stanley. A few remarks on the eligibility of extending the railway from Bray to the town of Wicklow, addressed to the directors and proprietors of the Kingstown Railroad.
appendix with tables. 16 pp. Dublin, R. Graisberry, 1836
A.

4743 A brief sketch of a proposed new line of communication between Dublin and London, via Portdynllaen (Carnarvonshire), Worcester, and Oxford, capable of being travelled in 12 hours, by means of steam packets and railways, to which are added the report of T. Rogers, esq., engineer, lighthouse-builder, &c. &c. to the rt. hon. the commissioners of his majesty's revenue in Ireland: and other documents published in 1807, showing its advantages at that time over the Holyhead line and demonstrating utility of Portdynllaen as an asylum harbour.
42 pp. Dublin, R. Milliken, 1836
A., N.

——. 52 pp. 2nd ed. with introduction. Dublin, R. Milliken, 1836
A., N.

4744 BURGH, Thomas John, dean of Cloyne. Some remarks on the appropriation clause of lord Morpeth's tithe bill and national education.
36 pp. Dublin, P. D. Hardy, 1836
A., N.

4745 BURGOYNE, John Fox. Letter from col. J. F. Burgoyne, chairman of the board of public works in Ireland to Daniel O'Connell, chairman of the parliamentary committee on the City of Dublin Steam Packet Company's bill; also a copy of the report of the commission for the improvement of the River Shannon.
16 pp. London, Brimmer, 1836
N.

4746 CAREY, Matthew. Vindication of the small farmers, the peasantry and the labourers of Ireland—from the injurious opinions too generally entertained of them, proving from the report of the late commissioners of investigation, that they will bear advantageous comparison with similar classes in any part of Christendom. Dedication to Daniel O'Connell, M.P.
appendix. 20 pp. Philadelphia, Carey and Hart, etc., 1836
D.

4747 [CASSELS, Walter Gibson.] Remarks on the formation and working of banks called joint stock, with observations on the policy and conduct of the Bank of England towards these establishments.
30 pp. London, Effingham Wilson, 1836
A.

4748 The charter party; or articles of agreement of the Tontine Buildings Company of the town of Ennis; with a list of the subscribers names, and also of their nominees.
20 pp. Ennis, Talbot, 1836
A.

4749 CHRISTIAN, George Ogle. An essay upon tithes in Ireland, addressed to the commons house of parliament; accompanied by a few words of advice to the members of that honorable house to whom it is submitted with great deference and respect.
48 pp. London, 1836
A.

4750 CLEMENTS, Hill. Plan for improving the port and quays of Limerick.
tables. 16 pp. Dublin, Coyne, 1836
N.

4751 COBBETT, William. Doom of the tithes.
120 pp. London, J. Oldfield, 1836
A., T.

4752 CONNERY, James. An essay on charitable economy, upon the loan bank system, called on the continent 'Mont de Piété', that is, the mount, or rather the heap, for the distribution of charity; being an antidote to counteract the baneful effects of pawnbroking, and other rapacious systems of money lending, which have entailed misery on the poor. Second edition.
84 pp. Dublin. John Cumming, 1836
A., N.

4753 ——. The reformer or, an infallible remedy to prevent pauperism and periodical returns to famine…
illustrations. table of contents. 70 pp. 6th ed. London, J. Murray, Dublin, J. Cumming, 1836
A.
See 4158, 4408, 4874.

4754 CRAWFURD, John. The newspaper stamp, and the newspaper postage; compared.
tables. 22 pp. London, J. Reed, 1836
T.

4755 CROSTHWAIT, Leland. On the failure of the potato crop, and the best means to avert a recurrence of the evil; founded on practical experiments made by the writer, and on the cultivation of green crops.
12 pp. Dublin, J. Hoare, 1836
A.

4756 [CROSTHWAITE, John Clarke.] Observations on a memorial to his majesty, and petition to both houses of parliament, from certain of the clergy of the Church of Ireland. By a churchman.
appendix. 76 pp. Dublin. R. Milliken, London, B. Fellowes, 1836
K., T.

4757 CUBITT, William. The report of William Cubitt, esq., F.R.S., M.R.I.A., civil engineer, etc. etc. to the provisional committee of the Dublin and Drogheda or Grand Northern Trunk Railway.
16 pp. Dublin, G. Folds, 1836
A.

4758 DICKENSON, Charles. Vindication of a memorial respecting church property in Ireland, together with the memorial itself, and protests against it.
72 pp. Dublin, R. Milliken, London, B. Fellowes, 1836
A., K., T.

4759 Deed of partnership of the Agricultural and Commercial Bank of Ireland.
76 pp. Belfast, A. Markham, 1836
A., N.

4760 Direct communication between Dublin and London in 12 hours. Short statement and proposal to the government.
4 pp. (2 broadsheets.) London, J. Nichols, 1836
A.

4761 Eighteenth annual report of the managing committee of the Association for the suppression of mendicity in Dublin. For the year 1835.
appendices. 140 pp. Dublin, the Association, 1836
N.

4762 An essay to shew the advantages that will follow the progressive formation of railways throughout the kingdom. By E. P. author of some anonymous fugitive pieces.
46 pp. London, Pelham Richardson, 1836
T.

4763 The establishment of a general packet station, on the south west coast of Ireland, connected by railways with Dublin and London, considered with reference to the advantages which it would afford, in facilitating the intercourse between Europe and America; in extending the commerce, and increasing the revenue of the united kingdom, and in promoting the improvement of Ireland.
map. 34 pp. London, Baldwin & Cradock, Dublin, Hodges & Smith, 1836
A., N.

4764 EVANS, H. Observations on the local advantages and security of Holyhead harbour, as a station for H.M. packets, and an asylum port for the trade of the Channel.
map. 16 pp. Liverpool, J. Jones, 1836
A., N.

4765 Facts and feelings, relative to the necessity of church building throughout England, and the means of forming an association for the collection and distribution of funds to this end. By a lay member of the University of Oxford.
tables. 18 pp. Oxford, W. Baxter, London, J. H. Parker, [etc.], 1836
T.

4766 FAIRBAIRN, Henry. A treatise on the political economy of railroads; in which the new mode of locomotion is considered in its influence upon the affairs of nations.
264 pp. London, John Weale, 1836
T.

4767 [FAIRBAIRN, William.] Reservoirs on the River Bann in the county of Down, Ireland, for more effectually supplying the mills with water.
tables. maps. plans. 24 pp. Manchester, Robert Robinson, 1836
U.

4768 FIELDEN, John. The curse of the factory system; or a short account of the origin of factory cruelties; of the attempts to protect the children by law; of their present sufferings; our duty towards them; injustice of Mr. Thomson's bill; the folly of the political economists; a warning of sending the children of the south into the factories of the north.
tables. 78 pp. London, A. Cobbett, 1836
N., T.

4769 Fourth annual report of the County and City of Cork General Annuity Endowment Society. Instituted October, 1831.
tables. 24 pp. Cork, printed by Jackson, 1836
A.

4770 GASKELL, P. Artisans and machinery: the moral and physical condition of the manufacturing population considered with reference to mechanical substitutes for human labour.
tables in appendix. 400 pp. London, John W. Parker, 1836
T.

4771 GILBART, James William. A history of banking in Ireland.
tables. 156 pp. London, Longman, Rees, Orme, Brown, Green & Longman, 1836
T.

4772 [GORDON, G. J.] Address to the people of Great Britain, explanatory of our commercial relations with the empire of China, and of the course of policy by which it may be rendered an almost unbounded field for British commerce. By a Visitor to China.
appendix. 132 pp. London, Smith, Elder, & Co., 1836
K., T.

4773 GORDON, John. Enquiry into the expediency and practicability of reducing the interest on the national debt; and a plan for effectuating that measure, with the concurrence of the fundholders.
32 pp. Edinburgh, John Gordon, 1836
T.

4774 GORDON, Richard. A review of the trade of banking in England and Ireland with a summary of the laws relating to banking and bills of exchange. Also, a summary of the evidence taken before the secret committee on joint stock banks during the last session of parliament.
82 pp. Dublin, R. Milliken, London, B. Fellowes, 1836
A., T.

4775 GORDON, Samuel. Advice to the Reformers, in reference to the taxes on food.
28 pp. Dublin, M. West, 1836
A.

4776 [HANNAY, ——.] Letter to William Clay, esq., M.P. containing strictures on his late pamphlet on the subject of joint stock banks, with remarks on his favourite theories. By Vindex.
36 pp. London, J. Ridgway, 1836
T.

4777 [HEATH, Joseph.] The currency, and its connection with national distress. By 'H. Θ.
tables. 140 pp. London, John van Voorst, 1836
T.

4778 [HICKEY, William.] An address to the landlords of Ireland on subjects connected with the melioration of the lower classes. By Martin Doyle.
appendix. 136 pp. 2nd ed. enlarged. Dublin, W. Curry, jr., 1836
A.

4779 HILLARY, Sir William. National importance of a great central harbour for the Irish Sea accessible at all times to the largest vessels, proposed to be constructed at Douglas in the Isle of Man.
appendix. 20 pp. 3d. ed. Douglas, Walls & Farqher, 1836
N.

4780 HILLYARD, Clarke. A summary of practical farming, observations on the breeding and feeding of sheep and cattle; on rents and tithes; and on the present state of agriculture.
tables. 56 pp. Northampton, T. E. Dicey, [1836]
T.

4781 HOARE, Edward Newenham. A letter to Thomas Fowell Buxton, esq., M.P. in reply to his speech on the Irish tithe bill.
52 pp. London, James Nisbet, 1836
B., K., N., T.

4782 HODGSON, Christopher. Practical directions and suggestions concerning the voluntary commutation of tithes: with the act of parliament.
52 pp. London, W. Clowes, 1836
A.

4783 House valuation and taxation of the parish of Saint Mark. Revised by the overseers of deserted children for that parish.
74 pp. Dublin, L. McDermot, 1836
A.

4784 Information for emigrants; or, a description of Guatemala, (one of the federal states of Central America) including the British colony of Verapaz. Drawn from authentic sources.
16 pp. London, Pelham Richardson, 1836
T.

4785 Instructions for the establishment of loan societies with a form of rules, etc. applicable thereto.
16 pp. London, W. Clowes, 1836
N.

4786 Irish church. A letter to the right honourable Lord Holland, or a reply to the 'Parliamentary Talk' of a disciple of Selden. By a pupil of Canning.
46 pp. London, J. Hatchard, 1836
K.

4787 Irish Eastern & Western, or Great Central Railroad, from Dublin by Athlone to Galway.
tables. 32 pp. London, Blades & East, 1836
A.

Contains engineers' report from W. Bald and D. J. Henry.

4788 JONES, Richard. Remarks on the government bill for the commutation of tithe.
58 pp. London, J. Murray, 1836
K., T.

4789 JORDAN, Andrew. Prospectus of Grand Junction Railway, for connecting Dublin with the ports of Galway, Sligo, and the intermediate and contiguous districts.
map. 4 pp. Dublin, 1836
A.

4790 KEATING, Michael I. Emigration. [A letter] to the right hon. lord Morpeth, M.P.
10 pp. Limerick, 1836
N.

4791 KINAHAN, Daniel. Digest of the Bankruptcy Act. With notes and an index.
table of contents. index. 158 pp. Dublin, R. Milliken, 1836
N.

4792 LEFEVRE, Charles Shaw, later first baron Eversley. Remarks on the present state of agriculture. In a letter addressed to his constituents.
42 pp. 10th ed. London, J. Ridgway, 1836
A.

4793 LESLIE, John. Further illustrations of the principles upon which a metropolitan poor rate is administered in the parish of St. George, Hanover sq., with a few desultory observations on the principle upon which poor laws are founded; and on the proposed extension of that system to Ireland.
tables, 38 pp. London, J. Ridgway [etc.], 1836
A., D.

4794 A letter to the subscribers to the Customs' Annuity and Benevolent Fund. [Signed T.G.W.]
20 pp. London, Charles Skipper and East, [1836]
T.

4795 LEWIS, Sir George Cornewall. Report on the state of the Irish poor in Great Britain.
104 pp. London, C. Knight, 1836
K.

A reprint of 1836 [40] xxxiv, App. G to Royal Commission on condition of poorer classes in Ireland.

4796 LINDSAY, Henry L. An essay on the agriculture of Co. Armagh.
36 pp. Armagh, M'Watters, 1836
A., N., T.

4797 LLOYD, William Forster. Two lectures on poor-laws, delivered before the university of Oxford, in Hilary term, 1836.
72 pp. London, Roake and Varty, Oxford, J. H. Parker, 1836
K.

4798 London and Dublin direct communication. St. George's harbour and Chester Railway Co.
map. 4 pp. (2 broadsheets.) London, Baily, 1836
A.

4799 [McCULLOCH, John Ramsay.] Observations illustrative of the practical operation and real effect of the duties on paper showing the expediency of their reduction or repeal.
tables. appendix. 38 pp. London, Longman, Rees, Orme, Brown, Green & Longman, 1836
N.

4800 [——.] Reasons for the establishment of a new bank in India; with answers to the objections against it.
44 pp. London, Longman, Rees, Orme, Brown, Green and Longman, 1836
T.

4801 MATHESON, Sir James, bart. The present position and prospects of the British trade with China; together with an outline of some leading occurrences in its past history.
tables. 148 pp. London, Smith, Elder & Co., 1836
K., T.

4802 Mining company of Ireland. Report for half-year ending 1st December, 1835.
tables. 16 pp. Dublin, Chambers, 1836
A.

4803 MORETON, Augustus Henry. Civilization; or, a brief analysis of the natural laws that regulate the numbers and condition of mankind.
220 pp. London, Saunders and Otley, 1836
T.

4804 Most important to grocers and spirit retailers. The only full report of the interesting proceedings of two great meetings, held on the 23rd and 26th of August, 1836, to protect the Irish grocers: with an exposure of Shaw's pernicious scheme.
16 pp. Dublin, 1836
A.

4805 MUNDELL, Alexander. Four letters addressed to the chairmen of the agricultural committees of both houses of parliament, showing the operation of the corn laws, and of the appreciation of money.
tables. 46 pp. London, Longman, Rees, Orme, Brown, Green, & Longman, 1836
T.

4806 NIMMO, Alexander. Great Central Irish Railway: Report of Alexander Nimmo Esq. to the directors.
tables. 12 pp. Dublin, Chambers, 1836
N.

4807 Nineteenth annual report of the managing committee of the Association for the Suppression of Mendicity in Dublin, for the year 1836: with resolutions upon the subject of poor laws.
Tables. 32 pp. Dublin, Warren, 1836
A

4808 Observation explanatory of the principles and practical results of the system of assurance proposed by the Family

Endowment Society, and demonstrative of its advantages over the system of life insurance, as a means of securing a provision for children.
tables. 16 pp. London, Baily, 1836

A.

4809 Observations on the habits of the labouring classes in Ireland, suggested by Mr. G. C. Lewis' report on the state of the Irish poor in Great Britain.
tables. 42 pp. Dublin, R. Milliken, 1836

C., T., U.

4810 O'FLYNN, James. Extracts from a pamphlet on the present state of the Irish poor. To which is added the means of profitable employment for the whole population, both of England and Ireland.
16 pp. London, Warr, 1836

N., U.

4811 Our natural rights: a pamphlet for the people by one of themselves. Dedicated, by permission to Wm. Sharman Crawford, esq., M.P.
44 pp. Belfast, Tate, 1836

N.

4812 PALMER, John Horsley. Reasons against the proposed Indian joint-stock bank; in a letter to G. G. de H. Larpent, esq. from J. Horsley Palmer.
30 pp. London, Pelham Richardson, 1836

T.

4813 PAYNE, John. To the freeholders of England and Wales. Reasons for opposing the compulsory commutation of tythes for money; and on the impolicy of the freeholders of England and Wales suffering their estates to be mortgaged for ever by a money annual payment.
16 pp. London, W. Dinnis, Nottingham, H. Wild, 1836

K., T.

4814 PETTIGREW, Thomas Joseph. The pauper farming system. A letter to the Right Hon. Lord John Russell, his majesty's secretary of state for the home department on the condition of the pauper children of St. James, Westminster; as demonstrating the necessity of abolishing the farming system.
94 pp. London, T. Rodd, 1836

T.

4815 Prospectus of the Dublin and Limerick Railway, being the second extension of the Leinster and Munster Railway, with the report of the government commissioners on the importance of the Shannon, and observations as to the western packet station, also a letter from the president of the chamber of commerce at Limerick, to Mr. Barrington, and his reply.
26 pp. Dublin, Coyne [etc.], 1836

A., N.

4816 Prospectus of the Great Leinster & Munster Railway. First extension from the city of Dublin to the city of Kilkenny, with estimated annual revenue, engineers' report, etc.
26 pp. London, Minerva press, 1836

A., N.

4817 Remarks on the salt monopoly of Bengal and the report from the Board of Customs (Salt and opium) of 1832.
tables. 68 pp. London, T. Savill, 1836

D.

4818 Report of the agricultural seminary at Templemoyle co. of Londonderry, Ireland. Estd. May, 1827.
tables. 14 pp. Londonderry, Hempton, 1836

A.

4819 Report of the council of the chamber of commerce of Dublin to the annual assembly of the members of the association, held 1st March, 1836.
40 pp. Dublin, P. D. Hardy, 1836

A.

4820 Report of the deputation appointed by the honourable the Irish society to visit the city of London's plantation in Ireland in the year 1836. Printed by order of the court.
fold. maps and plan. 146 pp. London, Charles Skipper & East, 1836

B.

4821 Reports and returns made to parliament, on the communication between London and Dublin, since the public meeting held in Dublin on the 22nd January, 1836; with the chancellor of the exchequer's reply to the deputation of M.P.s who waited on him in pursuance of the resolutions entered into at said meeting.
tables. 32 pp. n.p., 1836

A.

4822 REYNOLDS, F. R. An appendix to the act for the commutation of tithes in England and Wales; containing tables for calculating the rent-charge payable in lieu of tithes. Third edition.
tables. 12 pp. London, Whittaker [etc.], 1836

T.

4823 [RICHARDS, James.] Thirty years' observations on the effects of taxing provisions instead of income; with a just scale to tax income, derived from real property. By a farmer.
tables. tables in appendix. 90 pp. London, Effingham Wilson, [etc.], 1836

T.

4824 ROGERS, John. A brief statement of the origin, the regulations, and the proceedings of the board of governors of queen Anne's bounty for the augmentation of small livings; with suggestions for the more efficient application of the revenues placed at their disposal to the spiritual benefit of populous and laborious parishes, addressed to his grace, the archbishop of Canterbury.
tables. 32 pp. Falmouth, J. Trathan, [etc., etc.], 1836

T.

4825 Royal Bank of Ireland. Report from the provisional committee of the Royal Bank of Ireland to the subscribers. [Wednesday, 11th May, 1836.]
2 pp. Dublin, 1836

N.

4826 SCHOMBERG, Joseph Trigge. The act for the commutation of tithes in England and Wales: with notes, observations, and an epitome of the law of tithes, embracing all the latest decisions in the courts of law and equity, and the recent acts relating to tithes, with a copious index.
120 pp. London, Henry Butterworth, 1836

T.

4827 SCOVELL, John, with SCOVELL, Henry and SCOVELL, George. A letter to the Dublin merchants, dated 11th January, 1836.
12 pp. Dublin, 1836
A.

Refers to docks controversy.

4828 SPENCER, Thomas. The successful application of the new poor law to the parish of Hinton Charterhouse. Containing: 1. The aspect of pauperism prior to the passing of the new poor law. 2. The removal of abuses, and the reduction of the rates from £700 to £200 a year. 3. Some of the causes of the outcry against the new poor law. 4. An address to the higher classes in behalf of the industrious poor.
60 pp. London, J. Ridgway, 1836
N.

4829 Stability of parliamentary securities, railway, canal shares, paving bonds, &c., &c., affected. A letter to capitalists, with an appendix suggested by a bill now in parliament for repealing certain acts for paving, &c. and for abolishing the present boards of commissioners in the parish of St. Pancras, under which acts intended to be repealed, monies have been borrowed upon the security of the rates thereby authorized to be made and levied. By a mortgagee of the rates.
appendix. 56 pp. London, Charles Skipper & East, 1836
K.

4830 STANLEY, J. Ireland and her evils. Poor laws fully considered—their introduction into Ireland destructive of all landed interest.
116 pp. Dublin, R. Milliken, London, B. Fellowes, 1836
A., T.

4831 A statement of persecutions on the part of certain Tory landlords in co. Carlow, referred to in a petition of Nicholas Aylward Vigors, esq. presented to the house of commons, 15th February, 1836.
60 pp. London, J. Ridgway, 1836
A., N., U.

4832 Statistics of the Church of England, as developed in the reports of the ecclesiastical commissioners: with notes and comments thereon, and on the church reform bills introduced by his majesty's ministers.
tables. appendix. 86 pp. London, Effingham Wilson, 1836
T.

4833 Statistical Society of London. First series of questions circulated by the Statistical Society of London.
tables. table of contents. 32 pp. (not pag.) London, W. Clowes, 1836
N.

4834 Statistical Society of London. Second annual report, with the regulations of the society and a list of the fellows etc. March, 1836.
table of contents. table. 40 pp. London, Calder, 1836
N.

4835 STENT, William. Practical remarks on the failure of the potatoe crop. With instructions how to remedy the evil.
frontisp. 20 pp. London, Simpkin, Marshall, Gainsburgh, J. Drury, 1836
T.

4836 STEPHEN, Sir George. A letter to the Rt. Hon. lord John Russell, &c. &c. &c., on the probable increase of rural crime, in consequence of the introduction of the new poor-law and railroad systems.
54 pp. London, Saunders and Ottley, [1836]
T.

4837 [STOPFORD, Edward, archdeacon of Armagh.] A brief review of parliamentary acts and bills relating to compositions for tithes in Ireland.
66 pp. London, J. G. & F. Rivington, 1836
K., T.

4838 Third annual report of the Gorey Charitable Loan, established 8th April 1833 the earl of Courtown, patron. Robert Owen, esq., chairman.
12 pp. Dublin, T. White, 1836
A.

4839 What will parliament do with the railways? Third edition.
16 pp. London, Henry Renshaw, 1836
T.

4840 WHITE, John Meadows. The act for the commutation of tithes in England and Wales. With an analysis, explanatory notes, and an index.
tables. 142 pp. London, B. Fellowes, 1836
T.

4841 What would be an equitable assessment of the local taxes of Dublin? A brief inquiry exemplified by a suggested scale of applotment on the new valuation. By a rate payer.
tables. 32 pp. Dublin, Chambers, 1836
A.

4842 WHITE, William, and BARRINGTON, Mathew. On a western packet station at Limerick, and a railroad between that city and Dublin. (Correspondence between William White, esq., and Mathew Barrington, esq.)
10 pp. (no. t.p.) Limerick and London, 1836
N.

4843 WIGGINS, John. Report on three cases of successful improvement of people and property in Ireland effected between the years 1815 and 1835.
diagrams. 32 pp. London, H. Arnold, 1836
A.

4844 WILLIAMS, Charles Wye. Reasons in favour of the city of Dublin Steam Co.'s bill for an increase of capital, with a letter from colonel J. F. Burgoyne, chairman of the board of public works in Ireland, to Daniel O'Connell, esq., M.P. chairman of the parliamentary committee on the city of Dublin steam packet company's bill. Also a copy of the report of the commissioners for the improvement of the River Shannon.
52 pp. London, J. Brimmer, 1836
A.

1837

4845 Abstract of the final report of the commissioners of Irish poor inquiry; & also letters written to ministers by Messrs. N. W. Senior, & G. C. Lewis, in consequence of

applications from government for their opinions on that report. With remarks upon the measures now before parliament for the relief of the destitute in Ireland.
appendix. 66 pp. 2nd ed. London, F. C. Westley, 1837

A., B., N.

4846 Agricultural and Commercial Bank of Ireland: The former management and present future prospects of the Agricultural and Commercial Bank of Ireland, considered. In a brief letter to its shareholders. (Signed 'A Shareholder'.)
20 pp. Dublin, 1837

N.

4847 Annual report of the strangers' friend society (founded in 1790) for visiting and relieving distressed strangers, and the resident sick poor, in Dublin and its vicinity; with an account of some of the cases relieved, and list of subscribers for 1836.
table. 36 pp. Dublin, Thomas I. White, 1837

N.

4848 [BAGOT, J. J. ?] A short treatise on political economy. The poor man's bank.
appendices. 48 pp. Dublin, W. Frazer, 1837

N.

A collection of short pieces on charitable banks and loan funds, paginated separately.

4849 [BAILEY, Samuel.] Money and its vicissitudes in value; as they affect national industry and pecuniary contracts: with a postscript on joint-stock banks. By the author of 'The rationale of political representation', 'A critical dissertation on value' etc.
228 pp. London, Effingham Wilson, 1837

T.

4850 BAIN, Donald. The substance of two letters to a noble lord on the situation of Ireland.
36 pp. London, Smith, Elder, [etc., etc.], 1837

N.

4851 BARNES, Ralph. A letter on church rates.
34 pp. London, J. G. & F. Rivington, Exeter, W. Roberts, 1837

T.

4852 ——. A letter to Sir John Campbell on the law of church rates.
20 pp. London, J. G. & F. Rivington, Exeter, W. Roberts, 1837

A.

4853 BARRINGTON, Mathew. An address to the inhabitants of Limerick on the opening of the Mont de Piété, or Charitable Pawn Office for the support of Barrington's hospital in that city. Also, a report of a public meeting, held for the purpose of explaining the objects of the Mont de Piété and the intended system of management.
40 pp. 3rd ed. Dublin, W. Holden, 1837

A.

4854 [BERNARD, Sir Thomas.] Case on the 43rd Elizabeth for the relief of the poor. For the opinion of Mr. Serjeant Snigge, Galway, attorney.
26 pp. London, Longman, Orme, Brown, Green and Longmans, 1837

T.

4855 BIRT, John. Official responsibility affirmed and enforced, in a letter to Sir George Grey, bart., M.P., under-secretary of state for the colonies, on the administration of the act for the abolition of British colonial slavery.
16 pp. London, J. Hatchard, 1837

N.

4856 BLACKER, William. An essay on the improvements to be made in the cultivation of small farms by the introduction of green crops, and house-feeding the stock thereon.
table of contents. prefaces. 114 pp. 5th ed. Dublin, W. Curry, jr., London, J. Ridgway, 1837

A., N.

4857 ——. Prize essay, addressed to the agricultural committee of the Royal Dublin Society, on the management of landed property in Ireland; the consolidation of small farms, employment of the poor etc. etc.
52 pp. 2nd ed. Dublin, W. Curry, jr., [etc.], 1837

B.

4858 ——. Review of Charles Shaw Lefevre, esq.'s letter to his constituents, as chairman of the select committee appointed to inquire into the present state of agriculture.
table of contents. appendix. 84 pp. Dublin, W. Curry, jr., London, J. Ridgway, 1837

A., N., T.

4859 Brief remarks respecting steam communication with India and suggestions on the best mode of establishing it, offered by the London committee for establishing steam communication with India via the Red Sea.
map. 20 pp. London, Smith, Elder & Co., 1837

A.

4860 BRUNTON, Benjamin S. Objections to the present state of the co. Dublin roads: with systematic plans designed for their improvement.
plans. 32 pp. Dublin, Richard Moore Tims, [etc.], 1837

A., N.

4861 BUCHANAN, A. C. Outline of a practical plan for the immediate, effective and economical relief of the starving and destitute poor of Ireland; but more particularly the unemployed labouring classes by A. C. Buchanan esq. submitted in the following pages to the consideration of the Rt. Hon. lord Melbourne.
tables. 28 pp. Brighton, Fleet, 1837

N.

4862 [BURKE, St. George.] Remarks on the standing orders and resolutions of the last session of parliament relating to railways with practical instructions for their observance and some suggestions for their amendment. By a parliamentary agent.
appendix. 172 pp. London, J. Bigg, 1837

T.

4863 BUTT, Isaac. An introductory lecture, delivered before the University of Dublin, in Hilary term, 1837.
appendix. 72 pp. Dublin, W. Curry, jr., London, B. Fellowes, 1837

A., N., T.

4864 ——. The poor law bill for Ireland examined, its provisions and the report of Mr. Nicholls contrasted with the facts proved by the poor inquiry commission, in a letter to lord viscount Morpeth M.P., his majesty's principal secretary of state for Ireland.
appendix with table. 44 pp. Dublin, W. Curry, jr., London, B. Fellowes, 1837

A., N., T.

4865 CAMPBELL, Sir John. Letter to the right hon. lord Stanley, M.P. for North Lancashire, on the law of church rates.
42 pp. London, J. Ridgway, 1837

D.

4866 Cases with the opinions of the attorney-general of England, Edward Pennefather K.C., R. B. Warren, K.C., and D. R. Pigot, K.C., showing the defective state of the law regulating joint stock banks, as it now stands and the total want of protection afforded to shareholders against the mismanagement or misconduct of directors as exemplified by the facts stated in respect to the Agricultural and Commercial Bank of Ireland.
106 pp. Dublin, Cox, 1837

N.

4867 Charter of the Delaware Rail Road Company, with the report of the commissioners and engineers, acting by order of the legislature, and the estimates and proposed route of the road.
map. table. index. 54 pp. Delaware, Kimmey, 1837

N.

4868 [CHAYTOR, Joshua M.] Monetary system. The injury, insufficiency and inconvenience of a gold standard and circulating medium fairly stated with a proposed substitute. By J.M.C.
32 pp. London, R. Groombridge, Dublin, R. Milliken, 1837

A., N., T.

4869 The church establishment considered in its relation to the state and the community. By a layman.
appendix. 60 pp. London, J. Hatchard, 1837

T.

4870 [CLARK, Charles.] A few words on the subject of Canada. By a Barrister.
52 pp. London, Longman, Orme, Brown, Green & Longman, [1837]

N.

4871 CLAY, William. Speech of William Clay, esq., M.P. on moving for the appointment of a committee to inquire into the operation of the act permitting the establishment of joint-stock banks. To which are added, reflections on limited liability, paid-up capital, and publicity of accounts as applied to such associations; With some remarks on an article on joint stock companies in the last number of the Edinburgh Review.
tables. Appendix. 144 pp. 2nd edition. London, J. Ridgway, 1837

T.

4872 CLIBBORN, Edward. American prosperity. An outline of the American debit or banking system; to which is added, a justification of the veto of the late president [i.e. Andrew

Jackson]: also an explanation of the true principles of banking, with a paper currency in the United Kingdom.
46 pp. London, R. Groombridge, Dublin, Hodges & Smith, 1837

A., D., N., T.

4873 CONNERY, James. An essay on charitable economy...
84 pp. 2nd ed. Dublin, J. Cumming, 1837

N.

See 4752 and 4989.

4874 ——. The reformer, or an infallible remedy to prevent pauperism and periodical returns of famine...
62 pp. 5th ed. Limerick, G. & J. Goggin, 1837

N.

72 pp. 6th ed. Dublin, J. Cumming, 1837

N., P.

See 4158, 4408, 4753.

4875 Constitution and regulations of the Glasgow and Clydesdale Statistical Society. Instituted April, 1836.
20 pp. Glasgow, 1837

N.

4876 [CORRIE, J.] Remarks on the poor law for Ireland. By Philo-Hibernus.
26 pp. London, J. Ridgway, 1837

N.

4877 [——.] Remarks on the bill for the more effectual relief of the destitute poor in Ireland. By Philo-Hibernus. Second edition, revised and enlarged.
48 pp. London, J. Ridgway, 1837

A., B., N., U.

4878 [COSENS, Thomas.] A new treatise on agriculture and grazing: clearly pointing out to landowners and farmers the most profitable plans. To which are added remarks on the poor rates, the employment of the poor etc. and on the destruction of the black palmer. By an experienced farmer. Second ed.
62 pp. London, Longman, Orme, Brown, Green and Longmans, 1837

T.

4879 CRAMP, John Mockett. Letters on church rates. Addressed to the Rev. J. E. N. Molesworth, M.A. of Canterbury.
36 pp. London, George Wightman, [1837]

T.

4880 CRAWFORD, William Sharman. Observations showing the necessity of an amendment in the laws of landlord and tenant, in conjunction with a total repeal of the duties on foreign corn; and also showing the propriety of all classes of the people, in the United Kingdom, joining in the call for these two measures of practical reform.
52 pp. Belfast, F. D. Finlay, 1837

A.

4881 CREIGHTON, John Croker. The acts relating to insolvent debtors in Ireland with notes and a copious index.
132 pp. Dublin, Hodges & Smith, 1837

A.

4882 DENISON, William. Abstract of evidence taken before the committee appointed by the house of commons, the 27th February, 1837 to inquire into the operation and effect of the Poor Law Amendment Act with introductory remarks, etc.
tables. 132 pp. London, G. B. Whittaker, 1837
T.

4883 DIXON, Thomas. Who pays the taxes and who ought to pay them? A controversy between the man who has money and the man who has none, as well as between the owner of the soil and the eater of its produce.
tables. 16 pp. Dublin, printed by William Warren, [1837]
A., U.

4884 [ENDERBY, Charles.] The metallic currency the cause of the present crisis in England and America. By the author of 'Money, the representative of value'.
tables. 34 pp. London, Pelham Richardson, 1837
T.

4885 [——.] Money the representative of value. With considerations on the bank question, railway companies, savings banks, and the national debt.
84 pp. London, Pelham Richardson, 1837
T.

4886 GALE, Peter. A letter to the commissioners of railway inquiry in Ireland, on the advantages to the empire, from increased facilities of international communication, also, observations on the proper position for a main trunk, to the south & west of Ireland.
fold. table. 35 pp. 2nd ed. Dublin, R. Milliken, London, J. Ridgway, 1837
A., B., N., T.

4887 A geographical, statistical and commercial account of the Russian ports of the Black Sea, the sea of Asoph and the Danube: also an official report of the European commerce of Russia in 1835. From the German. With a map.
tables. appendix. plate. 48 pp. London, A. Schloss, P. Richardson, 1837
T.

4888 GILBART, James William. A history of banking in America: with an inquiry how far the banking institutions of America are adapted to this country: and a review of the causes of the recent pressure on the money market.
tables. appendix. 220 pp. London, Longman, Rees, Orme, Brown, Green & Longman, 1837
T.

4889 GORDON, Alexander. Observations addressed to those interested in either rail-ways or turnpike-roads; showing the comparative expedition, safety, convenience, and public and private economy of these two kinds of road for internal communication.
tables. 32 pp. London, John Weale, 1837
T.

4890 [GREG, Robert Hyde.] The factory question, considered in relation to its effects on the health and morals of those employed in factories. And the 'ten hours bill', in relation to its effects upon the manufactures of England, and those of foreign countries.
tables. appendices. 156 pp. London, J. Ridgway, 1837
T.

4891 GRINDLAY, Robert Melville. A view of the present state of the question as to steam communication with India. With a map, and an appendix, containing the petitions to parliament, and other documents.
map. appendix. tables. 102 pp. London, Smith, Elder, 1837
N.

4892 [HALL, John.] A letter to the right hon. Thos. Spring Rice, chancellor of her majesty's exchequer, etc. etc., containing a new principle of currency and plan for a national system of banking. By a Liverpool merchant.
tables. 28 pp. London, Effingham Wilson, 1837
T.

4893 HILL, Sir Rowland. Post office reform; its importance and practicability.
appendices. tables. 112 pp. 2nd ed. London, C. Knight & co., 1837
T.

106 pp. 3rd ed. London, C. Knight & co., 1837
N.

4894 Irish poor. A word for Mr. Nicholls. By a looker on.
54 pp. 2nd ed. London, Lumley, 1837
N.

4895 The Irish tithes bill, with explanatory notes.
26 pp. 2nd ed. London, James Ridgway, 1837
T.

4896 JOPLIN, Thomas. An examination of the report of the joint stock bank committee, to which is added an account of the late pressure in the money market, and embarrassment of the Northern and Central Bank of England.
table of contents. 128 pp. 2nd ed. London, J. Ridgway, 1837
A.

——. 128 pp. 3rd ed. London, J. Ridgway, 1837
A., N., T.

——. 128 pp. 4th ed. London, J. Ridgway, 1837
A.

4897 KENNEDY, John Pitt. Analysis of projects proposed for the relief of the poor of Ireland; more especially that of Mr. George Nicholls, embodied in a bill now before parliament; that of the commissioners for inquiring into the condition of the poorer classes in Ireland and that which has been brought into partial operation by the author.
tables. 56 pp. London, Thomas and William Boone, [etc. etc.], 1837
A., C., N., T.

4898 ——. 2. Memorandum of agreement between John Pitt Kennedy and James Moore relative to the Loughash Institution, established with a view to promote the instruction and employment of the Irish poor.
4 pp. n.p. [1837?]
U.

4899 ——. 4. Memorandum of agreement between John Pitt Kennedy, on behalf of Sir Thomas Charles Style, bart., M.P. on the one part and Charles McLoughlin, on the other

part, relative to the management of the Cloghan Agricultural School.
4 pp. Dublin, Alexander Thom, [1837?]
U.
See 5025 &c.

4900 ——. 3. Regulations for the boarding class of male pupils at the Loughash National Agricultural Model School.
4 pp. Dublin, Alexander Thom, 1837
U.

4901 KNOWLES, Sir Francis Charles, bart. 'The monetary crisis considered', being incidentally a reply to Mr. Horsley Palmer's pamphlet 'on the action of the Bank of England, etc.' and a defence of the joint-stock banks against his accusations.
80 pp. London, Pelham Richardson, 1837
A.

4902 The land tax, its origin, progress, and inequality, stated in a letter to the chancellor of the exchequer, with a view to its equalization. By a citizen of Westminster.
tables. 24 pp. 2nd ed. London, Daniel, 1837
N.

4903 LEFEVRE, Charles Shaw, afterwards first baron Eversley. Remarks on the present state of agriculture, in a letter addressed to his constituents.
42 pp. 11th ed. London, J. Ridgway, 1837
A., T.

4904 LEIGH, W. Church rates. Letter III. in which are examined the doctrines asserted in the letter to the Rt. Hon. lord Stanley, by Sir John Campbell.
26 pp. 2nd. ed. corrected, enlarged. Exeter, Pollard, 1837
A.

4905 A letter to the rt. hon. lord Hatherton on the projected improvements in the navigation of the River Severn. By a shareholder.
18 pp. Worcester, H. Deighton & Co., 1837
A.

4906 A letter to Right Hon. lord J. Russell, on the principles of the Irish poor law bill. By the chairman of an English poor law union.
22 pp. London, Houlston & Hughes, Bailey, 1837
N.

4907 A letter to the hon. the secret committee of the house of commons, upon joint-stock banks. The second edition, with observations in reply to Col. Torrens, Mr. Jones Loyd, Mr. Horsley Palmer, and Mr Samuel Clay. By Alfred.
32 pp. 2nd edition. London, Hatchard, 1837
T.

4908 LEWIS, George Cornewall. Remarks on the third report of the Irish poor inquiry commissioners; drawn up by the desire of the chancellor of the Exchequer, for the purpose of being submitted to his majesty's government. With an appendix and supplementary remarks.
tables. appendix. 58 pp. London, C. Knight & co., 1837
T.

4909 LOYD, Samuel Jones, afterwards 1st baron Overstone. Reflections suggested by a perusal of Mr. J. Horsley Palmer's pamphlet on the causes and consequences of the pressure on the money market.
tables. 56 pp. London, Pelham Richardson, 1837
T.

4910 ——. Further reflections on the state of the currency and the action of the Bank of England.
52 pp. London, Pelham Richardson, 1837
A., T.

4911 MACNAGHTEN, Sir Francis Workman, bart. Some observations upon the present state of Ireland.
78 pp. London, J. Ridgway, 1837
N., T.

4912 MANNING, James. Letter to earl Fitzwilliam upon the power of compelling the assessment of a church rate, by proceedings in courts of law. Third edition, enlarged with a postscript on ecclesiastical censures.
48 pp. 3rd ed. London, J. Ridgway, 1837
T.

4913 MERIVALE, Herman. An introductory lecture on the study of political economy.
38 pp. London, Longman, Orme, Brown, Green and Longmans, 1837
T.

4914 MOONEY, Thomas. The banking system; a letter addressed to the farmers of Ireland.
40 pp. Dublin, Keene, London, J. Ridgway, 1837
A.

4915 MORRISON, William Hampson. Observations on the system of metallic currency adopted in this country.
tables. 86 pp. London, Joseph Capes, 1837
T.

4916 MORTIMER, R. Untitled broadsheet containing suggestions for levying new taxes to raise the money necessary for a poor law system.
4 pp. Dublin, printed by G. Folds, 1837
A.

4917 MUDGE, Richard Z. Observations on railways, with reference to utility profit, and obvious necessity for a national system.
map. tables. 74 pp. London, Gardner, 1837
N.

4918 NAPER, James Lenox William. An address to the landlords and landholders of co. Meath in particular, and those of Ireland in general, on the new poor law bill.
36 pp. 2nd ed. Dublin, W. Curry, jr., 1837
A., N.

4919 National Loan Fund Life Assurance and Reversionary Interest Society, for granting assurances and annuities on lives and survivorships; endowments; and for the purchase and sale of reversionary property and life interests.
tables. 16 pp. Dublin, Chambers, 1837
A.

4920 New light on the Irish tithe bill; or the appropriate clause recommended by the heads of the Irish church. In a series of letters by Alienus.
table of contents. 70 pp. London, J. Ridgway, 1837
A., N., T.

4921 NICHOLLS, George. Poor laws, Ireland. Report of George Nicholls esq., to his majesty's principal secretary of state for the home department.
70 pp. London, C. Knight & co., 1837
A., N., T.

4922 Nineteenth annual report of the managing committee of the association for the suppression of mendicity in Dublin for the year 1836: with resolutions upon the subject of poor laws.
appendices. 182 pp. Dublin, the Association, 1837
N.

4923 Observations on the crisis, 1836–37, with suggestions for a remedy against commercial pressures. By a merchant.
tables. 24 pp. London, S. Highley, 1837
N., T.

4924 O'MALLEY, Thaddeus. Poor laws—Ireland. An idea of a poor law for Ireland.
86 pp. 2nd ed. London, Hooper, 1837
A., N.

4925 ——. Poor laws—Ireland. To lord John Russell, No. ii.
4 pp. (2 large sheets.) Dublin, 1837
A.

4926 [——.] A word or two on the Irish poor relief bill, and Mr. Nicholls' report; or a postscript to the Revd. Mr. O'Malley's 'Idea of a poor law for Ireland'.
24 pp. London, Hooper, 1837
A.

4927 O'ROURKE, Daniel. A voice from Ireland upon matters of present concern. Addressed to legislators & ministers of state.
82 pp. London, J. Ridgway, 1837
B.

4928 PALMER, John Horsley. The cause and consequences of the pressure upon the money-market; with a statement of the action of the Bank of England from 1st October 1833 to the 27th December 1836.
66 pp. London, Pelham Richardson 1837
A., T., U.

4929 ——. Reply to the reflections etc. etc. of Mr. Samuel Jones Loyd on the pamphlet entitled 'Causes and consequences of the pressure upon the money market'.
24 pp. London, Pelham Richardson, 1837
A., N., T.

4930 The parish and the union; or, the poor and the poor laws under the old system and the new: being an analysis of the evidence contained in the twenty-two reports of the select committee of the house of commons, appointed in the session of 1837, to inquire into the administration of the relief of the poor, under the orders and regulations issued by the commissioners under the provisions of the Poor Law Amendment Act. The whole digested under the various heads of complaint preferred before the committee, with illustrative facts and observations. To which are added the report of the committee; and a summary of petitions and addresses.
tables. appendix. 254 pp. London, C. Knight & co., 1837
A., T.

4931 The Poor Law Amendment Act. The case between the East Preston incorporation and the poor law commissioners, plainly stated; with some observations on a few of the numerous extraordinary misrepresentations and fallacies, respecting the Gilbert incorporations, put forth by the commissioners, in their last report.
tables. 68 pp. Worthing, G. Mackenzie, [1837]
T.

4932 POWELL, H. Townsend. Tithe commutation in 1969; or the working of the tithe act illustrated by an example of commutation in 1705.
tables. appendix. 34 pp. London, J. G. & F. Rivington, 1837
T.

4933 Prospectus of the Dundalk Western Railway to connect the western and north western counties of Ireland with the port of Dundalk.
illustrations. map. 16 pp. London, Roake & Varty, 1837
A., N.

4934 Prospectus of the Great Central Irish Railway, for connecting Dublin with the west and north west of Ireland.
tables. maps. 24 pp. Dublin, Chambers, 1837
A., N.

4935 PYNE, Henry. Tithe commutation. Table, shewing the amount of the corn rent chargeable in lieu of tithes, to be inserted in apportionments made under the act for the commutation of tithes in England and Wales.
tables. 24 pp. London, C. Knight & co., 1837
T.

4936 Remarks on the application of the workhouse system with other modes of relief to the Irish poor. By an assistant commissioner.
70 pp. London, J. Ridgway, 1837
A.

4937 Report of proceedings of, and resolutions passed at, a half-yearly meeting of shareholders, of the Agricultural & Commercial Bank of Ireland, held at Morrison's Gt. Rooms, Nassau-street, pursuant to requisition, on the 17th day of April, 1837; and also, the proceedings at a meeting of shareholders of said bank, held at 13, Dawson-street, on the 18th of April, 1837; and the resolutions passed thereat, and report of the committee of twenty-one, appointed on the 17th. April, verifying that one-fourth of the paid up capital of the company has been lost.
52 pp. Dublin, printed by G. Folds, 1837
A.

4938 Report of the council of the chamber of commerce of Dublin, to the annual assembly of the members of the association, held the 1st of March, 1837.
26 pp. Dublin, printed by P. D. Hardy, 1837
A.

4939 Report of the statement made by James Dwyer esq. B.L., chairman of the board of directors of the Agricultural and Commercial Bank of Ireland on the subject matter contained in the auditor's report, 17th April, 1837. To which is annexed the accountant's subsequent remarks.
32 pp. Dublin, Chambers, 1837
A.

4940 REVANS, John. Evils of the state of Ireland: their causes and their remedy—a poor law.
tables. 152 pp. London, J. Hatchard, [1837]
C.

170 pp. 2nd ed. London, J. Hatchard, 1837
A., N.

4941 RICARDO, Samson. Observations on the recent pamphlet of J. Horsley Palmer on The causes and consequences of the pressure on the money market etc.
table. 44 pp. London, C. Knight & co., 1837
N., T.

4942 ROGERS, John. A brief statement of the origin, the regulations, and the proceedings, of the board of governors of queen Anne's bounty, for the augmentation of small livings; with suggestions for the more efficient application of the revenues placed at their disposal to the spiritual benefit of populous and laborious parishes. Addressed to his grace the archbishop of Canterbury.
tables. appendices. 82 pp. 2nd ed. Falmouth, J. Trathan, 1837
T.

4943 Royal Irish Mining Company. Half-yearly report of the board of directors to January 1st, 1837.
4 pp. (2 broadsheets.) Dublin, 1837
A.

4944 SALOMONS, Sir David, 1st bart. A defence of the joint-stock banks; an examination of the causes of the present monetary difficulties, and hints for the future management of the circulation.
tables in appendix. 46 pp. 2nd ed. London, Pelham Richardson, 1837
T.

4945 ——. The monetary difficulties of America, and their probable effects on British commerce, considered.
table. 46 pp. London, Pelham Richardson, 1837
T.

4946 SCROPE, George Julius Duncombe Poulett. Remarks on the government Irish Poor-Law Bill in a letter to lord John Russell.
24 pp. London, J. Ridgway, 1837
N.

4947 A second letter to Sir Robert Peel, bart. M.P. on railway legislation. By Cautus.
24 pp. London, James Fraser, 1837
T.

4948 Second report of the Western Australian Association.
tables. 52 pp. London, Simpkin & Marshall, 1837
A.

4949 SENIOR, Nassau William. Letters on the Factory Act, as it affects the cotton manufacture, addressed to the right honourable the president of the board of trade, by N. W. Senior. To which are appended, a letter to Mr. Senior from Leonard Horner, esq. and minutes of a conversation between Mr. Edmund Ashworth, Mr. Thomson and Mr. Senior.
52 pp. London, B. Fellowes, 1837
N., T.

4950 Sketch of the commercial resources and monetary and mercantile system of British India, with suggestions for their improvement, by means of banking establishments.
tables. 118 pp. London, Smith Elder, 1837
T.

4951 STANLEY, J. Poor laws—Ireland. The injustice of assessing landlords, and the impracticability of assessing landholders.
16 pp. Dublin, R. Milliken, London, B. Fellowes, 1837
A., N.

4952 STANLEY, William. Remarks on the government measure for establishing poor laws in Ireland; chiefly with reference to the existing amount of pauperism, as stated in the report of the Irish poor inquiry commissioners; and the necessary extent and character of the means for its relief.
42 pp. 2nd ed. London, C. Knight & co., 1837
A., N., T.

4953 A statement of facts, illustrating the administration of the abolition law, and the suffering of the negro apprentices in the island of Jamaica.
38 pp. London, Haddon, 1837
A., N.

4954 A statement of the objects of the New Zealand Association, with some particulars concerning the position, content, soil and climate, natural productions and natives of New Zealand.
map. 8 pp. London, Black and Armstrong, 1837
N.

4955 Strictures on the proposed poor law for Ireland as recommended in the report of George Nicholls, esq.
92 pp. London, J. Ridgway, 1837
B., D., T.

4956 SWAN, Robert. The principle of church rates; from the earliest evidences of their existence to the present time, comprising a period of nearly twelve hundred years.
appendix. 80 pp. London, J. G. & F. Rivington, 1837
A.

4957 THEOBALD, William. A supplement to Theobald's practical treatise on the poor laws; containing an expository and critical statement of all the poor law cases reported since that publication; together with the poor law statutes, 7 Wm. IV & I Vict. and notes upon them.
52 pp. London, S. Sweet, V. & R. Stevens, 1837
T.

4958 Thoughts on the means of preventing abuses in life assurance offices and joint stock banks.
16 pp. 4th ed. Norwich, J. Sharpe, London, Pickering, 1837
N.

4959 Tobacco question. A statement, shewing that, under the sanction of the present enormous duty, a sum of money is raised on the labouring classes, by government and smuggling, sufficient to pay the whole expense of the effective service of the navy, army, customs, excise, and the pension list. Compiled from parliamentary evidence, the reports of the commissioners of revenue and excise enquiry, Sir Henry Parnell on Financial Reform, and other authentic documents.
tables. 16 pp. 3rd ed. London, C. Skipper and East, 1837
N.

4960 To the farming labourers of Great Britain and Ireland.
8 pp. London, Elliot, 1837
A.

4961 To the proprietors of Grand Canal stock (a letter, signed 'Proprietor').
4 pp. (2 broadsheets.) n.p., 1837
A.

4962 TORRENS, Robert. A letter to the rt. hon. lord John Russell, on the ministerial measure for establishing poor laws in Ireland, and on the auxiliary means which it will be necessary to employ in carrying that measure into effect.
152 pp. London, Longman, Rees, Orme, Brown & Green, 1837
A., T.

4963 ——. A letter to the right honourable lord viscount Melbourne on the causes of the recent derangement in the money market, and on bank reform. Second edition, with additions.
Tables. appendix. 82 pp. London, Longman, Rees, Orme, Brown, and Green, 1837
T.

4964 Twentieth annual report of the managing committee of the association for the suppression of mendicity in Dublin for the year 1837.
180 pp. Dublin, printed by W. Warren, 1837
A.

4965 TYLDEN, Sir John M. On Irish poor laws. Addressed to lord viscount Morpheth [sic].
30 pp. Sittingbourne, Coulter, 1837
N.

4966 WARD, Sir Henry George. The first step to a poor law for Ireland.
50 pp. London, J. Ridgway, 1837
A., N., U.

4967 WATT, Peter. Progress and present state of the science of life insurance, with thermometrical tables. Also, observations on health insurance, etc.
graph. tables. 80 pp. Edinburgh, John Anderson, London, Smith, Elder, 1837
T.

4968 WHITE, John Meadows. 1 Vict. c. 69. Act to amend an act for the commutation of tithes in England and Wales. (6 & 7 William IV., c. 71) With an introduction, notes, and an index.
34 pp. London, B. Fellowes, 1837
T.

4969 WILLICH, Charles M. Tithe commutation tables, for ascertaining, at sight, the amount of corn-rent in bushels, (as directed by the act of 6 and 7 William IV. Cap. 71), equivalent to the tithe-rent, fixed as the basis in the draft of apportionment: also, shewing the amount of tithe rent-charge payable for the year 1837, according to the average prices of wheat, barley, and oats for the seven preceding years, to Christmas 1836, as declared in the London Gazette of 13th January, 1837.
tables. 12 pp. London, Longman, Rees, Orme, Brown, Green, and Longman, 1837
T.

4970 YELLOLY, John. Observations on the arrangements connected with the relief of the sick poor; addressed in a letter to the right honourable the lord John Russell, secretary of state for the home department.
appendix. 44 pp. London, Longman, Rees, Orme, Brown, Green and Longman, 1837
T.

1838

4971 An address to the lords, embodying the spirit of the Irish grand juries' petitions on the poor relief bill; with an appeal in favour of the aged, infirm, and destitute agricultural labourers.
16 pp. London, J. Hatchard, 1838
T.

4972 AISLABIE, William James. A letter to lord John Russell, on the church bills.
12 pp. London, Longman, Orme, Brown, Green & Longman, 1838
T.

4973 Annual report of the strangers' friend society, (founded in 1790,) for visiting and relieving distressed strangers, and the resident sick poor, in Dublin and its vicinity; with an account of some of the cases relieved, and list of subscribers for 1837.
32 pp. Dublin, Thomas I. White, [1838]
N.

4974 ASHURST, William Henry. Facts and reasons in support of Mr. Rowland Hill's plan for a universal penny postage.
tables. 162 pp. 2nd ed. London, H. Hooper, 1838
N.

4975 ATKINSON, William. The state of the science of political economy investigated; wherein is shown the defective character of the arguments which have hitherto been advanced for elucidating the laws of the formation of wealth.
tables. 82 pp. London, Whittaker & co., 1838
T.

4976 The Bank of Ireland charter. Remarks on the proposed renewal of the charter of the Bank of Ireland.
26 pp. London, H. Hooper, 1838
A.

4977 BARRINGTON, Matthew. An address to the inhabitants of Limerick, on the opening of the Mont de Piété, or

charitable pawn-office, for the support of Barrington's Hospital in that city.
appendix. 40 pp. 3rd ed. Dublin, W. Holden, 1838
A.
First ed. 1836. See 4739.

4978 BENTHAM, Jeremy. Canada, emancipate your colonies! An unpublished argument by J. Bentham, with a dedication to the right hon. lord viscount Melbourne, signed by a Philo-Bentham.
34 pp. London, Effingham Wilson, 1838
N.

4979 BEVAN, William. A letter to the rt. hon. lord Brougham on the alleged breach of the colonial apprenticeship contract.
16 pp. Liverpool, D. Marples, [etc., etc.], 1838
N.

4980 BORRETT, W. P. Three letters upon a poor law and public medical relief for Ireland to Daniel O'Connell esq. M.P.
24 pp. London, J. Hatchard, Dublin, Robertson, 1838
N.

4981 BOSWORTH, Joseph. The contrast; or, the operation of the old poor laws contrasted with the recent poor law amendment act, and the necessity of a legal provision for the poor generally, but especially for Ireland.
44 pp. London, Longman, Rees, Orme, Browne, & Green, 1838
T.

4982 BURGES, George. A commentary on the act for the commutation of tithes in England and Wales.
138 pp. London, J. G. and F. Rivington, Norwich, Matchett, Stevenson & Matchett, 1838
T.

4983 BUTT, Isaac. Rent, profits and labour. A lecture delivered before the University of Dublin in Michaelmas term 1837
32 pp. Dublin, W. Curry, jr., London, Holdsworth, 1838
A., N.

4984 BUXTON, Thomas Fowell. A letter to the right hon. lord John Russell, from Thomas Fowell Buxton, esq., on certain allegations recently made in the house of commons in the debate on Sir George Strickland's motion for the abolition of negro apprenticeship.
16 pp. London, J. Hatchard, 1838
T.

4985 CATOR, Charles. Protest against the commutation of tithes, and correspondence, with the tithe commissioners.
12 pp. London, J. G. & F. Rivington, 1838
T.

4986 Circular to the ladies. Abstract history of the musical society of Ireland, and of the progress of the small loan system, founded by that society before 1747.
26 pp. Dublin, Clarke, 1838
A.

4987 CLEMENTS, Robert Birmingham Clements, viscount. The present poverty of Ireland convertible into the means of her improvement, under a well-administered poor law, with a preliminary view of the state of agriculture in Ireland.
table of contents. 186 pp. London, C. Knight & co., 1838
A., N., T.

4988 Communication between Dublin and London by short sea in fourteen hours.
4 pp. n.p., 1838
A.

4989 CONNERY, James. An essay on charitable economy...
98 pp. 3rd ed. Dublin, J. Cumming, 1838
A.
See 4752 and 4873.

4990 CUBITT, William, and others. London and Dublin direct communication. Opinions of William Cubitt, George Stephenson and George Roskell respecting the St. George's harbour and Chester railway.
4 pp. London, Baily, 1838
A.

4991 DAY, John. A few practical observations on the new poor law, showing the demoralizing & enslaving effects of this anti-christian enactment, containing various facts, illustrating the working of the new law; addressed to the rate-payers and labourers of England.
appendix. 32 pp. London, A. Redford, 1838
T.

4992 Digest of the act of parliament for the relief of the poor in Ireland, 1º & 2º Victoriae, Chapter 56; with an index, and the act. Second ed., to which is added a supplement, fully exemplifying, by calculations, the operation of the rate-paying clauses.
tables. supplement. 120 pp. Dublin, George and John Grierson, 1838
A., T.

4993 Digest of the act of parliament to abolish compositions for tithes and to substitute rent-charges in lieu thereof; divided into seven parts with introductions to each part, and full instructions for filling the schedules as required; with a comprehensive analytical index.
100 pp. Dublin, George and John Grierson, 1838
A., T.

4994 Direct communication between London & Dublin.
32 pp. n.p., 1838
A.
A series of accounts of meetings and reports, 1836–38.

4995 DREWRY, Charles Stewart. The patent-law amendment act: with notes and cases, and an appendix of rules and forms.
appendix. 62 pp. London, John Richards, 1838
T.

4996 DYOTT, W. H. A vindication of the tradesmen of Dublin from the late calumnious charges of Daniel O'Connell esq. M.P. being a letter addressed to that hon. and learned gentleman.
16 pp. Dublin, D. O'Brien, 1838
A.

19

4997 ELMORE, F. H. and BIRNEY, James G. The anti-slavery examiner no. 8. Correspondence between the hon. F. H. Elmore, one of the South Carolina delegation in Congress, and James G. Birney, one of the secretaries of the American anti-slavery society.
appendices. 68 pp. New York, American anti-slavery society, 1838
A.

4998 An essay on populousness. By Marcus.
28 pp. Printed for private circulation, London, 1838
A., T.

'The reader is requested to consider the following piece as being the fourth chapter of the foregoing tract'—i.e., *On the possibility of limiting populousness*, by the same author. See 5051, 5298.

4999 A few general observations on the principal railways executed, in progress, and projected in the midland counties and north of England with the author's opinion upon them as investments.
table of contents. maps. tables. 80 pp. London, Longman, Rees, Orme, Brown & Green, Liverpool, Cannell, 1838
N., T.

5000 First report and proceedings of the general railway committee appointed at a public meeting held at the Commercial Buildings, on Friday the 22nd day of November, 1838.
map. 24 pp. Dublin, W. Warren, 1838
A.

5001 A full and concise report of the speeches delivered on the occasion of opening the Dublin mechanics institution June 22nd, 1838, in the lecture room of the above institution, Royal Exchange.
24 pp. Dublin, D. O'Brien, 1838
A.

5002 FULTON, Henry. Grand canal. First letter to the proprietors of stock.
24 pp. Dublin, G. Folds, 1838
A., N.

5003 ——. Grand canal. Second letter to the proprietors of stock.
22 pp. Dublin, G. Folds, 1838
A., N.

5004 ——. Grand canal. Third letter (and possibly the last) to the proprietors of stock.
24 pp. Dublin, G. Folds, 1838
A., N.

5005 The ghost of John Bull; or, the devil's railroad. A marvellously strange narrative. Dedicated (without permission) to such members of parliament as may feel inclined to turn their coats, poor law commissioners, and railroad directors in particular.
72 pp. London, James Pattie, 1838
T.

5006 GOODE, William. A brief history of church-rates, proving the liability of a parish to them to be a common-law

liability; including a reply to the statements on that subject in Sir John Campbell's letter to the right hon. lord Stanley on the law of church-rates. Second edition, considerably enlarged.
appendix. 78 pp. 2nd ed. London, J. Hatchard, 1838
T.

5007 Great Leinster and Munster Railway. First extension from Dublin to Kilkenny. First report.
16 pp. London, Teape, 1838
A.

5008 GREGG, Francis. The law and practice of bankruptcy, as connected with the choice, appointment, duties, liabilities, remuneration, costs, death, or removal of official assignees.
100 pp. London, V. and R. Stevens, 1838
T.

5009 [HALIDAY, Charles.] Necessity of combining a law of settlement with local assessment in the proposed bill for the relief of the poor of Ireland.
60 pp. Dublin, R. Milliken, London, J. Ridgway, 1838
T.

5010 HANCOCK, Walter. Narrative of twelve years' experiments, (1824–1836,) demonstrative of the practicability and advantage of employing steam-carriages on common roads; with engravings and descriptions of the different steam-carriages constructed by the author, his patent boiler, wedge-wheels, and other invention.
illustrations. plates. tables. appendix. 106 pp. London, John Weale, and J. Mann, 1838
T.

5011 HANDLEY, Henry. A letter to earl Spencer (president of the Smithfield Club) on the formation of a national agricultural institution.
38 pp. London, J. Ridgway, 1838
A.

5012 HANKEY, William Alers. Letters to Joseph Sturge, esq., in answer to his statements relating to the Arcadia estate in Jamaica, in the journal of his visit to the West Indies.
28 pp. London, Thomas Ward, 1838
T.

5013 Hints to the directors and shareholders of the Great Western Railway, with reference to the probable loss of traffic by adopting the broad gauge, intended as a companion to the reports of Mr. Wood and Mr. Hawkshaw; to be submitted to the general meeting of proprietors to be held on the 9th January, 1839.
68 pp. London, R. Midleton, 1838
U.

5014 Historical review of the poor and vagrant laws, from the earliest period upon record to the present time, affording data for legislation from experience.
92 pp. 2nd ed. London, Henry Kent Causton, 1838
A., T.

5015 HOARE, Edward Newenham, archdeacon of Ardfert. Practical observations on church reform, the tithe question, and national education in Ireland.
table of contents. 72 pp. Dublin, W. Curry, jr., 1838
A., B., N., T.

5016 [HOBSON, Samuel.] The justice and equity of assessing the net profits of the land for the relief of the poor, maintained, in a letter to the poor law commissioners: with some remarks on the celebrated case of Rex *v.* Jodrell. By a Norfolk clergyman.
tables. 36 pp. London, Roake and Varty, [1838]
T.

5017 An impartial examination of all the authors on Australia; official documents and the reports of private individuals as evidences of the advantages of emigration, and as a guide to the selection of the colony best calculated to secure the welfare of settlers. By an intending emigrant.
96 pp. London, Smith & Elder, 1838
A.

5018 Information respecting the eastern township of lower Canada, addressed to emigrants and others, in search of lands for settlement.
10 pp. Sherbrooke, Walton, 1838
N.

5019 Instructions for the establishment of benefit building societies, with rules and forms of mortgages, etc. applicable thereto.
36 pp. London, Her Majesty's Stationery Office, 1838
N.

5020 Irish landlords, as they are, and the poor law bill accompanied as it ought to be; respectfully addressed to the right honourable and honourable the members of the imperial parliament; with a few words on landowners and slave-owners, wastelands, and weighty debts.
44 pp. Dublin, Hodges & Smith, 1838
A., T.

5021 The Irish poor-law bill. Two letters to Daniel O'Connell, esq. M.P. in reply to his letters to his constituents on the Irish poor-law bill.
Reprinted from 'the Courier' with notes. 20 pp. London, H. Hooper, 1838
P.

5022 JOHNSON, Cuthbert. On population.
table. 4 pp. n.p., 1838
N.

5023 JOHNSON, James F. W. The economy of a coal-field; an exposition of the objects of the Geological and Polytechnic Society of the West Riding of Yorkshire, and of the best means of obtaining them.
table of contents. tables. 78 pp. Durham, Andrews, 1838
A., N.

5024 JONES, Richard. Remarks on the manner in which tithe should be assessed to the poor's rate, under the existing law, with a protest against the change which will be produced in that law by a bill introduced into the house of commons by Mr. Shaw Lefevre.
64 pp. London, Shaw & sons, 1838
N.

5025 KENNEDY, John Pitt. 9. Regulations for the management of the Cloghan Agricultural Loan Fund, established by Sir Charles Style, bart., M.P. for improving the condition of his tenantry.
4 pp. Dublin, Alexander Thom, 1838
U.

5026 ——. 5. Regulations for the boarding class of male pupils, at the Cloghan National Agricultural Model School.
4 pp. Dublin, Alexander Thom, 1838
U.

See 4898 & 4899.

5027 KIDD, John. An act for the more effectual relief of the destitute poor in Ireland with prefatory remarks and a copious index.
182 pp. Dublin, R. Milliken, 1838
A.

5028 KINAHAN, Daniel. A digest of the act for the abolition of tithes. With notes and index, and an appendix containing the act.
appendix. index. 90 pp. Dublin, R. Milliken, 1838
T.

5029 LEEKE, William. A few suggestions for increasing incomes of many of the smaller livings, for the almost total abolition of pluralities, and for promoting the residence of ministers in the several parishes; more particularly addressed to the members of both houses of parliament.
12 pp. Derby, W. Bemrose, London, J. Hatchard, [etc.], 1838
A., N.

5030 [LEGRAND, Daniel.] Messieurs, Votre sollicitude pour l'amélioration physique et morale de la classe ouvrière, et vos expériences comme chefs d'un des premiers établissements industriels de la France, vous mettent a même de jeter une grande lumière sur toutes les questions qui ont rapport a ce sujet si important pour le présent et pour l'avenir d'une portion aussi notable de la population, qui ne doit être sacrifiée, ni à sa propre cupidité, qui l'aveugle, ni a celle de ceux des industriels qui voudraient l'exploiter.
[lacking t-p., or any heading.] 18 pp. dated at end: Gorges des Vosges, ce 31 mars 1838.
T.

5031 A letter to the marquess of Lansdowne on the report of the Irish railway commissioners, by a shareholder in the Kilkenny Railway.
appendix with tables. 38 pp. London, Pelham Richardson, 1838
A., N.

5032 LYNCH, A. H. An address to the electors of Galway on the poor-law bill for Ireland. With an appendix containing extracts from the evidence taken before the commissioners of poor inquiry. Ireland.
144 pp. London, C. Knight & co., 1838
A., N., T., U.

5033 MCCULLAGH, William Torrens. Letter to the representative peers of Ireland on the ministerial measure of Irish poor laws.
12 pp. Dublin, R. Milliken, London, J. Ridgway, 1838
A., N.

5034 MacGregor, Alexander. On the causes of the destitution of food in the highlands and islands of Scotland in the years 1836, 1837.
40 pp. [no t.p.] [1838?]

N.

5035 MacNaghten, Sir Francis Workman, bart. Poor laws—Ireland. Observations upon the report of George Nicholls, esq.
58 pp. London, Longman, Rees, Orme, Brown & Green [etc., etc.], 1838

A., N., T.

5036 M'Queen, James. A letter to the right hon. lord Glenelg, on the West Indian currency, commerce, African slave trade, &c. &c.
tables. 52 pp. London, B. Fellowes, 1838

T.

5037 Marcescheau, ——. Proposition d'une loi pour la conversion des rentes 4½, 4 et 3 pour cent en rentes 5 pour cent non remboursables pendant vingt ans.
tables. 62 pp. 2nd ed. Paris, Delaunay, 1838

N.

5038 Maunsell, Henry. The only safe poor law experiment for Ireland. A letter to the rt. honourable lord viscount Morpeth.
16 pp. Dublin, Fannin, 1838

A., N.

5039 Merivale, Herman. Five lectures on the principles of a legislative provision for the poor in Ireland. Delivered in 1837 and 1838.
118 pp. London, C. Knight & co., 1838

T.

5040 Molesworth, Robert. An essay upon the law regarding the registration of deeds and conveyances in Ireland.
tables. appendix. 176 pp. Dublin, R. Milliken, 1838

T.

5041 Morris, Jeffery. A complete abstract of the new Irish poor law act with all its clauses, disencumbered of legal technicality and repetition and the entire rendered familiar and instructive to every class of readers.
folding table. 40 pp. Dublin, L. Shaw, T. Hall, 1838

A.

5042 Morton, John. On the nature and property of soils: their connexion with the geological formation on which they rest: the best means of permanently increasing their productiveness, and on the rent and profits of agriculture.
tables. 255 pp. London, J. Ridgway, 1838

T.

5043 [Myers, Sir Francis.] Hints to the legislature, and, to the nation, on the provisions, character, and defects of the imprisonment for debt bill, as sent down from the house of lords to the house of commons, June 12, 1838.
86 pp. London, J. Ridgway, 1838

A., N.

5044 National interests. Part V. By a member of the Labourers' Friend Society.
8 pp. [pag. 17–24.] Dublin, 1838

N.

5045 [Nevile, Christopher.] Brief remarks on the justification of the new poor law, by the Rev. Christopher Nevile, an ex-officio guardian of the Lincoln Union. Wherein is given the opinion of John McCulloch, esq., on the principles of the same law. By one of the Thompson family.
20 pp. Newcastle, Currie and Bowman, London, J. G. and F. Rivington, [etc.], 1838

T.

5046 Nicholls, Sir George. Poor laws—Ireland. Third report of G. Nicholls to H.M. secretary of state for the home department containing the result of an inquiry into the condition of the labouring classes and the provision for the relief of the poor, in Holland and Belgium.
24 pp. London, C. Knight & Co., 1838

N.

5047 Norman, George Warde. Remarks upon some prevalent errors, with respect to currency and banking, and suggestions to the legislature and the public as to the improvement of the monetary system.
110 pp. London, Pelham Richardson, 1838

T.

5048 Observations explanatory of the orders of the poor law commissioners regulating the first election of guardians; and of some of the provisions of the Irish poor law.
32 pp. Dublin, A. Thom, 1838.

A.

5049 Observations on foreign mining in Mexico. By a resident.
48 pp. London, Pelham Richardson, 1838

T.

5050 O'Donnell, Mathew. A brief treatise on the law of combination, on unlawful societies and on the administration of unlawful oaths, in which the present state of the common and statute law in Ireland, affecting both master and workman, is fully explained.
appendix. table of contents. 76 pp. Dublin, Hodges & Smith, 1838

A., N., P.

5051 On the possibility of limiting populousness. By Marcus.
table of contents. 54 pp. London, J. Hill, 1838

A., T.

See 4998, 5298.

5052 [Perceval, Arthur Philip.] Working of the tithe commutation act.
table. 12 pp. London, J. G. & F. Rivington, 1838

T.

5053 Phillpotts, John. A letter to the Right Hon. Lord J. Russell, in answer to the pamphlet of the Rev. Richard Jones, one (o)f the tithe commissioners for England and Wales, on the manner in which tithe should be assessed to the poor rate.
30 pp. London, J. Hatchard, 1838

T.

5054 Portlock, Joseph E. An address explanatory of the objects and advantages of statistical enquiries, delivered at

the second general meeting of the statistical society of Ulster, 18th May, 1838.
28 pp. Belfast, Hodgson, 1838

A., N.

5055 Prices and wages in New South Wales and Van Diemen's Land. (Government Emigration office.)
tables. 8 pp. (no t.p.) London, Her Majesty's Stationery Office, 1838

N.

5056 Proposed prospectus for forming a tontine company, for building the new intended street from Richmond bridge to the Temple in the Queens Inns between Henrietta St. and Constitution Hill...
10 pp. Dublin, Corbet, 1838

A.

5057 Report by the directors of the Provincial Bank of Ireland to the proprietors assembled at the thirteenth yearly general meeting, on Thursday, May 16, 1838; with a list of the directors and branches, and an alphabetical list of the proprietors, at the 17th of May, 1838.
42 pp. London, Thomas, 1838

A.

5058 Report, from the select committee of the legislative council of Upper Canada, on the state of the province.
appendices. 152 pp. n.p., Stanton, 1838

N.

5059 Report of the deputation appointed by the honourable the Irish society to visit the city of London's plantation in Ireland, in the year 1838.
fold. map & diag. 104 pp. London, W. Tyler, 1838

A., B.

5060 RICARDO, Samson. A national bank the remedy for the evils attendant upon our present system of paper currency.
68 pp. London, Pelham Richardson, 1838

A., N., T.

5061 RODGERS, William. The mutual relations of landlord and tenant. A pamphlet wherein the true interest of the landowners of Ireland is shown to consist in a more liberal treatment of their tenantry.
table of contents. 74 pp. Derry, Derry Journal Office, 1838

N.

5062 ROSS, Sir John. On communication to India, in large steamships, by the Cape of Good Hope. Printed by order of the India steam-ship company, and addressed to the British public.
map. plan. tables. appendix. 64 pp. London, Smith and Elder, 1838

T.

5063 RUBIDGE, Charles. Plain statement of the advantages attending emigration to Upper Canada.
appendix. tables. 86 pp. London, Simpkin, Marshall, 1838

N.

5064 Rules and orders to be observed by the marchioness Wellesley Female Tontine Society.
12 pp. Dublin, Warren, 1838

A.

5065 RYAN, P. B. Manual for loan societies, respectfully submitted to the public.
30 pp. Dublin, W. Frazer, 1838

A., U.

5066 [——.] A substitute for poor laws in Ireland, affording all the relief necessary, without any additional taxation. Dedicated to Daniel O'Connell esq. M.P. Who is censured because he did not support a measure which he conscientiously believed would be injurious to his country. by P.B.R.
16 pp. n.p., [1838?]

A.

5067 [——.] Provision for the poor in Ireland, without any additional taxation.
appendices. 36 pp. notes. appendix revised and corrected. Dublin, W. Frazer, [1838?]

A., N.

5068 ——. Provision for the poor of Ireland, without any additional taxation, on the principles of the Musical Charitable Loan Society.
table of contents. appendices. 76 pp. 2nd ed. notes. appendix revised, corrected. Dublin, W. Frazer, 1838

A., N.

5069 SANKEY, William S. Villiers. The rights of labour to protect itself.
22 pp. Edinburgh, the author, 1838

A.

5070 SCOBLE, John. British Guiana. Speech delivered at the anti-slavery meeting, in Exeter Hall, on Wednesday, the 4th of April, 1838
36 pp. London, Central Negro Emancipation Committee, 1838

A,

5071 [SLIGO, Howe Peter Browne, 2nd marquess of.] Jamaica under the apprenticeship system. By a proprietor.
tables. appendix. 172 pp. London, J. Andrews, 1838

T.

5072 SMITH, Herbert. A letter to the bishops and parochial clergy in behalf of the deserving poor.
8 pp. London, J. G. & F. Rivington, [etc., etc.], [1838]

T.

5073 SMYTH, George Lewis. Aids to the Irish poor law in reclamation of Irish waste lands. A letter to the Rt. Hon. lord John Russell, on the propriety of reclaiming the waste lands of Ireland, upon the authority of a commission from the crown.
24 pp. London, H. Hooper, 1838

N.

5074 Society for the Encouragement of Arts, Manufactures, and Commerce: premiums for the sessions 1838–1839, 1839–1840.
16 pp. London, Moyes, 1838.

N.

5075 Steam navigation of England, Ireland, etc.
maps. 36 pp. Edinburgh, Thompson, 1838.

A.

5076 STEPHENSON, George.   Report of George Stephenson upon the proposed railway communications with Ireland.
4 pp. (2 large sheets.) Chester, Spence, 1838
A.

5077 STOKER, William.   Brief observations on the contemplated Irish poor law and medical charities' Bills...a supplement to his treatise on medical reform.
12 pp. Dublin, P. D. Hardy, 1838
A.

5078 Strictures on the proposed poor law for Ireland, as recommended in the report of George Nicholls esq., with an appendix, being remarks on the second report.
108 pp. 2nd ed. London, J. Ridgway, 1838
A.

5079 Tithe Commutation Act. Some observations on the dangerous principles and tendency of the Tithe Act: a letter to George Palmer, esq. M.P. of Nazing Part. By one of his clerical constituents.
50 pp. London, J. G. & F. Rivington, 1838
T.

5080 TORRENS, Robert.   A letter to the rt. hon. lord John Russell on the ministerial measure for establishing poor laws in Ireland.
97 pp. 2nd ed. London, Longman, Orme, Brown and Green, 1838
N.

5081 ——.   Plan of an association in aid of the Irish poor law.
36 pp. London, Longman, Orme, Brown & Green, 1838
A., N., U.

5082 [WAUGH, James.]   Three years' practical experience of a settler in New South Wales; being extracts from letters to his friends in Edinburgh, from 1834 to 1837. With a preface by the editor, and an appendix containing notes and information for all classes of intending emigrants, from the latest authorities, and public documents.
map. 72 pp. 8th ed. Edinburgh, Johnstone, 1838
A.

5083 WHALLEY, George Hammond.   The Tithe Act, and the Tithe Amendment Act, with notes on the principal points which have presented difficulties to parties during the operation of the measure, together with the report of the tithe commissioners, ordered by the act to be presented to one of her majesty's principal secretaries of state, before the first day of May, 1838, as to the cases which will receive an increase or decrease upon the average receipts; cases which will be specially adjudicated upon, and the principles upon which the tithe of coppice wood is to be commuted, with explanatory notes.
plans. tables. appendix. 398 pp. London, Shaw, 1838
T.

5084 YOUNG, George R.   A statement of the 'Escheat Question', in the island of Prince Edward; together with the causes of the late agitation, and the remedies proposed.
table in appendix. 72 pp. London, R. & W. Swale, 1838
T.

1839

5085 American slavery as it is: testimony of a thousand witnesses.
table of contents. appendix. 228 pp. New York, American Anti-slavery Society, 1839
A.

5086 ARABIN, Henry.   A plan for extending the paper currency on the security of the nation.
16 pp. London, J. G. & F. Rivington, 1839
A., N., T.

5087 BARBER, James.   Statement of facts relating to steam communication, with India, on the comprehensive plan.
tables. 16 pp. London, Smith, Elder & co., 1839
A.

5088 BELL, John.   A vindication of the rights of British landowners, farmers, and labourers, against the claims of the cotton capitalists to a free trade in corn.
tables. 48 pp. London, Hatchard, 1839
T.

5089 [BERMINGHAM, Thomas.]   A report of the proceedings at two public meetings held at the Thatched House Tavern, 13th & 20th April, 1839 for the purpose of taking into consideration the necessity of forming railways throughout Ireland. Called by Thomas Bermingham esq., chairman of the general Irish railroad committee.
tables. 50 pp. London, Smith, Elder & co. [etc.], 1839
A.

5090 ——.   A statistical account of foreign and English railways; extracted from synopses of German railways, and from the statistical journal of London, as referred to by able articles in the Railway Times and Mining Journal of May 18th, 1839.
map. 24 pp. London, Smith, Elder & co. [etc.], 1839
A.

5091 BLACKBURNE, Jonathan.   Some remarks upon the nature and origin of the tithes in London, with the view of suggesting a remedy for the present inadequate endowment of many populous places by similar payments out of houses. With an appendix.
appendix. 96 pp. Cambridge, T. Stevenson, 1839
T.

5092 BLACKER, William.   The evils inseparable from a mixed currency, and the advantages to be secured by introducing an inconvertible national paper circulation, throughout the British Empire and its dependencies, under proper regulations.
75 pp. London, R. Groombridge, J. Ridgway, [etc.], 1839
A., L., T.

5093 BLAKE, William.   Observations in reply to a pamphlet by the Rev. Richard Jones, one of the tithe commissioners for England and Wales, on the assessment of tithes to the poor rate.
64 pp. London, John Murray, 1839
T.

5094 BUXTON, Thomas Fowell.   The African slave trade.
tables. 255 pp. second ed. London, John Murray, 1839
                                                    T.

5095 CARMICHAEL SMYTH, David.   Zumeendaree accounts:
translated from the original, together with a few explanatory
remarks.
tables. 144 pp. 2nd ed. London, W. H. Allen, 1839
                                                    T.

5096 CHANNING, William Ellery.   Remarks on the slavery
question, in a letter to Jonathan Phillips, esq.
80 pp. London, Wiley and Putnam, 1839
                                                    T.

5097 Combinations defended; being a commentary upon,
and analysis of the evidence given before the parliamentary
committee of inquiry into combinations of employers and
workmen, appointed by the house of commons, February,
1838. By the London Trades' Combination committee.
64 pp. London, printed by Hartwell, 1839
                                                    A.

5098 Corn and currency; or, how shall we get through the
winter? By a merchant.
32 pp. London, Pelham Richardson, 1839
                                                    T.

5099 The corn laws. An authentic report of the late important discussions in the Manchester chamber of commerce
on the destructive effects of the corn laws upon the trade and
manufactures of the country. With notes and prefatory remarks explanatory of the character and position of some of
the members who were present, or took a part in the proceedings.
116 pp. London, J. Ridgway, 1839
                                                    A., T.

5100 CRAWFORD, William Sharman.   A defence of the small
farmers of Ireland.
132 pp. Dublin, Porter, 1839
                                                    A.

5101 CURTIS, T. A.   Appendix. Copies of correspondence
between T. A. Curtis and the India board and East India
company
32 pp. [paginated 50–82.] London, 1839.
                                                    A.
Appendix to 'State of the question of steam communication
with India, via the Red Sea', by T. A. Curtis.

5102 DAHLMANN, T.   A refutation to Cobbett's doctrine of
paper money being incompatible with the co-existence of gold;
comprising a scheme projected for regulating, improving, and
increasing, the stability of the currency through the aid of a
paper circulation of a competitive character.
24 pp. London, Simpkins, 1839
                                                    T.

5103 DAVIS, George Evan.   A letter addressed to the commissioners of Irish railways on transatlantic steam navigation,
by their desire and by their permission.
table. 40 pp. Dublin, W. Curry, jr., 1839
                                                    A.

5104 DE BARY, R. B.   A charm against chartism; in which
the title of the operative is set forth, and his estate ascertained:
comprising thoughts on education, and the expediency of
instituting public games.
20 pp. London, Harry Renshaw, 1839
                                                    U.

5105 DE MORGAN, Augustus.   Statement, on behalf of the
Liberal Annuity Company, of Dublin, submitted to Augustus
de Morgan, esq. Trinity college, Cambridge, professor of
mathematics, University college London, and secretary to
the Royal astronomical society, with his report thereon.
tables. 18 pp. Dublin, printed by Chambers, 1839
                                                    A.

5106 DICKSON, Stephen Fox.   The case and claims of the
licensed victuallers of Ireland briefly stated with notes and
observations.
72 pp. Dublin, McDermott, 1839–1840
                                                    A.

5107 DIXON, William.   Facts, established by authentic documents, bearing upon agriculture, as influenced by incautious
legislation; particularly applicable to seasons of actual or
apprehended scarcity.
table of contents. tables. 64 pp. London, Longman & co.,
[etc., etc.], 1839
                                                    A.

5108 DRUMMOND, Henry.   Causes which lead to a bank
restriction bill.
24 pp. London, J. Frazer, 1839
                                                    A., T.

5109 DUDGEON, George.   The duties of overseers of the
poor, and assistant overseers. [As the law now stands.]
M.DCCC. XXXIX. Pointed out in plain language.
72 pp. second edition. London, C. Knight & co., [1839]
                                                    T.

5110 A few cursory observations relating to the public
works of the county Kildare. Intended chiefly for the use of
the cess-payers in the southern part of the county. By Enna.
18 pp. Ballinasloe, French, 1839
                                                    N.

5111 FITZWILLIAM, Charles William Wentworth-Fitzwilliam, 5th earl.   First, second and third addresses to the landowners of England on the corn laws.
tables. 24 pp. new ed. London, Ridgway, 1839.
                                                    A., R.

5112 FLYNN, Henry E.   An appeal to the wisdom, justice
and mercy of the imperial parliament, in behalf of the Irish
peasantry, on the subject of a national system of railways in
Ireland.
8 pp. Dublin, G. Folds, 1839.
                                                    A.

5113 FRENCH, FitzStephen.   The question, Are the government entitled to the support of the Irish liberal members at
the present crisis? Considered in relation to the past and with
reference to the future.
50 pp. London, Ridgway, 1839
                                                    A., N.

5114 GILES, John Eustace. Socialism in its moral tendencies, compared with Christianity. The second of three lectures on socialism, (as propounded by Robert Owen and others) delivered in the baptist chapel, South-Parade, Leeds, September 30, 1838.
appendix. 48 pp. London, Simpkin, Marshall & co., Leeds, John Heaton, 1839
T.

5115 GLADSTONE, Sir John. The repeal of the corn laws with its probable consequences, briefly examined and considered.
20 pp. London, J. Hatchard, 1839
N.

——. 20 pp. 2nd ed. London, J. Hatchard, 1839
T.

5116 GLORNEY, B. The stimulus, or a proposition of a principle for employing population, extending trade, and lessening the expense of poor rates.
16 pp. Dublin, 1839
A.

5117 Great Leinster and Munster Railway. First extension from Dublin to Kilkenny. Second half-yearly report, 2nd March, 1839.
tables. folding plans. 42 pp. London, Teape, 1839
A.

5118 Great Leinster and Munster Railway. First extension from Dublin to Kilkenny. Report of special general meeting, 22nd July, 1839.
8 pp. Dublin, Chambers, 1839
A.

5119 Great Leinster & Munster Railway. First extension from Dublin to Kilkenny. 3rd half yearly report, August, 1839.
maps. 8 pp. London, Teape, 1839
A.

5120 GREGG, St. George. The currency; its evils, and their remedies.
8 pp. 2d. ed. London, Effingham Wilson, 1839.
A.

5121 HARLEY, James. The currency: its influence on the internal trade of the country: in a letter addressed to the drapers of Scotland. With a section from a valuable work recently published entitled 'A history of prices' by Thos. Tooke, esq., F.R.S.
tables. appendix. 116 pp. Glasgow, John Smith, 1839
T.

5122 HENCHY, John. General observations on the state of Ireland, and plans for its improvement, with remarks on poor laws.
24 pp. 2d. ed. Dublin, J. Kirkwood, 1839
A., N.

5123 HOARE, Edward N. Letters on subjects connected with Ireland, addressed to an English clergyman.
110 pp. Dublin, R. Milliken, London, J. Ridgway, 1839
A., T.

5124 HORTON, Sir Robert John Wilmot, bart. Correspondence between the rt. hon. Sir Robert Wilmot Horton, bart. and J. B. Robinson, chief justice of Upper Canada upon the subject of a pamphlet lately published entitled 'Ireland and Canada'.
32 pp. London, J. Murray, 1839
N.

5125 HUNT, Thornton Leigh. Canada and South Australia. A commentary on that part of the earl of Durham's report which relates to the disposal of wastelands and emigration. In three papers, delivered at the South Australian rooms No. 5 Adam St., Strand.
96 pp. London, Cole, 1839
A.

5126 An important problem having been solved by the Labourers' Friends' Society, is respectfully addressed to her most gracious majesty, the Queen; patroness.
diagrams. tables. 16 pp. London, Lee, 1839
N.

5127 The Irish Municipal Corporations Bill. A few words in time on the subject of reformed corporations, and of their powers of taxation. Addressed to all who are liable to the payment of poor-rates in Ireland.
tables. 32 pp. London, Kinder, 1839
A., K., N.

5128 Irish railways. Proceedings of the deputation.
8 pp. London, S. W. Fores [etc.], 1839
A.
Deputation to viscount Morpeth, then chief secretary.

5129 JACKSON, Samuel. Commercial distress temporary; arising from natural and periodical causes, and not from the effects of the corn laws.
36 pp. London, Longman, Orme and Co., 1839
T.

5130 Justice to corn-growers and to corn-eaters.
28 pp. London, James Fraser, 1839
T.

5131 The late commercial crisis; being a retrospect of the years 1836 to 1838: with tables representing a safe, speedy, and equitable plan for the abolition of the corn laws. By a Glasgow manufacturer.
tables. 114 pp. Glasgow, John Symington, 1839
T.

5132 LECOUNT, Peter. The history of the railway connecting London and Birmingham: containing its progress from the commencement. To which are added, a popular description of the locomotive engine: and a sketch of the geological features of the line.
122 pp. London, Simpkin, Marshall, Charles Tilt, [1839]
T.

5133 [LEGRAND, Daniel.] Nouvelle lettre d'un industriel des montagnes des Vosges à M. François Delessert, membre de la chambre des deputés, pour être communiqué à M. le ministre du commerce.
8 pp. Strasbourg, Levrault, 1839
T.

5134 Letter to the duke of Buckingham, on the corn laws. By a practical farmer.
tables. 40 pp. London, T. Cadell, 1839
T.

5135 Letterkenny Loan Fund Society: second annual report, 1839.
appendices. tables. 30 pp. Derry, at the Sentinel Office, 1839
N.

5136 LOYD, Samuel Jones, later 1st baron Overstone. Remarks on the management of the circulation and on the condition and conduct of the Bank of England and of the country issues, during the year 1839.
136 pp. London, Pelham Richardson, 1839
A.

5137 LYNCH, A. H. Measures to be adopted for the employment of the labouring classes in Ireland; detailed in an address to the electors of Galway; with an appendix, containing abstracts of the reports of some of the provincial assemblies in Belgium.
tables. appendix. 254 pp. London, Charles Knight, 1839
T.

5138 MADDEN, R. R. A letter to W. E. Channing, D.D. on the subject of the abuse of the flag of the United States in the island of Cuba, and the advantage taken of its protection in promoting the slave trade.
32 pp. Boston, Ticknor, 1839
A.

5139 MEARS, Edwin Hartley. On British colonization; particularly in reference to South Australia. The substance of the following essay was delivered as a lecture at the Greenwich Literary Society, on the 31st January, 1839.
appendix. 32 pp. 2nd. ed. London, Mann, Reynolds, 1839
N.

5140 METCALFE, William. The principle and law of assessing property to the poor's rate, under the 43rd of Elizabeth, cap. 2, stated and illustrated by numerous adjudged cases, and the method of assessment practised in Glasgow and Paisley, with remarks on the 'parochial assessment Act', Mr. Shaw Lefevre's declaratory bill, and the means for obtaining an equitable settlement of the rating question. In a letter, addressed, (by permission), to the right honourable the earl of Hardwicke.
46 pp. London, Whittaker [etc.], 1839
T.

5141 MILLER, Charles. The principles of Mr. Shaw Lefevre's parochial assessments bill, and the tithe commutation act, compared, in a letter to the Rev. Richard Jones, M.A., one of the tithe commissioners for England and Wales.
table. 52 pp. London, J. G. & F. Rivington, 1839
T.

5142 MILLER, John. On the present unsettled condition of the law and its administration.
tables. appendix. 176 pp. London, J. Murray, 1839
T.

5143 MILLER, Samuel. Suggestions for a general equalization of the land tax: with a view to provide the means of reducing or abolishing the malt duties: and a statement of the legal rights and remedies of persons unequally assessed to land tax in particular districts or places.
tables. 62 pp. London, H. Butterworth, 1839
T.

5144 MILNER, Thomas Hughes. The present and future state of Jamaica considered.
96 pp. London, H. Hooper [etc.], 1839
T.

5145 MORETON, Augustus Henry, later Macdonald-Moreton. Thoughts on the corn laws, addressed to the working classes of the county of Gloucester.
24 pp. London, Simpkin Marshall & co., 1839
T.

5146 MORRIS, Jeffery. A complete digest of the new Irish Poor Law Act with all its clauses; disencumbered of legal technicality and repetition: with numerous notes, illustrations, and a general index; rendering the entire a useful and necessary compendium, indispensable to rate payers.
folding table. 52 pp. 2nd ed. Dublin, Coyne, 1839
A.

5147 NAPIER, Sir Charles James. An essay on the present state of Ireland, showing the chief cause of, and the remedy for, the existing distresses in that country, dedicated to the Irish absentee landed proprietors as proving that, although their absence is injurious to Ireland, it is not the primary cause of the sufferings endured by the Irish people.
maps. 72 pp. London, J. Ridgway, 1839
A., N.

5148 Nineteenth report of the United East Lothian agricultural society, with a selection of reports of experiments on various subjects since its institution, and a list of the present members.
table of contents. tables. 120 pp. Haddington, Wood, 1839
N.

5149 On the public debt, with a plan for its final extinction.
tables. 32 pp. London, Pelham Richardson, 1839
T.
'Doubtfully attributed by Foxwell to Abbott'-Kress, C.4953.

5150 Order of the poor law commissioners for government of the workhouse and keeping of the accounts of the —— union.
tables. 58 pp. n.p., [1839?]
Q.

5151 Orders of the poor law commissioners regulating the meetings of the boards of guardians, and their proceedings thereat, and defining the duties of some of the officers appointed by the guardians; with some instructions relative to valuation and rating.
table of contents. 46 pp. Dublin, Her Majesty's Stationery Office, 1839
A.

5152 PAGE, Richard. A critical examination of the twelve resolutions of Mr. Joseph Hume, respecting the loan of fifteen millions for slave compensation: also, a review of the financial

operations of the British government since 1794; and an introductory discourse on the nature of annuities, and on the
obstacles interposed by the corn laws and the English system
of currency to a reduction of the interest on the national debt.
tables. appendices. 288 pp. London, Pelham Richardson, 1839

T.

5153 [PEPPERCORNE, J. Watts.] The rights of necessity and
the treatment of the necessitous by various nations.
tables. illustr. 88 pp. [various paging.] London, Pelham
Richardson, 1839

T.

5154 PIM, James. Irish railways. A letter to the Rt. Hon.
Frederick Shaw, M.P.
16 pp. London, Cox, 1839

A., N.

5155 PORTER, George Richardson. The effect of restrictions
on the importation of corn, considered with reference to
landowners, farmers, and labourers.
tables. appendix. 44 pp. London, H. Hooper, 1839

N.

5156 [PUNNETT, J. ?] Corn laws or no corn laws: an appeal
to the farmers and labourers of the parish of —— by 'Ruri-
cula'.
12 pp. Hayle, Huthnance and Ashwin, 1839

T.

The name of the parish is completed in ms. as 'St. Erth' and
the author as 'J. Punnett'.

5157 [PYM, John.] A remedy for the evils of banking.
32 pp. London, Smith Elder & co., 1839

T.

5158 Report of the directors of the Dublin and Drogheda
Railway Company to the shareholders at their general meeting, 1st March, 1839, with an appendix containing the correspondence with government and statements explanatory of
the traffic on the route of the line.
tables. appendices. 20 pp. Dublin, G. Folds, 1839

N.

5159 Report of the general committee of management of the
Children's Friend Society presented at their 9th annual
meeting 1839.
appendix. tables. 64 pp. London, Adlard, 1839

N.

5160 The report on the taxation of Dublin, and the petition
to parliament, adopted at a general meeting of the inhabitants,
held at the Royal Exchange, on the 24th March 1829, the right
hon. the lord mayor in the chair; to which are added a preface,
appendices, and tables, proving and illustrating the several
allegations and complaints therein contained.
tables. 60 pp. Dublin, printed by Porteous, 1839

A.

5161 ROBERTS, Samuel. The Rev. Dr. Pye Smith and the
new poor law.
70 pp. London, Whittaker, 1839

T.

5162 ROBINSON, Daniel. Irish Waste Land Improvement
Society. Report by Colonel Robinson of his visit to Ireland
as a director of the society in October and November, 1838.
30 pp. London, Blades & East, 1839

A., D.

5163 ROLPH, Thomas. Canada v Australia; their relative
merits considered in answer to a pamphlet by Thornton Leigh
Hunt esq., entitled 'Canada and Australia'.
48 pp. London, Smith, Elder & Co., 1839

N.

5164 The rules and regulations of the Agricultural and horticultural provident and scientific society instituted August,
1839.
24 pp. Dublin, M. Goodwin, 1839

A.

5165 Rules and regulations of the Ripon Operative conservative Benefit Association. Established May 7th, 1839
tables. 24 pp. Ripon, printed by Proctor & Vickers, 1839

A.

5166 RUSSELL, John Russell, 1st earl. Letter to the electors
of Stroud, on the principles of the reform act, by lord John
Russell.
44 pp. fifth edition. London, J. Ridgway, 1839

T.

5167 RYAN, Charles. An essay on Scottish husbandry,
adapted to the use of the farmers of Ireland.
table of contents. 148 pp. Dublin, Porter, 1839

A., N.

5168 [RYAN, P. B.] Abstract history of the Musical Loan
Society in Ireland.
14 pp. Dublin, Porter, 1839

A.

5169 SHULDHAM, W. L. Remarks on the small loan-fund
system addressed to the duke of Wellington.
folding table. 36 pp. London, Parker, 1839

A., K.

5170 SMYTH, George Lewis. Observations upon the report
of the Irish railway commissioners, with a review of the failures which have already occurred under the different government boards and commissions connected with public works in
Ireland. Addressed to the right honourable the viscount
Duncannon.
map. tables. 86 pp. London, H. Hooper, 1839

A., N.

5171 Speeches delivered at a public meeting for the formation of a British India Society; held in the Freemason's Hall,
Saturday, July 6th, 1839.... Lord Brougham in the chair.
table of contents. 76 pp. London, the British India Society,
1839

A.

Speakers included: Brougham, O'Connell, and the Nabob of
Oudh.

5172 St. George's harbour and railway project.
4 pp. Chester, Fletcher, 1838

A.

An attack on the project.

5173 STANLEY, J. The home market, Englands' treasure. Thoughts on corn laws and on Ireland.
90 pp. Dublin, Hodges & Smith, [etc.], 1839
A.

5174 STEPHENS, John. South Australia. An exposure of the absurd, unfounded, and contradictory statements in James's 'Six months in South Australia'.
54 pp. (various paging.) 3rd ed. London, Smith, Elder, 1839
T.

5175 SYMONS, J. The tendency of the tithe act considered with reference to the corn law question. Accompanied by a plain statement of the point at issue with respect to tithe-rate assessments.
16 pp. London, J. G. and F. Rivington, 1839
T.

5176 The tenth report of the Royal National Institution for the preservation of life from shipwreck. Supported by donations and voluntary contributions. Established in 1824.
appendix. tables. 124 pp. London, Metcalfe, 1839
A.

5177 THOMPSON, Henry. Free corn ruinous to England.
20 pp. 4th edition, London, Simpkin Marshall, 1839
T.

5178 [THOMPSON, Thomas Perronet.] Catechism on the corn laws; with a list of fallacies and the answers. To which is added the article on free trade, from the Westminster Review, No. XXIII; with a collection of objections and the answers. By a member of the University of Cambridge.
82 pp. 19th ed. London, Effingham Wilson, 1839
T.

5179 TORRENS, Robert. Emigration from Ireland to South Australia.
32 pp. London, Brettell, 1839
A., N., T., U.

5180 ——. Three letters to the marquis of Chandos, on the effects of the corn laws.
tables. 46 pp. London, Longman & Co., 1839
T.

5181 Twenty-first annual report of the managing committee of the Association for the Suppression of Mendicity in Dublin. For the year 1838.
appendices. 172 pp. Dublin, the Association, 1839
A., N.

5182 VAUGHAN, William. Tracts on docks and commerce, printed between the years 1793 & 1800, and now first collected; with an introduction, memoir, and miscellaneous pieces.
tables. 142 pp. London, Smith, Elder, 1839
T.

——. Memoir of William Vaughan, esq., F.R.S. with miscellaneous pieces relative to docks, commerce, etc.
tables. 142 pp. London, Smith, Elder, 1839
A.
This ed. has a different t.p. but the text appears to be the same. See 1990.

5183 VIGNOLES, Charles. Copy of Mr. Vignoles' observations on Mr. Stephenson's report to the Chester and Crewe railway directors.
4 pp. Dublin, A. Thom, 1839
A.

5184 VILLIERS, Charles Pelham. Mr. Villiers' speech on the corn laws.
24 pp. Manchester, Anti-Corn Law Association, 1839
A.

5185 WESTERN, Charles Callis Western, baron. The maintenance of the corn laws essential to the general prosperity of the empire.
34 pp. London, Ridgway, 1839
A.

5186 WESTHEAD, J. P. A letter to the Rt. Hon. Sir Robert Peel, bt., on the corn laws.
tables. 20 pp. London, Simpkin & Marshall, Manchester, Love & Barton, 1839
A.

5187 WHALLEY, George Hammond. Tithe amendment act, 2 & 3 Vict. cap. 62, with notes and index.
80 pp. London, Shaw, 1839
T.

5188 WHITE, John Meadows. 2 & 3 Vict. c. 62. An act to explain and amend the acts for the commutation of tithes in England and Wales; with an introduction, notes, and index.
72 pp. London, B. Fellowes, 1839
T.

5189 WILSON, James. Influences of the corn laws, as affecting all classes of the community, and particularly the landed interests.
tables. appendices. 144 pp. London, Longman, Orme, Brown, Green and Longmans, 1839
T.

5190 YOUNG, A. A. The poor law. Is any alteration of it necessary or tolerably practicable?
24 pp. London, J. Hatchard, 1839
T.

1840

5191 An abridged account of the Thames tunnel.
16 pp., Azulay, Thames Tunnel [London, 184–?]
N.

5192 BEASLEY, J. Richardson B. The Tipperary tenant farmers' charter and foundation for Ireland's power. Arranged with the assistance of the tenant farmers of the Tipperary Midland and Union of Cashel agricultural society.
56 pp. n.p., [184–?]
A.

5193 Half an ounce of advice to the labouring classes on the repeal of the corn laws. By a plain dealer.
14 pp. Doncaster, printed by R. Hartley, [184–?]
T.

5194 Incumbered estates (Ireland) Bill. Objections, by the attornies and solicitors, and answers by a member of the English Bar.
4 pp. London, printed by Newman, [184–?]

A.

5195 Instructions to the officers and servants of the Workhouse of the City of Dublin (No t. p.)
20 pp. [184–?]

N.

5196 A letter on the policy and expediency of protection to the corn trade of Great Britain, &c. &c.
36 pp. n.p. [184–?]

K.

5197 Address of the committee of the Northern Central British India Society. (established in Manchester Aug. 26th 1840.)
8 pp. Manchester, 1840

A.

5198 AINSLIE, Robert. An examination of socialism.
72 pp. London, L. & G. Seeley, 1840

T.

5199 ALISON, William Pulteney. Observations on the management of the poor in Scotland and its effects on the health of the great towns.
table of contents, table, 212 pp. Edinburgh, W. Blackwood, London, T. Cadell, 1840

A., N., T.

5200 ——. Reply to the pamphlet entitled 'Proposed alteration of the Scottish poor law considered and commented on, by David Monypenny, Esq., of Pitmilly.'
tables. 76 pp. Edinburgh, W. Blackwood; London, T. Cadell, 1840

T.

See 5268

5201 [ALLEN, John.] Letter to the editor of the Edinburgh Review, in reply to the Rev. Mr. Goode. By the author of the articles on church rates that appeared in the 134th and 141st numbers of the Edinburgh Review.
32 pp. London, Edward Moxon, 1840

T.

5202 ATKINSON, William. Principles of political economy; or the laws of the formation of national wealth: developed by means of the christian law of government; being the substance of a case delivered to the Hand-loom weavers' commission.
tables. 266 pp. London, Whittaker & Co., 1840

T.

5203 [BAILEY, Samuel.] A defence of joint stock banks and country issues. By the author of money and its vicissitudes in value.
104 pp. London, J. Ridgway, 1840

A.

5204 The Bank of England and other banks.
16 pp. London, Whittaker & Co., 1840

T.

5205 BARRETT, C. P. The overseer's guide and assistant, containing plain instructions to overseers of parishes in poor law unions.
tables. 72 pp. London, Shaw, 1840

T.

5206 BELL, Gavin Mason. The philosophy of joint stock banking.
114 pp. London, Longman, Orme, Brown, Green and Longmans, 1840

T.

5207 BERNARD, John. Thoughts on emigration as connected with Ireland, in a series of letters.
54 pp. Dublin, R. Milliken, 1840

A., N.

5208 BIRMINGHAM, James. A memoir of the very Rev. Theobald Matthew, with an account of the rise and progress of temperance in Ireland.
84 pp. 2nd ed. Dublin, Milliken & Son, 1840

Q.

5209 BOUCHERETT, Ayscoghe. A few observations on corn, currency, etc. with a plan for promoting the interests of agriculture and manufactures.
table in appendix. 22 pp. London, J. Hatchard, 1840

T.

5210 BRIGGS, John. The cotton trade of India. part I. Its past and present condition; part II. Its future prospects. With a map of India, coloured to indicate the different spots whereon all the varieties of cotton which are brought into the British market have been successfully cultivated.
map. tables. 90 pp. London, John W. Parker, 1840

T.

5211 British Colonization of New Zealand. Report of the proceedings of the public meeting of the citizens of Glasgow held in the assembly rooms, on Friday the 15th day of May 1840.
24 pp. Glasgow, Robertson, 1840

N.

5212 BUTT, Isaac. Irish Municipal Reform. The substance of a speech delivered at a meeting of protestants and freemen held in the King's room at the Mansion house, Dublin, on the 13th February, 1840.
32 pp. Dublin, W. Curry, 1840

T.

5213 [BUXTON, Sir Thomas Fowell, bart.] Abridgment of Sir T. Fowell Buxton's work on the African slave trade and its remedy. With an explanatory preface and an appendix. Published under the sanction of the 'Society for the extinction of the slave trade and for the civilization of Africa.'
tables. appendix. 68 pp. London, J. Murray, 1840

T.

5214 A catechism on the duty, advantages and means of promoting Irish manufacture, agriculture, trade and commerce.
16 pp. Dublin, printed by Powell, 1840

A., N.

5215 CAZENOVE, John. An elementary treatise on political economy; or a short exposition of its first and fundamental principles.
appendix. 158 pp. London, A. H. Baily, 1840
T.

5216 CHANNING, William Ellery. Lectures on the elevation of the labouring portion of the community. Fifth edition.
56 pp. London, J. Green, 1840
U.

5217 CONNER, William. The axe laid to the root of Irish oppression; and a sure and speedy remedy, for the evils of Ireland.
28 pp. Dublin, Samuel J. Machen, 1840
A., C., N.

5218 COOK, James. Remarks on the law of principal and factor, with suggestions for remedying its defects.
42 pp. London, Pelham Richardson, 1840
A.

5219 CUBITT, George. The power of circumstances.
62 pp. London, L. and G. Seeley, 1840
T.

5220. DALY, Thomas. The cash payment bill of 1819 and the Bank of England.
appendix. 116 pp. London, Pelham Richardson, 1840
A.

5221 Debate in the legislative council of New South Wales, and other documents on the subject of immigration to the colony. October, 1840. Published under the direction of the Australian Immigration Association.
table. 58 pp. Sydney, printed by Tegg, 1840
N.

5222 DUDGEON, George. The duties of overseers of the poor and assistant overseers.
tables. appendix. 80 pp. London, C. Knight, 1840
T.

5223 DUPIN, Charles, baron. Du travail des enfants qu' emploient les ateliers les usines et les manufactures, considéré dans les intérêts mutuels de la société, des familles et de l'industrie.
64 pp. Paris, Bachelier, 1840
T.

5224 ELIOT, William. A letter to the right honourable the Chancellor of the exchequer on the question concerning the country banks of issue of England and Wales; with remarks on the projected establishment of 'One general bank of issue'.
22 pp. London, Longman, Orme, Brown, Green, and Longmans, 1840
T.

5225 ENSOR, George. The origin, policy and consequences of the corn laws. Third letter.
62 pp. London, Effingham Wilson, 1840
T.

5226 Exhibition of articles of Irish manufacture, produce and invention, at the Royal Dublin Society's House, June 1st, 1841. List of premiums proposed.
12 pp. Dublin, R. Graisberry, 1840
A.

5227 Extracts from the new poor law: with a few short explanations as affecting landlord and tenant.
tables. 18 pp. Cork, printed by Morton, 1840
T.

5228 FARR, Thomas. A remedy for the distresses of the nation; showing a saving of fifty millions a year sterling, by an equitable adjustment of the corn laws, an increase of revenue of five millions, and a short plan for taking off half the assessed taxes, custom and excise duties.
tables. 96 pp. London, J. Ridgway, 1840
T.

5229 Feudal slavery broken and Ireland freed by temperance.
42 pp. Belfast, printed by Wilson, 1840
A.

5230 A few words on the promoting and encouraging of free emigration to the West India colonies, addressed to the rt. hon. Lord John Russell, secretary of state for the colonial department.
26 pp. Liverpool, printed by Carter, 1840
A., N.

5231 FILGATE, FitzHerbert. A practical treatise on thorough draining, accompanied by remarks on the various materials employed, their probable expenses, the comparative utility of the new and old methods, and its applicability to Ireland.
table of contents. tables. 68 pp. Dublin, Porter, 1840
A., N.

5232 First report of the directors of the New Zealand company presented to the first general meeting of the shareholders, on the 14th May, 1840
appendices. tables. 42 pp. London, Thompson and McKewan, 1840
N.

5233 First report of the loyal national repeal association upon absenteeism.
20 pp. n.p., [1840?]
L.

5234 First series of reports, of the loyal national repeal association of Ireland. With a dedication to the people of Ireland by Daniel O'Connell, esq., M.P.
tables. 132 pp. Dublin, printed by J. Browne, 1840
A., K., N.

5235 FLANAGAN, Mathew. Report of the Irish board of trades for the revival and encouragement of Irish manufactures.
30 pp. Dublin, printed by Underwood, 1840
A.

5236 FRY, William Storrs. Facts and evidence relating to the opium trade with China.
tables. 64 pp. London, Pelham Richardson, 1840
A.

5237 A general priced catalogue of implements, seeds, plants etc. sold at the Agricultural Museum and warehouse of W. Drummond & Sons, seedsmen and nursery men, Stirling.
16 pp. Stirling, Drummond, 1840

A.

5238 GILBART, James William. An inquiry into the causes of the pressure on the money market during the year 1839.
tables. appendix. 64 pp. London, Longman, Orme, Brown, Green and Longmans, 1840

T.

5239 GILLET, M. Quelques réflexions sur l'emploi des enfants dans les fabriques et sur les moyens d'en prévenir les abus.
102 pp. Paris, Lethune et Plon, 1840

T.

5240 GORE, Montague. Thoughts on the corn laws.
56 pp. [various paging.] London, Saunders and Otley, 1840

T.

5241 GRAHAM, Alexander. The right, obligation, and interest of the government of Great Britain to require redress from the government of China, for the late forced surrender of British-owned opium at Canton.
appendix. 40 pp. Glasgow, Robert Stuart [etc.], 1840

T.

5242 HEAD, Sir Francis Bond, bart. An address to the house of lords, against the bill before parliament for the union of the Canadas; and disclosing the improper means by which the consent of the legislature of the upper province has been obtained to the measure.
56 pp. London, J. Murray, 1840

T.

5243 HENRY, James. A letter to the secretaries of the Dublin Mendicity Institution. Reprinted from the Dublin Evening Post of January 20th, 1831.
18 pp. Dublin, P. Kennedy, 1840

T.

5244 HOLLAND, George Calvert. An exposition of corn-law repealing fallacies and inconsistencies.
tables. 202 pp. London, Longman, Orme, Brown, Green, and Longmans, 1840

T.

5245 HORNER, Leonard. On the employment of children, in factories and other works in the United Kingdom and in some foreign countries.
appendices. 142 pp. London, Longman, Orme, Brown, Green, and Longmans, 1840.

T.

5246 HORTON, Sir Robert John Wilmot, bart. Observations upon taxation as affecting the operative and labouring classes, made at the Crown and Anchor on the evening of the 6th of August, 1839. To which is added a letter to Joseph Hume, esq., M.P.
36 pp. London, J. Murray, 1840

T.

5247 HOUGHTON, Henry. The poor rate payer's guide exhibiting the various scales by which the payment of the rate is distributed between landlord & tenant.
tables. 18 pp. Dublin, printed by Walsh, 1840

A., N.

——. 46 pp. 2nd ed. Dublin, printed by Walsh, 1840

A.

5248 HULL, William. Remarks on the corn laws, in connection with the Germanic Confederation, or Prussian League:
table. 14 pp. London, Smith & Elder, 1840

N.

5249 JACKSON, James. A treatise on agriculture and dairy husbandry.
table of contents. diagrams. tables. appendix. 116 pp. Edinburgh, Chambers, 1840

N., T.

5250 JAMIESON, Robert. An appeal to the government and people of Great Britain, against the proposed Niger expedition: a letter, addressed to the Right Hon. Lord John Russell, principal secretary of state for the colonies, &c. &c. &c.
tables. appendix. 38 pp. London, Smith, Elder, 1840

T.

See 5293.

5251 JEVONS, Thomas. The prosperity of the landholders not dependant on the corn laws.
tables. 68 pp. London, Longmans, 1840

T.

5252 KELL, Edmund. The injurious effects of the corn-laws, on all classes of the community, including the farmer and the landowner. A lecture.
44 pp. London, Smallfield, Huddersfield, T. Smart, [etc.], 1840

T.

5253 LEATHAM, William. Letters on the currency, addressed to Charles Wood, esq., M.P. Chairman of the committee of the house of commons, now sitting; and ascertaining for the first time, on true principles, the amount of inland and foreign bills of exchange in circulation for several consecutive years, and out at one time.
tables in appendix. 68 pp. London, Pelham Richardson, 1840

T.

5254 [LEE, Daniel.] The policy of piracy as a branch of national industry, and a source of commercial wealth; with illustrations—statistical, geographical, and moral. Expounded and enforced in the evidence before the select committee of the house of commons, appointed to inquire into the expediency of extending the copyright of designs, of Daniel Lee, esq. Magistrate of the borough of Manchester, etc. etc.
36 pp. London, Bell, Manchester, Sims & Frazer, 1840

A.

5255 [LEGRAND, Daniel.] Lettre adressée à M. le Baron Charles Dupin, rapporteur de la commission de la chambre des pairs chargée de l'examen du projet de loi sur le travail des enfants dans les manufactures etc. [Together with other letters etc. on the same subject.]
no. t.p. 24 pp. Strasbourg, 1840

T.

5256 [——.] Mémoire d'un industriel des montagnes des Vosges adressé à m. le ministre du commerce et des manufactures.
16 pp. Strasbourg, Berger-Levrault, 1840
T.

5257 [——.] Projet de loi sur le travail et l'instruction des enfants employés dans les manufactures, usines et ateliers; en réponse à la circulaire de m. le ministre secrétaire d'état de l'agriculture et du commerce, du 1er juillet 1840. Par un industriel des montagnes des Vosges.
16 pp. Strasbourg, Berger-Levrault, 1840
T.

5258 LINGARD, John. To the British nation. On the propriety and justice of the corn laws, as now regulated.
tables. 48 pp. 2nd ed. London, W. Clowes, 1840
T.

5259 LOTT, Thomas. Observations as to rating stock in trade to the relief of the poor, and the decisions in relation thereto under the 43. Eliz. C.2.
24 pp. London, E. Spettigue, 1840
T.

5260 LOWNDES, Matthew Dobson. Review of the Joint Stock Bank acts and of the law as to joint stock companies generally: with the practical suggestions of a solicitor for their amendment; in a letter to the right honourable the chancellor of the exchequer.
50 pp. London, W. Pickering, 1840
T.

5261 LOYD, Samuel Jones, afterwards baron OVERSTONE. Effects of the administration of the Bank of England. A second letter to J. B. Smith, esq., president of the Manchester Chamber of Commerce.
58 pp. London, Pelham Richardson, 1840
A.

5262 ——. A letter to J. B. Smith, esq., president of the Manchester Chamber of Commerce.
28 pp. London, Pelham Richardson, 1840
A.
See 5287

5263 [LUBBOCK, Sir John William, 3rd bart.] On currency.
table of contents. appendix. tables. 78 pp. London, C. Knight, & co., 1840
N., T.

5264 The martyr age of the United States of America, with an appeal on behalf of the Oberlin Institute in aid of the abolition of slavery. Re-published from the London and Westminster review, by the Newcastle-upon-Tyne Emancipation and Aborigines Protection Society.
64 pp. Newcastle-upon-Tyne, Finlay and Charlton, 1840
A.

5265 Memorial of the Chamber of Commerce of Dublin to the lords of the treasury. 23rd April, 1839. (printed for private use.)
12 pp. London, W. Clowes, 1840
A.

5266 MILLER, Charles. The petition of the Rev. Charles Miller, vicar of Harlow, Essex, respecting the tithe commutation act, presented to the house of lords, by the bishop of London, during the session of MDCCCXL.
10 pp. London, J. G. F. & J. Rivington, 1840
T.

5267 Monetary currency; or the operation of money shown to be a perfect science, and that the unlimited amount and uncertain issue of paper, or other fictitious money is the sole and fundamental cause of all the commercial evils that now afflict the trading world.
34 pp. London, Effingham Wilson, 1840
A.

5268 MONYPENNY, David. Proposed alteration of the Scottish poor laws, and of the administration thereof, as stated by Dr. Alison, in his 'Observations on the management of the poor in Scotland'.
tables in appendices. 126 pp. Edinburgh, William Whyte, 1840
T.
See 5200.

5269 MORRIS, Jeffrey. Tables compiled for the use of valuators, guardians, rate payers, etc. under the Irish Poor Relief Act; also supplying a mode of distributing the annual value of a holding or tenement let in parts, after being valued as a whole, without requiring a new valuation.
tables. 32 pp. Dublin, A. Thom, 1840
N.

5270 [PEASE, Elizabeth.] Society of Friends in the United States: their views of the anti-slavery question, and treatment of the people of colour. Compiled from original correspondence.
26 pp. Darlington, printed by Wilson, 1840
A.
Not published.

5271 PINKUS, Henry. Prospectus of a new agrarian system.
tables. 32 pp. London, R. and J. E. Taylor, 1840
P.

5272 PORTER, F. Thorpe. 6 & 7 William IV Chap. 116. An act to consolidate and amend the laws relating to the presentment of public money by Grand Juries in Ireland, with notes and an index.
230 pp. 2d ed. Dublin, R. Milliken, 1840
A.

5273 Proceedings at the first public meeting of the society for the extinction of the slave trade and for the civilisation of Africa, held at Exeter Hall, on Monday, 1st June, 1840.
appendices. 74 pp. London, printed by W. Clowes, 1840
D.

5274 Proceedings of a public meeting for the formation of the Northern Central British India Society, held in the corn exchange, Manchester, on Wednesday evening, August 26th, 1840.
48 pp. Manchester, printed by Cave and Sever, 1840
A.

5275 Prospectus of the society for the extinction of the slave trade, and for the civilization of Africa: instituted June, 1839.
table. 8 pp. London, printed by W. Clowes, [1840]
N.

5276 PUTT, Charles. Observations on the corn laws, or bread for thirty millions of inhabitants; without the importation of a single grain of corn: without loss to the farmer, the landlord, or the fund-holder.
tables. 32 pp. London, J. Ollivier, [1840]
T.

5277 REECE, George. Owenism an imposition on the working classes; in a second letter addressed to the operatives' of Manchester.
24 pp. Manchester, printed by White & Carter, 1840
A.

5278 Report of the directors of the Dublin and Drogheda Railway Company at their sixth general meeting held at the Northumberland buildings, 4th March, 1841.
tables. 14 pp. Dublin, printed by G. Folds, 1840
A.

5279 Resolutions of the Irish distillers, passed June, 1840.
2 pp. Dublin, 1840
A.

5280 Review of the Neapolitan sulphur question. By a British merchant.
tables. 44 pp. n.p. 1840
N.

5281 RUDALL, Edward. The complaints of the manufacturers against the corn laws, considered and answered in a lecture, read to the Launceston Farmers Assoc.
tables. 32 pp. 2nd ed. Launceston, Cater and Maddox, London, Simpkin, Marshall, 1840
N.

5282 Rules and regulations of the County and City of Dublin widows' fund, and general annuity endowment society, instituted November, 1837.
16 pp. Dublin, printed by W. Frazer, 1840
A.

5283 SALOMONS, Sir David, 1st bart. Reflections on the operation of the present scale of duty for regulating the importation of foreign corn addressed to the borders of Kent and Sussex agricultural associations. Second edition with a supplement.
tables. appendices. 96 pp. London, Pelham Richardson, 1840
T.

5284 SCHOMBURGK, Sir Robert Hermann. A description of British Guiana, geographical and statistical: exhibiting its resources and capabilities, together with the present and future condition and prospects of the colony.
map. tables. table of contents. 160 pp. London, Simpkin Marshall & co., 1840
A., T.

5285 SCOTT, Henry. A letter to the proprietors of bank stock on the recent proceedings of the board of directors, in removing him from the office of agent to their establishment in Waterford.
36 pp. Waterford, printed by Smith, 1840
A.

5286 Second series of reports of the loyal national repeal association of Ireland.
tables. 122 pp. Dublin, J. Browne, 1840
A., C., K., N.

5287 SMITH, James Benjamin. Effects of the administration of the Bank of England. Reply to the letter of Samuel Jones Loyd, esq.
22 pp. London, Pelham Richardson, [etc.], 1840
A.
See 5262

5288 SMITH, Thomas. The old poor law and the new poor law contrasted.
tables. 34 pp. London, Simpkin, Marshall, [etc.], 1840
T.

5289 Society for the encouragement of arts, manufactures, and commerce: premiums for the sessions 1840–1841, 1841–1842.
16 pp. London, printed by Moyes and Barclay, 1840
N.

5290 Some pros and cons of the opium question; with a few suggestions regarding British claims on China.
44 pp. London, Smith, Elder, 1840
T.

5291 SPENCER, Thomas. The pillars of the Church of England; or, are intemperance and ignorance, bigotry and infallibility, church rates and corn laws, essential to the existence of the establishment? Together with a supplement to a speech delivered by the Rev. R. McGhee, at the anniversary of the Bath protestant association. Sixth thousand.
16 pp. London, John Green, Bath, Samuel Gibbs, 1840
T.

5292 ——. The prayer book opposed to the corn laws; or who are the non-conformists? Also a supplement to a speech delivered by R. McGhee at the anniversary of the Bath protestant association.
12 pp. London, Green, 1840
A.

5293 STEPHEN, Sir George. A letter to the Rt. Hon. Lord John Russell, &c. &c. &c. In reply to Mr. Jamieson, on the Niger expedition.
36 pp. London, Saunders and Otley, [1840]
T.
See 5250.

5294 STRACHAN, James Morgan. The connexion of the East India company with the superstitious and idolatrous customs and rites of the natives of India. The present state of the question.
appendix. 44 pp. London, W. Crofts, [etc.], 1840
T.

5295 STURGE, John. Report on free labour, presented to the general anti-slavery convention.
32 pp. London, Johnson & Barrett, [1840]
A.

5296 STURMER, Frederick. Socialism, its immoral tendency; or a plain appeal to commonsense.
24 pp. London, T. Ward, 1840
T.

5297 Suggestions for carrying into effect the act for establishing a reduced and uniform rate of postage as forwarded to the lords of the treasury, pursuant to their lordships minute of the 23rd August, 1839. By W.H.C.
26 pp. Dublin, printed by Corbet, 1840
A.

5298 Suppressed work! On the possibility of limiting populousness. An essay on populousness. To which is added the theory of painless extinction. By Marcus.
table of contents. 50 pp. 4th ed. London, printed by Dugdale, 1840
A.
See 4998, 5051.

5299 THORP, Robert. Practical conservatism: its nature and uses. With an appendix on conservative statesmen in parliament.
appendix. 50 pp. London, W. E. Painter, 1840
T.

5300 TORRENS, Robert. A letter to Thomas Tooke, esq., in reply to his objections against the separation of the business of the bank into a department of issue, and a department of deposit and discount: with a plan of bank reform.
48 pp. London, Longman, Orme, Brown, Green, and Longmans, 1840
T.

5301 TYRCONNEL, John Delaval Carpenter, 4th earl of. An address to the people of the United Kingdom on the corn laws.
tables. 32 pp. London, J. Ridgway, 1840
T.

5302 A voice for China to my countrymen, the government, and my church. By a minister of the established church, M.A., Cantab.
40 pp. London, Nisbet, 1840
T.

5303 WADE, John. Glances at the times, and reform government.
72 pp. London, Effingham Wilson, 1840
T.

5304 WARD, John. Information relative to New Zealand, compiled for the use of colonists.
maps. table of contents. appendix. 178 pp. 2nd ed. London, Parker, 1840
N.

5305 WARD, William. On monetary derangements, in a letter addressed to the proprietors of bank stock.
40 pp. London, Pelham Richardson, 1840
A.

5306 WARREN, Samuel. The opium question.
134 pp. 4th ed. London, J. Ridgway, 1840
T.

5307 WILSON, James. Fluctuations of currency, commerce, and manufactures; referable to the corn laws.
tables. appendix. 152 pp. London, Longman, Orme, Brown, Green, and Longmans, 1840
T.

1841

5308 Abstract of the accounts of the South Dublin Union, for the half-year ended 29th September, 1840; with the auditor's report to the Board of Guardians.
tables. 20 pp. Dublin, printed by A. Thom, 1841
A., N.

5309 ALISON, William Pulteney. Reply to Dr. Chalmers' objections to an improvement of the legal provision for the poor in Scotland.
62 pp. Edinburgh and London, William Blackwood, 1841
T.

5310 ALTON, John Bindon. The evils of Ireland and their only remedy.
84 pp. Limerick, printed by O'Brien, 1841
A.

5311 BERMINGHAM, Thomas. A letter on the corn laws, addressed to the land-owners and occupiers of land in Ireland, with extracts from Mr. Jacob's report on foreign agriculture and foreign corn, as also communications from other persons; with a petition to the house of commons, recommended for general adoption.
36 pp. Dublin, R. Milliken, London, J. Ridgway, 1841
A., U.

5312 [——.] Statistical evidence in favour of state railways in Ireland, with the speech of Thomas Bermingham, esq., of Caramana, Kilconnel, County of Galway, late chairman of the General Irish Railway committee, and author of 'The good of England and Ireland identified', and of several works on Irish railways, and enforcing the advantage of employing the poor; also an appendix, containing above twenty statistical tables, including returns on the Belgian State and other foreign railways, with extracts from the evidence before committees of both houses of parliament on western harbours, and returns compiled from parliamentary documents and from British and foreign statistical authorities, proving the facility of constructing state railways in Ireland, and the advantages to be derived therefrom to the manufactures, commerce, agriculture and general condition of the Irish people; also a plan whereby collision of railways may be altogether avoided; with a map of Ireland, reduced and engraved by Kirkwood, shewing the density of population, exports and imports, and the lines of the Irish Railway Commissioners, with additions recommended by the author.
appendix with tables. diag. map. 116 pp. Dublin, printed by John Chambers, 1841
A., N., U.

5313 BERWICK, William. Landlord oppression exemplified: in a letter to Daniel O'Connell, esq., M.P. regarding landlord & tenant.
8 pp. Edinburgh, printed by Anderson & Bryce, 1841
A., B., N.

5314 BIGGS, Henry Report on the industrial plan of education under the directions of the poor law commissioners, in England.
26 pp. Cork, George Ridings, 1841
U.

5315 British India: her claims upon the attention of the promoters of commerce and the friends of equal justice. Tables drawn from official sources, and opinions of eminent men, showing the comparative insignificant amount of our present commercial intercourse with India, and the capacity of that country to supply, to an unlimited extent, almost every important article of tropical produce, and to receive the varied manufactures of Great Britain.
tables. 16 pp. Manchester, printed by Cave and Sever, 1841
A.

5316 Brussels: exposition de 1841: catalogue des produits de l'industrie belge admis á l'exposition de 1841.
298 pp. 2nd ed. Bruxelles, Wahlen, 1841
N.

5317 BUTTERWORTH, Edwin. A statistical sketch of the county palatine of Lancaster.
tables. 208 pp. London, Longman, 1841
T.

5318 The carriers' case, considered in reference to railways.
36 pp. London, printed by Norris, 1841
A.

5319 Catalogue of articles of Irish manufacture, produce, and invention, exhibited at the Royal Dublin Society's house 8th June, 1841. and following days.
38 pp. Dublin, printed by Graisberry & Gill, 1841
A.

5320 CHAMBERLAIN, Ayling. A treatise on the commercial system and stamp laws of Great Britain; showing that by the reduction of the duties on imported commodities, by the abolition of all monopolies, and by revising the stamp laws affecting probates of wills, mortgages, conveyances, bonds, bills, appraisements, advertisements, etc. provisions would be cheapened, the revenue greatly increased, and the threatened imposition of additional taxes rendered unnecessary.
tables. 24 pp. London, Whittaker, 1841
T.

5321 Cheap bread and its consequences. A plain statement.
tables. 16 pp. 9th edition. London, William E. Painter, 1841
T., U.
Signed: A British farmer and landowner.

5322 CLARKSON, Thomas. A letter to the clergy of various denominations, & to the slave-holding planters, in the southern parts of the United States of America.
64 pp. London, printed by Johnston & Barrett, 1841
B.

5323 COOK, John. A brief view of the Scottish system for the relief of the poor; and of some proposed changes on it.
tables. 80 pp. Edinburgh, John Johnstone, 1841
T.

5324 'Corn-colonies' an effectual remedy for the distress of the working classes, and for the embarrassments of commerce, manufactures and trade.
52 pp. London, J. Ridgway, 1841
U.

5325 Corn laws. A letter addressed to the plain understanding of the people, on the operation of the proposed reduction of duty upon imported wheat to eight shillings per quarter, in lieu of the present graduated scale. By Candidus.
12 pp. London, George Bell, 1841
U.

5326 Corn laws. The farmer's case, shown from the evidence of the following agriculturists: . . .
16 pp. London, J. Ridgway, 1841
A.

5327 The corn question. Mr. McCulloch's pamphlet on the corn laws critically analysed; with a postscriptum on the latest fallacies of radicalism. By the author of 'the cost price of growing foreign corn', and 'an essay on free trade'.
tables. 20 pp. London, William E. Painter, 1841
A., T.

5328 CROSLEY, Henry. Hints to the landed proprietary and agriculturists of Great Britain and Ireland.
24 pp. London, Crosland, 1841
A.

5329 CURTIS, John. America and the corn laws; or facts and evidence showing the extensive supply of food which may be brought from America, and the effects of the restrictive system on the British and American trade.
tables. 36 pp. Manchester, J. Gadsby, 1841
A.

5330 DELANY, Patrick. The evils of Ireland, being the observations of a resident country gentleman, humbly inscribed to William Smith O'Brien, M.P.
52 pp. 1st ed. Limerick, printed by R. Canter, 1841
A., N.

5331 DENNIS, Jonas. Influence of corn laws on manufactures and commerce. A letter to the most noble the duke of Buckingham and Chandos, &c. &c. &c.
20 pp. Exeter, W. Roberts, 1841
T.

5332 DICKSON, Stephen Fox. The case and claims of the licensed victuallers of Ireland under the 6th and 7th articles of the union, to be placed on the same footing with respect to rights and privileges to trade, and burthens of taxation, with their fellow-traders in England and Scotland, briefly stated, with the opinions of eminent counsel, respectfully addressed to the right hon. the lords of her majesty's treasury, the honourable the commissioners of her majesty's excise, to Frank Thorpe Porter, esq., barrister-at-law, and the other justices of the peace of the city of Dublin.
appendix. Dublin, printed by Grace, 1841
A.

5333 ——. Supplementary appendix to the case and claims of the licensed victuallers of Ireland.
16 pp. Dublin, printed by Brady, 1841
A.

5334 DUDLEY, William. Ireland and the earl of Shrewsbury. Answer to his lordship's letter.
32 pp. Manchester, J. Gadsby, London, R. Groombridge, 1841
A.

5335 An exposure of the injurious effects of the present system of the bankruptcy law, in London and in the country; with suggestions for its improvement in a series of observations upon the most important of the reforms proposed by her majesty's commissioners of inquiry into bankruptcy and insolvency. By a barrister.
60 pp. London, John W. Parker, 1841
T.

5336 FAGAN, M. J. The repeal of the union would be separation, and must lead either to the re-conquest of Ireland, or the destruction of the British Empire: in which the question of Irish grievances and justice to Ireland is incidentally discussed.
56 pp. Dublin, Samuel J. Machen, 1841
T.

5337 The farmers of England. Foreign corn. The cost price of producing wheat in some foreign countries, and matters therewith connected. By a merchant, formerly a farmer of sixty thousand acres on the continent.
tables. 28 pp. 2nd ed. London, William E. Painter, 1841
T., U.

5338 First report of the Agricultural Improvement Society of Ireland.
appendix, 34 pp. Dublin, printed by John Hoare, 1841
A., N., T.

——. 3rd ed. 44 pp. Dublin, printed by John Hoare, 1841
A.

5339 FORSTER, R. W. E. The copyhold and customary tenure, commutation, enfranchisement, and improvement act, 4 & 5 Vict. c. 35, with an introduction and analytical digest of the act: The forms of procedure, issued by the copyhold commissioners, and an appendix, notes, and index.
tables. index. 226 pp. London, V. & R. Stevens & G. S. Norton, 1841
T.

5340 GLIDDON, George Robins. A memoir on the cotton of Egypt (No. 1.)
tables. appendix. 64 pp. London, J. Madden & co., 1841
N.

5341 GORDON, Alexander. Observations on railway monopolies, and remedial measures.
58 pp. London, J. Weale, 1841
T.

5342 HAUGHTON, James. Four letters to the Irish people, on the use of articles produced by the labour of slaves, particularly tobacco.
28 pp. Dublin, 1841
A.

5343 [HICKEY, William.] The Farmers' Guide, compiled for the use of the small farmer and cotter tenantry of Ireland.
table of contents. 188 pp. Dublin, Her Majesty's Stationery Office, 1841
A., RM.

5344 [HICKSON, William Edward H.] Hints to employers. 'The elevation of the labouring class', from the Westminster

Review, No. LXVII. Including two letters to Leonard Horner, esq. on the capabilities of the factory system.
24 pp. London, H. Hooper, 1841
T.

5345 An historical examination of the corn laws.
30 pp. Dublin, Hodges & Smith, London, J. Ridgway, 1841
A., T.

5346 HOLLAND, George Calvert. An analysis of the address of F. H. Fawkes, esq. to the landowners of England.
tables. 44 pp. 2nd ed. enlarged, revised. London, J. Ollivier, 1841
A,

5347 ——. Letter to J. R. McCulloch, esq., in answer to his statements on the corn laws.
tables. 28 pp. 2nd edition. London, J. Ollivier, 1841
T.

5348 ——. Suggestions towards improving the present system of corn-laws. Inscribed, by permission, to the Right Hon. Sir R. Peel, bart.
tables. 40 pp. London, J. Ollivier, 1841
T.

5349 How fares the agricultural labourer under the present corn-law?
tables. 4 pp. London, J. Ridgway, 1841
A.

5350 Information respecting the settlement of New Plymouth, in New Zealand, from the testimony of eye-witnesses, together with term of purchase for lands, regulations for labouring emigrants, etc. etc. Compiled under the direction of the West of England Board of the New Zealand Co.
appendix. table. 24 pp. London, Smith, Elder & co., [etc., etc.], 1841
A.

5351 JOHNSON, Cuthbert William. On increasing the demand for agricultural labour.
illustrations. 64 pp. London, J. Ridgway, 1841
A., N.

5352 JONES, Charles. Letter to Charles Wood, esq., M.P., chairman of the committee of the house of commons on banks of issue, in reply to the doctrine of George Warde Norman, esq. 'On money and the means of economizing the use of it.'
66 pp. London, A. Bailey, Birmingham, Barlow, 1841
A.

5353 JONES, William Bence. A letter to the tenants of Aghalusky, Lisilane and Cloheen.
20 pp. London, C. Richards, 1841
U.

5354 JOPLIN, Thomas. The cause and cure of our commercial embarrassments.
78 pp. London, J. Ridgway 1841
T.

5355 LEATHAM, William. Second series. Letters to William Rayner Wood, merchant, Manchester containing remarks on

the evidence of the members of the Manchester Chamber of commerce and others given before the committee of the house of commons, on the currency; in the sitting of 1840. Also, some comparative statements of the amounts of bills of exchange, to illustrate their practical effects on the currency.
38 pp. London, Pelham Richardson, 1841
A., T.

5356 [LEGRAND, Daniel.] Très humble requête d'un industriel des montagnes des Vosges adressée à M. le Chancelier de France et à MM. les membres de la chambre des pairs.
8 pp. Strasbourg, Berger-Levrault, 1841
T.
[On child labour.]

5357 A letter to the earl of Listowel, M.P. for St. Albans; one of the lords of the bedchamber to her majesty, by 'A joint of the tail'.
38 pp. London, J. Ridgway, 1841
A.
[On the economic effects of the Act of Union of 1800.]

5358 LEY, James Peard. Letters addressed to the people on the currency.
60 pp. London, H. Hooper, 1841
A.

5359 LLOYD, Humphrey. Praelection on the studies connected with the School of Engineering. Delivered, on the occasion of the opening of the School, the 15th of November, 1841.
32 pp, Dublin, A. Milliken, 1841.
A.

5360 MACARTHUR, Edward. Colonial policy of 1840 and 1841, as illustrated by the governor's despatches, and proceedings of the legislative council of New South Wales.
map. tables. 84 pp. London, J. Murray, 1841
T.

5361 McCULLOCH, John Ramsay. Statements illustrative of the policy and probable consequences of the proposed repeal of the existing corn laws, and the imposition in their stead of a moderate fixed duty on foreign corn when entered for consumption.
appendix with tables. 48 pp. 5th ed with a postscript. London, Longman, Orme, Brown, Green & Longmans, 1841
A., U.

———. 48 pp. 6th ed. London, Longman, Orme, Brown, Green and Longmans, 1841
N.

5362 MacGREGOR, John. The commercial and financial legislation of Europe and America, with a pro-forma revision of the taxation and the customs tariff of the United Kingdom.
tables. 320 pp. London, H. Hooper, 1841
T.

5363 MARSHALL, John. Letter to the rt. honorable lord John Russell, etc. on Australian emigration.
26 pp. London, printed by Eccles, 1841
N.

5364 MASLEN, Decimus. A new decimal system, of money, weights, measures, and time, proposed for adoption in Great Britain.
tables. 150 pp. London, Smith, Elder & co., 1841
T.

5365 MILLER, Charles. A second letter to the Rev. Richard Jones, M.A. one of the tithe commissioners for England and Wales, on the rating and commutation of tithes.
16 pp. London, J. G. F. & J. Rivington, 1841
T.

5366 MONYPENNY, David. Additional remarks on the proposed alteration of the Scottish poor laws, and the administration thereof.
appendices. 176 pp. Edinburgh, William Whyte, 1841
T.

5367 NAPIER, Sir William Francis Patrick. Observations on the corn law, addressed to lord Ashley, because his persevering efforts to protect the factory children give him a just title to the respect of all persons who acknowledge the value of justice and benevolence in national policy.
16 pp. 2nd ed. London, T. & W. Boone, 1841
T.

5368 NEVILE, Christopher. The sliding scale, or a fixed duty.
34 pp. London, J. Ridgway, 1841
T.

5369 The new tariff. Tables of new duties of customs, payable on goods, wares, and merchandise, imported into the United Kingdom from foreign parts & from British possessions; to which are prefixed the new clauses of the act of parliament for regulating the same; with the old duties, and the nett amount received on each article in 1840; together with the new corn duties. Authentically compiled from official documents.
tables. 42 pp. London, J. Gilbert, & H. Hooper, [1841]
T.

5370 NIXON, Edward. Temperate defence of the loan fund system, being a reply to a pamphlet put forward by the Revd. Wm. McCormick, Roman catholic curate of Nobber, addressed to the inhabitants of Castletown—Kilpatrick & its vicinity.
24 pp. Dublin, printed by Goodwin and Nethercott, 1841
A.

5371 NOEL, Baptist Wriothesley. A plea for the poor, showing how the proposed repeal of the existing corn laws will affect the interest of the working classes.
36 pp. London, J. Nisbet, 1841
A.

5372 NORMAN, George Warde. Letter to Charles Wood, M.P. on money, and the means of economizing the use of it.
106 pp. London, Pelham Richardson, 1841
A.

5373 O'BRIEN, William. The fishery case. A report of the case, Poole Gabbet, esq., v. Thomas Clancy & Thomas

Dwyer, tried before Mr. Justice Ball, and a special jury, at Limerick summer assizes, 1841 and which occupied the court for over five days.
104 pp. Limerick, George M'Kern, 1841

A., N.

5374 Official assignees. Reform in bankruptcy. Remarks and suggestions by an accountant.
22 pp. London, Pelham Richardson, 1841

T.

5375 PEMBERTON, Benjamin. An address to the nobility, gentry, and mercantile classes, on the extension of railway communications to the west of Ireland, by the formation of a line from the steam packet station on the North Wall, to the town of Trim in the county of Meath with casual observations etc.
appendices. 22 pp. Dublin, Dirham, 1841

N.

5376 PIESSE, Charles. Sketch of the loan-fund system of Ireland and instructions for the formation of a new society; with the loan fund acts, and an index thereto.
tables. 84 pp. Dublin, A. Thom, 1841

A., N.

5377 PIM, James, jr. The atmospheric railway. A letter to the right hon. the earl of Ripon president of the Board of Trade &c. &c. &c.
folding plates. 26 pp. London, printed [by Cox] for private circulation, 1841

A., N.

5378 ———. Irish railways. The atmospheric railway. A letter to the right hon. lord viscount Morpeth.
16 pp. London, printed by Cox, 1841

A.

5379 ———, and CUBITT, William. Letters to Joseph Kincaid, chairman of the Dublin-Kingstown railway, on the subject of the proposed atmospheric railway.
4 pp. Dublin, 1841

A.

5380 A plea for the rich showing how the proposed repeal of the existing corn laws will affect the interests of the upper and richer classes. In reply to the hon. and rev. Baptist W. Noel, M.A.
24 pp. London, W. Brittain, [1841 ?]

T.

5381 A plea from the poor versus many canting pleas for the poor; showing the ignorant and absurd notions of anti-protection and free-trade mania being advantageous to the commercial polity of the British nation, but on the contrary, particularly injurious to the working-classes. By Jacobus Veritas.
tables. 12 pp. London, W. Clowes, 1841

T.

5382 Pour et contre. A few humble observations upon the new poor law: with a short notice of a remedial measure for the labourer in sickness: a letter to the right hon. lord John Russell, secretary of state. By Clericus.
24 pp. London, J. G. F. & J. Rivington, 1841

T.

5383 The present state of banking in England considered in a letter addressed to the right hon. earl Fitzwilliam. By a Scotch banker.
44 pp. London, Smith, Elder, & co., 1841

A.

5384 Questions for the consideration of farmers. Exorbitant rents the true cause of agricultural distress.
8 pp. London, J. Ridgway, 1841

A.

5385 Questions for the consideration of farmers. No. II. The farmer uninjured by foreign competition.
table. 8 pp. London, J. Ridgway, 1841

A.

5386 Questions for the consideration of farmers. No. III. Ruinous prices periodically produced by the sliding scale.
tables. 8 pp. London, J. Ridgway, 1841

A.

5387 Railways for Ireland. From the 'Railroad monthly journal' for June 1841.
map. 16 pp. London, Drury, 1841

A.

5388 Read, compare and judge, facts. Addressed to all classes.
tables. 8 pp. London, H. Hooper, 1841

A.

[refers to public finance since 1792.]

5389 REID, George. Tables of exchange of sterling money and of dollars reduced into each other; I.—At from $460 to $505 per £100 sterling. II.—At from 3s. 10d. to 4s. 4d. per dollar. III.—At from $3\frac{1}{2}$ to $13\frac{1}{2}$ premium of North American currency: with an appendix containing tables of the currency of different colonies, reduced into dollars, and conversely.
tables. appendix. 304 pp. London, Pelham Richardson, 1841

T.

5390 A religious and moral view of the corn laws, etc. etc. with an appendix.
tables in appendices. 20 pp. London, J. Ridgway, 1841

T.

5391 Remarks on the law and present state of the corn measures and weights in Ireland: and the practice of buying and selling corn in Dublin and other places throughout Ireland. Addressed to the directors of the Dublin Corn Exchange Buildings by an inhabitant of the City of Dublin.
16 pp. Dublin, printed by T. White, 1841

A.

5392 Remarks on 'the old principle' of assessment to the poor rate, as it affected the tithe-owner and the occupier of land, and as compared with the present state of the law of rating. By a bystander.
tables. 68 pp. London, J. Burns, 1841

T.

5393 RENNY, James H. Reflections upon the corn laws, and upon their effects on the trade, manufactures, and agriculture of the country, and on the conditions of the working classes.
112 pp. London, Smith, Elder & co., 1841

T.

5394 The repealer repulsed! A correct narrative of the rise and progress of the repeal invasion of Ulster: Dr. Cooke's challenge and Mr. O'Connell's declinature, tactics, and flight. With appropriate poetical and pictorial illustrations. Also, an authentic report of the great conservative demonstrations in Belfast, on the 21st and 23rd of January, 1841.
illustrs. 160 pp. Belfast, William McComb, [etc.], 1841
B., N.

5395 A reply to the prize essays of the anti-corn law league. By a Lincolnshire landowner.
32 pp. London, printed by W. E. Painter, 1841
A.

5396 Report of the conference of ministers of all denominations on the corn laws, held in Manchester. August 17th, 18th, 19th, and 20th, 1841. With a digest of the documents contributed during the conference.
tables. 264 pp. Manchester, J. Gadsby, London, T. Ward and R. Groombridge, 1841
T.

5397 Report of the council of the chamber of commerce of Dublin, to the annual assembly of the members of the association.
appendix. 16 pp. Dublin, printed by P. D. Hardy, 1841
A.

5398 Report of the deputation appointed by the honourable the Irish Society, to visit the city of London's plantation in Ireland, in the year 1840.
108 pp. London, printed by W. Tyler, 1841
A., B.

5399 Report of the directors to a special general meeting of the chamber of commerce and manufactures at Manchester of the injurious effects of restrictions on trade, and the necessity of immediate changes in our commercial policy, arising out of the report and evidence of the select committee of the house of commons on import duties during the last session of parliament.
24 pp. London, Pelham Richardson, 1841
A.

5400 Report of the Moate agricultural society for the year 1841, with the premiums offered by the society for the year 1842, &c., &c., &c.
tables. appendices. 48 pp. Dublin, printed by P. D. Hardy, 1841
U.

5401 Report on the statistics of Western Australia in 1840; with observations by the Colonial committee of correspondence.
tables. appendix. 76 pp. Perth, printed by Lochee, 1841
N.

5402 ROCHE, Edmond Burke. A letter to the working farmers and agricultural labourers of Co. Cork. Showing the injurious effects to the people of Ireland of a fluctuating scale of duties upon imported grain.
22 pp. Cork, Bradford, 1841
A.

5403 ROGERS, Jasper W. Plan for road and steam communication.
16 pp. Dublin, 1841
A.

5404 ROUSE, Rolla. The copyhold commutation and enfranchisement Act, 4 & 5 Victoria, Cap. 35; with an introduction and explanatory notes, the practice and forms (upwards of one hundred in number) in the proceedings, and court-keeping entries under the Act, rules for calculating the more complicated values, and practical suggestions, pointing out the best course to be adopted by lords, stewards, and copyholders, in the promoting their respective interest. Forming also a supplement to Mr. Rouse's copyhold and court-keeping practice, and remarks, tables and rules on enfranchisement.
tables. appendix. 310 pp. London, E. Spettigue, 1841
T.

5405 SALOMONS, Sir David, 1st bart. The corn laws. Their effects on the trade of the country considered, with suggestions for a compromise.
tables. 88 pp. London, Pelham Richardson, 1841
T.

5406 SAMUDA, J. D'A. A treatise on the adoption of atmospheric pressure to the purposes of locomotion on railways.
diagrams. tables. 52 pp. London, J. Weale, 1841
N.

5407 Second report of the Royal Agricultural Improvement Society of Ireland.
appendix. 78 pp. Dublin, printed by A. Thom, 1841
A.

5408 [SENIOR, Nassau William.] Remarks on the opposition to the Poor Law Amendment Bill. By a guardian.
116 pp. London, printed by W. Clowes, 1841
N.

5409 SHREWSBURY, John Talbot, earl. A second letter to Ambrose Lisle Phillips, esq. from the earl of Shrewsbury. On the present posture of affairs.
58 pp. London, Charles Dolman, 1841
A., L., N.

5410 Six letters to Sir Robert Peel, bart., on the reaction in favour of a tory government, and on the vast improvement in the condition of the manufacturers, which may be expected to result from a sliding scale ministry, and a monopolist majority: with other incidental matters, comical as well as tragical. By a friend to the monarchy.
30 pp. London, Effingham Wilson, 1841
U.

5411 A sketch of the state of affairs in Newfoundland. By a late resident in that colony.
68 pp. London, Saunders and Otley, 1841
T.

5412 Slavery and the slave trade in British India; with notices of the existence of these evils in the island of Ceylon, Malacca and Penang, drawn from official documents.
tables. 80 pp. London, T. Ward, 1841
A.

5413 SPENCER, Thomas. The new poor law; its evils and their remedies.
tables. 16 pp. Bath, S. Gibbs, London, J. Green, 1841
N.

5414 ——. Objections to the new poor laws answered. Parts I, II, III and IV. [4 pamphlets.]
all are 64 pp. London, J. Green, Bath, S. Gibbs, 1841
N.

5415 ——. The outcry against the new poor law or who is the poor man's friend?
tables. 16 pp. London, J. Green, Bath, S. Gibbs, 1841
N.

5416 [——.] The parson's dream and the Queen's speech, or, the corn laws and the national debt. By a Somersetshire clergyman. Tenth thousand.
16 pp. London, J. Green, Bath, S. Gibbs, 1841
N., T.

5417 ——. The prayer book opposed to the corn laws: also, the repeal of the corn laws, a religious question; freedom of correspondence & freedom of trade; and the anti-corn-law grace.
16 pp. [ninth thousand.] London, J. Green, Bath, S. Gibbs, 1841
N.

5418 STANSFELD, Hamer. Monopoly and machinery: which is the real enemy of the working classes? A lecture, delivered before the Leeds Parliamentary Reform Association on Monday, November 8, 1841.
table. appendix. 12 pp. Leeds, printed by Hobson & Smiles, 1841
A.

5419 A statement of the satisfactory results which have attended emigration to Upper Canada, from the establishment of the Canada company until the present period; comprising statistical tables, and other important information, communicated by respectable residents in the various townships of Upper Canada; with a general map of the province.
64 pp. London, Smith, Elder and Co., 1841
D.
See 5532.

5420 Statements illustrative of the policy and probable consequences of the proposed repeal of the existing corn laws, and the imposition in their stead of a moderate fixed duty on foreign corn when entered for consumption.
tables in appendices. 38 pp. London, Longman, Orme, Brown, Green & Longmans, 1841
T.

5421 THIERS, Adolfe. (No. 36) Chambre des Députés—Session 1841. Rapport fait au nom de la Commission chargée de l'examen du projet de loi tendant à ouvrir un crédit de 140 million pour les fortifications de la ville de Paris.
tables. appendix. 136 pp. Paris, printed by Henry, 1841
N.

5422 This country must be governed.
72 pp. London, James Fraser, 1841
T.

5423 THOMPSON, Thomas Perronet. Corn laws. Extracts from the works of Col. T. Perronet Thompson, author of the 'Catechism on the corn laws'. Selected & classified by R. Cobden, esq., M.P., & published with the consent of the author.
16 pp. Manchester, J. Gadsby, [1841?]
L.

5424 THOMSON, James. Notes on the present state of calico printing in Belgium: with prefatory observations on the competition and tariff of different countries.
tables. appendix. 96 pp. 2nd ed. London, printed by Smith and Elder, 1841
N.

5425 Thoughts on the corn laws.
22 pp. London, Rivingtons, 1841
T.

5426 [TORRENS, Robert.] The Budget. A series of letters on financial, commercial and colonial policy. By a member of the Political Economy Club. No. I.
22 pp. London, Smith Elder, & co., 1841
T.

5427 [——.] The Budget. A series of letters on financial, commercial and colonial policy. By a member of the Political Economy Club. No. II.
22 pp. London, Smith Elder, & co., 1841
T.

5428 [——.] The Budget. A series of letters on financial, commercial and colonial policy. By a member of the Political Economy Club. No. III.
36 pp. London, Smith Elder, & co., 1841
T.

5429 TRENCH, Sir Frederick. Letter to the viscount Duncannon, first commissioner of woods and forests.
diagrams. 12 pp. London, J. Ollivier, 1841
N.

5430 WARDLEY, William. Observations on the resolutions of the Irish distillers agreed to in London, and presented to the chancellor of the exchequer by a deputation of Irish distillers, in July, 1840
30 pp. Dublin, printed by Stephens, 1841
A.

5431 WESTERN, Charles Callis Western, 1st baron. A letter from lord Western to lord John Russell, on his proposed alteration of the corn laws, and on the causes of commercial distress.
44 pp. 2nd ed. London, J. Ridgway, Smith and Elder, 1841
T.

5432 WHITMORE, William Wolryche. A letter to the agriculturists of the county of Salop.
24 pp. 3d. ed. London, Houlston & Stoneman, 1841
A.

5433 ——. A second letter to the agriculturists of the county of Salop.
tables. 48 pp. London, Houlston & Stoneman, 1841
A.

5434 WILCOCKS, J. B. Emigration, its necessity and advantages.
24 pp. 2nd ed. Exeter, printed by Trewman, 1841
A.

5435 YATES, John Ashton. A letter on the present depression of trade and manufactures. Addressed to the landowners and farmers of the county of Carlow.
tables. 36 pp. London, H. Hooper, 1841
N.

1842

5436 Abstract of the accounts of the North Dublin Union for the half years ended 29th September, 1841, and 25th March, 1842.
tables. 20 pp. Dublin, printed by Clarke, 1842
A.

5437 An address to farmers, on the way in which their families are to be provided for. [by] a farmer's son.
4 pp. Manchester, National anti-corn law league, [1842?]
L.

5438 Address to the people of Scotland on the principle and operations of the corn and provision laws, by the ministers and members of dissenting churches.
16 pp. Belfast, printed by M'Kendrick, 1842
A.

5439 ADSHEAD, Joseph. Distress in Manchester. Evidence (tabular and otherwise) of the state of the labouring classes in 1840–42.
tables. Appendix. 56 pp. London, H. Hooper, 1842
T.

5440 Anti-corn law conference: statistical committee: the report of the statistical committee appointed by the Anti-corn law conference held in London on the 8th, 9th, 10th, 11th and 12th of March, 1842
tables. 50 pp. London, C. Fox, 1842?
N.

5441 Appropriation of the proceeds of the sales of public waste lands in the Australasian colonies.
16 pp. London, 1842
N.

5442 ARCHBOLD, John Frederick. The new poor law amendment act, and the recent rules and orders of the poor law commissioners. With a practical introduction, notes, and forms.
tables. appendix. 170 pp. London, J. Richards, 1842
T.

5443 Authorities against the corn laws.
4 pp. Manchester, J. Gadsby, [1842]
L., N.

5444 BASSET, John. Observations on Cornish mining, as it is likely to be affected by the present tariff proposed by Sir R. Peel.
tables. 20 pp. London, John Rodwell, 1842
T.

5445 BEAUCLERC, G. The operation of monopolies on the production of food, as illustrated by the corn laws: for which the only adequate remedies are moral government and free trade.
106 pp. London, J. Ridgway, 1842
A.

5446 BLAND, W. Objections to the project of H. E. Sir George Cribbs, for raising a loan to be secured on the ordinary revenue of the colony; submitted by his excellency to the legislative council of New South Wales, 1841.
tables. 20 pp. Sydney, printed by Tegg, 1842
N.

5447 BLISS, Henry. Memoir upon the resolutions proposed by Mr. Gladstone for the future regulation of the trade of the British possessions in America. By the agent for New Brunswick.
table. 24 pp. London, printed by Roworth, 1842
N.

5448 BRIERLY, Thomas. Thoughts on currency, banking, and the funds, home and foreign. A letter to the Right Hon. Henry Goulburn, chancellor of her majesty's exchequer, etc.
18 pp. Dublin, printed by William Warren, 1842
A., K., N.

5449 BROTHERS, Thomas. The rights and the wrongs of the poor in a series of letters: addressed to the working classes of all denominations. To which, on the same subject, are appended six letters to the noblemen of England.
138 pp. London, Longman, Brown, Green and Longmans, 1842
A.

5450 BURR, J. Henry Scudamore. A petition presented to both houses of parliament during the session of 1842, also a protest against the principles of the tithe commutation act delivered to Charles Pym, esq., assistant tithe commissioner. Together with a schedule showing its probable results.
18 pp. Chepstow, printed by Clark, 1842
A.

5451 The case of the bona fide holders of the repudiated Exchequer Bills, briefly stated.
14 pp. London, W. Blackwood, 1842
N.

5452 CAWDOR, John Frederick, earl. Letter to the Rt. Hon. Sir R. Peel, bart. On a southern communication with Ireland.
16 pp. London, J. Ridgway, 1842
N.

5453 CLARKSON, Thomas. Not a labourer wanted for Jamaica: to which is added, an account of the newly erected villages by the peasantry there, and their beneficial results; and of the consequences of re-opening a new slave trade, as it relates to Africa, and the honour of the British Government in breaking her treaties with foreign powers: in a letter addressed to a member of parliament, appointed to sit on the West India committee, by Thomas Clarkson.
16 pp. London, T. Ward, 1842
T.

5454 CLIFFORD, Hugh Charles Clifford, 7th baron. The Magic Pot or a letter to the editor of the Tablet newspaper on

the extracts published in that newspaper, February 19, 1842, from the lord mayor of Dublin's 'Meek and modest reply to the second letter of the earl of Shrewsbury, Waterford and Wexford to Ambrose Lisle Phillips esq.'
facsimiles. appendix. 164 pp. London, T. Jones, 1842
U.

5455 [COCKBURN, Robert.] Remarks on prevailing errors respecting currency and banking.
86 pp. London, J. Murray, Edinburgh, W. Blackwood, 1842
A.

5456 The condition and treatment of the children employed in the mines and collieries of the United Kingdom.
tables. frontisp. 94 pp. London, William Strange, 1842
T.
Sometimes attributed to William Carpenter.

5457 CONNER, William. The prosecuted speech; delivered at Montmellick in proposing a petition to parliament in favour of a valuation and perpetuity on his farm to the tenant. With an introductory address on the nature and spirit of toryism.
62 pp. Dublin, Samuel J. Machen, 1842
A., B., N.

5458 Constitution of the Dublin typographical provident society, instituted 1827.
table of contents. 36 pp. revised & amended. Dublin, 1842
A.

5459 Corn laws. Selections from Mrs. Loudon's Philanthropic economy.
4 pp. Manchester, National Anti-Corn-Law League, [1842?]
L.

5460 Correspondence between the Right Hon. William Pitt and Charles duke of Rutland, lord lieutenant of Ireland. 1781–1787. Not published, and only one hundred copies printed.
178 pp. London, printed by A. Spottiswoode, 1842
G.

5461 Dialogue on the corn laws, between a gentleman & a farmer.
8 pp. Manchester, National Anti-corn-law League, [1842?]
L.

5462 DUDLEY, William. Two letters to her majesty, two letters to two dukes, analysis of lord John Russell and of Sir Robert Peel, letter to a celebrated lady philanthropist, and one to the elder member for Tipperary county; with a plea for the restoration of the parliament of Ireland.
48 pp. Manchester, J. Gadsby, London, R. Groombridge, 1842
A.

5463 DUPIN, Charles, baron. Sur l'importation des cereales dans la Grande-Bretagne (1) (Extrait de la Revue Britannique, numero de janvier 1842.)
tables. 12 pp. Paris, printed by Dondey-Dupré, 1842
N.

5464 ENDERBY, Charles. Currency: inquiry solicited; but general declamation, without reasoning disregarded.
44 pp. London, Hatchard & Son, 1842
T.

5465 England and China: their future duty, interest, and safety. In a letter to the right hon. Sir R. Peel, bart. &c. &c. &c. By an Englishman.
24 pp. London, Smith, Elder & co., Nisbet, 1842
T.

5466 Eighth annual report of the Glasgow Emancipation Society: with an appendix, list of subscribers etc.
tables. appendix. 90 pp. Glasgow, printed by Russell, 1842
A.

5467 Expenditure of the land-fund of New South Wales in the colony and principally on public works; as a means of promoting and supporting immigration. 1842.
appendix. 24 pp. Sydney, printed by Welch, 1842
N.

5468 Fox, William. Colonisation and New Zealand.
28 pp. London, Smith, Elder, & co., 1842
A.

5469 GILLY, W. S. The peasantry of the border: [Northumberland etc.] an appeal on their behalf.
illus. tables. appendices. 98 pp. 2nd ed. London, J. Murray, 1842
D., T.

5470 GRAHAME, James. Who is to blame? or, cursory review of 'American apology for American accession to negro slavery'.
112 pp. London, Smith Elder & co., 1842
T.

5471 [GREG, J. R.] Observations on the proposed duties on the exportation of coals; with tables and statements from parliamentary returns and other authentic sources. April 1842.
table of contents. tables. appendices. 42 pp. London, J. Ridgway, P. Richardson, 1842
N.

5472 GREG, Robert Hyde. A letter [to] the Right Hon. Henry Labouchere, on the pressure of the corn laws and sliding scale more especially upon the manufacturing interests and productive classes.
tables. 32 pp. 2nd ed. London, J. Ridgway, 1842
N.

5473 GREG, William Rathbone. Agriculture and the corn law. Prize essay. Showing the injurious effects of the corn law upon tenant farmers and farm labourers.
18 pp. Manchester, National Anti-Corn-Law League, 1842.
[The three prize essays on agriculture and the corn law.]
A., L., T., U.

5474 GUTTERIDGE, Thomas. Church rates: means proposed for surmounting the obstacles to the granting and collecting of them.
16 pp. London, Rivingtons, 1842
T.

5475 [HABICH, Edward.] The American churches, the bulwarks of American slavery. By an American. Revised by the author.
44 pp. 2nd ed. Newburyport, Whipple, 1842
N.

5476 [HICKEY, William.] A cyclopaedia of practical husbandry. By Martin Doyle.
52 pp. n.p. 1842
A.

5477 [——.] The farmer's guide, compiled for the use of the small farmers and cotter tenantry of Ireland.
table of contents. 192 pp. 2nd ed. Dublin, A. Thom, 1842
A.

5478 HOPE, George. Agriculture & the corn law. Prize essay. Showing the injurious effects of the corn law upon tenant farmers & farm labourers.
16 pp. Manchester, National Anti-corn-law League, 1842.
[The three prize essays on agriculture & the corn law.]
B., L., T., U.

5479 HOWMAN, Edward John. Thoughts on the rating question, in a letter, addressed to the hon. & rev. William Capel.
24 pp. London, J. G. F. & J. Rivington, 1842
T.

5480 HUDSON, J. S. Home slavery or, an earnest appeal, to the common sense of the nation, on the oppressive effects of the food laws.
tables. 20 pp. London, S. Gilbert, 1842
T.

5481 Information for emigrants to Canada.
tables. 16 pp. London, printed by Marchant, Singer and Smith, 1842
N.

5482 Ireland and Irish questions considered. By a fellow of the Dublin Law Institute.
appendices. 92 pp. London, J. Hatchard, Dublin, W. Curry, 1842
N.

5483 JAMES, Edwin. The act for the amendment of the law in bankruptcy.
appendix. 108 pp. London, John Richards, 1842
T.

5484 JOHNSTON, Hugh H. Letters on emigration to the United States and Canada.
24 pp. Downpatrick, printed at the Recorder Office, 1842
Y.

5485 JOHNSTON, James Finlay Weir. What can be done for English agriculture? A letter to the most noble the Marquis of Northampton, president of the Royal Society, by Jas. F. W. Johnston.
40 pp. London, W. Blackwood, 1842
D.

5486 KINGSLEY, Jefferies. The new county book of Tipperary, constructed on the principles of 'The standard or model county book' detailing the taxation and expenditure of the several counties of Ireland under the grand jury system. Vol. I For private circulation.
tables. 24 pp. Dublin, printed by Graisberry & Gill, 1842
A.

5487 LANG, Gabriel H. Letter to the Right Hon. Henry Goulbourn, M.P. chancellor of the exchequer, etc. etc. on the unequal pressure of the railway passenger tax.
tables. 16 pp. Glasgow, printed by Hedderwick, 1842
N.

5488 Letter to his grace the duke of Wellington on the present state of affairs in India.
tables. 32 pp. London, Saunders and Otley, 1842
N.

5489 A letter to the shareholders in the bank of India. By Aristides. Reprinted from a copy received from Bombay by the last mail.
appendix. 52 pp. London, Pelham Richardson, 1842
T.

5490 The London & Dublin Bank.
18 pp. Dublin, printed by Grace, 1842
A.

5491 McCULLOCH, John Ramsay. Memorandums on the proposed importation of foreign beef and live stock, addressed to Alexander Murray, esq., M.P.
10 pp. London, Longman, Brown, Green, and Longmans, 1842
T., U.

5492 MACKENZIE, J. Improvement of highland crofts.
tables. 16 pp. [no t.p.] Edinburgh, printed by W. & R. Tofts, [1842]
U.

5493 M'LAWS, Colin Sharp. Statement explanatory of the independent system of emigration.
20 pp. Glasgow, Edward Khull, 1842
T.

5494 MANGLES, Ross Donnelly. How to colonise: The interest of the country and the duty of the government.
table. 68 pp. London, Smith, Elder & co., 1842
A.

5495 MARSHALL, Henry Johnson. On the tendency of the new poor law seriously to impair the morals and condition of the working classes.
48 pp. London, J. G. F. & J. Rivington, 1842
T.

5496 Memoir on the colonial timber trade, presented to the Right Honourable Sir Robert Peel, bart. By the committee of the North American colonial association.
tables. 28 pp. London, Roworth, 1842
N.

5497 MILLER, Charles. A catalogue of authorities, ecclesiastical and civil, taken from the writings of the ancient fathers, from the laws of England, and from other sources, bearing uniform witness to the system of tithes, as a divine institution of perpetual obligation: with introductory observations.
appendix. 52 pp. London, J. G. F. & J. Rivington, 1842
T.

5498 ——. A letter of remonstrance to the Right Hon. Sir Robert Peel, M.P., bart. first lord of the treasury, on the proposed renewal of the tithe commission.
12 pp. London, J. G. F. & J. Rivington, 1842
T.

5499 ——. The offertory, and the duty of the legislature in the present relation between the poor and the state briefly considered in a letter to George Palmer, esq., M.P.
20 pp. London, J. G. F. & J. Rivington, 1842
T.

5500 ——. Prospectus of a publication entitled a catalogue of authorities, ecclesiastical and civil, taken from the writings of the ancient fathers, from the laws of England, and from other sources, bearing uniform witness to the system of tithes, as a divine institution of perpetual obligation.
10 pp. London, J. G. F. & J. Rivington, 1842
T.

5501 ——. The tithe system briefly considered: in a letter to the Right Hon. lord Stanley, M.P. secretary of state for the colonies.
10 pp. London, J. G. F. & J. Rivington, 1842
T.

5502 MORSE, Arthur. Agriculture & the corn law. Prize essay. Shewing the injurious effects of the corn law upon tenant farmers, & farm labourers.
16 pp. Manchester, National Anti-corn-law League, [1842]. [The three prize essays on agriculture & the corn law.]
A., L., T., U.

5503 NEVILE, Christopher. The new tariff.
36 pp. London, J. Ridgway, 1842
T.

5504 NICHOLSON, William. The income tax act, epitomized and simplified. Sixteenth thousand.
24 pp. London, Smith, Elder & co., 1842

T.

5505 Nine letters on the corn laws. Originally published in the 'Morning Chronicle', the 'Sun', the 'Manchester Guardian' and the 'Manchester Times'.
tables. 72 pp. (corrected and revised by the author.) London, H. Hooper, 1842
A.

5506 NOEL, Baptist Wriothesley. Corn laws. Selections from 'A plea for the poor'.
8 pp. Manchester, National Anti-corn-law League, [1842?]
L.

5507 [NOTT, Charles, ed.] The new American tariff; passed 30th August, 1842, alphabetically arranged, and shewing the old and new duties in juxta-position, payable on all goods, wares, and merchandise imported into the United States of America; with the legal provisions relative thereto, and a variety of other useful information. Officially compiled from authentic documents.
tables. 90 pp. London, James Gilbert, [1842]
T.

5508 NUNNS, Thomas. A letter to the right hon. lord Ashley, on the condition of the working classes in Birmingham, considered in reference to improvement in the condition of the same classes in manufacturing districts and large towns generally.
62 pp. Birmingham, Henry C. Langbridge, 1842
T.

5509 Observations on the proposed measure for the regulation of the corn trade, in respect to the encouragement it offers for the importation of foreign flour in preference to wheat.
tables. 16 pp. London, Vacher and Sons, 1842
N.

5510 O'CONNELL, Daniel. Observations on corn laws, on political pravity & ingratitude, & on clerical & personal slander, in the shape of a meek & modest reply to the second letter of the earl of Shrewsbury, Waterford, & Wexford, to Ambrose Lisle Phillips, esq.
182 pp. Dublin, Samuel J. Machen, 1842
A., L., N., U.

5511 On the application of Mutual Insurance to education.
tables. 16 pp. London, Chapman & Hall, 1842
N.

5512 Proceedings of the first annual general meeting of the society for the promotion and improvement of the growth of flax in Ireland, with a list of subscribers' names, treasurer's statement of accounts, and instructions to farmers.
appendix. 56 pp. Belfast, printed by Hugh Clark, 1842
N., RM.

5513 Proceedings of the second annual general meeting of the society for the promotion and improvement of the growth of flax in Ireland with an appendix, a list of subscribers' names, and treasurer's statement of accounts.
appendix. 52 pp. Belfast, printed by F. D. Finlay, 1842
D.

5514 Proposed new plan of a general emigration society. By a catholic gentleman.
32 pp. London, Dolman, Dublin, Coyne, 1842
A., N., U.

5515 Railways; their uses and management.
tables. 66 pp. London, Pelham Richardson, 1842
T.

5516 A reply to the prize essays of the anti-corn law league. By a Lincolnshire landowner.
32 pp. London, W. E. Painter, [1842]
T.

5517 Report of the court of directors of the Canada Company to the proprietors.
map. tables. 16 pp. London, Marchant, Singer and Smith, 1842
N.

5518 Report of the Hibernian auxiliary to the society for the extinction of the slave trade, and for the civilization of Africa. Held at the Rotunda, on Monday, the 18th of July, 1842.
54 pp. Dublin, printed by Thomas I. White, 1842
L.

5519 Report of the Newtown-Barn agricultural school near Moate. For the year ending 6th May, 1842.
appendices. 14 pp. Dublin, Purdon, 1842
U.

5520 RICHARDSON, Christopher. Transport service and Trinity House light dues: particulars of the illegal transfers to the Trinity House, by lord viscount Melbourne's administration, of certain balances of freight, left by several transport owners, at the conclusion of the late war, in her majesty's treasury: and of the virtual fraud committed upon the depositors by this proceeding. With an appendix, giving some useful information with respect to the corporation of the Trinity House.
appendix. 24 pp. London, Effingham Wilson, 1842
T.

5521 [ROGERS, Samuel Baldwin.] Samarias or working benefit societies; and a magnificent bridge across the mouth of the river Severn, at the new passage, in Gloucestershire. An effectual plan for abolishing the evils of pauperism, vagabondry, and slavery, and for accomplishing certain great and important national improvements, with the wasting energies of the United Kingdom: without expense to the state, or to any party or individual whatever.
40 pp. London, Simpkin, Marshall, [1842]
U.

5522 ROLPH, Thomas. Comparative advantages between the United States and Canada, for British settlers, considered in a letter addressed to captain Allardyce Barclay, of Ury.
32 pp. London, Smith Elder & co., 1842
T.

5523 ROWLAND, Charles. Abstract of the laws and regulations relating to shipping in the Port of London.
index. tables. 94 pp. London, Rowsell, 1842
A.

5524 RUTHVEN, Edward. A plan for the sale and profitable investment of capital, to be secured on land, proposed, and the loughs, lakes and shores of Ireland, commented on.
32 pp. London, Baily, 1842
N.

5525 A scale of prices for compositors and pressmen agreed upon by the employers and journeymen printers of the city of Dublin...1829.
16 pp. Dublin, 1842
A.

5526 SHIEL, John B. Observations on the salmon fisheries of Ulster; urging their claims to legislative protection.
62 pp. London, printed by Clay, 1842
A.

5527 SHREWSBURY, John Talbot, 19th earl of. A third letter to Ambrose Lisle Phillips. Chiefly in reference to his former letter 'On the present posture of affairs'.
appendix. 532 pp. London, Dolman, 1842
A.

5528 SHUTTLEWORTH, J. G. The hydraulic railway; being a carefully digested but plain statement of the advantages to be derived and impediments removed in establishing hydraulic propulsion, on railways.
folding plans. table of contents. 112 pp. London, J. Weale, 1842
A., N.

5529 SILVER, Thomas. A letter to his grace the duke of Marlborough, and the right hon. baron Churchill, lay-rectors of the manor and parish of Charlbury, on the sacrilege and impolicy of the forced commutation of tithes.
col. illustration. 190 pp. Oxford, W. Baxter, 1842
T.

5530 SIMPSON, William Wooley. A letter to his excellency the earl de Grey, lord lieutenant of Ireland, on the ameliorated condition of that country, more particularly as regards the agricultural classes; with suggestions for their further improvement; to which is subjoined an appendix, containing original and other interesting papers.
tables in appendix. 124 pp. London, Sherwood, Gilbert & Piper, Dublin, Curry, 1842
A., D., N., T., Y.

5531 SMITH, Thomas Sharpe. On the economy of nations.
140 pp. London, James Carpenter, 1842
T.

5532 A statement of the satisfactory results which have attended emigration to Upper Canada, from the establishment of the Canada company until the present period: comprising statistical tables and other important information communicated by respectable residents in the various townships of Upper Canada.
118 pp. 3rd ed. London, Smith Elder & co., 1842
N., P.

————. 118 pp. 4th ed. London, Smith Elder & co., 1842
A.
See 5419.

5533 TAYLOR, George. An enquiry into the principles which ought to regulate the imposition of duties on foreign corn, in answer to 'Statements illustrative of the policy and probable consequences of the proposed repeal of the existing corn-laws' by J. R. McCulloch, esq.
56 pp. London, J. Murray, 1842
T.

5534 Testimonials in reference to the sale of Irish estates; and minutes of evidence taken before a committee of the house of Lords, on the state of crime in Ireland.
28 pp. London, printed by Marchant, Singer and Smith, 1842
A.

5535 Thoughts on the currency.
64 pp. London, J. Ridgway, 1842
T.

5536 [TORRENS, Robert.] The Budget. A series of letters on financial, commercial and colonial policy. By a member of the Political economy club. No. IV.
24 pp. London, Smith Elder & co., 1842
T.

5537 [——.] The Budget. A series of letters on financial, commercial and colonial policy. By a member of the Political economy club. No. V.
36 pp. London, Smith Elder & co., 1842
T.

5538 [——.] The Budget. A series of letters on financial, commercial and colonial policy. By a member of the Political economy club. No. VI.
32 pp. London, Smith Elder & co., 1842
T.

5539 [——.] The Budget. A series of letters on financial, commercial and colonial policy. By a member of the Political economy club. No. VII.
20 pp. London, Smith, Elder & co., 1842
T.

5540 [——.] The Budget. A series of letters on financial, commercial and colonial policy. By a member of the Political economy club. No. VIII.
appendix, with tables. 38 pp. London, Smith, Elder & co., 1842
T.

5541 Tracts for farmers.
4 pp. Manchester, National anti-corn-law league, [1842?]
L.

5542 TRIPP, George. The Egremont ejectments; or, an appeal to the public, in a letter to the right hon. the earl of Egremont, against his proceedings at law, to eject a vast number of leaseholders for lives from his estates in Somersetshire and Devonshire, upon a point of form.
appendix. 42 pp. London, W. Lake, 1842
U.

5543 Twenty-fourth annual report of the managing committee of the association for the suppression of mendicity in Dublin. For the year 1841.
appendix. tables. 28 pp. Dublin, printed by Corbet, 1842
A.

5544 VYVYAN, Sir Richard, bart. A letter from Sir Richard Vyvyan, bart. M.P. to his constituents, upon the commercial and financial policy of Sir Robert Peel's administration.
54 pp. London, J. Bohn, 1842
T.

5545 WADE, John. History and political philosophy of the middle and working classes.
appendix. 176 pp. 4th ed. Edinburgh, William and Robert Chambers, 1842
T.

5546 WALKER, Thomas. Observations on the utility of savings' banks.
8 pp. Newcastle, printed at the Courant Office, 1842
N.

5547 WARNES, John, junior. Suggestions on fattening cattle with native instead of foreign produce.
appendix. 40 pp. London, Longman, 1842
D., T.

5548 WHYTOCK, Richard. An inquiry into the cause of the present depression of trade and a remedy proposed in a measure calculated at the same time to obviate the necessity of an income tax.
table of contents. 68 pp. London, Simpkin Marshall, Glasgow, Robertson, 1842
A.

1843

5549 Abstract of the accounts of the Cork union for the half-year ended 29th September, 1842.
table. 8 pp. Cork, printed by Nash, 1843
A.

5550 An address to the landowners and the public on the large farm system. By an observer.
tables. 62 pp. London, Simpkin, Marshall, 1843
T.

5551 An address to the right hon. Sir Robert Peel, bart., etc. etc. etc. in reply to Mr. Montgomery Martin's recently published pamphlet, entitled 'Ireland before and after the union', wherein it has been attempted to demonstrate the declining state of Ireland since the union, and to point out the real source of (& remedies for) that country's misfortunes; & an appeal is made to the first lord of the treasury to abandon the pending state trials. By Juverna.
fold. tables. 82 pp. Dublin, Samuel J. Machen, [1843?]
A., B.

5552 ALMACK, John, Jr. Character, motives and proceedings of the anti-corn law leaguers, with a few general remarks on the consequences that would result from a free trade in corn.
98 pp. London, J. Ollivier, 1843
T.

5553 Analysis of the deed of settlement as executed by the London & Dublin bank.
12 pp. Dublin, printed by Chambers, 1843
A.

5554 ANDERSON, Arthur. Communications with India, China, etc. via Egypt. The political position of their transit through Egypt considered.
28 pp. n.p. ['not printed for sale'], [1843?]
A.

5555 ANKETEL, William Robert. The effects of absenteeism briefly considered in the following pages, which are respectfully dedicated to the resident proprietors of Ireland, as a trifling but sincere tribute of respect, and addressed to the absentees as a short expostulation.
38 pp. London, Hatchard & co., 1843
A., N., T.

5556 Annual report of the Royal Agricultural Improvement Society of Ireland. For the year 1842.
76 pp. Dublin, printed by A. Thom, 1843
A.

5557 [BANFIELD, Thomas Charles.] Six letters to the right honourable Sir Robert Peel, bart., being an attempt to expose

the dangerous tendency of the theory of rent advocated by Mr. Ricardo, and by the writers of his school. By a political economist.
60 pp. London, printed by R. & J. E. Taylor, 1843
A.

5558 [BIGGS, Henry.] Annals of the county and city of Cork; commencing with an abridged report of the transactions of the British association at its thirteenth meeting: and treating of various other subjects of local interest to the south of Ireland. By a member of the association.
tables. 56 pp. Cork, Savage and Son, [etc.], 1843
U.

5559 BISCHOFF, James. Foreign tariffs; their injurious effect on British manufactures, especially the woollen manufacture; with proposed remedies. Being chiefly a series of articles inserted in the Leeds Mercury, from October 1842 to February 1843.
tables. 70 pp. London, Smith, Elder; Leeds, Baines & Newsome, 1843
T.

5560 BURGER, Johann. The economy of farming, transl. from the German of J. Burger; with many additional notes from the German of Thaer, Veit, Schwertz, Sprengel, Petri etc. and a copious index: by E. Goodrich Smith.
tables. 144 pp. New York, Leavitt & Frow, [etc.], 1843
N.

5561 BUTT, Isaac. Repeal of the union: the substance of a speech delivered in the corporation of Dublin, on the 28th February, 1843, on Mr. O'Connell's motion for a repeal of the legislative union.
70 pp. Dublin, W. Curry, London, Longman, Brown, Green & Longmans, 1843
A., B., K., N., T.,

5562 The catholic emigration society, its necessity, objects and advantages; to which is added a letter from the very revd. Stephen Badin, V.G. (of Kentucky and Ohio), to the British catholics.
16 pp. London, Brown, 1843
A.

5563 CHARNOCK, John Henry. Suggestions for the more general extension of land-draining, by the judicious and equitable application of collective capital.
20 pp. London, Longman, Brown, Green & Longmans, [etc., etc.], 1843
T.

5564 CHRISTIE, Robert. Letters relative to the affairs of the clerical provident society, diocese of Armagh.
appendix. tables. 36 pp. Armagh, McWatters, 1843
A.

5565 COCKBURN, Sir George. A dissertation on the state of the British finances, the debt, currency, and banking; with a plan for raising 30 millions, or more, without loan or increased taxation. Also, some observations on Ireland.
tables. 94 pp. London, Hatchard & Son, Dublin, Hodges & Smith, 1843
A.

5566 Communications between the Royal Dublin society and the lords of the treasury relative to an application for supplementary grants, in aid of the objects of the society, founded on the recommendation of the select committee of the house of commons in 1836
22 pp. Dublin, printed by Gill, 1843
N.

5567 CONNER, William. A letter to the right honourable the earl of Devon, chairman of the land commission, on the rackrent system of Ireland: showing its cause, its evils, and its remedy.
20 pp. Dublin, Samuel J. Machen, 1843
A., B.

5568 Corn v. cotton. An attempt to open the case between the manufacturers and the landlords. Respectfully inscribed to his grace, the duke of Buckingham. By the — S.S.C.
16 pp. London, J. Ollivier, 1843
T.

5569 [COWARD, William C.] Victoriaism; [sic] or, a reorganisation of the people: moral, social, economical, and political: suggested as a remedy for the present distress. Respectfully addressed to the right hon. Sir Robert Peel, bart. [Signed W.C.C.] 28 pp.
London, J. Clements, Knightsbridge, Charles Westerton, 1843
T.

5570 COWELL, John Welsford. Letters to the right honourable Francis Thornhill Baring on the institution of a safe and profitable paper currency.
appendix, with table of contents therefor. 130 pp. London, Pelham Richardson, 1843
A., T.

5571 CREWE, Sir George, bart. A word for the poor, and against the present poor law, both as to its principle and practice: by Sir George Crewe, bart., late M.P. for the southern division of the county of Derby.
38 pp. Derby, W. Rowbottom, 1843
T.

5572 A cry from Ireland; or landlord and tenant exemplified. A narrative of the proceedings of Richard Shee, esq., of Blackwell Lodge, co. of Kilkenny against his tenantry at Bennet's bridge; to which are added several other cases and singular documents relative to the intimidation of witnesses in lawsuits.
48 pp. London, Allen, 1843
A., N.

5573 DAUNT, William Joseph O'Neill. Letters of W. J. O'Neill Daunt in answer to Wm. Sharman Crawford, esq., on the repeal of the union. Republished by order of the Loyal National repeal association.
36 pp. Dublin, printed by J. Browne, 1843
N.

5574 ——. Mr. Daunt's speech at the repeal association, in refutation of the anti-repeal fallacies adopted from Spring Rice and others by lord Shrewsbury. Also, Mr. Daunt's speech at the meeting held in Edinburgh for repeal.
44 pp. Dublin, J. Browne [by order of the repeal association], 1843.
A., B., N.

5575 ——. Speech delivered by Mr. Daunt, at the great repeal demonstration, held in the amphitheatre, Liverpool, 12th Sept., 1843.
18 pp. [no t.p.] Dublin, printed by J. Browne, 1843
N.

5576 DAY, George Game. Defeat of the anti-corn-law league in Huntingdonshire. The speech of Mr. George Game Day on that occasion, at Huntingdon, June 17, 1843, (published by request) with notes and additions. Seventh edition.
tables. 40 pp. London, J. Ollivier, 1843
T.

5577 DICKSON, Stephen Fox. The violations of the act of union in the personal rights and properties of the licensed victuallers and tea dealers of Ireland, demonstrating that upwards of £3,753,000 of money, has been levied off these traders in Ireland, more than off their fellow-traders of England: and that agreeably to her majesty's speech to parliament, the monies and rights of the Irish traders are to be maintained inviolate. With the opinion of eminent counsel. And an address to the right hon. lord Eliot, M.P. &c. &c. &c.
tables. 32 pp. Dublin, printed by Brady, 1843
A.

5578 Discussion on the repeal. The only impartial and correct report of the important discussion in the Corporation of Dublin on the motion of Alderman O'Connell to petition parliament for a repeal of the union.
tables. 98 pp. Dublin, Dowling & Shea, 1843
A., N.

5579 DUCPÉTIAUX, Édouard. De la condition des ouvriers mineurs dans la Grande-Bretagne et en Belgique. Analyse de l'enquête ordonné par le parlement anglais sur le travail des enfants dans les mines.
tables. illustrations. 64 pp. Bruxelles, Vandooren, 1843
N.

5580 EASBY, John. Repeal! or sketches of the league,* its leaders, its members, and its foes!
24 pp. London, R. Groombridge, Manchester, Wood, 1843
A.
* i.e., the Anti-corn-law league.

5581 EDWARDS, Henry. Address to agriculturists and others, in one of the rural districts, on the nature and effects of the present corn laws as bearing on their interests.
62 pp. London, Effingham Wilson, 1843
T.

5582 Facts and arguments for the repeal of the legislative union examined.
tables. 82 pp. Dublin, Samuel J. Machen, London, Simpkin, Marshall, 1843
A., T.

5583 FANE, Henry. The distress and the remedy.
20 pp. London, J. Ridgway, 1843
T.

5584 Final report of the committee, appointed at a general meeting of the wine trade, held at the commercial sale rooms, Mincing Lane, London, on Tuesday, 26th July, 1842, to take into consideration the measures to be adopted in consequence of the reduction in the duties on wine, expected to take place, on conclusion of the commercial treaty with Portugal: George Barnes, esq. in the chair.
appendices. 16 pp. London, Smith, Elder & co., 1843
T.

5585 FLETCHER, Walter. Letter on free trade, addressed to the right hon. lord John Russell, M.P.
tables. 24 pp. 3rd ed. Liverpool, Joshua Walmsley, 1843
T.

5586 GALE, R. Protection of labour and land, closely allied with Britain's destiny.
appendix. 42 pp. London, J. Ollivier, 1843
T.

5587 [GALT, William.] Railway reform; its expediency and practicability considered. With a copious appendix containing a description of all the railways in Great Britain and Ireland; fluctuations in the price of shares; statistical and parliamentary returns; financial calculations, extracts from writers on political economy.
tables. appendix. 120 pp. London, Pelham Richardson, 1843
N.

See also 5714.

5588 GLADSTONE, Sir John, bart. A review of Mr. Cobden's corn politics submitted for the consideration of the landlords, farmers, and manufacturers of the United Kingdom, in a letter dated London, May 18th, 1843, addressed to the editor of the 'Morning Herald'.
8 pp. [½ t.p.] London, W. Blackwood, 1843
T.

5589 GODLEY, John Robert. A letter on the subject of poor rates, addressed to the landholders of the county of Leitrim.
8 pp. Dublin, printed by Folds & Patton, 1843
N.

5590 GORDON, Hunter. The right of search question.
28 pp. London, J. Ridgway 1843
T.

5591 GORE, Montague. Letter to his grace the duke of Wellington, etc. etc. etc. on the present state of affairs in India.
tables. 48 pp. 3rd ed. London, Saunders and Otley, 1843
T.

5592 The great cause of the present distress, and the remedy. By a friend to the home trade.
tables. 16 pp. Chelmsford [etc.], H. Guy, 1843
T.

5593 HALL, John. The iron trade, with remarks, pointing out the true cause and cure for its existing state of depression.
32 pp. London, Simpkin Marshall, Manchester, Thomas Forrest, 1843
T.

Criticism of Mackelcan: Suggestions to Iron masters: see 5611.

5594 HARWOOD, Philip. Six lectures on the corn-law monopoly and free trade: delivered at the London Mechanics Institution.
126 pp. London, John Green, 1843
T.

5595 HASLETT, William.   Address delivered to the corporation ... 7th August, 1843, on the subject of the relative duties of the city of Londonderry, and the hon. the Society of the Governors and Assistants, London, of the New Plantation in Ulster, commonly called the Irish Society.
tables. appendix. 78 pp. Londonderry, printed at the Standard Office, 1843
A., N.

5596 HAYES, ——.   Speech of Alderman Hayes on the discussion in the town council of Cork, upon the motion to petition parliament for a repeal of the union on Wednesday, April 19th, 1843.
76 pp. Dublin, printed by J. Browne, 1843
A., N.
Edited for the Loyal national repeal association of Ireland, by William O'Brien.

5597 HENSLOW, John Stevens.   Letter to the farmers of Suffolk, with a glossary of terms used, and the address delivered at the last anniversary meeting of the Hadleigh farmers' club.
tables. 116 pp. London, R. Groombridge, [1843]
T.

5598 HEYWORTH, Lawrence.   On the corn laws, and other legislative restrictions. Seventh edition. Containing new matter in refutation of popularly received fallacies on the monetary system, and additional evidences, that the tendency of a corn law is, to bring ruin on the agriculture, and the revenue, as well as on the manufactures and commerce of England.
12 pp. Manchester, J. Gadsby, 1843
T.

5599 HILDITCH, R.   The income tax criticised and epitomised; containing some plain statements on the income and property tax, showing that it falls most heavily on the industrious classes; with full instructions for filling up the tax papers.
tables. 36 pp. London, Charles Gilpin, 1843
T.

5600 HILL, James.   The defeater defeated: being a refutation of Mr. Day's pamphlet, entitled 'Defeat of the anti-corn law league in Huntingdonshire'.
60 pp. 4th edition. London, Effingham Wilson, 1843
T.
See 5576.

5601 [——.]   Hunger and Revolution. By the author of 'Daily bread'.
40 pp. [various paging.] 4th edition. London, Effingham Wilson, [c. 1843]
T.

5602 HUBBARD, John Gellibrand, later 1st baron ADDINGTON.   The currency and the country.
table of contents, tables. appendix. 120 pp. London, Longman, Brown, Green, and Longmans, 1843
A., T.

5603 The Instow tithe case, as made special, under the act for the commutation of tithes in England and Wales.
tables. 40 pp. London, Edwards and Hughes, 1843
T.

5604 Irish landlords, rents, and tenures. With some observations on the effects of the voluntary system, by which their church is supported, on the moral and social condition of the Roman catholic population. By an Irish Roman catholic landowner.
34 pp. London, J. Murray, 1843
N., T.

5605 [JOPLIN, Thomas.]   An essay upon the condition of the National Provincial Bank of England, with a view to its improvement: in a letter to the shareholders, by the founder of the establishment.
appendix. 73 pp. London, Richardson, 1843
T.

5606 KINAHAN, Daniel.   To the tenants and under-tenants of the townland of Ballyvowen, barony of Owna and Arra, and county of Tipperary.
2 pp. Dublin, printed by Goodwin & Nethercott, 1843
A.

5607 ——.   To the tenants of the townland of Annagh, barony of lower Ormond County Tipperary.
4 pp. Dublin, printed by Goodwin & Nethercott, 1843
A.
Two letters on sub-letting.

5608 Laws and regulations for the government of the Dublin district funeral, and widow and orphan's fund, of the loyal independent order of Odd Fellows, Manchester Unity.
34 pp. Dublin, printed by Johnson, 1843
A.

5609 A letter to the farmers of England, on the relationship of manufactures and agriculture. By one who has whistled at the plough.
16 pp. London, J. Ridgway, 1843
L.

5610 LUSHINGTON, William John.   Six letters lately addressed to the agriculturists of the county of Kent, on the doctrines of the anti-corn-law league, and the subject of free trade.
tables. 34 pp. Sittingbourne, J. E. Coulter, London, Longman, Brown, Green & Longmans, 1843
T.

5611 MACKELCAN, F. P.   Suggestions to iron-masters on increasing the demand for iron; also to the iron-masters of Staffordshire, on competing with those of Scotland and Wales.
36 pp. London, Simpkin Marshall, 1843
T.
See 5593.

5612 MACNEILL, Sir John.   Report on a proposed line of railway from Dublin to Cashel, being the first division of a main trunk to the south and south-west of Ireland, including a branch therefrom to Athy and Carlow.
tables. 16 pp. Dublin, printed by A. Thom, 1843
A.

5613 MADDEN, Richard Robert.   The slave trade and slavery: the influence of British settlements on the west coast of Africa, in relation to both: illustrated by extracts from the

letters of Dr. R. R. Madden, in the *Morning Chronicle*, the *United Service Gazette*, etc.
table of contents. appendices. 82 pp. London, James Madden, 1843

N.

5614 Manufacturing districts. Replies of Sir Charles Shaw to lord Ashley, M.P. regarding the education, and moral and physical condition of the labouring classes.
56 pp. London, J. Ollivier, 1843

T.

5615 MARINER, William. Exchequer bills forgery. A statement.
90 pp. 2nd ed. London, Pelham Richardson, 1843

T.

5616 A memoir of the union, and the agitations for its repeal; in which that measure, its causes and its consequences, are historically and politically reviewed; and its indissolubility demonstrated from many great authorities, and particularly by that of Daniel O'Connell, esq., M.P. By an Irish catholic.
table of contents. appendix. 144 pp. Dublin, W. Curry, Jun., London, Longman, Brown, Green and Longmans, 1843

A., T.

5617 MILLER, Samuel. Suggestions for a general equalization of the land tax; with a view to provide the means of reducing the malt duties: and a statement of the legal rights and remedies of persons unequally assessed to land tax in particular districts or places.
tables. 58 pp. (3rd. ed.) London, H. Butterworth, 1843

T.

5618 MORRIS, W. Three letters to the rt. hon. Sir Robert Peel, bt., first lord of the British treasury etc., on the repeal of the present system of revenue and protections, imports, excise, stamps, assessed taxes etc. and the adoption of a general system of income tax with present exemptions, or, income tax for trade and parish rate for land.
42 pp. Exeter, A. Holden, 1843

T.

5619 MUNTZ, George Frederick. The true cause of the late sudden change in the commercial affairs of the country.
tables. 18 pp. 2nd ed. Birmingham, Richard Peart, 1843

T.

5620 National distress; its causes and remedies.
44 pp. London, Sherwood, Gilbert and Piper, 1843

T.

5621 Observations and strictures on the present Irish poor law, with suggestions and outlines for an amended one. By an Irish magistrate. (signed 'J.P.')
24 pp. Dublin, John Cumming, London, Hatchard & co., 1843

A., N.

5622 O'CONNELL, Daniel. A full and revised report of the three day's discussion in the corporation of Dublin on the repeal of the union, with dedication to Cornelius MacLouglin, esq., and an address to the people of Ireland by Daniel O'Connell, M.P. To which are added a valuable appendix, and

21

the petition from the corporation to the imperial parliament, for the restoration of Ireland's domestic legislature.
tables. appendix. 220 pp. Dublin, Duffy, 1843

T.

5623 O'CONNELL, John. Letters to friends in Connaught, respectfully addressed to various parties in that province.
index. 54 pp. Dublin, printed by J. Browne, 1843

A., N.

5624 [——.] The 'commercial injustices'. Extract from appendix of a report to the Repeal Association, on the general case of Ireland for a repeal of the legislative union.
tables. 98 pp. Dublin, printed by J. Browne, 1843

A., D., K., N.

5625 [——.] The 'taxation injustice'. Extract from appendix of a report to the Repeal Association on the general case of Ireland for a repeal of the legislative union.
tables. 58 pp. Dublin, printed by J. Browne, 1843

C., K., Q., U.

See 6047.

5626 OGLE, Nathaniel. Direct or indirect taxation? or, should the corn laws, customs and excise duties be abolished, how is the revenue now obtained from them to be replaced?
tables. appendix. 24 pp. London, J. Ollivier, 1843

T.

5627 The opinions of the London press respecting the amount of opium compensation offered by her majesty's government.
64 pp. London, S. Clarke, 1843

N.

5628 The physical and moral condition of the children and young persons employed in mines and manufactures. Illustrated by extracts from the reports of the commissioners for inquiring into the employment of children and young persons in mines and collieries, and in the trades and manufactures in which numbers of them work together, not being included under the terms of the factories regulation act.
280 pp. London, John W. Parker, 1843

T.

5629 PIGOTT, Elizabeth. The waste of the revenue in the excise department, illicit distillation produced by high duties, and the illegality of the revenue police force; abridged from the reports of Sir Henry Parnell's commission, and the papers of the late Robert Pigott, esq.
28 pp. Dublin, the author, 1843

A., K., N.

5630 Plan for substituting wood pavement for 'macadamizing', to carry into effect the establishment of steam carriages on the common roads of Ireland. By an engineer.
14 pp. Dublin, printed by Wilson, 1843

A., D., N.

5631 PLUNKETT, Edward. Address to the landowners of Ireland upon the present agitation for a repeal of the union.
20 pp. London, J. Ridgway, 1843

T.

5632 PORTER, John Grey V.   Some agricultural and political Irish questions calmly discussed.
table of contents, appendix with tables. 140 pp. London, J. Ridgway, Dublin, Keene, 1843
A., C., N., T.

5633 PORTLOCK, Joseph E.   Notes on agricultural schools, in reference to Templemoyle Agricultural Seminary; from the report on the geology of the county of Londonderry etc.
tables. 28 pp. Dublin, A. Thom, 1843
D., U.

5634 POSTANS, Thomas.   A few observations on the increase of commerce by means of the river Indus.
appendix. 32 pp. London, Pelham Richardson, 1843
T.

5635 Proceedings of the third annual meeting of the society for the promotion and improvement of the growth of flax in Ireland; with report of the committee, an appendix, a list of subscribers' names, and treasurer's statement of accounts.
74 pp. Belfast, printed by F. D. Finlay, 1843
A.

5636 Prospectus of the Great Southern and Western railway. First division from Dublin to Cashel, with a branch to Athy and Carlow.
4 pp. n.p. [1843?]
A.

5637 Railway contracts in France, under the administration of the Ponts et Chaussées; with the condition, schedule of prices, and formulae, taken from the last lettings of the line from Paris to Belgium. Also, some remarks on railroads, from the Journal des Connaissances Utiles, for 1843.
tables. 44 pp. London, Simpkin, Marshall, 1843
T.

5638 [READE, Philip?]   Letter to an English M.P. upon the subject of the present state of Ireland. By an Irish country gentleman.
26 pp. Dublin, Grant & Bolton, London, Nickisson, 1843
A.

5639 Remarks on the present state of the coal trade, with a retrospective glance at its history: addressed to the marquess of Londonderry, K.C.B., lord lieutenant of the county of Durham, etc., etc., etc. By anti-monopolist.
52 pp. London, Smith Elder & co., Newcastle-on-Tyne, E. and T. Bruce, 1843
T.

5640 Report of the Agricultural Seminary at Templemoyle for the year 1843.
appendix. tables. 16 pp. Londonderry, Hempton, 1843
A., U.

5641 Report of the directors of the Dublin and Drogheda Railway Company, at their eleventh general meeting, held at the company's office, 2nd March, 1843; with the engineer's reports, and statement of the accounts.
table. 24 pp. Dublin, printed by G. Folds, 1843
A.

5642 Report of the general committee of the Loyal national repeal association upon the various remedies proposed for the evils complained of under the existing system of poor laws in Ireland.
16 pp. Dublin, printed by J. Browne, 1843
N.

5643 Report of the Newtown-Barn Agricultural School, near Moate, for the year ending 5th May, 1843, with a statement of the accounts, and an appendix, containing the rules of the institution, and lists of the subscribers and pupils.
table. appendix. 12 pp. Dublin, Purdon, 1843
U.

5644 Report of the proceedings of the North Walsham farmers' club, from its commencement to the present time. 1843.
illustrations. tables. 44 pp. Norwich, Bacon, Kinnebrook, 1843
T.

5645 ROBINSON, Daniel.   Irish waste land improvement society. [1st annual report.]
appendices. tables. 30 pp. London, printed by Bentley, Wilson & Fley, 1843
D., N.

5646 ROBINSON, George Richard.   Facts versus theory: a retrospect of our past policy, with hints for future improvement.
80 pp. London, Smith, Elder & co., 1843
T.

5647 SALOMONS, Sir David, 1st bart.   Reflections on the connexion between our gold standard and the recent monetary vicissitudes; with suggestions for the addition of silver as a measure of value.
tables. 100 pp. London, Pelham Richardson, 1843
T.

5648 Sir Robert Peel and his era: being a synoptical view of the chief events and measures of his life and time.
table of contents. 288 pp. London, Cotes, 1843
A.

5649 SLEIGH, William Willcocks.   Free trade and its consequences.
appendix. 32 pp. 2nd ed. London, J. Ollivier, 1843
T.

5650 SMITH, Sydney.   Letters on American debts. First printed in the 'Morning Chronicle'.
table of contents. 22 pp. London, Longman, Brown, Green & Longmans, 1843
A.

5651 Some of the difficulties of Ireland in the way of an improving government, stated. In a letter to Sir R. Peel by a clergyman of the Archdiocese of Canterbury.
30 pp. London, J. Ollivier, 1843
A., N., T.

5652 The south of Ireland and her poor.
tables. appendix. 144 pp. London, Saunders and Otley, 1843
T.

5653 STAPLETON, Augustus G. The real monster evil of Ireland.
42 pp. London, Hatchard & co., 1843
A., N., T.

5654 ——. Sequel to the real monster evil of Ireland.
46 pp. London, Hatchard & co., 1843
A., T.

5655 Statement as to local taxation of the city of Dublin, and suggested amendments of the Municipal Act, 3rd and 4th Victoria, cap. 108, 109, presented to his excellency the earl de Grey, in pursuance of an act of assembly of the corporation of the borough of Dublin, 10th January, 1843.
24 pp. Dublin, O'Neill & Duggan, 1843
A.

5656 STAUNTON, Michael. Speech of Michael Staunton, esq., on the state of Ireland, considered especially with reference to the neglected resources of its unreclaimed lands, delivered at a meeting of the corporation of Dublin, June 20th, 1843.
28 pp. Dublin, printed by J. Browne, 1843
A., N., U.

5657 STOKER, William. An address on the present state of the poor laws, to the parliament and the Irish government.
8 pp. Dublin, printed by Downes, 1843
A.

5658 Strictures on the speech of lord Ducie, on the corn laws, delivered at the meeting held at the hall of commerce in the City of London, on Monday, May 29, 1843; in the form of a letter, addressed to the editor of the Mark Lane Express.
22 pp. London, J. Ollivier, 1843
T.

5659 Suggestions for checking the repeal agitation. Addressed to the landlords of Ireland by one of themselves.
56 pp. Dublin, R. Milliken, London, J. Ridgway, 1843
A., N., T.

5660 [TAYLOR, John.] The minister mistaken; or the question of depreciation erroneously stated by Mr. Huskisson.
tables. 40 pp. London, S. Clarke, 1843
N.

5661 Things as they are and things as they ought to be; being a report of the committee of the Cambridgeshire and Isle of Ely farmer's association.
appendices. 16 pp. London, J. Ollivier, 1843
T.

5662 Thoughts on traits of the ministerial policy. By a very quiet looker-on.
32 pp. London, William Aylott, 1843
T.

5663 TORRENS, Robert. A letter to Nassau William Senior, esq., in reply to the article, 'Free trade and retaliation' in the Edinburgh review, no. clvii.
104 pp. London, Smith, Elder & co., 1843
T.

5664 ——. A letter to the right honourable Sir Robert Peel, bart., M.P. etc. etc. etc. on the condition of England, and on the means of removing the causes of distress.
96 pp. London, Smith, Elder & co., 1843
T.

5665 ——. Postscript to a letter to the right honourable Sir Robert Peel, bart., M.P. etc. etc. etc., on the condition of England and on the means of removing the causes of distress. Second edition. [Second title page]. The budget. A series of letters on financial, commercial, and colonial policy. By a member of the political economy club. Postscript to No. IX.
56 pp. London, Smith, Elder & co., 1843
T.

5666 TOWNSEND, William R. Directions on practical agriculture for the working farmers in Ireland. Originally published in the Cork Southern Reporter under the signature of 'Agricola'.
index. 72 pp. 2d. ed. revised. Dublin, W. Curry, jr., London, Longman, Brown, Green & Longmans, 1843
A.

5667 TWISS, Travers. On money and currency. A lecture delivered before the University of Oxford, in Lent term, 1843. With an appendix on the paper money of the Chinese.
appendix. 40 pp. Oxford, J. H. Porter, London, J. Murray, 1843
T.

5668 The unemployed, and the proposed new poor-law. A letter from a Renfrewshire heritor, to the holders of real property in that county, and other manufacturing districts of Scotland.
52 pp. Glasgow, J. Smith, Edinburgh & London, W. Blackwood, 1843
T.

5669 URE, Andrew. The revenue in jeopardy, from spurious chemistry, demonstrated in researches upon wood-spirit and vinous-spirit.
36 pp. London, J. Ridgway, 1843
A., T.

5670 WARNES, John. Reasons for the cultivation of flax in Great Britain and Ireland; or, a voice for the poor. Profits of the work to be appropriated to the promotion of the cultivation of flax.
appendix. 76 pp. London, Edwards and Hughes, Norwich, Matchett, Stevenson, & Matchett, 1843
T.

5671 WATSON, James. Remarks on the opening of the British trade with China, and the means of its extension. Being the substance of a paper read to the Literary and commercial society of Glasgow.
tables. 24 pp. Glasgow, J. Smith, Edinburgh & London, W. Blackwood, 1843
T.

5672 WEST, J. An agricultural tract for the times. The question, 'What can be done for British agriculture?' proposed a second time, with an attempt at an answer, in a letter to the landowners of Great Britain.
36 pp. Newark, J. Perfect, London, Longman, Brown, Green & Longmans, 1843
T.

5673 WILLIAMS, Albert. The law, or the league? Which? A letter to Robert Palmer, esq., M.P.
40 pp. London, J. Ollivier, 1843
T.

i.e., the Anti-corn law league.

1844

5674 [ABBOTT, Joseph.] The emigrant to North America, from memoranda of a settler in Canada. Being a compendium of useful practical hints to emigrants, with an account of every day's doings upon a farm for a year. By an emigrant farmer of twenty years' experience.
tables in appendix. 128 pp. Edinburgh & London, William Blackwood, 1844
T.

5675 Abstracts of the accounts of the South Dublin Union.
tables. 28 pp. Dublin, A. Thom, 1844
A.
Covers 25th March, 1842–25th March, 1844.

5676 The administration of the post office, from the introduction of Mr. Rowland Hill's plan of penny postage up to the present time, grounded on parliamentary documents, and the evidence taken before the select committee on postage at the conclusion of the last session of parliament. To which are added the last returns to the house of commons.
tables. 220 pp. London, J. Hatchard, 1844
T.

5677 ALISON, William Pulteney. Remarks on the report of her majesty's commissioners on the poor laws of Scotland, presented to parliament in 1844, and on the dissent of Mr. Twisleton from that report.
tables. 312 pp. Edinburgh and London, W. Blackwood, 1844
T.

5678 ALMACK, John. Printed for the agricultural protection society. Cheap bread and low wages. Extracted from a pamphlet, by John Almack, jun.
16 pp. London, J. Ollivier, 1844
T.

5679 ANKETEL, William Robert. The conduct of the resident landlords of Ireland contrasted with that of the absentees, and taxation as a remedy for absenteeism, demonstrated to be necessary, just and constitutional.
tables. 44 pp. London, J. Hatchard, 1844
T.

5680 Annual report and transactions of the Royal agricultural improvement society of Ireland. For the year 1843.
tables. folding plans. 160 pp. Dublin, A. Thom, 1844
T.

5681 BARRINGTON, Sir Mathew, bart. Letter of Matthew Barrington, esq. to the right hon. Sir Robert Peel, bart.
32 pp. Dublin, 1844
A.
Suggests system of land purchase.

5682 BAYLEY, George. Tables shewing the progress of the shipping interest of the British Empire, United States, and France compiled from parliamentary papers and other sources.
tables. 86 pp. London, Smith Elder & co., 1844
T.

5683 [BEAMISH, N. Ludlow.] Visit to the Gleneask estate of the Irish waste land improvement society, by a proprietor. With report and analysis by Professor Kane, M.D., M.R.I.A. By N.L.B.
28 pp. Cork, Purcell, 1844
A., N.

5684 BLACKER, William. The evils inseparable from a mixed currency, and the advantages to be secured by introducing an inconvertible national paper circulation, throughout the British Empire and its dependencies under proper regulations.
table of contents. tables. appendix. 138 pp. 2d. ed. London, Pelham Richardson, 1844
A., T.

5685 BRAY, Charles. An essay upon the union of agriculture and manufactures, and upon the organization of industry.
tables. 114 pp. London, Longman, Brown, Green, and Longmans, 1844
T.

5686 Canals and railways.
tables. 4 pp. London, printed by Stevens, [c. 1844]
A.

5687 CANNON, William J. The effect the repeal of the corn laws would have upon prices and rents, briefly considered by William J. Cannon.
8 pp. London, Effingham Wilson, [1844]
T.

5688 CAYLEY, Edward Stillingfleet. Reasons for the formation of the Agricultural protection society, addressed to the industrious classes of the United Kingdom.
table. 24 pp. London, J. Ollivier, 1844
T.

5689 CHARNOCK, John Henry. On thorough-draining; and its immediate results to the agricultural interest, as well as its probable effects on the general condition of the people. Being a paper read before the Wakefield farmers' club, January 5, 1844. Second edition.
illustration. 26 pp. London, Longman, Brown, Green & Longmans, 1844
T.

5690 CLAY, Sir William, bart. Remarks on the expediency of restricting the issue of promissory notes to a single issuing body.
92 pp. London, J. Ridgway, 1844
T.

5691 The constitutional rights of landlords; the evils springing from the abuse of them in Ireland; and the origin and effects of banks, of funds and of corn laws, considered.
48 pp. Dublin, 1844
T.

5692 Corn-laws defended; or, agriculture our first interest, and the main-stay of trade and commerce. A letter addressed to the Anti-corn-law league; demonstrating the dependence of trade upon agriculture, and the reciprocal agency of these great interests, and proving, by sober argument, the wild proceedings of the league to be founded upon false and selfish views, destructive, if realized, of the general welfare, and by consequence, fatal to their own. By Britannicus.
tables. 30 pp. Leeds, T. Harrison, [c. 1844]
T.

5693 DAUBENY, Charles. A lecture on institutions for the better education of the farming classes, especially with reference to the proposed Agricultural College near Cirencester, with some remarks on experimental farms, and on the class of inquiries for which they are more particularly designed. Delivered at the Botanic Garden, Oxford, on Tuesday, May 14th, 1844.
tables. 32 pp. Oxford, printed by Combe, 1844
N., T.

5694 D'AUBREE, Paul. Colonists and manufacturers in the West Indies.
plans. diags. 104 pp. London, J. Bain, 1844
T.

5695 DAVIS, Hewitt. The resources farmers possess for meeting the reduced prices of their produce.
46 pp. London, F. Walker, 1844
T.

5696 DAY, George Game. Defeat of the Anti-corn law league in Huntingdonshire. The speech of Mr. George Game Day on that occasion, at Huntingdon, June 17, 1843 (published by request) with notes and additions.
tables. 40 pp. 12th ed. London, J. Ollivier, 1844
A.

5697 DAY, William. Correspondence with the poor law commissioners, with observations on the working of certain points of the poor law, and on Sir James Graham's proposed alteration in the law of settlement.
52 pp. London, Longman, Brown, Green, and Longmans, Shrewsbury, John Davies, 1844
T.

5698 Deed of agreement of the liberal annuity company of Dublin, established in the year 1780. With a copious index containing all the rules of the company.
table of contents. tables. index. 76 pp. Dublin, printed by Chambers, 1844
A. N.

5699 Delusions and fallacies in the bill brought into the house of commons for the renewal of the charter of the Bank, and in the statements and arguments in support of it. By the author of 'An attempt to give a popular explanation of the theory of money'.
tables. 60 pp. London, Pelham Richardson, J. Ollivier, 1844
T.

5700 DICKSON, Stephen Fox. The rights of the licensed victuallers of Ireland to receive and hold, (and to enforce by action if refused) licenses for the sale of tea, concurrently with their licenses for selling spirits by retail to be consumed on one and the same premises (where tea may be sold) in common with their fellow traders of England and Scotland: vindicated and established by the opinion of eminent counsel. Respectfully addressed to the traders of Ireland etc. etc. etc.
appendix. 8 pp. Dublin, printed by P. W. Brady, 1844
N.

5701 EDWARDS, D. O. The National Diet Roll; or, an improved method of insuring to the lower ranks of the people a due supply of food, in a letter to Luke Thomas Flood esq.
tables. 32 pp. London, Miland, Miller, 1844
N.

5702 Emancipation of Industry. By M.M.
8 pp. London, printed by Wertheimer, 1844
A.

5703 England and Ireland. A political cartoon.
74 pp. London, J. Ridgway, 1844
T.

5704 ENSOR, George. Of property and of its equal distribution as promoting virtue, population, abundance.
188 pp. London, Effingham Wilson, 1844.
RM.

5705 FARREN, Edwin James. Historical essay on the rise and early progress of the doctrine of life contingencies in England, leading to the establishment of the first life-assurance society in which ages were distinguished.
tables. 94 pp. London, Smith, Elder & co., 1844
T.

5706 First report of the committee of the Loyal national repeal association on the glass duties.
tables. appendix. 16 pp. Dublin, printed by J. Browne, 1844
A., N.

5707 First report of the sub-committee of the Loyal national repeal association entitled 'Commercial tariffs and regulations of the several states of Europe and America'.
tables. appendix. 34 pp. Dublin, printed by J. Browne, 1844
A.

5708 First report of the sub-committee of the Loyal national repeal association on the estimates for 1844–5.
tables. 42 pp. Dublin, printed by J. Browne, 1844
A., N.

5709 FITZPATRICK, Thomas. Outline of a plan of an Irish parliament, with remarks, addressed chiefly to Englishmen; in which their objections to separate legislation are met & combated.
40 pp. Dublin, J. Duffy, 1844
B., M., N.

5710 FLETCHER, Walter. Letter on free trade, addressed to the right hon. lord John Russell, M.P.
tables. 32 pp. 4th ed. Liverpool, Joshua Walmsley, 1844
T.

5711 The fourth annual report and transactions of the Society for the promotion and improvement of the growth of flax in Ireland.
appendices. 72 pp. Belfast, printed by F. D. Finlay, 1844
A., N.

5712 GALE, Charles James. A letter to the right hon. the earl of Dalhousie, president of the board of trade, on railway legislation.
32 pp. London, J. Murray, 1844
T.

5713 [GALT, William.] Railway reform; its expediency and practicability considered. People's edition, printed textually from the third edition; the appendix only being omitted.
tables. 80 pp. London, Pelham Richardson, 1844
T.

5714 [——.] Railway reform; its expediency and practicability considered. With a copious appendix containing a description of all the railways in Great Britain and Ireland; fluctuations in the prices of shares; statistical and parliamentary returns; financial calculations, extracts from writers on political economy.
table of contents. tables. appendix. 120 pp. 3d. ed. London, Pelham Richardson, 1844
A.

5715 A general priced catalogue of implements, seeds, plants etc. sold by W. Drummond & Sons, seedsmen and nurserymen, agricultural museum, Stirling & Dublin.
22 pp. n.p. 1844
A., D.

5716 Grand canal atmospheric railway company.
4 pp. Dublin, 1844
A.

A prospectus.

5717 Grand canal company, Ireland: In parliament. Dublin and Cashel Railway; and Grand canal company, (Ireland). Statement on behalf of the Grand Canal Company.
map. 14 pp. Dublin?, Whitaker, 1844
A., N.

5718 GRANT, John. A few remarks on the large hedges and small enclosures of Devonshire, and the adjoining counties.
table. 16 pp. Exeter, W. Roberts, 1844
T.

5719 HAGEN, Karl Heinrich. System of political economy. By Charles Henry Hagen. Translated from the German by John Prince Smith.
96 pp. London, Longman, Brown, Green and Longmans, [1844]
T.

5720 The hand book to the Dublin and Drogheda railway.
tables. map. plate. 88 pp. Dublin, Walsh, 1844
A.

5721 HEAD, George Head. Protection to British industry. The speech of George Head Head, esq. of Rickerby House, at a public meeting held in Carlisle, on Saturday, the 3rd February, 1844, for the formation of the East Cumberland Agricultural protection society. Second edition, with notes. [Taken in short-hand.]
tables. 24 pp. London, J. Ollivier, 1844
T.

5722 HILL, James. The farmers and the anti-league: in answer to 'Mr. Day's second speech', published under the title of 'The farmers and the league'.
tables. 58 pp. London, Effingham Wilson, 1844
T.

5723 HILL, Sir Rowland. The state and prospects of penny postage, as developed in the evidence taken before the postage commission of 1843: with incidental remarks on the testimony of the post-office authorities; and an appendix of correspondence.
table of contents. appendices. 88 pp. London, C. Knight, 1844
N., T.

5724 Is the strong heart of England broken that she does not rise? being a few words upon the want of high principle exhibited by the public men of the present day; and some remarks upon the tergiversation of the periodical press.
42 pp. London, J. Ridgway, 1844
B.

5725 JAMES, Sir Walter, bart. The poor of London. A letter to the lord bishop of the diocese.
78 pp. London, W. H. Dalton, 1844
T.

5726 JOPLIN, Thomas. Currency reform: improvement not depreciation.
tables. 96 pp. London, Richardson, 1844
T.

5727 ——. An examination of Sir Robert Peel's currency bill of 1844, in a letter to the bankers of the United Kingdom, proposing arrangements for their adoption, to prevent the evils in which it will otherwise involve the country.
tables. appendices. 98 pp. London, Pelham Richardson, 1844
T.

5728 Kane's 'Industrial resources of Ireland'.
table. 24 pp. Dublin, William Curry, jr., 1844
T.

5729 KELLY, William. An essay on the general management of villa farms, the manures attainable and applicable to such farms, also a mode of cultivating two acres of ground whereby eight cows can be fed throughout the year, with some remarks on the management of small farms in general.
plans. 80 pp. Dublin, J. Porter, 1844
A.

5730 KENT, James Henry. Remarks on the injuriousness of the consolidation of small farms, and the benefit of small occupations and allotments; with some observations on the past and present state of the agricultural labourers: in two letters, inscribed, by permission, to his grace the duke of Grafton.
tables. 92 pp. Bury St. Edmund's, Gedge & Barker, London, J. Ridgway, [1844]

5731 KERR, R. Building societies, their advantages: a refutation of the attacks made upon them, an explanation of their rules, and the acts of parliament on which they are founded; with tables of calculations, shewing the working and duration of the same.
tables. appendices. 104 pp. London, G. and J. Watson, 1844
T.

5732 LAING, Samuel. Atlas prize essay. National distress; its causes and remedies.
178 pp. London, Longman, Green, Brown, and Longmans [etc., etc.], 1844

T.

5733 LAIRD, Macgregor. The effect of an alteration in the sugar duties on the condition of the people of England and the negro race considered.
tables. tables in appendices. 92 pp. 3rd ed. London, Effingham Wilson, 1844

T.

5734 LAWSON, James Anthony. Five lectures on political economy; delivered before the university of Dublin in Michaelmas term, 1843.
appendix. 160 pp. London, John W. Parker, Dublin, Andrew Milliken, 1844

T.

5735 The league and the beleagued. A free discussion of the points at issue.
56 pp. London, J. Hatchard, 1844

T.

5736 A letter from a crow to Mr. Cobden. Translated from the original by a Northamptonshire squire.
10 pp. London, J. Ollivier, 1844

T.

5737 Letter to the members of both houses of parliament, on the Bank Charter, and the evil consequences resulting from the fluctuations of paper money; with a remedy to prevent future evils, of the same sort, by redeeming the prerogative of the crown, so unjustly *pawned* by William the Third. By A. R. R. Second edition, with additional statistical information.
tables. 20 pp. London, Effingham Wilson, [1844]

T.

5738 A letter to right hon. W. E. Gladstone, M.P. President of the board of trade, on railway legislation.
tables. 60 pp. London, G. W. Nickisson, 1844

T.

5739 Letter to the right honourable Sir Robert Peel, bart. on free trade and finance. By a member of the Middle Temple.
28 pp. London, J. Hatchard, 1844

T.

5740 A letter to the rt. hon. Thomas B. C. Smith, M.P. H.M. attorney-general for Ireland, suggesting the propriety of extending to Ireland the several reforms recently adopted in England, particularly in the courts of common law and bankruptcy. By a solicitor.
48 pp. Dublin, printed by Leckie, 1844

A., N., U.

5741 LOYD, Samuel Jones, afterwards 1st baron OVERSTONE. Thoughts on the separation of the departments of the Bank of England.
tables. 56 pp. London, Pelham Richardson, 1844

T.

5742 MACDONNELL, R. P. The social and political condition of Ireland from the year 1782, when its parliament became independent of the British Legislature, until the legislative union in 1800, and the results to be anticipated from its repeal, examined in a letter addressed to Daniel O'Connell.
60 pp. Dublin, W. Curry, jr., London, Longman, Brown, Green and Longmans, 1844

A.

5743 MACNEILL, Sir John. Report on a proposed line of railway from Dublin to Cashel being the first division of a main trunk to the South and South-West of Ireland, including a branch therefrom to Athy and Carlow.
map. tables. 16 pp. Dublin, printed by A. Thom, 1844

N.

5744 The ministry and the sugar duties.
tables. 50 pp. London, J. Murray, 1844

T.

5745 NAPER, James Lenox William. Suggestions for the more scientific and general employment of agricultural labourers, together with a plan which would enable the landlords of Ireland to afford them suitable houses and gardens, with applotments, at a fair rent, being observations on chapter X. of Dr. Kane's 'Industrial resources of Ireland'.
table. 24 pp. Dublin, W. Curry, jr., 1844

T.

5746 NEWNHAM, Henry. Agriculture; its practice with profit, elucidated by a contrast of Oriental & British usages: in a correspondence with the Royal agricultural society of England. Second edition, with notes and additions.
52 pp. 2nd ed. London, Roake & Varty, 1844

T.

5747 O'CONNELL, John. Speech of J. O'Connell, M.P. suggesting outlines of fiscal arrangements between Great Britain and Ireland after repeal.
36 pp. Dublin, printed by J. Browne, 1844

A., N.

5748 O'NEILL, John A. Ireland's case, disease and remedy, respectfully stated to the people, the legislature and the aristocracy of the British Empire.
72 pp. Dublin, J. Duffy, London, Strange, 1844

A., D.

5749 OSBORNE, Sidney Godolphin. A view of the low moral & physical condition of the agricultural labourer.
tables. 30 pp. London, T. & W. Boone, 1844

T.

5750 Poor rates reduced by self-supporting reading, writing, and agricultural schools. From Johnson and Shaw's 'Farmers' almanack' for 1844.
illustrations. 10 pp. London, J. Ridgway, 1844

N.

5751 PORTER, John Grey V. Ireland. The union of 1801, 41 Geo. III., Cap. 47, (all on one side), does and always will draw away from Ireland her men of skill, genius, capital, and rank; all who raise, strengthen and distinguish a nation. A federal (the only fair) union between Great Britain and Ireland

inevitable, and most desirable for both islands. Lord John Russell and the Whigs better conservatives than Sir Robert Peel & the tories.
2nd ed. 72 pp. London, Ridgway & Fisher, Dublin, Keene, [1844?]

A., D., L., M., N., T.

5752 PRINSEP, Henry Thoby.   Notions on the corn-laws and customs' duties.
64 pp. 2nd ed. London, Wm. H. Allen, 1844

T.

5753 PRITCHARD, Andrew.   English patents; being a register of all those granted for inventions in the arts, manufactures, chemistry, agriculture, etc. in the year 1843: with a copious index.
appendix. 74 pp. London, Whittaker, 1844

T.

5754 Proceedings of the special general meeting of the shareholders of the Agricultural and Commercial Bank of Ireland. 12th September, 1844.
18 pp. Dublin, printed by Webb & Chapman, 1844

A.

5755 Prospectus of the North and North-Western railway, as proposed by the government railway commissioners, namely, from Dublin to Armagh, and from Dublin to Enniskillen.
4 pp. Dublin, 1844

A.

5756 RASHLEIGH, William.   Stubborn facts from the factories, by a Manchester operative. Published and dedicated to the working classes by Wm. Rashleigh, esq., M.P.
tables. 88 pp. London, J. Ollivier, 1844

T.

5757 READE, Philip.   Whig and Tory remedies for Irish evils, and the effect a repeal of the corn laws would have on the legislative union, considered in a letter to the right honorable lord Eliot, M.P.
54 pp. Dublin, Grant & Bolton, London, G. Nickisson, 1844

A., N., T.

5758 Reasons against legislative interference with the present system of circulation, submitted to Sir Robert Peel, bart., by the committee of private country bankers.
24 pp. London, J. Ollivier, 1844

T.

5759 Reasons for dissent from the scheme of reduction of interest on the three-and-a-half per cents. as proposed by government; and for assent to such reduction only upon an equitable principle.
tables. 28 pp. London, Pelham Richardson, 1844

T.

5760 Reciprocity. By a manufacturer.
tables. 74 pp. Leeds, Baines and Newsome, London, Simpkin, Marshall, [1844?]

T.

5761 Remarks by a junior to his senior, on an article in the Edinburgh review of January 1844, on the state of Ireland, and the measures for its improvement.
84 pp. London, J. Ridgway, 1844

M., T.

5762 Remarks by the public journals, on the advantages and distinguishing features of the Medical, Invalid, and General life assurance society, 25, Pall Mall, London.
16 pp. London, printed by Collis, 1844

N.

5763 Report (as taken by Messrs. W. B. Gurney and Sons) of an extraordinary meeting of the shareholders of the North American colonial association of Ireland, held at the company's office, Broad Street Buildings, on Thursday the 23rd May, 1844
120 pp. London, printed by G. McKewan, [1844]

U.

5764 Report of the committee of the Loyal national repeal association appointed to inquire into the state of 'joint stock banking in Ireland', particularly as regards the effects of the Bank of Ireland monopoly, upon the general prosperity of Ireland.
20 pp. Dublin, printed by J. Browne, 1844

A., N.

5765 Report of the committee of the Loyal national repeal association on the Commissariat accounts.
tables. 8 pp. [pag. 119–126.] Dublin, printed by J. Browne, 1844

A., N.

5766 Report of the committee of the Loyal national repeal association on the industrial resources of Ireland; founded on Dr. Kane's treatise on that subject.
tables. appendix. 70 pp. Dublin, printed by J. Browne, 1844

A., N.

5767 Report of the committee of the Loyal national repeal association upon the commissioners' report on the ordnance memoir of Ireland.
8 pp. Dublin, printed by J. Browne, 1844

A., N.

5768 Report of the parliamentary committee of the Loyal national repeal association on the army estimates for 1844–5.
tables. 68 pp. [pag. 43–110.] Dublin, printed by J. Browne, 1844

A., N.

5769 Report of the parliamentary committee of the Loyal national repeal association on the navy estimates for 1844–5.
tables. 20 pp. [pag. 151–170.] Dublin, printed by J. Browne, 1844

A., N.

5770 Report of the parliamentary committee of the Loyal national repeal association on the ordnance estimates for 1844–5.
tables. 24 pp. [pag. 127–150.] Dublin, printed by J. Browne, 1844

A., N.

5771 Report of the proceedings of a meeting of paper manufacturers, relative to obtaining relief from the excise duties, held at the London coffee house, on 19th of December, 1844.
16 pp. London, Longman, Brown, Green & Longmans, 1844
N.

5772 Report of a sub-committee to whom it was referred to enquire and report upon the removal of Irish poor from England. Read at a meeting of the Loyal national repeal association.
8 pp. Dublin, printed by J. Browne, 1844
A.

5773 Report of a sub-committee to which was referred the subject of the fiscal relations between Great Britain and Ireland, read at a meeting of the Loyal national repeal association.
4 pp. Dublin, printed by J. Browne, 1844
A., N.

5774 Report of the sub-committee of the Loyal national repeal association on the Irish fisheries.
appendices with tables. 34 pp. Dublin, printed by J. Browne, 1844
A., N.

5775 ROBINSON, Daniel. Irish waste land improvement society. The second annual report of the system pursued in the management of the Irish waste land improvement society's estates in Ireland, during the year 1843; with an estimate of their present position and future prospects.
tables. appendix. 24 pp. London, Bentley, Wilson and Fley, [1844]
N., U.

5776 Rules and regulations of the Dublin mercantile guardian association for the protection of trade.
8 pp. Dublin, printed by Goodwin, 1844
A.

5777 SALMON, John C. Assessing cottages to the poor rates. On the justice and fairness of assessing cottages to the poor rates; the unfairness and injustice of making excused lists; and the oppressiveness and impracticability of collecting the assessments from the cottage tenants. Shewing the propriety and necessity of a legislative enactment, authorising the rating of the proprietors, and to empower thr (sic) parish officers to enforce payment of the rates from them.
16 pp. London, C. Knight, [1844]
T.

5778 SHREWSBURY, John Talbot, 19th earl of. Hints towards the pacification of Ireland: addressed, more particularly, to the ruling powers of the day. By John, earl of Shrewsbury.
94 pp. London, C. Dolman, 1844
D.

——. 2nd ed., revised, corrected and enlarged. 118 p. London, C. Dolman, 1844
A.

5779 SIMPSON, W. W. A defence of the landlords of Ireland, with remarks on the relation between landlord and tenant.
appendix. 30 pp. London, J. Ollivier, Dublin, S. J. Machen, 1844
T.

5780 ——. A defence of the landlords of Ireland, with remarks on the relation between landlord and tenant. Second edition with a postscript, containing an extract from a speech delivered on the 7th Nov. by the rt. hon. the earl of Devon referring to the condition of Ireland.
appendix. 40 pp. Dublin, S. J. Machen, London, J. Ollivier, 1844
D., N.

5781 SMITH, John. Currency. Money the moral power of exchange. A lesson for young England.
76 pp. London, Pelham Richardson, 1844
T.

5782 SMYTH, George Lewis. Ireland historical and statistical. Part I.
116 pp. London, Whittaker, 1844
A.
'To be published in eight parts'. The complete work was published in three volumes, 1844–49.

5783 SOPWITH, Thomas. The national importance of preserving mining records.
60 pp. London, J. Weale, Newcastle-on-Tyne, Finlay and Charlton, 1844
T.

5784 STERNE, William. Landlord and tenant in Ireland.
appendix. plan. 46 pp. Enniskillen, Erne packet office, 1844
A.

5785 STOURTON, William Joseph Stourton, 18th baron. Some remarks on the social relations of Great Britain and Ireland at the present day, by the right hon. lord Stourton.
22 pp. (pagination irregular.) London, C. Dolman, 1844
T.

5786 SWAINE, Edward. Law and conscience: or the duty of dissenters on church taxes. Remarks opposed to recent advice in the Eclectic Review, in an article entitled 'Sir Robert Peel'.
20 pp. London, Snow, 1844
T.

5787 SWEET, George. The Statute 7 and 8 Vict. cap. 76 intitled an act to simplify the transfer of property with a commentary and forms.
32 pp. London, S. Sweet, Dublin, Hodges and Smith, 1844
U.

5788 A system, proposed and recommended for the better management and improvement of landed estates, in Liverpool and its neighbourhood.
22 pp. Liverpool, printed by D. Marples, 1844
T.

5789 TALBOT, James Beard. The miseries of prostitution.
tables. 84 pp. London, James Madden, 1844
T.

5790 [TAYLOR, John.] Currency fallacies refuted and paper money vindicated, by the author of 'An essay on money', and 'An essay on the standard and measure of value'.
table of contents. tables. appendix. 84 pp. 2d. ed. London, S. Clarke, 1844

A.

5791 TAYLOR, William Cooke. Factories and the factory system; from parliamentary documents and personal examination.
table of contents. tables. 126 pp. London, J. How, 1844

N., T.

5792 TOOKE, Thomas. An enquiry into the currency principle; the connection of the currency with prices, and the expediency of a separation of issue from banking.
appendix. 154 pp. London, Longman, Brown, Green & Longmans, 1844

A.

——. 172 pp. 2nd ed. London, Longman, Brown, Green and Longmans, 1844

N., T.

5793 TORRENS, Robert. The Budget. On commercial and colonial policy with an introduction, in which the deductive method, as presented in Mr. Mill's system of logic, is applied to the solution of some controverted questions in political economy.
52 pp. London, Smith Elder & co., 1844

T.

5794 ——. Reply to the objections of the Westminster Review to the government plan for the regulation of the currency.
tables. 40 pp. London, Smith, Elder & co., 1844

T.

5795 Transactions of the Royal agricultural improvement society of Ireland, with the report of the council for the year 1843.
table of contents. plate. tables. maps. 152 pp. Dublin, W. Curry, 1844

A., D.

5796 Twelfth report of the directors of the New Zealand Company presented to an adjourned special court of proprietors held on the 26th April, 1844.
38 pp. London, printed by Palmer & Clayton, 1844

N.

5797 Twenty-sixth annual report of the managing committee of the Association for the suppression of mendicity in Dublin. For the year 1843.
tables. appendices. 32 pp. Dublin, printed by Dowling and Shea, 1844

A.

5798 Two letters to the right hon. Sir R. Peel, bart., M.P. &c., &c., &c., on his proposed banking measures. By an ex-M.P.
table. 34 pp. London, J. Hatchard, 1844

T.

5799 VERNEY, Sir Harry, bart. A letter to the farmers of Buckinghamshire.
16 pp. London, J. Ridgway, [1844]

T.

5800 The voice of the nation. A manual of nationality.
100 pp. Dublin, J. Duffy, 1844

B.

5801 WALSH, J. An epitome of the grievances of Ireland, emanating, indisputably, from a griping landed aristocracy, sustained by a hostile alien parliament.
34 pp. Dublin, the author, [1844?]

A.

5802 Waterford and Limerick railway, connecting the two important rivers of the Shannon and Suir, and passing through one of the richest districts of Ireland.
4 pp. Waterford, printed by Harvey, 1844

A.

5803 What is to be done? or past, present, and future.
tables. 128 pp. 3rd ed. London, J. Ridgway, 1844

T.

Attack on the policies of Sir Robert Peel.

5804 What is to be done with the Irish church?
tables. 18 pp. London, J. Ridgway, 1844

T.

5805 WHEELWRIGHT, William. Observations on the Isthmus of Panama; as comprised in a paper read at a meeting of the Royal Geographical Society on 12th February, 1844, illustrated with a map of the various routes which have been proposed for connecting the two oceans.
map. 32 pp. London, J. Weale, 1844

A.

5806 WIGGINS, John. The 'monster' misery of Ireland; a practical treatise on the relation of landlord and tenant, with suggestions for legislative measures, and the management of landed property.
table of contents. 304 pp. London, S. & J. Bentley, 1844

A.

5807 WILLIAMS, Albert. Great facts concerning free trade and free trade essays.
30 pp. London, J. Ollivier, 1844

T.

5808 WILSON, Robert. Outlines of a plan for adapting the machinery of the public funds to the transfer of real property. Respectfully inscribed to the president and council of the society for promoting the amendment of the law.
appendix. 70 pp. London, Thomas Blenkarn, 1844

T.

5809 WOOLLGAR, J. W. Friendly societies' security. An essay on testing the condition of a Friendly Society, by valuation of all policies at annual or other short periods, without resorting to a professional actuary. Also, observations on the rates of contribution, and an entirely new series of elementary calculations applicable thereto; with other practical points connected with such societies.
tables. 32 pp. Lewes, R. W. Lower, 1844

T.

5810 Wyse, Francis. Federalism. Its inapplicability to the wants and necessities of the country; its assumed impracticability considered with remarks and observations on the rise and progress of the present repeal movement in Ireland; in reply to J. G. V. Porter, esq.
44 pp. Dublin, Keene, London, Fisher, 1844
A., D., N., T., U.

1845

5811 Alloway, Robert M. Peat coal versus pit coal.
16 pp. Dublin, Oldham, 1845
N., T.

5812 America and her slave-system.
appendix. 104 pp. London, Simpkin, Marshall, 1845
T.

5813 Andrews, Henry George. An address to the farmers of Great Britain, on the present state of the corn laws, and the necessity of agricultural protection.
tables. 40 pp. London, J. Ollivier, 1845
T.

5814 Barker, Charles Fiott. Memoir on Syria: Designed to illustrate the condition of that country before and subsequent to the evacuation of the Egyptian army, and its position under the Ottoman yoke. To which are added, remarks on its produce and resources, its climate and capabilities, the cultivation of silk, the purchase and tenure of land and the working of the old and new tariff. Being the result of personal observations made during a residence of seventeen years in the Levant.
tables. appendix. 56 pp. London, Madden and Malcolm, [1845]
T.

5815 Barry, Michael Joseph. Ireland, as she was, as she is, and as she shall be.
120 pp. Dublin, James Duffy, 1845. [First prize repeal essay.]
A., B., D., S.

5816 Baths and wash-houses for the labouring classes. Statement of the preliminary measures adopted for the purpose of promoting the establishment of baths and wash-houses for the labouring classes, including a report of the proceedings at a public meeting held in the Mansion House, Wednesday October 16th, 1844, the right hon. the lord mayor in the chair; with lists of the committees, officers and contributors.
48 pp. London, printed by Blades and East, 1845
A., N.

5817 Blacker, William. An essay on the improvement to be made in the cultivation of small farms by the introduction of green crops, and house-feeding the stock thereon: originally published in an address to the small farmers on the estates of the earl of Gosford and Colonel Close, in the county of Armagh. With a preface, addressed to landlords giving full information to those who may be inclined to adopt the plan recommended, as to the best mode of introducing it, and the results attending its introduction, together with the expenses likely to be incurred thereby.
124 pp. Dublin, W. Curry [etc.], 1845
A., B.

5818 [Bramly, T. J.] Loans by private individuals of Great Britain to foreign states, shewn to be entitled to protection, or indemnity, by the principles on which states are founded, laid down by public jurists, and by the law of the land.
appendix. 120 pp. London, J. Ridgway, 1845
T.

5819 Brodigan, Thomas. Statement of special services rendered to the Dublin and Drogheda Railway Company by Thomas Brodigan. Addressed to the directors.
42 pp. Dublin, printed by Walsh, 1845
A.

5820 Brodribb, Edward. A letter to the right hon. Sir Robert Peel, bart., first lord of her majesty's treasury, etc., on the tea duties. By a member of the Liverpool East India and China association.
30 pp. Liverpool, Webb, London, Simpkin, Marshall, 1845
A.

5821 ——. Abstract of a letter to the right hon. Sir Robert Peel, bart., first lord of her majesty's treasury, etc., on the tea duties.
14 pp. Liverpool, T. Baines, 1845
N.

5822 Bushe, Gervase Parker. Some considerations on the income tax.
tables. 36 pp. London, J. Ridgway, 1845
N., T.

5823 Cargill, William. The currency, showing how a fixed gold standard places England in permanent disadvantage in respect to other countries, and produces periodical domestic convulsions.
60 pp. London, J. Ollivier, 1845
T.

5824 Cavour, count Emille de. Considerations on the present state and future prospects of Ireland. Translated from the French, by a friend to Ireland.
142 pp. London, Longman, Brown, Green and Longmans, 1845
T.

5825 Claxton, Christopher. A description of the Great Britain steamship, built at Bristol, for the proprietors of the Great Western Steamship Company, with remarks on the comparative merits of wood and iron as materials for shipbuilding and reports of her experimental trips and voyage round to London.
plate. tables. plans. 16 pp. 4th ed. Bristol, printed by Taylor, 1845
N.

——. 16 pp. 5th ed. Bristol, printed by Taylor, 1845
A., T.

5826 Cochrane, George. On the employment of the poor in Great Britain and Ireland.
16 pp. London, J. Hatchard, 1845
A., T.

5827 The currency question.
14 pp. 2nd ed. London, J. Ridgway, 1845
N.

5828 The currency theory reviewed in a letter to the Scottish people on the menaced interference by government with the existing system of banking in Scotland. By a Banker in England.
appendix. 80 pp. Edinburgh, W. Tait [etc., etc.], 1845
A., T.

5829 DAVENPORT, Edward Davies. How to improve the condition of the labouring classes.
30 pp. London, J. Ridgway, 1845
T.

5830 DAWSON, Edward. First letter to the tradesmen and labourers of Ireland on the repeal of the union, etc. containing an account of the rise and decline of the trade and manufactures of this country.
tables. 70 pp. Dublin, printed by Daly, 1845
A., N.

5831 DORAN, Larry. Five letters on the Irish railways, projected in 1844, and to be produced to parliament in 1845. Addressed to the right honourable the earl of Dalhousie, vice-president of the board of trade.
map. 28 pp. London, Pelham Richardson, Dublin, Walsh, 1845
A., E., T.

5832 Dublin and Drogheda Railway. Report of the directors and of the engineer-in-chief; statement of the accounts, and list of share-holders; published preparatory to the half-yearly meeting to be held on the 5th March, 1845.
map. tables. 26 pp. Dublin, printed by Walsh, 1845
A.

5833 Dublin and Liverpool Steam-Ship Company (provisionally registered).
4 pp. Dublin, 1845
A.

Company prospectus.

5834 FARRELL, Isaac. The Archimedean Railway. A letter to Peter Purcell, esq., chairman of the Great Southern and Western Railway.
diagrams. 10 pp. Dublin, 1845
A.

5835 First general report of the trade and commerce committee of the Loyal national repeal association. Second report.
12 pp. (2 pamphlets.) Dublin, printed by J. Browne, 1845
A., N.

5836 First report of the parliamentary committee of the Loyal national repeal association on the land question, with appendix of evidence on the Ulster tenant-right. Read at a meeting of the association on Monday 14th April, 1845. (Signed by Daniel O'Connell.)
6 pp. (paginated 295–299.) no title page, [1845]
A., N., T.

For Appendix, see 5884.

5837 FITZPATRICK, Richard William. Railway rights and liabilities arising before an act of incorporation is obtained.
28 pp. London, Thomas Blenkarn, 1845
T.

5838 FORD, William. A letter addressed to the resident landed proprietors, merchants, farmers, mill owners, shop-keepers, mechanics and labourers of the county of Meath, on the important subject of railway communication between the county of Meath and the city of Dublin.
26 pp. Dublin, A. Thom, 1845
A.

See 6002.

5839 FORTESCUE, T. Knox. General remarks on steam communication, with reference to the United Kingdom as the centre.
20 pp. Dublin, S. J. Machen, 1845
A., N.

5840 GEALE, Hamilton. Ireland and Irish questions.
appendix. 94 pp. 2d. ed. London, J. Hatchard, 1845
A., N.

5841 GILBART, James William. The London bankers. An analysis of the returns made to the commissioners of stamps and taxes, by the private and joint stock banks of London in January, 1845, pursuant to the act 7 & 8 Victoria, C. 32.
16 pp. London, Smith, Elder & co., 1845
T.

5842 GIRDLESTONE, Charles. Letters on the unhealthy condition of the lower class of dwellings, especially in large towns. Founded on the first report of the health of towns commission. With notices of other documents on the subject, and an appendix, containing plans and tables from the report (inserted by permission).
illustrations. tables. appendix. 104 pp. London, Longman, Brown, Green, and Longmans, 1845
T.

5843 GLADSTONE, William Ewart. Remarks upon recent commercial legislation suggested by the expository statement of the revenue from customs and other papers lately submitted to parliament.
table of contents. tables. 66 pp. London, J. Murray, 1845
T.

——. 3rd ed. 66 pp. London, J. Murray, 1845
A.

5844 The Glasgow and Belfast Union Railway, connecting Edinburgh and Glasgow with Belfast and Dublin.
prospectus. (1 large folding sheet, including map.) Dublin, 1845
A.

5845 GODKIN, J. The rights of Ireland; third prize repeal essay.
184 pp. Dublin, James Duffy, 1845
A., B., D., G.

5846 [GRAYDON, William.] Suggestions on the best modes of employing the Irish peasantry, as an anti-famine precaution: a letter to the right hon. Sir Robert Peel, bart. By Agricola.
32 pp. London, J. Hatchard, 1845
A., T.

5847 Great Southern and Western Railway, Ireland: remarks on the Dublin terminus of the Cashel, or Great Southern & Western Railway.
16 pp. Dublin, printed by Folds, 1845

N.

5848 Great Southern and Western Railway, Ireland. Second half-yearly report. 19th March, 1845.
table. 4 pp. Dublin, printed by A. Thom, 1845

A.

5849 Great Southern and Western Railway, Ireland. Third half-yearly report. 20th September, 1845.
table. 4 pp. Dublin, printed by A. Thom, 1845

A.

5850 GRIFFITH, Charles. The present state and prospects of the Port Phillip district of New South Wales.
plate. table of contents. tables. 208 pp. Dublin, W. Curry, jr., London, Longman, Brown, Green & Longmans, 1845

A.

5851 HANCOCK, William Neilson. The tenant-right of Ulster, considered economically, being an essay read before the Dublin University Philosophical Society, with an appendix containing the evidence of John Hancock, esq., taken before the landlord and tenant commissioners.
96 pp. Dublin, Hodges & Smith, 1845

A., C., N., T., U.

5852 HANSARD, Luke James. Good! A proposition on the national debt, with the ways and means of the riddance from all oppressive taxes.
table of contents. tables. appendix. 46 pp. London, L. Hansard, 1845

A., T.

5853 ——. Sources or means of appropriation for the human creature's property of pecuniary possessions or increasings, now offered in lieu of the unsound, the unreal national funding system.
table of contents. appendix. 28 pp. London, L. Hansard, 1845

A.

5854 Heads of a joint stock company for the investment of capital combining landed security with facility of transfer, equal to Government funded property.
4 pp. n.p. [c. 1845]

A.

5855 HENCHY, John. Observations on the state of Ireland, with remarks on her resources and capabilities, and plans for carrying into effect the remedies necessary for the commissioners' report under the late land commission.
24 pp. Dublin, printed by L. Shaw, 1845

A.

5856 HEYWORTH, Lawrence. On economic fiscal legislation. To the honourable members of both houses of parliament.
16 pp. London, Palmer and Clayton, 1845

L.

5857 HILL, William Alfred. Remarks upon the late alterations in the law of imprisonment for debt; with suggestions for

their amendment and removal, in a letter addressed to the right hon. Henry lord Brougham.
56 pp. London, S. Sweet, 1845

T.

5858 HUTCHISON, Graham. Observations intended to point out the only effectual means of arresting the existing railway panic and of preventing future gambling in projected railways.
table of contents. 16 pp. Glasgow, printed by Bell & Bain, 1845

A.

5859 Irish Great Western, Dublin and Galway Railway. Speech of W. C. Rowe, esq., recorder of Plymouth, on the petition of the Grand Canal Company, with notes and an appendix.
tables. 56 pp. London, printed by W. Stevens, 1845

A.

5860 Irish railways and the board of trade, considered in a letter to the rt. hon. lord Brougham. Accompanied by a railway map of Ireland (signed 'Locomotive').
map. 66 pp. Dublin, Hodges & Smith, London, Effingham Wilson, 1845

A., N.

5861 The Isle of Wight system of roads, and system of guardians of the poor, not a model, but a warning to the legislature; especially as to the abuses arising from the incompatible functions of magistrates: and a proof that the maintenance of the highways is not one of the peculiar burdens of land.
94 pp. Southampton, Fletcher, Forbes and Fletcher, London, Longman, Brown, Green and Longmans, 1845

T.

5862 JAMESON, D. D. The sugar question.
tables. 28 pp. 2nd ed. London, Smith, Elder & co., 1845

T.

5863 JOHNSTON, James Finlay Weir. The potato disease in Scotland; being results of investigations into its nature and origin. Parts I, II, III, IV and V.
190 pp. Edinburgh and London, W. Blackwood, 1845

T.

5864 JOPLIN, Thomas. An examination of Sir Robert Peel's currency bill of 1844, in a letter to the bankers of the United Kingdom. Second edition. With supplementary observations.
appendices. tables. 110 pp. London, Pelham Richardson, 1845

T.

5865 KING, Edward. Bliss not riches. Love one another or you will torment one another. Colonisation on principles of pure Christism, designed to render perfect human character, and earthly bliss, affording glimpses on earthly happiness for the destitute and wretched, and hints to the damned, on the way to be blessed. In which is contained a reply to correspondents, concerning the essay upon the same subject published last winter; and to which are subjoined suggestions or a prospectus of a South Africa Colonisation Society, now under consideration.
52 pp. London, the author, 1845

A.

5866 LAMBERT, Joseph. Agricultural suggestions to the proprietors and peasantry of Ireland, on thorough-draining and subsoiling: the size, divisions and the fences of holdings; the dwellings of the peasantry; the improvement of agriculture: the house-feeding and manure-making; the alternative and restorative systems: on turnips, clover, and manures: and the improvement of the breed of stock.
diagrams. 96 pp. Dublin, W. Curry, jr., 1845
A., N., T.

5867 LAWSON, William John. History of banking in Scotland, embracing a brief review of the revenues of Scotland, with a copy of the act of the Scottish parliament establishing the Bank of Scotland.
tables. 50 pp. London, Richardson, 1845
T.

5868 A letter to the right hon. Sir Robert Peel, bart., on the law proposed for regulating the issue of bank notes in Ireland.
16 pp. Dublin, 1845
A.

5869 LEWIS, George Henry. The liabilities incurred by the projectors, managers, and shareholders of railway and other joint-stock companies considered: and also the rights and liabilities arising from transfers of shares. Written expressly for non-professional use.
table of contents. 84 pp. 2d. ed. London, Smith Elder & Co., 1845
A., N., T.

5870 LOWNDES, Matthew Dobson. The Liverpool stock exchange considered; with suggestions for its re-constitution on a safe footing.
24 pp. Liverpool, G. and J. Robinson, London, Longman, Brown, Green, and Longmans, 1845
T.

5871 M'KENNA, Joseph N. A chapter on railways and railway schemes, considered with a view to their social and political effects. Addressed to the people of England.
30 pp. London, Houlston & Stoneman, Dublin, S. J. Machen, 1845
A., N.

5872 MALLET, Robert. On the artificial preparation of turf, independent of season or weather, and with economy of labour and time.
diagrams. 58 pp. Dublin, Oldham, London, Whittaker, 1845
A., T.

5873 MAYDWELL, Isaac. The labourer's mine and the lord's security. Respectfully dedicated to the agricultural protection societies of England.
tables. 24 pp. London, J. Ollivier, 1845
T.

5874 ——. Letter to the queen, shewing the awful and alarming sacrifice of national property, exceeding the whole amount of the taxes of the empire, stated by deputation to Sir Robert Peel, and now most humbly presented in a letter to the queen's most excellent majesty.
8 pp. London, J. Ollivier, 1845
T.

5875 MECHI, John Joseph. A series of letters on agricultural improvement; with an appendix.
tables. illustrations. 128 pp. London, Longman, Brown, Green and Longmans, 1845
T.

5876 MILBURN, Matthew Marmaduke. Prize essay on Guano. Report on experiments with guano, to which the prize of the Yorkshire agricultural society was awarded. Extracted from the society's transactions, and published with the permission of the council.
tables. 18 pp. London, Simpkin and Marshall, 1845
T.

5877 MORTON, John, and TRIMMER, Joshua. An attempt to estimate the effects of protecting duties on the profits of agriculture.
tables. 90 pp. 4th ed. London, J. Ridgway, 1845
T.

5878 MULOCK, Thomas. Railway revelations, being letters on the subject of the proposed direct London and Manchester railways.
46 pp. London, Vickers, 1845
N.

5879 The Mutual accumulation society, established 31st December, 1839.
tables. 14 pp. Edinburgh, printed by T. Constable, 1845
A.
Prospectus of an endowment insurance society.

5880 NAPER, James Lenox William. A short commentary on the report of the land commissioners. Addressed to the consideration of the landlords and landholders of Ireland.
18 pp. Dublin, W. Curry, jr., 1845
A.

5881 National land-draining company for England, Ireland, and Scotland. Thoughts upon supplying food and employment for the working population of the United Kingdom. Published in connection with the prospectus of the above company.
18 pp. London, printed by W. Clowes, 1845
N.

5882 O'BEIRNE, James Lyster, and MALLEY, James. Dublin and Enniskillen Railway. (a letter.)
2 pp. Dublin, 1845
A.

5883 Observations of the provisional directors of the Mullingar, Athlone and Longford Railway on the report of the board of trade, on railways proposed to be made in Ireland, westward from Dublin.
folding maps. appendix. tables. 54 pp. Dublin, printed by Webb and Chapman, 1845
A., N.

5884 [O'CONNELL, John.] Appendix, being extracts of evidence relative to the custom of tenant-right in the North of Ireland, taken from the reports of the parliamentary committee of 1844, on Townland valuation of Ireland, and of the

commissioners of inquiry into the occupation of land in Ireland, 1845.
104 pp. Dublin, printed by J. Browne, 1845
N., T.
See 5836.

5885 [——.] The repeal dictionary. Part I. (From A to M inclusive.)
tables. appendix. 292 pp. Dublin, printed by J. Browne, 1845
A., L., N.

5886 O'CONNOR, Feargus. The employer and employed. The Chambers' philosophy refuted.
56 pp. London, printed by M'Gowan, 1845
A.

5887 O'DONOHOE, P. Irish wrongs & English misrule: or, the repealer's epitome of grievances.
82 pp. Dublin, A. C. Baynes, 1845
A., L.

5888 O'MALLEY, Thaddeus. An address to the mechanics, small farmers, and working classes generally, upon a feasible means of greatly improving their condition; with a word in their behalf to employers and landlords.
table of contents. 52 pp. Dublin, A. Thom, 1845
A.

5889 PALIN, William. Cheshire farming. A report on the agriculture of Cheshire. (The essay to which the premium of the Royal Agricultural Society of England was awarded.)
illustrations. tables. appendix. 68 pp. London, Simpkin and Marshall, Chester, Seacome and Prichard, 1845
T.

5890 Parliament and the railway schemes. Suggestions for an improved method of railway legislation.
30 pp. London, J. Ridgway, 1845
T.

5891 [PELHAM, Dudley.] Remarks as to measures calculated to promote the welfare and improve the condition of the labouring classes; and to provide for the maintenance of the increasing population, more particularly in connexion with the future prospects and the interests of landed proprietors and agriculturists. By a member of the aristocracy.
98 pp. London, W. H. Dalton, 1845
T.

5892 PHILLIPS, G. The potato disease; its origin, nature, & prevention, with a chemical and microscopical analysis of the sound and diseased tubers.
58 pp. London, S. Highley, 1845
T.

5893 Poor law commission. Skibbereen union. Abstract of the separate accounts of each electoral division, and number of paupers relieved, etc. For half-year ended 29th September, 1844.
tables. 6 pp. Cork, Nash, 1845
A.

5894 PORTER, John Grey V. Some calm observations on Irish affairs. Letter B.
48 pp. Dublin, Hodges and Smith, 1845
D., U.

5895 PRATT, John Tidd. Progress of savings banks. An account of the number of depositors and of the sums deposited in savings banks in Great Britain and Ireland, divided into classes, on the 20th of November in each of the years from 1829 to 1844 both inclusive and the increase or decrease in each year.
tables. 28 pp. London, Her Majesty's Stationery Office, 1845
A.

5896 Preliminary prospectus of the Great Hibernian Central Junction railway.
(1 large folding sheet, including map.) 2 pp. Dublin, 1845
A.

5897 Prospectus of the Dublin and Enniskillen Railway. (provisionally registered.)
2 pp. Dublin, printed by Charles, [1845?]
A.

5898 Railways in India; being four articles reprinted from the Railway Register for July, August, September, and November, 1845. Illustrated by a map.
map. tables. 56 pp. London, Madden and Malcolm, 1845
T.

5899 RAMSAY, George. A proposal for the restoration of the Irish parliament.
46 pp. Dublin, James Duffy, 1845. [Supplemental repeal essay. Printed by order of the Repeal Association.]
B., D., S.

5900 RAY, Thomas Mathew. To the trade and commerce committee of the Loyal national repeal association. Report of T. M. Ray, being the result of his inquiries in such towns as he visited on the repeal mission 1842–3.
26 pp. (3 pamphlets.) Dublin, printed by J. Browne, 1845
A.

5901 Report of the committee of the board of trade, on the various railways projected and in progress. With an introductory preface and general index.
tables. 126 pp. London, Simpkin Marshall, 1845
T.

5902 Report of the committee of the Loyal national repeal association on the Valuation (Ireland) bill.
6 pp. Dublin, printed by J. Browne, 1845
A.

5903 Report of the parliamentary committee of the Loyal national repeal association on the general Grand Jury laws of Ireland.
appendix with tables. 30 pp. Dublin, printed by J. Browne, 1845
A.

5904 Report of the parliamentary committee of the Loyal national repeal association on the provisions of the bill recently introduced into the house of commons, to regulate the issue of bank notes in Ireland. Read 2nd June, 1845.
8 pp. [pag. 355–362.] Dublin, printed by J. Browne, 1845
A.

5905 Report of the parliamentary committee of the Loyal national repeal association on the subject of having the enquiries connected with Irish Railway legislation transacted in Dublin.
appendices with tables. 12 pp. Dublin, printed by J. Browne, 1845

A.

5906 Report of the parliamentary committee of the Loyal national repeal association on the Tenants' compensation bill (sessional paper, no. 196) presented to the house of peers by the lord Stanley.
tables. 10 pp. Dublin, printed by J. Browne, 1845

A.

5907 Report of the trade and commerce committee of the Loyal national repeal association on the hosiery trade.
6 pp. Dublin, printed by J. Browne, 1845
A.

5908 Report of the trade and commerce committee of the Loyal national repeal association, on the soap and candle trade.
tables. 8 pp. Dublin, printed by J. Browne, 1845
A., N.

5909 ROBINSON, Daniel. Irish waste land improvement society. The third annual report of the system pursued in the management of the Irish waste land improvement society's estates in Ireland, during the year 1844; with an estimate of their present position and future prospects.
tables. appendix. 18 pp. London, printed by Bentley, Wilson and Fley, 1845

N., U.

5910 Rules and regulations adopted by a general meeting of the members of the Dublin mercantile guardian association, for the protection of trade.
10 pp. Dublin, printed by Goodwin, 1845
A.

5911 Rules and regulations of the Dublin stock and share brokers' association.
14 pp. Dublin, 1845
A.

5912 Ruminations on railways. No. I. Railway speculation.
14 pp. London, J. Weale, 1845
T.

5913 Ruminations on railways. No. II. The railway board of trade.
32 pp. London, J. Weale, 1845
T.

5914 Second report of the parliamentary committee of the Loyal national repeal association on the land question read 21st April, 1845.
12 pp. [pag. 317–328.] Dublin, printed by J. Browne, 1845
A., N.
This also includes the third report read 12th May, 1845.

5915 Second report of sub-committee on removal from England of poor persons born in Ireland. Adopted at a meet-ing of the Loyal national repeal association, held in Concilia-tion hall on Monday, March 10th, 1845.
no. t.p. 20 pp. Dublin, J. Browne, 1845
A., N., R., T.

5916 SEDGWICK, James. Letters addressed to the rt. hon. lord Granville Somerset; the rt. hon. Frankland Lewis; the rt. hon. the earl of Ripon; and the rt. hon. Henry Goulburn; on the extraordinary proceedings connected with the sudden and hitherto unexplained dissolution of the late board of stamps; with an address to the British public, containing strictures on the conduct of Sir John Easthope, as proprietor of the Morning Chronicle.
114 pp. London, J. Ridgway, 1845
T.

5917 SPOONER, Lucius H. Observations on the present decay among the potatoes, with particular reference to the extraction of starch, remarks on the value of this substance as food, with a detailed account of the method of obtaining it, its cost, and the sketch of a machine.
diagram. 16 pp. London, J. Ridgway, 1845
N.

5918 Statistics of South Australia, 1845. Comprehending a series of official returns, compiled by order of the government, and now published by permission of his excellency the gover-nor. To which are added, several tables of statistics derived from official and other authentic sources.
68 pp. Adelaide, Andrew Murray, 1845
T.

5919 STAUNTON, Michael. Second repeal prize essay. Reasons for a repeal of the legislative union between Great Britain and Ireland.
table of contents. tables. appendix. 160 pp. Dublin, J. Duffy, 1845
A., B., D., G., N.

5920 STEPHENSON, Robert, and Ross, Alex. M. To the provisional committee of the Dublin and Enniskillen Railway.
2 pp. London, 1845
A.

5921 [STRONG, Robert.] The emancipation of the soil, and free trade in land. By a landed proprietor.
46 pp. Edinburgh, John Johnstone, London, R. Groombridge, 1845
T.

5922 SWEETMAN, H. S. A plain and impartial exposition of the Act of Charitable Donations and Bequests; with incidental remarks on religious differences in Ireland.
42 pp. Dublin, J. Cumming, 1845
D., T.

5923 TOMPKINS, H. Building societies, their formation and management; with instructions for preparing rules, etc. etc. to which is annexed the Building Societies Statute, 6 & 7, Will. 4, c. 32.
tables. 42 pp. London, Shaw & sons, 1845
T.

5924 TOWNSEND, R. W. Report on the proposed Cork, Passage and Kinsale Railway, and its expected advantages as a main trunk line leading from Cork to the west of the country. map. folding plans. 12 pp. Cork, printed by Purcell, 1845
A.

5925 Trade between Dublin and Limerick.
4 pp. Dublin, 1845
A.
A complaint by merchants against the high charges of the City of Dublin Steam Packet Company, 'the one carrying company' on the Dublin-Limerick Canal.
See 5934.

5926 Traffic statement of the Irish Great Western (Dublin to Galway) Railway.
tables. 4 pp. London, 1845
A.
Statistics of number of passengers and volume of freight.

5927 Transactions of the Royal agricultural improvement society of Ireland with the report of the council for 1844.
tables. diagrams. maps. 100 pp. Dublin, W. Curry, jr., 1845
D.

5928 UDNY, George. A word on 'the currency'.
tables. 64 pp. London, Pelham Richardson, 1845
T.

5929 URQUHART, David. Wealth and want: or taxation as influencing private riches and public liberty, being the substance of lectures on pauperism delivered at Portsmouth, Southampton, etc. in February and March, 1845.
114 pp. London, J. Ollivier, 1845
N., T.

5930 Wexford, Carlow and Dublin Junction Railway. The evidence given before the committee on the bill in the house of commons. Printed from the short-hand writers' notes.
238 pp. London, printed by W. Stevens, 1845
A.

5931 What should be the policy of the government and the people in the present corn crisis: embodying conclusions deduced from a careful investigation of the extent of our deficiency, and the general results of the present harvest. By a true friend of the labouring classes.
table. 18 pp. London, J. Hatchard, 1845
T.

5932 WHITE, John Meadows. Suggestions for the rating of tithe commutation rent-charge.
tables. appendices. 48 pp. London, B. Fellowes, 1845
T.

5933 WILLIAMS, Albert. Facts upon facts against the league.
124 pp. London, J. Ollivier, 1845
T.
Refers to the Anti-corn law league.

5934 WILLIAMS, Charles Wye. Remarks on the alleged contrast of freights and tolls on the navigations from Dublin to Limerick and to Waterford.
20 pp. Dublin, printed by W. Underwood, 1845
A.
See 5925.

5935 [WILLIAMS, John.] Sub-railways in London. Letters to her majesty's ministers, the commissioners for metropolitan improvements, and the commissioners for the health of towns, in 1844 and 1845, respecting a great improvement in the streets of London, which is equally necessary in all the cities and towns in the kingdom: to which is added a proposal for sub-railways in the metropolis.
36 pp. London, Effingham Wilson, [1845?]
T.

5936 WILLIS, Thomas. Facts connected with the social and sanitary condition of the working classes in the city of Dublin together with some gleanings from the census returns of 1841.
folding map with statistics. 60 pp. Dublin, O'Gorman, 1845
A., N.

5937 WILSON, Henry. Hints to railroad speculators, together with the influence railroads will have upon society, in promoting agriculture, commerce, and manufactures.
table. 12 pp. London, Henry Wilson, 1845
T.

5938 YOUNGER, Samuel. Strictures on the policy of the bank of England with some remarks on the foreign exchanges and the corn laws; the whole suggested by the power of railway and marine steam; respectfully addressed to the first lord of the treasury.
42 pp. London, Pelham Richardson, 1845
T.

1846

5939 Abstract of the accounts of the Waterford Union for the half-year ended September 29th, 1845.
tables. 8 pp. Wexford, Greene, 1846
A.

5940 An address on the corn laws. By a protectionist.
44 pp. London, J. Hatchard, 1846
T.

5941 ALMACK, Bawgh. Hints to landowners. On tenure, prices, rents, etc.
appendix. 72 pp. London, Longman, Brown, Green, and Longmans, 1846
T.

5942 The amalgamation of railways considered as affecting the internal commerce of the country.
16 pp. London, Simpkin, Marshall, Manchester, Simms and Dinham, 1846
T.

5943 [ANDREW, Sir William Patrick.] Indian railways; as connected with the power, and stability of the British Empire in the east; the development of its resources, and the civilization of its people: with a brief analysis of the projects now claiming public confidence. By an old Indian postmaster.
map. table. 96 pp. London, T. C. Newby, 1846
T.

5944 Annual report of the Royal agricultural improvement society of Ireland for the year 1845.
tables. 102 pp. Dublin, A. Thom, 1846
N.

5945 ARCHBOLD, John Frederick. The act to amend the laws relating to the removal of the poor, 19 Vict. cap. 66; with notes and observations, etc., fourth edition.
table. 28 pp. London, Shaw & son, 1846
T.

5946 AYRES, H. To landlord and tenant farmers. The repeal of the malt tax: and its effect on land labour and commerce. With an explanation of the art of making malt and the mode of calculating the duty; also a statistical account of the malting trade for the last hundred years.
tables. appendix. 32 pp. London, J. Ollivier, 1846
T.

5947 Ballineen Agricultural Society.
48 pp. London, Marshall, 1846
N.

5948 The battle of the ploughshares. Price, profit and rent: their mutual relation in the prospects of British agriculture. By a landowner and a farmer.
34 pp. London, J. Ollivier, 1846
T.

5949 BEAMISH, N. Ludlow. Remedy for the impending scarcity; suggested by a visit to the Kilkerrin estate of the Irish waste land improvement society.
appendix. tables. 56 pp. Cork, Bradford & Co., 1846
N.

5950 BERMINGHAM, Thomas. Letter addressed to lord John Russell, containing facts illustrative of the good effects from the just and considerate discharge of the duties of a resident landlord in Ireland; with practical suggestions for legislative enactments necessary to induce, if not to compel, the fulfillment of similar duties by all landlords.
32 pp. 2d. ed. London, T. Saunders, 1846
A.

5951 BIRCH, James. The usury plague: a letter to the people of Ireland, on the system of usurious moneylending in Dublin. As developed in the progress of the various prosecutions instituted against the World newspaper, by Richard Woodroffe, Robert Gray etc., with an appendix, disclosing the frightful spread of usury in the provinces, suggestions for the suppression of that evil, &c., &c.
16 pp. Dublin, at the 'World' office, [1846]
A., L., N.

5952 BLACKALL, S. W. Labour on the land; containing a plan for the employment of the destitute poor on agricultural occupations; with observations on the workings of the present systems.
36 pp. Dublin, W. Curry, jr., 1846
A., N.

5953 BLACKER, William. An essay on the best mode of improving the condition of the labouring classes of Ireland.
table of contents. appendix. 60 pp. London, R. Groombridge, [etc., etc.], 1846
A., B., N.

5954 BLACKHAM, John, and HICKEY, A. Advice to promoters, subscribers, scripholders, and shareholders, of joint-stock and railway companies pointing out the rights and liabilities arising from signing parliamentary contracts, holding and transferring scrip, letters of allotment, and shares etc. Intended principally for the use of non-professional persons.
42 pp. Dublin, A. Milliken, 1846
A.

5955 Brief considerations with reference to the corn laws, and on the theory of protection generally.
40 pp. London, J. Ollivier, 1846
T.

5956 [BRIGHT, Henry Arthur?] Our free trade policy examined with respect to its real bearing upon native industry, our colonial system, and the institutions and ultimate destinies of the nation. By a Liverpool merchant.
tables. appendix. 46 pp. London, Whittaker, Liverpool, Lace & Addison, 1846
A., N., T.

5957 The broad gauge the bane of the Great Western Railway Company. With an account of the present and prospective liabilities saddled on the proprietors by the promoters of that peculiar crotchet. By £. s. d.
tables. 60 pp. 4th ed. London, John Ollivier, 1846
T.

5958 BRODRIBB, Edward. Published by the Liverpool Association for the reduction of the duty on tea. Abstract of a letter to ... Sir Robert Peel ... on the tea duties.
folding table. 14 pp. Liverpool, T. Baines, London, Simpkin, Marshall, 1846
A., N.
See 5821.

5959 BURNETT, (John J.). The Chemico-Agricultural Society of Ulster. On rotations of cropping.
8 pp. Belfast, F. D. Finlay, 1846
N.

5960 BUTT, Isaac. Protection to home industry: some cases of its advantages considered. The substance of two lectures delivered before the University of Dublin, in Michaelmas Term, 1840. To which is added, an appendix, containing dissertations on some points connected with the subject.
140 pp. Dublin, Hodges & Smith, London, John W. Parker, 1846
A., K., L., N., T., U.

5961 CAHILL, Daniel Williams. The lecture on slavery; delineating its rise, progress, and present awful prevalence, notwithstanding its nominal abolition by legislative enactment. Delivered by the Rev. Dr. Cahill, in the Town Hall, Waterford, January 15th, 1846.
20 pp. Waterford, printed by Harvey, 1846
A.

5962 Case of the tenant farmers; as illustrated in a series of letters, originally published in the Cork Examiner; by 'a tenant farmer', and leading to a proposition for the formation of a Tenant League: to which is added an article from the Cork Examiner.
28 pp. Cork, printed by Nash, 1846
A.

5963 Cases of tenant eviction, from 1840 to 1846 extracted from the public journals. (Not for publication.)
20 pp. n.p. [1846?]

L.

5964 CAYLEY, Edward Stillingfleet. Letters to the right honourable lord John Russell, M.P., on the corn laws.
32 pp. London, J. Ollivier, 1846

T.

5965 [CHUTON, Charles P. P.?] Berehaven Harbour as a naval station, and fortifications on the south-west coast of Ireland.
38 pp. Bath, Jennings, 1846

A.

5966 CLARKE, Hyde. Contributions to railway statistics, in 1845.
tables. 46 pp. London, J. Weale, 1846

T.

5967 ——. Theory of investment in railway companies.
tables. 38 pp. London, J. Weale, 1846

T.

5968 COLLINS, Charles James. The projected new railways. An epitome of the new lines of railway in England, which parliament will probably sanction, with reasons for their doing so.
tables. 32 pp. London, Effingham Wilson, 1846

T.

5969 COLLINS, Robert. Two letters, addressed to the right hon. Henry Labouchere, chief secretary of Ireland, on the extreme destitution of the poor in consequence of the total loss of the potato crop: with suggestions as to sources of employment, and other measures for their relief. Also, an appendix on the use of rice and turnips as a wholesome and excellent substitute for the potato.
20 pp. Dublin, Hodges & Smith, 1846

A., N.

5970 COLTHURST, Charles. How to make money and employ the people. A practical essay on the reclamation of the waste lands of Ireland, in connexion with irrigation.
tables. plan. 18 pp. Cork, Purcell, 1846

A., N.

5971 CONNER, William. Two letters to the editor of The Times, on the rackrent oppression of Ireland, its source—its evils—and its remedy, in reply to the Times commissioner, with prefatory strictures on public men and parties in Ireland, showing their perfidy to the people. Also, on lord Lincoln's three bills, showing their unfairness and utter futility.
60 pp. Dublin, S. J. Machen, 1846

A., B., T.

5972 A contrast between the rival systems of banking. By a country manager.
tables. 52 pp. London, Longman & co., Nottingham, Dearden, 1846

T.

5973 COOKE, William Robert. Peace Act dedicated with profound and awful devotion to God, and with due respect to man.
40 pp. London, the author, 1846

T.

5974 Corn and consistency. A few remarks in reply to a pamphlet entitled 'Sir Robert Peel and the corn law crisis'.
54 pp. London, J. Hatchard, 1846

T.

5975 Corn laws. Popkin's protest: addressed to the house of lords.
16 pp. London, J. Ollivier, 1846

T.

5976 CORRIGAN, D. J. On famine and fever as cause and effect in Ireland; with observations on hospital location, and the dispensation in outdoor relief of food and medicine.
36 pp. Dublin, Fannin, 1846

A., N.

5977 [CREWE, Henry Robert.] The repeal of the corn laws, and other measures of these latter days, considered in their relation to the rights of God and the rights of man. By one who fears God, and regards man.
32 pp. Derby, Bemrose, London, Hatchard, 1846

N.

5978 DAUNT, William Joseph O'Neill. Repeal of the union. Letter from W. J. O'Neill Daunt, esq., of Kilcascan, county Cork, to the landlords of Ireland.
16 pp. Dublin, republished by order of the Loyal national repeal association, 1846

A., L., N.

5979 DAVIES, Richard. A defence of the agricultural interest; comprising, also, a refutation of the statements of the anti-corn-law league: addressed to the landed proprietors, etc., etc.; to which is added a letter to lord John Russell.
tables. 64 pp. London, Simpkin, Marshall, [1846]

T.

5980 Deed of co-partnership of the Lurgan Gas-Light Company. Dated 13th day of August, 1845
index. 38 pp. Lurgan, printed by Evans, 1846

N.

5981 Deed of partnership of the Portadown Gas-Light Company. Dated the 1st of March, 1846.
14 pp. Dublin, printed by Corbet, 1846

N.

5982 DICKSON, Stephen Fox. Case on behalf of the grocers of Ireland, retailers of foreign grapes, currants, raisins and figs, being the grocers within the meaning of the excise laws, in force in Ireland at and before the passing of 6 George IV, c. 81 with the opinions of Daniel O'Connell, esq., Q.C., M.P., and William Mackey, esq., barrister-at-law. Concurrently agreeing that such grocers rights, to have their licenses to retail spirituous and other liquors, are still in full force.
24 pp. Dublin, P. W. Brady, 1846

A.

5983 ——. Case, with the opinion of eminent counsel thereon, demonstrating that, by petition of right the spirit retailer and tea dealers of Ireland can recover the large sums of money which the officers of the Crown have illegally and wrongfully levied off them. Also compensation for all the injuries they have suffered from the wrongful acts of the officers of the crown.
16 pp. Dublin, P. W. Brady, 1846
A.

5984 Distress in Ireland.
4 pp., London, 1846
A.
Appeal from the Central Committee for famine relief of the Society of Friends in Ireland.

5985 Distress in Ireland. Address of the committee to the members of the Society of Friends in Ireland.
4 pp. Dublin, 1846
A.

5986 DOUGLAS, John. Life and property in Ireland assured as in England, by a poor-rate on land, to provide employment for the destitute poor on the wastelands of Ireland.
tables. 40 pp. London, J. Ridgway, Glasgow, Smith, 1846
A., N., T.

5987 DRUMMOND, Henry. Letter to the bishop of Winchester on free trade.
44 pp. London, J. Hatchard, 1846
T.

5988 Dublin and Drogheda Railway. Report of the directors, with statement of the accounts and list of shareholders; published preparatory to the half-yearly meeting to be held on the 26th February, 1846.
tables. 28 pp. Dublin, printed by N. Walsh, 1846
A.

5989 Dublin and Drogheda Railway. Report of the directors with statement of the accounts, published preparatory to the half-yearly meeting, to be held on the 27th August, 1846.
tables. 12 pp. Dublin, printed by N. Walsh, 1846
A.

5990 The Dublin trades' guilds. To the citizens and tradesmen of Dublin.
2 pp. Dublin, 1846
A.

5991 DUNCAN, Jonathan. How to reconcile the rights of property, capital and labour. Tract 1 of the Currency reform association.
56 pp. London, J. Ollivier, 1846
T.

5992 ENSOR, Thomas. Ireland made happy and England safe. Two letters addressed to the rt. hon. Sir Robert Peel, bart., M.P. and a letter to Daniel O'Connell, esq., M.P.
appendix. 36 pp. London, J. Ridgway, 1846
T.

5993 An essay, suggestive of the safest way of carrying out the scheme of a decimal system of money; as a preliminary to the subsequent adoption of decimal weights, measures, and months.
table. 24 pp. London, Smith Elder & co., 1846
T.

5994 EVANS, Eyre. State and prospects of Ireland.
26 pp. Liverpool, printed by Whitley and Ellis, 1846
A., N.

5995 EVANS, George. Report upon the present condition and relative merits of the harbours of Larne, Loch Ryan, Port Patrick, Donaghadee, and Belfast; surveyed by order of the lords commissioners of the admiralty.
18 pp. London, printed by Spottiswoode, 1846
N.
See 6069

5996 A familiar treatise on taxation, free trade, etc. comprising facts usually unnoticed or unconsidered in theories of those subjects. With notes on subjects arising incidentally.
tables. 46 pp. London, P. Richardson and J. Ollivier, 1846
T.

5997 A few words on the corn laws. By a landowner.
40 pp. London, J. Ridgway, 1846
T.

5998 A few words on the repeal of the corn laws.
48 pp. London, J. Ollivier, 1846
T.

5999 The fifth annual report and transactions of the society for the promotion and improvement of the growth of flax in Ireland.
Appendices. tables. 70 pp. Belfast, Simms & M'Intyre, 1846
A., N.

6000 FITZGERALD, James Edward. A letter to the noblemen, gentlemen and merchants of England.
14 pp. London, F. and J. Rivington, 1846
T.

6001 FITZGERALD, lord William. Some suggestions for the better government of Ireland, addressed to the marquess of Kildare, by lord William Fitzgerald.
52 pp. London, J. Ridgway, 1846
A., B., D., G., T.

6002 FORD, William. A letter addressed to the resident landed proprietors, merchants, farmers, mill-owners, shopkeepers, mechanics, and labourers of the county, on the important subject of railway communication between the county of Meath, and the counties north of it, and the city of Dublin, containing suggestions as to the mode whereby such communication should now be effected, and be made subsidiary to giving employment during the present state of the country, owing to the destruction of the food of the people.
appendices. 40 pp. Dublin, A. Thom, 1846
N.
See 5838.

6003 FORTESCUE, Thomas Knox. Remarks on the deep sea fisheries of Ireland, as a source of national prosperity.
16 pp. Dublin, S. Machen, 1846.
A.

6004 FYFE, Alexander Gordon. Suggestions for separating the culture of sugar from the process of manufacture; with a plan for establishing a central sugar factory at Annotto Bay, Jamaica.
map. tables. appendix. 46 pp. London, Effingham Wilson, 1846

T.

6005 GLADSTONE, Sir John. Plain facts intimately connected with the intended repeal of the corn laws, its probable effects on the public revenue, and the prosperity of this country. Addressed to all classes, in the United Kingdom and her colonies, by John Gladstone, esq.
36 pp. London, J. Murray, 1846

T.

6006 God's laws versus corn laws. A letter to his grace the archbishop of Canterbury. From a dignitary of the English church.
52 pp. London, Houlston & Stoneman, 1846

T.

6007 Great Southern and Western Railway, Ireland. Fourth half-yearly report. 20th March, 1846
tables 6 pp. Dublin, printed by A. Thom, 1846

A.

6008 Great Southern and Western Railway, Ireland. Fifth half-yearly report. 12th August, 1846.
tables. 4 pp. Dublin, printed by A. Thom, 1846

A.

6009 GREENHOW, C. H. An exposition of the danger and deficiencies of the present mode of railway construction, with suggestions for its improvement.
diags. 30 pp. London, J. Weale, 1846

T.

6010 [GREVILLE, Charles Cavendish Fulke.] Sir Robert Peel and the corn law crisis.
34 pp. 3rd ed. London, J. Ridgway, 1846

T.

6011 GUY, William A. On the health of towns, as influenced by defective cleansing and drainage. And on the application of the refuse of towns to agricultural purposes.
appendices. 48 pp. London, Renshaw, 1846

A.

6012 HAINWORTH, William. Free trade fallacies refuted. Remarks on a pamphlet by Mr. John Morton, F.G.S., and Mr. Joshua Trimmer, F.G.S., entitled 'An attempt to estimate the effects of protecting duties on the profits of agriculture'.
28 pp. London, J. Ollivier, 1846

T.

6013 HAMILTON, Charles William. Short hints to the small farmers in Ireland, on the question what shall we substitute for the potato?
table of contents. 34 pp. Dublin, W. Curry, jr., 1846

A., N.

See 6202.

6014 HARVEY, Daniel Whittle. An address upon the law and liabilities of railway speculation, with hints for legislative interference.
32 pp. London, Simpkin and Marshall [etc.], 1846

T.

6015 Health of towns association. Report of the committee to the members of the association on lord Lincoln's sewerage, drainage, etc., of towns bill.
122 pp. London, C. Knight, 1846

A., N.

6016 HICKEY, William. The labouring classes in Ireland: an inquiry as to what beneficial changes may be effected in their condition by the legislature, the landowner, and the labourer respectively.
table of contents. 86 pp. Dublin, J. McGlashan [etc., etc.], 1846

A.

6017 HOGAN, William. On the means of escaping the ravages of the potato disease, by raising fully-grown healthy potatoes from seed in one season.
4 pp. Dublin, 1846

A., D.

6018 [HOLLOWAY, N.] Essay on the repeal of the malt-tax, for which a prize of twenty pounds was awarded by the association, established at 39, New Bridge St., Blackfriars, London [i.e. the 'Total repeal of the malt tax association'].
tables. 28 pp. London, J. Rogerson, 1846

N.

6019 HUNT, Thornton. The rationale of railway administration, with a view to the greatest amount of accommodation, cheapness, and safety.
table. 78 pp. London, Smith, Elder & co., 1846

T.

6020 HUTCHINSON, S. A letter to the agricultural tenants of the rt. hon. the earl Brownlow upon the drainage of land.
diagrams. 16 pp. 2d. ed., enlarged and improved. Grantham, printed by S. Ridge, 1846

A.

6021 Industry, education, and public virtue; or measures for a new parliament to complete under a liberal and enlightened government; suggested by Amor Patriae, in three letters to lord John Russell, prime minister of England.
tables. 32 pp. London, J. Ridgway, [1846]

T.

6022 Ireland, its evils and their remedy for the present and the future; being a letter by a magistrate of Clare, to his excellency the lord lieutenant of Ireland.
38 pp. Limerick, Goggin, 1846

A., N.

6023 The Irish turf, peat-coal, and charcoal company, to be incorporated by act of parliament.
2 pp. Dublin, printed by G. Folds, 1846

A.

Prospectus.

6024 JOHNSON, George W. The potato murrain and its remedy.
16 pp. 2d. ed. London, Baldwin, 1846
A.

6025 KING, Peter King, 7th baron. A short history of the job of jobs.
18 pp. London, J. Ridgway, 1846
T.

Written in 1825.

6026 A letter addressed to the right honorable lord Stanley, on the proposed repeal of the corn laws: being a reply to a letter addressed to the same noble lord by Mr. Wyse of Waterford, on the same subject. By Agricola.
10 pp. Dublin, P. D. Hardy, London, R. Groombridge, 1846
A.

6027 Letter to A. B., esq., on the impolicy of repealing the present corn laws.
28 pp. Bury Saint Edmund's, G. Thompson, London, Longman, Brown, Green and Longmans, 1846
T.

6028 A letter to British agriculturists. By a British merchant.
16 pp. London, Pelham Richardson, 1846
T.

6029 A letter to the right hon. lord John Russell. [Signed Auctor.]
12 pp. Dublin, printed by W. Frazer, 1846
A.

On landlord-tenant relations.

6030 A letter to the shareholders of the Irish Great Western Dublin to Galway Railway, on the present crisis in their affairs.
18 pp. London, printed by Smith, 1846
A.

6031 A list of the sizes of rod, skain, and brown basket work, with the journeyman's prices affixed, for the city of Dublin, compiled by a committee of six journeymen, and agreed to at a general meeting of the trade, held in ... Dublin, March 17th, 1846.
tables. 70 pp. Dublin, printed by O'Donohoe, 1846
A.

6032 Lord Grey and lord Palmerston. A letter addressed to the right hon. T. B. Macaulay, M.P. on occasion of his letter to Mr. McFarlane, from a free trader.
32 pp. London, J. Ollivier, 1846
T.

6033 LUMLEY, William Golden. The act to amend the laws relating to the removal of the poor, 9 & 10 Vic. c. 66; with a practical commentary and index. Second edition with additional observations, and the poor law commissioner's circular letter, (dated 17th September, 1846).
48 pp. 2nd ed. London, C. Knight, 1846
T.

6034 MAEREN, Corr van der. Coup d'œil sur le tarif des douanes Belges, à propos du libre échange. Par un Négociant de Bruxelles.
tables. 30 pp. Bruxelles, Perichon, 1846
N.

6035 MAHONY, Cornelius. Every man his own landlord, or building societies, their objects, principles and advantages familiarly explained, and their importance as a mode of profitable investment to the tradesman, the shopkeeper, the small capitalist, and the industrious classes of society in general, plainly demonstrated.
tables. 14 pp. Dublin, Le Mesurier, 1846
A., C.

6036 [MATHER, James.] Ships and railways.
tables. 40 pp. London, Longman, Brown, Green and Longmans, 1846
T.

6037 Moral force. An appeal to the wisdom, justice and mercy of her most gracious majesty Queen Victoria, and of the peers and commons of parliament, on the present state of Ireland. By H. E. F. Juvernae.
tables. 14 pp. Dublin, S. J. Machen, 1846
A., N.

6038 MORRISON, James. Observations illustrative of the defects of the English system of railway legislation and of its injurious operation on the public interests with suggestions for its improvement.
tables. 42 pp. London, Longman, Brown, Green & Longmans, 1846
N., T.

6039 MULLINS, Bernard, and MULLINS, M. B. The origin and reclamation of peat bog, with some observations on the construction of roads, railways and canals in bog.
plans. 52 pp. Dublin, Oldham, 1846
A., T.

6040 MULOCK, Thomas. Three letters on the present destitution of the Irish peasantry.
16 pp. Dublin, R. M. Tims, 1846
A.

6041 NAPER, James Lenox William. Observations in answer to Mr. G. Poulett Scrope's question of 'How is Ireland to be governed?' addressed to him by J. L. W. Naper, esq.
16 pp. Dublin, J. McGlashan, London, J. Ridgway, 1846
A.

6042 NEISON, Francis Gustavus Paulus. Observations on the questions at present pending in the Manchester unity of the Independent Order of Oddfellows. With some suggestions for the settlement of the same.
tables. 56 pp. London, Simpkin, Marshall, 1846
T.

6043 NELSON, Thomas. Remarks on the slavery and slave trade of the Brazils.
tables. 86 pp. London, J. Hatchard, 1846
T.

6044 NEVILE, Christopher. Corn and currency, by the Rev. Christopher Nevile. In a letter to A. Alison, esq.
44 pp. 2nd. ed. London, J. Ridgway, 1846
T.

6045 New South Wales, as it was, as it is, and as it will be; or colonial dreams. Also, three letters on the Bank of New South Wales, signed Nobody, originally published in the 'Sydney Morning Herald'. By the hermit in Australia.
36 pp. Carnarvon, James Rees, 1846
T.

6046 NIVEN, Ninian. The potato epidemic, and its probable consequences; a letter to his grace the duke of Leinster, as president of the Royal agricultural improvement society of Ireland.
44 pp. Dublin, James M'Glashan, London, W. S. Orr, 1846
A., N., U.

6047 [O'CONNELL, John.] Appendix, No. VI. 'The taxation injustice'.
tables. 84 pp. Dublin, printed by J. Browne, 1846
A.
A Loyal national repeal association pamphlet. See 5625.

6048 OGIER, J. C. H. Proposal for a general metropolitan railway. A letter addressed to the commissioners appointed to investigate projects for metropolitan railway termini.
map. 12 pp. London, J. Weale, 1846
T.

6049 On the drainage of land.
16 pp. Dublin, printed by A. Thom, 1846
A.
A collection of Royal agricultural improvement society papers on the subject.

6050 Origin and results of the clearing system which is in operation on the narrow gauge railways with tables of the through traffic in the year 1845.
tables. 26 pp. London, printed by Smith & Ebbs, 1846
N.

6051 PARKIN, John. The cause of blight and pestilence in the vegetable creation with suggestions for the development of other supplies of foodstuffs during the present crisis.
16 pp. London, J. Hatchard, 1846
A., T.

6052 PEARSON, W. Wilberforce. Suggestions for improved railway legislation at the present crisis in Great Britain and Ireland in a letter to the committee of the house of commons.
8 pp. London, Blanchard, 1846
N.

6053 The petition of the guardians of the poor of the North Dublin Union.
2 pp. Dublin, 1846
A.

6054 PIESSE, Charles. Sir Robert Peel as wrong upon currency as he states himself to have been, heretofore, upon corn.
36 pp. Dublin, 1846
A., P.

6055 PIM, James, jr. A letter to George Carr, esq., chairman of the Great Southern and Western Railway of Ireland (for private circulation only).
24 pp. Dublin, Webb & Chapman, 1846
A., C., N.

6056 A popular treatise on our financial system.
40 pp. London, J. Hatchard, 1846
T.

6057 PORTER, John Grey V. Some calm observations on Irish affairs. Letter C.
appendix. 30 pp. Dublin, Hodges & Smith, London, J. Ridgway, 1846
A., D., N.

6058 POWELL, Henry Buckworth. A description and explanation of an invention for obviating the difficulties experienced by the break of gauge, and at the same time doing away with the necessity for a central terminus; with many other advantages.
illustrations. 30 pp. London, Pelham Richardson, 1846
T.

6059 Practical hints towards improving the merchant marine service. Dedicated to the committee of the general shipowners' society. By a merchant captain.
40 pp. London, Smith, Elder & co., 1846
T.

6060 Present condition and future prospects of the country, in reference to free trade and its recent application. By F. C.
48 pp. London, W. E. Painter, 1846
T.

6061 The present ship-building controversy; or, which is the misrepresented party? Illustrated by a few examples, shewing the difference between 'facts' and 'fictions'. By a naval architect.
tables. 46 pp. London, C. Letts, 1846
T.

6062 Protection and free-trade; or, the interests of an empire, and not of a party, considered, in a letter to lord viscount Sandon, M.P. for Liverpool.
tables. 40 pp. London, F. & J. Rivington, 1846
T.

6063 Railway eccentrics. Inconsistencies of men of genius exemplified in the practice and precept of Isambard Kingdom Brunel, esq., and in the theoretical opinions of Charles Alexander Saunders, esq., secretary to the Great Western Railway. By Vigil.
30 pp. London, J. Ollivier, 1846
T.

6064 Rates and regulations of the Grand Canal Company's floating and graving docks at Ringsend. In the port of Dublin.
index. tables. 16 pp. Dublin, printed by Porter, 1846
A.

6065 RAY, Thomas Matthew. Report on the Irish Coercion Bill, the causes of discontent in Ireland, condition of the people, comparative criminality with England, remedial measures etc.
286 pp. Dublin, printed by J. Browne, 1846
A., N.

6066 Reasons for a tax on property in substitution for duties of excise and customs.
8 pp. London, Longman, Brown, Green and Longmans, 1846
T.

6067 REDMOND, S. Landlordism in Ireland. Letters on the Gerrard tenantry. A portion of which appeared originally in the 'Freeman's Journal'.
48 pp. Dublin, printed by Lowe, 1846
A., N.

6068 Remarks on the anti-corn-law mania, in a letter to his grace the duke of Buckingham. By Cincinnatus.
74 pp. London, J. Ollivier, 1846
T.

6069 RENNIE, Sir John. Observations on the report of Capt. G. Evans, R.N. upon the present condition and relative merits of the harbours of Larne, Loch Ryan, Port Patrick, Donaghadee and Belfast.
14 pp. London, printed by W. Clowes, 1846
N.
See 5995.

6070 Report of a select committee appointed to inquire into the statistics of distress in the parishes of Mallow and Rahan, and to give information and offer suggestions to government, on its nature and causes, and the means of its amelioration.
tables. appendix. 96 pp. Mallow, printed at the Albion Office, 1846
A.

6071 Report of the committee of the society for the improvement of Ireland, as adopted at the public meeting of the citizens of Dublin, and others interested in the welfare of Ireland, held 21st May, 1846.
appendix. Dublin, Hodges and Smith, 1846
A.

6072 Report of the Mansion house committee on the potato disease.
fold. tabs. 14 pp. Dublin, printed by J. Browne, 1846
A., D., L., T.

6073 Report of the proceedings of the public meeting on the tea duties, held in the Borough Sessions house, Liverpool, on the 25th November, 1846. Published by the committee of the Liverpool Association for the reduction of the duty on tea.
tables. 80 pp. Liverpool, Carter, 1846
A., N.

6074 RIPLEY, W. R. The present state of the law of tithes, under lord Tenterden's act, and the act for the limitation of actions and suits relating to real property. With reference to tithe commutations.
160 pp. London, J. Hatchard, 1846
T.

6075 ROBINSON, Daniel. Irish waste land improvement society. The fourth annual report of the system pursued in the management of the Irish waste land improvement society's estates in Ireland, during the year 1845; with an estimate of their present position and future prospects.
appendices. tables. 38 pp. London, printed by Bentley, Wilson & Fley, 1846
N.

6076 ——. Practical suggestions for the reclamation of waste lands, and improvement in the condition of the agricultural population of Ireland. With an introductory letter to the chancellor of the Exchequer from the earl of Devon.
tables. 22 pp. London, printed by Darling, 1846
N.

6077 ROGERS, Jasper W. Letter to the landlords and rate-payers of Ireland, detailing means for the permanent and profitable employment of the peasantry, without ultimate cost to the land or the nation, and within the provisions of the Act 10 Vict. c. 107.
table. appendix. 78 pp. London, J. Ridgway, 1846
A., T.

6078 ——. Proposition for the permanent employment of the Irish peasantry without cost to the nation by which a large revenue may be produced; also, facts respecting the value and advantages of peat and charcoal, as a fuel and fertilizer.
tables. 42 pp. Dublin, N. Walsh, 1846
N.

6079 ROWCROFT, Charles. Currency and railways; being suggestions for the remedy of the present railway embarrassments.
26 pp. London, Smith Elder & co., [1846?]
N. T.

6080 RUMFORD, Benjamin Thompson, count. Essay on food, and particularly on feeding the poor. Published in the year 1795 and now reprinted for the friends of the poor.
table of contents. 52 pp. Youghal, printed by Lindsay, 1846
A.

6081 Schools of industry.
32 pp. n.p., [1846]
B.
Education for pauper children.

6082 Scottish widows' fund and life assurance society, founded A.D. 1815 for assurances on lives and survivorships etc. on the principle of mutual contribution.
table of contents. tables. appendix. 76 pp. Edinburgh, [1846]
N.

6083 SCROPE, George Julius Duncombe Poulett. How is Ireland to be governed? A question addressed to the new administration of lord Melbourne in 1834 with a postscript in which the same question is addressed to the administration of Sir Robert Peel in 1846.
68 pp. London, J. Ridgway, 1846
A., N.

——. 70 pp. 2nd ed. London, J. Ridgway, 1846
T.

6084 ——. Letters to the right hon. lord John Russell on the expediency of enlarging the Irish Poor Law to the full extent of the Poor Law of England.
92 pp. London, J. Ridgway, 1846
A., N., T.

6085 SMEE, William Ray. The income tax: its extension at the present rate proposed to all classes: abolishing the malt tax, window tax and other taxes, with some observations on the tea duties.
tables. appendix. 30 pp. 2nd edition. London, Pelham Richardson, [1846]
T.

6086 Some considerations suggested by the loss of the potato, as a staple of food in Ireland, and its consequences as affecting the moral and domestic position of the peasantry addressed to Corry Connellan, esq., private secretary to his excellency the earl of Bessborough, by a resident rector in the province of Leinster.
26 pp. Dublin, S. Machen, 1846
A., N.

6087 Some remarks on the state of the leather trade in 1846.
12 pp. n.p., 1846
A., N.

6088 SPARKHALL, Edward. A broad hint to the manufacturers, on the subject of corn, coals, steam, and machinery. Or a first impression from a seal intended for the lips of the free-trade advocates. Entered at Stationers' Hall.
24 pp. London, the author, 1846
T.

6089 The sugar duties. Free and slave labour.
20 pp. London, Smith, Elder & co., 1846
T.

6090 SYMONS, Jelinger Cookson. Railway liabilities as they affect subscribers, committees, allottees, and scripholders inter se, and third parties.
80 pp. London, William Benning, 1846
T.

6091 Third general report of the parliamentary committee of the Loyal national repeal association.
42 pp. Dublin, printed by J. Browne, 1846
A.

6092 [TRAILL, Catherine Parr.] The backwoods of Canada: being letters from the wife of an emigrant officer, illustrative of the domestic economy of British America.
illust. 244 pp. 2nd ed. London, C. Knight, 1846
T.

6093 Transactions of the Royal agricultural improvement Society of Ireland for the year 1845.
table of contents. tables. diagrams. 58 pp. Dublin, W. Curry, jr., 1846
N.
Contains essays and reports.

6094 TROUP, James. Railway reform, and rights of shareholders and the public in the railway highways of the United Kingdom.
40 pp. London, Pelham Richardson, 1846
N., T.

6095 TRULOCK, George. Remedies suggested to meet the present state of Ireland. A letter addressed to lord John Russell.
appendix. 28 pp. Dublin, Grant and Bolton, 1846
N.

6096 Upon the probable influence of a repeal of the corn laws, upon the trade in corn.
tables. 46 pp. London, J. Ridgway, 1846
T.

6097 WALKER, James. Admiralty. Mr. Walker's report on the Wexford and Valentia Railway, and Valentia Harbour.
appendices. 22 pp. London, printed by Vacher, 1846
A.

6098 WARD, James. Railways for the many and not for the few; or, how to make them profitable to all.
34 pp. London, Smith, Elder & co., 1846
T.

6099 WATSON, James. A paper on the present railway crisis; read at a meeting of the Literary and commercial society of Glasgow, held on the 26th March, 1846, Charles Hutchison, esq., in the chair, and ordered by the society to be printed, by permission of the author.
22 pp. Glasgow, William Lang [etc., etc.], 1846
T.

6100 WILLIAMS, Sir Erasmus, bart. A letter of remonstrance to his grace the duke of Richmond, on the repeal of the corn laws.
24 pp. London, Longman, Brown, Green and Longmans, 1846
T.

6101 WOLSELEY, John. 'The difficulty' met. A letter to the labouring poor of Ireland.
24 pp. 2d. ed. Dublin, W. Curry, jr., 1846
A., N.

6102 WYSE, Francis. A letter addressed to the right honourable lord Stanley, late secretary of state for the colonies, on the proposed repeal of the corn laws, and its injurious consequences to the well-being and prosperity of Ireland.
14 pp. Dublin, Arthur B. Keen, 1846
A.

1847

6103 ADAIR, Sir Robert Alexander Shafto, bart., later baron Waveney. The winter of 1846–7 in Antrim, with remarks on outdoor relief and colonization.
70 pp. London, J. Ridgway, 1847
A., N.

——. 3rd edition. table. 72 pp. London, J. Ridgway, 1847
T.

6104 ALCOCK, T. St. Leger. Observations on the Poor relief bill for Ireland, and its bearing on the important subject of emigration with some remarks on the great public works projected in the British North American colonies.
30 pp. London, J. Ridgway, 1847
A., T.

6105 ALISON, Sir Archibald, bart. Free trade and a fettered currency.
tables. 82 pp. Edinburgh & London, W. Blackwood, 1847
T.

6106　ALISON, William Pulteney.　Observations on the famine of 1846–7 in the Highlands of Scotland, and in Ireland, as illustrating the connection of the principle of population with the management of the poor.
table of contents. 78 pp. Edinburgh & London, W. Blackwood, 1847

A., T.

6107　ANDERSON, Alexander.　The recent commercial distress; or the panic analysed: showing the cause and cure.
48 pp. London, Effingham Wilson, 1847

T.

6108　ANDREWS, William.　On the fisheries of the coasts of Ireland, addressed to rear admiral Sir Thomas Ussher, K.C.H.
16 pp. [no tp.] Dublin, printed by T. Browne, 1847

C., N.

6109　ANTISELL, Thomas.　Suggestions towards the improvement of the sanitary condition of the metropolis [i.e. Dublin].
plan. tables. 28 pp. Dublin, J. McGlashan, 1847

N.

6110　ASHBURTON, Alexander Baring, 1st baron.　The financial and commercial crisis considered.
40 pp. 2nd ed. London, J. Murray, 1847

A.

——.　3rd. ed. 40 pp. London, J. Murray, 1847

T.

6111　AYLWIN, D. C.　A letter on cotton cultivation in India, as affected by the East India Company's salt monopoly.
16 pp. London, J. Madden, 1847

A., N.

6112　——.　A letter to George Frederick Young, esq. (deputy chairman of the Shipowners' Association) . . . in reply to certain questions regarding the operation of the navigation laws on the trade of Calcutta.
18 pp. London, J. Madden, 1847

A.

6113　AYTOUN, James.　The railways and the currency as connected with the present monetary crisis.
36 pp. Edinburgh, Adam and Charles Black, 1847

T.

6114　BAINES, Thomas.　The agricultural resources of Great Britain, Ireland, and the colonies considered in connection with the rise in the price of corn, and the alarming condition of the Irish people.
tables. appendix. 72 pp. Liverpool, Times Office, London, Longman & co., 1847

A.

6115　BALLANTINE, Michael Ward.　An appeal to the public but especially to the supporters of the London City Mission, concerning the extent of its capabilities as to the advancements of the interests of the poor.
32 pp. London, F. & J. Rivington, 1847

T.

6116　[BANISTER, Thomas.] Memoranda relating to the present crisis as regards our colonies, our trade, our circulating medium, and railways. Thomas Retsinab.
8 pp. London, John Ollivier, 1847

T.

6117　BENNETT, William.　Narrative of a recent journey of six weeks in Ireland, in connection with the subject of supplying small seed to some of the remoter districts: with current observations on the depressed circumstances of the people, and the means presented for the permanent improvement of their social condition.
table of contents. appendix. 194 pp. London, C. Gilpin, Dublin, W. Curry, jr., 1847

A.

6118　BERMINGHAM, Thomas.　The Thames, the Shannon, and the St. Lawrence or the good of Great Britain, Ireland and British North America identified and promoted: in the development of the vast resources of Ireland and British North America, by the employment, for the next 10 years, of 250,000 families of the destitute peasantry of Ireland, improperly called redundant population.
tables. 32 pp. London, S. & W. Fores, 1847

N.

6119　BISHOP, Daniel.　The Constitution of society as designed by God.
136 pp. London, Arthur Hall, 1847

T.

6120　BLUNT, Walter.　Ecclesiastical restoration and reform No. 1. Considerations and practical suggestions on Church rates,—parish officers,—education of the poor,—cemeteries.
appendix. 50 pp. London, Joseph Masters, 1847

T.

6121　BOOTH, Henry.　The rationale of the currency question; or, the plea of the merchant and the shareholder for an improved system of national banking.
24 pp. London, J. Weale, Liverpool, T. Baines, 1847

T.

6122　BRODIGAN, Thomas.　A letter written by Thomas Brodigan, esq., to George A. Hamilton, M.P., respecting his claims against the Dublin and Drogheda Railway Company, including, in an appendix, a report of the trial of the cause of Brodigan against the company, August 1847.
appendix. 32 pp. Dublin, Webb & Chapman, 1847

A.

6123　BROWN, Edward.　Practical remarks on a new and unfailing method of increasing the potato plant, with full directions thereon.
12 pp. London, Chapman and Hall, 1847

T.

6124　BROWN, Francis Carnac.　Free trade and the cotton question with reference to India, being a memorial from the British merchants of Cochin, to the right hon. Sir John Hobhouse, bart., M.P., president of the board of control with a letter and appendix.
appendices. 126 pp. London, Effingham Wilson, 1847

T.

6125 BROWN, James. The present state and future prospects of the Monmouthshire canal company considered; in a letter addressed to the committee of management.
tables. diags. 42 pp. London, J. Weale, 1847
T.

6126 BROWNE, Joseph Houston. The navigation laws: their history and operation.
54 pp. London, Smith, Elder, & co., 1847
A., T.

6127 BROWNE, William John. The real el dorado; or, true principles of currency developed.
30 pp. London, Effingham Wilson, Liverpool, Wareing Webb, 1847
T.

6128 BROWNELL, Charles. A letter to the right hon. the earl of Clarendon, president of the board of trade, on the copper ore duties, in reply to the letter of Sir Charles Lemon, bart.
tables. 34 pp. London, J. Ridgway [1847]
T.

6129 BURGES, George. Native guano the best antidote against the future fatal effects of a free trade in corn.
tables. 48 pp. London, Effingham Wilson, 1847
T.

6130 BURKE, James Henry. India salt. Scinde versus Cheshire, Calcutta, and Bombay.
map. tables. 32 pp. London, Smith, Elder & co., 1847
N.

6131 BURRITT, Elihu. A journal of a visit of three days to Skibbereen, and its neighbourhood.
16 pp. London, C. Gilpin, Birmingham, J. Whitehouse, 1847
T.

6132 BUTT, Isaac. A voice for Ireland. The famine in the land. What has been done, and what is to be done.
68 pp. Dublin, J. McGlashan, London, Orr, 1847
A , N.
Reprinted from the Dublin University Magazine. April 1847

6133 CARROLL, Peter. A letter from Peter Carroll to John Bull, on the origin, nature, and conduct of the landlords of Ireland, and on the best method of preventing them in future from starving 'Patrick' and robbing 'John'.
24 pp. Liverpool, Kenny, 1847
N.

6134 CHAPMAN, Sir Montagu L., bart. Rough notes on the present and future state of Ireland, addressed to the members of the Reproductive employment society.
22 pp. Dublin, Hodges and Smith, 1847
D., T.

6135 CHARD, Henry. Spanish bonds. A statement of the present position of the Spanish bondholders: with the opinions of eminent counsel and jurists on their case; and petitions, appealing to the justice and protection of the British parliament and government, for such interposition with Spain as will obtain a settlement of the claims of the bondholders.
tables. 80 pp. London, J. Ollivier, 1847
N., T.

6136 CHISHOLM, Mrs. Caroline. Emigration and transportation relatively considered in a letter, dedicated, by permission, to earl Grey.
appendix. 46 pp. London, J. Ollivier, 1847
A.

6137 CLARKE, E. Hyde. Prophetic letters, on the West Indian interest.
20 pp. London, Simpkin, Marshall, 1847
T.

6138 COLLES, Edward Richards Purefoy, and COLLES, Henry. The clauses of acts affecting public works in Ireland abstracted and arranged in dictionary order as an index for the use of the commissioners of public works.
120 pp. Dublin, Hodges and Smith, 1847
T.

6139 COLLINS, Robert. A proposal to the rt. hon. earl Grey, to establish a charge upon estates, as in drainage, etc., to enable landlords to promote emigration, as the only means of preserving the lives of one million of our fellow creatures.
8 pp. Dublin, Hodges and Smith, 1847
N.

6140 COLQUHOUN, J. C. The effects of Sir R. Peel's administration on the political state and prospects of England.
44 pp. London, Rivington, 1847
A.

6141 COOPER, Henry G. Condition of the working classes; and the anomaly of the people wanting necessaries whilst there are abundant means of producing them, considered with a view to its removal.
table. 32 pp. Grantham, S. Ridge, London, R. Groombridge, 1847
T.

6142 A correct monetary system essential to a free-trade system. By the author of 'No trust, No trade'.
32 pp. London, Effingham Wilson, 1847
T.

6143 The currency question. Currency records; being extracts from speeches, documents, &c., &c., &c., illustrating the character and consequences of the acts of 1819 and 1844.
50 pp. 2nd. ed. London, Simpkin, Marshall, [1847]
T.

6144 DAYMAN, John. Observations on the justice and policy of regulating the trade in corn.
34 pp. London, Pelham Richardson, 1847
T.

6145 DEANE, J. C. A paper on the importance of encouraging the Irish Fisheries as an industrial resource. Read at an evening sectional meeting, [of the Royal Dublin Society], 23rd January, 1847.
16 pp. Dublin, University Press, 1847
D., N.

6146 Depositor's pass book with the Drogheda Savings Bank, together with the rules of management, etc.
12 pp. Drogheda, 1847
N.

6147 DERCSENYI, baron. Researches for a philanthropical remedy against Communism; or, a system of philanthropy applied to national economy, national education, and the political life of the people. Translated from the German.
table of contents. 124 pp. London, Shillinglaw, 1847
A.

6148 DESMOND, Daniel. Project for the creation of a sound paper currency, based on the security of real property, to be vested in a government commission, which should license banking companies to issue notes of legal tender to the value of all property so deposited, which notes, thus protected, should be a safe medium for home circulation, to represent transactions of trade, manufactures and agriculture, as well as of purchase and sale, in all respects as secure as a metal currency, which should therefore only be required to discharge our adverse foreign balances of commerce or of treaty, wherever such should arise.
16 pp. Cheltenham, printed by T. Withey, 1847
A.

6149 [——.] Project for the reclamation of one million acres of waste lands, in Ireland, by colonies of the present surplus and unemployed population, whose labour should, in the first instance, render those lands available for their own support, and finally, in a period of 21 years, convert them into a considerable and permanent item of revenue in the shape of Crown lands, while the habits and condition of that population should be progressively and essentially improved.
tables. 34 pp. Dublin, printed by Folds, 1847
A., N., N.

6150 [DEVON, William Courtenay, 10th earl of.] Letter from an Irish proprietor to the ministers of religion of the district.
24 pp. Dublin, Hodges & Smith, Limerick, G. McKern, 1847
A., N., T., U.

6151 DE WITTE, G. J. Financial plan for the relief of Ireland and the landlords of Ireland.
tables. 22 pp. London, Saunders and Otley, 1847
T.

6152 Distress in Ireland. Extracts from correspondence published by the Central Relief Committee of the Society of Friends. No. 1.
appendix. 34 pp. Dublin, printed by Webb & Chapman, 1847
A., N.

6153 Distress in Ireland. Extracts from correspondence published by the Central Relief Committee of the Society of Friends. no. II.
appendices with tables. 64 pp. Dublin, printed by Webb & Chapman, 1847
A., N.

6154 Distress in Ireland. Extracts from correspondence published by the Central Relief Committee of the Society of Friends. No. III.
appendices. 24 pp. Dublin, printed by Webb & Chapman, 1847
A.

6155 Distress in Ireland. Irish Relief Association for the destitute peasantry, being a re-organisation of the association formed during the period of famine in the west of Ireland in 1831.
appendix. 32 pp. Dublin, P. D. Hardy, 1847
N.

6156 Distress in Ireland. Outlines of a plan for employing funds to be raised by subscription in England, in such a manner, that in relieving the destitute, their condition may be so far improved as to prevent the necessity for aid in future years.
table. appendix. 16 pp. London, J. Ridgway, 1847
T.

6157 Distress in Ireland. Report of the trustees of the Indian Relief fund showing the distribution of £13,919/14s/2d. Commencing the 24th April, and ending the 31st December, 1846.
tables. 24 pp. Dublin, printed by Browne, 1847
A., N.

6158 DOOLAN, Thomas. Practical suggestions on the improvement of the present condition of the peasantry of Ireland.
table. 34 pp. London, printed by Barclay, 1847
N.

6159 Dublin & Drogheda Railway. Report of the directors, with statement of accounts, and list of shareholders; published preparatory to the half yearly meeting, to be held on Thursday 4th March, 1847.
tables. 28 pp. Dublin, printed by N. Walsh, 1847
A.

6160 Dublin and Drogheda Railway. Report of the directors with statement of accounts, published preparatory to the half-yearly meeting, to be held 27th August, 1847
tables. 8 pp. Dublin, printed by Falconer, 1847
A.

6161 DUFFERIN AND AVA, Frederick Temple Hamilton-Temple-Blackwood, 1st marquess of, and BOYLE, George Frederick, earl of Glasgow. Narrative of a journey from Oxford to Skibbereen during the year of the Irish famine.
plate. appendix. 30 pp. 2nd ed. Oxford, J. H. Parker, 1847
T.

6162 DUKINFIELD, Sir Henry R., bart. A letter to the inhabitants of the parish of St. Martin-in-the-Fields.
24 pp. London, W. H. Dalton, 1847
T.

On poor relief.

6163 DUNCAN, Jonathan. The national Anti-gold law league. The principles of the league explained, versus Sir R. Peel's currency measures, and the partial remedy advocated by the Scottish Banks, in a speech delivered at the City Hall, Glasgow, 7th August, 1847.
16 pp. London, J. Ollivier, 1847
T.

6164 DUNN, James. An address to the working classes of the United Kingdom on the necessity of acting in unison for a great object during the ensuing general election.
2 pp. (broadsheet.) Sunderland, printed by Smith, 1847
A.

6165 ELLERMAN, Charles F. Disinfection; or, remarks on the health of towns, and the manufacture of odourous azotiscal manure from animal and vegetable matters. appendix. 24 pp. London, Perice, 1847

A.

6166 ELLIS, Hercules. A report of the arguments and proceedings in the case of John Jackson in the years 1846–47. 42 pp. Dublin, Grant & Bolton, 1847

A.

6167 ENDERBY, Charles. England in 1830: being a letter to (the late) earl Grey, laying before him the condition of the people as described by themselves in their petitions to parliament. Reprinted. tables. 154 pp. London, Simpkin, Marshall, 1847

T.

See 4175.

6168 ——. The fallacy of our monetary system, as deduced from its author's, Sir Robert Peel's, definition of a 'pound'. 16 pp. London, Pelham Richardson, 1847

T.

6169 ——. Our money laws the cause of the national distress. 46 pp. London, Pelham Richardson, 1847

T.

6170 ——. Proposal for re-establishing the British Southern Whale Fishery, through the medium of a chartered company, and in combination with the colonisation of the Auckland Islands, as the site of the company's whaling station. (Being in reply to a letter [by T. R. Preston] addressed to him on behalf of certain parties connected with the British shipping interest, inviting the expression of his sentiments on the first-named subject.) table of contents. maps. tables. appendix. 72 pp. London, E. Wilson, 1847

N.

6171 The English poor-law, and poor-law commission, in 1847. tables. appendix. 56 pp. London, J. Murray, 1847

T.

6172 Evidence and opinions on the harbour of Valentia (Ireland) as to its fitness for a western packet station. Submitted to the right hon. lord John Russell first lord of the treasury, compiled by the solicitors of the Waterford and Valentia Railway Company. map. index. 54 pp. London, Wilson, 1847

A., N.

6173 Extracts from the views of W. H. Gregory, M.P., on Romanism in connection with colonisation. With the opinions of lord Roden and the bishop of Cashel of the same. 2 pp. London, 1847

A.

6174 FAGAN, James. Wastelands of Ireland: suggestions for their immediate reclamation, as a means of affording reproductive employment to the able-bodied destitute. 38 pp. Dublin, J. McGlashan, 1847

A., N., U.

6175 [FEATHERSTONHAUGH, George William?] Observations on the application of human labour under different circumstances, when employed on reproductive industry, or for national objects, in various parts of the British empire. By a field officer. tables. 58 pp. London, Smith Elder, 1847

T.

6176 FERGUSON, Samuel. On the expediency of taking stock. A letter to James Pim jr. table. 16 pp. Dublin, J. McGlashan, 1847

A., N., U.

6177 A few words on behalf of the middle classes of England on the subject of the income tax. 22 pp. London, J. Ollivier, 1847

T.

6178 FITZWILLIAM, Charles William Wentworth-Fitzwilliam, 5th earl. A letter to the rev. John Sargeaunt, rector of Stanwick, Northamptonshire. 30 pp. London, J. Ridgway, 1847

T.

See 6433.

6179 FLETCHER, John. Letter to the right hon. earl Grey, on the subject of emigration; with a short history of the colony of Port Phillip, its past reverses, present circumstances, and future prospects; shewing its peculiar fitness for a large and extensive scheme of colonization. table. appendix. 44 pp. Edinburgh & London, W. Blackwood, 1847

T.

6180 General order of the Poor-law Commissioners for regulating the administration of out-door relief. table of contents. tables. 24 pp. Dublin, Thom, 1847

A., N.

6181 GLYNN, Henry. A reference book to the incorporated railway companies of Ireland, alphabetically arranged, including a list of their directors, offices and officers, constitution, and capital. Gauge of way 5 feet 3 inches. map. table. 100 pp. London, J. Weale, Newcastle, R. Currie, 1847

T.

6182 ——. Reference book to the incorporated railway companies of Scotland, alphabetically arranged, including a list of their directors, offices and officers, constitution and capital. Gauge of way 4 feet 8½ inches. map. table. 100 pp. London, J. Weale, Newcastle, R. Currie, 1847

T.

6183 ——. Reference book to the incorporated railway companies of England and Wales, alphabetically arranged, including a list of their directors, offices and officers, constitution, and capital, shewing also the lines suspended in Session 1847, and applications for bills in 1848. Gauge of way National, . . . 4 feet 8½ inches. Exceptional, . . . 7 feet. Mixed, . . . the two combined. map. table. 240 pp. London, J. Weale, Newcastle, R. Currie, 1847

T.

6184 GODDARD, Samuel A. Miscellaneous letters on currency, free trade, etc.
46 pp. London, Simpkin, Marshall, 1847
A., T.

6185 GODLEY, John Robert. An answer to the question— What is to be done with the unemployed labourers of the United Kingdom?
60 pp. London, Stewart & Murray, 1847
N.

6186 ——. Observations on an Irish poor law. Addressed to the committee of landed proprietors, assembled in Dublin, January, 1847.
32 pp. Dublin, Grant & Bolton, London, Nickisson, 1847
A., N., T.

6187 [——.] To the right honourable lord John Russell, first lord of the treasury, the Memorial of the noblemen, gentlemen and landed proprietors of Ireland.
53 pp. London, Stewart and Murray, 1847
A.

6188 GOOLD, Henry. Thoughts on a judicious disposition of land in Ireland. Calculated to promote the best interests of landlord and tenant, while securing equitable remunerative employment for the entire labouring population, communicated in a letter to Richard S. Guinness esq., an Irish landlord and land agent.
tables. 24 pp. London, Effingham Wilson, Dublin, Madden & Hare, 1847
A., T.

6189 GORE, Montague. Suggestions for the amelioration of the present condition of Ireland.
tables. appendix. 70 pp. London, J. Ridgway, 1847
C., T.

6190 GRAHAM, Francis James. On the potato disease. Prize essay.
London, printed by W. Clowes, 1847
T.

6191 GRANT, Henry. Post office management. Cypher scheme developed, mail arrival hours adjusted to immediate delivery.
58 pp. 3rd. ed. London, J. Hatchard, 1847
A.

6192 GRAY, John. The currency question. A rejected letter to the editor of 'The Times', on the subject of the currency: to which is added the above-named offer repeated; failing the acceptance of a challenge to 'The Times' to discuss the subject for the sum of five hundred guineas.
24 pp. Edinburgh, A. and C. Black, London, Longman, Brown, Green and Longmans, 1847
A., T.

6193 [GRAYDON, William.] Relief for Ireland, prompt and permanent, suggested in a letter to the rt. hon. lord John Russell, by Agricola.
20 pp. London, J. Ridgway, 1847
U.

6194 [——.] On the reduction of taxes, and increase of food and revenue for the united kingdom of Great Britain and Ireland. By Agricola.
tables. appendices. 24 pp. 2nd edition. London, J. Ridgway, 1847
T.

6195 [——.] An oppressed poor in an insolvent nation. A letter to the members of the new parliament. By Agricola.
28 pp. London, J. Ollivier, 1847
T.

6196 The Great Britain steam ship. Extracts from the letters of Capt. Claxton, R.N., to I. K. Brunel, esq., and the directors of the Great Western steam ship company, giving a detailed account of the manner in which the Great Britain was first protected through the winter of 1847 in and afterward released from Dundrum Bay, with a report from the chairman to the shareholders of the company, and copies of documents relating to the breakwater, moved for and laid before parliament on the motion of the earl of Roden.
appendices. 76 pp. London, Longman, Brown, Green and Longmans [1847]
T.

6197 Great Southern and Western Railway, Ireland. Sixth half-yearly report.—1st February, 1847.
tables. 6 pp. Dublin, printed by A. Thom, 1847
A.

6198 Great Southern and Western Railway, Ireland. Seventh half-yearly report.—8th September, 1847.
tables. 8 pp. Dublin, printed by A. Thom, 1847
A.

6199 HAGGARD, William Debonaire. Observations on the standard of value, and the circulating medium of this country.
36 pp. 2nd ed. London, P. Richardson, 1847
A., T.

6200 [HALIDAY, Charles.] An appeal to his excellency the lord lieutenant on behalf of the labouring classes.
54 pp. Dublin, printed by P. D. Hardy, [1847]
A., U.

6201 HALL, John Charles. Facts which prove the immediate necessity for the enactment of sanitary measures, to remove those causes which at present increase most fearfully the bills of mortality, and seriously affect the health of towns.
60 pp. London, Longman, Brown, 1847
T.

6202 HAMILTON, Charles William. Short hints to the small farmers in Ireland on the question what shall we substitute for the potato?
table of contents. 34 pp. Dublin, W. Curry, jr., 1847
A.

See 6013.

6203 HAMILTON, John. On poor law and labour rate. A letter from a resident Irish landowner.
14 pp. Dublin, J. McGlashan, London, J. Ridgway, 1847
C., N.

6204 HANCOCK, William Neilson. Three lectures on the questions, should the principles of political economy be disregarded at the present crisis? and if not, how can they be applied towards the discovery of measures of relief? Delivered in the theatre of Trinity College, Dublin, in Hilary term 1847. 64 pp. Dublin, Hodges & Smith, London, B. Fellowes, 1847
A., N., T.

6205 HAYWARD, A., and BRASSINGTON, C. P. Report on the Dublin Improvement Bill.
56 pp. London, L. Hansard, 1847
A.

6206 [HIGGINS, Matthew James.] Is cheap sugar the triumph of free trade? A letter to the rt. hon. lord John Russell, etc., etc., etc. By Jacob Omnium.
20 pp. 2nd ed. London, J. Ridgway, 1847
T.
See 6457.

6207 A history of the Holyhead harbours of refuge, showing the circumstances under which these works originated: their present progress, their probable cost, and questionable utility when completed. Compiled from parliamentary records.
maps. 32 pp. n.p. [1847]
A.

6208 HOARE, Edward Newenham. The duty and expediency on the part of the landed proprietors of Ireland, of co-operating with the board of national education; considered in a letter to a deputy-lieutenant of the Co. Sligo.
36 pp. Dublin, Hodges & Smith, London, John W. Parker, 1847
B., N.

6209 HOLMES, Robert. The case of Ireland stated.
102 pp. 2nd ed. Dublin, James McGlashan; etc., 1847
B., D., N.

——. 102 pp. 3rd ed. Dublin, James McGlashan, 1847
B., T.

6210 HUGHES, John, bishop of New York. A lecture on the antecedent causes of the Irish famine in 1847 ... at the Broadway tabernacle, March 20th, 1847.
24 pp. 2nd ed. New York, E. Dunigan, 1847
A., U.

6211 The Irish council. [Rules, reports, etc.]
28 pp. Dublin, 1847
A.
The 'Irish Council' represented an attempt by landlords to combat the effects of the potato famine.

6212 The Irish Fishing and Fishing-boat Company. To be incorporated by letters patent or by royal charter. Prospectus.
4 pp. London, printed by Madden, 1847
A.

6213 Irish improvidence encouraged by English bounty; being a remonstrance against the government projects for Irish relief, and suggestions of measures by which the Irish poor can be speedily and effectually fed, relieved, employed and elevated above their present degraded position, without taxing English industry for this purpose. By an ex-member of the British parliament.
16 pp. London, [1847?]
N.

6214 Irish poor law question. A letter to the rt. hon. lord John Russell. From an Irish landlord.
10 pp. London, Smith, Elder & co., 1847
T.

6215 JAMES, Sir Walter, bart. Thoughts upon the theory and practice of the poor-laws. Being a series of letters originally written to the editor of the 'Spectator'.
94 pp. London, J. Murray, 1847
N., T.

6216 JAY, Charles. A few words on West Indian troubles; with a brief examination of England's West Indian policy.
8 pp. London, J. Ollivier, 1847
T.

6217 ——. Observations on the manufacture of sugar, sugar-making machinery, central works, and government restrictions: with suggestions for the improvement of manufacturing processes.
28 pp. London, Effingham Wilson, 1847
T.

6218 ——. Observations on the present state and future prospects of the West Indies, considered as national, commercial, and financial questions.
38 pp. London, Effingham Wilson, 1847
T.

6219 JOPLING, Thompson R. Vital statistics. Part 1. On the computing a rate of mortality among persons affected with various diseases, and on a set of tables prepared by the author.
tables. 14 pp. London, King, [1847]
T.

6220 KELLY, William. The Irish small farmer of 1847; containing ample directions for the cultivation of the soil during the present crisis.
table of contents. diagrams. 32 pp. Dublin, Cumming & Ferguson, 1847
A.

6221 KENNEDY, Henry. Observations on the connection between famine and fever in Ireland, and elsewhere.
54 pp. Dublin, Hodges & Smith, 1847.
A., N.

6222 KENNEDY, John Pitt. Correspondence on some of the general effects of the failure of the potato crop and the consequent relief measures, with suggestions as to the reconstruction of the poor law electoral or rateable divisions, as a means of arresting the impending national dangers, by substituting reproductive enterprise and industry for almsgiving.
tables. plan. 48 pp. Dublin, A. Thom, 1847
A., N., U.

6223 KINAHAN, Daniel. The system of relief for the poor as used in the Dublin Mendicity Institution, adapted to general use, considered in a letter.
10 pp. Dublin, R. M. Tims, 1847

A., N.

6224 KING, George. Holyhead Harbour. Reply to letter addressed by Charles Wye Williams esq. to the rt. hon. viscount Sandon, M.P.
20 pp. London, 1847

A.

6225 KINNEAR, George. Banks and exchange companies: a letter to Alexander Blair, esq., treasurer of the Bank of Scotland, in answer to the prospectus issued by the proposed British trust company.
appendix. 24 pp. Glasgow, David Robertson [etc., etc.], 1847

T.

6226 KINNEAR, John Gardiner. The crisis and the currency: with a comparison between the English and Scottish systems of banking.
86 pp. London, J. Murray, 1847

T.

Second edition with a postscript.
16 pp. London, J. Murray, 1847

T.

This contains only the postscript.

6227 KNIGHT, James. Private and public guarantee for persons appointed to offices of trust considered.
24 pp. London, Effingham Wilson [etc.], 1847

T.

6228 LANE, John. An appeal to the freemasons of England, on behalf of the starving poor of Ireland.
16 pp. London, S. Highley, 1847

T.

6229 LECKIE, William. A letter to the rt. hon. Sir Robert Peel, bart., M.P., on the bank charter bill: with a view to its modification or repeal.
24 pp. London, Pelham Richardson, 1847

T.

6230 LEMON, Sir Charles, bart. A letter to the right hon. the earl of Clarendon on the copper ore duties.
tables. 36 pp. London, J. Ridgway, 1847

T.

6231 A letter to the congestive bankerhood of Great Britain with a proposition for a new currency. By a traveller (not from Geneva).
20 pp. London, Effingham Wilson, 1847

T.

6232 A letter to the rt. hon. lord John Russell on the future prospects of Ireland.
16 pp. London, Cleaver, 1847

A., T.

6233 A letter to the right hon. the marquess of Lansdowne, lord president of Her Majesty's privy council, on the endowment of parochial schools. By a clergyman of the Church of England.
table. 20 pp. London, J. Hatchard, 1847

T.

6234 A letter to the shareholders of the East Indian and Great Western of Bengal railways, on their present position and future prospects. By one of themselves.
16 pp. London, Smith, Elder & co., 1847

T.

6235 MACADAM, James, jr. An economic review of the linen industry, with observations on the duties imposed on the import of linens and linen yarns by the continental states, and their effects upon the employment of the working classes. Read at the 'Congrès des économistes de tous les pays' at Brussells, 18th September, 1847.
24 pp. Belfast, printed by F. D. Finlay, 1847

A., N.

6236 M'NEILE, Hugh. The famine a rod of God; its provoking cause—its merciful design. A sermon preached in Liverpool February, 28th, 1847.
appendix. 48 pp. London, Seeley, Liverpool, Newling, 1847

A.

6237 MABERLEY, Mrs. K. C. The present state of Ireland, and its remedy.
32 pp. London, J. Ridgway, 1847

A.

———. 2nd ed. 32pp. London, J. Ridgway, 1847

D., N., T.

———. 3rd ed. 32 pp. London, J. Ridgway, 1847

A., C., N.

6238 MAITLAND, John. National savings banks. Suggestions for rendering such savings banks self-supporting; to increase efforts through them for the promotion of moral and provident habits in the classes of the community for whose behoof savings banks were instituted, and to remove from the public funds the present evil influence of savings banks.
tables. appendix. 32 pp. London, J. Johnstone, 1847

T.

6239 MANN, William. A plan for relieving the landed interest of the empire from the necessity of granting out-door relief to able-bodied paupers, etc. [by emigration to Australia] in a letter addressed to the Reproductive labour committee, College Green, Dublin.
12 pp. 3rd ed. (with additions). Dublin, printed by Dyott, 1847

N.

6240 MARSH, Sir Henry, bart. On the preparation of food for the labourer: in a letter to Joshua Harvey, M.D.
10 pp. Dublin, J. McGlashan, 1847

A., N.

6241 [MARTIN, Robert Montgomery.] British possessions in Europe, Africa, Asia, & Australasia connected with England by the India and Australia mail steam packet company.

Prepared at the request of the committee by the author of the 'History of the British colonies'.
map. tables. 58 pp. London, W. H. Allen, 1847

N., T.

6242 MARTINEAU, James. Ireland and her famine: a discourse preached in Paradise Street Chapel, Liverpool, on Sunday, Jan. 31, 1847.
22 pp. London, Chapman, 1847

N., U.

6243 MASSEY, Benjamin. The money crisis; its causes, consequences, and remedy. In a letter to the rt. hon. Sir Robert Peel, bart.
tables. 42 pp. London, W. H. Allen, 1847

T.

6244 [MATHER, James.] An address to the electors of the sea-ports of the United Kingdom on the Navigation laws: and their duties at this critical juncture. By the author of 'Ships and railways'.
24 pp. South Shields, printed by Hewison, 1847

A.

6245 Measures adopted in Boston, Massachusetts, for the relief of the suffering Scotch and Irish.
24 pp. Boston, printed by Eastburn, 1847

A.

6246 The measures which can alone ameliorate effectually the condition of the Irish people.
68 pp. London, J. Hatchard, 1847

T.

6247 MEEKINS, Robert. Plan for the removal of pauperism, agrarian disturbances, and the poor's rate in Ireland, by liberally providing for the destitute, free of expence. With other important improvements.
plan. tables. 32 pp. Dublin, J. McGlashan, London, J. Ridgway, 1847

A., N.

6248 MEYER, H. L. Treatise on a method of managing the potato plant, with a view to saving the present crop from the ravages of the disease; being the substance of a communication made before the president and council of the royal society of agriculture of England.
illust. 12 pp. London, Simpkin, Marshall & co., 1847

T.

6249 MILLER, Charles. The neglect of the poor the real danger of the nation. A letter on the scripture principle of church endowment, and its relation to the poor. Addressed to the right hon. Sir George Grey, bart., M.P., Her Majesty's secretary of state for the home department.
appendix. 36 pp. London, J. Ollivier, 1847

T.

6250 MILLS, Arthur. Systematic colonization.
48 pp. London, J. Murray, 1847

T.

6251 MILNE, David. Observations on the probable cause of the failure of the potato crop, in the years 1845 and 1846.
tables. 56 pp. Edinburgh and London, W. Blackwood, 1847

A., T.

6252 MITCHEL, John. The Irish Confederation. No. 4. Report on the levy of rates in Ireland for the repayment of government loans.
12 pp. Dublin, printed by Charles, 1847

A.

6253 The 'money market'; a brief, lucid, and intelligible exposition. By a country accountant.
tables. 16 pp. London, Arthur Hall, 1847

T.

6254 MONTEAGLE, Thomas Spring Rice, 1st baron. *Confidential*. Letter from lord Monteagle to the duke of Leinster respecting agricultural schools. Suggestions for the establishment and government of agricultural schools.
12 pp. Foynes, (Co. Limerick), 1847

A.

6255 MOORE, Arthur. The poor law unions and electoral divisions in Ireland, and the baronies in which they are situate; showing their population, area, and net annual value: With summaries of the unions, counties, and provinces, and a list of the marriage registrars' districts, showing their population, area, counties in which situate, etc. Compiled from official returns.
table of contents. tables. 84 pp. Dublin, Hodges and Smith. 1847

N., T.

6256 MOORE, William Prior. The case of Ireland; and remedies suggested for the amelioration of the condition of her people; contained in two letters to the rt. hon. Henry Labouchere, chief secretary of Ireland.
28 pp. Dublin, W. Curry, 1847

A.

6257 MORGAN, William. Pitt, Peel, and equitable adjustment. A plan of equitable adjustment, submitted as a remedy for the monetary condition of the country at the present time; and deduced as necessary from the present state of our finances, trade and commerce; and also from a comparison of Sir Robert Peel's monetary legislation, with that of Pitt's in 1797, when the Bank of England ceased to pay its notes in gold and silver.
16 pp. Bristol, W. Parsons, [1847?]

T.

6258 [MURE, David.] The commercial policy of Pitt and Peel. 1785–1846.
68 pp. London, J. Murray, 1847

A., T.

6259 [——.] Reply to the Quarterly Review. By the author of the 'Commercial policy of Pitt and Peel'.
38 pp. London, J. Murray, 1847

T.

6260 MURRAY, Robert. Ireland, its present condition and future prospects. In a letter addressed to the right honourable Sir Robert Peel, baronet.
24 pp. Dublin, J. McGlashan, London, J. Ridgway, 1847

A., G., N., T.

23

6261 NAPER, James Lenox William. On reproductive employment: being a paper addressed to the Reproductive committee.
12 pp. Dublin, J. McGlashan, 1847
A.

6262 National industry, the basis of national wealth, being a dissertation on the present state of the currency.
table. 26 pp. Liverpool, printed by Whitly and Ellis, 1847
A.

6263 Navigation laws. Report of a public meeting held at the Eastern Institution, Commercial Road, London, in support of the principle of the Navigation laws.
appendix. 64 pp. London, printed by Nias, 1847
A.

6264 NEWLAND, Henry. An address to the Relief committee of the Gorey electoral division on the close of their operations.
tables. 12 pp. Dublin, printed by A. Thom, 1847
N.

6265 NICHOLLS, George. On the condition of the agricultural labourer; with suggestions for its improvement.
diag. appendices. 82 pp. Second edition. London, C. Knight, 1847
T.

6266 OASTLER, Richard. Brougham *versus* Brougham, on the new poor law, with an appendix, consisting of a letter to lord John Russell. Dedicated to the duke of Wellington.
72 pp. London, W. J. Cleaver, 1847
T.

6267 O'BRIEN, William Smith. Reproductive employment; a series of letters to the landed proprietors of Ireland; with a preliminary letter to lord John Russell.
52 pp. Dublin, J. McGlashan, London, J. Ridgway, 1847
A., N., T., U.

6268 Observations on Mr. Strutt's railway bill.
56 pp. Westminster, J. Bigg, 1847
T.

6269 Observations on the law and present practice of bankruptcy and insolvency. By a registrar of a district court of bankruptcy.
table in appendix. 24 pp. Liverpool, D. Marples, 1847
T.

6270 Observations upon Ireland, and how her present destitute condition may be benefitted, addressed to lord John Russell. By T. F.
18 pp. Youghal, printed by Lindsay, 1847
N.

6271 O'CONNELL, John. An argument for Ireland.
table of contents. tables. appendices. index. 498 pp. 2nd. ed. Dublin, printed by Browne, 1847
A.

6272 On the currency. A letter to the right honourable lord John Russell, M.P., etc. By 'one who has seen better days'.
8 pp. London, B. Kimpton, 1847
T.

6273 OSBORN, John T. The food question: shewing the effects which steam power applied to agriculture would have on increasing the supply of food throughout Great Britain Ireland and the colonies.
tables in appendix. illustr. 36 pp. London, Smith, Elder & co., 1847
T.

6274 OWEN, James Eugene. The causes of the potato disease explained, with a statement of the means for its prevention, as indicated by such causes. Also, an account of seawater for agricultural and other purposes.
36 pp. London, Sherwood, Gilbert & Piper, 1847
A.

6275 Paper versus gold-money; or a new system of currency and banking, to render paper as secure as specie, and to unite the Bank of England, joint stock and private banks in one harmonious plan. By Spectator. [in 2 separate parts.]
64 pp. 2nd. ed. London, P. Richardson, 1847
N.

6276 PARKIN, John. The prevention and treatment of disease in the potato and other crops.
appendix. 92 pp. London, Wood, 1847
A.

6277 PARRY, John William, editor. The yeoman philosophizing on his poverty. The cause and the cure, familiarly exhibiting the origin of distress in England and destitution in Ireland, by an atrocious monopoly of the monetary system of coining bank notes. By a Welsh plebeian of the nineteenth century. (edited by John William Parry.)
table of contents. tables. 80 pp. London, Dyson, 1847
N.

6278 PEEL, Sir Robert, 2d. bart. To the electors for the borough of Tamworth.
36 pp. Drayton Manor, 1847
N.

6279 PHIPPS, Edmund. The monetary crisis, with a proposal for present relief, and increased safety in future.
16 pp. London, J. Ridgway, 1847
T.

6280 [PIM, Jonathan.] Observations on the evils resulting to Ireland, from the insecurity of title and the existing laws of real property; with some suggestions towards a remedy.
32 pp. Dublin, Hodges and Smith, 1847
A., N., T.

6281 A plan for a domestic currency, rendered independent of the foreign exchanges, and measured in standard gold. By a banker.
tables. 14 pp. London, Letts, Son & Steer, 1847
T.

6282 PORTER, John G. V. Irish railways. A few observations upon our present railway system in Ireland.
tables. appendix. 32 pp. Dublin, Hodges and Smith, 1847
N.

6283 The potato blight famine. Questions and replies between two travellers, on its causes and results, edited by one of them.
4 pp. Dublin, printed by Webb, [1847]
N.

6284 Practical information on the best method of brewing from sugar; in which is given the history of the trade from 1769, to the present time, with an account of the price of raw material and the selling price of beer. By a practical brewer.
32 pp. Burnley, printed by Waddington, 1847
T.

6285 The present state of the currency practically considered; proving the justice and necessity of immediately and effectually revising the currency measures of 1819 and 1844.
tables. appendices. 92 pp. London, G. Biggs, 1847
A., N.

6286 Railways in India. By an Engineer.
tables. appendix. 132 pp. London, J. Williams, 1847
T.

6287 RAWSTORNE, Lawrence. The cause of the potato disease ascertained by proofs; and the prevention proved by practice. With some remarks added on Irish affairs.
32 pp. 3rd ed. London, Simpkin, Marshall, Preston, Oakey,
N., T.

6288 RAYNBIRD, Hugh. Essay on measure work, locally known as task, piece, job, or grate work, (in its application to agricultural labour,) for which the prize was awarded by the Royal agricultural society. Re-printed from the society's journal with additional information.
tables. 32 pp. London, Henry Wright [etc., etc.], 1847
T.

6289 Relief to Ireland, under the recent calamity, from the general funds of the state. Extract of a letter (signed Selden).
18 pp. Dublin, printed by G. Folds, 1847
N.

6290 Remarks on the consequences of the entire change of our colonial policy in British North America.
58 pp. Edinburgh & London, W. Blackwood, 1847
A., T.

6291 The report and adjudication of the judges on the exhibition of Irish manufacture, produce and invention, held at the Royal Dublin Society's house, 30th June, 1847, and following days.
index. 52 pp. Dublin, Hodges and Smith, 1847
N.

6292 Report of the acting committee to the standing committee of West India planters and merchants. 13th January, 1847.
appendix. tables. 56 pp. London, Maurice, 1847
A.

6293 Report of the general executive committee of the city and county of Philadelphia, appointed by the town meeting of February 17th, 1847, to provide means to relieve the sufferings in Ireland.
42 pp. Philadelphia, printed by Crissy & Markley, 1847
A.

6294 REVANS, John. A per centage tax on domestic expenditure, to supply the whole of the public revenue.
42 pp. London, J. Hatchard, 1847
T.

6295 REYNOLDS, John. Dublin improvement bill. A letter to the earl of Lincoln, M.P., on the bill before the house of commons for the improvement of the Borough of Dublin.
tables. 52 pp. London, printed by Palmer, 1847
A.

6296 RICHMOND, William. A condensed and comparative view of the population, navigation and trade of the United Kingdom for 1816 and 1846 both years of profound and continuous peace, with a glance at the progressive increase of the shipping of the United States of America, and the kingdoms of Russia, Prussia, Sweden, Norway and Denmark, in the carrying trade of the commodities of the consumption of the British empire for the same periods, carefully extracted from authentic parliamentary documents, save where otherwise the exception is noted, compiled for the express purpose of shewing that the increase in the merchant shipping of England, on which rests the base of her power, bears no proportion to the increased means she possesses of affording them employment. Why it is so has yet to be shewn.
tables. 2 pp. (broadsheet.) London, 1847
A.

6297 ROBINSON, Daniel. Irish waste land improvement society. 5th annual report [for 1846].
appendix. 26 pp. London, printed by Darling, 1847
N.

6298 ROBINSON, W. W. The dawn of Ireland's prosperity. General employment; blight of the potato crop. A visitation! In a series of lectures.
appendix. 32 pp. Dublin, Robertson, 1847
N.

6299 ROGERS, Jasper Wheeler. An appeal for the Irish peasantry, with facts of paramount advantage to the ironmasters, manufacturers, and agriculturists of England, respecting the value of peat and peat-charcoal as a fuel and a fertiliser.
table of contents. tables. 116 pp. London, E. Wilson, 1847
A., N., U.

6300 ——. An appeal for the peasantry of Ireland, and objects of the Irish Amelioration Society. With heads of the amended Act.
table of contents. tables. 108 pp. 2nd ed. London, E. Wilson, 1847
A., N.

6301 ——. Employment of the Irish peasantry the best means to prevent the drain of gold from England. Originally published in 'The Mark Lane Express', with an appendix containing notes, and observations on the letters of his excellency the lord lieutenant of Ireland, and Sir John Burgoyne, bart., K.C.B.
appendix. 32 pp. London, T. Saunders, 1847
A., N.

6302 ——. Facts for the kind-hearted of England as to the wretchedness of the Irish peasantry, and the means for their regeneration.
40 pp. new ed. London, J. Ridgway, 1847
A., N., Q., T.

6303 ——. The potato truck system of Ireland, the main cause of her periodical famines and of the non-payment of her rents.
20 pp. 2nd ed. London, J. Ridgway, 1847
A., N., T.

6304 ROSSE, William Parsons, 3rd earl. Letters on the state of Ireland. By the earl of Rosse.
appendix. 36 pp. 2nd ed. London, J. Hatchard, 1847
A., D., N., T.

6305 Royal Charter of Incorporation, sanctioned by Her Majesty on the 20th May, and passed the great seal on the 6th August, 1847, for the India and Australia Mail Steam Packet Company from England to India, Australia, etc., etc., etc. Extension of the whole Line granted on the 24th August, 1847.
16 pp. London, Offices of the company, 1847
N.

6306 RUFFY, Daniel William. Rules of the United patriots' and patriarchs' equitable land and building benefit society.
tables in appendix. 34 pp. London, H. Morton, 1847
T.

6307 Rules and regulations of the benevolent society of the law clerks of the City of Dublin. Founded 1847.
20 pp. Dublin, printed by Hogan, 1847
A.

6308 Rules of the Irish metropolitan mutual benefit building and investment society. Established according to Act of Parliament 6 & 7 William IV., C.32.
index. tables. 24 pp. Dublin, 1847
N.

6309 RUSSELL, Archibald. Account of the eleven thousand schools in the state of New York. Being a letter to Sir William Hamilton, bart., Advocate.
tables. 60 pp. Edinburgh, A. and C. Black, London, Longman, Brown, Green and Longmans, 1847
T.

6310 SALOMONS, Sir David, 1st bart. Railways in England and in France: being reflections suggested by Mr. Morrison's pamphlet, and by the report drawn up by him for the Railway acts committee.
tables. 80 pp. London, P. Richardson, 1847
A., T.

6311 SANDERSON, Henry. A plan for an effectual general system of sewage for the cities of London and Westminster, and their suburbs: with a view chiefly to permanent sanitary results; and subordinately, to further pecuniary advantages in the reduction of parochial and sewer rates, respectfully referred to the common sense of acting commissioners of sewers, and the common prudence of working members of parliament; on behalf of his fellow-ratepayers and the rising generation.
32 pp. London, John Williams 1847
T.

6312 SCROPE, George Julius Duncombe Poulett. Extracts of evidence taken by the late commission of inquiry into the occupation of land in Ireland, on the subject of wastelands reclamation; with a prefatory letter to the right honourable lord John Russell.
tables. 112 pp. London, J. Ridgway, 1847
A., N.

6313 ——. A letter to the landed proprietors of Ireland, on the means of meeting the present crisis, by measures of a permanent character.
24 pp. London, J. Ridgway, 1847
A., C., N.

6314 ——. Letters to lord John Russell, M.P., etc., on the further measures required for the social amelioration of Ireland.
64 pp. London, J. Ridgway, 1847
A., N., T.

6315 ——. Remarks on the Irish poor relief bill.
32 pp. London, J. Ridgway, 1847
N., T.

6316 ——. Reply to the speech of the archbishop of Dublin, delivered in the house of lords, on Friday, 26th March, 1847, and the protest signed R. Dublin, Monteagle, Radnor, Mountcashel, against the poor relief (Ireland) bill.
44 pp. London, J. Ridgway, 1847
A., N., T.

6317 SENIOR, Nassau William. A lecture on the production of wealth, delivered before the University of Oxford, in Michaelmas term, 1847.
20 pp. Oxford, J. H. Parker, London, Rivington, 1847
T.

6318 The settlement and removal of the poor considered.
60 pp. London, J. Ollivier, 1847
T.

6319 SHAEN, Samuel, Junr. A review of railways and railway legislation at home and abroad.
tables. 108 pp. London, William Pickering, 1847
T.

6320 SHARPE, B. Plan for an extension of the currency; proposed in a letter to the right hon. Sir Charles Wood, bart., chancellor of the exchequer, &c., &c., &c.
16 pp. London, Smith, Elder & co., 1847
T.

6321 SHREWSBURY, John Talbot, 16th earl of. Thoughts on the poor relief bill for Ireland: together with reflections on her miseries, their causes and their remedies.
tables in appendix. 86 pp. London, Charles Dolman, 1847
P., T.

6322 SIGSTON, W. H. A lecture on Ireland: delivered in the Binfield-House school-room, by W. H. Sigston, on Tuesday evening, March 16, 1847.
70 pp. London, Bell, 1847
A.

6323 [SIMPSON, James.] A letter to the right honourable Henry Labouchere, chief secretary of Ireland: on the more effective application of the system of relief by means of soup kitchens.
tables. 14 pp. London, Whittaker, 1847
A., N., T.

6324 Sketches of popular tumults: illustrative of the evils of social ignorance.
238 pp. London, C. Cox, 1847

L.

6325 SLIGO, George John Browne, 3rd marquess of. A few remarks and suggestions on the present state of Ireland.
36 pp. London, Andrews, 1847

A., N.

6326 SMITH, Arthur. The eastern counties railway viewed as an investment: With statistical information taken from parliamentary papers, showing the powers possessed by this company of raising money. With remarks on the present and prospective outlay on the eastern counties district. Illustrated by references to authorities with a view of facilitating inquiry.
tables. 24 pp. London, Smith Elder & co., 1847

T.

6327 [——.] Railways as they really are: or, facts for the serious consideration of railway proprietors. No. I. London, Brighton and South Coast railway.
tables. 42 pp. London, Sherwood, Gilbert, and Piper, 1847

T.

6328 [——.] Railways as they really are: or, facts for the serious consideration of railway proprietors. No. VII. Lancashire and Yorkshire railway.
40 pp. 2nd ed. London, Sherwood, Gilbert, and Piper, 1847

T.

6329 SMITH, Edward. A treatise on the navigation laws, founded on facts, combined with close practical observation during the last thirty years. British naval supremacy, commercial prosperity and maritime rights.
appendix. tables. 48 pp. London, Pelham Richardson, 1847

A., T.

6330 The state of Ireland, and the measures of government for its relief, considered with reference to the interests of the poor.
tables. 28 pp. London, J. Ridgway, 1847

N.

6331 Statement of the directors of the Dublin and Drogheda railway respecting the claims of Mr. Thomas Brodigan for special services.
36 pp. Dublin, MacDonnell, 1847

A.

6332 Statement of the income and expenditure of James Fanning's Charitable institution, for the year ending 31st December, 1846.
tables. 12 pp. Waterford, printed by Harvey, 1847

A.

6333 STEEL, Samuel H. A report on the sanitary condition of the town of Abergavenny: with remedial suggestions, founded chiefly upon the reports of the health of towns commission.
tables. 70 pp. Abergavenny, James Hiley Morgan, 1847

T.

6334 STODDART, George Henry. The true cure for Ireland, the development of her industry: being a letter addressed to the right honourable lord John Russell, M.P., with a notice of the Irish Amelioration society, as organised upon the plan of Mr. Jasper Rogers.
appendix. tables. 24 pp. London, Saunders, 1847

A., C., N.

6335 Substance of the reports and evidence of the several authorities, who have reported on the comparative merits of Holyhead and Portdynllaen, as a harbour of refuge, showing that all who have so reported have decided against Holyhead and in favour of Portdynllaen.
8 pp. London, the Milton Press, [1847?]

A.

6336 Suggestions for a domestic currency founded upon philosophic and unerring principles: preceded by a few thoughts on the economy of order and industry, the harmony of which becomes permanent only by an equitable measure of exchange.
72 pp. London, Wiley and Putnam, 1847

T.

6337 Suggestions to small farmers in the barony of Farney, on substitute for potato crop. Published for the Farney relief committee.
8 pp. Dublin, printed by A. Thom, 1847

A.

6338 Third address of the Liverpool association for the reduction of the duty on tea.
tables. 4 pp. [no. t.p.] Liverpool, printed by Whitty & Ellis, 1847

N.

6339 THOMAS, John Harries. A new kind of money, and a new system of currency, based on real property, whereby the nation would be saved £10,000,000 sterling per annum; exhibited in a letter to the right hon. lord Stanley, and lord George Bentinck, M.P.; being the substance of a lecture delivered by the rev. J. H. Thomas, B.A., incumbent of Millbrook; wherein the defects of the present monetary system are exposed, and the advantages of the proposed one explained.
28 pp. London, C. Mitchell, 1847

T.

6340 THOMPSON, T. A few words respecting the currency, the bank of England, and the new banking act.
18 pp. London, Pelham Richardson, 1847

T.

6341 THORBURN, David. The divinely prescribed method for the support of the clergy, the ordinances of religion, and the poor. Written for, and partially read at the monthly conference of the free presbytery of Edinburgh, Wednesday, September 2nd, 1846
68 pp. Edinburgh and London, John Johnstone, 1847

T.

6342 Thoughts on Ireland.
48 pp. London, J. Ridgway, 1847

T.

6343 To the parliamentary electors throughout the United Kingdom and especially to the constituencies of maritime boroughs. Address of the Central Committee for upholding the principles of the Navigation laws.
12 pp. London, Nias, 1847

A.

6344 To the subscribers to the Irish relief fund of the Society of Friends. Address to Friends in North America from the committee of the Society of Friends in London, appointed on the subject of the distress existing in Ireland.
4 pp. London, 1847

A.

6345 TORRENS, Robert.   On the operation of the bank charter act of 1844, as it affects commercial credit.
40 pp. 2nd ed. London, J. Ridgway [etc., etc.], 1847

T.

6346 ———. Self-supporting colonization. Ireland saved without cost to the imperial treasury.
32 pp. London, J. Ridgway, 1847

A., N.

6347 TRELAWNY, Sir Jonathan Salusbury, bart.   Sketch of existing restrictions on banking, and doubts of the soundness of the principles on which they rest.
26 pp. London, Longman, Brown, Green and Longmans, 1847

T.

6348 TRYE, Tristram (pseudonym).   Tract for the times—No. II. The incubus on commerce; or, the false position of the Bank of England: a practical enquiry. By Tristram Trye, esq.
100 pp. London, Smith Elder, Liverpool, Thomas Baines, 1847

T.

6349 ———. Appendix to tract for the times, No. II entitled, the incubus on commerce; or, the false position of the Bank of England. By Tristram Trye, esq.
40 pp. London, Smith Elder, Liverpool, Thomas Baines, 1847

T.

6350 ———. Why trade is at a stand-still; or, the influence of the bank of England on property, commerce and labour; a practical enquiry.
tables in appendices. 48 pp. London, Simpkin and Marshall, Liverpool, Thomas Baines, 1847

T.

6351 URQUHART, David.   The parliamentary usurpations of 1819 and 1844, in respect to money, considered: in a letter to the burgesses and electors of Stafford.
20 pp. London, J. Ollivier, 1847

T.

6352 WALKER, William Stuart.   The drainage act. An analysis and exposition of the act 9 & 10 Victoria, cap. 101. With an appendix, containing the act, and official forms and documents.
tables in appendix. 96 pp. Edinburgh & London, W. Blackwood & sons, 1847

T.

6353 WARD, James.   The bank of England justified in their present course.
36 pp. London, Smith, Elder & co., 1847

T.

6354 ———. How to re-construct the industrial condition of Ireland: a letter to lord J[ohn] Russell.
36 pp. London, Smith Elder & co., 1847

T.

6355 ———. Railways for the many, and not for the few, or, how to make them profitable to all. Second edition, enlarged. With some remarks on building and other benefit societies.
tables. 70 pp. London, Smith Elder & co., 1847

T.

6356 ———. Remedies for Ireland. A letter to the right hon. lord Monteagle, on the fallacy of the proposed poor law, emigration, reclamation of waste lands, as remedies: being a postscript to 'How to reconstruct the industrial condition of Ireland'.
22 pp. London, Smith, Elder & co., 1847

T.

6357 ———. The true policy of organizing a system of railways for India. A letter to the right hon. the president of the board of control.
38 pp. London, Smith, Elder & co., 1847

T.

6358 WARD, William.   Remarks on the commercial legislation of 1846.
tables. 86 pp. London, Pelham Richardson, 1847

T.

6359 ———. Remarks on the monetary legislation of Great Britain.
appendix. 74 pp. London, Pelham Richardson, J. Ollivier, 1847

T.

6360 WASON, Peter Rigby.   Letter to the right honourable lord John Russell, M.P., etc., etc., etc., suggesting that the mode adopted for the reclamation of waste land at Corwar, should be pursued in Ireland.
18 pp. London, J. Ridgway, Edinburgh, W. Watson, 1847

N., T.

6361 Where has our cash gone? And how are we to get it? In order to benefit trade and remove the increasing distress of Great Britain and Ireland; exposing the great and unsuspected causes of our pauperism, with the only safe, fair, and certain remedies applicable.   The author's name in anagram: Cash v. Larder is wealth.
tables. 24 pp. London, J. Ollivier, 1847

T.

6362 WHITEHEAD, John.   Railway and government guarantee. Which is preferable? Facts and arguments to shew that guaranteed railway stock offers a better investment than do government securities. Second edition, with additions, alterations, and corrections.
tables. 56 pp. London, Smith, Elder & co., 1847

T.

6363 WHITMORE, William Wolryche. Letter to lord John Russell on railways.
tables. 22 pp. London, J. Ridgway, 1847
T.

6364 WILLIAMS, Albert. Antagonistic anomalies. Inconvertible paper and free trade, free trade and bullion, and inconvertible paper and protection.
16 pp. London, J. Ollivier, 1847
T.

6365 ——. The crisis and the crash. A letter to the free traders of England.
16 pp. London, J. Ollivier, 1847
T.

6366 WILLIAMS, Charles Wye. Holyhead harbour, and its contemplated monopoly. Chester and Holyhead railway bill.
4 pp. London, 1847
A.

6367 ——. Remarks on the proposed asylum harbour at Holyhead, and the monopoly contemplated by the Chester and Holyhead Railway company, in a letter addressed to viscount Sandon, M.P.
folding maps. 46 pp. Liverpool, 1847
A.

6368 ——. Further remarks on the proposed asylum harbour at Holyhead, and the monopoly contemplated by the Chester and Holyhead Railway company, in a second letter addressed to viscount Sandon, M.P.
folding maps. 40 pp. Liverpool, 1847
A.

6369 [WILLIAMS, W.] A plan for regulating the circulation on the principle of Sir Robert Peel's celebrated currency bill of 1819. By a man of business.
appendix. 36 pp. (various paging.) 2nd ed. with additions. London, Pelham Richardson, 1847
T.

6370 A word in season to the Liberal electors of Ireland. By a graduate of Dublin University.
40 pp. London, J. Ridgway, Dublin, J. M'Glashan, 1847
A., N.

6371 WRIGHT, Ichabod Charles. The evils of the currency, an exposition of Sir Robert Peel's bank charter act.
22 pp. Nottingham, Dearden, London, Longman, Brown, Green and Longmans, 1847
T.

1848

6372 The act to facilitate the sale of incumbered estates in Ireland, with a copious index and directions for proceeding (under the provision of the act) for the sale of lands subject to incumbrances. By a practising solicitor.
table of contents. appendix. 74 pp. Dublin, A. Milliken, London, W. G. Benning, 1848
A., N.

6373 Address to the proprietors of the south Devon railway. By the chairman of the board of directors.
tables in appendix. 60 pp. London, Effingham Wilson, 1848
T.

6374 Address to the protestants of Ireland on the Repeal movement.
16 pp. Dublin, Oldham, 1848
A.

6375 ALCOCK, T. The tenure of land in Ireland considered.
appendix. 34 pp. London, J. Ridgway, 1848
A., T.

6376 [ALEXANDER, James.] A letter to Sir R. A. Ferguson, bart., M.P., on the relative rights of landlord and tenant, proposing an adjustment of their interests on the basis of certain principles already recognised in India, and held to be applicable to the present condition of Ireland. By an Irish landholder and member of the Bengal civil service.
22 pp. London, B. Fellowes, 1848
N., T.

6377 The anti-panic monetary system. Relief to the commercial classes and to shareholders in public works.
14 pp. London, Simpkin Marshall, 1848
T.

6378 Anti-revolutionary tracts. By Sosthenes. Employment of the people. No. 6.
16 pp. London, Joseph Masters, [c. 1848]
T.

6379 ANTROBUS, Edmund Edward. Anarchy and order. Facts for the consideration of all classes of the community, more especially for the mechanic artisan etc.
tables. 26 pp. London, Staunton, 1848
T.

6380 ARCHBOLD, John Frederick. Buller's Acts, 11 & 12 Victoria, cc. 82, 91, 110, 114; relating to the payment of parochial debts, the audit of accounts, the chargeability of paupers upon unions, and the education of the infant poor, with practical notes and index.
index. 58 pp. London, Shaw, 1848
T.

6381 ——. The new Poor law amendment Act, 11 & 12 Vict. c. 31, relating to orders of removal, grounds of removal, and appeals, with a practical introduction and notes.
42 pp. London, Shaw, 1848
T.

6382 BABBAGE, Charles. Thoughts on the principles of taxation, with reference to a property tax and its exceptions.
tables. 24 pp. London, J. Murray, 1848
T.

6383 BEASLEY, J. Richardson B. The Guardian of landlord and tenant, of trade and poor man, and convertor of poor-rates into capital. With the plan for applying the capital, with science and safety, to cultivating the resources, effecting the social and general reformation of Ireland, rendering poor-rates—except for those unable from infirmities to provide for themselves—unnecessary; arranging the tenant-right question:

and showing how to pay the tithe-rent charge, to the satisfaction of all parties, without expense to anyone: as lately laid, by a Tipperary deputation, before his excellency the earl of Clarendon, arranged with the assistance of the Tipperary Midland and Union of Cashel trade and agricultural society.
48 pp. Dublin, J. Duffy, 1848

A., N.

6384 BIDDELL, H. T. Hand book of financial statistics comprising 168 tables of the public revenue, expenditure, customs, excise, stamps (etc.) of Great Britain and Ireland, in the year of 1820; and from 1840 to 1846. Taken from the public annual "finance accounts" and other official authorities. To which are added numerous miscellaneous notices of matters of public interest, with a diagram, showing the yearly average prices of wheat from 1793 to 1846; and a comparative view of the weekly prices of 1846 and 1847. Compiled and alphabetically arranged.
tables. 16 pp. Chelmsford, 1848

N.

6385 BLACKALL, Samuel Wensley. Suggestions for relieving distress, by stimulating private and public employment.
24 pp. Dublin, J. M'Glashan, 1848

T.

6386 BLACKER, William. Currency. [a letter which had been refused by the Morning Chronicle.]
4 pp. Armagh, 1848

A.

6387 BLEST, Albert. Letter to his excellency, George William Frederick earl of Clarendon, lord lieutenant general and general governor of Ireland containing suggestions for the further development of the system of instruction in practical husbandry, instituted by his excellency, and for the establishment of small farmers' loan societies.
20 pp. Dublin, J. McGlashan, 1848

N.

6388 The Blue book of the British manufacturers; or, the money-monger's true picture: a companion to the Black book! containing also an exposure of the money received by romanists and dissenters; and a Black list of commissions, etc., under the centralisation system; and remarks on taxation, representation, manufacturers, migration, corn law repeal, etc. By Squire Auty.
tables. 54 pp. 2nd ed. London, Parry, 1848

N.

6389 BOSANQUET, Samuel Richard. A letter to lord John Russell, on the safety of the nation.
34 pp. London, J. Hatchard, 1848

T.

6390 BOURNE, John. An introduction to the second edition of Railways in India; illustrative of the practicability of rendering available existing works in diminution of the cost of such undertakings, whereby their profits may be greatly increased.
map. table. 24 pp. London, J. Williams, 1848

N.

6391 BOWEN, C. H. Mortgage banks considered as the means of providing employment in Ireland. In a letter to lord John Russell.
16 pp. Dublin, J. McGlashan, 1848

A.

6392 BOYLE, Thomas. Hope for the canals! Showing the evil of amalgamations with railways to public and private interests, and the means for the complete and permanent restoration of canal property to a position of prosperity, upon its present basis of original and independent enterprise.
diags. 44 pp. London, Simpkin, Marshall, 1848

T.

6393 British spirits. Comments upon the evidence affecting the spirit trade, given before the committee of the house of commons, upon sugar and coffee planting. By a Scotchman.
82 pp. London, Effingham Wilson, 1848

A., T.

6394 BROWN, Humphrey. Irish wants and practical remedies. An investigation on practical and economical grounds as to the application of a government system of railways in Ireland.
table of contents. tables. 76 pp. London, Barnett, 1848

A., N.

6395 BROWNE, Joseph Houston. The navigation laws, a national question. A brief examination of Mr. Ricardo's 'Anatomy of the navigation laws'.
32 pp. London, Smith, Elder & co., 1848

T.

6396 A budget of two taxes only. A stamp tax with the legacy duty equalised and extended to real property; and a property tax, applied to all realised property, with an equitable proportion on income.
12 pp. London, Effingham Wilson, 1848

T.

6397 CATLIN, George. Catlin's notes for the emigrant to America.
16 pp. London, the author, 1848

T.

6398 CHARNOCK, John Henry. On land drainage; with some remarks on meteorological influences as connected therewith.
tables. 32 pp. London, Longman, Brown, Green and Longmans, 1848

T.

6399 CLEVELAND, Robert Frank. The London and north western railway. Are railways a good investment? The question considered by an examination of the last half yearly statements of the six leading companies.
tables. plate. appendix. 60 pp. (various paging.) London, Effingham Wilson, 1848

T.

6400 Commerce and free trade promoted in the Indian archipelago. By 'Philopatris'.
24 pp. London, Smith Elder & co., 1848

T.

6401 Competence in a colony contrasted with poverty at home; or, relief to landlords and labourers held out by Australian colonization and emigration. A memorial addressed to the right hon. lord John Russell, etc., etc.
tables. 30 pp. London, J. Murray, 1848.

A., T.

6402 COOPER, Thomas, ed. and tr. The land for the labourers, and the fraternity of nations: a scheme for a new industrial system, just published in Paris, and intended for proposal to the national assembly.
16 pp. London, Effingham Wilson, 1848
T.

6403 COOPER, W. Waldo. Mr. Feargus O'Connor's land scheme. An examination of the principles and ultimate results of the national land company scheme, projected by Mr. Feargus O'Connor.
12 pp. London, F. and J. Rivington, 1848
T.

6404 COURT, Major Henry. A digest of the realities of the Great Western railway.
tables. 24 pp. London, Pelham Richardson, 1848
T.

6405 DAVIS, Hewitt. Farming essays.
tables. 108 pp. London, J. Ridgway, 1848
T.

6406 Defects in the practice of life assurance, and suggestions for their remedy, with observations on the uses and advantages of life assurance, and the constitution of offices.
tables. 42 pp. London, W. S. Orr, [1848?]
T.

6407 DENMAN, Thomas, 1st baron. A letter from lord Denman to lord Brougham, on the final extinction of the slave-trade. Second edition, corrected.
90 pp. London, J. Hatchard, 1848
T.
See 6618.

6408 [DENNIS, James Blatch Piggot.] A letter to lord John Russell, relative to some allusions in his lordship's speech concerning the appropriation of the revenues of the Irish church. By Lucius.
16 pp. London, F. and J. Rivington, 1848
T.

6409 DIGWELL, Philip. Modern agriculture as peculiarly applicable to Ireland, including draining, sub-soiling, manuring, rotation of crops and house-feeding.
tables of contents. table. diagrams. appendix. 96 pp. Dublin, J. McGlashan, 1848
A., N.

6410 DRUMMOND, Henry. Elementary propositions on currency.
14 pp. London, T. Bosworth, 1848
T.

6411 Dublin & Drogheda Railway. Report of the committee appointed at the half-yearly meeting, held 2nd and 3rd March, 1848, to investigate into the affairs of the company.
tables. 16 pp. Dublin, Falconer, 1848
A.

6412 [DUNCAN, Jonathan.] Letters on monetary science. By Aladdin. [Revised and reprinted from 'Douglas Jerrold's Weekly Newspaper'.]
tables. 80 pp. London, J. Ollivier, and Effingham Wilson, 1848
T.

6413 Dundalk and Enniskillen railway company. Reports of the directors and engineer, with statement of accounts, submitted to the shareholders at the half-yearly meeting, August 31st, 1848.
tables. 62 pp. Dublin, printed by Charles, 1848
A.

6414 [ELLIOT, John Lettsom.] A letter to the electors of Westminster. From a protectionist.
tables. 84 pp. 2nd edition. London, John Hearne, 1848
T.

6415 ELLY, Sandham. Potatoes, pigs and politics, the curse of Ireland and the cause of England's embarrassments. This essay is most earnestly recommended to the serious reflection of every Irish landlord, and every member of parliament.
36 pp. London, Kent and Richards, 1848
A., N.

6416 The emigrant's guide, by an experienced traveller; (corrected, revised and enlarged:) containing all the necessary instruction for persons leaving Ireland for New York, or other parts of the United States of North America. Together with truly important and recent information respecting Canada.
table of contents. 24 pp. Dublin, printed by Scott, 1848
A.

6417 The emigrants' guide to California, describing its geography, agricultural and commercial resources. Containing a well-arranged list of the commodities most desirable for exporting to that country, with a table of the duties. Also, some useful information for commanders of vessels, and for the overland travellers through Texas. Together with a valuable map, on which the various routes are traced, and an authentic sketch of San Francisco; to which is appended the governor of California's (Colonel Mason's) official despatches concerning the gold districts. By a traveller recently returned from California.
map. appendix. 78 pp. London, Pelham Richardson, [1848?]
T.

6418 Emigration and superabundant population considered in a letter to lord Ashley. By Amicus Populi.
16 pp. London, P. Richardson, 1848
A.

6419 England, a self-supporting country, or, a method of turning every perfect grain into a plant, and preserving each plant till harvest, whereby a saving of two bushels of seed out of every three, is effected. By a practical farmer.
36 pp. (various paging.) London, J. Hatchard, [etc., etc.], 1848
T.

6420 The evils of monopoly and its remedies. By Eight Seven.
half title only. 16 pp. [London?], 1848
N.

6421 'Facts and figures': a letter to the proprietors of the Sambre and Meuse railway. By an engineer and shareholder.
tables. 22 pp. London, Effingham Wilson, 1848.
T.

6422 Facts from the fisheries, contained in two reports from the Ring district, Co. Waterford.
20 pp. Waterford, printed by Harvey, 1848
A.

6423 Facts from the fisheries contained in four quarterly reports from the Ring district, Co. Waterford.
tables. 48 pp. Waterford, printed by Harvey, 1848
A.

6424 The famine as yet in its infancy; or, 1847 compared with the prospects of 1848, 1849, &c. Addressed to every-body.
tables. 24 pp. London, Hamilton, Adams, [1848?]
T.

6425 FANE, C. Bankruptcy reform: in a series of letters addressed to William Hawes, esq., chairman of the London committee for promoting the amendment of the law of bankruptcy and insolvency.
28 pp. London, printed by Spottiswoode and Shaw, 1848
T.

6426 FARRELL, Henry. Letters to lord John Russell on the Improvement Bill for Ireland, and on the legal maintenance of the able-bodied poor; also a letter to lord Devon.
12 pp. Dublin, printed by L. Shaw, 1848
A., N.

6427 FARRELL, Isaac. Suggestions on the Dublin improvements.
tables. 36 pp. Dublin, J. McGlashan, 1848
A., N., T.

6428 A few words of remonstrance and advice addressed to the farming and labouring classes of Ireland, by a sincere friend.
14 pp. Dublin, A. Thom, 1848
A., N., T., U.

6429 A few words on a state endowment for the Irish clergy. By a catholic ecclesiastic.
tables. 32 pp. London, J. Ridgway, 1848
T.

6430 Financial reform imperative: or, remarks relative to the possibility of an equitable adjustment of the national debt.
16 pp. London, Effingham Wilson, 1848
T.

6431 First report of the county of Kildare Independent Club. Instituted 30th August, 1847.
24 pp. Dublin, printed by Webb and Chapman, 1848
A.
Club concerned with tenant-right.

6432 FITZGERALD, James Edward. Irish migration. A letter to Wm. Monsell, M.P.
24 pp. London, F. & J. Rivington, 1848
A., N., T.

6433 FITZWILLIAM, Charles William Wentworth-Fitzwilliam, 5th earl. A letter to the Rev. John Sargeaunt, rector of Stanwick, Northamptonshire.
44 pp. 3rd ed. London, J. Ridgway, 1848
N.
Mainly on the poor law. See 6178.

6434 Free trade and no colonies. A letter addressed to the right hon. lord John Russell, prime minister of England.
20 pp. Edinburgh, W. Blackwood & Son, 1848
T.

6435 The French revolution & the repeal of the union; an address to the people of Ireland. By an Irishman.
24 pp. Dublin, Mullen, Corbet & Hodges, 1848
A., L., N.

6436 The friendly brothers of St. Andrew Tontine society instituted January, 1848.
index. table. 18 pp. Dublin, printed by Hogan, 1848
A.

6437 GERNON, William. The act to amend the law of imprisonment for debt and to facilitate the recovery of possession of tenements in cities and towns in Ireland: with commentary, notes, forms and index.
appendix. 88 pp. Dublin, A. Milliken, London, W. G. Benning, 1848
A.

6438 GIBSON, William Sidney. A letter to the lord chancellor on the amendment of the law of bankruptcy, with comments on the existing regulations, and suggestions for their improvement.
32 pp. London, H. Butterworth, 1848
A.

6439 A glance at the effects produced on trade by the existing banking laws.
table of contents. 16 pp. London, Smith, Elder, 1848
A., T.

6440 The gold standard.
28 pp. London, J. Ollivier, 1848
T.

6441 GORE, Montague. Reflections on the present state and prospects of the British West Indies.
40 pp. London, J. Ridgway, 1848
T.

6442 ——. Suggestions for the amelioration of the present condition of Ireland. Third edition.
tables. appendix. 72 pp. London, J. Ridgway, 1848
T.

6443 GRAY, M. Wilson. Self-paying colonization in North America: being a letter to Capt. John P. Kennedy. From a forthcoming volume, supplemental to Captain Kennedy's digest of evidence on occupation of land in Ireland.
tables. 66 pp. Dublin, printed by A. Thom, 1848
N.

6444 The great industrial exhibition, in 1851. The disastrous consequences which are likely to arise to the manufacturing trade of this country, from the carrying out of the proposed great industrial exhibition of all nations, in 1851. Addressed to all ranks of society, more particularly the manufacturers and working classes of Great Britain and Ireland. By a late manufacturer.
16 pp. n.p. [1848?]
T.

6445 Great Southern and Western Railway, Ireland. Eighth half-yearly report Wednesday, 15th March, 1848.
tables. 6 pp. Dublin, printed by A. Thom, 1848
A.

6446 Great Southern and Western Railway, Ireland. Ninth half-yearly report Tuesday, 19th September, 1848.
tables. 8 pp. Dublin, printed by A. Thom, 1848
A.

6447 GUINNESS, Arthur Lunden Olave. Is agitation useful? And when?
46 pp. Dublin, Hodges and Smith, 1848
T.

6448 HAMILTON, John. Ireland's recovery and Ireland's health.
table of contents. appendix. 56 pp. Dublin, J. McGlashan, 1848
A., N., RM.

6449 HANCOCK, John. Observations on tenant-right legislation: being an answer to a deputation of lord Lurgan's tenantry, given on 16th March, 1848
8 pp. Dublin, Hodges & Smith, 1848
A., R.

6450 HANCOCK, William Neilson. On the compulsory use of native manufactures, a paper read before the Dublin Statistical society.
14 pp. Dublin, Hodges & Smith, 1848
A., C., T.

6451 ——. On Laissez-Faire, and the economic resources of Ireland. A paper read before the Dublin Statistical society.
18 pp. Dublin, Hodges & Smith, 1848
A., C., T.

6452 ——. On the condition of the Irish labourer: being a paper read before the Dublin Statistical society.
12 pp. Dublin, Hodges & Smith, 1848
A., T.

6543 ——. On the economic causes of the present state of agriculture in Ireland: Part I. A paper read before the Dublin Statistical society.
14 pp. Dublin, Hodges & Smith, 1848
A., C., N., T.

6454 ——. On the effects of the usury laws on the funding system. A paper read before the Dublin Statistical society, January 1848.
6 pp. Dublin, Hodges & Smith, 1848
A., C., N., T.

6455 ——. A notice of the theory 'that there is no hope for a nation which lives on potatoes'. A paper read before the Dublin Statistical society, April, 1848.
4 pp. Dublin, Hodges & Smith, 1848
A., C., N., T.

6456 HARLE, William Lockey. The total repeal of the navigation laws, discussed and enforced, in a letter to the right honourable the earl Grey.
34 pp. London, Whittaker, 1848
T.

6457 [HIGGINS, Matthew James.] Is cheap sugar the triumph of free trade? A second letter to the rt. hon. lord John Russell, etc., etc., etc. By Jacob Omnium.
tables in appendix. 64 pp. London, J. Ridgway, 1848
T.
See 6206.

6458 [——.] A third letter to lord John Russell, containing some remarks on the ministerial speeches delivered during the late sugar debates. With an appendix, containing copies of the despatches of Sir C. Grey and lord Harris. By Jacob Omnium.
appendices. 42 pp. London, J. Ridgway, 1848
T.

6459 Highland destitution. Third report of the Edinburgh section of the central board for the relief of destitution in the Highlands and islands of Scotland, for 1848. Containing documents illustrative of their relief operations.
tables. 120 pp. Edinburgh, W. Blackwood & Son, 1848
T.

6460 HILL, Laurence. A letter from the New Forest, on its present state and proposed improvement, to the lord chief commissioner of her majesty's woods and forests, etc.
appendix. 36 pp. London, J. Murray; Ringwood, W. Wheaton, 1848
T.

6461 Hints to emigrants. By an emigrant.
24 pp. Dublin, Carrick, 1848
N.

6462 HODGKIN, Thomas. A letter to Richard Cobden, M.P., on free trade and slave labour.
no t.p. 16 pp. London, W. Watts, 1848
T.

6463 HODGSON, Adam. A letter to the right honourable Sir Robert Peel, bart., on the currency.
20 pp. London, J. Ridgway, Liverpool, Wareing Webb, 1848
T.

6464 HUBBARD, John Gellibrand, later baron Addington. A letter to the right honourable Sir Charles Wood, bart., M.P., chancellor of the exchequer, on the monetary pressure and commercial distress of 1847.
tables. 50 pp. London, Longman, Brown, Green, and Longmans, 1848
T.

6465 An income tax, a remedy for all political and social abuses: with flying remarks de omnibus rebus. By John Hampden the Younger.
38 pp. Dublin, J. McGlashan, 1848
A.

6466 Ireland in reality, or the true interest of the labourer; embracing rights of landlord and tenant, universal suffrage in practice, not theory, and a project whereby to satisfy the people at the expense of the authors of their discontent.
16 pp. Dublin, Grant & Bolton, 1848
A.

——. 16 pp. 2nd ed. Dublin, Grant & Bolton, 1848
N.

6467 The Irish amelioration society: for employing the peasantry in reproductive labour, and improving their social condition.
tables. 18 pp. London, T. Saunders, 1848
A., N.

6468 JACKSON, Warren H. R.   An address to the honourable the members of the house of commons on the landlord and tenant question.
38 pp. Cork, Purcell, 1848
T.

6469 JERNINGHAM, Frederick.   Steam communication with the Cape of Good Hope, Australia, and New Zealand, suggested as the means of promoting emigration to those colonies.
map. tables. appendix. 44 pp. London, C. Dolman, 1848
T.

6470 KINGSFORD, Philip.   Two lectures upon the study of political philosophy; delivered at the college of preceptors, in November 1848.
appendix. 48 pp. London, C. H. Law, 1848
T.

6471 The landlord's address: in two letters for the encouragement and instruction of farmers, and the benefit of the labouring classes. By a landed proprietor.
table of contents. 36 pp. Dublin, printed by Downes, 1848
A.

6472 LATTIMORE, Charles Henry.   A plea for tenant right, addressed to the farmers of Hertfordshire and of the United Kingdom: shewing the existing obstructions to an improved system of agriculture, and the necessity of legal security for the capital of the occupiers of the soil, in a statement of facts connected with the late occupation of Bride Hall farm, Herts.
20 pp. London, J. Ridgway, 1848
T.

6473 LAWSON, James Anthony.   On commercial panics; A paper read before the Dublin Statistical society.
8 pp. Dublin, Hodges & Smith, 1848
A., C., N., T.

6474 ——.   On the connexion between statistics and political economy, a paper read before the Dublin Statistical society. 10 pp. Dublin, A. Thom, 1848
A., T.

6475 LEA, Nathaniel.   What is a pound?
18 pp. London, Simpkin Marshall, 1848
T.

6476 LE DOCTE, Henri.   Exposé général de l'agriculture Luxembourgeoise.
table of contents. 182 pp. Bruxelles, Hayez, 1848
A.

6477 LENNON, Bernard.   Tenant-right or tenant-compensation. (A letter to the honourable lord viscount Castlereagh.)
16 pp. (no t.p.) Belfast, printed by Read, 1848
N.

6478 A letter from a rejected member of a late parliament, to the earl of Clarendon, the Queen's viceroy.
48 pp. London, J. Ollivier, 1848
T.

6479 A letter on the West India question, addressed to the British people. By a free trader.
16 pp. London, Smith, Elder & co., 1848
T.

6480 A letter to the right honourable lord John Russell, M.P., etc., etc., etc., on the subject of Indian railways. By an East India merchant.
126 pp. London, Smith, Elder & co., 1848
T.

6481 A letter to the shareholders of the East India railway, and to the commercial capitalists of England and India. By Transit.
16 pp. London, Smith, Elder & co., 1848
T.

6482 LE QUESNE, Charles.   Ireland and the Channel Islands; or, A remedy for Ireland.
tables. 142 pp. London, Longman, Brown, Green & Longmans, 1848
A.

6483 LINDSAY, Henry.   The way from want to plenty.
92 pp. Dublin, printed by Berry, [1848?]
A.

6484 LINKINWATER, Timothy.   How to right the nation by an equitable adjustment of its capital as a compromise under free trade and cash payments, in times of adverse exchanges to the wants of the people; together with a few plain reasons for the potato rot and the present depreciation of property.
tables. 40 pp. London, Pelham Richardson, 1848
T.

6485 LOCKE, Joseph.   A letter to the right hon. lord John Russell, M.P., on the best mode of avoiding the evils of mixed gauge railways and the break of gauge.
folding map. tables. 16 pp. London, J. Ridgway, 1848
T.

6486 [LOVELACE, William King-Noel, 1st earl of.]   Review of the agricultural statistics of France: with a notice of the works of MM. Rubichon, Mounier, and Passy, respecting its produce and the condition of its rural population.
tables. 44 pp. London, D. Batten, 1848
N.

6487 LUMLEY, William Gordon.   The act to amend the procedure in respect of orders for the removal of the poor in England & Wales, and appeals therefrom, (11 & 12 Vict. c. 31); with a commentary and notes.
index. 30 pp. London, C. Knight, 1848
T.

6488 ——.   The minute of the poor law board for the repression of vagrancy: with introductory observations, and a statement of the penal provisions now in force for this object.
56 pp. London, C. Knight, [1848]
T.

6489 MAC DONNELL, Eneas. Irish sufferers, and anti-Irish philosophers, their pledges and performances.
tables. appendix. 60 pp. London, J. Ollivier, [1848]

T.

6490 MACDOUGALL, Sir Patrick Leonard. Emigration; its advantages to Great Britain and her colonies. Together with a detailed plan for the formation of the proposed railway between Halifax and Quebec, by means of colonization.
tables. 32 pp. London, T. & W. Boone, 1848

T.

6491 M'KNIGHT, James. The Ulster tenants' claim of right; or, landownership a state trust; the Ulster Tenant-Right an original grant from the British crown, and the necessity of extending its general principle to the other provinces of Ireland, demonstrated; in a letter to the rt. hon. lord John Russell.
72 pp. Dublin, J. McGlashan, 1848

A., N.

6492 MACONOCHIE, Alexander. Emigration, with advice to emigrants; especially those with small capital; addressed to the society for promoting colonization.
appendix. 24 pp. London, J. Ollivier, 1848

T.

6493 MAHONY, Pierce. Letter to Sir John Romilly, knt, H.M. solicitor-general for England; on the incumbered estates bill Ireland.
40 pp. London, Trelawney Wm. Saunders, 1848

A.

6494 [MALEY, A. J.] To the noblemen and gentlemen resident in Ireland (an open letter (by) A. J. M.).
4 pp. (no t.p.) Dublin, 1848

N.

6495 MARTIN, James. Observations on the evils and difficulties of the present system of poor laws in Ireland; with suggestions for removing or obviating them considered.
30 pp. Dublin, A. Thom, 1848

C.

6496 [MARTIN, Robert Montgomery.] The sugar question: being a digest of the evidence taken before the committee on sugar and coffee plantations. Which was moved for by lord George Bentinck, M.P., 3rd February, 1848. By one of the witnesses. Part I. The East Indies and the Mauritius.
tables. 60 pp. London, Smith, Elder & co., 1848

T.

6497 [——.] The sugar question: being a digest of the evidence taken before the committee on sugar and coffee plantations. Which was moved for by lord George Bentinck, M.P., 3rd February, 1848. By one of the witnesses: Part II. The British West Indies, and foreign sugar growing countries.
tables. 166 pp. London, Smith, Elder & co., 1848

T.

6498 MATSON, Henry James. Remarks on the slave trade and African squadron.
table. appendix. 94 pp. 3rd ed. London, J. Ridgway, 1848

T.

6499 MAXWELL, James. Remarks on the present state of Jamaica, with a proposal of measures for the resuscitation of our West Indian colonies.
tables. 52 pp. London, Smith, Elder & co., 1848

T.

6500 MILLER, Charles. Tithes or heathenism: reasons for not accepting the tithe commissioners award, most dutifully and respectfully submitted to the Queen of England, her parliament, and her people, in a second letter to the right hon. Sir George Grey, M.P., Her Majesty's secretary of state for the home department.
appendix. 24 pp. London, J. Ollivier [etc.], 1848

T.

6501 MILLER, Samuel. Suggestions for a general equalisation of the land tax and the abolition of the income and real property taxes and the malt duty.
34 pp. London, S. Sweet, 1848

T.

6502 MILNER, Thomas Hughes. On the regulation of floating capital, and freedom of currency: with an attempt to explain practically the general monetary system of the country.
tables. 126 pp. London, Smith, Elder & co., 1848

T.

6503 The miseries of our time, and their remedies; a work for the people, and dedicated to them by a catholic merchant.
48 pp. London, J. Brown, 1848

P.

6504 MOORSOM, Richard. A letter to the earl of Mulgrave, M.P., on the currency, and the monetary crisis; with some remarks on Mr. Cayley's letter to lord John Russell.
18 pp. London, Simpkin, Marshall, [1848]

T.

6505 NAPER, James Lenox William. An appeal to Irishmen to unite in supporting measures formed on principles of common justice and common sense for the social regeneration of Ireland.
26 pp. London, J. Ridgway, 1848

A., D., N., T.

6506 NEVILE, Christopher. The justice and expediency of tenant-right legislation considered, in a letter to P. Pusey, esq.
34 pp. London, J. Ridgway, 1848

T.

6507 NEWMAN, Charles. On the importance of a legislative enactment uniting the interests of landlord and tenant, to facilitate the culture of the land, and promote an increase of food and employment for the millions.
20 pp. 2nd ed. London, J. Ridgway, 1848

T.

6508 NEWMAN, Francis W. An appeal to the middle classes on the urgent necessity of numerous radical reforms, financial and organic.
28 pp. London, Taylor and Walton, 1848

T.

6509 NICHOLSON, Samuel. Observations upon the operation of the present poor law in Ireland with suggestions for its improvement.
14 pp. Dublin, A. Thom, 1848
A.

6510 NOAKES, John. The right of the aristocracy to the soil considered.
16 pp. London, Effingham Wilson, 1848
N.

6511 O'BRIEN, Sir Lucius, bart. Ireland. The late famine, and the poor laws.
12 pp. London, J. Hatchard, 1848
T.

6512 ———. Ireland in 1848. The late famine and the poor laws.
48 pp. London, J. Hatchard, 1848
A., D., N., U.

6513 PARKES, Josiah. Essays on the philosophy and art of land-drainage.
tables. 88 pp. London, Longman, Brown, Green, and Longmans, 1848
T.

6514 [PERCEVAL, Arthur Philip.] Suggestions for the relief of British commerce; addressed, with permission, to the chancellor of the exchequer. By a clergyman.
16 pp. London, John Leslie, 1848
T.

6515 PETERS, William. A local index to the list of proprietors of East India stock.
66 pp. London, G. Bligh, [1848]
T.

6516 PHIPPS, Edmund. The adventures of a £1000 note; or, railway ruin reviewed.
34 pp. London, J. Murray, 1848
T.

6517 PICKERING, William. The currency, its defects and cure.
18 pp. Liverpool, Wareing Webb, London, Simpkin Marshall, 1848
T.

6518 PORTER, John Grey V. A letter to shareholders in Irish railway companies.
tables. 16 pp. Dublin, Hodges & Smith, 1848
A., T.

6519 PORTER, W. H. Savings Banks: their defects—the remedy. The position respectively of the commissioners for the reduction of the national debt, the trustees and managers and the depositors in savings banks, explained; also containing copious statistical information, and an exposition of Mr. Craig's system of savings bank book-keeping, together with some account of the failure of St. Peter's Parish Savings Bank, Dublin, its past and present position and history.
188 pp. Dublin, Hodges and Smith, 1848
A., N.

6520 Property tax versus income tax in a letter addressed to the representatives of the United Kingdom.
16 pp. London, J. Hatchard, 1848
T.

6521 Proposition for fitting up baths and washhouses for the use of the poor of the Mendicity Institution and adjacent district of the city, submitted to the public.
diagrams. tables. 12 pp. Dublin, printed by Shea, 1848
A.

6522 The question of the repeal of the union, in connexion with the prosperity of Ireland; discussed in a conversation between two Dublin shopkeepers. By a patriot.
24 pp. Dublin, Hodges and Smith, 1848
A., N.

6523 Railway policy. A letter to George Carr Glyn, esq., M.P., chairman of the London and north-western railway company, on the correspondence addressed to him by Captain Huish and Mr. John Whitehead: from a sufferer.
12 pp. London, Smith, Elder & co., 1848
T.

6524 Railway property as it is, and railway property as it should be: or, an examination into the causes of its depression, and the means necessary to retrieve it. Addressed to all railway shareholders and more especially the directorates. By a member of the institution of civil engineers.
16 pp. 2nd ed. London, Effingham Wilson, 1848
T.

6525 Railway rescue: a letter addressed to the directorates of Great Britain, by a traveller of many lands.
20 pp. London, Effingham Wilson, 1848
T.

6526 REARDON, William. Some remarks on a question very current at the present time 'what is to be done with Ireland?'
28 pp. London, Simpkin Marshall, 1848
N.

6527 Regulations of the Madras military fund. Amended edition for 1848. Published by authority of the directors.
tables. appendix. 72 pp. London, Grindlay, 1848
T.

6528 Supplement to the regulations of the Madras military fund. Amended edition for 1848. Published by authority of the directors.
tables. 18 pp. London, Grindlay, 1848
T.

6529 Remarks on the present state of our West Indian colonies, with suggestions for their improvement.
48 pp. London, Smith, Elder & co., 1848
T.

6530 Report of the address on the conclusion of the first session of the Dublin Statistical society, delivered by his grace the archbishop of Dublin, president of the society. Together with the report of the council, read at the annual meeting, 19th June, 1848.
table. 12 pp. Dublin, Hodges and Smith, 1848
A., N., T.

6531 Report of the directors of the Dublin and Drogheda Railway company, to the proprietors; published preparatory to the half yearly meeting to be held on the 1st September, 1848.
tables. 16 pp. Dublin, printed by Falconer, 1848
A.

6532 Report of the proceedings of the General central relief committee for all Ireland, from its formation on the 29th December, 1846, to the 31st December, 1847.
tables. appendix. 24 pp. Dublin, printed by Browne, 1848
A., U.

6533 Report of the proceedings of the Irish relief association for the destitute peasantry; being a reorganisation of the association formed during the period of famine in the West of Ireland in 1831; with a list of subscribers, an audited statement of income and expenditure.
appendix. tables. 76 pp. Dublin, P. D. Hardy, 1848
A., U.

6534 Report of the Society of St. Vincent de Paul in Ireland, for the year 1847.
tables. 40 pp. Dublin, printed by Wyer, 1848
A.

6535 Report of the trustees of the Lurgan loan fund to the commissioners of the loan fund board of Ireland, read before the Dublin Statistical society, March, 1848.
8 pp. Dublin, Hodges & Smith, 1848
A., C.

6536 Review of four months proceedings in aid of the destitute and unemployed fishermen of Ballycotton, Co. Cork.
12 pp. Cork, printed by Purcell, 1848
A.

6537 [ROBERTSON, Frederick W.] The Irish difficulty: Addressed to his countrymen, by an Englishman.
tables. 40 pp. London, Saunders and Otley, 1848.
A., N., T.

6538 Royal agricultural improvement society of Ireland. Dialogues on improved husbandry with a practical instructor, under lord Clarendon's letter. Approved and circulated by the council.
24 pp. Dublin, J. McGlashan, 1848
A., N.

6539 Royal agricultural improvement society of Ireland. Management of small farms, house-feeding, etc. By Ninus. To which the Gold Medal of the society was awarded.
24 pp. Dublin, J. McGlashan, 1848
A.

6540 Royal agricultural improvement society of Ireland. Practical instructions for small farmers. Approved and circulated by the council.
24 pp. Dublin, J. McGlashan, 1848
A., N.

6541 RYLEY, E. A statement of facts connected with an anonymous circular, and the proceedings at certain meetings lately held of actuaries and others officially connected with life assurance companies.
appendix. 28 pp. London, Smith, Elder & co., 1848
T.

6542 SCHMIT, J. P. A few words addressed to the labouring classes.
16 pp. London, Effingham Wilson, 1848
T.

6543 SCHOMBERG, John Duff. An enquiry into the currency; in which the measures of 1819 and 1844 are fully considered; the schemes of lord Ashburton and Mr. Cayley examined; and suggestions made towards an improvement of the system.
34 pp. London, William Edward Painter, [1848]
T.

6544 [SCROPE, George Julius Duncombe Poulett.] How to make Ireland self-supporting; or, Irish clearances, and improvement of waste lands. From the 'Westminster and foreign quarterly review' for October, 1848. With a postscript.
40 pp. London, J. Ridgway, 1848
T.

6545 ——. The Irish relief measures, past and future.
102 pp. London, J. Ridgway, 1848
N., T., U.

6546 ——. A plea for the rights of industry in Ireland. Being the substance of letters which recently appeared in the Morning Chronicle, with additions.
table of contents. 96 pp. London, J. Ridgway, 1848
A., T., U.

6547 ——. The rights of industry, or The social problem of the day, as exemplified in France, Ireland, and Britain.
46 pp. London, J. Ridgway, 1848
A., N.

6548 ——. The rights of industry. Part III. On the best form of relief to the able-bodied poor.
24 pp. London, J. Ridgway, 1848
A.

6549 SHAW, Charles. An extensive system of emigration considered, with a practical mode of raising the necessary funds.
tables. 20 pp. 2nd ed. London, Effingham Wilson, 1848
T.

6550 SIDNEY, Samuel. The commercial consequences of a mixed gauge on our railway system examined.
tables. 50 pp. London, Smith Elder & co., 1848
T.

6551 SMITH, Arthur. An appendix to the second edition of the bubble of the age; or fallacies of railway investment, railway accounts, and railway dividends.
tables. 22 pp. London, Sherwood, Gilbert and Piper, 1848
T.

6552 ——. The bubble of the age; or, the fallacies of railway investment, railway accounts, and railway dividends.
tables. 62 pp. 2nd edition. London, Sherwood, Gilbert and Piper, 1848
T.

6553 [——.] Railways as they really are: or, facts for the serious consideration of railway proprietors. No. V. The Great Western railway, and all broad gauge lines.
tables. 84 pp. London, Sherwood, Gilbert, and Piper, 1848
T.

6554 SMITH, George.   The case of our West-African cruisers and West-African settlements fairly considered.
table. 74 pp. London, J. Hatchard, 1848
T.

6555 Some talk about the repeal of the union, cheap food, employment of the people by government, and the agricultural instructors: in a dialogue between two small farmers. By a patriot.
22 pp. Dublin, Hodges and Smith, 1848
U.

6556 SPROULE, John.   Model farms, as leading to an improved system of cultivation, the appropriate remedy for the present distressed condition of Ireland. In a letter to his grace the duke of Leinster.
16 pp. Dublin, J. McGlashan, London, J. Ridgway, 1848
A., E., N., U.

6557 [STARKEY, Digby Pilot.]   The game's up! by Menenius.
64 pp. Dublin, Hodges & Smith, 1848
B., N.

——.   64 pp. 2nd ed. Dublin, Hodges and Smith, 1848
T.

6558 [——.]   Menenius to the people.
58 pp. Dublin, Hodges & Smith, 1848
B., N., T.

6559 State of New York. No. 46. In assembly, Jan. 8th, 1848. Resolution in relation to printing the report of the select committee of the assembly of 1847, to investigate frauds upon emigrants.
tables. 170 pp. New York, 1848
A.

6560 Statistics of Ireland. From Thom's Irish Almanac and official directory for 1848.
table of contents. tables. 102 pp. Dublin, A. Thom, 1848

A.

6561 STEWART, J. C.   Facts and documents relating to the affairs of the union bank of Calcutta, during his service as secretary to that institution, by J. C. Stewart.
tables in appendices. 116 pp. Calcutta, W. Thacker, London, Smith, Elder & Co., 1848
T.

6562 STURGEON, Charles.   The protection of the Court of Bankruptcy to persons not in trade, under the 7 & 8 Vict. cap. 70. An act to facilitate arrangements between debtors and creditors.
tables. index. 70 pp. London, Shaw, 1848
T.

6563 Suggestions for the repeal of the assessed taxes, and the substitution of an equitable property and income tax.
8 pp. London, J. Ollivier, 1848
T.

6564 SYNGE, Millington Henry.   Canada in 1848. Being an examination of the existing resources of British North America, with considerations for their further and more per-fect development as a practical remedy by means of colonisation, for the prevailing distress in the United Empire, and for the defence of the colony.
appendix. 38 pp. London, E. Wilson, 1848
A.

6565 TAYLOR, William Cooke.   On the changes in the locality of textile manufactures. A paper read before the Dublin Statistical society.
10 pp. Dublin, Hodges & Smith, 1848
A., C., N., T.

6566 The tea duties. Report of the second public meeting, held in the sessions house Liverpool on the 14th January, 1848 to which is prefixed the report of the parliamentary committee of last session. Published by the Liverpool association for the reduction of the duty on tea.
tables. 60 pp. Liverpool, printed by Smith, Rogerson, 1848
A., N.

6567 THIMBLEBY, John.   What is money? Or man's birthright, 'Time', the only real wealth; its representative forming the true medium of exchange.
appendix. 20 pp. London, Effingham Wilson, [1848?]
T.

6568 A third letter to the electors of Great Britain on the income tax, etc., etc. Together with an appendix, containing the two former letters on that subject.
appendix. 28 pp. 2nd ed. London, J. Ollivier, 1848
T.

6569 To the honourable the members of the house of commons. [Letter.]
16 pp. n.p. [1848?]
N.

On the Irish land question.

6570 TORRENS, Robert.   The principles and practical operation of Sir Robert Peel's Bill of 1844 explained, and defended against the objections of Tooke, Fullarton, and Wilson.
table of contents. 182 pp. London, Longman, Brown, Green & Longmans, 1848
A.

6571 Transactions of the Dublin University Philosophical society. Vol. III.
22 pp. Dublin, Hodges & Smith, 1848
A.

contains a two-part paper on *conacre* by W. N. Hancock.

6572 A treatise on the necessity of social and political reform, with a proposed method for accomplishing the same. By Veritas et Justitex.
28 pp. Dublin, J. Duffy, 1848
A.

6573 TUKE, James Hack.   A visit to Connaught in the autumn of 1847. A letter addressed to the Central relief committee of the Society of Friends, Dublin. With notes of a subsequent visit to Erris.
72 pp. 2d. ed. London, Gilpin, York, Linney, 1848
A., C., T.

6574 Two letters to a member of parliament containing suggestions for a property tax. By R. S. B.
40 pp. London, J. Ollivier, 1848
T.

6575 VANCE, Robert. On the English and Irish analyses of wages and profits. A paper read before the Dublin Statistical society.
10 pp. Dublin, Hodges & Smith, 1848
A., C., N., U.

6576 VEREKER, John P. Absenteeism considered in its economical and social effects upon Ireland.
table of contents. tables. appendix. 210 pp. Dublin, Ponsonby, 1848
A.

6577 WADDILOVE, William. The system of discriminating duties investigated according to the proposals made to several of the North-Sea-States of Germany, for establishing a German navigation- and trade-union.
tables. 128 pp. Leibzic, E. F. Steinacker, [1848]
T.
Copy of the proposals is adjoined.

6578 WELCH, James. Tenant-right: its nature and requirements; together with a plan for a legislative act for the readjustment of the relationship between landlord and tenant, and for the promotion of agriculture.
40 pp. London, J. Ridgway, 1848
T.

6579 WELFORD, Richard Griffiths. The impolicy of the present high duties on tobacco and their injurious effects on the trade and morals of the country.
table of contents. tables. 68 pp. London, J. Gadsby, 1848
N.

6580 What have the West Indian planters a right to expect? A dialogue between Mercator and Colonus. Containing a practical suggestion for an equitable settlement of the sugar question.
16 pp. London, J. Ridgway, W. J. Adams, 1848
T.

6581 WHITEHEAD, John. Railway management. Letter to George Carr Glyn, esq., M.P., chairman of the London and north western railway company.
tables. 24 pp. 2nd ed. London, Smith, Elder & co., 1848
T.

6582 ——. Railway management. A second letter to George Carr Glyn, esq., M.P., chairman of the London and north western railway company; in reply to Capt. Huish's letter.
18 pp. London, Smith, Elder & co., 1848
T.

6583 WRIGHT, Ichabod Charles. The evils of the currency, no. 2.
20 pp. 3rd ed. (enlarged). London, Simpkin, Marshall, Nottingham, Dearden, 1848
T.

24

6584 YULE, A. The importance of spade husbandry and general manual agriculture as a certain means of removing Irish distress.
index. 84 pp. Dublin, J. McGlashan, 1848
A.

1849

6585 An account of the meeting of the Hinckford agricultural and conservative club, in the baronial hall, Hedingham Castle, on Friday, October 5th, 1849. Ashhurst Majendie, esq., F.R.S. in the chair. Together with a corrected report of the speeches of Benjamin Disraeli, esq. Sir John Tyrell, Major Beresford, Rev. John Cox, &c., &c., delivered on the occasion.
illust. 64 pp. Sudbury, Williams Fulcher, London, Longman, Brown, 1849
T.

6586 ALLEN, Robert Mahon. Irish legislation; or, two ways to meet a crisis.
table. 68 pp. Dublin, printed by Jolly, 1849
A.

6587 ALLEN, William. A plan for the immediate extinction of the slave trade, for the relief of the West India colonies, and for the diffusion of civilization and Christianity in Africa, by the co-operation of Mammon with Philanthropy.
38 pp. London, J. Ridgway, 1849
T.

6588 ARCHBOLD, John Frederick. The whole of the new practice in poor law removals and appeals.
46 pp. 2nd edition. London, Shaw, 1849
T.

6589 The Ardeley petition for alteration in the poor law; or, a plan for every parish managing its own poor, police, registration, etc., by means of vestry committees; thereby saving at once about two millions per annum of local taxation, and nearly the whole expense of the board at Somerset House, with a prospect of much more extensive economy, including a just and constitutional substitute for church rates, in an appendix: being a letter to M. T. Baines, esq., M.P., president of the Poor Law Board, from the chairman of the Ardeley vestry.
appendices. 32 pp. London, Shaw, 1849
T.

6590 An 'article' for lord Brougham's bankruptcy digest, being remarks upon a recent letter. By a practical man.
28 pp. London, Shaw, 1849
T.

6591 BALL, John. What is to be done for Ireland?
appendices with tables. 126 pp. London, J. Ridgway, 1849
A., N.

——. 126 pp. 2nd ed. London, J. Ridgway, 1849
N., T.

6592 BAMPTON, A. Hamilton. The drainage of towns. A lecture delivered at the Athenaeum, Plymouth, January 25, 1849.
diag. 28 pp. Plymouth and Devonport, Roger Lidstone [etc., etc.], 1849
T.

6593 BARROW, John.   Facts relating to north-eastern Texas, condensed from notes made during a tour through that portion of the United States of America, for the purpose of examining the country, as a field for emigration.
map. 68 pp. London, Simpkin, Marshall, 1849
T.

6594 BEASLEY, J. Richardson B.   The constitutional or King Alfred Parish Governor, destroyer of rates and taxes, crime and starvation; promoter of trade, and protector of agriculture; opposer of oppression, asserter of the people's rights, and defender of the crown from the danger it is placed in.
88 pp. Dublin, printed by Goodwin and Nethercott, 1849
A., U.

6595 BEESLEY, George.   A report of the state of agriculture in Lancashire; with observations on the political position and general prospects of the agricultural classes; and a tabular statement of the prices of corn and wages of husbandry, etc., at various periods since the Norman conquest; by George Beesley, land agent.
tables. appendix. 76 pp. Preston, Dobson, 1849
T.

6596 BEGG, James.   Pauperism and the poor laws; or, our sinking population and rapidly increasing public burdens practically considered.
tables. appendix. 96 pp. Edinburgh, John Johnstone, 1849
T.

——.   104 pp. 2nd ed. Edinburgh, Johnstone and Hunter, 1849
T.

6597 BLAIKIE, William G.   Six lectures addressed to the working classes on the improvement of their temporal condition.
appendix. 64 pp. 3rd ed. Edinburgh and London: John Johnstone, 1849
T.

6598 BODINGTON, George.   Letters: I. A new year's gift to Ireland. II. Irish prospects. III. On political expediency, colonial unjustice, and Irish misgovernment. IV. On Irish agriculture and manufactures. The dislocation and misdirection of capital. V. The defects of the Irish Act of Union. VI. The effects of free trade on wages. The Irish question solved. VII. On the principle which should defend or protect the position of the relative interests of any given community from clashing with those of any other.
32 pp. London, J. Ridgway, W. W. Robinson, Birmingham, Benjamin Hall, 1849
T.

6599 BRIDGES, William.   Three practical suggestions for the colonisation of Ireland.
appendix. 16 pp. London, Bailliere, 1849
A., N.

6600 BROWNE, T. S.   A treatise on the laws and practice relating to patents of invention, and the registration of designs, with remarks on the patent laws of foreign countries.
72 pp. Manchester, J. & J. Thompson and J. Haycroft, 1849
T.

6601 BRYANT, Edwin.   What I saw in California: its soil, climate, production, and gold mines.
table of contents. 144 pp. London, Routledge, 1849
A.

6602 BURGESS, Henry.   The duty of the state to its infant poor. A letter to lord John Russell, occasioned by the recent disclosures respecting the infant poor at Tooting.
16 pp. London, C. Cox, 1849
T.

6603 BURKE, James.   12 and 13 Vict. c. 77. An act further to facilitate the sale and transfer of incumbered estates in Ireland with an introductory analysis and a copious index.
108 pp. 2nd edition. Dublin, Hodges and Smith, 1849
T.

6604 ——.   26 Vict. c. 105. An act for converting the renewable leasehold tenure of lands in Ireland into a tenure in fee, with an introductory analysis, practical directions, forms and an index.
72 pp. Dublin, Hodges & Smith, 1849
A., T.

6605 BUTT, Isaac.   'The rate in aid'. A letter to the earl of Roden.
76 pp. Dublin, J. McGlashan, London, W. Orr, 1849
A., B., N., T.

6606 CAIRD, Sir James.   High farming under liberal covenants, the best substitute for protection.
table of contents. 34 pp. 3d. ed. Edinburgh and London, W. Blackwood, 1849
T.

——.   36 pp. 5th ed. Edinburgh and London, W. Blackwood, 1849
A., N.

6607 CALVERT, Frederic.   A letter to the right hon. Sir Charles Wood, bart., M.P., upon certain laws affecting agriculture, by Frederic Calvert, esq., Q.C.
32 pp. 2nd ed. London, J. Ridgway, 1849
T.

6608 CAMPBELL, W. F.   Will Mr. Labouchere's navigation measure pass the house of lords? In a letter to a protectionist peer.
30 pp. London, F. & J. Rivington, 1849
T.

6609 CANNON, William J.   Outline of a plan for the relief and improvement of Ireland.
12 pp. London, Mann, 1849
A., D.

6610 CAVE, Stephen.   A few words, on the encouragement given to slavery and the slave trade, by recent measures, and chiefly by the sugar bill of 1846.
appendix. 36 pp. London, J. Murray, 1849
T.

6611 The christian's key to the philosophy of socialism; being hints and aids towards an analytical inquiry into the principles of social progress, with a view to the elucidation of

the great practical problem of the present day,—the improvement of the condition of the working classes. In ten propositions by Upsilon.
34 pp. London, J. Chapman, 1849

T.

6612 Church rates. A short address both to those who oppose them, and to those who are of opinion that they ought to be supported. By B.
12 pp. London, Longman, Brown, Green & Longmans, Wakefield, John Stanfield, 1849

T.

6613 [COLCHESTER, Charles Abbot, 2nd baron.] Some observations on the importance of the Navigation laws. By a member of parliament.
tables. 40 pp. London, J. Rodwell, 1849

T.

6614 COMBE, John. Remarks on the state and prospects of the flax yarn manufacture.
16 pp. Leeds, R. Slocombe, London, Longman, Brown, Green & Longmans, 1849

T.

6615 CRAWFORD, William Sharman. Depopulation not necessary. An appeal to the British members of the imperial parliament against the extermination of the Irish people.
tables. postscript. 46 pp. London, C. Gilpin, 1849

A.

6616 CREAGH, Pierce. Correspondence between the Irish poor law commissioners and Pierce Creagh. 'Relative to a crisis being brought about by heavy and destructive poor-rates by the imposition of which the present landlords and tenants could be got rid of'.
32 pp. Dublin, printed by Daly, 1849

N.

6617 Cui Bono? The endowment scheme.
64 pp. Dublin, Hodges & Smith, 1849

B., N., T.

6618 DENMAN, Thomas, 1st baron. A second letter from lord Denman to lord Brougham, on the final extinction of the slave trade, with remarks on a late narrative of the Niger expedition in 1841.
34 pp. London, J. Hatchard, 1849

T.

See 6407.

6619 [DEVON, William Courtenay, 10th earl of.] Irish estates: hints for 1850.
8 pp. (no t.p.) (signed in m.s., Devon.) London, printed by Macintosh, 1849

N.

6620 DIBB, John Edward. The landed interest. An examination of the new General Registry Bill; setting forth I. Objections to a registry of titles; II. Advantages of county registries of deeds; and III. Suggestions for their improvement and extension.
18 pp. London, Longman, Brown, Green & Longmans, 1849

T.

6621 Direct taxation. Prize essay; to which has been awarded the premium offered by the National Confederation, for the best essay on the equitable adjustment of national taxation.
tables. 68 pp. London, Simpkin Marshall [etc., etc.], [1849?]

T.

6622 The disease and the remedy: or, parochial and national emigration, versus parochial and national pauperism. By Philo-humanitas.
30 pp. London, J. Ollivier, 1849

T.

6623 DOBBS, Conway Edward. Some observations on the tenant right of Ulster. A paper read before the Dublin Statistical society.
12 pp. Dublin, Hodges & Smith, 1849

A., C., N., T., U.

6624 DUNCAN, Jonathan. The principles of money demonstrated, and bullionist fallacies refuted.
52 pp. London, R. Groombridge, 1849

T.

6625 EDGAR, John. The women of the west. Ireland helped to help herself.
76 pp. Belfast, printed at the Banner of Ulster Office, 1849

B.

6626 The emigrant's almanack for 1849.
table of contents. tables. 58 pp. London, C. Gilpin, 1849

N.

6627 ENDERBY, Charles. The Auckland Islands: a short account of their climate, soil, & productions; and the advantages of establishing there a settlement at Port Ross for carrying on the southern whale fisheries. With a panoramic view of Port Ross, and a map of the islands.
map. plate. tables. appendix. 58 pp. London, Pelham Richardson, 1849

T.

6628 ENSOR, Thomas. The case decided: protectionists and free traders reconciled: a letter addressed to the electors of Somerset, occasioned by the county meeting held at Bridgwater, on the 28th June, 'to take into consideration the depressed condition of the agricultural interest'. To which is added, a letter to the editor of the Times entitled 'Ireland living: protection dead'.
tables. appendix. 44 pp. London, J. Ridgway, Sherborne, E. M. Kingdon, 1849

T.

6629 FARRELL, Henry. A series of letters addressed to the British cabinet on the subject of the corn bill, free trade, and the improvement bill for Ireland. Continued and carried down to December, 1849.
20 pp. Dublin, Bull, 1849

A., T.

6630 [FERGUSON, Sir Samuel.] Inheritor & economist; a poem.
32 pp. Dublin, J. McGlashan, 1849

B.

Satire on economic doctrines.

6631 A few words of advice to tories, whigs, radicals, and churchmen; being the second edition, much enlarged of 'the revolution in France, a warning to the aristocracy and middle classes of England'.
appendix. 72 pp. London, Effingham Wilson, 1849
T.

6632 A few words on the endowment of the Roman catholic clergy in Ireland. By an English protestant.
tables. 16 pp. London, J. Ollivier, 1849
U.

6633 FITZGERALD, Henry. The timber merchant and builders guide. Containing calculations of timber, deals and battens, showing the relative prices they bear to each other, from £2.10.0 to £22.10.0, the Petersburgh standard, with the duties on timber, and other useful tables.
tables. 36 pp. London, Grant and Griffith, 1849
T.

6634 Fox, Richard Maxwell. Poor laws in England and Ireland.
appendix. 84 pp. Dublin, W. Curry, 1849
A., N., T.

6635 Free-trade a Bunya's owl; to which is added a literal version of the original Hindu satire of Meerza Rufee-oos-souda. [By F.C.]
36 pp. London, W. H. Allen, 1849
T.

6636 Free trade in negroes.
table. 54 pp. London, J. Ollivier, 1849
T.

6637 GIBBS, Joseph. Considerations relative to the sewage of London, and suggestions for improving the sanatory conditions of the metropolitan districts; together with some remarks on the production of periodic disease arising from bad drainage and the want of sufficient water.
tables. appendices. 88 pp. London, John Weale, 1849
T.

6638 [GILDEA, George Robert.] Reproductive relief spinning in the West of Ireland. A letter to his excellency the earl of Clarendon, lord lieutenant of Ireland, etc., etc., etc.
diag. 24 pp. London, Samuel Bagster, 1849
T.

6639 GLEN, William Cunningham. The poor law board act, 12 and 13 Vict., cap. 103, for charging the costs of certain relief upon the common fund; and for amending the laws for the relief of the poor. With notes.
26 pp. London, Shaw, 1849
T.

6640 The gold regions of California; describing the geography, topography, history, and general features of that country, from the official reports transmitted to the American government by Colonel Mason, Lieutenant Emory, T. O. Larkin, esq., Rev. Walter Colton, J. S. Folsom, esq., and Lieutenant-Colonel Fremont. Together with exclusive authentic particulars, and a coloured map of the country. Second edition.
map. tables. 80 pp. 2nd ed. London, Baily [etc., etc.], [1849]
T.

6641 GORDON, Lewis. Railway economy. An exposition of the advantages of locomotion by locomotive carriages instead of the present expensive system of steam tugs.
tables. appendices. 68 pp. Edinburgh, Sutherland and Knox, 1849
T.

6642 GORE, Montague. Thoughts on the present state of Ireland.
tables. 36 pp. 3rd edition. London, J. Ridgway, 1849
T.

6643 Great Southern and Western Railway, Ireland. An account of the proceedings of the meeting of the shareholders of the Great Southern and Western railway—Ireland—which was held at their terminus, Kingsbridge, Dublin, on Monday, 19th March, 1849.
4 pp. Dublin, 1849
A.

6644 Great Southern and Western Railway, (Ireland). Eleventh half-yearly report, Wednesday 19th September, 1849.
tables. 8 pp. Dublin, printed by Falconer, 1849
A.

6645 HANCOCK, William Neilson. An introductory lecture on political economy. Delivered in the theatre of Trinity College, Dublin, in Trinity term, 1848.
36 pp. Dublin, Hodges & Smith, London, J. Ridgway, 1849
A., N.

6646 ——. On the economic causes of the present state of agriculture in Ireland: Part II. A paper read before the Dublin Statistical society.
14 pp. Dublin, Hodges & Smith, 1849
A., C., N., T.

6647 ——. On the economic causes of the present state of agriculture in Ireland. Part III. A paper read before the Dublin Statistical society.
12 pp. Dublin, Hodges & Smith, 1849
A., C., N., T.

6648 ——. On the economic causes of the present state of agriculture in Ireland: Part IV. A paper read before the Dublin Statistical society.
16 pp. Dublin, Hodges & Smith, 1849
A., C., N., T.

6649 ——. On the economic causes of the present state of agriculture in Ireland. Part V. A paper read before the Dublin Statistical society.
10 pp. Dublin, Hodges & Smith, 1849
A., C., N., T.

6650 ——. On the economic causes of the present state of agriculture in Ireland, Part VI. A paper read before the Dublin Statistical society.
8 pp. Dublin, Hodges & Smith, 1849
A., C., T.

6651 ——. On the utility of making the ordnance survey the basis of a general register of deeds and judgements in Ireland: a paper read before the Dublin Statistical society.
12 pp. Dublin, Hodges & Smith, 1849
A., N., T.

6652 HARDINGE, William Henry. Summary of authorities relating to the nine turnpike trusts on the north side of the City of Dublin.
table of contents. tables. 40 pp. Dublin, printed by Goodwin, Son & Nethercott, 1849

N.

6653 HEADLAM, Thomas Emerson. A speech on limited liability in joint stock banks delivered by Thomas Emerson Headlam, esq., M.P., in the house of commons, May 8, 1849: together with a proposed act of parliament on the subject.
table. appendix. 28 pp. London, Trelawney Saunders, 1849

T.

6654 HEATHFIELD, Richard. Means of extensive relief from the pressure of taxation, on the basis of a charge of five per cent. on all property in the United Kingdom, real and personal. With some prefatory notes on the early history of taxation by G. P. R. James, esq.
tables. appendices. 32 pp. London, J. Ridgway, 1849

T.

6655 HENCHY, John. Ireland, its present and future prospects considered, with plans for its improvement.
38 pp. Dublin, printed at the Commercial Journal Office, 1849

A., N.

6656 Highland destitution. First report of the Edinburgh section of the central board for the relief of destitution in the highlands and islands of Scotland, for 1849. Containing documents illustrative of their relief operations. Published for the committee.
tables. 68 pp. Edinburgh, William Blackwood & son, [1849]

T.

6657 Highland destitution. Second report of the Edinburgh section of the central board for the relief of destitution in the highlands and islands of Scotland, for 1849. Containing documents illustrative of their relief operations.
tables. 190 pp. Edinburgh, William Blackwood & son, [1849]

T.

6658 HILLARY, Sir Augustus W. A letter to the right honourable lord John Russell, first lord of the treasury, suggesting a plan for the adjustment of the relation between landlord and tenant in Ireland.
56 pp. London, Effingham Wilson, Dublin, A. Milliken, 1849

A., N., T., U.

6659 HINCKS, Sir Francis. Canada: its financial position and resources.
tables. appendix. 38 pp. London, J. Ridgway, 1849

T.

6660 HODGSON, Arthur. A lecture on colonization and emigration, delivered at a public meeting, at Walsall, Staffordshire, on Tuesday evening, March 20th, 1849, by Arthur Hodgson, esq., member of the committee of the London colonization society, who has resided ten years in Australia, and is now on a visit to this country.
30 pp. Walsall, J. R. Robinson, London, Simpkin, Marshall, [1849]

T.

6661 HOGAN, William. The dependence of national wealth on the social and sanatory condition of the labouring classes:

on the necessity for model lodging houses in Dublin, and the advantages they would confer on the community. Read before the Dublin Statistical society, Feb. 1849.
illustration. 20 pp. Dublin, Hodges & Smith, 1849

A., K.

——. Another issue. 10 pp. Dublin, Hodges & Smith, 1849

A., K., N., T.

6662 HUNTLEY, Sir H. V. Observations upon the free trade policy of England, in connexion with the sugar act of 1846, showing the influence of the latter upon the British tropical possessions, and its direct operation to perpetuate the slave trade. (Derived from official and authentic sources.)
tables. 104 pp. London, Simpkin, Marshall, 1849

T.

6663 Ignorance, serfdom, and the worship of the golden image.
32 pp. London, J. Ridgway, 1849

T.

6664 Instructions to agents, sub-agents and clerks at Bank of Ireland branches.
index. 34 pp. Dublin, printed by Chambers, 1849

A.

6665 Ireland as she ought to be: being practical suggestions for putting an end to the system of early and improvident marriages amongst the Irish peasantry, and thus diminishing the mass of pauperism in Ireland. By a Catholic layman.
table. 24 pp. Dublin, J. McGlashan, 1849

A.

6666 Ireland imperialized: a letter to his excellency the earl of Clarendon.
20 pp. Dublin, J. McGlashan, 1849

T.

6667 Irish grievances, real and imaginative, with some suggestions thereon; an address to the orderly and peaceable members of society, by a wellwisher to his country.
32 pp. Dublin, J. McGlashan, 1849

A.

6668 Irish poor law: past, present and future.
tables. 60 pp. London, J. Ridgway, 1849

A., N., T., U.

6669 JERROLD, W. Blanchard. The old woman who lived in a shoe; being conversations with Britannia on her colonial shoes, for the instruction of emigrants. To which is added an essay on colonial government. With copious notes, and an authentic comparative list of the prices of land, labour, and provisions in the colonies.
tables. 112 p. London, H. Hurst, 1849

T.

6670 KENNEDY, John Pitt. A railway caution!! or exposition of changes required in the law and practice of the British Empire to enable the poorer districts to provide for themselves the benefits of railway intercourse; and to forewarn the government and the capitalists of British India, who now appear disposed to introduce this most important class of national improvement; that they may avoid those fatal errors

which have occurred elsewhere, and so secure their respective interests as well as the rapid development of this vast country's resources. Illustrated in reports addressed to the proprietors and directors of the Waterford and Limerick Railway company.
table of contents. plate. tables. appendices. 72 pp. Calcutta, R. C. Lepage, 1849

A., T.

6671　KINNAIRD, George William Fox Kinnaird, 9th baron. Profitable investment of capital, or 11 years' practical experience in farming: a letter from lord Kinnaird to his tenantry; with lecture by W. White, esq., and a speech of Mr. Finnie of Swanston, on the application of chemistry to agriculture. Second edition, with a few remarks addressed to the landlords and tenants of England.
tables. 44 pp. Dundee, Frederick Shaw [etc., etc.], 1849

T.

6672　KNIGHT, James. Public guarantee and private suretyship.
40 pp. London, Longman, Brown, Green & Longmans, 1849

T.

6673　LAING, S. Railway taxation.
24 pp. Westminster, Vacher, 1849

T.

6674　LATTIMORE, Charles Henry. Another plea for tenant right, on the grounds of justice! An antidote in reply to Mr. J. V. Shelley's pamphlet misnamed A plea for truth.
tables. 48 pp. London, J. Ridgway, 1849

T.

6675　LAWSON, James Anthony. On the policy of direct or indirect taxation: a paper read before the Dublin Statistical society.
8 pp. Dublin, Hodges & Smith, 1849

A., C., N., T., U.

6676　——. The over-population fallacy considered: a paper read before the Dublin Statistical society.
10 pp. Dublin, Hodges & Smith, 1849

A., N., T.

6677　A letter addressed to the shareholders in the Chester and Holyhead railway company, and the London and North Western railway company, on the doings of directors, in the case of the Chester and Holyhead railway, and the Mold railway. By a shareholder.
tables. folding map. 48 pp. London, E. Wilson, 1849

A.

6678　Letter to Robertson Gladstone, esq., on the publications of the Financial reform association.
16 pp. London, Effingham Wilson, 1849

T.

6679　A letter to the landowners of England. By a man of Surrey.
8 pp. London, J. Ollivier, 1849

T.

6680　A letter to the rt. hon. Sir John Cam Hobhouse, bt., M.P., president of the board of control, on the existing Indian Railway companies, and particularly the Great Indian Peninsular Railway company; showing that their projects would be useless to the country, expensive to the government, and unprofitable to the shareholders. By a friend to Indian Railways.
16 pp. London, printed by Johns, 1849

A.

6681　LEVI, Leone. Chambers and tribunals of commerce, and proposed general chamber of commerce in Liverpool. Dedicated, by permission, to the right honorable the earl of Harrowby, &c., &c., &c.
appendix. 40 pp. London, Simpkin, Marshall, 1849

T.

6682　LIFFORD, James Hewitt, 3rd viscount. Thoughts on the present state of Ireland.
appendix. 30 pp. London, J. Murray, 1849

T.

6683　LONGFIELD, Mountifort. Report of the address on the conclusion of the second session of the Dublin Statistical society. Together with the report of the council.
appendix. table. 22 pp. Dublin, Hodges & Smith, 1849

A., C., T.

6684　LUMLEY, William Gordon. Emigration of the poor. Practical instructions to boards of guardians & parish officers as to proceedings to be taken in respect to the emigration of poor persons at the cost of the poor rate.
tables. appendix. 68 pp. London, Charles Knight, 1849

T.

6685　Lurgan union. Report of the committee appointed by order of the board 14th Sept., 1848.
tables. 44 pp. Dublin, printed by Kirkwood, 1849

A.

6686　LYONS, John. Act further to facilitate the sale of incumbered estates, 12 & 13 Victoria, chapter 77. With explanatory comments, rules and orders under the act, as confirmed by privy council and a general index.
164 pp. Dublin, A. Milliken, 1849

N.

6687　MACADAM, James, jun. On industrial, educational & scientific progress in the north of Ireland: being an address, delivered at the opening of the twenty-ninth session of the Belfast Natural History & Philosophical society.
24 pp. Belfast, Francis D. Finlay, 1849

A., B., N.

6688　——. On schools of design in Ireland: a paper read before the Dublin Statistical society.
12 pp. Dublin, Hodges & Smith, 1849

A., N., T.

6689　MCCULLOCH, John Ramsay. Supplement to the edition of Mr. McCulloch's Commercial Dictionary published in 1847.
tables. 106 pp. London, Longman, Brown, Green, and Longmans, 1849

T.

6690 MACDONNELL, Eneas. County of Mayo: its awful condition and prospects and present insufficiency of local relief.
26 pp. London, J. Ollivier, 1849
A.

6691 MACFARLANE, Henry James. On the economic levying and application of the Irish poor rate: being a paper read before the Dublin Statistical society.
tables. appendix. 12 pp. Dublin, Hodges & Smith, 1849
A., C., N., T.

6692 MACGREGOR, John. Financial reform: a letter to the citizens of Glasgow.
tables. appendices. 72 pp. London, J. Ridgway, 1849
T.

6693 [McLAUCHLAN, Thomas.] The depopulation system in the highlands: its extent, causes, and evil consequences, with practical remedies. By an eye-witness.
24 pp. Edinburgh and London, Johnstone and Hunter, 1849
T.

6694 MACLEOD, John Macpherson. Remarks on some popular objections to the present income tax.
32 pp. London, J. Murray, 1849
T.

6695 MAITLAND, John Gorham. Church leases.
16 pp. London, F. & J. Rivington, 1849
T.

6696 MALET, William Wyndham. The tithe redemption trust. A letter to the lord Lyttleton.
appendix. 30 pp. London, W. J. Cleaver, 1849
T.

6697 [MALEY, A. J.] Observations upon the inutility of exterminating the resident landlords of Ireland, by Act of Parliament, or otherwise; and some suggestions for their self-preservation.
32 pp. Dublin, Hodges & Smith, 1849
A., N., U.

6698 MASON, John. An inquiry into the economy, exchange, and distribution of wealth. Part second.
tables. 64 pp. London, Simpkin, Marshall, Birmingham, E. C. Osborne, and J. Tonks, 1849
T.

6699 [MEDCALF, William.] A plea for Ireland; or a proposal to form an association for the purchase and improvement of Irish lands, and the re-sale thereof, on the freehold assurance principle or otherwise. By a member of the Manchester Corporation.
28 pp. Manchester, printed by Harrison, 1849
N.

6700 MILNER, Thomas Hughes. Some remarks on the Bank of England; its influence on credit; and the principles upon which the bank should regulate its rate of interest.
tables. appendix. 62 pp. London, Smith, Elder & co., 1849
T.

6701 MITCHELL, J. M. On British commercial legislation, in reference to the tariff or import duties, and the injustice of interfering with the navigation laws. Being the substance of a speech at a meeting of the chamber of commerce and manufactures, Edinburgh.
tables. 60 pp. Edinburgh and London, William Blackwood, 1849
A., T.

6702 MONRO, David. 'Landlords' rents' and 'tenants' profits'; or corn-farming in Scotland.
tables. 32 pp. Edinburgh and London, William Blackwood, 1849
T.

6703 [MOORE, James.] Guide for emigrants to the United States of America, particularly the north-western states.
tables. map. 28 pp. Dublin, Grant and Bolton, 1849
T.

6704 MUDIE, George. A solution of the portentous enigma of modern civilization, now perplexing republicans as well as monarchs with fear of change. Addressed to Charles Louis Napoleon Bonaparte, president of the French Republic and author of a work on the Extinction of pauperism, as being the probable harbinger of a golden age of universal prosperity.
36 pp. London, C. Cox, 1849
T.

6705 MUGGERIDGE, Richard M. Notes on the Irish 'difficulty'; with remedial suggestions.
98 pp. Dublin, J. McGlashan [etc., etc.], 1849
A., N.

6706 MURLAND, James W. Observations on Irish railway statistics: a paper read before the Dublin Statistical society.
tables. 14 pp. Dublin, Hodges & Smith, 1849
A., C., N., T.

6707 MURPHY, Walter. Remarks on the Irish Grand Jury system, illustrated by tables, showing the monies presented by the grand juries of the County of Cork, under their different heads, during the last twenty-six years.
tables. 18 pp. Cork, printed by Roche, 1849
N., U.

6708 NAPER, James Lenox William. The present circumstances of the union of Oldcastle submitted to the consideration of the parliamentary committees now sitting for the reconstruction of the Irish poor laws; with some propositions for their amendment.
26 pp. Dublin, J. McGlashan, 1849
A.

6709 NASH, Richard West. Suggestions on the subject of colonization, viewed as the especial mission of England, and the allotted task of the nineteenth century.
60 pp. London, T. W. Saunders, 1849
T.

6710 National association for the protection of British industry and capital. Report of the proceedings and speeches at the great public meeting of this association, held at the Theatre Royal, Drury Lane, London, on Tuesday, the 26th June, 1849.
48 pp. London, J. Ollivier, Chelmsford, Meggy and Chalk, 1849
T.

6711 NEALE, Edward Vansittart. Thoughts on the registration of the title to land: its advantages and the means of effecting it. With observations upon the bill to facilitate the transfer of real property brought in by Mr. Henry Drummond and Mr. Wood.
table. appendix. 72 pp. London, Stevens & Norton, 1849
T.

6712 NEWDEGATE, Charles Newdigate. A letter to the right hon. H. Labouchere, M.P., &c., &c., by C. N. Newdegate, esq., M.P., on the balance of trade, ascertained from the market value of all articles imported during the last four years.
tables. 52 pp. London, R. R. & G. Seeley, 1849
T.

6713 ——. Two letters to the right hon. H. Labouchere, M.P., etc., etc., on the balance of trade. Ascertained from the market value of all articles imported, as compared with the market value of all articles exported during the last four years.
tables. 142 pp. 2nd ed. London, R. R. & G. Seeley, 1849
T.

6714 NEWMAN, Francis W. On the constitutional and moral right or wrong of our national debt.
36 pp. London, Taylor, Walton, and Maberley, 1849
T.

6715 NORREYS, D. Jephson. Letter to the earl of Clarendon on a better organisation of Ireland, for local and general government.
16 pp. London, 1849
A., B., N.

6716 [NORTHCOTE, Sir Henry Stafford.] A short review of the history of the navigation laws of England, from the earliest times; to which are added a note on the present state of the law; and an account of the acts and parts of acts proposed to be repealed by the bill now before parliament. By a barrister. Second edition.
tables. 86 pp. London, J. Ridgway, 1849
T.

6717 NOTLEY, Samuel. Suggestions for the management of railway accounts and a word or two on audit.
tables. 28 pp. London, Effingham Wilson, 1849
T.

6718 Observations on the board of works, the new poor-law and other topics of present interest and importance in Ireland. By a resident proprietor and magistrate.
appendix. 38 pp. London, printed by Vizetelly, 1849
N.

6719 OGILVY, Thomas. Statistical evidence affecting the question of the navigation laws.
tables. 20 pp. Edinburgh and London, W. Blackwood & son, 1849
T.

6720 OKEOVER, Nigel. National taxation, a national poor-rate, and their equitable adjustment. A letter to Ernest Ricardo, esq., showing how the million may be relieved from the oppressive inequality of taxation, without a shadow of

injustice to any. Embracing at the same time the most ample and comprehensive 'Justice to Ireland'.
tables. 14 pp. Walsall, J. R. Robinson [etc.,] etc.], 1849
T.

6721 OWEN, Robert. A supplement to the revolution in mind and practice of the human race; shewing the necessity for and the advantages of, this universal change.
appendix. 84 pp. London, Effingham Wilson, 1849
T.

6722 Paddy's leisure hours in the poor-house; or, priests, parsons, potatoes, and poor rates.
appendix. 94 pp. London, J. W. Parker, Dublin, Hodges & Smith, 1849
A., N.

6723 Pauperism: is it the effect of a law of nature, or of human laws and customs which are in opposition to nature?
table. 96 pp. London, Effingham Wilson, 1849
T.

6724 PORTER, John Grey V. Moderate fixed duties for the sake of revenue on foreign breadstuffs, cattle, meat, etc. Notes on the present customs duties on articles of food, which come into competition with similar articles grown by our own farmers.
table of contents. tables. 62 pp. Dublin, Hodges & Smith, London, J. Ridgway, 1849
A., N., T.
See 6902.

6725 Practical financial reform.
tables. 30 pp. London, J. Ridgway, 1849
T.

6726 PYNE, Henry. Table showing the value of tithe rent-charges for the year 1849.
table. 8 pp. London, Shaw, 1849
T.

6727 Reflections on the manner in which property in Great Britain may be affected by a large influx of gold from California and suggestions as to the means by which such effects may be neutralised, and any material disturbance in the currency prevented. By a merchant.
16 pp. London, E. Wilson, 1849
A., N., T.

6728 Remarks on Ireland; as it is;—as it ought to be;—and as it might be: Sir Robert Peel's plantation scheme, etc. Suggested by a recent article in 'The Times'; and addressed to the capitalists of England. By a native.
42 pp. London, Law, Dublin, J. McGlashan, 1849
A., T.

6729 Report and proceedings of the general relief committee of the Royal Exchange, from 3rd May to 3rd September, 1849, with the speeches, etc., at the great general meetings.
tables. 60 pp. Dublin, printed by Shea, 1849
A., N.

6730 Report of the British association for the relief of the extreme distress in Ireland and Scotland.
table of contents. folding map. folding tables. 192 pp. London, printed by Clay, 1849
A.

6731 Report of the directors of the Dublin & Drogheda Railway co., to the proprietors, published preparatory to the half yearly meeting, to be held . . . 1st March, 1849.
tables. 24 pp. Dublin, printed by Falconer, 1849
A.

6732 Report of the directors of the Dublin and Drogheda railway, to the proprietors, for the half year ending 30th June, 1849.
tables. 8 pp. Dublin, printed by Falconer, 1849
A.

6733 Report of the discussions in parliament on the Customs' duty reduction acts, (corn, rum and other colonial spirits) passed in sessions 1847 & 1848, with observations thereon, in a letter to the distillers of Ireland. By an Irish trader.
70 pp. Dublin, printed by T. White, 1849
A.

6734 Report of the General central relief committee for all Ireland, from 1st July, 1848, to 1st September, 1849, and audited statement of receipts and disbursements from 1st January, 1848.
tables. appendix. 20 pp. Dublin, printed by Browne & Nolan, 1849
A., U.

6735 Report of the sub-committee appointed on the 21st December, 1848, by the 'Grand Jury of the City of Dublin', the 'Wide Street Commissioners', the 'Sanatory Board', the 'Chamber of Commerce', and the 'Municipal Corporation', to consider the best means of remedying admitted evils in the city.
8 pp. no. t.p. [1849?]
U.

6736 REVANS, John. England's navigation laws no protection to British shipping.
tables. 28 pp. London, J. W. Parker, 1849
T.

6737 RICHARDSON, James. The cruisers: being a letter to the marquess of Lansdowne, lord president, &c., &c., &c., in the defence of armed coercion for the extinction of the slave trade.
40 pp. London, J. Hatchard, 1849
T.

6738 Ross, Thomas. Lord Kinnaird's letter to his tenantry, on 'profitable investment of capital, or eleven years practical experience in farming', answered by Thomas Ross, farmer, Wardheads, and revised by lord Kinnaird.
24 pp. Perth, Thomas Richardson, 1849
T.
See 6671.

6739 [ROWAN, A. B.] What's to be done? or, a collection of the various suggestions for amending the poor law, with observations.
28 pp. Tralee, 1849
A.

6740 Rules and regulations adopted by the Macclesfield silk trade board: together with the list of prices fixed upon to be paid for weaving the various fabrics hereafter enumerated.
tables. 136 pp. Macclesfield, printed by Swinnerton and Brown, 1849
T.

6741 RUTTER, J. O. N. Gas-lighting: its progress and its prospects; with remarks on the rating of gas-mains, and a note on the electric-light.
70 pp. London, J. W. Parker, 1849
T.

6742 SCALLY, M. The surest road to Ireland's prosperity; dedicated to the ministry of England, the landlords of Ireland, and the catholics of the United Kingdom.
appendix. 24 pp. London, C. Dolman [etc., etc.], 1849
T.

6743 SCRIVENOR, Harry. Government intervention in railway affairs. A letter to the right hon. H. Labouchere, M.P., president of the board of trade, upon the right, necessity and duty of government interference in railway affairs; with especial reference to the establishing a uniform system of railway accounts, and an independent audit of such accounts, as an effectual remedy for existing evils.
tables and diag. in appendices. 62 pp. London, Smith Elder and co., 1849
T.

6744 SCROPE, George Julius Duncombe Poulett. The Irish difficulty; and how it must be met. From the 'Westminster and foreign quarterly review' for January, 1849. With a postscript.
38 pp. London, J. Ridgway, 1849
A., N.

6745 ——. The Irish poor law. How far has it failed? And why? A question addressed to the common sense of his countrymen. (With extracts from and references to the evidence given before the committees of the two houses of parliament now sitting on the subject.)
60 pp. London, J. Ridgway, 1849
T.

6746 ——. A labour rate recommended in preference to any reduction of the area of taxation, to improve the operation of the Irish poor-law. In three letters to the editor of the 'Morning Chronicle'.
24 pp. London, J. Ridgway, 1849
A., T.

6747 ——. Some notes of a tour in England, Scotland and Ireland, made with a view to the inquiry, whether our labouring population be really redundant? in letters to the editor of the 'Morning Chronicle'.
table of contents. 44 pp. London, J. Ridgway, 1849
A., T.

6748 ——. Suggested legislation with a view to the improvement of the dwellings of the poor.
26 pp. London, J. Ridgway, 1849
T.

6749 ——. Votes in aid, and rates in aid of the bankrupt Irish unions. Two speeches delivered in the house of commons by G. Poulett Scrope, esq., M.P., on Friday, 16th February, and Tuesday, 27th March, 1849.
26 pp., London, J. Ridgway, 1849
A.

6750 SHEE, William. Three letters addressed to the Reverend James Fitzpatrick, of Castletownroche, in the diocese of Cloyne, on the justice and policy of appropriating a portion of the revenues of the Irish protestant church to the increase and maintenance of church accommodation for the catholic people of Ireland.
46 pp. London, J. Ridgway, 1849
T.

6751 SHELLEY, John Villiers. A plea for truth, addressed to the tenant farmers of Hertfordshire and of the United Kingdom: exposing the mis-statement of facts advanced by Mr. C. H. Lattimore in his pamphlet entitled 'A plea for tenant right'.
20 pp. London, J. Ridgway, 1849
T.

6752 SHORT, Thomas Keir. On the cultivation and management of flax, and the best method of consuming the seed.
tables. appendix. 36 pp. London, R. Groombridge, H. Wright, 1849
T.

6753 SINCLAIR, Sir George, bart. Observations on the new Scottish poor law.
appendix. 92 pp. Edinburgh, Adam & Charles Black, London, Longman, Brown, Green, & Longmans, 1849
T.

6754 Slop shops and slop workers.
28 pp. London, printed by Phipps, 1849
A.

6755 SMILES, Samuel. Railway property: its condition and prospects.
tables. 64 pp. London, Effingham Wilson, [1849]
T.

6756 SMITH, Richard Baird. Agricultural resources of the Punjab; being a memorandum on the application of the waste waters of the Punjab to purposes of irrigation.
tables. map. 36 pp. London, Smith, Elder & co., 1849
T.

6757 [SMITH, Samuel.] A word in season; or, how the corn-grower may yet grow rich, and his labourer happy. Addressed to the stout British farmer.
16 pp. London, J. Ridgway, 1849
T.

6758 Some effects of the Irish poor-law: with a plan for emigration from Ireland. By an Englishman.
tables. 34 pp. London, Saunders and Otley, 1849
T.

6759 STANSFELD, Hamer. A remedy for monetary panics and free trade in currency suggested in a brief view of the currency question.
134 pp. London, Effingham Wilson, 1849
T.

6760 [STARKEY, Digby Pilot.] Ireland. The political tracts of Menenius.
236 pp. Dublin, Hodges & Smith, 1849
A.
collected ed.—cf. 6557, 6558.

6761 The state of the nation, considered with reference to the condition of the working-classes.
tables. 108 pp. London, Smith, Elder & co., 1849
T.

6762 The state of the nation: or, an inquiry into the effects of free trade principles upon British industry and taxation; in which the arguments of Sir Robert Peel in reply to Mr. Disraeli, in the house of commons, July 6, 1849, on the question of free trade, are carefully investigated and refuted. By Anglicanus.
tables. 64 pp. London, J. Hearne, 1849
F.

6763 Statistics of Ireland from Thom's Irish almanac and official directory for 1849.
index. tables. 96 pp. [not paginated.] Dublin, A. Thom, 1849
A.

6764 STEPHEN, Sir George. A letter from Sir George Stephen to Sir E. F. Buxton, bart., M.P., on the proposed revival of the English slave trade.
16 pp. London, Simpkin, Marshall, 1849
T.

6765 ——. The Niger trade considered in connexion with the African blockade, illustrated by a map compiled from recent travels.
map. 72 pp. London, Simpkin, Marshall, 1849
T.

6766 STEPHENS, John. Sanitary reform: its general aspect and local importance considered in a lecture.
table of contents. 72 pp. Adelaide, J. Stephens, 1849
A.

6767 STEWART, John Vandeleur. A letter to the earl of Clarendon on the subject of poor laws, with an appendix.
appendix. tables. folding table. 44 pp. Letterkenny, printed by Maddock, 1849
A., N.

6768 STIRLING, Thomas Henry. The question propounded: or, how will Great Britain ameliorate and remedy the distresses of its workmen, and others, out of employment.
appendix. 28 pp. London, J. Ollivier, 1849
T.

6769 Tables for calculating the quantity of provisions consumed by any number of persons according to the workhouse dietary; and also the loss incurred in cooking, cutting, and weighing provision, etc. Under the sanction of the poor law board.
tables. 16 pp. London, C. Knight, [1849]
T.

6770 THOROLD, William. An essay on the present and future prospects of farming in Great Britain.
inset plan. 24 pp. London, J. Ridgway, C. Fox, 1849
T.

6771 Thoughts on church endowment and church patronage. In their relationship to church extension, and to each other. By a solicitor.
32 pp. London, R. R. & G. Seeley, 1849
T.

6772 The true statement of the church leasehold question.
24 pp. London, Longman, Brown, Green, and Longmans, 1849
T.

6773 TUCKER, Jedediah Stephens. Naval financial reform. A letter addressed to the right hon. Sir F. T. Baring, bart., M.P., first lord of the admiralty, etc., on portions of the naval report of the finance committee.
tables. 66 pp. London, Richard Bentley, 1849

T.

6774 VEREKER, John Prendergast. An economic consideration of the Irish judgement acts: a paper read before the Dublin Statistical society, March, 1849.
12 pp. Dublin, Hodges & Smith, 1849
A., C., N., T., U.

6775 WAKEFIELD, Felix. Colonial surveying with a view to the disposal of waste land: in a report to the New Zealand company.
96 pp. London, John W. Parker, 1849
T.

6776 WASON, Peter Rigby. Letter to the right honourable lord John Russell, M.P., etc., etc., etc., suggesting a plan for the reclamation of waste lands in Ireland, securing the government from any loss.
tables. 20 pp. Ayr, printed by McCormick & Gemmell, 1849
A.

6777 WEBB, C. Locock. A letter to the right hon. Henry Labouchere, M.P., president of the board of trade, etc., etc., on railways, their accounts and dividends, their progress, present position and future prospects; their effects on trade and commerce, with suggestions for government assistance, and the amendment of the general railway acts of 1845.
tables. 64 pp. London, Smith, Elder & co., 1849.
T.

6778 WELTON, Cornelius. Substance of a lecture delivered at a quarterly meeting of the Wickham Market farmers' club, upon the mutual relation between landlord and tenant; on the 10th of April, 1849. Published at the request of the president, John Moseley, esq., and the members.
table. 28 pp. London, Effingham Wilson, [1849]
T.

6779 WHITE, George Preston. A tour in Connemara, with remarks on its great physical capabilities.
folding map. table of contents. tables. appendix. 188 pp. London, Smith, 1849
A.

6780 ——. Letter to the right honourable lord John Russell on the expediency of promoting railways in Ireland.
tables. 40 pp. London, John Weale, 1849
A., N., T.

6781 WHITEHEAD, John. Railway and government guarantee. Which is preferable? Facts and arguments to shew that guaranteed railway stock offers a better investment than do government securities.
tables. 56 pp. 6th ed. 'completely remodelled'. London, printed by Davy, 1849
A.

6782 ——. Railway management. The proof! A third letter to George Carr Glyn, esq., M.P., chairman of the London and North Western railway company.
tables. 50 pp. London, Smith, Elder & co., 1849
T.

6783 ——. Railway prostration. Causes and remedies. Letter to the right hon. Sir Robt. Peel, bart., M.P.
26 pp. London, Smith, Elder & co., 1849
T.

6784 WILLIAMS, Charles Wye. A letter to his excellency the earl of Clarendon, K.G., lord lieutenant of Ireland, on the completion of the works in connection with the improvement of the river Shannon.
18 pp. Dublin, printed by Underwood, 1849
A.

6785 WILLIAMS, Theophilus. Political equity: or, a fair equalization of the national burdens. Comprised in some intermingled and scattered thoughts, suggesting an anti-destitution policy; a graduated system of taxation on real property and regular incomes; a non-inquisitorial mode of collecting the tax on trade; a gradual liquidation and an ultimate extinction of the national debt, etc.
tables. appendix. 96 pp. London, C. Gilpin, 1849
T.
See 7102.

6786 WILLIAMS, William. An address to the electors and non-electors of the United Kingdom on the defective state of the representative system, and the consequent unequal and oppressive taxation, and prodigal expenditure of the public money.
tables. 32 pp. London, Effingham Wilson, 1849
A.

6787 WORTLEY, W. N. A plan for the extension of the savings bank system, with a view to a more economical management and the greater security of trustees and depositors; in a letter to . . . the chancellor of the exchequer. With additional observations.
tables. appendices. 26 pp. London, Letts, 1849
A.

1850

6788 ANCONA, J. S. Hints for the valuation of ecclesiastical and other property: whether held in fee, on life or other limited interest, or in reversion. To which are added a few useful observations and directions for parties contemplating either a purchase or sale.
tables. 32 pp. London, W. E. Painter, [185–?]
T.

6789 The building strike. Trial and verdict in the great case of Potterabout versus Wollop. Containing a fair statement of both sides of the question, and some good advice in the present time of difficulty.
16 pp. London, Ward and Lock, [185–?]
T.

6790 Farmers estate company (Ireland). Prospectus.
tables. 4 pp. London, printed by Palmer, [185–?]
A.

6791 Financial Reform Tracts. New series. no. VII. The way the public money goes on place-holders and sinecurists; being an analysis of salaries, pensions, etc., in the civil services of Great Britain and Ireland. By the Liverpool Financial Reform Association.
tables. 34 pp. Liverpool, Wilmer & Smith, [185–?]
A.

6792 GAMBLE, Richard Wilson. Abstract of a proposed bill for securing compensation to tenants in Ireland for improvements on their farms. (Prepared by W. Gamble, esq., Baggot St., Dublin, and printed for private circulation only.)
16 pp. Dublin, Porteous and Gibbs, [185–?]
N.

6793 Holyhead Refuge Harbour. Reasons which are submitted to show the necessity for an immediate inquiry into the capabilities of Holyhead for a refuge harbour, and against any further expenditure of the public money upon the works now in progress there pending the results of such inquiry.
36 pp. n.p., [185–?]
A.

6794 The landlord and tenant question.
folding plan. tables. 66 pp. n.p., [185–?]
A.

Includes (1) commentary on various land measures. (2) text of several land bills.

6795 POWNALL, Henry. The maintenance of the aged and necessitous poor a national tax and not a local poor rate. A subject for the consideration of all ratepayers.
23 pp. London, John Hearne, [185–?]
B.

6796 Proposal for establishing a small proprietors' society of Ireland.
24 pp. n.p., [185–?]
A.

6797 WARD, James. A history of gold as a commodity and as a measure of value. Its fluctuations both in ancient and modern times, with an estimate of the probable supplies from California and Australia. With a coloured geological map.
map. tables. 142 pp. London, W. S. Orr, Dublin, J. McGlashan, [185–?]
T.

6798 ADAMS, William Bridges. Road progress; or amalgamation of railways and highways for agricultural improvement, and steam farming in Great Britain and the colonies, also practical economy in fixed plant and rolling stock for passenger and goods trains.
folding plans. tables. 76 pp. London, Luxford, 1850
A.

6799 ALISON, William Pulteney. Observations on the reclamation of waste lands, and their cultivation by croft husbandry considered with a view to the productive employment of destitute labourers, paupers and criminals.
table of contents. 92 pp. Edinburgh and London, W. Blackwood & son, 1850
A., T.

6800 The attorney-general, at the relation of Frederick Jackson, vs. the mayor, aldermen, and burgesses of the city of Dublin.
22 pp. Dublin, G. & J. Grierson, 1850
A.

6801 [BARTY, James Strachan.] Caird's high farming harrowed by Cato the censor. Reprinted from Blackwood's magazine with an appendix.
tables in appendix. 38 pp. Edinburgh and London, W. Blackwood & son, 1850
T.

See 6813.

6802 [——.] Peter Plough's letters to the right honourable lord Kinnaird, on high farming and free trade.
appendix. 62 pp. 2nd ed. Edinburgh & London, W. Blackwood & son, 1850
T.

6803 BELL, John. The usurer *versus* the producer; or free trade illustrated.
32 pp. London, J. Ollivier, 1850
T.

6804 BERKELEY, Grantley F. Two letters addressed to the landed and manufacturing interests of the United Kingdom of Great Britain and Ireland, on the just maintenance of free trade.
14 pp. London, J. Bigg, 1850
T.

6805 BLACKER, William. Pro-corn law tracts No. III. Is it the producer or consumer who pays a protecting duty? Or is it paid, according to circumstances, partly by each? And if so, by what rules are their respective proportions regulated?
16 pp. London, R. Groombridge [etc.], 1850
N.

6806 BOWEN, C. H. What would be the effect of Sir John Romilly's bill 'for facilitating the sale of encumbered estates in Ireland'?
24 pp. Dublin, J. McGlashan, London, J. Ridgway, 1850
N.

6807 BOWEN, John. The Russell predictions on the working class, the national debt, and the new poor law, dissected.
tables. 74 pp. London, J. Hatchard, 1850
T.

6808 BRADLEY, Richard Beadon. The expected budget; or how to save more than twelve millions a year, not only without detriment, but with manifest advantage to existing interests.
tables. 42 pp. London, Whittaker, Teignmouth, D. Westcott, 1850
T.

6809 BRANDON, Woodthorpe. An inquiry into the freedom of the city of London in connection with trade, and into the laws and ordinances within the city respecting wholesale and retail traders, and the power of the corporation over persons carrying on trade within the city, not being free.
62 pp. London, H. Butterworth, 1850
T.

6810 BRODIE, William. Modern slavery and the slave trade. A lecture delivered at the Cheshunt literary and scientific institution.
56 pp. London, J. Hatchard, 1850
T.

6811 BROWN, Abner W. Village provident societies. Rules, tables, and history of the provident society established in 1836, for Pytchley, Isham, and Broughton, in Northamptonshire. Rules certified and enrolled according to act of parliament. With introductory suggestions on the formation, working, and improvement of similar local self-supporting institutions for the welfare and comfort of the labouring classes; and a few remarks addressed to the members of such societies.
82 pp. London, Wertheim and Macintosh, 1850
T.

6812 The building societies' directory, and almanack for 1850, containing a full and ample digest of the laws relating to them. With a diary of dates of subscriptions.
tables. 84 pp. London, Effingham Wilson, 1850
T.

6813 CAIRD, James. High farming vindicated and farther illustrated.
tables. 48 pp. 4th ed. enl. Edinburgh, A. & C. Black, London, Longman, Brown, Green & Longmans, 1850
A.
See 6801.

6814 CALVERT, Frederic. Second letter to the rt. hon. Sir Charles Wood, bart., M.P., upon certain laws affecting agriculture, by Frederick Calvert, esq., Q.C.
42 pp. 2nd ed. London, J. Ridgway, 1850
T.

6815 CALVERT, John William. The merits and tendencies of free-trade and protection respectively investigated. And measures of amendment suggested.
94 pp. London, J. Hearne, 1850
T.

6816 Colonization assurance corporation. A report of their agent in Western Australia; including the new discoveries to the northward, of rich pasturable and tillage lands, mines of silver-lead, copper, and coal. Authenticated by a copy of government survey, and confirmed by private letters.
16 pp. London, Thoms, 1850
N.

6817 Colonization assurance corporation: Short sketch of the means offered by the Colonization assurance corporation to assist the enterprise and promote the prosperity of farmers, artisans, and other small capitalists wishing to emigrate.
tables. 12 pp. London, T. Saunders, 1850
N.

6818 CONNER, William. A letter to the tenantry of Ireland, containing an exposition of the rackrent system; and pointing out a valuation and perpetuity as its only effectual remedy.
24 pp. Dublin, B. Gilpin, 1850
B.

6819 Copy of correspondence between the governors and directors of the Bank of Ireland, and James Hamilton, late agent at Kilkenny.
22 pp. Glasgow, Troup, 1850
A.

6820 COTTERILL, Charles Foster. Agricultural distress, its cause and remedy; with a preliminary inquiry concerning the civil law of the freedom of private enterprise.
tables. 156 pp. London, Effingham Wilson, 1850
T.

6821 CRAWFORD, William Sharman. Depopulation not necessary. An appeal to the British members of the imperial parliament, against the extermination of the Irish people.
44 pp. 2nd ed. London, C. Gilpin, Dublin, J. B. Gilpin, 1850
B., N.

6822 A cry from the middle passage; or the act of 1846, and its effects on the slave trade.
tables. appendix. 162 pp. London, Seeleys, 1850
T.

6823 Dublin Savings Bank established in School St., February 11th, 1818. Report and general statement of account, 20th November, 1850.
appendices and tables. 60 pp. Dublin, Goodwin, Son & Nethercott, 1850
N.

6824 Emigrants letters: being a collection of recent communications from settlers in the British colonies.
map. appendix. 138 pp. London, T. Saunders, 1850
T.

6825 EVERARD, Robert. The effects of free trade on the various classes of society, in a letter addressed to the members of the Spalding protection society, by the president, Robert Everard, esq.
32 pp. London, Simpkin, Marshall, 1850
T.

6826 FALCONER, David. The agricultural crisis: or landlords' duties, and tenants' rights.
tables. 50 pp. Edinburgh, A. & C. Black, 1850
T.

6827 The Farmer's title to his rights; or the truth in opposition to the 'cry' of 'confiscation'. By P. O'F.
44 pp. Belfast, printed by Henderson, 1850
A.

6828 A few words addressed to the agriculturists of England.
8 pp. London, W. Pickering, 1850
T.

6829 The freedom of the farmer not his boast nor glory; or, the church that costs nothing.
appendix. 20 pp. 3rd ed. London, J. Hughes, 1850
T.

6830 Free trade and its so-called sophisms: a reply to 'Sophisms of free trade, etc., examined by a barrister'.
table of contents. 106 pp. 2d. ed. London, J. W. Parker, 1850
A.

6831 GALLOWAY, A. An insight to the assessed taxes, giving the exemption, and the manner of claiming the same, also general observations to avoid surcharge, with a new and complete set of tables, (including the additional duty of ten per cent) shewing the total charge per annum for any number of windows, and every article.
diag. tables. 36 pp. London, printed by Causton & Hogberg, [1850]
T.

6832 GIBBON, Alexander. Past and present delusions in the political economy and consequent errors in the legislation of the United Kingdom.
tables. 184 pp. Edinburgh & London, W. Blackwood & son, 1850
T.

6833 [GRANT, Henry.] Ireland's hour.
appendix. 114 pp. Dublin, Hodges & Smith, London, J. Hatchard, 1850
A., N.
On measures for recovery after the Great Famine.

6834 [GRAYDON, William.] An address to the people on the subject of free-trade. The theory upon which free-trade cheapness rests is unsound; and that cheapness is not, in itself, a national blessing, as it is generally represented and supposed to be: it is either a national loss, or it is an effect which wears all the appearance of a domestic injustice; or rather it is a combination of both. By Agricola.
40 pp. London, Longman, Brown, Green and Longmans, 1850
T.

6835 Great Southern and Western Railway (Ireland). Twelfth half-yearly report, 19th March, 1850.
4 pp. Dublin, printed by Falconer, 1850
A.

6836 Great Southern and Western Railway (Ireland). Thirteenth half-yearly report,—9th September, 1850.
tables. 4 pp. Dublin, printed by Falconer, 1850
A.

6837 Great Southern and Western Railway. Statement of accounts, 30th June, 1850.
tables. 2 pp. (1 large sheet.) Dublin, printed by Falconer, 1850
A.

6838 GREENE, Jeremiah Greene Jones. Land and its laws! A few observations upon the evils resulting from the existing system of the laws relating to real property.
10 pp. London, J. Ridgway, 1850
T.

6839 GREER, Samuel M'Curdy. Freedom of agriculture: or the necessity of adequate compensation for permanent improvements.
table of contents. 80 pp. Dublin, J. McGlashan, London, J. Ridgway, 1850
A.

6840 ——. Law of landlord and tenant. Amount of compensation for tenants' improvements. To the tenant farmers of Great Britain and Ireland.
table of contents. 78 pp. Coleraine, printed at the Coleraine Chronicle Office, 1850
A.

6841 HANCOCK, William Neilson. Impediments to the prosperity of Ireland.
table of contents. 188 pp. London, Simms & McIntyre, 1850
A., L., U.

6842 ——. On Irish absenteeism. A paper read before the Dublin Statistical society, 23rd January, 1850.
12 pp. Dublin, Hodges & Smith, 1850
A., C., N., T.

6843 ——. On the causes of distress at Skull and Skibbereen, during the famine in Ireland, a paper read before the statistical section of the British association at Edinburgh, August, 2nd, 1850.
10 pp. Dublin, Hodges and Smith, 1850
A., N., T.

6844 ——. On the cost of patents of invention in different countries. A paper read before the statistical section of the British association, at Edinburgh, 1850.
table. 12 pp. Dublin, Hodges & Smith, 1850
A., N., T.

6845 ——. Statistics respecting sales of incumbered estates in Ireland. A paper read before the statistical section of the British association at Edinburgh, August 6th, 1850.
tables. 10 pp. Dublin, Hodges & Smith, 1850
A., N., T.

6846 ——. The usury laws, and the trade of lending money to the poor in Ireland. A paper read before the Dublin Statistical society, 18th February, 1850.
12 pp. Dublin, Hodges & Smith, 1850
A., C., N., T.

6847 HERON, Denis Caulfield. Three lectures on the principles of taxation, delivered at Queen's College Galway, in Hilary Term, 1850.
table of contents. 118 pp. Dublin, J. McGlashan, 1850
A., T., U.

6848 Highland destitution. Third report of the Edinburgh section of the central board for the relief of destitution in the Highlands and islands of Scotland, for 1849. Containing documents illustrative of their relief operations.
tables. 200 pp. Edinburgh, W. Blackwood & son, [1850]
T.

6849 Histoire de la fondation de la Société d'encouragement pour l'industrie nationale, ou recueil des procés-verbaux des

séances de cette société, depuis l'époque de sa fondation, le 9 Brumaire An X (1er novembre 1801), jusqu'au 1er Vendémiaire An XI (22 septembre 1802).
148 pp. Paris, Madame Veuve Bouchard-Huzard, 1850

T.

6850 HOWELL, Thomas. A day's business in the port of London. A lecture delivered at a meeting of the Clapham Athenaeum, April 29, 1850.
appendix. 48 pp. London, Simpkin, Marshall, D. Batten, 1850

T.

6851 HUBERT, Henry Samuel Musgrave. Ruin, and not prosperity, must be the fate of every country, whose trade and commerce are not subservient to the promotion of native agriculture: a patriotic essay—No. 2.
22 pp. London, Longman, Brown, Green & Longmans, 1850

T.

6852 ——. To protect native industry is a national duty, as well as a national benefit: a patriotic essay.
26 pp. London, Longman, Brown, Green & Longmans, 1850

T.

6853 HUXTABLE, Anthony. The 'present prices'.
appendix 54 pp. 6th ed. Blandford, W. Shipp, London, J. Ridgway, 1850

T.

6854 Incumbered estates in Ireland.
tables of contents. 118 pp. London, Bradbury & Evans, 1850

A.

6855 India v. America. A letter to the chairman of the Hon. East India company, on cotton. By Anti-Cant.
8 pp. London, Aylott & Jones, 1850

T.

6856 Irish Amelioration Society: Report of a special meeting of the Irish Amelioration Society held in London, on Saturday, August 3, 1850, on the subject of peat charcoal, as an immediate deodorizer, and valuable manure.
24 pp. Dublin, Farmer's Gazette Office, 1850

N.

6857 JOHNSON, William. A letter on protection to the rt. hon. lord Stanley, in which is discussed the probable duration of the British Empire under the present laws.
tables. 12 pp. Dublin, printed by Webb & Chapman, 1850

A., T.

6858 KINGDOM, William. Suggestions for improving the value of railway property, and for the eventual liquidation of the national debt.
16 pp. London, Whittaker, [1850]

T.

6859 [KINGSLEY, Charles.] Cheap clothes and nasty. By Parson Lot.
36 pp. London, William Pickering, Cambridge, Macmillan, 1850

T.

6860 KINNAIRD, George William Fox Kinnaird, 9th baron. Profitable investment of capital, or 11 years practical experience in farming: a letter from lord Kinnaird to his tenantry;

with lecture by W. White, esq., and a speech of Mr. Finnie, of Swanston, on the application of chemistry to agriculture. Third edition, with a few remarks addressed to the landlords and tenants of England.
tables. 44 pp. Dundee, Frederick Shaw, 1850

T.

6861 KNIGHT, Charles. The struggle of a book against excessive taxation.
16 pp. 2d. ed. London, printed by W. Clowes, 1850

A.

6862 [KNOTT, John M.] The currency and the late Sir Robert Peel.
24 pp. [no t.p.] London, [1850]

T.

6863 LANDOR, Henry. The best way to stop the slave trade.
24 pp. London, Longman, Brown, Green and Longmans, 1850

T.

6864 LARCOM, Thomas Aiskew. The address on the conclusion of the third session of the Dublin Statistical society. With the report of the council, read at the annual general meeting, 18th June, 1850.
tables. appendix. 24 pp. Dublin, Hodges & Smith, 1850

A., C., N.

6865 The law of landlord and tenant familiarly explained, so far as applicable to Ireland, including all the late enactments on the subject; giving full directions relative to tenancies at will and the notice to quit; lodgings; proceedings by distress for recovery of rent; taxes, rates, and assessments; repairs, cultivation, and fixtures.
table. 88 pp. 4th ed. Belfast, John Henderson, 1850

T.

6866 LEE, Thomas Gardiner. A plea for the English operatives: being a competing essay for the prize offered by John Cassell, esq., in which the means of elevating the working classes are humbly suggested.
table. 132 pp. London, Simpkin, Marshall, [1850]

T.

6867 LEE, James. Repeal of the navigation laws. A practical digest of the Act 12 & 13 Victoria, c. 29, being the new navigation act, with notes.
table. 30 pp. London, Simpkin, Marshall, [etc.], Liverpool, George Philip, 1850

T.

6868 A letter addressed to the country party. By a country gentleman.
8 pp. London, J. Ridgway, 1850

T.

6869 A letter on the rent-charge in commutation for tithe, as settled by the Acts 6th and 7th Will. IV. c. 71, etc.: showing the object and operation of that law; especially with reference to the question of an immediate diminution of the rent-charge.
12 pp. London, W. E. Painter, 1850

T.

6870 A letter to the right hon. lord John Russell, M.P., in favour of a protective duty on the importation of foreign grain. By D. K.
tables. 24 pp. London, C. Mitchell, 1850
T.

6871 A letter to the right hon. Sir Charles Wood, bt., M.P., etc., etc., etc., chancellor of the exchequer, on the assessed taxes, with suggestions for a general revision of the duties. By an officer of the Tax Department of the Board of Inland Revenue.
tables. 42 pp. London, Simpkin, Marshall, 1850
T.

6872 A letter to the right hon. Sir Robert Peel on the establishment of a state bank, the repeal of his currency measure of 1844, and free trade in banking. By a free trade banker.
52 pp. Glasgow, Robertson, Edinburgh, A. & C. Black, 1850
A.

6873 Low, David. Appeal to the common sense of the country regarding the present condition of the industrious classes; and exposition of the effects of what is called free trade on British agriculture and the classes dependent upon it, as well as on the general prosperity of the empire.
140 pp. Edinburgh & London, W. Blackwood & son, 1850
T.

6874 Low, William. Letter to the rt. hon. lord John Russell, first lord of the treasury, explanatory of a financial system for extending railways in Ireland, and for restoring confidence in railway property generally.
tables. 16 pp. London, Hamilton, & Adams, 1850
A.

6875 McCalmont, Robert. Letter to the right hon. lord John Russell, on communication with Ireland.
folding plate. plate. tables. 22 pp. London, T. Saunders, Dublin, Hodges & Smith, 1850
A., N.

6876 Mackey, William. Depopulation illegal and a crime.
32 pp. Dublin, J. Duffy, 1850
A., U.

6877 McLauchlan, Thomas. Recent Highland ejections considered: in five letters. With an appendix.
table. appendix. 28 pp. Edinburgh and London, Johnstone and Hunter, 1850
T.

6878 Macqueen, James. Statistics of agriculture, manufactures and commerce drawn up from official and authentic documents.
tables. 44 pp. Edinburgh & London, W. Blackwood & son, 1850
T.

6879 Macqueen, John Fraser. A lecture or reading on the recent Bankruptcy Act, (12 & 13 Vict. cap. 106,) delivered (with the permission of the Benchers) at Lincoln's Inn, on the 28th January, 1850.
24 pp. London, S. Sweet, 1850
T.

6880 Malet, William Wyndham. The funds of the church; their appropriation and alienation the cause of ignorance, heresy, and schism: and church self-government the only remedy for these evils. A letter to the archbishop of Canterbury.
appendix. 22 pp. London, J. Masters, 1850
T.

6881 Maley, A. J. Observations on the economic effects of absenteeism upon Ireland; a paper read before the Dublin Statistical society.
8 pp. Dublin, Hodges & Smith, 1850
A., C., T.

6882 Mechi, John Joseph. Copy of a paper on the subject of British agriculture. Read before the Society of arts, by Mr. J. J. Mechi, Nov. 27, 1850.
tables. 32 pp. London, Longman, Brown, Green & Longmans, 1850
T.

6883 ——. On the principles which ensure success in trade: a lecture, delivered at the Witham Literary Institute, on Tuesday, February 12th, 1850.
14 pp. London, Whittaker, [etc.], Royston, S. and J. Warren, 1850
T.

6884 Milne, David. Report of a visit to the farms of Mr. Rigden, Sussex; Rev. Mr. Huxtable, Dorset; and Mr. Morton, Gloucestershire. With remarks on agricultural improvement. By David Milne, esq., of Milnegarden, read to a meeting of the east of Berwickshire farmers' club. To which is added, the discussion and opinions of the club thereon.
tables. appendix. 80 pp. Berwick-upon-Tweed, printed by the Warder Office, 1850
T.

6885 Mongredien, A. Report on the consumption of Indian corn, etc., in Ireland in 1849.
6 pp. London, 1850
A.

6886 ——. Report on the potato crop in Ireland for the year 1850.
tables. 16 pp. London, printed by Skipper & East, 1850
A.

6887 Monro, Edward. Agricultural colleges and their working. A letter to A. J. B. Hope, esq., M.P., from the Rev. E. Munro, M.A., incumbent of Harrow Weald, Middlesex.
appendix. 74 pp. Oxford and London, J. H. Porter, 1850
U.

6888 Mr. Hemans' report on the port of Galway as a packet station, in communication with America.
tables. folding map. 14 pp. Dublin, printed by Leckie, 1850
A.

6889 Mr. Huxtable and his pigs. By Porcius.
tables. 32 pp. Edinburgh & London, W. Blackwood & son, 1850
A., N., T.

6890 Mr. Huxtable's sophisms exposed: By Holdfast, reprinted from the Dorset County Chronicle, with notes and additions.
44 pp. (pagination irregular.) London, W. Blackwood & son, 1850
T.

6891 MOONEY, Thomas. Nine years in America by Thomas Mooney, a traveller for several years in the United States of America, the Canadas, and other British provinces, in a series of letters to his cousin Patrick Mooney, a farmer in Ireland.
tables. 36 pp. Dublin, J. McGlashan, 1850
A.

6892 NORMAN, George Warde. An examination of some prevailing opinions, as to the pressure of taxation in this, and other countries.
appendix with tables. 96 pp. London, T. & W. Boone, 1850
T.

6893 OASTLER, Richard. Richard Oastler's reply to Richard Cobden's speech at Leeds, 18th December, 1849.
48 pp. 2nd ed. London, Pavey, 1850
A.

6894 O'RORKE, Edward. Speech of Edward O'Rorke, esq., on the bill for relieving Belfast from county cess, for roads and bridges, and for the further improvement of that borough, as delivered by him in the town hall of the said borough, on Monday and Tuesday, the 15th and 16th days of April, 1850, at an inquiry held by George Archibald Leach, esq., Captain Royal Engineers, the surveying officer appointed by the commissioners of woods and forests, and which inquiry commenced on Tuesday, the 2d April, 1850.
154 pp. Belfast, printed by W. & G. Agnew, 1850
A., B.

6895 OSBORNE, Robert W. The transfer of land considered in relation to the rights of judgement creditors. A paper read before the Dublin Statistical society on the 10th March, 1850.
10 pp. Dublin, Hodges & Smith, 1850
A., C., N., T.

6896 OUSELEY, William Gore. Notes on the slave-trade, with remarks on the measures adopted for its suppression. To which are added: a few general observations on slavery, and the prejudices of race and colour, as affecting the slave-trade, and some suggestions on the means by which it may be checked.
80 pp. London, John Rodwell, 1850
T.

6897 OUTRAM, Joseph. Nova Scotia. Its conditions and resources. In a series of six letters.
36 pp. Edinburgh and London, W. Blackwood & Son, 1850
T.

6898 PEARSON, Robert. A reply to 'Sophisms of free trade, and popular political economy examined. By a barrister'. Dedicated to William Hills, esq.
tables. 48 pp. London, Effingham Wilson, 1850
T.

6899 PELHAM, Dudley. Suggestions on immediate legislative requirements, addressed more particularly to the landed interests.
tables. 16 pp. London, W. H. Dalton, 1850
T.

6900 PIM, James. Ireland. 'Incumbered estates commission.' A letter to Sir John Romilly, M.P., Her Majesty's solicitor-general.
16 pp. London, printed by C. Cox, 1850
A.

6901 A plan for the systematic colonization of Canada, and all other British colonies. By an officer of rank, nearly twenty years resident in Canada.
map. diag. tables. 88 pp. London, J. Hatchard, 1850
T.

6902 PORTER, John Grey V. Moderate fixed duties, for the sake of revenue, on foreign breadstuffs, cattle, meat, &c. Notes on the present customs' duties on articles of food, which come into competition with similar articles grown by our own farmers.
tables. 62 pp. Dublin, J. McGlashan, 1850
T.
See 6724.

6903 Prospectus of the Irish Amelioration society. Incorporated by Royal Charter.
16 pp. London, printed by Rogerson, 1850
N.

6904 'Protection to British industry' considered, as it was represented at an entertainment, performed at the court house, Warwick, on the 14th of January, 1850: to which are added some observations upon the condition and treatment of the agricultural-labouring class. By Barnaby Breakbread.
64 pp. Warwick, Henry Sharpe, 1850
T.

6905 PURDON, W. A. South-western packet station, Ireland, and communication with America. 1850.
14 pp. Dublin, G. Ponsonby, London, Simpkin, Marshall, 1850
A.

6906 PYNE, Henry. Pyne's tithe table. Table showing the value of tithe rent-charges for the year 1850.
tables. 8 pp. London, Shaw, 1850
T.

6907 Remarks on Indian corn; its preservation and manufacture. With receipts for cooking, etc. Published gratuitously for the use of consumers by the Atlantic Dock Mills company, New York.
illustrations. 26 pp. New York, printed by Van Norden, 1850
A.

6908 Reply to Professor Low's 'Appeal', showing the true causes of rent. By Justitia.
62 pp. London, C. Gilpin, 1850
T.
See 6873.

6909   Report and account of the Crichton Loan Fund.
tables. 8 pp. Dublin, 1850

A.

6910   Report of the auditors of the Dublin and Drogheda Railway company.
2 pp. Dublin, 1850

A.

6911   Report of the directors of the Dublin and Drogheda Railway co. to the proprietors; published preparatory to the half yearly meeting, to be held 28th Feb. 1850.
tables. 24 pp. Dublin, printed by Falconer, 1850

A.

6912   Report of the directors of the Dublin-Drogheda Railway, to the proprietors, for the half year ending 30th June, 1850.
tables. 8 pp. Dublin, printed by Falconer, 1850

A.

6913   Report of the directors to the proprietors of the City of Dublin steam packet company.
8 pp. Dublin, 1850

A.

6914   Report of the sub-committee on currency to the acting committee of the National association for the protection of industry and capital throughout the British empire.
18 pp. n.p. 1850

G.

6915   ROBERTS, Owen Owen.   Protection a pretext: or home truths for tenant farmers.
table. 32 pp. Carnarvon, printed by Rees, 1850

A.

6916   ROLFE, John.   The injustice of the present free trade policy towards the high taxed English farmer; being the substance of a speech delivered by Mr. John Rolfe, of Wattleton Farm, Beaconsfield, at a meeting held at Great Marlow, Bucks, January 8th, 1850.
tables. 16 pp. London, Whittaker, [c. 1850]

T.

6917   ROTHWELL, William.   Report of the agriculture of the county of Lancaster, with observations on the means of its improvement: being a practical detail of the peculiarities of the county, and their advantages or disadvantages duly considered. Written for the Royal agricultural society of England, 1849. Together with an appendix, containing reports of crops, cultivation, general improvements, &c., for 1849; and other subsidiary remarks. By William Rothwell, Winwick, land agent, surveyor and valuer.
map. tables in appendix. 240 pp. London, R. Groombridge, [etc.], 1850

T.

6918   Rules of the Irish Metropolitan Building and Investment society. No. 2.
index. tables. 40 pp. Dublin, Mullany, 1850

A.

6919   SALVUCCI, F.   A few brief observations upon England.
72 pp. London, W. E. Painter, [1850]

T.

6920   SANDARS, Samuel.   Observations on the elements of taxation, and the productive cost of corn, etc., etc.
tables. appendix. 60 pp. London, J. Ollivier, 1850

T.

6921   SCROPE, George Julius Duncombe Poulett.   Draft report proposed to the select committee of the house of commons on the Kilrush union, by the chairman, G. Poulett Scrope, esq., M.P., with prefatory remarks.
32 pp. London, J. Ridgway, 1850

A., N.

6922   SCULLY, Vincent.   Poor rate (Ireland). Present system of collection, its evils and the remedy.
table of contents. 46 pp. Dublin, Hodges & Smith, London, J. Ridgway, 1850

A., N., T.

6923   SHACKLETON, Ebenezer.   Thoughts on reading the hon. John P. Vereker's paper on absenteeism: a paper read before the Dublin Statistical society, 18th March, 1850.
6 pp. Dublin, Hodges & Smith, 1850

A., C., N., T.

6924   The shortest way with the free traders, in a letter to the editor of the Standard, by Daniel De Foe, Jun.
30 pp. Yarmouth, C. Barber, [1850]

T.

6925   A sketch of cheap corn; or the wealth of agriculture. By a barrister.
tables. 72 pp. London, J. Hatchard, 1850

T.

6926   Slop shops, and slop workers.
table. 28 pp. 2nd ed. London, J. Ollivier, 1850

T.

6927   SLOPER, John.   A letter to the agriculturists of England.
8 pp. London, Simpkin, Marshall, Newbury, J. Blacket, 1850

T.

6928   SMITH, Arthur.   The railway returns made to the special orders of the house of lords, 1849–1850, prefaced with the results of previous returns, with the view to a complete comprehension of the nature of railway investment, and the restoration of confidence, by the adoption of a sound policy and management.
tables. 52 pp. London, Effingham Wilson, 1850

T.

6929   SMITH, Edmund James.   The error of mistaking net rental for permanent income.
12 pp. London, J. Ollivier, 1850

T.

6930   SMITH, Hugh.   Free farming to meet free trade.
32 pp. London, J. Ridgway, 1850

T.

6931 [SMITH, Samuel.] A word in season; or, how the corn-grower may yet grow rich and his labourer happy. Addressed to the stout British farmer. Sixth edition, much enlarged; with an illustration of implements for carrying out the plan with ease, economy, and expedition, to any extent.
tables. illustrations. 34 pp. London, J. Ridgway, 1850
T.

6932 Somerville's Manchester school of political economy. (Edited by 'one who has whistled at the plough'.) No. 1. June, 1850.
table of contents. 70 pp. London, Strange, Manchester, Heywood, etc., 1850
A.

6933 STARK, Archibald G. How to render pauperism self-supporting; with practical hints for developing the system of re-productive employment, as a substitute for idleness and useless tests, suggested by a visit to the Cork Union Workhouse. Extracted by permission of the author, from 'The South of Ireland in 1850', and re-published by the Poor law association.
16 pp. [London, 1850?]
N.

6934 Statement. To the City of Dublin Steam Packet company.
4 pp. Dublin, 1850
A.

6935 STAUNTON, Sir George Thomas, bart. Observations on our Chinese commerce, including remarks on the proposed reduction of the tea duties, our new settlement at Hong Kong, and the opium trade.
52 pp. London, J. Murray, 1850
T.

6936 Stock exchange, Dublin. Rules and regulations of the society of the stock exchange, approved of on the 12th February, 1850, by his excellency the lord lieutenant.
24 pp. Dublin, printed by A. Thom, 1850
A.

6937 STONEY, Sadleir. Remarks on the adjustment of the poor-rate taxation in Ireland: a paper read before the Dublin Statistical society, on the 18th of February, 1850.
8 pp. Dublin, Hodges & Smith, 1850
A., C., N., T.

6938 STRANG, John. The progress of Glasgow, in population, wealth, manufactures, etc., being the substance of a paper read before the statistical section of the British association for the advancement of science, in Edinburgh, on Tuesday the 6th August, 1850.
tables. 18 pp. Glasgow, printed by Hedderwick, 1850
A.

6939 Taxation and rents. A short address to all concerned. By T. R.
tables. 8 pp. London, Simpkin, Marshall, J. G. Caborn, [1850]
T.

6940 THOMSON, Thomas Richard Heywood. The Brazilian slave trade and its remedy: shewing the futility of repressive force measures. Also, how Africa and our West Indian colonies may be mutually benefited.
88 pp. Douglas (Isle of Man), John Mylrea, London, Simpkin, Marshall, 1850
T.

6941 The tithe-owner's tale; or, a bleat from the pastures. By a black sheep.
40 pp. London, J. Ridgway, 1850
T.

6942 Tracts on protection. No. 1. Introductory tract.
16 pp. London, J. Ollivier, 1850
T.

6943 Tracts on protection no. 2. The occupations of the people. London. Published for the National association for the protection of industry and capital throughout the British Empire.
tables. 136 pp. London, J. Ollivier, 1850
T.

6944 Tracts on protection. no. 3. An abstract of political opinions. London. Published for the National association for the protection of industry and capital throughout the British Empire.
16 pp. no. t.p. London, J. Ollivier, 1850
T.

6945 Tracts on protection no. 4. The war of classes. London. Published for the national association for the protection of industry and capital throughout the British Empire.
16 pp. no. t.p. London, J. Ollivier, 1850
T.

6946 Tracts of the British anti-State-Church association. New series.—No. 1. Church property and revenues in England and Wales.
tables. 32 pp. [London], the British anti-State-Church association, 1850
T.

6947 Tracts of the British anti-State-Church association. New series.—no. 5. Facts and figures relating to the Irish Church.
tables. 12 pp. London, the British anti-State-Church association, 1850
T.

6948 Transatlantic packet station. Replies of the joint committee appointed by the town council, harbour commissioners, and committee of merchants of the city of Cork, to the queries of the Transatlantic packet station commissioners.
22 pp. Cork, Purcell, 1850
A.

6949 URQUHART, William Pollard. Agricultural distress and its remedies.
16 pp. Aberdeen, D. Wyllie, Edinburgh and London, W. Blackwood & son, 1850
T.

6950 VEREKER, John P. Absenteeism economically considered: a paper read before the Dublin Statistical society, December 17th, 1849.
20 pp. Dublin, Hodges & Smith, 1850
A., C., N., T.

6951 VINCENT, Robert. Life assurance as bearing on social economy.
tables. 50 pp. London, Longman, Brown, Green, and Longmans [etc., etc.], 1850

T.

6952 WARD, James. How to regenerate Ireland; or facts from the fisheries.
tables. 36 pp. London, J. Ridgway, 1850

A., N.

6953 WARNES, John. Flax versus cotton; or the two-edged sword against pauperism and slavery.
tables. appendix. 58 pp. London, J. Ridgway, 1850

T.

6954 What are things coming to?
30 pp. London, W. Pickering, 1850

T.

6955 WOODHOUSE, J. O. Justice to the landed interest. Free trade for farmers. Growth of beet-root for sugar, and culture of tobacco in Ireland.
16 pp. Dublin, printed by Corbett, 1850

A., N.

6956 WYSE, Francis. The Irish tenant league: the immoral tendency and entire impracticability of the measures considered, in a letter addressed to John O'Connell, M.P.; with observations on the character and constitution of the Loyal repeal association of Ireland.
20 pp. Dublin, J. McGlashan, London, J. Ridgway, 1850

A.

6957 YEATMAN, Henry Farr. A speech in favour of protection to British capital and industry.
tables. notes. 64 pp. London, J. Ollivier, [1850?]

T.

6958 YULE, Alexander. Spade husbandry and manual labour, with low or cheap farming, a certain means of removing Irish distress; applicable to England and Scotland.
table of contents. tables. diagrams. 94 pp. 2nd ed. Edinburgh & London, W. Blackwood & son, 1850

N.

6959 YULE, Henry. The African squadron vindicated.
tables. appendices. 44 pp. 2nd ed. London, J. Ridgway [etc., etc.], 1850

T.

1851

6960 Abstract of the seventh census. (Third edition.)
tables. 8 pp. 3rd ed. [Philadelphia], Lippincott, Grambo, [1851]

T.

7th Census of the U.S.A.

6961 An account showing the quantity and value of work done in the several industrial departments of the Enniscorthy union workhouse, during the half year ending March 25th, 1851.
tables. 12 pp. Eniscorthy, printed at the General printing establishment, 1851

A.

6962 Agriculture retrieved. An address to landowners. By a small proprietor.
32 pp. Dublin, P. Hardy, 1851

A.

6963 ALISON, William Pulteney. Letter to Sir John McNeill, G.C.B., on Highland destitution and the adequacy or inadequacy of emigration as a remedy.
48 pp. Edinburgh and London, W. Blackwood & son, 1851

T.

6964 Association for the abolition of the duty on paper—Tract no. 1.
4 pp. Dublin, printed by J. Falconer, 1851

A.

6965 Association for the abolition of the duty on paper. Tract no. 2.
4 pp. Dublin, printed by J. Falconer, 1851

A.

6966 Association for the abolition of the duty on paper. Article no. 1.
6 pp. Dublin, printed by J. Falconer, 1851

A.

T.p. headed: 'Taxes upon knowledge'.

6967 Association for the abolition of the duty on paper. Article no. 2.
4 pp. Dublin, printed by J. Falconer, 1851

A.

6968 Association for the abolition of the duty on paper: Circular letter from Robt. Heron, sec., Dublin, 1851, together with:—Tract no. 1, Jan. 1851. Article no. 1, Jan. 1851. Tract no. 2, Jan. 1851. Article no. 2, Jan. 1851. [Broadsheet no. 1, n.d. 'Taxation upon knowledge'.]
24 pp. Dublin, 1851

N.

6969 BABBAGE, Charles. Thoughts on the principles of taxation, with reference to a property tax, and its exceptions. Second edition with additions.
28 pp. London, J. Murray, 1851

T.

6970 BAKER, Robert. The present condition of the working classes, generally, considered: in two lectures, delivered before the members of the Bradford Church institution, and published at their request.
tables. 64 pp. London, Longman, Brown, Green & Longmans, 1851

T.

6971 BARLOW, Henry Clark. Industry on Christian principles.
36 pp. London, Seeleys, 1851

T.

6972 BATSON, Thomas. How to improve the condition of the agricultural labourer. A self-supporting system, by which boys may be trained in acts of industry, and at the same time receive a suitable education.
tables. 30 pp. London, R. Groombridge, 1851

T.

6973 BEGG, James. Social reform. How every man may become his own landlord; or, a way by which to elevate the condition of the masses of Britain, and develop the resources of the country: being a lecture delivered in Newington Free Church, at the request of the 'Scottish social reform association', on the 6th of March, 1851. (Taken in shorthand and revised by the author.)
table. 22 pp. London and Edinburgh, Johnstone and Hunter, 1851

T.

6974 BINNS, Jonathan. Notes on the agriculture of Lancashire, with suggestions for its improvement.
tables in appendices. illusts. 164 pp. Preston, Dobson, London, Simpkin, Marshall, 1851

T.

6975 BLAKELY, F. Letters on the relation between landlord and tenant.
8 pp. Belfast, printed by Mayne, 1851

N.

6976 Board of Irish manufactures and industry. Tract No. 1. Flax culture and manufacture.
tables. 16 pp. Dublin, printed at the Office of 'the Commercial Journal', 1851

A.

6977 A brief inquiry into the evils attendant upon the present method of erecting, purchasing, and renting dwellings for the industrial classes, with suggestions for their remedy; being an apology for the formation of the Metropolitan buildings purchase company. By one of its promoters.
plans. 20 pp. London, Houlston and Stoneman, 1851

T.

6978 The British electric telegraph company. Prospectus.
4 pp. London, printed by Unwin, 1851

A.

6979 The British electric telegraph company. Statement.
8 pp. London, printed by Unwin, 1851

A.

6980 CAPPER, Henry. Capper's colonial calendar, for 1851, being a comprehensive summary of the colonial possessions of Great Britain, containing a description of each settlement, its situation, extent and acquisition, chief town and trade, amount of imports and exports, revenue and expenditure, government, religion, education, number of churches and schools, population, chronological events. Also the civil, military and ecclesiastical officers, official colonial salaries, public companies, newspapers, list of parliamentary colonial papers, public companies and associations connected with the respective colonies, government colonial land regulation, &c., &c.
146 pp. London, C. Cox, T. Saunders, [1851]

T.

6981 The case of the farmer and labourer stated, in a letter to Benjamin D'Israeli, esq., M.P.
50 pp. London, J. Ridgway, 1851

T.

6982 [CLEMENTS, Jacob.] The farmers' case with regard to education, plainly stated, in a letter, addressed to the farmers and other parishioners of Upton St. Leonards, by the incumbent of the parish.
24 pp. London, F. & J. Rivington, [1851]

T.

6983 COOKE, George. A statement of facts in reference to the farm of Rossena; and illustrative of the evils of the present land system of Ireland.
tables. appendix. 30 pp. Dublin, C. Gilpin, 1851

A., K., N.

6984 CRAIG, William. Correspondence of Rev. William Craig, Dromara, containing his entire negociation for obtaining acceptance of the surrender of his lease, on 20th May, 1850, with an appendix, containing extracts from subsequent correspondence relating thereto, and his letter to the tenant right meeting at Flow Bog.
20 pp. Dublin, Hodges & Smith, 1851

A.

6985 CROSLEY, H. Reasons for the introduction of the manufacture of beet root sugar into Ireland.
tables. 8 pp. London, Buck & Straker, 1851

N.

6986 DAY, George Game. The effects of free trade. The speech of Mr. George Game Day, at a public dinner, given to him and the Rev. James Linton, in the Town Hall, Huntingdon, July 29, 1851. Second edition.
18 pp. London, J. Ollivier, 1851

T.

6987 DEAN, George Alfred. The compulsory enfranchisement and commutation of copyhold property considered, with suggestions for ascertaining the value of existing interests in such a property. To which is appended the 'copyhold enfranchisement bill' just brought before the legislature, with remarks thereon.
96 pp. London, Atchley, 1851

T.

6988 Debt and surplus. A letter to the right honourable lord John Russell, M.P., March, 1851.
6 pp. London, S. Johnson, 1851

T.

6989 DEERING, James. Valuation of Ireland. Observations on Mr. Griffith's letter to lord Clarendon, 23rd Dec. 1850.
30 pp. Cork, printed by Guy, 1851

A.

6990 DEERING, William. A brief account of the origin, establishment and working of the office for the registration and regulation of coal whippers, of the Port of London.
48 pp. London, Arthur Hall, [etc.], 1851

T.

6991 The Dublin & Kingstown, the Waterford, Wexford, Wicklow & Dublin, and the Dublin, Dundrum and Rathfarnham railway companies.
folding map. 12 pp. London, printed by C. Roworth, 1851

A.

6992 Dublin Savings Bank. Report and general statement of account, with appendix, including schedule of depositors balances, at 20th November, 1850.
table of contents. appendix. tables. 60 pp. Dublin, Goodwin & Nethercott, 1851
A.

6993 DUMAS, J. Crédit Foncier. Rapport à M. le Président de la République par Mon. Dumas, Ministre de l'Agriculture et du Commerce suivi d'un rapport sur la publication de nouveaux documents relatifs aux institutions de crédit foncier qui existent dans les divers états Européens par Mon. J. B. Josseau.
54 pp. Paris, Imprimérie Nationale, 1851
N.

6994 DUNCAN, John. Observations on the affairs and policy of the Eastern Counties' railway company.
tables. appendix. 52 pp. London, Effingham Wilson, [1851]
T.

6995 EARPS, Joseph. A treatise on the relative interests of landlord, tenant, and labourer, connected with the market value of agricultural produce. Sep. 30, 1851. Re-published with additions and corrections, Dec. 31, 1851.
tables. 32 pp. London, Simpkin, Marshall, 1851
T.

6996 England's western, or America's eastern shore? Old Ireland a new state? With their various complexities and perplexities discussed. By an old and almost obsolete loyalist.
50 pp. Dublin, J. Falconer, 1851
T.

6997 The equalisation of the poor rates. A sketch by Brittanicus.
16 pp. London, printed by Odell, 1851
A.

6998 Examination of the landlords' and tenants' case, illustrated by reference to the revaluation of the earl Romney's farms, as published in 'The Times', April 11th, 1851, by one of Sir James Graham's shopkeepers.
28 pp. London, C. Gilpin, [1851]
T.

6999 FERRAND, W. Busfield. Protection to native industry. The speech of W. Busfield Ferrand, esq., at Aylsham, in Norfolk, March 4th, 1851. The right hon. the earl of Oxford in the chair.
28 pp. London, J. Ollivier, 1851
T.

7000 A few words from John Bull, in reply to letters received from Sir E. Bulwer Lytton, bart. By a landowner.
tables. 40 pp. London, J. Ollivier, 1851
T.

7001 The first report of the committee appointed by the town council of Dublin, on the 2nd December, 1850, to report upon the powers of the corporation, the state of their finances, and their resources; and also the powers conferred by the Dublin improvement act, and of the acts incorporated there-with, and the collection of rates act, and to suggest the best means of carrying out such powers, to the right hon. the lord mayor, aldermen, and burgesses of Dublin.
tables. 24 pp. Dublin, printed by Grierson, 1851
A.

7002 FISHER, Joseph. Ireland, past and present. Being a speech delivered at the provincial meeting of deputies from the boards of guardians of Munster.
tables. appendix. 38 pp. Dublin, J. McGlashan [etc., etc.], 1851
A., N.

7003 FORTESCUE, Hugh Fortescue, 2nd earl. Official salaries. Letters to the electors of Plymouth and to lord John Russell, from viscount Ebrington, M.P. Late secretary to the poor law board.
60 pp. 2nd ed. London, J. Ridgway, 1851
T.

7004 FOSTER, John Fitzgerald Leslie. The new colony of Victoria, formerly Port Philip: Together with some account of the other Australian colonies. [Second thousand, 8 pp. additional material.]
tables. 100 pp. London, T. Saunders, 1851
T.

7005 Galway transatlantic steam-packet company. Nautical and statistical report with time and traffic tables.
tables. 16 pp. Dublin, Mullany, 1851
A., N.

7006 GIBBON, Alexander. Taxation: its nature and properties, with remarks on the incidence and the expediency of the repeal of the income-tax.
tables. appendix. 138 pp. London, Henry Colburn, 1851
T.

7007 GIRDWOOD, William. A letter to the tenant farmers of the county of Armagh.
12 pp. Lurgan, Evans, 1851
A.

7008 Great Southern and Western railway, statement of accounts, 31st December, 1850
tables. 2 pp. Dublin, printed by J. Falconer, 1851
A.

7009 Great Southern and Western railway. (Ireland.) Fifteenth half-yearly report, Wednesday 10th September, 1851.
tables. 6 pp. Dublin, printed by J. Falconer, 1851
A.

7010 GREY, W. H. Church leases; or the subject of church leasehold property considered with a view to place it on a firmer basis.
106 pp. 3d ed. enl. London, J. Ridgway, 1851
A., T.

7011 HANCOCK, William Neilson. Is the competition between large and small shops injurious to the community? Being a lecture delivered in Trinity College, Dublin, in Trinity term, 1851.
32 pp. Dublin, Hodges & Smith, 1851.
A., N., Q., T., U.

7012 ——. Is there really a want of capital in Ireland? A paper read before the Statistical section of the British association, at Ipswich, July 3rd, 1851.
tables. 16 pp. Dublin, Hodges & Smith, 1851
A., N., T.

7013 ——. On the general principles of taxation, as illustrating the advantages of a perfect income tax. A paper read before the Dublin Statistical society, 18th November, 1850.
table. 16 pp. Dublin, Hodges & Smith, 1851
A., C., N., T.

7014 ——. Should boards of guardians endeavour to make pauper labour self-supporting, or should they investigate the causes of pauperism? A paper read before the Statistical section of the British association, at Ipswich, 1851.
16 pp. Dublin, Hodges & Smith, 1851
A., C., N., T., U.

7015 HARVEY, James. Remunerative price the desideratum, not cheapness.
44 pp. London, Effingham Wilson, [1851]
T.

7016 HEARN, William Edward. The Cassell prize essay on the condition of Ireland.
134 pp. London, (Cassell?), 1851
N.

7017 ——. On cottier rents: a paper read before the Dublin Statistical society.
8 pp. Dublin, Hodges & Smith, 1851
A., C., N., T.

7018 HEATHFIELD, Richard. Fallacies of taxation.
tables. 18 pp. London, Pelham Richardson, 1851
T.

7019 HERON, Denis Caulfield. Taxes on the administration of justice. A paper read before the Dublin Statistical society, . . . 20th January, 1851.
8 pp. Dublin, Hodges & Smith, 1851
A., N., T., U.

7020 Highland destitution. First report of the Edinburgh section of the central board for the relief of destitution in the Highlands and islands of Scotland, for 1850. Containing documents illustrative of their relief operations.
tables. appendix. 128 pp. Edinburgh, W. Blackwood & son, [1851]
T.

7021 Highland destitution. Second report of the Edinburgh section of the central board for the relief of destitution in the highlands and islands of Scotland, for 1850. Being their concluding report. Containing documents illustrative of their relief operations, and a map of the districts under their charge.
map. tables. appendix. 176 pp. Edinburgh, W. Blackwood, & son, 1851
T.

7022 HINDMARCH, William Matthewson. Observations on the defects of the patent laws of this country with suggestions for the reform of them.
table of contents. tables. 60 pp. London, Benning, 1851
N.

7023 HOGAN, William. On the advantages and disadvantages of indirect taxation; and a scheme for direct taxation, which would be equitable and combine the advantages of an indirect tax. A paper read before the Dublin Statistical society, on the 16th December, 1850
8 pp. Dublin, Hodges & Smith, 1851
A., C., N., T.

7024 [HOWE, James.] Howe's two systems for relieving the farmers; one, without interfering with the freedom of trade, or causing any tax upon food; and pointing out the dangerous position that trade and agriculture are both placed in under the present system; also, to what extent agriculture has been and may expect to be benefited by the use of machinery. The other, 'The sliding scale'; and shewing the cause of its failing to give satisfaction, and the necessity of petitioning the parliament for relief in some way. By the author of 'A treatise upon leasing land'; 'A treatise upon an elucidation of assessment'; and 'A treatise upon copyholds and the adjustment of copyhold tenures';—(the principles of which have passed the house of commons the second time) and 'A treatise pointing out the absolute necessity of some enactment to relieve the agriculturalists, and elucidating the position of landlord and tenant'
26 pp. London, A. Hall, Chesham, I. S. Garlick, [1851]
T.

7025 HURSTHOUSE, Charles, jr. New Zealand. The emigration field of 1851. An account of New Plymouth; or guide to the garden of New Zealand. 3rd edition. And an article on the Canterbury settlement.
map. table of contents. 202 pp. Aberdeen, printed by Chalmers, 1851
A.

7026 Ireland. Its landlords: Its poor law: and its system of national education. By an English clergyman.
48 pp. Dublin, Hodges & Smith, 1851
A., T., U.

7027 Is distinct trading or the 'monster house' system most conducive to the public interest?
46 pp. Dublin, printed by Carrick, 1851
A.

7028 KANE, Sir Robert. The address on the opening of the fifth session of the Dublin Statistical society, delivered by Sir Robert Kane, vice-president of the society with the report of the council, read at the annual meeting, 19th November, 1851.
20 pp. Dublin, Hodges & Smith, 1851
A., T.

7029 KNIGHT, Charles. The case of the authors as regards the paper duty.
tables. 24 pp. London, printed by W. Clowes, 1851
A.

7030 [LAMBERT, Henry.] A memoir of Ireland in 1850. By an ex.-M.P.
tables. appendix. 150 pp. Dublin, J. McGlashan, London, J. Ridgway, 1851
A.

7031 LAWRENCE, Charles. A letter on agricultural education. Addressed to a youth who had resolved on farming as his future occupation.
16 pp. London, J. Ridgway, 1851
T.

7032 LAWSON, James Anthony. Society for promoting scientific inquiries into social questions. Report on the Patent laws.
table of contents. 30 pp. Dublin, Hodges & Smith, London, J. Ridgway, 1851

A., N.

7033 LE FANU, William R. Report to the directors of the Great Southern and Western railway, on the port of Cork as a packet station for communication with America.
folding map. 16 pp. Dublin, printed by C. Bull, 1851

A., N.

7034 LESLIE, Thomas Edward Cliffe. On the self dependance of the working classes under the law of competition: a paper read before the Dublin Statistical society.
12 pp. Dublin, Hodges & Smith, 1851

A., C., T.

7035 A letter on the 'Monster house series', written for newspaper publication.
no tp. 8 pp. Dublin, 1851

N.

Signed 'Censor'. A defence of large establishments in trade.

7036 LEVI, Leone. International code of commerce in connection with the law of nature and nations.
24 pp. London, Simpkin, Marshall [etc.], 1851

N.

7037 [LOCKE, John.] Ireland. Observations on the people, the land and the law in 1851; with especial reference to the policy and practice of the Incumbered estates court.
appendix with tables. 60 pp. Dublin, Hodges & Smith, London, Simpkin & Marshall, 1851

A., N.

7038 LONG, Henry Lawes. Enclosure and irrigation. A letter addressed to the landowners of certain portions of the hundreds of Farnham and Godalming.
28 pp. London, Longman, Brown, Green, and Longmans, [1851]

T.

7039 LONGFIELD, Robert. Society for promoting scientific inquiries into social questions. Report on the legislative measures requisite to facilitate the adoption of commercial contracts respecting the occupation of land in Ireland.
table of contents. 46 pp. Dublin, Hodges & Smith, London, J. Ridgway, 1851

A., C., N., U.

7040 LUDLOW, John Malcolm. Christian socialism and its opponents: a lecture, delivered at the office of the Society for promoting working men's associations, 76, Charlotte street, Fitzroy square, on Wednesday, February 12th, 1851.
appendices. 96 pp. London, John W. Parker, 1851

T.

7041 LYNE, Francis. Tribunals of commerce. A letter to the merchants, bankers, traders, and others, of Great Britain.
24 pp. London, Effingham Wilson, 1851

T.

7042 LYSAGHT, Edward. A consideration of the theory that the backward state of agriculture in Ireland, is a consequence of the excessive competition for land. A paper read before the Dublin Statistical society, 24th March, 1851.
8 pp. Dublin, Hodges & Smith, 1851

A., T.

7043 BULWER LYTTON, Sir Edward, bart. Letters to John Bull, esq., on affairs connected with his landed property and the persons who live thereon. Seventh edition.
tables. 106 pp. London, Chapman and Hall, 1851

T.

——. 48 pp. eleventh ed. Edinburgh and London, W. Blackwood & son, 1851

A., D.

7044 McCULLOCH, John Ramsey. London in 1850–1851. From the geographical dictionary of J. R. McCulloch, esq.
132 pp. London, Longman, Brown, Green & Longmans, 1851

B.

7045 McDONALD, J. H. England rescued from her present dilemma, or free trade and protection reconciled in our deliverance from the burden of the national debt. Explained in a series of letters, addressed to the merchants, manufacturers, agriculturists, and tradesmen of Great Britain.
126 pp. London, Seeleys, 1851

T.

7046 MACKENZIE, John. Letter to lord John Russell on Sir John McNeill's report on the state of the west highlands and islands of Scotland.
table. 24 pp. Edinburgh and London, W. Blackwood & son, 1851

T.

7047 MAKGILL, George. Rent no robbery. An examination of some erroneous doctrines regarding property in land.
table. 38 pp. Edinburgh & London, W. Blackwood & son, 1851

T.

7048 [MALEY, A. J.] Suggestions for immediate establishment of a direct communication by steam navigation between Ireland and the United States of North America without the aid of the British government. (signed 'A.J.M.')
12 pp. 2nd ed. Dublin, Hodges & Smith, 1851

A.

7049 MARTIN, Samuel. True christianity—pure socialism. A lecture.
24 pp. London, T. Ward, 1851

T.

7050 MECHI, John Joseph. A second paper on British agriculture, with an account of his own operations at Tiptree Hall farm: read before the Society of arts, manufactures, and commerce, by Mr. J. J. Mechi, 11th December, 1851.
tables. tables in appendices. 44 pp. London, Longman, Brown, Green & Longmans, 1851

T.

7051 MONGREDIEN, A. Report on Indian corn and Mediterranean wheat.
tables. 16 pp. London, printed by Skipper & East, 1851

A.

7052   The 'monster house' system and the small trade system considered and compared.
30 pp. Dublin, printed by Carrick, 1851
A., N., U.

7053   NEWDEGATE, Charles Newdigate.   Third letter to the right hon. H. Labouchere, M.P., &c., &c. On the balance of trade, ascertained from the market value of all articles imported, as compared with the market value of all articles exported, during the five years ending January 1850. Further tested by reference to the balance of trade between the United Kingdom and her colonies, which has been similarly ascertained.
tables. 160 pp. London, Seeleys, [1851]
T.

7054   ——.   Fourth letter to the right hon. H. Labouchere, M.P., etc., by C. N. Newdegate, esq., M.P., on the balance of trade, ascertained from the market value of all articles imported, as compared with the market value of all articles exported, during the year 1850.
tables. 28 pp. London, Seeleys, 1851
T.

7055   Notices of the proposed small proprietor society of Ireland. By the Irish & English press.
table of contents. 72 pp. n.p. 1851
N.

7056   Observations with reference to the *past* and *present* condition of the medical charities in Ireland, and suggestions as to the best means for ensuring future efficient and economical administration of medical relief to the sick poor. By Medicus.
tables. appendix. 96 pp. Dublin, J. McGlashan, 1851
T.

7057   Official catalogue of the Great Exhibition of the works of industry of all nations. 1851.
table of contents. 324 pp. London, 1851
N.

7058   The origin and progress of 'monster house' monopoly; and its ruinous effects upon the community considered. By 'Edward'.
24 pp. Dublin, printed by Carrick, 1851
A., U.

7059   PARKES, Josiah.   Fallacies on land-drainage exposed. A refutation of a letter by lord Wharncliffe to Philip Pusey, esq., M.P., published in the journal of the Royal agricultural society of England, Vol. XII. Part I. 1851.
diags. 18 pp. London, Longman, Brown, Green, and Longmans, 1851
T.

7060   PORTER, John Grey V.   A regular commercial system of keeping the accounts of a tillage farm, with an appendix, on the repayment of outlay.
tables. appendix. 16 pp. Dublin, J. McGlashan, 1851
U.

7061   A present-day pamphlet. Condition of the labouring poor considered, with suggestions for their amelioration, physical and moral. By ΧΡΙΣΤΟΦΕΡΟΣ.
tables. 40 pp. London, Whittaker, Birkenhead, Crichton and Marshall, 1851
T.

7062   PUSEY, Philip.   The improvement of farming. What ought landlords and farmers to do? Being the reprint of an article 'On the progress of agricultural knowledge during the last eight years', from the journal of the Royal agricultural society, no. 26.
maps. tables. 64 pp. London, J. Murray, 1851
N., T.

7063   PYNE, Henry.   Table showing the value of tithe rent-charges for the year 1851. To which is added, another table showing the extent of the yearly fluctuation in the prices of wheat, barley, and oats, since 1835.
tables. 8 pp. London, Henry Shaw, 1851
T.

7064   The Queen and constitution, the producer and consumer, or Protection, what is it, and where to put it; addressed to all classes of her majesty's subjects, from the wealthy proprietors of the 'Times' newspaper, to the agricultural laborer who weeds the wheat. By Iustitio.
12 pp. London, W. Hopcraft, [1851?]
T.

7065   RAMSAY, Thomas.   Is Christian socialism a church matter? A lecture, delivered in Blagrove's rooms, Mortimer street, Cavendish square, on Friday evening, August 8th, 1851, at the invitation of the central co-operative agency.
44 pp. London, J. Ollivier, J. J. Bezer, 1851
T.

7066   Remarks on the customs establishment as at present constituted, regarding the promotion of its officers, and connection with the mercantile world. By an impartial hand.
tables. 24 pp. London, Aylott and Jones, 1851
T.

7067   Report of proceedings in Newfoundland, with a view to making St. John's a port of call for a transatlantic line of steamers, 1851.
tables. 50 pp. St. John's, printed at the office of the 'Morning Post', 1851
A.

7068   Report of the directors of the Dublin and Drogheda railway company, to the proprietors; published preparatory to the half-yearly meeting, to be held on Saturday, the 1st of March, 1851.
tables. 24 pp. Dublin, printed by J. Falconer, 1851
A.

7069   Report of the directors of the Dublin and Drogheda railway, to the proprietors, for the half-year ending 30th June, 1851.
tables. 8 pp. Dublin, printed by J. Falconer, 1851
A.

7070   Report of the directors to the proprietors of the City of Dublin steam-packet company for half-year ended 1st March, 1851.
8 pp. Dublin, 1851

A.

7071   Retford currency society. Currency, agriculture, and free trade.
8 pp. London, Simpkin, Marshall, 1851

T.

7072   Retford currency society. How can paper money increase the wealth of a nation?
12 pp. London, Simpkin, Marshall, 1851

T.

7073   Retford currency society. Market Bosworth farmers' association meeting, held October 2nd, 1850, at the Dixie arms inn.
18 pp. London, Simpkin, Marshall, 1851

T.

7074   Retford currency society. Second address to the farmers of England.
4 pp. [no t.p.] [London, Simpkin, Marshall, 1851]

T.

7075   Retford currency society. To the farmers of England.
4 pp. London, Simpkin, Marshall, 1851

T.

7076   Retford currency society. What has Peel's bill of 1844 done? And what has it not done?
4 pp. [no t.p.] [London, Simpkin, Marshall, 1851]

T.

7077   Rules and regulations of the Commercial permanent benefit building society. Enrolled pursuant to Act of Parliament, 6 & 7 William IV., cap. 30.
tables. appendix. 40 pp. London, Bruce and Ford, 1851

T.

7078   Rules and tables of the Witham permanent benefit building society. Established December, 1850, pursuant to act of parliament 6 and 7 Wm. IV, c. 32. Shares: Investors . . . Class 1, £60; Class 2, £30. Subscriptions . . . Class 1, 5s.; Class 2, 2s. 6d. Borrowers . . . Class 1, £50; Class 2, £25. Repayments regulated by number of years over which loan is to extend. Tables based on equitable principles—Rules duly certified and enrolled. Subscriptions payable the last Monday in every month, from half-past 6 to 8 p.m. at the literary institution, Witham.
tables. 36 pp. Chelmsford, H. Rayner, 1851

T.

7079   Rules of the Braintree and Bocking permanent benefit building society, established January 14, 1851, and enrolled pursuant to act of parliament, 6 and 7 William 4, C. 32.
tables. 20 pp. Braintree, printed by Joscelyne, 1851

T.

7080   SANDERS, Samuel.   Suggestions for monetary reform, respectfully addressed to his royal highness Prince Albert.
tables. appendix. 36 pp. London, J. Ollivier, 1851

T.

7081   SCULLY, Vincent.   The Irish land question, with practical plans for an improved land tenure, and a new land system.
table of contents. notes. 286 pp. Dublin, Hodges & Smith, London, J. Ridgway [etc.], 1851

A.

7082   ——.   Mutual land societies, their present position and future prospects.
32 pp. Dublin, Hodges and Smith, 1851

A.

7083   Second report of the emigrants protection society, read at a general meeting of the society of St. Vincent de Paul held at the presbytery, Essex-street, Dublin, on Sunday the 20th day of July 1851.
18 pp. Dublin, printed by Browne & Nolan, 1851

A.

7084   SEYMOUR, William Digby.   How to employ capital in Western Ireland: being answers to a few practical questions upon the manufacture of beet-sugar, flax, and chicory, in connexion with a land investment in the west of Ireland. Third ed.
tables. appendix. 296 pp. London, John Hearne [etc.], Dublin, Hodges & Smith, 1851

T.

7085   SMIRKE, Edward.   A letter to lord Campbell, lord chief justice of the Court of Queen's Bench, on the rating of railways.
28 pp. London, Bradbury & Evans, 1851

T.

7086   [SMITH, Samuel.]   A word in season; or, how the corn-grower may yet grow rich, and his labourer happy. Addressed to the stout British farmer. Eighth edition, re-arranged and revised; with full directions for carrying out the plan of growing wheat.
illustration. tables. 38 pp. London, J. Ridgway, 1851

T.

7087   Society for promoting scientific inquiries into social questions.
4 pp. Dublin, [1851]

A.

Contains objects and laws of the society.

7088   STANLEY, Edmund H.   What are tribunals of commerce? Addressed to the commercial community.
16 pp. London, Effingham Wilson, 1851

T.

7089   STEPHENSON, Robert.   The Great Exhibition, its palace and its principal contents. With notices of the public buildings of the metropolis, places of amusement, etc.
plate. table of contents. 224 pp. London, Routledge, 1851

A.

7090   STOPFORD, James E., and ANDREWS, William.   Royal Irish fisheries company. Second report to his excellency the earl of Clarendon, lord lieutenant of Ireland.
32 pp. Dublin, printed by Browne & Nolan, 1851

A.

7091 SULLIVAN, William K.   The manufacture of beet-root sugar in Ireland.
tables. 36 pp. Dublin, J. McGlashan, 1851
D., N., T.

——.   52 pp. 2nd. ed. Dublin, J. McGlashan, 1851
A., N.

7092 TAIT, William.   Slave trade overruled for the salvation of Africa.
map. 44 pp. London, Seeleys, 1851
T.

7093 TIMOTHY, Evan.   Banks; their construction, purposes, and effects. A digest of the law of agreements & guarantees, bills of exchange and bankers cheques, I.O.U.'s and cash notes, and an abstract of the recent stamp act. With plain directions how to keep a cash, deposit, or current banking account; hints to merchants, manufacturers, and tradesmen, including all the material sections of the bankrupt law consolidation act, 1849. What constitutes an act of bankruptcy; who are liable to the bankruptcy laws; and an abstract of the law of attachments and equity of the lord mayor's court against garnishees, with respect to cash and property. With an appendix, containing forms of bonds, guarantees, etc., etc.
tables. appendix. 94 pp. London, W. Fitch, 1851
T.

7094 Tracts of the British anti-state-church association. New series.—No. 4. Scotland and its Kirk.
tables. 30 pp. London, the British anti-State-Church association, 1851
T.

7095 Tracts of the British anti-State-Church association. New series.—No. 6. The Church establishment in Wales: its past history and present condition.
tables. 36 pp. London, the British anti-State-Church association, 1851
T.

7096 URQUHART, William Pollard.   The substitution of direct for indirect taxation necessary to carry out the policy of free trade.
12 pp. Edinburgh & London, W. Blackwood & son, 1851
T.

7097 'Vates'' railway prospects for 1851 investigated.
8 pp. London, Effingham Wilson, [1851]
T.

7098 Visit to the great exhibition by one of the exhibitors.
illustrations. 30 pp. London, Cundall and Addey, 1851
N.

7099 What have the whigs done for Ireland? Or, the English whigs and the Irish famine. By a barrister.
42 pp. Dublin, A. Milliken, London, Longman, Brown, Green & Longmans, 1851
A., T.

7100 [WHATELY, Richard, archbishop of Dublin.] Easy lessons on money matters, for the use of young people. Published under the direction of the committee of general litera-

ture and education, appointed by the Society for promoting Christian knowledge.
72 pp. 9th ed. Wellington, N.Z., at the 'Independent' office, 1851
T.

Note on t.p. 'Translated into the New Zealand (Maori) language under the direction of the Government.' Reprinted from the 1845 London edition.

7101 WHITE, George Preston.   Three suggestions for the investment of capital.
tables. 48 pp. London, T. Saunders [etc., etc.], 1851
A., N.

7102 WILLIAMS, Theophilus.   Political equity: or a fair equalisation of the national burdens. Comprised in some intermingled and scattered thoughts, suggesting an anti-destitution policy; a graduated system of taxation on real property and regular incomes; a non-inquisitorial mode of collecting the tax on trade; a gradual liquidation and an ultimate extinction of the national debt, etc.
tables. 96 pp. London, Ward, 1851
T.

See 6785.

7103 YOUNG, George Frederick.   Speech of George Frederick Young, esq., at a public meeting at Framlingham, Suffolk, on Thursday, the 9th of January, 1851
table. 36 pp. London, J. Ollivier & J. Madden, 1851
T.

1852

7104 An address to the nobility and gentry, and great landed proprietors of England; also, to farmers and agriculturalists, whether merely tenants or proprietors of their own farms; for all are more or less concerned and interested in the following narrative; which is a statement of facts of very recent occurrence, and which has been the result of, and entirely owing to the corn laws, or laws of protection; in the first place, to their unwise and unjust enactment; and then, in the second place, to the sudden and total and precipitate repeal of those laws; and which laws have been the fruitful source of all the mischief, sorrow, loss, and suffering, among the farmers and agriculturalists of late years; and which sorrow, loss, and suffering has not yet terminated or come to an end. Written by a sufferer, by one who has incurred great loss, and has been a great sufferer, and who has published this narrative from his own sorrowful, but through the mercy of the Lord, salutary experience.
36 pp. London, Hamilton, Adams, [1852]
T.

7105 ALISON, Alexander.   To the electors. Universal free trade; by A. Alison, esq., author of 'The Future', etc.
tables in appendix. 80 pp. London, J. Ridgway, 1852
T.

7106 ALISON, William Pulteney.   On the present state of the law of settlement & removal of paupers in Scotland. Read at the Statistical section of the British Association at Belfast, on Monday 6th September, 1852.
16 pp. Dublin, Hodges & Smith, 1852.
A., C., L., N., T.

7107 An appeal for a charitable trusts act of parliament which is absolutely required to turn the abuses of most of the now rich endowed charitable trusts, and also cathedral and corporation foundations of Great Britain, to the maintenance and relief of the respectable aged poor, instead of their enormous estates and funds being misapplied to the income of the managers and not to the extension and further relief of the poor and needy.
tables. 28 pp. n.p., 1852

T.

7108 Australia: who should go;—how to go;—what to do when there. With a map and latest information.
map. tables. appendix. 48 pp. Liverpool, Gabriel Thomson, [1852]

T.

7109 BARRINGTON, Sir Matthew, bart. Reasons for the formation of the Farmers' estate company in Ireland, suggested in a correspondence of Sir Matthew Barrington, bart., with the late Sir Robert Peel, bart.
29 pp. Dublin, Browne & Nolan, 1852

B.

7110 BASTIAT, Frédéric. Protection & communism. With a preface, by the translator.
92 pp. London, J. W. Parker, 1852

T.

7111 BAXTER, William Edwin. Notes on the practical effects of repealing the newspaper stamp duty, the advertising duty, and the excise duty on paper.
16 pp. London, Simpkin, Marshall, 1852

T.

7112 BAYLIS, Edward. Reply of the Professional life assurance company to the attacks of its assailants; together with remarks, illustrative and explanatory of the new system of life assurance.
52 pp. 2d. ed. London, John Teulon, 1852

A., T.

7113 BEARN, William. Prize essay on the farming of Northamptonshire.
map. tables. 74 pp. London, Hamilton, Adams, 1852

T.

7114 BRIGHT, John. Great demonstration in Belfast. Speech of John Bright, esq., M.P., on Monday, October 4th, 1852.
12 pp. Manchester, T. Smith, [1852?]

L.

On the Irish land and church questions.

7115 BROUGH, Arthur. The coming election, or, what has been done? what should be done? and what can be done? A letter to the farmers and other electors of the United Kingdom.
66 pp. London, Houlston and Stoneman, 1852

T.

7116 BROUN, Sir Richard, bart. Letter to the rt. hon. the earl of Derby on the imperial Halifax and Quebec railway, and Anglo-Asian steam transit project.
34 pp. London, T. W. Saunders, 1852

N.

7117 BROWN, David Stevens. America in 48 hours, India and back in a fortnight, being suggestions for certain improvements in the construction of steam vessels, by D. S. Brown.
diag. 18 pp. [London,] T. Saunders, 1852

T.

7118 BROWN, John Bailey. The evils of our present joint stock banking system considered, with a few practical and practicable suggestions for its improvement.
table. 14 pp. London, Effingham Wilson, Liverpool, Webb and Hunt, 1852

T.

7119 BROWN, William. The social condition of Ireland; or the land question historically and economically considered.
tables. appendix. 96 pp. Magherafelt, Richardson, 1852

A.

7120 BROWNE, Edmund Head. A few words on the gold question: showing that the value of gold will *not* become depreciated by the large discoveries of that metal.
22 pp. London, W. N. Wright, and Pelham Richardson, 1852

T.

7121 BULLER, Thomas Wentworth. The hare and many friends. Remarks on the monopoly of guano, addressed to the agriculturists and shipowners of Great Britain.
appendix. 44 pp. London, J. Ridgway, 1852

T.

7122 CAPPER, John. The emigrants' guide to Australia, containing the fullest particulars relating to the recently-discovered gold-fields, the government regulations for gold seeking, etc. With a new map of the gold-fields, comprising the recent discoveries of Mr. Hargraves, Mr. Hunter, Rev. W. Clark, and others.
92 pp. London, Whittaker, Liverpool, Henry Young, 1852

T.

7123 The case of the free-labour British colonies, submitted to the British legislature and British nation for an impartial re-hearing.
tables in appendices. 172 pp. London, J. Madden, 1852

T.

7124 CASSELL, John. Cassell's emigrants' handbook: being a guide to the various fields of emigration in all parts of the globe. With an introductory essay, on the importance of emigration, and the danger to which emigrants are exposed. To which is added, a guide to the gold fields of Australia, with copious instructions, government regulations, etc., accompanied by a map of Australia, in which the gold regions are clearly indicated.
plate. tables. 92 pp. London, John Cassell, 1852

T.

7125 CHRISTIE, Robert. Letter to the right hon. Joseph W. Henley, M.P., president of the board of trade, regarding life assurance institutions, with abstracts of all the accounts registered by London life assurance companies from the passing of the act 7 & 8 Vict. cap. 110, (5th September 1844), to 5th February 1852.
tables. 48 pp. Edinburgh, Thomas Constable, 1852

A., T.

7126 CLARKE, John Algernon.   On the farming of Lincoln-shire. Prize report.
map. illustrations. 158 pp. London, printed by W. Clowes, 1852
T.

7127 COLLES, Henry. Social inquiry society of Ireland. An inquiry as to the policy of limited liability in partnerships. 26 pp. Dublin, J. M'Glashan, 1852
C.

7128 COLVIN, Alexander. Actuarial figments exploded. A letter to the right hon. J. W. Henley, M.P., president of the board of trade, in defence of the life assurance offices registered under 7 and 8 Vic., cap. 110.
tables. appendix. 38 pp. London, C. and E. Layton, 1852
T.

7129 COMBE, George. Secular instruction or extension of church endowments? Letter by George Combe, esq., to his grace the duke of Argyle.
no t.p. 8 pp. [Revised.] [Glasgow, John Robertson, 1852]
T.

7130 Correspondence between the board of trade and T. Grahame, esq., late chairman of the Grand Junction Canal Company, on railway & canal combination.
44 pp. London, J. Ridgway, 1852
T.

7131 CULLEN, Edward. The isthmus of Darien ship canal. map. table of contents. appendix. 68 pp. London, Effingham Wilson, 1852
N.

7132 DALE, Thomas. Five years of church extension in St. Pancras; being an address to the parishioners on the proposed application to the legislature for an act to amend the local acts, and to place on a permanent and equitable basis the ecclesiastical administration of the parish with an outline of the proposed act and an appendix, containing a report of the proceedings in vestry, &c., &c., &c.
appendix. 84 pp. London, F. and J. Rivington, 1852
T.

7133 Dublin Corporation. Rules and regulations for the guidance of assistant supervisor, overseers, gangers, and depot keepers in the employment of the corporation of Dublin.
24 pp. Dublin, Kirkwood, 1852
A.

7134 The Egyptian railway; or, the interest of England in Egypt.
42 pp. London, Hope, 1852
T.

7135 ELLIS, George M. B. Irish ethnology socially and politically considered; embracing a general outline of the celtic and saxon races; with practical inferences.
table of contents. 164 pp. Dublin, Hodges & Smith, London, Hamilton & Adams, 1852
A.

7136 The emigrant in Australia or gleanings from the gold-fields. By an Australian journalist. With illustrations, taken on the spot, by J. S. Prout, esq., and four maps.
plates. illust. 96 pp. London, Addey, 1852
T.

7137 European and North American Railway Co. [various documents and correspondence].
table. appendix. 48 pp. n.p., 1852
N.

7138 An examination of statements made during a recent debate at the East India House, in a letter to Lieut.-General Welsh, and the 220 service memorialists of the Indian army. By a proprietor.
20 pp. London, Smith, Elder & co., 1852
T.

7139 FAUCHER, Leon. Remarks on the production of the precious metals and on the demonetization of gold in several countries in Europe. Translated by T. Hankey, Jun.
table. 110 pp. London, Smith, Elder & co., 1852
T.

7140 FERGUSON, William Dwyer. Social inquiry society of Ireland. Report on the law of debtor and creditor so far as relates to proceedings subsequent to final judgment.
appendix. 24 pp. Dublin, J. McGlashan [etc., etc.], 1852
A., C., N., T.

7141 A few words on the effect of the increase of gold upon the currency.
16 pp. London, J. Ridgway, 1852
T.

7142 A few words upon the merits and demerits of the question of free trade.
28 pp. London, Pelham Richardson, 1852
T.

7143 The finances and trade of the United Kingdom at the beginning of the year 1852.
tables. 60 pp. 3rd ed. London, J. Ridgway, 1852
T.

7144 FISHER, Joseph. Taxation of Ireland; its causes, extent, and effects: being a speech delivered at the aggregate meeting of magistrates and poor law guardians of Ireland, assembled at the Rotunda, in Dublin, on the 30th January, 1852. Sir Lucius O'Brien, bt., M.P., in the chair.
tables. 28 pp. Dublin, J. McGlashan, London, J. Ridgway, 1852
N.

7145 Forty-seventh annual report of the Charitable Association, being for the year 1851.
table. 16 pp. Dublin, George Drought, 1852
T.

7146 Free thoughts on free trade.
88 pp. London, J. Ollivier, 1852
T.

7147   Free trade: its moral, social, commercial, agricultural, and political results. An essay for the prize offered by the anti-corn-law league. By F.C.
44 pp. London, W. E. Painter, 1852
T.

7148   GALE, R.   The first principles of labour, property, and money, demand primary consideration for home agriculture.
32 pp. London, J. Ollivier, 1852
T.

7149   [GANN, Amos John.]   The New Zealand emigration circular for 1852.
map. tables. 28 pp. no t.p. London, T. Saunders, 1852
T.

7150   GILBART, James William.   The elements of banking; with ten minutes' advice about keeping a banker.
fspce. 104 pp. London, Longman, Brown, Green, and Longmans, 1852
T.

7151   [GISBORNE, Thomas, the younger.]   Agricultural drainage: an essay reprinted from the 'Quarterly Review', No. CLXXI.
illust. 48 pp. 2nd ed. London, J. Murray, 1852
T.

7152   ——.   Thoughts on an income tax, and on a property tax; principally founded on the evidence taken by the house of commons committee in the session 1851.
68 pp. London, J. Murray, 1852
T.

7153   GOOD, William Walter.   The politics of agriculture. With an appendix: are Mr. Mechi's intentions honourable?
tables. appendix. 100 pp. London, J. Ridgway, 1852
T.

7154   [GRAYDON, William?]   Letters on free trade addressed to the public. By Agricola.
40 pp. London, Seeleys, [1852]
T.

7155   The guide to Australia and the gold regions, containing the most recent and complete accounts of the gold fields, together with advice to intending emigrants. By a Liverpool merchant. With a coloured map, carefully corrected from the latest authorities.
116 pp. London, Whittaker, Liverpool, Henry Young, 1852
T.

7156   GUTTERIDGE, John Rowton.   The disease and the remedy. An essay on the present state of the working classes; including a true description of the degraded character of our railway labourers.
tables. 84 pp. London, Wertheim and Macintosh, 1852
T.

7157   HAMBER, Frederick M.   The 'En commandite', 'Anonyme' and 'En nom collectif' partnerships, extracted from the French code of commerce (Articles 18 to 64) and translated into English. Together with an appendix illustrating the liabilities of partners under the French and English systems.
appendix. 16 pp. London, Effingham Wilson, 1852
T.

7158   HAMILTON, William Tighe.   The land question for England and Ireland; together with a measure for its settlement.
56 pp. Dublin, Hodges & Smith, 1852
A.

7159   Hammers and ploughshares. A book for the labourer, in the workshop and by the fireside.
100 pp. London, Partridge & Oakey, 1852
T.

7160   HANCOCK, William Neilson.   Belfast Social inquiry society. What are the causes of the prosperous agriculture in the Lothians of Scotland? A paper read before the society on the 23rd December, 1851.
16 pp. Belfast, Henry Greer, 1852
A., C., N., Q., T.

7161   ——.   The abolition of slavery considered, with reference to the state of the West Indies since emancipation. A paper read before the Statistical section of the British Association at Belfast, September 2nd, 1852.
15 pp. Dublin, Hodges & Smith, 1852
A., L., N., T.

7162   ——.   What are the causes of the distressed state of the highlands? A paper read before the Belfast Social inquiry society, 1852.
16 pp. Belfast, H. Greer, 1852
A., Q., T.

7163   [HARCOURT, Sir William George Granville Venables Vernon Harcourt.]   The morality of public men. A letter to the right hon. the earl of Derby.
48 pp. [signed 'An Englishman'.] 3rd ed. London, J. Ridgway, 1852
A., T.

7164   HAWARD, Charles. Currency reform; the true remedy for our present agricultural depression, and the proper complement of our late free trade legislation.
48 pp. Chelmsford, Fry [etc., etc.], [1852]
T.

7165   HEMMING, George Wirgman.   A just income tax how possible, being a review of the evidence reported by the income tax committee, and an inquiry into the true principle of taxation.
40 pp. London, John Chapman, 1852
T.

7166   HERON, Denis Caulfield.   Should the tenant of land possess the property in the improvements made by him? A paper read before the Dublin Statistical society on the 23rd April, 1850, and 17th May, 1852.
28 pp. Dublin, Hodges & Smith, 1852
A., N., T.

7167   HOPE, Horace.   The crimes and confiscations of the Russell Whigs in Ireland, illustrated in letters to the rt. hon. the earl of Derby, etc., etc., Letter I.
36 pp. Dublin, J. McGlashan, 1852
A., U.

7168 HUBBARD, John Gellibrand, later baron Addington. How should an income tax be levied? considered in a letter to the right honourable Benjamin Disraeli, M.P., chancellor of the exchequer.
tables. appendix with tables. 56 pp. London, Longman, Brown, Green and Longmans, 1852
A., T.

7169 HUGHES, W. A few particulars for the guidance of intending emigrants, describing the principal fields of emigration, and showing the rate, distance, and cost of passing to each place, with the class of labour to which it is best suited.
maps. 8 pp. [London], H. G. Collins, [1852]
T.

7170 The humble appeal of Piers Plowman the younger, to the archbishops and bishops of the Church of England.
16 pp. London, John Hughes, 1852
T.

7171 HURSTHOUSE, Charles, Jun. Emigration: *where* to go, and *who* should go. New Zealand & Australia (as emigration fields) in contrast with the United States & Canada. Canterbury and the diggings. Dedicated to Mrs. Chisholm.
tables. appendices. 148 pp. London, T. Saunders, [1852]
N., T.

7172 Irish transatlantic packet station. Report of the Dublin committee considered, and Mr. Whiteside's statement reviewed, with remarks on the relative advantages of the Shannon and Galway Bay.
68 pp. Dublin, Browne & Nolan, 1852
A., N.

7173 JAMES, Mrs. A.[nne]. The Australian emigrant's companion, containing practical advice to intending emigrants, especially to those of the working class. Entered in Stationers Hall.
48 pp. London, H. Green, 1852
T.

7174 JOHNSON, Andrew. Some observations on the recent supplies of gold, with remarks on Mr. Scheer's letter to Sir F. Baring.
tables. appendix. 36 pp. London, Pelham Richardson, 1852
T.
See 7230.

7175 JONES, Richard. Text-book of lectures on the political economy of nations, delivered at the East India College, Haileybury.
140 pp. Hertford, Stephen Austin, 1852
T.

7176 'Justice to John Bull'; or the fallacies of the existing policy, called 'free trade'. Addressed to the 'pupils' of the 'Manchester School', and to the working portion generally of 'John Bull's family'. By 'one of the latter class', author of 'An essay on mental, moral, and social improvement', etc.
tables. 48 pp. London, Hope, [1852]
T.

7177 KENNEDY, Joseph Camp Griffith. Statistics of American railroads, prepared by J. C. G. Kennedy at the U.S. census office, at the request of the French department of public works.
tables. 6 pp. Washington, Gideon, 1852
T.

7178 LAWSON, James Anthony. Statistics to illustrate the kinds of business which joint stock companies are suited to carry on, especially with respect to investments in land. A paper read before the Dublin Statistical society, 16th Feb., 1852.
tables. 14 pp. Dublin, Hodges & Smith, 1852
A., C., N., T.

7179 Letter from the Dublin Steamship association, to the hon. secretary of the chamber of commerce, Dublin.
14 pp. Dublin, P. Hardy, 1852
A., N.

7180 A letter to the right hon. the earl of Derby, first lord of the treasury, and prime minister on the currency, money, and labour; with suggestions for a revision of the currency, calculated to ensure security to the fundholder, advance the interests and facilitate the operations of trade and commerce, and provide for the rights and necessities of labour. By the author of 'The land and the loom briefly contrasted; or, a plea for the plough and the people; with observations, embodying letters to the right hon. lord John Russell, on the relative value of home and foreign trade'.
24 pp. London, Whitaker and Co., 1852
T.

7181 Life assurance: its schemes, its difficulties and abuses.
32 pp. London, Pateman, 1852
A.

7182 Liverpool chamber of commerce. Report of the special committee on mercantile law reform and tribunals of commerce, read at a special meeting of the council, and ordered to be printed, 16th August, and adopted by the council, Sept. 6, 1852.
tables. 32 pp. London, Effingham Wilson, [1852?]
T.

7183 [LOCKE, John.] Ireland. Observations on the people, the land and the law, in 1851; with especial reference to the policy, practice and results of the incumbered estates court.
appendices. tables. 106 pp. 3rd ed. Dublin, Hodges & Smith, London, Simpkin, Marshall, 1852
A., N., U.

7184 ——. On Irish emigration, with especial reference to the working of the incumbered estates commission. Read before the statistical section of the British Association, at Belfast, 3rd September, 1852, *bound together with* Additional observations on the valuation and purchase of land in Ireland. Read before the Statistical Society of London, 15th November, 1852.
tables. 12 pp. London, Harrison, 1852
N.

——. 16 pp. 2nd ed. London, J. W. Parker, 1852
N.

7185 MACDONALD, Duncan George Forbes. What the farmers may do with the land: or, practical hints for their and its improvement.
52 pp. 2nd ed. London, Henry Adams, 1852
T.

7186 [MacLaren, James.] Observations on the effect of the Californian and Australian gold; and on the impossibility of continuing the present standard, in the event of gold becoming seriously depreciated.
32 pp. London, Thomas Bumpus, Aylott and Jones, 1852
T.

7187 Major, R. H. A speech on the treaty of navigation and commerce between Sardinia and France, delivered in the house of deputies at Turin by the minister of finance on the 8th and 9th of April, 1852. Translated from the French by R. H. Major, esq.
tables. 64 pp. (pagination irregular.) London, W. Pickering, 1852
T.

7188 Malcolm, Andrew George. The sanitary state of Belfast, with suggestions for its improvement: a paper read before the statistical section of the British Association, at Belfast, September 7, 1852.
col. plans. 31 pp. Belfast, H. Greer, 1852
A., L., N.

7189 [Maley, A. J.] Observations upon the policy and provisions of the act for facilitating the sale of incumbered estates, considered with reference to their supposed economic effects upon the condition of Ireland.
22 pp. [signed 'A.J.M.'] Dublin, J. McGlashan, 1852
A., K., N., T.

7190 Marryat, Frank. Gold quartz mining in California. Practical observations during a residence of two years, 1850–1, and 52, in the mining districts of that country. With coloured plates of gold veins.
plates. tables. 24 pp. London, Smith, Elder & co., 1852
T.

7191 Maxwell, Sir John, bart. Suggestions arising out of the present want of employment for labour and capital.
tables. appendix. 40 pp. Edinburgh and London, W. Blackwood & son, 1852
T.

7192 Mayne. Edward Graves. Social inquiry society of Ireland. An inquiry into the foreign systems of registering dealings with land by means of maps and indexes.
24 pp. Dublin, J. McGlashan, 1852
A., N.

7193 Mechi, John Joseph. A lecture, delivered at the Chelmsford literary institute, by Mr. J. J. Mechi, of Tiptree Hall, Dec. 1, 1852. 'On the present position of British agriculture, as compared with our other industrial occupations.'
28 pp. [London], Longman, Brown, Green & Longmans, 1852
T.

7194 Meekins, T. C. Mossom. Report to the attorney-general for Ireland, on compensation to the tenant for improvements.
tables. 22 pp. London, J. Ridgway, 1852
A., N., T.

7195 Memorial regarding amendments in the Scottish poor-law, proposed by William P. Alison, M.D., &c., revised and adopted by a committee formed from the managers of several charitable institutions in Edinburgh. With appendix.
table of contents. appendices. 58 pp. Edinburgh & London, W. Blackwood & son, 1852
A.

7196 Money, Edward. A letter on the cultivation of cotton, the extension of internal communication, and other matters connected with India, addressed to Sir Harry Verney, bart., M.P.
42 pp. London, J. Ridgway, 1852
T.

7197 Moorsom, W. S. London & South-Western Railway. [a letter to his 'fellow-shareholders'].
tables. 18 pp. London, Metchim & Burt, 1852
A.

7198 Mossman, Samuel. The gold regions of Australia: a descriptive account of New South Wales, Victoria, and South Australia, with particulars of the recent gold discoveries.
map. 104 pp. London, W. S. Orr, Dublin, J. McGlashan, [1852]
T.

7199 Naper, James Lenox William. The landlord and tenant bills; a letter to the attorney-general.
8 pp. Dublin, J. McGlashan, 1852
A.

7200 Neville, Parke. Report to the right honourable the lord mayor, aldermen and councillors of the borough of Dublin, on the state of the public works of the city.
tables. 82 pp. Dublin, Kirkwood, 1852
A.

7201 Newcastle-under-Lyme, Henry Pelham Pelham-Clinton, 5th duke of. The duke of Newcastle and his tenantry. Speeches delivered by his grace the Duke of Newcastle, to his tenantry at the rent-audit for Michaelmas, MDCCCLI.
32 pp. London, J. Murray, Nottingham, Job Bradshaw, 1852
T.

7202 Newdegate, Charles Newdigate. A letter to the right hon. J. W. Henley, M.P., on the balance of trade, ascertained from the market value of all articles imported, as compared with the market value of all articles exported, during the year 1851, in continuation of his previous letters on this subject.
tables. 34 pp. London, Seeleys, 1852
T.

7203 Nisbet, Harry C. Prize essay on life assurance.
10 pp. Uxbridge, John Mackenzie, 1852
T.

7204 Notman, Robert Russell. Railway amalgamation: addressed to the shareholders of the Aberdeen, Scottish, Midland, Dundee and Arbroath, Scottish Central, and Caledonian railway companies.
30 pp. London, Smith, Elder & co., 1852
T.

7205 O'Hagan, John, and Jackson, Arthur S. Social inquiry society of Ireland. An inquiry into taxes on law proceedings in Ireland.
appendix. tables. 28 pp. Dublin, J. McGlashan, 1852
A., N.

7206 PIM, Jonathan. On partnerships of limited liability. A paper read before the Dublin Statistical society, 6th Feb., 1852.
table. 16 pp. Dublin, Hodges & Smith, 1852
A., C., T.

7207 A plan for the equitable settlement of the guano question, in which the interests of the agriculturists, the Peruvian government, and the bondholders are duly considered.
tables. 8 pp. [London], Letts, Son & Steer, J. Ridgway, [1852]
T.

7208 Plan of economy for government, farming, manufactures, and trade.
appendix. 32 pp. London, Effingham Wilson, 1852
T.

7209 PLAYFAIR, Lyon. Industrial instruction on the continent.
tables. appendices. 54 pp. London, Longman, Brown, Green & Longmans, 1852
E.

7210 Preliminaries of peace between protection and free trade: or, cheap bread compatible with both. By F.C.
36 pp. London, W. E. Painter, 1852
T.

7211 Property and income tax. Schedule A and schedule D.
72 pp. London, J. Ridgway, 1852
T.

7212 PRYME, George. A syllabus of a course of lectures on the principles of political economy. Third edition, corrected and altered.
44 pp. Cambridge, University Press, 1852
T.

7213 The repeal of the land tax essential to an equitable adjustment of taxation.
tables. 40 pp. London, Effingham Wilson, [1852]
T.

7214 Reply (principally founded on parliamentary returns) to Mr. S. Gurney's pamphlet in favor [sic] of free trade. Addressed to the protectionists of Essex. By SX.
tables. 12 pp. 2nd ed. London, Simpkin, Marshall, 1852
T.

7215 Report and suggestions addressed to the mercantile community, of the united kingdom, by the London committee of merchants, and others associated for the improvement of the commercial and bankruptcy laws of Scotland, and the assimilation of those laws in England and Scotland.
42 pp. London, Longman, Brown, Green and Longmans, Edinburgh, A. and C. Black, 1852
T.

7216 Report of the directors of the Dublin and Drogheda Railway, to the proprietors, for the half-year ending 30th June, 1852.
tables. 8 pp. Dublin, printed by John Falconer, 1852
A.

7217 Report of the directors of the Dublin and Drogheda Railway Company to the proprietors; published preparatory to the half-yearly meeting, to be held on Tuesday the 2nd March, 1852.
tables. 24 pp. Dublin, printed by John Falconer, 1852
A.

7218 A report of the proceedings of a meeting (consisting chiefly of authors), held May 4th, at the house of Mr. John Chapman, 142, Strand, for the purpose of hastening the removal of the trade restrictions on the commerce of literature.
30 pp. London, J. Chapman, 1852
T.

7219 Report of the Strangers' friend society (founded 1790) [year ending 1851].
table. 16 pp. Dublin, T. White, 1852
N.

7220 Report of the tithe redemption trust, for the church in England and Wales, for the year 1852.
table. appendix. 20 pp. London, F. & J. Rivington, 1852
T.

7221 Report of the transatlantic packet station committee appointed at a meeting held on the 21st August, 1851, at the Mansion House, Dublin.
table of contents. appendices. 94 pp. Dublin, J. McGlashan, London, J. Ridgway, 1852
A.

7222 RICKARDS, Sir George Kettilby. Three lectures delivered before the University of Oxford, in Michaelmas term, 1852. Lecture I. The harmonies of the social economy. Lecture II. On the operation of self-interest in the social economy. Lecture III. On the operation of competition.
96 pp. Oxford and London, J. H. Parker, 1852
T.

7223 RIVINGTON, William. Church extension in St. Pancras. A comparative statement of the increase of houses, population and church accommodation, in the parish of St. Pancras, Middlesex, from 1801 to 1851; with a brief summary of the measures taken and in progress to provide for the spiritual wants of the parish.
tables. appendix. 24 pp. London, F. and J. Rivington, 1852
T.

7224 ROBERTSON, Alexander. Periodical savings, applied to provident purposes: with remarks on the constitution and practice of friendly, odd-fellows', building, freehold land, loan societies, and savings' banks. And suggesting a plan of self-protecting life insurance.
appendix. 64 pp. London, W. S. Orr, 1852
T.

7225 Rules of the Andrean Freehold Investment and Mutual Benefit Building Society.
16 pp. Dublin, J. Birmingham, 1852
A.

7226 Rules of the Belfast Permanent Building and Investment Society. Established under 6 and 7 Wm. IV. c. 32.
tables. appendix. 24 pp. Belfast, Welsh, 1852
N.

7227 Rules of the Edinburgh Holy Gild of St. Joseph Friendly Society. Instituted at Edinburgh in 1842, under the sanction of the right reverend the vicar apostolic of the eastern district in Scotland. [Ed. by bishop Gillis.]
table of contents. tables. appendix. 62 pp. Edinburgh, printed by Hogg, 1852
A.

7228 RUSSELL, lord John.   Speeches of the right honourable lord John Russell, delivered at Stirling and at Perth, September, 1852.
24 pp. London, Longman, Brown, Green, and Longmans, 1852
T.

7229 SANDARS, Samuel.   Suggestions for monetary reform, and a national currency, with observations on the influence of corn laws and indirect taxation on the currency. Second edition.
tables. appendix with tables. 48 pp. London, W. Blackwood & son, 1852
T.

7230 SCHEER, Frederick.   A letter to Thomas Baring, esq., M.P., on the effects of the Californian and Australian gold discoveries.
tables. appendices with tables. 38 pp. London, Effingham Wilson, 1852
T.

7231 SCULLY, Vincent.   Notes on Ireland and the land question. Note 1. Free trade in land.
40 pp. Dublin, Hodges & Smith, London, Simpkin, Marshall [etc.], 1852
A., N.

7232 ——.   Notes on Ireland and the land question. Note II. The Channel Islands.
32 pp. Dublin, Hodges & Smith, London, Simpkin, Marshall, [etc.], 1852
A., N.

7233 SENIOR, Nassau William.   Four introductory lectures on political economy, delivered before the University of Oxford.
76 pp. London, Longman, Brown, Green & Longmans, 1852
N.

7234 SHARPE, B.   Fair play and no extra taxes for the farmers. An appeal for the removal of the rates and taxes which are exclusively levied on land. In a letter addressed to the right hon. the earl of Derby, first lord of the treasury, etc., etc., etc.
12 pp. London, J. Ollivier, 1852
T.

7235 SHAW, William and CORBET, Henry.   A digest of evidence taken before a committee of the house of commons, appointed to inquire into the agricultural customs of England and Wales in respect of tenant-right. With a portrait of Philip Pusey, esq., and a sketch of his career.
portrait. index. 270 pp. [various paging.] 2nd ed. London, Rogerson and Tuxford, 1852
E.

7236 Ships, colonies, and commerce, being the substance of a letter addressed to the late right hon. Sir Robert Peel, bart., previous to his removal of the duties on corn. Now for the first time printed. By Philopatris.
16 pp. London, T. & W. Boone, 1852
T.

7237 Sketch of an institution to be called the board of supply and demand; consumers' protective institution.
tables. 18 pp. London, J. Unwin, [1852]
T.

7238 SMYLIE, Samuel.   Circular addressed by Mr. Samuel Smylie to the leading members of the legal profession, and others, in reference to establishing a medium for diffusing information in Scotland and England regarding Irish estates and investments.
16 pp. Dublin, A. Thom, 1852
A.

7239 Special report of the Bristol and Clifton ladies' anti-slavery society; during eighteen months, from January, 1851, to June, 1852; with a statement of the reasons of its separation from the British and foreign anti-slavery society.
tables. 68 pp. London, J. Snow, 1852
T.

7240 STEPHEN, Sir George.   Bankruptcy and credit trade.
60 pp. London, J. Crockford, 1852
T.

7241 SULLIVAN, William K.   Facts and theories; or, the real prospects of the beet-sugar manufacture in Ireland.
tables. 104 pp. Dublin, J. McGlashan, London, J. Ridgway [etc.], 1852
A., N.

7242 SWINEY, William.   A letter to the right hon. Benjamin D'Israeli, M.P., her majesty's chancellor of the exchequer, in reply to several anonymous articles and letters in the 'Times' and 'Morning Chronicle' newspapers; respecting certain life assurance companies established since the passing of the act 7 & 8 Vict.
appendices. 24 pp. London, J. Cookes, 1852
T.

7243 TAYLOR, James.   Political economy illustrated by sacred history.
80 pp. London, Seeleys, 1852
T.

7244 THIERS, Louis Adolphe.   Speech of M. Thiers on the commercial policy of France and in opposition to the introduction of free-trade into France, delivered in the National Assembly of France, on the 27th of June, 1851. Translated by M. de Saint Felix, and to which translation has been added a note on Russian wheat, and also a letter of one of the first manufacturers of France, in opposition to free-trade.
tables. 82 pp. London, J. Ollivier, 1852
T.

7245 THOMAS, Frederick Samson.   Correspondence with right honourable lord John Russell, and with right honorable earl Derby, relative to the gold in Australia, the currency of the realm, and the national defences. Second edition.
diags. appendix. 92 pp. London, Effingham Wilson, 1852
T.

7246 THOMSON, William Thomas. Further suggestions with reference to the amendment of the joint stock companies registration act as regards life assurance institutions. Contained in a letter addressed to Francis Whitmarsh, esq., registrar of joint stock companies.
tables. folding table. 20 pp. Edinburgh, W. Blackwood & son, 1852.
T.

7247 ——. On the present position of the life assurance interests of Great Britain. A letter to the right hon. Joseph W. Henley, M.P., president of the board of trade.
tables. 16 pp. Edinburgh, William Blackwood & son, 1852
T.

7248 TORRENS, Robert. Tracts on finance and trade, submitted to the consideration of the electors of the United Kingdom No. I. 1. On the equalisation of taxation between land and trade. 2. On the maintenance of a differential duty in favour of colonial sugar, considered as an act of justice to the planters, and as a means of suppressing slave cultivation.
tables. 44 pp. London, Chapman and Hall, 1852
T.

7249 ——. Tracts for electors on finance and trade, submitted to the consideration of the constituencies of the United Kingdom. No. II. On the question, should the income tax be continued, and the import duties diminished; or should the income tax be abolished, and the import duties on non-necessaries be increased?
tables 54 pp. London, Chapman and Hall, 1852
T.

7250 Transactions of the relief committee of the Society of Friends.
table of contents. tables. 152 pp. Dublin, 1852
A.

7251 TRELAWNY, Sir John Salusbury. An epitome of the evidence given before the select committee of the house of commons, on church-rates, in the session of 1851. With an historical sketch of recent proceedings on the same subject.
tables. appendix. 96 pp. London, R. Theobald, 1852
T.

7252 TROUP, George. The revenue and commerce of the united kingdom for 1851, contrasted with the transactions of previous years.
tables. 158 pp. [various paging.] London, T. Saunders [etc.], 1852
T.

7253 [WALLACE, Robert.] History of the steam engine, from the second century before the Christian era.
illust. diags. 140 pp. [various paging.] London, Cassell, Petter and Galpin, [1852?]
T.

7254 WALLBRIDGE, Alfred A. Public health. A popular exposition of the advantages and benefits to be derived from the adoption of the Public Health Act, 1848: and showing its non-interference with local self-government.
24 pp. London, C. Knight, [1852]
T.

7255 The war of parties and waste of the national resources, with a peep into the policy of European cabinets: or the history and mystery of increasing taxation, commercial difficulties, pauperism and crime, since the revolution of 1688, in a series of dialogues between John Bull and Brother Jonathan. In this work, to be continued in parts, will be developed a plan for easing the national burdens and improving the condition of the agricultural, commercial, and manufacturing classes.
table. 34 pp. London, J. Robinson, 1852
T.

7256 WEBB, C. Locock. Suggestions on the present condition of Ireland, and on government aid for carrying out an efficient railway system.
index. tables. 46 pp. London, Smith & Elder, Dublin, Hodges & Smith, 1852
A., T.

7257 WEBSTER, William Bullock. Ireland considered as a field for investment or residence.
table of contents. tables. notes. index. map. 136 pp. Dublin, Hodges & Smith, 1852
A.

7258 WILD, Justus. England as it is, and as it might and ought to be.
tables. 62 pp. London, W. Thacker, Calcutta, Thacker, Spink [etc.], 1852
T.

7259 A word or two on the condition of our agricultural labourers. By a farmer's son.
32 pp. London, Hope, 1852
T.

7260 WRIGHT, John. Projects for constructing railways in Algeria. Dedicated to his highness the Prince President of France.
folding map. 32 pp. London, Myers, 1852
A.

7261 WYATT, Harvey. On the repeal of the Malt Tax.
18 pp. Stafford, R. and W. Wright, London, Longman, Brown, Green & Longmans, 1852
T.

7262 YOUNG, George Frederick. Free-trade fallacies refuted; in a series of letters to the editor of the Morning Herald.
48 pp. London, J. Madden, J. Ollivier, 1852
T.

1853

7263 American and English oppression, and British and American abolitionists: a letter addressed to R. D. Webb, esq., by an American in his fatherland.
68 pp. London, O. C. Marcus, 1853
T.

7264 Arterial drainage, (Ireland). One word to Irish landed proprietors, and two to British taxpayers.
tables. 28 pp. London, Stanford, 1853
A., N.

7265 The Australian. Practical hints to intending emigrants. By a passenger in June, 1852
80 pp. London, Eyre and Williams, 1853
T.

7266 BASTIAT, Frédéric. Essays on political economy. Part I. Capital and interest.
54 pp. London, C. Gilpin, [1853?]
T.

7267 BECK, Richard L. Practical hints on life assurance.
table. 18 pp. London, W. & F. G. Cash, 1853
T.

7268 BENNOCH, Francis. The bridges of London. 'Are more bridges needed?' answered affirmatively.
map. tables. 56 pp. London, Effingham Wilson, 1853
T.

7269 [BORRADAILE, Harry.] A table for a decimal system of account, adapted to the current coinage of the realm.
4 pp. and folding table. London, Smith, Elder & co., 1853
T.

7270 [BOURNE, Stephen.] The British West India colonies in connection with slavery, emancipation, etc. By a resident in the West Indies for thirteen years. With an introduction and concluding remarks by a late stipendiary magistrate in Jamaica.
44 pp. London, T. Bosworth, 1853
T.

7271 [——, and CAMPBELL, Mrs.] The importance, necessity, and practicability of thorough drainage in the British West India colonies, in order to restore prosperity to those countries; as well as to render compulsory labour unnecessary to the production of an adequate supply of sugar and cotton. A letter to the right hon. the earl of Aberdeen, by a late stipendiary magistrate in Jamaica.
appendix. 16 pp. London, T. Bosworth, 1853
T.

7272 [——, ——.] Suggestions relative to the improvement of the British West India colonies, by means of instruction by ministers of religion and schools. The relations of property and labour. Agricultural and other industrial improvements, &c., &c. With especial reference to the increased cultivation of the sugar cane and cotton in Jamaica and British Guiana. By a resident in the West Indies for thirteen years. With an introduction and concluding remarks by a late stipendiary magistrate in Jamaica.
84 pp. London, T. Bosworth, 1853
T.

7273 [BRIGHT, Henry Arthur.] Free blacks and slaves. Would immediate abolition be a blessing? A letter to the editor of the Anti-slavery advocate. By a Cambridge man.
table. 28 pp. London, Arthur Hall Virtue, Liverpool, Deighton & Laughton, 1853
T.

7274 [BRUMELL, John.] British Guiana. Demerara after fifteen years of freedom. By a landowner.
tables. appendix. 122 pp. London, T. Bosworth, 1853
T.

7275 BUCKINGHAM, James Silk. Plan for the future government of India.
64 pp. London, Partridge and Oakey, 1853
N.

7276 BULLEN, Edward. Modern views on the relations between landlord and tenant, tenant-right, and compensation for improvements.
32 pp. London, Saunders & Stanford, 1853
A., U.

7277 BURKE, James. The Income Tax act: with explanatory introduction and copious table of contents.
table of contents. 48 pp. Dublin, O'Gorman, 1853
A., N.

7278 Cathedral property. Substance of a letter addressed to a member of the commons house of parliament on the subject of a scheme recently concluded between the dean and chapter of Carlisle and the ecclesiastical commissioners, for the transfer and future management of the capitular estates, with reference also to the past and future management of capitular property generally throughout England and Wales. Also an appendix, containing the scheme and her majesty's order in council, ratifying the same, as published in the London Gazette of the 17th December last.
tables. appendix. 40 pp. London, Seeleys, 1853
T.

7279 Centurion's letter on the present government of India.
46 pp. Calcutta, Thacker, Spink, Bombay, Thacker, [1853?]
T.

7280 CHESHIRE, Edward. The results of the census of Great Britain in 1851; with a description of the machinery and processes employed to obtain the returns. Also an appendix.
tables. appendix. 56 pp. London, J. W. Parker, 1853
N., T.

7281 ——. Statistics of poor relief in England and Wales for the year 1851. Compiled from the fourth annual report of the Poor Law Board, and read before the Dublin Statistical society, on Monday, March 21st, 1853.
tables in appendix. 18 pp. Dublin, Hodges & Smith, 1853
C., T.

7282 CHEVALIER, Michel. Remarks on the production of the precious metals, and on the depreciation of gold.
tables. appendix. 114 pp. London, Smith, Elder & co., 1853
T.

7283 COBDEN, Richard. 1793 & 1853, in three letters.
140 pp. 2nd ed. London, J. Ridgway, 1853
T.

On French politics & economics.

——. 140 pp. 4th ed. London, J. Ridgway, 1853
A., L.

7284 COCQUIEL, Chevalier de. Industrial instruction in England, being a report made to the Belgian Government. Translated into English, by Peter Berlyn.
table of contents. appendix. 90 pp. London, Chapman and Hall, 1853
N.

7285 COLEMAN, John. Some observations on direct taxation, in reference to commercial reform.
tables. 128 pp. London, J. Ridgway, 1853
T.

7286 COURT, Major Henry. A review of the income tax in its relation to the national debt; with suggestions for removal of its present inequalities by a more uniform mode of assessment.
tables. 44 pp. London, T. Hatchard, 1853
T.

7287 DERECOURT, Henry. Derecourt on taxes and duties, in a letter to her majesty's chancellor of exchequer previous to his forming 'The Budget', (and partly adopted).
tables. 14 pp. (no pagination.) London, J. and W. Robins, 1853
T.

7288 DICKINSON, John, jun. India: its government under a bureaucracy.
tables in appendices. 218 pp. London, Saunders and Stanford, 1853
T.

7289 Dublin Savings' Bank established in School St. Feb. 11th, 1818. Report and general statement of account, 20th November, 1853
appendices and tables. Dublin, Goodwin, Son & Nethercott, 1853
N.

7290 DUNCKLEY, Henry. 'Strikes', viewed in relation to the interests of capital and labour; a few thoughts on the present industrial crisis.
36 pp. Salford, George Wiley, London, Hall, Virtue, 1853
T.

7291 EARDLEY-WILMOT, Arthur Parry. A letter to the rt. honourable viscount Palmerston, M.P., one of her majesty's secretaries of state, etc., on the present state of the African slave trade, and on the necessity of increasing the African squadron.
16 pp. London, J. Ridgway, 1853
T.

7292 The Eastern Archipelago Company and Sir James Brooke. Memorandum. The following letters from the chairman of the Eastern Archipelago Company to the duke of Newcastle and the earl of Aberdeen, form part of a series of documents which will shortly be laid on the table of the house of commons. They are now printed and circulated in order publicly to contradict and refute certain false statements, relative to the affairs of the Eastern Archipelago Company recently promulgated by Sir James Brooke in a pamphlet called, 'Vindication of his character'.
tables. 14 pp. no t.p. [1853?]
T.

7293 Elements of taxation; to which are added, a summary of the evidence adduced before the parliamentary committee on the property and income tax, and also a complete analysis of the finance accounts of the United Kingdom for the year 1851, ended January 5, 1852. By X + Y., authors of the prize essay on direct taxation.
tables. appendix. 94 pp. London, Simpkin Marshall, [1853]
A., R., T.

7294 The fashionable philanthropy of the day. Some plain speaking about American slavery. A letter addressed to the Stoweites of England and Scotland. By a Briton.
32 pp. London, Hope, 1853
T.

7295 FERGUSON, William Dwyer. Literary appropriations and the Irish Land Bills of the late government.
44 pp. Dublin, E. Milliken, 1853
A., T.
Reply to W. T. Hamilton's 'The Irish land bills of the late government'—see 7305.

7296 A few remarks on the railways of the north of Ireland, with special reference to the proposed railway from Armagh to Cavan via Clones.
folding map. 20 pp. Dublin, J. Duffy, 1853
A.

7297 GAEL, Samuel H. Considerations on the present state of copyholds, and on their enfranchisement.
190 pp. London, C. Knight, [1853]
T.

7298 GALBRAITH, Joseph A. On a decimal currency. A paper read before the Dublin Statistical society, on Monday, May 16th, 1853.
tables. 24 pp. Dublin, Hodges and Smith, 1853
C., T.

7299 General report of James Fanning's Charitable Institution, Waterford: to the end of the tenth year of its establishment; with a statement of the origin of the institution.
plate. appendix. table. table of contents. 66 pp. Waterford, Harvey, 1853
N.

7300 GIBBON, Alexander. Taxation: its nature and properties. Second edition. Showing by analysis, that a land-tax, a house-tax, and a tax upon commodities, are comprised in the impost called the income-tax; and that such impost is repudiation of public debt.
tables. appendix. 112 pp. London, Pelham Richardson, 1853
T.

7301 GREEN, James. Emigration considered: or, a general description of the leading countries most adapted to emigration; and a comparison of their relative positions of advantage over the other leading countries of the world, with general information to all classes of emigrants, on the most advantageous country to settle in, and to the people at large, on the advantages of emigration, and the best means of securing them.
tables. 80 pp. London, G. Vickers, 1853
T.

7302 GREER, Samuel M'Curdy. On the relation between landlord and tenant in Ireland. A paper read before the Dublin Statistical society, on Monday, April 18th, 1853
10 pp. Dublin, Hodges and Smith, 1853
C., T.

7303 GRINSTED, John. Correspondence with the National Provident Institution upon the insecurity of a nomineeship in the event of bankruptcy or insolvency of the assured, with

counsel's opinion, and remarks of the press thereon: also a letter to the rt. hon. the chancellor of the exchequer: and letters and articles on life assurance companies' receipts and expenditure.
tables. 32 pp. London, C. and E. Layton, 1853
T.

7304 HAMILTON, Walter Kerr. The cathedral commission. A letter to the very rev. the dean of Salisbury by the Rev. Walter Kerr Hamilton, M.A., precentor and canon residentiary of the cathedral church of Salisbury, and chaplain of the bishop of Salisbury.
table. 36 pp. London, F. & J. Rivington, Salisbury, G. Brown, 1853
T.

7305 HAMILTON, William Tighe. The Irish land bills of the late government considered with reference to sounder legislation for England and Ireland, in a letter to the members of both houses of parliament.
76 pp. Dublin, Hodges & Smith, 1853
A., N., T.
See 7295.

7306 HANCOCK, William Neilson. Observations on the question, how can Sir Robert Peel's income tax be made more equitable?
8 pp. Dublin, Hodges & Smith, 1853
C., N.

7307 HERON, Denis Caulfield. Celtic migrations; a paper read before the Dublin Statistical society.
tables. 14 pp. Dublin, Hodges & Smith, 1853
A., N., T.

7308 HIGGINS, Joseph Napier. The gold companies and the cost-book system, second edition.
36 pp. London, Effingham Wilson, Dublin, Hodges & Smith, 1853
T.

7309 HINTON, John Howard. Secular tracts, no. 4. On social inequalities; a lecture delivered at Devonshire square chapel, London, April 3rd, 1853.
20 pp. London, Houlston and Stoneman, 1853
T.

7310 How to do without customs and excise, by basing the parliamentary representation, of all classes and interests, home and colonial, on contributions from all parts of the empire. By a landed proprietor.
tables. 26 pp. London, Smith, Elder & co., 1853
T.

7311 HUBBARD, John Gellibrand, later baron Addington. Reform or reject the income-tax. Objections to a reform of the income-tax considered, in two letters to the editor of The Times. With additional notes.
tables. 52 pp. London, Longman, Brown, Green and Longmans, 1853
T.

7312 HUMPHRY, Joseph Thomas. Registration of assurances bill: its peculiar system and practical consequences considered.
32 pp. London, V. & R. Stevens and G. S. Norton, 1853
T.

7313 HURSTHOUSE, Charles, Jun. Emigration. Emigration fields contrasted. The diggings. Practical hints on emigration. Mechanics. Farmers. Small-capital families. Younger sons. Clerks, and shopmen. Female emigrants. Outfit. Voyage. New Zealand.
tables. 62 pp. London, Robert Hardwicke, 1853
T.

7314 INGRAM, Thomas Dunbar. The wine duties and their effects on the commercial relations between the British dominions and France. A paper read before the Dublin Statistical society on Monday, April 18th, 1853.
12 pp. Dublin, Hodges and Smith, 1853
C., E., T.

7315 (The Irish land bills.) No. I. Land Improvement Bill.
table of contents. 12 pp. London, T. Harrison, 1853
A., N.

7316 (The Irish land bills.) No. II. Leasing powers Bill.
table of contents. 16 pp. London, T. Harrison, 1853
A.

7317 (The Irish land bills.) No. III. Tenants' improvements compensation Bill.
table of contents. 14 pp. London, T. Harrison, 1853
A., N.

7318 (The Irish land bills.) No. IV. Landlord and tenant law amendment Bill.
table of contents. 18 pp. London, T. Harrison, 1853
A.

7319 JAMES, James Henry. Modern assurance companies vindicated: being a review of the late controversy, and of the report of the select committee of the house of commons.
24 pp. London, Simpkin, Marshall & Co., [1853]
T.

7320 JERVIS, Thomas Best. India in relation to Great Britain. Considerations on its future administration.
appendix. 96 pp. London, J. Petheram, 1853
T.

7321 JOHNES, Arthur James. Popular proofs of the fallacy of recent government plans for the reform of the superior courts, and of the unjust application of the public taxes on which they are founded; with remarks on the necessity of a local administration of the law in chancery, common law, bankruptcy, and other cases; in a letter to lord Brougham and Vaux.
24 pp. London, V. & R. Stevens & G. S. Norton, 1853
T.

7322 JONES, T. D. Record of the great industrial exhibition of 1853, being a brief and comprehensive description of the different objects of interest contained in that temple of industry.
plate. table of contents. 120 pp. Dublin, J. Falconer, 1853
A., N.

7323 JOPLIN, William. A letter on fluctuations in the money market, chiefly with the view of explaining the nature of those violent pressures termed panics, addressed to the bankers of England.
22 pp. London, Hamilton, Adams, Reading, E. Blackwell, 1853

T.

7324 KAY, Joseph. The condition and education of poor children in English and in German towns. Published by the Manchester Statistical society.
tables. appendices. 80 pp. London, Longman, Brown, Green and Longman, 1853

T.

7325 KER, H. Bellenden. On the reform of the law of real property: in a letter to the right hon. lord Lyndhurst, &c., &c., &c.
126 pp. London, V. & R. Stevens, and G. S. Norton, 1853

T.

7326 ——. Shall we register our deeds? A letter to the right hon. lord Lyndhurst, etc., etc., etc.
24 pp. London, V. & R. Stevens and G. S. Norton, 1853

T.

7327 KINGSMILL, Sir John. Taxation in Ireland in connexion with the extension of the property and income tax acts to that kingdom.
tables. 32 pp. Dublin, J. McGlashan, 1853

T.

7328 The landlord and tenant question in Ireland, argued, in a dialogue between Tom and Dick.
44 pp. Dublin, Kelly, 1853

A., T.

7329 Landlordism in Ireland, with its difficulties; a sketch of the tenant-right of Ulster; the duties of agent and bailiff in Ireland, defined, &c., &c. By one late an agent.
tables in appendices. 64 pp. London, Longman, Brown, Green, and Longmans, Belfast, H. Greer, 1853

T.

7330 LANKTREE, John. The elements of land valuation, with copious instructions as to the qualifications and duties of valuators.
tables. 96 pp. London and Liverpool, William S. Orr, [etc.], 1853

U.

7331 The Leinster and Ulster united mines of the British and Irish mining company, in the counties of Dublin, Meath, Armagh, Louth, Wicklow and Tyrone, on the system of the cost book.
26 pp. Dublin, O'Toole, 1853

A.

7332 LENDRICK, William Edmonstone. Sugar-trade and slave-trade. The West India question considered.
tables. appendix. 136 pp. London, Saunders & Otley, 1853

A., K., T.

7333 LESLIE, Thomas Edward Cliffe. Trades' unions and combinations in 1853. A paper read before the Dublin Statistical society, on Monday, May 16th, 1853.
16 pp. Dublin, Hodges and Smith, 1853

C., T.

7334 A letter to those ladies who met at Stafford House in particular, and to the women of England in general, on slavery at home. By an Englishman.
23 pp. London, J. Ridgway, 1853

T.

7335 LEVI, Leone. An introductory lecture on the law of shipping and marine insurance, delivered at King's College, London, November, 1853.
tables. 16 pp. London, Smith, Elder & co., 1853

T.

7336 LOCKE, John. Ireland. Emigration and valuation and purchase of land in Ireland.
tables. 22 pp. 2nd ed. London, J. W. Parker, 1853

A., N.

See 7184.

7337 ——. Ireland's recovery, or excessive emigration and its reparative agencies in Ireland. An essay read September 10, 1853, before the British Association for the advancement of science, at their twenty-third meeting held at Hull, with additions, and numerous statistical tables, illustrating and substantiating the conclusions deduced.
index. appendices with tables. 44 pp. London, J. W. Parker, 1853

A., N., T.

7338 LONGFIELD, Robert. Report on the alterations and amendments necessary in the present system of sale and mortgage of land in Ireland.
26 pp. Dublin, J. M'Glashan, 1853

C., U.

7339 LUCAS, H. Journal of a voyage from London to Port Phillip, in the Australian Royal Mail Steam Navigation company's ship 'Australian', being the first voyage by steam between England and the Australian colonies; containing some useful hints to intending emigrants.
tables. 30 pp. London, Clarke, Beeton, 1853

T.

7340 LUSHINGTON, Henry. The double government, the civil service, and the India reform agitation.
100 pp. London, W. H. Allen, 1853

T.

7341 M'CORMAC, Henry. Moral-sanatory economy. Education, health, order, progress, competence.
appendix. 154 pp. London, Longman, Brown, Green and Longmans, Dublin, J. M'Glashan, 1853

T.

——. Another issue. 162 pp. Belfast, Alexander Mayne, 1853

L.

7342 MACGREGOR, John. A synthetical view of the results of recent commercial and financial legislation.
tables. 32 pp. 2nd ed. London, J. Ridgway, 1853

T.

7343 MACKENZIE, David. The gold digger: a visit to the gold fields of Australia in February, 1852; together with much useful information for intending emigrants.
map. tables. 78 pp. London, W. S. Orr, Dublin, J. McGlashan, [1853?]
T.

7344 MACLAREN, James. The effect of a small fall in the value of gold upon money; the secret progress of a depreciation of the currency; and the power which capitalists have of protecting themselves.
40 pp. London, Thomas Bumpus [etc.], 1853
T.

7345 ——. On the impolicy of providing for a family by life assurance, since the recent discoveries in California and Australia; with a proposal for the establishment of a new office, upon a plan which would secure the assured from the effects of a fall in the value of gold.
82 pp. London, Thomas Bumpus, 1853
T.

7346 MACLEOD, Alexander Charles. State-paper taxation, with an analysis of the nature and relations of gold, paper, and credit.
table. 74 pp. London, J. Ridgway, 1853
T.

7347 MAITLAND, John Gorham. Property and income tax. The present state of the question.
46 pp. London, J. Ridgway, 1853
A., T.

7348 [MALEY, A. J.] Who beggared Ireland? British statesmen, Irish landlords, or Irish agitators? Submitted for the consideration of all ranks and classes of her remaining inhabitants. By A. J. M.
22 pp. Dublin, Hodges and Smith, 1853
A., N., T.

7349 MARSHMAN, John Clark. Letter to John Bright, esq., M.P., relative to the recent debates in parliament, on the India question. Second edition.
52 pp. London, W. H. Allen, T. Hatchard, 1853
T.

7350 MEARS, Robert. Decimal coinage tables for simplifying and facilitating the introduction of the proposed new coinage.
36 pp. London, W. J. Adams, 1853
T.

7351 Meath Loan Office Board Room, 37 Thomas Court, 18 January, 1853. At a meeting of the committee of managers held this day. John Abbott, esq., in the chair. Ordered:—that the following report be printed.
6 pp. Dublin, 1853
A.

7352 MEREWETHER, Francis. A reply to lord Stanley's pamphlet on church rates.
22 pp. London, F. and J. Rivington, 1853
T.

7353 MILWARD, A. The decimal coinage. A letter to the rt. hon. the chancellor of the exchequer, advocating, as a preliminary step, the issue of a five-farthing piece.
tables. 48 pp. London, George Bell, 1853
T.

7354 Minutes of correspondence between the directors of the Grand Canal Company and the directors of the Great Southern and Western and of the Midland Great Western Railway companies.
28 pp. Dublin, Porter, 1853
A.

7355 Money: how to get, how to keep, and how to use it. A guide to fortune.
tables. 158 pp. London, Ingram, Cooke, 1853
T.

7356 MULOCK, Thomas. Disenthralment of incurably-involved Irish estates: in two letters to his excellency the earl of Clarendon, K.G., &c., &c., &c.
16 pp. Dublin, J. McGlashan, 1853
A., N., T.
'published anterior to the Incumbered Estates Act'.

7357 NAPER, James Lenox William. The cause of the operatives of Ireland advocated in a letter to Sir Robert Kane.
8 pp. Dublin, J. McGlashan, 1853
A.

7358 NAPIER, Joseph. The landlord and tenant bills. Reply of the right honourable Joseph Napier, M.P., to the letter of the earl of Donoughmore on the landlord and tenant bills of the last session.
32 pp. Dublin, G. and J. Grierson, 1853
A., K., N., T.

7359 The National freehold land society as it is and as it must be: illustrated by that much desired picture 'the inside of a freehold land society'. Respectfully recommended to shareholders in general, and to small shareholders in particular; and dutifully inscribed, by an ardent, a thankful, but much disappointed admirer, to Richard Cobden, esq., M.P.
24 pp. London, Effingham Wilson, [1853]
T.

7360 NEVINS, Robert. Letters addressed particularly to the Greek and other foreign mercantile houses importing breadstuffs into this country.
tables. 46 pp. London, Nissen & Parker, 1853
A.

7361 NEWMARCH, William. The new supplies of gold; facts and statements, relative to their actual amount; and their present and probable effects. Revised edition, with five additional chapters.
tables. 130 pp. London, Pelham Richardson, 1853
T.

7362 NORWOOD, John. A summary of transactions relative to the proposed formation of a new and wide street, from the terminus of the Midland Great Western Railway and the King's Inns, to Richmond Bridge and the Four Courts.

Compiled from original documents, etc., at the request of the committee for the promotion of that project. 1833–1853. tables. 58 pp. Dublin, Charles, 1853

A., N.

7363 Observations on the communication between London and Dublin, in connection with the report of the select committee of the house of commons, and the minutes of evidence on that subject, ordered to be printed. tables. 30 pp. Dublin, J. Falconer, 1853

A.

7364 Observations on the fundamental principles of monetary circulation and the necessity for a national deposit bank of issue. Third edition. 68 pp. Glasgow, J. Maclehose, 1853

T.

7365 O'HANLON, W. M. Walks among the poor of Belfast, and suggestions for their improvement. table of contents. 168 pp. Belfast, H. Greer, Dublin, P. Hardy, 1853

A.

7366 Pantomime budgets, and by special command a tête-à-tête between Sir John Barleycorn and the old lady of Threadneedle street. 74 pp. [various paging.] London, J. Cross, [1853]

T.

7367 The people's gold diggings; or practical methods of improving the commerce of communities, and the status of individuals. By one of the people. table. 34 pp. Wiveliscombe: The People's unitive association for promoting the establishment of mutual improvement societies, and provincial exhibitions of industry, [1853?]

T.

7368 PEYTON, Alex. J. The emigrant's friend; or hints on emigration to the United States of America, addressed to the people of Ireland. 56 pp. Cork, O'Brien, 1853

A.

7369 PIM, Jonathan. On the connection between the condition of tenant farmers and the laws respecting the ownership and transfer of land in Ireland. A paper read before the Dublin Statistical Society, on 23rd February, 1853. 10 pp. Dublin, Hodges & Smith, 1853

C., N., U.

7370 PLAYFAIR, Lyon. Science in its relations to labour. Being a speech delivered at the anniversary of the people's college, Sheffield, on the 25th October, 1853. 24 pp. London, Chapman and Hall, 1853

E.

7371 POLLARD-URQUHART, W. A short account of the Prussian land credit companies: with suggestions for the formation of a land credit company in Ireland. appendices. 38 pp. Dublin, Hodges & Smith, 1853

A., T.

7372 The present state of the finances and currency in Austria. By an impartial observer. Translated from the second edition of a German original. 64 pp. Leipzic, J. M. C. Armbrustier, London, Dulau [etc.], 1853

T.

7373 PRINSEP, Henry Thoby. The India question in 1853. 114 pp. London, W. H. Allen, 1853

T.

7374 The problem of the age: or the abolition of American slavery considered in a physical and moral aspect. Dedicated to Mrs. Harriet Beecher Stowe. 32 pp. London, Houlston and Stoneman, Edinburgh, Thomas Grant, 1853

T.

7375 RATHBONE, Theodore W. An examination of the report and evidence of the committee of the house of commons, on decimal coinage, with reference to a simpler, sounder, and more comprehensive mode of proceeding. Second edition with a preface. 60 pp. London, J. Ridgway, 1853

T.

7376 Remarks on the present state of the Metropolis Churches' Fund. By a layman. Illustrated with a plan of the London district. plan. tables. appendix. 32 pp. London, F. & J. Rivington, 1853

T.

7377 The report of the committee appointed to take measures for the abolition of the tolls on the Dublin and Mullingar turnpike road. 24 pp. Dublin, A. Thom, 1853

A.

7378 Report of the council of the chamber of commerce of Dublin to the members of the association, at the annual assembly held on 12th April, 1853. tables. appendix. 46 pp. Dublin, J. Falconer, 1853

A.

7379 Report of the directors of the Dublin and Drogheda railway company to the proprietors, published preparatory to the half-yearly meeting, to be held on Friday, 25th February, 1853. tables. 24 pp. Dublin, J. Falconer, 1853

A.

7380 Report of the directors of the Dublin and Drogheda railway to the proprietors, for the half-year ending 30th June, 1853. tables. 8 pp. Dublin, J. Falconer, 1853

A.

7381 RHODES, George John. Remarks on the purchase value, management and letting of landed property; with several useful tables, by which the rental value may be ascertained of any number of acres, roods, or perches. tables. 65 pp. London, Effingham Wilson, 1853

T.

7382 ROBINSON, Francis Horsley. What good may come out of the India bill; or, notes of what has been, is, and may be, the government of India.
48 pp. London, Hurst and Blackett, 1853
T.

7383 Savings banks. Ought government to make good past losses in savings banks? The opinion of eminent writers and authorities on the security depositors stated.
16 pp. Rochdale, Hartley & Howorth, London, Longman, Brown, Green & Longmans, 1853
T.

7384 Scale of prices for compositors and pressmen agreed upon by the employers and journeymen printers of the city of Dublin, February 9, 1829, reprinted in September, 1853, with explanatory notes, showing the general practice of the trade.
table of contents. tables. appendix. 40 pp. Dublin, G. Drought, 1853
A.

7385 Shall we simplify our titles? A letter to the lord high chancellor of England, from a conveyancing barrister.
20 pp. London, Wildy, 1853
A.

7386 Shareholders' key to the London and North Western railway company, containing full particulars of all the subsidiary and other lines in which the proprietors of the London and North Western railway company are interested. By a member of the Stock Exchange.
map. tables. 48 pp. London, Pelham Richardson, 1853
T.

7387 [SHOWERS, Charles.] Proposal of a plan for remodelling the government of India. Respectfully submitted to the consideration of her majesty's ministers, and both houses of parliament.
46 pp. London, Smith, Elder & Co., Bombay, Smith, Taylor, 1853
T.

——. 52 pp. 2nd ed. London, Smith, Elder & co., Bombay, Smith, Taylor, 1853
T.

7388 SHREWSBURY, Charles John Chetwynd-Talbot, 19th earl of. Social evils: their causes and their cure. A lecture delivered before the Bilston Institute in connection with St. Mary's National Schools.
tables. 20 pp. Wolverhampton, William Parke, London, Simpkin Marshall, 1853
T.

7389 STOPFORD, Edward A., archdeacon of Meath. A reply to Sergeant Shee on the Irish Church: its history and statistics; being a statement of the income and requirements of the Irish Church; and showing why Sergeant Shee avoided stating either, while professing to show a surplus of income above requirements.
table of contents. tables. Appendix. 122 pp. London, F. & J. Rivington, Dublin, Hodges and Smith, 1853
D., N.
See Stopford's 'The income and requirements of the Irish Church', which is the same work as this, with a different title page.

7390 STUART, Harry. Agricultural labourers, as they were, are, and should be, in their social condition; being an address, delivered to a general meeting of the Forfarshire agricultural association, June 1853, and published at the request of the association.
appendix. 90 pp. Edinburgh and London: W. Blackwood & son, 1853
T.

7391 SUMNER, Charles. Freedom national; slavery sectional. Speech of hon. Charles Sumner, of Massachusetts, on his motion to repeal the fugitive slave bill, in the senate of the United States, August 26, 1852.
62 pp. Edinburgh, reprinted from the American edition by Johnstone and Hunter, 1853
T.

7392 SYMONS, Jelinger. A scheme of direct taxation, for 1853.
tables. 46 pp. London, W. Parker, 1853
T.

7393 Ten per cent or a few words on the subject of money abatements. By a landlord.
28 pp. London, T. Harrison, 1853
T.

7394 Tenure and peerage. 'By Barony'. An essay.
44 pp. London, V. & R. Stevens and G. S. Norton, 1853
T.

7395 THOMS, Peter Perring. The Emperor of China v. the Queen of England. A refutation of the arguments contained in the seven official documents transmitted by her majesty's government at Hong-Kong, who maintain that the documents of the Chinese Government contain insulting language.
70 pp. London, P. P. Thoms, 1853
T.

7396 Thoughts on the temporalities of the church in Ireland, and ministers' money, occasioned by the recent change of administration. By a clergyman.
tables. 32 pp. Dublin, E. J. Milliken, 1853
T.

7397 To the public. The poor law and its medical officers. Published at the request of a society of union surgeons in Bishops Stortford, Herts. and its neighbourhood.
10 pp. London, Churchill, Bishops Stortford, J. M. Mullinger, 1853
T.

7398 WAKEFIELD, Edward Thomas. The feasibility of constructing a new system of registering title deeds which shall supersede the costly process of searches, and insure the discovery of all documents registered against each estate, considered.
38 pp. London, S. Sweet, 1853
T.

7399 Waterford and Kilkenny Railway. [letter from a shareholder.]
tables. 20 pp. Dublin, 1853
A.

7400 [WHITEHEAD, John.] An essay on the resources of Portugal, and especially considered as to her relations with foreign countries. Sent to Benjamin Oliveira, esq., M.P., F.R.S. (to compete for the premium of fifty guineas offered by that gentleman,) with an envelope, containing the name and residence of the writer, on which envelope is the following motto: '*Fiat Justitia ruat mundus.*'
68 pp. London, J. Ridgway, 1853
T.

7401 WILSON, Robert. A letter to the right hon. lord John Russell on the transfer of landed property.
map. plan. illustration. table. forms. 76 pp. London, T. Blenkarn, 1853
T.

7402 WILSON, Thomas, Jottings on money; or a few remarks on currency, coinage, and a new decimal system with the theory of annular coinage.
tables. illust. 110 pp. London, Effingham Wilson, [1853]
T.

1854

7403 ASHWORTH, Henry. The Preston strike, an enquiry into its causes and consequences. The substance of which was read before the statistical section of the British Association, at its meeting, held in Liverpool, September, 1854.
tables. 100 pp. Manchester, G. Simms, 1854
T.

7404 BAINES, Edward. Education best promoted by perfect freedom, not by state endowments. With an appendix, containing official returns of education, in 1818, 1833, and 1851.
appendix. 48 pp. London, J. Snow, Leeds, R. Newsome, 1854
T.

7405 BAKER, Benjamin. The national debt: should the revenues of the church be applied towards its extinction?
table. 36 pp. London, Houlston and Stoneman, 1854
T.

7406 The bank charter ought not to be renewed. A letter to the right hon. W. Gladstone, M.P., chancellor of the exchequer. By an ex-M.P.
26 pp. London, J. Ridgway, Ayr, J. Maclehose, 1854
T.

7407 The bank screw: or, war and the gold discoveries in connexion with the money market. With a proposition of a new, simple and thorough reform of the English currency. In a letter to the right hon. W. E. Gladstone, M.P., by Malagrowther the less.
40 pp. London, Houlston & Stoneman, 1854
T.

7408 BAYLIS, Edward, BERMINGHAM, George, and ERITH, Francis Norton. An essay upon life assurance: illustrative of the modern application of its principles to the requirements of the living.
table. 24 pp. London, the authors, 1854
T.

7409 BEAUCLERC, G. Abstract of an address on the advantages of rendering Ardglass port a safety harbour, as delivered in the Commercial Rooms, Belfast.
appendix. 48 pp. Dublin, Webb, 1854
A.

7410 BOURDIN, Mark A. An exposition of the land tax: its assessment and collection. And rights and advantages conferred by the redemption acts.
86 pp. London, T. F. A., Day, 1854
T.

7411 BOWDEN, James. A review of the testimony of friends on tithes and tithe rent-charge, more particularly impropriate tithes.
tables. 20 pp. London, W. and F. G. Cash, 1854
T.

7412 BRADY, Cheyne. The practicability of improving the dwellings of the labouring classes, with remarks on the law of settlement and removal of the poor.
tables. 60 pp. London, E. Stanford, 1854
A., D., N.

7413 BRANCH, John. A national system of finance; an adjustment of property between the landowner and the fundowner, by a reform of the monetary system of finance, in conformity with the late Sir R. Peel's currency bill of 1844.
32 pp. 2nd ed. London, Hamilton and Adams, 1854
T.

7414 BREARY, Frederick William. Suggestions for the formation of two assurance offices, upon novel principles.
4 pp. London, H. Baynes, 1854
T.

7415 BRIDGES, William. The prudent man: or, how to acquire land, and bequeath money, by means of co-operation.
tables in appendix. 142 pp. London & New York, H. Bailliere, 1854
T.

7416 BRIGHT, Henry S. Statistics of the corn trade 1825–1853. In a series of diagrams arranged and drawn under the superintendence of Henry S. Bright, Hull.
tables. diags. 34 pp. London, Longman, Brown, Green & Longmans, [1854]
T.

7417 BROWN, Sir Richard. Further exposition of Sir Richard Brown's great scheme for direct Anglo-Asian intercourse by route of British North America and the monarchical settlement of the vacant territory between the Atlantic and Pacific Oceans.
table of contents. tables. 14 pp. London, E. Stanford, 1854
N.

7418 BROWN, William. A letter from William Brown, esq., M.P., to Francis Shand, esq., chairman of the Liverpool Chamber of Commerce. With additional remarks and suggestions to his letter of the 13th December, 1853: and a copy of an order of the committee of council on education to H.M. inspectors of training schools.
tables. 20 pp. London, J. Ridgway, 1854
T.

7419 BROWNE, George. Transfer of land. Proposal for an assurance of title to real property. With a view to facilitating the transfer of land and reducing the cost of conveyances.
16 pp. London, R. Hardwicke, 1854
T.

7420 BUCKLAND, James M. Agricultural statistics. Practical suggestions for a national system of annual agricultural statistics, with observations on the experiments made in October and November, 1853, and the parliamentary reports in March, 1854, by Sir John Walsham, bart., Mr. Hawley, and Mr. Maxwell. Also an appendix, with tables and forms elucidating the proposed system.
tables. appendix. 42 pp. London, J. Ridgway, [1854]
T.

7421 CAIRNES, John Elliot. An examination into the principles of currency involved in the Bank Charter Act of 1844.
78 pp. Dublin, Hodges & Smith, London, J. Ridgway, 1854
A., C., N., T.

7422 ——. On the best means of raising the supplies for a war expenditure. A paper read before the Dublin Statistical society on the 20th March, 1854.
tables. 26 pp. Dublin, Hodges and Smith, 1854
C., T.

7423 CARGILL, W. M. The Bank Charter Act of 1844 and its effects upon industry and commerce.
22 pp. London, Bagot & Thompson, 1854
A.

7424 CASTLE, Henry James. Contributive value a necessary element in the parochial principle of railway assessments, what it is, and how it can be measured; shewing how to ascertain the contributive as well as the special earnings of a parish, whether that parish be upon a branch, or upon a main line; with a brief history of railway rating.
tables. 64 pp. London, W. Maxwell Shaw, 1854
T.

7425 CHILDS, Robert Walker. A letter to R. B. Crowder, esq., M.P., on mining partnerships, upon the cost-book system, as carried on within the stannaries of Cornwall and Devon.
24 pp. London, Simpkin, Marshall, 1854
T.

7426 COATES, Thomas. Notes on the present condition of railway legislation.
46 pp. London, J. Bigg, 1854
A.

7427 Correspondence between the directors of the Midland Great Western and Great Southern and Western Railway Companies, and Grand Canal Company.
44 pp. Dublin, Leckie, 1854
A.

7428 COWPER, Henry Augustus. Statement of the case of the 'Condor's' gold dust, addressed to her majesty's consuls, and to all British merchants residing in foreign ports.
appendices. 32 pp. Westminster, J. Bigg, 1854
T.

7429 Decimal coinage. A short and easy method of changing the present currency into the decimal system. By a retired merchant.
14 pp. London, J. Ridgway, 1854
T.

7430 DE MORGAN, Augustus. Decimal Association. (Formed June 12, 1854.) Proceedings: with an introduction, by Professor de Morgan: and notes.
78 pp. London, M. S. Rickerby, 1854
L.

7431 DERECOURT, Henry. Colonial and international postage. A collection of extracts, ideas, and information on postal affairs, and post office anomalies.
tables. 62 pp. London, C. Cawley, 1854
T.

7432 ENDERBY, Charles. A statement of facts connected with the failure of the southern whale fishery company at the Auckland islands; with a vindication of the measures proposed to be adopted for its success.
appendix. 68 pp. London, P. Richardson, 1854
T.

7433 ERITH, Francis Norton. Stray thoughts on life assurance: or, the great principles of the modern system succinctly explained, and rendered familiar.
54 pp. London, W. Tweedie, 1854
T.

7434 Exposure of the stock exchange and bubble companies. Dedicated to the victims of time bargains and the public generally.
tables. 20 pp. London, Piper, Stephenson and Spence, 1854
T.

7435 A farming tour, or hand book on the farming of Lincolnshire. By a Lindsey yeoman.
maps. table. 54 pp. London, Simpkin, Marshall, Market Rasen, J. G. Coborn, 1854
T.

7436 FFOOKS, Woodforde. The law of partnership an obstacle to social progress.
32 pp. London, W. G. Benning, 1854
T.

7437 FIELD, Edwin Wilkins. Observations of a solicitor on the right of the public to form limited liability partnerships, and on the theory, practice, and cost of commercial charters.
appendices. 104 pp. London, Longman, Brown, Green and Longmans, 1854
T.

7438 FLEURY, Charles M. The destitute classes: our duty towards them. A lecture by the Rev. Charles M. Fleury, A.M., chaplain to the Molyneux Asylum. Delivered before the Young Men's Christian Association in the Rotunda (Josiah Smyly, esq., M.D., in the chair), November 14, 1854.
12 pp. Dublin, 1854
A., N.

7439 Foreign loans and their consequences considered, in a letter to Benjamin Oliveira, esq., M.P. By a member of the stock exchange, London.
tables. 38 pp. London, Pelham Richardson, 1854
T.

7440 GOODEVE, Joseph. Shall we transfer our lands by register? A letter to the lord chancellor on the contemplated transfer of land by register.
74 pp. London, W. G. Benning, 1854
T.

7441 [GREY, John Edward.] Decimal coinage: what it ought and what it ought not to be. By one of the million.
tables. appendix. 48 pp. London, J. Ridgway, 1854
T.

7442 [HASLAM, John.] The impediments to the manufacturing prosperity of Dublin considered; with suggestions for their removal. By 'Turgot'.
48 pp. London, W. & F. G. Cash, Dublin, J. B. Gilpin, 1854
A., N., T., U.

7443 [——.] Proposal to establish an additional bank in Dublin considered. By 'Turgot'.
8 pp. Dublin, 1854
A.
Reprinted from the Dublin Monthly Journal of Industrial Progress, October, 1854.

7444 HAUGHTON, James. Statistics of Australia: a paper read before the Dublin Statistical society on Monday, 28th November, 1853.
tables. 14 pp. Dublin, Hodges and Smith, 1854
C., T.

7445 HAUGHTON, Samuel. The pretensions of the museum of Irish industry considered; in a letter to the right hon. viscount Palmerston, secretary of state for the home department.
tables. 48 pp. Dublin, Hodges & Smith, 1854
A., N.

7446 HILL, lord George Augustus. Facts from Gweedore.
frontisp. maps. tables. appendix. 52 pp. 3rd edition. Dublin, P. D. Hardy, 1854
C., T.

7447 [HOLLAND, J. Simon.] Aslits' decimal coinage; with a proposal for decimalizing our weights & measures of length and capacity. Also a copious appendix of the present French and English weights and measures.
tables. frontispiece. 58 pp. London, H. Silverlock, 1854
T.

7448 HUTTON, William. Stanford's emigrants' guides. Canada: its present condition, prospects, and resources, fully described for the information of emigrants.
map. tables. 142 pp. London, E. Stanford, [1854]
T.

7449 Improvement of the City of Dublin. Copy of memorial presented by the right honorable the lord mayor & the municipal council of Dublin, to his excellency the lord lieutenant upon the 26th December, 1853, praying for a grant of money for the purpose of opening a new street, and effecting other improvements in the city of Dublin and extract from the correspondence between his excellency the lord lieutenant of Ireland and the lords commissioners of her majesty's treasury, in relation thereto.
table. 14 pp. Dublin, O'Neill & Duggan, 1854
A.

7450 Incumbered Estates Court, Ireland. List of petitions filed from the commencement of proceedings October 25th, 1849, to July 28th, 1853.
tables. appendix. 58 pp. Dublin, Allnutt, 1854
A., T.

7451 KAY, Alexander. Hulme's charity. A letter to Benjamin Nicholls, esq., mayor of Manchester, on the past management of this charity, with suggestions for the future application of its large surplus income.
tables in appendix. 42 pp. London, Longman, Brown, Green, and Longmans, 1854
T.

7452 KEATING, Michael George. Life assurance.
44 pp. London, George E. Petter, [1854]
A.

7453 KEENE, Thomas Pacey. The annihilation of past titles considered as the only effectual amelioration of present titles; with a scheme for its accomplishment. A letter to the lord high chancellor.
20 pp. London, T. Blenkarn, 1854
T.

7454 KNIGHT, Frederic Winn. A statistical report to the poor law board on the subject of close and open parishes.
table of contents. tables. appendix. 148 pp. London, H. Shaw, 1854
A.

7455 LAURIE, James. Decimal coinage. A practical analysis of the comparative merits of one pound and tenpence as the ruling integer of a decimal currency for the united kingdom, shewn by tables of merchandise, produce, French merchandise, universal profits per cent, marine and other insurances, etc.; to which is added, £ s. d. and f. reduced into twenty-eight of the principal countries of the world; the division of the moneys, and value in decimals of the £, &c.
tables. 46 pp. London, A. Hall, Virtue, 1854
T.

7456 LAWSON, James Anthony. On the agricultural statistics of Ireland. A paper read before the Dublin Statistical society, 27th April, 1854.
tables. 8 pp. Dublin, Hodges & Smith, 1854
A., N., T.

7457 A letter to the rt. hon. M. T. Baines, president of the poor law board, on the bill for the alteration of the law of settlement and removal. By a county magistrate.
14 pp. London, J. Ridgway, 1854
T.

7458 LOCKE, John. Ireland's recovery; or, excessive emigration, and its reparative agencies in Ireland, an essay with appendix containing useful information, and numerous statistical tables.
index. appendices with tables. 68 pp. London, J. W. Parker, 1854
A., C.
Another edition of 7337.

7459 McARTHUR, John, and ORMSBY, C. M. Incumbered estates court, Ireland. Summary of proceedings from the filing of the first petition, October 21st, 1849, to the 13th July, 1854 (inclusive) being the last day of sale by public auction in court previous to the recess, and of the fifth session of the sittings of the court; also, the names of the staff of the commission and a selection of the opinions of the London, Dublin, and Irish provincial press as to the operations of the court; with an appendix of the names of solicitors (alphabetically arranged), with their residences, who have had the carriage of sales (sold) in the incumbered estates court, containing above six hundred names. The statistics furnished by C. M. Ormsby, statistics office, Incumbered estates court.
38 pp. fold. sheet. tables. Dublin, 1854
A., N.

7460 McDONNELL, G. Railway management, with and without railway statistics.
38 pp. London, Simpkin, Marshall, Liverpool, Geo. J. Poore, [1854]
T.

7461 MAGUIRE, John Francis. Removal of Irish poor from England and Scotland; showing the nature of the law of removal, the mode in which it is administered, the hardships which it inflicts, and the necessity for its absolute and unconditional repeal.
134 pp. London, W. & F. G. Cash, Dublin, J. McGlashan, 1854
A.

7462 [MEAGHER, Thomas?] The Roman law of landlord and tenant; with suggestions for its application to Irish tenures. By an Irish priest.
table of contents. 42 pp. Dublin, J. Duffy, 1854
A., T.

7463 NAPER, James Lennox William. The necessity of domestic and sound education as a preliminary step to parliamentary purification.
16 pp. Dublin, W. Curry, 1854
B., N., T.

7464 [NEWMARCH, William.] Should the money required to pay the expenses of the war be raised by loans or by taxes?
tables. 62 pp. London, Binns and Goodwin, [1854]
T.

7465 Nouveau traité d'agriculture, avec planches des outils, et la manière de s'en servir; suivi d'un traité sur le baillage de terres, lu et approuvé par lord Erskine et plusieurs des juges les plus éminents; et qui montre la nécessité de changer presque tous les contrats dont on s'est servi jusqu'a présent, et qui l'on trouvera finalement être de la plus grande utilité tant au propriétaire qu'au tenancier.
illust. 30 pp. (various paging.) 2nd ed. Chesham, J. S. Garlick, 1854
T.

7466 O'HAGAN, Thomas. The future of Ireland in some of its industrial and social aspects. A lecture delivered for the benefit of the Belfast Working Classes Association in the Music-hall, Belfast, on the 28th October, 1853.
appendix. 40 pp. Dublin, J. McGlashan, 1854
U.

7467 On the whig project for abolishing the removal of the poor and the vicious system of centralization. By a clerk to one of the metropolitan unions.
26 pp. London, Butterworths, 1854
T.

7468 One or two remarks on the law relating to combinations. By a member of the Temple.
8 pp. London, W. G. Benning, 1854
T.

7469 PARE, William. The claims of capital and labour: with a sketch of practical measures for their conciliation. A paper read before the Dublin Statistical society.
table of contents. 40 pp. London, Ward & Lock, Dublin, W. Robertson, 1854
A.

7470 PASHLEY, Robert. Observations on the government bill for abolishing the removal of the poor and redistributing the burden of poor-rate with a proposal for more equitably re-distributing that burden. Second edition revised.
table. appendix. 32 pp. London, Longman, Brown, Green and Longmans, 1854
T.

7471 The past and present ministries, a political essay, in two chapters.
tables. 72 pp. London, T. Harrison, 1854
T.

7472 PRENDERGAST, John P. Letter to the earl of Bantry: or, a warning to English purchasers of the perils of the Irish incumbered estates court; exemplified in the purchase by lord Charles Pelham Clinton, M.P., of two estates in the barony of Bere, county of Cork.
24 pp. Dublin, James McGlashan, 1854
A., U.

——. 22 pp. 2nd ed. Dublin, J. McGlashan, 1854
N., P.

7473 PRICE, George. Combinations and strikes their cost and results. Comprising a sketch of the history, and present state of the law respecting them. With a few suggestions for remedying the evils arising therefrom.
tables. 32 pp. London, Houlston & Stoneman, 1854
T.

7474 Proceedings on a deputation relative to the construction of a harbour of refuge at the River Tyne.
32 pp. Gateshead, Douglas, 1854
A.

7475 Prospectus and tables of rates of the Patriotic Assurance Company of Ireland. Established in the year 1824, for all descriptions of life and fire insurances, and for purchasing and granting annuities.
table of contents. tables. 38 pp. Dublin, Chapman, 1854
N.

7476 Province de la Flandre Orientale. Budget de la ville de Gand pour l'exercice 1854.
tables. 84 pp. (no tp.) n.p., 1854

N.

7477 The ragged school shoe-black society. An account of its origin, operations, and present condition. By the committee.
tables. 20 pp. London, Seeleys, [etc., etc.], 1854

T.

7478 Railway extension to Mayo. Exposition of the fallacy of the proposed scheme called 'The Grand Junction Railway of Ireland'. With a county guarantee.
12 pp. Dublin, Leckie, 1854

A.

7479 RATHBONE, Theodore W. Comparative statement of the different plans of decimal accounts and coinage; which have been proposed by the witnesses examined before the committee of the house of commons, and others. Paper prepared for the statistical section of the British Association for the advancement of science, at their meeting at Liverpool, Sept., 1854.
tables. 116 pp. London, J. Ridgway, 1854

T.

7480 Remarks on the laws of settlement and removal; being a review of the speech of the rt. hon. M. T. Baines, M.P., delivered in the house of commons, 10th Feb., 1854, with practical observations on the present system, by a metropolitan poor law officer.
20 pp. London, Truscott, 1854

A.

7481 Remarks on the proposed Bromley branch. By a South-eastern proprietor.
10 pp. London, M. Pelham Richardson, 1854

T.

7482 RONAYNE, Joseph P. The supply of water to Cork, and its application to the production of motive power within the city.
tables. map. appendix. 24 pp. Cork, Purcell, 1854

N., T.

7483 The routes to Australia, considered in reference to commercial and postal interests, by the directors of the Australian Direct steam navigation company, via Panama. In a letter to the right hon. viscount Canning, her majesty's postmaster-general. With a map and distance tables, explanatory of routes.
map. tables in appendices. 48 pp. London, E. Stanford, 1854

T.

7484 SCOTT, Thomas. Ireland estimated as a field for investment.
tables. table of contents. index. plans. 56 pp. London, T. Harrison, 1854

A.

7485 SCULLY, Vincent. Free trade in land explained.
table of contents. map. 60 pp. Dublin, Hodges & Smith, London, Simpkin, Marshall, 1854

A., E., K., N., U.

7486 SELFE, H. S. The accounts of the Canterbury Association: with explanatory remarks, in a letter to lord Lyttleton.
82 pp. London, J. W. Parker, 1854

T.

7487 SLATER, Robert, junior. Tables showing the value of gold at £3:17:9 per oz. standard, from two carats worseness to pure gold.
tables. 8 pp. London, Longman, Brown, Green, and Longmans, 1854

T.

7488 Strikes prevented. By a Preston manufacturer.
18 pp. London, Whittaker, 1854

T.

7489 The sugar duties. By a West Indian.
22 pp. London, Pelham Richardson, Liverpool, C. & J. Robinson, [1854]

T.

7490 The suppressed pamphlet. The curious and remarkable history of the Royal Irish Bank, showing 'how we got it up' and 'how it went down'. By one behind the scenes.
72 pp. n.p. [1854?]

A.

7491 TANNER, Henry. The cultivation of Dartmoor.
tables. 60 pp. London, Longman, Brown, Green and Longmans, 1854

T.

7492 TAUNTON, Edmund. A lecture on the permanent national measure of value, and all its various influences on our nation, in thirty-eight chapters, by Edmund Taunton, a Manchester foreign merchant of 1807; delivered in the town hall, Birmingham, on Tuesday, July 4, 1854; unfolding incredible causes, effects, and future happy results for Great Britain. With perfect free trade by impartial taxation, reducing all taxes to only 2 per cent and paying off the national debt the fifth time over in eight years more, and the surprising anomaly that protection gives free trade, through the patriot Pitts' till hitherto lost secret system of finance.
40 pp. London, Everett, [etc., etc.] [1854]

T.

7493 The thirteenth annual report and transactions of the Royal Society for the promotion and improvement of the growth of flax in Ireland; with an appendix, treasurer's statement of accounts and list of subscriptions and donations, for the year ending 31st October, 1853.
72 pp. Belfast, at the 'Mercury' Office, 1854

D.

7494 THOMSON, H. Byerley. The laws of war, affecting commerce and shipping.
52 pp. London, Smith, Elder & Co., 1854

T.

7495 TOMLINS, Frederick Guest. A proposition to introduce into life assurance transactions, a completely novel document, entitled a post obit assurance note: by which invention the capital sums assured may be made easily negotiable, and converted into a money currency.
8 pp. (no t.p.) [1854]

T.

7496 Under the superintendence of the anti-centralisation union. Law of settlement and removal of the poor. Reasons showing the impolicy and injurious consequences of the bill introduced by Mr. Baines.
10 pp. London, printed by Taylor and Francis, 1854
A.

7497 The United Kingdom waste lands' improvement company.
tables. 12 pp. London, printed by T. Baron, 1854
T.

7498 WILKINS, Edward. Man his own benefactor; or the value of waste land, and capability for producing two crops annually, (superior in quality to those grown on good land), by means of an improved system of cultivation, as proved by actual experiments at Wokingham, Berkshire, where potatoes were raised free from spot or defect in eleven weeks; and swedes grew three inches round in one week; some of which, with other roots, etc., were exhibited at the Smithfield Club Cattle Show, with some suggestions for improving the condition of the industrious classes, and affording at the same time a profitable investment for capital.
illustrative engraving. tables. 28 pp. London, 1854
T.

7499 WILKINSON, William Francis. A plea for national education with religion and without rates.
54 pp. London, J. W. Parker, 1854
T.

1855

7500 Australia a mistake. New Brunswick for the emigrant. By a retired officer, late a resident in New Brunswick.
30 pp. London, E. Stanford, 1855
T.

7501 BANFIELD, Thomas Charles. A letter to William Brown, esq., M.P., on the advantages of his proposed system of decimal coinage.
16 pp. London, R. Hardwicke, 1855
T.

7502 BEAL, James. Free trade in land: an inquiry into the social and commercial influence of the laws of succession and the system of entails, as affecting the land, the farmer, and the laborer: with observations on the transfer of land.
132 pp. London, J. Chapman, 1855
T.

7503 BISHOP, JAMES. The limited liability act. (18 and 19 Vict. cap. 133.) Received the royal assent, August 14th, 1855. With plain instructions how to proceed in the formation of a company or partnership, and the conditions upon which complete registration may be obtained, with limited liability.
18 pp. London, Dean and Son, [1855?]
T.

7504 BOOTH, J. P. Gold a delusion.
2 pp. Dublin, 1855
A.

7505 BOWEN, Christopher. Suggestions respecting church rates.
10 pp. London, Seeley, Jackson, and Halliday, 1855
T.

7506 BRADY, Cheyne. On schools of industry.
24 pp. Dublin, Hodges & Smith, 1855
A., D., N.

7507 [BURNS, Richard.] Commercial facts affecting the present condition of Great Britain. By a practical man.
tables. 24 pp. Manchester, Wheeler, 1855
A.

7508 Canada as a field for emigration. [Extracts from newspapers reprinted.]
plate. map. tables. 12 pp. n.p., [1855?]
N.

7509 Chancery and the incumbered estates. Observations and suggestions on the expediency of restoring the sale of land in Ireland to the court of chancery.
52 pp. Dublin, Herbert, 1855
A.

7510 CHASE, Drummond Percy. The question, should industrial schools erected at the cost of the poor-rates be made available, (on payment), to children not chargeable to the poor-rates? Considered in a letter to the guardians of the Oxford incorporation.
14 pp. Oxford and London, J. H. and J. Parker, 1855
T.

7511 COOKE, Layton. Bread for the people! secured by the skilful cultivation and efficient supervision of estates.
tables. 20 pp. London, W. H. Dalton, 1855
T.

7512 DE LESSEPS, Ferdinand. The isthmus of Suez question.
table of contents. tables. appendices. maps. 228 pp. London, Longman, Brown, Green & Longmans, Paris, Galignani, 1855
N.

7513 [ELLICE, Edward, jun.] A letter to the right honourable Sir George Grey, bart., M.P., etc., etc., etc., in reply to a report upon the administration of the poor law in the highlands of Scotland.
London, J. Ridgway [etc., etc.], 1855
T.

7514 ERITH, Francis Norton. The mission of life assurance. An essay by Francis Norton Erith, esq., manager and actuary, of the 'British Nation' life assurance association.
8 pp. (no t.p.) [1855?]
T.

7515 ——, and ORAM, John White. The progress of life assurance; developed in the principle of sustentation, or the prevention of policies from lapse. An essay: illustrative of the method of popularizing the system, and adapting it to the exigencies of all classes.
12 pp. Bath, Wood, 1855
T.

7516 EVANS, H. B. Our West Indian colonies. Jamaica a source of national wealth and honour.
tables. 84 pp. London, Effingham Wilson, 1855
T.

7517 EVEREST, R. Statistical details respecting the republic of Lübeck, compared with those of some other European states.
tables. folding tables. 42 pp. London, T. Harrison, [1855?]
A.

7518 FEARON, John Peter. The endowed charities: With some suggestions for further legislation regarding them.
table. 88 pp. London, Longman, Brown, Green and Longmans, 1855
T.

7519 A few words about the inmates of our union workhouses.
16 pp. London, Longman, Brown, Green, and Longmans, 1855
T.

7520 First steps towards a universal system of decimal coinage.
tables. appendix. 30 pp. London, Smith, Elder & co., 1855
T.

7521 FISHER, Joseph. The position and prospects of Ireland. Being a series of articles originally published in the Waterford Mail.
table of contents. tables. appendix. 68 pp. Waterford, the Waterford Mail Office, 1855
A., D., N.

7522 FOSTER, Vere. Work and wages; or, the penny emigrant's guide to the United States and Canada, for female servants, laborers, mechanics, farmers, etc. Containing a short description of those countries, and most suitable places for settlement; rates of wages, board and lodging, house rent, price of land, money matters, etc.; together with full information about the preparations necessary for the voyage, instructions on landing, and expenses of travelling in America. With an appendix.
illust. tables. appendix. 18 pp. (partly unpaginated.) London, W. & F. G. Cash, [c. 1855]
T.

7523 GAYER, Arthur E. Money; what it is worth, and what it is not worth. A lecture by Arthur E. Gayer, esq., Q.C., LL.D. delivered before the Young Men's Christian Association, in the Rotunda (Timothy Turner, esq., in the chair), January 9, 1855.
44 pp. n.p. [1855]
T.

7524 GIRDLESTONE, Charles. The South Staffordshire Colliery District, its evils and their cure; two letters of which the former appeared in 'The Times' of April 18th, 1855; to which is prefixed, by permission, the letter of the Messrs. Walker, to 'The Times', on the same subject.
18 pp. London, Simpkin, Marshall, 1855
T.

7525 GOODFELLOW, James. The decimal coinage; showing its commercial advantages, and exhibiting prominently the immense decrease of clerical labor; also its utility in the promotion of national education, more especially if accompanied with a decimal standard of weights and measures. The new coins required confirmed by calculations; (on this head the author differs with all the witnesses examined before the select committee). A really necessary table, very simply constructed for the general use of the public, namely a table of sterling money, and of the proposed decimal coinage, compared from one farthing to one pound of the former, and from one mil to one hundred cents, or ten florins, of the latter. Also, a few simple short tables for converting the present prices of goods sold by weight into that of a decimal standard. A lengthy comment on the evidence given before the select committee. Commercial illustrations in arithmetic for the use of all classes, and well adapted for schools.
tables. 78 pp. London, Simpkin, Marshall, [1855]
T.

7526 Great Southern and Western Railway. Report of directors, statement of accounts, and proceedings at the 22nd half-yearly general meeting, held at Kingsbridge terminus, Dublin, on Saturday, 24th February, 1855.
tables. 32 pp. Dublin, J. Falconer, 1855
A.

7527 Great Southern and Western Railway. Report of directors, statement of accounts, and proceedings at the 23rd half-yearly general meeting, held at Kingsbridge terminus, Dublin, on Saturday, 25th August, 1855.
tables. 20 pp. Dublin, J. Falconer, 1855
A.

7528 HANNAM, John. Agricultural statistics: a lecture, delivered at the literary institute, Thorner, February, 1855.
tables. 28 pp. London, Longman, Brown, Green & Longmans, 1855
T.

7529 HARE, John Middleton. The decimal coinage question. A letter addressed to the right honourable the chancellor of the exchequer.
tables. 16 pp. London, T. Ward, 1855
T.

7530 HINCKS, Sir Francis. Reply to the speech of the hon. Joseph Howe, of Nova Scotia, on the union of the North American provinces, and on the right of British colonists to representation in the imperial parliament.
tables. 64 pp. London, J. Ridgway, 1855
T.

7531 HOGAN, J. Sheridan. Canada. An essay to which was awarded the first prize by the Paris exhibition committee of Canada.
index. tables. 110 pp. Montreal, Lovell, 1855
A.

7532 HOWE, Joseph. Speech of the hon. Joseph Howe on the union of the North American provinces and on the right of British colonists to representation in the imperial parliament, and to participation in the public enjoyments and distinctions of the empire.
tables. 64 pp. London, J. Ridgway, 1855
T.

27

7533 HUMBERT, Chas. F. On the advantages that would accrue to the landed and agricultural interest of the United Kingdom, from a general act of parliament, (analogous in principle to the private money drainage act of 1849) to enable owners of settled and encumbered estates to borrow money for their improvement upon the security of the estates themselves. A letter to the right honourable the earl of Essex.
14 pp. London, Piper, Stephenson and Spence, Watford, Peacock, 1855

T.

7534 JAMES, George Coulson. Pseudo cost-book mines. A letter to a shareholder.
56 pp. London, Effingham Wilson, 1855

T.

7535 JAMES, James Henry. Dedicated to the right hon. viscount Palmerston. What should be the price of bread? And how can it be regulated? Being an inquiry into the growth, consumption, and cost of wheat: and suggestions for an amended system of corn returns.
tables. 36 pp. London, J. Moore, 1855

T.

7536 KENNEDY, Tristram, and SULLIVAN, William K. On the industrial training institutions of Belgium, and on the possibility of organising an analogous system in connection with the national schools of Ireland.
tables. 78 pp. Dublin, Browne & Nolan, 1855

A., N.

7537 KING, James. A letter to the right honourable lord Cranworth, lord chancellor of England, &c., &c., &c., on the practical injustice and impolicy of the proceedings under the Irish encumbered estates' acts.
46 pp. Cork, G. Purcell, 1855

K.

7538 KINGDOM, William. Suggestions for the liquidation of the national debt, by means of railway property, and for the increase at the same time of railway dividends.
table. 14 pp. 2nd ed. London, Whittaker, 1855

T.

7539 LAWSON, James Anthony. Duties and obligations involved in mercantile relations. A lecture delivered before the Young Men's Christian Association in the Rotunda, (Jonathan Pim, esq., in the chair), January 16, 1855.
20 pp. Dublin, 1855

N.

7540 LENDRICK, William Edmonstone. Cabinets reviewed. A political sketch.
58 pp. London, T. and W. Boone, 1855

K., T.

7541 LOCKE, John, A.B. Ireland's recovery; or excessive emigration and its reparative agencies in Ireland, an essay, with appendix, containing useful information, and numerous statistical tables, illustrating and substantiating the conclusions deduced.
tables. appendix. 96 pp. London, J. W. Parker, 1855

N., U.

See 7337, 7458.

7542 McCONVERY, James. A letter on tenant-right. Second letter.
table. 18 pp. Belfast, at 'the Advertiser' Office, 1855

A.

7543 MACDONALD, J. H. The errors and evils of the bank charter act of 1844, as divulged by lord Overstone, (late Samuel Jones Loyd, esq.,) in his lordship's evidence before the select committee of the houses of parliament appointed to enquire into the causes of the commercial distress in the year 1847.
28 pp. London, P. Richardson, 1855

T.

7544 M'SWEENY, C. Help each other.
8 pp. Dublin, 1855.

A.

A scheme to raise money for purchase of small holdings through 'penny-a-week' savings.

7545 MARRIOTT, Charles. The cooperative principle not opposed to a true political economy, or remarks on some recent publications on subjects relative to the intercommunion of labour, capital, and consumption.
86 pp. Oxford and London: J. H. Parker, 1855

T.

7546 MARTINEAU, Harriet. The factory controversy: a warning against meddling legislation. Issued by the National association of factory occupiers.
56 pp. Manchester, A. Ireland, 1855

T.

7547 Mene, Mene, Tekel Upharsin.
table. 16 pp. London, Waterlow, 1855

A., T.

On banking.

7548 NAPLETON, John Charles. The present condition of the working classes. A lecture delivered and published at the request of the Odd Fellows of Leominster, March 29, 1955.
appendix. 36 pp. London, Longman, Brown, Green and Longmans, [1855?]

T.

7549 NEWMARCH, William. On the loans raised by Mr. Pitt during the first French war, 1793–1801; with some statements in defence of the methods of funding employed.
tables. appendix. 88 pp. London, Effingham Wilson [etc., etc.], 1855

T., U.

7550 OASTLER, Richard. Factory legislation. A letter, caused by the publication of the special report of the executive committee of the National association of factory occupiers. (July, 1855.)
16 pp. London, Wertheim & MacIntosh, [1855]

T.

7551 On the amendment of the bankrupt law.
tables. appendix. 82 pp. Dublin, Hodges & Smith, 1855

A., N., T.

7552 Notes for home circulation. By A, B, and C.
32 pp. London, Effingham Wilson, 1855

T.

7553 Opinions of the press on a pamphlet by Thomas Edward Symonds, R.N., dedicated, by kind permission, to his excellency the right honourable the earl of Carlisle, K.G., lord-lieutenant of Ireland, &c., &c., on which is based the proceedings of the London and West of Ireland fishing company.
index. 36 pp. London, Chapman and Hall, Dublin, J. McGlashan, W. Kelly, 1855

A.

7554 Our staple manufactures: a series of papers on the history and progress of the linen and cotton trades in the north of Ireland. By a manufacturer.
table of contents. tables. 232 pp. Belfast, McComb, Shepherd & Aitchison, 1855

A., T.

7555 PARSONS, Arthur. The limited liability act, 18th and 19th Victoria, c. 133, and its legal interpretation.
16 pp. London, Simpkin, Marshall, 1855

T.

7556 Past and present policy of the Bank of England; the banking acts of 1844–45; or free trade in banking? By an old banker.
22 pp. Edinburgh, Sutherland and Knox, 1855

T.

7557 [PAULSON, K. J. W.] Decimalism. Part I. Remarks on the proposed decimalization of the weights, measures and moneys of Great Britain. With explanatory hints and suggestions. By a commercial traveller.
tables. 46 pp. London, Longman, Brown, Green and Longmans, 1855

T.

7558 POOR, John A. Commercial, railway, and ship-building statistics of the city of Portland, and the state of Maine. Prepared to accompany the second report of the commissioners on Portland harbours.
tables. map. 50 pp. Portland, Tucker, 1855

N.

7559 Railways in India: their present state and prospects; considered with reference to the field they present for English capital. With observations upon the terms of the guarantee granted to the railway companies, by the hon. East India Company.
tables. 44 pp. London, W. H. Allen, 1855

T.

7560 Rationale of our present subdivision of the pound sterling, with strictures on a decimal coinage.
tables. 44 pp. London, Houlston & Stoneman, Bristol, J. Wright, [1855]

T.

7561 Report of the council of the chamber of commerce of Dublin to the members of the association at the annual assembly held on 17th May, 1855.
tables. appendix. 104 pp. Dublin, J. Falconer, 1855

A.

7562 Report of the Directors of the Dublin and Drogheda Railway, to the proprietors, for the half-year ending 30th June, 1855.
tables. 8 pp. Dublin, J. Falconer, 1855

A.

7563 Report of the directors of the Dublin and Drogheda Railway Company, with statement of accounts, for six months ending December 31st, 1854, published preparatory to the half-yearly meeting to be held on Thursday the 1st March, 1855.
tables. 24 pp. Dublin, J. Falconer, 1855

A.

7564 Report of the directors of the Portadown Mont de Piété and loan fund, to the central board in Dublin; shewing the formation, progress and winding up of the Portadown Loan Fund Society.
tables. 18 pp. Portadown, Wilson, 1855

N.

7565 Report of the proceedings of a commission of inquiry into the local charges on shipping within the port of Dublin; held at the city assembly house, Jan., 1855.
tables. appendix. 92 pp. Dublin, Webb, 1855

A., N.

7566 RICKARDS, Sir George Kettilby. The financial policy of war. Two lectures, on the funding system, and on the different modes of raising supplies in time of war, delivered before the University of Oxford, in Trinity term, 1855. By George K. Rickards, M.A., professor of political economy. To which are added some remarks on Mr. Newmarch's recent publication, 'On the loans raised by Mr. Pitt during the first French war.'
appendix. 82 pp. London, J. Ridgway, 1855

T.

7567 ROCHE, Charles Mills. The transfer of land and judicial registration. A letter to Sir Richard Bethell, M.P., her majesty's solicitor general, on the defects of the present system of transferring land.
28 pp. London, Butterworths, 1855

T.

7568 Rules of the Lurgan Building Society. Established under 13 & 14 Victoria, Cap. 115.
tables. 14 pp. Lurgan, Evans, 1855

N.

7569 [SHEE, William.] The tenants' improvements compensation (Ireland) bill.
38 pp. London, J. Ridgway, 1855

A., T.

7570 SOLLY, Edward. On the mutual relations of trade and manufactures. A lecture delivered before the Society of Arts on the 23rd May, 1855, on the opening of the animal department of the Trade Museum.
appendix. 40 pp. London, Longman, Brown, Green & Longmans, 1855

D., T.

7571 STEPHENS, Henry. Catechism of practical agriculture.
table of contents. illustrations. 80 pp. Edinburgh & London, W. Blackwood & son, 1855

N.

7572 SWEET, George. Observations on the existing and the proposed rules for ascertaining the debtor in mercantile dealings.
44 pp. London, H. Sweet, 1855
T.

7573 SYMONDS, Thomas Edward. Observations on the fisheries of the west coast of Ireland, having reference more particularly to the operations of the London and West of Ireland fishing co.
72 pp. Dublin, J. McGlashan, London, Chapman & Hall, 1855
A., N.

——. 96 pp. 2nd ed. Dublin, J. McGlashan, London, Chapman & Hall, 1855
N.

7574 SYMONS, Jelinger. The industrial capacities of South Wales.
tables. 46 pp. London, Longman, Brown, Green and Longmans, 1855
T.

7575 TAYLOR, George Ledwell. Programme and plan of the metropolitan general junction railways and roads.
tables. 2. plates. 26 pp. London, Longman, Brown, Green & Longmans, 1855
T.

7576 [TONGUE, Cornelius.] Hints on agriculture adapted to a midland county.
tables. 26 pp. London, Hamilton, Adams, Leicester, Crossley and Clarke, 1855
T.

7577 [TORRENS, Robert.] Political economy and representative government in Australia.
112 pp. London, J. Ridgway, 1855
T.

7578 To the right hon. lord John Russell, etc. On money, morals, and progress. By Anglo-Americana.
table. 64 pp. London, Sampson Low, 1855
T.

7579 VINING, C. A system of decimal coinage and currency, without fractions of the lowest denomination, in exchanging for sterling money.
tables. appendix. 48 pp. London, Hamilton Adams, Bristol, Oldland and May [etc.], [1855]
T.

7580 WILKINS, Edward. Man his own benefactor; or the value of wasteland, two crops have been produced on the poorest land not worth 2s. 6d. per acre. Potatoes grown in saw-dust, also in sand, in separate beds, and in less than twelve weeks free from disease, spot, or defect. Suggestions for improving the industrious classes; hot house improvements, flowers grown in chandeliers, standards for halls, etc. Second ed.
appendix. 18 pp. Reading, E. Wilkins, 1855
T.

7581 WILSON, John. The agriculture of the French exhibition. An introductory lecture delivered in the University of Edinburgh, session 1855–6.
34 pp. Edinburgh, A. and C. Black, 1855
T.

1856

7582 ALEXANDER, Robert. The rise and progress of British opium smuggling, and its effect upon India, China, and the commerce of Great Britain. Four letters addressed to the right honourable the earl of Shaftesbury.
tables. 70 pp. London, Seeley, Jackson and Halliday, 1856
T.

7583 The Atlantic telegraph.
appendix. 16 pp. London, Bradbury & Evans, 1856
A.
Gives prospectus of Atlantic Telegraph Co. Ltd.

7584 [BAINES, M. A.] A comprehensive view of national education schemes; their past fallacies and future prospects: being a review of education measures during the session of 1856. By the author of 'A short essay on the education question', 'Rules and reasons', etc.
16 pp. London, Wertheim and Macintosh, T. Hatchard, 1856
T.

7585 BEGGS, Thomas. Dear bread and wasted grain. A lecture delivered at the Broadmead rooms, Bristol, on Thursday evening, December 20th, 1855, by Thomas Beggs, Fellow of the Statistical Society. Robert Charleton, esq., in the chair. Published by request.
tables. appendices. 20 pp. London, W. Tweedie, 1856
T.

7586 Birmingham Income Tax Reform Association. Condensed summary of the income tax and property tax question.
18 pp. Birmingham, Ragg, 1856
A.

7587 BOTT, William Eagle. A letter to lord Campbell, lord chief justice of the Queen's Bench, etc., etc., suggesting alterations in the law of rating railways and in the apportionment of their assessable value among parishes.
16 pp. London, J. Weale, 1856
T.

7588 BRICKDALE, Matthew Inglett. The leases and sales of settled estates act, (19 and 20 Victoria, cap. 120) and the general order of the 15th November, 1856, made in pursuance thereof. With an introduction and notes.
98 pp. London, Stevens and Norton [etc.], 1856
T.

7589 Circular of the board of trade of Portland, Maine.
tables. 8 pp. Portland, Foster, 1856
N.

7590 CLAYTON, John. Observations on the proposed decimal coinage.
tables. appendix. 24 pp. London, P. Richardson, 1856
T.

7591 COBDEN, Richard.   What next and next?
tables. 50 pp. London, J. Ridgway, 1856
T.

7592 COLOMBINE, David Elwin.   A word to the share-holders and depositors in the Royal British bank, containing a scheme for the arrangement of its affairs without litigation. To which is added an appendix of the names of shareholders who have sold out since February, 1855, and are still liable, as well as those last returned to the stamp office.
24 pp. London, P. Richardson, [1856]
T.

7593 CROSS, William.   A standard pound versus the pound sterling. A project for rendering the measure of value inde-pendent of the price of gold, and establishing the monetary system on a secure foundation.
32 pp. Edinburgh, Sutherland & Knox, Glasgow, Griffin [etc.], 1856
T.

7594 Cuffe Street Savings Bank, Dublin. Memorial to his excellency the lord lieutenant presented by a deputation, 7th April, 1856. With the reply of his excellency, 17th September, 1856.
22 pp. Dublin, 1856
N.

7595 DE LESSEPS, Ferdinand, ed.   New facts and figures relative to the isthmus of Suez canal; with a reply to the Edinburgh Review by M. Barthelemy St. Hilaire.
table of contents. tables. 224 pp. London, Effingham Wilson, 1856
N.

7596 DE STRZELECKI, P. E.   Gold and silver: a supplement to Strzelecki's physical description of New South Wales and Van Diemen's land.
34 pp. London, Longman, Brown, Green, and Longmans, 1856
T.

7597 DICK, Robert.   On the evils, impolicy, and anomaly of individuals being landlords, and nations tenants; together with twelve propositions on labour, wages, etc.
32 pp. London, J. Chapman, 1856
T.

7598 DIXON, Thomas.   Observations on the management of the North Dublin Union, and the ruinous expenses conse-quent thereupon.
20 pp. Dublin, Powell, 1856
A., N.

7599 The elements of the currency plainly stated and prac-tically discussed. By F. C.
34 pp. London, R. Hardwicke, 1856
T.

7600 A few words of importance to the directors and share-holders of land and building societies. Designed to render them all more successful, and more beneficial to the working classes.
tables. 24 pp. London, Simpkin, Marshall, 1856
T.

7601 A few words on the sound dues.
tables. 16 pp. London, J. Ridgway, 1856
T.
Refers to dues payable to the Danish government by ships entering the Baltic sea.

7602 The fourth report of the Tribunal of Commerce Association. With an appendix giving a few cases illustrative of the hardships and absurd cruelties inflicted on suitors by the present state of the law. The copies of letters from the arch-bishop of Canterbury, the bishop of Chichester, Dr. Thorpe, D.D., lord Brougham, lord Overstone, lord John Russell, the earl of Harrington, lord Wharncliffe, lord Stanley, lord Elrington, and the copy of a letter to Kirkman D. Hodgson, esq., a bank director, the opinions of the press, and the ex-cuses of certain rich men of the city of London for not sup-porting the movement, etc., etc.
table. appendix. 36 pp. London, Effingham Wilson, 1856
T.

7603 FRAZER, Edward.   The banking laws of Ireland. A full and accurate report of the judgment of the lord chan-cellor of Ireland in the case of O'Flaherty and others v. McDowell and others, (the Tipperary bank case), taken ver-batim from the shorthand notes, and all authorities, carefully collected.
32 pp. Dublin, E. J. Milliken, 1856
T.

7604 GIBBON, Alexander.   A paper on the circulating medi-um, on seignorage on gold coin, and on the statute the 7th and 8th of the Queen, cap. XXXII, entitled, An act to regulate the issue of bank notes, and for giving to the governor and company of the Bank of England certain privileges for a limited period.
tables. appendices. 128 pp. London, T. Hatchard, 1856
T.

7605 GRANT, John Miller.   To emigrants. Canada: its advantages to settlers.
plate. tables. 16 pp. London, Algar and Street, W. Wesley, 1856
T.

7606 Great Southern and Western Railway. Report of directors, statement of accounts and proceedings at the 24th half-yearly general meeting held at Kingsbridge terminus, Dublin, on Saturday, 23rd February, 1856.
tables. 28 pp. Dublin, J. Falconer, 1856
A.

7607 Great Southern and Western Railway. Report of directors and statement of accounts to be submitted to the proprietors at the half yearly general meeting to be held at Kingsbridge terminus, Dublin, on Saturday, 30th Aug., 1856.
tables. 16 pp. Dublin, 1856
A.

7608 Great Southern and Western Railway. Report of directors, statement of accounts, and proceedings at the 25th half-yearly general meeting, held at Kingsbridge terminus, Dublin, on Saturday, 30th August, 1856.
tables. 26 pp. Dublin, J. Falconer, 1856
A.

7609 HALL, Edward Hepple. Ho! For the West! ! ! The traveller and emigrant's handbook to Canada and the north-west states of America, for general circulation. Containing useful information on all important points, gathered during a residence of eight years in both countries. Compiled from the latest authentic sources, and designed particularly for the use of travellers, emigrants and others.
tables. 64 pp. London, Algar & Street, 1856
T.

See 7779.

7610 HARRISON, William George, & CAPE, George A., jun. The Joint Stock Companies Act, 1856. With remarks legal and practical, and a copious index.
appendix. 94 pp. London, Baily, 1856
T.

7611 HASLAM, John ['late Turgot']. The paper currency of England dispassionately considered, with suggestions towards a practical solution of the difficulty.
tables. 80 pp. London, E. Wilson, Dublin, McGlashan & Gill, 1856
A.

7612 [——.] Proposal to establish an additional bank in Dublin considered (second article) by 'Turgot'. To the editor of the Journal of Social Progress.
table. 8 pp. n.p., [1856]
A.

7613 HOSKYNS, Chandos Wren. Agricultural statistics; a reprint.
tables. 58 pp. London, J. Murray, 1856
T.

7614 HUTTON, Henry Dix. A statement of the principal reasons in support of the accompanying resolutions submitted to the Congress for commercial reform assembled at Brussels on behalf of the 'Tribunal of Commerce Association' at London.
30 pp. Paris, Thunot, 1856
A.

7615 An inquiry into the national debt and sinking fund. By F. C.
tables. 32 pp. London, R. Hardwicke, 1856
T.

7616 JOHNSON, Andrew. Currency principles versus banking principles; being strictures on Mr. Tooke's pamphlet on the bank charter act of 1844.
50 pp. London, P. Richardson, 1856
T.

7617 JOHNSON, William Forbes. An inquiry into the nature of a conveyance by the commissioners for the sale of incumbered estates.
14 pp. Dublin, Hodges, Smith, 1856
U.

7618 KETTLE, Rupert. A note on rating to the poor for non-productive land. (Suggested by the case of Heaton, appellant, and parish of Harborne, respondents, Q. B. Hilary, 1856).
28 pp. London, V. & R. Stevens and G. S. Norton, 1856
T.

7619 A letter from a proprietor of East-India stock to his fellow-proprietors.
24 pp. London, P. Richardson, 1856
T.

7620 A letter to the right hon. Benjamin Disraeli, M.P., for the county of Buckingham, on the culture of the field. By Agricola.
36 pp. London, Lovell Reeve, 1856
T.

7621 MACDONALD, J. H. Mr. George Combe's doctrine on the currency question, examined and refuted, by Lieut-Colonel J. H. Macdonald.
appendix. 44 pp. London, P. Richardson, 1856
T.

7622 MACKEY, William. Why are four million acres of the soil of Ireland kept in privileged barrenness? An essay.
30 pp. Dublin, J. Duffy, 1856
A., U.

7623 MACLAREN, James. A letter to those who have insured their lives, on the evidence afforded by the present extraordinary movement of the precious metals of the necessity and possibility of protecting their property against the effects of the continued production of gold.
24 pp. London, Aylott and Jones, Thomas Bumpus [etc.], 1856
T.

7624 MECHI, John Joseph. On the principles which ensure success in trade. A lecture delivered by Mr. J. J. Mechi, at the Crosby Hall Literary Institution, Bishopsgate Street, London, 1856.
20 pp. London, Longman, Brown, Green & Longmans, 1856
T.

7625 The mines of Wicklow.
table of contents. tables. plans. illustration. 114 pp. London, Law, 1856
A.

7626 Morality: and its practical application to social institutions. By the author of 'Adaptability, an exposition of the law of all phenomena'.
16 pp. London, J. Chapman, 1856
T.

7627 [NUTTING, H.] A few plain remarks on decimal currency, respectfully submitted to the consideration of the public. By a Cypher.
tables. 16 pp. Luton, J. Wiseman, London, Royston & Brown, 1856
T.

7628 O'FLYNN, James. Popular Social Philosophy. Part I. Being an inquiry into the material causes of social misery.
86 pp. Dublin, McGlashan & Gill, 1856
A., T., U.

7629 PASLEY, Sir Charles William. Plan for simplifying and improving the measures, weights and money of this country, without materially altering the present standards. Read before section F—Economic Science and statistics—of the British Association.
tables. 16 pp. London, Cox & Wyman, 1856
A.

7630 PATTEN, Robert. Report of the locating survey of the St. Croix and Lake Superior Railroad.
appendix. tables. 24 pp. Madison, Calkins and Proudfit, 1856
N.

7631 PHILLIPS, Edmund. A letter on the currency and Bank of England charter.
16 pp. London, Nissen & Parker, 1856
A.

7632 ——. Bank of England charter, currency, limited liability companies, and free trade.
tables. 48 pp. London, P. Richardson [etc.], 1856
T.

7633 POTTER, Edmund. A picture of a manufacturing district. A lecture delivered in the town hall, Glossop, to the Littlemoor & Howard Town mechanics' institution, on Tuesday evening, January 15th, 1856.
58 pp. London, J. Ridgway, 1856
T.

7634 Poverty with relation to the state; or, a glance at the monetary system.
20 pp. 2nd ed. London, Hamilton, Adams, Bristol, Chilcott, 1856
T.

7635 Prospectus of the Templemoyle Seminary and Agricultural National Model School.
18 pp. Londonderry, Hempton, 1856
D., N.

7636 Reduction of the wine duties. Report of the meeting of the wine duties reduction committee and the Anglo-French free trade association, at the Crystal Palace, July 9th, 1856; debate in the house of commons on Mr. Oliveira's motion for the wine duties reduction, on the 15th July, 1856; a list of the general committee; and other particulars connected with the reduction of the import duty upon wines.
64 pp. London, Ward and Lock, [1856]
T.

7637 Remarks on the expediency of some of the private banks of London being formed into joint-stock companies.
28 pp. London, Simpkin, Marshall, [1856]
T.

7638 A reply to Mr. George Combe's pamphlet, on the currency, and the Bank of England restriction act. By Civis.
16 pp. London, Smith, Elder & co., 1856
T.

7639 Report of the committee of inquiry appointed by the Royal Agricultural Improvement Society of Ireland, at their half-yearly meeting, held on 21st Dec., 1855.
12 pp. Belfast, printed at the Northern Whig Office, 1856
U.

7640 Report of the directors of the Dublin and Drogheda Railway Company, to the proprietors, for the half-year ending 30th June, 1856.
tables. 8 pp. Dublin, J. Falconer, 1856
A.

7641 Report of the directors of the Dublin & Drogheda Railway Company, with statement of accounts for six months ending December 31, 1855, published preparatory to the half-yearly meeting to be held on Thursday, the 28th February, 1856.
tables. 24 pp. Dublin, J. Falconer, 1856
A.

7642 Report of the tithe redemption trust for the church in England and Wales, for the year 1856.
tables. 24 pp. London, F. & J. Rivington, 1856
T.

7643 A review of the London and North Western Railway accounts, for the last ten years. By a Manchester shareholder.
tables. 40 pp. Manchester, Joseph Thomson, London, Simpkin, Marshall, 1856
T.

7644 RIDLEY, William Henry. Clerical incomes and clerical taxation. A letter addressed to the right hon. W. E. Gladstone, M.P., with especial reference to Dr. Phillimore's bill for the assessment of tithe commutation rent-charge.
tables. 36 pp. London, Bell and Daldy, 1856
T.

7645 ROSS, Alexander Goudy. An address to his tenantry and an appeal to the British public, on behalf of the tenant farmer.
28 pp. Belfast, J. Reed, 1856
R.

7646 Rules of the Portadown loan fund.
10 pp. n.p., 1856
N.

7647 SIMPSON, John Hawkins. An Englishman's testimony to the urgent necessity for a tenant right bill for Ireland. After a residence of five years in that country.
46 pp. Westport, Bole, 1856
A., N., T.

7648 SMITH, William. A letter on steam cultivation, to Edmund Greaves, esq., of Haversham; chairman of Newport Pagnell division of the Royal Bucks Agricultural Association.
12 pp. London, J. Wesley, Newport Pagnell, E. H. Croydon, 1856
T.

7649 A speech delivered at Midnapore on the amelioration of the conditions of the ryot population of Bengal. By a native.
24 pp. Bhowanipore, Shama Churn Sircar, 1856
T.

7650 STATTER, Richard Dover. The decimal system as a whole, in its relation to time, measure, weight, capacity, and money, in unison with each other.
tables. 38 pp. London, R. Groombridge, Liverpool, Joshua Walmsley, 1856
T.

7651 STAUNTON, Michael. Report of the collector general of rates in the city of Dublin, for the year ending 31st December, 1855.
tables. 22 pp. Dublin, 1856
A.

7652 Tennant, Charles. Suggestions for the renewal of the Bank of England charter and for a decimal coinage.
tables. 112 pp. London, Chapman and Hall, 1856
T.

7653 Torrens, Robert. Letter to the right honble R. Vernon Smith; with a review of documents relating to revenue administration in India, published by order of the house of commons.
26 pp. London, C. Westerton, 1856
T.
'By Robert Torrens, retired Bengal Civil Service.'

7654 The trade spirit versus the religion of the age: a discourse.
40 pp. Edinburgh, J. Hogg, 1856
T.

7655 Traill, James Christie. A letter to the most honourable the marquess of Blandford, on the management of church property, and the distribution of its revenues through the medium of the ecclesiastical commission.
44 pp. London, Simpkin, Marshall, 1856
T.

7656 Van Sandau, Andrew. An exposition of the author's experience as one of the assured in the 'Alliance' British and foreign life and fire assurance company: showing how it has happened that an assurance in that company has proved a disastrous investment; and suggesting useful hints for the guidance of such persons as may be desirous of assuring their lives, in their selection of the office.
tables. appendix. 48 pp. (various paging.) London, C. A. Bartlett, 1856
T.

7657 Warren, Samuel. Labour: its rights, difficulties, dignity, and consolations. A paper read before the Hull Mechanics' Institute on Thursday, January 3, 1856.
32 pp. London, Longman, Brown, Green & Longmans, 1856
T.

——. Another issue. 18 pp. 'reprinted from the Morning Chronicle.' London, J. Pattie. 1856
T.

7658 Wilson, James Moncrieff. Civil service superannuation. A paper read before the Dublin Statistical society, 21st April, 1856.
tables. 24 pp. Dublin, McGlashan & Gill, London, J. Ridgway, 1856
A.
Paper not published in the society's journal.

7659 Wordsworth, Charles. New joint stock company law, with instructions how to form a company; and herein of the liabilities of persons engaged in so doing.
index. tables. 104 pp. 5th ed. with additions. London, H. Shaw, 1856
N., T.

7660 Worthington, Robert. The fisheries, considered as a national resource, with comments upon the laws relating to them: being a collection of articles on the state of the Irish fisheries published at different periods.
table of contents. appendix. 214 pp. Dublin, E. Milliken, 1856
N.

7661 Yates, James. Narrative of the origin and formation of the International Association for obtaining a uniform decimal system of measures, weights, and coins.
appendices. 56 pp. 2nd ed. London, Bell and Daldy, Paris, Librairie Internationale Universelle, 1856
N., T.

1857

7662 Alexander, Robert. Contraband opium traffic, the disturbing element in all our policy and diplomatic intercourse with China.
28 pp. London, Seeley, Jackson and Halliday, 1857
T.

7663 ——. Opium revenue of India. The question answered, that it is not right to break the laws of England and of China, and injure the commerce of both countries, for the sake of temporarily obtaining £3,000,000 sterling, by destroying the lives, morality, and commercial reciprocity, of 300,000,000 of our fellow-men.
20 pp. London, Seeley, Jackson & Halliday, 1857
T.

7664 Andrew, Sir William Patrick. The Punjaub railway. A selection from official correspondence regarding the introduction of railways into the Punjaub, with map of Scinde and the Punjaub.
folding map. tables. 32 pp. London, W. H. Allen, 1857
T.

7665 Arbuthnot, G. Sir Robert Peel's act of 1844, regulating the issue of bank notes, vindicated.
table in appendix. 120 pp. London, Longman, Brown, Green, Longmans, and Roberts, 1857
T.

7666 Ayrton, Edward Nugent. Suggestions for an act to give an indefeasible title in land. Addressed to the legislature.
42 pp. London, W. Walker, [1857]
T.

7667 Bain, Donald. Notes on the government security savings' banks bill. No. 2.
20 pp. London, Vacher, 1857
A.

7668 Baynes, John. The cotton trade. Two lectures on the above subject, delivered before the members of the Blackburn Literary, Scientific, and Mechanics' Institution by Mr. Alderman Baynes, (of that town); first,—April 2nd, 1857, The origin, rise, progress and present extent of the cotton trade; second—June 11th, 1857, its mission; politically, socially, morally, and religiously; James Pilkington, esq., M.P. Blackburn, and John Livesey, esq., (late chairman of the Master Cotton-Spinners and Manufacturers' Association of the Blackburn district,) respectively presided on the occasions. Dedicated by permission to the right hon. lord Cavendish, M.P., North Lancashire.
tables. 119 pp. Blackburn, J. N. Haworth, 1857
T.

7669 Bowring, Cobden and China; a memoir. By Lammer Moor [pseud.].
32 pp. Edinburgh, J. Menzies, London, Houlston and Wright, 1857
T.

7670 BRAY, Charles. The industrial employment of women: being a comparison between the condition of the people in the watch trade in Coventry, in which women are not employed; and the people in the provision trade, in which they are employed. A paper partly read before the British Association for the Advancement of Science, October, 1857.
tables. 18 pp. London, Longman, Brown, Green, Longmans & Roberts, [1857]
T.

7671 BROWN, William Keer. On neutral trade and right of search, five letters, written in 1854. With a preliminary essay on a revision of the law of nations, and on the necessity of incorporating the western with the eastern hemisphere in the general administration of that law.
tables. appendix. 70 pp. London, J. Ridgway, Faversham, J. Sherwood, 1857
T.

7672 BUTT, Isaac. The transfer of land by means of a judicial assurance: its practicability and advantages considered in a letter to Sir Richard Bethell, M.P., H.M. attorney-general for Ireland.
appendices. 130 pp. Dublin, Hodges & Smith, London, J. Ridgway, 1857
A., N., T.

7673 CAHILL, D. W. Dr. Cahill on Irish emigration, tenant-right and sectarian animosity.
12 pp. Dublin, Nugent, 1857
A.

7674 ——. Dr. Cahill on tenant right.
12 pp. Dublin, Nugent, 1857
A.

7675 ——. Letter on the eviction of the Irish tenantry. Extermination of the Irish small farmers. Tenant-right.
12 pp. Dublin, Nugent, 1857
A.

7676 ——. Letter on the Irish emigrants to America returning to Ireland.
12 pp. Dublin, Nugent, 1857
A., N.

7677 CAIRNS, John. The Indian crisis, viewed as a call to prayer: a discourse.
16 pp. Berwick, Melrose & Plenderleith, 1857
T.

7678 Church-rate commutation; or, the outline of a plan for an equitable settlement of the church-rate question. By Laicus Urbanus.
8 pp. London, Bell and Daldy, 1857
T.

7679 CLINTON, Henry. The best possible government at the least possible cost impossible until commerce is regulated.
16 pp. London, Effingham Wilson, 1857
T.

7680 CROKER, John Dillon. Letter of J. Dillon Croker, esq., auditor of the Cork and Youghal Railway Company, to the shareholders of the said company.
table. 8 pp. London, printed by S. Geoghegan, 1857
A.

7681 DAYNES, Samuel. The Manchester Unity. Attack by lord Albemarle on the Manchester Unity friendly society; with the reply in defence of the order. With extracts from the leading articles of the Norfolk Chronicle.
48 pp. Norwich, 1857
T.

7682 The decimal system adapted to our present coinage. By J. S., barrister-at-law.
tables. 24 pp. London, R. Groombridge, 1857
T.

7683 DE LESSEPS, Ferdinand. Inquiry into the opinions of the commercial classes of Great Britain on the Suez ship canal.
illustr. diags. 156 pp. London, John Weale, 1857
A., P.

7684 Dublin and Drogheda Railway. Report of the directors and statement of accounts, published preparatory to the half-yearly meeting to be held on Friday, the 27th February, 1857.
tables. 26 pp. Dublin, J. Falconer, 1857
A.

7685 EVELYN, Frederic. The 'Dublin Traders' Alliance' versus the monster houses.
appendix. 40 pp. Dublin, G. Ponsonby, 1857
A., N.

7686 FITZGERALD, John. The duty of procuring more rest for the labouring classes; the earlier closing of shops, and the Saturday half-holiday.
table. 78 pp. London, W. H. Dalton, [1857]
T.

7687 GAMGEE, Joseph Sampson. The cattle plague and diseased meat, in their relations with the public health, and with the interests of agriculture. A letter to the rt. hon. Sir George Grey, bart., G.C.B., secretary of state for the home department.
42 pp. London, T. Richards, 1857
T.

7688 ——. The cattle plague and diseased meat, in their relations with the public health, and with the interests of agriculture. A second letter. To the rt. hon. Sir George Grey, bart., G.C.B., secretary of state for the home department.
26 pp. London, T. Richards, 1857
T.

7689 General Sir Charles Napier, and the directors of the East India Company.
45 pp. London, C. Westerton, 1857
T.

7690 GODDARD, Samuel A. Letters to the Edinburgh chamber of commerce, &c., &c., upon the monetary system; embracing a reply to the pamphlet of Mr. George Combe, on the same subject.
44 pp. London, Arthur Hall, Virtue, Birmingham, John W. Showell, 1857
T.

7691 Great Southern and Western Railway. Report of directors and statement of accounts, to be submitted to the proprietors at the half-yearly general meeting to be held at Kingsbridge terminus, Dublin, on Saturday, 28th February, 1857.
tables. 14 pp. Dublin, 1857

A.

7692 Great Southern and Western Railway. Report of directors and statement of accounts, to be submitted to the proprietors at the half-yearly general meeting to be held at Kingsbridge terminus, Dublin, on Saturday, 29th August, 1857.
tables. 12 pp. Dublin, 1857

A.

7693 GUTHRIE, George. A safe, effective, and simple reform of currency and banking, submitted to the select committee of inquiry.
appendix. 32 pp. 2nd ed. Glasgow, D. Bryce, 1857

T.

7694 HALIBURTON, Thomas Chandler. An address on the present condition, resources and prospects of British North America, delivered by special request at the city hall, Glasgow, on the 25th of March, 1857.
44 pp. London, Hurst and Blackett, 1857

T.

7695 HANNAM, William. A gift to the uninsured. Thirty short replies to 30 common objections.
10 pp. London, W. Penny, 1857

T.

7696 HUTTON, Henry Dix. Commercial courts: comprising the resolutions and explanatory statement submitted to the Brussels Free Trade Congress of 1856; an address prepared for the consideration of that assembly; and an appendix containing a concise view of the constitutions and procedure of the French tribunals of commerce.
appendix. 50 pp. Dublin, McGlashan & Gill, 1857

A., E., T.

7697 International association for obtaining a uniform decimal system of measures, weights and coins. British branch. First report of the council to the general meeting, held February 26th, 1856: with an appendix to the report, a statement of receipts and expenditure, the proceedings of the general meeting, a list of contributions, etc.
tables in appendices. 24 pp. London, The Association, 1857

T.

7698 Isthmus of Suez Ship Canal. Report and plan of the international scientific commission, with appendix containing the latest official documents.
table of contents. tables. appendix. 192 pp. London, J. Weale, 1857

A.

7699 JONES, William Arthur. The decimal system of measures, weights, and money.
tables. 16 pp. 2nd ed. London, Bell and Daldy, 1857

T.

7700 KELLY, James. A letter from Mr J. Kelly, formerly of Cushima, King's County, to his late landlord, Doctor Tabuteau, of Portarlington.
12 pp. (no t.p.) n.p., 1857

N.

7701 KENNY, Charles Lamb. The gates of the east. Ten chapters on the isthmus of Suez canal.
illustrations. plan. maps. tables. 72 pp. London, Ward and Lock, 1857

T.

7702 [KINGDON, William Nicholson.] God and the country robbed, or the non-conformist movement for the abolition of church rates briefly exposed.
16 pp. Launceston, P. D. Maddox, London, Simpkin, Marshall, 1857

T.

7703 KINNAIRD, Arthur FitzGerald, baron. Bengal: its landed tenure and police system. Speech on a motion for inquiry in the house of commons, June 11, 1857. With an appendix.
appendix. 70 pp. London, J. Ridgway, 1857

T.

7704 KNIGHT, James. The London joint stock banks: their progress, resources, and constitution.
tables. 38 pp. London, P. Richardson, 1857

T.

7705 LANGE, Daniel Adolphus. Lord Palmerston and the Isthmus of Suez Canal. Two letters addressed to the editor of 'the Times'.
map. illustration. 16 pp. London, P. Richardson, 1857

A.

7706 A letter on the fiscal affairs of Ireland, respectfully submitted to the consideration of his excellency the lord lieutenant of Ireland, by his obedient servant, the author.
20 pp. Dublin, J. Falconer, 1857

A.

7707 LEWIN, Malcolm. The government of the East India Company and its monopolies; or, the Young India party, and free trade?
24 pp. London, J. Ridgway, 1857

T.

7708 ——. Has Oude been worse governed by its native princes than our Indian territories by Leadenhall Street?
26 pp. London, J. Ridgway, 1857

T.

7709 MACKENZIE, James Thompson. Suggestions for the reconstruction of the government of India; with some remarks upon its monetary, commercial, social, and religious aspects.
56 pp. London, Jones & Causton, 1857

T.

7710 McPHIN, William Lyon. Report of evidence submitted to the committee of the house of commons now sitting on the bank acts of 1844–45.
tables. 76 pp. London, P. Richardson, 1857

T.

7711 ———. The true principles of currency; explained in a report of evidence submitted to the committee of the house of commons now sitting on the bank acts of 1844–45.
28 pp. London, P. Richardson, 1857
T.

7712 MARRIOTT, Saville. India: the duty and interest of England to inquire into its state.
80 pp. 2nd ed. London, Longman, Brown, Green, Longmans & Roberts, Frome, Harvey, 1857
T.

7713 MATHESON, Donald. What is the opium trade.
20 pp. Edinburgh, T. Constable, 1857
T.

———. 28 pp. 2nd ed. Edinburgh, T. Constable, 1857
T.

7714 Metropolitan work houses and their inmates.
tables. appendix. 78 pp. London, Longman, Brown, Green, Longmans & Roberts, 1857
T.

7715 [MIDDLETON, Henry.] Economical causes of slavery in the United States, and obstacles to abolition. By a South Carolinian.
60 pp. London, R. Hardwicke, 1857
T.

7716 [NORTON, Edward.] The Bank Charter Act of 1844 truthfully considered in connexion with the dearness of money, free trade, the currency, and the fair employment of labour. By Honestus.
tables. 34 pp. London, William Skeffington, 1857
T.

———. 62 pp. 2nd edition, enlarged, corrected and signed with author's name. London, W. Skeffington, 1857
T.

———. 62 pp. 3rd edition. London, W. Skeffington, 1857
T.

7717 NORTON, George. A new financial scheme for India: the first step towards political reform; in a letter to the rt. hon. the president of the board of control.
24 pp. London, P. Richardson, 1857
T.

7718 Observations on the general grand jury act, 6 & 7 William IV, Chap. 116, with reference to the arrangements thereby provided for the execution of county works. In a letter to the rt. honourable E. Horsman, M.P., chief secretary for Ireland. By Justitia.
tables. 30 pp. Dublin, Hodges & Smith, 1857
N.

7719 'Open sesame'; or, the key to national wealth: being a short analysis of views and opinions entertained as to the operation of our present banking and currency laws.
table. 16 pp. London, Arthur Hall, Virtue, 1857
T.

7720 The opium revenue of India. Is it right to take three millions sterling from the Chinese beyond the cost price of the drug, as the condition of their enjoying the forbidden indulgence of opium smoking?
tables. 38 pp. London, W. A. Allen, 1857
T.

7721 Our monetary system. Why does it break down under the growth of capital and the expansion of commerce?
table. 34 pp. London, Seeley, Jackson, and Halliday, & B. Seeley, 1857
T.

7722 Our national relations with China. Being two speeches delivered in Exeter Hall and in the Free-trade Hall, Manchester, by the bishop of Victoria.
23 pp. London, J. Hatchard, 1857
T.

7723 PASLEY, Sir Charles William. Plan for simplifying and improving the measures, weights, and money of this country, without materially altering the present standards.
16 pp. London, W. H. Dalton, 1857
T.
See 7629.

7724 Past and proposed legislation on the presentment of public money by grand jury presentments for public works in Ireland.
20 pp. Dublin, A. Thom, 1857
N.

7725 PHILLIPS, J. H. The life assurance agents' manual.
60 pp. London, W. Tweedie, 1857
T.

7726 PLATT, Alexander. A new financial scheme; or, proposals for readjusting the balance of taxation, in favour of the poor.
48 pp. London, J. Ridgway, 1857
T.

7727 PONJIS, Bole. The Marcy Convention. Capture or no capture? 'That is the question', reverentially submitted to the two houses of parliament.
32 pp. London, W. Thacker, Calcutta, Thacker, Spink [etc.], 1857
T.

7728 RAMSAY, Edward Bannerman. Two lectures on some changes in social life and habits.
114 pp. Edinburgh, Edmonston & Douglas, 1857
T.

7729 RATHBONE, Theodore William. Comments on the preliminary report, evidence of the witnesses, and information obtained from countries in which the decimal system has been more or less fully brought into practical use, submitted to her majesty and the houses of parliament, by the decimal coinage commission, with the evidence, verbal and in reply to a series of questions, touching the only plan of proceeding it seems expedient and practicable to adopt in this country. By the author of 'An examination of the report and evidence of the committee of house of commons', etc.
118 pp. London, J. Ridgway, 1857
T.

7730 Report of the directors of the Dublin and Drogheda Railway Company to the proprietors, for the half-year ending 30th June, 1857.
tables. 8 pp. Dublin, J. Falconer, 1857
A.

7731 Report of the directors of the National Bank to the twenty-second annual meeting, held at 13, Old Broad Street, May 27th, 1857.
tables. 8 pp. London, 1857
N.

7732 Report on the Templemoyle Seminary and Agricultural National Model School, for year ending 31st Dec., 1856.
tables. 12 pp. Londonderry, Hempton, 1857
A., D.

7733 A review of the case of the civil servants of the crown, with reference to the question of their superannuation and salaries. By Investigator.
84 pp. London, J. Ridgway, 1857
T.

7734 The savings bank system. Suggestions for its re-organization, extension, and future safety. By a savings bank reformer.
tables. 28 pp. London, R. Groombridge, 1857
T.

7735 SHEPHERD, George. London sewerage, and its application to agriculture. The London drainage, and how to apply the sewerage to the land with advantage to the farmer and the capitalist; the only comprehensive plan yet proposed for applying the sewerage to the land.
tables. 64 pp. London, Effingham Wilson, 1857
T.

7736 [SMITH, James Alexander.] Monetary panics and their cure, with hints to investigators. By the author of 'Atheisms of geology'.
24 pp. London, Houlston and Wright, 1857
T.

7737 STANSFELD, Hamer. Comments on the currency fallacies of lord Overstone avowed by him in his evidence before the bank committee of the house of commons of 1857 to be the principles on which the Bank Charter Act of 1844 was founded.
18 pp. London, Simpkin, Marshall [etc., etc.], 1857
A., T.

7738 [STEVENS, Francis Worrell.] Liability of parties depositing money 'at call'.
10 pp. n.p., M. Lownds, [1857]
T.

7739 ——. The proposed new circulating medium, as suggested to the rt. hon. the chancellor of the exchequer.
10 pp, London, F. W. Stevens, 1857
T.

7740 SULLIVAN, Robert. A chapter on the present condition and prospects of the Australian colonies.
table. 14 pp. Dublin, Sullivan, 1857
N.

7741 SUTTON, Richard Lindsay. The British workman's legacy or political, moral, & social regeneration.
72 pp. Edinburgh, W. Blackwood & son, 1857
T.

7742 Thoughts on the Indian crisis, and its bearings on the freedom of the press. To which is added the metropolitan sewage question, considered in reference to Dr. Hawkesley's letter, and the agriculture of the country. By 'Civicus'.
16 pp. London, Effingham Wilson, 1857
T.

7743 TODD, William G. The Irish in England. Reprinted with additions from the Dublin Review.
46 pp. London, C. Dolman, 1857
U.

7744 TOLHAUSEN, Alexander. A synopsis of the patent laws of various countries. Comprising the following heads: 1. law, date, and where recorded; 2. kinds of patents; 3. previous examination; 4. duration; 5. government fees; 6. documents required, and where to be left; 7. working and extension; 8. assignments; 9. specifications, inspection and copies of; 10. list of patents delivered; 11. specifications published; 12. originals of specifications (models).
appendix. 36 pp. London, Taylor and Francis, 1857
T.

7745 TWEEDIE, William. Temperance and high wages. Total abstinence from intoxicating beverages a practical and efficient remedy for scarcity of employment and low wages. Lowering the intensity of competition and restoring commercial prosperity. A lecture. Fifty-fifth thousand.
tables. 18 pp. London, W. Tweedie, 1857
T.

7746 Twenty-eighth annual report of the Orphan refuge, or Charitable protestant orphan union, for the education and support of the destitute orphans of mixed marriages, adopted at the annual meeting of the society, held at the Rotundo, on Tuesday, 6th April, 1858, with a statement of income and expenditure, etc., from December 31, 1856, to December 31, 1857. Founded A.D. 1830. Office, 9, Upper Sackville Street.
table. 70 pp. Dublin, J. Charles, 1857
T.

7747 WILLOUGHBY, Sir Henry, bart. A few words on the question, whether there is by law any effective control over the public expenditure, addressed to the members of the house of commons.
18 pp. London, J. Ridgway, 1857
T.

7748 WYLIE, Macleod. The commerce, resources and prospects of India.
tables. 108 pp. London, W. H. Dalton, 1857
T.

1858

7749 Advice to the embarrassed. With the most important provisions of the bankrupt and insolvent laws affecting debtors.
appendix. 62 pp. London, Cooper, 1858
T.

7750 Agricultural education in Ireland: Its organization and efficiency; with a reply to recent criticisms.
table of contents. tables. 22 pp. Dublin, J. Falconer, 1858
D., E., N., T.

7751 Annual report and transactions of the Royal Agricultural Improvement Society of Ireland. For the years 1857–8.
tables. 160 pp. Dublin, at the "Farmers' Gazette" Office, 1858
A., D., N.

7752 Atlantic Telegraph Company. Report of the directors to the ordinary general meeting of shareholders, to be held on the 18th day of February, 1858.
tables. 28 pp. London, Royston & Brown, 1858
A.

7753 BAIN, David. (A letter to) his grace, the duke of Buccleuch and Queensberry &c., &c., &c. Governor of the Bank of Scotland.
8 pp. Edinburgh, 1858
A.

7754 ——. A plan for preventing the recurrence of monetary panics similar to those of 1847 and 1857.
part second. 24 pp. London, James, 1858
A.

7755 The Bank Charter Act of 1844/Its theory and practical effects on commerical and monetary transactions/also the evils of the exclusive system of bank management.
table. 52 pp. London: Houlston & Wright, 1858
T.

7756 BAYLISS, Thomas H., and SCOTT, George. An explanation of the life assurance classes, originated by Thomas H. Baylis and George Scott.
tables. 14 pp. [London?, 1858]
T.

7757 BOTTS, ——. Mr. Botts' Address.
40 pp. [no t.p.] n.p., 1858
N.
An address to the Order of United Americans, criticising the U.S. Government's economic policies.

7758 CAHILL, D. W. How can the question of tenant-right be settled?
12 pp. Dublin, Nugent, 1858
A.

7759 CAMPBELL, Norman. Report of the registrar general on the progress and statistics of Victoria from 1851 to 1858. Compiled from authentic official records.
tables. appendix. 46 pp. Melbourne, J. Ferres, 1858
N., T.

7760 CANSDELL, Charles Stuart. A new method of life assurance.
tables. 16 pp. London, C. Hatchett, 1858
T.

7761 CAW, John Young. On banking liability.
28pp. London, E. Wilson, Manchester, Johnson & Rawson, 1858
A.

7762 CLARKE, S. H. The Scinde railway and Indus flotilla companies: their futility and hollowness demonstrated. Also an exposure of the delusion which exists respecting the five per cent guarantee, which insures no dividend whatever to the respective shareholders.
36 pp. London, P. Richardson, 1858
T.

7763 COMBE, George. The currency question considered in relation to the Bank Restriction Act. Revised by the author, with comments upon the present suspension of the Bank Charter Act and remarks upon the bank note question in Scotland.
appendix. tables. 10th ed. 48 pp. London, E. Wilson, Edinburgh, A. & C. Black, 1858
A., T.

7764 COOK, John. The speech in extenso, the substance of which was delivered at the East India-House, 13th March, 1858, by John Cook Esq., one of the proprietors, against the transference of the company to the crown.
24 pp. London, Whittaker, [1858]
T.

7765 COWELL, John Welsford. Further letters on currency, to the right hon. sir F. T. Baring, bart., M.P.
appendix. 58 pp. London, J. Ridgway, 1858
T.

7766 CRAWFURD, John. China and its trade. A paper read by John Crawfurd, F.R.S. to the Philosophical and Literary Society of Leeds, of which he is an honorary member, on Wednesday the 17th November, 1858.
24 pp. London, Reynell, 1858
N.

7767 Currency explosions, their cause, and cure.
16 pp. New York, 1858
N.

7768 DICKSON, Stephen Fox. The case of the spirit grocers of Ireland briefly stated and most respectfully addressed to the right hon. lord Naas, M.P., her majesty's chief secretary of state for Ireland, etc., etc., etc.
12 pp. Dublin, I. & E. MacDonnell, 1858
B.

7769 A discourse upon the obligation of tithe, delivered in the Catholic and Apostolic Church Gordon Square on Tuesday, October 5, 1858.
24 pp. London, Bosworth and Harrison, 1858
T.

7770 DOMER, John. New British gold fields. A guide to British Columbia and Vancouver Island, with coloured map showing the gold and coal fields, collected from authentic sources.
map. table. table of contents. 58 pp. London, Angel, [1858]
N.

7771 EVEREST, George. An address to the proprietors of East India stock.
appendix. 32 pp. London, F. W. Calder, 1858
T.

7772 FAWCETT, John. Letter to the right hon. lord Brougham on his bill to facilitate the transfer of real estate.
14 pp. London, J. Ridgway, 1858
T.

7773 First annual report of the Monkstown and Kingstown Charitable Inquiry Society. Established August 1st, 1857.
20 pp. Dublin, G. Ponsonby, 1858
A.

7774 Financial Reform Tracts. New Series, No. XXIII. To be continued periodically. Governmental model farming: its history, its cost, and its results. By the Liverpool Financial Reform Association.
tables. 32 pp. Liverpool, the Association, London, King, 1858
A., N., T.

7775 FORSTER, William Edward. How we tax India: a lecture on the condition of India under British Rule, more especially as affected by the mode of raising the India revenue: delivered before the Leeds Philosophical & Literary Society, March 30th, 1858.
table. 42 pp. London, A. W. Bennett, [1858]
T.

7776 FREELAND, Humphry William. Church leaseholds. A letter to the earl of Derby.
appendix. 63 pp. 2nd ed. London, J. Ridgway, 1858
T.

7777 FREEMAN, John. A reply to the memorandum of the East-India Company: or, an insight into British India.
70 pp. London, R. Hardwicke, 1858
T.

7778 GALBRAITH, Joseph A. A statement in explanation of evidence given before a committee of the house of commons, relative to the Boyne viaduct.
appendices. 16 pp. Dublin, Gill, 1858
N.

7779 HALL, Edward Hepple. Ho! For the west!! The traveller and emigrants' hand-book to Canada and the northwest of the American union: comprising the states of Illinois, Wisconsin, and Iowa, and the territories of Minnesota, and Kansas; with a description of their climate, resources, and products; and much other useful information compiled from the latest authentic sources, and designed particularly for the use of travellers, emigrants, and others. To which is added, a list of railway stations, routes and distances, stage coaches in connection with the railways, etc.
32 pp. 3rd ed. London, Algar and Street, [etc., etc.], 1858
T.

See 7609

7780 HAMILTON, P. S. Nova-Scotia considered as a field for emigration.
map. 96 pp. London, J. Weale, 1858
T.

7781 HANNAM, William. Proposition for a change in the system of working life assurance societies. Calculated very considerably to promote their extension and usefulness.
8 pp. Manchester, W. Hannam, 1858
T.

7782 HASKINS, Edmund Henry. The problem solved: or, a practicable scheme of decimal coinage for the people. With answers to lord Overstone's questions.
tables. 50 pp. London, W. H. Dalton, 1858
T.

7783 HAYES, James. Irish waste land settlements versus emigration and foreign wild land settlements. Specially addressed to the Poor Law Guardians of Ireland.
tables. 32 pp. Dublin, Kelly, 1858
A., N.

7784 HENNESSY, Henry. On a uniform system of weights, measures and coins for all nations. Published by the International Association for obtaining a uniform decimal system of measures, weights and coins.
30 pp. London, Bell and Daldy, 1858
A., N.

7785 How to abolish slavery in America, and to prevent a cotton famine in England, with remarks upon coolie and African emigration. By a slave-driver.
plate. 16 pp. London, A. W. Bennett, 1858
T.

7786 Incentives to emigration, consisting of a borrowed preface; leaves from an extraordinary black book; parliamentary reports; anonymous letters to the editor of the 'Times;' comments of the 'Spectator' on the ungracious sentiments of an ex-governor general; Mr. John Bright's letter on emigration; letters from Dr. E. Cullen to the compiler on the formation of an Irish colony in the Valle Dupar, Republic of New Granada, South America. By a member of the Universal Institute.
28 pp. Dublin, printed by Mullany, 1858
A.

7787 INCHBALD, John. The Bank Act: what it is and what it does, and the laws which regulate the price of money briefly explained.
24 pp. London, E. Wilson, 1858
A.

7788 International Association for obtaining a uniform decimal system of measures, weights and coins. British branch. Second report of the council adopted by the general meeting, held Feb. 25, 1858, with a statement of receipts and expenditure, the proceedings of the general meeting, a list of contributions, etc.
15 pp. London, the association, 1858
L.

7789 KEMP, Robert. The Thames. Great scheme for profitable investment, metropolitan improvement, and national benefit.
8 pp. London, printed by H. Kemshead, 1858
T.

7790 KINGSMILL, Sir John. Imperialisation without centralisation. Practical suggestions submitted to the Government at various times on several subjects connected with public affairs in Ireland.
table of contents. 88 pp. Dublin, A. Thom, 1858
A.

7791 KINNEAR, John Boyd. A comparison of the bankruptcy systems of England and Scotland with reference to the proposed changes in England: to which is added an abstract of the procedure in Scotland, and glossary of Scottish law terms.
48 pp. London, W. Maxwell, 1858
T.

7792 LAING, Seton. An address to the creditors of Joseph Windle Cole, in reference to the proceedings in bankruptcy arising out of the great city frauds of Cole, Davidson, & Gordon.
appendices. 130 pp. (various paging.) London, the author, 1858
T.

7793 Let every man read. The three social evils of manufacturing towns, and the remedy considered. By a struggling man.
56 pp. London, A. Hall, Virtue, Birmingham, John Whitehouse Showell, 1858
T.

7794 LISTER, John. Suggestions for the improvement of railway property in a letter to the right hon. the chancellor of the exchequer.
table. 16 pp. Edinburgh, J. Menzies, 1858
T.

7795 LLOYD, Edward. The Bank Charter Act cannot be maintained without a relaxing clause. A suggestion addressed to the rt. hon. Sir G. Cornewall Lewis, bart., M.P. Chancellor of the exchequer.
20 pp. London, Effingham, Wilson, 1858
A.

7796 ——. The requirements and resources of the sick poor.
tables. 56 pp. London, Longman, Brown, Green, Longmans, & Roberts, 1858
T.

7797 LOCKE, John. Land Question. Expediency of facilitating the sale and transfer of land in Great Britain. An essay read before the 'Association for promotion of Social Science,' Department of Jurisprudence, Liverpool, October 15th, 1858.
16 pp. Belfast, Reed, 1858
N.

7798 [MILL, John Stuart] Memorandum of the Improvements in the administration of India during the last thirty years and the petition of the East-India Company to Parliament.
table of contents. tables. appendices. 134 pp. London, W. Allen, 1858
N.

7799 MILLER, Thomas. The agricultural and social state of Ireland in 1858, being the results of the experience of Englishmen and Scotchmen who have settled in Ireland in relation to the people, climate, soil, productions, and the progress of agricultural improvement in the country. With an appendix, consisting of letters from Scotch and English proprietors and farmers resident in Ireland.
appendix. 62 pp. Dublin, A. Thom, 1858
A., N., U.

7800 Money, its use and abuse. A summary view of the currency question.
26 pp. London, Bosworth and Harrison, 1858
T.

7801 MORGAN, Henry Lloyd. Personal liabilities of directors of joint-stock companies under the Fraudulent Trustees' Act (20 & 21 Vict. c. 54), with remarks on limited liability.
22 pp. London, E. Wilson, 1858
A.

7802 O'BRIEN, W. The prize essay on canals and canal conveyance for which a premium of £100 was awarded by the Canal association.
tables. appendix. 42 pp. London, J. Weale 1858
T.

7803 Our policy in China, or a glance at the past, present, and future of China, in its foreign relations and commerce.
142 pp. London, Bell and Daldy, 1858
T.

7804 PARKER, Henry Meredith. The empire of the middle classes. Being nos. 1 and 2 of short sermons on Indian texts.
32 pp. London, W. Thacker, 1858
T.

7805 Rail and waterway competition. Pleasing dividends. No reserve fund. Praiseworthy shareholders. Directorial self satisfaction. What happened in England. Audit. Who is to blame? Moral. By Tiresias.
16 pp. Dublin, J. Falconer, McGlashan & Gill, 1858
A., N.

7806 Report of the council of the chamber of commerce of Dublin, to the members of the association, at the annual assembly held on 13th April, 1858.
tables. appendix. 46 pp. Dublin, printed by J. Falconer, 1858
A.

7807 The republic of New Granada as a field for emigration.
tables. 22 pp. Dublin, Mullany, 1858
A., N.

7808 Ross, George. Analysis of the titles to land act. With the act appended.
48 pp. Edinburgh, T. Constable, 1858
T.

7809 [SANDYS, Richard Hill?] Thoughts on the present state and prospects of legal discontent in relation to the registration of titles.
48 pp. London, V. & R. Stevens and G. S. Norton, 1858
T.

7810 SCOTT, John. The recent banking crisis as applicable to the Bank of England, the Western Bank of Scotland, and City of Glasgow Bank.
appendix. tables. 16 pp. London, E. Wilson, 1858
A.

7811 Selections No. II from the public correspondence, petitions and memorials of the British Indian association. Contents: I—A petition relative to the Chowkeedary bill; II—Ditto relative to the lands appropriation bill. III—A memorial for the repeal of the lands' appropriation act. IV—Ditto for the repeal of the Chowkeedary act. V—The reply of the Court of Directors. VI—A petition relative to the cattle trespass bill. VII—Ditto relative to the bill to extend the provisions of regulation VI of 1810 of the Bengal Code. VIII—Ditto relative to the suburbs bill.
40 pp. Calcutta, I. C. Bose, 1858
T.

7812 Seventeenth annual report and transactions of the Society for the promotion and improvement of the growth of flax in Ireland; with an appendix. Annual statement of accounts, and list of subscriptions and donations for the year ending October 31st 1857.
tables. appendix. diagram. 74 pp. Belfast, at 'The Daily Mercury' Office, 1858
N.

7813 Shannon as a Transatlantic packet port. Printed by authority of the Corporation, Chamber of Commerce and Harbour Board of Limerick.
16 pp. Limerick, McKern, 1858
N.

7814 A statement of the claims of the officers of the excise branch of the Inland Revenue to an increase of salary. As presented to members of the house of commons. By a committee of the service.
table. 26 pp. Dublin, J. Falconer, 1858
A.

7815 STOKES, William. Indian Reform Bills; or legislation for India, from 1766 to 1858. Also, an argument for a representative government in India, in a letter to the right hon. B. Disraeli, M.P., chancellor of the exchequer, etc. to which is added an appendix on the present state and commercial importance of the Indian market.
table. appendix. 48 pp. London, A. W. Bennett, 1858
T.

7816 The tax upon paper: the case stated for its immediate repeal.
tables. 48 pp. [London]: Published under the direction of the committee of the newspaper and periodical press association for obtaining the repeal of the paper duty, 1858
T.

7817 Thoughts on the bank charter act; with suggestions for a revised system of convertible and regulated currency. By a student.
54 pp. London, Seeley, Jackson, and Halliday, 1858
T.

7818 TUCKER, Henry. An address upon the 'condition of the agricultural labourer,' by Henry Tucker, delivered at the annual dinner of the Faringdon agricultural library, on the 25th November, 1858. E. M. Atkins, Esq., in the chair and published, in compliance with a request of the committee, and the company present on the occasion.
28 pp. London, Longman, Brown, Green, Longmans & Roberts, Faringdon, T. Knapp, [1858?]
T.

7819 TYLER, J. Talbot. The national annuity fund, a plan for securing annuities to persons in their declining years, or under physical infirmity, founded upon the principle of deferred annuities, but rendered more popular by an easier mode of payment, and provision for other contingencies not contemplated in deferred annuities, with rules and tables.
16 pp. London, J. Teulon, 1858
T.

7820 WALKER, James, and WOLFE, P. Report on Valentia Harbour, as a western packet station. Together with evidences and opinions of various naval and scientific authorities on the same subject.
map. index. 56 pp. London, Cope, 1858
A.

7821 WARMINGTON, R. Railroad mismanagement; its evils and remedy; showing how the dividends of shareholders can be greatly augmented, and railroad property put on a sound and solid basis.
24 pp. London, Ward and Lock, [1858?]
T.

7822 WESTON, H. W. Protection without imprisonment for all embarrassed debtors. Why not? Dedicated by permission to Charles Dickens, Esq.
20 pp. London, W. Freeman, 1858
T.

7823 WHITE, F. Meadows. A report of the cases R. *v.* Goodchild, R. *v.* Lamb, R. *v.* Goodchild and Lamb, R. *v.* Hawkins, recently decided by the court of Queen's Bench, on rating of tithe commutation rent-charge, with an appendix of observations.
tables. 86 pp. London, H. Shaw, 1858
T.

7824 WHITEHEAD, John. Guaranteed securities: their merits as investments considered. Second edition.
tables. 148 pp. London, Effingham Wilson, 1858
T.

7825 WOODS, Joseph. Newfoundland Almanack, for the year of Our Lord 1859, containing astronomical, statistical, commercial, local and general information, derived from the most authentic sources.
tables. table of contents. 68 pp. St. John's, J. Woods, 1858
N.

7826 WORDSWORTH, Charles. The new joint stock company law, [of 1856, 1857, & 1858] with the acts for banking companies, and instructions how to form a company; and herein of the liabilities of persons engaged in so doing.
130 pp. 6th ed. London, H. Shaw, 1858
T.

7827 WRIGLEY, Thomas. Railway management. The official view refuted, being a reply to objections urged against a plan for the government and working of a railway.
44 pp. London, Simpkin, Marshall, 1858
T.

7828 What is the best unit of length? An inquiry, addressed to the international association for obtaining a uniform decimal system of measures, weights, and coins; with answers from the British branch of the association, shewing that the best unit of length is the metre.
tables. 92 pp. London, Bell and Daldy, 1858
T.

1859

7829 An address to the landed gentry of England on the land bills before Parliament. Will you expose your estates to taxation? Will you bar your entails? Will you create a gigantic land speculation, by means of a land register? First part.
22 pp. London, J. R. Smith, 1859
T.

7830 AITKEN, R. Hints, suggestions, and reasons for the provisional adjustment of the church-rate for the reformation of the Church's external administration, and for the union of Church and Dissent. Published by an association of laymen (chiefly for special distribution).
58 pp. London, Longman, Brown, Green, Longmans, & Roberts, 1859
T.

7831 ALDRICH, John Cobbold. Church rates and the parochial system. A pamphlet dedicated to his grace the duke of Marlborough. With appendix containing copious references to the minutes of evidence brought before the house of commons in 1851, and the house of lords in 1859.
table. appendices. 52 pp. London, J. Masters, 1859
T.

7832 Annual report and transactions of the Royal Agricultural Improvement Society of Ireland for the years 1858–59.
tables; plans (of houses). 88 pp. Dublin, at the office of the 'Farmers' Gazette', 1859
D.

7833 ARNOTT, Sir John. The investigations into the condition of the children in the Cork Workhouse, with an analysis of the evidence.
tables. appendix. 68 pp. Cork, Brothers, 1859
A., N.

7834 Articles of association of the Connorree Mining Company (limited) being the rules and resolutions for the government and regulation of said company.
30 pp. Dublin, A. Thom, 1859
A.

7835 BAKER, Robert. The Factory Acts made easy: or how to work the law without the risk of penalties. Including the Acts of 1853 and 1856. New ed. carefully revised.
tables. illustration. 116 pp. Leeds, Alice Mann, London, Simpkin, Marshall, [1859]
T.

7836 BALDWIN, Thomas. Agricultural education in Ireland. To Richard Deasy, Esq. M.P.
12 pp. Dublin, J. Falconer, 1859
T.

7837 Bankruptcy law reform. A letter to Sir Richard Bethell, Knt., her majesty's attorney-general. By a registrar of the court of bankruptcy, London.
20 pp. London, V. & R. Stevens and G. S. North, 1859
T.

7838 BLAIR, Frank P., jr. Destiny of the races of this continent. An address delivered before the Mercantile Library Association of Boston, Massachusetts, on the 26th of January, 1859.
appendix. 38 pp. Washington D.C., Buell & Blanchard, 1859
N.

7839 BRIGGS, Frederick. A plan for the economical management of the Mutual Life Assurance Association system.
table. 8 pp. London, the author, [1859?]
T.

7840 BROWNING, Reuben. The finances of Great Britain considered. Comprising an examination of the property and income tax, and succession duty act of 1853. Part I.
tables. 36 pp. London, P. Richardson, 1859
T.

7841 CANSDELL, Charles Stuart. A new method of banking, based on government securities.
tables. 66 pp. London, Mann, 1859
T.

7842 CAYLEY, George John. The working classes; their interest in administrative, financial and electoral reform.
38 pp. London, D. F. Oakey, 1859
T.

7843 Church rates. The present state of the Church rate question, with an authentic report of the lords' debate, July 8, 1858. And an appendix. Published under the sanction of the committee of laymen.
tables. appendices. 98 pp. London, Seeley, Jackson, and Halliday; [etc., etc.,] 1859
T.

7844 CLARKE, Henry. Penny banks: their formation and management.
index. tables. appendix. diagram. 26 pp. Southampton, Forbes & Bennet, London, R. Groombridge, 1859
N., T.

7845 CLARKE, J. Erskine. Plain papers on the social economy of the people. No. II. Penny banks.
tables. 46 pp. London, Bell & Daldy, 1859
N.

7846 COLLINS, J. J. Pawnbrokers' charges. Important to the public. By an omission of the legislature, for protection of the indigent, a calculation of interest, established by the statute. With observations on a few of the sections affecting the needy, exposing illegal and unauthorized charges, producing, in the aggregate, a vast fund raised by unlawful

exactions. Being an antidote to counteract the illegal charges made by many pawnbrokers in town and country. Dedicated to the indigent.
tables. 28 pp. London, 1859
                                                    T.

7847 [CRANE, John.] Remarks on coinage; with an explanation of a decimal coinage proposed to be introduced into this country. By 'Jacia'.
tables. appendix. 24 pp. London, Simpkin, Marshall, Birmingham, R. Matthison, 1859
                                                    T.

7848 [DANIEL, Evan.] A prize essay on the reduction of the hours of labour, as proposed by the nine-hours movement.
32 pp. London, Sampson Low, 1859
                                                    T.

7849 DRUMMOND, Henry. A letter to the working classes in trades and manufactures.
30 pp. London, Bosworth and Harrison, 1859
                                                    T.

7850 ENDERBY, Charles. Redress of national grievances, whereby every man will obtain full and constant employment, with liberal support to the aged and infirm.
106 pp. London, P. Richardson, 1859
                                                    T.

7851 The experiences of a landholder and indigo planter in Eastern Bengal.
22 pp. Aberdeen, J. Smith, London, Simpkin, Marshall, 1859
                                                    T.

7852 First report of the committee of the drapers' Early Closing Association.
16 pp. Dublin, Bowles, 1859
                                                    A.

7853 GIRDLESTONE, Charles. The questions of the day by the creature of an hour or social subjects discussed on scripture principles; new ed.
198 pp. London, Longman, Brown, Green, Longmans, & Roberts and W. H. Dalton, [1859]
                                                    T.

7854 Harbour of Refuge on the north-east coast of Ireland; a short view of the claims of the different positions for government works, as asylum harbours for ships in distress. By the author of 'The deep sea and coast fisheries of Ireland.'
map. 16 pp. Dublin, Hodges and Smith, 1859
                                                    A.

7855 HINCKS, Sir Francis. The results of negro emancipation. A speech delivered at a public meeting, held in London, August 1, 1859, the twenty-fifth anniversary of the abolition of slavery by the parliament of Great Britain; the right hon. lord Brougham in the chair.
30 pp. London, W. M. Watts, 1859
                                                    B.

7856 HOBBS, W. Fisher. Landlord, tenant, and labourer, in a series of papers affecting their interests, (as read before the members of the central farmers' club).
52 pp. London, J. Ridgway, 1859
                                                    T.

7857 HOLROYD, Edward Dundas. Retrograde legislation in bankruptcy, as it affects the public through the official assignees. A letter addressed to George Carr Glyn, Esq., M.P. by Edward Dundas Holroyd, M.A. of Gray's Inn, Barrister-at-law.
16 pp. London, V. & R. Stevens and G. S. Norton, 1859
                                                    T.

7858 How to mismanage a bank: a review of the Western Bank of Scotland.
tables. 48 pp. Edinburgh, A. and C. Black, J. Maclaren, 1859
                                                    T.

7859 The Irremovable Poor Bill.
table. no. t.p. 8 pp. [1859?]
                                                    T.

7860 JAMIESON, Robert. Commerce with Africa. The inefficacy of treaties for the suppression of the African slave trade, and their influences on British commercial interests in Africa, with suggestions for the development of the commercial resources of Western Central Africa; and a short notice of the kingdom of Benin.
map. appendix. 46 pp. 2nd ed. London, Effingham Wilson, 1859
                                                    T.

7861 JONES, W. Henry. A letter to the right hon. the earl of Shaftesbury on the question of 'church rates', chiefly as it concerns our populous parishes.
28 pp. London, T. Hatchard, 1859
                                                    T.

7862 LAW, William John. Comments on the Bankruptcy and Liquidation Act, 1858.
56 pp. London, V. & R. Stevens and G. S. Norton, 1859
                                                    T.

7863 LAWRANCE, Edward. Bankruptcy-law reform. A letter to the lord chancellor, containing practical suggestions on the law of bankruptcy.
14 pp. London, Hamilton, Adams, 1859
                                                    T.

7864 LEVINGE, W. J. Reasons for extending the land improvement act to improve the Irish labourers' dwellings. Addressed to the earl of Bandon.
16 pp. Dublin, Hodges & Smith, 1859
                                                    N.

7865 London v. New York. By an English workman.
96 pp. London, Bosworth and Harrison, 1859
                                                    T.

7866 MACCARTHY, John George. Letters on land tenures.
index. 28 pp. Cork, Mulcahy, 1859
                                                    N.

7867 MACKENZIE, James Thompson. The trade and commerce of India: being a paper read by J. T. Mackenzie, before the British Association, at Aberdeen, in September, 1859. With an appendix, since added, containing a few remarks on the land tenures, and general government of India, and the question of an imperial guarantee.
tables. appendix. 48 pp. London, Jones & Causton, 1859
                                                    T.

7868 MORTIMER, R. Suggestions for the gradual payment of the national debt.
8 pp. n.p., 1859

N.

7869 NEATE, Charles. Two lectures on the currency, delivered in the year 1858.
48 pp. Oxford and London, J. H. and J. Parker, 1859

T.

7870 The Ottoman bank. An address to the shareholders on its present position.
52 pp. London, Baily, 1859

T.

7871 PHELAN, Denis. Reform of the poor law system in Ireland; or facts and observations on the inadequacy of the existing system of poor relief.
table of contents. tables. 72 pp. Dublin, A. Thom, 1859

A., N.

7872 Philanthropy versus Phelanthropy; or, a short reply to the observations of Denis Phelan, M.D., on reform of the poor laws in Ireland. By a Union clerk.
tables. 14 pp. Dublin, A. Thom, 1859

A.

7873 PIESSE, Charles. Sketch of the loan-fund system of Ireland, and instructions for the formation of a new society.
tables. 56 pp. Dublin, Webb, 1859

A.

First published 1841; see 5376.

7874 PLUMMER, John. Dedicated to the members of the London building trades. Reduction of the hours of labour, as proposed by the nine hours movement. A reply to the prize essay of the united building trades. To which are appended, some remarks on the contemplated strike to effect the same.
20 pp. London, W. Tweedie, 1859

T.

7875 ——. Strikes: their causes and their evils; especially with regard to the machine question in Northamptonshire, Staffordshire and other places.
16 pp. London, W. Tweedie, 1859

T.

7876 The present state of the church rate question exhibited, in an abstract of the evidence contained in the report of a select committee of the house of lords, appointed to enquire into the present operation of the law and practice respecting the assessment and the levy of church rates, and which was ordered to be printed, Aug. 5, 1859.
64 pp. London, F. & J. Rivington, 1859

T.

7877 Prospectus of the Portadown penny savings bank.
4 pp. Portadown, Farrell, 1859

N.

7878 PRYME, George. A syllabus of a course of lectures on the principles of political economy.
30 pp. 4th ed. Cambridge, Deighton, Bell, London, Bell and Daldy, 1859

T.

7879 Report of the council of the chamber of commerce of Dublin to the members of the association, at the annual assembly, held on 26th May, 1859.
appendix. table. 34 pp. Dublin, J. Falconer, 1859

A.

7880 Report of the directors of the National Bank presented at the twenty-fourth annual meeting of proprietors held at the Head Office, 13, Old Broad Street, London, on Tuesday, 24th May, 1859.
tables. 8 pp. [London?] 1859

N.

7881 Report of the tithe redemption trust for the church in England and Wales for the year 1859.
tables. 24 pp. London, F. & J. Rivington, [1859]

T.

7882 Reports of the several departments of the city government of Portland for the municipal year 1858–9.
tables. index. 104 pp. Portland, Maine, at the Advertiser Office, 1859

N.

7883 SAVILE, Bourchier Wrey. A letter to the right hon. viscount Palmerston, M.P., K.G., G.C.B., first lord of the treasury, on church rates, with a proposal for a suitable equivalent in the event of their being totally abolished.
table. 30 pp. London, Longman, Green, Longmans, and Roberts, 1859

T.

7884 SEYMOUR, William Digby. The wail of Montrose; or the wrongs of shipping.
tables. 72 pp. London, Effingham Wilson and W. Benning, 1859

T.

——. 72 pp. 2nd ed., London, Effingham Wilson and W. Benning, 1859

T.

7885 SIKES, C. W. Post Office Savings Banks. A letter to the right honourable W. E. Gladstone, M.P. chancellor of the exchequer.
tables. 18 pp. London, R. Groombridge, 1859

T.

7886 SIMPSON, John Hawkins. 'Men groan from out of the city': robbed by laws of the rich.
tables. 46 pp. Edinburgh, Thomas C. Jack, London, Hamilton, Adams, [etc., etc.], 1859

T.

7887 Social *versus* political reform. The sin of great cities; or, the great social evil a national sin. Illustrated by a brief enquiry into its extent, causes, effects, and existing remedies.
60 pp. London, A. W. Bennett, 1859

T.

7888 STANSFELD, Hamer. Outline of a system of direct taxation, for superseding customs and excise duties, and establishing perfect freedom of trade. A letter to the president and council of the Liverpool Financial Reform Association.
tables. 24 pp. London, Simpkin, Marshall, [etc.], [1859]

T.

7889 STEPHENSON, Sir Macdonald. Railways in Turkey. Remarks upon the practicability and advantage of railway communication in European and Asiatic Turkey.
tables. map. 96 pp. London, J. Weale, 1859
T.

7890 TORRENS, Robert R. The English law of property its principles and consequences contrasted with the South Australian system of conveyancing by registration of title; description of the method in which transactions in land are conducted under the real property act, now in successful operation in that colony, with instructions for the guidance of parties dealing, illustrated by copies of the books and forms in use in the lands titles office, by Robert R. Torrens, to which is added, the South Australian real property act as amended in the sessions of 1858, with a copious index by Henry Gawler, Esq., barrister, solicitor to the lands titles commissioners.
tables. 144 pp. Adelaide, printed at the Register and Observer General printing offices, 1859
T.

7891 ——. The South Australian system of conveyancing by registration of title, with instructions for the guidance of parties dealing, illustrated by copies of the books and forms in use in the lands titles office, by Robert R. Torrens, to which is added, the South Australian real property act as amended in the sessions of 1858, with a copious index by Henry Gawler, Esq., barrister, solicitor to the lands titles commissioners.
tables. 144 pp. Adelaide, printed at the Register and Observer General Printing Offices, 1859
T.

7892 WARD, Elijah. Atrato Ship Canal. Its importance to the commerce of the United States and other nations. Speech delivered in the house of representatives, February 15th, 1859.
appendix. tables. 16 pp. n.p., [1859]
N.

7893 WORDSWORTH, Charles. The new joint stock company law, [of 1856, 1857, and 1858] with all the statutes, and instructions how to form a company; and herein of the liabilities of persons engaged in so doing.
tables. 158 pp. London, H. Shaw, 1859
T.

1860

7894 An account of the Chorleywood Association for the improvement of the labouring classes.
16 pp. London, Longman, Green, Longman and Roberts, 1860
T.

7895 American Anti-Slave society: American Anti-Slave tracts. No. 4. New Series. The new 'Reign of Terror' in the slaveholding States, for 1859–60.
144 pp. New York, the society, 1860
N.

7896 American securities. Practical hints on the tests of stability and profit. For the guidance and warning of British investors. By an Anglo-American. Second edition revised, with illustrative map.
tables. appendix. 48 pp. London, Mann Nephews, W. P. Metchim, 1860
T.

7897 BALDWIN, Thomas. Agricultural Essays. No. 2. Manures.
tables. 32 pp. Dublin, Robertson, 1860
D.

7898 The bank of England and the discount houses. By A. B. C.
8 pp. London, P. Richardson, 1860
T.

7899 [BARTHOLOMEW, John.] The census and the church rate: a charge delivered by the venerable the archdeacon of Barnstable.
table. appendix. 22 pp. London, J. Murray, 1860
T.

7900 BELL, Henry Glassford. On the bankruptcy law of England and Scotland. Also, expenses in bankruptcy, and the best means of lessening these consistent with security, by George Auldjo Esson.
tables. 44 pp. Glasgow, J. Maclehose, [etc., etc.], 1860
T.

7901 BICKERSTETH, Robert, Bishop of Ripon. The physical condition of the people and its bearing upon their social and moral welfare.
20 pp. London, Hamilton, Adams, 1860
T.

7902 BOHN, Henry George. The paper duty considered in reference to its action on the literature and trade of Great Britain: showing that its abolition on the terms now proposed in parliament would be prejudicial to both. In two letters to a public journal.
12 pp. London, H. G. Bohn, 1860
T.

7903 BROWNING, Reuben. The finances of Great Britain considered. Examination of the land tax. Part II.
tables. 60 pp. London, P. Richardson, 1860
T.

7904 The budget and the income-tax.
tables. 12 pp. London, T. Hatchard, 1860
T.

7905 BURN, Charles. On the construction of horse railways for branch lines in England and the colonies.
tables. appendix. illusts. 62 pp. London, J. Weale, 1860
T.

7906 BUSTEED, Thomas M. Trades' Unions, combinations and strikes.
42 pp. London, V. & R. Stevens, W. Walker, Dublin, McGlashan and Gill, 1860
A., E., N., T.

7907 CAIRNES, John Elliott. Political Economy as a branch of general education; being an inaugural lecture delivered in Queen's College, Galway, in Michaelmas term, 1859.
38 pp. London, J. W. Parker, Dublin, McGee, 1860
A., N.

7908 CLARKE, John Erskine. Plain papers on the social economy of the people. No. IV. The children of the people.
table. 34 pp. London, Bell and Daldy, 1860
T.

7909 CLIBBORN, Edward. The Dublin water question. The springs of Dublin and fountains of Ath Cliath and Dublinia, attributed to St. Patrick: proposed as an auxiliary to the present and any future supply of water to the city. With remarks, historical, statistical, and economical, in relation to the further utilisation of the Liffey water.
diag. appendix. 50 pp. Dublin, McGlashan & Gill, 1860
G., N.

7910 The connexion between industry and wealth.
26 pp. London, Saunders, Otley, 1860
T.

7911 [COTTON, Sir William J. R.] Smash: a sketch of the times, past, present, and again to come. Smash—smashing—smashed, an active verb (*very*). Kite flying—gives to airy nothings local habitation (*value*) and a name.
38 pp. London, Houlston and Wright, 1860
T.

7912 COURTNEY, Leonard Henry. Direct taxation: an inquiry.
tables. 36 pp. London, Bell and Daldy, 1860
T.

7913 Debt and taxation of Ireland.
34 pp. Dublin, W. B. Kelly, 1860
T.

7914 The defects of the Grand Jury Laws and their proper remedies pointed out. By a County Officer.
32 pp. Dublin, Hodges and Smith, 1860
N.

7915 DYER, ——. A lecture on the state of some of the charities of Belfast.
28 pp. Belfast, Johnson, 1860
N.

7916 EDEN, Ashley. Evidence of the honourable Ashley Eden taken before the Indigo Commission, sitting in Calcutta.
40 pp. Calcutta, C. H. Manuel, 1860
N., T.

7917 Extracts from the records of the government of Bengal, No. XXXIII. Containing the opinions of several officers of government in various districts of Bengal on the indigo planting system.
64 pp. Calcutta, C. H. Manuel, 1860
T.

7918 FENDALL, James. Exemption from the payments of church rates on personal grounds considered in a letter to J. G. Hubbard, Esq., M.P. Together with some suggestions for the amendment of the laws on this subject.
20 pp. Cambridge & London, Macmillan, 1860
T.

7919 A few questions and answers on the science of exchanges. By an M.A. of Trinity College, Oxford.
52 pp. London, J. Ridgway, 1860
T.

7920 GIBBON, Alexander. The income tax; its causes and incidence: showing by analysis that it is a land-tax, a house-tax, a tax upon commodities, and a repudiation of public-debt.
tables. tables in appendices. 64 pp. London, T. Hatchard, 1860
T.

7921 ——. Remarks on the report of July 1858, of the select committee of the house of commons on the Bank Acts; on the passage in that report on seignorage on coinage of gold; on the circulating-medium of the United Kingdom; and on the policy and expediency of the establishment by law of a national bank.
appendix. 64 pp. London, T. Hatchard, 1860
T.

The appendix takes the form of a supplementary pamphlet entitled *On the coins and on seignorage on the gold coins of the realm.*

7922 Grand trunk railway of Canada. Might it not pay better?
16 pp. London, P. Richardson, 1860
T.

7923 HALE, William Hale, archdeacon of London. An address to the clergy of the Archdeaconry of London, at the annual visitation, May 23, 1860, on the subject of church rates: with a supplement and documents illustrative of the Bishops Burton church rate case, 44 Ed. III., A.D. 1370.
46 pp. London, F. & J. Rivington, 1860
T.

7924 HEWITT, William. A code of laws, containing abstracts from Acts of Parliament, and original rules arranged expressly for the permanent endowment of the 'Ancient Blue' friendly society, North Walsham, Norfolk.
tables. 16 pp. 2nd ed. London, Jarrold, 1860
T.

7925 ——, ed. Rules of the Ancient Blue friendly society, North Walsham, Norfolk. Certified by John Tidd Pratt, Esq., registrar general: being the sequel to the North Walsham 'Code of Laws', for the permanent endowment of friendly societies. Entered at Stationers' hall.
tables. 22 pp. Norwich, Jarrold, 1860
T.

7926 HILL, George. Vital statistics of Stirling, and some lessons which they teach.
tables. 30 pp. Edinburgh, Sutherland & Knox, Stirling, R. S. Shearer, 1860
T.

7927 HODGSON, William Ballantyne. Two lectures on the conditions of health and wealth educationally considered. appendix. 68 pp. Edinburgh, J. Gordon, London, Hamilton, Adams, 1860

T.

7928 HOLLAND, Thomas Erskine. The advantages and disadvantages of charitable endowments, especially for purposes of education. A prize essay read in the theatre, Oxford, June 20th, 1860. 36 pp. Oxford, T. and G. Shrimpton, 1860

T.

7929 HOPLEY, Thomas. Wrongs which cry for redress. A letter to the men and women of the United Kingdom. Written with a view to the formation of a popular opinion upon solemnly momentous questions. 42 pp. London, Houlston and Wright, [etc., etc.], 1860

A.

Refers to factory conditions and the employment of women.

7930 HUGHES, Thomas. Account of the lock-out of engineers, &c. 1851–2. Prepared for the National Association for the promotion of social science, at the request of the committee of trade societies. table. appendices. 48 pp. Cambridge & London, Macmillan, 1860

T.

7931 HUNTER, Sylvester Joseph. The Act to further amend the law of property (23 & 24 Vict. c. 38), with introductions and practical notes, and with further notes on 22 & 23 Vict. c. 35. index. 46 pp. London, Butterworths, Dublin, Hodges & Smith, 1860

T.

7932 ——. Observations on real property law reform. 20 pp. London, Butterworths, 1860

T.

7933 Ireland: her landlords, her people and their homes. By an Irish landlord. 108 pp. Dublin, G. Herbert, 1860

U.

7934 The Irish question. Translated from the French by J. P. L. 56 pp. Dublin, A. M. Sullivan, 1860

P., T.

Possibly John P. Leonard?

7935 JONES, G. W. Life assurance, 'What it is, what it ought to be, and how to make it so'. A lecture by G. W. Jones delivered at Exeter Hall, Strand, on Wednesday, May 16th, 1860. tables. 48 pp. London, Davies, [1860]

T.

7936 The labour question in the West Indies. Three letters from Baptist Noel, Esq. (Son of the hon. and rev. Baptist Noel,) and also, extracts from the correspondent of the New York Times. 40 pp. Birmingham, Hudson, [1860]

T.

7937 The lace trade and the factory act. Reprinted from the 'New Quarterly Review'. Revised and enlarged. 34 pp. 3rd edition. London, R. Hardwicke, [1860]

T.

7938 LANE, C. B. Railway communication in London and the Thames embankment. 24 pp. 2nd ed. London, J. Ridgway, 1860

N., T.

7939 LEVINGE, William. The agricultural statistics of Ireland (1860) considered; in a letter addressed to his excellency the earl of Carlisle. 8 pp. Dublin, Hodges & Smith, 1860

N.

7940 M'ALEER, John. The social condition of the population of Ireland from the year 1850: their progressive prosperity. Illustrated by statistics and three beautifully engraved union maps, in four colours, exhibiting the density of the population, the relative valuation of property and the pressure of distress. tables. maps. 40 pp. Dublin, A. Thom, 1860

E., T.

7941 McCULLOCH, John Ramsay. An article, practical and theoretical, on taxation. Written for the eighth edition of the Encyclopaedia Britannica. tables. 38 pp. Edinburgh, A. and C. Black, 1860

T.

7942 MACLEAN, Alexander Walker. Observations on the fundamental principles of monetary circulation: and the necessity for a national deposit bank of issue. tables. appendix. 84 pp. 6th ed. Glasgow, R. Weir, 1860

T.

7943 MACPHERSON, Alexander. Report of a committee of the working-classes of Edinburgh on the present overcrowded and uncomfortable state of their dwelling-houses. appendices, Plan. 40 pp. Edinburgh, Paton & Ritchie, 1860

T.

7944 MARRIOTT, William Thackeray. Some real wants and some legitimate claims of the working classes. 32 pp. London, George Manwaring, 1860

T.

7945 MAXWELL, Sir John, bart. True reform: or character a qualification for the franchise. appendix. tables. 50 pp. Edinburgh, T. Constable, London, Hamilton, Adams, 1860

T.

7946 Memorandum and articles of association of the National Credit and Exchange Company (Limited). Incorporated 17th April, 1860. 40 pp. n.p., [1860?]

T.

7947 [MUIR, Francis.] Property and income tax tables. By a surveyor of taxes, 1857–61. tables. 16 pp. Edinburgh, A. & C. Black, Glasgow, Thomas Murray, 1860

T.

7948 NAPER, James Lenox William. Observations on our social condition; addressed to the members of the Irish Farmers' Club.
appendix. 22 pp. Dublin, McGlashan & Gill, 1860
N.

7949 ———. To the tenant farmers, land stewards, and others superintending the work of the labouring classes.
16 pp. Dublin, McGlashan & Gill, 1860
N.

7950 NEALE, Edward Vansittart. The co-operator's handbook, containing the laws relating to a company of limited liability, with model articles of association, suitable for co-operative purposes.
tables. 32 pp. London, G. Holyoake, 1860
T.

7951 NEATE, Charles. Two lectures on the history and conditions of landed property. Being the first of a series delivered in the years 1859–60, in the University of Oxford.
34 pp. Oxford & London, J. H. & J. Parker, 1860
T.

7952 NEWMAN, Charles. On the importance of a legislative enactment, uniting the interest of landlord and tenant, to facilitate the culture of the land, and promote an increase of food and employment for the millions. Third edition, revised and enlarged.
table. 88 pp. London, J. Ridgway, 1860
T.

7953 OSBORNE, R. W. The landlord and tenant Acts of the last session, with introduction, practical observations, and a copious index.
appendix. index. 144 pp. Dublin, McGlashan and Gill, 1860
N.

7954 Papers relating to the case of the journeymen bakers published for the information of the clergymen, merchants and citizens, who have joined in the requisition to the lord mayor of Dublin, to convene a meeting to consider their case.
table of contents. 24 pp. Dublin, J. Falconer, 1860
N.

7955 Penny Savings Banks for Ireland. Their nature and advantages, with suggestions for their formation and management. By A Manager.
table of contents. tables. appendix. 46 pp. Monaghan, Robinson, 1860
N.

7956 Portadown Loan Co. Limited. Copy memorandum, articles of association, and extracts 19 & 20 Victoria, Chapter 47. Dated 25th May, 1860.
26 pp., Portadown, at the 'Portadown News' office, 1860
N.

7957 PORTER, H. W. An essay on life assurance: being a popular exposition of the subject, and a plea for its more general adoption.
16 pp. London, C. & E. Layton, 1860
T.

7958 La question Irlandaise.
32 pp. Paris, E. Dentu, 1860
T.

7959 Report of the tithe redemption trust for the church in England and Wales, for the year 1860.
tables. 24 pp. London, F. & J. Rivington, 1860
T.

7960 Report of the workhouse visiting society upon the proposed industrial home for young women and the correspondence with the poor law board.
appendix. 16 pp. London, Longman, Brown, Green, Longman & Roberts, 1860
T.

7961 Reports of Sir John MacNeill and Messrs. Barton and Hawkshaw, to the board of directors of the Dublin and Belfast junction railway company.
18 pp. Dublin, A. Thom, 1860
N.

7962 The reviewer reviewed: in an answer to the Edinburgh review, on 'British Taxation'.
tables. 84 pp. London, Routledge, Warne, and Routledge, 1860
T.

7963 RITHERDON, North. Savings banks, as they are, and as they ought to be; with a proposal for the establishment of an institution wherein the prudent may invest on deposit their savings with an absolute security.
12 pp. London, Blades, East and Blades, 1860
T.

7964 Ross, Malcolm. An address to trades' unionists, on the question of strikes.
tables. 26 pp. London, W. Tweedie, [1860]
T.

7965 [ROY, Henry.] The stock exchange; strictures on the evidence in the report of the royal commission of inquiry into the corporation of the city of London, on the regulation of brokers and stock brokers, and the proposed repeal of Sir John Barnard's act.
36 pp. London, Houlston and Wright, 1860
T.

7966 SANDFORD, John. The church rate and the census. A charge addressed to the clergy and churchwardens of the Archdeaconry of Coventry, at the visitations held at Birmingham, Coventry, and Southam, in June 1860.
32 pp. Birmingham, W. J. Sackett, London, J. Masters, 1860
T.

7967 Selections from papers on indigo cultivation in lower Bengal, with an introduction and a few notes by a ryot. No. II.
172 pp. Calcutta, C. H. Manuel, 1860
T.

7968 Sixty-fourth half yearly report of the directors of the City of Dublin Steam Packet Company. Established in 1828, and empowered by Act of Parliament in 1828.
12 pp. Dublin, 1860
A.

7969 SMEE, William Ray. A proposal to increase the smaller salaries under government.
tables. appendix. 32 pp. [London], Pelham Richardson, [1860]

T.

7970 Some thoughts of an octogenarian upon public matters.
20 pp. London, Hookham, 1860

T.

Including emancipation and employment of women.

7971 STANSFELD, Hamer. Money and the money market explained and the future rate of discount considered. With an appeal to Richard Cobden, Esq., M.P. & John Bright, Esq., M.P., to fulfil their great mission, by procuring from the legislature, free trade in sound money. Also, the correspondence with the honourable Amasa Walker, late secretary of state for Massachusetts, on monetary panics.
40 pp. London, Simpkin, Marshall, Leeds, Webb, Millington, [1860]

T.

7972 ——. A plan for a national bank of issue; whereby the convertibility of the bank note into gold will be made more secure than at present; a revenue of upwards of £1,000,000 obtained, and monetary panics prevented: respectfully submitted to the consideration of chambers of commerce and the nation.
14 pp. London, Simpkin, Marshall, Leeds, Webb, Millington, [1860]

T.

7973 STEPHENSON, Nash. On benefit societies. A paper read before the National association for the promotion of social science, (President right hon. lord Brougham,) at their third annual meeting, Bradford, 1859.
tables. 12 pp. London, R. Groombridge, Birmingham, W. J. Sackett, [etc.], 1860

T.

7974 Strikes and the rights of labour. By a Conservative.
16 pp. London, Houlston & Wright, 1860

T.

7975 TAYLOR, George, (continued by). Pyne's table, showing the value of tithe rent charges for the year 1860. To which is added, another table showing the extent of the yearly fluctuation in the prices of wheat, barley, and oats, since 1835.
8 pp. London, H. Shaw, 1860

T.

7976 TREVELYAN, Sir Charles Edward. Statement by Sir Charles Trevelyan of the circumstances connected with his recall from the government of Madras.
tables. appendix. 58 pp. London, Longman, Green, Longman and Roberts, 1860

T.

7977 TYLER, J. Talbot. Christian finance; or, the church's exchequer augmented, so as to raise funds for the evangelization of the world, upon a plan both easy and practicable.
table. 12 pp. London, T. Ward, [1860]

T.

7978 WALKER, James. Remarks addressed to the landlords and tenant farmers of Ireland.
12 pp. Belfast, printed by the Ulster printing company, 1860

N., R.

7979 Why did you let the cat out of the bag? Four letters to the political dissenters of England, on their proposed abolition of church-rates and church property. By Philip Plainspoken.
table. 56 pp. Oxford & London, J. H. and J. Parker, 1860

T.

7980 WILSON, James. Financial measures for India. Speech of the right hon. James Wilson, delivered before the legislative council of Calcutta on the 18th February, 1860.
44 pp. London, W. H. Allen, 1860

T.

7981 WORDSWORTH, Charles. The new Joint Stock Company Law, [of 1856, 1857, and 1858,] with all the statutes, and instructions how to form a company; and herein of the liabilities of persons engaged in so doing; also remarks on the French Association, La Société en Commandite.
tables. 165 pp. 8th ed. London, Shaw and Sons, 1860

T.

1861

7982 ABRAHALL, Bennet Hoskyns. Reform of the laws relating to bankruptcy and insolvency. A second letter to Sir Richard Bethell, knt., M.P., her majesty's attorney-general.
50 pp. London, V. & R. Stevens, 1861

T.

7983 ANDREWS, William A. Remarks on the formation and progress of the Royal Irish Fisheries Company, with notes on trawling on the west coast and its effects, and on the ling and cod fisheries of Ireland, to which is added 'Notes on trawling on the east coast of Ireland'.
plate. table of contents. tables. 66 pp. Dublin, Browne and Nolan, 1861

N.

7984 Annual report and transactions of the Royal Agricultural Society of Ireland for the years 1860–61.
tables. plans [of houses]. 40 pp. Dublin, at the office of the 'Farmers' Gazette', 1861

D.

7985 ARCHBOLD, John Frederick. The statutes 24 & 25 Victoria, cc. 55, 76, 59, relating to the irremovability of paupers from unions; to the passing of paupers to Ireland; and to vaccination: with notes.
54 pp. London, H. Shaw, 1861.

T.

7986 ARCHER, Hannah. A scheme for befriending orphan pauper girls.
appendix. 16 pp. London, Longman, Green, Longman and Roberts, 1861

T.

7987 BAKER, Robert. New edition. Carefully revised. The factory acts made easy: or, how to work the law without the risk of penalties. Including the acts of 1853 and 1856. Entered at Stationers' hall.
illustrations. tables. 116 pp. Leeds, Alice Mann, London, Simpkin, Marshall, [c. 1861]
                                                                    T.

7988 BALDWIN, Thomas. Handbook to the model farm, Glasnevin, and of agricultural education in Ireland.
plan, tables. illustrations. 80 pp. 2nd ed. Dublin, McGlashan and Gill [etc., etc.], 1861
                                                                    N.

7989 BENNETT, William J. E. Why church rates should be abolished.
70 pp. London, Whittaker, 1861
                                                                    T.

7990 BENSON, Robert. Indian resources applied to the development of India; in letters addressed to the right honourable Sir Charles Wood, bart., M.P., secretary of state for India, his grace the duke of Sutherland, and the honourable Arthur F. Kinnaird, M.P.
32 pp. London, Smith, Elder & Co., 1861
                                                                    T.

7991 BOHN, Henry George. The paper duty considered in reference to its action on the literature and trade of Great Britain; showing that its abolition on the terms now proposed in parliament would be prejudicial to both. In letters addressed to the public journals. Third edition, containing four additional letters.
30 pp. London, H. G. Bohn, 1861
                                                                    T.

7992 BOOTH, Henry. The struggle for existence; a lecture addressed to the working classes. Delivered at the school room at the Hope Street church, Liverpool, on Friday, 23rd November, 1860.
table. 32 pp. London, E. Whitfield, Liverpool, H. Young, 1861
                                                                    T.

7993 BOUVERIE, P. Pleydell. Vindication of a churchman for desiring the abolition of church rates, shewing how the legitimate object in levying church rates is, and may be supplied.
table. 12 pp. London, 1861
                                                                    T.

7994 BRICKDALE, Matthew Inglett Fortescue. A supplement to the leases and sales of settled estates act, (19 & 20 Victoria, Cap. 120), containing the amending act, 21 & 22 Victoria, Cap. 77, and additional notes.
77 pp. London, V. & R. Stevens [etc.], 1861
                                                                    T.

7995 British settlers in India. [copy] [sic] memorial delivered to the secretary of state for India in answer to a minute by the lieut.-governor of Bengal, shewing the fallacy of the statements and calculations contained in that minute, and setting forth the true present condition of British settlers in Bengal.
appendices. 82 pp. London, J. Ridgway, 1861
                                                                    T.

7996 Church rates and convocation. A letter to his grace the lord archbishop of Canterbury, in which is shown reform of convocation might be made the basis of a settlement of the church-rate question. By a clergyman.
26 pp. London, R. Hardwicke, 1861
                                                                    T.

7997 CLARKSON, Samuel. Church rates, [in] lectures on voluntaryism; delivered in the Mechanics' Institution, Manchester.
30 pp. Manchester, J. Heywood, London, Simpkin, Marshall, [1861]
                                                                    T.

7998 COLWELL, Charles. Fiery facts: or, the city coal tax exposed! Being a new year's gift to the corporation of the city of London; with suggestions to ameliorate the social condition of coal-miners and their families.
tables. 40 pp. London, Effingham Wilson, 1861
                                                                    T.

7999 The cotton question: some remarks, with extracts from pamphlets on the subject; and Mr. Bazley's paper on cotton statistics, read at the meeting of the British Association, Manchester, Sept. 6, 1861; also, the Indian finance minister's speech, at Manchester, Sept. 19, 1861; also extracts from Mr. James Johnstone's pamphlet on the opium trade.
120 pp. London, J. Caudwell, 1861
                                                                    T.

8000 The cotton supply. A letter to John Cheetham, esq., president of the Manchester cotton supply association. By a fellow of the Royal Geographical Society.
appendices. 40 pp. London, R. Hardwicke, 1861
                                                                    T.

8001 CRAWFORD, John. 'Social Science'. A lecture on land and money; or emigration and colonization, and reform of our money laws, the true remedies for social evils.
tables. 28 pp. London, R. Hardwicke, Paisley, R. Stewart, 1861
                                                                    T.

8002 DE GASPARIN, comte Agenor. The uprising of a great people: the United States in 1861. Abridged from the French of count Agenor de Gasparin. With appendices.
tables in appendices. 86 pp. London, Sampson Low, 1861
                                                                    T.

8003 DENISON, George Anthony. Church rate. What ought parliament to do?
30 pp. London, Saunders, Otley, 1861
                                                                    T.

8004 DENTON, William. Observations on the displacement of the poor, by metropolitan railways and by other public improvements.
appendices. tables. 43 pp. London, Bell and Daldy, 1861
                                                                    T.

8005 DUPANLOUP, —., bishop of Orleans. Discours prononcé en faveur des pauvres catholiques d'Irlande, à Paris, dans l'église Saint Roch, le 25e Mars, 1861. Se vend au profit des pauvres catholiques Irlandais.
78 pp. Paris, Douniel, 1861
                                                                    N.

——. English translation by Rev. W. H. Anderson.
41 pp. Dublin, J. F. Fowler, 1861

B.

8006 The East India government guarantee on railways, with lord Canning's speech on the opening of the railway from Calcutta to the Ganges, &c., &c., &c.
34 pp. 3rd ed. London, W. H. Allen, 1861

T.

——. 34 pp. 4th ed. London, W. H. Allen, 1861

T.

8007 [EBURY, Robert Grosvenor, 1st baron.] The only compromise possible in regard to church rates. By a former member of the house of Commons.
14 pp. London, J. Murray, 1861

T.

——. 2nd ed., with preface and giving author's name. 18 pp. London, J. Murray, 1861

T.

8008 [EDDIS, William U.] A letter to Sir Charles Wood, bart., G.C.B., her majesty's secretary of state for India, on the policy of the hon. J. P. Grant, governor of Bengal, towards British settlers, during 1860–61.
28 pp. London, J. Ridgway, 1861

T.

8009 Emancipation in the West Indies. Two addresses by E. B. Underhill, esq., and the Rev. J. T. Brown, the deputation from the Baptist missionary society to the West Indies, delivered at a public meeting, held at Willis's Rooms, 20th February, 1861.
36 pp. London, British and foreign anti-slavery society, 1861

T.

8010 The government guarantee on Indian railways, as officially explained and recognized. By the railway boards, the government, and the stock exchange. Compiled by the chairman of the Scinde Railway Company.
tables. 16 pp. London, W. H. Allen, 1861

T.

8011 The great cotton question: where are the spoils of the slave? Addressed to the upper and middle classes of Great Britain. By Λ.
22 pp. Cambridge & London, Macmillan, 1861

T.

8012 GROVE, George. Nine caveats against church rates, church-stateism and state-churchism. Entered by George Grove.
36 pp. London, Pewtress & Co., Worcester, John Grainger, 1861

T.

8013 HARE, Thomas. The development of the wealth of India. Reprinted from Macmillan's Magazine, with notes on the different administrative and judicial systems required for the Asiatic races and the British inhabitants.
74 pp. Cambridge & London, Macmillan, 1861

T.

8014 HARROP, John. Eureka, an unlimited source of national wealth, an antidote to the great sanitary evils and nuisances of cities and towns. The great fertilizer of the soil, and promoter of the growth of all kinds of vegetation,—as corn, grass, potatoes, garden plants, fruits, etc.
tables. 20 pp. London, Simpkin, Marshall, Manchester, J. Heywood, [1861?]

T.

8015 HAUGHTON, James. Observations upon a paper on poor relief, by Dr. Dowling, of Tipperary.
4 pp. n.p., [1861]

P.

8016 HECTOR, Alexander. Remarks on the salmon fisheries of Scotland.
tables. 28 pp. Edinburgh, Oliver and Boyd [etc., etc.], 1861

A.

8017 [HOBSON, Samuel?] A letter to the rt. hon. W. E. Gladstone, esq., M.P., the chancellor of the exchequer, on free trade in table beer of a limited price, together with the repeal of the duty on hops, and a reduction of the duty on malt, as a means of improving the moral and physical condition of the labouring classes, by substituting the use for the abuse of malt liquors, and also of increasing the revenue. By a Norfolk clergyman.
8 pp. 2nd. ed. London, J. Ridgway, 1861

N., T.

8018 HOPE, A. J. B. Beresford. Church rates and dissenters. A speech delivered at the council of the Church Institute, January 21, 1861, and revised by the author.
26 pp. London, J. Ridgway, 1861

M.

8019 HUBBARD, John Gellibrand, later first baron Addington. The church and church-rates. A letter to the electors of the borough of Buckingham.
20 pp. London, J. Ridgway, 1861

T.

8020 HUTTON, James. Suggestions as to the appointment by the legislature of public accountants, to audit the accounts of all joint-stock companies.
20 pp. London, C. Letts, 1861

T.

8021 IRONS, William J. He gave tithes of all. A sermon, preached before the Tithe Redemption Trust, at their anniversary service in the church of St. Michael, Burleigh Street, June 19th, 1861. Published at the request of the meeting.
24 pp. London, F. & J. Rivington, 1861

T.

8022 KINGSLEY, J. Church property—national property, [in] Lectures on voluntaryism; delivered in the Mechanics' Institution, Manchester.
30 pp. Manchester, J. Heywood, London, Simpkin Marshall, [1861]

T.

8023 The labour question. I. A letter from a French working man [i.e. F. Magain] on 'the present strike'. II. A report on the labour question presented to the Positivist Society [dated 1848]. Translated from the French.
24 pp. London, Manwaring, 1861

N.

8024 LESTGARENS, Jules. La situation économique et industrielle de l'Espagne en 1860.
tables. 110 pp. Bruxelles: A. Lacroix, Van Meenen, 1861

T.

8025 Letterkenny Railway Company: report of the proceedings at the second ordinary general meeting of shareholders, held on Tuesday, 30th April, 1861. As reported in 'The Londonderry Sentinel'.
12 pp. Londonderry, at the Sentinel Office, 1861

N.

8026 LEWIS, Charles Edward. The Bankruptcy Manual; being a plain summary of the present statute law of bankruptcy as affecting traders and non-traders. Second ed.
tables. 144 pp. London, P. Richardson, 1861

T.

8027 LIÉBERT, Eugene. L'Irlande en 1861.
33 pp. Paris, Revue Nationale, 1861

N.

Extract from *Revue Nationale et étrangère*, vol. VI, Oct. 1861.

8028 The London dock companies: an inquiry into their present position and future prospects, with suggestions for improvement of revenue and dividends.
tables. 64 pp. London, P. Richardson, 1861

T.

8029 LONG, James. Strike, but hear! Evidence explanatory of the indigo system in lower Bengal.
appendix. 110 pp. Calcutta, R. C. Lepage, 1861

N., T.

8030 LONGFIELD, Mountifort. A proposal for an act to authorize the issue of land debentures in connection with sales made by the landed estates court. With a copy of the proposed act.
34 pp. Dublin, A. Thom, 1861

N.

8031 MACRAE, David, Jun. The social hydra; or, the influences of the traffic of pawnbrokers and brokers on the religious, moral, and social condition of the working classes and the poor.
tables. appendix. 42 pp. Glasgow, Gallie, 1861

T.

8032 MORTON, John Chalmers. Handbook of farm labour.
tables. appendix. index. 136 pp. London, Longman, Green, Longman, and Roberts, 1861

T.

8033 Musings on money matters; or crotchets on currency. By a merchant trader,
8 pp. London, Ash and Flint, 1861

T.

8034 NEATE, Charles. Three lectures on taxation, especially that of land, delivered at Oxford, in the year 1860.
65 pp. Oxford and London, J. H. and J. Parker, 1861

T.

8035 NICHOLSON, Nathaniel Alexander. The science of exchanges.
96 pp. London, Effingham Wilson, 1861

T.

8036 O'CONNOR, Denis Charles. Seventeen years' experience of workhouse life: with suggestions for reforming the poor-law and its administration.
82 pp. Dublin, McGlashan & Gill, 1861

T.

8037 OSBORNE, Lord Sidney Godolphin. The respective duties of landlords, tenants, and labourers. An address delivered to a farmers' club. Published by request.
56 pp. London, J. Ridgway, [1861]

T.

8038 PALI, Baldassare. Sull'Insegnamento dell'economia politica e sociale in Inghilterra. Letta nella tornata del 5 dicembre 1861 di esse Istituto. (Estratta dal vol II degli Atti de R. Istituto Lombardo.)
16 pp. Milan, Bernardoni, 1861

N.

8039 PATTON, William. The American crisis; or, the true issue, slavery or liberty?
tables. 40 pp. London, Sampson Low, 1861

T.

8040 Penny banks for villages and small towns. Guide for their formation and management, both as branches of larger penny banks, and under the new post office savings bank act, with a simple and accurate system of books for either case. By the honorary secretary of the Gloucester penny bank.
tables. 42 pp. London, Longman, Green, Longman & Roberts, 1861

T.

8041 PEVERLY, B., and HATT, Charles. The new bankruptcy law. The act to amend the law relating to bankruptcy and insolvency arranged and simplified with an explanatory introduction.
66 pp. London, Houlston and Wright, 1861

T.

8042 PHILIPS, Edmund. A plea for the reform of the British currency and Bank of England charter.
28 pp. London, Whittaker, 1861

T.

8043 PIKE, William Patrickson. Form of mortgage in fee and of freeholds and leaseholds, with borrowing clause; and of mortgage to secure an account current, and equitable mortgage, with memorial, notes, and costs.
26 pp. Dublin, W. Leckie, 1861

T.

8044 POCOCK, George. Remarks on a pamphlet by H. S. Selfe, entitled 'The United Kingdom mutual annuity society and benevolent annuity fund, a narrative'.
16 pp. London, P. Richardson, 1861

T.

8045 The projected railways in connection with Lough Derg, considered, in reference to their amalgamation. By Pax.
10 pp. Dublin, at the Farmers' Gazette Office, 1861.

A.

8046 Public expenditure considered in connection with public works & buildings.
tables. 48 pp. London, L. Booth, 1861

T.

8047 PULMAN, John. The extradition treaty. 'The church of the poor' and church rates; or, a national religion the bulwark of religious and civil liberty: With suggestions to clergymen in the election of churchwardens.
50 pp. London, Simpkin, Marshall, 1861

T.

8048 Real and un-real life assurance considered. Letter, the manager of the Indisputable Life Assurance Company of Scotland, to the actuary of the Standard and Colonial life assurance companies.
16 pp. Edinburgh, T. and T. Clark, 1861

T.

8049 Remarks on the anticipated cotton crisis, in a letter to Tim Bobbin, esq., cotton spinner of Miln Row, near Manchester. By an ex-Indian cotton collector.
20 pp. London, E. Wilson, 1861

T.

8050 Report of the tithe redemption trust for the church in England and Wales, for the year 1861.
24 pp. London, F. & J. Rivington, [1861]

T.

8051 ROBERTS, Martyn J. Our poor law. Its defects and the way to mend them.
16 pp. London, Bosworth and Harrison, 1861

T.

8052 ROBINSON, Christopher. Second series of church questions. Practical methods for the arrangement of easter-dues, church-rates, an increased episcopate, places in prayer-book, hymnal, third service, rubrics, &c.
26 pp. London, T. Hatchard, 1861

T.

8053 SHARMAN, H. Riseborough. A handy book on post office savings banks: giving clear and complete instructions for opening, transferring, and closing accounts in them, with every necessary detail, including copies of the act by which they are created, and of the official regulations, under which they are conducted. [Entered at Stationers' Hall.]
52 pp. London, G. J. Stevenson, [1861]

T.

8054 SKINNER, James. Facts and opinions concerning statute hirings respectfully addressed to the landowners, clergy, farmers and tradesmen of the East Riding of Yorkshire.
tables. appendices. 28 pp. 2nd ed. London, Wertheim and Macintosh, 1861

T.

8055 The slave trade to Cuba, as set forth in an address to marshal Espartero, from the committee of the British and foreign anti-slavery society, on the 2nd March, 1855. With additional facts to the present date.
22 pp. London, British and foreign anti-slavery society, 1861

T.

8056 SMEE, William Ray. Three letters to the chancellor of the exchequer. Letter I. The gold discoveries—silver and gold—prices. Letter II. The gold discoveries—paper and credit—joint stock banks. Letter III. The civil service—the abolition of the shuttings of the national debt—the post office savings banks.
20 pp. London, P. Richardson, 1861

T.

8057 [SMITH, Samuel.] A word in season; or, how to grow wheat with profit. By the author of 'Lois Weedon husbandry'. Eighteenth edition; with a practical farmer's view of the plan.
tables. 64 pp. London, J. Ridgway, 1861

T.

8058 SMYTH, P. J. Notes on direct communication between Ireland and France.
tables. 30 pp. Dublin, Fowler, 1861

A.

8059 Social science made easy. Illustrated with two charts, representing the present political conditions of England and France in contrast, with a clear definition of those agencies which promote social freedom and commercial progress, and also of those which beget and sustain despotic power. Embracing also, short, concise and practical views on the French invasion, the cotton supply, and that great mechanical requirement a practical steam plough. By the author of 'Free trade in gold'.
diags. 14 pp. London, P. Richardson, 1861

T.

8060 STEPHENSON, George Robert. 'High speeds.' A letter to the right. hon. T. M. Gibson, M.P., president of the board of trade.
36 pp. London, R. Clay, 1861

A.

On railways.

8061 TARBERNER, John Loude. The Northfleet docks: the past, present, and future wet and dry dock accommodation of the port of London; with remarks on the new inland bonding act and the French treaty. And also on an anonymous pamphlet entitled 'the London dock companies'.
tables. 70 pp. + 3 plates. 3rd ed. London, Effingham Wilson, 1861

T.

See 8028.

8062 Tariff annexed to the conventions concluded on the 12th October and 16th November, 1860, between Great Britain and France.
tables. 20 pp. London, P. S. King, Waterlow & Sons, 1861

T.

8063 THORP, Thomas. Church-rates. A village sermon preached at Kemerton on the fourth Sunday after Epiphany, 1860.
16 pp. London, F. & J. Rivington, 1861

T.

8064 The true principles of taxation; an essay submitted to the British association for the advancement of science, by the council of the financial reform association. At Manchester, Sept., 1861.
tables. appendix. 32 pp. Liverpool, J. R. Williams, 1861
T.

8065 UDNY, George. A letter to the secretary of state for India, on the expediency of an income tax for the purpose of revenue, and the inexpediency of a government bank-note issue for that purpose: whether in India or elsewhere.
tables. 30 pp. London, P. Richardson, 1861
T.

8066 WALKER, James C. Seventh annual report of the directors of the association for promoting improvement in the dwellings and domestic condition of agricultural labourers in Scotland: and supplementary report, with specification and designs for cottages, &c., by James C. Walker, architect and secretary to the association.
diags. plate. appendix. 28 pp. Edinburgh, W. Blackwood & son, 1861
T.

8067 WATHERSTON, James H. A letter to the right hon. W. E. Gladstone, M.P., chancellor of the exchequer, on the trial of the pix, in her majesty's mint.
34 pp. London, Effingham Wilson, 1861
T.

8068 WATTS, John. The workman's bane & antidote: comprising the essay on strikes, read at the British Association for the advancement of science, 1861; the history of a mistake; being a tale of the Colne strike, 1860–1; and a lecture on the power and influence of co-operative effort, delivered at the Mechanics' Institution, Manchester, November 6th, 1861.
68 pp. Manchester, A. Ireland, [1861]
T.

8069 The workhouse orphan. By the author of 'A plea for the helpless'.
28 pp. London, T. Hatchard, 1861
T.

1862

8070 An address to the young men of Ireland, of all classes & creeds, by their countrymen the nationalists.
35 pp. Dublin, John F. Fowler, 1862
B.
Includes references to agriculture and land tenure.

8071 The American question. Secession. Tariff. Slavery.
74 pp. Brighton, H. Taylor, 1862
T.

8072 The American struggle. An appeal to the people of the north. By Philo-Americanus.
32 pp. London, Effingham Wilson, Liverpool, Webb & Gunt, 1862
T.

8073 BADGER, George Percy. A visit to the isthmus of Suez canal works. With a map.
map. illustration. 72 pp. London, Smith, Elder & co., 1862
T.

8074 BAGEHOT, Walter. Count your enemies and economise your expenditure.
28 pp. London, J. Ridgway, 1862
T.

8075 BIDEN, William Downing. Practical rules for valuers; with notes on the valuation of freeholds, leaseholds for lives or for years, copyholds, advowsons and next presentations; also on claims for compensation for property taken or damaged by the construction of railways and other public works.
tables. 50 pp. London, C. & E. Layton, 1862
T.

8076 BLACK, Morrice A. The assurance of diseased and doubtful lives on a new principle, more advantageous and equitable to policy-holders than the system hitherto adopted. With observations on the characteristics of assurable and non-assurable lives, by A. P. Stewart, M.D., F.R.C.P., physician to the [London and Yorkshire Assurance] Company.
illust. 40 pp. 2nd ed. London, W. S. D. Pateman, 1862
T.

8077 BRABAZON, H. B. (Letter) to Sir Robert Peel, bart., chief secretary for Ireland.
16 pp. London, 1862
N.
On land tenure.

8078 [BUCHANAN, John.] Banking in Glasgow during the olden time. In two sections. By Glasguensis.
tables. appendix. 64 pp. Glasgow, D. Robertson, 1862
T.

8079 CAIRNES, John Elliott. The revolution in America: a lecture delivered before the Dublin Young Men's Association on October 30th, 1862.
43 pp. n.p., 1862
B.

8080 Canada: the land of hope for the settler and artisan, the small capitalist, the honest, and the persevering. With a description of the climate, free grants of land, wages, and its general advantages as a field for emigration. By the editor of the 'Canadian News'.
map. 16 pp. 3rd ed. London, F. Algar, 1862
T.

8081 The Canadian native oil; its story, its uses, and its profits, with some account of a visit to the oil wells.
52 pp. London, Ashley, 1862
T.

8082 Canadian railways: Great Western Railway of Canada, Buffalo and Lake Huron, and Grand Trunk Railway of Canada, considered in reference to the proposed fusion of the lines.
24 pp. Glasgow, J. Maclehose, 1862
T.

8083 CARPENTER, William. The perils of policy-holders, and the liabilities of life offices. A second letter addressed to the right hon. William Ewart Gladstone, M.P., chancellor of the exchequer.
46 pp. London, W. Carpenter, 1862
T.

8084 CHARLEY, William. Flax and its products in Ireland. frontisp. 233 pp. London, Bell & Daldy, 1862
B.

8085 The church rate question in the parish of St. George the Martyr, Queen Square, W.C. tables. 24 pp. London, J. Stenson, 1862
T.

8086 Circular letter of Poor Law Board to Boards of Guardians, as to the Union Assessment Committee Act, 1862. 18 pp. London, H. Shaw, 1862
T.

8087 Circular letter of the Poor Law Board as to irremovable poor and common fund chargeability. 24 & 25 Vict. c. 55. Dated 24th March, 1862. 12 pp. London, H. Shaw, 1862
T.

8088 Cotton supply from the Ottoman empire. 72 pp. London, J. E. Taylor, 1862
T.

8089 CURLING, John. The church rate question examined, upon its true grounds. 16 pp. London, J. Ridgway, 1862
T.

8090 DAY, William Ansell. Famine in the west; being an enquiry into the crisis impending in the western districts of Ireland. With some suggestions for the amelioration of the condition of the poor in those parts. 58 pp. Dublin, Hodges & Smith, London, J. Ridgway, 1862
N.

8091 DE VINCENZI, Giuseppe. On the cultivation of cotton in Italy. Report to the minister of agriculture, industry, and commerce of the kingdom of Italy. tables. appendix. illust. plate. 48 pp. London, W. Trounce, 1862
T.

8092 The distress in Lancashire. A visit to the cotton districts. tables. 92 pp. London, Jackson, Walford, and Hodder, [1862]
T.

8093 DOBSON, William. An account of the celebration of Preston guild, in 1862. tables. 96 pp. Preston, W. and T. Dobson, London, Simpkin, Marshall, [1862?]
T.

8094 DOBSON, William, & HARLAND, John. A history of Preston guild; the ordinances of various guilds merchant, the custumal of Preston, the charters to the borough, the incorporated companies, list of mayors from 1327, etc., etc. tables. 116 pp. Preston, W. and J. Dobson, London, Simpkin, Marshall, [1862]
T.

8095 DUFFY, Sir Charles Gavan. The land law of Victoria (Australia). map. tables. 36 pp. London, W. H. Smith, 1862
B., N.

8096 EASTWOOD, T. F. Observations on the fishery laws for Ireland, or A plea for the salmon. 48 pp. Dublin, Hodges & Smith, 1862
N.

8097 The eighteenth annual report of the society for improving the condition of the labouring classes. tables. 42 pp. London?, W. Watts, 1862
T.

8098 État actuel de l'Algérie d'après les documents officiels. Geographie, produits, administration, statistique. tables. appendix. 88 pp. map. Alger, Imprimerie et papeterie Bouyer, 1862
T.

8099 FINNEY, S. G. Hints on agriculture, for landlords and tenants. plans. tables. 198 pp. London, Ward and Lock, 1862
T.

8100 FISHER, Joseph. How Ireland may be saved; or, the injurious effects of the present system of agriculture, on the prosperity of Ireland, and the social position of the Irish people. diagrams. tables. table of contents. 104 pp. [various paging.] London, J. Ridgway, 1862
A., C., N., P.

8101 GORDON, Margaret Maria. Prevention or an appeal to economy and common sense. 20 pp. Edinburgh, Edmonston and Douglas, 1862
T.

8102 GRADY, Standish Grove. The diminution of the poor rate by improved legislation and a more just distribution of the burden; being a manual for members of parliament, county magistrates, boards of guardians, and ratepayers. Second edition, with an appendix containing 'The Union Aid Relief Act'. appendix. 188 pp. London, Wildy, 1862
T.

8103 GREY, Thomas Belgrave. Tables showing the superannuation allowance to the civil servants of the crown, as authorized by 4 and 5 William IV, cap. 24, and 22 Victoria, cap. 26. tables. 70 pp. London, T. Harrison, 1862
T.

8104 GURDON, William. Bankruptcy for the million; or, a plea for the pauper debtor of the county courts. 18 pp. London, V. & R. Stevens, 1862
T.

8105 HANCOCK, William Neilson. A History of the Irish poor laws, and the differences between the administration of the English and Irish systems: being a lecture delivered in the Mechanic's Institute, Lurgan, on Monday evening, 12th May, 1862 tables. 16 pp. Lurgan, Evans, 1862
N.

8106 Handbook to Vancouver island and British Columbia, with map.
map. 16 pp. London, F. Algar, 1862
T.

8107 HECTOR, Alexander. Statement of facts relative to the Irish fishery question, as compared with the procedure in the house of lords in the recent enquiry into the Scotch fisheries, before proceeding to legislation thereon.
22 pp. London, Vincent and Skeen, 1862
A.

8108 HOLMES, Sir William Henry. Free cotton; how and where to grow it. With a map of British Guiana.
appendix. 44 pp. London, Chapman and Hall, 1862
T.

8109 HORRY, Sidney Calder. The people's edition of the lord chancellor's new bankruptcy & insolvency act. With notes and explanations to the respective clauses, and an historical sketch of the laws of bankruptcy from the earliest period.
120 pp. London, Henry Lea, [1862]
T.

8110 HOUSTON, Arthur. The emancipation of women from existing industrial disabilities: considered in its economic aspect.
appendix. 52 pp. London, Longman, Green, Longman, and Roberts, 1862
T.

8111 How can the amount of the grants for education be kept under the control of parliament?
tables. appendix. 12 pp. London, J. Ridgway, 1862
T.

8112 How shall we supply our cotton market? A letter addressed to the right hon. Thomas Milner Gibson, president of the board of trade.
16 pp. London, J. H. and J. Parker, 1862
T.

8113 INCHBALD, John. The price of money: the laws that regulate it, and the working of the bank act, briefly explained.
28 pp. 2nd ed. London, Effingham Wilson, 1862
T.

8114 JELLICOE, Anne. The condition of young women employed in manufactories in Dublin.
8 pp. London, Emily Faithfull and Co., 1862
A.

8115 JERVIS, William George. The hardships and sufferings of the poor clergy. A sequel to 'Startling facts'.
50 pp. London, E. Thompson, [etc.], 1862
T.

8116 JONES, John. Self-supporting dispensaries, their adaptation to the relief of the poor and working classes, with directions for the establishment and management of such institutions.
tables. 24 pp. London, J. Churchill, Derby, Bemrose, 1862
T.

8117 LAW, William John. Remarks on the Bankruptcy Act, 1861, concerning the transfer of officers from the insolvent court.
52 pp. London, W. & R. Stevens, 1862
T.

8118 LORD, John. The commercial compendium: an epitome of the law of bankruptcy, with full and copious abstracts of the 'Bankruptcy Act, 1861', and the acts of parliament preceding it; and the schedules and rules and orders used in the bankruptcy and county courts; to which is added, a popular treatise on the law of bankruptcy.
tables. 76 pp. London, Simpkin, Marshall, 1862
T.

8119 LOUREIRO, P. New tea table showing the cost of tea with all charges (minus freight), as bought by the pecul, for taels of sycee or dollars, and sold by the pound avoirdupois in England, exchange from 4s. to 9s. tea from 1 to 60 taels or dollars. Second edition.
tables. 26 pp. London, W. Brown, 1862
T.

8120 LYSAGHT, William. A reply to the letter of William L. Joynt, esq., on Mr. McMahon's fishery bill.
10 pp. Limerick, 1862
N.

8121 MAGILL, D. Lecture on the American conflict.
24 pp. Belfast, at the 'Banner' office, 1862
B.
Extracted from 'Banner of Ulster', Tuesday, April 1, 1862.

8122 MARSHMAN, John. Canterbury, New Zealand, in 1862. Published with the approval of the provincial government.
map. tables. 68 pp. London, G. Street, [1862]
T.

8123 MERMILLOD, G., abbé. Discours prononcé en faveur des pauvres d'Irlande à Paris, dans l'église Sainte-Clotilde, 22e Mai, 1862. Se vend au profit des pauvres catholiques d'Irlande.
78 pp. Paris, Lesort, 1862
N.

8124 NAPER, James Lenox William. The state of parties: labour and wages: as connected with the social education and condition of the labouring classes: addressed to the rt. hon. Sir Robert Peel, bt.
appendix. tables. 36 pp. Dublin, McGlashan and Gill, 1862
A., N.

8125 NEATE, Charles. Two lectures on trades unions, delivered in the University of Oxford, in the year 1861.
52 pp. Oxford and London, J. H. and J. Parker, 1862
T.

8126 NIXSON, A. F. On the walk-collection of London bankers. A letter to the London bankers upon a plan for the more economical collection of walks, for a general system of clearing among all London bankers, and for the earlier collection of walk-articles received in country remittances.
20 pp. London, Waterlow, 1862
T.

8127 PASSY, Frédéric. Conférences d'Économie Politique faites à Bordeaux sous le patronage de la société philomathique. Discours d'ouverture.
56 pp. Bordeaux, Feret, Paris, Guillaumin, [etc.], 1862
U.

8128 PIGOTT, Grenville. The laws of settlement & removal; their evils and their remedy.
52 pp. London, J. Ridgway, 1862
T.

8129 A plan for the complete and final settlement of the question of the sale and transfer, mortgage and registration of land, which provides for the total abolition of receivers exclusively over real estate, except in the case of charges without a power of sale, or of entry and distraint, applicable to England and Wales, as well as to Ireland. Containing, among other most important additions, three letters from Edward Lytton, esq., to the author, giving a complete approval of the plan. By an Irish landowner.
table of contents. appendix. 96 pp. 2nd ed. Dublin, Robertson, 1862
N., T.

8130 POTTER, Rupert. A few observations upon the bill introduced by the lord chancellor in the house of lords; entitled, 'A bill to facilitate the proof of title to, and the conveyance of, real estates'.
appendix. 116 pp. London, W. Draper, 1862
T.

8131 Principia pauperismatis. Considerations regarding paupers.
56 pp. London, Emily Faithfull & co., 1862
T.

8132 Proposal for a national life assurance fund. (1) The facilities of the post office for the collection and transmission of the premium. (2) The security of the government for payment of the sum assured on proof of death. A letter to the right hon. the chancellor of the exchequer.
16 pp. London, W. Kent, [1862]
T.

8133 REID, Hugo. The American question in a nutshell; or, why we should recognize the confederates.
32 pp. London, R. Hardwicke, 1862
T.

8134 Report of the Mansion House committee for the relief of distress in Ireland, 1862.
appendix. tables. 38 pp. Dublin, Browne and Nolan, 1862
B., N.

8135 Report of the tithe redemption trust for the church in England and Wales, for the year 1862.
tables. 24 pp. London, F. & J. Rivington, [1862?]
T.

8136 ROBINSON, Nugent. Homes for the working poor.
tables. 26 pp. Dublin, Goodwin and Nethercott, 1862
A., N.

8137 RUSSELL, James. Sugar duties. Digest and summary of evidence taken by the select committee appointed to inquire into the operation of the present scale of sugar duties, by J. Russell, dedicated by permission to the right honourable W. E. Gladstone, M.P., chancellor of the exchequer.
tables. appendices. 156 pp. London, W. Dawson, 1862
T.

8138 SANDARS, Samuel. Condensed observations on the elements of money, &c., &c.
tables. 20 pp. London, P. Richardson, 1862
T.

8139 Savings' banks. The old system and the new post office system, impartially explained by an old actuary.
table. 8 pp. London, Whittaker, 1862
T.

8140 SEDGWICK, John. An essay on the rights of owners and occupiers of property required by a railway company to compensation, and the way to obtain it.
10 pp. London, G. & J. W. Taylor, 1862
T.

8141 SHARMAN, H. Riseborough. The fire duty. The duty on fire insurances: reasons for its abolition or reduction. Second ed. issued by 'The Association for the abolition or reduction of the duty on fire insurance'.
tables. 18 pp. London, A. C. Hailes, 1862
T.

8142 [SMITH, Samuel.] Lois Weedon husbandry as it is. Third edition,—including 'A word in season about growing wheat',—corrected and condensed.
tables. 78 pp. London, J. Ridgway, 1862
T.

8143 Spain and the African slave-trade. An address to Spaniards; from the committee of the British and foreign anti-slavery society, 1862.
6 pp. London, 1862
T.

8144 Suggestions for a 'Church rate relief bill'. A letter addressed [by permission] to the right hon. Sir George Grey, bart., M.P., G.C.B., her majesty's secretary of state for the home department.
30 pp. London, T. Hatchard, 1862
T.

8145 The twenty-third annual report of the British and Foreign Anti-Slavery Society, for the abolition of slavery and the slave-trade throughout the world; presented to the meeting of subscribers held at the society's rooms, 27 New Broad Street, London, on the 30th of June, 1862, George William Alexander, esq., in the chair.
tables 26 pp. London, the society, 1862
T.

8146 TWINING, Elizabeth. A lecture on cotton, given at the working people's rooms, Portugal-street, Lincoln's Inn. Sold for the benefit of the suffering cotton workers.
18 pp. London, 1862
T.

8147 VINER, Henry. Experience of an amateur miner. A letter to the Wheal Alfred Consols Adventurers.
20 pp. London, W. Strange, [1862]
T.

8148 ——. Third series. Experience of an amateur miner: a letter to the adventurers in Wheal Margery.
appendix. 24 pp. London, W. Strange, 1862
T.

8149 WIGHT, Robert. Notes on cotton farming, explanatory of the American and East Indian methods, with suggestions for their improvement.
table. 44 pp. Reading, G. Lovejoy, London, Whittaker, 1862
T.

8150 WILLIAMS, Joshua. On the true remedies for the evils which affect the transfer of land: a paper read before the Juridical Society, on Monday the 24th March, 1862.
46 pp. London, H. Sweet, Dublin, Hodges, Smith, 1862
T.

8151 WRIGHT, William. The improvements in the farming of Yorkshire since the date of the last reports in the journal of the Royal Agricultural Society. Prize essay.
tables. 48 pp. Hull, J. Mosley Stark, 1862
T.

1863

8152 Annual report and transactions of the Royal Agricultural Society for the years 1862-3.
tables. 72 pp. Dublin, at the office of the 'Farmers Gazette', 1863
D.

8153 BLAKE, John A. The Irish salmon fisheries. Replies to arguments advanced against the bill now before parliament for assimilating the fishery laws of Ireland to England.
map. 28 pp. London, R. Hardwicke, Dublin, McGlashan & Gill, 1863
N.

8154 The case of the West Hartlepool harbour and railway company. Debenture stock no security: an act of parliament no protection.
tables. appendix. 16 pp. London, Effingham Wilson, 1863
T.

8155 CHESTER, Harry. Education and advancement for the working classes. A speech delivered at a public meeting at the Hackney Working Men's Institute, on January 20th, 1863.
16 pp. London, Bell and Daldy, [1863]
T.

8156 A churchman's protest against church rates; being a speech delivered in the parish vestry of Egham. Second edition.
16 pp. Egham, W. F. Larkin, London, E. Marlborough, 1863
T.

8157 Circular letter of the poor law board as to the rating of tithes. Dated 9th May, 1859.
12 pp. London, H. Shaw, 1863
T.

8158 COWELL, John Welsford. Lancashire wrongs and the remedy: two letters addressed to the cotton operatives of Great Britain.
34 pp. London, R. Hardwicke, 1863
T.

8159 DE HAERNE, Désiré P. The American question. Translated by Thomas Ray.
tables. 116 pp. London, W. Ridgway, 1863
U.

8160 Direct taxation and freedom of trade; paper submitted by the council of the Financial Reform Association, to the National association.
28 pp. Liverpool, J. R. Williams, 1863
E.

8161 Report on taxation: direct and indirect. Adopted by the Financial Reform Association, Liverpool, and presented at the annual meeting of the National Association for the Promotion of Social Science, held at Bradford, October, 1859.
appendix. 30 pp. Liverpool, J. R. Williams, [1863]
T.

8162 DIXON, Henry Hall. Appendix to the second edition of the law of the farm.
142 pp. London, V. and R. Stevens, 1863
T.

8163 [DRYSDALE, George.] The land question; containing remarks on the rights of property in land, on land tenure, large and small farms, peasant proprietors, cottiers, the laws of primogeniture and entail, the land transfer act, and other matters relating to landed property. By G. R.
52 pp. London, E. Truelove, 1863
T.

8164 EDGE, Frederick Milne. The destruction of the American carrying trade. A letter to earl Russell, K.G., her majesty's principal secretary of state for the foreign departments.
tables. 28 pp. London, W. Ridgway, 1863
T.

8165 ELLIS, Thomas. The metropolitan sewage. Is it 'an engineering and commercial impossibility to utilise, in the liquid state, the sewage of the metropolis', as has been stated by Mr. Thomas Wicksteed, C.E., in his report to the metropolitan commissioners of sewers? The question is answered in a letter to the chairman of the metropolitan board of works; in which is also given a plan for utilising, in its liquid state, the sewage of the metropolis; together with a detailed estimate of cost and suggestions for division of profits between the metropolitan board of works and a projected company, by which there would be placed at the disposal of the board of works for the reduction of local taxation over the metropolitan area, an annual sum of not less than £700,000.
appendices. 62 pp. n.p., [1863?]
T.

8166 España, y el trafico de negros. Observaciones que dirige la sociedad Britanica y estrangera contra la esclavitud, a los Señores Españoles. Año 1862.
8 pp. London, [1863?]
T.

8167 FALK, Robert, PHIPSON, Thomas Lamb. The use of salt in agriculture: prize essays published by the salt chamber of commerce of Northwich.
tables. 56 pp. Liverpool, G. J. Poore, London, Simpkin Marshall, 1863
T.

8168 FELLOWS, Frank P. On the impediments to the introduction of the metrical system of weights and measures, and the best way to remove them: a lecture, delivered December 13, 1860, in the hall of the Society of Arts, Adelphi, London—second ed. with notes and appendices.
tables. 56 pp. London, Smith, Elder & co., 1863
T.

8169 FFENNELL, William J. Remarks on past and present legislation for protection of salmon fisheries of Ireland.
28 pp. London, Crockford, 1863
N.

8170 The Gravesend inland bonding docks. An exposition of the past and present wet and dry dock accommodation of the port of London, and of the objects of the Gravesend docks and inland bonding company, (limited): with remarks on the Inland Bonding Act of 1860, and the French Treaty. By the projector of the Gravesend docks and inland bonding undertaking.
tables. 70 pp. London, Day, 1863
T.

8171 HANCOCK, William Neilson. Report on the supposed progressive decline of Irish prosperity.
tables. 93 pp. Dublin, A. Thom, 1863
N., Q., T., U.

8172 HARVEY, William Wigan. The assessment of tithe rent charge, stated in accordance with the various judgements of the court of Queen's Bench.
appendix with tables. 34 pp. London, Bell and Daldy, 1863
T.

8173 HERON, Denis Caulfield. Historical statistics of Ireland.
tables. 48 pp. 2nd ed. London, Parker, Son, & Bourn, 1863
B., C., N., P., U.

8174 HEYWORTH, Lawrence. Fiscal policy. Direct and indirect taxation contrasted; or, the immeasurably preferable policy of an income tax, to customs and excise duties, eliminated.
table. 36 pp. Liverpool, J. R. Williams, [1863]
T.

8175 HUGHES, Samuel. London and its gas companies. State and condition of the companies supplying gas to the metropolis, described in a letter to her majesty's principal secretary of state for the home department, with reference to the first accounts made out by each company in accordance with the metropolis gas act, 1860.
tables. appendix. 64 pp. London, Waterlow, 1863
T.

8176 HUTCHINSON, Simon. Fire and water, versus corn and hay. An essay on the effects of steam cultivation.
tables. 18 pp. London, Simpkin, Marshall, Grantham, L. Ridge, 1863
T.

8177 JAMES, Frank. Remarks on the highway act: addressed to Thomas Falconer, esq., judge of the county courts of Glamorganshire and Brecknockshire; and one of the magistrates of the counties of Glamorganshire, Brecknockshire and Monmouthshire, etc.
tables. 14 pp. 2nd ed. Merthyr-Tydfil, M. W. White, 1863
T.

8178 JEVONS, William Stanley. A serious fall in the value of gold ascertained, and its social effects set forth. With two diagrams.
tables. diagrams, appendix. 78 pp. London, E. Stanford, 1863
Q., T.

8179 LEVY, John. Summer rambles to the west: employment for the people—harbours of refuge—tramways.
32 pp. Dublin, Hodges, Smith, 1863
N.
Reprints of letters to various papers.

8180 LYSAGHT, William. Some remarks upon Mr. McMahon's bill, entitled 'A bill to assimilate the law of Ireland as to salmon fisheries, to that of England', With a map of Lower Shannon, showing the number of fixed engines in that river in 1862.
map. table. appendix. 32 pp. London, Cox & Wyman, 1863
N.

8181 MACDONNELL, Sir Richard Graves. Australia: what it is, and what it may be: a lecture by Sir Richard Graves MacDonnell, C.B., late chief governor of South Australia. Delivered before the Dublin Young Men's Christian Association, May the 7th, 1863.
tables, map, 68 pp. n.p., 1863
B., N.

8182 MACFIE, Robert Andrew. The patent question: a solution of difficulties by abolishing or shortening the inventor's monopoly, and instituting national recompenses. A paper submitted to the congress of the Association for the promotion of social science, at Edinburgh, October, 1863, by Robert Andrew Macfie, president of the Liverpool Chamber of Commerce. To which are added translations of recent contributions to patent reform by M. Chevalier and other continental economists.
96 pp. London, W. J. Johnson, 1863
T.

——. 2nd ed. with title beginning *The patent question under free trade*.
96 pp. London, W. J. Johnson, 1863
T.

8183 MARTIN, John. Letters on the Irish national question.
table of contents. 58 pp. Dublin, Harding, 1863
A.

8184 The maze of banking. The Bank Act. Joint-stock banks. Banking plant—capital, circulation, deposits. Scotch bank reports. Aberdeen Town and county bank; North of Scotland banking company; Union Bank of Scotland; Clydesdale banking company. Their physiology and anatomy. Banker's profits—expenditure—losses. The chartered banks. By a depositor.
diagram. tables. 62 pp. Edinburgh and Glasgow, W. P. Nimmo, London, Simpkin, Marshall, 1863
T.

8185 Money, and its responsibilities. A tract on proportionate and regulated giving, for religious and charitable purposes. Issued by a committee of churchmen.
8 pp. Manchester, Hale and Roworth, London, Whittaker, [1863]

T.

8186 NAPER, James Lenox William. Papers on Ireland for the consideration of lords Derby, Russell and Palmerston.
24 pp. Dublin, McGlashan & Gill, 1863

U.

8187 NELSON, Henry. The sugar duties discussed.
20 pp. London, Smith, Elder & co., 1863

T.

8188 NELSON, Isaac. The American war in relation to slavery. A lecture delivered to the Presbyterian Young Men's Society, Donegall Street, Belfast, 24th November, 1863.
52 pp. Belfast, A. Mayne, 1863

L.

8189 Observations on the theory and practice of taxation, submitted by the council of the Financial Reform Association, Liverpool, to the National association for the promotion of social science, at the annual congress held at London, June, 1862.
12 pp. Liverpool, J. Holme, [1863]

T.

8190 OLIVEIRA, Benjamin. A few observations upon the works of the isthmus of Suez canal made during a visit in April, 1863.
34 pp. London, T. Harrison, 1863

D., T.

8191 Report of the special committee of the municipal council of Dublin on the state of the public accounts between Ireland and Great Britain.
tables. 54 pp. Dublin, Dollard, 1863

N.

8192 The Royal Dublin Society & its privileges versus imperial policy & Irish public right.
24 pp. Dublin, D. Webb, 1863

B., D., N.

8193 RUSSELL, James. The sugar duties. Letter to the right hon. W. E. Gladstone, M.P., chancellor of the exchequer.
tables. 32 pp. London, W. Dawson, 1863

T.

8194 SINCLAIR, William. The Irish fishery laws. A letter to Sir Robert Peel, bt., chief secretary for Ireland.
14 pp. London, Cox & Wyman, 1863

N.

8195 Slave-traders in Liverpool. Extracts from the correspondence on the slave-trade, published by command, and presented to parliament in April, 1862, setting forth the case of the slaver 'Nightingale', fitted out at Liverpool in October and November, 1861.
8 pp. London, British and foreign anti-slavery society, [1863]

T.

8196 SMITH, Samuel. The cotton trade of India, being a series of letters written from Bombay in the spring of 1863.
tables. map. 72 pp. London, Effingham Wilson, Liverpool, Webb & Hunt, 1863

T.

8197 SMITH, William. Ireland's right & need: self-government. A letter to the earl of Carlisle.
52 pp. Dublin, W. B. Kelly, 1863

B., N.

8198 SMYTH, P. J. Ireland's capacities for foreign commerce.
26 pp. Dublin, Fowler, 1863

A., N.

8199 Steam in the farm-yard: its adaptation to agricultural purposes.
tables. 26 pp. London, W. Kent, 1863

T.

8200 Sugar duties. The sugar duties considered, extract from the annual report of the committee of the Mercantile Law Amendment Society, 1863.
16 pp. London, W. Dawson, [1863]

T.

8201 TAYLOR, George. Tithe table, showing the value of tithe rentcharges for the year 1863. To which is added, another table showing the extent of the yearly fluctuation in the prices of wheat, barley, and oats, since 1835.
8 pp. London, H. Shaw, 1863

T.

8202 TORRENS, Robert R. Transportation considered as a punishment, and as a mode of founding colonies. A paper read before the British Association for the Advancement of Science at Newcastle, 29th August, 1863.
24 pp. London, W. Ridgway, 1863

A.

8203 TRIMBLE, Robert. The negro, north and south: the status of the coloured population in the northern and southern states of America compared.
34 pp. London, Whittaker [etc., etc.], 1863

T.

8204 WALKER, Robert J. American finances and resources. Letter no. I.
appendix. 46 pp. London, W. Ridgway, 1863

T.

8205 ——. American finances and resources. Letter no. II.
tables. 24 pp. London, W. Ridgway, 1863

T.

8206 ——. Jefferson Davis. Repudiation, recognition and slavery. Letter of hon. Robert J. Walker, M.A.
58 pp. 2nd ed. London, W. Ridgway, 1863

T.

8207 WHITEHEAD, James. The rate of mortality in Manchester. With emendations and additions.
tables. 66 pp. 2nd ed. London, Simpkin Marshall, Manchester, A. Ireland, 1863

T.

8208 WILLIAMS, W. Mattieu. The intellectual destiny of the working man; an address delivered on the 28th May, 1863, to the members of the 'Institute chemical society'.
24 pp. London, Cornish [etc.], [1863?]
                                                              T.

1864

8209 ABRAHAM, Robert John. A popular explanation of the system of land registration under lord Westbury's act; to which is added the report of the recent debate in the house of lords, etc.
tables. 44 pp. 2nd ed. London, Routledge, Warne & Routledge, 1864
                                                              T.

8210 Anent the North American continent.
tables. 16 pp. London, W. Ridgway, 1864
                                                              T.

8211 ARTHUR, Henry. Suggestions for raising and securing a general fund to provide annuities for the widows and orphans of all the ministers of the established church in Ireland.
appendices. 64 pp. Dublin, Hodges and Smith, 1864
                                                              A.

8212 BEHIC, Armand, minister of agriculture, commerce and public works. Rapport a l'émpereur sur l'agriculture.
46 pp. Paris, Panckoucke, 1864
                                                              N.

8213 BEWICK, Robert. The advantages and practicability of applying co-operation to the wants of farmers.
28 pp. London, Simpkin, Marshall [etc., etc.], 1864
                                                              T.

8214 CHADWICK, Edwin. Association for the promotion of social science. Address to the meeting at York, Sept. 26, 1864, on the effect of manufacturing distress, on manufacturing progress, and on the improvement of the condition of the wage classes, in agriculture as well as in manufacture.
40 pp. London, R. Hardwicke, 1864
                                                              T.

8215 [CHAMBERS, George W.] Everybody's question; or a few words on banking and currency. By one who for more than thirty years has dealt largely with money.
32 pp. London, Smith, Elder & co., 1864
                                                              T.

8216 CLANCARTY, William Thomas Le Poer Trench, 7th earl. Ireland: her present condition, and what it might be.
38 pp. Dublin, G. Herbert, 1864
                                                              A., T.

8217 COATES, Thomas. Railways construction facilities, railway companies—powers, bills. Railways and the board of trade again discussed.
16 pp. London, P. S. King, 1864
                                                              T.

8218 CONN, John L. Reform of the grand jury laws of Ireland.
tables. 26 pp. Dublin, Ponsonby, 1864
                                                              A.

8219 The cotton question.
tables. 28 pp. London, H. F. Mackintosh, [1864]
                                                              T.

8220 DANIELS, William Henry. Introduction to the science of wealth.
40 pp. London, R. Hardwicke, 1864
                                                              T.

8221 DENISON, Sir William. Roads and railways in New South Wales and India, with remarks explanatory of the advantages likely to result from the employment under certain circumstances, of animal power, instead of steam power.
tables. appendix. 78 pp. Madras, J. Higginbotham, 1864
                                                              T.
See 8718.

8222 DENNEHY, Cornelius. Letters on the banking systems and industrial resources of Ireland, taxation of Ireland, etc., etc.
tables. 38 pp. Dublin, Dollard, 1864
                                                              A., P.

8223 Dialogue between a doctor of laws and a student, touching the reasons why the lord chancellor's 'Land Transfer Act' is not generally used.
18 pp. London, H. Sweet, 1864
                                                              T.

8224 DUREAU, M. B. The sugar question as it affects the consumer.
tables. 80 pp. London, Longman, Green, Longman, Roberts and Green, 1864
                                                              T.

8225 The financial exigencies of Ireland before and after the legislative union.
table of contents. tables. 26 pp. Dublin, A. Thom, 1864
                                                              A., N.

8226 FINLAY, Alexander Struthers. Our monetary system. Some remarks on the influence of the bullion in the Bank of England on commercial credit and on the rate of interest.
32 pp. London, Willis and Sotheran, 1864
                                                              T.

8227 FISHER, Henry. Bank audits: the practicability of a thorough independent system considered. Dedicated by permission to Edward Baines, esq., M.P.
tables. 46 pp. London, Simpkin, Marshall, Leeds, E. Baines, [1864]
                                                              T.

8228 FRYER, Alfred. The sugar duties. An examination of the letter addressed by Edmund Potter, M.P., to the rt. hon. W. E. Gladstone, M.P.
tables. 44 pp. Manchester, Galt, 1864
                                                              T.

8229 GRAY, J. McFarlane. Arithmetic of building societies: what they profess to be; what they are; what they ought to be; with extensive tables and illustrations of well known societies.
tables. 34 pp. Liverpool, H. Young, London, Virtue, 1864
                                                              T.

8230 HANCOCK, William Neilson. Report on the state of public accounts between Great Britain & Ireland.
tables. 68 pp. Dublin, A. Thom, 1864
E., N., Q., T., U.

8231 HANN, William. Chapel and other trust debts. Letters shewing the means of management and certain liquidation.
table. appendix. 28 pp. London, H. J. Tresidder, 1864
T.

8232 [HOPE, W., & NAPIER, W.] The sewage of the metropolis. A letter to John Thwaites, esq., chairman of the metropolitan board of works, in reply to the report of the coal, corn, & finance committee, to the corporation of the city of London.
12 pp. London, E. Stanford, 1864
Q., T.

8233 HORSFALL, J. H. Remarks on the Salmon Fisheries' bill, (1861) and the necessity for amended legislation, illustrated with a design for a salmon ladder.
plan. 36 pp. London, Longman, Green, Longman, Roberts & Green, 1864
T.

8234 How 'nicely' we are (locally) governed. Dedicated to (and especially worthy the attention of) the ratepayers resident in Shoreditch, St. Luke's, and Bethnal Green. By one who knows.
24 pp. London, [1864?]
T.

8235 HUME, A. Results of the Irish census of 1861, with a special reference to the condition of the church in Ireland.
table of contents. tables. maps. diagrams. graph. appendix. 68 pp. London, F. & J. Rivington, Dublin, Hodges, Smith, 1864
N., T.

8236 HUNTER, W. A. The origin of the criminal laws affecting the working-classes. Glasgow Tracts for Trades' Unionists—No. 1.
4 pp. Glasgow, Executive for the repeal of the Criminal Law Amendment Act, [1864?]
N.

8237 ——. Glasgow Tracts for Trades Unionists—No. II.
4 pp. [no t-p.] Glasgow, Executive for the repeal of the Criminal Law Amendment Act, [1864?]
N.

8238 HUTTON, Henry Dix. Registration of Title Association. Private conveyancing reformed; or, dealings with land rendered secure, simple, and easy, by registration of title. A lecture delivered on the invitation of the council of the chamber of commerce of Belfast, the 18th March, 1864.
60 pp. Dublin, Hodges & Smith, Belfast, H. Greer, 1864
N.

8239 The land and the agricultural population.
44 pp. Arundel, 'West Sussex Gazette' office, 1864
A.
A series of letters to the 'West Sussex Gazette' on Cobden and Bright's Rochdale speeches.

8240 The law of limited liability, in its application to joint stock banking, advocated.
tables. 44 pp. London, Whittaker, [1864]
T.

8241 LEES, F. R. The condensed argument for the legislative prohibition of the liquor traffic.
table of contents. tables. 160 pp. London, J. Caudwell, Manchester, United Kingdom Alliance, 1864
A.

8242 A letter to George Twycross, esq., in reply to his speech on the church-rate question at Wokingham. By a parishioner.
14 pp. London, Houlston and Wright, 1864
T.

8243 LUMLEY, William Golden. The Union Assessment Committee Act, 1862; with introduction, notes, and an appendix, containing the circular letters of the poor law board upon the act. Sixth edition, with additional notes, the amendment act of 1864, and an explanatory preface.
appendix. 166 pp. London, H. Shaw, 1864
T.

8244 LYTTLETON, William Henry. Church establishments: their lawfulness and advantages, social and religious: a lecture. Published under the direction of the trade committee.
50 pp. London, Society for Promoting Christian Knowledge, [1864]
T.

8245 McEVOY, John. Reasons for the establishment of a free library, and an industrial college, on the foundation of some of the so-called scientific institutions of Dublin.
table of contents. tables. appendix. 46 pp. Dublin, Kelly, 1864
A., T.

8246 MACSWINEY, Peter Paul. Lecture on Irish manufactures, delivered by the right hon. Peter Paul MacSwiney, lord mayor of Dublin (at the request of the managing committee in the exhibition building of the Royal Dublin Society) for the Catholic Young Men's Society.
tables. 48 pp. Dublin, Browne & Nolan, 1864
U.

8247 The metric system. By a British resident in France.
tables. 54 pp. London, T. Harrison, 1864
T.

8248 MILLER, Marmaduke. A lecture to working men on work and wages: co-operation and strikes.
18 pp. Darlington, Rapp and Dresser, 1864
T.

8249 MOORE, Edward Wells. An address on the condition of the agricultural labourer and his cottage home. Delivered at a meeting of the Oxford Farmers' Club.
illustration. tables. 60 pp. Faringdon, C. Luker, 1864
T.

8250 The moral, social, and political effects of revenue from intoxicating drinks. By a temperance politician.
table. 16 pp. London, J. Caudwell, 1864
T.

8251 Musings on money matters; or crotchets on currency: By a merchant trader. Second edition. Dedicated to the right honourable the chancellor of the exchequer.
16 pp. London, Ash and Flint, 1864
T.

See 8033.

8252 National and other public debts. Letters addressed to the editors of the 'Leeds Mercury'. shewing the means of their ultimate and certain liquidation. By Indicator.
tables. 36 pp. London, W. Macintosh, 1864
T.

8253 NELSON, Henry. The sugar duties discussed. Second edition, with additional notes.
24 pp. London, Smith Elder & co., 1864
T.

8254 NORMAN, George Warde. An examination of some prevailing opinions, as to the pressure of taxation in this, and other countries. Fourth edition. With a supplementary chapter, continuing the financial review to the present time.
tables. appendices, with tables. 142 pp. London, T. and W. Boone, 1864
T.

8255 Observations on the Torrens registration scheme; with remarks upon the proposed 'Recording of Titles Act (Ireland)' (prepared and issued by Robert R. Torrens, esq.). By Mentor.
74 pp. Dublin, Hodges and Smith, 1864
N.
See 8269.

8256 POTTER, Edmund. The sugar duties. A letter to the rt. hon. W. E. Gladstone, M.P., chancellor of the exchequer. Second edition, with additions.
tables. 28 pp. London, Dawson and Sons, Manchester, Johnson and Rawson, 1864
T.

8257 RAINES, William. Observations on the Highway Act of 1862 and the management of highways, addressed to the ratepayers of Middle Holderness by William Raines.
table [in] appendix. 16 pp. Hull, Goddard, 1864
T.

8258 REEVES, Robert William Cary. Some remarks on the Irish Fishery Acts, and the construction now put upon them by the special commissioners appointed under the provisions of the 26 & 27 Vic. c. 114.
22 pp. 2nd ed. Dublin, Hodges & Smith, 1864
N.

8259 Regulations of the Railway Clearing House, January, 1864
tables. index. appendix. 180 pp. London, Truscott, Son & Simmons, 1864
T.

8260 Remarks on the London (City) Tithes Bill, now before parliament. By a layman.
28 pp. London, J. Gilbert, [1864]
T.

8261 Report of the central committee for relief of distress in Ireland 1862–3.
tables. appendices. 108 pp. Dublin, Browne and Nolan, 1864
L., N., U.

8262 Rules and regulations of the Hibernian Williamite Society.
12 pp. Dublin, Warren, 1864
A.

8263 SCRATCHLEY, Arthur. Handy-book on life assurance law, for the use of policy-holders and agents. With a preliminary statement of some amendments that are desirable.
76 pp. London, V. & R. Stevens, 1864
T.

8264 Society for the encouragement of arts, manufactures and commerce, president: H.R.H. the Prince of Wales. Report addressed to the council by the special committee on the statistics of dwellings improvement in the metropolis.
tables. appendix. 48 pp. London, Simpkins, 1864
T.

8265 Stock farming in Canada.
24 pp. London, 1864
T.

8266 A supplement to the statement of the financial exigencies of Ireland before and after the legislative union, published in January, 1864.
tables. 18 pp. Dublin, A. Thom, 1864
N., U.

8267 TAYLOR, George. Tithe table showing the value of tithe rent-charges for the year 1864. To which is added, another table showing the extent of the yearly fluctuation in the prices of wheat, barley, and oats, since 1835.
8 pp. London, Shaw and Sons, 1864
T.

8268 TOMKINSON Frederick William, and TOMKINSON, T. H. The Factory Acts, as applied to the manufacture of earthenware, (including the act of 1864,) with notes and forms.
tables. appendices. 56 pp. Burslem, 1864
T.

8269 TORRENS, Robert R. Lectures on dealings with land by registration of title. As proposed to be applied to Ireland. With the proceedings of the meeting held on the 1st Feb. in Dublin. Published by the direction of the committee of the Registration of Title Association.
32 pp. Dublin, Hodges and Smith, 1864
N.

8270 TURNER, T. The three gilt balls: or, my uncle, his stock-in-trade and customers. A lecture.
34 pp. London, E. Marlborough, Hoxton, J. Rose, [1864?]
T.

8271 The twentieth annual report of the society for improving the condition of the labouring classes, 1863–64.
tables. 46 pp. n.p., [1864?]
T.

8272 WALKER, Robert J. American finances and resources, Letter no. V.
tables. 26 pp. London, W. Ridgway, 1864
T.

8273 ——. Jefferson Davis, repudiation of Arkansas bonds. Letter III.
14 pp. London, W. Ridgway, 1864
T.

8274 WILDE, Sir William Robert Wills. Ireland, past & present; the land & the people. A lecture.
52 pp. Dublin, McGlashan & Gill, 1864
B., T.

8275 WRAY, G. The farmer's difficulties: protection the only remedy.
24 pp. London, W. Ridgway, 1864
T.

8276 YOOL, George Valentine. Compensation to landowners: being a practical digest of the law of compensation.
56 pp. London, W. Maxwell, Dublin, Hodges, Smith, Edinburgh, Bell & Bradfute, 1864
T.

1865

8277 The agricultural value of the sewage of London examined in reference to the principal schemes submitted to the metropolitan board of works. With extracts from the evidence of chemists, engineers, and agriculturists.
frontisp. tables in appendix. 82 pp. London, E. Stanford, 1865
Q., T.

8278 ARRIVABENE, Carlo, count. The finances of Italy. A letter addressed by count Arrivabene to lord Stratford de Redcliffe.
tables. 12 pp. London, W. Ridgway, 1865
T.

8279 The assurance register: being a record of the progress and financial position of various life assurance associations in Great Britain as reported in the year 1864. Also the progress of fire insurance companies, as shown in the duty collected by government, and the sums insured on farming stock, in the years 1862 and 1863, respectively. By a fellow of the statistical society.
tables. 26 pp. London, W. Dawson, 1865
T.

8280 AVELING, Thomas. Road locomotives. An epitome of the new road locomotive acts, for the use of owners and drivers. With an introductory preface. By homas Aveling.
32 pp. London, E. and F. N. Spon, 1895
T.

8281 BEATSON, D. Notes on New South Wales.
60 pp. London, W. Kent, 1865
T.

8282 BRADY, William Maziere. Remarks on the Irish Church Temporalities.
tables. 32 pp. Dublin, McGee, 1865
A., T.

8283 BRAME, S. Voices from New Zealand: being a compilation of authentic letters from emigrants who have located in New Zealand since 1863; also, a series of questions answered.
illustrations. tables. 64 pp. London & Birmingham, James Upton, [1865]
T.

8284 BROWN, John. Jacob: a sermon on emigration.
23 pp. Londonderry, Standard Steam Book-Printing House, [1865]
B.

8285 BUCKLE, Fleetwood. Vital and economic statistics of the hospitals, infirmaries, etc., of England and Wales, for the year 1863.
tables. 86 pp. London, J. Churchill, 1865
T.

8286 BURGES, Ynyr H. A plea for the 'Irish Enemy'.
table of contents. 60 pp. Dublin, Hodges & Smith, 1865
N., T.

8287 CALLOW, John. A letter to the shareholders and policy holders of the European assurance society, on the subject of its recent amalgamation with the British nation life assurance association.
16 pp. London, W. Dawson, 1865
T.

8288 Canada: Bureau of Agriculture: A geographical, agricultural, and mineralogical sketch.
table of contents. 36 pp. Quebec, 'Le Canadien', 1865
N.

8289 CHADWICK, Edwin. Address on railway reform.
tables. 50 pp. London, Longman, Green, Longman, Roberts & Green, 1865
T.

8290 [CLARKE, Henry.] Workingmen's clubs. Hints for their formation, with rules, bye-laws, etc., by the author of 'Penny Banks.' Price fourpence.
table. 22 pp. Wolverhampton, J. McD. Roebuck, 1865
T.

8291 Cotton: the present and prospective position of supply and demand considered. By an onlooker.
tables. 24 pp. London, Effingham Wilson, 1865
T.

8292 COWELL, John Welsford. France and the Confederate States.
38 pp. London, R. Hardwicke, Paris, E. Dentu, 1865
T.

8293 The farmer's hour of trial. In four chapters: I To the general public. II To the tenant farmers. III To the landed proprietors. IV To the factors. By a friend to the agriculturist.
48 pp. London, Simpkin, Marshall, Manchester, John Heywood, [etc., etc.], 1865
T.

8294 A few words about Ireland. By an Englishman.
24 pp. London and Cambridge, Macmillan, 1865
T.

8295 FIELDEN, Joshua. Malt tax. A letter to the members of the house of commons, showing some of the effects of the malt tax on the labouring people of this country, and exposing the mis-statements of the chancellor of the exchequer and Mr. Milner Gibson, as to the relative pressure of the duties on wine, tea, coffee, and sugar, and the tax on malt.
tables. 36 pp. London, R. Hardwicke, 1865
                         T.

8296 Final report of the Central Relief Committee of the Society of Friends, established during the famine in Ireland in 1846 and 1847, and dissolved in 1865.
tables. appendices. 56 pp. Dublin, Hodges and Smith, London, A. W. Bennett, 1865
                         A.

8297 FRY, Henry. Henry Fry's shilling guide to the London charities for 1865–6; showing in alphabetical order the name, date of foundation, address, objects, and annual income, number of people benefited by, mode of application to, and chief officers of every charity in London.
192 pp. (various paging). 3rd ed. London, R. Hardwicke, 1865
                         T.

8298 GERRARD, Samuel. Prize essay. On the mode of managing farms in Ireland, under 40 statute acres, but applicable to farms of any size. Awarded a prize by the Royal Agricultural Society of Ireland. Third edition.
diags. 28 pp. Dublin, R. S. Magee, 1865
                         T.

8299 GILL, G. R. Remarks on the oppressive working of the game laws. By the late G. R. Gill, sometime schoolmaster in the village of Rowland's Castle, Hants.
34 pp. Southsea, T. Whitehorn, [1865]
                         T.

8300 HALL, John Charles. The trades of Sheffield as influencing life and health, more particularly file cutters and grinders. Read before the National Association for the promotion of social science, October 6th, 1865.
tables. 22 pp. London, Longman, Green, Longman, Roberts & Green, [1865]
                         T.

8301 HANCOCK, William Neilson. Report on the alleged violence of the working classes in Irish towns, as an impediment to the employment of capital.
tables. 13 pp. Dublin, A. Thom, 1865
                         N., Q., T.

8302 HARVEY, James. The exchequer note versus the sovereign: the great want of the country a state paper money expanding with population and wealth.
illust. appendix. 24 pp. Liverpool, Howell, London, Simpkin, Marshall, 1865
                         A., T.

8303 [HASLAM, John.] The real wants of the Irish people. By a member of the Statistical & Social Inquiry society of Ireland.
50 pp. Dublin, R. D. Webb, 1865
                         C., P., Q., T.

8304 HAYMAN, James. England. A word about the income tax; or, the difficulties in making a correct return explained and made easy.
tables. 2 pp. + fold-out. London, Briscoe, [1865]
                         T.

8305 HAYNES, John Bishop. How to supply the agricultural labourer with good beer at a low price, involving an argument for the repeal or reduction of the malt tax.
table. 14 pp. Evesham; W. & H. Smith, 1865
                         T.

8306 HENCHY, John. Ireland; its past and present condition since the termination of the French War, in 1815; and the remedial measures necessary for its improvement.
30 pp. Dublin, Forster, 1865
                         N.

8307 [HOWARD, James.] The evils of England, social and economical. By a London physician.
168 pp. 2nd ed. London, H. Renshaw, 1865
                         T.

8308 HUNTER, Adam. The fruits of amalgamation exhibited in the correspondence of a Palladium policy-holder with Charles Jellicoe, Esq., actuary of the Eagle assurance company of London.
tables. 42 pp. Edinburgh, Edmonston & Douglas, London, Hamilton, Adams, 1865
                         T.

8309 The Imperial Railway of Great Britain. By M. A.
12 pp. Oxford and London, J. H. and J. Parker, 1865
                         T.

8310 The Indian land question: a timely warning. Two series of papers. Reprinted from the 'Times of India.'
tables. 108 pp. London, Smith, Elder & Co., 1865
                         T.
Signed 'Indopolite'.

8311 The Irish Regium Donum; its history, character and effects.
tables. appendix. 56 pp. London, Miall, 1865
                         T.
Deals with finances of Presbyterian church in Ireland.

8312 JENNINGS, Francis M. The present & future of Ireland as the cattle farm of England, and her probable population. With legislative remedies.
110 pp. 2nd ed. Dublin, Hodges & Smith; London, Simpkin, Marshall, 1865
                         N., Q.

8313 JOYNT, William Lane. Suggestions for the amendment of the arterial drainage laws of Ireland.
table in appendix. 44 pp. Dublin, M. H. Gill, 1865
                         A., E., T.

8314 [KINCAID, William?] On contracts between landlord and tenant in Ireland. By a Leinster agent.
14pp. Dublin, Hodges and Smith, 1865
                         N.

8315 LARMUTH, George H. Practical information for landlords, tenants, lodgers, agents, and others; treating on the law of landlord and tenant, purchasing, valuing, letting, collecting, repairing, and the general management of property, etc., with an appendix, containing useful forms of agreements, notices, etc.
tables. appendix. 64 pp. London, Simpkin, Marshall, [1865]
T.

8316 LIFFORD, James Hewitt, 4th viscount. 'Who is Blacker?' Speech of Sir Robert Peel, February 24th, 1865.
16 pp. Dublin, Hodges & Smith, 1865
T.

8317 LIVESEY, J. Malt, malt liquor, malt tax, beer, and barley being a reply to Sir Fitzroy Kelly M.P. for East Suffolk, Mr. Everett, Mr. Smee and other gentlemen, on the repeal of the malt tax.
tables. 16 pp. London, Tweddie, [1865]
N., T.

8318 Loan societies: their history, formation, & management.
tables. 84 pp. London, printed at 'Marylebone Mercury' offices, [1865?]
T.

8319 McEVOY, John. The fiscal and social injustice of the Irish pawnbroking system. A report prepared for the general committee of the united trades' association by John McEvoy, honorary secretary to the St. Stephen's Green committee, the births and deaths registration committee, etc.
appendices. 16 pp. Dublin, R. D. Webb, 1865
P.

8320 McHAFFIE, Michael J. Eighteen years statistical tables giving monthly price and yearly average of money, corn, cotton and cotton goods. Also stocks of cotton on last Friday each month. 1847 to 1864.
34 pp. London, Effingham Wilson, Manchester, Thomson, [1865]
T.

8321 Minnesota as a home for immigrants. Being the first and second prize essays awarded by the board of examiners appointed pursuant to an act of the legislature of the state of Minnesota, approved March 4, 1864.
tables. 80 pp. Saint Paul, Minn., 1865
P.

8322 Money to any amount advanced at one hour's notice; or the vampires of London.
appendix. 34 pp. London, G. Wells, 1865
T.

8323 MOORE, William Armitage. Opinions on Mr. Dalton and Mr. Carden's pamphlets on the Irish question.
12 pp. Cavan, Fegan, 1865
A.

8324 NAPER, James Lenox William. An address to the ratepayers of the County of Meath.
tables. 20 pp. Dublin, McGlashan and Gill, 1865
A.

8325 O'CONOR DON, The. A few remarks on the evidence received by the Irish Taxation Committee together with a brief review of the subject.
tables. 102 pp. Dublin, Fowler, 1865
N., U.

8326 On exorbitant rate of discount, and showing how the malt tax might be repealed without creating a deficiency in the revenue. A letter addressed to the working-classes. By an ex-M.P.
22 pp. London, R. Hardwicke, 1865
T.

8327 Our currency. By a merchant.
tables. 48 pp. London, Effingham Wilson, 1865
T.

8328 PLUNKETT, Wm. Conyngham, later archbishop of Dublin and 4th baron Plunket. The church and the census in Ireland. An address (reprinted by permission from the report of the church congress held in Manchester, October, 1863).
appendix. tables. 40 pp. Dublin, Hodges and Smith, 1865
A., E., N.

8329 Portadown Loan Co., Limited. Fifth annual report.
tables. 4 pp. Portadown, Farrell, 1865
N.

8330 Rates of carriage. Report of the proceedings of a public meeting of the inhabitants of the borough of Liverpool.
appendix. tables. 44 pp. Liverpool, Lee & Nightingale, 1865
N.

8331 Report of the committee of the Registration of Title Association (Ireland).
20 pp. Dublin, Hodges and Smith, 1865
A.

8332 RIDLEY, William Henry. An address to the people of a country parish on friendly societies and benefit clubs.
12 pp. Oxford and London, J. H. and J. Parker, 1865
T.

8333 SPARGO, Thomas. The mines of Cornwall and Devon: statistics and observations. Illustrated by maps, plans, and sections of the several mining districts in the two counties.
maps. plans. appendix. tables. 202 pp. London, Emily Faithfull & Co., 1865
T.

8334 The statements of earl Russell K.C. respecting the revenues of the Irish Church in the new edition of his essay on 'The English Government and Constitution', examined by an Englishman resident in Ireland.
tables. 24 pp. London, J. Parker, Dublin, Hodges & Smith, 1865
N., T.

8335 Total repeal of the malt tax. By Julio, Tunbridge Wells.
22 pp. London, W. Ridgway, 1865
N., T.

8336 TRAVERS, S. Smith.   On the sugar duties: a paper read before the meeting of the associated chambers of commerce, London, February 23rd, 1865.
tables. appendix. 46 pp. London, Longman, Green, Longman, Roberts, & Green, 1865

T.

8337 WETHERFIELD, George Manley.   How to arrange embarrassed affairs. A plain guide for debtors and creditors in bankruptcy and trust deeds.
14 pp. London, J. Moore, 1865

T.

8338 WILSON, Edward Thomas.   Sanitary statistics of Cheltenham. A paper read before the British association for the advancement of science—Bath, Sept. 1864.
tables. appendix. 46 pp. London, Longman, Green, Longman, Roberts and Green, Cheltenham, G. A. Williams, 1865

T.

1866

8339 ADAIR, Sir Robert Alexander Shafto, bart. later baron Waveney.   Ireland and her servile war.
table. 72 pp. London, W. Ridgway, Dublin, Hodges & Smith, 1866

A., N., T., U.

8340 ANNAND, William.   Confederation. A letter to the right honourable the earl of Carnarvon, principal secretary of state for the colonies.
42 pp. London, E. Stanford, 1866

T.

8341 [ASTON, C. Penrhyn.]   A letter to the working men of England, from one of themselves.
8 pp. Chelsea, at the office of the 'West Middlesex Advertiser', 1866

T.

8342 ATKINS, William.   The consideration of certain changes in the distribution and management of church property which would tend to render the Irish branch of the United Church more efficient.
tables. 40 pp. London, F. & J. Rivington, Dublin, Hodges and Smith, 1866

N., T.

8343 AYTOUN, James.   Does the Bank Charter Act of 1844 need modification? A paper prepared at the request of the Council of the National Association for the promotion of Social Science, and read at a meeting of that body at Manchester, October 5, 1866.
23 pp. London, R. Hardwicke, 1866

T.

8344 ——.   The Irish difficulty, in five letters to 'The Examiner'.
24 pp. London, R. Hardwicke, Dublin, McGlashan & Gill, 1866

T.

8345 BATH, John.   On the insurance of merchants' and wholesale traders' commercial debts.
24 pp. London, Effingham Wilson, 1866

N.

8346 BAXTER, Robert Dudley.   The re-distribution of seats and the counties.
tables. appendix. 38 pp. London, E. Stanford, 1866

T.

8347 [BENTLEY, Joseph.]   How to get plenty of cotton, good and cheap. The second cotton famine, and how to prevent a third; by the oldest school inspector; being his 34th work, designed to teach people how to become 'well off'. Nobody believes the manufacturing districts can be 'well off', without plenty of good cheap cotton.
98 pp. London, J. Bentley, [1866?]

T.

8348 BRERETON, Joseph Lloyd.   Employers and employed.
28 pp. London, W. Ridgway, 1866

T.

8349 BUSBY, James.   Our colonial empire and the case of New Zealand.
tables. appendix. 206 pp. London, Williams and Norgate, [1866]

T.

8350 BUTT, Isaac.   Fixity of tenure; heads of a suggested legislative enactment; with an introduction & notes. To which are added queries, proposed for the consideration of all who desire to solve the problem of Ireland's social condition.
48 pp. Dublin, J. Falconer, 1866

C., Q., T., U.

8351 ——.   Land tenure in Ireland: a plea for the Celtic race.
118 pp. Dublin, J. F. Fowler, 1866

A., L., N., T., U.

8352 CAMPBELL-WALKER, A.   Proper free trade and when are we to have it?
32 pp. 2nd edition. London, Chapman & Hall, 1866

T.

8353 COLE, Henry Warwick.   The middle classes and the borough franchise.
88 pp. London, Longmans, Green, Reader and Dyer, 1866

T.

8354 COPLAND, Samuel.   Black and white; or, the Jamaica question.
64 pp. London, W. Freeman, 1866

T.

8355 Credit and its bearings upon the crisis of 1866.
44 pp. London, Effingham Wilson, 1866

T.

8356 DE VERE, Aubrey.   The church settlement of Ireland, or, Hibernia Pacanda.
96 pp. London, Longmans, Green, Reader, and Dyer, Dublin, J. Duffy, 1866

T.

8357 DOUBLEDAY, Thomas.   The war, the balance of trade and the Bank Acts, in a series of letters addressed to the editor of 'The Newcastle Chronicle', with a preface and appendix.
62 pp. London, Effingham Wilson, 1866

T.

8358 DUFFERIN AND AVA, Frederick Temple Hamilton-Temple-Blackwood, 1st marquess of. Contributions to an inquiry into the state of Ireland.
table of contents. appendices. tables. 224 pp. London, J. Murray, 1866
N., T., U.

8359 DUNLOP, Charles. Brazil as a field for emigration: its geography, climate, agricultural capabilities, and the facilities afforded for permanent settlement.
tables. 32 pp. London, Bates, Hendy, Trubner, [1866]
T.

8360 DWYER, Philip. Work and its reward in the Irish church.
tables. 56 pp. Dublin, Hodges & Smith, 1866
T.

8361 EAGAR, Geoffrey. Financial statement. Speech of the hon. Geoffrey Eagar, colonial treasurer, in moving the first resolution, in committee of ways and means, in the legislative assembly, on Thursday the 27th of September, 1866. With an appendix, containing the project, for the establishment of a national bank.
appendix. tables. 50 pp. Sydney, Sands, 1866
N.

8362 [ELLIS, William.] Three letters from a London merchant to a country friend on the late 'Monetary crisis'.
38 pp. London, J. Gilbert. 1866
T.

8363 The evils of Ireland considered, with a view to possible remedies. In a letter to the right hon. Chichester Fortescue, chief secretary for Ireland. With the draft of a bill on the land question. By Scamperdale.
appendix. 50 pp. Dublin, Hodges & Smith, 1866
T.

8364 FISHER, Joseph. The land question.
62 pp. Dublin, McGlashan & Gill, London, Longmans, Green, Reader & Dyer, 1866
B.

8365 FOWLER, William. The crisis of 1866: a financial essay.
tables. appendices. 60 pp. London, Longmans, Green, Reader & Dyer, 1866
T.

8366 GAMBLE, Richard W. Suggestions as to why the legislature should interfere to secure to the tenant compensation for his improvements, as to how far they should interfere, and the principles by which they should be guided in doing so.
8 pp. Dublin, Warren, 1866
N.

8367 General hints to emigrants containing notices of the various fields for emigration, with practical hints on preparation for emigrating—outfit for the voyage—the voyage—landing—obtaining employment—purchase and clearing of land etc; together with various directions and recipes useful to the emigrant.
map. index. tables. 214 pp. London, Virtue, 1866
N.

8368 GIBBON, Alexander. Principia in the science, and errors in the practice of political economy in the United Kingdom.
30 pp. tables. London, W. Ridgway, 1866
T.

8369 La grève des charbonniers d'Anzin en 1866. Ordre et progrès.
44 pp. Paris, Picard, 1866
N.

8370 [GUTHRIE, George.] Guthrie's bank reform. Letter to the right hon. Benjamin Disraeli, M.P., chancellor of the exchequer, on money, capital, banking.
16 pp. Edinburgh & London, W. Blackwood, & Son, 1866
T.

8371 Half-yearly reports and transactions of the Royal Agricultural Society of Ireland, 42, Upper Sackville Street, Dublin, Dec., 1863 to May 1866.
tables. plans [of houses]. 56 pp. Dublin, at the office of the 'Farmers' Gazette', 1866
D.

8372 HANCOCK, William Neilson. Report on deposits in joint stock banks in Ireland, 1863–1865, with deposits, 1840–1865, annexed.
6 pp. Dublin, A. Thom, 1866
Q.

8373 ——. Report on the landlord & tenant question in Ireland, from 1860 till 1866; with an appendix, containing a report on the question from 1835 till 1859.
86 pp. Dublin, A. Thom, 1866
C., N., Q., T.

8374 HEMANS, George Willoughby, and HASSARD, Richard. On the future water supply of London.
tables. 34 pp. London, E. Stanford, 1866
N.

8375 HEYWORTH, Lawrence. Glimpses at the origin, mission, and destiny of man; with miscellaneous papers on taxation, peace, war, the Sabbath, intoxicants, etc., shewing that unwise fiscal legislation is the great impediment of our day to universal commerce, to social amelioration, and to intellectual advancement. Customs duties are human barriers, nefariously erected everywhere, across the heaven-designed channels of humanising commerce.
230 pp. London, Williams and Norgate, 1866
T.

8376 HORRY, Sidney Calder. The new partnership amendment act, with notes on each clause, included in a general exposition of the laws relating to common partnerships, and companies, under the acts for joint-stock companies, railways, banking, mining and letters patent, and showing the liabilities of all partners and shareholders.
tables. 104 pp. London, Darton and Hodge, [1866]
T.

8377 The Irish poor in English prisons and workhouses. A letter to a member of parliament.
tables. 14 pp. London, Burns, Lambert, and Oates, 1866
T.

8378 Irish railways. Government loans. Memorial of certain of the companies to the lords commissioners of H.M. Treasury, praying for legislation to enable government to lend money in order to pay off their debts, etc. and to finish the construction of their railways; also financial and statistical statement in relation thereto. April, 1866.
tables. 36 pp. Limerick, McKern, 1866
N.

8379 JACKSON, Robert [compiler]. Hand book on Irish railway reform: containing copy of memorial addressed to the Lords Commissioners of H.M. Treasury, by the people of Ireland; together with the resolutions passed at public meetings, extracts from the evidence given before the Royal Commissioners on railways, and the plan, as submitted to them by the Irish Railway Reform Committee, for improving and developing Irish railways, and the debate in the house of commons on the motion of W. H. Gregory Esq. M.P. July 23, 1866 and other data (see Contents).
table of contents. tables. 66 pp. Dublin, Farmers' Gazette Office, 1866
N.

8380 JENNINGS, Francis M. An inquiry into the causes of the poverty & discontent in Ireland, with suggestions for their removal.
tables. 36 pp. Dublin, Hodges & Smith, London, Simpkin, Marshall & Co., 1866
A., C., Q., T.

8381 JOHNES, Arthur James. Remarks on the late report from the select committee on bankruptcy and the bankruptcy bill now pending; in a letter to lord Brougham and Vaux.
26 pp. London, Wildy, 1866
T.

8382 ——. Postscript to Mr. A. J. Johnes's letter on bankruptcy.
8 pp. Aberystwyth, printed by Cox [1866?]
T.

8383 KETTLE, Rupert. Strikes and arbitrations: with the procedure and forms successfully adopted in the building trade at Wolverhampton. Written at the request of the working men's club.
appendix. 48 pp. London, Simpkin, Marshall, Wolverhampton, W. Parke, 1866
T.

8384 KINGDOM, William. Suggestions for the liquidation of the national debt.
12 pp. London, Whittaker, 1866
T.

8385 KNIGHT, Robert. Speech on Indian affairs, delivered before the Manchester chamber of commerce, on the 24th January, 1866.
table. 64 pp. London, W. J. Johnson, 1866
T.

8386 LAMB, Arthur. The statutes relating to friendly, industrial and provident societies; with an introduction and notes.
tables. index. 128 pp. London, R. Hardwicke, [1866]
T.

8387 LEES, Henry. The North British Railway, its past and future policy with remarks on the duties and responsibilities of directors in reference to accounts.
20 pp. Edinburgh, A. and C. Black, 1866
T.

8388 LEVI, Leone. On the wine trade and wine duties. A lecture, delivered at King's College, London, February 26th 1866.
tables. 20 pp. London, Effingham Wilson, 1866
T.

8389 LINDO, Abraham. Dr. Underhill's testimony on the wrongs of the negro in Jamaica examined in a letter to the editor of 'The Times'.
table. 32 pp. London, Effingham Wilson, 1866
T.

8390 LIVESEY, William. A financial scheme for the relief of railway companies, submitted to directors, shareholders, and the public for their consideration. In two parts.
tables. 38 pp. London, Waterlow, [1866]
T.

8391 London, Chatham, and Dover Railway Company. Complication made clear; or the exact condition of each interest defined. For the use of the debenture-holders, shareholders and the public.
index. tables. 28 pp. London, Effingham Wilson, 1866
N.

8392 LONGE, Francis D. A refutation of the wage-fund theory of modern political economy as enunciated by Mr. Mill, M.P. and Mr. Fawcett, M.P.
84 pp. London, Longmans, Green, Reader & Dyer, 1866
T.

8393 Lord Dufferin refuted. Tenant-right on expiration of a lease, established on arbitration in Co. Down, before the agents of colonel Forde and lord Hill Trevor.
map. 14 pp. Dublin, Hodges & Smith, 1866
T.

8394 MACBAY, W. The United Kingdom really united (Ireland to England): how to obtain good and cheap beef and unfailing crops.
map. 20 pp. London, E. Stanford, 1866
N.

8395 MILLER, William. A plan for a national currency, in a letter to the chamber of commerce of Glasgow.
tables. 32 pp. Glasgow, J. Smith, 1866
T.

8396 MILLS, John. The bank charter act and the late panic: A paper read before the economic section of the national social science association, at Manchester, October 5th, 1866. With notes added.
24 pp. London, Simpkin, Marshall, Manchester, A. Ireland, 1866
T.

8397 MURCHISON, John Henry. The conservatives and 'liberals,' their principles and policy.
52 pp. London, Saunders & Otley, 1866
T.

8398 Notes on some statements in the evidence and accounts received by the select committee of the house of commons on the taxation of Ireland in 1864 and 1865, compiled by a retired comptroller of revenue.

table of contents. tables. 24 pp. 2nd issue, with corrections and additions. Dublin, A. Thom, 1866

N.

8399 O'HARA, H. Report on the supply of fuel in Ireland: an inquiry into the character and extent of the Irish coal fields, peat marshes, etc.

maps. diags. tables. appendix. 28 pp. Dublin, McGlashan and Gill, 1866

U.

8400 Our next money panic. It may not come for three years, and it may come in three months! Being a short inquiry into the natural laws which govern coined money in its relation to bullion, and showing the necessity for any early revision of our present currency laws.

appendix. 24 pp. Lewes, printed at 'Sussex Express', [1866?]

T.

8401 Overend, Gurney, & Co. Birchin-Lane book-keeping; or the new knack of muddling through millions: addressed not only to existing contributories, but also to shareholders, that have been, and to creditors, that are; and dedicated by permission, as a pilot and a beacon, to young honesty, present and prospective, in the city of London. Second ed.

20 pp. London, Effingham Wilson, 1866

T.

8402 Overend, Gurney, & Coy., or the saddle on the right horse, in a letter to the shareholders from one of themselves, '1915'.

16 pp. 3rd ed. London, Effingham Wilson, 1866

T.

8403 The panic; a second sketch from nature. By A. Fitz-adam (pseud.)

48 pp. London, W. Ridgway and Mann, [1866]

T.

——. 2nd ed.

52 pp. (various paging). London, W. Ridgway and Mann, [1866]

T.

8404 PETRIE, Francis William Henry. The Irish poor law rating as it affects tithe rent-charge property.

8 pp. London, F. & J. Rivington, [etc.], 1866

N., T.

8405 The present position, prospects, and duties of the Scottish farmer, viewed in relation to the landlord's right of hypothec, the operation of the game laws on grass and corn lands, and the new reform bill.

14 pp. Edinburgh, Bell and Bradfute, 1866

T.

8406 The prevention of panics; or, suggestions for an economical system of national finance in connexion with the construction of public works in any country in the world, without either subscriptions, loans, mortgages, bonds, or interest. By a civil engineer.

58 pp. 3rd ed. London, A. H. Baily, 1866

T.

8407 RAWLINGS, Thomas. What shall we do with the Hudson's Bay territory? Colonize the 'fertile belt' which contains forty millions of acres.

tables. 84 pp. London, A. H. Baily, 1866

T.

8408 RENNIE, C. G. Colleton. Reform considered in connection with the Government Bill.

tables. 50 pp. London, E. Stanford, 1866

T.

8409 SANKEY, William H. Villiers. Railway reform. Being the essence of a larger work which will appear shortly, containing apposite suggestions for adopting certain requisite measures with a view to ensure, firstly: security of life and immunity from personal injury, so far as human foresight can provide, to those who travel by or have to do with the working of railways; and, secondly: security of capital and receipt of fair reliable returns to those who invest their money in, or in any way contribute to, those necessary and useful undertakings.

46 pp. London, Effingham Wilson, 1866

N.

8410 Scottish Chamber of Agriculture. Discussion on the report of her majesty's commissioners on the law relating to the landlord's right of hypothec in Scotland, in so far as regards agricultural subjects, and the minutes of evidence on which it is based.

48 pp. Edinburgh, Seton & Mackenzie, 1866

T.

8411 SHAW, Sir Charles, ed. The abuses of the Irish church verified by historical records, by a member of the Church of England.

74 pp. London, W. Ridgway, 1866

T.

8412 SHUTTLEWORTH, Sir James Kay, bart. A scheme for general and local administration of endowments, especially those for middle-class education. Read at the meeting of the national association for the promotion of social science at Manchester, October 5, 1866.

22 pp. London, Faithfull & Head, 1866

T.

8413 SMITH, George Henry. Outlines of political economy, designed chiefly for the use of schools and of junior students.

76 pp. London, Longmans, Green, Reader, and Dyer, 1866

T.

8414 SMITH, John Benjamin. An inquiry into the causes of money panics, and of the frequent fluctuations in the rate of discount: a letter addressed to Malcolm Ross, Esq., president of the Manchester chamber of commerce.

table. 20 pp. London, Simpkin, Marshall, Manchester, A. Ireland, 1866

T.

8415 SMITH, William. Ireland's own verdict on the Irish question. Letters to lord Wodehouse & earl Russell. With a postscript to the gentlemen of Ireland.

12 pp. Dublin, J. White, 1866

B., T.

8416 SMYTH, R. Brough. Intercolonial Exhibition, 1866. Mining and Mineral Statistics.
tables. 42 pp. Melbourne, Blundell and Ford, 1866
N.

8417 STIRLING, James. Practical considerations on banks and bank management.
tables in appendix. 68 pp. 2nd ed. Glasgow, James Maclehose, [etc., etc.], 1866
T.

8418 TAPPING, Thomas. Joint stock companies, how to form them; being the second edition of the handy book on public companies. Designed as a practical guide for projectors, promoters, directors, shareholders, creditors, solicitors, secretaries, and other officers.
tables. 84 pp. 2nd ed. London, Mining Journal Office, 1866
T.

8419 [THOMSON, William Thomas.] The Bank of England the Bank Acts and the currency by Cosmopolite.
tables. appendices. 72 pp. Edinburgh & London, W. Blackwood & Son, 1866
T.

8420 Thoughts upon church reform in Ireland. By a beneficed clergyman.
table. 40 pp. Dublin, G. Herbert, 1866
T.

8421 Unfair assessment of the clergy. A letter to the right honourable C. P. Villiers, M.P. on the unjust and mischievous operation of the Union Assessment Committee Act of 1862, as it affects the clergy. With a report of two cases of appeal, and suggestions for the amendment of the act. By a country rector.
tables. appendix. 100 pp. London, [etc.], F. & J. Rivington, 1866
T.

8422 WARD, James. The Continental crisis: its probable causes and effects.
tables. 104 pp. London, Houlston and Wright, 1866
T.

8423 WASON, Peter Rigby. An effectual remedy for an usurious rate of discount, also exposing its baneful effects upon the agricultural, commercial, manufacturing, trading, and railway interests. And upon the working classes, on whom it operates with crushing severity.
66 pp. 3rd ed. London, R. Hardwicke, 1866
T.

8424 WETHERFIELD, George Manley. A handy book, or plain guide for debtors and creditors in bankruptcy and trust deeds. With short forms of assignments and composition deeds and scales of costs. Also suggestions for practical improvements.
tables in appendix. 40 pp. 2nd ed. London, Smith, 1866
T.

1867

8425 ANDERSON, George. The reign of bullionism.
tables. 66 pp. Glasgow, T. Murray, 1867
T.

8426 ASHBURTON, Alexander Baring, 1st baron. The financial and commercial crisis considered. By lord Ashburton. Also, the letter of a London banker on the currency question to the editor of the Times.
32 pp. London, reprinted by P. S. King, 1867
N.

2nd ed. published London 1847: see 6110

8427 ATKINSON, Edward. On the collection of revenue.
tables. appendices. 70 pp. Boston, Williams, 1867
T.

8428 BAKER, T. B. Vagrancy. To be read at the Social Science Meeting, at Belfast, September 19th, 1867.
12 pp. Gloucester, Bellows, 1867
N.

8429 BAYMAN, Robert. A letter to the right reverend the lord bishop of London, on the dwellings of the poor. New Year's Eve, 1866.
tables. appendix. 14 pp. London, W. Ridgway, 1867
T.

8430 BIRD, Henry Edward. Railway accounts: a comprehensive analysis of the capital and revenue of the railways of the United Kingdom; with a few observations thereon.
tables. 30 pp. [London, Dean, 1867?]
T.

8431 BUTT, Isaac. Fixity of tenure; heads of a suggested legislative enactment; with an introduction and notes.
40 pp. 2nd ed. Dublin, J. Falconer, London, W. Ridgway, 1867
N., Q., U.

8432 ——. The Irish querist: a series of questions proposed for the consideration of all who desire to solve the problems of Ireland's social condition.
40 pp. Dublin, J. Falconer, 1867
C., T.

8433 Capital and labour. By a member of the Manchester Chamber of Commerce.
table. 78 pp. London, E. Stanford, 1867
T.

8434 The case of Ireland stated, irrespective of party considerations. By Mentor.
70 pp. Dublin, the Official Printing Company, 1867
A., N.

8435 CLEMINSHAW, Charles Graham. A few remarks on the pamphlet entitled 'Metropolitan Gas legislation past and prospective'.
22 pp. London, Longmans, Green, Reader & Dyer, 1867
T.

8436 COLERIDGE, Derwent. Compulsory education and rate-payment. A speech delivered at a meeting of the London Diocesan Board of Education at London House, on Thursday, February 28th, 1867. Corrected and enlarged, with a postscript.
30 pp. London, E. Moxon, 1867
T.

8437 Consolidation of Irish Railways: A letter to the rt. hon. the earl of Derby, K.G. etc. first lord of the treasury. By a member of the Institution of Civil Engineers.
tables. 14 pp. Dublin, McGlashan & Gill, London, C. Letts, 1867

N.

8438 CRAWFORD, Robert Wigram. Railway legislation. Speech delivered by Robert Wigram Crawford, Esq., in the house of commons, on Tuesday, April 2nd, 1867; together with the debate and opinions of the press.
table. 90 pp. London, Effingham Wilson, 1867

T.

8439 The Credit Foncier of Mauritius, Limited.
table of contents. tables. 72 pp. London, Causton, 1867
N.
Includes Prospectus, Reports, etc.

8440 DALTON, Gustavus Tuite. Irish peers on Irish peasants. An answer to lord Dufferin and the earl of Rosse. 48 pp. Dublin, Hodges, Smith, London, W. Ridgway, 1867
N.
Deals with emigration and the land question.

8441 A demurrer to Mr. Butt's plea. By an Irish land agent.
tables. 44 pp. Dublin, Hodges, Smith, 1867

T.

8442 DE VERE, Aubrey. Ireland's church property, and the right use of it.
60 pp. London, Longmans, Green, Reader, and Dyer, Dublin, J. Duffy

B., N., P., T.

8443 DICKSON, Stephen Fox. Address to the honourable the commons of the United Kingdom of Great Britain and Ireland, more especially the Irish members. On the elevation of Ireland, by the international fiscal terms, conditions and stipulations made and fixed by the parliament of Ireland, with the parliament of Great Britain, in the seventh article of union.
fold. tabs. 92 pp. Dublin, I. MacDonnell, 1867

A., B., L., N.

8444 Emigration to Natal, and conditions of government land grants, with full description of the colony and its industries. [Incomplete.]
map. tables. 64 pp.
Appendix to the pamphlet 'Emigration to Natal', August, 1866. [Should read 1867.] 12 pp. [Published separately.] London, Jarrold, [1867]

N.

8445 A few remarks on Mr. Butt's pamphlet, land tenure, and relation of landlord and tenant: with an appendix, containing some remarks on the Roman catholic priesthood, education, and the established church.
appendix. 66 pp. Dublin, G. Herbert, 1867

E.

8446 The financial lessons of 1866. A letter addressed, by permission, to the right hon. W. E. Gladstone, M.P., by a city manager.
tables in appendix. 82 pp. London, Smith, Elder & co., 1867

T.

8447 FITZ-WYGRAM, Loftus. Limited liability made practical. Reduction of capital of companies and the subdivision of shares; with remarks on the 12th section of 'the Companies Act, 1862,' and suggestions as to 'shares to bearer.'
22 pp. London, Effingham Wilson, 1867

T.

8448 Fox, Charles Douglas. On the construction of future branch railways in the United Kingdom.
tables. 16 pp. London, published at 8 New Street, Spring Gardens, 1867

T.

8449 FRANCE, R. S. Lord Redesdale and the new railways: a review of his lordship as a railway legislator.
24 pp. London, Witherby, 1867

N.

8450 The franchise: freemen: free-trade. By the author of the people's blue book.
table. 24 pp. London, Longmans, Green, Reader, and Dyer, 1867

T.

8451 GASSIOT, John P. Monetary panics and their remedy, with opinions of the highest authorities on the Bank Charter Act.
tables. appendix. 50 pp. 2nd ed. (enlarged). London, Effingham Wilson, 1867

N., T.

8452 GRAHAME, James. Financial fenianism and the Caledonian railway.
appendix with tables. 32 pp. Glasgow, John Smith, [etc., etc.], 1867

T.

8453 HARVEY, Thomas, & BREWIN, William. Jamaica in 1866. A narrative of a tour through the island, with remarks on its social, educational and industrial condition.
map. tables. appendix. 134 pp. London, A. W. Bennett, 1867

T.

8454 How to relieve the poor of Edinburgh without increasing pauperism. A tried, economical, and successful plan.
28 pp. Edinburgh, Edmonston and Douglas, 1867

T.

8455 HUTTON, Henry Dix. The Prussian land-tenure reforms and a farmer proprietary for Ireland. Two papers read at the annual meeting of the National Association for the promotion of social science, held in Belfast, September, 1867. Published by permission of the council.
tables. appendixes with tables. 46 pp. Dublin, J. Falconer, London, W. Ridgway, 1867

T.

8456 ——. The record of title in Ireland, its working and advantages, illustrated by practical examples. A paper read at the annual meeting of the National Association for the promotion of social science, held at Belfast, 1867 and published with the permission of the council.
16 pp. Dublin, Hodges, Smith, London, W. Ridgway, 1867

U.

8457 Ireland: her present condition; its causes and remedies. tables. 78 pp. Dublin, J. Falconer, London, W. Ridgway, 1867.

U.

8458 The Irish difficulty. By an Irish peer. 106 pp. Dublin, Hodges, Smith, 1867

A., N., T.

8459 Irish railways. Should government purchase the Irish railways? A question for the shareholders and the public. 18 pp. Dublin, W. B. Kelly, 1867

T.

8460 Jamaica: its state and prospects; with an exposure of the proceedings of the freed-man's aid society, and the Baptist missionary society. 24 pp. London, W. Macintosh, 1867

T.

8461 JONES, Ernest. Democracy vindicated. A lecture delivered to the Edinburgh working men's institute, on the 4th January 1867, in reply to Professor Blackie's lecture on democracy, delivered on the previous evening. 24 pp. Edinburgh, A. Elliot, London, W. Ridgway, [1867?]

T.

8462 KITTO, R. L. M. The gold fields of Victoria; with statistics, gathered from the various departments of the Victorian government, & other sources; showing an immense opening for the safe investment of capital in the Australian gold mines. tables. 64 pp. London, Effingham Wilson, 1867

T.

8463 LAMB, Arthur. The statutes relating to friendly, industrial and provident societies; with an introduction and notes. index. tables. 128 pp. London, R. Hardwicke, [1867]

T.

8464 LE MERCHANT, Henry D. Trades' unions and the commission thereon. 34 pp. London, R. Bentley, 1867

T.

8465 LEVY, John. Seven letters on the Irish land question and the Prussian land laws. 72 pp. Dublin & London, J. Duffy, 1867

U.

8466 Liabilities of shareholders and the rights of creditors, under the 'Limited Liability Act, 1862,' considered in a series of letters published in a leading weekly commercial journal, and having reference more particularly to the matter of Overend, Gurney, and Co., Limited. 24 pp. London, Effingham Wilson, 1867.

T.

8467 LIFFORD, James Hewitt, 4th viscount. A plea for Irish landlords. A letter to Isaac Butt Q.C. 20 pp. Dublin, Hodges, Smith, 1867

A., N.

8468 LOND, T. Destitution in Poplar. A letter to the right hon. the earl of Derby, K.G., on the present destitute condition of the shipbuilding trades in the Port of London; with some practical suggestions for their present and future wellbeing with especial reference to the operation of trades unions. table. 18 pp. London, W. Tweedie, 1867

T.

8469 The London, Chatham and Dover Railway (Main Line) Beckenham to Dover. Consisting of first or Dover preference stock, ordinary consolidated stock, and debentures secured on the general undertaking. Report of the committee of the main line shareholders, appointed the 3rd December, 1866. tables. 30 pp. London, Effingham Wilson, 1867

T.

8470 Lord Elcho and the miners. Employers & employed. table. 18 pp. London, T. Harrison, 1867

T.

8471 MAESTRI, Pierre. Rapport soumis à la Junte Organisatrice sur le programme de la VIme session du Congrès International de Statistique. table of contents. 70 pp. Florence, Barbera, 1867

N.

8472 MALONE, Sylvester. Tenant wrong illustrated in a nutshell; or a history of Kilkee in relation to landlordism during the last seven years. In a letter addressed to the right hon. W. E. Gladstone, M.P. 60 pp. Dublin, W. B. Kelly, 1867

A., N., Q., T.

8473 The Midland railway. Another word to the proprietors. By a large shareholder. 8 pp. London, Effingham Wilson, 1867

T.

8474 MITCHELL, Joseph. Railway finances, being suggestions for the resuscitation and improvement of the railway companies at present in financial difficulties in a letter addressed to the right hon. Benjamin Disraeli H.M. Chancellor of the Exchequer. tables. appendix. 28 pp. London, E. Stanford, 1867

T.

8475 MONCREIFF, James. Extension of the suffrage. An address delivered by James Moncreiff, Esq., M.P., LL.D., dean of the faculty of advocates, in the Music-hall, Edinburgh, on Monday, December 10, 1866. 40 pp. Edinburgh, Edmonston and Douglas, 1867

T.

8476 NAPER, James Lenox William. Irish proprietors and Irish peasantry. table. 26 pp. Dublin, McGlashan and Gill, 1867

N.

8477 NEISON, Frances G. P. Observation on odd fellow and friendly societies. Fourteenth ed. much enlarged and extended. tables. 150 pp. London, Simpkin Marshall, 1867

T.

8478 NICHOLSON, Nathaniel Alexander. One reserve or many? Thoughts suggested by the crisis of 1866.
22 pp. London, Trübner, 1867
T.

8479 Notes on the investment of trust funds in East India stock. By a barrister.
16 pp. London, Stevens, 1867
T.

8480 O'BRIEN, James Thomas. Bishop of Ossory, Ferns, and Leighlin. The case of the established church in Ireland.
72 pp. London, [etc.], F. & J. Rivington, Dublin, G. Herbert, 1867
T.

8481 Overend, Gurney, & Co. (Limited). A plain statement of the case, by a barrister.
20 pp. London, J. Gilbert, 1867
T.

8482 Overend, Gurney, & Co., Ltd. Report of the committee of the defence association.
tables. appendix. 86 pp. London, 1867
T.

8483 PETRIE, Francis William Henry. The Irish poor law rating, as it affects tithe rent-charge property. Fourth edition.
table. appendix. 8 pp. London, F. & J. Rivington, Dublin, Hodges, Smith, 1867
T.

8484 PIM, Jonathan. The land question in Ireland: suggestions for its solution by the application of mercantile principles to dealings with land.
64 pp. Dublin, Hodges, Smith, 1867
N., T.
Includes text of 'The Landed Property (Ireland) Improvement Act, 1867'—a proposed Bill, written by Pim.

8485 ROBERTSON, Alexander. Our deer forests. An inaugural lecture delivered to the members of the Highland Economic Society, at the Religious Institution Rooms, Glasgow, on 5th March, 1867. By the president.
50 pp. London, Longmans, Green, Reader & Dyer, 1867
T.

8486 RONEY, Sir Cusack P. The alps and the Eastern Mails.
tables. map. 58 pp. London, Effingham Wilson, 1867
T.

8487 ROSSE, William Parsons, 3rd earl of. A few words on the relation of landlord and tenant in Ireland, and in other parts of the United Kingdom.
tables. 54 pp. London, J. Murray, 1867
A., N., T.

8488 [RUSSELL, R.] London railways: a contribution to the parliamentary papers of the session. By a middle-aged citizen.
36 pp. London, Effingham Wilson, 1867
T.

30

8489 ST LEONARDS, Edward Burtenshaw Sugden, 1st baron. Observations on an Act for amending the law of auctions of estates. By lord St. Leonards.
appendix. 28 pp. [London], J. Murray, Henry Sweet, 1867
T.

8490 SCROPE, George Julius Duncombe Poulett. No vote no rate, or household suffrage made at once safe and popular. A proposal made to Parliament in 1850, and renewed in 1867.
14 pp. London, W. Ridgway, 1867
T.

8491 STONE, Lewis. Some notes on the writings of professor Fawcett, Mr. Leslie, and professor Newman on the land laws of England. With an appendix consisting of further comments by another hand.
appendix. 50 pp. London, T. Bosworth, 1867
T.

8492 TARRANT, Henry Jefferd. Lloyd's bonds: their nature and uses.
appendix. 20 pp. London, Stevens and Haynes, 1867
T.

8493 TAYLOR, John Robert. The past, present, and future of the London auxiliary of the United Kingdom alliance. In a series of letters addressed to the 'Temperance Star', with preface and notes.
tables. 40 pp. London, J. Caudwell, 1867
T.

8494 TUPPER, Charles. A letter to the right honourable the earl of Carnarvon, principal secretary of state for the colonies. In reply to a pamphlet entitled *Confederation*, considered in relation to the interests of the Empire.
appendix. 78 pp. London, C. Westerton, 1867
U.

8495 [TWELLS, John.] How can paper money increase the wealth of a nation? Fourth Thousand (revised).
14 pp. London, W. Skeffington, 1867
T.

8496 United States bonds and securities. What they are—their cost—and the interest they pay—with illustrations of the exchange of sterling into American currency, and vice-versa; and many other items which may be of interest to those desirous of information concerning American finances and exchange.
table. appendix. chart. 24 pp. London, Cassell, Petter, and Galpin, 1867
N., T.

8497 WALTON, William. A plea for shareholders, or, shareholders' guide to building societies, containing necessary information respecting the method of investing shares in such societies; also building societies' tables simplified, and calculated at $4\frac{1}{2}$ per cent per annum compound interest on the monthly deposits paid when they become due; and at 3 per cent per annum compound interest on the monthly payments in advance; with rules explanation and examples, shewing how any person may arrive at the proper amount of deposits, interest, and amount due upon such deposits, at any stated period or number of months.
tables. 16 pp. Leeds, T. Harrison, [etc., etc.], 1867
T.

8498 WASON, Peter Rigby. Monetary panics rendered impossible under a note issued from the mint.
40 pp. London, R. Hardwicke, 1867

T.

8499 Work for laymen: or, working men's clubs and institutes; with hints and suggestions for their management. By the hon. secretary of S. George's Mission Working Men's Club, S. Peter's, Old Gravel Lane, S. Georges-in-the-East.
24 pp. London, G. J. Palmer, 1867

T.

8500 WREY, W. Long. New Zealand in 1867, considered as a field for investment of capital.
tables. 36 pp. London, Bates, Hendy, [1867]

T.

1868

8501 ALEXANDER, John. The real remedies for Ireland, tenant right, the church, and the bible, to make her happy, prosperous, and loyal: dedicated to his royal highness the Prince of Wales, and the people of England, by a loyal Irishman.
12 pp. Shrewsbury, J. Alexander, [1868]

T.

8502 ANDREWS, Michael, jr. A statistical review of the present state of flax culture in Ireland.
fold. tab. 10 pp. Belfast, 'Northern Whig' office, 1868

L.

8503 BARUCHSON, Arnold. Beetroot sugar: remarks upon the advantages derivable from its growth and manufacture in the United Kingdom; together with a description of the rise, progress, and present position of that industry on the continent of Europe, and some practical directions to agriculturists and manufacturers for conducting it successfully.
tables. illustrations. appendix. 120 pp. London, Effingham Wilson, Liverpool, Webb, Hunt and Ridings, 1868

T.

8504 BEGG, James. The proposed disestablishment of protestantism in Ireland; its bearings upon the religion & liberties of the empire.
32 pp. Edinburgh, James Nichol, [etc.], 1868

B.

8505 BLAKE, John A. The history and position of the sea fisheries of Ireland, and how they may be made to afford increased food and employment.
tables. table of contents. 142 pp. Waterford, J. H. McGrath, 1868

A., E.

8506 BOOTH, Arthur John. Popular remedies for poverty; [a speech, later privately printed].
28 pp. London, Taylor, 1868

T.

8507 BOWDITCH, William Renwick. Church questions: No. 2. Who pays the tithe?
36 pp. London, E. & F. N. Spon, 1868

T.

8508 ——. Church questions: No. 3. Voluntary church work in Ireland contrasted with liberationist neglect and failure.
tables. 92 pp. London, E. & F. N. Spon, 1868

T.

8509 BRADY, William Maziere. Two letters in reply to certain 'observations' of the Ecclesiastical Commissioners for Ireland on a letter to the Times, concerning Irish church revenues.
20 pp. London, Longmans, Green, 1868

A.

8510 BRANDRETH, Henry. Wastethrifts and workmen. Of the mode of producing them, and their relative value to the community.
16 pp. London, Longmans, Green, 1868

T.

8511 BRIGGS, Thomas. Proposal for an Indian policy under the new reform Parliament, read at a meeting of the East India Association, February 1st, 1868.
The Development of the Dormant Wealth of the British Colonies and Foreign Possessions, read at the Social Science Congress, Birmingham, October 6th 1868.
tables. 16 pp. London, Head, 1868

N.

8512 BROOKE, Charles L. Remarks on the pamphlet entitled 'Reasons why the Baroda goods terminus should not be at Colaba.' With some suggestions regarding extensions and improvements necessary to enable the Bombay, Baroda, and Central Indian railway to pay and maintain its guaranteed interest.
16 pp. London, Effingham Wilson, 1868

T.

8513 BROWNING, Reuben. Addenda to a pamphlet on the currency, considered with a view to the effectual prevention of panics.
16 pp. London, E. & F. N. Spon, 1868

T.

8514 BRYSON, John. An address, delivered in the corporation hall, Londonderry, on Wednesday evening, May 20, 1868, by the rev. John Bryson, LL.D., of the presbyterian church in Ireland; with an introductory letter, by the right reverend the lord bishop of Derry & Raphoe.
18 pp. Derry, Hempton; Belfast, Phillips, 1868

B.

8515 [BUTLER, Thomas.] An Irish answer to lord Stanley, abbreviated reprint from the Irish National Review, of December 6th, 1868.
8 pp. Dublin, 1868

A.

8516 BUTT, Isaac. Land tenure in Ireland. A plea for the Celtic race. Third edition with a preface commenting on some objections that have been made.
120 pp. Dublin, J. Falconer, London, W. Ridgway, 1868

N.

8517 CAIRD, James. Our daily food, its price, and sources of supply. Second edition.
tables. appendix. 40 pp. London, Longmans, Green, Reader & Dyer, 1868

T.

8518 CALLENDER, Henry. The post-office and its money-order system, with proposal for a cheap system of conducting money order business by private enterprise.
tables. 24 pp. Edinburgh, Edmonston and Douglas, 1868

T.

8519 CLARK, William George. A few words on Irish questions.
28 pp. London & Cambridge, Macmillan & co., 1868

Q.

8520 CLEMINSHAW, Charles Graham. The gas supply of the metropolis. A word to the public, the companies, and the shareholders.
10 pp. London, Longmans Green, Reader & Dyer, 1868

T.

8521 The clergy of the church in Ireland weighed in the balance, & the true cause of the condition of Ireland explained.
15 pp. London, W. MacIntosh, 1868

B.

8522 CROFT, Cyrus W. Commercial panics and their causes, with some practical suggestions for the true basis of a national currency.
tables. 24 pp. London, Waterlow, 1868

T.

8523 DAVIES, H. D. A new proposal for the gradual creation of a farmer proprietary in Ireland.
9 pp. London, Longmans, Green, Reader & Dyer, 1868

N., Q., T.

8524 DENNEHY, Cornelius. Three letters on banking and currency; clearly showing that the panic of 1866 and the monetary paralyses [sic] of 1867 were owing to the present state of the laws relating to banking and currency.
34 pp. Dublin, J. Dollard, 1868

P.

8525 ——. Three letters on taxation, industrial resources, and banking systems of Ireland.
32 pp. Dublin, J. Dollard, 1868

L., P.

8526 DENTON, J. Bailey. The agricultural labourer.
appendix. tables. 48 pp. London, E. Stanford, 1868

N.

8527 DODD, John. Railway reform: a public necessity, with practical suggestions.
map. 24 pp. Belfast, Adair, Dublin, Ponsonby, 1868

N.

8528 DUFFERIN and AVA, Frederick Temple Hamilton-Temple-Blackwood, 1st. marquess of. Mr. Mill's plan for the pacification of Ireland examined.
appendix. 50 pp. London, J. Murray, 1868

A., N., T.

8529 East-African slave-trade. [No title page.]
map. 32 pp. [London], W. M. Watts, [1868]

T.

8530 Endowment debate in the general assembly. Resolutions on the endowment question, amendments, lists of voters, protest of the minority, reply, etc.
16 pp. Belfast, C. Aitchison, 1868

B., L.

8531 The Established church in Ireland: its relation to other religious bodies in that country. By an Irish protestant.
32 pp. London, Whittaker, Liverpool, Henry Young, [etc.], 1868

Q.

8532 FERRAR, William Hugh. Tracts on the Irish church question. No. I. The title of the Irish church to her property, and the consequences of disendowment. A lecture delivered in Rathmines parochial schoolhouse, on March 6, 1868. With an introduction, and notes, by the author.
16 pp. Dublin, G. Herbert, Belfast, G. Philips, 1868

T.

8533 ——. No. II. The antagonism of the church of Rome to intellectual and social liberty.
12 pp. London, William Macintosh, [etc., etc.], 1868

T.

8534 FITZGIBBON, Gerald. Ireland in 1868, the battle-field for English party strife; its grievances, real and factitious; remedies, abortive or mischievous: confined to the church question.
84 pp. London, Longmans, Green, Reader and Dyer, 1868

R.

8535 GAYER, Arthur Edward. Fallacies & fictions relating to the Irish church establishment exposed in a letter to the right hon. the attorney-general for Ireland, M.P. for the University of Dublin.
24 pp. Dublin, Hodges, Smith & Foster, 1868

B., D.

8536 GLADSTONE, William Ewart. A chapter of autobiography.
62 pp. London, J. Murray, 1868

T.

8537 ——. Speeches of the right hon. W. E. Gladstone, M.P., delivered at Warrington, Ormskirk, Liverpool, Southport, Newton, Leigh, & Wigan, in October, 1868.
98 pp. London, Simpkin, Marshall; Kent, [1868]

Q.

8538 A gold coinage for India; and the principles upon which its introduction should be regulated
10 pp. London, Effingham Wilson, 1868

T.

8539 GOSCHEN, George J. Speech on bankruptcy legislation and other commercial subjects, delivered before the Liverpool Chamber of Commerce, February 7th, 1868.
30 pp. London, Effingham Wilson, 1868

T.

8540 GRAHAM, Archibald. The industrial improvement by European settlers of the resources of India.
appendix. 38 pp. London, Smith, Elder & co., [etc., etc.], 1868
T.

8541 GRANT, Brewin. 'Gladstone & justice to Ireland.' The Liberal cry examined on liberal principles. A repertory of of arguments for all true Liberals, liberationists, protestants, & patriots.
72 pp. Sheffield, Pawson & Brailsford, London, Elliot Stock, 1868
B.

8542 Havre international maritime exhibition.
14 pp. London, W. J. Johnson, 1868
N.

8543 HAYES, William. 'Free trade in land.' Comments on the speech of professor Fawcett, at Brighton, on the 27th January, 1868, as respects some passages in reply to the letters of 'A Hertfordshire incumbent', and others, in the *Times*.
12 pp. London, H. Sweet, 1868
T.

8544 [HUTTON, Henry Dix.] Proposals for the gradual creation of a farmer-proprietary in Ireland.
tables. appendices. 16 pp. London, W. Ridgway, Dublin, W. B. Kelly, 1868
N., T.

8545 ——. The Prussian land-tenure reforms and a farmer proprietary for Ireland. Two papers read at the annual meeting of the National Association for the promotion of social science, held in Belfast, September, 1867. Published by permission of the council. Second Edition.
table. appendices with tables. 48 pp. Dublin, J. Falconer, London, W. Ridgway, 1868
N., U.

8546 ——. The Stein-Hardemberg land-legislation: its basis, development and results in Prussia. [and] Plan for the gradual creation of a farmer-proprietary in Ireland.
tables. appendices. 52 pp. [lacks title page]. 2nd ed. Dublin, 1868
T.

8547 The Irish difficulty. (1) The church question. (2) The land question. (3) The education question. Being a review of the debate in the house of commons on Mr. Maguire's motion (March 10th, 1868), 'That this House will immediately resolve itself into a Committee, with the view of taking into consideration the condition and circumstances of Ireland'. By an observer.
52 pp. London, F. & J. Rivington, 1868
N.

8548 The Irish land question and the twelve London companies in the county of Londonderry.
appendix with table. 30 pp. Belfast, 'Northern Whig' office, 1868
C., U.

See also 8635.

8549 JEPHSON, Robert H. The Irish civil service and general (permanent benefit) building society, its principles, objects and advantages, briefly explained.
tables. 24 pp. Dublin, the Society, 1868
N.

8550 JOHNES, Arthur James. Should the law of imprisonment for debt in the superior courts be abolished or amended? In a letter to the right hon. lord Brougham & Vaux.
12 pp. London, Wildy, [1868]
T.

8551 KEANE, Marcus. The Irish land question: suggestions for legislation. A letter addressed to Colonel C. M. Vandeleur, M.P.
14 pp. Dublin, Hodges, Smith, 1868
N., T.

8552 KELLY, William. A letter stating and reviewing 'The Irish Difficulty' and suggesting a few simple expedients towards its eventual abatement.
table. 46 pp. London, Longmans, Green, Reader & Dyer, 1868
T.

8553 KIRK, James. Britain's drawbacks: a brief review of the chief of those national errors which retard the prosperity of our country.
32 pp. Glasgow, Christian News Office, Edinburgh, A. Muir, 1868
Q.

8554 LAWES, Sir John Bennet, & GILBERT, Sir Joseph Henry. On the home produce, imports, & consumption of wheat.
fold. table. tables. 40 pp. London, Longmans, Green, Reader & Dyer, 1868
Q., T.

8555 LEE, Alfred T. Facts respecting the present state of the church in Ireland.
table of contents. tables. appendix. 32 pp. London, F. & J. Rivington, Dublin, Hodges, Smith & Foster, 1868
A., N.

8556 MANNING, Henry Edward, cardinal. Ireland. A letter to earl Grey.
44 pp. London, Longmans, Green, Reader & Dyer, 1868
A., B., N., T.

8557 MARUM, Mulhallen. A narrative of landlord oppression and tenant wrong, in 1868 in Co. Kilkenny.
tables. 20 pp. Dublin, J. M. O'Toole, 1868
P.

8558 ——. Protestant ascendancy in Ireland: its cause and cure and the right of Irish tenants, under the British constitution, to fixity of tenure, vindicated.
102 pp. Dublin, J. M. O'Toole, 1868
U.

8559 The metropolitan railway. Its public convenience, its capital, its traffic, its dividends. By Veritas.
tables. 16 pp. London, Effingham Wilson, 1868
T.

8560 The metropolitan railway. What dividend will it really pay? An unexaggerated statement.
24 pp. London, Effingham Wilson, 1868
T.

8561 MILL, John Stuart. England & Ireland.
28 pp. London, Longmans, Green, Reader, & Dyer, 1868
N., Q., T.

——. 2nd ed.
42 pp. London, Longmans, Green, Reader, & Dyer, 1868
A., B., C., D., N.

8562 A model manufacturing town (Bessbrook, Co. Armagh).
10 pp. Dublin, Irish Permissive Bill Association, [1868]
A.

8563 NEVILE, Christopher. The Irish difficulty. A letter to the right hon. W. E. Gladstone, M.P.
28 pp. London, A. Miall, 1868
N., T.

8564 NICHOLSON, Nathaniel Alexander. The controversy on free banking. Being a few observations on an article in 'Frazer's Magazine', January, 1868.
32 pp. London, Trübner, 1868
T.

8565 ——. Observations on coinage, and our present monetary system. Second edition, revised and enlarged.
tables. 36 pp. London, Trübner, 1868
T.

8566 ——. Observations on coinage seignorage, etc., etc.
tables. 22 pp. London, Trübner, 1868
T.

8567 NUGENT, Richard. The church in Ireland & her assailants.
20 pp. London, W. MacIntosh, 1868
B.

8568 On the pollution of the rivers of the kingdom; the enormous magnitude of the evil, & the urgent necessity in the interest of the public health & the fisheries for its suppression by immediate legislative enactment.
52 pp. London, Fisheries Preservation Association, 1868
Q.

8569 PICTET, Francis. The railways of England, Scotland, and Ireland. A comprehensive scheme for the redemption of capital; a general reduction in the fares to uniform rates; and reform in management and expenses.
tables. 16 pp. London, E. Marlborough, [1868]
T.

8570 PORTER, James. Billy Bluff and squire Firebrand: in six letters; which appeared in the 'Northern Star', 1796.
28 pp. Belfast, 1868
B.

8571 Report on the condition of the poorer classes of Edinburgh and of their dwellings, neighbourhoods, and families. Prepared by order of a public meeting of the inhabitants, held in the council chamber, under the presidency of the right honorable the lord provost, on the 15th April 1867, and adopted and ordered to be published, at a meeting held on the 28th of February 1868.
tables. appendix. 150 pp. Edinburgh, Edmonston and Douglas, London, Hamilton, Adams, [etc., etc.], 1868
T.

8572 ROGERS, James Edwin Thorold. The political situation. A speech delivered at Wigan, October 30, 1868, by James E. Thorold Rogers, M.A. . . . Published under the auspices of the Wigan liberal registration association.
16 pp. Wigan, Wall, [1868?]
Q.

In support of Gladstone.

8573 RUSSELL, John, 1st earl Russell. A letter to the right hon. Chichester Fortescue M.P. on the state of Ireland.
tables. 98 pp. 3rd ed. London, Longmans, Green 1868
A., B., C., N., T.

8574 St. Pancras parochial rates reduction association. Ratepayers v. guardians, being a critical examination of the 'Facts & Observations' issued by the guardians, November 19th, 1868.
16 pp. London, 1868
Q.

8575 SEYD, Ernest. The question of seignorage and charge for coining, and the report of the royal commission on international coinage.
60 pp. London, Effingham Wilson, 1868
T.

8576 SHEIL, Sir Justin. French thoughts on Irish evils.
72 pp. London, Longmans, Green, 1868
B.

8577 SHERVILL, G. R. Unadulterated liquors. A few observations on the adulteration of the malt liquors and spirits of the community, more especially with reference to the value of pure genuine porter: also extracts from parliamentary evidence, newspaper criticism, &c.
table. 16 pp. London, Harp Tavern, 1868
T.

8578 SILLAR, William Cameron. Usury: its character further investigated.
appendix. 72 pp. London, Effingham Wilson, 1868
T.

8579 SLATER, Robert, Jun. International coinage critically considered.
tables. 24 pp. London, Effingham Wilson, 1868
T.

8580 SMITH, Goldwin. The Irish question. Three letters to the editor of the Daily News.
24 pp. London, W. Ridgway, 1868
Q., T.

8581 STRATTON, J. Y. Suggestions for legislation relating to friendly societies, and for a system of insurances for the wage-paid classes by means of the Post Office.
30 pp. London, W. Ridgway, 1868
T.

8582 STURGEON, Charles. Letters to the trades' unionists and the working classes, on the recent bill brought in to repeal the combination laws, and enslave the working classes by Sir J. F. Buxton, bart. and Mr. Young.
8 pp. London, Heywood, 1868
T.

8583 SWANSTON, Clement T. Observations on proposed changes in the law of debtor and creditor.
48 pp. London, Davis, 1868
T.

8584 Times of India. An appeal to the electors of Great Britain & Ireland. By the 'Times of India'.
18 pp. Bombay, 'Times of India' Office, 1868
Q.

8585 'To be, or not to be?' A few observations on joint stock companies.
8 pp. London, W. Ridgway, 1868
T.

8586 The value of insurance companies' shares, as an investment. By a member of the stock exchange.
tables. 10 pp. London, W. Macintosh, [1868?]
T.

8587 WALDEGRAVE, Samuel, bishop of Carlisle. Justice to Ireland. The maintenance of the Irish branch of the United church necessary, in the interests not of Great Britain only but of Ireland also.
16 pp. London, W. Hunt & W. MacIntosh, 1868
B.

8588 WALTON, H. M. To the shareholders of the Crystal Palace. Facts and figures; a retrospect of the cost of maintenance for nine years; with a few observations on the Sunday opening question, addressed to Thomas Hughes, Esq., M.P.
28 pp. London, Effingham Wilson, 1868
T.

8589 [WARWICK, R. V.] The government, the Bank of England, and the public: their relations briefly discussed, and important alterations suggested, in a recent correspondence with the right hon. W. E. Gladstone, M.P.
14 pp. London, Effingham Wilson, 1868
T.

8590 WRIGLEY, Thomas. Railway reform. A plan for the effectual separation of capital from revenue.
24 pp. London, Effingham Wilson, 1868
T.

1869

8591 ADAIR, Sir Robert Alexander Shafto, bart., later baron Waveney. The established church of Ireland, past & future. With a reprint of 'Ireland & her servile war', 1866.
108 pp. Dublin, Hodges, Smith & Foster, London, W. Ridgway, 1869
Q.

8592 Address of the Minnesota Irish emigration convention held in the city of Saint Paul, Minnesota, Jan. 20th, 1869. To the people of Ireland.
tables. 22 pp. no t.p. [n.p., 1869?]
N., P.

8593 AINSLIE, Alex. Colvin. Self-help, or pauperism? Suggestions for obviating the evils of the present poor law.
16 pp. London, Longmans, Green, Reader, and Dyer, Taunton, F. May, 1869
T.

8594 ANDREW, Sir William Patrick. On the completion of the railway system of the valley of the Indus. A letter to his grace the duke of Argyll, K.T. (Secretary of State for India in council), etc., etc., etc., with appendix and maps.
maps. tables. appendix. 128 pp. London, W. H. Allen, 1869
T.

8595 ANKETELL, William Robert. Landlord and tenant: Ireland. Letters by a land agent on I agricultural leases. II tenants' improvements. III tenant right. IV fixity of tenure. V tenant's claims. VI covenants. VII capricious evictions. VIII valuation rents; corn rents. IX peasant proprietorship. X settled estates—Montgomery's act. XI Scotch land tenure. XII the Irish land—Mr. Campbell's proposals. XIII landlord and tenant—an agent's proposal. Appendix: a model case of Ulster tenant-right.
table in appendix. 40 pp. Belfast, Archer, 1869
U.

8596 ATHERTON, Henry. An acre of land in his native parish the right of every British subject, if he can pay for it and if there be room for him, with remarks on the state of the country in general and Ireland in particular.
16 pp. Battle, F. W. Ticehurst, [1869]
T.

8597 [ATKINSON, Edward?] An inquiry into the causes of the present long-continued depression in the cotton trade; with suggestions for its improvement. By a cotton manufacturer.
tables. 16 pp. Bury, Fletcher, Manchester, Heywood, 1869
N.

8598 BAGEHOT, Walter. A practical plan for assimilating the English and American money, as a step towards a universal money. Reprinted from the *Economist*, with additions and a preface.
tables. 72 pp. London, Longmans, Green, Reader, and Dyer, 1869
T.

8599 BAXTER, Robert Dudley. The Irish tenant-right question examined by a comparison of the law and practice of Ireland; with suggestions on the basis of legislation, and the consequences which would follow the adoption of fixity of tenure or the Ulster tenant-right.
42 pp. London, E. Stanford, 1869
L., T., U.

8600 BRADY, William Maziere. Some remarks on the Irish church bill, etc.
30 pp. London, Longmans, Green, Reader & Dyer, 1869
T.

8601 BROWNING, Reuben. Reflections on the currency, with a view to the effectual prevention of panics. tables. 54 pp. London, E. & F. N. Spon, 1869
T.

8602 CAIRD, Sir James. The Irish land question. 32 pp. 2nd ed. London, Longmans, Green, Reader & Dyer, 1869
N., T.

8603 CHENERY, Thomas. Suggestions for a railway route to India. 24 pp. London, R. Hardwicke, 1869
T.

8604 CHEVALIER, Michel. The history of political economy taught by the history of the freedom of labour. To which is added an account of the negociation of the commercial treaty between France and England. Translated by William Bellingham. 48 pp. London, Effingham Wilson, 1869
T.

8605 Circular from the general land office showing the manner of proceeding to obtain title to public lands, by purchase, by location with warrants or agricultural college scrip, by pre-emption and homestead. 26 pp. Washington, Government printing office, 1869
N., T.

8606 CLIVE, Archer. A few remarks by the Rev. Archer Clive, on a pamphlet by Chandos Wren Hoskins, Esq., M.P., on the tenure of land in England and Ireland. 16 pp. London, Simpkin, Marshall, Hereford, Head and Hull, 1869
T.

See 8632.

8607 COLLINS, Clifton W. Chancellor's Latin Essay, 1869, Trades Unions. Utrum prosint an obsint reipublicae operariorum societates, censendum est. 28 pp. Oxford and London, J. Parker, 1869
T.

8608 COOPER, Robert Jermyn. Eighth letter to the Conservatives of England. On the spoliation of the Irish church, and social disorganization, &c., &c. 50 pp. London, W. MacIntosh, 1869
T.

8609 DEAN, G. A. A treatise on the land tenure of Ireland, and influences which retard Irish progress. table of contents. 92 pp. London, Longmans, Green, Reader & Dyer, York, Sampson, 1869
N.

8610 DETHRIDGE, Frank. Building societies: their objects, principles and advantages. To which are added, useful household hints. tables. 36 pp. London, Simpkin, Marshall, 1869
T.

8611 DIRCKS, Henry. Patent monopoly as affecting the encouragement, improvement, and progress of sciences, arts and manufactures. A letter with accompanying statements and statistics, addressed to the right hon. lord Stanley, M.P., etc., etc., etc., tables. 32 pp. London, E. & F. N. Spon, 1869
T.

8612 DIXON, Joshua. London, Chatham, & Dover railway. Considerations on the position and prospects of the company, addressed to its debenture-holding & other creditors. 24 pp. London, Effingham Wilson, 1869
T.

8613 EDGE, Frederick Milne. Great Britain and the United States. A letter to the right honourable William Ewart Gladstone, M.P. her majesty's first lord of the treasury. tables. 38 pp. London, W. Ridgway, 1869
T.

8614 [ELLIS, William.] A chart of industrial life with some instructions for its use. 34 pp. London, Simpkin & Marshall, Manchester, A. Ireland, 1869
N.

8615 FERGUSON, Robert. A tenant right for Ireland. 18 pp. Dublin, McGlashan & Gill, 1869
N., U.

8616 A few practical suggestions for a land bill. By an Ulsterman. 8 pp. Dublin, J. O'Toole, [1869?]
N.

8617 FITZGIBBON, Gerald. The land difficulty of Ireland, with an effort to solve it. 84 pp. London, Longmans, Green, Reader and Dyer, Dublin, McGlashan, 1869
C., N., T., U.

8618 FOWLER, William. Thoughts on 'Free trade in land'. tables. 64 pp. London, Longmans, Green, Reader & Dyer, 1869
T.

8619 FRESTON, William, ed. Report of the conference presided over by the duke of Manchester, on the question whether colonization and emigration may be made self-supporting or even profitable to those investing capital therein. (13th July, 1869). With appendix. tables. appendix. 64 pp. London, J. T. Wheeler, 1869
T.

8620 GOOD, W. Walter. Where are we now? A politico-agricultural letter to the chairman of the central chamber of agriculture (Clare Sewell Reid, Esq., M.P.). 48 pp. London, the author, 1869
T.

8621 GRAHAME, James. A popular survey of the life assurance statistics of the year 1868, with a chapter upon the capital of proprietary companies. tables. 24 pp. Edinburgh, Bell & Bradfute, 1869
T.

8622 GREY, Sir George.   The Irish land question.
20 pp. London, Hall and Foster, 1869
R., T.

8623 HAGGARD, Frederick T.   A mile of railway in the United Kingdom.
tables. 40 pp. London, Effingham Wilson, 1869
T.

8624 ——.   Railway facts and lower fares.
tables. 32 pp. London, Effingham Wilson, 1869
T.

8625 Half-yearly reports and transactions of the Royal Agricultural Society of Ireland, 42, Upper Sackville Street, Dublin. November, 1866–November, 1868.
tables. plans [of houses]. 78 pp. Dublin, at the office of the 'Farmers' Gazette', 1869
D.

8626 HANCOCK, William Neilson. Two reports for the Irish government on the history of the landlord & tenant question in Ireland, with suggestions for legislation. First report made in 1859;—second, in 1866.
72 pp. Dublin, A. Thom, 1869
C., N., P., Q.
See 8373

8627 HAWKINS, F. Vaughan.   Optional mobilisation of land: a scheme for simplifying title and land transfer.
14 pp. London, W. Maxwell, 1869
T.

8628 HAWKSLEY, Thomas.   The charities of London, and some errors in their administration: with suggestions for an improved system of private and official charitable relief. (Read at a meeting of the association for the prevention of pauperism and crime in the metropolis, in the rooms of the society of arts, December 17th, 1868: the earl of Shaftesbury, K.G., in the chair.)
tables. 20 pp. London, J. Churchill, 1869
T.

8629 HILL, Alsager Hay.   Our unemployed: an attempt to point out some of the best means of providing occupation for distressed labourers; with suggestions on a national system of labour registration; and other matters affecting the well-being of the poor.
appendices. 50 pp. London, W. Ridgway, [1869]
T.

8630 HILL, Florence. The boarding-out system distinguished from baby-farming and parish apprenticeship: a paper read before the National Association for the promotion of social science, at Bristol, October 5th, 1869.
12 pp. London, Macmillan, Bristol, Arrowsmith, 1869
T.

8631 HINCKS, Sir Francis. Religious endowments in Canada. The clergy reserve and rectory questions. A chapter of Canadian history.
108 pp. London, Dalton & Lucy, 1869
T.

8632 HOSKYNS, Chandos Wren.   Land in England, land in Ireland, and land in other lands.
58 pp. London, Longman, 1869
T.
See 8606.

8633 IMRAY, John.   British railways, as they are and as they might be. Suggestions as to cheap and uniform fares, with increased and guaranteed dividends.
tables. 32 pp. London, E. & F. N. Spon, 1869
T.

8634 The insurance register: being a record of the yearly progress and the present financial position of the life insurance associations of Great Britain. Second edition. By a Fellow of the Statistical Society.
tables. appendix. 56 pp. London, W. Kent, 1869
T.

8635 The Irish land question and the twelve London companies in the county of Londonderry.
tables. appendices. 88 pp. Belfast, at the Northern Whig Office, 1869
R., T.
See 8548.

8636 The Irish land question. By a member of the council. Published by the council.
18 pp. [London] [The National Union of conservative and constitutional associations], 1869
T.
Publications of the National Union—No. IX.

8637 Irish landlordism: a plea for the crown. By an Irish Landowner.
128 pp. 2nd ed. London, the author, 1869
B.

8638 JELLETT, Morgan Woodward.   The Irish Church Act. The compensation and commutation clauses considered, with which are combined opinions of Sir Roundell Palmer, M.P., D.C.L. and references to the rules and orders of the commissioners. Second edition—revised and enlarged.
tables. 52 pp. Dublin, Hodges, Foster, [1869]
T.

8639 JENKINS, Edward.   State emigration; an essay.
tables. 54 pp. London, E. Stanford, 1869
T.

8640 JONES, George William. G. W. Jones's plan of universal penny railways, by the application of turnpikes to railways. A practical plan, suitable to the genius of the people, and calculated to satisfy the locomotive requirements of the country.
appendix. 64 pp. London, Davies, 1869
T.

8641 JONES, William Bence.   The future of the Irish church.
table of contents. 48 pp. Dublin, Hodges, Foster, 1869
N.

8642 Justice to Ireland. Tenant right versus landlord wrong. An Irish land measure. By an Irishman.
appendix. 16 pp. London & Dublin, Moffat, 1869
B., N., U.

8643 LAMBERT, Brooke. East London pauperism. A sermon preached before the University of Oxford, on Sunday, December 20th 1868.
16 pp. London, J. Parker, 1869
T.

8644 LAMBERT, James. The 'Land Question' solved being part of a plan for making Ireland a rich and prosperous country. In a series of letters to a local journal.
table of contents. appendix. 56 pp. Dublin, G. Herbert, 1869
N.

8645 LEE, Alfred Theophilus. The Irish Church bill. An abstract of Mr. Gladstone's bill for the proposed disendowment and disestablishment of the church in Ireland, with observations thereon.
tables. 20 pp. London, J. B. Nichols, [1869]
T.

8646 A letter on pauperism and crime, addressed to the members of the house of commons by a guardian of the poor.
12 pp. London, F. & J. Rivington, 1869
T.

8647 LUBBOCK, Sir John, bart. A proposal to extend the system pursued by her majesty's civil service commissioners to candidates for commercial appointments. A letter to the bankers, merchants, and directors of public companies in the city of London.
appendix. 32 pp. London, Effingham Wilson, 1869
T.

8648 LYNN, W. Frank. Canada. Pamphlet for working men on emigration, labour, wages, and free grants of land.
tables. 16 pp. London, 'Canadian News' Office, 1869
T.

8649 McCOMBIE, William. The Irish land question practically considered. A letter to the right honourable William Ewart Gladstone, M.P., first lord of the treasury.
38 pp. Aberdeen, Wyllie, 1869
N.

8650 MACDONNELL, John Cotter. Shall we commute? A question for the Irish clergy, with an answer.
table. appendix. 28 pp. Dublin, Hodges, Foster, 1869
T.

8651 MACIVOR, James. Dis-endowment or co-endowment? A letter to the right hon. W. E. Gladstone and the right hon. John Bright.
appendix. 32 pp. London, Longmans, Green, Reader & Dyer, 1869
T.

8652 McKENNA, Sir Joseph Neale. Statement to the shareholders of the National Bank.
tables. 74 pp. London, 1869
A.

8653 MACLAGAN, Peter. Land culture and land tenure in Ireland. The result of observations during a recent tour in Ireland.
tables. 74 pp. Edinburgh, W. Blackwood & Son, Dublin, Hodges, Foster, 1869
A., C., N., T., U.

8654 MAGUIRE, John Francis. America in its relation to Irish emigration: A lecture delivered at Cork and Limerick.
appendix. 32 pp. Cork, Mulcahy, 1869
N.

8655 MILL, John Stuart. England and Ireland. Fifth edition.
46 pp. London, Longmans, Green, Reader, and Dyer, 1869
T.

8656 MORGAN, Henry Lloyd. Accounts and audits: remarks on the new 'Regulation of railways Act'. Fifth edition, with appendix.
tables. appendix. 40 pp. London, Effingham Wilson, 1869
T.

8657 NEWMAN, Francis W. The cure of the great social evil, with special reference to recent laws delusively called Contagious Diseases Acts.
40 pp. London, Trübner, 1869
T.

8658 NICHOLSON, Nathaniel Alexander. Observations on coinage, and our present monetary system.
48 pp. 3rd ed. London, Trübner, 1869
T.

8659 NOBLE, John. Free trade, reciprocity and the revivers: an inquiry into the effects of the free trade policy upon trade, manufactures, and employment.
tables. 40 pp. London, Simpkin, Marshall, 1869
T.

8660 Notes for the new parliament. By Alpha.
18 pp. London, R. J. Bush, 1869
T.

8661 O'BRIEN, James Thomas, bishop of Ossory, Ferns, and Leighlin. The disestablishment and disendowment of the Irish branch of the united church, considered. Part I. Effects, immediate and remote.
70 pp. London, [etc.], Rivingtons, Dublin, G. Herbert, 1869
T.

8662 ——. The disestablishment and disendowment of the Irish branch of the united church, considered. Part II. Reasons for and against.
appendix. 150 pp. London, Rivingtons, Dublin, G. Herbert, 1869
T.

8663 ——. The appendix to the disestablishment and disendowment of the Irish branch of the united church, considered. With a preface and table of contents.
[Preface and table of contents only.] 16 pp. London, Rivingtons, Dublin, G. Herbert, 1869
T.

8664 O'LOUGHLIN, Edward. The National Bank; its wrongs, its rights, and its remedies. Being an address to the shareholders, in reply to the statement of Sir Joseph Neale McKenna Knight.
48 pp. Dublin, 1869
A.

8665 Our colonies and their future. By the author of monarchy *versus* republic. A political tract for the times. No. 2.
12 pp. Bristol, I. E. Chillcott, 1869
T.

8666 Pauperism and emigration. By a fellow of the colonial society.
54 pp. London, E. Stanford, 1869
T.

8667 PICTET, Francis. The railways of England, Scotland, and Ireland. A comprehensive scheme for the redemption and consolidation of capital; a complete reform in the constitution, management, and working expenses, and a general reduction in the passenger fares and traffic charges of 28 & 10 per cent. to uniform rates throughout the United Kingdom, with tables. To which is now added a letter to the editor of the 'Money Market Review', in reply to criticism on scheme, giving further extensive particulars of present management and expenses; and numerous extracts from various journals bearing on the question.
tables. 32 pp. London, W. Tweedie, [1869]
T.

8668 PLUNKETT, William. Commutation considered especially with a view to compensation for diminished security. A paper read at a meeting of the standing committee of the Irish church conference, on Wednesday, June 23rd, 1869.
40 pp. Dublin, Hodges and Foster, 1869
N., T.

8669 A scheme of county administration, embracing the management of the poor, the highways, and the county finances, with notes and explanations. By a county magistrate.
18 pp. London, Longmans, Green, Reader, and Dyer, 1869
T.

8670 SCOTT, Benjamin. Church finance; a plea for pure voluntaryism, the only scriptural and efficient source of church sustentation. The substance of a paper prepared for and read before the Surrey congregational union, at Guildford, in June, 1869.
16 pp. London, Elliot Stock, 1869
B., T.

8671 SHAEN, Samuel. The assault at Lambeth workhouse. A letter to the parishioners of Lambeth.
20 pp. London and Edinburgh, Williams and Norgate, 1869
T.

8672 ——. The assault at Lambeth workhouse. Letter to the president of the poor law board, from Samuel Shaen.
appendix. 200 pp. London, Williams and Norgate, 1869
T.

8673 ——. Workhouse management and workhouse justice. A further letter to the president of the poor law board.
56 pp. London and Edinburgh, Williams and Norgate, 1869
T.

8674 SHERIFF, D. Suggestions on the land question of Ireland. The subject of a paper read at the meeting of the Social science association in Birmingham, October 6th, 1868.
32 pp. Dublin, McGee, London, Simpkin, Marshall, 1869
N.

8675 SPENCE, William. The public policy of a patent law.
34 pp. London, Downing, 1869
N.

8676 STALLARD, Joshua Harrison. Pauperism, charity, & poor laws. Being an inquiry into the present state of the poorer classes in the metropolis, the resources and effects of charity, and the influence of the poor-law system of relief; with suggestions for an improved administration. (Read before the Social science association, February 17th, October 1st, and December 21st, 1868).
tables. 50 pp. London, Longmans, Green, Reader, and Dyer, [1869]
T.

8677 Statistics: exhibiting the history, climate and productions of the state of Wisconsin.
map. tables. 56 pp. Madison, Wisconsin, Atwood and Rublee, 1869
N.

8678 STEPHENS, William W. The settlement of the Alabama question with self-respect to both nations being a speech on the exemption from seizure of all private property on sea delivered before the Edinburgh chamber of commerce, 6th May, and the joint chambers of Edinburgh and Leith, 21st May 1869.
25 pp. Edinburgh, Edmonston and Douglas, 1869
T.

8679 The Suez maritime canal. A sketch of the undertaking, from notes, &c., taken during a personal visit, by the Chevalier De W. Stoess, Bavarian consul, &c., &c., &c.
maps. plans. tables. 58 pp. Liverpool, Webb, Hunt, and Ridings, 1869
T.

8680 TAYLOR, N. S. United Irishmen; or, a plan for retaining for Irish religious use sixteen millions sterling of Irish ecclesiastical property now about to be wasted or destroyed and also for forming a nation church in Ireland free from English mismanagement and rule.
20 pp. Dublin, Hodges, Smith and Foster, 1869
D.

8681 TENNANT, Charles, FFOULKES, Edmund S. Two opinions (Protestant and Roman Catholic) on the Irish church question. Disestablish and disendow none. By Charles Tennant, and Disendow all or none. In a letter from Edmund S. Ffoulkes, B.D.
42 pp. London, Longmans, Green, Reader, and Dyer, 1869
T.

8682 THOM, Adam. Overend and Gurney prosecution: in its relation to the public as distinguished from the defendants.
16 pp. London, Effingham Wilson, 1869
T.

8683 TODD, Charles Hawkes. The Irish church; its disestablishment & disendowment.
52 pp. London, Rivingtons, 1869
B., T.

8684 ——. Observations on the Irish church bill.
48 pp. London, Rivingtons, Dublin, Hodges, Foster, 1869
T.

8685 TRAILL, Anthony. Commutation.
4 pp. (no t.p.). n.p., 1869
N.

8686 TRENCH, Thomas Cooke. Reconstruction of the church in Ireland and the uses of commutation. Second edition, revised.
table. 28 pp. Dublin, Hodges, Foster, 1869
T.

8687 TREVELYAN, Sir Charles. Three letters on the Devonshire labourer.
16 pp. London, Bell and Daldy, 1869
N.

8688 VALENTINE, William. Commutation: its safety and advantages.
tables. appendix. 28 pp. 2nd ed. Dublin, G. Herbert, 1869
D., N.

8689 WATTS, Edmund W. The land question: or, equitable ownership defined; its universality and practicability. With the true province of accumulation.
52 pp. London, Longmans, Green, Reader, and Dyer, 1869
T.

8690 YOUNG, Frederick. Transplantation the true system of emigration. Second edition.
table. 16 pp. London, R. Elkins, Simpkin, Marshall, 1869
T.

1870

8691 Justice to Ireland. Tenant right *versus* Landlord right. An Irish land measure. By an Irishman.
table of contents. appendix. 16 pp. Dublin & London, Moffat, [187–?]
N.

8692 RÉMUSAT, Charles François Marie de, count. Du paupérisme et de la charité légale; lettre adressée à M. les préfets du royaume. Suivie d'observations de M. A-P. de Candolle sur un traité de la bienfaisance publique.
108 pp. Paris, Renouard, [187–?]
T.

8693 SLAGG, John, Junr. The cotton trade of Lancashire and the Anglo-French commercial treaty of 1860, being a report of the English evidence at the French commercial enquiry of 1870, translated and edited, with an introduction and appendix.
tables. appendices. 124 pp. London, Longmans, Green, Reader, and Dyer, [187–?]
T.

8694 Strikes and their cost.
24 pp. London, Society for the promotion of Christian knowledge, [187–?]
T.

8695 Suggestions for a settlement of the Irish land question or, at least a large step towards it.
24 pp. Dublin, Nicholson, [187–?]
N.

8696 WATTS, John. The catechism of wages and capital.
32 pp. Manchester, J. Heywood, [187–?]
T.

8697 Mr. Gladstone's Irish land bill. (Dedicated to the earl of Granard.)
26 pp. Carlow, Price, [1870?]
N.

8698 The new land bill; or, Ireland governed according to Irish ideas; a dialogue between an Irish landlord and his agent.
24 pp. Glasgow, Cameron & Ferguson, [1870?]
N.

8699 Plan of 'parliamentary tenant right', applicable equally to all parts of Ireland. Explained; with letters, opinions of the press, etc., etc.
72 pp. Dublin, [1870?]
B., N., Q.

8700 All about California and the inducements to settle there. [For gratuitous circulation.]
maps. tables. appendix. 80 pp. San Francisco, California immigrant union, 1870
T.

8701 ALVAREZ, J. The foreign debt of Spain. 1822–1870. A review of its conversions, with tabular statements of the result to the government and the bondholders.
tables. appendix. 24 pp. London, Effingham Wilson, 1870
T.

8702 BARRY, James F. A chapter of Irish history; or, land tenure in Ireland.
40 pp. London, Dublin, Moffat, [1870]
N.

8703 BISSET, Thomas. The national debt considered, in a letter to the right hon. Hugh C. E. Childers, M.P., first lord of the Admiralty.
tables. 16 pp. London, J. Nisbet, 1870
T.

8704 BRABROOK, Edward William. Legislation on life assurance: a statement of the principles on which it should proceed.
20 pp. London, Butterworths, 1870
T.

8705 British Empire. If people put a face on things, who shall take off the mask?
table of contents. tables. appendix. 134 pp. n.p., 1870
N.

On labour and emigration.

8706 BROOKE, William G., ed. Handy-book of the Irish land act. Landlord and tenant (Ireland) act 1870, with introduction, notes, explanations, and an index.
index. table. 58 pp. Dublin, Hodges, Foster, 1870
N.

8707 BROWN, Joseph. The evils of the unlimited liability for accidents of masters and railway companies, especially since lord Campbell's act. Second edition. Enlarged and corrected.
46 pp. London, Butterworth's, 1870
T.

8708 BUCHANAN, Robert. The finance of the free church of Scotland. A paper read before the statistical society of London on the 15th March, 1870.
tables. 38 pp. London, Harrison & sons, 1870
A., T.

8709 BUTT, Isaac. The handbook of the land: selections from Mr. Butt's tracts on the land question. Part I.
72 pp. Dublin, J. Falconer, London, W. Ridgway, 1870
N.

8710 ——. Irish federalism! its meanings, its objects, and its hopes.
70 pp. 2nd ed. Dublin, The Irish Home Rule League, 1870
N.
See 8794.

8711 CAMPBELL, George. The progress of the land bill.
32 pp. London, Trübner, 1870
N., U.

8712 CHURCHILL, Fleetwood. Church finance.
appendices. tables. 22 pp. Dublin, Hodges, Foster, 1870
N., T.

8713 CLIVE, George. Some evidence on the Irish land question.
36 pp. Hereford, J. Hull, 1870
R., T.

8714 Companies and the men who make them. By one of themselves.
38 pp. London, 1870
T.

8715 A complete abstract of the new bankruptcy act; with an index by a barrister.
32 pp. Manchester, A. Heywood, 1870
T.

8716 Conference on night refuges, held at 15 Buckingham St., Strand, June 8th, 1870.
appendix. 24 pp. London, society for organising charitable relief and repressing mendicity, 1870
A.
See 8771.

8717 COVENTRY, Andrew. A method of economizing our currency. Read before the Royal Society, on 3rd January, 1870.
16 pp. Edinburgh, Edmonston & Douglas, 1870
T.

8718 DENISON, Sir William. Roads and railways in New South Wales and India. With remarks explanatory of the advantages likely to result from the employment, under

certain circumstances, of animal power, instead of steam power.
tables. 78 pp. London, Longmans, Green, Reader & Dyer, 1870
T.
First published in Madras, 1864, see 8221

8719 DIXON, Robert V. Commutation and government annuties.
16 pp. Dublin, Hodges, Foster, 1870
T.

8720 DUFFERIN AND AVA, Frederick Temple Hamilton Temple-Blackwood, 1st Marquess of. The case of the Irish tenant as stated sixteen years ago, in a speech delivered in the house of lords, February 28, 1854.
26 pp. London, Willis, Sotheran, 1870
U.

8721 ——. Irish emigration and the tenure of land in Ireland.
tables. 88 pp. new ed. Dublin, J. Falconer, 1870
T., U.

8722 ——. The tenure of land in Ireland, abridged from the work of the right hon. lord Dufferin, K.B., on that subject; with additions and alterations.
tables. 72 pp. Dublin, J. Falconer, 1870
N., U.

8723 FILIPOWSKI, Herscheu E. Universal table of exchange for comparing the coins of all nations with one another, in a simple and easy manner.
tables. 8 pp. London, E. & F. N. Spon, 1870
T.

8724 Fixity of tenure. A dialogue. By an Irish landlord.
36 pp. London, W. Ridgway, 1870
T.

8725 GIBBS, Frederick Waymouth. English law and Irish tenure.
tables. 116 pp. London, W. Ridgway, 1870
N., T.

8726 GRAY, Sir John. The Irish land bill as it is and as it was: an address to the citizens of Kilkenny.
24 pp. Dublin, J. Falconer, 1870
U.

8727 GUINNESS, Henry. Irish land question. Practical suggestions.
12 pp. Dublin, Hodges, Foster, 1870
N.

8728 Half-yearly reports and transactions of the Royal Agricultural Society of Ireland, 42, Upper Sackville Street, Dublin. December, 1868 to December, 1869.
tables. diagrams. 88 pp. Dublin, at the office of the 'Farmers' Gazette', 1870
D.

8729 HAMILTON, William Tighe. The mechanical difficulties of the Irish land question.
table of contents. 64 pp. Dublin, Hodges, Foster, London, W. Ridgway, 1870
N.

8730 HANCOCK, William Neilson. Plan of encouraging commutation of clerical incomes of the church of Ireland, under the Irish church act.
16 pp. Dublin, Hodges, Foster, 1870
N.

8731 ——. Report on deposits and cash balances in joint stock banks in Ireland, 1840–1869.
tables. 8 pp. Dublin, A. Thom, 1870
N.

8732 Hand book for emigrants to Queensland, Australia. By authority of the agent general for the government of Queensland.
map. tables. appendix. 16 pp. London, E. Stanford, 1870
T.

8733 HANNYNGTON, John Caulfield. Commutation. Remarks on the conditions of safety.
tables. appendix. 16 pp. Dublin, Hodges, Foster, 1870
N., T.

8734 HASTINGS, William. The lucifer match, and post office monopoly; being the substance of a paper read at the Huddersfield literary & scientific society.
table. 20 pp. London, Effingham Wilson, 1870
T.

8735 HAYES, James. Suggestions for the organisation of co-operative farming associations in Ireland. Read before the Royal Dublin society, March 21, 1870.
12 pp. [no t.p.] n.p., 1870
U.

8736 HENDERSON, W. D. The Irish land bill.
24 pp. Belfast, Ward Bros., 1870
N., Q.
Headed, 'For private circulation'.

8737 HILL, John, ed. The railway problem, 1870. A series of papers. I. The power of railways and their evils.—The separation of passenger and goods traffic. II. How to make railways pay.—Light lines. III. Railway reform.—Abolition of tickets. IV. By whom ought railways to be managed—by 4,000 oligarchs or one central board? V. How railways may be acquired gratis by the state. VI. Railways of the future.—Convertible carriages for road and rail. VII. The railway league.
72 pp. London, Hicks, 1870
T.

8738 HOEY, John Cashel. Is Ireland irreconcilable? An article reprinted from the Dublin Review. [Together with:] Why is Ireland poor and discontented? A lecture delivered in the Polytechnic Hall, Melbourne, on the 23rd February, 1870, by Sir Charles Gavan Duffy.
48 pp. London, Burns, Oates, Dublin, J. Duffy, 1870
A., N., U.

8739 HURSTHOUSE, Charles Flinders. 'Australian independence'. Remarks in favour of the six Australian colonies (inspired by the magnificent career of those kindred ones which raised the 'stars and stripes') meeting England's 'new attitude' against them—not by humiliating prayer or protest —but by wholesome *separation* from a blinded, waning,

power and federation into an *independent state*. Respectfully submitted to Australian colonists by Charles Flinders Hursthouse, an old colonist, and observer of colonies and colonization in Canada, Australia, Cape Colony, New Zealand, and United States.
appendix. 26 pp. London, E. Stanford, 1870
T.

8740 HUTTON, Henry Dix. History, principle, and fact; in relation to the Irish question. Letters addressed to the 'Manchester Examiner and Times'.
64 pp. London, W. Ridgway, [etc., etc.], 1870
T.

8741 Information for emigrants to the British colonies, issued by H.M. emigration commissioners.
map. tables. appendix. 60 pp. London, her majesty's stationery office, 1870
T.

8742 The Irish land question. [A series of letters, dated March, 1870.]
72 pp. [no t.p., 1870?]
T.

8743 IRVINE, Henry Mervyn D'Arcy. Letters to the rt. hon. Wm. E. Gladstone on the Irish land bill and the state of Ireland for the last twenty years.
24 pp. Enniskillen, the 'Advertiser' office, 1870
N.

8744 JERDEIN, Arthur. The Argentine Republic, as a field for the agriculturist, the stock-farmer, and the capitalist.
28 pp. London, E. Stanford, 1870
T.

8745 KEMP, W. C. The A.B.C. guide to the new bankruptcy system, and to the law abolishing imprisonment for debt with a list of the local bankruptcy courts shewing the jurisdiction of each.
appendix. 48 pp. London, Simpkin Marshall, 1870
T.

8746 Key to the Irish land bill, showing what it purposes to do for the Irish tenantry.
12 pp. [n.p., 1870]
P.

8747 KINCAID, Joseph. Practical observations on the Irish Land Act 1870. (33 & 34 Vic. cap. 46.) With a copious index.
48 pp. Dublin, McGlashan & Gill, 1870
E., N.

8748 KINLOCH, Arthur. The Andaman Islands, their colonization, etc. A correspondence addressed to the India office.
16 pp. London, R. J. Bush, 1870
T.

8749 The land question. An outline of social history, showing how to reconcile the rights of landlord and tenant on constitutional principles.
tables. appendix. 84 pp. London, P. Richardson, 1870
N., T., U.
Signed 'E.'

8750 The land question in Ireland, viewed from an Indian stand-point. By a Bombay civilian.
76 pp. Dublin, Hodges, Foster & Co., London, Trübner & Co., 1870

N., Q., T., U.

8751 LAWES, Sir John Bennet. Exhaustion of the soil in relation to landlords' covenants and the valuation of unexhausted improvements. Read before the London farmers' club, April 4th, 1870.
tables. 32 pp. London, Rogerson & Tuxford, 1870

N.

8752 LEIGH, Evan. Plan for conveying railway trains across the straits of Dover: showing the origin of the idea.
plans. 8 pp. Manchester, A. Ireland, 1870

T.

8753 LLOYD, Humphrey. On the financial results of commutation: being the substance of a communication made to the general convention of the church of Ireland.
table. 14 pp. Dublin, Hodges, Foster, 1870

T.

8754 LONGFIELD, Mountifort. Remarks on the safety and advantages of commutation, if accepted by the clergy generally.
20 pp. Dublin, A. Thom, 1870

N., T.

8755 LOWE, Robert, and REYNOLDS, Henry. Revision of the stamp duties. Correspondence between the right honourable Robert Lowe, M.P., chancellor of the exchequer, and Henry Reynolds, solicitor, Birmingham. With appendix.
40 pp. London, Butterworths, 1870

T.

8756 McCABE, Charles. Supplement to the tithe commutation tables for ascertaining, at sight, the tithe rent-charge payable for the year 1870 according to the average prices of wheat, barley, and oats for the seven preceding years to Christmas, 1869 as declared in the 'London Gazette' of 4th January, 1870. Accompanied by tables showing the annual average prices of wheat, barley, and oats, from 1790 to 1868. Septennial average prices from 1835. Report of progress made in the commutation of tithes.
tables. 8 pp. London, [etc.], Rivingtons, 1870

T.

8757 [MacCOLL, Malcolm.] Is liberal policy a failure? By Expertus.
tables. 54 pp. London, Longmans, Green, Reader & Dyer, 1870

T.

8758 McGEE, Thomas D'Arcy. A history of the Irish settlers in America from the earliest period.
table of contents. index. 226 pp. Dublin, J. Mullany, 1870

A.

8759 MACKAY, H. W. Boyd. An apology for the present system of conveyancing, as contrasted with those of registration and record of title.
appendix. 66 pp. London, Longmans, Green, Reader and Dyer, 1870

T.

8760 McKENNA, Sir Joseph Neale. The National Bank, a case with proofs.
index. tables. 130 pp. London, Wertheimer and Lea, 1870

A.

8761 ——. To the shareholders of the National Bank.
44 pp. London, Wertheimer and Lea, 1870

A.

8762 Minnesota: its resources and progress; its beauty, healthfulness and fertility; and its attractions and advantages as a home for immigrants.
tables. 72 pp. St. Paul Minn., Press Printing Company, 1870

P.

8763 MURPHY, Joseph John. Commutation and compounding.
tables. 24 pp. Belfast, Phillips, 1870

N.

8764 NELSON, Joseph. Published by authority. Handbook of emigration to the western states of America. The shortest, cheapest, and best routes, and cost of passage; the mode of acquiring land by purchase or free grant; and copies of the pre-emption and homestead laws, and latest land office circular. With maps. Entered at Stationers' Hall.
maps. tables. 114 pp. London, at the passenger and forwarding office, via Pennsylvania Central Railway, 1870

T.

8765 NEWMAN, G. G. A summary of the law relating to cheques on bankers.
44 pp. 2nd ed. London, Effingham Wilson, 1870

T.

8766 NOBLE, John. Our imports and exports: with some remarks upon the balance of trade.
tables. 68 pp. London, Longmans, Green, Reader, and Dyer, 1870

T.

8767 PETRIE, Francis William Henry. The Irish poor law rating as it affects tithe rent-charge property.
appendix. table. 8 pp. 3rd ed. London, Rivingtons, Dublin, Hodges & Smith, 1870

N.

8768 The province of Quebec, and european emigration. Published by order of the government of Quebec.
tables. appendix. table of contents. 146 pp. Quebec, at the office of 'L'Événement'. 1870

N.

8769 The 'Question of the Hour' or why is Ireland poor and discontented and how she can be made contented and rich, by a Leinster Man.
tables. 14 pp. Dublin, Warren, 1870

N.

8770 REARDEN, P. J. This, or separation. A plan to establish & guarantee Irish national independent home rule, and a federal army and navy.
80 pp. Glasgow, Cameron & Ferguson, [1870?]

A., B.

8771 Report of the committee on night refuges, appointed at the conference held at the rooms of the society for organising charitable relief and repressing mendicity, on the 8th June, 1870.
8 pp. London, the society, 1870

A.

See 8716.

8772 Report of the Kilkenny tenant league to the president, George Bryan, Esq., M.P., embodying their views generally upon land tenure in Ireland and upon the land bill.
16 pp. Kilkenny, at the 'Journal Office', 1870

N., U.

8773 Rules for the management of the Abbeyleix savings bank.
14 pp. Maryborough, 'Leinster Express', 1870

N.

8774 RUSSELL, Robert. Ulster tenant-right for Ireland or notes upon notes, taken during a visit to Ireland in 1868, with additional notes, analysing the Irish land bill. Second Edition.
appendix. 106 pp. Edinburgh, A. and C. Black, London, Longmans, Green, Reader & Dyer, 1870

T., U.

8775 SCRIVEN, J. E. An Irish farmer on the land question. Reprinted from the 'Examiner'. With a plan for applying the law as now administered to the settlement of the question.
16 pp. Dublin, McGee, 1870

N.

——. 16 pp. 2nd ed. Dublin, McGee, 1870

N.

8776 SHEPPARD, Thomas. Local taxation and parochial government: poor relief and pauper management.
60 pp. London, Longmans, Green, Reader & Dyer, 1870

T.

8777 SPROULE, John. Facts and observations on the Irish land question; collected and arranged by the direction and under the supervision of the Irish land owners' committee: also observations on the new Irish land bill.
index. tables. 60 pp. Dublin, 1870

A.

8778 TAYLOR, George. Tithe commutation. Table showing the value of tithe rent-charges for the year 1870. To which is added other tables, showing the effect of the yearly fluctuation in the prices of wheat, barley, and oats, since 1835.
tables. 8 pp. London, H. Shaw, 1870

T.

8779 THORP, Robert. Cashmere misgovernment.
tables. 78 pp. London, Longmans, Green, Reader & Dyer, 1870

T.

8780 TREVELYAN, Sir Charles. Address delivered by Sir Charles Trevelyan on the 27th of June, 1870 at a conference of the society for organizing charitable relief and suppressing mendicity on the systematic visitation of the poor in their own homes, an indispensable basis of an effective system of charity, and report on the same subject, by a sub-committee of the same society, adopted by the council July 18, 1870.
table. 20 pp. London, Bell & Daldy, [1870]

T.

8781 WARBURTON, William, dean of Elphin. Speech on the land question.
16 pp. Dublin & London, Moffat, 1870

N.

8782 WATSON, James Harvey. Irish railway reform: a scheme for amalgamating the different railway companies in Ireland. Proving that uniform fares of—first class 2s., second class 1s., third class 6d., for any distance above 10 miles; and 6d. 3d. and 1d. for distances not exceeding 10 miles, would be profitable to the state.
tables. tables in appendix. 24 pp. London, J. H. Watson, 1870

T.

8783 WILLIAMS, Arthur John. The appropriation of the railways by the state. A popular statement.
tables. appendix. 152 pp. London, Cassell, Petter, and Galpin, 1870

T.

8784 WRAY, G. Depression of trade and the French treaty.
tables. 24 pp. London, W. Ridgway, 1870

T.

1871

8785 ABINGTON, S. J. The 'Great West'. The question of emigration—where to? Extent and resources of the United States. States and territories west of the Mississippi. Iowa and Nebraska as peculiarly adapted to English colonization. Land for farms—free homesteads, etc. Easy accessibility—railroad communication. Rapid growth of towns—facilities for emigrants. Prospects for the industrious of all classes in the 'Great West'.
20 pp. London, The educational trading company, (limited), 1871

T.

8786 Address of the Home Government Association to the people of Ireland.
4 pp. Dublin, J. Falconer, 1871

B.

8787 ARMSTRONG, Richard, and others. The new land act explained, for the use of the tenant farmers of Ireland. By Richard Armstrong, Denis Caulfield Heron, and William O'Brien.
32 pp. Dublin, Browne & Nolan, 1871

B., N., P.

8788 BARRINGTON, William L. Tramways in Dublin: a letter addressed to the citizens.
16 pp. Dublin, R. D. Webb, 1871

A., L., N.

8789 BARRY, James F. The state of parties in Ireland.
110 pp. Dublin, J. Falconer, London, W. Ridgway, 1871

B.

8790 The beet-root sugar manufacture in Ireland, by K. P. Printed for private circulation.
tables. appendix. 52 pp. Glasgow, Renfrew, 1871
D.

8791 BORDMAN, Thomas J. C. L. The plain guide in bankruptcy and private arrangements between debtors and creditors.
London, Bell, 1871
T.

8792 BUND, John William Willis. The ancient land settlement of England. A lecture delivered at University College, London, October 17, 1871.
34 pp. London, Butterworths, 1871
T.

8793 BUTLER, Thomas Ambrose. The state of Kansas and Irish immigration.
38pp. Dublin, McGlashan and Gill, 1871
A.

8794 BUTT, Isaac. Irish Federalism! its meanings, its objects, and its hopes.
70 pp. 3rd ed. Dublin, The Irish Home Rule League, 1871
N.
See 8710.

8795 ——. Speech of Isaac Butt, esq., Q.C., M.P., at Glasgow, November 14th, 1871, on home rule for Ireland.
16 pp. Dublin, The Irish Home Rule Association, 1871
B., N.

8796 [CHAMBERS, George.] A tribute to the principles, virtues, habits and public usefulness of the Irish and Scotch early settlers of Pennsylvania. By a descendant.
172 pp. Chambersburg, Pennsylvania, M. A. Foltz, 1871
B.
First published 1856.

8797 CHAPMAN, Henry Cleaver. A brief review of the shipping bills of 1870–71. Dedicated to the members of the Mercantile Marine Association.
tables. appendix. 22 pp. London, G. Philip, Liverpool, H. Greenwood, 1871
T.

8798 COX, Edward. Pocket notes on the use of adhesive stamps on receipts, agreements, and other legal and commercial documents.
26 pp. London, Cox, 1871
T.

8799 DASHWOOD, Fredk. Loftus. On local rating in England, Scotland & Ireland; and how to enlist the cooperation of owners and occupiers, both large and small, in advancing primary education, and diminishing pauperism. Being a reprint of a paper read in April, 1869, revised from the journal of the London Farmers' Club.
tables. 28 pp. London, W. Ridgway, 1871
T.

8800 DILLON, James. On the railways of Ireland, and the causes which have led to the stoppage of railway enterprise, and the best way of providing for the improvement and extension of the railway system, read before the Royal Dublin Society.
map. tables. appendix. 32 pp. Dublin, G. Ponsonby, 1871
A., N.

8801 DIXON, Robert V. Remarks on the probable financial results of diocesan sustentation funds.
appendix. tables. 32 pp. Dublin, Hodges, Foster, 1871
T.

8802 DUNN, George. A case of real hardship, and no relief under the New Land Bill.
14 pp. Cork, the Cork Printing Works, 1871
N.

8803 EAGLE, William. Tithes. The ancient law of tithes, shewing that tithes are the property of the public, and of the poor.
32 pp. London, Whittaker, [1871]
T.
This is a new edition of a pamphlet published about 1831 entitled *A legal argument shewing that tithes are the property of the public and of the poor.* . . .

8804 ELMHIRST, Edward. Leicestershire. A report on the highway districts. The results of the system during the last eight years; and suggestions for the more effectual working of it. A comparative cost of the old and the new systems showing, in the year 1870, a saving in the actual outlay over the county. Third ed. Revised, corrected, and enlarged.
table. 24 pp. London, Hamilton, Adams, Leicester, Crossley and Clarke, 1871
T.

8805 FRASER, Julia Agnes. Universal equality: or Jonathan Baxter's peep into the future.
32 pp. Edinburgh, J. Menzies, 1871
T.

8806 GABBETT, William. Irish National Mutual Cattle Insurance. A letter to the 'Irish Farmers' Gazette'.
16 pp. Dublin, "Farmers' Gazette", 1871
N.

8807 GALLWEY, Thomas. A plea for union rating.
tables. 14 pp. Dublin, Hodges, Foster, 1871
N.

8808 GRANT-DUFF, Sir Mountstewart Elphinstone. Mr. Grant-Duff on the teachings of Richard Cobden, Dec. 20th, 1871.
32 pp. London, Cassel, Petter and Galpin, 1871 (Cobden Club Pamphlet)
T.

8809 HULL, Hugh Munro. Practical hints to emigrants intending to proceed to Tasmania: and a full description of the several counties and their products; with a paper on local industries written by E. C. Nowell.
tables. 56 pp. Hobart, Fletcher, 1871
A.

8810 The increase of capital.
30 pp. London, B. M. Pickering, 1871
T.

8811 Irish railways and the Irish board of public works: Being a review of some of the unused powers of the loan commissioners, with suggestions for their practical employment.
table of contents. tables. appendix. 44 pp. Dublin, Hodges, Foster, 1871

N. T.

8812 Jamaica and its governor during the last six years. By a fellow of the Royal Geographical Society.
32 pp. London, E. Stanford, 1871

B.

8813 JEVONS, William Stanley. The match tax: a problem in finance.
tables. appendix with tables. 66 pp. London, E. Stanford, 1871

T.

8814 JONES, William Bence. Letter to an assistant barrister on unexhausted tillages and manures, under the Land Act (1870, Ireland).
20 pp. Dublin, Hodges, Foster, 1871

E., N., T.

8815 KING, George. Modern pauperism and the Scottish poor laws, including hints for the amendment of the poor law act of 1845. With some suggestions for the amelioration and social elevation of the people. Inscribed to the right honourable W. E. Gladstone.
76 pp. Aberdeen, J. Murray, 1871

T.

8816 LACOIN, Paul. Programme de constitution par voie de réformes successives ou synthèse de Principes économiques administratifs politiques et religieux. Conclusion d'enquête auprès des Membres de l'Assemblée nationale. (Projet de réorganisation financière et morale soumis aux conseils généraux). Troisième edition.
appendix. 56 pp. Paris, Librarie Guillaumin, 1871

U.

8817 Letter to the policy-holders and annuitants of the European Assurance Society. By a former director and present policy-holder of the society. With an appendix.
120 pp. London, C. and E. Layton, 1871

8818 LEVI, Leone. The liquor trades. A report to M. T. Bass, esq., M.P., on the capital invested and the number of persons employed therein.
tables. 24 pp. London, W. Ridgway, 1871

T.

8819 MACCARTHY, John George. The Munster farmers' guide to the new Land Act.
table of contents. 36 pp. Cork, Guy, 1871

N.

8820 MACFIE, Robert Andrew. Colonial questions pressing for immediate solution, in the interest of the nation and the empire. Papers and letters.
tables. 136 pp. London, Longmans, Green, Reader, and Dyer, Edinburgh, Edmonston & Douglas, 1871

T.

8821 MACLEAN, James Mackenzie. The Indian deficit and the income tax.
18 pp. London, F. Algar, 1871

T.

8822 MILNE, R. L. Money and Christianity; or a way to make charity as well as money profitable; addressed to the Christian and un-Christian world.
18 pp. London, Shaw & co., 1871

T.

8823 Minnesota: its resources and progress, its beauty, healthfulness and fertility; and its attractions and advantages as a home for immigrants, with a map, compiled by the commissioner of statistics, and published by direction of Horace Austin, governor.
map. tables. 82 pp. Minneapolis, Tribune Printing Co., 1871

N.

8824 NICHOLSON, Nathaniel Alexander. A shilling's worth of political economy.
52 pp. London, Williams and Norgate, 1871

T.

8825 The ninth annual report of the West Clare Agricultural Society, for the year ending October, 1871
4 pp. Kilrush, at the 'Clare Advertiser' Office, 1871

N.

8826 O'LOUGHLIN, Edward. Sir Joseph McKenna and his financing operations: comprising correspondence which appeared in the 'Nation' newspaper, with an explanatory statement and appendix, showing the manner in which he most improperly turned his position in the National Bank to his own account, and the enormous losses sustained by the proprietors through his misconduct.
tables. appendix. index. 200 pp. Dublin, 1871

A., U.

8827 Our railway system viewed in reference to invasion. Being a translation of a memoir entitled the training of railways for war, in time of peace, by baron M.M. Von Weber, K. K. Hoffrath. With an introduction and notes by Robert Mallet, M.I.C.E., F.R.S.
116 pp. London, Chapman and Hall, 1871

T.

8828 PALMERSTON, Henry John Temple, 3rd viscount. Selections from private journals of tours in France in 1815 & 1818.
58 pp. London, R. Bentley, 1871

L.

8829 PIM, Jonathan. Ireland & the imperial parliament.
22 pp. Dublin, Hodges, Foster, London, W. Ridgway, 1871

B., N.

8830 Preparatory programme of the national University for industrial and technical training, with a summary of subjects for discussion at a conference to be held at the Guildhall early in May, under the auspices of the lord mayor, the city authorities, and the municipal and industrial representatives of the United Kingdom.
table of contents. 86 pp. London, printed by H. Simpkins, 1871

A.

31

8831 Programme of the Land Tenure Reform Association. With an explanatory statement by John Stuart Mill.
16 pp. London, Longmans, Green, Reader & Dyer, 1871
N.

8832 ROBINSON, Isaac. Steam cultivation: two papers read before the Wisbech District Chamber of Agriculture, October 20th, & November 23rd, 1870.
tables. appendix. 38 pp. Wisbech, Leach, London, Simpkin Marshall, 1871
T.

8833 Roumanian railway bonds and intervention in foreign bonds. Correspondence between the right hon. earl Granville, K.G., H.M's. secretary of state for foreign affairs, and the council of foreign bond holders.
16 pp. London, Council of foreign bond holders, 1871
T.

8834 The royal mint: altered returns, presented to parliament. A letter from the right hon. lord Kinnaird to the right hon. W. E. Gladstone, M.P.
tables. 8 pp. London, Effingham Wilson, 1871
T.

8835 Rules of the Franklin emigration, land, investment, and industrial society (limited). Incorporated pursuant to act of parliament. Registered offices: 30 Hope Street, Glasgow.
16 pp. Glasgow, Bell and Bain, 1871
T.

8836 SALMON, George. Commutation, not a speculative transaction.
32 pp. Dublin, Hodges, Foster, 1871
N.

8837 SAMUELSON, James. Trade unions and public-houses. A letter to the right honourable H. A. Bruce, M.P., etc., H.M. chief secretary of state for the home department.
16 pp. London, Longmans, Green, Reader & Dyer, 1871
T.

8838 SIEGFRIED, Jules. Les cités ouvrières du Havre. Conférence faite à l'Élysée le 25 juin 1871.
table. diagrams. 28 pp. Le Havre, Santallier, 1871
N.

8839 [SKELTON, Sir John.] Boarding out pauper children. A re-print of the Memorial of Ladies and subsequent orders, observations, and forms issued by the poor law board, to which is appended suggestions by a lady, forming complete instructions for carrying out the system. Second edition. With several new forms.
36 pp. London, Simpkin, Marshall, Windermere, J. Garnett, [1871]
T.

8840 SMITH, George. The cry of the children from the brickyards of England: a statement and appeal, with remedy, illustration. appendix. 96 pp. London, Simpkin, Marshall. Leicester, Spencer, 1871
A.

8841 SMYTH, P. J. A plea for a peasant proprietary in Ireland.
20 pp. Dublin, Fowler, 1871
A., U.

8842 SUTTIE, Sir George Grant, bart. On land tenure and the cultivation of the soil.
14 pp. Edinburgh and London, W. Blackwood & son, 1871
T.

8843 TODD, Charles Hawkes. The rights of tenants of ecclesiastical lands under the Irish Church Act (1869).
42 pp. Dublin, Hodges, Foster, 1871
B., T.

8844 TRAVIS, Henry. The co-operative system of society, or, the change from evil to good in man and in social affairs. A pamphlet for the Owen centenary.
tables. appendix. 32 pp. London, Longmans, Green, Reader & Dyer, 1871
T.

8845 TUCKER, Henry Carre. Thoughts on poverty and pauperism.
48 pp. London, Dalton & Lucy, 1871
T.

8846 TURNBULL, W. Wilson. Law and liquor: the whole case against the Gothenburg proposal of Mr. Chamberlain; the permissive bill, with a syllabus of 100 reasons why it should not become law; and the licensing boards bill.
tables. 80 pp. London, Weldon, [1871?]
T.

8847 Unbiassed notes on life assurance. Illustrated by seven original fables for popular use.
tables. 42 pp. London, Houlston, 1871
T.

8848 Union rating in Ireland; the question discussed.
table. 28 pp. Dublin, J. M. O'Toole, 1871
B.

8849 WATTS, Isaac. The cotton supply association: its origin and progress.
tables. appendix. 174 pp. Manchester, Tubbs & Brook, 1871
T.

1872

8850 ADAMS, Thatcher A. A letter addressed to A. H. Brown, esq., M.P., on the settlement of land and system of land transfer in the United States.
appendix. 56 pp. London, D. Lane, 1872
T.

8851 The Alabah claims, and how the Ya-kees 'fixed' the Yn-gheesh. Being a fragment of some lately discovered annals of monkeydom.
32 pp. London, Simpkin Marshall, 1872
T.

8852 BENSON, Robert. The amalgamation of railway companies or the alternative of their purchase by the state considered.
tables. 30 pp. London, Longmans, Green, Reader & Dyer, 1872
N.

8853 BIGG, James. Supplement to the twelfth edition of the general railway acts: containing the enactments affecting railways in England and Ireland, passed in sessions 1867, 1868, 1869, 1870, and 1871. With index. 4th edition. 136 pp. Westminster, Waterlow, 1872

T.

8854 BOTLY, William. The land question. 52 pp. London, E. Owen, 1872

T.

8855 BRYAN, George. Chatsworth and Clough; or falsehood and cowardice unmasked. 34 pp. Kilkenny, Coyle Bros., 1872

A.

On a land dispute in Kilkenny.

8856 BUTT, Isaac. Irish government and Irish railways: an argument for home rule. A speech delivered at the meeting of the Home Government Association, on Monday, May 27th, 1872. 20 pp. Dublin, The Home Government Association, 1872

B., C., N.

8857 DE AULA, Hugh. A new theory of poverty. 16 pp. London and Edinburgh, Williams and Norgate, 1872

T.

8858 Diddledom, or tonics for co-operative society fever. By R. L. tables. 38 pp. London, Bell, [1872]

T.

8859 DONNELL, Robert Cather. Chapters on leasehold tenant-right and other tenant-right questions. Supplemental to the author's guide to the land act. With reports of the judges and chairmen's decisions. 142 pp. Dublin, J. Falconer, 1872

E.

8860 ELMHIRST, Edward. Leicestershire. A report on the highway districts. The results of the system during the last nine years; and suggestions for the more effectual working of it. A comparative cost of the old and the new systems showing, in the year 1871, a saving in the actual outlay over the county, of nearly £2,000. Fourth edition, revised, corrected, and enlarged. tables. 26 pp. London, Hamilton, Adams, Leicester, Crossley and Clarke, 1872

T.

8861 FERGUSON, Thomas Pattinson. Letter to the chairman of the Billericay board of guardians. 12 pp. London, Rivingtons, 1872

T.

8862 A few remarks on the present state of the commercial relations of England with Portugal, Spain and Italy, and on the means of improving them. table of contents. tables. 118 pp. London, Spottiswoode, 1872

A.

8863 FORNEY, John Wien. What I saw in Texas. map. 92 pp. Philadelphia, Ringwalt & Brown, [1872]

N.

8864 FOWLER, William. The present aspect of the land question. tables. 70 pp. London, Cassell, Petter, and Galpin, 1872

T.

8865 FOX, Charles H. Out-door relief as a cause of pauperism. tables. 12 pp. London, Simpkin Marshall, 1872

T.

8866 GRIFFITH, George Sandham. Pauper or provident: which? A plea for the industrious poor. A letter addressed to his grace the duke of Marlborough. 16 pp. Oxford & London, J. Parker, 1872

A.

8867 Half-yearly reports and transactions of the Royal Agricultural Society of Ireland, 42, Upper Sackville Street, Dublin. January, 1870, to December, 1871. tables. 68 pp. Dublin, at the office of the 'Farmers' Gazette', 1872

D.

8868 HEAD, Jeremiah. Retail traders and co-operative stores. Being a paper read, September 14, 1872, in the economy and trade department of the Social Science Congress at Plymouth, Sir John Bowring presiding. tables. 22 pp. Middlesbrough, Reid, 1872

N.

8869 Hints and suggestions for the formation and management of working men's clubs and institutes. 16 pp. 12th ed. London, W. J. Johnson, 1872

A.

8870 HUMFREY, R. H. Blake. Wages. A lecture given by R. H. Blake Humfrey on August 6th, 1872. 24 pp. London, Jarrold, 1872

T.

8871 LALOR, William. Remarks in connection with a proposal for extending the railway accommodation of Dublin; with a map and sections. 14 pp. Dublin, McGlashan & Gill, 1872

L.

8872 LEGG, R. How to prevent monetary panics by reform in banking. 42 pp. London, Effingham Wilson, [1872]

T.

8873 LEIGHTON, Sir Baldwyn, bart. Agricultural Labour. Being a paper read before the social science congress at Plymouth, September 13th, 1872. 20 pp. London, R. Bentley, 1872

T.

8874 ——. The farm labourer in 1872. 32 pp. London, R. Bentley, 1872

T.

8875 A letter to the parliamentary and select committee of the house of commons on the Truck Bill, from the Flat Pressers executive committee, by W. R. C. 2 pp. (no t.-p.) Colbridge, 1872

N.

8876 MacCarthy, John George. A plea for the home government of Ireland.
114 pp. Dublin, A. M. Sullivan, 1872
B.

8877 Manchester Chamber of Commerce. Hours of labour in factories. Report of speeches delivered at the quarterly meeting of the chamber, held April 22nd, 1872.
24 pp. Manchester, Cave and Sever, 1872
A.

8878 Martin, John. The quarrel between Ireland and England; a lecture delivered in Dundalk on 3rd October, 1871.
18 pp. Dublin, the Home Government Association, 1872
A., B.

8879 Martineau, John. City, country, and colony: who ought to emigrate and how many.
30 pp. London, Longmans, Green, Reader & Dyer, 1872
T.

8880 Massingham, John Deacon. Mr. Alderman Carter, M.P., and the Liberation Society. A reply lecture, for the Leeds Mechanics' Institute, Nov. 30th, 1871.
appendix. 24 pp. London, W. Macintosh, [1872]
T.

8881 Maxse, Frederick Augustus. The causes of social revolt. A lecture delivered in London, Portsmouth, Bradford, Nottingham, Derby and Greenwich.
appendix. 108 pp. London, Longmans, Green, Reader & Dyer, 1872
A.

8882 Mr. Bull and his family troubles; especially in relation to 'The Case', Jonathan versus Bull.
30 pp. London, E. Stanford, 1872
T.

8883 Nash, Francis Herbert. A letter to the small farmers of Ireland. [Profit without outlay, and improvement without capital.]
36 pp. Dublin, Hodges Foster, 1872
L.

8884 Old monarchy or new republic. Conversations about constitutions, communism, capital and liberty.
68 pp. London, Hamilton, Adams, 1872
T.

8885 Overland communications with Western China. A brief statement of how the matter stands at present. By R. G. With a map.
map. 10 pp. Liverpool, Webb, Hunt & Ridings, [1872]
T.

8886 Perrin, J. Beswick. Labour and capital: shewing some of the consequences of the nine hours movement.
18 pp. London, R. Hardwicke, 1872
T.

8887 The private speculator on the stock exchange. By Grobecker, Son and Co.
18 pp. London, August Siegle, 1872
T.

8888 Rules, regulations and forms of the Canada Patent Office, 1st September, 1872.
diagrams. 28 pp. n.p., Taylor, 1872
N.

8889 Sullivan, Sir Edward, bart. Our economic Catos.
92 pp. London, E. Stanford, 1872
T.

8890 Teetgen, Alexander T. A pamphlet reporting the proceedings of 'the House of ('little') Commons', held at Westminster, for the discussion of commercial & political grievances and for self-improvement.
28 pp. [London], 1872
T.

8891 Torrens, Sir Robert R. Transfer of land by registration of title. (A paper read at the recent Congress of the Social Science Association.) With the discussion and concluding remarks of the attorney-general, Sir John Coleridge.
table. 24 pp. London, Head & Hole, 1872
N.

8892 Turner, Patrick. Home rule explained.
43 pp. Dublin, J. Mullany, 1872
B.

8893 Twelve months at the South African diamond fields. By 'Fossor'.
illustrations. map. 68 pp. London, E. Stanford, 1872
T.

8894 [Vanderbilt, Lincoln.] The new and wonderful explorations of Professor Lincoln Vanderbilt the great American traveller, in the territories of Colorado, Arizona and Utah, and the states of California, Nevada, and Texas, adapted for the emigrants, settlers, mine speculators, fortune hunters, and travellers. Showing the cheapest and best ways of transit, the most consistent and genuine means of making money. Including a full description of Utah, Salt Lake City, Mormonism and polygamy, exhibiting startling revelations and extraordinary facilities for accumulating a fortune, coupled with the most authentic, valuable, and essential information ever published. Also a most interesting description of the various routes from New York to San Francisco, via Niagara Falls, the Pennsylvania Mountains, and the Pacific railroads, including the gorgeous scenery of the Rocky Mountains and the Sierra Nevadas. (Entered at Stationers' Hall.)
40 pp. London, J. W. Last, [1872]
T.

8895 Watts, John. The power and influence of co-operative effort.
16 pp. London, Labour News, 1872
T.

8896 White, William. The insurance register, 1872; containing, with other information, a record of the yearly progress and the present financial position of British insurance associations.
tables. 66 pp. London, C. and E. Layton, New York, J. H. & C. M. Goodsell, 1872
T.

1873

8897 The agricultural labourer, by a farmer's son.
56 pp. London, W. Macintosh, 1873
T., U.
Preface is signed F.H.D.

8898 ALCOCK, Thomas St. Leger. The relative equality of men, considered with reference to the wants of the industrious classes and the deserving poor.
appendices. 80 pp. London, Williams & Norgate, 1873
T.

8899 ARCHER, Charles P. A common sense remedy for Ireland, based on the practice of civilised nations, and on an approved custom within the kingdom.
80 pp. 2nd ed. Dublin, R. D. Webb, 1873
N.

8900 BARTLEY, Sir George Christopher Trant. The poor law in its effects on thrift with suggestions for an improved out-door relief. Paper read and discussed at the British Association for the advancement of science at Bradford on the 22nd September, 1873.
24 pp. 2nd ed. London, Bell, [1873]
T.

8901 BOND, Francis T. The home of the agricultural labourer: its defects and how to remedy them; being the substance of a paper read at the Social Science Congress at Norwich, October, 1873.
24 pp. Gloucester, J. Headland, [1873?]
T.

8902 CHAMBERLAIN, Joseph. Speech of Mr. Joseph Chamberlain, of Birmingham, delivered at the Temperance Hall, Townhead Street, Sheffield, on September 23rd, 1873.
12 pp. Sheffield, Taylor & Winterbottom, 1873
N.

8903 CLARKE, Hyde. On the financial resources of our colonies.
18 pp. London, Unwin Bros., 1873
A.

8904 COBDEN, Richard. Mr. Cobden on the land question. [Reprinted from 'The Morning Star', Jan. 22, 1864.]
14 pp. London, P. S. King, 1873
T.

8905 COLT, Frederick Hoare. Remarks on the land transfer question; with a sketch of a plan for a general register.
34 pp. London, H. Sweet, 1873
T.

8906 CROMPTON, Henry. The Criminal Law Amendment Act, and other laws affecting labour. Published by authority of the congress.
8 pp. Leeds, Goodall, 1873
N.

8907 CULLEY, Samuel Hall. Schedule 'D' of the income tax and how to kill or cure it.
12 pp. London, E. Stanford, 1873
T.

8908 DE ROS, William L. Lascelles FitzGerald, 23rd baron. The Land Act of 1872 and its results.
20 pp. Belfast, W. & G. Baird, 1873
N.
Includes cutting from 'Freeman's Journal', reviewing the work. The review draws attention to the error of lord de Ros in referring to the act of '1872'.

8909 Emigration to the Province of Ontario, Dominion of Canada. The capitalist, the farmer, the labourer, and every other class will find the new dominion to be the best field in the world for improving their position.
24 pp. Belfast, W. & G. Baird, 1873
N.

8910 A farmer's views on the agricultural labour question. By one of them.
18 pp. Norwich, Fletcher and Son, 1873
T.

8911 A few remarks upon certain practical questions of political economy. By a former member of the Political Economy Club.
24 pp. London, Simpkin, Marshall, 1873
T.

8912 HANCOCK, William Neilson. Report on statistics of savings invested in Ireland in joint stock banks and in savings banks, and in government funds; and on statistics of bank note circulation in Ireland 1860–1872.
tables. 10 pp. Dublin, Her Majesty's Stationery Office, 1873
N.

8913 HENRY, James P. Resources of the state of Arkansas with description of counties, railroads, mines, and the city of Little Rock.
table of contents. tables. 136 pp. 3rd. ed. Little Rock, Arkansas, Price & McClure, 1873
N.

8914 JEFFERIES, Richard. Jack Brass, emperor of England.
12 pp. London, T. Pettit, 1873
T.

8915 KENNEDY, Edward. The present hard times and how to mend them.
32 pp. Manchester, J. Heywood, [1873]
T.

8916 KINGLAKE, Robert Arthur. Land, landlord, lawyer, labourer. A letter to Chandos Wren Hoskyns, esq., M.P., from a magistrate of the county of Somerset in which is described a safe simple expeditious and cheap mode of transferring land.
appendices. 40 pp. Weston-super-mare, C. Robbins, [1873]
T.

8917 LEVI, Leone. Estimate of the amount of taxation falling on the working classes of the United Kingdom.
appendix. 32 pp. London, W. Ridgway, 1873
T.

8918 LEWIS, Bailie. The Gothenburg licensing system. Lecture delivered at a public meeting in Edinburgh, 14th July, 1873. With report of a meeting convened for the purpose of hearing reply by Mr. Carnegie.
tables. 44 pp. Edinburgh, Oliphant, 1873
T.

8919 The London gas stokers. A report by the committee of their trial for conspiracy, of their defence, and of the proceedings for their liberation.
tables. 50 pp. London, Foster, 1873
N.

8920 MAGNUS, Philip. Labourers and capitalists. How related; how separated; how united. A study for working men.
40 pp. London, E. Stanford, 1873
T.

8921 MEADOWS, J. McC. Turf industry; with suggestions for its promotion and extension in Ireland.
33 pp. Dublin, McGlashan & Gill, 1873
L.

8922 Miners' National Association: Proceedings of the Miners' National Association conference, held at Leeds, on the 18th, 19th, 20th, 21st and 22nd Nov., 1873.
tables. 80 pp. Glasgow, at the 'Sentinel' Office, 1873
N.

8923 Notes on Texas and the Texas and Pacific Railway. Compiled from official and other authentic data.
tables. 48 pp. Philadelphia, Ringwalt & Brown, 1873
N.

8924 Ought the state to buy the railways? A question for everybody. Reprinted, with additions, from the 'British Quarterly Review'. By a midland shareholder.
44 pp. London, Longmans, Green, Reader & Dyer, 1873
T.

8925 A peep through home-rule spectacles at English rule in Ireland.
54 pp. Dublin, Hodges Foster, 1873
R.

8926 READWIN, T. A. On the Leitrim Coal (Ireland).
map. table. 6 pp. Manchester, A. Ireland, 1873
N.
Includes also a prospectus of the Irish Midland Coal Consumers Company.

8927 Report of the committee appointed by the council of the Home Government Association to examine the financial relations between Great Britain and Ireland, and the pressure of taxation upon Irish resources.
tables. appendix. 28 pp. Dublin, R. Chapman, 1873
B., C., N.

8928 ROBINSON, Charles. New South Wales: the oldest and richest of the Australian colonies.
maps. table of contents. tables. appendix. 114 pp. Sydney, Richards, 1873
A.

8929 SCHULTZ, Charles W. H. New York in September, 1873.
tables. 62 pp. London, J. & W. Rider, 1873
T.

8930 Sea coast fisheries. Report of the trustees for bettering the condition of the poor of Ireland, for the year to 31st December, 1872.
appendices. tables. 36 pp. Dublin, Browne and Nolan, 1873
N.

8931 SPROULE, J. A chapter of Irish landlordism comprising an account of the operations on the estate of the late John Armitage Nicholson, esq., of Balrath, in the County of Meath, with an appendix illustrating some of the difficulties to be encountered in the management of landed property in Ireland.
appendix. 32 pp. Dublin, 1873
N.

8932 Tenth annual report of the West Clare Agricultural Society. Treasurer's account of the receipts and disbursements 1873.
8 pp. Kilrush, at the 'Clare Advertiser' Office, 1873
N.

8933 TRENCH, W. le Poer. A plea for the agricultural population residing in the undeveloped districts in the West of Ireland. With remarks on the motion, notice of which was given on Thursday, July 10, 1873.
10 pp. London, Buck, 1873
N.

8934 WHITCOMBE, George. Transfer of land. Suggestions as to a convenient form of index applicable to any system of registration and as to a plan for registration of assurances.
tables. appendices. 24 pp. London, G. R. Stevens, 1873
T.

1874

8935 ANKETELL, William Robert. The Irish Land Act, 1870. Observations on the Ulster custom and proposed amendments to the act.
12 pp. [London?], 1874
U.

8936 BROWN, William. The labour and money questions: a new catechism on political economy.
70 pp. Montreal, J. Lovell, 1874
T.

8937 BUTT, Isaac. The Irish deep sea fisheries. A speech delivered at a meeting of the Home Government Association of Ireland, on Tuesday 17th of October, 1871.
table. 26 pp. Dublin, Irish Home Rule League, 1874
N.

8938 ——. Irish federalism! its meanings, its objects, and its hopes.
68 pp. 4th ed. Dublin, The Irish Home Rule League, 1874
B., N.

8939 Capital and wages: what are they?
24 pp. London, Social Science Committee of the Society for promoting Christian knowledge, [1874]
T.

8940 CROMPTON, Henry. (Tracts for Trades Unionists—No. IV.) The National Federation of Associated Employers of Labour. Report upon the memorial presented to the home secretary by the National Federation of Associated Employers of Labour, December 13th, 1873. Together with the correspondence between Mr. Henry Crompton and Mr. T. R. Jackson.
22 pp. London, Foster, 1874

N.

8941 DODD, Joseph. The land question viewed from a church aspect.
66 pp. Oxford, J. Parker, 1874

T.

8942 DONNELL, Robert. C. A scheme of land transfer for small properties by local registry of title.
tables. 36 pp. Dublin, E. Ponsonby, 1874

C.

8943 DUNN, Archibald J. The bankers' clearing house. Some suggestions as to its extension and further development.
16 pp. London, Houlston, 1874

T.

8944 [ESSINGTON, Robert William.] The coming finance, or no income-tax. By A. Kingsman.
30 pp. London, Simpkin Marshall, 1874

T.

8945 FILGATE, Fitzherbert. Tenant-right and the land act.
22 pp. Dublin, Hodges, Foster, 1874.

R.

8946 Full report of the sixth annual Trades Congress held in the Temperance Hall, Sheffield, Jan. 12th, 13th, 14th, 15th, 16th, and 17th, 1874.
40 pp. Salford, Salford Steam Printing Co., 1874

N.

8947 GREGG, Robert S., dean of Cork. The Irish clergy and the representative church body. Remarks upon the financial position of the church of Ireland.
tables. 36 pp. Dublin, Hodges, Foster, 1874

A., N., T.

8948 GRIMSHAW, Thomas Wrigley. Remarks on the Public Health (Ireland) Bill, 1874.
8 pp. Dublin, Browne & Nolan, 1874

L.

8949 GWYNN, John. The church of Ireland and her censors: a vindication of the conduct of the clergy and of the representative church body.
60 pp. Dublin, Hodges, Foster, 1874

T.

8950 Half-yearly reports and transactions of the Royal Agricultural Society of Ireland, 42, Upper Sackville Street, Dublin. January, 1872, to December, 1873.
tables. 94 pp. Dublin, at the office of the 'Farmers' Gazette', 1874

D.

8951 HAMLY, C. H. Burbidge. Competition or co-operation. A lecture delivered before the members of S. Matthew's Guild, Leicester, on December 1st 1873.
50 pp. London, Hamilton Adams, [1874]

T.

8952 HANCOCK, William Neilson. Report on the state of Ireland in 1874.
table of contents. tables. 56 pp. Dublin, A. Thom, 1874

N.

8953 HARRISON, Frederic. (Tracts for Trades Unionists, No. I.) Imprisonment for breach of contract; or the Master and Servant Act [1867].
8 pp. London, the Trades Union Congress, [1874?]

N.

8954 ——. (Tracts for Trades Unionists, No. II.) Workmen and the law of conspiracy.
8 pp. London, the Trades Union Congress, [1874?]

N.

8955 ——. (Tracts for Trades Unionists—No. III.) The Criminal Law Amendment Act.
8 pp. (from the 'Times' of June 2nd, 1873). London, the Trades' Union Congress, [1874?]

N.

8956 HUNTER, W. A. A lecture on the criminal laws affecting labour. Glasgow tracts for trade unionists—No. IV.
16 pp. Edinburgh, Criminal Law Amendment Act Repeal Association, 1874

N.

8957 JONES, George William. The million on the rail; a few statistics, showing the expediency of encouraging the third-class passenger to travel.
tables. 20 pp. London, Davis, 1874

T.

8958 LLOYD, George A. Ways and means. The financial statement of George A. Lloyd, colonial treasurer of New South Wales.
tables. 60 pp. Sydney, Richards, 1874

N.

8959 LUDLOW, J. U. Amalgamated Society of Engineers. Registration of the society under the Trades' Union Act, 1871. Case submitted to J. U. Ludlow and opinion thereon.
12 pp. London, Kenny, 1874

N.

8960 MURRAY, Henry. Road reform: lecture by Henry Murray, hon. sec. to the 'Scottish National Toll Abolition Association', discussion thereon, and appendix of expired acts. January 19th, 1874.
appendix. 24 pp. Edinburgh, Seton and Mackenzie, Glasgow, Murray, 1874

T.

8961 On 'Tenant-Right', or 'Good will' within the barony of Farney and Co. of Monaghan in Ireland.
22 pp. London, Whittingham and Wilkins, 1874

A.

8962 PLIMSOLL, Samuel. A letter addressed to his grace the duke of Somerset, chairman of the Royal Commission on Unseaworthy Ships.
16 pp. London, printed (for private circulation only) by Virtue and Co., 1874
N.

8963 PRICE, John. Homes for the people! Our greatest want, and how to supply it. Together with an abstract of a paper on the industrial dwellings at Newcastle-upon-Tyne, read at the Social Science Congress, at Glasgow, October, 1874.
32 pp. London, E. & F. N. Spon, 1874
T.

8964 RHODES, John G. Four essays on subjects comprised in the science of political economy.
tables. appendix. 78 pp. London, Longman, Green, Reader & Dyer, 1874
T.

8965 SCOTT, Charles. The royal commission on the labour laws. Letter to the labour laws commissioners.
40 pp. Edinburgh, W. Blackwood & son, 1874
N.

8966 Toll gaspings. The last speeches of the toll-men to the right honourable the home secretary, reviewed by a road trustee.
10 pp. Edinburgh, Seton and Mackenzie, 1874
T.

8967 TRYE, H. Norwood. Trye v. Leinster; or, an Englishman's experience of the working of the Landlord & Tenant (Ireland) Act, 1870.
map. 62 pp. Dublin, W. J. Dunbar, 1874
B.

8968 URLIN, Richard Denny. Transfer of land and registration of title: as the question now stands in England and Ireland. A paper contributed to the Social Science Congress, Norwich, 1873.
10 pp. London, Spottiswoode, 1874
T.

8969 WHITCOMBE, George. Land Titles and Transfer Bill. Suggestions as to a convenient form of index to the register.
16 pp. London, V. & R. Stevens 1874
T.

1875

8970 BARRINGTON, William L. North Dublin tramways: A letter to those interested in the prosperity of Dublin.
map. 10 pp. Dublin, R. D. Webb, 1875
N.

8971 British Columbia. Information for emigrants.
map. illustrations. tables. appendix. index. 106 pp. London, 1875
N.

8972 BUTT, Isaac. The parliamentary policy of home rule: an address delivered to the electors of the city of Limerick, on the evening of Thursday, September 23rd, 1875.
46 pp. Dublin, McGlashan and Gill [etc.], 1875
B., N.

8973 CARNEGY, Patrick. Notes on the indebtedness of the agricultural classes of India.
24 pp. [London?], Charles Dickens and Evans, 1875
U.

8974 The charity organisation society. Its objects and mode of operation.
20 pp. 4th ed. London, Longmans, Green, Reader & Dyer, 1875
A.

8975 Co-operative Credit Bank, London: Articles on the credit bank, reprinted from the Co-operative and Financial Review. Conducted by R. B. Oakley, F.R.G.S., manager of the Co-operative Credit Bank.
table. 64 pp. London, 1875
N.

8976 Dublin Mendicity Association. 57th and 58th annual reports for the years 1874–5.
34 pp. Dublin, printed by Lyons, 1875
A.

8977 FALKINER, Frederick R. Lecture on the land question.
34 pp. Belfast, at the 'News Letter' Office, 1875
R.

8978 FOSTER, Balthazar. How we die in large towns. A lecture on the comparative mortality of Birmingham & other large towns.
24 pp. London, Statham, [1875]
B.

8979 Half-yearly reports and transactions of the Royal Agricultural Society of Ireland, 42, Upper Sackville Street, Dublin. January, 1874, to December, 1874.
tables. 78 pp. Dublin, at the office of the 'Farmers' Gazette', 1875
D.

8980 HENRY, Mitchell. The financial and economical condition of Ireland: a speech delivered at the Rotunda.
appendix. 36 pp. Dublin, The Irish home rule league, 1875.
B., N.

8981 PURDON, C. D. Longevity of flax mill and factory operatives; length of time they are able to work under present sanitary arrangements, with such suggestions as will render them more useful to their employers and their own families. Read at the annual meeting of the association of certifying medical officers of Great Britain and Ireland, held in Edinburgh, on August 5th, 1875
fold. tables. 8 pp. Belfast, H. Adair, 1875
L.

8982 RUSSELL, John, 1st earl Russell of Kingston. Some thoughts on national education for the United Kingdom, June, 1875.
18 pp. 2nd ed. London, Longmans, Green, Reader & Dyer, 1875
B.

8983 Sea coast fisheries. Report of the trustees for bettering the condition of the poor of Ireland, chiefly in promoting the coast fisheries, for the year to 31st December, 1874.
tables. 16 pp. Dublin, Browne & Nolan, 1875
N.

8984 Thirty-sixth annual report of the committee of the night asylum for houseless poor, no. 8 Bow-street, for the year 1874.
14 pp. Dublin, A. Thom, 1875
A.

8985 TORRENS, Sir Robert R. An essay on the transfer of land by registration under the duplicate method operative in British colonies.
appendix. 88 pp. London, Cassell, Petter and Galpin, [1875]
T.

Cobden Club Pamphlet.

1876

8986 ARCH, Joseph. Joseph Arch on the church and the labourers. A speech delivered at a working men's meeting at Sheffield, February 1, 1876.
8 pp. London, Society for the liberation of religion from state-patronage and control, 1876
B.

8987 BASS, Michael Thomas. A circular from M. T. Bass, M.P., to Great Eastern [Railway] shareholders, with a financial report.
tables. appendix. 34 pp. London, Longmans, Green, 1876
T.

8988 ——. Second circular from M. T. Bass to the shareholders of the Great Eastern Railway, in reply to the directors' special report.
14 pp. London, Longmans, Green, 1876
T.

8989 BEAR, William E. The relations of landlord & tenant in England & Scotland.
tables. 132 pp. London, Cassell, Petter & Galpin, 1876
B., T.

Cobden Club pamphlet.

8990 BOOTHBY, Josiah. Statistical sketch of South Australia. Published by authority of the government of South Australia.
table of contents. map. tables. 86 pp. London, Sampson Low, Marston [etc.], 1876
N.

8991 BRADY, Thomas Francis. Irish fisheries—digest of the principal sections in the acts of parliament relating to the Irish fisheries, with appendices.
tables. appendices. index. 116 pp. Dublin, Her Majesty's Stationery Office, 1876
N.

8992 CERNUSCHI, Henri. Silver vindicated. Paper read before the 'Trade & economy section' of the National Social Science Association, Liverpool meeting, 1876.
26 pp. London, P. S. King, 1876
Q.

8993 DANSON, John Towne. Of the proposed legislation touching maritime contracts.
24 pp. Liverpool, H. Young, 1876
T.

8994 [Emigration to Queensland.]
map. tables. 16 pp. [no t.-p.] Dublin, McGlashan and Gill, [1876?]
N.

8995 FITZGERALD, Sir Peter George, 19th Knight of Kerry, bart. Irish landlords and tenants. Recent letters to 'The Times', and further correspondence on the above subject.
table. 38 pp. Dublin, Browne & Nolan, 1876
A., B., N., T.

8996 HANCOCK, William Neilson. Report on statistics of savings in Ireland, December, 1875.
table of contents. tables. 14 pp. Dublin, A. Thom, 1876
A.

8997 Is credit capital? A letter addressed to the public of England. In two parts. By Kuklos.
14 pp. London, W. Ridgway, 1876
T.

8998 McKENNA, Sir Joseph Neale. The incidence of imperial taxation on Ireland: a speech delivered at the Rotunda, Dublin, on Tuesday, 2nd November, 1875.
16 pp. Dublin, The Irish Home Rule League, 1876
B., N.

8999 Memorandum for the guidance of societies under the Friendly Societies Acts (38 and 39 Vict. c. 60, and 39 and 40 Vict. c. 32) followed by the principal provisions of the acts and of the treasury regulations.
54 pp. London, Her Majesty's Stationery Office, 1876
A.

9000 Oregon. Facts regarding its climate, soil, mineral and agricultural resources, means of communication, commerce and industry, laws, etc. For the use of immigrants.
maps. tables. 44 pp. Portland, Oregon State Board of Immigration, 1876
N.

9001 PARSONS, Charles Edward. Clerks; their position and advancement. Addressed to parents, employers, and employed.
44 pp. London, Provost, 1876
T.

9002 Political economy club. Revised report of the proceedings at the dinner of 31st May, 1876, held in celebration of the hundredth year of the 'Wealth of Nations'. Rt. hon. W. E. Gladstone, in the chair.
table of contents. appendices. 88 pp. London, Longmans, Green, Reader & Dyer, 1876
N., T.

9003 Poplin; a short history of its manufacture, and introduction into Ireland. In English, French and German.
tables. 52 pp. Dublin, R. Atkinson and Co., poplin manufacturers, 1876
A.

9004 PORTER, John Grey Vere. Free sale of tenant-right with fair but strict terms by mutual agreement between landlord and tenant: a practical settlement of the land question in Ireland; just and useful to landlord and tenant and the country at large, as proved by several cases on my estate in Fermanagh, since 1873. Second edition.
tables. 92 pp. Dublin, Hodges & Foster, 1876
U.

9005 RAVENSTEIN, E. G. Birthplaces of the people and the laws of migration.
map. tables. appendix. 58 pp. London, Trübner, 1876
N.

9006 RAWLINGS, Edmund Charles. Davis prize essay 1876 of the United Law Students Society on the best system of land transfer.
16 pp. London, V. & R. Stevens, [1876]
T.

9007 SMITH, James Walter. Handy book on the law of bills, cheques, notes and I.O.U.'s; containing new stamp act.
table of contents. index. 8 pp. London, Effingham Wilson, 1876
N.

9008 Stock exchange syndicates. A guide to small speculators.
14 pp. London, J. Abbott, 1876
T.

9009 STUART, James Montgomery. The history of free trade in Tuscany, with remarks on its progress in the rest of Italy.
126 pp. London, Cassell, Petter and Galpin, 1876
T.
Cobden Club pamphlet.

9010 Thoughts on various subjects. Representation and taxation, large and small farms, etc.
48 pp. 2nd ed. Dublin, Roe, 1876
A.

9011 WILLIAMSON, Stephen. Depreciation in the value of silver. A letter addressed to Samuel Smith, esq., president of the Liverpool chamber of commerce.
26 pp. London, Simpkin, Marshall, 1876
T.

1877

9012 ANDREWS, Christopher Columbus. Report from Mr. Andrews, minister resident of the United States at Stockholm on pauperism and poor laws in Sweden and Norway. Reprinted from 'Foreign relations of the United States', 1876.
32 pp. London, J. S. Levey, 1877
T.

9013 The annals of Ulster tenant-right; by an Antrim tenant farmer. A political discussion between the secretary of the Ulster constitutional association, and the secretary of the tenant-right league, to effect a compromise between the parties.
illustrations. 54 pp. Belfast, Aitchison, 1877
B., N.

9014 ARGYLL, George Douglas Campbell, 8th duke of. Essay on the commercial principles applicable to contracts for the hire of land.
96 pp. London, Cassell, Petter & Galpin, 1877
B.
Cobden Club pamphlet.

9015 A crack with his grace of Argyll anent the commercial principles the noble duke applies to contracts for the hire of land in Scotland. By a Clodhopper.
56 pp. Edinburgh, Seton and Mackenzie, 1877
T.

9016. FINLAY, James Fairbairn. Essay to which was awarded the first Mackenzie prize for the best essay on the best means of improving the relations between capital and labour.
60 pp. Edinburgh, D. Douglas, 1877
T.

9017 GARDEN, Guillaume, comte de. A state crime and secret revelation of great financial forgeries in connection with the first Napoleonic aggression ... Translated [from the work entitled: 'Un Éclair d'histoire'] and preceded by an introduction by Ernest Glendower Ottley.
62 pp. London, Chapman & Hall, 1877
B.

9018 Histoire des corporations ouvrières.
128 pp. Paris, Librairie de la Société Bibliographique, 1877
T.

9019 Half-yearly reports and transactions of the Royal Agricultural Society of Ireland, 42, Upper Sackville Street, Dublin. January, 1875, to December, 1876.
tables. 100 pp. Dublin, at the office of the 'Farmers' Gazette', 1877
D.

9020 HANCOCK, William Neilson. Notes on the failure of the Bright clauses of the Irish land act of 1870; with suggestions of further facilities to be given for the purchase by tenants of their holdings.
18 pp. Dublin, E. Ponsonby, 1877
T.

9021 HARRISON, W. B. Premium debentures.
32 pp. London, London co-operative printing, [1877]
T.

9022 HENDERSON, W. D. Lecture on the history and origin of Ulster tenant-right by W. D. Henderson, Belfast. Delivered before the National Reform Union, Manchester, March 20, 1877. [Reprinted from the Manchester Critic & N.R.U. Gazette.]
48 pp. Manchester, National Reform Union, 1877
L.

9023 LAWES, Sir John Bennet. Freedom in the growth and sale of the crops of the farm, considered in relation to the interests of the landowner and the tenant farmer. A paper read before the society of arts, December 12th, 1877.
tables. 26 pp. London, printed by W. Trounce, 1877
D.

9024 MALLET, Sir Louis. Reciprocity: a letter addressed to Mr. Thomas Bayley Potter, M.P., as chairman of the committee of the Cobden club.
tables. appendices. 32 pp. London, Cassell, Petter and Galpin, 1877
T.

Cobden Club pamphlet.

9025 Observations on the object and effect of section 38 of the Companies Act, 1867. By a solicitor.
28 pp. London, V. & R. Stevens, 1877
T.

9026 PROBYN, John Webb, ed. Correspondence relative to the budgets of various countries.
136 pp. London, Cassell, Petter and Galpin, 1877
T.

Cobden Club pamphlet.

9027 PURDON, C. D. The sanitary state of the Belfast factory district, during ten years (1864 to 1873 inclusive), under various aspects.
fold. map. and tables. 50 pp. Belfast, H. Adair, 1877
L.

9028 Statement of the objects and operations of the Dublin Mendicity Association, Moira House, Usher's Island.
8 pp. Dublin, Charles, 1877
A.

9029 Stock options. The key to stock exchange speculation.
tables in appendices. 22 pp. London, Madison Reeves, 1877
T.

9030 THOMPSON, Robert Ellis. Hard times and what to learn from them. A plain talk with the working people.
42 pp. Philadelphia, E. Stern & Co., 1877
U.

9031 WATSON, William. Pauperism, vagrancy, crime, and industrial education in Aberdeenshire 1840–1875.
tables. 62 pp. Edinburgh and London, W. Blackwood & son, Aberdeen, John R. Smith, 1877
T.

9032 WOOD, John. Free trade. A labour question for working men.
58 pp. London, Simpkin Marshall, 1877
T.

9033 WOODS, W. Fell. Letters on oyster fisheries: the causes of scarcity; the remedies, etc.
44 pp. London, E. Bumpus, 1877
B.

1878

9034 BAXTER, William Edwin. Our land laws of the past.
34 pp. London, Cassell, Petter and Galpin, [1878]
T.

Cobden Club pamphlet.

9035 DE VERE, Stephen E. Thoughts on the grand jury system of Ireland, in a letter to the right honourable lord Emly, her majesty's lieutenant for the county of Limerick.
10 pp. Dublin, 1878
N.

9036 DIEBL, C. Economisten. System einer Reform der gewerblichen Oekonomik und der politischen Oekonomie.
table of contents. 62 pp. Vienna, Faesy & Frick, 1878
N.

9037 Half-yearly reports and transactions of the Royal Agricultural Society of Ireland, 42, Upper Sackville Street, Dublin. January, 1877, to December, 1877.
tables. 88 pp. Dublin, at the office of the 'Farmers' Gazette', 1878
D.

9038 HELD, Adolf. Grundriss für vorlesungen über Nationalökonomie.
index. 92 pp. Bonn, Strauss, 1878
N.

9039 INGRAM, John Kells. The present position and prospects of political economy; being the introductory address delivered in the section of economic science and statistics of the British Association for the advancement of science, at its meeting in Dublin, 1878.
32 pp. revised, with notes & additions. London, Longmans Green, Dublin, E. Ponsonby, 1878
N., T.

9040 LEACH, George A. Proposed mode of land registration.
maps. table. 14 pp. London, Harrison, 1878
T.

9041 LOCKHART, M. J. Something about saving.
16 pp. Manchester, J. Heywood, 1878
T.

9042 NEUMANN-SPALLART, F. X. von. Sociologie und Statistik. [Separat—Abdruck aus der 'Statistischen Monatschrift', iv. Jahrgang, i Heft.]
34 pp. Vienna, Holden, [1878]
N.

9043 NICHOLSON, J. Shield. Effects of machinery on wages. (Being the Cambridge Cobden prize essay for 1877).
64 pp. Cambridge, Deighton Bell, London, Bell, 1878
N.

9044 [O'BRIEN, William.] Christmas on the Galtees: an inquiry into the condition of the tenantry of Mr. Nathaniel Buckley. By the special correspondent of the *Freeman's Journal*.
56 pp. Dublin, Central Tenants Defence Association, 1878
B., N.

9045 One-sided free trade with wreck and ruin, or fair trade with prosperity. The commercial crisis and the remedy considered. By a public auditor.
24 pp. Manchester, J. Heywood, 1878
T.

1879

9046 The act relating to bills of sale, rendered into plain English and revised with explanatory notes by a barrister-at-law.
10 pp. London, F. E. Longley, [1879?]
T.

9047 ARNOLD, Arthur. An address on Ireland, delivered at the town hall, Salford, October 22, 1879.
16 pp. Chapel St., Salford, Salford Liberal Association, 1879
B.

9048 ASHTON, Samuel Elkanah. Commercial depression; its cause and remedy. A plea for reciprocity.
appendix. 32 pp. London, Simpkin Marshall, 1879
T.

9049 BLACKLEY, William Lewery. Independence versus pauperism: a national cure for a national curse.
8 pp. London, Moseley, 1879
A.

9050 British commerce: its past, present, and future by W. E. W.
tables in appendix. 96 pp. 2nd edition, Hull, Goddard, 1879
T.

9051 CAZALET, Edward. Bimetallism and its connection with commerce.
32 pp. London, Effingham Wilson, 1879
T.

9052 CHADWICK, Edwin. On county government in combination with union organisation, for the improvement of local administration.
52 pp. London, C. Knight, 1879
T.

9053 COWLARD, John Lethbridge. The present agricultural depression in Devon and Cornwall and how to meet it.
16 pp. London, printed by W. Clowes, 1879
T.

9054 DAVISON, T. R. R. Bankruptcy reform: prefatory remarks and two letters reprinted from 'the Economist'.
12 pp. London, Effingham Wilson, 1879
T.

9055 Depression in agriculture. Protection, Limited, alias self-preservation, versus free-trade, limited, alias good-natured tomfoolery. (signed Matje.)
32 pp. London, Waterlow, 1879
T.

9056 DERBY, Edward Henry Stanley, 15th earl of. Verbatim report of the speech of the right hon. the earl of Derby at the anniversary of the Rochdale workmen's club, held at the Town Hall, Rochdale, January 2nd, 1879.
12 pp. Rochdale, printed by Wrigley, 1879
T.

9057 The distress in the country: its true cause and remedy. By Vox Veritatis.
20 pp. London, E. W. Allen, [1879]

9058 ELLIOT, Nenion. The conversion into money of grain and victual payments in Scotland.
tables in appendices. 58 pp. Edinburgh, T. & T. Clark, 1879
T.

9059 FIELDEN, John C. Lecture on the government and the state of trade, delivered at Blackley, October 14th, 1879, under the auspices of the National Reform Union.
16 pp. Manchester, A. Heywood, 1879
T.

9060 Five years of tory rule: a lesson and a warning. By 'Nemesis'.
64 pp. London, Hodder & Stoughton, 1879
B.

9061 [GIFFEN, Sir Robert.] The approaching general election. The new protection cry. By 'Economist'.
58 pp. London, H. J. Infield, 1879
T.

9062 GLADSTONE, Robert. What is money? In question and answer.
26 pp. London, Effingham Wilson, 1879
T.

9063 Half-yearly reports and transactions of the Royal Agricultural Society of Ireland, 42, Upper Sackville Street, Dublin. January, 1878, to December, 1878.
tables. 76 pp. Dublin, at the 'Farmers' Gazette' office, 1879
D.

9064 HANKEY, Thomson. On bi-metallism. A reply to Mr. Cazalet and Mr. Gibbs.
8 pp. London, Effingham Wilson, 1879
T.

9065 HOOPER, F. Bodfield. Reciprocity, overproduction v. overconsumption, commercial depression, political economy, etc. A review of four articles in 'the Nineteenth Century' and 'the Contemporary'.
52 pp. London, Elliot Stock, 1879
T.

9066 Ireland as it is and as it might be: being three letters on the land question. By a 'Scot'.
22 pp. Dundee, printed by J. Leng, 1879
Q.

9067 JOASS, Edward C. A brief review of the silver question, 1871 to 1879.
tables. appendix. 30 pp. Edinburgh, D. Douglas, 1879
T.

9068 MELSHEIMER, Rudolph E. The law of bills of exchange. An English version of the German code.
appendix. 32 pp. London, H. Sweet, 1879
T.

9069 MILWARD, Dawson A. Report on the butter manufacture of Denmark and other countries.
30 pp. Dublin, printed by Chambers, 1879
D.

9070 Minnesota, her agricultural resources, commercial advantages and manufacturing capabilities, being a concise description of the state of Minnesota, and the inducements she offers to those seeking homes in a new country. Published by the state board of immigration.
table of contents. map. tables. 36 pp. St. Paul, Minn., printed by Smith, 1879

N.

9071 MONGREDIEN, Augustus. Free trade and English commerce.
tables. 106 pp. London, Cassell, Petter and Galpin, [1879?]

B., T.

Cobden Club pamphlet.

9072 MURRAY, Gilbert. Agricultural depression: its causes and remedies.
16 pp. London, Bemrose, 1879

T.

9073 NICOLL, T. M. Our land laws and the agricultural situation.
16 pp. Edinburgh, Seton & Mackenzie, 1879

T.

9074 Our banking system: the interests involved, and suggestions for their security. A scheme contributing to the relief of shareholders, security of depositors and protection of bankers. By a banker.
32 pp. London, Effingham Wilson, 1879

T.

9075 Report on statistics of bank-note circulation in Ireland, 1st October (1844 to 1879)
6 pp. Dublin, the Queen's printer [A. Thom], 1879

N.

'Confidential' printed on t.p.

9076 RICCA SALERNO, Giuseppe. Teoria generale dei prestiti pubblici.
tables. 168 pp. Milan, Hoepli, 1879

N.

9077 SHAW-LEFEVRE, George John. The working of the Bright clauses of Irish Land Act, 1870, enabling occupiers to purchase their holdings.
table. 62 pp. Dublin, A. Robertson, 1879

T., U.

9078 WATHERSTON, Edward J. Our railways: should they be private or national property?
tables. 60 pp. London, E. Stanford, 1879

T.

9079 WILLSON, H. BOWLEY. Industrial crises, their causes and remedies. (from the report of the Congressional committee on depression in labor and business).
14 pp. Washington, United States Government printing office, 1879

N.

1880

9080 DOUGLAS, afterwards DIXIE, lady Florence Caroline. An address to the tenant farmers and people of Ireland, with advice and warning.
8 pp. 6th ed. [n.p., 188–?]

R.

9081 FOX, J. A. The Irish absentees.
8 pp. [no t.p.] [n.p., 188–?]

P.

9082 Ireland. No. 4. Resistance to Evictions.
16 pp. Dublin, Irish loyal and patriotic union, [188–?]

C.

9083 KINGSLEY, F. J. The three 'F's' for Ireland. A few words on the Irish land question.
16 pp. Manchester, National Reform Union, [188–?]

N.

9084 MECREDY, Thomas Tighe. Scheme of a proposed act of parliament for the abolition of dual ownership of land in Ireland.
8 pp. Dublin, Abbey Printing Works, [188–?]

N.

9085 RICCA-SALERNO, Giuseppe. Del metodo in economia politica.
36 pp. [no t.p.] [n.p., 188–?]

N.

9086 An address to the tenant farmers of Ireland. By an Irishman.
16 pp. Dublin, Hodges, Foster & Figgis, 1880

A.

9087 Audi alteram partem. Irish land as viewed from British shores. A short catechism on Irish land legislation.
16 pp. Edinburgh and London, W. Blackwood & son, 1880

N.

9088 BAGENAL, Philip Henry Dudley. The Irish agitator in parliament and on the platform: a complete history of Irish politics for the year 1879; with a summary of conclusions and an appendix, containing documents of political importance published during the year.
192 pp. Dublin, Hodges, Foster, & Figgis, 1880

B., D.

9089 ——. Parnellism unveiled; or the land-and-labour agitation of 1879–80, with an index.
72 pp. Dublin, Hodges, Foster, & Figgis, London, Simpkin, Marshall, 1880

A., B., C., N., T.

9090 BERNARD, William Leigh. The Irish land question. Suggestions for the extended establishment of a peasant proprietary in Ireland.
table of contents. 22 pp. Dublin, Hodges, Foster & Figgis, 1880

N., U.

9091 Bonaparte-Wyse, William C. Vox clamantis: or, letters from the land league. By William C. Bonaparte-Wyse, J.P. for the County of Waterford. With a letter from James Anthony Froude on the present crisis in Ireland.
62 pp. London, W. Ridgway, 1880
C.

9092 Bonfield, Robert. On imperial and local taxation.
tables. 32 pp. Crewkerne, at the 'West of England Express' Office, 1880
T.

9093 Chaytor, Henry. Agricultural and trade depression. An exposition of the principles by which home and foreign trade, and agriculture should be carried on and on which our national finances should be managed.
50 pp. London, Simpkin, Marshall, 1880
T.

9094 Chichester, C. Raleigh. The land question in Ireland, the land act of 1870, the interests of the state, considered.
46 pp. Dublin, Hodges, Foster and Figgis, 1880
A., N.

9095 Davison, T. R. R. Bankruptcy reform.
tables in appendix. 88 pp. London, Effingham Wilson, 1880
T.

9096 Donisthorpe, Wordsworth. The claims of labour; or, serfdom, wagedom and freedom.
58 pp. London, S. Tinsley, 1880
T.

9097 Dunraven, Thomas Wyndham Quin, 4th earl of. The Irish question examined in a letter to the 'New York Herald', a speech in parliament, and additional notes.
80 pp. London, E. Stanford, 1880
N., T.

9098 Errington, George. The Irish land question, a problem in practical politics. A letter to the right hon. H. C. E. Childers, M.P., secretary of state for war, from George Errington, M.P.
appendix. 28 pp. London, Wyman, Dublin, M. H. Gill, 1880
A., N., T., U.

9099 Evidence on the cause of the present agricultural depression obtained from practical and bona-fide farm labourers, issued by the authority of the executive committee of the National Agricultural Labourers Union.
tables. 32 pp. Leamington, Curtis and Beamish, 1880
U.

9100 Fox, J. A. Reports on the condition of the peasantry of the county of Mayo, during the famine crisis of 1880.
46 pp. Dublin, Browne & Nolan, 1880
Q., U.

9101 Further report of the land tenure reform committee. December 1880.
table of contents. tables. appendix. 36 pp. Dublin, Hodges, Foster & Figgis, London, W. Ridgway, 1880
N.

9102 Greig, John Kinloch. Bank note and banking reform with suggestions for a new banking act.
26 pp. London, Effingham Wilson, 1880
T.

9103 Heygate, Sir Frederick William, bart. Ireland since 1850 and her present difficulty.
22 pp. 2nd ed. London, Rivingtons, 1880
N., T.

9104 Hooper, F. I. Bodfield. 'Free trade & English commerce' (the 'unanswerable little book' of rt. hon. J. Bright) by Mr. Mongredien answered: with a reply also to his 'Western farmer of America'.
88 pp. London, Draper, 1880
B.

9105 Hopkinson, Alfred. Definite reform in English land law.
table in appendix. 24 pp. London, Simpkin Marshall, 1880
T.

9106 Humphrys, David. The justice of the land league.
18 pp. London, Kegan Paul, 1880
R.

9107 An impartial survey of the land question with special reference to proposed legislation.
52 pp. London, V. & R. Stevens, 1880
T.

9108 Ireland in A.D. 1900. By Votes.
20 pp. Dublin, Hodges, Foster, & Figgis, 1880
B., N.
Prophetic satire on home rule.

9109 Irish agitation: I. Land league speeches. II. Agrarian crime. III. Opinions of public men.
44 pp. Dublin, Hodges, Foster and Figgis, 1880
U.

9110 Irish extermination schemes: A reply to 'Leo', one of Father Nugent's defenders, by a member of the Liverpool Irish relief committee. (signed N.F.)
appendix. 116 pp. Liverpool, 1880
N.

9111 John Abbott's analysis of British railways.
tables. 68 pp. London, J. Abbott & Co., 1880
T.

9112 Jones, Lloyd. Co-operation in danger! An appeal to the British public.
28 pp. London, Simpkin Marshall, 1880
T.

9113 The land conference, Thursday, April 29th, 1880
118 pp. Dublin, M. H. Gill, 1880
N.

9114 The land question in Ireland: Confiscation or contract. November, 1880. Irish land committee, 31 South Frederick St., Dublin.
40 pp. Dublin, Hodges, Foster & Figgis, London, W. Ridgway, 1880
C., N., T., U.

9115 The land question, Ireland. No. I. Notes upon the government valuation of land in Ireland, commonly known as 'Griffith's valuation'.
38 pp. 2nd. ed.

C., N., T., U.

——. No. II. The anarchy in Ireland.
48 pp.

T., U.

——. No. III. Facts and figures, December, 1880.
tables. 40 pp.

C., D., N., T., U.

——. No. IV. French opinion on the Irish crisis.
28 pp.

D., N., Q., T., U.

Series issued by the Irish Land Committee, 31, South Frederick Street, Dublin.
Dublin, Hodges, Foster & Figgis, London, W. Ridgway, 1880

9116 Land tenure reform committee. Further report. Dec., 1880.
table of contents. tables. appendix. 34 pp. Dublin, Hodges, Foster & Figgis, London, W. Ridgway, 1880

N., U.

9117 McDONNELL, Robert. Parliamentary tenant-right, or the Longfield system of land tenure explained: being letters to the 'Freeman's journal'.
appendix. 26 pp. Dublin, M. H. Gill, 1880

T.

9118 MACFARLANE, D. H. Ireland versus England.
38 pp. London, W. Ridgway, 1880

N.

9119 [MacIVOR, Rev. Dr. —.] The Union programme for 1880. Constructive, not destructive Irish legislation.
32 pp. Londonderry, at the 'Sentinel' office, 1880

A.

Contains sketches of bills, for purchase and consolidation of Irish railways and for improving Irish education.

9120 [MAHONY, Richard John.] A short statement concerning the confiscation of improvements in Ireland. Addressed to the right hon. W. E. Forster, M.P., chief secretary to the lord lieutenant of Ireland. By a working landowner.
appendix. 64 pp. Dublin, Hodges, Foster & Figgis, 1880

C., T., U.

9121 MAN, E. Garnet. The commerce and prospects of England, and a review of the agricultural iron and cotton trades.
tables. 30 pp. London, W. Ridgway, 1880

T.

9122 MARSHALL, J. J. Half an hour with the English land laws showing their baneful effects on all classes, and the proposed reforms.
24 pp. London, E. W. Allen, 1880

T.

9123 MOFFAT, Robert Scott. On the regulation of production; or, regulated versus unregulated production. A letter to Lord Justice Bramwell.
32 pp. London, S. Tinsley, 1880

T.

9124 MOLINARI, Gustav de. French spectacles in an Irish case. Letters on the state of Ireland. Translated by L. Colthurst.
36 pp. Dublin, Hodges, Foster & Figgis, London, W. Ridgway, 1880

A., N.

9125 MONGREDIEN, Augustus. The western farmer of America.
table. 28 pp. London, Cassell, Petter, Galpin, 1880

B., N., T.

Cobden Club pamphlet.

9126 MUSGRAVE, James. Letter to James H. Tuke, esq., author of Irish distress and its remedies, having reference to that portion of his pamphlet which describes the county of Donegal.
16 pp. n.p., 1880

N.

9127 NEWCOME, Frederick N. Plan to liquidate the national debt with less than the cost of interest. A paper on diminishing sinking funds partly read before the British association at Swansea, August 30th, 1880.
tables. 22 pp. London, Effingham Wilson, 1880

T.

9128 O'BRIEN, Richard Barry. The Irish land question and English public opinion.
tables. 60 pp. London, Cameron and Ferguson, Dublin, T. D. Sullivan, 1880

T.

9129 Observations on the state of Ireland in April, 1880. By 'Rabirius.'
68 pp. Dublin, Hodges, Foster, & Figgis, 1880

B.

9130 [PILKINGTON, William?] Help for Ireland by an 'Anglo-Irishman' of forty years' farming experience in Ireland.
80 pp. London, Kirby & Endean, 1880

N., T.

9131 PIM, Joseph Todhunter. Ireland in 1880, with suggestions for the reform of her land laws.
tables. 32 pp. Dublin, Hodges, Foster & Figgis, 1880

U.

9132 PROBYN, Lesley Charles. A proposal for re-establishing and maintaining the value and position of silver.
16 pp. 2nd ed. London, Effingham Wilson, 1880

T.

9133 Report of the Irish relief fund, South Australia. Reprinted from the 'South Australian Register', October 12th, 1880.
table. 10 pp. Adelaide, Thomas, 1880

N.

9134 RIVINGTON, Francis. A new proposal for providing improved dwellings for the poor upon an adequate scale in the metropolis and other populous places.
appendix. 24 pp. London, W. Skeffington, 1880
T.

9135 SAUNDERS, William. Land laws and their results at home and abroad.
appendix. 64 pp. Hull, Eastern Morning News, 1880
T.

9136 SINCLAIR, W. J. Irish peasant proprietors. Facts and misrepresentations. A reply to the statements of Mr. Tuke.
tables. 30 pp. Edinburgh, W. Blackwood & son, 1880
A., C., N., Q., R.

9137 Some thoughts on strikes, free trade, and protection.
14 pp. London, Stanesby, 1880
T.

9138 STRACHAN, T. Y. Protection, reciprocity, free trade; a paper read before the liberal clubs of Newcastle-on-Tyne and Tynemouth.
tables. 20 pp. Newcastle-on-Tyne, Franklin, London, Kent, 1880
T.

9139 Suggestions for establishing a British Zollverein.
16 pp. London, W. Clowes, 1880
T.

Preface signed W.G.

9140 SULLIVAN, Sir Edward, bart. Joint-stock farming: a suggestion.
36 pp. London, E. Stanford, 1880
T.

9141 Trinity College, Dublin, as landlords of Cahirciveen. Statement by the provost and senior fellows in reply to the letter of Charles Russell, Q.C., M.P., in the 'Daily Telegraph'.
24 pp. Dublin, Hodges, Foster & Figgis, 1880
A., N., Q., T., U.

9142 TUKE, James Hack. Irish distress.
20 pp. London, West, Newman, 1880
B., R.

9143 ——. Irish distress & its remedies. The land question. A visit to Donegal & Connaught in the spring of 1880.
map. 128 pp. London, W. Ridgway, Dublin, Hodges, Foster & Figgis, 1880
A., B., C., N., R., T.

9144 WALTERS, John T. Tory or Liberal: for which shall I vote? A letter to the middle-class & operative electors.
32 pp. London, Hodder & Stoughton, 1880
Q.

9145 WALTON, Alfred A. Agricultural depression and distress: the causes and remedy.
18 pp. London, Simpkin, Marshall, 1880
T.

9146 Wealth or weal? A word on the political aspect of free trade and the land question.
24 pp. London, Sampson Low, Marston, Searle and Rivington, 1880
T.

9147 Why pay poor rates? Or the abolition of poor rates a social necessity. By T. S. P.
40 pp. London, W. Ridgway, 1880
T.

1881

9148 BARCLAY, Robert. Essay and letters on bimetallism.
tables. 36 pp. London & Manchester, J. Heywood, 1881
T.

9149 BEESLY, Edward Spencer. The social future of the working class. A lecture delivered to a meeting of trades' unionists, May 7, 1868.
16 pp. 3rd ed. London, Reeves & Turner, 1881
N.

9150 BEHAN, John. Why Ireland has no manufactures: a lecture delivered in the hall of St. Nicholas catholic total abstinence league.
18 pp. Dublin, printed by R. D. Webb, 1881
A., B.

9151 BLACKBURNE, Edward. Causes of the decadence of the industries of Ireland: a retrospect.
66 pp. Dublin, McGee, 1881
A., N., R.

9152 BOURCICAULT afterwards BOUCICAULT, Dionysius Lardner. The fireside story of Ireland.
26 pp. Dublin, M. H. Gill, [1881]
B.

9153 BUXTON, Sidney Charles. A manual of political questions of the day: with the arguments on either side.
126 pp. London, social & political education league, 1881
B.

9154 CAIRD, Sir James. The British land question.
table. 48 pp. London, Cassell, Petter, Galpin, 1881
T.

9155 CARROLL, William George. The Lansdowne Irish estates.
tables. 40 pp. Dublin, M. H. Gill, London, Simpkin, Marshall, Whittaker, 1881
N., U.
Gives history of Sir William Petty's connections with Ireland.

9156 CERNUSCHI, Henri. Bi-metallism at 15½ a necessity for the Continent, for the United States, for England.
42 pp. London, P. S. King, 1881
T.

9157 CHALMERS, Sir Mackenzie Dalzell Edwin Stewart. Bills of exchange bill, 1881, with notes.
tables. appendices. 48 pp. London, Waterlow, 1881
T.

9158 CLARKE, C. B. A letter to the right hon. W. E. Gladstone upon a land scheme for Ireland.
20 pp. London, MacMillan, 1881
B., N.

9159 COWEN, Joseph. The Irish crisis. Speech of Joseph Cowen, M.P.
8 pp. Dublin, Irish national land league, [1881?]
B.

9160 CRESSWELL, Mrs. Gerard. How the farming in Great Britain can be made to pay.
30 pp. 2nd ed. London, Simpkin, Marshall, 1881
T.

9161 Deputation of Cleveland miners: Report on the state of Ireland. (From the Middlesbrough (Yorkshire) North-Eastern Daily Gazette June 21st 1881.)
14 pp. Dublin, Irish national land league, 1881
N.

9162 DERBY, Edward Henry Stanley, 15th earl of. Lord Derby on the commercial condition and prospect of the country. An address delivered (after the opening of the new markets) at the Cambridge Hall. Southport, Sept. 7th, 1881 in reply to the toast of his health, proposed by the mayor.
4 pp. London, Cobden Club, 1881
T.

9163 DOUGLAS, James. The prospects of Britain.
104 pp. 2nd ed. Edinburgh, A. & C. Black, 1881
B.

9164 A dream of the nineteenth century, upon the decline and fall of British agriculture.
28 pp. London, E. Stanford, 1881
T.

9165 ECROYD, W. Farrer. The policy of self-help. Suggestions towards the consolidation of the Empire and the defence of its industries and commerce.
30 pp. 4th ed. London, Hamilton Adams, Bradford, J. Dale, 1881
T.

9166 EVARTS, William Maxwell. Speech of Mr. Evarts, a delegate of the United States at the international monetary conference at Paris on the 19th day of May 1881.
34 pp. London, Chiswick Press, 1881
T.

9167 Extracts from parliamentary speeches on the Irish land question. April, 1881.
106 pp. Dublin, issued by the Irish land committee, [1881]
T.

9168 Fair rents? The only test is free contract, proved by agricultural experience, economic laws, legal right, abstract justice, and political consequences. The report of the Royal commission on the land act, 1870: its errors as to fair rent and the Ulster custom. By 'Political Economy'.
table of contents. tables. 88 pp. Dublin, Hodges, Figgis, London, W. Ridgway, 1881
A., C., N.

9169 Fair trade v. free trade or, which system will best promote the financial and commercial interests of Great Britain. By Pelekus.
appendix. 52pp. London, Kerby and Endean, 1881
T.

9170 FERGUSON, John. The land for the people: an appeal to all who work by brain or hand.
32 pp. Glasgow & London, Cameron & Ferguson, [1881?]
Q.

9171 FIELDEN, John C. Free trade v. reciprocity.
tables. 36 pp. 2nd ed. Manchester, Thomas J. Day, 1881
T.

9172 FISHBOURNE, Edmund Gardiner. The injustice of free trade policy.
20 pp. London, Harrison and Sons, 1881
T.

9173 FISHER, Henry. Opening, conducting and closing of special banking accounts.
10 pp. London, Waterlow, 1881
T.

9174 FITZGERALD, James F. V. A practical guide to the valuation of rent in Ireland: with an appendix containing some extracts from the instructions issued to valuators in 1853, by the late Sir R. Griffith, bart.
tables. appendix. index. 176 pp. Dublin, E. Ponsonby, 1881
D.

9175 ——. Some practical suggestions concerning the land law (Ireland) bill. [For private circulation only.]
24 pp. Dublin, M. H. Gill, 1881
T.

9176 ——. Thoughts on the nature and value of the tenant's interest, and on part V of the land law bill.
tables. 40 pp. Dublin, Hodges, Figgis and Co., 1881
C.

9177 FITZPATRICK, Bernard. The ABC of the Irish land question.
tables. 40 pp. London, W. Ridgway, 1881
C.

9178 ——. Ireland's brighter prospects.
28 pp. London, E. Stanford, 1881
D.

9179 Free trade and political economy.
22 pp. London, Simpkin Marshall, 1881
T.

9180 Free trade and trades' unionism. By a shipowner.
table. 68 pp. London, Simpkin, Marshall, 1881
T.

9181 GAMBLE, Richard Wilson. Fixity of tenure incompatible with freedom of contract, and shown to be unjust and impolitic.
table of contents. tables. 86 pp. Dublin, Hodges, Figgis, London, W. Ridgway, 1881
N.

9182 GEORGE, Henry. The Irish land question: what it involves & how alone it can be settled. An appeal to the land leagues.
66 pp. London, Cameron & Ferguson, 1881
B., N., U.

32

9183 A 'good' landlord & his tenants. Colonel King-Harman's tenants. (From our special commissioner.)
25 pp. Dublin, Irish national land league association, 1881
B.

9184 GRANT, Daniel.   Land tenure in Ireland.
tables. 36 pp. London, W. Ridgway, 1881
N.
A lecture delivered in London, December 10th, 1880.

9185 GREEN, Thomas Hill.   Liberal legislation and freedom of contract.
22 pp. Oxford, Slatter & Rose, 1881
T.

9186 Half-yearly reports and transactions of the Royal agricultural society of Ireland, 42, Upper Sackville Street, Dublin. January, 1879, to December, 1880.
tables. 100 pp. Dublin, at the 'Farmers' Gazette' office, 1881
D.

9187 HAMILTON, William Tighe.   The mechanism of land tenure.
appendix. 40 pp. Dublin, Hodges, Figgis, London, W. Ridgway, 1881
A.U.

9188 HEALY, T. M.   The tenant's key to the land law act, 1881.
table of contents. 112 pp. Dublin, M. H. Gill, 1881
A.

9189 ——.   Why there is an Irish land question and an Irish land league: published for the Irish national land league.
table of contents. tables. index. 140 pp. 2nd ed. Dublin, M. H. Gill, London, Simpkin, Marshall, 1881
A., N.

9190 HUTTON, Henry Dix.   Registration of title indispensable for peasant proprietorship. A paper read at the annual meeting of the National association for the promotion of social science, held in Dublin, October, 1881. (Published by permission of the council.)
10 pp. Dublin, printed by R. D. Webb, 1881
N.

9191 JENKS, Edward.   A scheme for the immediate compulsory enfranchisement of lands the subject of copyhold tenure.
40 pp. London, V. & R. Stevens, 1881
T.

9192 KEHOE, Daniel.   College historical society, University of Dublin. Free trade and the fair trade movement. An address delivered in the dining-hall of Trinity College at the opening meeting of the 112th Session, 9th November, 1881 by the auditor.
18 pp. Dublin, printed by Browne and Nolan, 1881
N.

9193 Key to the new land bill, showing, in plain language, how the bill proposes to give free sale, fixed rents, and secure tenure, and establish peasant proprietorship. By Lex.
22 pp. n.p., 1881
Q.

9194 KINNEAR, John Boyd.   Ireland in 1881.
52 pp. London, Smith, Elder & co., 1881
R.

9195 Land act (Ireland) 1881. Benefits conferred on Irish tenant-farmers by the land act (Ireland) 1881.
8 pp. Dublin, printed by A. Thom, 1881
A., C.

9196 Land-law reform and its relation to work, wages, and population. By a member of the Tyldesley liberal club.
16 pp. Manchester, A. Heywood, [1881]
T.

9197 The land question, Ireland.
——.   No. V. Arrested progress, January 1881.
26 pp. signed 'W.'
C., D., N., T., U.

——.   No. VI. Lord Dufferin on the three Fs.
32 pp. signed 'W.'
D., N., T., U.

——.   No. VII. Mr. Gladstone and the three Fs. February 1881.
46 pp. signed 'W.'
D., N., T., U.

——.   No. VIII. Mr. Bonamy Price and the three Fs. February, 1881. signed 'W.'
16 pp.
D., N., Q.

——.   No. IX. Mr. Gladstone's commissioners and Mr. Gladstone. March 1881.
42 pp., signed 'W.'
C., D., N., Q., T.

——.   No. X. Mr. Gladstone's bill. April, 1881.
40 pp., signed 'W.'
D., N., Q., T.

——.   No. XI. Foregone conclusions; the Bessborough commission, April, 1881.
68 pp.
D., N., T.

——.   No. XII. The Richmond Commission. Notes on lord Carlingford's report, June, 1881.
36 pp.
D., N.

——.   No. XIII. More facts and figures. Evictions, July 1881.
20 pp.
D., N.
Continuation of series issued by the Irish Land Committee, 31, South Frederick St., Dublin. Dublin, Hodges, Figgis, London, W. Ridgway, 1881.
See 9115 and 9256.

9198 Landlords, land laws and land leagues in Scotland being a humble contribution to contemporary politics by Aliquis.
tables. appendix. 68 pp. Edinburgh, D. Douglas, 1881
T.

9199 LAVELEYE, Émile de. International bimetallism and the battle of the standard. [An address read before the French Institute (academy of moral and political sciences), Paris May 10, 1881.]
88 pp. London, P. S. King, 1881
T.

9200 MACDEVITT, E. O. The land bill explained.
24 pp. Dublin, M. H. Gill, 1881
B.

9201 MANNING, Henry Edward, cardinal. Ireland. Portions of a letter on the land question, addressed to earl Grey, in 1868. With an introductory preface by Henry Bettingham, Esq., M.P.
32 pp. London, W. Ridgway, 1881
B.

9202 MEDLEY, George W. England under free trade. An address delivered to the Sheffield junior liberal association, 8th November, 1881.
36 pp. London, Cassell, Petter, Galpin, 1881
B., T.
Cobden Club pamphlet.

9203 ——. The reciprocity craze. A tract for the times.
36 pp. London, Cassell, Petter, Galpin, 1881
B., T.
Cobden Club pamphlet.

9204 Monetary relief through the Paris international conference. By Nemo.
28 pp. London, Effingham Wilson, 1881
T.

9205 MONTGOMERY, Hugh de F. Irish land and Irish rights. By an Ulster landlord.
42 pp. London, E. Stanford, 1881
N.

9206 More elbow-room in Scotch banking; or free trade for Scotland on the basis of consols. By Scrutator.
12 pp. Glasgow, Porteous Brothers, 1881
T.

9207 MORRIS, Alfred. England's progress in prosperity examined by the light of the national statistics, with illustrative tables.
24 pp. (folding tables). London, Effingham Wilson, 1881
T.

9208 MURRAY, Henry. Poor law administration and proposed legislative amendments.
24 pp. Edinburgh, Bell and Bradfute, 1881
T.

9209 NAZZIANI, Emilio. Saggi di economia politica. i) La scuola classica di economia politica. ii) Sulla rendita fondiaria. iii) Del propitto. iv) Alcuni quesiti sulla domanda di lavoro.
index. 184 pp. Milan, Hoepli, 1881
N.

9210 NICHOLSON, Joseph Shield. Political economy as a branch of education. Inaugural address.
28 pp. Edinburgh, D. Douglas, 1881
T.

9211 NULTY, Thomas, bishop of Meath. The land agitation in Ireland. Letter to the clergy and laity of the Diocese of Meath.
12 pp. Manchester, A. Heywood, London, Grattan, Marshall, 1881
N.

9212 O'BRIEN, Richard Barry. Coercion or redress, a chapter from the Melbourne administration, with a sketch of the political career of Thomas Drummond.
28 pp. Manchester, A. Heywood, London, Grattan, Marshall, 1881
B.

9213 Our trade with France under the Cobden treaty, in imports and exports of each article for 22 years, year by year, from 1859 to 1880.
tables. 12 pp. London, P. S. King, [1881 ?]
T.

9214 Peasant proprietors in Ireland. By Spes.
16 pp. London, Pickering, 1881
A., N., T.

9215 PEEL, Thomas G. The land: Whose is it, and whose should it be? Being a lecture delivered in the protestant hall, Armagh, to the Orangemen of that district, on the 22nd December, 1880.
20 pp. Belfast, printed by W. & G. Baird, 1881
N.

9216 SAWYER, Frederick E. Land tenure and division in Brighton and the neighbourhood. A paper read at the annual provincial meeting of the Incorporated law society held at Brighton on the 11th and 12th October, 1881.
8 pp. London, Spottiswoode & Co., [1881]
U.

9217 SCULLY, Vincent. Occupying Ownership (Ireland), by the late Vincent Scully, with appendix containing Free trade in land (1854) and The Transfer of land bill (1853) by the same author. Edited by his son.
tables of contents. map. 116 pp. London, E. Stanford, 1881
A., T.

9218 SINCLAIR, William. The Irish land question. Gladstonian legislation: its prompters and proclivities. Letters to A.Z.
90 pp. Dublin, Hodges, Figgis, London, W. Ridgway, 1881
A.

9219 SLAGG, John. Free trade and tariffs. A speech delivered on July 20, 1881, to the Penge and Anerley liberal association.
tables (in) appendix. 16 pp. London, Cassell, Petter & Galpin, 1881
T.
Cobden Club pamphlet.

9220 SPENCER, Edward. Artisans' and labourers' dwellings, with an appendix on the operations in London and other large cities and towns of the United Kingdom, under the Artisans' and labourers' dwellings improvement Act, 1875 and local acts with similar objects.
tables. appendix. 20 pp. London, printed by Spottiswoode, 1881
A.

9221 STAPLES, James Head.   Solutions of the land question in Ireland.
table. 40 pp. London, Hamilton Adams, Belfast, A. F. Tait, 1881

R.

9222 Suggestions on the land question (Ireland), etc. By 'Slug'.
8 pp. Naas, printed by the 'Leinster Leader', 1881

N.

9223 SULLIVAN, Alexander Martin.   The new land bill: what it proposes to do, and how it is to be done, what tenants it proposes to protect, and how they are to be protected. Explained in clear and simple terms, for the information of the Irish tenant farmers by A. M. Sullivan, M.P., to which is appended the full text of the bill. In corresponding lines and pages, with the official parliamentary print.
76 pp. 2nd ed. Dublin, T. D. Sullivan, London, Cameron and Ferguson, 1881

Q.

9224 The 'suppressed' pamphlet. How to become the owner of your farm. Why Irish landlords should sell and Irish tenants should purchase and how they can do it under the land act of 1881.
16 pp. Dublin, 'Freeman's Journal', 1881

N.

9225 A synopsis of the grounds and reasons for land reform. With suggestions and reflections, social and political, by an Anglo-Saxon.
32 pp. London, Elliott Stock, 1881

T.

9226 Thoughts on the questions agitated at farmers' meetings in Aberdeenshire.
32 pp. Edinburgh, W. Blackwood & Son, 1881

T.

9227 TRENCH, George F.   The land question. Are the land-lords worth preserving? Or, forty years management of an Irish estate.
60 pp. Dublin, Hodges, Figgis, London, W. Ridgway, 1881

N., R.

9228 URLIN, Richard Denny.   The history and statistics of the Irish incumbered estates court, with suggestion for a tribunal with similar jurisdiction in England. Read before the Statistical Society, May 17th, 1881.
table of contents. tables. 36 pp. London, E. Stanford, 1881

A.

9229 WALSH, William J.   A plain exposition of the Irish land act of 1881.
148 pp. Dublin, Browne & Nolan; & Gill, 1881

B.

9230 WALTERS, John T.   Ireland's wrongs and how to mend them. With a postscript on the land bill. A letter to the middle-class & operative electors.
48 pp. London, Hodder & Stoughton, 1881

N., Q.

9231 WESTGARTH, William.   A reconsideration of the silver question and the double standard.
32 pp. London, Effingham Wilson, 1881

T.

9232 WILLOUGHBY, F. S.   Free trade v. fair trade: Patent laws! England v. America. An appeal to the working classes of Great Britain.
32 pp. Stockport, Claye and son, 1881

T.

1882

9233 BAGENAL, Philip Henry Dudley.   Foreign land tenures and the Irish tenant.
48 pp. Dublin, Hodges, Figgis, [1882]

N., T., U.

9234 Bank of England: Tales of the Bank of England, with anecdotes of London bankers. Illustrated by portraits and engravings.
plates. table of contents. 128 pp. London, Hogg, 1882

N.

9235 BARCROFT, Henry.   Newry and its trade, as it might be.
tables. illustration. 22 pp. Newry, Warnock, 1882

N.

9236 BASTIAT, Frédéric.   Popular fallacies regarding trade and foreign duties: being the 'Sophismes économiques' of Frédéric Bastiat, adapted to the present time by Edward Robert Pearce.
80 pp. London, Cassell, Petter and Galpin, 1882

B., T.

Cobden Club pamphlet.

9237 BATTERSBY, T. S. Frank.   The secret policy of the land act. Compensation to landlords the corollary to the land act.
appendix. 56 pp. Dublin, Carson Bros., London, Simpkin, Marshall, 1882

A., C., N.

9238 The difficulties of Ireland and the way to overcome them. (By) A cosmopolitan.
appendix. 18 pp. Toledo, Ohio, printed by Timmers, 1882

N.

9239 EARDLEY-WILMOT, Sir John E., bart.   Free or fair trade?
tables. appendix. 48 pp. London, E. Stanford, 1882

T.

9240 England, happy England once more. No more taxes.
32 pp. London, C. A. Bartlett, 1882

T.

9241 An enquiry into the terminal charges of railway companies.
40 pp. London, V. & R. Stevens, 1882

T.

9242 FARRER, Thomas Henry.   Free trade and fair trade.
190 pp. London, Cassell, Petter, Galpin, 1882

T.

Cobden Club pamphlet.

9243 FIELD, William. The Dublin victuallers *re* the press, the public health committee, the corporation, the abattoir, & the dejeuner attack.
8 pp. n.p., [1882?]

B.

9244 FINDLATER, John. Free trade, protection and fair trade.
appendix. 52 pp. London, Marcus Ward, 1882

T.

9245 FISHBOURNE, Ernest H. An answer to Mr. T. H. Farrer and the Cobden club. With a preface by Admiral Fishbourne, C.B.
24 pp. London, Harrison & Son, [1882]

T.

9246 [FORSTER, Hugh Oakeley Arnold.] The truth about the land league, its leaders, & its teaching. By 'one who knows'.
68 pp. London, National press agency, 1882

B.

9247 Free trade; an appeal to the public.
tables. map. appendix. 30 pp. London, E. & F. N. Spon, 1882

T.

9248 GOTOBED, Henry. Remarks on Mr. Chamberlain's bankruptcy bill with suggestions for the amendment of the present law.
20 pp. Cambridge, Macmillan and Bowes, 1882

T.

9249 GRATTAN, Richard. Repeal or ruin; which is it to be? A petition to the English Parliament, and letters to the local government board and to Messrs. Gladstone and Forster, on the misgovernment of Ireland. Parts I–III.
40 pp. Dublin, Fogarty, 1882

N.

9250 HAUPT, Ottomar. Bi-metallic England.
32 pp. Paris, J. Lecuir, London, Effingham Wilson, 1882

T.

9251 HENRY, T. Bimetallism exposed.
38 pp. London, Waterlow, 1882

T.

9252 HOLMES, Frederic Morrell. The history of the Irish land league impartially reviewed.
frontisp. 154 pp. London, F. E. Longley, [1882]

B.

9253 JAMAR, Joaquin. A brief review of the treaty negotiations between Spain and England.
tables. 94 pp. Manchester, J. Heywood, 1882

T.

9254 JORDAN, William Leighton. The standard of value; Lord Liverpool's oversight and its consequences.
appendix. 30 pp. Buenos Ayres, Lowe, Anderson y Ca, 1882

T.

9255 Justice to British farming.
36 pp. London, P. S. King, 1882

T.

9256 The land question, Ireland. No. XIV: The working of the land law act. February, 1882.
tables. 50 pp. Dublin, Hodges, Figgis, London, W. Ridgway, 1882

C., D., N., T.

Conclusion of the series issued by the Irish Land Committee, 31, South Frederick Street, Dublin. See 9115 & 9197.

9257 LYNCH, John. The land laws of Ireland. A paper read before the Ballarat eclectic association, on 7th August, 1882.
36 pp. Ballarat, Luphu, Herwood & Rider, 1882

U.

9258 MACKAY, George Grant. The land and the land laws.
40 pp. Inverness, R. Carruthers, 1882

T.

9259 MITCHEL, John. An apology for the British government in Ireland.
32 pp. Dublin, J. J. Lalor, 1882

B., N.

9260 MONGREDIEN, Augustus. Pleas for protection examined.
48 pp. London, Cassell, Petter and Galpin, 1882.

T.

Cobden Club pamphlet.

9261 My lords unmasked, by Athos.
54 pp. London, National press agency, 1882

N.

9262 NOBLE, John. Fifty three years' taxation and expenditure. 1827–28 to 1879–80.
tables. 64 pp. London, P. S. King, 1882

T.

9263 O'GRADY, Standish. The crisis in Ireland.
56 pp. Dublin, E. Ponsonby, London, Simpkin & Marshall, 1882

B., N.

9264 [O'HARA, Robert.] The Bright clauses of the Irish land acts of 1870 & 1881. Two letters to 'The Times' (reprinted by permission) with an appendix. By R. O'H.
44 pp. London, P. S. King, 1882

Q.

9265 POLSON, John. Affluence, poverty and pauperism.
44 pp. London, Elliot Stock, 1882

T.

9266 Practical politics & moonlight politics. Letters to a grand old man, & certain cabinet ministers, lately our confederates, By Rory-o'-the-hills, some time national schoolmaster, now a moonlighter.
64 pp. London, Tinsley, 1882

B., C., N.

9267 Report of the proceedings at the great aggregate meeting of Irish landlords held in Dublin, on Tuesday, 3rd January, 1882.
64 pp. Dublin, Hodges, Figgis, 1882
N.

9268 RUSSELL, Charles (later Lord Russell of Killowen). Letter to the electors of Dundalk on the condition of Ireland.
28 pp. London, Wyman, 1882
Q.

9269 SHAW-LEFEVRE, George John. The purchase clauses of the Irish land acts. Speech made in the house of commons, on the 2nd of May, 1879, & papers written on the same subject.
40 pp. London, National press agency, 1882
Q.

9270 STEVENS, C. A. Fluctuations of prices, 1835 to 1880, in relation to the value of tithe rent-charge and land-rent, from parliamentary returns.
tables. diagram. 34 pp. London, P. S. King, 1882
T.

9271 SMITH, Arthur M. Want: a vindication of protection.
74 pp. London, W. Ridgway, 1882
T.

9272 Vagrancy and mendicancy. A report based on a general inquiry instituted by the committee of the Howard association with communications (from a number of individuals and public bodies).
appendix. 26 pp. London, printed by Wertheimer and Lea, 1882
N., T.

9273 VAIZEY, John Savill. Settlement of land; being an enquiry whether they hinder husbandry.
36 pp. London, H. Sweet, 1882
T.

9274 WESTGARTH, William. The silver question, as viewed from the bimetallic standpoint. (Paper read at the social science [congress?] at Nottingham, 26th Sept. 1882, together with preface and notes, relative to the subsequent discussion which arose out of the paper.)
tables. appendix. 36 pp. London, Effingham Wilson, 1882
T.

9275 Who are the farmer's friends? Being some considerations for British tenant farmers in view of the coming general election.
40 pp. London, P. S. King, 1882
T.

9276 WILSON, Darcy Bruce. The bills of sale act (1878) amendment act, 1882, with notes.
appendix. 30 pp. London, Cox, 1882
T.

9277 WOODWARD, T[homas?] B[ert?]. What parliament should do for the farmers; or constitutional reform of the land laws.
40 pp. London, E. Stanford, [1882?]
T.

1883

9278 ARMFIELD, William Nathaniel. The money question considered.
16 pp. London, E. W. Allen, [1883]
T.

9279 BALDWIN, Thomas. Introduction to suggestions on the state of Ireland, with opinions thereon of the Irish press, and of the Roman catholic bishops of the congested districts.
28 pp. Dublin, M. H. Gill, 1883
A.

9280 ——. Suggestions on the state of Ireland chiefly given in evidence by Professor Baldwin.
212 pp. Dublin, M. H. Gill, 1883
B.

9281 BONIS, Carlo. Inghilterra ed Irlanda. Studio storico sociale.
table of contents. index. 90 pp. Ferrara, Bresciani, 1883
N.

9282 BOURKE, Ulick J. A plea for the evicted tenants of Mayo.
appendices. 32 pp. Dublin, Browne & Nolan, 1883
A., B.

9283 BOYD, J. F. State directed emigration. With a prefatory letter from his excellency the right hon. the earl of Dufferin, K.P., K.C.B., G.C.M.G.
36 pp. Manchester, J. Heywood, 1883
T.

9284 BRAMWELL, George William Wilsher, baron Bramwell. Nationalisation of land: a review of Mr. Henry George's 'Progress and Poverty'.
16 pp. London, Liberty and property defence league, 1883
T.

9285 BRETT, Edwin. The London Chartered Bank of Australia: its policy and management.
tables. 22 pp. London, Blades, East and Blades, 1883
T.

9286 BRODERICK, George C. The reform of the English land system.
28 pp. London, Cassell, Petter & Galpin, 1883
T.
Cobden club pamphlet.

9287 CASHIN, T. F. The inutility of bankruptcy laws. With a prefatory dissertation on bankruptcy, by the right hon. lord Sherbrooke.
48 pp. London, Sampson Low, 1883
T.

9288 CHALLIS, Henry W. A short exposition of the settled land act, 1882.
54 pp. London, Reeves and Turner, 1883
T.

9289 [Crory, William George?] Industry in Ireland: a treatise on the agricultural powers, manufacturing capabilities, and commercial advantages of Ireland.
174 pp. Dublin, office of the 'Irish Builder', 1883
P.

9290 The demands of agriculture, by Oppidan.
50 pp. London, W. Ridgway, 1883
T.

9291 Douglas, James. Address on slavery, sabbath protection, & church reform.
70 pp. Edinburgh, A. & C. Black, 1883
B.

9292 Eardley-Wilmot, Sir John E., bart. Free or fair trade? or, Is our free trade fair trade?
tables. appendices. 60 pp. 4th ed. London, E. Stanford, 1883
A.

9293 Fawcett, Henry. State socialism and the nationalisation of the land.
24 pp. London, Macmillan, 1883
T.

9294 Field, William. Suggestions for the improvement of the Irish poor law.
26 pp. Dublin, R. D. Webb, 1883
B.

9295 Fisher, Havelock. The English land question.
28 pp. London, Simpkin Marshall, 1883
T.

9296 Flach, Jacques. Collège de France. Histoire du régime agraire de l'Irlande.
20 pp. Paris, printed by Chamerot, 1883
N.

9297 Forster, Hugh Oakeley Arnold. The truth about the land league, its leaders, and its teaching. 3rd ed. with additional chapter.
tables. appendix. 88 pp. London, The National press agency, Limited, 1883
N., T., U.

9298 Gladstone, William Ewart. The conservative legacy, 1880. Liberal work, 1880–1883. Speech by the right hon. W. E. Gladstone, M.P. at the inaugural banquet, National liberal club, May 2nd, 1883.
16 pp. London, National liberal club, 1883
Q.

9299 Goschen, George Joachim, 1st viscount. Address by the right hon. G. J. Goschen to the members of the philosophical institution at Edinburgh on laissez-faire and government interference.
36 pp. London, Macmillan, 1883
T.

9300 Greening, William Berry. The people's guide to the new law of bankruptcy, comprising the bankruptcy act 1883 (which comes into operation on 1st January 1884) with pre-

liminary observations on the still existing act, plainly written for the information of the general public, and also forming a complete pocket guide for solicitors.
20 pp. London, Tanner, 1883
T.

9301 ——. The people's guide to the new law of bankruptcy, comprising the bankruptcy act, 1883, with preliminary observations thereon, with which is incorporated arrangements with creditors, shewing the various and only legal means by which they can be effected.
18 pp. 2nd ed. London, Tanner, [1883]
T.

9302 Half yearly reports and transactions of the Royal Agricultural Society of Ireland, 40, Dawson Street, Dublin, January, 1881, to December, 1883.
tables. 92 pp. Dublin, at the 'Farmers' Gazette' office, 1883
D.

9303 Hedley, Thomas F. Local taxation. Observations on the rating of railways, and suggestions for the amendment of the law.
tables. 18 pp. Sunderland, printed by Hills, 1883
T.

9304 Hyndman, Henry Mayers. Socialism versus Smithism. An open letter from H. M. Hyndman to Samuel Smith, M.P.
15 pp. London, the Modern Press, 1883
T.

9305 Kilbourn, J. K. Fish preservation and refrigeration. (International fisheries exhibition London, 1883.)
index. 28 pp. London, W. Clowes, 1883
N.

9306 The landlords and tenants bill now before parliament. Commented on by a landlord.
16 pp. London, E. Stanford, 1883
T.

9307 McKenna, Sir Joseph. Imperial taxation. The case of Ireland plainly stated for the information of the English people and of those others whom it may concern.
46 pp. London, Rivingtons, 1883
B., N.

9308 Mathieson's vade mecum for investors, giving the latest information regarding all classes of stocks, shares and bonds.
tables. 16 pp. London, Simpkin, Marshall, 1883
T.

9309 Mearns, Andrew. The bitter cry of outcast London.
20 pp. [no. t.p.] London, J. Clark, 1883
T.

9310 Muir, James. Money, being a review of economic theories with regard to money and the precious metals.
40 pp. Glasgow, J. Maclehose, 1883
T.

9311 Mundahl, C. M. Line fishing. International fisheries exhibition, London, 1883.
24 pp. London, W. Clowes, 1883
N.

9312 NEALE, John Alexander. The principles of land law reform reconsidered.
32 pp. London, P. S. King, 1883
T.

9313 NETTLETON, J. A. A study of the history and of the art of brewing; being a descriptive and historical essay on the arts of brewing and malting, and comprising a sketch of brewing legislation and taxation with the appropriate statistics.
62 pp. London, Ford, Shapland, 1883
T.

9314 NEWMAN, F. W. The land as national property. With special view to the scheme of reclaiming it for the nation proposed by Alfred Russel Wallace, LL.D.
16 pp. London, the Land Nationalisation society, [1883]
U.

9315 NEWTON, A. V. Analysis of the patents, designs, and trade marks act, 1883, with remarks on its working.
24 pp. London, Trübner, 1883
N.

9316 The Oxford handbook of political economy. Specially prepared for the use of candidates for examination.
28 pp. Oxford, Shrimpton, London, Simpkin, Marshall, 1883
T.

9317 PEARSON, Hugh W. The agricultural holdings (England) act, 1883, 46 & 47 Vict. cap 61; with introduction, notes and forms for the use of landlords, tenants and others.
66 pp. London, Hamilton, Adams, [1883?]
T.

9318 PETERS, Charles R. Building societies explained and compared, with information and advice on property, and bases of valuing same, together with definitions of some terms used in the building trade.
tables. 32 pp. London, Eden Fisher, 1883
T.

9319 Premium loans, their security and advantages. By 'Thrift'.
tables. 16 pp. London, printed by Dunn, Collin, 1883
T.

9320 Public companies from the cradle to the grave, or how promoters prey on the people. By Jaycee.
112 pp. London, Wyman, 1883
T.

9321 RAWLINSON, Sir Robert. The social and national influence of the domiciliary condition of the people. Three addresses by Sir Robert Rawlinson.
100 pp. London, P. S. King, 1883
T.

9322 REID, W. S. The enhancing value of gold and the industrial crisis.
28 pp. London, Effingham Wilson, 1883
T.

9323 SILLAR, Robert George. Usury. A paper read before the London junior clergy society at the vestry hall St. Martin's in the fields, 14th November 1882.
18 pp. London, A. Southey, [1883?]
T.

9324 ——. Usury. A paper read before the 'Somerville Club', Mortimer Street, Cavendish Square. 12th December, 1882.
16 pp. London, A. Southey, [1883?]
T.

9325 Socialism made plain, being the social and political manifesto of the democratic federation.
8 pp. London, W. Reeves, 1883
T.

9326 STANLEY, Henry. A popular summary of the agricultural holdings (England) act, 1883, for the use and information of landlords, tenants, valuers and others.
44 pp. Wolverhampton, printed by Barford and Newitt, 1883
T.

9327 WAKEFIELD, Edward Thomas. State-aided emigration made self-supporting. Three letters addressed to the earl of Derby.
66 pp. London, E. Stanford, 1883
T.

9328 WALSH, R. F. On improved facilities for the capture, economic transmission and distribution of sea fishes and how these matters affect Irish fisheries. (International Fisheries Exhibition, London 1883.)
38 pp. London, W. Clowes, 1883
N.

9329 WESSLAU, O. E. Current questions popularly explained. Free trade and protection.
56 pp. London, Elliot Stock, 1883
T.

9330 WRIGHT, Edward A. Irish industries: their promotion and development. A lecture.
52 pp. Cork, Francis Guy, 1883
C.

1884

9331 The approaching messiah of co-operation, entitled 'the millenium of industry'. A work upon co-operation; showing what co-operation is today, and what it is not. Also an illustration of the glorious future of the working classes upon the adoption of the Halidavian system of distribution; on the theory of pay no rent upon your own property. By H. S. Theoriss Plentifralle.
62 pp. Manchester, J. Heywood, 1884
T.

9332 BALDWIN, Thomas. A remedy for the congested districts of Ireland. Migration versus emigration.
30 pp. Dublin, M. H. Gill, 1884
Q., U.

9333 BASTABLE, Charles Francis. An examination of some current objections to the study of political economy: being an introductory lecture delivered in Trinity College, during Trinity term, 1884.
30 pp. Dublin, Hodges, Figgis & Co., 1884

N.

9334 BEAL, James. Practical guide to administration orders under section 122 of the bankruptcy act 1883.
tables. 32 pp. Exeter, Godfrey, 1884

T.

9335 BERMINGHAM, J. A. The rise and decline of Irish industries.
76 pp. Dublin, Hodges, Figgis, London, Simpkin, Marshall, 1884

B., U.

9336 BLENNERHASSETT, Sir Rowland, bart. Peasant proprietors in Ireland. Memorandum.
28 pp. London, printed by Strangeways & sons, 1884

Q., T.

Headed, 'confidential'; underneath, 'for private circulation'.

9337 BRAMWELL, Sir Frederick. State monopoly or private enterprise? An address delivered at the second annual meeting of the Liberty and property defence league.
24 pp. London, Liberty and property defence league, 1884

T.

9338 BRAMWELL, George William Wilsher, baron Bramwell. Nationalisation of land: A review of Mr. Henry George's 'progress and poverty'.
20 pp. 2nd ed. London, Liberty and property defence league, 1884

A., N.

9339 BROCKELBANK, Duncan. Exhibit of bankruptcy and county court debts law as altered by the bankruptcy act 1883 and the bankruptcy rules 1883.
42 pp. London, J. Kempster, [1884]

T.

9340 BROWNE, Frederick W. Figures and facts: or suggestions to tradesmen and others, in the present depressed times, with regard to the proper oversight of their affairs.
tables. 16 pp. London, printed by A. Napier, [1884]

T.

9341 BRUCE, F. J. Mr. Henry George's unproved assumption or the pauperism of capital, being a politico-economical sonata in four movements.
30 pp. London, Kegan Paul, Trench, 1884

T.

9342 BRYCE, James. England and Ireland. An introductory statement.
56 pp. London, Committee on Irish affairs, 1884

B., N.

9343 CAMPBELL, Dugald. The land question in the highlands and islands with observations on the administration of Scotch affairs.
76 pp. Paisley, J. & R. Parlane, [1884?]

T.

9344 Can a sufficient mid-day meal be given to poor school children at a cost for material of less than one penny?
tables. 24 pp. London, printed by Causton, 1884

T.

9345 CHARLES, George. Scheme for a parochial relief committee and some remarks on its working and results in S. Paul's, Paddington. With a preface by the Rev. H. V. H. Cowell, B.A., vicar of S. Paul's Paddington.
tables. 20 pp. London, Hatchards, 1884

T.

9346 EDWARDS, William. The people's edition of Debtor and Creditor; shewing the insolvent debtor how to obtain release from debt without bankruptcy and solvent traders how they may carry on their business without the possibility of ever coming within the range of the new bankruptcy act.
12 pp. Liverpool, J. Wilson, 1884

T.

9347 ELLIOT, Nenion. Teind law reform.
tables. appendices. 26 pp. Edinburgh, W. Green, 1884

T.

9348 FAIRMAN, Frank. Herbert Spencer on socialism. A reply to the article entitled 'the coming slavery' in the 'Contemporary Review' for April 1884.
16 pp. London, the Modern Press, 1884

T.

9349 FORSTER, Joseph. Stay and starve or go and thrive.
16 pp. Manchester, J. Heywood, 1884

T.

9350 Gallop of poverty, illustrated by John Proctor.
tables. 34 pp. London, Association for defence of British industry, 1884

T.

9351 GIFFEN, Sir Robert. The progress of the working classes in the last half century.
tables. 32 pp. London, Bell, 1884

N., T., U.

9352 HARPER, Archibald. The national debt and paper currency; or how to save the taxpayers seven millions a year.
16 pp. Revised edition, Glasgow, printed by John Crawford, 1884

T.

9353 HEDLEY, Thomas F. Observations on the incidence of local taxation. The exemption of stock-in-trade and the attempts to get machinery exempted from rateability.
28 pp. Sunderland, Hills, 1884

T.

9354 HYNDMAN, Henry Mayers, and BRADLAUGH, Charles. Will socialism benefit the English people? Verbatim report of a debate between H. M. Hyndman and Charles Bradlaugh.
40 pp. London, Free thought publishing co. 1884

T.

Printed by Annie Besant and Charles Bradlaugh.

9355 INGRAM, John Kells. Work and the workman; being an address to the Trades Union Congress in Dublin, September, 1880.
44 pp. 2nd ed. London, Longmans, Green & Co., Dublin, E. Ponsonby, 1884

N.

9356 Land Corporation of Ireland, Limited. Report of extraordinary general meeting held in Molesworth Hall, Dublin, on Thursday, January 24th, 1884.
28 pp. Dublin, 1884

N.

9357 LASSALLE, Ferdinand. The working man's programme (Arbeiter-Programm). Translated by Edward Peters.
60 pp. London, the Modern Press, 1884

T.

9358 LONG, J. Edmond. The hopeful cry of outcast London.
122 pp. London, Skeffington, 1884

T.

9359 LYSTER, H. Cameron. College Historical Society; University of Dublin. The functions of government. An address delivered in the dining hall of Trinity College at the opening meeting of the 115th session, November 12th, 1884.
28 pp. Dublin, Ponsonby & Weldrick, 1884

N.

9360 McCREE, George Wilson. Sweet herbs for the bitter cry.
illustr. 38 pp. London, National temperance publication depot, 1884

T.

9361 [MAHONY, Richard John.] The crime and penalty of ownership. A chapter in the history of the Irish land act of 1881, addressed to the right hon. W. E. Gladstone, M.P., first lord of the treasury, by one of the proscribed.
26 pp. Dublin, J. L. Dixon, 1884

C.

9362 MASON, M. H. Classification of girls and boys in workhouses and the legal powers of boards of guardians for placing them beyond the workhouse.
32 pp. London, Hatchards, 1884

T.

9363 MEDLEY, Dudley J. Socialism as a moral movement. A short consideration of its value and its dangers.
28 pp. Oxford, B. H. Blackwell, 1884

T.

9364 MENGER, Carl. Die Irrthümer des Historismus in der deutschen Nationalökonomie.
table of contents. 98 pp. Wien, Hölder, 1884

N.

9365 MOLESWORTH-HEPWORTH, E. N. British free trade versus the world's protection. Letters and illustrations showing how to raise wages and profits and lower taxation.
illustr. 24 pp. Manchester and London, J. Heywood, 1884

T.

9366 NEALE, John Alexander. An enquiry into the principles of free trade.
50 pp. London, P. S. King, 1884

T.

9367 The new bankruptcy act. Administration orders as they affect tradesmen, shopkeepers and the working classes. By L. E. X., clerk to one of the official receivers.
14 pp. Manchester, J. Heywood, [1884?]

T.

9368 New Brunswick as a home for the farmer emigrant. Published by authority of the Government of Canada.
tables. 56 pp. Ottawa, Dept. of agriculture, 1884

N.

9369 O'BRIEN, Edward W. Proposal for a guarantee to facilitate the purchase of their holdings by tenants in Ireland.
8 pp. Limerick, G. M'Kern & sons, 1884

Q.

'For private circulation only.'

9370 Overlegislation in 1884. Review of the bills of the session by the parliamentary committee of the Liberty and property defence league.
46 pp. London, Liberty and property defence league, 1884

A.

9371 A pen'orth o' poetry for the poor, by Peter Primrose.
124 pp. London, Harrison, 1884

B.

9372 POSNETT, Hutcheson Macaulay. The Ricardian theory of rent.
94 pp. London, Longmans, Green & co., 1884

R.

9373 RICHARD, Henry. The recent progress of international arbitration.
32 pp. London, Hodder and Stoughton, [1884]

T.

9374 ROBERTSON, Edward Stanley. Communism.
32 pp. London, Liberty and property defence league, 1884

A.

9375 ——. The state and the slums.
22 pp. London, Liberty and property defence league, 1884

A.

9376 SANDIFORD, T. Henry. Permanent reduction of the poor-rates in Ireland, by three pence in the pound. To be effected by the formation of a new public health service.
table. 12 pp. Dublin, Hodges, Figgis & co., 1884

Q.

9377 SMITH, Samuel. The nationalisation of land.
tables. appendix. 48 pp. London, Kegan Paul and Trench, 1884

T.

9378 Socialism a curse. Being a reply to a lecture delivered by Edward A. Aveling entitled 'The curse of capital', by 'Humanitas'.
44 pp. London, Freethought publishing co. 1884

T.

Printed by Annie Besant and Charles Bradlaugh.

9379 Socialism at St. Stephen's in 1883. Work done during the session by the parliamentary committee of the Liberty and property defence league.
table of contents. 56 pp. London, Central offices of the league, 1884

N., T.

9380 The socialist revolution of 1888. By an eye-witness.
36 pp. London, Harrison, 1884

T.

9381 SORGE, F. A. Socialism and the worker.
16 pp. London, the Modern Press, 1884

T.

9382 TWISS, Sir Travers. Belligerent right on the high seas since the declaration of Paris (1856).
32 pp. London, Butterworths, 1884

T.

9383 Two Irelands: or, loyalty versus treason. Part I. History of the 'New departure'. Part II. The attempted invasion of Ulster. Part III. Extracts from speeches, crime returns, etc.
96 pp. London, P. S. King, Dublin, Hodges & Figgis, 1884

B., N.

9384 [UPWARD, Allen.] The truth about Ireland by an English liberal.
56 pp. London, Kegan Paul, Trench, 1884

B.

9385 What is state-aided emigration? by an Irishman who knows.
40 pp. Dublin, Browne & Nolan, 1884

N.

9386 WILLIAMS, John. The angel's foot; or John Bull's only remedy.
48 pp. Evesham, the author, 1884

T.

1885

9387 ARBUTHNOT, F. F. Free trade in land; a few remarks on the English land question in the shape of an address to the Wonersh district liberal association.
16 pp. London, printed by Cassell, 1885

T.

9388 BRAY, John. Facts for the new electorate.
44 pp. London, E. Stanford, 1885

T.

9389 CERNUSCHI, Henri. The great metallic powers.
30 pp. London, P. S. King, 1885

T.

9390 CHICHESTER, C. Raleigh. What is amiss with the cattle trade? Printed and circulated by order of the Irish cattle association.
16 pp. Dublin, printed by Browne and Nolan, 1885

N.

9391 CLARK, Gavin Brown. The Highland land question. An abstract of the report of the royal commission to enquire into the condition of the crofters and cottars in the highlands and islands of Scotland.
40 pp. London, W. Reeves, [1885]

T.

9392 COLEBROOKE, Sir Edward, bart. Small holdings and school fees.
50 pp. Edinburgh, D. Douglas, 1885

T.

9393 CURROR, David. Industrial depression.
28 pp. Edinburgh, Bell and Bradfute, 1885

T.

9394 DE VERE, Sir Stephen Edward. Extract from a letter to a private friend on the present conditions and prospects of Ireland.
16 pp. London, printed by Skipper and East, 1885

T.

Title page bears statement 'not published'.

9395 DUFFY, Sir Charles Gavan. The price of peace in Ireland. A letter to his excellency the earl of Carnarvon. With some extracts from 'An appeal to the conservative party', by the same writer.
26 pp. Dublin, Hodges and Figgis, J. Duffy, London, W. Ridgway, [1885?]

T.

9396 Fair trade economically justified.
16 pp. Manchester, J. Heywood, 1885

T.

9397 FERGUSON, Robert J. The land tenure of Ireland, past, present and future, a practical guide for landlords, agents and tenants.
32 pp. Dublin, J. Falconer, 1885

U.

9398 FULLER, Morris. The alleged tripartite division of tithes in England for maintaining 'the clergy', 'the poor' and the 'fabric of the church'.
appendices. 62 pp. London, Bosworth, 1885

T.

9399 GEDDES, Patrick. An analysis of the principles of economics. (Part 1.) Read before the Royal society of Edinburgh, 17th March, 7th April, and 7th July, 1884.
diagrams. 40 pp. London & Edinburgh, Williams and Norgate, 1885

N.

9400 GOADBY, Edwin, and WATT, William. The present depression in trade: Its causes and remedies. The 'Pears' prize essays (of one hundred guineas). By Edwin Goadby and William Watt. With an introductory paper by Professor Leone Levi (one of the adjudicators) read at the British Association for the advancement of science, in Aberdeen, September, 1885.
tables. appendices. 130 pp. 10th ed. London, Chatto & Windus, 1885

N.

9401 HANNA, Hugh, and WALLACE, Bruce. Verbatim report of the debate upon land and nationalisation between the Rev. Hugh Hanna and the Rev. Bruce Wallace, A.M.
28 pp. Belfast, printed at the Ulster Echo steam-printing works, 1885
B.

9402 HART, Ernest. Local government as it is and as it ought to be.
tables. appendix. 78 pp. London, Smith Elder & co., [1885]
T.

9403 HODGSON, Charles D. Land reform, social and financial.
24 pp. London, P. S. King, 1885
T.

9404 HOEY, David George. 'Bulling and bearing' or 'operating', otherwise betting or gambling on the stock exchange, being two letters addressed to a prominent member of her majesty's privy council with observations on the same subject appended to an official communication to the Lord advocate for Scotland, and a glance at reform in legal procedure.
32 pp. Glasgow, printed by R. Maclehose, 1885
T.

9405 JAMIESON, George Auldjo. The present agricultural and financial depression. Some of its causes, influences and effects.
tables in appendices. 70 pp. Edinburgh, W. Blackwood & Son, 1885
T.

9406 JONES, Alfred. The homes of the poor in Westminster.
34 pp. 2nd edition. London, Rivington, 1885
T.

9407 JONES, Alfred Orlando. Falling markets: their cause.
32 pp. London, F. Hodgson, 1885
T.

9408 Land corporation of Ireland, limited. Report of directors for year 1885.
18 pp. Dublin, printed at the University press, 1885
N.

9409 A land purchase scheme. By an Irish landowner.
12 pp. Dublin, W. McGee, 1885
A., T.

9410 LEAKE, Robert. The tale of an Ulster tenant. Reprinted from the Manchester 'Examiner and Times' of January 24, 1881, to which are now added letters from the tenant (Patrick M'Atavey) and Mrs. M'Atavey and reports of his case before the land court. Being the first case adjudicated upon under the Irish Land Act of 1881, and the first instance of a Fair Rent made statutory.
16 pp. Manchester, A. Ireland, 1885
U.

9411 LYNCH, Stanislaus J. How to open the Irish land market. Suggestions for the simplification of the procedure in relation to the sale of land in Ireland. To which is annexed a bill further to facilitate the sale and transfer of land in Ireland.
32 pp. Dublin, W. McGee, 1885
U.

9412 MACDONALD, Rowland Hill. The emigration of highland crofters.
44 pp. Edinburgh, W. Blackwood & son, 1885
T.

9413 MALLET, Sir Louis. The national income and taxation.
48 pp. London, Cassell, 1885
T.
Cobden Club pamphlet.

9414 MAN, E. Garnet. The present trade crisis critically examined.
48 pp. London, Effingham Wilson, 1885
T.

9415 The Manifesto of the Socialist league signed by the provisional council at the foundation of the league on 30th Dec. 1884, and adopted at the general conference held at Farringdon Hall, London, on July 5th, 1885. New ed. annotated by Wm. Morris and E. Belfort Bax.
16 pp. London, Socialist League Office, 1885
N.

9416 MASON, Stephen. Agricultural and industrial depression in connection with free versus fair trade.
tables. 28 pp. Published by request for the Glasgow chamber of commerce. Glasgow, J. Maclehose, 1885
T.

9417 MEARNS, Andrew. London and its teeming toilers. Who they are and how they live. Facts and figures suggested by recent statistics of the census and charities commission.
tables. 74 pp. London, printed by Warren Hall & Lovitt, [1885]
T.

9418 MEDLEY, George W. The trade depression: its causes and its remedies.
tables. 48 pp. London, [etc.] Cassell & co., 1885
U.

9419 MONGREDIEN, Augustus. Free trade and English commerce.
tables. 96 pp. 2nd ed. London, [etc.] Cassell & Co., 1885
U.

9420 ——. Trade depression, recent and present.
tables. 24 pp. 2nd ed. London, Cassell, Petter & Galpin, 1885
T.
Cobden Club pamphlet.

9421 MONTEAGLE, Thomas Spring-Rice, 2nd baron. Liberal policy in Ireland.
16 pp. London, printed by Mackie, 1885
N., T.

9422 O'BRIEN, George. Supplement to a treatise on gold and silver. To show a chief cause of present depression in trade and shrinkage in value of all produce and property.
8 pp. London, printed at 'Mining Journal' Office, 1885
T.

9423 OELSNER, Ludwig. Ueber den Volkswirtschaftlichen Unterricht. Beilage zum Osterprogramm der Wöhlerschule (Realgymnasium nebst Handelsschule).
18 pp. Frankfurt a.M., C. Adelmann, 1885
N.

9424 O'REILLY, Thomas M. The marquess of Waterford and his Wicklow Estate. With an analysis of the affidavits of R. C. Heighington, A. J. Owen, Michael Dunne (Peeler) Patrick Burke (Mouser), and Patrick Traynor (the 'lord') in the famous Halpin case. Compiled by Thomas M. O'Reilly, Ballyknockan.
22 pp. Naas, printed at the office of the Leinster Leader. [1885?]
U.

9425 The Oxford handbook of political economy. Specially prepared for the use of candidates for examination.
40 pp. 2nd ed. Oxford, Shrimpton, London, Simpkin, Marshall, 1885
T.

9426 Parnellism unmasked: its finances exposed, by an Irish nationalist.
tables. 56 pp. Dublin, 1885
R., T.

9427 POWELL, Joseph. How to make simple the transfer of land.
40 pp. London, W. Clowes, 1885
T.

9428 The questions put by the royal commissioners on the depressed state of trade, dealt with in an independent but sympathetic spirit by a former M.P.
24 pp. Edinburgh, T. & T. Clark, 1885
T.

9429 ROBERTSON, John. Socialism and Malthusianism.
16 pp. London, Freethought publishing co., 1885
T.

9430 SAYCE, S. J. Anti corn-law league, free trade, and general depression.
14 pp. Bristol, I. E. Chillcott, 1885
T.

9431 SIDGWICK, Henry. The scope and method of economic science. An address delivered to the economic science and statistics section of the British Association at Aberdeen, 10th September, 1885.
60 pp. London, Macmillan, 1885
D.

9432 SILLAR, Robert George. Usury. A paper read before some members of the University of Cambridge in the lecture room, St. John's College, 12th February, 1885.
16 pp. London, printed by Exeter Hall Printing Works, 1885
T.

9433 TODD, Charles Hawkes. The unearned increment. Observations on Ricardo's theory of rent.
20 pp. London, Kegan Paul, Trench, 1885
T.

9434 TRAILL, Anthony. A proposed solution of the land question in Ireland: a paper read before the Fortnightly club, Dublin, on March 12th, 1884.
16 pp. Dublin, Ponsonby and Weldrick, 1885
T.

9435 UNDERDOWN, Emanuel M. Registration of titles and deposit of deeds: a letter addressed to baron Halsbury, lord high chancellor of England.
16 pp. London, Stevens and Haynes, 1885
T.

9436 WALLACE, Robert. Agricultural education in its various aspects.
24 pp. Edinburgh, Oliver and Boyd, 1885
T.

9437 WILKINSON, Henry B. and others. Letters to the bishop of Manchester on thrift and on co-operation.
16 pp. Manchester, J. Heywood, 1885
T.

9438 WILLIAMS, H. Depression of trade and want of employment. A search after a sound basis of political economy.
table of contents. 56 pp. London, Cull, 1885
T.

9439 WILLOUGHBY, F. S. The depression in trade: true fair trade proposals.
16 pp. Manchester, J. Heywood, 1885
T.

9440 YOUNG, Edmund J. Literary and historical society, University College, Dublin. The labour question: an address delivered at the inaugural meeting of the session, November, 1885.
18 pp. Dublin, printed by Browne and Nolan, 1885
N.

1886

9441 APPLETON, Lewis. The gradual progress of international arbitration.
32 pp. London, Appleton, 1886
T.

9442 'As it was said.' Extracts from prominent speeches and writings of the Parnellite party, 1878–1886, with classification and index and a sketch of the Separist movement, illustrated with 'agrarian crimes' map and a parliamentary map of Ireland.
tables. maps. appendix. 196 pp. Dublin & London, Irish Loyal and Patriotic Union, 1886
D., T.

9443 BAILEY, William F. Fiscal relations of the United Kingdom and Ireland, with special reference to the state purchase of land.
18 pp. Dublin, Hodges, Figgis, 1886
A., N., Q., U.

9444 BALL, William Platt. Mrs. Besant's socialism: an examination and an exposure.
36 pp. London, Progressive publishing co., [1886]
B., T.

9445 BARBOUR, Sir David Miller. Bimetallism. An address delivered in Belfast.
32 pp. Eastbourne, The Southern publishing company ltd., [1886]

Q.

9446 BARTLETT, E. Ashmead. Union or separation: Analysis of Mr. Gladstone's Irish policy.
146 pp. London, Irish Loyal and Patriotic Union, [1886?]

T.

9447 BARTY, Thomas. Scottish agriculture in distress. Some facts and suggestions.
14 pp. Edinburgh, W. Blackwood & Son, 1886

T.

9448 BELLOWS, John. Chapters of Irish history. I—Ireland before its connection with England. II—Irish land tenures under English rule.
32 pp. London, Trübner, [1886]

T.

9449 BIRD, Henry Edward. Railway accounts: a concise view for the last four years, 1881 to 1884, and an estimate for 1885. With remarks on the relation of capital to revenue and on vital statistics of the working of railways.
tables. 20 pp. London, Effingham Wilson, 1886

T.

9450 BRADLAUGH, Charles. A letter to the right hon. lord Randolph S. Churchill, M.P., chancellor of the exchequer.
16 pp. London, Freethought publishing company, 1886

B.

9451 BRETT, John. Free trade. Cobden Bright Gladstone Fawcett, etc., etc., collated and examined.
tables. 64 pp. London, Effingham Wilson, 1886

T.

9452 BROWN, Thomas Craig. Foreign tariffs. Their effect on British commerce.
14 pp. Edinburgh, W. Blackwood & son, 1886

T.

9453 BROWNFIELD, Arthur. A concise lesson in Irish history contained in a letter to Mr. H. T. Davenport.
14 pp. London, [etc.], Burns & Oates, [1886]

Q.

9454 BURCKHARDT, William. The currency problem. A proposal for the rehabilitation of silver.
tables. 26 pp. London, Effingham Wilson, 1886

T.

9455 BURN, Francis W. A commercial guide to the court practice in debt recovery, etc. with a treatise on bankruptcy, administration orders, bills of sale, assignments, landlord and tenant, wills and sundry legal information and forms.
40 pp. Manchester, printed by the Guardian, 1886

T.

9456 BUXTON, Sydney Charles, earl. Mr. Gladstone's Irish bills: what they are and the arguments for them.
32 pp. 2nd ed. London, the National press agency, [1886]

N., Q.

9457 CASHIN, T. F. Free trade fallacies; or Cobden confuted. An exposition of the existing phase of progress and poverty.
tables. 88 pp. London, Wyman, 1886

T.

9458 CERNUSCHI, Henri. Anatomy of money.
26 pp. London, P. S. King, 1886

T.

9459 CHADWICK, Edwin. Alternative remedies for Ireland; with note on Professor Dicey's 'England's case against home rule'.
34 pp. n.p., 1886

T.

9460 The city companies and their property. A plea for fair play.
16 pp. no. t.p. London, Hamilton Adams, 1886

T.

9461 CLANCY, John J. No. 7. The Irish question. Irish Industries and English legislation.
32 pp. London, Irish press agency, 1886

N.

9462 COGNETTI DE MARTIIS, Salvatore. L'economia come scienza autonoma.
40 pp. Roma, [etc.] Fratelli Bocca, 1886

N.

9463 A critical analysis of the sale and purchase of land (Ireland) bill.
26 pp. Dublin & London, Irish Loyal and Patriotic Union, [1886]

D.

9464 DAVIS, C. Deep sea fisheries of Ireland.
32 pp. Dublin, M. H. Gill, 1886

P., Q.

9465 DERBY, Edward Henry Stanley, 15th earl of. The Irish question. A speech delivered at Liverpool, June 29th, 1886.
16 pp. London, Liberal unionist committee, 1886

T.

9466 DE RICCI, J. H. Liberal misrule in Ireland.
40 pp. London, E. Stanford, 1886

R.

9467 DE VERE, Sir Stephen Edward. Ireland. A letter addressed to lord Monteagle.
12 pp. London, printed by Mackie, 1886

T.

T.p. bears statement 'printed for private circulation'.

9468 DICK, George Handasyde. Bi-metallism popularised.
tables. appendix. 62 pp. Glasgow, printed by McCorquodale, 1886

A.

9469 DODD, Joseph. The land question viewed from a church aspect.
66 pp. 2nd edition. Oxford, J. Parker, 1886

T.

9470 DOYLE, John P. The Ireland of the past and of the future. Being a letter to the rt. hon. W. E. Gladstone, M.P., Prime Minister, on 1. A home rule parliament sitting in Dublin. 2. The settlement of the land question by buying out the landlords. 3. A great system of public works for opening up and developing the resources of the country.
20 pp. Dublin, J. Duffy, 1886

N.

9471 The duty of Irish landlords at this imperial crisis, April 1886.
16 pp. London, E. Allen, Dublin, W. McGee, 1886

T.

9472 EDEN, Frederick Morton. There is no god but free trade, and Cobden is his prophet; or, food and free trade.
22 pp. London, E. Stanford, 1886

T.

9473 ERCK, Wentworth. Returns of sales of tenant-right in agricultural holdings, Ireland.
tables. 24 pp. Dublin, W. McGee, London, P. S. King, 1886

T.

9474 ——. Suggestions towards a measure for the settlement of the Irish land question.
16 pp. 2nd ed. Dublin, printed by C. W. Gibbs, 1886

N.

9475 EWAN, Alexander. The Irish problem solved: and the remedy found: the land monopoly broken up, and the unity, antiquity, and stability of the British empire consolidated on a true basis.
16 pp. Banchory-Teman, A. Ewan, [1886]

Q.

9476 FEVERHEERD, H. L. A cry for more money. The depression of trade; the cause and the remedy. By a London merchant.
24 pp. London, Effingham Wilson, 1886

T.

9477 FISHBOURNE, Edmund Gardiner. Protection for her people and her industries the cure for Irish discontent.
table. 16 pp. London, Harrison, [1886]

T.

9478 FITZPATRICK, T. E. The existing manufactures of Ireland, with suggestions for their development.
82 pp. Dublin, Mara, 1886

N.

9479 FORSSELL, Hans. The appreciation of gold, and the fall in prices of commodities.
tables. 32 pp. London, Effingham Wilson, 1886

T.

9480 FORSTER, Hugh Oakeley Arnold. The truth about the land league; its leaders and its teaching.
tables. appendix. additional chapter. 96 pp. 4th ed. Dublin, University Press, 1886

D.

9481 FOWLER, William. Appreciation of gold. An essay. tables. diagrams. appendices. 72 pp. London, Cassell & Co., 1886

T.

Cobden Club pamphlet.

9482 GLADSTONE, William Ewart. Gladstone's measures for the pacification of Ireland: the full text of I.—the premier's two speeches on the home rule scheme; II—the home rule bill; III—the premier's speech on land purchase; IV—the land purchase bill.
48 pp. Belfast & Dublin, Morning news and Freeman's journal, 1886

Q.

9483 ——. The Irish question. i.—History of an idea. ii.—Lessons of the election.
58 pp. London, J. Murray, 1886

B., D., L., N., T.

9484 GOUBAREFF, D. N. Le socialisme à notre époque.
20 pp. Beaulieu-sur-mer, Imprimerie Niçoise, 1886

T.

9485 HADDON, Caroline. Where does your interest come from? A word to lady investors.
16 pp. Manchester, J. Heywood, 1886

T.

9486 Half-yearly reports and transactions of the Royal Agricultural Society of Ireland, 40 Dawson Street, Dublin. January, 1884, to May 1886.
tables. 92 pp. Dublin, at the 'Farmers' Gazette' office, 1886

D.

9487 HOARE, Henry. The appreciation of gold and its connexion with the depression of trade.
54 pp. London, E. Stanford, 1886

T.

9488 HODGSON, James M. Socialism.
16 pp. Manchester, Brook & Chrystal, 1886

T.

9489 Home rule and what next?
16 pp. Dublin, [1886?]

D., N., Q.

9490 HUBBARD, John Gellibrand, later 1st baron Addington. Our fiscal future.
26 pp. London, Effingham Wilson, 1886

T.

9491 HUTCHINSON, L. W. Letter to the president of the gold and silver currency commission.
8 pp. London, Stewart, 1886

T.

9492 Information for intending emigrants to the Province of Nova Scotia, (Dominion of Canada). Issued by the Government of Nova Scotia.
maps. tables. 64 pp. Halifax, N.S., Commissioner of Public Works and Mines, 1886

N.

9493 The Irish parliament and Irish property. Railways.
14 pp. Dublin, E. Ponsonby, 1886

A., N.

9494 The Irish question: a dilemma. By a Liberal.
16 pp. London, Alexander and Shepheard, 1886

T.

9495 An Irish tenant's privileges.
4 pp. Dublin & London, Irish Loyal and Patriotic Union.
[1886?]

A., T.

9496 KINNEAR, John Boyd.   The urgent needs of Ireland.
14 pp. London, Bale, 1886

N.

9497 KROPOTKIN, Peter Alexeivich, Prince.   Expropriation.
An anarchistic essay. Translated by Henry Glasse.
8 pp. London, International publishing company, 1886

T.

9498 ——.   Law and authority; an anarchist essay.
24 pp. London, International publishing co., 1886

T.

9499 ——.   The place of anarchism in socialistic evolution.
An address delivered in Paris. Translated by Henry Glasse.
8 pp. London, International publishing co., 1886

T.

9500 Land transfer. Published by order of the Bar committee.
104 pp. London, Butterworths, 1886

T.

9501 MADDEN, John.   A few remarks upon the Irish crisis.
appendices. 32 pp. Dublin, Hodges, Figgis, 1886

D.

9502 MAYNE, John D.   Home rule: an examination of the
government of Ireland bill.
36 pp. Dublin, Hodges, Figgis, 1886

D.

9503 MILWARD, Dawson A.   Advice to small farmers on
the management of farms. An essay by Dawson A. Milward.
Published by authority of the Royal Agricultural Society of
Ireland.
28 pp. Dublin, printed at the 'Farmers' Gazette' office, 1886

D.

9504 MONGREDIEN, Augustus.   On the displacement of
labour and capital: a neglected chapter in political economy.
36 pp. London, Cassell, Petter, & Galpin, 1886

T.

Cobden Club pamphlet.

9505 MONTAGUE, Francis Charles.   The old poor law and
the new socialism: or pauperism and taxation.
66 pp. London, Cassell, Petter and Galpin, 1886

T.

Cobden Club pamphlet.

9506 MONTGOMERY, H. de F.   Gladstone and Burke.
appendix. 60 pp. Dublin, Hodges Figgis, London, P. S. King,
1886

D.

9507 O'CONNELL, Mary Anne, [Mrs. Morgan John
O'Connell].   Munster land-owning.
46 pp. London, W. Ridgway, Dublin, Hodges, Figgis, 1886

T., U.

9508 Parnellism. By an Irish nationalist.
54 pp. Dublin, 1886

D.

9509 Pauper and destitute children 1886.
4 pp. London, printed by Wertheimer and Lea, 1886

N.

Issued by the Howard Association, London.

9510 PHEAR, Henry Herbert.   Emigration: a summary of
the acts that have been passed for assisting emigration from
England, Scotland and Ireland with a few facts and figures
connected therewith.
28 pp. London, Stevens, 1886

T.

9511 PILLING, William.   Money: the question of to-day.
24 pp. Liverpool, G. Walmsley, 1886

T.

9512 POYNTER, S. W.   Our national dangers and our need.
A scheme for the full and proper cultivation of the land of
Great Britain and Ireland, and the production of the larger
proportion of our food supplies.
tables (in) appendices. 62 pp. London, Hamilton, Adams,
1886

T.

9513 A radical scheme for a land act and a land registration
act by M.A., barrister-at-law.
24 pp. no t.p. London, William Maxwell. [Common sense
tract.] [c. 1885]

T.

9514 RAFFALOVICH, Arthur.   La ligue pour la défence de la
liberté et de la propriété en Angleterre et le socialisme agraire
de M. Chamberlain.
90 pp. Paris, Guillaumin, 1886

T.

9515 The repeal of the union conspiracy; or Mr. Parnell,
M.P., and the I.R.B.
58 pp. London, W. Ridgway, 1886

B., D., N., T.

9516 Report on the present state of the Irish land question.
By a land valuer.
32 pp. London, Kegan Paul & Trench, 1886

N., Q., U.

9517 Returns of sales of tenant-right in agricultural holdings, Ireland.
tables. 24 pp., 4th ed. Dublin, W. McGee, London, P. S. King,
1886

D., N., Q.

9518 RUXTON, George W. Home rule for Ireland under a Parnellite government.
16 pp. Dublin, Hodges, Figgis, 1886
D.

9519 SAY, Léon. Municipal and state socialism.
28 pp. London, Liberty and property defence league, 1886
T.

9520 The silver pamphlet, by Specie.
tables. 40 pp. London, Effingham Wilson, 1886
T.

9521 The silver question, plainly and practically considered by a free-trader.
tables. 32 pp. Liverpool, Walmsley, London, Hamilton, Adams, 1886
T.

9522 SMITH, John Chaloner. On the practicability of reducing railway rates in Ireland.
tables. 72 pp. Dublin, printed by J. Falconer, 1886
N.

9523 Some observations on the government of Ireland bill, with an analysis of its chief provisions.
46 pp. n.p., [1886]
D.

9524 STUART, H. Villiers. Prices of farm products in Ireland from year to year for thirty-six years, illustrated by diagrams, with observations on the prospects of Irish agriculture, including the substance of letters addressed to the rt. hon. W. E. Gladstone, M.P., in February and March of this year.
fold. diag. tables. 32 pp. Dublin, Hodges, Figgis, London, P. S. King & son, 1886
C., D., N., Q.

9525 Thirty nine articles of belief proposed as the profession and programme of Christian socialists by one of them.
32 pp. Bristol, J. W. Arrowsmith, 1886
T.

9526 TUKE, James Hack. Achill and West of Ireland. Report of the distribution of the seed potato fund in the spring of 1886. With some suggestions for the permanent relief of the districts.
map. tables. 40 pp. London, W. Ridgway, 1886
N.

9527 TWAMLEY, William. The cause of the Dublin poor.
32 pp. Dublin, printed by White, 1886
N.

9528 WARNER-JONES, F. Where are we? or the remedy for depressed trade.
64 pp. London, Griffith, Farran Okeden & Welsh, 1886
T.

9529 WILLIAMS, S. D. Trade depression and the appreciation of gold.
10 pp. Birmingham, Cornish, 1886
T.

33

9530 WILLIAMSON, Stephen. The silver question, considered especially in relation to British trade and commerce. An address to the philosophical society of Dumbarton, delivered on 22nd November, 1886.
28 pp. Liverpool, Walmsley, London, Chapman & Hall, 1886
T.

1887

9531 The ABC of the Irish land question. Revised and brought down to date, by competent legal authorities.
tables. 32 pp. London, McCorquodale, 1887
D., N.

9532 ARMOUR, Samuel Crawford. Christianity and socialism.
24 pp. Liverpool, A. Holden, 1887
T.

9533 BESANT, Annie, & FOOTE, George William. Is socialism sound? Verbatim report of a four nights' debate between Annie Besant and G. W. Foote, at the hall of science, Old St., London, E.C., on February 2nd, 9th, 16th, & 23rd, 1887.
180 pp. London, Freethought publishing company, 1887
B.

9534 BRADLAUGH, Charles. The channel tunnel: ought the democracy to oppose or support it?
20 pp. London, A. Bonner, 1887
B.

9535 BROWNRIGG, Bookey. The best solution of the land-problem.
16 pp. Dublin, W. McGee, London, Simpkin, Marshall, 1887
N.

9536 BULL, H. The instability of gold as a standard of value. An essay on the divergence of value between gold and silver.
26 pp. London, Hamilton, Adams, 1887
T.

9537 BUTCHER, S. H. Irish land acts and their operation. An address delivered to the liberal unionist association of the College division of Glasgow, 14th January, 1887.
tables. 24 pp. Glasgow, J. Maclehose, 1887
T.

9538 CARPENTER, Edward. England's ideal and other papers on social subjects.
150 pp. London, Swan, Sonnenschein and Lowrey, 1887
N.

9539 CERNUSCHI, Henri. The bimetallic par. (Notes submitted to the gold and silver commission.)
46 pp. London, P. S. King, 1887
T.

9540 CHAMBERLAIN, Joseph. On the privileges of Irish tenants.
2 pp. Dublin, Irish Loyal and Patriotic Union, 1887
A.

9541 COOKE-TRENCH, Thomas. Irish landowners convention. Replies to queries on the subject of the sale and purchase of land.
32 pp. Dublin, printed by Humphrey & Armour, 1887
N.

9542 CRILLY, Daniel. No. 13. The Irish question. Irish evictions.
tables. 20 pp. London, Irish Press Agency, 1887
C., N.

9543 CUNNINGHAM, William. Political economy treated as an empirical science. A syllabus of lectures.
32 pp. Cambridge, Macmillan and Bowes, 1887
T.

9544 Dominion of Canada Pacific Railway and North-West territories.
map. table of contents. table. 34 pp. n.p., [1887]
N.

9545 ERCK, Wentworth. Dr. Erck's report (submitted to No. 2 committee, [Irish landowners' convention], but not adopted) on compensation and public charges.
16 pp. Dublin, printed by Gibbs, 1887
D.

9546 ——. On Irish mortgages and family charges.
16 pp. Dublin, printed by Gibbs, 1887
D.

9547 ——. Some remarks on purchase [of land].
8 pp. Dublin, printed by Gibbs, 1887
D.

9548 EVANS, Frederick W. A workman's view of the Irish question. A letter to English working men on the Irish difficulty in the aspect of a great labour question, and on their interest in a just and satisfactory settlement of it.
16 pp. London, National Press Agency, 1887
B.

9549 Evictions in Ireland from 1st January to 30th June, 1886. Preliminary statement and returns (with appendices).
table of contents. tables. appendices. 24 pp. London & Dublin, Irish Loyal and Patriotic Union, 1887
D., N.
See 9604.

9550 FERRÉ, Emmanuel. L'Irlande. La crise agraire et politique. Ses causes—ses dangers—sa solution.
64 pp. Paris, Perrin, 1887
N.

9551 FOOTE, George William. Royal paupers: a radical's contribution to the jubilee. Showing what royalty does for the people and what the people do for royalty.
32 pp. 2nd ed. London, Progressive Publishing Company, 1887
B.

9552 FRASER, William. Profitable farming for bad times. Prize essay of the Royal Agricultural Society of Ireland.
38 pp. Dublin, printed at 'Farmer's Gazette' office, 1887
N.

9553 GILES, Richard W. A few words to railway passengers and railway proprietors. By one of themselves.
tables. 22 pp. London, T. G. Johnson, 1887
T.

9554 HALL, Wilhelmina L. Boarding-out, as a method of pauper education and a check on hereditary pauperism. A paper read at the Birmingham meeting of the British association for the advancement of science, Sept., 1886.
appendices. 58 pp. London, Hatchards, 1887
T.

9555 HARRISON, Frederick. Mr. Gladstone!—or anarchy!
16 pp. London, National Press Agency, [1887?]
B., Q.

9556 HARVEY, Frederick Burn. Tithes and tithe rent charge. Paper read at the rural-decanal conference of Ivinghoe in the diocese of Oxford.
44 pp. London, E. W. Allen, 1887
T.

9557 HILL, lord George Augustus. Facts from Gweedore.
tables. appendices. 50 pp. 5th ed. Londonderry, Sentinel Office, 1887
N.
See 7446.

9558 HODGKIN, Thomas. Think it out. A lecture on the question of home rule for Ireland.
40 pp. London, Scott, 1887
N.

9559 Ireland in 1887. Part I. Proceedings at assizes. Part II. Extracts from proceedings of national league branches.
100 pp. Dublin & London, Irish Loyal and Patriotic Union, 1887
D.

9560 Irish home industries association.
32 pp. Dublin, 1887
A.

9561 The Irish land question. Proceedings and speeches at the landowners' convention, held on September 14th and 15th, 1887. At the Leinster Hall, Molesworth St., Dublin.
24 pp. Dublin, 1887
N.

9562 Irish landowners' convention: Preliminary report of the executive committee, to be submitted to the Irish landowners' convention, on Tuesday, 13th December, 1887.
20 pp. Dublin, 1887
D., N., Q.

9563 Irish press agency. Leaflets nos. 4, 17, 18, 20, 35.
London, [1887?]
B.
Leaflets on the land question in Ireland.

9564 JACKSON, M. B. Foreign loans and depression of trade. Article No. 2. Local government. And the Irish problem.
8 pp. Ilfracombe, Twiss, 1887
T.

——. Another issue, described as 'Article no 3'.
8 pp. London, P. S. King, 1887
T.

9565 JONES, E. Brandram. Political economy of agriculture or the puzzle of today.
table [in] appendix. 82 pp. London, W. Ridgway, 1887
T.

9566 Land law (Ireland) Act, 1887, with new rules under the land act.
32 pp. Dublin, Humphrey & Armour, 1887
Q.

9567 LEVIN, T. Woodhouse. 'The logic of money'. An essay on the principles of currency, and the theory of bi-metallism.
42 pp. London, G. Bell, 1887
T.

9568 Local government in Ireland.
24 pp. n.p., [1887?]
Q., T.

9569 Low prices in connection with free trade, gold and silver and the Manchester ship canal, by a successful business man.
24 pp. London, J. Heywood, 1887
T.

9570 M'KENNA, Sir Joseph Neale. The Irish land question. Where the requisite funds for its solution are to be found, without trenching on or imperilling the proceeds of British taxes. The question considered and answered in connection with Mr. Gladstone's taxation of Ireland from 1853 to the present time.
tables. 38 pp. London, W. Ridgway, 1887
N., T.

9571 MANNING, Henry Edward, cardinal. The rights and dignity of labour. By the cardinal archbishop of Westminster.
24 pp. London, Burns, 1887
G.

9572 MEDLEY, George W. Fair trade unmasked; or, notes on the minority report of the royal commission on the depression of trade & industry.
96 pp. London, printed by Cassell, 1887
B.

Cobden Club pamphlet.

9573 MONTAGUE, Francis Charles. Technical education. A summary of the report of the royal commission appointed to inquire into the state of technical instruction. With a preface by Sir Bernhard Samuelson, bart., M.P., chairman of the commission.
68 pp. London, Cassell, 1887
B.

Cobden Club pamphlet.

9574 MOORE, Harold E. Agricultural co-operation: being a paper read at the Shire Hall, Chelmsford, at a meeting of the Essex chamber of agriculture, on January 7th, 1887.
28 pp. London, Simpkin, Marshall, 1887
T.

9575 NEUMAN, B. Paul. Home rule. An address to working men.
40 pp. London, National Press Agency, 1887
B.

9576 NEYMARCK, Alfred. Les dettes publiques européennes.
tables. 104 pp. 2nd ed. Paris, Guillaumin, 1887
T.

9577 [NICKERSON, D.] Is free trade a mistake? Dedicated to the production of England, both capital and labour. By Don't Care.
28 pp. Southsea, 'Hampshire Post', 1887
T.

9578 NORMAN, Sir Henry. Bodyke. A chapter in the history of Irish landlordism. Reprinted with several additional chapters from the 'Pall Mall Gazette' and illustrated with sketches from instantaneous photographs by the author.
tables. illustrations. 78 pp. London, T. Fisher Unwin, 1887
B., N., Q., U.

9579 PEARSON, Karl. The moral basis of socialism.
32 pp. London, W. Reeves, [1887]
T.

9580 ——. Socialism, its theory and practice.
32 pp. 2nd ed. London, W. Reeves, 1887
T.

9581 PETRIE, Alfred Ernest. Labour and independence: or profitable work for those in need of it.
40 pp. London, E. Stanford, 1887
T.

9582 PHELPS, Lancelot Ridley. Poor law and charity: a paper read in the common room of Keble College, March 9th, 1887.
16 pp. Oxford, B. H. Blackwell, 1887
T.

9583 PILKINGTON, William. Help for Ireland.
92 pp. 5th ed. London, J. Heywood, 1887
T.

On agricultural improvement.

9584 Proceedings and speeches of the landowners' convention held on September 14th and 15th, 1887, at the Leinster Hall, Molesworth St., Dublin.
24 pp. Dublin, 1887
N.

9585 RAWLINSON, Joshua. Bimetallism for beginners. A paper read to the Burnley literary and scientific club. February 8th, 1887.
tables. 24 pp. Manchester & London, J. Heywood, 1887
T.

9586 RELTON, William. Saving and growing money; with practical instructions for judging some investment accounts.
36 pp. Manchester & London, J. Heywood, 1887
T.

9587 ROUNDELL, Charles Savile. A plea for the Irish people. An address delivered before the Bentham liberal association, on November 11th, 1887.
46 pp. Skipton, Edmundson, [1887]

B.

9588 SARGANT, George Herbert. Farthing dinners.
20 pp. 2nd ed. London, Simpkin Marshall, Birmingham, Cornish Bros., 1887

T.

9589 A short study of the land question. How it may be settled by the Irish parliament. By 'Concordia'.
26 pp. Dublin, Sealy, Bryers & Walker, 1887

N.

9590 SINTON, John. The Irish question: a threefold question: home government, land, and drink: by an Irish quaker tenant farmer.
12 pp. Dublin, R. D. Webb, 1887

Q.

9591 SMITH, Arthur M. The creed of a political economist.
40 pp. London & Edinburgh, Williams and Norgate, 1887

T.

9592 SMITH, C. M. Trade depression and wasted resources: with some remarks on popular government in New South Wales.
42 pp. Sydney, Turner & Henderson, 1887

T.

9593 SMITH, W. Compton. The social democrats.
32 pp. London, J. Byland, 1887

T.

9594 ——. Socialism. An address delivered to the Stratford new town conservative working men's club.
30 pp. London, J. Byland, 1887

T.

9595 SPENCE, J. C. Freedom—our birthright. A protest against taxes.
50 pp. Newcastle-upon-Tyne, Lambert, 1887

T.

9596 TERRELL, Arthur à Beckett. Trade and currency.
30 pp. London, Effingham Wilson, 1887

T.

9597 The tithe, the parson and the farmer, with ancient fables, mainly applicable to the tithe agitation amongst the Welsh farmers and labourers, by a countryman.
48 pp. London, Griffith, Farran, Okeden and Welsh, 1887

T.

9598 TWINING, Louisa. A letter on some matters of poor law administration, addressed (by kind permission) to the right hon. the president of the local government board.
appendices. 70 pp. London, W. Ridgway, 1887

T.

9599 UNDERHILL, Arthur. Leasehold enfranchisement.
46 pp. 2nd ed. London, Cassell, [1887]

B.

9600 WESSLAU, O. E. Rational banking (the remedy for depression in trade) versus bank monopoly, by O. E. Wesslau. Edited by Bancroft Cooke.
76 pp. London, Elliot Stock, 1887

T.

9601 WESTGARTH, William. Sketch of the nature and limits of a science of economics.
table of contents. 50 pp. London, printed by Mathieson, 1887

N.

9602 WILSON, John. A cottage tenant's views concerning the transfer of land by registration.
32 pp. London, Alexander and Shepheard, [1887]

T.

9603 WRIGHT, Buchan W. Inventive genius versus free trade or fair trade and no favour.
8 pp. London, W. Dawson, 1887

T.

9604 A year's evictions in Ireland. January to December 1886. Statement and returns; with appendices.
tables. 24 pp. Dublin, Irish Loyal and Patriotic Union, 1887

A., D.

See 9549.

1888

9605 Arran relief fund, 1888. Report of committee.
4 pp. Dublin, 1888

A.

9605 BAILEY, William F. Local and centralized government in Ireland. A sketch of the existing systems.
64 pp. London, Cassell, Dublin, Hodges, Figgis, 1888

D., Q.

9607 Bimetallism and agriculture.
24 pp. Manchester, printed by 'Courier' printing works, 1888

T.

9608 BOND, Henry Simon. Handbook to the stamp duties. A treatise upon the stamp acts and the law and practice of stamping documents.
tables and appendices. 44 pp. London, Waterlow, 1888

T.

9609 BULL, H. Problems in fixed ratio bimetallism.
16 pp. London, Effingham Wilson, 1888

T.

9610 The Canadian Pacific Railway.
illustrations. map. 48 pp. Montreal, 1888

N.

9611 CARTER, Joseph Robert. Stock exchange securities in 1877 and 1887 compared.
tables. 14 pp. London, F. Mathieson, 1888

T.

9612 CLANCY, John J. The position of the Irish tenant. A reply.
12 pp. London, Irish Press Agency, 1888

N.

9613 The diminution of pauperism. Holland and poverty.
4 pp. London, Howard Association, 1888
N.

9614 DONELAN, Dermot O'C. Irish industrial resources. Young forests and their industries. Paper from wood, chemical products, charcoal, wicker trades, pine wool, etc.
48 pp. Dublin, M. H. Gill, 1888
A.

9615 Dublin portland cement. A few facts about a successful Irish industry.
table of contents. diagram. 74 pp. Dublin, printed by Browne and Nolan, 1888
A.

9616 [ERCK, Wentworth.] Scheme for dealing with Irish mortgages. Together with a proposed amendment, extension, & continuance of lord Ashbourne's purchase act. Note on the result to owners of any large measure of purchase. [by W.E.]
12 pp. Dublin, printed by C. W. Gibbs, 1888
Q.

9617 The facts and fallacies of National League finance brought up to date.
10 pp. Dublin and London, Irish Loyal and Patriotic Union, 1888
D.

The Recess series, 1887–8.

9618 Facts for Englishmen and Scotchmen about Ireland, being an answer to Irish Press Agency leaflet no. 8, by a member of the executive committee of the Ulster loyalist anti-repeal union.
tables. appendices. 24 pp. n.p., 1888
T.

9619 FIELDEN, John C. The silver question, considered in relation to the wages, employment and cost of living of the working classes; an address by J. C. Fielden, esq., at the Bi-metallic conference, Manchester, 4th April, 1888.
14 pp. Manchester, Bimetallic League, 1888
N., U.

9620 GRAY, J. C. How to start co-operative stores. A paper prepared with a view to facilitate the formation of co-operative societies.
8 pp. Manchester, Co-operative Union Ltd., [1888]
N.

9621 GUYOT, Yves. The French corn laws. Translated by J. W. Probyn.
tables. 32 pp. London, Cassell, 1888
T.

Cobden Club pamphlet.

9622 HARRIMAN, D. G. Protection vs. free trade. The trial of both doctrines in the United States from 1783 to 1888. Historical statement of the results. Reprinted by the courtesy of the Union League Club of Brooklyn.
tables. 20 pp. New York, The American Protective Tariff League, 1888
U.

9623 HARRIS, Alfred. The revival of industries in Ireland. Notes made during a tour in October, 1887.
table of contents. 40 pp. London, P. S. King, Dublin, M. H. Gill, 1888
N., U.

9624 Ireland from one or two neglected points of view. By the author of 'Hints to country bumpkins', etc.
appendix. 194 pp. London, Hatchards, 1888
T.

9625 Irish home industries association (founded by the countess of Aberdeen). Report of the executive committee for the year ending April, 1888, to the central council of the association.
12 pp. [Dublin, 1888]
N.

9626 Irish landowners' convention. Second report of the executive committee [to be submitted to the Irish landowners' convention, on Friday, 27th April, 1888].
tables. appendices. 52 pp. Dublin, printed by Humphrey and Armour, 1888
D.

9627 Irish Loyal and Patriotic Union: Conspicuous moderation.
12 pp. Dublin & London, [c. 1888]
Q.

9628 Irish Loyal and Patriotic Union. The year's work, 1887. An account of the operations of the Irish Loyal and Patriotic Union, during the year 1887, with details of the meetings and publications and a specially prepared map.
tables. appendices. map. 54 pp. Dublin, Irish Loyal and Patriotic Union, 1888
D.

9629 The London companies and their Irish tenantry.
tables. 28 pp. Dublin, 'Freeman's Journal', 1888
D.

9630 MACDOWALL, Alex. B. Facts about Ireland. A curve-history of recent years.
table of contents. tables. graphs. 32 pp. London, E. Stanford, 1888
N.

9631 MARGETTS, J. W. Downfall of Mammon.
40 pp. London, Alexander and Shepheard, 1888
T.

9632 MAVOR, James. On wage statistics and wage theories. A paper read before the economic section of the British association at Bath, September, 1888.
appendices. 20 pp. Edinburgh, W. Brown, 1888
T.

9633 MAXWELL, William. Lecture on wholesale co-operation a necessity.
28 pp. Manchester, Central Co-operative Board, 1888
T.

9634 MENGER, Carl. Contribution à la théorie du capital. Traduction par Charles Secretan. Extrait de la Revue d'Économie politique Novembre-Decembre, 1888.
20 pp. Paris, Larose et Forcel, 1888
N.

9635 MILLER, E. P.   Number 6. The American protective tariff league. Fallacies of free trade. Protection the farmer's only security.
tables. 32 pp. 4th edition. New York, 1888
U.

9636 MILLER, Edward.   Free trade? Protection? or encouragement? A letter to the right hon. lord Randolph Churchill, M.P.
16 pp. London, Hatchards, 1888
T.

9637 Mr. Gladstone on the rejection of Mr. Parnell's tenant relief bill of 1886 and the plan of campaign.
14 pp. Dublin and London, Irish Loyal and Patriotic Union, 1888
D.

9638 MONTAGUE, Francis Charles.   Local administration in the United States and in the United Kingdom.
32 pp. London, Cassell, 1888
T.

Cobden Club pamphlet.

9639 MONTGOMERY, Hugh de F.   An Irish landowners' view of purchase. Speech by H. de F. Montgomery at the Irish landowners' convention, Dublin, December 13th, 14th and 15th, 1887.
6 pp. no t.p. n.p., [1888]
D.

9640 NICHOLSON, Joseph Shield.   The joint standard consistent with sound political economy. An address at the Bimetallic conference, Manchester, 4th April, 1888.
14 pp. Manchester, Bimetallic League, 1888
N.

9641 NULTY, Thomas, bishop of Meath.   Cause of poverty explained. Land nationalization the only true remedy. An essay on the land question.
8 pp. Cork [etc.], Eagle Printing Works, [1888]
S.

9642 PATTERSON, Richard.   Mercantile Ireland versus home rule, by a Belfast merchant. Reprinted by permission from the 'National Review' of January, 1888.
tables. 16 pp. Belfast, Ulster Liberal Unionist Association, 1888
D.

9643 The plan of campaign illustrated. An account of the Ponsonby, Kingston, Lansdowne, O'Grady and Brooke estates.
tables. 24 pp. Dublin and London, Irish Loyal and Patriotic Union, 1888
D., T.

9644 PRENDERGAST, Segismundo Moret y.   The financial policy of William Pitt.
40 pp. London, Hatchards, 1888
T.

9645 The present position and claims of Irish landowners. By a member of the executive committee of the Irish landowners' convention.
16 pp. Dublin, printed by Humphrey and Armour, 1888
D.

9646 The proceedings of the Bimetallic conference, held at Manchester 4th and 5th April, 1888.
table. 128 pp. Manchester, the Bimetallic League, 1888
U.

9647 [REID, Herbert Lloyd.]   The budget proposals of 26th March, 1888; being a criticism subjointed to a work on taxation, now in the press, entitled, 'The British taxpayer and his wrongs'. By 'Finance'.
12 pp. London, Effingham Wilson, 1888
T.

9648 Remarks on the bill in relation to joint stock companies introduced into parliament by the right honourable the lord chancellor in the year 1888 and on contemplated legislation in reference to those corporations.
14 pp. London, printed by Ford & Turner, 1888
T.

9649 RICCA-SALERNO, Giuseppe.   Le dottrine finanziarie in Inghilterra tra la fine del Secolo XVII e la prima metà del XVIII. (estratto dal Giornale degli Economisti. Vo. III. Fasc. 6.)
26 pp. Bologna, Garagnani, 1888
N.

9650 ROLLESTON, T. W.   Boycotting. A reply to Mr. Laing.
16 pp. Dublin, E. Ponsonby, 1888
C.

9651 Sales of tenants interests in Ireland. Extracted from the daily press, January, 1887, to April, 1888.
tables. 20 pp. Dublin and London, Irish Loyal and Patriotic Union, 1888
D.

9652 SCHELLING, P. M.   Pauperism, its cause and remedy.
78 pp. London, W. Reeves, [1888]
T.

9653 SEYMOUR, Henry.   Anarchy; theory and practice.
12 pp. London, the author, 1888
T.

9654 SHAW, James Johnston.   Mr. Gladstone's two Irish policies: 1868 and 1886. A letter to an Ulster liberal elector.
40 pp. London, Marcus Ward, Belfast, Royal Ulster Works, 1888
B., D., L., N.

9655 SHAW-LEFEVRE, George John.   Incidents of coercion. A journal of visits to Ireland in 1882 and 1888. Second edition.
202 pp. London, Kegan Paul, Trench, 1888
U.

9656 VAN DEN BERG, H. P. J.   An inquiry into the influence of falling exchange on the prosperity of a nation.
tables. 32 pp. London, Effingham Wilson, 1888
T.

9657 WEBB, Sidney.   The Hampstead society for the study of socialism. (In correspondence with the Fabian Society) Tract no. 1. The progress of socialism: a lecture.
18 pp. London, printed by Foulger & Co., 1888
U.

9658 ——. What socialism means; a call to the uncon-
verted.
7 pp. 4th ed. London, W. Reeves, 1888
N.

9659 WHITE, C. Arnold. The Deeds of Arrangement Act,
1887, with rules, forms, and scales of fees; also an introduction
and practical notes.
tables in appendix. 54 pp. London, H. Shaw, 1888
T.

9660 WOOD, James. Farmers and the tariff. Remarks made
at Bedford, N.Y., September 15th, 1888.
14 pp. n.p., 1888
U.

1889

9661 AVELING, F. W. The Irish question from the conquest
of Ireland to the suicide of Pigott, 1169–1889.
table of contents. index. appendices. 66 pp. 3rd ed. Taunton,
printed by 'Somerset Express', 1889
D.

9662 BOTELLA, Cristobal. Naturaleza y estado actual de la
economía política. Discurso leido en el Alteneo de Madrid
con motivo de la apertura de la seccion de Ciencias Morales y
Politicas. Curso de 1888 á 1889.
36 pp. Madrid, de los Rios, 1889
N.

9663 BOUSFIELD, Edward Tenney. The bread supply of the
United Kingdom; a question of national defence.
14 pp. London, Courier co., 1889
T.

9664 CLEAVER, T. E. Every working-man his own landlord. Containing a reprint of 'an act to enable every working-
man to become his own land-lord'.
32 pp. London, Simpkin, Marshall, Hamilton, Kent, 1889
T.

9665 Co-operation versus private trading. A public discussion held in the Waterloo rooms, Glasgow, Feb. 5th, 1889,
between Mr. J. Deans, of Kilmarnock (representing the
Central co-operative board) and Mr. R. Walker, of Glasgow
(representing the Traders' defence association of Scotland).
32 pp. Manchester, Central co-operative board, 1889
N.

9666 CUNNINGHAM, William. The Comtist criticism of
economic science.
10 pp. London, printed by Spottiswoode, 1889
N.

9667 DONOVAN, Robert. Trades' unionism: its principles,
its history and its uses.
24 pp. Dublin, 'The Nation' office, 1889
B.

9668 ERCK, Wentworth. A review of the present position
of landlords and incumbrancers, with the object of shewing
that a readjustment of private charges on land has been
rendered necessary by recent legislation, and indicating how

such readjustment may be equitably and beneficially made,
and any gigantic purchase scheme avoided.
tables. diag. appendix. 80 pp. Dublin, W. McGee, London,
P. S. King, 1889
U.

9669 FARRER, Thomas Henry, 1st baron. The sugar convention.
136 pp. London, Cassell, 1889
T.

Cobden Club pamphlet.

9670 FISHER, J. Greevz. Voluntary taxation.
30 pp. Leeds, the author, 1889
T.

9671 FREAM, W. Agricultural Canada: a record of progress.
maps. illust. tables. 76 pp. London, printed by McCorquodale,
1889
P.

9672 [GARSON, William.] Should feu-duties be taxed? By
Vindex.
40 pp. Edinburgh, D. Douglas, 1889
T.

9673 GRAY, J. C. The system of credit as practised by co-
operative societies.
tables. 32 pp. Manchester, Central co-operative board, [1889]
T.

9674 High wages. Respectfully dedicated to the working men
of the United Kingdom.
tables. appendix. 72 pp. Dundee, W. Kidd, London, Simpkin,
Marshall, 1889
T.

9675 HURTADO, Jose M. Piernas y. Estudios economicos;
dos escritos sobre el concepto y estado actual de la economia
politica y otros tres acerca de la llamada cuestion social.
table of contents. 174 pp. Madrid, Polo, 1889
N.

9676 The incidence of local taxation. The national remedy.
By a member of the college of justice.
tables. appendix. 46 pp. Edinburgh, W. Blackwood & son,
1889
T.

9677 Interest: is it just or not? A letter addressed to the
native traders of West Africa by G. B. Ollivant & Co.
tables. 8 pp. Manchester, Taylor, Garnett, Evans, 1889
T.

9678 The limits of free trade. By a liberal.
tables. 54 pp. London, Trübner, 1889
T.

9679 Local taxation. An inquiry into the proposal to
subject feu-duties and ground rents to local rates. By H. H. S.
62 pp. Edinburgh, D. Douglas, 1889
T.

9680 M'FADDEN, James. The present and the past of the agrarian struggle in Gweedore with letters on railway extension in Donegal.
tables. appendices. 150 pp. Londonderry, printed at the Derry Journal works, 1889

U.

9681 MARSHALL, Alfred. Inaugural address delivered at the twenty-first annual co-operative congress held at Ipswich, June 10, 11 & 12, 1889.
32 pp. Manchester, Central co-operative board, 1889

T., U.

9682 MENGER, Carl. Grundzüge einer Klassifikation der Wirtschaftswissenschaften. Sonderabdruck aus der Jahrbüchern für Nationalökonomie und Statistik, herausgeg. von Prof. J. Conrad, N.F. Bd. XIX.
32 pp. Jena, G. Fischer, 1889

N.

9683 [PATTERSON, Hugh Gill.] A new invention. Eviction by proxy in Ireland. Is it good law? The Irish farmer partially protected by late legislation from direct landlord spoliation, but still wholly in the power of estate mortgagees, as demonstrated by the Scottish Provident Institution v. Hugh Gill Patterson.
52 pp. Belfast, Circle co-operative printing co., 1889

U.

9684 PLAMER, Charles John. Money: prices and the report of the currency commission on Bi-metallism. A paper read before the Ipswich scientific society, February 6th, 1889.
tables. 16 pp. Ipswich, printed by S. & W. J. King, 1889

T.

9685 PRASCHKAUER, Maximilian. Antimetallism.
20 pp. London, the author, 1889

T.

9686 RAWLINSON, Joshua. The silver question as it affects the cotton trade. A paper read before the Manchester chartered accountants students' society, 1889.
26 pp. Manchester, J. Heywood, 1889

T.

9687 The remedy for landlordism or, a free land fund with home rule.
appendix. 142 pp. 2nd ed. London, Kegan Paul, Trench, Trübner & Co., 1889

T.

9688 RUSSELL, T. W. Disturbed Ireland. The plan of campaign estates.
illustrations. table of contents. tables. 152 pp. London, Truslove & Shirley, 1889

N.

9689 STIRLING, James. Trade unionism: with remarks on the report of the commissioners on trades' unions. Reprinted from the second edition, 1869.
tables. 56 pp. Glasgow, J. Maclehose, 1889

U.

9690 SWALLOW, William. Credit trading in relation to co-operative societies.
8 pp. Manchester, Central co-operative board, 1889

T.

9691 TUKE, James Hack. The condition of Donegal. Letters reprinted from 'the Times' of May 20th, 28th and June 29th, 1889 with further suggestions for the improvement and development of the congested districts of Ireland and promotion of light railways, fisheries etc.
map. table of contents and tables. 50 pp. London, W. Ridgway, Dublin, Hodges, Figgis, 1889

N.

9692 VALPY, R. A. An inquiry into the conditions and occupations of the people in central London.
tables. 28 pp. London, E. Stanford, 1889

T.

9693 Verbatim report of the debate in St. James's Hall, July 2nd, 1889. The single tax v. social-democracy: which will most benefit the people? Between Henry George and H. M. Hyndman.
28 pp. London, printed at the 'Justice' printery, 1889

T.

9694 WATSON, Reuben. The causes of deficiencies in friendly societies, and some remarks on hazardous occupations.
tables. 24 pp. Manchester, J. Heywood, 1889

T.

9695 What is rent? How should the Irish land question be settled?
48 pp. Dublin, M. H. Gill, 1889

P., U.

9696 A word to investors of fifty pounds to fifty thousand pounds. By E. M.
table in appendix. 28 pp. Edinburgh, Bell and Bradfute, 1889

T.

1890

9697 BIRKMYRE, William. Old age pensions.
appendices. 44 pp. 3rd ed. Glasgow, Aird & Coghill, [189–?]

T.

9698 CRAWFORD, Robert F. Letters and leaflets on usury, also extracts from fathers of the church, bishops, philosophers, poets and historians denouncing this infamous national sin, the cause of poverty, grinding toil, anxious care and the social and moral tyranny that debases all men.
appendix. 28 pp. London, the author, [189–?]

T.

9699 ——. A political essay on money: advocating the desirability of forcing its circulation through society.
diags. 16 pp. London, the author, [189–?]

T.

9700 EDGEWORTH, Francis Ysidro. Syllabus of lectures on political economy. Delivered for King's College, the London society for university extension, and other institutions.
8 pp. n.p., [189–?]

N.

9701 Fabian tracts, no. 1. Why are the many poor?
4 pp. London, [189–?]

Q.

'According to tradition . . . [this pamphlet] was drafted by W. L. Phillips'—PEASE, E. R. *History of the Fabian Society.* First issued 1884; this edition after 1890 according to advertisement on back.

9702 NICHOLSON, Joseph Shield. State management of land.
8 pp. (no. t.p., not paginated, uncorrected proof). n.p., [189–?]

N.

9703 Purchase of land acts. Memorandum for the information of tenants as to obtaining advances from the Irish land commission for the purchase of their holdings; the terms for repayment of the same; and the conditions imposed while such advances are outstanding.
tables. appendix. 18 pp. Dublin, Her Majesty's Stationery Office, [189–?]

N.

9704 ROSS, Owen Charles Dalhousie. The depression in agriculture and trade: its cause and remedy.
tables. 16 pp. London, W. Ridgway, [189–?]

T.

9705 Social restoration.
30 pp. London, E. Marlborough, [189–?]

T.

9706 THOMPSON, Alexander M. That blessed word— Liberty.
16 pp. London, 'Clarion' newspaper, [189–?]

T.

'Clarion' pamphlet No. 4.

9707 [WEBB, Beatrice.] Committee of inquiry on the control of industry.
12 pp. Letchworth, Garden City press, [189–?]

U.

9708 WEBB, Sidney, and WEBB, Beatrice. Principles of the labour party.
4 pp. (no t.p.) London, [189–?]

N.

9709 ASPDIN, James. 'Our boys': what shall we do with them? Or, emigration the real solution of the problem.
illus. 32 pp. Manchester, J. Heywood, [1890?]

T.

9710 BRECKON, John Robert. North eastern railway company. An analysis of the capital expended from 1868 to 1889 showing the annual outlay upon the numerous works constructed during that period; also the profits derived from passenger goods and mineral traffic during those years.
tables. appendix. 42 pp. Newcastle-upon-Tyne, Lambert, London, Simpkin, Marshall, Hamilton, Kent, 1890

T.

9711 BYCRAFT, E. S. Labour, capital and consumption.
12 pp. Manchester, the Co-operative union, 1890

T.

9712 DUFFY, Sir Charles Gavan. The land purchase bill. Two letters addressed to the archbishop of Cashel.
36 pp. Dublin, Browne and Nolan, 1890

N.

9713 GIDE, Charles. L'école Nouvelle. Conférence faite à Genève le 28 Mars 1890 par M. Charles Gide. Tiré de l'ouvrage intitulé *Quatre écoles d'Économie sociale* publié par la Société Chrétienne Suisse d'Économie Sociale.
60 pp. Genève, Richter, 1890

N.

9714 The government land bill and Mr. Chamberlain's proposal (Being letters to the Times, Economist, and Scotsman). By an Irish Landlord.
32 pp. London, P. S. King, 1890

N.

9715 HYNDMAN, Henry Mayers. Socialism and slavery.
14 pp. London, W. Reeves, [1890]

T.

9716 Irish loyal and patriotic union. Publications issued during the year 1889.
tables. 452 pp. Dublin & London, 1890

Q.

9717 Irish protestant home rule leaflets.—no. 10. Mr. T. W. Russell's plantation scheme: A plain statement for Ulster farmers.
4 pp. Dublin, printed by R. D. Webb, [1890]

U.

9718 LINTON, E. Lynn. About Ireland.
tables. 74 pp. London, Methuen, 1890

D.

9719 MACKAY, T. Working class insurance.
tables. 78 pp. London, E. Stanford, 1890

T.

9720 O'CONNELL, John Robert. A plea for a peasant proprietary for Ireland.
28 pp. Dublin, Warren, 1890

N.

9721 [PENTLAND, William.] A warning from Westmeath!! The great Irish-American confidence trick. Startling facts!! Newspaper patriots and the mighty dollar. By an evicted tenant.
22 pp. Mullingar, 1890

C.

9722 The plan of campaign. The Ponsonby estate.
28 pp. Dublin, Liberal union of Ireland, 1890

A., N.

9723 PLAYFAIR, Sir Lyon, later 1st baron Playfair of St. Andrews. The tariffs of the United States in relation to free trade. Speech delivered in Leeds, 13th November, 1890.
32 pp. London, Cassell, 1890

T.

Cobden Club pamphlet.

9724 ROBARTS, N. F. Strikes and lock-outs.
20 pp. London, Whittingham, 1890
T.

9725 ROBERTSON, John M. Over-population.
24 pp. London, R. Forder, 1890
T.

9726 ROUNDELL, Charles Savile. The progress of the working classes during the reign of the queen: 'a goodly record'.
appendix. 50 pp. Skipton, printed by Edmondson, [1890]
T.

9727 STAREY, John Helps. The paddy tax in Ceylon. A letter addressed to the Cobden club, with preface.
appendix. 30 pp. London, Cassell, 1890
T.

Cobden Club pamphlet.

9728 Travelling tax abolition committee. Two memorials to the Prime Minister and the Chancellor of the exchequer, to which is prefixed a brief history of the railway passenger duty.
tables. 12 pp. London, printed by Bedford Press, 1890
T.

9729 The triumph of free trade. The annual general meeting of the Cobden club 1890, including an address by Mr. G. W. Medley on 'the triumph of free trade' and speeches by Mr. T. B. Potter, M.P., Mr. I. S. Leadam, Mr. C. S. Seale-Hayne and other members.
tables. 40 pp. n.p. 1890
T.

Cobden Club pamphlet.

9730 TURNER, William. Revival of trade.
tables. appendix. 68 pp. London, Elliot Stock, 1890
T.

9731 TUSTIN, Frank. The great war between capital and labour and how to emancipate the working classes within twelve months.
8 pp. London, printed by Thos. Williams, 1890
T.

9732 [WHITE, J. C.] London and Londonderry. Transactions of three centuries considered from a historical and legal standpoint.
80 pp. London, Marcus Ward, 1890
B.

1891

9733 BANCROFT, Hubert. England and free trade versus the United States and protection.
12 pp. London, the Authors' publishing association, [1891?]
T.

9734 The Companies (winding-up) act, 1890. Table shewing principal steps to be taken from presentation of petition to winding-up order.
4 pp. Manchester, G. Floyd, [1891?]
T.

9735 COSTELLOE, Benjamin Francis Conn. The reform of the poor law.
16 pp. London, Catholic truth society, 1891
T.

9736 DAWSON, Joshua. Injustice of recent and present (1891) tithes, by Joshua Dawson, a Yorkshire farmer.
24 pp. Bradford, M. Field, 1891
T.

9737 ELLISSEN, Adolf. Banking questions asked by the chancellor of the exchequer with an attempted reply.
tables. appendices. 16 pp. no t.p. London, Gilbert & Field, [1891]
T.

9738 English land restoration league. Special Report 1891. Among the Suffolk labourers with the 'red van'.
appendix. 20 pp. London, offices of the English land restoration league, 1891
T.

9739 FOTRELL, George, and FOTRELL, John George. The land purchase acts explained.
tables. 60 pp. Dublin, M. H. Gill, 1891
T.

9740 Further remarks on suggested alterations in the Bank act of 1844 by an ex-bank manager.
20 pp. n.p., 1891
T.

9741 [GARBETT, Edward Lacy.] War on capital: With the necessary tables.
tables. 20 pp. London, W. Reeves, 1891
T.

9742 GIBSON, William. The future of political economy.
14 pp. Oxford & London, J. Parker, 1891
T.

9743 GORST, Sir John. The labour question. A speech by Sir John Gorst, M.P., at Chatham, February 12th, 1891.
12 pp. Birmingham, 'Birmingham Daily Gazette', 1891
T.

9744 HALL, W. H. Bullock. Fruit-growing and market-gardening as Irish industries.
14 pp. Cambridge, printed at the University Press, 1891
D.

9745 HAYNES, Thomas Henry. International fishery disputes.
maps. 24 pp. London, Cassell, 1891
T.

9746 HERBERT, Auberon. The rights of property.
appendices. 50 pp. London, Liberty and property defence league, [1891]
T.

9747 [HITCHINGS, J. J.] Income tax to pay or not? By the ex-crown surveyor of the income tax enquiry office.
70 pp. London, The income tax enquiry office, [1891]
T.

9748 INNES, ——. Technical instruction in agriculture. Suggestions to county councils.
24 pp. Edinburgh, W. Blackwood & son, 1891
T.

9749 KINGSMILL MOORE, H. £200,000 a year for Irish education: how may it be spent? Written at the request of the standing committee of the general synod of the church of Ireland.
56 pp. Dublin, Educational depository of the Church of Ireland Training college, 1891
L.

9750 LAMBERT, Agnes. School savings banks. A paper read at the catholic conference 1891.
8 pp. London, Catholic truth society, 1891
T.

9751 Memorandum on valuations of friendly societies.
8 pp. 2nd ed. London, Her Majesty's Stationery Office, 1891
T.

9752 NOLAN, Edmond. Catholic benefit societies. A paper read at the catholic conference 1891.
14 pp. London, Catholic truth society, 1891
T.

9753 An official handbook of information relating to the dominion of Canada.
table of contents. tables. map. plates. 84 pp. n.p., Government of Canada (Dept. of Agriculture), 1891
N.

9754 Ought landowners to bear a share of local taxation? By Justitia.
46 pp. Edinburgh, W. Green, 1891
T.

9755 RHODES, John Milson. Pauperism, past and present.
maps. tables. 112 pp. London, C. Knight, 1891
T.

9756 SAMUELSON, James. Boards of conciliation and arbitration for the settlement of labour disputes.
32 pp. London, Kegan Paul, Trench, Trübner, 1891
T.

9757 United British provinces. A sequel to the remedy for landlordism or, a free land fund with home rule. With extracts on the analysis of land values and their taxation from 'An essay on the right of property in land' by William Ogilvie.
12 pp. London, Sheppard and St. John, 1891
T.

9758 WATSON, John. Tenancy and ownership: Cobden club prize essay.
120 pp. London, Cassell, 1891
T.

Cobden Club pamphlet.

9759 The way out of it or how the working community may quickly become millionaires. By J. W. M.
36 pp. London, Kegan Paul, Trench, Trübner, 1891
T.

1892

9760 ARMSDEN, John. Trade depressions, or the cause of 'cutting', and its remedy. Being an appeal to the commercial world.
32 pp. London, Wm. Reeves, [1892?]
T.

9761 BAKER, A. F. Banks and banking.
tables. 30 pp. London, 1892
T.

9762 BARRINGTON, Richard Manliffe. Eleven graphs showing prices of various Irish agricultural products for various periods between 1784 and 1892.
16 pp. Dublin, Walpole, 1892
N.

9763 BATE, John. Work, workers and wages.
appendix. 120 pp. London, Simpkin, Marshall, Hamilton, Kent, 1892
T.

9764 BOSANQUET, Bernard Tindal. Our banking system: and the sufficiency or insufficiency of our cash reserves.
34 pp. London, Effingham Wilson, 1892
T.

9765 BROWNFIELD, Arthur. The lock-out. A potters' guild. Proposal by Arthur Brownfield, (Master potter).
44 pp. Hanley, printed by the New Press printing co., 1892
T.

9766 CARRUTHERS, George Thompson. The units in exchange and a free currency: being suggestions for the employment of a unit of value in political economy, and the abolition of legal tenders in currency.
66 pp. London, E. Stanford, 1892
T.

9767 COATES, Charles. Capital and labour or how to avert strikes. Being a few suggestions and words of advice to masters and the working classes.
16 pp. Bristol, Arrowsmith, London, Simpkin, Marshall, Hamilton, Kent, 1892
T.

9768 COBB, Arthur Stanley. Metallic reserves and the meeting of parliament.
28 pp. London, Effingham Wilson, 1892
T.

9769 Congested districts board for Ireland: List of electoral divisions that are congested.
16 pp. Dublin, Her Majesty's Stationery Office, 1892
N.

9770 Congested districts board for Ireland. Report for 1892.
tables. maps. appendices. 56 pp. Dublin, Her Majesty's Stationery Office, 1892
N.

9771 CRAWFORD, William Sharman. Suggestions with reference to the necessity of constituting a national body to manage the local interests and local taxation of Ireland, in

connection with the imperial parliament, by W. Sharman Crawford, 1833. Published by John Cumming and S. Archer, Belfast. Re-printed, with preface, by W. H. Dodd, Q.C.
44 pp. Dublin, Sealy, Bryers and Walker, 1892
N., Q.

9772 [DE BRATH, Stanley.] Commerce and currency, two object lessons in ethics addressed to the British public. By V. C. Desertis.
tables. 78 pp. Allahabad, printed at the Pioneer press, 1892
T.

9773 DERFEL, Robert Jones. Common misconceptions about socialism.
16 pp. no. t.p. Manchester, the author, [1892?]
T.

9774 [——.] Socialism and the pope's encyclical. By Munullog.
56 pp. Manchester, the author, [1892?]
T.

9775 DOUGLAS, John Monteath. Gold and silver money: A vital British home question; loss and danger in present system, and remedies proposed; with tables of average prices of commodities and silver from 1846 till 1892.
appendix. tables. table of contents. 34 pp. London, Effingham Wilson, 1892
N., T.

9776 FOGG, William. Workers in cotton factories and the eight hours' day. An address delivered on November 16th, 1892.
64 pp. Manchester, J. Heywood, 1892
T.

9777 FOWLE, Thomas Welbanke. The friendly societies, and old age destitution. A proposed solution.
24 pp. Oxford, J. Parker, 1892
T.

9778 GRAHAME, James. Mr. Goschen's one pound note. A digest of parliamentary opinion on bank note issues, etc., 1797–1819. Also two letters, signed 'Liberal Unionist' (in the *Scotsman* newspaper) upon the note circulation of the kingdom in connection with Mr. Goschen's small note proposal.
tables. 32 pp. London, P. S. King, 1892
T.

9779 The Ground values delusion.
24 pp. London, Witherby, 1892
T.

'This pamphlet is taken from the proof now in the press of the forthcoming book entitled 'Land: its attractions and riches' which will be ready next April.'

9780 HART, C. Constitutional socialism.
26 pp. London, W. Reeves, [1892?]
T.

——. 24 pp. 2nd ed. London, W. Reeves, [1892?]
T.

9781 HILL, James. How to solve the labour problem.
12 pp. London, W. Ridgway, 1892
T.

9782 How to establish a fixed ratio between gold and silver. By F. A. A.
24 pp. London, Effingham Wilson, 1892
T.

9783 JENNINGS, H. J. The silver crisis.
28 pp. London, Effingham Wilson, 1892
T.

9784 JOYCE, P. W. The teaching of manual work in schools.
36 pp. London & Liverpool, G. Philip, [etc., etc.], 1892
N.

9785 KROPOTKIN, Peter Alexeivich, Prince. Le Salariat.
38 pp. 2nd ed. Paris, Bureau de la Revolte, 1892
N.

9786 Liberal Union of Ireland: Then and now. Ireland in 1886 and 1892.
tables. 40 pp. Dublin, the Liberal union of Ireland, 1892
N.

9787 MADDEN, Dodgson Hamilton. Land transfer and registration of title (Ireland) act, 1891.
50 pp. Dublin, W. McGee, London, W. Ridgway, 1892
N.

9788 MAZEPPA, Herman Taxis, count. A new yet ancient system of politics or problems of Great Britain at home.
60 pp. London, Simpkin, Marshall, Hamilton, Kent, 1892
T.

9789 The national philanthropic co-operative society. This book explains a new money making method for philanthropic and other special uses. By Uncle John's nephew.
50 pp. London, New Parcel Post, [1892?]
T.

9790 PALMER, Francis B. Private companies and syndicates, their formation and advantages; being a concise popular statement of the mode of converting a business into a private company, and of establishing and working private companies and syndicates for miscellaneous purposes.
50 pp. 7th ed. London, Stevens, 1892
T.

——. 58 pp. 10th ed. London, Stevens, 1892
T.

9791 PEEK, Francis. The workless, the thriftless and the worthless.
76 pp. 2nd ed. London, Isbister, 1892
T.

9792 PICOT, Georges Marie Réne. Self-help for labour. An address to the members of the Liberty and property defence league, Tuesday, Dec. 8th, 1891.
34 pp. London, Liberty and property defence league, 1892
T.

9793 The plan of campaign. Irish landlords and tenants. table of contents. tables. 52 pp. Dublin, Liberal union of Ireland, 1892

N.

9794 PLUNKETT, Horace. Report upon emigration to Canada.
table. 20 pp. Dublin, Her Majesty's Stationery Office, 1892

N.

9795 RAFFALOVICH, Arthur. Les socialistes allemands. Le programme d'Erfurt et la satire de M. Richter.
28 pp. Paris, Guillaumin, 1892

T.

9796 Rates and ground values. A review of 'The taxation of ground values' by J. Fletcher Moulton, Q.C.
24 pp. London, W. Ridgway, 1892

T.

Preface signed P.M.T.

9797 Register of charity organisation and relief societies in correspondence with the London Charity organisation society.
table. 68 pp. London, Charity organisation society, 1892

T.

9798 Report of the council of the chamber of commerce of Dublin for the year 1891 to the members of the association at the annual assembly held on the 26th of January, 1892.
tables. appendix. 76 pp. Dublin, printed by J. Falconer, 1892

D.

9799 SHARP, David. A scheme for a national system of rest-funds (or pensions) for working people.
16 pp. London, G. Philip, 1892

T.

9800 SHAW, George Bernard. The Fabian society; what it has done and how it has done it.
34 pp. London, Fabian society, 1892 (Fabian society tract, no. 41)

T.

9801 The silver problem: how it has arisen; its influence on trade; and a suggestion for its solution.
24 pp. London, Effingham Wilson, 1892

T.

9802 SWEENEY, Edward. The labour question as it is, with its solution.
10 pp. Liverpool, printed by S. R. Jones, 1892

T.

9803 TAYLOR, William. State pensions. A paper read before the Bath liberal association, on March 18th, 1892.
10 pp. Bristol, W. Lewis, 1892

T.

9804 TULLIS, John. Old age pensions: a scheme for the formation of a citizens' national union. A contribution towards the solution of the problem of pauperism.
appendix. 40 pp. London, P. S. King, 1892

T.

1893

9805 BAIN, Francis William. The unseen foundation of the 'unseen foundations of society'.
16 pp. London, J. Parker, 1893

T.

9806 BEKEN, George. The taxation of ground-rents, and the division of rates between occupiers and owners. (Reprinted from 'the Liberty Annual'.)
12 pp. London, the Liberty and property defence league, 1893

U.

9807 Commercial Ulster and the home rule movement. Profusely illustrated. Portraits of all the Ulster unionist members of parliament.
64 pp. Belfast, Olley, 1893

B.

9808 COSTELLOE, Benjamin Francis Conn. The incidence of taxation.
tables in appendix. 40 pp. London, Ward and Foxlow, 1893

T.

9809 English land restoration league. Special report 1892. Among the agricultural labourers with the 'red vans'.
22 pp. London, Offices of the English land restoration league, 1893

T.

9810 'The future of the Irish nationalists' with other contributions towards the solution of the Irish question (being letters to the daily press) by an Irish unionist.
78 pp. Dublin, W. McGee, 1893

T.

9811 GIDE, Charles. L'Idée de solidarité en tant que programme économique. [Extrait de la Revue Internationale de Sociologie.]
18 pp. Paris, Giard et Briere, 1893

N.

9812 Government of Ireland bill. Belfast Chamber of commerce and Mr. Gladstone, Report, including premier's reception and speech to the deputation, etc., with the original report of the Chamber.
appendices, etc. 40 pp. London, Marcus Ward, 1893

L., N., T.

9813 GRIMSHAW, Thomas Wrigley. Facts and figures about Ireland. Part I. Comprising a summary and analysis of the principal statistics of Ireland for the fifty years 1841–1890.
tables. 60 pp. Dublin, Hodges, Figgis, London, Simpkin, Marshall, [etc.], 1893

D., N., T.

9814 ——. Facts and figures about Ireland. Part II. Comprising comparative statistics of Irish counties; with tables of the principal statistics of the counties for each of the six decennial census years, 1841–1891; and a summary and analysis.
tables. 28 pp. Dublin, Hodges, Figgis, London, Simpkin, Marshall, 1893

D., N., T.

9815 HOARE, H. N. Hamilton. On the development of the English poor law.
28 pp. London, W. Ridgway, 1893
T.

9816 The home rule bill of 1893: a plain statement of its provisions with notes and comments.
24 pp. London, Liberal unionist association, [1893?]
T.

9817 HOWELL, J. H. Bimetallism; or currency reform. A paper read at the Bristol liberal club, February 9th, 1893.
tables. appendix. 48 pp. 5th ed. Bristol, Arrowsmith, 1893
T.

9818 LEAVER, J. C. Money: its origin, its internal and international use and development.
32 pp. London, Effingham Wilson, 1893
T.

9819 ——. Review of the rt. hon. Leonard Courtney's article [in 'the Nineteenth Century'] 'Bimetallism once more', by the Author of 'Money'.
10 pp. London, Effingham Wilson, 1893
T.

9820 MAYHEW, Athol. Railway enterprise of the United Kingdom.
8 pp. London, Eyre and Spottiswoode, 1893
T.

9821 PAMPERL, Karl. Grammgeld oder das zukünftige Welt-Munz System.
tables. 24 pp. Zürich, Ed. Leemann, 1893
T.

9822 PYKE, Vincent. The land laws of New Zealand, as enacted by the land act, 1892.
table. 30 pp. Wellington, printed by Costall, 1893
T.

9823 Report of the council of the chamber of commerce of Dublin for the year 1892 to the members of the association at the annual assembly, held 31st January, 1893.
tables. appendix. 84 pp. Dublin, printed by J. Falconer, 1893
D.

9824 Report of the council of the Irish industries association, for the year ending December 31st, 1893.
tables. 20 pp. Dublin, J. Dollard, 1893
P.

9825 SALISBURY, Robert Arthur Talbot Gascoyne Cecil, 3rd marquess of. The reform of local taxation. Extracts from the speeches of the Marquess of Salisbury, K.G.
8 pp. London, Property protection society, 1893
T.

9826 SYNGE, A. H. Plan for developing the resources of North-West Donegal. Together with a report thereon by hon. R. C. Parsons, M.I.C.E., with chart and plan attached.
maps. tables. 20 pp. London, printed by Whitehead and Morris, 1893
N.

9827 TWIGG, John Hill. A plain statement of the currency question, with reasons why we should restore the old English law of bimetallism.
24 pp. London, Effingham Wilson, 1893
T.

9828 WALSH, William J., archbishop of Dublin. Bimetallism and monometallism. What they are, and how they bear upon the Irish land question.
table of contents. tables. 136 pp. 2nd ed. Dublin, Browne and Nolan, 1893
N., U.

9829 WARREN, G. O. Freedom. Rent, interest, profit and taxes, the true causes of wage-slavery, discussed and exploded. An address on the labour question. Delivered before the Dublin ethical society on 16th Nov., 1893.
16 pp. London, W. Reeves, 1893
T.

9830 WEMYSS, Francis Charteris-Douglas, 7th earl of. Modern municipalism. An address to the Paddington rate-payers' defence association.
appendices. 28 pp. London, Liberty and property defence league, 1893
T.

1894

9831 BANCROFT, Hubert. Stored silver and stored goods.
16 pp. London, Effingham Wilson, 1894
T.

9832 BARKER, W. H. Gold fields of Western Australia.
index. map. tables. 100 pp. 2nd ed. London, Simpkin, Marshall, 1894
N.

9833 BEETON, Henry R. The case for monetary reform.
appendix. 48 pp. 2nd edition. London, Effingham Wilson, 1894
T.

9834 Bimetallic league. Official statement of the Bimetallic league.
8 pp., n.p. [1894?]
N.

9835 BRICKDALE, Sir Charles Fortescue. Notes on land transfer in various countries.
66 pp. London, H. Cox, 1894
T.

9836 CHAMBERLAIN, Joseph. Friendly Societies and 'Old-age pensions'. Important speech by the rt. hon. Joseph Chamberlain M.P., to a representatives' meeting of friendly societies, in the Town Hall, Birmingham. 6th December, 1894.
20 pp. Handsworth, Handsworth Chronicle, 1894
N.

9837 DOYLE, John P. Report on the bay and harbour of Galway, Drawn up with the view of showing how they may be utilised as a great transatlantic steam packet station for the

carriage of mails, passengers and goods by a first-class line of Irish steamships, proposed to run between Galway, New York, Boston, Halifax and Liverpool.
tables. 46 pp. Dublin, Sealy, Bryers & Walker, 1894
N.

9838 English land restoration league, special report, 1893. Among the agricultural labourers with the 'red vans'.
24 pp. London, offices of the English land restoration league, 1894
T.

9839 FARRER, Thomas Henry, 1st baron. The weakness of bimetallism, and the folly of a conference.
8 pp. London, Cassell, [1894?]
T.
Gold standard defence association (pamphlet) no. 2.

9840 GREER, Edward. A scheme for the compulsory purchase of the lands of Ireland.
14 pp. Dublin, Hodges, Figgis, London, Simpkin, Marshall, Hamilton, Kent, 1894
U.

9841 HOULDSWORTH, Sir William H., bart. The fall in prices of commodities with special reference to trade depression and bimetallism. An address to the Bradford chamber of commerce November 19th, 1894. E. P. Arnold-Forster, Esq., President, in the chair. Being a reply to the right hon. G. J. Shaw-Lefevre, M.P.
tables. 24 pp. London, Effingham Wilson, 1894
U.

9842 HOVENDEN, Frederick. The A.B.C. of international bimetallism.
tables. 16 pp. London, Effingham Wilson, 1894
T.

9843 Irish justice exhibited in three specimens of the procedure of the Irish land commission.
20 pp. London, Vacher, 1894
R., T.

9844 Irish mail service. Pledges and promises of the Post-Master-General and of the Chief Secretary for Ireland.
table. 26 pp. Dublin, 1894
N.

9845 Irish mails question. A review of the history of the mail contracts for postal and passenger communication between England and Ireland, Via Holyhead. [printed for the council of the Chamber of commerce]
tables. 58 pp. Dublin, printed by J. Falconer, 1894
N.

9846 KENNY, P. D. How to prevent strikes: Applied economics.
76 pp. Manchester, J. Heywood, 1894
T.

9847 LAMOND, Robert Peel. The taxation of land. An address.
20 pp. [Glasgow? 1894]
T.

9848 LESLIE, R. J. A tract upon tithes for clergy and laity.
32 pp. London, J. Masters, 1894
T.

9849 LOFFT, R. E. The great experiment: mock free trade.
16 pp. Bury St. Edmund's, the author, 1894
T.

9850 [MCKEEVER, C. Constantine?.] Scheme to abolish poverty.
62 pp. New York, the New Era publishing co., 1894
T.

9851 MCKENNA, Sir Joseph Neale. Silver, the burning question of the century: an analysis and exposition of it.
32 pp. London, Chapman and Hall, 1894
T.

9852 Mr. Morley's land acts committee report, and Mr. Kilbride's land tenure bill, with the official record of the Irish votes in the division against the second reading of the bill (11th April, 1894), and an introduction by Mr. Sexton M.P.
144 pp. Dublin, Irish national federation, [1894?]
P.

9853 MOLESWORTH, Sir Guilford L. Silver and gold: the money of the world.
tables. diagrams. appendices. 136 pp. 3rd ed. London, Bimetallic league, 1894
D.

9854 NYLAND, J. Report on the social condition of the people. With a map. The result of fifteen years' researches.
map. 8 pp. London, J. Davy, 1894
T.

9855 Report of the council of the chamber of commerce of Dublin for the year 1893 to the members of the association at the annual assembly, held 30th January, 1894.
tables. appendix. 84 pp. Dublin, J. Falconer, 1894
D.

9856 ROBINSON, Thomas, and BURROWS, Joseph. The next revolution; or an agricultural remedy for the present distress in the United Kingdom.
plans (of houses). 12 pp. London, C. H. Kelly, 1894
T.

9857 SCHRAUT, Max von. Currency and international banking.
48 pp. London, Effingham Wilson, 1894
T.

9858 SMART, William. Miners' wages and the sliding scale.
34 pp. Glasgow, J. Maclehose, 1894
T.

9859 SMITH, John Chaloner. Financial relations: Great Britain and Ireland. Proceedings and report of select committee on the taxation of Ireland, 1864–5, with remarks.
18 pp. Dublin, J. Falconer, 1894
N.

9860 SPENCE, John D. A shorter catechism of the land question.
12 pp. London, Liberty and property defence league, 1894
T.

9861 Suggestions for rendering a silver note currency available as a medium of exchange in the wholesale and foreign trade of states whose silver currency has only a restricted legal tender value.
12 pp. London, printed by Wertheimer, Lea, 1894
T.

9862 The taxation of ground values. Questions for electors, with the answers supplied by 'progressive' leaders.
8 pp. London, Property protection society, 1894
T.

9863 Les transactions de M. Gustave Eiffel avec la liquidation de Panama.
28 pp. Paris, Maretheux, 1894
A.

9864 WALKER, Francis Amasa. Bimetallism: A tract for the times.
26 pp. Boston, 1894
A., N.

1895

9865 BEETON, Henry R. Bimetallism; its advantages and what we suffer by the loss of it. An address delivered at the invitation of the Bristol committee of the Bimetallic league, in the Lesser Colston Hall, Bristol, on 18th April, 1895.
diagrams. table [in] appendix. 28 pp. London, Effingham Wilson, 1895
T.

9866 The Bimetallic league and the Gold standard defence association. The scientific theory of bimetallism.
18 pp. London, Bimetallic league, [1895?]
N.

9867 The Bimetallic league and the Gold standard defence association, no. 7. The measure of value and the metallic currency.
18 pp. London, Bimetallic league, [1895?]
T.

9868 Bimetallism in parvo; or the whole controversy focussed, by 'Short, please!'
14 pp. Manchester & London, J. Heywood, [c. 1895]
T.

9869 COLLINS, John Hoar. A plea for the bimetallic amalgamation of the currencies of Great Britain and Hindustan, including, inter alia, tables of proposed new imperial coinage, a plan for the issue of full weight silver, on a basis of actual value, without expense to the imperial exchequer, and a scheme for the equitable adjustment of the sterling indebtedness of India in accordance with the proposed fixed ratio without loss to the British investor.
tables. 20 pp. London, Trapps, Holmes, 1895
T.

9870 COSSA, Luigi. I trattati e compendii Inglesi d' economia politica. Saggio bibliografico. (Estratto dal Giornale degli Economisti, Agosto, 1895.)
20 pp. Bologna, Garagnani, 1895
N.

9871 CREE, T. S. A criticism of the theory of trade unions. Paper read before the economic guidance section of the Philosophical society of Glasgow. 12th Nov., 1890.
Appendices. 50 pp. 4th ed. Glasgow, Bell and Bain, 1895
T.

9872 DE VERE, Sir Stephen Edward. A letter on legislation for restoration of evicted tenants in Ireland, with some remarks on the policy of English government in Ireland up to the present century.
56 pp. London, printed by Skipper and East, 1895
N., T.

9873 Dividend; What it is, and how it is made: a paper to be read at members' meetings or social gatherings. Issued by the educational committee of the Co-operative union limited.
4 pp. Manchester, Co-operative printing society, 1895
N.

9874 ELLIS, Guy. Appreciation of gold and its effect on investments.
32 pp. London, Effingham Wilson, 1895
N., T.

9875 ELLISSEN, Adolf. The errors and fallacies of bimetallism.
tables. 32 pp. London, Effingham Wilson, 1895
T.

9876 An essay on the mysteries of excessive taxation written by a poor man.
20 pp. London, D. Dickson, 1895
T.

9877 FARADAY, Frederick J. The Bimetallic league and the Gold standard defence association, no. 4. The fictions of the Gold standard defence association.
tables. 10 pp. London, Bimetallic league, [1895?]
T.

9878 GAINSFORD, William Dunn. What bimetallism really is. A simple explanation of that system of currency in theory and practice.
tables. 42 pp. Nottingham, F. Murray, 1895
T.

9879 GARSTIN, John Ribton. Memorandum as to the terms on which government loans are made for public works in Ireland and particularly for the building &c. of lunatic asylums. Submitted by desire of the governors of the 'Richmond' (or Metropolitan) district, to the Royal commission on the financial relations between Great Britain and Ireland, May, 1895.
tables. 12 pp. Dublin, J. Dollard, 1895
U.

9880 GHOSH, Augustin Stanislas. What is bimetallism? or how to restore England's loss of £5,000,000,000?
tables. appendix. 42 pp. Calcutta, Patrick Press, 1895
U.

9881 GIBBS, Henry Hucks, baron Aldenham. The Bimetallic league and the Gold standard defence association, No. 9. The Gresham law.
26 pp. London, Bimetallic league, [1895?]
T.

9882 GIBBS, Herbert Cokayne, baron Hunsdon. Address on bimetallism, delivered before the Bristol chamber of commerce, 9th April, 1895.
32 pp. London, Effingham Wilson, 1895
T.

9883 ——. Address on international bimetallism, delivered before the London Institution, 8th May, 1895.
48 pp. London, Effingham Wilson, 1895
T.

9884 Gold standard defence association, No. 11. The scientific theory of bimetallism.
8 pp. London, Gold standard defence association, [1895]
T.

9885 GRENFELL, Henry Riversdale. The Bimetallic league and the Gold standard defence association, No. 8. England's adoption of the gold standard.
tables. 20 pp. London, Bimetallic league, [1895]
T.

9886 ——. The Bimetallic league and the Gold standard defence association, No. 12. The facts as to French bimetallism.
16 pp. London, Bimetallic league, [1895?]
T.

9887 GRENFELL, William Henry, later 1st baron Desborough. An address on Bimetallism, delivered at the junior Constitutional Club on November 22nd, 1895.
tables. appendices. 30 pp. London, McCorquodale, 1895
N., T.

9888 GUESDE, Jules. Collectivism.
16 pp. London, 'Clarion' newspaper, 1895
T.
'Clarion' pamphlet No. 5.

9889 GUNDRY, R. S. English Industries and Eastern competition. Read before the British association, at Ipswich, on the 13th of September, 1895, and published afterwards in an abbreviated form, in the October number of the Fortnightly Review.
tables. 34 pp. London, Effingham Wilson, 1895
N., T.

9890 HOWELL, J. H. Bi-metallism: or currency reform. A paper read at the Bristol liberal club, February 9th 1893, Mr. Carey Batten in the Chair.
tables. appendix. 48 pp. 7th ed. Birmingham, Cornish Bros., [etc., etc.], 1895
N., U.

9891 ——. How Bimetallism will affect the working classes. Read at a meeting held at the Oddfellows' hall, Rupert St., Bristol, March 14th, 1895. Mr. J. W. Renwick in the chair.
16 pp. London, printed by Hamilton Bros., 1895
N.

9892 HULL, Charles Henry. Cornell University syllabus of lectures on the history of economic theories with references.
12 pp. New York, 1895
N.

9893 JAMIESON, George. The silver question. Injury to British trade and manufactures. The paper by George Jamieson, Esq. (H.B.M.'s Consul-general at Shanghai, China), which won the bimetallic prize offered by Sir Henry M. Meysey-Thompson in 1894; together with two other papers on the same subject by Thomas Holyoake Box (Yokohama); and David Octavius Croal (London). Also a preface and a sequel by Sir Henry M. Meysey-Thompson, bart., M.P.
88 pp. London, Effingham Wilson, 1895
N., Q., T.

9894 LEVY, J. H., ed. A symposium on value. Edited by J. H. Levy and consisting of papers by 1. Ernest Belfort Bax. 2. Wordsworth Donisthorpe. 3. George Bernard Shaw. 4. J. C. Spence. 5. J. Armsden. 6. Philip H. Wicksteed. 7. H. M. Hyndman. 8. Clara E. Collet. 9. J. H. Levy.
58 pp. London, P. S. King and son; Personal Rights Association, [1895]
T.

9895 LINDSAY, C. Seton. Negotiable bond policy.
30 pp. no t.p. [London, C. J. Thynne, 1895]
T.

9896 MACLEOD, Henry Dunning. Gold standard defence association, no. 12. Bimetalism [sic] in France. (From 1803 to 1874.)
8 pp. London, Gold standard defence association, 1895
T.

9897 MANN, Tom. The programme of the I.L.P. and the unemployed.
16 pp. London, 'Clarion' newspaper, 1895
T.
'Clarion' pamphlet No. 6.

9898 MERRIMAN, Frank. Gold and silver: or, some of the alleged effects of a legal ratio.
14 pp. Manchester, Palmer Howe, [1895]
T.

9899 MEYER, Edward. Die wirtshaftliche Entwicklung der Altertums. Ein Vortrag, gehalten auf der dritten Versammlung Deutscher Historiker in Frankfurt a M. am 20 April, 1895.
table of contents. 76 pp. Jena, G. Fischer, 1895
N.

9900 Mr. Morley's land acts committee report, and Mr. Kilbrides' land tenure bill, with the official record of the Irish votes in the division against the second reading of the bill (11th April, 1894) and an introduction by Mr. Sexton, M.P.
index. 144 pp. Dublin, Irish national federation, 1895
N.

9901 Monometallism unmasked; or the gold mania of the nineteenth century showing the defects of our present monetary system with some suggestions for a remedy. By a Senior Optime.
30 pp. London, Effingham Wilson, 1895
T.

9902 NORMAN, John Henry. Prices and monetary and currency exchanges of the world.
tables. 32 pp. London, Effingham Wilson, 1895
N.

9903 ——. The science of money: with investigations into bimetallism and four of its alternatives: also the probable future national ratio between the two standard substances; and gold and silver measured by wheat and labour.
tables. 42 pp. (no t.p.) n.p., 1895
N.

9904 PLAYFAIR, Sir Lyon, later 1st baron Playfair of St. Andrews. The working of bimetallism in the United States.
table. 8 pp. London, Cassell, 1895
T.
Gold standard defence association, [pamphlet] no. 13.

9905 POWELL, Thomas E. The Bimetallic league and the gold standard defence association No. 10. Bimetallism and legal tender.
26 pp. London, Bimetallic league, [1895]
T.

9906 Report of the council of the chamber of commerce of Dublin for the year 1894 to the members of the association at the annual assembly, held 29th January, 1895.
tables. appendices. 76 pp. Dublin, printed by J. Falconer, 1895
D.

9907 Report of the council of the Irish industries association, for the period of thirteen months ending January 31st, 1895.
appendices. 36 pp. Dublin, Weller, 1895
P.

9908 SAMUELS, H. B. A contribution on communism.
24 pp. London, W. Reeves, (Bijou Library No. 6), [1895]
T.

9909 SCHÜLLER, Richard. Die Klassische Nationalökonomie und ihre Gegner. Zur Geschichte der Nationalökonomie und social politik seit A. Smith.
table of contents. 76 pp. Berlin, Heymanns, 1895
N.

9910 TALLACK, William. Poor relief and the diminution of pauperism. A British desideratum. The following letter appeared in the 'Times', London, January 25th 1895:—The problem of poor relief.
4 pp. (no t.p.) London, printed by Wertheimer and Lea, 1895
N.

9911 TRITTON, J. Herbert. The assault on the standard.
tables. 36 pp. London, Eden Fisher, 1895
T.

9912 WETHERED, H. L. International Bimetallism: a cure for agricultural depression. A lecture delivered at Tetbury, November 16th, 1894, under the auspices of the Kingscote agricultural association. Revised and with additions.
diagrams. tables. 32 pp. London, Effingham Wilson, Bristol, Hayward, 1895
N., U.

9913 ZORN, John C. L. Theory of bimetallism.
8 pp. London, Effingham Wilson, 1895
T.

1896

9914 BEAR, William E. Agriculture and the currency. A paper read at the Imperial institute, London, on the 5th of December, 1895.
table. 24 pp. 2nd. ed. London, Effingham Wilson, [1896]
N., T.

9915 ——. No. 17. The Bimetallic league and the Gold standard defence association. Reply to leaflet no. 17 of the G.S.D.A., Bimetallism and agricultural depression, by the rt. hon. G. Shaw-Lefevre (late chairman of the Royal commission on agriculture).
tables. appendices. 28 pp. London, printed by the Argus printing co., [1896]
N.

9916 The bimetallic panacea practically discussed, by Messrs. Goldney—monometallist, Silverton—bimetallist and Barker —a cynic.
36 pp. London, Effingham Wilson, 1896
T.
Pamphlet is signed 'Senex'.

9917 CUDMORE, P. B. Cleveland's maladministration. Free trade, protection and reciprocity.
illustration. tables. 44 pp. New York, Kennedy, 1896
A.

9918 Fabian tract No. 29. What to read; A list of books for social reformers.
table of contents. 46 pp. 3rd. ed. London, Fabian society, 1896
N.

9919 HARMEL, Léon. A key to labour problems: being an adapted translation of the Catéchisme du patron by Léon Harmel, with an introduction by Virginia M. Crawford.
76 pp. London, Catholic truth society, 1896
T.

9920 HAYNES, Thomas Henry. An imperial customs union or commercial federation of the British Empire.
tables. 34 pp. London, Hayman, Christy, and Lilly, [1896]
T.

9921 HELFFERICH, Karl Theodor. Germany and the gold standard.
8 pp. London, Cassell [1896]
T.
Gold standard defence association, [pamphlet] no. 2.

9922 HIRD, Dennis. Jesus the socialist.
28 pp. London, Clement Wilson, 1896
T.

9923 Increased armaments protest committee. Empire, trade, and armaments. An exposure.
tables. 26 pp. London, Bonner, 1896
N.

9924 LECKY, William Edward Hartpole. Memorandum—Irish land bill, 1896.
4 pp. London, printed by Spottiswoode, 1896
T.

9925 LORIMER, J. Campbell. The death-duty clauses of the finance act, 1896, (sections 14 to 24) with text of statute and notes, being supplement to 'The new death duties under the finance act, 1894'.
52 pp. Edinburgh, W. Green, 1896
T.

9926 LOUGH, Thomas. England's wealth, Ireland's poverty. With nine diagrams. A new edition.
diags. appendix with tables. 240 pp. London, Downey, New York, G. P. Putnam, [etc., etc.], 1896
U.

9927 LOWTHER, James P. William. Fiscal reform. Address in the Festival concert room, York, on Saturday, March 21st, 1896.
18 pp. York, printed by 'Yorkshire Herald', 1896
T.

9928 LUBBOCK, Sir John, 4th baronet, afterwards baron Avebury. Bimetallism considered.
8 pp. London, Cassell, 1896
T.
Gold standard defence association, [pamphlet] no. 16.

9929 McGRATH, William. Irish local government. An address delivered in the dining-hall, Kings Inns, Dublin, at the inaugural meeting of the 66th session, Wednesday, 23rd October, 1895.
appendix. 44 pp. Dublin, Ponsonby & Weldrick, 1896
T.

9930 MANISTY, George Eldon. Currency for the crowd; or, Great Britain herself again.
tables. 56 pp. London, Effingham Wilson, 1896
T.

9931 MULHALL, Michael G. Report of inquiries concerning state-aid to agriculture and industry in Bavaria.
tables. 10 pp. Dublin, printed by Browne & Nolan, 1896
N.
MS note: 'never published'.

9932 ——. Reports of inquiries concerning state-aid to agriculture and industry in Würtemberg and Switzerland.
tables. 32 pp. Dublin, printed by Browne & Nolan, 1896
N.

9933 PALMER, J. E. How to cheapen inland transit. Reprinted from 'the New Ireland Review' March, 1896, and revised by the author.
12 pp. Dublin, Hodges, Figgis, 1896
T.

9934 PLAYFAIR, Sir Lyon, 1st baron Playfair of St. Andrews. What is the appreciation of gold, and what is its effect on the prices of commodities and labour?
8 pp. London, Cassell, 1896
T.
Gold standard defence association, [pamphlet] no. 14.

9935 Report of the council of the chamber of commerce of Dublin for the year 1895 to the members of the association at the annual assembly, held 28th January, 1896.
tables. appendix. 66 pp. Dublin, printed by J. Falconer, 1896
D.

9936 RÜHLAND, G. The ruin of the world's agriculture and trade. International fictitious dealings in 'futures' of agricultural produce and silver with their effect on prices.
tables. appendix. 76 pp. London, Sampson, Low and Marston, 1896
T.

9937 SHAW-LEFEVRE, George John. Bimetallism and agricultural depression.
tables. appendices. 12 pp. London, Cassell, 1896
T.
Gold standard defence association, [pamphlet] no. 17.

9938 SWITZER, R. W. A short review of free trade legislation with reference to its injurious influence on British trades particularly on Irish industries and interests: (industrial and agricultural).
table. 40 pp. Limerick, Guy, 1896
U.

9939 THÉRY, Edmond. Monsieur Paul Leroy-Beaulieu on Bimetallism: Reply by Monsieur E. Théry.
12 pp. London, Bimetallic league, 1896
T.

9940 WHITELAW, T. N. A contribution to the constant standard and just measure of value.
appendices. 88 pp. Glasgow, Donegan, 1896
T.

1897

9941 BLYTH, Edmund Kell. The German and Austrian systems of land registry and their application to England.
34 pp. London, Stevens and sons, 1897
T.

9942 CHAMBERS, Trant. A land of promise. A brief and authentic account of the conditions and resources of Western Australia.
table of contents. 60 pp. Fremantle, printed by Cant, 1897
N.

9943 DALE, Bernard. How are profits for the year to be ascertained? Or what is capital of a company, within the meaning of the prohibition that dividends may not be paid out of capital.
56 pp. 2nd ed. rev. London, Effingham Wilson, 1897
T.

9944 DILLON, James. Address read before the institute of Civil Engineers of Ireland by the president James Dillon, Esq., M.Inst.C.E., on the public works that Ireland needs.
42 pp. Dublin, printed by J. Falconer, 1897
T.

9945 DONEGAN, J. H. The new Irish policy. Limited or extended local government for 'our Irish enemies': which is the better?
30 pp. Dublin, Hodges, Figgis, London, Simpkin, Marshall, 1897
T.

9946 FATKIN, Thomas. Observations on the 'Poor law officers superannuation act' for the consideration of the Leeds board of guardians.
tables. 18 pp. Leeds, printed by Goodall and Suddick, 1897
T.

9947 FLÜRSCHEIM, Michael. The real history of Money Island.
table of contents. appendix. 96 pp. London, 'Clarion' office, Manchester, Labour press ltd., 1897
N.

9948 GIDDINGS, Franklin Henry. The theory of socialisation. A syllabus of sociological principles for the use of college and university classes.
appendix. maps. 62 pp. New York, the Macmillan co., 1897
T.

9949 HURTADO, Jose M. Piernas y. Principios elementales de la ciencia economica. Segundo cuaderno que comprende parte general—Libro I La vida economica en si misma, Libro II Los actos economicos; teoria de la production.
index. 142 pp. Madrid, Suarez, 1897
N.

9950 INGLIS, John. On the workmen's compensation act of 1897. Paper read before the Civic society of Glasgow.
16 pp. n.p., 1897
T.

9951 Irish financial reform league. Concise memorandum, made by Sir Joseph Neale McKenna, D.L., to exemplify the inequality of the imperial taxation of Ireland, irrespective of all stipulations in the act of union which purported to secure equality in proportion to the taxable ability of Great Britain and Ireland respectively.
tables. 4 pp. (no t.p.) Dublin, [1897?]
N.

9952 Irish financial reform league. The financial relations between Great Britain and Ireland. The terms of reference.
4 pp. Dublin, [1897?]
N.

9953 'Irish Homestead' special. Some Irish Industries.
illustrations, 120 pp. Dublin, the 'Irish Homestead,' 1897
U.

9954 Irish Landowners' Convention. Twelfth report of the executive committee, 1895–1896.
appendices. 38 pp. Dublin, printed by Humphrey and Armour, 1897
T.

9955 MARX, Karl, et ENGELS, Frédéric. Manifeste du parti communiste.
60 pp. Paris, reprinted by Giard et Brière, 1897
T.

9956 O'CONOR DON, The. The over-taxation of Ireland. Speech of the rt. hon. O'Conor Don, in answer to the English case. Delivered at the Mansion house, Dublin, on Wednesday, 8th December, 1897.
16 pp. Dublin, Irish financial reform league, 1897
N., U.

9957 REID, Charles. A criticism of five years' work by the Congested districts board. Written specially for the 'Irish Times' and 'Irish farming world' and reproduced in pamphlet form. September, 1897.
18 pp. Dublin, printed by Humphrey and Armour, 1897
N.

9958 The reform of currency.
78 pp. London, Effingham Wilson, 1897
T.

9959 Report of the council of the chamber of commerce of Dublin, for the year 1896 to the members of the association at the annual assembly, held 26th January, 1897.
tables. 70 pp. Dublin, J. Falconer, 1897
D.

9960 SAMUELS, Arthur W. The financial relations report. What it finds. A summary; compiled for the Irish financial reform league.
20 pp. Dublin, Eason, [1897?]
N.

9961 Western Australia. The land selectors guide to the crown lands of Western Australia, being explanatory notes respecting land selection under the land regulations and the Homestead acts, with a description of the surveyed agricultural areas and lands open to free selection before survey. Also notes of the Agricultural Bank act, 1894, and amendment act, 1896. Issued by direction of the hon. George Throssell.
map. 32 pp. Perth, Pether, 1897
N.

9962 WOODWORTH, Arthur V. Report of an inquiry into the condition of the unemployed conducted under the Toynbee trust, Winter 1895–6, by Arthur V. Woodworth. Based on information collected from local inquirers by Viscount Fitzharris, B.A.
tables. 68 pp. London, J. M. Dent, 1897
T.

1898

9963 AUSTIN, William. What bimetallism means.
16 pp. London, Nelthropp, 1898
T.

9964 BLANDFORD, Thomas. Co-operative workshops in Great Britain, 1898.
tables. 54 pp. London, Labour Association, 1898
T.

9965 CREE, T. S. Evils of collective bargaining in trade unions.
30 pp. Glasgow, Bell and Bain, 1898
T.

9966 CURRY, John. A compilation of the Glebe loan question in Ireland.
94 pp. Dublin, Browne and Nolan, 1898
T.

9967 Distress in the west and south of Ireland. 1898. Report on the work of the Mansion house committee by rt. hon. Daniel Tallon, lord mayor. A visit to the distressed districts and a report thereon, with suggestions for their permanent improvement.
illustrations. table of contents. tables. 110 pp. Dublin, M. H. Gill, 1898
N.

9968 FARRER, Thomas Henry, 1st baron. Sugar-bounty conference 1898. A retrospect and a warning.
8 pp. (no. t.p.) London, Cassell, 1898
T.
Cobden Club leaflet no. 112.

9969 FIELD, William. Irish railways compared with state-owned and managed lines.
22 pp. Dublin, printed by the Irish Independent, 1898
A.

9970 GRETH, August. The extinction of poverty.
112 pp. San Francisco, the author, 1898
T.

9971 HACKETT, E. A. The Irish grand jury system, with a note on the Irish poor law system, 1898.
40 pp. London, P. S. King, 1898
T.

9972 IRVING, Charles J. An essay of public granaries.
tables. appendix. 28 pp. Edinburgh and London, W. Blackwood & son, 1898
T.

9973 LAKE, J. H. The knell of free trade or, the great mistake and the cost of it upwards of 120 millions per annum.
table. 48 pp. London, Homewood, 1898
T.

9974 LEROY, Lucien. Mexique. Les colonies française, suisse et belge et l'état economique, politique et financier du Mexique en 1898.
photographs. tables. 66 pp. Mexico, printed by Bouligny and Schmidt, [1898]
N.

9975 NEUMANN, Franz Josef. Wirtschaftliche Gesetze nach früherer und jetziger Auffassung. [Abdruck aus den Jahrbüchern für Nationalökonomie und Statistik.]
42 pp. Jena, G. Fischer, 1898
N.

9976 PLUNKETT, Horace Curzon. Help for self-help in Ireland.
16 pp. Dublin, the 'Irish Homestead', 1898
T.

9977 Report of the council of the chamber of commerce of Dublin for the year 1897 to the members of the association at the annual assembly held, 25th January, 1898.
tables. appendix. 96 pp. Dublin, printed by J. Falconer, 1898
D.

9978 ROCHFORD, Thomas. Suggestions on the constitution of a board of agriculture.
20 pp. Nenagh, Gleeson, 1898
T.

9979 ROSEBERY, Archibald Philip Primrose, 5th earl of. Speech on the anti-corn law league and free trade, delivered at the Free Trade Hall, before the Manchester Chamber of Commerce, on the 1st November, 1897.
20 pp. n.p., The Cobden Club, 1898
N., T.

9980 STONE, Henry. Public companies and the duties of shareholders, in great part published as correspondence in the 'Irish Times' over the signature of 'Fair Play', and eulogised in a leading article as having aroused widespread attention etc. etc.
appendix. tables. 48 pp. Dublin, M. H. Gill, 1898
N.

9981 Suggested alterations in the Bank act of 1844, by an ex-bank manager.
36 pp. Revised edition. London, Effingham Wilson, 1898
T.

9982 VIVIAN, Henry. Partnership between capital and labour as a solution of the conflict between them.
12 pp. London, the Labour association, 1898
T.

9983 WOLFF, Henry W. Co-operative credit banks a help alike economic and educational for the labouring and cultivating classes.
58 pp. London, P. S. King, 1898
T.

1899

9984 BOOTH, Charles. Old age pensions and the aged poor.
table of contents. tables. 84 pp. London & New York, Macmillan, 1899
N.

9985 BRYSON, W. G. Crofters Holdings (Scotland) Act, 1886 reviewed.
12 pp. Banff, Banffshire Journal Office, 1899
T.

9986 BUSCH, Arthur P. Nationalization by instalments, A project of land reform.
appendix. 16 pp. London, Burnett and Russell, 1899
T.

9987 CAIRD, Sir James. High farming, under liberal covenants, the best substitute for protection.
plan (of farmstead). 34 pp. 6th ed. Edinburgh & London, W. Blackwood & son, 1899
T.

9988 Copy of a note showing the Brewers of Dublin in 1756 and in 1825 and statistics of their business lent by Mr. Edmund Sweetman of Longtown Clane co. Kildare to Col. G. T. Plunket April 22nd, 1899 on the occasion of purchase of part of panelling of old house in Sweetman's brewery for the Dublin museum.
tables. 6 pp. [3 typed sheets], 1899
N.

9989　CORREA, Alberto.　Reseña economica del estado de Tabasco.
tables. illustrations. map. index. 166 pp. Mexico, Oficina tip. de la Secretaria de Fromento, 1899

N.

9990　FARRER, Thomas Henry, 1st baron.　Protection within the empire.
12 pp. no. t.p. London, Cassell, 1899

T.

Cobden Club leaflet no. 116.

9991　——.　What is a bounty?
32 pp. London, Cassell, 1899

T.

Cobden Club pamphlet.

9992　FIELD, William.　High rates and railway monopoly in Ireland.
50 pp. Dublin, Sealy, Bryers and Walker, 1899

A.

9993　Handbook of Tasmania with list of reference works on the agricultural, pastoral, horticultural and mineral resources of the colony. Published under the authority of the Government.
map. index. tables. 32 pp. Tasmania, Examiner Office, 1899

N.

9994　LAW, John.　Imperial Credit.
40 pp. Adelaide, printed by Vardon & Pritchard, 1899

T.

9995　MAKATO, Tentearo.　Japanese notions of European political economy, being a summary of a voluminous report upon that subject forwarded to the Japanese Government. Preceded by a sketch of a preliminary enquiry into the same subject by Mr. Teremoto, of the Japanese Legation. Third edition, revised.
appendix. 146 pp. Camden, N. J., James Love, Glasgow, Scottish single tax league, [1899]

U.

9996　The money-lenders bill from a money-lender's point of view.
20 pp. London, printed by Bonner, 1899

T.

9997　PHEAR, Sir J. B.　Notes on money and international exchanges.
40 pp. London, Effingham Wilson, 1899

T.

9998　Report of the council of the chamber of commerce of Dublin for the year 1898 to the members of the association at the annual assembly held on the 31st January, 1899.
tables. 52 pp. Dublin, printed by J. Falconer, 1899

D.

9999　SANTALO RODRIGUEZ, José.　Las cooperativas y los obreros.
tables. index. 136 pp. 2nd ed. Santiago, Fernandez, 1899

N.

10000　SYNNOTT, Nicholas J.　Financial relations between Great Britain and Ireland. Overtaxation and local expenditure.

A review of a speech delivered by the rt. hon. A. J. Balfour, M.P., in the house of commons on the 5th July, 1898.
tables. 30 pp. Dublin, Sealy, Bryers and Walker, 1899

U.

10001　WRIGHT, J. Cooke.　Old age pensions.
20 pp. London, P. S. King, 1899

T.

1900

10002　The agricultural holdings bill of 1900; by a small Scottish farmer.
16 pp. Edinburgh, Constable, 1900

T.

10003　BARRINGTON, Cecil V.　Agricultural and technical instruction (Ireland) act, 1899. The new department.
table of contents. 40 pp. Dublin, E. Ponsonby, 1900

N.

10004　Both sides of the question [i.e., the moneylending bill.] reviewed by the Yorkshire moneylenders defence association.
appendix. 32 pp. 2nd ed. Leeds, printed by Goodall & Suddick, 1900

T.

10005　CARPENTER, William Boyd, bishop of Ripon.　Co-operation, character and culture.
16 pp. Manchester, Co-operative union, [1900?]

T.

10006　Grand canal company. Address to the shareholders by the chairman on the occasion of the last meeting of the century.
36 pp. Dublin, printed by Cherry & Smalldridge, 1900

N.

10007　Postal reform. How to accomplish it.
10 pp. London, Jordan, 1900

N.

10008　Report of [the] committee on wage-earning children. A statement of the existing laws for their protection, with suggestions of possible amendments.
16 pp. London, printed by G. Reynolds, 1900

T.

10009　Report of the council of the chamber of commerce of Dublin for the year 1899 to the members of the association at the annual assembly held on the 30th of January, 1900.
tables. 52 pp. Dublin, printed by J. Falconer, 1900

D.

10010　RUSSELL, Thomas Wallace.　The land question and compulsory sale: the problem stated. Speech at Clogher, on 20th September, 1900
16 pp. Belfast, printed at the Northern Whig Office, 1900

N.

10011　Sixty years against slavery. A brief record of the work and aims of the British and Foreign Antislavery society, 1839–1899. With an article on the abolition of the legal status of slavery. By Joseph G. Alexander LL.B.
18 pp. London, the Society, 1900

N.

AUTHOR INDEX

A

A, B, and C. 7552
A., F. 565
A., F.A. 9782
A., M. 8309
A., M., barrister-at-law. 9513
A., N. 112
A***, T. 1745
ABBOTT, Joseph. 5674
ABINGDON, Bertie Willoughby, 4th earl of. 990, 1170
ABINGTON, S. J. 8785
ABITBOL, M. 4731
Abolitionist, an (pseud. of Thomas Fisher). 3530
ABRAHALL, Bennet Hoskyns. 7982
ABRAHAM, Robert John. 8209.
Accountant, an. 5374
ADAIR, Sir Robert Alexander Shafto, bart., later baron Waveney. 6103, 8339, 8591
ADAMS, John. 1799
ADAMS, Philip. 2494
ADAMS, Samuel. 947
ADAMS, Thatcher A. 8850
ADAMS, William Bridges. 6798
ADAMSON, Lawrence. 3701
ADDINGTON. See HUBBARD, John Gellibrand, 1st baron Addington.
ADSHEAD, Joseph. 5439
Advocate for justice, an. 1344
Agent for New Brunswick, the. 5447
Agricola. 1685, 6026, 7620
Agricola (pseud. of William Graydon). 5846, 6193, 6194, 6195, 6834, 7154
Agricola (pseud. of Richard Kirwan). 1883
Agricola (i.e. William R. Townsend). 5666
AIKIN, John, and PERCIVAL, Thomas 768
AINSLIE, Alex. Colvin. 8593
AINSLIE, John. 1645
AINSLIE, Robert. 5198
AINSWORTH, William H. 3597
AISLABIE, William James. 4972
AITKEN, R. 7830
Aladdin (pseud of Jonathan Duncan). 6412
ALCOCK, Thomas. 6375
ALCOCK, Thomas St. Leger. 6104, 8898
ALDENHAM, Henry Hucks Gibbs, 1st baron. 9881
ALDBOROUGH, Edward Augustus Stratford, 2nd earl of. 1227
ALDRICH, John Cobbold. 7831
ALEXANDER, joint author. See MAUNSELL and ALEXANDER. 2358
ALEXANDER, James. 6376
ALEXANDER, John. 8501
ALEXANDER, Robert. 7582, 7662, 7663
ALEXANDER, William. 3790
Alfred. 4907
Alienus. 4920
Aliquis. 9198
ALISON, Alexander. 7105
ALISON, Archibald. 6105
ALISON, William Pulteney. 5199, 5200, 5309, 5677, 6106, 6799, 6963, 7106

ALLARDYCE, A. 1946
ALLEN, John. 5201
ALLEN, Robert Mahon. 6586
ALLEN, William. 3598, 3702, 3791, 4132, 4284, 4393, 6587
ALLEY, Rev. Jerome. 1741, 2495
ALLOWAY, Robert M. 5811
ALMACK, Bawgh. 5941
ALMACK, John. 5552, 5678
Alpha. 8660
ALTON, John Bindon. 5310
ALVAREZ, J. 8701
American, an (pseud. of Joseph Galloway). 1249
American, an (pseud. of Edward Habich). 5475
American in his fatherland, an. 7263
American merchant, an. 4616
Ami des hommes de toutes les couleurs, un (pseud. of Henri Gregoire). 2867
Amicus Populi. 6418
Amor Patriae. 6021
ANCONA, J. S. 6788
ANDERSON, Alexander. 6107
ANDERSON, Arthur. 5554.
ANDERSON, George (1760–1796). 1742
ANDERSON, George (fl. 1867). 8425
ANDERSON, James. 2289
ANDERSON, Sir James. 992, 1172, 1947
ANDERSON, James, joint author. See PALLAS, Peter Simon, and ANDERSON, James. 1851
ANDERSON, W. 1948, 1949
ANDERSON, W. H. (translator). 8005
ANDERSON, William. 3599
ANDREW, Sir William Patrick. 5943, 7664, 8594
ANDREWES, George Payne. 3793
ANDREWS, Christopher Columbus. 9012
ANDREWS, Francis. 317
ANDREWS, Harry George. 5813
ANDREWS, Michael, Jr. 8502
ANDREWS, William A. 6108, 7983
Anglicanus. 6762
Anglo-American, an. 7896
Anglo-Americana. 7578
Anglo-Irishman, of forty years' farming experience in Ireland, an (? pseud. of William Pilkington). 9130
Anglo-Saxon, an. 9225
Anglus. 3519
ANKETEL, William Robert. 5555, 5679, 8595, 8935
ANNAND, William. 8340
Annuitant, an (pseud. of James Carey). 2675
Another hand. 2358
Another Irish country gentleman. 2504
Anti-Cant. 6855
Anti-monopolist. 5639
ANTISELL, Thomas. 6109
Antrim tenant-farmer, an. 9013
ANTROBUS, Edmund Edward. 6379
APPLETON, Lewis. 9441
ARABIN, Henry. 5086
ARBUCKLE, James. 308
ARBUTHNOT, F. F. 9387
ARBUTHNOT, G. 7665

ARBUTHNOT, John. 833, 1228, 1688
ARBUTHNOT, John, joint author. See GREER John and ARBUTHNOT, John. 1328
ARCH, Joseph. 8986
ARCHBOLD, John Frederick. 5442, 5945, 6380, 6381, 6588, 7985
ARCHDALL, Nicholas. 31, 87
ARCHER, Charles P. 8899
ARCHER, Hannah. 7986
ARCHER, Thomas. 4287
Ardent, thankful, but much disappointed admirer (i.e. of Richard Cobden). 7359
ARGYLL, George Douglas Campbell, 8th duke of. 9014
Aristides. 5489
ARMFIELD, William Nathaniel. 9278
ARMOUR, Samuel Crawford. 9532
ARMSDEN, John. 9760
ARMSTRONG, Richard, HERON, Denis Caulfield, and O'BRIEN, William. 8787
ARNOLD, Arthur. 9047
ARNOTT, Sir John. 7833
ARRIVABENE, Carlo, count. 8278
ARTHUR, Henry. 8211
Artophagos. 3641
Asellus. 2604
ASHBURTON, Alexander Baring, 1st baron. 2552, 6110, 8426
ASHBURTON, John Dunning, 1st baron. 520
ASHE, Isaac. 1950
ASHTON, Samuel Elkanah. 9048
ASHURST, William Henry. 4974
ASHWORTH, Henry. 7403
ASHWORTH, Samuel. 2191
ASPDIN, James. 9709
ASSER, John. 3981
Assistant commissioner, an. 4936
ASTON, C. Penrhyn. 8341
ASTON, Richard. 488
ATHERLEY, Edmund Gibson. 3601
ATHERTON, Henry. 8596
Athos. 9261
ATKINS, William. 8342
ATKINSON, Edward. 8427, 8597
ATKINSON, Jasper. 2335, 2625, 2672
ATKINSON, William. 4975, 5202
Atticus. 3750
Attorney, an. 2044, 4720
Attorney-at-law, an. 1573
ATTWOOD, Thomas. 2991, 2992, 3053, 3212, 3795
AUCKLAND, William Eden, 1st baron. 1034, 1035, 1036, 1075, 1140, 1441, 1860, 1903, 1904, 2046, 2047
Auctor. 6029
AUSTIN, Gilbert. 1905, 1951
AUSTIN, William. 9963
Australian journalist, an. 7136
Authenticus. 1580
Author of an appeal to the justice and interests of Great Britain, the (pseud. of Arthur Lee?). 925
Author of a letter to a member of the Irish h(ous)e of c(ommon)s on the present crisis of affairs, the. 187

Author of a letter to Edmund Burke, the (i.e. William Drennan). 1147
Author of A plea for the helpless, the. 8069
Author of a scheme for a constitutional association. 1114
Author of Adaptability, an exposition of the law of all phenomena, the. 7626
Author of four former letters to the people of England, the. 315
Author of free trade in gold, the. 8059
Author of Junius's letters, the (pseud. of Denis O'Bryen). 1267
Author of letters to a nobleman on the conduct of the American war, the (i.e. Joseph Galloway). 1097, 1099, 1101
Author of Lois Weedon Husbandry, the (i.e. Samuel Smith). 8057
Author of 'Monarchy versus republic', the. 8665
Author of 'No trust, no trade', the. 6142
Author of Observations on the present state of the East India Company, etc., the (i.e. Alexander Dalrymple). 812
Author of 'Penny Banks', the (pseud. of Henry Clarke). 8290
Author of the case fairly stated, the (pseud. of John Leland). 175
Author of the deep sea and coast fisheries of Ireland, the. 7854
Author of the Estimate, the. 345
Author of the farmer's letters to the people of England, the (i.e. Arthur Young). 765, 766
Author of the first, the (i.e. Arthur Lee). 924
Author of the historical essay on the English constitution, the (i.e. Alan Ramsay). 975
Author of the observations, etc., the (pseud. of David Bindon). 144
Author of the people's blue book, the. 8450
Author of the proposal for establishing a national bank, the. 494
Author of the remarks, the. 231
Author of the state of the nation, the (i.e. William Knox). 721
Author of tours through England, the (i.e. Arthur Young). 860
AUTY, Squire. 6388
AVEBURY. See LUBBOCK, Sir John, 4th baronet, later baron AVEBURY.
AVELING, F. W. 9661
AVELING, Thomas. 8280
AVONMORE, Barry Yelverton, 1st viscount. 2192
AYLWIN, D. C. 6111, 6112
AYRES, H. 5946
AYRTON, Edward Nugent. 7666
AYTOUN, James. 6113, 8343, 8344

B

B. 6612
B., G. 85
B., G. gent. 1060
B., L. haberdasher and citizen of Dublin (pseud. of John Gast). 161, 162
B., M. 43
B., N. L. (i.e. N. Ludlow Beamish). 5683
B., R. S. 6574
B., T. 3861
B., T. journeyman weaver. 381
BABBAGE, Charles. 6382, 6969
Backwoodsman, a (pseud. of Wm. Dunlop). 4300, 4422
BADGER, George Percy. 8073
BADNALL, Richard. 3796, 3891, 3982
BAGEHOT, Walter. 8074, 8598
BAGENAL, Philip Henry Dudley. 9088, 9089, 9233
BAGOT, David. 1690, 1839, 2845
BAGOT, J. J. 4848

BAILEY, Samuel. 3232, 3602, 4849, 5203
BAILEY, William. 343
BAILEY, William F. 9443, 9606
BAILLIE, George. 2594
BAIN, David. 7753, 7754
BAIN, Donald. 4850, 7667
BAIN, Francis William. 9805
BAINES, Edward, jun. 3983, 7404
BAINES, M. A. 7584
BAINES, Thomas. 6114
Baker, A. 110, 306, 603
BAKER, A. F. 9761
BAKER, Benjamin. 7405
BAKER, John Wynn. 309, 467, 547, 548, 579, 642, 643, 714, 715, 716, 717, 769, 770, 771, 772, 773, 774, 802, 835, 864
BAKER, Robert. 6970, 7835, 7987
BAKER, T. B. 8428
BALBERNIE, Arthur. 2918
BALD, William. 4737
BALDWIN, Thomas. 7836, 7897 7988, 9279, 9280, 9332
BALDWIN, Walter J. 3347
BALL, Charles. 1994, 2048
BALL, John. 2846, 6591
BALL, William Platt. 9444
BALLANCE, John. 3892, 3893
BALLANTINE, Michael Ward. 6115
BALLARD, John. 1230
BAMPTON, A. Hamilton. 6592
BANCROFT, Hubert. 9733, 9831
BANFIELD, Thomas Charles. 5557, 7501
BANISTER, Thomas. 6116
Banker, a. 6281, 9074
Banker, a (pseud. of Magens Dorrien Magens). 2019
Banker in England, a. 5828
BANKS, Sir Joseph. 1176
BANNATYNE, Dugald. 2919
BARBER, James. 5087
BARBER, Samuel. 1494, 1495
BARBOUR, Sir David Millar. 9445
BARCLAY, David. 2291
BARCLAY, Robert. 9148
BARCROFT, Henry. 9235
BARHAM, Joseph Foster. 3348
BARING, Alexander. See ASHBURTON, Alexander Baring, 1st baron.
BARING, Sir Francis. 1442, 1952, 2292
BARKER, Charles Fiott. 5814
BARKER, Thomas Michael. 1496
BARKER, W. H. 9832
BARLOW, Henry Clark. 6971
BARLOW, Joel. 2193, 2194
BARNARD, Sir John. 3
BARNES, George. 1995, 2049, 2337, 2376, 2673
BARNES, Ralph. 3984, 4738, 4851, 4852
Barony (pseud.). 7394
BARRET, —— 'of Jamaica'. 3797
BARRETT, C.P. 5205
BARRINGTON, Cecil V. 10003
BARRINGTON, Jonah. 2626
BARRINGTON, Sir Matthew, bart. 4739, 4853, 4977, 5681, 7109
BARRINGTON, Matthew, joint author. See WHITE, William and BARRINGTON, Matthew. 4842
BARRINGTON, Richard Manliffe. 9762
BARRINGTON, William L. 8788, 8970
Barrister, a. 2143, 3663, 3724, 4214, 4218, 4267, 4736, 5335, 6925, 7099, 8479, 8481, 8715
Barrister, a (pseud. of Charles Clark). 4870
Barrister, a (pseud. of William Johnstone). 2013, 2104
Barrister, a (pseud. of Theobald McKenna?). 1969
Barrister, a (pseud. of Sir Henry Stafford Northcote). 6716
Barrister, a (possibly J. W. Stokes). 1555

Barrister-at-law, a. 9045
Barrister of the honourable society of Lincoln's Inn, a. 2507
BARROW, John. 6593
BARRY, James F. 8702, 8789
BARRY, Michael Joseph. 5815
BARTHOLOMEW, John. 7899
BARTLETT, E. Ashmead. 9446
BARTLEY, Sir George Christopher Trant. 8900
BARTON, E. 3442
BARTON, John. 4396
BARTON, Richard B. D. 32
BARTY, James Strachan. 6801, 6802
BARTY, Thomas. 9447
BARUCHSON, Arnold. 8503
BASS, Michael Thomas. 8987, 8988
BASSET, John. 5444
BASTABLE, Charles Francis. 9333
BASTIAT, Frédéric. 7110, 7266, 9236
BATE, John. 9763
BATES, David. 1443
BATH, John. 8345
BATHURST, Henry. 4397
BATSON, Thomas. 6972
BATTERSBY, Leslie, joint author. See BARRINGTON, Jonah, and BATTERSBY, Leslie. 2626
BATTERSBY, T. S. Frank. 9237
BATTERSBY, W. J. 3985
BAXTER, Robert Dudley. 8346, 8599
BAXTER, Stafford Stratton. 4133
BAXTER, William Edwin. 7111, 9034
BAYLDON, J. S. 3350
BAYLEY, George. 5682
BAYLEY, John. 1609
BAYLEY, Thomas Butterworth. 834, 1906
BAYLIS, Edward. 7112
BAYLIS, Edward, BERMINGHAM, George and ERITH, Francis Norton. 7408
BAYLIS, Thomas H. and SCOTT, George. 7756
BAYLY, Edward. 1077
BAYLY, William Davis. 3174
BAYMAN, Robert. 8429
BAYNES, John. 7668
BEAL, James. 7502, 9334
BEAMISH, N. Ludlow. 5683, 5949
BEAR, William E. 8989, 9914, 9915
BEARBLOCK, James. 2595
BEARE, John. 3705
BEARN, William. 7113
BEASLEY, J. Richardson B. 5192, 6383, 6594
BEATSON, D. 8281
BEATSON, Jasper. 3351
BEATTY, J. 1610
BEAUCHAMP, Francis, viscount. 1177, 1232
BEAUCLERC, C. 5445, 7409
BEAUMONT, Augustus Hardin. 3603
BEAUMONT, George. 4649
BEAUMONT, John Thomas Barber. 2920, 2921, 3054
BECHER, John Thomas. 3798, 3799
BECK, Richard V. 7267
BEEKE, Henry. 2195
BEESLEY, George. 6595
BEESLY, Edward Spencer. 9149
BEETON, Henry R. 9833, 9865
BEGG, James. 6596, 6973, 8504
BEGGS, Thomas. 7585
BEHAN, John. 9150
BEHIC, Armand. 8212
BEKEN, George. 9806
BELDAM, ——. 803
BELL, Gavin Mason. 5206
BELL, Henry Glassford. 7900
BELL, John. 5088, 6803
BELL, Robert. 2419
BELLAMONT, Charles Coote, 1st earl of. 1231
BELLEW, Robert. 2377, 2378, 2553
BELLONI, Jerome. 59
BELLOWS, John. 9448
Beneficed clergyman, a. 2781, 8420

Beneficed clergyman, a (pseud. of Patrick Duigenan?). 1457
Beneficed clergyman, a (pseud. of J. W. Ormsby). 3398
Beneficed clergyman, a (pseud. of Henry Soames). 3424
Beneficed clergyman of the established church, a. 2929
Beneficed clergyman of the protestant church of Ireland, a. 4689
BENNETT, William. 6117
BENNETT, William J. E. 7989
BENNOCH, Francis. 7268
BENSON, Robert. 7990, 8852
BENTHAM, George. 4135
BENTHAM, Jeremy. 1800, 4978
BENTHAM, Sir Samuel. 3986
BENTINCK, William H. C., 3rd duke of Portland. See PORTLAND, William Henry Cavendish Bentinck, 3rd duke.
BENTLEY, Joseph. 8347
BENTLEY, Richard. 1907, 1996, 2050, 2051
BENTLEY, Thomas. 1178, 1746
BENWELL, James B. 3987
BERESFORD, John. 994, 2133, 2196
BERKELEY, George, bishop of Cloyne. 4, 60, 456
BERKELEY, Grantley F. 6804
Berkshire magistrate, a. 4130
BERLYN, Peter (translator). 7284
BERMINGHAM, George, joint author. See BAYLIS, Edward, BERMINGHAM, George and ERITH, Francis Norton. 7408
BERMINGHAM, T. A. 9335
BERMINGHAM, Thomas. 4542, 4650, 5089, 5090, 5311, 5312, 5950, 6118
BERNARD, Sir Francis. 865
BERNARD, John. 5207
BERNARD, Sir Thomas, bart. 2518, 2993, 2994, 4854
BERNARD, William Leigh. 9090
BERWICK, William. 5313
BESANT, Annie and FOOTE, George William. 9533
BESNARD, Peter. 3175
BETHEL, Isaac Burke. 2052
BEVAN, William. 4979
BEWICK, Robert. 8213
BEWLEY, Samuel. 4651
BEXLEY, Nicholas Vansittart, baron. 1833, 1938, 2770
Biblicus. 4265
BICHENO, James Ebenezer. 2995
BICKERSTETH, Robert, bishop of Ripon. 7901
BIDDELL, H. T. 6384
BIDEN, William Downing. 8075
BIGG, James. 8853
BIGGS, Henry. 5314, 5558
BIGNOLD, Thomas. 3056
BIGSBY, John Jeremiah. 4740
BINDON, David. 5, 88, 144, 145
BINGHAM, Sir Charles. 644
BINNS, Jonathan. 6974
BIRCH, James. 5951
BIRD, Henry Edward. 8430, 9449
BIRD, Robert. 1078
BIRKETT, M. 1747
BIRKMYRE, William. 9697
BIRMINGHAM, James. 5208
BIRNEY, James G., joint author. See ELMORE, F. H. and BIRNEY, James G. 4997
BIRT, John. 4855
BISCHOFF, James. 3800, 5559
BISH, Thomas. 4543
BISHOP, Daniel. 6119
BISHOP, James. 7503
BISSET, Thomas. 8703
BIZOTT, Dr. 344
Black sheep, a. 6941
BLACK, Adam. 4652
BLACK, Morrice A. 8076

BLACK, Robert. 2742
BLACK, William. 1748
BLACKALL, Samuel Wensley. 5952, 6385
BLACKBURNE, ——, archdeacon. 737
BLACKBURNE, Edward. 9151
BLACKBURNE, Jonathan. 5091
BLACKER, William. 4544, 4545, 4741, 4856, 4857, 4858, 5092, 5684, 5817, 5953, 6386, 6805
BLACKHALL, John. 866
BLACKHAM, John and HICKEY, A., joint authors. 5954
BLACKLEY, William Lewery. 9049
BLACKWOOD, John. 580
BLAIKIE, William G. 6597
BLAIR, Frank P. jr. 7838
BLAKE, Sir Francis, 2nd bart. 1233, 1444
BLAKE, John A. 8153, 8505
BLAKE, William. 2627, 3352, 5093
BLAKELY, F. 6975
BLAKEMORE, Richard. 3111
BLAKISTON, Peyton. 4136
BLAND, W. 5446
BLANDFORD, Thomas. 9964
BLANE, Sir Gilbert, bart. 4137
BLANE, William Newnham. 3443
BLANSHARD, Richard. 3604
BLENNERHASSETT, Sir Roland, bart. 9336
BLESSINGTON, Charles John Gardiner, earl of. 3259, 3260, 3261
BLEST, Albert. 6387
BLIGH, Richard. 4546
BLISS, Henry. 3605, 4398, 5447
BLOMFIELD, Charles James. 3353
BLOOMFIELD, S. T. 4399
BLOUNT, William. 3606
BLUNT, Walter. 6120
BLYTH, Edmund Kell. 9941
BOASE, Henry. 2338, 2379, 2420, 2674
BODINGTON, George. 6598
BOHN, Henry George. 7902, 7991
BOLES, William. 56
Bolingbroke. 1895
BOLLMAN, Erick. 3112, 3113
Bombay civilian, a. 8750
BONAPARTE-WYSE, William C. 9091
BOND, Francis T. 8901
BOND, Henry Simon. 9608
BOND, Sir Thomas, bart. 1861, 2053, 2293, 2380, 2461
BONFIELD, Robert. 9092
BONIS, Carlo. 9281
BOOTH, Arthur John. 8506
BOOTH, Charles. 9984
BOOTH, David. 3354
BOOTH, George. 2800, 2847
BOOTH, Henry. 4138, 4400, 6121, 7992
BOOTH, J. P. 7504
BOOTHBY, Sir Brooke. 1646, 1749
BOOTHBY, Josiah. 8990
BORDMAN, Thomas J. C. L. 8791
BORRADAILE, Harry. 7269
BORRETT, W. P. 4980
BOSANQUET, Bernard Tindal. 9764
BOSANQUET, Charles. 2519, 2628
BOSANQUET, Samuel Richard. 6389
BOSWELL, George. 1037, 1750, 2294
BOSWORTH, Joseph. 4981
BOTELLA, Cristobal. 9662
BOTLY, William. 8854
BOTT, William Eagle. 7587
BOTTS, ——. 7757
BOUCHERETT, Ayscoghe. 5209
BOUCICAULT, Dionysius Lardner (formerly BOURCICAULT). 9152
BOURCICAULT, Dionysius Lardner. See BOUCICAULT.
BOURDIN, Mark A. 7410
BOURKE, Ulick J. 9282
BOURNE, John. 6390
BOURNE, Richard. 4288

BOURNE, Stephen. 7270
BOURNE, Stephen and CAMPBELL, Mrs. 7271, 7272
BOUSFIELD, Benjamin. 1692, 2054
BOUSFIELD, Edward Tenney. 9663
BOUSTEAD. ——. 2197
BOUVERIE, P. Pleydell. 7993
BOWDEN, C. H. 6391, 6806
BOWDEN, James. 7411
BOWDITCH, William Renwick. 8507, 8508
BOWDLER, John. 1997
BOWEN, Christopher. 7505
BOWEN, John. 4653, 6807
BOWLES, John. 1801, 1802, 1840, 1862, 1908, 2996
BOYD, Charles. 2596
BOYD, Hugh. 6, 949
BOYD, J. F. 9283
BOYD, Walter. 2295, 3801, 3802
BOYES, John. 3213
BOYLE, George Frederick, earl of Glasgow, joint author. See DUFFERIN and AVA, Frederick Temple Hamilton-Temple-Blackwood and BOYLE, George Frederick. 6161
BOYLE, Thomas. 6392
BRABAZON, H. B. 8077
BRABROOK, Edward William. 8704
BRADLAUGH, Charles. 9450, 9534
BRADLAUGH, Charles, joint author. See HYNDMAN, Henry Mayers and BRADLAUGH, Charles. 9354
BRADLEY, Richard Beadon. 6808
BRADY, Cheyne. 7412, 7506
BRADY, Thomas Francis. 8991
BRADY, W. E. 4654
BRADY, William Maziere. 8282, 8509, 8600
BRAME, S. 8283
BRAMLY, T. J. 5818
BRAMSTON, Thomas Gardiner. 3262, 3706
BRAMWELL, Sir Frederick. 9337
BRAMWELL, George William Wilsher, baron Bramwell. 9284, 9338
BRANCH, John. 7413
BRAND, John. 2198
BRANDON, Woodthorpe. 6809
BRANDRETH, Henry. 8510
BRASSINGTON, C. P., joint author. See HAYWARD, A. and BRASSINGTON, C. P. 6205
BRAY, Charles. 5685, 7670
BRAY, John. 9388
BREAKBREAD, Barnaby. 6904
BREAKEY, James, joint author. See O'CONNOR, Roderick and BREAKEY, James. 1269
BREARY, Frederick William. 7414
BRECKON, John Robert. 9710
BREED, ——, of Liverpool. 4401
BRENTON, Edward Pelham. 3988, 4139, 4289, 4547
BRERETON, Charles David. 3444, 3707
BRERETON, Joseph Lloyd. 8348
BRETT, Edwin. 9285
BRETT, John. 737
BRETT, John. 9451
BREWIN, William, joint author. See HARVEY, Thomas and BREWIN, William. 8453
BRICKDALE, Sir Charles Fortescue. 9835
BRICKDALE, Matthew Inglett. 7588, 7994
BRICKWOOD, John. 3803, 3989, 3990
BRIDE, Arthur Stanley. 4742
BRIDGES, George W. 4655
BRIDGES, William. 6599, 7415
BRIERLY, Thomas. 5448
BRIGGS, Frederick. 7839
BRIGGS, John. 3991, 5210
BRIGGS, Thomas. 8511
BRIGGS, William. 4141
BRIGHT, Henry Arthur. 5956, 7273
BRIGHT, Henry S. 7416
BRIGHT, John. 7114
BRINDLEY, James. 581, 582
BRINKLEY, John. 2462

HERRIES, John Charles. 2692
HERRIES, Sir Robert, bart. 1963
HEWITT, William. 7924, 7925
HEY, J. V. D. 1330
HEY, Richard. 957
HEYGATE, Sir Frederick William, bart. 9103
HEYWOOD, T. 4024
HEYWORTH, Lawrence. 5598, 5856, 8174, 8375
HIBBARD, John. 2435
Hibernia. 688
Hibernicus. 308, 3227
Hibernicus (pseud. of James Digges Latouche). 2109
Hibernicus (pseud. of Eneas MacDonnell). 3392
Hibernicus (pseud. of Theobald Wolfe Tone). 1682
HICKEY, A., joint author. See BLACKHAM, John and HICKEY, A. 5954
HICKEY, William. 3184, 3915, 4025, 4026, 4027, 4186, 4187, 4319, 4320, 4444, 4679, 4680, 4778, 5343, 5476, 5477, 6016
HICKSON, William Edward H. 5344
HIGGINS, Godfrey. 3633
HIGGINS, Joseph Napier. 7308
HIGGINS, Matthew James. 6206, 6457, 6458
HILDITCH, R. 5599
HILL, Adam. 4028
HILL, Alsager Hay. 8629
HILL, Florence. 8630
HILL, George. 7926
HILL, Lord George Augustus. 7446, 9557
HILL, James, (fl. 1844). 5600, 5601, 5722
HILL, James, (fl. 1892). 9781
HILL, John, ed. 8737
HILL, Lawrence. 6460
HILL, Sir Rowland. 4321, 4893, 5723
HILL, Waldron. 4188
HILL, William Alfred. 5857
HILLARY, Sir Augustus W., bart. 6658
HILLARY, Sir Wm. bart. 3535, 3536, 4779
HILLYARD, Clarke. 4780
HINCHY, John. 4574, 4681
HINCKS, Sir Francis. 6659, 7530, 7855, 8631
HINCKS, Thomas Dix. 2353, 2640
HINCKS, William. 3375
HINDMARCH, William Matthewson. 7022
HINTON, John Howard. 7309
HIRD, Dennis. 9922
HITCHINGS, J. J. 9747
HITT, Thomas. 452
HOARE, Edward Newenham. 4781, 5015, 5123, 6208
HOARE, H. N. Hamilton. 9815
HOARE, Henry. 9487
HOBBS, W. Fisher. 7856
HOBSON, Samuel. 5016, 8017
HODGKIN, Thomas, (1798–1866). 4447, 6462
HODGKIN, Thomas, D. C. L. 9558
HODGSON, Adam. 3377, 6463
HODGSON, Arthur. 6660
HODGSON, Charles D. 9403
HODGSON, Christopher. 4782
HODGSON, James M. 9488
HODGSON, John. 4032, 4190
HODGSON, Peter. 2307, 2778
HODGSON, P. Levi. 1057
HODGSON, P. Levi and Son. 1589, 2308
HODGSON, William Ballantyne. 7927
HODSON, Hartly. 3288
HOEY, David George. 9404
HOEY, John Cashel. 8738
HOGAN, J. Sheridan. 7531
HOGAN, William. 6017, 6661, 7023
Holdfast. 6890
HOLLAND, George Calvert. 5244, 5346, 5347, 5348
HOLLAND, J. Simon. 7447
HOLLAND, Thomas Erskine. 7928
HOLLINGSWORTH, S. 1463

HOLLOWAY, N. 6018
HOLMES, Frederic Morrell. 9252
HOLMES, Robert. 2098, 6209
HOLMES, William. 1882
HOLMES, William Anthony. 2748
HOLMES, Sir William Henry. 8108
HOLROYD, Edward Dundas. 7857
HOLROYD, John Baker. See SHEFFIELD, John Baker Holroyd, 1st baron and 1st earl.
HOLT, Francis Ludlow. 3827
HOLWELL, J. J. 1019
HOME, Francis. 318, 380
HOME, George. 3634
HOMER, Henry. 653
Honest Irishman, an. 179
Honestus (pseud. of Edward Norton). 7716
Honorary secretary of the Gloucester penny bank, the. 8040
HOOKE, Andrew. 38
HOOPER, F. Bodfield. 9065, 9104
HOPE, A. J. B. Beresford. 8018
HOPE, George. 5478
HOPE, Horace. 7167
HOPE, John. 1332
HOPE, William and NAPIER, William. 8232
HOPKIN, Evan. 2470, 2501
HOPKINS, Thomas. 2642, 3289, 3828
HOPKINSON, Alfred. 9105
HOPLEY, Thomas. 7929
HORAN, George. 1965
HORNER, Leonard. 5245
HORRY, Sidney Calder. 8109, 8376
HORSFALL, J. H. 8233
HORTON, Sir Robert John Wilmot, bart. 3635, 3829, 3830, 3916, 4033, 4034, 4035, 4036, 4037, 4191, 5124, 5246
HOSKYNS, Chandos Wren. 7613, 8632
HOUGHTON, Benjamin. 536
HOUGHTON, Henry. 5247
HOULDSWORTH, Sir William H., bart. 9841
HOULTON, Robert. 1199
HOUSTON, Arthur. 8110
HOVENDEN, Frederick. 9842
Howard (pseud.). 3659
HOWARD, Gorges Edmond. 105, 165, 166, 167, 168, 169, 170, 453, 497, 498, 746, 918, 919, 1394
HOWARD, James. 8307
HOWE, James. 2779, 7024
HOWE, Joseph. 7532
HOWELL, J. H. 9817, 9890, 9891
HOWELL, Thomas. 6850
HOWISON, William. 2397
HOWLETT, John. 1153, 1464, 1520, 1590
HOWMAN, Edward John. 5479
HOYTE, Henry. 3831
HUBAND, Joseph. 2936
HUBBARD, John Gellibrand, baron Addington. 5602, 6464, 7168, 7311, 8019, 9490, 9920
HUBBERSTY, J. L. 3186
HUBERT, Henry Samuel Musgrave. 6851, 6852
HUDDART, Joseph. 3832
HUDSON, J. S. 5480
HUGHES, John, bishop of New York. 6210
HUGHES, Samuel. 8175
HUGHES, Thomas. 7930
HUGHES, W. 7169
HULL, Charles Henry. 9892
HULL, Hugh Munro. 8809
HULL, John. 4577
HULL, John Simpson. 2235
HULL, William Winstanley. 4322, 5248
Humanitas. 9378
HUMBERT, Charles F. 7533
Humble patriot, an. 3772
HUME, A. 8235
HUME, James Deacon. 2869, 4682
HUME, Joseph. 4039
HUMFREY, R. H. Blake. 8870
HUMPHREY, John. 2008, 2099

HUMPHREYS, William. 3378
HUMPHRY, Joseph Thomas. 7312
HUMPHRYS, David. 9106
HUNSDON, Herbert Cokayne Gibbs, 1st baron. 9882, 9883
HUNT, Thornton Leigh. 5125, 6019
HUNTER, Adam. 8308
HUNTER, C. 2009
HUNTER, Sylvester Joseph. 7931, 7932
HUNTER, W. A. 8236, 8237, 8956
HUNTER, William. 2694
HUNTLEY, Sir H. V. 6662
HURSTHOUSE, Charles Flinders. 7025, 7171, 7313, 8739
HURTADO, José M. Piernas y. 9675, 9949
HUSKE, John. 224
HUSKISSON, William. 2606, 2643, 2780, 3733, 3734
HUTCHESON, Francis. 1521
HUTCHINSON, ——. 958
HUTCHINSON, Graham. 5858
HUTCHINSON, L. W. 9491
HUTCHINSON, S. 6020
HUTCHINSON, Simon. 8176
HUTTON, Henry Dix. 7614, 7696, 8238, 8455, 8456, 8544, 8545, 8546, 8740, 9190
HUTTON, James. 8020
HUTTON, William. 7448
HUXTABLE, Anthony. 6853
HYNDMAN, C. 878
HYNDMAN, Henry Mayers. 9304, 9715
HYNDMAN, Henry Mayers and BRADLAUGH, Charles. 9354

I

Iernus Cambriensis. 230
Impartial hand, an. 7066
Impartial looker-on, an. 3280
Impartial observer, an (pseud. of William Dennis). 741
Impartial observer, an. 3311, 7372
Impartial reporter, an. 2787
IMRAY, John. 8633
INCHBALD, John. 7787, 8113
Incumbent of a country parish, the. 4001
Incumbent of the parish (i.e. Jacob Clements—of Upton St. Leonards). 6982
Independent gentleman, an. 2968
Independent gentleman, an (pseud. of John Symmons). 2283
Independent Irish Whig, a (pseud. of Theobald Wolfe Tone). 1681
Independent observer, an (pseud. of Archibald Redfoord). 2259
Indicator. 8252
Individual of thirty years' practical experience in banking and commercial affairs, an (pseud. of Thomas Skinner Surr). 3685
Industriel des montagnes des Vosges, un (i.e. Daniel Legrand). 5257
INGLIS, John. 9950
INGRAM, John Kells. 9039, 9355
INGRAM, Robert Acklam. 2572
INGRAM, Thomas Dunbar. 7314
Inhabitant of Belfast, a. 1787
Inhabitant of Edinburgh, an. 2132
Inhabitant of the City of Dublin, an. 5391
INNES, ——. 9748
INNES, John. 4683
Intending emigrant, an. 5017
Investigator. 2528, 4232, 7733
IRELAND, John. 3075
Irish catholic, an. 5616
Irish catholic, an (pseud. of W. J. MacNeven). 2122
Irish country gentleman, an (pseud. of William Parnell). 2447, 2479
Irish country gentleman, an (pseud. of Philip Reade?). 5638
Irish gentleman, an, a member of the whig club (pseud. of William Burgh). 1363

MAGENS, Magens Dorrien. 2019, 2439
MAGILL, D. 8121
Magistrate and a clergyman of Chichester, a. 4229
Magistrate of Middlesex, a (pseud. of John Thomas Barber Beaumont). 2921
Magistrate of the county of *****. 3477
Magistrate of the county of Pembroke, a. 3226
MAGNUS, Philip. 8920
MAGUIRE, John Francis. 7461, 8654
MAHON, Charles Stanhope, styled viscount Mahon. 929
MAHONY, Cornelius. 6035
MAHONY, Pierce. 4594, 4595, 6493
MAHONY, Richard John. 9120, 9361
MAILLARD DE CHAMBURE, Charles Hippolyte. 3841
MAITLAND, John. 3078, 6238
MAITLAND, John Gorham. 6695, 7347
MAJOR, Henry. 2875
MAJOR, R. H. 7187
MAKATO, Tentearo. 9995
MAKGILL, George. 7047
MALAGROWTHER, Malachi (pseud. of Sir Walter Scott). 3672, 3673, 3674
Malagrowther the less. 7407
MALCOLM, Andrew George. 7188
MALCOLM, Sir John. 4466
MALET, Sir Alexander, bart. 4202
MALET, William Wyndham. 6696, 6880
MALEY, A. J. 6494, 6697, 6881, 7048, 7189, 7348
MALHAM, John. 2313
MALLET, Sir Louis. 9024, 9413
MALLET, Robert. 5872
MALLEY, James, joint author. See O'BEIRNE, James Lyster and MALLEY, James. 5882
MALONE, Anthony, joint author. See STONE, George and MALONE, Anthony. 763
MALONE, Sylvester. 8472
MALTHUS, Thomas Robert. 2245, 2530, 2822, 2876, 2877, 2878, 3393, 3926
Man of business, a. 3721
Man of business, a (pseud. of W. Williams). 6369
Man of no party, a. 4424
Man of Surrey, a. 6679
MAN, E. Garnet. 9121, 9414
Manager, a. 7955
Manchester manufacturer, a (pseud. of Richard Cobden). 4660
Manchester shareholder, a. 7643
MANGIN, Edward. 3842
MANGLES, Ross Donnelly. 4063, 5494
MANISTY, Geo. Eldon. 9930
MANN, Abraham. 2576
MANN, Tom. 9897
MANN, William. 6239
MANNING, Henry Edward, cardinal. 8556, 9201, 9571
MANNING, James. 4912
Manufacturer, a. 1801, 1802, 3731, 5760, 7554
MARCANDIER, ——, magistrate of Brouges. 539
MARCESCHEAU, ——. 5037
Marcus. 4998, 5051, 5298
MARGETTS, J. W. 9631
MARINER, William. 5615
MARJORIBANKS, Charles. 4467
MARRIAGE, Joseph. 4064
MARRIOTT, Charles. 7545
MARRIOTT, Saville. 7712
MARRIOTT, William Thackeray. 7944
MARRYAT, Frank. 7190
MARRYAT, Joseph. 2649, 2946, 2947, 3030, 3394
MARSH, Sir Henry, bart. 6240
MARSHALL, Alfred. 9681
MARSHALL, Henry Johnson. 5495

MARSHALL, Humphrey. 1398
MARSHALL, J. J. 9122
MARSHALL, John. 5363
MARSHALL, William. 2123
MARSHMAN, John. 8122
MARSHMAN, John Clark. 7349
MARTIN, James. 6495
MARTIN, John. 8183, 8878
MARTIN, Matthew. 2699
MARTIN, Richard. 2246
MARTIN, Robert Montgomery. 4065, 4332, 4333, 4468, 4469, 6241, 6496, 6497
MARTIN, Samuel. 7049
MARTINEAU, Harriet. 7546
MARTINEAU, James. 6242
MARTINEAU, John. 8879
MARUM, Mulhallen. 8557, 8558
MARX, Karl and ENGELS, Frédéric. 9955
MASCALL, Edward-James. 1530
MASERES, Francis, baron. 820, 848
MASLEN, Decimus. 5364
MASON, Henry J. M. 2879
MASON, I. M. 356
MASON, James. 2577
MASON, John. 6698
MASON, M. H. 9362
MASON, Stephen. 9416
MASON, W. Monck. 3547
MASON, William Shaw, SINCLAIR, Sir John bart. and LEDWICH, Edward. 2783
MASON, Wm. Shaw. 2823
MASSEY, Benjamin. 6243
MASSIE, Joseph. 286, 287, 323, ed. 357, 454
MASSINGBERD, Francis Charles. 4696
MASSINGHAM, John Deacon. 8880
MATHER, James. 6036, 6244
MATHESON, Donald. 7713
MATHESON, James. 4801
MATHISON, Gilbert. 2948, 3650
Matje. 9055
MATSON, Henry James. 6498
MAUDUIT, Israel. 455, 967
MAUDUIT, Jasper. 610
MAUGHAM, Robert. 3468
MAULE, Henry, bishop of Dromore. 324
MAUNSELL, Henry. 5038
MAUNSELL, William, and Alderman ALEXANDER. 2358
MAVOR, James. 9632
MAXSE, Frederick Augustus. 8881
MAXWELL, Henry. 235
MAXWELL, James. 6499
MAXWELL, Sir John, 8th bart. 4596, 7191, 7945
MAXWELL, William. 9633
MAY, Edward. 1663
MAYDWELL, Isaac. 5873, 5874
MAYHEW, Athol. 9820
MAYNE, Edward Graves. 7192
MAYNE, John D. 9502
MAZEPPA, Herman Taxis, count. 9788
MEADOWS, J. McC. 8921
MEAGHER, Thomas. 7462
MEARNS, Andrew. 9309, 9417
MEARS, Edwin Hartley. 5139
MEARS, Robert. 7350
MEASON, Gilbert Laing. 3395
Mechanic, a. 3035
MECHI, John Joseph. 5875, 6882, 6883, 7050, 7193, 7624
MECREDY, Thomas Tighe. 9084
MEDCALF, William. 6699
Medicus. 7056
Mediensis. 3436
MEDLEY, Dudley J. 9363
MEDLEY, George W. 9202, 9203, 9418, 9572
MEDWYN, John Hay Forbes, baron. 2880, 2949
MEEKINS, Robert. 6247
MEEKINS, T. C. Mossom. 7194
MELSHEIMER, Rudolf E. 9068

MELVILLE, Henry Dundas, 1st viscount. 1817, 1818, 2124, 2784
MELVILLE, Henry Dundas, 1st viscount and Wellesley, Arthur, 1st duke of WELLINGTON. 2785
Member for Lanarkshire, the (i.e. Sir John Maxwell). 4596
Member of a county committee, a. 4003
Member of a parochial poor relief Committee. 3741
Member of Lincoln's Inn, F.R.S., F.S.A., a (pseud. of John Lind). 963
Member of one of the inferior corporations, a. 575
Member of parliament, a. 542, 1048, 3670
Member of parliament, a (i.e. Charles Abbot, 2nd baron Colchester). 6613
Member of parliament, a (pseud. of Davies Gilbert). 2433
Member of parliament, a (pseud. of Lawrence Parsons, 4th earl of Rosse). 1828
Member of Parliament many years in the treasury, a. 517
Member of the aristocracy, a (pseud. of Dudley Pelham). 5891
Member of the [British] association, a (pseud. of Henry Biggs). 5558
Member of the British parliament, a (pseud. of Francis, viscount Beauchamp). 1232
Member of the college of justice, a. 9676
Member of the committee of agriculture of the Dublin Society, a. 1699
Member of the Council, a. 8636
Member of the Dublin Society, a. 2979
Member of the Dublin Society, a (pseud. of Sir John Hasler). 1055
Member of the established Church of Scotland, a. 4587
Member of the executive committee of the Irish landowners' convention, a. 9645
Member of the executive committee of the Ulster loyalist anti-repeal union, a. 9618
Member of the guild of merchants and a real lover of his country, a. 499
Member of the honourable society of Lincoln's inn. 3362
Member of the house of commons, a. 736, 1139
Member of the Institution of Civil Engineers, a. 6524, 8437
Member of the Irish parliament, a (pseud. of Hervey Redmond Morres, 2nd viscount Mountmorres). 1116, 1132
Member of the Labourers' Friend Society, a. 5044
Member of the last Irish parliament, a. 2390
Member of the late committee, a. 4617
Member of the late parliament, a. 1109, 3192, 3665
Member of the Liverpool East India and China association, a (i.e. Edward Brodribb). 5820
Member of the Lowestoft book-club, a. 2950
Member of the Manchester Chamber of Commerce, a. 8433
Member of the Manchester Corporation, a (pseud. of William Medcalf). 6699
Member of the Middle Temple, a. 5739
Member of the Political Economy Club, a (pseud. of Robert Torrens). 5426, 5427, 5428, 5536, 5537, 5538, 5539, 5665
Member of the revolution society, a. 1646
Member of the Royal College of Surgeons in Ireland, a. 1675, 1728
Member of the same, a (i.e. Society for the encouragement of arts, manufactures and commerce). 571
Member of the society, a (Dublin society). 919
Member of the Statistical and Social Inquiry Society of Ireland (pseud. of John Haslam). 8303

NAPER, James Lenox William. 4071, 4211, 4918, 5745, 5880, 6041, 6261, 6505, 6708, 7199, 7357, 7463, 7948, 7949, 8124, 8186, 8324, 8476
NAPIER, Sir Charles James. 5147
NAPIER, Joseph. 7358
NAPIER, William, joint author. See HOPE, W. and NAPIER, W. 8232
NAPIER, Sir William Francis Patrick. 5367
NAPLETON, John Charles. 7548
NASH, Francis Herbert. 8883
NASH, Richard West. 6709
National observer, a. 2449
Native, a. 2234, 6728
Native, a (i.e. of Bengal). 7649
Native of a common, now no more, a. 3869
Native of Ireland and a lover of the British empire, a. 1137
Native of the county of Meath, a. 1855
Naval architect, a. 6061
NAZZIANI, Emilio. 9209
NEALE, Edward Vansittart. 6711, 7950
NEALE, Erskine. 4213
NEALE, Francis. 3654
NEALE, John Alexander. 9312, 9366
NEATE, Charles. 7869, 7951, 8034, 8125
NECKER, Jacques. 1158, 1159, 1531, 1592
Negociant de Bruxelles, un (i.e. Corr van der Maeren). 6034
NEISON, Francis G. P. 6042, 8477
NELSON, Henry. 8187, 8253
NELSON, Isaac. 8188
NELSON, Joseph. 8764
NELSON, Robert. 74
NELSON, Thomas. 6043
Nemesis. 9060
Nemo. 9204
Neptune (pseud. of Benjamin Ogle). 1356
Nero. 3462
NETTLETON, J. A. 9313
NEUMAN, B. Paul. 9575
NEUMAN-SPALLART, F. X. von. 9042
NEUMANN, Franz Josef. 9975
NEVILE, Christopher. 5045, 5368, 5503, 6044, 6506, 8563
NEVILL, John. 1266
NEVILLE, or NEVILL, Arthur Jones. 477, 726
NEVILLE, Parke. 7200
NEVINS, Robert. 7360
NEWBERRY, Francis. 2128
NEWCASTLE-UPON-TYNE, Thomas Pelham-Holles, 4th duke of. 115
NEWCASTLE-UNDER-LYME, Henry Pelham-Clinton, 5th duke of. 7201
NEWCOME, Frederick N. 9127
NEWDEGATE, Charles Newdigate. 6712, 6713, 7053, 7054, 7202
NEWENHAM, Sir Edward. 615
NEWENHAM, Thomas. 2652
NEWHAVEN, William Mayne, baron. 1473
NEWLAND, Henry. 4344, 6264
NEWMAN, Charles. 6507, 7952
NEWMAN, Francis W. 6508, 6714, 8657
NEWMAN, F. W. 9314
NEWMAN, G. G. 8765
NEWMARCH, William. 7361, 7464, 7549
NEWNHAM, Henry. 4478, 5746
NEWTON, A. V. 9315
NEYMARCK, Alfred. 9576
NICHOLLS, Sir George. 4921, 5046, 6265
NICHOLLS, John. 2020
NICHOLS, Thomas. 1820
NICHOLSON, Joseph Shield. 9043, 9210, 9640, 9702
NICHOLSON, Nathaniel Alexander. 8035, 8478, 8564, 8565, 8566, 8658, 8824
NICHOLSON, Samuel. 6509
NICHOLSON, William. 5504
NICKERSON, D. 9577
NICOLL, S. W. 3032, 3081
NICOLL, T. M. 9073

NIGHTINGALE, Joseph. 2953
NIMMO, Alexander. 3082, 3554, 3655, 4806
Ninus. 6539
NISBET, Harry C. 7203
NIVEN, Ninian. 4701, 6046
NIXON, Edward. 5370
NIXSON, A. F. 8126
No Bigot. 2347
No landowner. 3711
No-Tithe-Gatherer (pseud. of Samuel Cooper). 840
NOAKES, John. 6510
NOBLE, John, publisher. 3143
NOBLE, John. 8659, 8766, 9262
Nobleman, a. 397, 2172
NOEL, Baptist Wriothesley. 5371, 5506
NOLAN, Edmond. 9752
NOLAN, George. 3849
NOLAN, Michael and HARTIGAN, ——. 2579
Non-beneficed clergyman, a. 4461
Norfolk clergyman, a (pseud. of Samuel Hobson). 5016, 8023
NORMAN, George Warde. 5047, 5372, 6892, 8254
NORMAN, Sir Henry. 9578
NORMAN, John Henry. 9902, 9903
NORREYS, D. Jephson. 6715
North-American, a (pseud. of Myles Cooper). 869
North Briton, a (pseud. of Thomas Gordon). 1326
NORTH, Richard. 425
NORTHCOTE, Sir Henry Stafford, bart. 6716
Northamptonshire squire, a. 5736
NORTON, Eardley. 4479
NORTON, Edward. 7716
NORTON, George. 7717
NORWOOD, John. 7362
NOTLEY, Samuel. 6717
NOTMAN, Robert Russell. 7204
NOTT, Charles, ed. 5507
Nottinghamshire farmer, a. 3231
NOWELL, Edwin Cradock. 8905
NOWLAN, Thomas. 2702
NUGENT, Richard. 8567
NUGENT, Robert. 426, 563
NULTY, Thomas, bishop of Meath. 9211, 9641
Number of linen-drapers in and near Lisburn and Belfast, a. 505
NUNNS, Thomas. 5508
NUTTING, H. 7627
NYLAND, J. 9854

O

O'F., P. 6827
O'H., R. (i.e. Robert O'Hara). 9264
OASTLER, Richard. 6266, 6893, 7550
O'BEIRNE, James Lister and MALLEY, James. 5882
O'BEIRNE, Thomas Lewis, bishop of Meath. 1117, 1118, 1119, 1402, 1403, 2021, 3303
O'BRIAN, John, joint author. See SLOAN, John, O'BRIAN, John, BYRNE, Terence, PRIVAT, J. 982, 1030
O'BRIEN, Edward W. 9369
O'BRIEN, George. 9422
O'BRIEN, James Thomas, bishop of Ossory, Ferns and Leighlin. 8480, 8661, 8662, 8663
O'BRIEN, Sir Lucius, bart. 6511, 6512
O'BRIEN, Sir Lucius Henry, bart., 1st baron Inchiquin. 969, 1404, 1405
O'BRIEN, Richard Barry. 9128, 9212
O'BRIEN, W., 'engineer' (B.M.). 7802
O'BRIEN, William. 5373
O'BRIEN, William., M.P. 9044
O'BRIEN, William, joint author, see ARMSTRONG, Richard, HERON, Denis Caulfield, and O'BRIEN, William. 8787

O'BRIEN, William Smith. 4074, 4075, 4216, 4217, 4480, 6267
O'BRYEN, Denis. 1267, 1532
Observer, an. 2418, 3691, 5550, 8547
Observer in an agricultural district, an. 4618
O'CALLAGHAN, J. 3556
OCHARIK, Desh-u-Lubun. 4077
O'CONNELL, Daniel. 2704, 3752, 4078, 5510, 5622
O'CONNELL, John. 5623, 5624, 5625, 5747, 5884, 5885, 6047, 6271
O'CONNELL, John Robert. 9720
O'CONNELL, Mary Anne (Mrs. Morgan John). 9507
O'CONNER, ——. 456
O'CONNOR, Arthur. 1971, 2022, 2443
O'CONNOR, Charles, joint author. See CURRY, John and O'CONNOR, Charles. 782, 811
O'CONNOR, Denis Charles. 8036
O'CONNOR, Feargus. 4348, 5886
O'CONNOR, Roderick and BREAKEY, James. 1269
O'CONOR, Charles. 118
O'CONOR DON, the. 8325, 9956
Oculus. 3714
O'DEDY, U. 2754
ODELL, William Butler. 1343
O'DONNELL, Mathew. 5050
O'DONOHOE, P. 5887
O'DRISCOL, John. 3471, 3557
O'DRISCOL, William. 1535
OELSNER, Ludwig. 9423
Officer, an (pseud. of Charles Kerr). 2014, 2108
Officer of rank, nearly twenty years resident in Canada, an. 6901
Officer of the customs of Ireland, a (pseud. of —— Symes). 3205
Officer of the late board of Irish fisheries, an (pseud. of William Stanley?). 4140
Officer of the service. 4540
Officer of the Tax Department of the Board of Inland Revenue, an. 6871
O'FLANAGAN, Phelim. 2580
O'FLATTERY, Patrick. 1406
O'FLYNN, James. 4703, 4810, 7628
OGIER, J. C. H. 6048
OGILVIE, Henry. 4483
OGILVIE, J. 2023
OGILVY, Thomas. 6719
OGLE, Nathaniel. 5626
O'GRADY, Standish. 9263
O'HAGAN, John and JACKSON, Arthur S. 7205
O'HAGAN, Thomas. 7466
O'HANLON, W. M. 7365
O'HARA, H. 8399
O'HARA, Robert. 9264
O'KELLY, P. 4607
OKEOVER, Nigel. 6720
Old actuary, an. 8139
Old and almost obsolete loyalist, an. 6996
Old banker, an. 7556
Old country gentleman, a (pseud. of —— Cockburn). 3064
Old farmer, an. 3778
Old friend, an. 2043
Old Indian postmaster, an (pseud. of Sir William Patrick Andrew). 5943
Old inhabitant of British America, an (pseud. of Sir Brenton Halliburton). 4183
Old member of parliament, an (pseud. of Arthur Lee). 923, 959
Old merchant, an. 3572
Old practitioner, an. 3909
Old sailor, an. 3208
Old scene-painter, an. 2933
Old tory, an. 3299
OLDBOTTOM, Hezekiah. 223
OLDBOTTOM, Obadiah. 180

SAWYER, Frederick E. 9216
SAY, Jean Baptiste. 3489
SAY, Léon. 9519
SAYCE, S. J. 9430
SCALÉ, Bernard and RICHARDS, William. 570
SCALLY, M. 6742
Scamperdale. 8363
SCARLETT, James, joint author. See SLANEY, Robert A. and SCARLETT, James. 3324
SCARTH, Michael. 2028
SCHEER, Frederick. 7230
SCHELLING, P. M. 9652
SCHLEGEL, August Wilhelm von. 2793
SCHMIT, J. H. 6542
SCHOMBERG, Alexander C. 1549
SCHOMBERG, John Duff. 6543
SCHOMBERG, Joseph Trigge. 4826
SCHOMBURGK, Robert Hermann. 5284
SCHRAUT, Max von. 9857
SCHÜLLER, Richard. 9909
SCHULTZ, Charles W. H. 8929
SCOBLE, John. 5070
'Scot', a. 9066
Scotch banker, a. 5383
Scotch banker, the. 3795
Scotchman, a. 6393
SCOTT, A. 4626
SCOTT, Benjamin. 8670
SCOTT, Charles. 8965
SCOTT, Sir Claude, bart. 3671
SCOTT, George, joint author. See BAYLIS, Thomas H. and SCOTT, George. 7756
SCOTT, Henry. 5285
SCOTT, J. 853
SCOTT, John, of Amwell. 854
SCOTT, John. 7810
SCOTT, Thomas. 7484
SCOTT, Sir Walter, bart. 3672, 3673, 3674
SCOTT, William. 3675
Scotus (pseud. of William Reid). 4496
Scourge. 1148
SCOVELL, John, SCOVELL, Henry and SCOVELL, George, joint authors. 4827
SCRATCHLEY, Arthur. 8263
SCRIVEN, J. E. 8775
SCRIVENOR, Harry. 6743
SCROPE, George Julius Duncombe Poulett. 3870, 3949, 4110, 4111, 4112, 4243, 4244, 4509, 4510, 4627, 4628, 4629, 4946, 6083, 6084, 6312, 6313, 6314, 6315, 6316, 6544, 6545, 6546, 6547, 6548, 6744, 6745, 6746, 6747, 6748, 6749, 6921, 8490
SCROPE, John. 855
Scrutator. 9206
SCULLY, Vincent. 6922, 7081, 7231, 7232, 7485, 9217
Seaman, a. 2671, 2680
Searcher after truth, a. 2257
Secretary and member of a friendly benefit society, a. 3047
Secretary to the Kellewerris and West Tresavean mining companies, 55 Old Broad Street, the. 4656
SEDGWICK, James. 3677, 3765, 4511, 5916
SEDGWICK, John. 8140
SEELY, John B. 3422
SEELEY, Robert B. 3421
SEFTON, William Philip Molyneux, 1st baron. 1115
Select vestryman of the parish of Putney (pseud. of William Carmalt). 3358
SELFE, H. S. 7486
Senex. 9916
Senior Optime, a. 9901
SENIOR, Nassau William. 3766, 3871, 3950, 4113, 4114, 4115, 4247, 4368, 4369, 4714, 4715, 4845, 4949, 5408, 6317, 7233
SERLE, Ambrose. 978
Servant of the crown in that kingdom, a. 254

SEYD, Ernest. 8575
SEYMOUR, Henry. 9653
SEYMOUR, William Digby. 7084, 7884
SHACKLETON, Ebenezer. 3492, 4370, 6923
SHAEN, Samuel. 6319, 8671, 8672, 8673
Shareholder, a. 4846, 4905, 6677, 7399
Shareholder in the Kilkenny Railway, a. 5031
SHARKEY, Richard F. 2514
SHARMAN, H. Riseborough. 8053, 8141
SHARP, David. 9799
SHARP, James. 1127
SHARP, R. 249
SHARPE, B. 6320, 7234
SHAW, Charles. 6549
SHAW, Sir Charles, ed. 8411
SHAW, George Bernard. 9800
SHAW, James Johnston. 9654
SHAW, William and CORBET, Henry. 7235
SHAW-LEFEVRE, George John. 9077, 9269, 9655, 9937
SHEAHAN, Thomas. 4513
SHEBBEARE, John. 298, 299, 300, 979, 980
SHEE, William. 6750, 7569
SHEEHY, P. 2157
SHEFFIELD, John Baker Holroyd, 1st baron and 1st earl. 1348, 1414, 1415, 1416, 1726, 1727, 2158, 2273, 2274, 2275, 2325, 2451, 2618, 2725, 2794, 2899, 3097, 3163
SHEIL, Sir Justin. 8576
SHELLEY, John Villiers. 6751
SHEPHERD, George. 7785
SHEPPARD, Thomas. 8776
SHERIDAN, Charles Francis. 1166, 1417
SHERIDAN, James. 3752
SHERIDAN, Richard. 1065
SHERIDAN, Richard Brinsley. 1418, 1600, 2159
SHERIDAN, Thomas. 731
SHERIFF, D. 8674
SHERLEY, Frederick. 3951
SHERVILL, G. R. 8577
SHIEL, John B. 5526
SHIPLEY, Jonathan, bishop of St. Asaph. 892
SHOLL, Samuel. 2726
'Short, please!' 9868
SHORT, Thomas Keir. 6752
SHOWERS, Charles. 7387
SHREWSBURY, Charles John Chetwynd-Talbot, 19th earl of. 7388
SHREWSBURY, John Talbot, 16th earl of. 5409, 5527, 5778, 6321
SHULDHAM, W. L. 5169
SHUTE, Hardwicke. 4716
SHUTTLEWORTH, Sir James Kay, bart. 8412
SHUTTLEWORTH, J. G. 5528
SIDGWICK, Henry. 9431
SIDNEY, Samuel. 6550
SIEGFRIED, Jules. 8838
SIGSTON, W. H. 6322
SIKES, C. W. 7885
SILENT, Paul. 2982
SILLAR, Robert George. 9323, 9324, 9432
SILLAR, William Cameron. 8578
SILVER, Thomas. 4717, 5529
SIMPSON, James. 6323
SIMPSON, John Hawkins. 7647, 7886
SIMPSON, Thomas. 2833, 2974
SIMPSON, William Wooley. 5530, 5779, 5780
Sincere friend, a. 6428
Sincere friend to humanity, to peace, and the constitution. 2162
Sincere unbiassed protestant, a. 1558
Sincere well-wisher to the trade and prosperity of Great Britain, a. 253
SINCLAIR, Sir George, bart. 6753
SINCLAIR, John. 1216, 1217, 1292, 2664
SINCLAIR, Sir John, bart. 1553, 1673, 1677, 1678, 1730, 1731, 1984, 1985, 2278, 2368, 2369, 2515, 2619, 2662, 2663, 2760, 2934, 3323, 3952, 4371, 4514

SINCLAIR, Sir John, bart., joint author. See MASON, William Shaw, SINCLAIR, Sir John, bart. and LEDWICH, Edward. 2783
SINCLAIR, William. 8194, 9218
SINCLAIR, W. J. 9136
SINTON, John. 9590
SIORDET, J. M. 2727
SISSON, Jonathan. 4248, 4372
SKELTON, Sir John. 8839
SKINNER, James. 8054
SLADE, John. 4116
SLAGG, John. 8693, 9219
SLANEY, Robert A. and SCARLETT, James. 3324
SLATER, Robert, jun. 7487, 8579
Slave-driver, a. 7785
SLEIGH, William Willcocks. 3678, 5649
SLIGO, George John Browne, 3rd marquess of. 6325
SLIGO, Howe Peter Browne, 2nd marquess of. 5071
SLOAN, John; O'BRIAN John; BYRNE, Terence; PRIVAT. J. 982, 1030
SLOPER, John. 6927
Slug. 9222
Small proprietor, a. 6962
Small Scottish farmer, a. 10,002
SMART, William. 9858
SMEE, William Ray. 6085, 7969, 8056
SMILES, Samuel. 6755
SMIRKE, Edward. 7085
SMITH, Arthur. 6326, 6327, 6328, 6551, 6552, 6553, 6928
SMITH, Arthur M. 9271, 9591
SMITH, C. M. 9592
SMITH, Charles. 362, 626
SMITH, Edmund James. 6929
SMITH, Edward. 6329
SMITH, George. 6554, 8840
SMITH, George Henry. 8413
SMITH, Goldwin. 8580
SMITH, Herbert. 5072
SMITH, Hugh. 6930
SMITH, James Alexander. 7786
SMITH, James Benjamin. 5287
SMITH, James Walter. 9007
SMITH, John. 5781
SMITH, John Benjamin. 8414
SMITH, John Chaloner. 9522, 9859
SMITH, Richard Baird. 6756
SMITH, Samuel, M.P. for Flintshire. 8196, 9377
SMITH, Samuel, vicar of Lois Weedon. 6757, 6931, 7086, 8057, 8142
SMITH, Sydney. 5650
SMITH, Thomas. 2453, 2730, 2762, 2834, 2975, 2976, 2977, 4249, 5288
SMITH, Thomas Sharpe. 4375, 5531
SMITH, W. Compton. 9593, 9594
SMITH, William (1727–1803). 983
SMITH, William, writer on agriculture, 1856. 7648
SMITH, William, writer on Irish affairs, 1866. 8197, 8415
SMITH, Sir William Cusac. 2163, 2164, 2165, 2279, 2901, 3423, 3494
SMYLIE, Samuel. 7238
SMYTH, George Lewis. 5073, 5170, 5782
SMYTH, Giles S. 2166
SMYTH, P. J. 8058, 8198, 8841
SMYTH, R. Brough. 8416
SNELLING, Thomas. 627
SOAMES, Henry. 3424
SOCKETT, Thomas. 4516
Solicitor, a. 3541, 3679, 4287, 5740, 6771, 9025
SOLLY, Edward. 3429, 4117, 4250, 7570
Solomon Second Sight (pseud. of James McHenry). 2698
Somersetshire clergyman, a (pseud. of Thomas Spencer). 5416

THOMAS, Daniel. 1559
THOMAS, Frederick Samson. 7245
THOMAS, John Harries. 6339
THOMPSON, Alexander. 3774
THOMPSON, Alexander M. 9706
THOMPSON, Henry. 5177
THOMPSON, Robert Ellis. 9030
THOMPSON, Thomas Perronet. 1899, 3688, 3775, 3886, 3957, 3958, 3959, 4125, 4264, 4636, 5178, 5423, 6340
THOMS, Peter Perring. 7395
THOMSON, H. Byerley. 7494
THOMSON, James. 5424
THOMSON, Thomas Richard Heywood. 6940
THOMSON, William Thomas. 7246, 7247, 8419
THORBURN, David. 6341
THORN, William. 4265
THORNTON, Edward. 2733
THORNTON, Henry. 2370
THORNTON, W. 80
THOROLD, William. 6770
THORP, Robert. 5299, 8779
THORP, Thomas. 8063
THORPE, Robert. 2907, 2908, 2909, 3103, 3166
Thrift. 9319
TICKELL, Richard. 1032, 1070, 1071
TIGHE, Robert Stearne. 1560, 1832
TIGHE, W. 1167
TILSON, James. 440
TIMOTHY, Evan. 7093
Tiresias. 7805
TODD, Charles Hawkes. 8683, 8684, 8843, 9433
TODD, William G. 7743
TOLHAUSEN, Alexander. 7744
TOMKINSON, Frederick William and TOMKINSON, T. H. 8268
TOMKINSON, T. H., joint author. See TOMKINSON, Frederick William and TOMKINSON, T. H. 8268
TOMLINS, Frederick Guest. 7495
TOMPKINS, H. 5923
TONE, Theobald Wolfe. 1681, 1682, 1737, 1791
TONGUE, Cornelius. 7576
TOOKE, John Horne. 1601
TOOKE, Thomas. 3689, 3776, 3961, 3962, 5792
TORRENS, Robert. 2591, 2983, 3167, 3777, 4269, 4525, 4637, 4962, 4963, 5080, 5081, 5179, 5180, 5300, 5426, 5427, 5428, 5536, 5537, 5538, 5539, 5540, 5663, 5664, 5665, 5793, 5794, 6345, 6346, 6570, 7248, 7249, 7577
TORRENS, Robert, 'retired Bengal Civil Service'. 7653
TORRENS, Sir Robert R. 7890, 7891, 8202, 8269, 8891, 8984
TOWERS, Joseph. 1738
TOWNSEND, Edmund. 3332
TOWNSEND, George. 4526
TOWNSEND, Horatio. 2411, 2984, 3249
TOWNSEND, Joseph. 1562, 1602, 3046
TOWNSEND, R. W. 5924
TOWNSEND, T. S. 4382
TOWNSEND, William R. 5666
Tracy, Darby (pseud.). 2175
TRAIL, John. 797
TRAILL, Anthony. 8685, 9434
TRAILL, Catherine Parr. 6092
TRAILL, James Christie. 7655
Transit. 6481
TRANT, Dominick. 1563
TRANT, James Phillip. 1007
Traveller (not from Geneva). 6231
Traveller of many lands, a. 6525
Traveller recently returned from California, a. 6417
TRAVERS, S. Smith. 8336
TRAVIS, Henry. 8844

TRELAWNY, Sir Jonathan Salisbury, bart. 6347, 7251
TRENCH, Sir Frederick. 5429
TRENCH, George F. 9227
TRENCH, Thomas Cooke. 8686
TRENCH, W. Le Poer. 8933
TRENCH, William. 3690
TRENOR, Keating. 3207, 3370, 3503
TREVELYAN, Sir Charles. 8687, 8780
TREVELYAN, Sir Charles Edward. 7976
TRIMBLE, Robert. 8203
TRIMMER, Joshua, joint author. See MORTON, John and TRIMMER, Joshua. 5877
TRIMMER, Joshua Kirby. 2620, 2765, 3335, 3887
TRIPP, George. 5542
TRITTON, J. Herbert. 9911
TROTTER, Coutts. 2670
TROTTER, John Benard. 2176
TROTTER, Thomas. 3169
TROUP, George. 7252
TROUP, James. 6094
True church of England-man, a. 462
True citizen, a. 606
True friend of the labouring classes, a. 5931
TRUEMAN, —— and COOK, ——. 4271
TRULOCK, George. 6095
TRUSLER, John. 1008, 1429
TRUSS, Charles. 1739
TRYE, H. Norwood. 8967
TRYE, Tristram. 6348, 6349, 6350
TUCKER, Henry. 7818
TUCKER, Henry Carre. 8845
TUCKER, Henry St. George. 3250, 3590
TUCKER, Jedediah Stephens. 6773
TUCKER, Josiah. 25, 54, 55, 81, 136, 137, 138, 253, 340, 368, 465, 635, 858, 899, 940, 941, 942, 985, 986, 1026, 1220, 1221, 1300, 1425, 1426, 1427, 1564, 1565, 2002
TUCKER, Josiah and CLARKE, Thomas Brooke. 2177
TUFNELL, Edward Carleton. 4639
TUKE, James Hack. 6573, 9142, 9143, 9526, 9691
TULLIS, John. 9804
TUNNARD, Charles Keightley. 3963
TUPPER, Charles. 8494
Turgot (pseud. of John Haslam). 7442, 7443, 7611, 7612
TURGOT, Anne Robert Jacques, baron de l'Aulne. 1136
TURNBULL, W. Wilson. 8846
TURNER, Edmund. 1222
TURNER, Patrick. 8892
TURNER, Samuel. 3170, 3336, 3591
TURNER, T. 8270
TURNER, William. 9730
TUSTIN, Frank. 9731
TWAMLEY, William. 9527
TWEEDIE, William. 7745
TWELLS, John. 8495
TWIGG, J. A. 3779
TWIGG, John Hill. 9827
TWIGG, T. (pub.). 4127
TWINING, Elizabeth. 8146
TWINING, Louisa. 9598
TWINING, Richard. 1357, 1358, 1430, 1431
TWISS, Richard. 987
TWISS, Travers. 5667, 9382
TYLDEN, Sir John M. 4965
TYLER, J. Talbot. 7819, 7977
TYRCONNEL, John Delaval Carpenter, 4th earl of. 5301

U

UDNY, George. 5928, 8065
Ulster landlord, an. 4215
Ulster landlord, an (pseud. of Hugh de F. Montgomery). 9205
Ulsterman, an. 8616

Ultra tory, an. 4049
Unbiassed Irishman, an. 1710
Uncle John's nephew. 9789
UNDERDOWN, Emanuel M. 9435
UNDERHILL, Arthur. 9599
Union clerk, a. 7872
Unitarian Clergyman, an. 4604
Upsilon. 6611
UPWARD, Allen. 9384
Urbanus, Laicus. 7678
URE, Andrew. 5669
URLIN, Richard Denny. 8968, 9228
URMSTON, Sir James Brabazon. 4640
URQUHART, David. 5929, 6351
URQUHART, Thomas. 2911, 2986, 2987
URQUHART, William Pollard. 6949, 7096

V

VAIZEY, John Savill. 9273
VALENTINE, William. 8688
VALPY, R. A. 9692
VANCE, Robert. 6575
VAN DEN BERG, H. P. J. 9656
VANDERBILT, Lincoln. 8894
VAN SANDAU, Andrew. 7656
VANSITTART, Nicholas, later 1st baron Bexley. 1833, 1938, 2770
VARLEY, Charles. 672
VAUGHAN, William. 1834, 1856, 1900, 1981, 1990, 2182, 5182
VAVASOUR, William. 2456
VEREKER, John P. 6576, 6774, 6950
Veritas. 3936, 8559
Veritas et Justitex. 6572
Veritas, Jacobus. 5381
VERNEY, Sir Harry, bart. 5799
Verus (pseud. of Sir James Bland Burgess). 1647
Very quiet looker-on, a. 5662
Viator (pseud. of Joseph Huband). 2936
VICARS, Richard. 4128
Vigil. 6063
VIGNOLES, Charles. 5183
VILLIERS, Charles Pelham. 5184
VINCENT, Robert, jun. 6951
Vindex. 3482, 3519
Vindex (pseud. of William Garson). 9672
Vindex (i.e. —— Hannay). 4776
Vindex, Julius (pseud. of Denis Taaffe). 2454
Vindicator. 1991
VINER, Henry. 8147, 8148
VINING, C. 7579
Visitor to China, a (pseud. of G. J. Gordon). 4772
VIVIAN, Henry. 9982
VIVIAN, Sir Hussey. 4527
VOGHT, Kaspar, freiherr von. 1901, 1941
Voice from Kent, a. 4606
VOLTAIRE, François Marie Arouet de. 443
Votes. 9108
VOUSDON, P. 4641
Vox Veritatis. 9057
VYVYAN, Sir Richard, bart., 3888, 5544

W

W. 9197
W., G. T. 4794
W., K. 3098
W., W. E. 9050
WADDILOVE, William. 6577
WADE, John. 3692
WADE, John. 5303, 5545
WADE, Walter. 2372
WADSTROM, C. B. 1641
WAKE, Bernard John. 3437
WAKEFIELD, David. 1942, 2331
WAKEFIELD, Daniel. 2457
WAKEFIELD, Edward Thomas. 7398, 9327
WAKEFIELD Felix. 6775

WILSON, John (fl. 1887). 9602
WILSON, Robert, 'Accountant' (B.M.). 2736, 2914
WILSON, Robert, 'Solicitor' (B.M.). 5808, 7401
WILSON, Thomas. 7402
Wiltshire Clothier, a. 1740
WINCHILSEA, George Finch, 9th earl. 1943
WINTER, John Pratt. 1944, 3699, 4388
WITHERSPOON, John. 1010
WODEHOUSE, Charles Nourse. 4389
WOLFE, P., joint author. See WALKER, James and WOLFE, P. 7820
WOLFF, Henry W. 9983
WOLLSTONECRAFT, Mary. 1683
WOLSELEY, John. 6101
WONTNER, Thomas. 4730
WOOD, Sir George. 4390
WOOD, James. 9660
WOOD, John. 9032
WOOD, Joseph. 4129
WOODCOCK, William. 3783
WOODFALL, William. 1433
WOODHOUSE, J. O. 4645, 6955
WOODROW, John. 4535
WOODS, Joseph. 7825
WOODS, W. Fell. 9033
WOODWARD, Henry. 4391
WOODWARD, Richard, bishop of Cloyne. 639, 710, 711, 832, 944, 945, 1570, 1605, 1606, 2593
WOODWARD, T[homas] B[ert?]. 9277
WOODWORTH, Arthur V. 9962
WOOLGAR, J. W. 5809
WORDSWORTH, Charles. 7659, 7826, 7893, 7981

Working landowner, a (pseud. of Richard John Mahony). 9120
Workman and employer, a. 3731
WORTHINGTON, Robert. 7660
WORTLEY, John Stuart. 4536
WORTLEY, W. N. 6787
WRAY, G. 8275, 8784
WRAY, John. 3107
WRENFORD, W. O. 3784
WREY, W. Long. 8500
WRIGHT, Buchan W. 9603
WRIGHT, Edward A. 9330
WRIGHT, Ichabod Charles. 6371. 6583
WRIGHT, J. Cooke. 10001
WRIGHT, John (fl. 1785). 1434
WRIGHT, John (fl. 1823). 3440
WRIGHT, John (fl. 1852). 7260
WRIGHT, Martin. 27
WRIGHT, T. 1796
WRIGHT, William, missionary (fl. 1831). 4281
WRIGHT, William (fl. 1862). 8151
WRIGLEY, Thomas. 7827, 8590
WYATT, Harvey. 3785, 7261
WYATT, J. 3700
WYLIE, Macleod. 7748
WYSE, Francis. 5810, 6102, 6956
WYVILL, Christopher. 1435

X

X. 8011
X (pseud. of William Ware). 4274
X+Y., authors of the prize essay on direct taxation. 7293
X. Y. Z. 4072

Y

Y., J. mathematician. 899
YATES, James. 7661
YATES, John Ashton. 3049, 3786, 5435
YEATMAN, Henry Farr. 4537, 6957
YELLOLY, John. 4970
Yeoman, a. 1923
Yeoman of Herts, a. 3204
YOOL, George Valentine. 8276
YORKE, Henry. 1857
Yorkshire freeholder, a. 2915
YOUNG, A. A. 5190
YOUNG, Arthur. 765, 766, 799, 860, 1072, 1304, 2039, 2621, 2767
YOUNG, Edmund J. 9440
YOUNG, Frederick. 8690
YOUNG, George Frederick. 7103, 7262
YOUNG, George R. 4646, 5084
YOUNG, John. 1858
YOUNG, Thomas. 3253
YOUNG, Sir W. 1638
YOUNGER, Samuel. 5938
YOUNGHUSBAND, Israel. 546
YULE, Alexander. 6584, 6958
YULE, Henry. 6959

Z

Zealous advocate for the abolition of the slave trade, a. 2938
Zeno (pseud. of Thomas McGrugar). 1264
ZORN, John C. L. 9913
ZUBLY, John. 946

INDEX OF TITLES

The addresses of Robert Owen. 4081

Addresses to the people of Ireland on the degradation and misery of their country, ... 3278

Administration of the affairs of Great Britain and Ireland and their dependencies ... 3389

The administration of the British Colonies. Part the second. 884

Administration of the poor laws. 4282

The administration of the post office. 5676

Admiralty. Mr. Walker's report on the Wexford and Valentia railway, and Valentia harbour. 6097

The advantages and disadvantages of charitable endowments. 7928

The advantages and disadvantages of inclosing waste lands and open-fields. 800

The advantages and method of watering meadows by art, with ... 1796

The advantages and practicability of applying co-operation to the wants of farmers. 8213

The advantages of the proposed national bank of England. 4457

The advantages of the revolution illustrated. 85

The adventures of a bale of goods from America. 574

The adventures of a £1,000 note. 6516

Advice and guide to emigrants. 4607

Advice to a newly elected member of parliament inscribed to the rt. hon. William Fitzgerald. 713

Advice to a newly elected member of parliament with observations on the legislative constitution, ... 1073

Advice to both the protestants and papists of this kingdom. 515

Advice to emigrants, or observations made during a nine months residence ... 2342

Advice to promoters, subscribers, scripholders, and shareholders. 5954

Advice to small farmers on the management of farms. 9503

Advice to the embarrassed ... 7749

Advice to the patriots of the Coomb. 370

Advice to the protestant clergy of Ireland; in which the present dispositions ... 1491

Advice to the reformers in reference to the taxes on food. 4775

Advice to the servants of the crown in the House of Commons of Ireland. 1437

Affluence, poverty and pauperism. 9265

The African squadron vindicated. 6959

The African slave trade. 5094

The age of gold not a golden age. 4283

Agrarian justice, opposed to agrarian laws, ... 1974

Agricola's letter to the right hon. the chancellor of the exchequer, ... 1685

Agricultural and commercial bank of Ireland. 4846

Agricultural and industrial depression in connection with free versus fair trade. 9416

The agricultural and social state of Ireland in 1858. 7799

Agricultural and technical instruction (Ireland) act, 1899. 10003

Agricultural and trade depression. 9093

Agricultural Canada: a record of progress. 9671

Agricultural colleges and their working. 6887

Agricultural co-operation ... 9574

The agricultural crisis. 6826

Agricultural depression and distress. 9145

Agricultural depression: its causes and remedies. 9072

Agricultural distress and its remedies. 6949

Agricultural distress, its cause and remedy. 6820

Agricultural drainage. 7151

Agricultural education in Ireland. 7836

Agricultural education in Ireland: its organization and efficiency. 7750

Agricultural education in its various aspects. 9436

Agricultural employment institution, founded 1832. 4647

Agricultural Essays No. 2. Manures. 7897

The agricultural holdings bill of 1900. 10002

The agricultural holdings (England) Act, 1883. 9317

Agricultural labour. 8873

The agricultural labourer. 8526

The agricultural labourer, by a farmer's son. 8897

Agricultural labourers. 7390

The agricultural resources of Great Britain, Ireland and the colonies considered. 6114

Agricultural resources of the Punjab. 6756

Agricultural society of Ireland. Essay on the recent failure of the potato crop. 4694, 4701

Agricultural society of Ireland. Report of the gentlemen who formed a deputation to inspect ... bog improvements. 4734

Agricultural statistics. A lecture delivered at the Literary institute. February 1855. 7528

Agricultural statistics, a reprint. 7613

The agricultural statistics of Ireland (1860) considered. 7939

Agricultural statistics. Practical suggestions for a national system ... 7420

Agricultural suggestions. 5866

An agricultural tract for the times. 5672

The agricultural value of the sewage of London examined. 8277

Agriculture and the corn law. Prize essay [by George Hope]. 5478

Agriculture and the corn law. Prize essay [by Arthur Morse]. 5502

Agriculture and the corn law. Prize essay [by William Rathbone Greg]. 5473

Agriculture and the currency. 2nd ed. 9914

Agriculture considered as a moral and political duty. 911

Agriculture; its practice with profit. 5746

The agriculture of the French exhibition. 7581

Agriculture retrieved. 6962

Agriculture the source of the wealth of Britain. 2587

Aids to the Irish poor law. 5073

The Alabah claims. 8851

The alarm: or, an address to the nobility, gentry, and clergy of the church of Ireland, as by law established. 1246

The alarm; or, the Irish spy. 1032

An alarm to the people of England. 307

Alarming distress in Ireland. 4131

The alarming state of the country considered. 4648

Alarming state of the nation considered. 3978

All about California. 8700

The alleged tripartite division of tithes in England. 9398

The alps and the Eastern Mails. 8486

Alternative remedies for Ireland. 9459

Amalgamated Society of Engineers. Registration of the society under the Trades' Union Act, 1871. 8959

The amalgamation of railway companies. 8852

The amalgamation of railways, considered. 5942

America and her slave-system. 5812

America and the corn laws. 5329

America in 48 hours. 7117

America in its relation to Irish emigration. 8654

American and English oppression. 7263

American Anti-slave Society: American Anti-slave Tracts. No. 4. The new "Reign of Terror" in the slaveholding states, for 1859–60. 7895

The American churches, the bulwarks of American slavery. 5475

The American crisis. 8039

American finances and resources Letter 1. 8204, 8205, 8272

The American museum or repository of ancient and modern fugitive pieces ... 1492

American prosperity. An outline of the American debit or banking system. 4872

The American querist ... 868

The American question. 8159

The American question in a nutshell. 8133

The American question. Secession. Tariff. Slavery. 8071

American securities. Practical hints on the tests of stability and profit. 7896

American slavery as it is. 5085

The American struggle. An appeal to the people of the North. 8072

The American war in relation to slavery. 8188

Americans against liberty, ... 978

The analysis of a new quack medicine. 575

Analysis of projects proposed for the relief of the poor in Ireland. 4897

An analysis of the address of F. H. Fawkes Esq. 5346

An analysis of the artificial wealth of England. 3792

Analysis of the deed of settlement as executed by the London and Dublin bank. 5553

Analysis of the defective state of turnpike roads. 4611

Analysis of the evidence taken before the factory commissioners. 4572

Analysis of the memorial presented by the secretary of the treasury ... 3509

Analysis of the money situation of Great Britain. 2623

Analysis of the patents, designs, and trade marks act, 1883. 9315

An analysis of the principles of economics (Part 1). 9399

Analysis of the titles to land act. 7808

The analysis of trade, commerce, coin, bullion, banks and foreign exchanges. 374

Analytical hints relative to the process of Ackermann, Suardy & Co's. 2288

Analytical hints relative to the process of Ackermann, Suardy and Co's. ... as now established by the Irish Company. 2333

An analytical view of a popular work, on a new plan, ... 2254

An analytical view of the principal plans of church reform. 4399

Anarchy and order. 6379

The anarchy in Ireland. 9115

Anarchy; theory and practice. 9653

Anatomy of money. 9458

The ancient land settlement of England. 8792

The ancient right of the English nation to the American fishery. 516

The Andeman Islands; their colonization, etc 8748

Anent the North American continent. 8210

The angel's foot. 9386

Animadversions on a pamphlet lately published entitled, The rights of the clergy of Ireland. 677

Animadversions on the conflicting interests of the church of Ireland as a chief cause of her disturbed state. 4541

Animadversions on the practice of tithing under the Gospel. 2024

Animadversions on the repeal of the act for regulating the wages of labour among the Spitalfield weavers. 3344

The conduct of the resident landlords of Ireland. 5679

Confederation. A letter to the right honourable the earl of Carnarvon. 8340

Conference on night refuges. 8716

Conférences d'économie politique faites à Bordeaux sous le patronage de la société philomathique. Discours d'ouverture. 8127

Congested districts board for Ireland: list of electoral divisions that are congested. 9769

Congested districts board for Ireland. Report for 1892. 9770

A congratulatory address to his majesty, from the peasantry of Ireland vulgarly denominated White Boys, or Right Boys. 1454, 1502

The connexion between industry and wealth. 7910

The connexion of the East India Company. 5294

The consequences of the proposed union. 2090

The conservative legacy, 1880. Liberal work, 1880–1883. 9298

The conservatives and 'liberals', their principles and policy. 8397

The consideration of certain changes in the distribution and management of church property which would tend to render the Irish Branch of the United Church more efficient. 8342

Consideration of the claims and conduct of the United States. 3605

A consideration of the population of Ireland. 4159

A consideration of the theory that the backward state of agriculture in Ireland, is a consequence of the excessive competition for land. 7042

Consideration on the propriety of granting protection to the agriculture of the United Kingdom, ... 3220

Considerations addressed to the clergy and laity. 4160

Considerations addressed to the landed proprietors of the county of Clare. 4216

Considerations on a commutation of tithes ... 3003

Considerations on a pamphlet lately published on the proposed pier and harbour at Dunleary, ... 2679

Considerations on behalf of the colonists. 565

Considerations on commerce, bullion and coin, circulation and exchanges. 2678

Considerations on joint-stock banking. 4409

Considerations on money, bullion and foreign exchanges. 803

Considerations on negro slavery. 3465

Considerations on public granaries. 589

Considerations on some of the more popular mistakes ... 4001

Considerations on taxes, as they are supposed to affect the price of labour in our manufactures. 551

Considerations on the abolition of negro slavery, ... 3348

Considerations on the act of parliament commonly called the Nullum Tempus Act. 838

Considerations on the acts of parliament relative to the highways in Scotland. 525

Considerations on the American Stamp act. 590

Considerations on the alarming increase of forgery on the Bank of England ... 3106

Considerations on the best means of affording immediate relief to the operative classes. 3597

Considerations on the bill now depending in the house of commons, for enabling parishes to grant life annuities to poor persons. 848

Considerations on the case of the bakers in Dublin. 62, 93, 312

Considerations on the currency and banking system of the United States. 4181

Considerations on the dependencies of Great Britain. 724

Considerations on the effects of protecting duties. 1252

Considerations on the effects which the bounties granted on exported corn, malt and flour, have on the manufactures of the kingdom. 348, 695

Considerations on the exorbitant price of provisions. 849

Considerations on the expediency of a national circulation bank at this time in Ireland. 1106

Considerations on the expediency of a Spanish war. 449

Considerations on the expediency of adopting certain measures for the encouragement and extension of the Newfoundland fishing. 2463

Considerations on the expediency of an improved mode of treatment of slaves ... 3177

Considerations on the fatal effects to a trading nation of the present excess of public charities. 492

Considerations on the intended modification of Poyning's Law. 1116

Considerations on the late and present state of Ireland, in refutation of observations and reflections thereon, ... 2426

Considerations on the late bill for payment of the remainder of the national debt. 189, 190

Considerations on the late disturbances by a consistent whig. 1117

Considerations on the means of preventing fraudulent practices on the gold coin. 929

Considerations on the measures carrying on with respect to the British colonies in North America. 890

Considerations on the merchantile character and conduct. 526

Considerations on the National Debt, & nett produce of the revenue. 1313

Considerations on the nature and objects of the intended light and heat company. 2556

Considerations on the necessity and importance of an asylum port in the bay of Dublin, ... 2680

Considerations on the necessity of lowering the exorbitant freight on ships ... 1446

Considerations on the negotiation for reducing the rate of interest on the national debt of Ireland. 1503, 1577

Considerations on the opinion stated by the committee of council, in a representation to the king, ... 1715

Considerations on the political and commercial circumstances of Great-Britain and Ireland ... 1504

Considerations on the poor laws. 3010

Considerations on the present and future state of France. 1697

Considerations on the present calamities of this kingdom. 399

Considerations on the present disturbances in the province of Munster. 1563

Considerations on the present German war. 455

Considerations on the present scarcity of silver coins ... 377

Considerations on the present state and future prospects of Ireland. 5824

Considerations on the present state of bank notes, specie and bullion. 2681

Considerations on the present state of copyholds. 7297

Considerations on the present state of Ireland. 3302

Considerations on the present state of the navigation of river Thames from Maidenhead to Isleworth. 1739

Considerations on the present state of public affairs. 1062

Considerations on the present state of the linen manufacture. 195

Considerations on the present state of the military establishment of this kingdom ... 683

Considerations on the present state of the silk manufacture in Ireland. 550

Considerations on the probable commerce and revenue, that may arise ... 2341

Considerations on the proposal for reducing interest on the national debt. 3

Considerations on the proposed renewal of the bank charter. 1151

Considerations on the proposed Southwark bridge, from Bankside to Queen Street, Cheapside. 2771

Considerations on the propriety of a general draining bill ... 2773

Considerations on the propriety of imposing taxes in the British colonies. 597

Considerations on the propriety of the bank of England resuming its payments in specie ... 2335

Considerations on the protection required by British agriculture. 2817

Considerations on the provisional treaty with America, and the preliminary articles of peace with France and Spain. 1254

Considerations on the removal of the Custom-House humbly submitted to the public. 1145

Considerations on the silk trade of Ireland. 1014

Considerations on the silver currency. 2386

Considerations on the silver currency relative to both the general evil as affecting the Empire, and the present enormous particular evil in Ireland. 2462

Considerations on the sinking fund. 3118

Considerations on the state of Ireland. 1022

Considerations on the state of Ireland; and on the impolity and impracticability of separation. 2069

Considerations on the state of the currency. 3689, 3776

Considerations on the state of the Roman catholics in Scotland. 1045

Considerations on the state of the Sugar Islands. 839

Considerations on the trade and finances of this kingdom. 638, 735

Considerations on the utility and necessity of a marine in every trading country. 265

Considerations on the value and importance of the British north American provinces. 4166

Considerations on the woollen manufactory of Ireland. 1373

Considerations, political, financial, and commercial, relative to the important subject of the public funds. 2361

Considerations relative to the renewal of the East India company's charter. 4074

Considerations relative to the sewage of London. 6637

Considerations respecting the necessity of increasing the circulating medium. 1911

Considerations submitted in defence of the orders in council for the melioration of slavery in Trinidad. 3519

Considerations submitted to the people of Ireland, on their present condition with regard to trade and constitution. 1140

Cottage husbandry, the utility and national advantage of alloting land for that purpose. 4663

A cottage tenant's views ... 9602

The cotton question. 8219

The cotton question: some remarks, with extracts from pamphlets on the subject. 7999

The cotton supply. A letter to John Cheetham, Esq. 8000

The cotton supply association. 8849

Cotton supply from the Ottoman empire. 8088

Cotton: the present and prospective position of supply and demand considered. 8291

The cotton trade of India, being a series of letters ... 8196

The cotton trade of India. Part I. Its past and present condition; Part II. Its future prospects. 5210

The cotton trade of Lancashire and the Anglo-French commercial treaty of 1860. 8693

The cotton trade. Two lectures on the above subject ... 7668

Count Rumford's experimental essays, ...
Essay I. 1932
Essay II. 1933
Essay III. 1934, 1935

Count your enemies and economise your expenditure. 8074

The counter address of a free citizen, to the right honourable the lord mayor of Dublin. 593

The counterpoise. Being thoughts on a militia and a standing army. 80

A country gentleman's reasons for voting against Mr. Wilberforce's question ... 1755

County of Kildare presentments lent assizes, March 23rd 1795. 1865

County of Mayo: its awful condition and prospects. 6690

Coup-d'œil historique et statistique sur l'état passé et présent de l'Irlande. 3841

Coup-d'œil sur les assignats, ... 1867

Coup d'œil sur le tarif des douanes Belges, à propos du libre échange. 6034

A course of experiments and improvements in agriculture. 400

A crack with His Grace of Argyll. 9015

Credit and its bearings upon the crisis of 1866. 8355

The Crédit Foncier of Mauritius Ltd. 8439

Crédit Foncier. Rapport à M. le Président de la Republique par Mon. Dumas, ... 6993

Credit pernicious. 3418

Credit trading in relation to co-operative societies. 9690

The creed of a political economist. 9591

The crime and penalty of ownership. 9361

The crimes and confiscation of the Russell Whigs in Ireland. 7167

The Criminal Law Amendment Act and other laws affecting labour. 8906

The crisis. 266

The crisis. A collection of essays written in the years 1792 & 1793, upon toleration, public credit, ... 1886

The crisis and the crash. 6365

The crisis and the currency. 6226

The crisis in Ireland. 9263

The crisis of 1866. 8365

The crisis of the monied and commercial interest. 2209

The crisis. Or, a full defence of the colonies. 594

The crisis; or immediate concernment of the British empire. 1375

The crisis; or, immediate concernments of the British Empire. Addressed to the Lord Loftus. 1448

A critical analysis of the sale and purchase of land (Ireland) bill. 9463

A critical examination of the twelve resolutions of Mr. Joseph Hume. 5152

A critical view of a pamphlet, intitled 'The West India question practically considered'. 3650

A critical view of the B ... of Cloyne's publication. 1505

A criticism of five years' work by the Congested Districts Board. 9957

A criticism of the theory of trade unions. 9871

Crofters Holdings (Scotland) Act, 1886 reviewed. 9985

The cruisers: being a letter to the marquis of Lansdowne. 6737

A cry for more money. 9476

A cry from Ireland; or landlord and tenant exemplified. 5572

A cry from the middle passage. 6822

The cry of the children from the brickyards of England. 8840

Cuffe Street Savings Bank, Dublin. Memorial to his excellency the lord lieutenant. 7594

Cui bono? or, an inquiry ... 1220

Cui bono? Or, the prospect of a free trade in tea. 4414

Cui bono? The endowment scheme. 6617

The cultivation of Dartmoor. 7491

Cultivation of the grasses best suited to Ireland. 3967

The cure of the great social evil. 8657

Currency. 6386

Currency and international banking. 9857

The currency and its connection with national distress. 4777

Currency and railways; being suggestions for the remedy of the present railway embarrassments. 6079

The currency and the country. 5602

The currency and the late Sir Robert Peel. 6862

Currency explosions. 7767

Currency fallacies refuted and paper money vindicated. 5790

Currency for the crowd. 9930

Currency: inquiry solicited; but general declamation, without reasoning, disregarded. 5464

The currency, its defects and cure. 6517

The currency; its evils, and their remedies. 5120

The currency: its influence on the internal trade of the country. 5121

Currency. Money the moral power of exchange. 5781

Currency principles versus banking principles. 7616

The currency problem. A proposal for the rehabilitation of silver. 9454

The currency question. 5827

The currency question. A rejected letter to the editor of 'The Times'. 6192

The currency question considered in relation to the Bank Restriction Act. 7763

The currency question. Currency records; being extracts from speeches, documents, etc. 6143

The currency question freed from mystery. 4110

Currency reform: improvement not depreciation. 5726

Currency reform; the true remedy. 7164

The currency, showing how a fixed gold standard places England in permanent disadvantage. 5823

The currency theory reviewed in a letter to the Scottish people. 5828

Current questions popularly explained. 9329

The curse of the factory system. 4768

Cursory inquiry into the expediency of repealing the Annuity Act ... 2763

Cursory observations on Ireland ... 1055

Cursory observations on the act for ascertaining the bounties, ... 2433

Cursory observations on the evidence and report of the Bullion committee and on the pamphlets of ... 2686

Cursory observations upon the proposed application to the legislature of these kingdoms for the grant of a charter to effect marine insurances. 2629

Cursory remarks on lord Sheffield's pamphlet. 1376

Cursory suggestions on naval subjects, with the outline of a plan ... 3269

A cursory view of the assignats, and remaining resources of French finance. 1868

A cyclopaedia of practical husbandry. 5476

D

A daily and alphabetical arrangment of all imports and exports. 1381

The danger of popery to the present government examined. 456

The danger of the resolutions relative to the bank charter. 4476

The dangerous situation of England ... 1481

Dangers from the policy of England in the depression of Ireland. 2630

Dangers of an entire repeal of the bank restriction act. 3107

The dangers of premature peace. 1862

The dangers of the country. 2545

Davis prize essay 1876 of the United Law Students Society on the best system of land transfer. 9006

The dawn of Ireland's prosperity. 6298

A day's business in the port of London. 6850

Dean Tucker's arguments on the propriety of an union. 2062

Dear bread and wasted grain. 7585

The death-duty clauses of the finance act, 1896, (Sections 14 to 24). 9925

The debate in the British house of commons, on the repeal of the corporation and test acts, March 2, 1790. 1654

Debate in the legislative council of New South Wales and other documents on the subject of immigration. 5221

Debates of the house of commons of Ireland, on a motion whether the king's most excellent majesty, ... 1086

Debates relative to the affairs of Ireland; in the years 1763 and 1764. 583

Debt and surplus. 6988

Debt and taxation of Ireland. 7913

Decimal association. 7430

The decimal coinage. A letter to the rt. hon. the chancellor of the exchequer. 7353

Decimal coinage. A practical analysis. 7455

Decimal coinage: a short and easy method of changing the present currency. 7429

The decimal coinage question. 7529

The decimal coinage; showing its commercial advantages. 7525

Decimal coinage tables. 7350

Decimal coinage: what it ought and what it ought not to be. 7441

The decimal system adopted to our present coinage. 7682

The decimal system as a whole. 7650

The decimal system of measures, weights, and money. 7699

Decimalism. Part I. 7557

The decline and fall of the English system of finance. 1928

Décret de l'assemblée nationale, du 16 Août 1792, ... 1756

England's western, or America's eastern shore? 6996

An English country gentleman's address to the Irish members of the imperial parliament, ... 2346

English industries and eastern competition. 9889

The English land question. 9295

English land restoration league: Special reports. 9738, 9809, 9838

English law and Irish tenure. 8725

The English law of property its principles and consequences contrasted with the south Australian system of conveyancing by registration of title. 7890

English patents; being a register ... in the year 1843. 5753

The English poor-law, and poor-law commission, in 1847. 6171

English union is Ireland's ruin. 2109

The English woollen manufacturers remarks ... on the present declining state of their trade ... 1190

An Englishman's testimony to the urgent necessity for a tenant right bill for Ireland. 7647

The enhancing value of gold and the industrial crisis. 9322

Enquiries relating to negro emancipation. 3908

An enquiry as to the practicability and policy of reducing the duties on malt and beer. 4008

An enquiry concerning the nature and end of a national militia. 327

An enquiry how far the restrictions laid upon the trade of Ireland, by the British acts of parliament, ... 1040

An enquiry into the advantages and disadvantages resulting from bills of inclosure. 1092

An enquiry into the causes and remedies of pauperism. First series. 4033

An enquiry into the causes of popular discontent in Ireland. 2479

An enquiry into the causes of the high prices of corn and labour, the depressions on our foreign exchanges ... 2914

An enquiry into the causes of the late increase of robbers, etc. 37

An enquiry into the causes that have impeded the increase and improvement of arable farms. ... 2864

An enquiry into the conduct of a late right honourable commoner. 592

An enquiry into the consumption of public wealth by the clergy. 3277

An enquiry into the currency; in which the measures of 1819 and 1844 are fully considered. 6543

An enquiry into the currency principle. 5792

An enquiry into the customary estates and tenant-rights. 686

An enquiry into the depreciation of Irish bank paper, its effects and causes, and a remedy proposed. 2429

An enquiry into the effects produced on the national currency and rates of exchange, by the Bank Restriction Bill. 2651

Enquiry into the expediency and practicability of reducing the interest on the national debt. 4773

An enquiry into the history of tithe, its influence upon the agriculture, population and morals of Ireland. 2579

An enquiry into the impediments to a free trade with the peninsula of India. 4024

An enquiry into the legality and expediency of increasing the Royal Navy by subscriptions for building county ships. 1304

An enquiry into the means of preserving and improving the publick roads of this kingdom. 653

An enquiry into the nature and qualities of English wools. 1191

An enquiry into the nature of the corn-laws; with a view to the new corn-bill proposed for Scotland. 992

An enquiry into the origin and increase of the paper currency of the kingdom. 3621

An enquiry into the poor laws and surplus labour. 4417

An enquiry into the principles of free trade. 9366

An enquiry into the principles which ought to regulate the imposition of duties on foreign corn. 5533

An enquiry into the progressive value of money in England ... 2767

An enquiry into the state of the public mind amongst the lower classes. 2039

An enquiry into the terminal charges of railway companies. 9241

The ensanguined strand of Merrion: or, a ... 2580

An epistle to the right honourable Philip earl of Chesterfield. 379

Epitome of a scheme of finance; whereby ... 2928

An epitome of the evidence given before the select committee of the house of commons. 7251

Epitome of the evidence on grand jury cess, taken ... 3456

An epitome of the grievances of Ireland. 5801

The equalisation of the poor rates. 6997

An equitable property tax. 4177

The error of mistaking net rental for permanent income. 6929

The errors and evils of the Bank Charter Act of 1844. 7543

The errors and fallacies of bimetallism. 9875

Errors in our funding system and the management of our money concerns, ... 3369

España, y el trafico de negros. 8166

Esprit de la revolution et de la constitution de France. 1725

Essai Historique Sur l'Origine des Dixmes. 1089

Essai sur l'etat actuel de l'administration ... 2228

Essay and letters on bimetallism. 9148

An essay concerning the establishment of a national bank in Ireland. 877, 1054

Essay in answer to the following question proposed by the Royal Irish Academy. 'What are the manures ...' 1883, 2356

An essay of public granaries. 9972

An esssay on a reduction of the interest of the national debt, proving, ... 2943

An essay on aerial navigation, with some observations on ships. 3466

An essay on aerostation. 1972

An essay on charitable economy. 4752, 4873, 4989

An essay on circulation and credit, in four parts. 870

An essay on civil liberty ... Delivered ... on Wednesday, May 29th 1776. 988

An essay on coin. 335

Essay on currency: being a serious research ... 3909

An essay on drill husbandry, by Lt. Col. Hardy, ... 2352

Essay on food, and particularly on feeding the poor. 6080

An essay on hospitals. 687

An essay on life assurance. 7957

Essay on measure work, locally-known as task, piece, job, or grate work. 6288

An essay on money. 3087

An essay on money-lending. 3654

An essay on paper circulation. 531

An essay on political economy. 3853

An essay on populousness. 4998

An essay on provident or parish banks for the security and improvement of the savings of tradesmen, ... 2920

An essay on raising potatoes from shoots, by the Rev. Dr. Maunsell. 2358

An essay on Scottish husbandry. 5167

An essay on the abolition of slavery throughout the British dominions. 4403

An essay on the actual resources for reestablishing the finances of Great Britain. 1374

An essay on the age of Louis XIV. 443

An essay on the agriculture of Co. Armagh. 4796

Essay on the agriculture of the county of Cork ... 2411

An essay on the antient and modern state of Ireland. 371, 393

Essay on the application of capital to land, ... 2912

An essay on the best mode of improving the condition of the labouring classes of Ireland. 5953

An essay on the cause of the decline of foreign trade. 35

An essay on the causes of the present high price of provisions. 841

An essay on the character and conduct of his excellency lord visc. Townshend. 776

Essay on the commercial principles applicable to contracts for the hire of land. 9014

An essay on the creation and advantages ... 3539

An essay on the East India trade. 742

An essay on the employment of the poor ... 3324

An essay on the employment which bridges, roads, and other public works ... 3149

An essay on the English national credit: or, an attempt ... 1977

An essay on the expediency of a national militia. 314

An essay on the general management of villa farms. 5729

An essay on the general principles and present practice of banking in England and Wales. 3292

An essay on the impolicy of the African slave trade ... 1575

An essay on the improvement of the great flow bogs of Ireland. 2539

An essay on the improvements to be made in the cultivation of small farms. 4544, 4856, 5817

An essay on the influence of a low price of corn on the profits of stock. 2891

An essay on the law of bailments. 1155

An essay on the management and mismanagement of the currency. 3527

An essay on the manufactures of Ireland, in which is considered, ... 2035

An essay on the means of discharging the public debt. 494

An essay on the mysteries of excessive taxation, written by a poor man. 9876

An essay on the national debt and finance of Great Britain. 4426

An essay on the national debt, and the national capital. 38

An essay on the nature of a loan ... 1189

An essay on the nature of credit ... 2809

An essay on the necessity of protecting duties. 1265

An essay on the origin, progress and establishment of national society. 980

An essay on the population of Dublin. 2491

An essay on the population of England, from the revolution to the present time, ... 1122

An examination of the report and evidence of the committee of the house of commons, on decimal coinage. 7375

An examination of the report of the Berbice commissioners, and an answer to the letters of James Stephen. 3030

An examination of the report of the joint stock bank committee. 4896

An examination of the rights of the colonies upon principles of law. 599

An examination of the scheme of church-power. 496, 1384

Examinator's letters, or, a mirror for British monopolists and Irish financiers. 1484

The example of France, a warning to Britain. 1836

Exchequer bills forgery. 5615

The exchequer note versus the sovereign. 8302

Exemption from the payments of church rates on personal grounds considered. 7918

Exhaustion of the soil in relation to landlords' covenants. 8751

Exhibit of bankruptcy and county court debts law. 9339

Exhibition of articles of Irish manufacture. 5226

The existing manufactures of Ireland. 9478

The expected budget. 6808

The expedience and method of providing assurances for the poor. 4068

The expediency and necessity of a local legislative body in Ireland. 4411

The expediency of a free exportation of corn at this time. 765

The expediency of giving the civil bill to the city of Dublin. 272

The expeditious discounter. 813

Expenditure of the land fund of New South Wales. 5467

Experience of an amateur miner. 8147, 8148

Experience preferable to theory. An answer to Dr. Price's observations on the nature of civil liberty . . . 958

The experiences of a landholder and indigo planter in Eastern Bengal. 7851

Experiments and observations on the constituent parts of the potato root. 1890

Experiments in agriculture, made under the direction of the right honourable and honourable Dublin Society. 547, 579, 642, 714, 715, 772, 773, 802, 864

Experiments on lime, united with wood-ash and kelp. 684, 810

Expert calculator; or counting house companion. 3467

An explanation of the life assurance classes. 7756

An explanation of the cause of the distress which pervades the civilised parts of the world . . . 3399

An explanation of the principles and proceedings of the provident institution at Bath for saving. 2935

An explanatory defence of the estimate of the manners and principles of the times. 345

Explanatory report on the plan and object of Mr. Buckingham's lectures. 3993

Exposé général de l'agriculture Luxembourgeoise. 6476

An exposition of corn-law repealing fallacies and inconsistencies. 5244

Exportation of cotton yarns. The real cause of the distress that has fallen upon the cotton trade . . . 2713

Exposition of facts and fallacies concerning Ireland. 4518

An exposition of fallacies on rent, tithes etc. 3688

An exposition of the act for a contribution on property, professions, trades and offices. 2391

An exposition of the author's experience. 7656

Exposition of one principal cause of the national distress, particularly in manufacturing districts. 3013

An exposition on the danger and deficiencies of the present mode of railway construction. 6009

An exposition of the land tax. 7410

An exposition of the principal terms of Union, and its probable effects on Ireland. 2219

An exposition of the real causes and effective remedies of the agricultural distress . . . 3280

Exposure of the fallacies contained in the letter to the rt. hon. Robert Peel M.P. 3173

An exposure of the injurious effects of the present system of the bankruptcy law. 5335

Exposure of the stock exchange and bubble companies. 7434

An exposure of the unjustifiable proceedings and unworthy motives . . . 3056

Expropriation. An anarchist essay. 9497

Extension of the suffrage. 8475

An extensive system of emigration considered. 6549

The extinction of poverty. 9970

Extra official state papers. Addressed to the right hon. lord Rawdon. 1620

Extract from an account of the funds . . . of the society in Scotland for propagating christian knowledge. 2398

Extract from a letter to a private friend on the present conditions and prospects of Ireland. 9394

Extract of rules on the revenue side of the Exchequer, from 1685. 1017

Extracts from letters written by a gentleman lately established on the Swan river. 4305

Extracts from parliamentary speeches on the Irish land question. 9167

Extracts from the records of the government of Bengal, No. XXXIII. 7917

Extracts from the reports of the English Society for bettering the condition of the poor. 2080

Extracts from a pamphlet, entitled, observations on the brewing trade of Ireland. 1049

Extracts from a pamphlet on the present state of the Irish poor. 4810

Extracts from publications relating to the culture and management of hemp. 2569

Extracts from the new poor law. 5227

Extracts from the several laws which have been at any time enacted in this kingdom, . . . 1699

Extracts from the views of W. H. Gregory, M.P. 6173

Extracts from the votes and proceedings of the American continental congress, . . . 874

Extracts of evidence taken by the late commission of inquiry into the occupation of land in Ireland. 6312

Extracts relative to the fisheries on the northwest coast of Ireland . . . 1513

The extradition treaty. 8047

The extraordinary case of James Ph. Trant. 1007

Extravagance supported on the principles of policy and philosophy. 1583

F

The Fabian Society; what it has done and how it has done it. 9800

Fabian tracts,
    No. 1. Why are the many poor? 9701
    No. 29. What to read. 9918

Faction's overthrow, or more fair warning and good advice. 220

Factories and the factory system. 5791

The Factory Acts, as applied to the manufacture of earthenware. 8268

The Factory Acts made easy. 7835

The factory acts made easy New ed. carefully revised. 7987

The factory controversy. 7546

Factory legislation. 7550

The factory question, considered in relation to its effects on the health and morals. 4890

Facts about Ireland. A curve-history of recent years. 9630

Facts: addressed to the landholders, stockholders, merchants, farmers, . . . 1094

Facts addressed to the serious attention of the people of Great Britain . . . 1926

Facts and arguments for the repeal of the legislative union examined. 5582

Facts and arguments respecting the great utility of an extensive plan . . . 2244

Facts and circumstances relating to the condition of the Irish clergy. 4382

Facts and documents relating to the affairs of the union bank of Calcutta. 6561

Facts and evidence relating to the opium trade. 5236

Facts and experiments on the use of sugar in feeding cattle. 2610

The facts and fallacies of National League finance brought up to date. 9617

Facts and feelings relative to the necessity of church building. 4765

'Facts and figures.' 6421

Facts and figures about Ireland. Part 1. 9813, 9814

Facts and figures Dec. 1880. 9115

Facts and illustrations for the labourers friend society. 4429

Facts and observations on the Irish land question. 8777

Facts and opinions concerning statute hirings. 8054

Facts and reasons in support of Mr. Rowland Hill's plan. 4974

Facts and their consequences . . . 1218

Facts and theories. 7241

The facts as to French bimetallism. 9886

Facts connected with the social and sanitary condition of the working classes in the City of Dublin. 5936

Facts established by authentic documents. 5107

Facts for Englishmen and Scotchmen about Ireland. 9618

Facts for the kind-hearted of England. 6302

Facts for the new electorate. 9388

Facts for the repealers. 4561

Facts founded upon parliamentary returns illustrative of the great inequaiity of the taxes. 4430

Facts from Gweedore. 7446, 9557

Facts from the fisheries, contained in two reports from the Ring district, Co. Waterford. 6422

Facts from the fisheries contained in four quarterly reports from the Ring district, Co. Waterford. 6423

Facts on Ireland. 4378

Facts relating to Chinese commerce. 3911

Facts relating to north-eastern Texas. 6593

Facts relative to a banking connexion between Thellusson Brothers and Co., . . . 1872

Facts respecting the present state of the church in Ireland. 8555

Facts upon facts against the league. 5933

Facts versus theory: a retrospect of our past policy. 5646

Facts which prove the immediate necessity for the enactment of sanitary measures. 6201

A fair and honest statement of the several humane institutions established within these last twenty-five years . . . 2252

Fifth annual report of the Cork ladies society. 3817

A fifth letter, by the author of four former letters to the people of England. 315

A fifth letter to the earl of Carlisle from William Eden, esq. on population. 1075

A fifth letter to the people of England. 300

Fifth number of the reports of the Society for promoting the comforts of the poor. 2348

Fifth report of the committee of the county of Limerick agricultural association. 3722

Fifth report of the Meath charitable loan. 2810

Fifth report of the society for promoting the education of the poor of Ireland. 3015

The Fifth report of the society, instituted in Edinburgh on 25th January, 1813, . . . 3016

Fifty three years' taxation and expenditure. 9262

Figures and facts: or suggestions to tradesmen and others. 9340

Final report of the Central Relief Committee of the Society of Friends. 8296

Final report of the committee . . . to take into consideration the measures to be adopted in consequence of the reduction in the duties on wine. 5584

Final report of the Irish Distress committee. 4670

The finance of the free church of Scotland. 8708

The finances and trade of the United Kingdom at the beginning of the year 1852. 7143

The finances of Great Britain considered. 7840, 7903

The finances of Italy. 8278

The financial and commercial crisis considered. 6110

The financial and commercial crisis considered, . . . also the letter of a London banker on the currency question . . . 8426

The financial and economical condition of Ireland. 8980

Financial and political facts of the eighteenth and present century. 2400

The financial exigencies of Ireland before and after the legislative union. 8225

Financial facts of the eighteenth century; or, a cursory view, . . . 2312

Financial fenianism and the Caledonian railway. 8452

The financial house that Jack built. 3129

The financial lessons of 1866. 8446

Financial measures for India. 7980

Financial plan for the relief of Ireland and the landlords of Ireland. 6151

The financial policy of war. 7566

The financial policy of William Pitt. 9644

Financial reform: a letter to the citizens of Glasgow. 6692

Financial reform imperative. 6430

Financial reform scrutinized. 3986

Financial Reform Tracts. New series.
    No. VII. 6791
    No. XXIII. 7774

Financial relations between Great Britain and Ireland . . . A review of a speech delivered by the rt. hon. A. J. Balfour, . . . 10000

The financial relations between Great Britain and Ireland. The terms of reference. 9952

Financial relations: Great Britain and Ireland. 9859

The financial relations report . . . A summary; compiled for the Irish financial reform league. 9960

A financial scheme for the relief of railway companies. 8390

Financial statement: speech of the hon. Geoffrey Eagar, colonial treasurer, in moving the first resolution, in committee of ways and means. 8361

The finishing stroke, being a supplement to the queries to the people of Ireland. 158

Fire and water, versus corn and hay. 8176

The fire duty. The duty on fire insurances: reasons for its abolition or reduction. 8141

The fireside story of Ireland. 9152

First annual report of the Association for the suppression of mendicity in the city of Waterford. 3282

First annual report of the County of Roscommon ladies' association, . . . 3457

First annual report of the Monkstown and Kingstown charitable inquiry society. 7773

First general report of the trade and commerce committee of the Loyal national repeal association. 5835

First half yearly report presented to the Mining Co. of Ireland. 3529

A first letter from R . . R . . s, esq., to the creditors of Burton's bank. 76

First letter to a noble lord, on the subject of the union. 2166

First letter to the tradesmen and labourers of Ireland on the repeal of the union. 5830

The first lines of Ireland's interest in the year 1780. 1050

The first number of the reports of the society for promoting the comforts of the poor. 2223

First part of the report of the Sub-committee of the same. 2224

The first principles of labour, property and money, . . . 7148

First report and proceedings of the general railway committee. 5000

First report and statement of accounts of the Sandymount loan-fund committee, January, 1832. 4306

First report of the agricultural improvement society of Ireland. 5338

The first report of the British-Irish ladies society . . . 3370

The first report of the committee appointed by the town council of Dublin. 7001

First report of the committee of the drapers' Early Closing Association. 7852

First report of the committee of the Limerick board of trade appointed to inquire into the present state and prospects of Irish manufactures . . . 3968

First report of the committee of the Loyal national repeal association on the glass duties. 5706

First report of the county of Kildare Independent club. 6431

First report of the directors of the New Zealand company. 5232

First report of the Loyal national repeal association. 5233

First report of the parliamentary committee of the Loyal national repeal association on the land question. 5836

The first report of the society for bettering the condition . . . of the poor. 2084

First report of the Society for the suppression of beggars. 2811

First report of the sub-committee of the Loyal national repeal association entitled 'Commercial tariffs . . .' 5707

First report of the sub-committee of the Loyal national repeal association on the estimates for 1844-5. 5708

First report on the object and effects of the house of recovery in Cork-street. 2498

First, second and third addresses to the landowners of England. 5111

First series of reports of the Loyal national repeal association of Ireland. 5234

The first step to a poor law for Ireland. 4966

First steps towards a universal system of decimal coinage. 7520

The fiscal and social injustice of the Irish pawnbroking system. 8319

Fiscal policy. Direct and indirect taxation contrasted. 8174

Fiscal reform. 9927

Fiscal relations of the United Kingdom & Ireland. 9443

Fish preservation and refrigeration. 9305

The fisheries, considered as a national resource. 7660

The fisheries revived: or, Britain's hidden treasure discovered. 13

The fishery case. 5373

The fitness of turnpike roads and highways. 4676

Five lectures on political economy . . . 5734

Five lectures on the principles of a legislative provision for the poor in Ireland. 5039

Five letters from a free merchant in Bengal to Warren Hastings, Esq. . . . 1279

Five letters on the Irish railways. 5831

Five years of church extension in St. Pancras. 7132

Five years of Tory rule. 9060

Fixity of tenure. A dialogue. 8724

Fixity of tenure; heads of a suggested legislative enactment. 8431

Fixity of tenure; heads of a suggested legislative enactment; . . . to which are added queries. 8350

Fixity of tenure incompatible with freedom of contract. 9181

Flax and its products in Ireland. 8084

Flax versus cotton. 6953

Fluctuations of currency, commerce and manufactures. 5307

Fluctuations of prices, 1835 to 1880. 9270

The following resolutions were proposed by Mr. Madison in the house of representatives of the United States, . . . 1848

The food question: shewing the effects which steam power applied to agriculture would have. 6273

Foregone conclusions; the Bessborough commission, April, 1881. 9197

The foreign debt of Spain. 8701

Foreign land tenures and the Irish tenant. 9233

Foreign loans and depression of trade. 9564

Foreign loans and their consequences. 7439

Foreign slave trade. Abstract of the information recently laid on the table . . . 3222

Foreign tariffs. Their effect on British commerce. 9452

Foreign tariffs; their injurious effects on British manufactures. 5559

The foreign trade of China divested of monopoly . . . 4308

Form of mortgage in fee and of freeholds and leaseholds. 8043

Form of the notices necessary to be given before the first day of July, 1799 . . . for the recovery . . of tithes . . . under the compensation act . . . 2085

Fortune's epitome of the stocks and public funds, . . . 3179

Forty-seventh annual report of the Charitable Association. 7145

The forty-shilling freeholder. 3724

Four essays on colonial slavery. 4192

Four essays on subjects comprised in the science of political economy. 8964

Four introductory letters on political economy. 7233

Four lectures on poor-laws, delivered before the University of Oxford . . . 4692

Four lectures on the poor laws. 4589

Four letters addressed to the chairman of the agricultural committee of both houses of parliament. 4805

G

The game's up! 6557
Gas lighting: its progress and its prospects. 6741
The gas supply of the metropolis. 8520
The gates of the east. 7701
Gauging unmasked, which shews all the necessary rules in vulgar and decimal arthmetic. 1230
General and equitable commutation of tithes. 4453
A general guide to the companies formed for working foreign mines . . . 3525
General hints to emigrants containing notices of the various fields for emigration. 8367
General observations on the state of Ireland, and plans for its improvement. 4681, 5122
The general opposition of the colonies to the payment of the stamp duty. 601
General order of the Poor Law Commissioners for regulating the administration of outdoor relief. 6180
A general priced catalogue of implements, seeds, plants, etc. 5237, 5715
General reflections on the system of the poor laws, with a short view of Mr. Whitbread's bill . . . 2532
General remarks on our commerce with the continent. 2500
General remarks on steam communication. 5839
General remarks on the British fisheries. 1326
General report of James Fanning's Charitable Institution. 7299
General Sir Charles Napier and the directors of the East India Company. 7689
General tariff of the customs for all ports and frontiers of the Russian Empire, . . . 1250
A general view of a plan of universal and equal taxation. 2009
A general view of the history and objects of the Bank of England. 3301
A general view of the variations which have been made in the affairs of the East-India Company, . . . 1742
The gentleman and builders assistant; containing . . . 2568
The gentleman and builder's director; . . . 977
A genuine account of Nova Scotia. 14
A geographical, statistical and commercial account of the Russian ports of the Black Sea. 4887
Geological and mining report on the Leinster coal district. 2812
Geological and mining surveys of the coal districts of the counties of Tyrone and Antrim. 3912
A Georgic of modern husbandry. In twelve parts. 2596
The German and Austrian systems of land registry and their application to England. 9941
Germany and the gold standard. 9921
The ghost of John Bull. 5005
A gift to the uninsured. 7695
Give us our rights! . . . 1180
Gladstone and Burke. 9506
'Gladstone & justice to Ireland.' 8541
Gladstone's measures for the pacification of Ireland. 9482
A glance at the effects produced on trade by the existing banking laws. 6439
A glance at the question of a ship-canal. 4566
Glances at the times. 5303
The Glasgow and Belfast Union Railway. 5844
Glasgow Tracts for Trades Unionists—No. II. 8237
A gleam of comfort to this distracted empire. 1402

Gleanings in Ireland; particularly respecting its agriculture, mines, and fisheries. 2351
Glimpses at the origin, mission, and destiny of men. 8375
Glympses accross the Irish Channel by a friend, not a flatterer. 3508
God and the country robbed. 7702
God's goodness visible in our deliverance from Popery. 324
God's laws versus corn laws. 6006
Gold a delusion. 7504
Gold and silver. 9898
Gold and silver: a supplement to Strzelecki's physical description of New South Wales . . . 7596
Gold and silver money. 9775
A gold coinage for India. 8538
The gold companies. 7308
The gold digger. 7343
The gold fields of Victoria. 8462
Gold fields of Western Australia. 9832
Gold quartz mining in California. 7190
The gold regions of Australia. 7198
The gold regions of California. 6640
The gold standard. 6440
Gold Standard Defence Association. 9884, 9896
The golden fleece: or some thoughts on the clothing trade of Ireland. 475
Good! A proposition on the national debt. 5852
A 'good' landlord & his tenants. 9183
The Gothenburg licensing system. 8918
The government guarantee on Indian railways. 8010
Government intervention in railway affairs. 6743
The Government land bill and Mr. Chamberlain's proposal (being letters to The Times, Economist, and Scotsman). 9714
Government of Ireland bill. Belfast Chamber of Commerce and Mr. Gladstone, Report. 9812
The government of the East India Company and its monopolies. 7707
The government, the Bank of England, and the public. 8589
The gradual progress of international arbitration. 9441
Grammgeld oder das zukünftige Welt-Munz System. 9821
Grand Canal Atmospheric Railway Company. 5716
Grand Canal Company. Address to the shareholders by the chairman on the occasion of the last meeting of the century. 10006
Grand Canal Company. At the half-yearly meeting of . . . 2434
Grand Canal Company, Ireland. 5717
Grand Canal Company. To the proprietors of Grand Canal stock 1815. 2866
Grand Canal. Defence of the court of directors, including a statement of . . . 2901
Grand canal. First lettters to the proprietors of stock. 5002
Grand Canal. Report of the court of directors at the half-yearly meeting of the Company. 3023
Grand canal. Second letter to the proprietors of stock. 5003
Grand canal. Third letter (and possibly the last) to the proprietors of stock. 5004
Grand trunk railway of Canada. 7922
The Gravesend inland bonding docks. 8170
Great Britain and the United States. 8613
The Great Britain steamship. 6196
Great Britain's crisis! 4275
The great case of tithes truly stated. 292
The great cause of the present distress and the remedy. 5592

Great central Irish railway. 4806
The great charter of the liberties of the city of Dublin. 750
The great cotton question: where are the spoils of the slave. 8011
Great demonstration in Belfast. Speech of John Bright, Esq., M.P., on Monday, October 4th 1852. 7114
The Great Exhibition, its palace and its principal contents. 7089
The great experiment: mock free trade. 9849
Great facts concerning free trade and free trade essays. 5807
The great importance and necessity of increasing tillage, by an act of parliament, in Ireland. 154, 211
Great importance of the Shannon navigation to the whole kingdom of Ireland. 221
The great industrial exhibition, in 1851. 6444
Great Leinster and Munster railway. First extension from Dublin to Kilkenny. First report. 5007
Great Leinster and Munster railway. First extension from Dublin to Kilkenny. Report of special general meeting. 5118
Great Leinster and Munster railway. First extension from Dublin to Kilkenny. Second half-yearly report. 5117
Great Leinster and Munster railway. First extension from Dublin to Kilkenny. 3rd half yearly report. 5119
The great metallic powers. 9389
Great Southern and Western Railway, Ireland. An account of the proceedings of the meeting of the shareholders . . . 19th March, 1849. 6643
Great Southern and Western Railway, Ireland. Half-yearly reports.

1845.	5848, 5849
1846.	6007, 6008
1847.	6197, 6198
1848.	6445
1849.	6644
1850.	6835, 6836
1851.	7009
1855.	7526, 7527
1856.	7606, 7607
1857.	7691, 7692

Great Southern and Western Railway, Ireland. Remarks on the Dublin terminus. 5847
Great Southern and Western Railway. Statement of accounts, 30th June, 1850. 6837
—— 31st December, 1850. 7008
The great war between capital and labour. 9731
The 'Great West'. 8785
Great Western Railway, England. An account of the proceedings. 4571
The green box of Monsieur de Sartine. 1071
The Gresham law. 9881
La grève des charbonniers d'Anzin en 1866. 8369
The grievances of Ireland, an address to all ranks of the people. 1878
The grievances of Ireland, their causes and their remedies. 3684
The grievances of the American colonies candidly examined. 637
The ground of national grievances examined. 3180
The ground values delusion. 9779
The grounds of an opinion on the policy of restricting the importation of foreign corn. 2876
Grundriss für vorlesungen über National ökonomie. 9038
Grundzüge einer Klassifikation der Wirtschaftswissenschaften. 9682
Guaranteed securities. 7824
The guardian of landlord and tenant. 6383

An inquiry into the connection between the present price of provisions and the size of farms. 833

An inquiry into the economy, exchange, and distribution of wealth. Part second. 6698

An inquiry into the effects of the Irish Grand Jury laws as affecting the industry of the people
  of Ireland. 2883
  of England. 2884

An inquiry into the expediency of the existing restrictions on the importation of foreign corn. 4396

An inquiry into the expenses of the collection of the revenue of Ireland, and the examination of the principal merchants of Dublin, ... 1877

An inquiry into the freedom of the city of London. 6809

An inquiry into the impolicy of the continuance of distillation from grain, ... 2632

An inquiry into the influence of falling exchange on the prosperity of a nation. 9656

An inquiry into the influence of the excessive use of spirituous liquors. 4022

A inquiry into the justice and policy of an union between Great Britain and Ireland, ... 1522

An inquiry into the late mercantile distresses in Scotland and England. 817

An inquiry into the legality of pensions. 501

An inquiry into the merits of the American colonization society. 4447

An inquiry into the merits of the poor law report of D. O. P. Okeden, esquire. 4537

An inquiry into the national debt and sinking fund. 7615

An inquiry into the nature & origin of public wealth & into the means & causes of its increase. 2437

An inquiry into the nature and progress of rent ... 2877

An inquiry into the nature of a conveyance. 7617

An inquiry into the nature of benevolence, chiefly with a view to elucidate the principles of the poor laws, ... 2995

Inquiry into the navigation laws. 4451

Inquiry into the opinion of the commercial classes of Great Britain on the Suez ship canal. 7683

An inquiry into the origin of copyhold tenure. 4649

An inquiry into the policy, efficiency, and consistency, of the alterations in our corn laws. 2815

An inquiry into the policy of the laws, affecting the popish inhabitants of Ireland ... 903

An inquiry into the political economy of the Irish peasantry. 3334

An inquiry into the practice of imprisonment for debt. 843

An inquiry into the present agricultural distress of this country, with suggestions for their relief ... 2937

An inquiry into the present state and means of improving the salmon fisheries. 3735

An inquiry into the present state of population in England & Wales. 1169

An inquiry into the principle and tendency of the bill now pending in parliament, ... 3073

An inquiry into the real difference between actual money consisting of gold and silver, and paper money of various descriptions. 2439

An inquiry into the state and progress of the linen manufacture of Ireland. 339

An inquiry into the state of the currency of the country, its defects and remedy. 3074

An inquiry into the state of the finances of Great Britain. 1938

An inquiry into those principles, respecting the nature of demand ... 3224

An inquiry whether the disturbances in Ireland have originated in tithes ... 3275

An insight to the assessed taxes. 6831

The instability of gold ... 9536

Institution for administering medical aid to the sick poor ... 2749, 2885

The Instow tithe case. 5603

Instruct; employ; don't hang them. 4685

Instructions for establishing friendly institutions upon the improved principle. 4041

Instructions for the establishment of benefit building societies. 5019

Instructions for the establishment of friendly societies. 4684

Instructions for the establishment of loan societies. 4785

Instructions for the gaugers of excise in Ireland. 1466

Instructions for travellers. 368

Instructions given by the commissioners appointed to enquire into the state of the poor of Ireland. 4578

Instructions to agents, sub-agents and clerks at Bank of Ireland branches. 6664

Instructions to the officers and servants of the workhouse of the city of Dublin. 5195

The insufficiency of the causes to which the increase of our poor ... 1590

The insurance register. 8634

The insurance register, 1872. 8896

The insurrection, or, a faithful narrative of the disturbances which lately broke out in the province of Munster ... 1523

The intellectual destiny of the working man. 8208

Intercolonial Exhibition, 1866. 8416

Interest: is it just or not? 9677

The interest of Great Britain considered, with regard to her colonies. 408

The interest of Great Britain, with regard to her American colonies, considered. 1172

The interest of the merchants and manufacturers of Great Britain, in the present contest with the colonies, stated and considered. 879, 922

Interesting extracts from the minutes of evidence taken before the committee of the whole house ... 2816

Interesting facts respecting the loans and lotteries of the years of 1788 and 1789, ... 1610

Interesting particulars, relative to that great national undertaking, ... 3187

The interests and present state of the nation, considered. 1969

The interests of agriculture and commerce, inseparable. 2575

The interests of Ireland considered ... 372

The interference of the British legislature in the internal concerns of the West India Islands, ... 2938

International Association for obtaining a uniform decimal system of measures, weights and coins. 7697, 7788

International bimetallism: a cure for agricultural depression. 9912

International bimetallism and the battle of the standard. 9199

International code of commerce. 7036

International coinage critically considered. 8579

International fisheries exhibition. 9311

International fishery disputes. 9745

Introduction to political economy lecture IX. 4387

Introduction to suggestions on the state of Ireland. 9279

An introduction to the law of tenure. 27

Introduction to the science of wealth. 8220

An introduction to the second edition of Railways in India. 6390

Introductory discourse to a few lectures on the application of chemistry to agriculture, ... 3546

An introductory lecture, delivered before the university of Dublin, in Hilary term 1837. 4863

An introductory lecture on political economy. Delivered in the theatre of Trinity College. Dublin, in Trinity term, 1848. 6645

An introductory lecture on political economy delivered at King's College, London, 27th February, 1833. 4455

An introductory lecture on political economy, delivered before the university of Oxford. 3766

An introductory lecture on the law of shipping and marine insurance. 7335

An introductory lecture on the study of political economy. 4913

Introductory lecture to a course of political economy. 4062

The inutility of bankruptcy laws. 9287

Inventive genius versus free trade. 9603

An investigation into the principles and credit of the circulation of paper money. 2397

An investigation of Mr. Morgan's comparative view of the public finances, ... 2331

An investigation of the causes of the present high price of provisions. 2245

An investigation of the legality and validity of a union. 2176

The investigations into the condition of the children in the Cork workhouse. 7833

Ireland. A letter addressed to lord Monteagle. 9467

Ireland. A letter to earl Grey. 8556

Ireland and her evils. 4830

Ireland and her famine. 6242

Ireland and her servile war. 8339

Ireland and Irish questions. 5840

Ireland and Irish questions considered. 5482

Ireland and the Channel Islands. 6482

Ireland and the earl of Shrewsbury. 5334

Ireland and the imperial parliament. 8829

Ireland as it is and as it might be. 9066

Ireland as it was,—is,—and ought to be. 4468

Ireland as she ought to be, being practical suggestions ... 6665

Ireland as she ought to be, or a serious and impressive call ... 3515

Ireland, as she was, as she is, and as she shall be. 5815

Ireland considered as a field for investment. 7257

Ireland disgraced, or the island of saints become an island of sinners. 349

Ireland. Emigration and valuation. 7336

Ireland estimated as a field for investment. 7484

Ireland from one or two neglected points of view. 9624

Ireland: her landlords, her people and their homes. 7933

Ireland: her present condition, and what it might be. 8216

Ireland: her present condition; its causes and remedies. 8457

Ireland historical and statistical. Part I. 5782

Ireland. Ignorance. 'Repeal'. 4452

Ireland imperialized. 6666

Ireland in A.D. 1900. 9108

Ireland in 1829; or the first year's administration of the duke of Northumberland. 4042

Ireland in 1831. Letters on the state of Ireland. 4148

A letter to the proprietors and occupiers of land in the parish of Bledlow in Buckinghamshire. 4520

A letter to the proprietors and occupiers of land, on the cause of, and the remedies for, the declension of agricultural prosperity. 3370

A letter to the proprietors of bank stock. 5285

A letter to the proprietors of East India stock ... 520

A letter to the proprietors of the East India Stock, from lord Clive. 524

A letter to the protestants of England. 3606

A letter to the public, containing some important hints relating to the revenue. 560

A letter to the publick, concerning bogs. 322

A letter to the publick on the present posture of affairs. 165

A letter to the publick: with some quaeries humbly offered to its consideration. 166, 167

Letter to the queen, shewing the awful and alarming sacrifice of national property. 5874

A letter to the rate-payers of Great Britain. 4511

Letter to the representative peers of Ireland. 5033

A letter to the rev. Doctor O'Leary. Found on the great road leading from the city of Cork ... 1535

A letter to the rev. Dr. Richard Price on his Observations on the nature of civil liberty, ... 961

A letter to the rev. H. F. Yeatman, LL.B. 4528

A letter to the rev. John Sargeaunt, rector of Stanwick. 6178, 6433

A letter to the rev. John T. Becher. 4554

A letter to the rev. Mr. John Wesley, occasioned by his calm address to the American colonies. 914

A letter to the rev. Samuel Barber, minister of the presbyterian congregation of Rathfryland, ... 1499

A letter to the rev. T. R. Malthus, M.A., F.R.S., being an answer to the criticism ... 3354

A letter to the right honorable and honorable the Dublin Society from the right rev. Doctor Coppinger, ... 2682

A Letter to the right honorable William Pitt ... [and] ... a short epistle to Wm. Pulteney ... 1202

A letter to the right hon. and honourable the trustees of the linen manufacture. 387, 1633

A letter to the right honourable and honourable the trustees of the linen manufacture, and also, to the trustees for distributing bounties, etc., etc. 1732

A letter to the right hon. Benjamin Disraeli, M.P. for the county of Buckingham. 7620

A letter to the right hon. Benjamin D'Israeli, M.P. her majesty's chancellor of the exchequer, in reply to several anonymous articles. 7242

A letter to the rt. hon. Charles Abbot ... 2393

A letter to the right honourable Charles B. Bathurst, M.P. on the subject of the poor laws. 3111

Letter to the right hon. Charles Grant president of the board of control on the present state of British intercourse with China. 4467

Letter to the right hon. Charles Grant. 4592

A letter to the right hon. Chichester Fortescue M.P. on the state of Ireland. 8573

A letter to the right honorable earl Grey, on colonial slavery. 4342

A letter to the right honourable earl Grey on the obligation of the coronation oath. 4488

Letter to the right hon. earl Grey, on the subject of emigration. 6179

A letter to the right honourable earl Grey Premier, chiefly respecting the established church of Ireland. 4587

Letter to the rt. hon. earl Grey proposing the appointment of a board of trade for Ireland. 4248

A letter to the right hon. Edmund Burke, in reply to his "Reflections on the revolution in France, etc." 1646

A letter to the right honourable Edmund Burke, on the present state of Ireland. 1866

A letter to the right honorable Edward G. Stanley. 4471

A letter to the rt. hon. E. G. Stanley etc etc in answer to Dr. Doyle's letter to Thomas Spring Rice esq. M.P. 4241

A letter to the rt. hon. E. G. Stanley on the state of church property in Ireland. 4196

A letter to the rt. hon. E. G. Stanley on tithes in Ireland. 4391

A letter to the rt. hon. Frederick Robinson, president of the board of trade, ... etc. 3139

A letter to the right honourable George Canning, M.P. relative to a free trade in corn ... 3514

A letter to the right honourable George Canning, on the principle and administration of the English poor laws. 3358

A letter to the right honourable George Canning, Secretary of State for foreign affairs. 3462

A Letter to the right hon. Henry Grattan, on the deplorable consequences resulting to Ireland from the very low price of spirituous liquors. 2697

A letter to the rt. hon. Henry Grattan, on the state of the labouring poor in Ireland, ... 1937

Letter to the right hon. Henry Goulbourn, M.P. ... 5487

A letter to the right hon. H. Labouchere, M.P. &c. &c. by C. N. Newdegate, esq., M.P. on the balance of trade. 6712

A letter to the right hon. Henry Labouchere, M.P. president of the board of trade, etc. etc. on railways. 6777

A letter to the right honourable Henry Labouchere, ... on the more effective application of the system of relief ... 6323

A letter [to] the right hon. Henry Labouchere on the pressure of the corn laws, ... 5472

A letter to the right honourable J--n L--d A---y. 846

A letter to the right honourable James, earl of Kildare, on the present posture of affairs. 178

A letter to the right honourable John Ponsonby, Esq. 411

A letter to the right hon. J. P. Esq.; in relation to a national affair ... 232

A letter to the right honourable J— P—, speaker of the house of commons in Ireland. 557

A letter to the right honourable J--n P-----y, s---r of the h----e of c----s in I-----d. 658

A letter to the right honourable J(oh)n P(onsonb)y, speaker of the house of commons in Ireland. 659

Letter to the rt. hon. Joseph W. Henley, M.P. president of the board of trade regarding life assurance institutions. 7125

A letter to the right hon. J. W. Henley, M.P. on the balance of trade. 7202

A letter to the rt. hon. lord Althorp, chancellor of the exchequer, etc., etc., on the subject of the duty on printed cottons. 3969

A letter to the rt. hon. lord Althorp chancellor of the exchequer, etc. etc. on the wine duties' bill. 4318

A letter to the right honourable lord Althorp on the bill for amending the poor laws. 4588

Letter to the rt. hon. lord Ashley on the cotton factory system ... 4433

A letter to the right hon. lord Ashley, on the condition of the working classes in Birmingham. 5508

A letter to the rt. hon lord Brougham on the alleged breach of the colonial apprenticeship contract. 4979

Letter to the right hon. lord Brougham on his bill to facilitate the transfer of real estate. 7772

Letter to the right honorable lord Castlereagh upon the subject of the present state of Great Britain. 2974

Letter to the rt. hon lord Cloncurry. 4048

A letter to the right honourable lord Cranworth, lord chancellor of England, &c. &c. &c. on the practical injustice and impolicy of the proceedings under the Irish encumbered estates' acts. 7537

A letter to the rt. hon. lord Erskine, lord high chancellor of Great Britain ... 2494

A letter to the right hon. lord Glenelg. 5036

A letter to the rt. hon lord Goderich. 3741

A letter to the rt. hon. lord Hatherton. 4905

A letter ... to the right hon. lord John Russell. 6029

A letter to the right honourable lord John Russell. By a beneficed clergyman of the protestant church of Ireland. 4689

Letter to the rt. hon. lord John Russell, first lord of the treasury, explanatory of a financial system for extending Railways in Ireland. 6874

A letter to the right honourable lord John Russell, first lord of the Treasury, suggesting a plan for the adjustment of the relation between landlord and tenant in Ireland. 6658

A letter to the right hon lord John Russell from Thomas Fowell Buxton. 4984

A letter to the right hon. lord J. Russell in answer to the pamphlet of the rev. Richard Jones. 5053

A letter to the right hon. lord John Russell, M.P., in favour of a protective duty on the importation of foreign grain. 6870

A letter to the rt. hon lord John Russell, &c &c &c. In reply to Mr Jamieson. 5293

Letter to the rt. honorable Lord John Russell, etc. on Australian emigration. 5363

Letter to the right hon lord John Russell on communication with Ireland. 6875

A letter to the right hon. lord John Russell M.P., on the best mode of avoiding the evils of mixed gauge railways and the break of the gauge. 6485

Letter to the right honourable lord John Russell on the expediency of promoting railways in Ireland. 6780

A letter to the rt. hon. lord John Russell on the future prospects of Ireland. 6232

A letter to the rt. hon. lord John Russell, on the ministerial measure for establishing poor laws. 4962, 5080

A letter to the right hon. lord J. Russell on the principles of the Irish poor law bill. 4906

A letter to the right hon. lord John Russell, etc. etc. etc. on the probable increase in rural crime. 4836

A letter to the right honourable lord John Russell, M.P., etc., etc., etc., on the subject of Indian Railways. 6480

A letter to the right hon. lord John Russell on the transfer of landed property. 7401

O

On the whig project for abolishing the removal of the poor. 7467

On the wine trade and wine duties. 8388

On the Workmen's Compensation Act of 1897. 9950

On thorough-draining; and its immediate results to the agricultural interest. 5689

On wage statistics and wage theories. 9632

On wages and combination. 4637

On wet docks, quays, and warehouses for the port of London. 1834

One more letter to the people of England, by their Old Friend. 479

One more specific for Ireland. 3560

One or two remarks on the law relating to combinations. 7468

One reserve or many? 8478

One-sided free trade with wreck and ruin, or fair trade with prosperity. 9045

I Vict. c. 69. Act to amend an act for the commutation of tithes. 4968

One year of the administration of his Excellency the marquess of Wellesley in Ireland. 3367

The only compromise possible in regard to church rates. 8007

The only safe poor law experiment for Ireland. 5038

'Open Sesame'; or, the key to national wealth. 7719

Opening, conducting and closing of special banking accounts. 9173

The operation of monopolies on the production of food. 5445

The operation of the corn laws. 4477

Opinion de M. Laffitte sur le projet de loi relatif aux finances pour 1817 ... 3026

Opinions of Henry Brougham, Esq. on negro slavery. 3658

The opinions of lords Wellesley and Grenville, on the government of India. 4349

Opinions of the hon. Mountstuart Elphinstone upon some of the leading questions connected with the government of British India. 4220

Opinions of the late lord Melville and marquess Wellesley upon an open trade to India. 2785

The opinions of the London press respecting the amount of opium compensation offered by her majesty's government. 5627

Opinions of the press on a pamphlet by Thomas Edward Symonds. 7553

Opinions on interesting subjects of public law and commercial. 1311

Opinions on Mr. Walton and Mr. Carden's pamphlets on the Irish question. 8323

Opinions on tithes, and on the state of Ireland, ... 4527

The opium question. 5306

Opium revenue of India. the question answered. 7663

The opium revenue of India. Is it right to take three millions sterling from the Chinese. 7720

The oppressed labourers, the means for their relief, ... 3147

An oppressed poor in an insolvent nation. 6195

The oppression of tithe exemplified. 1973

Oppression unmasked; being a narrative of the proceedings ... 1344

Oppressions and cruelties of Irish revenue officers. 3061

Optional mobilisation of land. 8627

An oration delivered at the State-house in Philadelphia, ... Thursday the 1st of August, 1776. 947

Order of the poor law commissioners for government of the workhouse. 5150

Orders appointed by his majestie (King Charles I) to be straitly observed. 357

The orders in council and the American embargo beneficial to the political and commercial interests of Great Britain. 2618

Orders in council, or an examination of the justice, legality, and policy of the new system of commercial, ... 2581

Orders of the poor law commissioners regulating the meetings of the board of guardians. 5151

Oregon. Facts regarding its climate, ... etc. 9000

The origin and principles of the agricultural and commercial bank of Ireland. 4705

Origin and proceedings of the agricultural associations in Great Britain, ... 3134

The origin and progress of 'monster house' monopoly. 7058

The origin and reclamation of peat-bog. 6039

Origin and results of the clearing system which is in operation on the narrow gauge railways. 6050

The origin of the criminal laws affecting the working classes. 8236

Origin of the new system of manufacture. 3860

The origin, policy and consequences of the corn laws. 5225

An original financial plan for the conversion of the foreign debt of Spain without interest. 4731

The Orphan-house: being a brief history of that institution, & ... 1777

Ostensible causes of the present state of Ireland considered and remedies suggested ... 3272

The Ottoman bank. 7870

Ought landowners to bear a share of local taxation? 9754

Ought the state to buy the railways? 8924

Our banking system: and the sufficiency or insufficiency of our cash reserves. 9764

Our banking system: the interests involved, and suggestions for their security. 9074

'Our boys': what shall we do with them. 9709

Our colonial empire and the case of New Zealand. 8349

Our colonies and their future. 8665

Our currency. 8327

Our daily food, its price, and sources of supply. 8517

Our deer forests. 8485

'Our economic Catos.' 8889

Our fiscal future. 9490

Our free trade policy examined. 5956

Our imports and exports. 8766

Our land laws and the agricultural situation. 9073

Our land laws of the past. 9034

Our monetary system. Why does it break down ... 7721

Our monetary system. Some remarks ... 8226

Our money laws the cause of the national distress. 6169

Our national dangers and our need. 9512

Our national relations with China. 7722

Our natural rights. 4811

Our next money panic. 8400

Our policy in China. 7803

Our poor law. Its defects and the way to mend them. 8051

Our railway system viewed in reference to invasion. 8827

Our railways: should they be private or national property? 9078

Our staple manufactures. 7554

Our trade with France under the Cobden treaty. 9213

Our unemployed. 8629

Our West Indian colonies. 7516

The outcry against the new poor law. 5415

Out-door relief as a cause of pauperism. 8865

Outline of a plan for an agricultural school. 4556

An outline of a plan for a new circulating medium. 4313

The outline of a plan for bringing the Scotch and English currency to the same standard bullion value ... 3652

Outline of a plan for employing the poor of Ireland. 4193

Outline of a plan for raising provincial capital 3931

An outline of a plan for relieving the poor of Ireland. 3918

Outline of a plan for the abolition of the tithes. 4557

An outline of a plan for the formation of a savings and Annuity bank. 4535

Outline of a plan for the general commutation of tithes. 4885

Outline of a plan for the relief and improvement of Ireland. 6609

Outline of a plan of an Irish parliament. 5709

Outline of a plan to pay off the nation. 4562

Outline of a practical plan for the immediate, effective economical relief of the starving and destitute poor of Ireland. 4861

Outline of a system of direct taxation. 7888

Outlines of a new budget. 4146

Outlines of a plan for adapting the machinery of the public funds to the transfer of real property. 5808

Outlines of a plan for the establishment of an agricultural model school. 3933

Outlines of a plan for the immediate settlement. 4492

Outlines of a plan of finance: proposed to be submitted to parliament. 2770

Outlines of political economy. 8413

Outlines of the fifteenth chapter of the proposed general report from the board of agriculture. 1896

Overend and Gurney prosecution. 8682

Overend, Gurney & Co. Birchin-Lane bookkeeping. 8401

Overend, Gurney & Co. (Limited). A plain statement of the case. 8481

Overend, Gurney, & Coy., or the saddle on the right horse. 8402

Overend, Gurney & Co., Ltd. Report of the committee of the defence association. 8482

Overland communications with Western China. 8885

Overlegislation in 1884. 9370

Over-population. 9725

The over-population fallacy considered. 6676

The overseer's guide and assistant. 5205

The over-taxation of Ireland. 9956

Owenism an imposition on the working classes. 5277

The Oxford Handbook of political economy. 9316

—— 2nd ed. 9425

P

The paddy tax in Ceylon. 9727

Paddy's leisure hours in the poor-house. 6722

A pamphlet containing reflections upon subjects suited to the nature of the present times. 4028

The pamphlet entitled, 'Taxation no tyranny,' candidly considered, and it's arguments, and pernicious doctrines exposed and refuted. 931

A pamphlet reporting the proceedings of 'the House of ("little") Commons'. 8890

The panic: a second sketch from nature. 8403

The panorama; or a journey to Munster. 2534

Plain truth: or, a letter to the author of dispassionate thoughts on the American war. 1101

Plain words addressed to members of the church of England. 4490

Plan and regulations of the society for promoting the comforts of the poor. 1891, 2142

A plan calculated to reduce the expenditure of the nation, ... 3069

A plan for abolishing pluralities. 4526

Plan for a complete harbour at Howth-town. 2465

A plan for a county provident bank. 2927

A plan for a domestic currency. 6281

A plan for an effectual general system of sewage from the cities of London and Westminster. 6311

Plan for an extension of the currency. 6320

A plan for a general enclosure bill, for commons of a limited extent, ... 2964

A plan for a modified system of poor laws. 4574

A plan for a national bank of issue. 7972

A plan for a national currency. 8395

A plan for benefitting [sic] the agricultural labourers. 4132

A plan for clothing and educating the destitute orphans and poor children of soldiers, ... 1873

Plan for conveying railway trains across the straits of Dover. 8752

Plan for developing the resources of North-West Donegal. 9826

A plan for diminishing the poor's rates in agricultural districts. 4393

Plan for establishing a board of agriculture and internal improvement. 1823

A plan for extending the paper currency. 5086

A plan for finally settling the government of Ireland ... 1391

Plan for forming parochial committees. 4086

A plan for immediately ameliorating the present distressed condition of the agricultural poor. 4012

A plan for improving the condition of the Irish peasantry. 4304

A plan for improving the condition of the peasantry ... 3545

Plan for improving the port and quays of Limerick. 4750

A plan for instructing youths in the knowledge of husbandry. 548

A plan for lessening pauperism. 3690

A plan for preventing the recurrence of monetary panics. 7754

A plan for procuring the residence of ministers. 4491

Plan for reclaiming the bog of Allen, and the other great morasses, in Ireland. 2617

A plan for redeeming the new four per cents. 3990

A plan for reducing the capital. 3803

A plan for regulating the currency on the principle of Sir Robert Peel's celebrated currency bill of 1819. 6369

A plan for relieving the landed interest of the empire from the necessity of granting outdoor relief. 6239

A plan for relieving the pressure of the poor rates. 4287

Plan for road and steam communication. 5403

Plan for simplifying and improving the measures, weights and money of this country. 7629, 7723

Plan for substituting wood pavement for 'macadamizing'. 5630

A plan for the amelioration of the condition of the poor. 4051

A plan for the complete and final settlement of the question of the sale and transfer, mortgage and registration of land. 8129

A plan for the detection and prevention of forgery, ... 3057

A plan for the economical management of the Mutual Life Assurance Association system. 7839

A plan for the equitable settlement of the guano question. 7207

Plan for the establishment of a national bank. 3485

Plan for the establishment of a small note circulation in England. 4514

A plan for the extension of the savings bank system. 6787

Plan for the future government of India. 7275

A plan for the general improvement of the state of the poor in Ireland. 2961

A plan for the immediate extinction of the slave trade. 6587

A plan for the improvement of Dublin harbour, together with a project for a new one denominated Dublin Life Harbour etc. 2607

Plan for the improvement of the condition of the people of Ireland. 3502

A plan for the improvement of Ireland by the union of English and Irish capital. 4553

A plan for the payment of the national debt and for the immediate reduction of taxation. 2940

Plan for the reconciliation of all interests in the emancipation of West India slaves. 4440

A plan for the redemption of the public debt. 4325

Plan for the relief of the poor and the emancipation of mankind. 3038

A plan for the relief of the poor in Ireland in a letter addressed to his grace the duke of Devonshire. 3694

Plan for the relief of the poor in Ireland with observations on the English and Scotch poor laws. 4075, 4217

Plan for the relief of the unemployed poor. 4055

Plan for the removal of pauperism. 6247

A plan for the sale and profitable investment of capital. 5524

A plan for the systematic colonization of Canada. 6901

Plan for three harbours, one, easterly from Howthtown, one due-east from the island at Holyhead, ... 2599

Plan for tranquillizing Ireland. 3408

Plan of a company to be established. 4226

A plan of a labour rate. 4071

Plan of an association in aid of the Irish poor law. 5081

Plan of an universal fishing company, in Ireland. 850

Plan of a poor-law for Ireland. 4510, 4629

The Plan of Campaign illustrated. 9643

The Plan of Campaign. Irish landlords and tenants. 9793

The Plan of Campaign. The Ponsonby estate. 9722

A plan of church reform. 4301

Plan of economy for government, farming, manufactures, and trade. 7208

A plan of education for the young nobility & gentry of Great Britain. 731

Plan of encouraging commutation of clerical incomes of the church of Ireland. 8730

A plan, of general and perpetual employment, ... 3029

Plan of 'parliamentary tenant right'. 8699

A plan of reconciliation between Great Britain and her colonies. 975

A plan of reconciliation with America. 1182

Plan of St. Georges dispensary for administering advice and medicines to the poor, ... 2318

Plan of the Chamber of Commerce, (in the building late the King's Arms Tavern, Corn Hill). 1223

Plan of the European Company for life insurances, ... 3116

Plan of the general dispensary in Aldersgate-Street, London, for the relief of the poor. 1273

Plan of the London-dock, with some observations respecting the river immediately connected with docks in general ... pt. II. 1856

A plan of reconciliation with America; ... 1189

Plan of the re-printed reports of the board of agriculture. 2508

Plan of the St. Mary-le-bone general dispensary, Margaret Street, Cavendish Square. 2405

Plan of the universal register office now opened. 44

Plan or proposed system by which above 150,000 poor in Ireland may not only be supported but lodged in comfort. 4224

Plan to liquidate the national debt. 9127

Plans respecting a survey made for a navigation and railroad ... 2819

A plea for a peasant proprietary for Ireland. 9720

A plea for a peasant proprietary in Ireland. 8841

A plea for Ireland; or a proposal ... 6699

A plea for Ireland, submitting the outline ... 4543

A plea for Irish landlords. 8467

A plea for national education. 7499

A plea for shareholders. 8497

A plea for tenant right. 6472

Plea for the abolition of slavery in England. 3949

A plea for the agricultural population residing in the undeveloped districts in the West of Ireland. 8933

A plea for the bimetallic amalgamation of the currencies of Great Britain and Hindustan. 9869

A plea for the church in Ireland, or a protest against sacrilege. 4612

A plea for the English operatives. 6866

A plea for the evicted tenants of Mayo. 9282

A plea for the home government of Ireland. 8876

A plea for the 'Irish Enemy'. 8286

A plea for the Irish people ... Nov. 11th, 1887. 9587

A plea for the poor. 5371

A plea for the poor ... By a merchant of the city of London. 382

A plea for the poor and industrious. Part I. 3150

A plea for the reform of the British currency and Bank of England charter. 8042

A plea for the rich. 5380

A plea for the rights of industry in Ireland. 6546

A plea for truth, addressed to the tenant farmers of Hertfordshire and of the United Kingdom. 6751

A plea for union rating. 8807

A plea from the poor. 5381

Pleas for protection examined. 9260

Pocket notes on the use of adhesive stamps on receipts, etc. 8798

A poem on the African slave trade. 1747

Policy and justice: an essay. 244

The policy of a poor law for Ireland analytically examined. 4718

Q

Reasons for an union between Ireland and Great Britain. 2105

Reasons for and against lowering the gold and silver of this kingdom. 404, 405

Reasons for dissent from the scheme of reduction of interest on the three-and-a-half per cents. 5759

Reasons for establishing a registry of slaves in the British colonies. 2905

Reasons for extending the land improvement act to improve the Irish labourer's dwellings. 7864

Reasons for extending the public wharfs in the port of London. 1981

Reasons for preventing the French under the mark of liberty, from trampling upon Europe. 1748

Reasons for the cultivation of flax in Great Britain and Ireland. 5670

Reasons for the establishment of a free library and an industrial college. 8245

Reasons for the establishment of a new bank in India. 4800

Reasons for the establishment of provident institutions, called savings' banks. 2996

Reasons for the foundation of the Agricultural Protection Society. 5638

Reasons for the formation of the Farmers' Estate Company. 7109

Reasons for the introduction of the manufacture of beet root sugar into Ireland. 6985

Reasons for the late increase of the poor-rates; or, a comparative view of the price of labour and provisions. 1004

Reasons for thinking that free trade will raise the rent of land as well as the profit of capital and the wages of labour. 3326

Reasons humbly offered to public consideration against the present scheme of reducing the interest of money in Ireland. 569

Reasons humbly offered, why heads of a bill for the regulating trades and manufactures in Ireland should not pass into a law. 706

Reasons, humbly submitted to the honourable members of both houses of parliament, for introducing a law, to prevent unnecessary and vexatious removals of the poor. 887

Reasons in favour of the city of Dublin Steam Co's bill. 4844

Reasons in favour of the London-docks. 1900, 1990

Reasons offered for erecting a bank in Ireland. 235

Reasons why the approaching treaty of peace should be debated in parliament. 436

Reasons why the Bank of England ought not to reduce the rate of discount to 4%. 3311

Reasons why the canal for the inland navigation . . . should be cut through the Bog of Allen. 296

The recent banking crisis as applicable to the Bank of England, the Western Bank of Scotland, and City of Glasgow Bank. 7810

The recent commercial distress; or the panic analysed. 6107

Recent Highland ejections considered. 6877

The recent progress of international arbitration. 9373

Recent scenes and occurrences in Ireland. 3423

Recherches sur divers objets de l'économie politique. 1142

Reciprocity. 9024

Reciprocity. By a manufacturer. 5760

The reciprocity craze. 9203

Recriprocity, overproduction v. overconsumption, commercial depression, political economy, etc. 9065

The reclaiming and cultivation of a bog in the county of Kildare . . . 835

A reconsideration of the silver question. 9231

Reconstruction of the church in Ireland. 8686

Record of the great industrial exhibition of 1853. 7322

The record of title in Ireland. 8456

The recorder's second letter to the gentry, clergy, freemen and free holders of the city of Dublin. 351

The re-distribution of seats and the counties. 8346

Redress of national grievances. 7850

Reduction of the wine duties. 7636

Reference book to the incorporated railway companies of England and Wales . . . 6183

Reference book to the incorporated railway companies of Ireland. 6181

Reference book to the incorporated railway companies of Scotland. 6182

Reflections and resolutions proper for the gentlemen of Ireland, . . . 2945

Reflections on national reformation . . . to which are prefixed congratulatory lines to the marquess of Buckingham. 1598

Reflections on slavery. 3663

Reflections on the abundance of paper in circulation and the scarcity of specie. 2638

Reflections on the bank paper currency, with a plan how to prevent forgeries, . . . 2918

Reflections on the best means of securing tranquillity. 1944

Reflections on the causes and probable consequences of the late revolution in France. 1672

Reflections on the connexion between our gold standard and the recent monetary vicissitudes. 5647

Reflections on the currency. 8601

Reflections on the domestic policy, proper to be observed on the conclusion of a peace. 508

Reflections on the employment, wages and condition of the poor. 3907

Reflections on the expediency of a law for the naturalization of foreign protestants. 55, 81

Reflections on the expediency of opening the trade to Turky (sic). 253

Reflections on the financial system of Great Britain. 3802

Reflections on the importance of the domestic growth of tobacco. 3946

Reflections on the lieutenancy of the marquess Wellesley, in a letter to a friend. 3494

Reflections on the manner in which property in Great Britain may be affected by a large influx of gold from California. 6727

Reflections on the nature and extent of the licence trade. 2706

Reflections on the operation of the present scale of duty. 5283

Reflections on the policy and necessity of encouraging the commerce of the citizens of the United States of America. 1410

Reflections on the post-master's demand of a halfpenny. 622

Reflections on the present crisis of publick affairs. 4137

Reflections on the present low price of coarse wools . . . 1221

Reflections on the present matters in dispute between Great Britain and Ireland. 1425, 1426, 1427

Reflections on the present state and prospects of the British West Indies. 6441

Reflections on the present state of England, and the independence of America. (Thos. Day). 1185, 1241

Reflections on the propriety of an immediate conclusion of peace. 1833

Reflections on the revolution in France, and on the proceedings in certain societies in London, relative to that event. 1648

Reflections on the state of Ireland in the 19th century. 3312

Reflections on the State of parties . . . 976

Reflections previous to the establishment of a militia. 274

Reflections suggested by a perusal of Mr J. Horsley Palmer's pamphlet. 4909

Reflections upon circulating medium. 3006

Reflections upon naturalization, corporations and companies. 124

Reflections upon the corn laws. 5393

Reflections upon the present state of affairs, at home and abroad, particularly with regard to subsidies . . . 935

Reflections upon the present state of England, and the independence of America. (Thos Hardy). 1198

Reflections upon the value of the British West Indian colonies . . . 3664

Reflections upon tithes, seriously addressed in behalf of the clergy. 855

Reflections upon tithes, with a plan for the general commutation of the same. 4327

Reflexions on the causes which influence the price of corn. 3723, 3818

Réflexions politiques, . . . 1186

Réflexions sur la guerre. 1869

Reform considered in connection with the government bill. 8408

The reform ministry and the reformed parliament. 4460

The reform of currency. 9958

The reform of local taxation. 9825

Reform of the bankrupt court. 3939

The reform of the English land system. 9286

Reform of the grand jury laws of Ireland. 8218

A reform of the Irish house of commons considered. 1289

Reform of the laws relating to bankruptcy and insolvency. 7982

The reform of the poor law. 9735

Reform of the poor law system in Ireland. 7871

Reform or reject the income-tax. 7311

Reform or ruin: take your choice! 1997

The Reformer: or an infallible remedy to prevent pauperism. 4158, 4408, 4753, 4874

A refutation of an article in the Edinburgh Review (No CII) entitled 'Sadler's Law of Population . . .' 4109

Refutation of Dr. Duigenan's appendix; or an attempt to . . . 2260

A refutation of the 'Remarks, on the agreement between the commissioners for making wide streets and Mr. Ottiwell,' . . . 1892

A refutation of the wage-fund theory of modern political economy as enunciated by Mr. Mill, M.P. and Mr. Fawcett, M.P. 8392

A refutation to Cobbett's doctrine of paper money being incompatible with the co-existence of gold. 5102

Register of charity organisation and relief societies in correspondence with the London charity organisation society. 9797

A register of the trade of the port of London. 989

Registration made easy; or, a concise plan for a general register . . . 4184

Registration of assurances bill. 7312

Registration of Title Association. Private conveyancing reformed. 8238

Registration of title indispensable for peasant proprietorship. 9190

Registration of titles and deposit of deeds. 9435

A regular commercial system of keeping the accounts of a tillage farm. 7060

Regulations for the boarding class of male pupils at the Loughash national agricultural model school. 4900, 5026

A report of the committee appointed at a meeting of gentlemen, merchants, and traders. 4503

Report of the committee appointed by the council of the Home Government Association to examine the financial relations between Great Britain and Ireland. 8927

Report of the committee appointed by the Royal Canal Company, 12th June, 1793, etc. 1825

Report of the committee appointed by the Royal Dublin Society . . . on reclaiming the bogs and waste lands . . . 3238

Report of the committee appointed to distribute relief to the poor of Dublin . . . 2828

Report of the committee appointed to enquire into the funds and conduct of the Norwich Union Society. 3092

The report of the committee appointed to take measures for the abolition of the tolls. 7377

Report of the committee for the relief of the distressed districts in Ireland, . . . 3412

Report of the committee of directors of the association for the suppression of mendicity in Dublin. 3093

Report of the Committee of Inquiry appointed by the Royal Agricultural Improvement Society of Ireland at their half-yearly meeting held on 21st December, 1855. 7639

Report of the committee of investigation. Arigna Iron & Coal Co. 3758

Report of the committee of the Board of Agriculture, appointed to extract information . . . 1893

Report of the Committee of the Board of Trade on the various railways projected and in progress. 5901

Report of the committee of the Carrickfergus Mendicity Association for the year ending
May 1st, 1827. 3759
May 1st, 1829. 3940
May 1st, 1830. 4097

Report of the committee of the commerce and navigation of the United States. 4098

Report of the committee of the Highland Society of Scotland, . . . 1673

Report of the committee of secrecy of the house of commons. 2147

Report of the Committee of the Loyal National Repeal Association appointed to enquire into the state of 'Joint Stock Banking in Ireland' . . . 5764

Report of the Committee of the Loyal National Repeal Association on the Commissariat Accounts. 5765

Report of the Committee of the Loyal National Repeal Association on the Industrial resources of Ireland . . . 5766

Report of the Committee of the Loyal National Repeal Association on the Valuation (Ireland) Bill. 5902

Report of the Committee of the Loyal National Repeal Association upon the Commissioners' Report on the Ordnance memoir of Ireland. 5767

Report of the committee of the Registration of Title Association (Ireland). 8331

Report of the committee of the Society for relief of the industrious poor, . . . January, 1819. 3155

Report of the committee of the society for the Improvement of Ireland . . . 21st May, 1846. 6071

Report of the committee of the Society of arts etc., . . . 3156

Report of the committee on night refuges. 8771

Report of [the] committee on wage-earning children. 10008

Report of the committee to the annual meeting of the society for promoting the education of the poor in Ireland. 4362

Report of the committee, to whom it was referred to examine the matter of the petition of Michael Keating, esq., . . . 805

Report of the conference of ministers of all denominations on the corn laws. 5396

Report of the conference presided over by the duke of Manchester. 8619

Report of the Council of the Chamber of Commerce of Belfast, 19th November, 1823. 3413

Report of the Council of the chamber of Commerce of Dublin to the Annual Assembly of the members of the association.
1821. 3239
1823. 3414
1825. 3575
1827. 3760
1828. 3864
1829. 3941
1830. 4099
1832. 4363
1833. 4504
1834. 4622
1836. 4819
1837. 4938
1841. 5397
1853. 7378
1855. 7561
1858. 7806
1859. 7879
1891. 9798
1892. 9823
1893. 9855
1894. 9906
1895. 9935
1896. 9959
1897. 9977
1898. 9998
1899. 10009

Report of the Council of the Irish Industries Association year ending December 31st, 1893. 9824
    13 months ending January 31st, 1895. 9907

Report of the Court of Directors of the Canada Company to the Proprietors. 5517

Report of the Court of Directors of the Grand Canal . . . 1805. 2481
                    1816. 2971

Report of the court of directors to the company of undertakers of the Grand canal. 3761

A report of the debate in the house of commons of Ireland, on Wednesday and Thursday the 15th and 16th of January, 1800. 2265

A report of the debate in the house of commons of Ireland on Wednesday and Thursday, the 5th and 6th of February 1800 . . . 2264

Report of the debate in the house of commons of Ireland, on Friday the 14th of February, 1800, . . . 2263

A report of the debate in the house of commons of Ireland, on Tuesday & Wednesday the 22nd & 23rd of January, 1799. 2149

A report of the debate of the Irish bar on Sunday the 9th December, 1798. 2148

Report of the deputation appointed by the honourable the Irish society to visit the city of London's plantation in Ireland in the year 1836. 4820
                    1838. 5059
                    1840. 5398

Report of the directors of the National Bank to the twenty-second Annual meeting held at 13 Old Broad Street, May 27th 1857. 7731

Report of the directors of the National Bank presented at the twenty-fourth annual meeting of proprietors . . . 24th May, 1859. 7880

Report of the directors of the Portadown Mont de Piété and loan fund. 7564

Report of the directors of the Royal Canal Company to a court of proprietors . . . 2789

Report of the directors to a special general meeting of the chamber of commerce and manufactures at Manchester. 5399

Report of the directors to the proprietors of the City of Dublin steam packet company. 1850. 6913

Report of the directors to the proprietors of the City of Dublin Steam-packet Company for half-year ended 1st March, 1851. 7070

Report of the discussions in parliament on the Customs' duty reduction acts, corn, rum and other colonial spirits passed in sessions 1847 & 1848. 6733

Report of the General Central Relief Committee for all Ireland, from 1st July, 1848 to 1st September 1849. 6734

Report of the general committee for the association for the suppression of mendicity 1820. 3240

Report of the general committee of management of the children's friend society. 5159

Report of the general committee of the association for the suppression of mendicity 1821. 3316

Report of the general committee of the Loyal national repeal association . . . 5642

[Fifth] Report of the General Committee of the Association for the suppression of mendicity in Dublin . . ., 1822. 3415

Report of the General Executive Committee of the City and County of Philadelphia. 6293

Report of the gold mines in the county of Wicklow. 2310

Report of the Grand Jury of Co. Cork . . . 2829

Report of the great commercial cause of Minet and Fector versus Gibson and Johnson. 1723

Report of the Hibernian auxiliary . . . 5518

A report of the important debate in the house of commons of Ireland, on Thursday, April 11, 1799, . . . 2150

Report of the Institution established at Fenagh, . . . 3198

Report of the Irish board of trades. 5235

Report on the Irish Coercion Bill, the causes of discontent in Ireland, condition of the people . . . 6065

Report of the Irish Relief Fund, South Australia. 9133

Report of the Kilkenny Tenant League to the president, George Bryan. 8772

Report of the late committee together with a list of subscribers who contributed to the support of the house of industry, Belfast for . . . 1829. 4100

Report of the locating survey of the St. Croix and Lake Superior Railroad. 7630

Report of the lords commissioners for trade and plantations on the petition of hon. T. Walpole, Benjamin Franklin, John Sargent and Samuel Wharton . . . 827

Report of the Mansion House committee for the relief of distress in Ireland. 8134

Report of the Mansion House committee on the potato disease. 6072

Report of the Mansion House relief committee appointed at a public meeting, held on the 25th September, 1829, . . . 4101

Report of the Moate Agricultural Society for the year 1841. 5400

Report of the Newtown-Barn agricultural school near Moate for the year ending 5th May 1842. 5519

—— for the year ending 5th May 1843. 5643

A report to the Farming Society of Ireland. 3318

Report to the right honourable the lord mayor, aldermen and councillors of the borough of Dublin, on the state of the public works of the city. 7200

Report upon emigration to Canada. 9794

Report upon the present condition and relative merits of the harbours of Larne, Loch Ryan, Port Patrick, Donaghadee and Belfast... 5995

Report upon the proposed railways between Dublin, Navan and Drogheda. 4737

The reports and observations of Robert Stephenson made to the right hon. and honourable the trustees of the linen manufacture for the years 1760 and 1761. 486

The reports and observations of Robert Stephenson for... the years 1762 and 1763. 512, 544

The reports and observations of Robert Stephenson... for the years 1764 and 1765. 631

Reports and returns made to parliament. 4821

Reports of a committee of proprietors of the new Royal Canal Company. 4623

Reports of inquiries concerning state-aid to agriculture and industry in Wurtemberg and Switzerland. 9932

Reports of the board of managers of the Pennsylvania colonisation society. 4238

Reports of the committee of St. Mary's parish, on local taxation. 3417

Reports of the committee of the house of commons respecting the Caledonian Canal. 2482

Reports of the several departments of the city government of Portland for the municipal year 1858–9. 7882

Reports of Sir John MacNeill and Messrs. Barton and Hawkshaw, to the board of directors of the Dublin and Belfast junction railway company. 7961

The reports of the society for bettering the condition and increasing comforts of the poor. Vol. I. 2027
       Vol. II. 2266

Reports on the condition of the peasantry of the county of Mayo. 9100

Reports on the fine wooled flocks of the Messrs. Nolan at Merino Cottage. 3193

Reports on the Grand Ship Canal from London to Arundel Bay and... 3521

Reports relative to Dublin harbour and adjacent coast, made in consequence of orders... 2316

The representation of the L(-----)s J(------)s of Ireland... 434

The representation of the L---s J----s of Ireland, touching the transmission of a privy-council money bill previous to the calling of a new parliament. 763

Representation of the lords of the committee of council,... 1674

A representation of the progress of the linen and hempen manufactures of Ireland,... 793

Representation of the state of government slaves and apprentices in the Mauritius. 4128

A representation of the state of the trade of Ireland... 12, 216

A representation to his majesty, moved in the House of Commons, by the right honourable Edmund Burke... 1309

Reprint of the statistical account of the town and parish of Thurso in Scotland,... 2783

Reproductive employment; a series of letters to the landed proprietors of Ireland... 6267

Reproductive relief spinning in the west of Ireland. 6638

The republic of New Granada as a field for emigration. 7807

The requirements and resources of the sick poor. 7796

Researches for a philanthropical remedy against communism... 6147

Reseña economica del estado de Tabasco. 9989

Reservoirs on the river Bann. 4767

Resolutions and regulations of the Committee for managing the Charitable Fund raised in the Parish of St. Peter. 2790

Resolutions of the committee of owners and occupiers of lands in the County of Lincoln... 1214

Resolutions of the Irish distillers. 5279

Resources of the state of Arkansas. 8913

Resources of the United Kingdom; or, the present distresses considered. 4084

The resources farmers possess for meeting the reduced prices of their produce. 5695

The respective charges given to the grand jury of the county of Armagh... 510, 1547

The respective duties of landlords, tenants, and labourers. 8037

The respective reports of John Greer Inspector-General for the province of Ulster and of John Arbuthnot,... 1328

The restoration of national prosperity, shewn to be immediately practicable. 3248

The result of the change of administration. 4104

The result of the pamphlets or, what the duke of Wellington has to look to. 4105

The results of negro emancipation. 7855

The results of the census of Great Britain in 1851. 7280

Results of the Irish census of 1861, with a special reference to the condition of the Church in Ireland. 8235

Retail traders and co-operative stores. 8868

Retford currency society. Currency, agriculture and free trade. 7071

——. How can paper money increase the wealth of a nation? 7072

——. Market Bosworth farmers' association meeting. 7073

——. Second address to the farmers of England. 7074

——. To the farmers of England. 7075

——. What has Peel's bill of 1844 done? 7076

Retrograde legislation in bankruptcy. 7857

A retrospective view of West India slavery. 4364

Return of all Charitable donations and bequests contained in the wills registered in the prerogative and consistorial offices of Dublin... 2538

Returns of sales of tenant-right in agricultural holdings, Ireland. 9473, 9517

The Rev. Dr. Pye Smith and the new poor law. 5161

The Rev. Mr. O'Leary's address to the common people of Ireland. 1474

The revenue and commerce of the United Kingdom for 1851. 7252

The revenue in jeopardy... 5669

The revenues of the church of England not a burden on the public. 4106

Review and examination of the statements reasoning and opinions... 2830

The review; being a short account of the doctrine, arguments and tendency of the writings offered to the public... 187

Review illustrative of various bearings peculiar to interests and discounts. 4290

Review of a publication entitled, the speech of the right honourable John Foster... 2164

Review of Charles Shaw Lefevre, esq.'s letter. 4858

A review of circumstances connected with the past and present state of the protestant and catholic interests in Ireland;... 4412

A review of Dr. Price's writings on the subject of the finances of this kingdom. 1775

Review of four months proceedings in aid of the destitute and unemployed fishermen of Ballycotton, Co. Cork. 6536

A review of Mr. Cobden's corn politics... 5588

A review of Mr. Grattan's answer to the earl of Clare's speech. Part the first. 2267

A review of Mr. Pitt's administration... 509

A review of part of the schemes proposed at different times by Robert Stephenson... 439

A review of railways and mining legislation at home and abroad. 6319

Review of the agricultural statistics of France. 6486

A review of the arguments and allegations. 3945

A review of the case of the civil servants of the crown. 7733

A review of the catholic question, in which the constitutional interests of Ireland,... 1771

A review of the conduct of administration during the seventh session of parliament. 1681

A review of the conduct of his excellency John, earl of Buckinghamshire, lord lieutenant general and general governor of Ireland,... 1164

Review of the controversy respecting the high price of bullion and the state of our currency. 2692

Review of the evidence taken before the Irish committees of both houses of parliament. 3557

A review of the evils that have prevailed in the linen manufacture of Ireland. 480.   Part II. 481

A review of the existing causes which at present disturb the tranquillity of Ireland. 3319

A review of the financial situation of the East India Company. 3590

A review of the income tax in its relation to the national debt. 7286

Review of the Joint Stock bank acts. 5260

A review of the London and North Western Railway accounts, for the last ten years. 7643

Review of the Neapolitan sulphur question. 5280

A review of the negociations between the United States of America and Great Britain. 3955

A review of the present position of landlords and incumbrancers. 9668

Review of the Quarterly Review. 3484

Review of the rt. hon. Leonard Courtney's article... "Bimetallism once more." 9819

A review of the speech of the right hon. William Pitt, in the British house of commons,... 2135

Review of the state of Ireland, with regard to the best means of employing... 3284

A review of the testimony of friends. 7411

A review of the three great national questions relative to a Declaration of Right, Poyning's Law and the Mutiny Bill. 1166

A review of the trade of banking in England and Ireland. 4774

The reviewer reviewed. 7962

Some hints to the right honourable and honourable the trustees of the linen manufactory, for promoting the growth of flax and seed in Ireland . . . 672

Some illustrations of Mr McCulloch's Principles of political economy. 3698

Some impartial observations on the proposed augmentation. 707

Some information respecting America, collected by Thomas Cooper, late of Manchester. 1842

Some Irish industries. 9953

Some notes of a tour in England, Scotland and Ireland. 6747

Some notes on the writings of Professor Fawcett, Mr. Leslie, and Professor Newman on the land laws of England. 8491

Some notices touching the present state of Ireland. 4251

Some observations and queries on the present laws . . . relative to the papists. 462

Some observations and remarks on a late publication, entitled travels in Europe, . . . 1293

Some observations on direct taxation. 7285

Some observations on the government of Ireland bill. 9523

Some observations on the importance of the navigation laws. 6613

Some observations on the original and late and present state of the excise establishment . . . 2902

Some observations on the proceedings in the Dublin Society, in the granting and disposing of premiums and bounties . . . 894

Some observations on the projected union between Great Britain and Ireland, . . . 2003

Some observations on the recent supplies of gold. 7174

Some observations on the subject of the debate in the house of commons, on Indian affairs. 2486

Some observations on the tenant right of Ulster. 6623

Some observations relative to the late bill for paying off the residue of the national debt of Ireland. 145

Some observations upon a pamphlet entitled, 'Remarks on the consumption of Public Wealth . . .' 3434

Some observations upon libels and laws relating thereto. 894

Some observations upon the present state of Ireland. 4911

Some of the difficulties of Ireland in the way of an improving government, stated. 5651

Some practical remarks on the effect of the usury laws on the landed interests. 3679

Some practical suggestions concerning the land law (Ireland) bill. 9175

Some proceedings of the Freeholder's-society. 338

Some pros and cons of the opium question. 5290

Some queries relative to the present state of popery in Ireland. 301

Some questions upon the legislative constitution of Ireland. 746

Some real wants and some legitimate claims of the working classes. 7944

Some reasons humbly offered to the consideration of parliament for preventing the delays of justice, . . . 830

Some reasons against raising an army of Roman catholics in Ireland. 484

Some reflections concerning the reduction of gold coin in Ireland. 1554

Some reflections of a church of England man, on the conduct of a chief secretary for Ireland. 4377

Some remarks on a question very current at the present time. 6526

Some remarks on Dr. Jebb's considerations on the expediency of a national circulation bank in Ireland. 1138

Some remarks on purchase. 9547

Some remarks on the apparent circumstances of the war in the fourth week of October, 1795. 1860, 1903

Some remarks on the appropriation clause of lord Morpeth's tithe bill. 4744

Some remarks on the Bank of England. 6700

Some remarks on the Irish church bill. 8600

Some remarks on the Irish Fishery Acts. 8258

Some remarks on the late negotiations. 4459

Some remarks on the present state of affairs; respectfully addressed to the Marquess of Lansdowne. 4255

Some remarks on the social relations of Great Britain and Ireland at the present day. 5785

Some remarks on the state of the leather trade in 1846. 6087

Some remarks on the statute law affecting parish apprentices. 3966

Some remarks upon Mr. McMahon's bill, entitled 'A bill to assimilate the law of Ireland as to salmon fisheries, to that of England.' 8180

Some remarks upon the nature and origin of the tithes in London. 5091

Somerville's Manchester school of political economy. 6932

Some seasonable thoughts, relating to our civil and ecclesiastical constitution. 53

Some short historical anecdotes with remarks relative to Ireland. 485

Some strictures on the conduct of administration during the session of Parliament, that opened under Charles, Marquess Cornwallis, . . . 2280

Some suggestions for the better government of Ireland. 6001

Some talk about the repeal of the union, cheap food, employment of the people by government, and the agricultural instructors. 6555

Some thoughts of an octogenarian upon public matters. 7970

Some thoughts on lowering the water of Lough Neagh and other great lakes in Ireland. 193, 385, 857

Some thoughts on national education for the United Kingdom June 1875. 8982

Some thoughts on strikes, free trade, and protection. 9137

Some thoughts on the bill for the relief of tenants holding leases for lives, renewable for ever. 1115

Some thoughts on the general improvement of Ireland. 364, 1130

Some thoughts on the importance of the linnen-manufacture (sic) to Ireland, & how to lessen the expence of it. 1637

Some thoughts on the interest of money in general. 251

Some thoughts on the nature of paper-credit, relative to the late failures of bankers and receivers in Ireland. 386, 438

Some thoughts on the present state of our trade to India. 365

Some thoughts on the present state of the linen trade, of Great Britain & Ireland. 895

Something about saving. 9041

The soul of Mr. Pitt. 3161

The source and remedy of the national difficulties deduced from principles . . . 3243

The source of the evil: or, the system displayed. 1351

Sources or means of appropriation for the human creature's property of pecuniary possessions or increasings. 5853

South Australia. 5174

The South Australian system of conveyancing by registration of title. 7891

The south of Ireland and her poor. 5652

South of Ireland. Hints to Irish landlords, on the best means of obtaining and increasing their rents. 3507

The South Staffordshire colliery district. 7524

South Wales association for improvement of roads, 1st June, 1808. 2586

South western packet station, Ireland. 6905

Spade husbandry. 4416

Spade husbandry and manual labour. 6958

Spain and the African slave-trade. 8143

Spanish bonds. A statement of the present position of the Spanish bondholders. 6135

Spanish war. An enquiry how far Ireland is bound, or right, to embark in the impending contest. 1682

Special directions for the government of persons interested in the new licence act. 4641

Special report of the Bristol and Clifton ladies' anti-slavery society. 7239

Special report of the directors of the African institution, made at the annual general meeting, . . . 2903

Special rules on the revenue side of the court of the exchequer. 1002

Specimen of the statistical account of Scotland. Drawn up . . . 1731

Spectacles for sans-culottes of full age. 1853

Speculations on our prospects under the present administration. 1897

Speculations on the state of Ireland. 1830

Speech etc. [MS note 'Rt. Hon. John Foster, answer to Lord Castlereagh, 5th Feb. 1800']. 2225

Speech against the proposed alteration of the corn laws. 2801

Speech against the suspending and dispensing prerogative. 652, 956

The speech (at length) of the Honourable Henry Grattan, . . . 2231

A speech delivered at a free conference between the honourable the council and assembly of Jamaica, held the 19th November, 1789. 1656

A speech delivered at Midnapore. 7649

A speech delivered by Mr Daunt at the great repeal demonstration, held in . . . Liverpool . . . 1843. 5575

The speech delivered by the order and in the presence of the king, in the assembly of the notables, . . . 1508

A speech, in behalf of the constitution, against the suspending and dispensing prerogative. 669

The speech in extenso, the substance of which was delivered at the East India-House, 13th March, 1858. 7764

A speech in favour of protection to British capital and industry. 6957

A speech intended to have been delivered in the House of Commons, in support of the petition from the General Congress at Philadelphia. 925

A speech intended to have been spoken on the bill for altering the charters of the colony of Massachusett's Bay. 892

Speech in the House of Commons of Ireland, 5th March, 1799 . . . 2074

Speech in the House of Commons, April 23rd, 1799. 2229

Speech in the House of Commons, on Friday July 2, 1784, on moving certain papers relative to the state of East India Company's affairs. 1324

Speech of Alderman Hayes on the discussion in the town council of Cork. 5596

The speech of a patriot prince. 302

Suggestions for establishing a British Zollverein. 9139

Suggestions for giving employment and permanent relief to the manufacturers now so distressed in the liberty. 3634

Suggestions for immediate establishment of a direct communication by steam navigation between Ireland and the United States. 7048

Suggestions for improved railway legislation. 6052

Suggestions for improving the condition of the industrious classes. 4020

Suggestions for improving the value of railway property. 6858

Suggestions for legislation relating to friendly societies. 8581

Suggestions for monetary reform. 7080, 7229

Suggestions for producing public improvements, . . . 2963

Suggestions for raising and securing a general fund to provide annuities for the widows and orphans of all the ministers of the established Church in Ireland. 8211

Suggestions for relieving distress. 6385

Suggestions for rendering a silver note currency available as a medium of exchange . . . 9861

Suggestions for separating the culture of sugar from the process of manufacture. 6004

Suggestions for the amelioration of the present condition of Ireland. 6189, 6442

Suggestions for the amendment of the arterial drainage laws of Ireland. 8313

Suggestions for the employment of the poor of the metropolis, . . . 3019

Suggestions for the formation of two assurance offices. 7414

Suggestions for the gradual payment of the national debt. 7868

Suggestions for the improvement of Ireland. By the author . . . 3500

Suggestions for the improvement of railway property. 7794

Suggestions for the improvement of the domestic policy. 4483

Suggestions for the improvement of the Irish poor law. 9294

Suggestions for the liquidation of the national debt. 8384

Suggestions for the liquidation of the national debt, by means of railway property, . . . 7538

Suggestions for the management of railway accounts and a word or two on audit. 6717

Suggestions for the more general extension of land-draining. 5563

Suggestions for the more scientific and general employment of agricultural labourers. 5745

Suggestions for the organisation of co-operative farming associations in Ireland. 8735

Suggestions for the rating of tithe commutation rent-charge. 5932

Suggestions for the reconstruction of the government of India. 7709

Suggestions for the regulations of the office of justice of the peace in Ireland. 3699

Suggestions for the relief of British commerce. 6514

Suggestions for the renewal of the Bank of England charter. 7652

Suggestions for the repeal of the assessed taxes. 6563

Suggestions on fattening cattle. 5547

Suggestions on immediate legislative requirements. 6899

Suggestions on the abolition of slavery in the British colonies. 4259

Suggestions on the best mode of relieving the present prevailing distress in the south of Ireland. 3088

Suggestions on the best modes of employing the Irish peasantry. 5846

Suggestions on the constitution of a board of agriculture. 9978

Suggestions on the Dublin improvements. 6427

Suggestions on the entire discharge of the national debt. 2661

Suggestions on the land question (Ireland), etc. 9222

Suggestions on the land question of Ireland. 8674

Suggestions on the necessity, and on the best mode of levying assessments for local purposes, in Ireland. 4156

Suggestions on the present condition of Ireland. 7256

Suggestions on the question of colonization. 6709

Suggestions on the slave trade, for the consideration of the legislature of Great Britain. 1960

Suggestions on the state of Ireland chiefly given in evidence . . . 9280

Suggestions relative to the improvement of the British West India colonies. 7272

Suggestions relative to the project of a survey and valuation of Ireland. 3547

Suggestions respecting church rates. 7505

Suggestions submitted to the consideration of the nobility, gentry and magistrates of Ireland, . . . 2979

Suggestions to iron-masters on increasing the demand for iron. 5611

Suggestions to small farmers in the barony of Farney. 6337

Suggestions towards a measure for the settlement of the Irish land question. 9474

Suggestions towards improving the present system of corn-laws. 5348

Suggestions towards the improvement of the sanitary condition of the metropolis. 6109

Suggestions with a view to ameliorate the condition of the poor. 3881

Suggestions with reference to the necessity of constituting a national body to manage the local interests and local taxation of Ireland. 9771

Sull' Insegnamento dell'economia politica e sociale in Inghilterra. 8038

Summary abstract of the evidence given by the manufacturers, before the committee of the house of lords of Great Britain against the Irish propositions. 1422

A summary explanation of the principles of Mr. Pitt's intended bill for amending the representation of the people in parliament. 1435

A summary of a treatise by major Cartwright. 1181

Summary of authorities relating to the nine turnpike trusts on the north side of the city of Dublin. 6652

A summary of practical farming. 4780

Summary of the administration of the Indian Government by the Marquess of Hastings . . . 3458

A summary of the law relating to cheques on bankers. 8765

A summary of transactions relative to the proposed formation of a new and wide street. 7362

A summary statement of the one pound note question. 3834

A summary view of the East-India Company of Great Britain. 1355

A summary view of the principal measures relating to Ireland, . . . 2327

A summary view of the report and evidence relative to the poor laws, . . . 3081

Summer rambles to the West. 8179

Summum bonum; or, a sponge for the taxes. 3204

Sun Assurance Co. Report of a Trial wherein Bernard Burgess was plaintiff, . . . 3247

Sun Life Assurance Society for effecting assurances on lives and survivorships. 3433

Sundry papers and reports, relative first, to the defense of the estate of Cherry Cobb Sands against the Humber. 1736

Supplement au Traité sur la Mendicité avec les objections qui ont été faites contre les projets de Réglemens, . . . 937

Supplement to an examination of the evidence taken before the committee of secrecy. 4341

Supplement to a treatise on gold and silver. 9422

A supplement to Lord Anson's voyage around the world. 64

A supplement to the annals of the coinage of Britain, &c. 3162

Supplement to the edition of Mr. McCulloch's Commercial Dictionary published in 1847. 6689

Supplement to the interests of Ireland. 373

A supplement to the leases and sales of settled estates act. 7994

Supplement to the regulations of the Madras military fund. 6528

A supplement to the remarks on a pamphlet entitled, Considerations on the late bill for paying the national debt. 196

A supplement to the remarks on the nature and operation of money &c. 3161

A supplement to the revolution in mind and practice of the human race. 6721

A supplement to the second edition of the treatise on reversionary payments, etc. . . . 825

Supplement to the seventh edition of Fairman on the funds. 3713

A supplement to the statement of the financial exigencies of Ireland before and after the legislative union. 8266

Supplement to the Tithe Commutation Tables. 8756

Supplement to the twelfth edition of the general railway Acts. 8853

A supplement to Theobald's practical treatise on the poor laws. 4957

Supplementary appendix to the case and claims of the licensed victuallers. 5333

Supplementary observations to the third edition of an essay on the general principles and present practice of banking. 3293

A supplementary section on the poor laws; and on a list of errata and omissions . . . 3007

The supply of water to Cork. 7482

Suppressed work! On the possibility of limiting populousness. 5298

Suppression of street-begging. Report. 3102

The suppressed pamphlet . . . 7490

The "suppressed" pamphlet . . . 9224

Suppression of the French nobility vindicated, in an essay on their origin, & qualities, . . . 1745

The supremacy of the British legislature over the colonies, candidly discussed. 936

Sur la Banque de France, les causes de la crise qu'elle a éprouvée, les tristes effets qui en sont resultés, . . . 2731

Sur l'importation des cereales dans la Grande-Bretagne. 5463

Sur le systeme continental et sur ses rapports avec la Suède. 2793

The sure road to prosperity; or the way to obtain wealth and increase it. 2293

The thirteenth annual report and transactions of the Royal Society for the promotion and improvement of the growth of flax in Ireland. 7493

Thirteenth report of the managing committee of the association for the suppression of mendicity in Dublin . . . for 1830. 4263

Thirty nine articles of belief proposed as the profession and programme of Christian socialists. 9525

Thirty-sixth annual report of the committee of the night asylum for houseless poor. 8984

Thirty years' observations on the effects of taxing provisions instead of income. 4823

This country must be governed. 5422

This, or separation. 8770

Thoughts and details on scarcity. 2200

Thoughts and facts relating to the increase of agriculture, manufactures, and commerce, by the extension of inland navigation in Ireland. 1879

Thoughts and suggestions on the means apparently necessary to be adopted by the legislature, . . . 2553

Thoughts and suggestions on the present condition of the country. 4061

Thoughts concerning the constitutional principles in points of finance and personal service, . . . 1485

Thoughts, English and Irish, on the pension-list of Ireland. 764

Thoughts explanatory of the pressure experienced by the British agriculturalist and manufacturer. 3960

Thoughts for the total abolition of tythes in Ireland, submitted with the utmost . . . 3487

Thoughts on a fund for the improvement of credit in Great Britain. 1133

Thoughts on a judicious disposition of land in Ireland. 6188

Thoughts on a late advertisement in the Dublin Evening Post. 2546

Thoughts on a letter addressed to the right hon. Thomas Conolly, as secretary to the Whig Club. 1679

Thoughts on a new coinage of silver, . . . 2019

Thoughts on an income tax. 7152

Thoughts on a question of importance proposed to the public. 572

Thoughts on a radical remedy for the present distresses of the country, . . . 3206

Thoughts on an union. 2031

Thoughts on church endowment and church patronage. 6771

Thoughts on church reform. 4322

Thoughts on circulation and paper currency. 2664

Thoughts on civil government: addressed to the disfranchised citizens of Sheffield. 1857

Thoughts on currency and the means of promoting national prosperity . . . 3952

Thoughts on currency, banking and the funds, home and foreign. 5448

Thoughts on emigration as connected with Ireland. 5207

Thoughts on emigration as the means of surmounting our present difficulties. 4266

Thoughts on equal representation; with hints for improving . . . 1333

Thoughts on finance, suggested by the measures of the present session. 1968

Thoughts on "Free Trade in Land". 8618

Thoughts on government: occasioned by Mr. Burke's Reflections etc. 1724

Thoughts on Hospitals. 768

Thoughts on inland navigation. 4338

Thoughts on Ireland. 6342

Thoughts on liberty and equality. 1828

Thoughts on news-papers and a free trade. 1091

Thoughts on penitentiaries. 1659

Thoughts on poverty and pauperism. 8845

Thoughts on protecting duties. 1329

Thoughts on reading the hon. John P. Vereker's paper on absenteeism. 6923

Thoughts on some late removals in Ireland. 197

Thoughts on taxation. 3772

Thoughts on taxation: in the course of which . . . 2128

Thoughts on the abolition of the slave trade, and civilization of Africa. 2947

Thoughts on the act for making more effectual provision for the government of the province at Quebec. 897

Thoughts on the affairs of Ireland: the speeches of the Lord Chancellor, Cardinal Wolsey and Gerald, earl of Kildare. 198

Thoughts on the Bank Charter act. 7817

Thoughts on the alarming state of the circulation, and on the means of redressing the pecuniary grievances in Ireland. 2474

Thoughts on the cause of the present discontents. 738

Thoughts on the causes and consequences of the present high price of provisions. 654, 670, 691

Thoughts on the causes of the present failures. 1826

Thoughts on the changes which have taken place in the navigation laws of England. 4474

Thoughts on the commencement of a new parliament. With an appendix, containing remarks . . . 1738

Thoughts on the commercial arrangements with Ireland; addressed to the people of Great Britain. 1423

Thoughts on the commutation, or abolition, of tithes. 2852

Thoughts on the conduct and continuation of the volunteers of Ireland. 1297

Thoughts on the corn laws [by M. Gore]. 5240

Thoughts on the corn laws [anon]. 5425

Thoughts on the corn laws addressed to the working classes . . . 5145

Thoughts on the corn laws, as connected with agriculture, commerce and finance. 2869

Thoughts on the currency. 5535

Thoughts on the difficulties and distresses in which the peace of 1783 has involved the people of England. 1253

Thoughts on the discontents of the people last year, respecting the sugar duties. 1154

Thoughts on the effects of the bank restrictions. 2436

Thoughts on the establishment of new manufactures in Ireland, occasioned by the late freedoms we have obtained. 1298

Thoughts on the expediency and means of improving the agriculture of Ireland. 2669

Thoughts on the expediency of adopting a system of national education . . . 1814

Thoughts on the expediency of forwarding the establishment of manufactures in Ireland. 1251

Thoughts on the expediency of legalizing the sale of game. 3435

Thoughts on the expediency of repealing the usury laws. 3067

Thoughts on the funding system and its effects. 3480

Thoughts on the grand jury system of Ireland. 9035

Thoughts on the Indian crisis. 7742

Thoughts on the inexpediency of continuing the Irish woollen ware-house. 1068

Thoughts on the late proceedings of government, respecting the trade of the West India Islands with the United States of North America . . . 1320

Thoughts on the letter of Edmund Burke, Esq.; to the sheriffs of Bristol, on the affairs of America. 990

Thoughts on the liquidation of the public debt. 3914

Thoughts on the management and relief of the poor. 2853

Thoughts on the manufacture and trade of salt on the herring fisheries, and on the coal-trade of Great Britain, . . . 1319

Thoughts on the means of preventing abuses in life assurance offices. 4958

Thoughts on the misery of a numerous class of females. 1835

Thoughts on the nature and value of the tenant's interest. 9176

Thoughts on the naval strength of the British Empire. 1216

Thoughts on the necessity and advantages of care and economy . . . [with] . . . manure. 1906

Thoughts on the necessity of improving the condition of the slaves in the British Colonies . . . 3361

Thoughts on the peace in a letter from the country. 1299

Thoughts on the pernicious consequences of borrowing money. 388

Thoughts on the policy of the proposed alteration of the corn laws. 3773

Thoughts on the poor of Ireland. 4267

Thoughts on the poor relief bill for Ireland. 6321

Thoughts on the present alarming crisis of affairs [1779]. 1069

Thoughts on the present commercial distress . . . 3604

Thoughts on the present depressed state of the agricultural interest of this kingdom. 3014

Thoughts on the present mode of taxation in Great Britain. 1318

Thoughts on the present political state of affairs, in a letter to a friend. 2694

Thoughts on the present prices of provisions, their causes & remedies. 2283

Thoughts on the present situation of Ireland. 1219

Thoughts on the present state and future commercial policy of the country. 3925

Thoughts on the present state and prospects of legal discontent. 7809

Thoughts on the present state of affairs with America and the means of conciliation . . . 1026

Thoughts on the present state of Ireland. 6642, 6682

Thoughts on the present state of the colliers & day labourers of this kingdom. 1855

Thoughts on the principles of taxation. 6382, 6969

Thoughts on the projected union between Great Britain and Ireland. 1988

Thoughts on the questions agitated at farmer's meetings in Aberdeenshire. 9226

Thoughts on the rating question. 5479

Thoughts on the registration of the title to land. 6711

Thoughts on the report of the committee appointed by the House of Commons to inquire into the agricultural distress. 3212

Thoughts on the restriction of payments in specie. 2399

Thoughts on the resumption of cash payments by the bank. 3115

Thoughts on the separation of the departments of the Bank of England. 5741

Thoughts on the strength of the British Empire. Part 2. 1217

Thoughts on the temporalities of the Church of Ireland. 7396

Thoughts on the use of machines, in the cotton manufacture. 1125

The United Kingdom Waste Lands' Improvement Company. 7497

United States bonds and securities. 8496

The units in exchange and a free currency. 9766

Universal equality. 8805

Universal table of exchange. 8723

The unseen foundation of the "Unseen foundations of Society." 9805

Upon the necessity of a commutation of tithes. 4581

Upon the probable influence of the repeal of the corn laws, upon trade in corn. 6096

The uprising of a great people. 8002

The urgent needs of Ireland. 9496

The usage of holding parliaments & of passing bills of supply, in Ireland, stated from record. 752

The usage of holding parliaments; & of preparing and passing bills of supply, in Ireland, stated from record. 749

The use of salt in agriculture. 8167

The usurer *versus* the producer. 6803

Usurpations of England the chief sources of the miseries of Ireland. 1137

Usury. A paper read before some members of the University of Cambridge. 9432

Usury. A paper read before the London junior clergy society. 9323

Usury. A paper read before the "Somerville Club." 9324

Usury: its character further investigated. 8578

The usury laws. 6846

Usury or interest proved to be repugnant to the divine and ecclesiastical laws, ... 3556

The usury plague. 5951

The utility of an early dispatch, of the inland mails, proved by a statement of facts, ... 1795

The utility of an union ... considered ... 1566, 1603

The utility of country banks considered. 2371

V

Vagrancy and mendicancy. 9272

Vagrancy. To be read at the Social Science Meeting at Belfast 1867. 8428

A valuation of annuities and leases. 173

Valuation of Ireland. 6989

The value of insurance companies' shares, as an investment. 8586

'Vates'' railway prospects for 1851 investigated. 7097

The Vaticination. As you will find it written in the 110th no. of Pue's Occurrences, Redivivus! 2181

Verbatim report of the debate in St. James' Hall, July 2nd, 1889. 9693

Verbatim report of the debate upon land and nationalisation. 9401

Verbatim report of the speech of the right hon. the earl of Derby at the anniversary of the Rochdale Workmen's Club. 9056

Verbum sapienti; or a few reasons for thinking that it is imprudent ... 2183

A very short letter to the right hon. R. Peel. 3171

Victoriaism (sic); or, a reorganization of the people. 5569

A view of evidence on the subject of tithes. 4423

View of our late and of our future currency. 3135

A view of the advantages of inland navigations. 673

A view of the agricultural state of Ireland, in 1815. 2984

A view of the British and Irish fisheries with recommendations ... 3208

A view of the British Empire, more especially Scotland. 1334

A view of the causes and consequences of the present war with France. 1958

A view of the comparative state of Great Britain and France in 1811. 2735

A view of the existing law affecting unincorporated joint stock companies. 3532

View of the financial affairs of the city of Edinburgh. 4652

A view of the injurious effects of the present bankrupt system. 3332

A view of the interests of Ireland. 2392

A view of the laws of landed property in Ireland. 2754

A view of the low moral and physical condition of the agricultural labourer. 5749

A view of the money system of England from the conquest. 3882

A view of the past and present state of the works for supplying Dublin with water. 3900

A view of the policy and methods of government. 1567

A view of the present increase of the slave trade, ... 3103

A view of the present state and future prospects of the free trade and colonisation of India. 3812, 3903

A view of the present state of Ireland. 1082

View of the present state of pauperism in Scotland. 4006

View of the present state of the manufactures of Ireland. ... 2286

A view of the present state of the question as to steam communication with India. 4891

A view of the present state of the salmon and channel fisheries, ... 3446

A view of the silk trade. 3796

A view of the state of agriculture in Ireland, with some remarks on the impediments to its prosperity. 3216

A view of the state of the nation, & of the measures of the last five years. 2684

A view of the treaty of commerce with France. 1532

View of the very great natural advantages of Ireland. 3357

Views on the corn bill of 1827. 3835

Views on the currency. 3836

Village politics. By Will Chip. 1819

Village provident societies. 6811

The village system, being a scheme for the gradual abolition of pauperism, ... 3021

Vindication of a churchman for desiring the abolition of church rates. 7993

Vindication of a memorial respecting church property. 4758

The vindication of Dominick Molloy, merchant. 26

A vindication of Gen. Richard Smith, chairman of the select committee ... 1285

A vindication of government. Addressed to the people of Ireland. 1307

A vindication of Mr. Owen's plan for the relief of the distressed working classes, ... 3209

A vindication of the case of the corporation of bakers. 306

A vindication of the church and clergy of England from the misrepresentations of the Edinburgh Review. 3424

A vindication of the conduct of Mr. John McCannon. 234

A vindication of the conduct of the clergy. 1568, 1604

A vindication of the enquiry into charitable abuses, with an exposure of the misrepresentations ... 3137

A vindication of the ministerial conduct of his grace the duke of Dorset in Ireland. 254

A vindication of the present ministry. 636

A vindication of the present order of friendly benefit societies, ... 3047

A vindication of the principles and statements advanced in the strictures of the Right Hon. Lord Sheffield ... 2495

A vindication of the r---t h--------e and h--------e l--ds and gentlemen who have been basely aspersed. 82

A vindication of the rights of British landowners, farmers & labourers, ... 5088

A vindication of the rights of men in a letter to the right honourable Edmund Burke. 1683

Vindication of the small farmers. 4746

A vindication of the tradesmen of Dublin. 4996

A vindication of Truth against craft. 201

Vindicators remarks on Sarsfield's letters, ... 1991

Vindiciae Gallicae. Defense of the French Revolution and its English admirers ... 1713

The violations of the act of union. 5577

A visionary letter to the free men of the city of Bagdad. 56

A visit to Connaught in the autumn of 1847. 6573

Visit to the Gleneask estate of the Irish waste land improvement society. 5683

Visit to the Great Exhibition. 7098

Visit to the Irish poor in the borough. 4384

A visit to the isthmus of Suez Canal works. 8073

A visit to the Philadelphia prison, etc. 1940

Vital and economic statistics of the hospitals, infirmaries, etc., of England and Wales, for the year 1863. 8285

Vital statistics of Stirling. 7926

Vital statistics. Part 1. 6219

A voice for China. 5302

A voice for Ireland. The famine in the land 6132

A voice from Ireland upon matters of present concern. 4927

The voice of the nation. A manual of nationality. 5800

The voice of the West Indies. 4385

Voices from New Zealand. 8283

Voluntary taxation. 9670

A volunteer's queries, humbly offered to the consideration of all descriptions of men in Ireland. 1322

A volunteer's queries, in Spring, 1780; humbly offered ... 1095

Votes in aid, and rates in aid of the bankrupt Irish Unions. 6749

Vox clamantis. 9091

W

Wages: a lecture. 8870

The wail of Montrose. 7884

Walks among the poor of Belfast. 7365

Want: a vindication of protection. 9271

War in disguise; or, the frauds of the neutral flags. 2517

The war of parties and waste of the national resources. 7255

War on capital. 9741

The war, the balance of trade and the Bank Acts. 8357

A warm appeal to the freemen of Ireland, on the present interesting crises of affairs. 1340

A warning from Westmeath. 9721

A warning voice to the legislators and landowners of the United Kingdom. 3251

The waste of the revenue in the excise department. 5629

INDEX OF SOCIETIES AND INSTITUTIONS

A

Abecedarian Society, Dublin. 1607

Abbeyleix Savings Bank. 8773

Ackermann, Suardy & Co. 2288, 2333

African Institution. 2637, 2903, 3222

Agricultural and Commercial Bank of Ireland. 4667, 4705, 4759, 4937, 4939, 5754

Agricultural Employment Institution, London. 4647

Agricultural Improvement Society of Ireland. (*See also* Royal Agricultural ...). 5338

Agricultural Protection Society. 5678, 5688

Agricultural Seminary, Templemoyle, Co. Londonderry. 4501, 4818, 5640, 7635, 7732

Agricultural School: Barrow. 3349

Agricultural Society of Ireland. 4690, 4694, 4701, 4734

Amalgamated Society of Engineers. 8959

American Anti-Slave Society. 7895

American Anti-slavery Society. 4997, 5085

American Protective Tariff League. 9622, 9635

American Society for the encouragement of domestic manufactures. 2988

Ancient Blue Friendly Society, North Walsham, Norfolk. 7924, 7925

Andrean Freehold Investment and Mutual Benefit Building Society, Dublin. 7225

Anti-Corn Law Conference. 5440

Anti-Corn Law League. *See* National Anti-Corn Law League

Arigna Iron and Coal Company. 2304, 2468, 3758, 3779, 4102, 4236

Arran Relief Fund. 9605

Association for defence of British Industry, London. 9350

Association for preserving liberty and property against republicans & levellers, London. 1667

Association for promoting improvement in the dwellings and domestic condition of agricultural labourers in Scotland. 8066

Association for promoting the employment of the poor and ameliorating their condition in Co. Kilkenny. 3094

Association for suppressing street-begging, Dublin. 3102

Association for the abolition of the duty on paper, Dublin. 6964, 6965, 6966, 6967, 6968

Association for the support of the rights and interests of the fishermen, Dublin. 1413

Association for the suppression of mendicity in Dublin. 3085, 3093, 3154, 3197, 3240, 3316, 3415, 3483, 3582, 3749, 3883, 3943, 4103, 4126, 4263, 4309, 4735, 4761, 4807, 4922, 4964, 5181, 5543, 5797, 8976, 9028

Association for the suppression of mendicity, in the city of Waterford. 3282, 3420, 3501, 3624

Atlantic Telegraph Company. 7583, 7752

B

Ballineen Agricultural Society. 5947

Bank of England. 1578, 9234

Bank of Ireland. 1239, 6664

Barrow Navigation Company. 1714, 2382

Bath Provident Institution for Savings. 2935

Bedford Society. 4240

Belfast Annuity Company. 779

Belfast Charitable Society. 4373

Belfast Natural History & Philosophical Society. 6687

Belfast Permanent Building and Investment Society. 7226

Belfast Social Inquiry Society. 7160, 7162

Belfast society for the relief of the destitute sick. 4512

Beneficent Annuity Company of the city of Dublin. 1451

Benevolent Annuity Company of Dublin. 780

Benevolent Society of St. Patrick. 3055

Benevolent Society of the law clerks of the city of Dublin. 6307

Bimetallic League. 9619, 9640, 9646, 9834, 9865, 9866, 9867, 9877, 9881, 9885, 9886, 9905, 9939

Birmingham Income Tax Reform Association. 7586

Board of Agriculture. 1859, 1893, 1984, 2480, 2508, 2515, 2612, 2621

Board of Irish manufactures and industry. 6976

Board of Trade of Portland, Maine. 7589

Braintree and Bocking Permanent Benefit Building Society. 7079

Bristol and Clifton Ladies' Anti-slavery Society. 7239

Bristol Chamber of Commerce. 4142

Bristol Samaritan Society. 4711

British and Foreign Anti-slavery Society. 8009, 8055, 8143, 8145, 8195, 10011

British and Foreign Philanthropic Society. 3401

British and Irish Mining Company. 7331

British anti-state-church association. 6946, 6947, 7094, 7095

British Association for the advancement of science. 6843, 6844, 6845, 6938, 7012, 7014, 7106, 7161, 7184, 7188, 7337, 7403, 7479, 7670, 8068, 8202, 8338, 8900, 9039, 9127, 9400, 9431, 9554, 9632

British Association for the relief of extreme distress in Ireland and Scotland. 6730

British Electric Telegraph Company. 6978, 6979

British India Society. 5171

British Indian Association. 7811

British-Irish Ladies Society for improving the condition and promoting the industry and welfare of the female peasantry of Ireland. 3371, 3491, 3686, 3817

Brotherly Annuity Company of Dublin. 1369

Bureau of Agriculture, Canada. 8288

C

Cambridgeshire and Isle of Ely Farmers' Association. 5661

Canada Company. 5517

Canada Patent Office. 8888

Canadian Pacific Railway. 9544, 9610

Canterbury Association. 7486

Carlow Charitable Society. 2383

Carrickfergus Mendicity Association. 3759, 3940, 4097

Castle Eden Friendly Society. 2028

Catholic Emigration Society. 5562

Catholic Truth Society. 9735, 9750, 9752, 9919

Central Board for the relief of destitution in the Highlands and Islands of Scotland. 6459, 6656, 6657, 6848, 7020, 7021

Chamber of Commerce of Belfast. 3413, 9812

Chamber of Commerce of the city of Dublin. 2477, 3225, 3239, 3295, 3414, 3575, 3760, 3864, 3941, 4099, 4363, 4504, 4622, 4710, 4819, 4938, 5265, 5397, 7378, 7561, 7806, 7879, 9798, 9823, 9845, 9855, 9906, 9935, 9959, 9977, 9998, 10009

Charitable Association, Dublin. 2768, 3455, 7145

Charitable protestant orphan union, Dublin. 7746

Charitable Repository and School of Industry, Bandon, Co. Cork. 2798

Charity Organisation Society, London. 8974, 9797

Chemico-Agricultural Society of Ulster. 5959

Children's Friend Society. 4669, 5159

Chorleywood Association for the improvement of the labouring classes. 7894

City of Dublin steam packet company. 5925, 6913, 6934, 7070, 7968

Cloghan Agricultural Loan Fund. 5025

Cloghan National Agricultural Model School. 4899, 5026

Clondalkin Institution for bettering the condition, and promoting the comforts of the poor of that parish. 3041

Clonmel Annuity Company. 1999

Cobden Club. 8989, 9009, 9014, 9024, 9026, 9034, 9071, 9125, 9202, 9203, 9219, 9236, 9242, 9260, 9286, 9413, 9420, 9481, 9504, 9505, 9572, 9621, 9638, 9669, 9723, 9727, 9729, 9758, 9968, 9979, 9990, 9991

College Historical Society, University of Dublin. 9192, 9359

Colonial Land and Emigration Commissioners. 8741

Colonization Assurance Corporation. 6816, 6817

Commercial Insurance Company, Dublin. 2210, 2711

Commercial Permanent Benefit Building Society, London. 7077

Commissioners of the Thames Navigation. 2734

Committee for the relief of the distressed districts in Ireland. 3317, 3412

Royal Dublin Society. 519, 547, 548, 578, 579, 624, 642, 643, 664, 676, 699, 704, 714, 715, 716, 729, 757, 769, 771, 772, 773, 802, 822, 835, 864, 972, 1025, 1476, 1542, 1597, 1631, 1669, 1719, 1784, 1930, 2256, 2362, 2480, 2655, 3196, 3238, 4712, 5226, 5319, 5566, 8800

Royal Exchange Insurance Company of Ireland. 1305, 2360, 2410, 2981

Royal Hospital of King Charles II, Dublin. 57

Royal Irish Academy. 1883, 3264

Royal Irish Fisheries Company. 7090, 7983

Royal Irish Mining Company. 4943

Royal National Institution for the preservation of life from shipwreck. 5176

Royal Society of Ireland. 1706

S

St. George's Parochial Charitable Loan Society, Dublin. 2835

St. Katharine Dock Company, London. 4379

St. Pancras Parochial Rates Reduction Association, London. 8574

St. Patrick Assurance Company of Ireland. 3450

St. Peter's Parochial Charitable Loan, Dublin. 2790, 2897

Sandymount Loan-fund Committee, Dublin. 4306

Savings Bank, School Street, Dublin. 3099, 6823, 6992, 7289

Scottish Benevolent Society of St. Andrew. 4724

Scottish Chamber of Agriculture. 8410

Scottish widows' fund and life assurance society. 6082

Shipwright Society in the city of Dublin. 2721

Sierra Leone Company. 1735, 1783

Sittingbourne Friendly Society. 4107

Social Annuity Company of Dublin. 149, 829

Social Inquiry Society of Ireland. 7032, 7039, 7087, 7127, 7140

Social Science Congress. 8511, 8868, 8873, 8891, 8901, 8963, 8968, 9274

Socialist League, London. 9415

Société Chrétienne Suisse d'Économie Sociale. 9713

Société d'encouragement pour l'industrie nationale. 6849

Society for bettering the condition and increasing the comforts of the poor. 2027, 2080, 2084, 2249, 2266, 2300, 2322, 2365, 2366, 2401, 2490

Society for bettering the condition of the poor in Ireland, by means of employment. 3325

Society for improving the condition of the Irish peasantry. 3425, 3426

Society for improving the condition of the labouring classes. 8097, 8271

Society for improving the condition of the poor in Ireland. 3427

Society for organising charitable relief and repressing mendicity, London. 8716, 8771, 8780

Society for promoting Christian knowledge, London. 7100, 8244, 8939

Society for promoting scientific inquiries into social questions. *See* Social Inquiry Society of Ireland

Society for promoting the comforts of the poor, Dublin. 1891, 2142, 2223, 2224, 2328, 2348, 2349, 2452, 2484

Society for promoting the education of the poor of Ireland. 3015, 4362

Society for propagating Christian knowledge. 2398

Society for relief of the destitute sick, Belfast. 4512

Society for the encouragement of the Arts, manufactures, and commerce, London. 331, 359, 571, 823, 828, 933, 1608, 2583, 3156, 3428, 4376, 5074, 5289, 7050, 8264

Society for the extinction of the slave trade and for the civilisation of Africa. 5273, 5275, 5518

Society for the improvement of Ireland. 3872, 3874, 3875, 3953, 6071

Society for the liberation of religion from state patronage and control, London. 8986

Society for the mitigation and gradual abolition of slavery throughout the British dominions. 3581, 3687

Society for the promotion and improvement of the growth of flax in Ireland. 5512, 5513, 5635, 5711, 5999, 7493, 7812

Society for the relief of sick and indigent roomkeepers in the city of Dublin. 1918, 3430, 3495, 3587, 3769, 3878, 4285, 4538

Society for the relief of the industrious poor, Dublin. 3155

Society for the suppression of beggars, instituted in Edinburgh. 2811, 2832, 3016, 3956

Society of Friends in Ireland: Central Relief Committee. 5984, 5985, 6152, 6153, 6154, 6334, 6573, 7250, 8261, 8296

Society of St. Vincent de Paul in Ireland. 6534

South Devon Railway. 6373

South Dublin [Poor Law] Union. 5308, 5675

South Wales association, for improvement of roads. 2586

Statistical Society of London. 4833, 4834, 7184, 8708, 9228

Stillorgan Charitable Institution for promoting the comforts of the poor, Co. Dublin. 2761

Stock Exchange, Dublin. 6936

Stranger's Friend Society, Dublin. 2271, 2290, 2409, 2990, 3109, 3510, 3704, 3890, 3979, 4096, 4286, 4394, 4502, 4847, 4973, 7219

Sun Life Assurance Society. 3247, 3433

T

Tithe Redemption Trust for the church in England and Wales. 7220, 7642, 7881, 7959, 8021, 8050, 8135

Tontine Buildings Society, Ennis, Co. Clare. 4748

Trades' Union Congress. 8940, 8946, 8953, 8954, 8955

Travelling tax abolition committee, London. 9728

Tribunal of Commerce Association, London. 7602

Trustees for bettering the condition of the poor of Ireland. 3576, 3676, 8983

Trustees for the encouragement of industry in the county of Cork. 3933

Trustees of the linen and hempen manufactures of Ireland. 486, 512, 544, 631, 793, 796, 1228, 1269, 1328, 1353, 1440, 1650, 1664, 2343, 2535, 2536, 2569, 2584, 2592, 2614, 2656, 2709, 2881, 3040, 3079, 3152, 3235, 3258

U

Unanimous Annuity Company of Dublin. 491

United East Lothian Agricultural Society. 5148

United Kingdom Waste Lands Improvement Company. 7497

United Patriots' and Patriarchs' Equitable Land and Building Benefit Society, London. 6306

W

Waterford and Kilkenny Railway. 7399

Waterford and Limerick Railway. 5802

Waterford Chamber of Commerce. 2851

Waterford [Poor Law] Union. 5939

Waterford, Wexford, Wicklow and Dublin Rail Company. 6991

West Clare Agricultural Society. 8825, 8932

West India Dock Company, London. 2458, 2624

Western Australian Association. 4948

Western committee for the relief of the Irish poor. 4252

Westminster Society for insurance on lives, etc. 2412

Wexford, Carlow and Dublin Junction Railway. 5930

Wigan Liberal Registration Association. 8572

Witham Permanent Benefit Building Society. 7078

Workhouse Visiting Society, London. 7960

Y

York Saving Bank. 3032